Collins

Portuguese
Dictionary

PORTUGUÊS-INGLÊS
INGLÊS-PORTUGUÊS

HarperCollins Publishers
Westerhill Road
Bishopbriggs
Glasgow
G64 2QT

Sixth Edition 2013

Reprint 10 9 8 7 6 5 4 3 2 1 0

ISBN 978-0-00-748552-9

www.collinslanguage.com

A catalogue record for this book is
available from the British Library

DISAL S.A.
Av. Marginal Direita do Tietê, 800
Jaguara – CEP 05118-100
São Paulo – SP – Brazil

www.disal.com.br

ISBN 978-0-00-751228-7 (vinyl)
ISBN 978-0-00-751229-4 (paperback)

Typeset by Davidson Publishing
Solutions, Glasgow

Printed in Italy by Lego SpA,
Lavis (Trento)

Acknowledgements

We would like to thank those
authors And publishers who
kindly gave permission for
copyright material to be used in the
Collins Corpus. We would also like
to thank Times Newspapers Ltd for
providing valuable data.

ABREVIATURAS

ABBREVIATIONS

singular	*sg*	singular
	sth	something
sujeito (gramatical)	*su(b)j*	(grammatical) subject
subjuntivo, conjuntivo	*sub(jun)*	subjunctive
superlativo	*superl*	superlative
também	*tb*	also
técnica, tecnologia	*Tec(h)*	technical term, technology
telecomunicações	*Tel*	telecommunications
tipografia, imprensa	*Tip*	typography, printing
televisão	*TV*	television
tipografia, imprensa	*Typ*	typography, printing
inglês americano	*US*	American English
ver	*V*	see
verbo	*VB*	verb
verbo intransitivo	*VI*	intransitive verb
verbo reflexivo	*VR*	reflexive verb
verbo transitivo	*VT*	transitive verb
zoologia	*Zool*	zoology
marca registrada	®	registered trademark
equivalente cultural	≈	cultural equivalent
linguagem ofensiva	!	offensive

PRONÚNCIA INGLESA

VOGAIS

	Exemplo Inglês	Explicação
[a:]	father	Entre o *a* de p*a*dre e o *o* de nó; como em f*a*da
[ʌ]	but, come	Aproximadamente como o primeiro *a* de c*a*ma
[æ]	man, cat	Som entre o *a* de l*á* e o *e* de p*é*
[ə]	father, ago	Som parecido com o *e* final pronunciado em Portugal
[ə:]	bird, heard	Entre o *e* aberto e o *o* fechado
[ε]	get, bed	Como em p*é*
[ɪ]	it, big	Mais breve do que em s*i*
[i:]	tea, see	Como em f*i*no
[ɔ]	hot, wash	Como em p*ó*
[ɔ:]	saw, all	Como o *o* de p*o*rte
[u]	put, book	Som breve e mais fechado do que em b*u*rro
[u:]	too, you	Som aberto como em j*u*ro

DITONGOS

	Exemplo Inglês	Explicação
[aɪ]	fly, high	Como em b*ai*le
[au]	how, house	Como em c*au*sa
[εə]	there, bear	Como o *e* de a*e*roporto
[eɪ]	day, obey	Como o *ei* de l*ei*
[ɪə]	here, hear	Como *ia* de companh*ia*
[əu]	go, note	[ə] seguido de um *u* breve
[ɔɪ]	boy, oil	Como em b*oi*a
[uə]	poor, sure	Como *ua* em s*ua*

CONSOANTES

	Exemplo Inglês	Explicação
[d]	mended	Como em *d*a*d*o, an*d*ar
[g]	get, big	Como em *g*rande
[dʒ]	gin, judge	Como em i*d*ade
[~]	sing	Como em ci*n*co
[h]	house, he	*h* aspirado
[j]	young, yes	Como em *i*ogurte
[k]	come, mock	Como em *c*ama
[r]	red, tread	*r* como em pa*r*a, mas pronunciado no céu da boca

xiv

[s]	sand, yes	Como em sala
[z]	rose, zebra	Como em zebra
[ʃ]	she, machine	Como em chapéu
[tʃ]	chin, rich	Como t em timbre
[w]	water, which	Como o u em água
[ʒ]	vision	Como em já
[θ]	think, myth	Sem equivalente, aproximadamente como um s pronunciado entre os dentes
[ð]	this, the	Sem equivalente, aproximadamente como um z pronunciado entre os dentes

b, f, l, m, n, p, t, v pronunciam-se como em português.

O sinal [*] indica que o r final escrito pronuncia-se apenas em inglês britânico, exceto quando a palavra seguinte começa por uma vogal. O sinal [¹] indica a sílaba acentuada.

BRAZILIAN PORTUGUESE PRONUNCIATION

CONSONANTS

c	[k]	café	c before a, o, u is pronounced as in cat
ce, ci	[s]	cego	c before e or i, as in receive
ç	[s]	raça	ç is pronounced as in receive
ch	[ʃ]	chave	ch is pronounced as in shock
d	[d]	data	as in English EXCEPT
de, di	[dʒ]	difícil	d before an i sound or final unstressed
		cidade	e is pronounced as in judge
g	[g]	gado	g before a, o, u as in gap
ge, gi	[ʒ]	gíria	g before e or i, as s in leisure
h		humano	h is always silent in Portuguese
j	[ʒ]	jogo	j is pronounced as s in leisure
l	[l]	limpo, janela	as in English EXCEPT
	[w]	falta, total	l after a vowel tends to become w
lh	[ʎ]	trabalho	lh is pronounced like the lli in million
m	[m]	animal, massa	as in English EXCEPT
	[ãw]	cantam	m at the end of a syllable preceded by a
	[ĩ]	sim	vowel nasalizes the preceding vowel
n	[n]	nadar, penal	as in English EXCEPT
	[ã]	cansar	n at the end of a syllable, preceded by a
	[ẽ]	alento	vowel and followed by a consonant, nasalizes the preceding vowel
nh	[˜]	tamanho	nh is pronounced like the ni in onion
q	[k]	queijo	qu before i or e is usually pronounced as in kick
q	[kw]	quanto	qu before a or o, and sometimes before
		cinquenta	e or i, is pronounced as in queen
-r-	[r]	compra	r preceded by a consonant (except n) and followed by a vowel is pronounced with a single trill
r-, -r-	[h]	rato, arpão	inital r, r followed by a consonant and
rr	[h]	borracha	rr are pronounced like h in house
-r	[r]	pintar, dizer	word-final r can sometimes be heard as a single trill, but usually it is not pronounced at all in colloquial speech
s-	[s]	sol	as in English EXCEPT
		escada	
		livros	
-s-	[z]	mesa	intervocalic s and s before b, d, g, l, m, n,
		rasgar,	r, and v, as in rose
		desmaio	

-ss-	[s]	nosso	double s is always pronounced as in boss
t	[t]	todo	as in English EXCEPT
te, ti	[tʃ]	amante tipo	t followed by an i sound or final unstressed e is pronounced as ch in cheer
x-	[ʃ]	xarope	initial x is pronounced like sh in ship
-x-	[s]	exceto explorar	x before a consonant is pronounced like s in sail
ex-	[z]	exame	x in the prefix ex before a vowel is pronounced as z in squeeze
-x-	[ʃ]	relaxar	x in any other position may be pronounced as in ship, axe or sail
	[ks]	fixo	
	[s]	auxiliar	
z	[z]	zangar cartaz	as in English

b, f, k, p, v, w are pronounced as in English.

VOWELS

a, á, à, â	[a]	mata	a is normally pronounced as in father
ã	[ã]	irmã	ã is pronounced approximately as in sung
e	[e]	vejo	unstressed (except final) e is pronounced like e in they, stressed e is pronounced either as in they or as in bet
-e	[i]	fome	final e is pronounced as in money
é	[ɛ]	miséria	é is pronounced as in bet
ê	[e]	pêlo	ê is pronounced as in they
i	[i]	vida	i is pronounced as in mean
o	[o]	locomotiva	unstressed (except final) o is pronounced as in local;
	[ɔ]	loja	stressed o is pronounced either as in local or as in rock
	[o]	globo	
-o	[u]	livro	final o is pronounced as in foot
ó	[ɔ]	óleo	ó is pronounced as in rock
ô	[o]	colônia	ô is pronounced as in local
u	[u]	luva	u is pronounced as in rule
	[w]	linguiça frequente	it is usually silent as in gue, gui, que, qui but in some words it is pronounced as a w sound in this position

DIPHTHONGS

ãe	[ãj] mãe	nasalized, approximately as in fly*ing*
ai	[aj] vai	as is r*i*de
ao, au	[aw] aos, auxílio	as is sh*ou*t
ão	[ãw] vão	nasalized, approximately as in r*ou*nd
ei	[ej] feira	as is th*ey*
eu	[ew] deusa	both elements pronounced
oi	[oj] boi	as is t*oy*
ou	[o] cenoura	as is l*o*cal
õe	[õj] aviões	nasalized, approximately as in 'b*oi*ng!'

STRESS

The rules of stress in Portuguese are as follows:

(a)   when a word ends in *a, e, o, m* (except *im, um* and their plural forms) or *s*, the second last syllable is stressed;
camara*da*; camara*das*
*par*te; *par*tem

(b)   when a word ends in *i, u, im* (and plural), *um* (and plural), *n* or a consonant other than *m* or *s*, the stress falls on the last syllable:
ven*di*, al*gum*, al*guns*, fa*lar*

(c)   when the rules set out in (a) and (b) are not applicable, an acute or circumflex accent appears over the stressed vowel:
*ó*tica, *â*nimo, in*glês*

In the phonetic transcription, the symbol [¹] precedes the syllable on which the stress falls.

EUROPEAN PORTUGUESE PRONUNCIATION

The pronunciation of Brazilian Portuguese differs quite markedly from the Portuguese spoken in Portugal itself and in the African and island states. The more phonetic nature of Brazilian means that words nearly always retain their set pronunciation; in European Portuguese, on the other hand, vowels can often be unpronounced or weakened and consonants can change their sound, all depending on their position within a word or whether they are being elided with a following word. The major differences in pronunciation of European Portuguese are as follows:-

CONSONANTS: as in Brazilian, except:

-b-	[β]	cuba	*b* between vowels is a softer sound, closer to *have*
d	[d]	dança, difícil	as in English EXCEPT *d* between vowels is softer,
-d-	[ð]	fado, cidade	approximately as in *the*
-g-	[ɣ]	saga	*g* between vowels is a softer sound, approximately as in la*g*er
gu	[ɣw]	aguentar	in certain words *gu* is pronounced as in *Gw*ent
qu	[kw]	tranquilo	in certain words *qu* is pronounced as in *quoits*
r-, rr	[ʀ]		initial *r* and double *r* are pronounced either like the
	[rr]		French *r* or strongly trilled as in Scottish *R*ory; pronunciation varies according to region
-r-, -r	[r]	rato, arma	*r* in any other position is slightly trilled
t	[t]	todo, amante	*t* is pronounced as in English
z	[ʒ]	zangar	as in English EXCEPT final *z* is pronounced as *sh* in fla*sh*
	[ʃ]	cartaz	

VOWELS: as in Brazilian, except:

a	[a]	falar	stressed *a* is pronounced either as in *father* or as
	[ɐ]	cama	*u* in f*u*rther
-a-, -a	[ə]	falar, fala	unstressed or final *a* is pronounced as *e* in furth*er*
e	[ə]	medir	unstressed *e* is a very short *i* sound as in rabb*i*t
-e	[ə]	arte, regime	final *e* is barely pronounced; these would sound like English *art* and *regime*
o	[u]	poço, poder	unstressed or final *o* is pronounced as in *foot*

PORTUGUESE SPELLING

In 2009, a spelling reform was introduced in all the Portuguese-speaking countries with the aim of eliminating the differences which existed between Brazilian and European Portuguese spelling. The following table summarizes these differences, which you will come across in texts written before the 2009 reform:

Description	Brazilian spelling pre-2009	European Portuguese spelling pre-2009	Universal spelling post-2009
The combinations -gue-, -gui-, -que-, -qui- when u is pronounced	With trema, e.g. lingüiça, freqüente etc.	Without trema, e.g. linguiça, frequente etc.	Without trema, e.g. linguiça, frequente etc.
Stressed -ei- and -oi- in penultimate syllables	With acute accent, e.g. idéia, heróico	Without acute accent, e.g. ideia, heroico	Without acute accent, e.g. ideia, heroico
Stressed o followed by unstressed o	First o has circumflex accent, e.g vôo, abençôo	No written accent, e.g. voo, abençoo	No written accent, e.g. voo, abençoo
First person plural preterite tense of -ar verbs	Without accent, e.g. amamos, jogamos	With acute accent, e.g. amámos, jogámos	Without accent, e.g. amamos, jogamos
comum + mente	comumente	comummente	comumente
com + nós	conosco	connosco	conosco
(h)úmido and derivatives	úmido, umidade	húmido, humidade	úmido, umidade
Latin consonant group -ct-	Simplified to -c-/-ç- or -t-, e.g. acionar, ação, ator	Silent -c- retained, e.g. accionar, acção, actor	Simplified spelling, e.g. acionar, ação, ator
Latin consonant group -pt-	Simplified to -ç- or -t-, e.g. exceção, ótimo	Silent -p- retained, e.g. excepção, óptimo	Simplified spelling, e.g. exceção, ótimo
Months of the year	e.g. janeiro, dezembro	e.g. Janeiro, Dezembro	e.g. janeiro, dezembro

One important difference between Brazilian and Portuguese spelling which still applies even after the reform is that, when a written accent is required on stressed e and o before m or n, Brazilian uses the circumflex while European uses the acute accent, reflecting the difference in the way the sounds are pronounced, e.g. tênis (BR), ténis (PT); econômico (BR), económico (PT). In addition, there are cases where two different spellings are permitted in European Portuguese to reflect two possible pronunciations, e.g. súdito/súbdito, sutil/subtil, anistia/amnistia.

English – Portuguese

Inglês – Português

A [eɪ] N (*Mus*) lá *m*

KEYWORD

a [eɪ, ə] INDEF ART (*before vowel or silent h*: **an**) **1** um(a); **a book/girl/mirror** um livro/uma menina/um espelho; **an apple** uma maçã; **she's a doctor** ela é médica
2 (*instead of the number "one"*) um(a); **a year ago** há um ano, um ano atrás; **a hundred/thousand** *etc* **pounds** cem/mil *etc* libras
3 (*in expressing ratios, prices etc*): **3 a day/week** 3 por dia/semana; **10 km an hour** 10 km por hora; **30p a kilo** 30p o quilo

aback [ə'bæk] ADV: **to be taken ~** ficar surpreendido, sobressaltar-se
abandon [ə'bændən] VT abandonar ▶ N: **with ~** com desenfreio
abbey ['æbɪ] N abadia, mosteiro
abbreviation N abreviatura
abdomen ['æbdəmən] N abdômen *m*

abduct [æb'dʌkt] VT sequestrar
ability [ə'bɪlɪtɪ] N habilidade *f*, capacidade *f*; (*talent*) talento
able ['eɪbl] ADJ capaz; (*skilled*) hábil, competente; **to be ~ to do sth** poder fazer algo
abnormal [æb'nɔːməl] ADJ anormal
aboard [ə'bɔːd] ADV a bordo ▶ PREP a bordo de
abolish [ə'bɔlɪʃ] VT abolir
aborigine [æbə'rɪdʒɪnɪ] N aborígene *m/f*
abort [ə'bɔːt] VT (*Med*) abortar; (*plan*) cancelar; **abortion** N aborto; **to have an abortion** fazer um aborto

KEYWORD

about [ə'baut] ADV **1** (*approximately*) aproximadamente; **it takes about 10 hours** leva mais ou menos 10 horas; **it's just about finished** está quase terminado
2 (*referring to place*) por toda parte, por todo lado; **to run/walk** *etc* **about** correr/andar *etc* por todos os lados
3: **to be about to do sth** estar a ponto de fazer algo
▶ PREP **1** (*relating to*) acerca de, sobre; **what is it about?** do que se trata?, é sobre o quê?; **what** *or* **how about doing this?** que tal se fizermos isso?
2 (*place*) em redor de, por

above [ə'bʌv] ADV em *or* por cima, acima ▶ PREP acima de, por cima de; **costing ~ £10** que custa mais de £10; **~ all** sobretudo
abroad [ə'brɔːd] ADV (*be abroad*) no estrangeiro; (*go abroad*) ao estrangeiro

abrupt [ə'brʌpt] ADJ (*sudden*) brusco; (*curt*) ríspido

abscess ['æbsɪs] N abscesso (BR), abcesso (PT)

absence ['æbsəns] N ausência

absent ['æbsənt] ADJ ausente; **absent-minded** ADJ distraído

absolute ['æbsəlu:t] ADJ absoluto; **absolutely** [æbsə'lu:tlɪ] ADV absolutamente

absorb [əb'zɔ:b] VT absorver; (*group, business*) incorporar; (*changes*) assimilar; (*information*) digerir; **absorbent cotton** (US) N algodão *m* hidrófilo

abstain [əb'steɪn] VI: **to ~ (from)** abster-se (de)

abstract ['æbstrækt] ADJ abstrato

absurd [əb'sə:d] ADJ absurdo

abuse [n ə'bju:s, vt ə'bju:z] N (*insults*) insultos *mpl*; (*misuse*) abuso; (*ill-treatment*) maus-tratos *mpl* ▶ VT insultar; maltratar; abusar; **abusive** [ə'bju:sɪv] ADJ ofensivo

abysmal [ə'bɪzməl] ADJ (*ignorance*) profundo, total; (*very bad*) péssimo

academic [ækə'dɛmɪk] ADJ acadêmico; (*pej: issue*) teórico ▶ N universitário(-a)

academy [ə'kædəmɪ] N (*learned body*) academia; **~ of music** conservatório

accelerate [æk'sɛləreɪt] VT, VI acelerar; **accelerator** N acelerador *m*

accent ['æksənt] N (*written*) acento; (*pronunciation*) sotaque *m*; (*fig: emphasis*) ênfase *f*

accept [ək'sɛpt] VT aceitar; (*responsibility*) assumir; **acceptable** ADJ (*offer*) bem-vindo; (*risk*) aceitável; **acceptance** N aceitação *f*

access ['æksɛs] N acesso; **accessible** [æk'sɛsəbl] ADJ acessível; (*available*) disponível

accessory [æk'sɛsərɪ] N acessório; (*Jur*): **~ to** cúmplice *m/f* de

accident ['æksɪdənt] N acidente *m*; (*chance*) casualidade *f*; **by ~** (*unintentionally*) sem querer; (*by coincidence*) por acaso; **accidental** [æksɪ'dɛntl] ADJ acidental; **accidentally** [æksɪ'dɛntəlɪ] ADV sem querer; **Accident and Emergency Department** N (BRIT) pronto-socorro

acclaim [ə'kleɪm] N aclamação *f*

accommodate [ə'kɔmədeɪt] VT alojar; (*subj: car, hotel, etc*) acomodar; (*oblige, help*) comprazer a; **accommodation** [əkɔmə'deɪʃən] N, (US) **accomodations** NPL alojamento

accompany [ə'kʌmpənɪ] VT acompanhar

accomplice [ə'kʌmplɪs] N cúmplice *m/f*

accomplish [ə'kʌmplɪʃ] VT (*task*) concluir; (*goal*) alcançar; **accomplishment** N realização *f*

accord [ə'kɔ:d] N tratado ▶ VT conceder; **of his own ~** por sua iniciativa; **accordance** [ə'kɔ:dəns] N: **in accordance with** de acordo com; **according** PREP: **according to** segundo; (*in accordance with*) conforme; **accordingly** ADV por conseguinte; (*appropriately*) do modo devido

account [ə'kaunt] N conta; (*report*) relato; **accounts** NPL (*books, department*) contabilidade *f*; **of no ~** sem importância; **on ~** por conta; **on no ~** de modo nenhum; **on ~ of** por causa de; **to take into ~, take ~ of** levar em conta; **account for** VT

FUS (*explain*) explicar; (*represent*) representar; **accountant** N contador(a) *m/f* (BR), contabilista *m/f* (PT); **account number** N número de conta

accumulate [əˈkjuːmjuleɪt] VT acumular ▶ VI acumular-se

accuracy [ˈækjurəsɪ] N exatidão *f*, precisão *f*

accurate [ˈækjurɪt] ADJ (*description*) correto; (*person, device*) preciso; **accurately** ADV com precisão

accusation [ækjuˈzeɪʃən] N acusação *f*; (*instance*) incriminação *f*

accuse [əˈkjuːz] VT: **to ~ sb (of sth)** acusar alguém (de algo); **accused** N: **the accused** o/a acusado/a

ace [eɪs] N ás *m*

ache [eɪk] N dor *f* ▶ VI (*yearn*): **to ~ to do sth** ansiar por fazer algo; **my head ~s** dói-me a cabeça

achieve [əˈtʃiːv] VT alcançar; (*victory, success*) obter; **achievement** N realização *f*; (*success*) proeza

acid [ˈæsɪd] ADJ, N ácido

acknowledge [əkˈnɔlɪdʒ] VT (*fact*) reconhecer; (*also*: **~ receipt of**) acusar o recebimento de (BR) or a receção de (PT); **acknowledgement** N notificação *f* de recebimento

acne [ˈæknɪ] N acne *f*

acorn [ˈeɪkɔːn] N bolota

acoustic [əˈkuːstɪk] ADJ acústico

acquire [əˈkwaɪəʳ] VT adquirir

acquit [əˈkwɪt] VT absolver; **to ~ o.s. well** desempenhar-se bem

acre [ˈeɪkəʳ] N acre *m* (= 4047 m²)

across [əˈkrɔs] PREP (*on the other side of*) no outro lado de; (*crosswise*) através de ▶ ADV: **to walk ~ (the road)** atravessar (a rua); **the lake is 12 km ~** o lago tem 12 km de largura; **~ from** em frente de

acrylic [əˈkrɪlɪk] ADJ acrílico ▶ N acrílico

act [ækt] N ação *f*; (*Theatre*) ato; (*in show*) número; (*Jur*) lei *f* ▶ VI tomar ação; (*behave, have effect*) agir; (*Theatre*) representar; (*pretend*) fingir ▶ VT (*part*) representar; **in the ~ of** no ato de; **to ~ as** servir de; **acting** ADJ interino ▶ N: **to do some acting** fazer teatro

action [ˈækʃən] N ação *f*; (*Mil*) batalha, combate *m*; (*Jur*) ação judicial; **out of ~** (*person*) fora de combate; (*thing*) com defeito; **to take ~** tomar atitude; **action replay** N (*TV*) replay *m*

activate [ˈæktɪveɪt] VT acionar

active [ˈæktɪv] ADJ ativo; (*volcano*) em atividade; **actively** ADV ativamente; **activity** [ækˈtɪvɪtɪ] N atividade *f*

actor [ˈæktəʳ] N ator *m*

actress [ˈæktrɪs] N atriz *f*

actual [ˈæktjuəl] ADJ real; **actually** ADV realmente; (*in fact*) na verdade; (*even*) mesmo

acute [əˈkjuːt] ADJ agudo; (*person*) perspicaz

ad [æd] N ABBR = **advertisement**

A.D. ADV ABBR (= *Anno Domini*) d.C.

adamant [ˈædəmənt] ADJ inflexível

adapt [əˈdæpt] VT adaptar ▶ VI: **to ~ (to)** adaptar-se (a)

add [æd] VT acrescentar; (*figures: also*: **~ up**) somar ▶ VI: **to ~ to** aumentar

addict [ˈædɪkt] N viciado(-a); **drug ~** toxicômano(-a); **addicted** [əˈdɪktɪd] ADJ: **to be/become addicted to** ser/ficar viciado em;

addiction N dependência;
addictive ADJ que causa
dependência
addition [ə'dɪʃən] N adição f; (thing
added) acréscimo; **in ~** além disso;
in ~ to além de; **additional** ADJ
adicional
additive ['ædɪtɪv] N aditivo
address [ə'drɛs] N endereço;
(speech) discurso ▶ VT (letter)
endereçar; (speak to) dirigir-se a,
dirigir a palavra a; **to ~ (o.s. to)**
enfocar
adequate ['ædɪkwɪt] ADJ (enough)
suficiente; (satisfactory) satisfatório
adhere [əd'hɪər] VI: **to ~ to** aderir a;
(abide by) ater-se a
adhesive [əd'hiːzɪv] N adesivo
adjective ['ædʒɛktɪv] N adjetivo
adjoining [ə'dʒɔɪnɪŋ] ADJ adjacente
adjourn [ə'dʒəːn] VT (session)
suspender ▶ VI encerrar a sessão;
(go) deslocar-se
adjust [ə'dʒʌst] VT (change) ajustar;
(clothes) arrumar; (machine) regular
▶ VI: **to ~ (to)** adaptar-se (a);
adjustment N ajuste m; (of engine)
regulagem f; (of prices, wages)
reajuste m; (of person) adaptação f
administer [əd'mɪnɪstər] VT
administrar; (justice) aplicar; (drug)
ministrar; **administration**
[ədmɪnɪs'treɪʃən] N administração f;
(us: government) governo;
administrative [əd'mɪnɪstrətɪv]
ADJ administrativo
admiral ['ædmərəl] N almirante m
admire [əd'maɪər] VT (respect)
respeitar; (appreciate) admirar
admission [əd'mɪʃən] N
(admittance) entrada; (fee) ingresso;
(confession) confissão f
admit [əd'mɪt] VT admitir; (accept)
aceitar; (confess) confessar; **admit**

to VT FUS confessar; **admittance** N
entrada; **admittedly** ADV
evidentemente
adolescent [ædəu'lɛsnt] ADJ, N
adolescente m/f
adopt [ə'dɔpt] VT adotar; **adopted**
ADJ adotivo; **adoption** N adoção f
adore [ə'dɔːr] VT adorar
Adriatic [eɪdrɪ'ætɪk], **Adriatic**
Sea N (mar m) Adriático
adrift [ə'drɪft] ADV à deriva
ADSL N ABBR (= asymmetric digital
subscriber line) ADSL m
adult ['ædʌlt] N adulto(-a) ▶ ADJ
adulto; (literature, education) para
adultos
adultery [ə'dʌltərɪ] N adultério
advance [əd'vɑːns] N avanço;
(money) adiantamento ▶ ADJ
antecipado ▶ VT (money) adiantar
▶ VI (move forward) avançar;
(progress) progredir; **in ~** com
antecedência; **to make ~s to sb**
fazer propostas a alguém;
advanced ADJ adiantado
advantage [əd'vɑːntɪdʒ] N
vantagem f; (supremacy)
supremacia; vantagem f; **to take ~**
of aproveitar-se de
adventure [əd'vɛntʃər] N aventura
adverb ['ædvəːb] N advérbio
adverse ['ædvəːs] ADJ (effect)
contrário; (weather, publicity)
desfavorável
advert ['ædvəːt] N ABBR =
advertisement
advertise ['ædvətaɪz] VI anunciar
▶ VT (event, job) anunciar; (product)
fazer a propaganda de; **to ~ for**
(staff) procurar; **advertisement**
[əd'vəːtɪsmənt] N (classified)
anúncio; (display, TV) propaganda,
anúncio; **advertising** N
publicidade f

advice [əd'vaɪs] N conselhos mpl; (notification) aviso; **piece of ~** conselho; **to take legal ~** consultar um advogado

advise [əd'vaɪz] VT aconselhar; (inform): **to ~ sb of sth** avisar alguém de algo; **to ~ sb against sth** desaconselhar algo a alguém; **to ~ sb against doing sth** aconselhar alguém a não fazer algo; **advisory** ADJ consultivo; **in an advisory capacity** na qualidade de assessor(a) or consultor(a)

advocate [vt 'ædvəkeɪt, n 'ædvəkɪt] VT defender; (recommend) advogar ▶ N advogado(-a); (supporter) defensor(a) m/f

Aegean [iː'dʒiːən] N: **the ~ (Sea)** o (mar) Egeu

aerial ['ɛərɪəl] N antena ▶ ADJ aéreo

aerobics [ɛə'rəubɪks] N ginástica

aeroplane ['ɛərəpleɪn] (BRIT) N avião m

aerosol ['ɛərəsɔl] N aerossol m

affair [ə'fɛər] N (matter) assunto; (business) negócio; (question) questão f; (also: **love ~**) caso

affect [ə'fɛkt] VT afetar; (move) comover; **affected** ADJ afetado

affection [ə'fɛkʃən] N afeto, afeição f; **affectionate** ADJ afetuoso

afflict [ə'flɪkt] VT afligir

affluent ['æfluənt] ADJ rico; **the ~ society** a sociedade de abundância

afford [ə'fɔːd] VT (provide) fornecer; (goods etc) ter dinheiro suficiente para; (permit o.s.): **I can't ~ the time** não tenho tempo; **affordable** ADJ acessível

afraid [ə'freɪd] ADJ assustado; **to be ~ of/to** ter medo de; **I am ~ that** lamento que; **I'm ~ so/not** receio que sim/não

Africa ['æfrɪkə] N África; **African** ADJ, N africano(-a)

after ['ɑːftər] PREP depois de ▶ ADV depois ▶ CONJ depois que; **a quarter ~ two** (US) duas e quinze; **what are you ~?** o que você quer?; **who are you ~?** quem procura?; **~ having done** tendo feito; **to ask ~ sb** perguntar por alguém; **~ all** afinal (de contas); **~ you!** passe primeiro!; **aftermath** N consequências fpl; **afternoon** N tarde f; **after-shave, after-shave lotion** N loção f após-barba; **aftersun** ['ɑːftəsʌn] N loção f pós-sol; **afterwards** ADV depois

again [ə'gɛn] ADV (once more) outra vez; (repeatedly) de novo; **to do sth ~** voltar a fazer algo; **~ and ~** repetidas vezes

against [ə'gɛnst] PREP contra; (compared to) em contraste com

age [eɪdʒ] N idade f; (period) época ▶ VT, VI envelhecer; **he's 20 years of ~** ele tem 20 anos de idade; **to come of ~** atingir a maioridade; **it's been ~s since I saw him** faz muito tempo que eu não o vejo; **~d 10** de 10 anos de idade; **aged** ['eɪdʒɪd] ADJ idoso ▶ NPL: **the aged** os idosos; **age group** N faixa etária; **age limit** N idade f mínima/máxima

agency ['eɪdʒənsɪ] N agência; (government body) órgão m

agenda [ə'dʒɛndə] N ordem f do dia

agent ['eɪdʒənt] N agente m/f

aggravate ['ægrəveɪt] VT agravar; (annoy) irritar

aggressive [ə'grɛsɪv] ADJ agressivo
AGM N ABBR (= *annual general meeting*) AGO f
ago [ə'gəʊ] ADV: **2 days ~** há 2 dias (atrás); **not long ~** há pouco tempo; **how long ~?** há quanto tempo?
agony ['ægənɪ] N (*pain*) dor f; **to be in ~** sofrer dores terríveis
agree [ə'griː] VT combinar ▶ VI (*correspond*) corresponder; **to ~ (with)** concordar (com); **to ~ to do** aceitar fazer; **to ~ to sth** consentir algo; **to ~ that** concordar or admitir que; **agreeable** ADJ agradável; (*willing*) disposto; **agreed** ADJ combinado; **agreement** N acordo; (*Comm*) contrato; **in agreement** de acordo
agricultural [ægrɪ'kʌltʃərəl] ADJ (*of crops*) agrícola; (*of crops and cattle*) agropecuário
agriculture ['ægrɪkʌltʃər] N (*of crops*) agricultura; (*of crops and cattle*) agropecuária
ahead [ə'hɛd] ADV adiante; **go right** or **straight ~** siga em frente; **go ~!** (*fig*) vá em frente!; **~ of** na frente de
aid [eɪd] N ajuda ▶ VT ajudar; **in ~ of** em benefício de; **to ~ and abet** (*Jur*) ser cúmplice de
AIDS [eɪdz] N ABBR (= *acquired immune deficiency syndrome*) AIDS f (BR), SIDA f (PT)
aim [eɪm] VT: **to ~ sth (at)** apontar algo (para); (*missile, remark*) dirigir algo (a) ▶ VI (*also*: **take ~**) apontar ▶ N (*skill*) pontaria; (*objective*) objetivo; **to ~ at** mirar; **to ~ to do** pretender fazer
ain't [eɪnt] (*inf*) = **am not; aren't; isn't**
air [ɛər] N ar m; (*appearance*) aparência, aspecto ▶ VT arejar; (*grievances, ideas*) discutir ▶ CPD aéreo; **to throw sth into the ~** jogar algo para cima; **by ~** (*travel*) de avião; **to be on the ~** (*Radio, TV*) estar no ar; **air bed** (BRIT) N colchão *m* de ar; **air conditioning** N ar-condicionado; **aircraft** N INV aeronave f; **airfield** N campo de aviação; **Air Force** N Força Aérea, Aeronáutica; **air hostess** (BRIT) N aeromoça (BR), hospedeira (PT); **airline** N linha aérea; **airliner** N avião *m* de passageiros; **airmail** N: **by airmail** por via aérea; **airplane** (US) N avião *m*; **airport** N aeroporto; **airsick** ADJ: **to be airsick** enjoar-se (no avião); **airtight** ADJ hermético; **airy** ADJ (*room*) arejado; (*manner*) leviano
aisle [aɪl] N (*of church*) nave f; (*of theatre etc*) corredor *m*
ajar [ə'dʒɑːʳ] ADJ entreaberto
alarm [ə'lɑːm] N alarme *m*; (*anxiety*) inquietação f ▶ VT alarmar; **alarm clock** N despertador *m*
album ['ælbəm] N (*for stamps etc*) álbum *m*; (*record*) elepê *m*
alcohol ['ælkəhɔl] N álcool *m*; **alcohol-free** ADJ sem álcool; **alcoholic** [ælkə'hɔlɪk] ADJ alcoólico ▶ N alcoólatra *m/f*
ale [eɪl] N cerveja
alert [ə'ləːt] ADJ atento; (*to danger, opportunity*) alerta ▶ N alerta *m* ▶ VT: **to ~ sb (to sth)** alertar alguém (de or sobre algo); **to be on the ~** estar alerta; (*Mil*) ficar de prontidão
Algarve [æl'gɑːv] N: **the ~** o Algarve
algebra ['ældʒɪbrə] N álgebra
Algeria [æl'dʒɪərɪə] N Argélia
alias ['eɪlɪəs] ADV também chamado ▶ N (*of criminal*) alcunha; (*of writer*) pseudônimo

alibi ['ælɪbaɪ] N álibi *m*

alien ['eɪlɪən] N estrangeiro(-a); (*from space*) alienígena *m/f* ▶ ADJ: **~ to** alheio a

alight [ə'laɪt] ADJ em chamas; (*eyes*) aceso; (*expression*) intento ▶ VI (*passenger*) descer (de um veículo); (*bird*) pousar

alike [ə'laɪk] ADJ semelhante ▶ ADV similarmente, igualmente; **to look ~** parecer-se

alive [ə'laɪv] ADJ vivo; (*lively*) alegre

(KEYWORD)

all [ɔːl] ADJ (*singular*) todo(-a); (*plural*) todos(-as); **all day/night** o dia inteiro/a noite inteira; **all five came** todos os cinco vieram; **all the books/food** todos os livros/toda a comida
▶ PRON **1** tudo; **all of us/the boys went** todos nós fomos/todos os meninos foram; **is that all?** é só isso?; (*in shop*) mais alguma coisa? **2** (*in phrases*): **above all** sobretudo; **after all** afinal (de contas); **not at all** (*in answer to question*) em absoluto, absolutamente não; **I'm not at all tired** não estou nada cansado; **anything at all will do** qualquer coisa serve; **all in all** ao todo
▶ ADV todo, completamente; **all alone** completamente só; **it's not as hard as all that** não é tão difícil assim; **all the more** ainda mais; **all the better** tanto melhor, melhor ainda; **all but** quase; **the score is 2 all** o jogo está empatado em 2 a 2

allegiance [ə'liːdʒəns] N lealdade *f*

allergic [ə'lɜːdʒɪk] ADJ: **~ (to)** alérgico (a)

allergy ['ælədʒɪ] N alergia

alleviate [ə'liːvɪeɪt] VT (*pain*) aliviar; (*difficulty*) minorar

alley ['ælɪ] N viela

alliance [ə'laɪəns] N aliança

all-in (BRIT) ADJ, ADV (*charge*) tudo incluído

allocate ['æləkeɪt] VT destinar

allot [ə'lɒt] VT: **to ~ to** designar para

all-out ADJ (*effort etc*) máximo ▶ ADV: **all out** com toda a força

allow [ə'lau] VT permitir; (*claim, goal*) admitir; (*sum, time estimated*) calcular; (*concede*): **to ~ that** reconhecer que; **to ~ sb to do** permitir a alguém fazer; **allow for** VT FUS levar em conta; **allowance** [ə'lauəns] N ajuda de custo; (*welfare, payment*) pensão *f*, auxílio; (*Tax*) abatimento; **to make allowances for** levar em consideração

all right ADV (*well*) bem; (*correctly*) corretamente; (*as answer*) está bem!

ally [*n* 'ælaɪ, *vt* ə'laɪ] N aliado ▶ VT: **to ~ o.s. with** aliar-se com

almighty [ɔːl'maɪtɪ] ADJ onipotente; (*row etc*) maior

almond ['ɑːmənd] N amêndoa

almost ['ɔːlməust] ADV quase

alone [ə'ləun] ADJ só, sozinho ▶ ADV só, somente; **to leave sb ~** deixar alguém em paz; **to leave sth ~** não tocar em algo; **let ~ ...** sem falar em ...

along [ə'lɒŋ] PREP por, ao longo de ▶ ADV: **is he coming ~?** ele vem conosco?; **he was hopping/ limping ~** ele ia pulando/ coxeando; **~ with** junto com; **all ~** o tempo tudo; **alongside** PREP ao lado de ▶ ADV encostado

aloof [ə'lu:f] ADJ afastado, altivo
▶ ADV: **to stand ~** afastar-se
aloud [ə'laud] ADV em voz alta
alphabet ['ælfəbɛt] N alfabeto
Alps [ælps] NPL: **the ~** os Alpes
already [ɔ:l'rɛdɪ] ADV já
alright ['ɔ:l'raɪt] (BRIT) ADV = **all right**
also ['ɔ:lsəu] ADV também;
(*moreover*) além disso
altar ['ɔltəʳ] N altar m
alter ['ɔltəʳ] VT alterar ▶ VI
modificar-se
alternate [*adj* ɔl'tə:nɪt, *vi* 'ɔltə:neɪt]
ADJ alternado; (US: *alternative*)
alternativo ▶ VI: **to ~ with**
alternar-se (com)
alternative [ɔl'tə:nətɪv] ADJ
alternativo ▶ N alternativa;
alternatively ADV: **alternatively
one could ...** por outro lado se
podia ...
although [ɔ:l'ðəu] CONJ embora;
(*given that*) se bem que
altitude ['æltɪtju:d] N altitude f
altogether [ɔ:ltə'gɛðəʳ] ADV
totalmente; (*on the whole*) no total
aluminium [ælju'mɪnɪəm] (BRIT)
N alumínio
aluminum [ə'lu:mɪnəm] (US) N =
aluminium
always ['ɔ:lweɪz] ADV sempre
Alzheimer's ['æltshaɪməz],
Alzheimer's disease N mal m de
Alzheimer
am [æm] VB *see* **be**
a.m. ADV ABBR (= *ante meridiem*) da
manhã
amateur ['æmətəʳ] ADJ, N
amador(a) m/f
amaze [ə'meɪz] VT pasmar; **to be
~d (at)** espantar-se (de or com);
amazement N pasmo, espanto;
amazing ADJ surpreendente;
(*fantastic*) fantástico

Amazon ['æməzən] N Amazonas m
ambassador [æm'bæsədəʳ] N
embaixador/embaixatriz m/f
amber ['æmbəʳ] N âmbar m; **at ~**
(BRIT Aut) em amarelo
ambiguous [æm'bɪgjuəs] ADJ
ambíguo
ambition [æm'bɪʃən] N ambição f;
ambitious ADJ ambicioso
ambulance ['æmbjuləns] N
ambulância
ambush ['æmbuʃ] N emboscada
▶ VT emboscar
amend [ə'mɛnd] VT emendar; **to
make ~s (for)** compensar
America [ə'mɛrɪkə] N (*continent*)
América; (*USA*) Estados Unidos mpl;
American ADJ americano; (*from
USA*) norte-americano,
estadunidense ▶ N americano(-a);
(*from USA*) norte-americano(-a)
amicable ['æmɪkəbl] ADJ amigável
ammunition [æmju'nɪʃən] N
munição f
among [ə'mʌŋ], **amongst**
[ə'mʌŋst] PREP entre, no meio de
amount [ə'maunt] N quantidade f;
(*of money etc*) quantia ▶ VI: **to ~ to**
(*total*) montar a; (*be same as*)
equivaler a, significar
amp ['æmp], **ampere** ['æmpɛəʳ] N
ampère m
ample ['æmpl] ADJ amplo;
(*abundant*) abundante; (*enough*)
suficiente
amplifier ['æmplɪfaɪəʳ] N
amplificador m
amuse [ə'mju:z] VT divertir;
(*distract*) distrair; **amusement** N
diversão f; (*pleasure*) divertimento;
(*pastime*) passatempo;
amusement park N parque m de
diversões
an [æn, ən, n] INDEF ART *see* **a**

anaesthetic [ænɪs'θεtɪk], (US)
anesthetic N anestésico
analyse ['ænəlaɪz], (US) **analyze**
VT analisar; **analysis** [ə'næləsɪs]
(pl **analyses**) N análise f; **analyst**
['ænəlɪst] N analista m/f;
(psychoanalyst) psicanalista m/f
analyze ['ænəlaɪz] (US) VT =
analyse
anarchy ['ænəkɪ] N anarquia
anatomy [ə'nætəmɪ] N anatomia
ancestor ['ænsɪstər] N
antepassado
anchor ['æŋkər] N âncora ▶ VI
(also: **to drop ~**) ancorar, fundear
▶ VT (fig): **to ~ sth to** firmar algo
em; **to weigh ~** levantar âncoras
anchovy ['æntʃəvɪ] N enchova
ancient ['eɪnʃənt] ADJ antigo;
(person, car) velho
and [ænd] CONJ e; **~ so on** e assim
por diante; **try ~ come** tente vir;
he talked ~ talked ele falou sem
parar; **better ~ better** cada vez
melhor
Andes ['ændiːz] NPL: **the ~** os
Andes
angel ['eɪndʒəl] N anjo
anger ['æŋgər] N raiva
angina [æn'dʒaɪnə] N angina (de
peito)
angle ['æŋgl] N ângulo;
(viewpoint): **from their ~** do ponto
de vista deles
Anglican ['æŋglɪkən] ADJ, N
anglicano(-a)
angling ['æŋglɪŋ] N pesca à vara
(BR) or à linha (PT)
angry ['æŋgrɪ] ADJ zangado; **to be
~ with sb/at sth** estar zangado
com alguém/algo; **to get ~**
zangar-se
anguish ['æŋgwɪʃ] N (physical) dor f,
sofrimento; (mental) angústia

animal ['ænɪməl] N animal m,
bicho ▶ ADJ animal
aniseed ['ænɪsiːd] N erva-doce f,
anis f
ankle ['æŋkl] N tornozelo
annex [n 'ænεks, vt ə'nεks] N
(BRIT: building) anexo ▶ VT anexar
anniversary [ænɪ'vɜːsərɪ] N
aniversário
announce [ə'naʊns] VT anunciar;
announcement N anúncio;
(official) comunicação f; (in letter
etc) aviso; **announcer** N (Radio, TV)
locutor(a) m/f
annoy [ə'nɔɪ] VT aborrecer; **don't
get ~ed!** não se aborreça!;
annoying ADJ irritante
annual ['ænjuəl] ADJ anual ▶ N
(Bot) anual f; (book) anuário
anonymous [ə'nɒnɪməs] ADJ
anônimo
anorak ['ænəræk] N anoraque m
(BR), anorak m (PT)
another [ə'nʌðər] ADJ: **~ book**
(one more) outro livro, mais um
livro; (a different one) um outro livro,
um livro diferente ▶ PRON outro;
see also **one**
answer ['ɑːnsər] N resposta; (to
problem) solução f ▶ VI responder
▶ VT (reply to) responder a;
(problem) resolver; **in ~ to your
letter** em resposta or
respondendo à sua carta; **to ~ the
phone** atender o telefone; **to ~
the bell** or **the door** atender à
porta; **answer back** VI replicar,
retrucar; **answer for** VT FUS
responder por, responsabilizar-se
por; **answer to** VT FUS (description)
corresponder a; **answering
machine** N secretária eletrônica;
answerphone N (esp BRIT)
secretária eletrônica

ant [ænt] N formiga

Antarctic [ænt'ɑːktɪk] N: **the ~** o Antártico

antenatal ['æntɪ'neɪtl] ADJ pré-natal

anthem ['ænθəm] N: **national ~** hino nacional

anticipate [æn'tɪsɪpeɪt] VT prever; (*expect*) esperar; (*look forward to*) aguardar, esperar; **anticipation** N expectativa; (*eagerness*) entusiasmo

anticlimax [æntɪ'klaɪmæks] N desapontamento

anticlockwise [æntɪ'klɔkwaɪz] (*BRIT*) ADV em sentido anti-horário

antics ['æntɪks] NPL bobices *fpl*; (*of child*) travessuras *fpl*

antifreeze ['æntɪfriːz] N anticongelante *m*

antihistamine [æntɪ'hɪstəmiːn] N anti-histamínico

antique [æn'tiːk] N antiguidade *f* ▶ ADJ antigo; **antique shop** N loja de antiguidades

antiseptic [æntɪ'sɛptɪk] N antisséptico

antisocial [æntɪ'səuʃəl] ADJ antissocial

antivirus ['æntɪ'vaɪərəs] ADJ antivírus *m inv*; **~ software** software antivírus

antlers ['æntləz] NPL esgalhos *mpl*, chifres *mpl*

anxiety [æŋ'zaɪətɪ] N (*worry*) inquietude *f*; (*eagerness*) ânsia; (*Med*) ansiedade *f*; **~ to do** ânsia de fazer

anxious ['æŋkʃəs] ADJ (*worried*) preocupado; (*worrying*) angustiante; (*keen*) ansioso; **~ to do/for sth** ansioso para fazer/por algo; **to be ~ that** desejar que

(KEYWORD)

any ['ɛnɪ] ADJ **1** (*in questions etc*) algum(a); **have you any butter/ children?** você tem manteiga/ filhos?; **if there are any tickets left** se houver alguns bilhetes sobrando

2 (*with negative*) nenhum(a); **I haven't any money/books** não tenho dinheiro/livros

3 (*no matter which*) qualquer; **choose any book you like** escolha qualquer livro que quiser

4 (*in phrases*): **in any case** em todo o caso; **any day now** qualquer dia desses; **at any moment** a qualquer momento; **at any rate** de qualquer modo; **any time** a qualquer momento; (*whenever*) quando quer que seja

▶ PRON **1** (*in questions etc*) algum(a); **have you got any?** tem algum?

2 (*with negative*) nenhum(a); **I haven't any (of them)** não tenho nenhum (deles)

3 (*no matter which one(s)*): **take any of those books (you like)** leve qualquer um desses livros (que você quiser)

▶ ADV **1** (*in questions etc*) algo; **do you want any more soup/ sandwiches?** quer mais sopa/ sanduíches?; **are you feeling any better?** você está se sentindo melhor?

2 (*with negative*) nada; **I can't hear him any more** não consigo mais ouvi-lo

anybody ['ɛnɪbɔdɪ] PRON qualquer um, qualquer pessoa; (*in interrogative sentences*) alguém

anyhow ['ɛnɪhau] ADV (*at any rate*) de qualquer modo, de qualquer maneira; **I shall go ~** eu irei de qualquer jeito; **do it ~ you like** faça do jeito que você quiser; **she leaves things just ~** ela deixa as coisas de qualquer maneira

anyone ['ɛnɪwʌn] PRON (*in questions etc*) alguém; (*with negative*) ninguém; (*no matter who*) quem quer que seja; **can you see ~?** você pode ver alguém?; **if ~ should phone …** se alguém telefonar; **~ could do it** qualquer um(a) poderia fazer isso

anything ['ɛnɪθɪŋ] PRON (*in questions etc*) alguma coisa; (*with negative*) nada; (*no matter what*) qualquer coisa; **can you see ~?** você pode ver alguma coisa?

anyway ['ɛnɪweɪ] ADV (*at any rate*) de qualquer modo; (*besides*) além disso; **I shall go ~** eu irei de qualquer jeito

anywhere ['ɛnɪwɛəʳ] ADV (*in questions etc*) em algum lugar; (*with negative*) em parte nenhuma; (*no matter where*) não importa onde, onde quer que seja; **can you see him ~?** você pode vê-lo em algum lugar?; **I can't see him ~** não o vejo em parte nenhuma; **~ in the world** em qualquer lugar do mundo

apart [ə'pɑːt] ADV à parte, à distância; (*separately*) separado; **10 miles ~** a uma distância de 10 milhas um do outro; **to take ~** desmontar; **~ from** além de, à parte de

apartment [ə'pɑːtmənt] (*US*) N apartamento

ape [eɪp] N macaco ► VT macaquear, imitar

aperitif [ə'pɛrɪtɪv] N aperitivo

aperture ['æpətʃuəʳ] N orifício; (*Phot*) abertura

APEX ['eɪpɛks] N (= *advance passenger excursion*) tarifa aérea com desconto por compra antecipada

apologize [ə'pɔlədʒaɪz] VI: **to ~ (for sth to sb)** desculpar-se or pedir desculpas (por or de algo a alguém); **apology** N desculpas *fpl*

apostrophe [ə'pɔstrəfɪ] N apóstrofo

app [æp] (*inf*) N ABBR (= *application program*) aplicativo (BR), aplicação f (PT)

appalling [ə'pɔːlɪŋ] ADJ (*shocking*) chocante; (*awful*) terrível

apparatus [æpə'reɪtəs] N aparelho; (*in gym*) aparelhos *mpl*; (*organization*) aparato

apparent [ə'pærənt] ADJ aparente; (*obvious*) claro, patente; **apparently** ADV aparentemente, pelo(s) visto(s)

appeal [ə'piːl] VI (*Jur*) apelar, recorrer ► N (*Jur*) recurso, apelação f; (*request*) pedido; (*plea*) súplica; (*charm*) atração f; **to ~ (to sb) for** suplicar (a alguém); **to ~ to** atrair; **to ~ to sb for mercy** pedir misericórdia a alguém; **appealing** ADJ atraente

appear [ə'pɪəʳ] VI aparecer; (*Jur*) apresentar-se, comparecer; (*publication*) ser publicado; (*seem*) parecer; **to ~ in "Hamlet"** trabalhar em "Hamlet"; **to ~ on TV** (*person, news item*) sair na televisão; (*programme*) passar na televisão; **appearance** N aparecimento; (*presence*) comparecimento; (*look, aspect*) aparência

appendicitis [əpɛndɪ'saɪtɪs] N apendicite f

appendix [ə'pɛndɪks] (*pl* **appendices**) N apêndice *m*

appetite ['æpɪtaɪt] N apetite m;
(fig) desejo

appetizer ['æpɪtaɪzəʳ] N (food)
tira-gosto; (drink) aperitivo

applaud [ə'plɔːd] VI aplaudir ▶ VT
aplaudir; (praise) admirar;
applause N aplausos mpl

apple ['æpl] N maçã f

appliance [ə'plaɪəns] N aparelho;
electrical or **domestic ~s**
eletrodomésticos mpl

applicant ['æplɪkənt] N: **~ (for)**
(for post) candidato(-a) (a); (Admin:
for benefit etc) requerente m/f(de)

application [æplɪ'keɪʃən] N
aplicação f; (for a job, a grant etc)
candidatura, requerimento; (hard
work) empenho; **application form**
N (formulário de) requerimento

apply [ə'plaɪ] VT (paint etc) usar;
(law etc) pôr em prática ▶ VI: **to ~ to**
(be suitable for) ser aplicável a; (be
relevant to) valer para; (ask) pedir; **to
~ for** (permit, grant) solicitar, pedir;
(job) candidatar-se a; **to ~ o.s. to**
aplicar-se a, dedicar-se a

appoint [ə'pɔɪnt] VT (to post)
nomear; **appointment** N
(engagement) encontro,
compromisso; (at doctor's etc) hora
marcada; (act) nomeação f; (post)
cargo; **to make an appointment
(with sb)** marcar um encontro
(com alguém)

appraisal [ə'preɪzl] N avaliação f

appreciate [ə'priːʃɪeɪt] VT (like)
apreciar, estimar; (be grateful for)
agradecer; (understand)
compreender ▶ VI (Comm)
valorizar-se; **appreciation** N
apreciação f, estima; (understanding)
compreensão f; (gratitude)
agradecimento; (Comm)
valorização f

apprehensive [æprɪ'hɛnsɪv] ADJ
apreensivo, receoso

apprentice [ə'prɛntɪs] N aprendiz
m/f

approach [ə'prəutʃ] VI
aproximar-se ▶ VT aproximar-se de;
(ask, apply to) dirigir-se a; (subject,
passer-by) abordar ▶ N aproximação f;
(access) acesso; (to problem,
situation) enfoque m

appropriate [adj ə'prəuprɪɪt, vt
ə'prəuprɪeɪt] ADJ (apt) apropriado;
(relevant) adequado ▶ VT
apropriar-se de

approval [ə'pruːvəl] N aprovação f;
on ~ (Comm) a contento

approve [ə'pruːv] VT (publication,
product) autorizar; (motion, decision)
aprovar; **approve of** VT FUS aprovar

approximate [ə'prɔksɪmɪt] ADJ
aproximado; **approximately** ADV
aproximadamente

apricot ['eɪprɪkɔt] N damasco

April ['eɪprəl] N abril m

apron ['eɪprən] N avental m

apt [æpt] ADJ (suitable) adequado;
(appropriate) apropriado; (likely):
~ to do sujeito a fazer

Aquarius [ə'kwɛərɪəs] N Aquário

Arab ['ærəb] ADJ, N árabe m/f

Arabian [ə'reɪbɪən] ADJ árabe

Arabic ['ærəbɪk] ADJ árabe;
(numerals) arábico ▶ N (Ling) árabe m

arbitrary ['ɑːbɪtrərɪ] ADJ arbitrário

arbitration [ɑːbɪ'treɪʃən] N
arbitragem f

arcade [ɑː'keɪd] N arcos mpl;
(passage with shops) galeria

arch [ɑːtʃ] N arco; (of foot) curvatura
▶ VT arquear, curvar

archaeology [ɑːkɪ'ɔlədʒɪ], (US)
archeology N arqueologia

archbishop [ɑːtʃ'bɪʃəp] N
arcebispo

archeology [ɑːkɪˈɔlədʒɪ] (US) N = **archaeology**

architect [ˈɑːkɪtɛkt] N arquiteto(-a); **architecture** N arquitetura

Arctic [ˈɑːktɪk] ADJ ártico ▶ N: **the ~** o Ártico

are [ɑː] VB see **be**

area [ˈɛərɪə] N (zone) zona, região f; (part of place) região; (in room, of knowledge, experience) área; (Math) superfície f, extensão f; **area code** (US) N (Tel) (código) DDD (BR), indicativo (PT)

aren't [ɑːnt] = **are not**

Argentina [ɑːdʒənˈtiːnə] N Argentina

arguably [ˈɑːgjuəblɪ] ADV possivelmente

argue [ˈɑːgjuː] VI (quarrel) discutir; (reason) argumentar; **to ~ that** sustentar que

argument [ˈɑːgjumənt] N (reasons) argumento; (quarrel) briga, discussão f

Aries [ˈɛərɪz] N Áries m

arise [əˈraɪz] (pt **arose**, pp **arisen**) VI (emerge) surgir

arithmetic [əˈrɪθmətɪk] N aritmética

arm [ɑːm] N braço; (of clothing) manga; (of organization etc) divisão f ▶ VT armar; **arms** NPL (weapons) armas fpl; (Heraldry) brasão m; **~ in ~** de braços dados

armchair N poltrona

armed ADJ armado

armour [ˈɑːməʳ], (US) **armor** N armadura

armpit [ˈɑːmpɪt] N sovaco

armrest [ˈɑːmrɛst] N braço (de poltrona)

army [ˈɑːmɪ] N exército

aroma [əˈrəumə] N aroma; **aromatherapy** N aromaterapia

arose [əˈrəuz] PT of **arise**

around [əˈraund] ADV em volta; (in the area) perto ▶ PREP em volta de; (near) perto de; (fig: about) cerca de

arouse [əˈrauz] VT despertar; (anger) provocar

arrange [əˈreɪndʒ] VT (organize) organizar; (put in order) arrumar ▶ VI: **to ~ to do sth** combinar em or ficar de fazer algo; **arrangement** N (agreement) acordo; (order, layout) disposição f; **arrangements** NPL (plans) planos mpl; (preparations) preparativos mpl; **home deliveries by arrangement** entregas a domicílio por convênio; **I'll make all the necessary arrangements** eu vou tomar todas as providências necessárias

array [əˈreɪ] N: **~ of** variedade f de

arrears [əˈrɪəz] NPL atrasos mpl; **to be in ~ with one's rent** estar atrasado com o aluguel

arrest [əˈrɛst] VT prender, deter; (sb's attention) chamar, prender ▶ N detenção f, prisão f; **under ~** preso

arrival [əˈraɪvəl] N chegada; **new ~** recém-chegado; (baby) recém-nascido

arrive [əˈraɪv] VI chegar

arrogant [ˈærəgənt] ADJ arrogante

arrow [ˈærəu] N flecha; (sign) seta

arse [ɑːs] (BRIT !) N cu m (!)

arson [ˈɑːsn] N incêndio premeditado

art [ɑːt] N arte f; (skill) habilidade f, jeito; **Arts** NPL (Sch) letras fpl

artery [ˈɑːtərɪ] N (Med) artéria; (fig) estrada principal

art gallery N museu m de belas artes; (small, private) galeria de arte

arthritis [ɑ:'θraɪtɪs] N artrite f
artichoke ['ɑ:tɪtʃəuk] N (globe artichoke) alcachofra; (also: **Jerusalem ~**) topinambo
article ['ɑ:tɪkl] N artigo; **articles** NPL (BRIT Jur: training) contrato de aprendizagem; **~s of clothing** peças fpl de vestuário
articulate [adj ɑ:'tɪkjulɪt, vt ɑ:'tɪkjuleɪt] ADJ (speech) bem articulado; (writing) bem escrito; (person) eloquente ▶ VT expressar
artificial [ɑ:tɪ'fɪʃəl] ADJ artificial; (person, manner) afetado
artist ['ɑ:tɪst] N artista m/f; (Mus) intérprete m/f; **artistic** [ɑ:'tɪstɪk] ADJ artístico
art school N ≈ escola de artes

(KEYWORD)

as [æz, əz] CONJ 1 (referring to time) quando; **as the years went by** no decorrer dos anos; **he came in as I was leaving** ele chegou quando eu estava saindo; **as from tomorrow** a partir de amanhã
2 (in comparisons) tão … como, tanto(s) … como; **as big as** tão grande como; **twice as big as** duas vezes maior que; **as much/many as** tanto/tantos como; **as much money/many books as** tanto dinheiro quanto/tantos livros quanto; **as soon as** logo que, assim que
3 (since, because) como
4 (referring to manner, way) como; **do as you wish** faça como quiser
5 (concerning): **as for** or **to that** quanto a isso
6: **as if** or **though** como se; **he looked as if he was ill** ele parecia doente
▶ PREP (in the capacity of): **he works as a driver** ele trabalha como motorista; **he gave it to me as a present** ele me deu isso de presente; see also **long, such, well**

a.s.a.p. ABBR = **as soon as possible**
asbestos [æz'bɛstəs] N asbesto, amianto
ash [æʃ] N cinza; (tree, wood) freixo
ashamed [ə'ʃeɪmd] ADJ envergonhado; **to be ~ of** ter vergonha de
ashore [ə'ʃɔ:ʳ] ADV em terra; **to go ~** descer à terra, desembarcar
ashtray ['æʃtreɪ] N cinzeiro
Asia ['eɪʃə] N Ásia; **Asian** ADJ, N asiático(-a)
aside [ə'saɪd] ADV à parte, de lado ▶ N aparte m
ask [ɑ:sk] VT perguntar; (invite) convidar; **to ~ sb sth** perguntar algo a alguém; **to ~ sb to do sth** pedir para alguém fazer algo; **to ~ (sb) a question** fazer uma pergunta (a alguém); **to ~ sb out to dinner** convidar alguém para jantar; **ask after** VT FUS perguntar por; **ask for** VT FUS pedir; **it's just ~ing for it** or **trouble** é procurar encrenca
asleep [ə'sli:p] ADJ dormindo; **to fall ~** dormir, adormecer
asparagus [əs'pærəgəs] N aspargo (BR), espargo (PT)
aspect ['æspɛkt] N aspecto; (direction in which a building etc faces) direção f
aspire [əs'paɪəʳ] VI: **to ~ to** aspirar a
aspirin ['æsprɪn] N aspirina
ass [æs] N jumento, burro; (inf) imbecil m/f; (us!) cu m (!)
assassinate [ə'sæsɪneɪt] VT assassinar

assault [ə'sɔːlt] N assalto ▶VT assaltar, atacar; (*sexually*) agredir, violar

assemble [ə'sɛmbl] VT (*people*) reunir; (*objects*) juntar; (*Tech*) montar ▶ VI reunir-se

assembly [ə'sɛmblɪ] N reunião f; (*institution*) assembleia

assert [ə'səːt] VT afirmar

assess [ə'sɛs] VT avaliar; **assessment** N avaliação f

asset ['æsɛt] N vantagem f, trunfo; **assets** NPL (*property, funds*) bens mpl

assign [ə'saɪn] VT (*date*) fixar; **to ~ (to)** (*task*) designar (a); (*resources*) destinar (a); **assignment** N tarefa

assist [ə'sɪst] VT ajudar; **assistance** N ajuda, auxílio; **assistant** N assistente m/f, auxiliar m/f; (BRIT: *also*: **shop assistant**) vendedor(a) m/f

associate [*adj* ə'səʊʃiɪt, *vt, vi* ə'səʊʃieɪt] ADJ associado; (*professor, director etc*) adjunto ▶ N sócio(-a) ▶ VI: **to ~ with sb** associar-se com alguém ▶ VT associar; **association** N associação f; (*link*) ligação f

assorted [ə'sɔːtɪd] ADJ sortido

assortment [ə'sɔːtmənt] N (*of shapes, colours*) sortimento; (*of books, people*) variedade f

assume [ə'sjuːm] VT (*suppose*) supor, presumir; (*responsibilities etc*) assumir; (*attitude, name*) adotar, tomar; **assumption** [ə'sʌmpʃən] N suposição f, presunção f

assurance [ə'ʃʊərəns] N garantia; (*confidence*) confiança; (*insurance*) seguro

assure [ə'ʃʊər] VT assegurar; (*guarantee*) garantir

asthma ['æsmə] N asma

astonish [ə'stɔnɪʃ] VT assombrar, espantar; **astonishment** N assombro, espanto

astound [ə'staʊnd] VT pasmar, estarrecer

astray [ə'streɪ] ADV: **to go ~** extraviar-se; **to lead ~** desencaminhar

astrology [əs'trɔlədʒɪ] N astrologia

astronaut ['æstrənɔːt] N astronauta m/f

astronomy [əs'trɔnəmɪ] N astronomia

asylum [ə'saɪləm] N (*refuge*) asilo; (*hospital*) manicômio; **asylum seeker** [-siːkər] N solicitante m/f de asilo

(KEYWORD)

at [æt] PREP **1** (*referring to position*) em; (*referring to direction*) a; **at the top** em cima; **at home/school** em casa/ na escola; **to look at sth** olhar para algo

2 (*referring to time*): **at 4 o'clock** às quatro horas; **at night** à noite; **at Christmas** no Natal; **at times** às vezes

3 (*referring to rates, speed etc*): **at £1 a kilo** a uma libra o quilo; **two at a time** de dois em dois

4 (*referring to manner*): **at a stroke** de um golpe; **at peace** em paz

5 (*referring to activity*): **to be at work** estar no trabalho; **to play at cowboys** brincar de mocinho

6 (*referring to cause*): **to be shocked/surprised/annoyed at sth** ficar chocado/surpreso/ chateado com algo; **I went at his suggestion** eu fui por causa da sugestão dele

▶ N (*symbol* @) arroba

ate [eɪt] PT *of* **eat**

atheist ['eɪθɪɪst] N ateu/ateia *m/f*

Athens ['æθɪnz] N Atenas

athlete ['æθliːt] N atleta *m/f*;
athletic [æθ'lɛtɪk] ADJ atlético;
athletics N atletismo

Atlantic [ət'læntɪk] ADJ atlântico
▶ N: **the ~ (Ocean)** o (oceano)
Atlântico

atlas ['ætləs] N atlas *m inv*

ATM ABBR (= *automated teller machine*) caixa eletrônico *m*

atmosphere ['ætməsfɪəʳ] N
atmosfera; (*fig*) ambiente *m*

atom ['ætəm] N átomo; **atomic**
[ə'tɔmɪk] ADJ atômico

attach [ə'tætʃ] VT prender;
(*document, letter*) juntar, anexar;
(*importance etc*) dar; **to be ~ed to**
sb/sth (*like*) ter afeição por alguém/
algo; **to ~ a file to an email** anexar
um arquivo a um e-mail

attachment [ə'tætʃmənt] N (*tool*)
acessório; (*to email*) anexo; (*love*):
~ (to) afeição *f* (por)

attack [ə'tæk] VT atacar; (*subj: criminal*) assaltar; (*task etc*)
empreender ▶ N ataque *m*; (*on sb's life*) atentado; **heart ~** ataque
cardíaco *or* de coração

attain [ə'teɪn] VT (*also*: **~ to**:
happiness, results) alcançar, atingir;
(: *knowledge*) obter

attempt [ə'tɛmpt] N tentativa ▶ VT
tentar; **to make an ~ on sb's life**
atentar contra a vida de alguém

attend [ə'tɛnd] VT (*lectures*) assistir
a; (*school*) cursar; (*church*) ir a;
(*course*) fazer; (*patient*) tratar;
attend to VT FUS (*matter*)
encarregar-se de; (*needs, customer*)
atender a; (*patient*) tratar de;
attendance N comparecimento;
(*people present*) assistência;

attendant N servidor(a) *m/f* ▶ ADJ
concomitante

attention [ə'tɛnʃən] N atenção *f*;
(*care*) cuidados *mpl* ▶ EXCL (*Mil*)
sentido!; **for the ~ of ...** (*Admin*)
atenção ...

attic ['ætɪk] N sótão *m*

attitude ['ætɪtjuːd] N atitude *f*

attorney [ə'tɜːnɪ] N (*US: lawyer*)
advogado(-a)

attract [ə'trækt] VT atrair, chamar;
attraction N atração *f*; **attractive**
ADJ atraente; (*idea, offer*)
interessante

attribute [*n* 'ætrɪbjuːt, *vt* ə'trɪbjuːt]
N atributo ▶ VT: **to ~ sth to** atribuir
algo a

aubergine ['əubəʒiːn] N beringela

auction ['ɔːkʃən] N (*also*: **sale by ~**)
leilão *m* ▶ VT leiloar

audience ['ɔːdɪəns] N (*in theatre, concert etc*) plateia; (*of writer, magazine*) público

audit ['ɔːdɪt] VT fazer a auditoria de

audition [ɔː'dɪʃən] N audição *f*

August ['ɔːgəst] N agosto

aunt [ɑːnt] N tia; **auntie** N titia;
aunty N titia

au pair ['əu'pɛəʳ] N (*also*: **~ girl**) au
pair *f*

Australia [ɔs'treɪlɪə] N Austrália;
Australian ADJ, N australiano(-a)

Austria ['ɔstrɪə] N Áustria;
Austrian ADJ, N austríaco(-a)

authentic [ɔː'θɛntɪk] ADJ autêntico

author ['ɔːθə] N autor(a) *m/f*

authority [ɔː'θɔrɪtɪ] N autoridade *f*;
(*government body*) jurisdição *f*;
(*permission*) autorização *f*; **the**
authorities NPL (*ruling body*) as
autoridades

authorize ['ɔːθəraɪz] VT autorizar

auto ['ɔːtəu] (*US*) N carro,
automóvel *m*

autobiography [ɔːtəbaɪˈɔgrəfɪ]
N autobiografia

autograph [ˈɔːtəgrɑːf] N
autógrafo ▶ VT (photo etc)
autografar

automatic [ɔːtəˈmætɪk] ADJ
automático ▶ N (gun) pistola
automática; (washing machine)
máquina de lavar roupa
automática; (car) carro
automático

automobile [ˈɔːtəməbiːl] (US) N
carro, automóvel m

autonomy [ɔːˈtɔnəmɪ] N
autonomia

autumn [ˈɔːtəm] N outono

auxiliary [ɔːgˈzɪlɪərɪ] ADJ, N
auxiliar m/f

available [əˈveɪləbl] ADJ
disponível; (time) livre

avalanche [ˈævəlɑːnʃ] N
avalanche f

Ave. ABBR (= avenue) Av., Avda.

avenue [ˈævənjuː] N avenida;
(drive) caminho; (means) solução f

average [ˈævərɪdʒ] N média
▶ ADJ (mean) médio; (ordinary)
regular ▶ VT alcançar uma média
de; **on ~** em média; **average
out** VI: **to ~ out at** dar uma
média de

avert [əˈvəːt] VT prevenir; (blow,
one's eyes) desviar

avocado [ævəˈkɑːdəu] N (BRIT:
also: **~ pear**) abacate m

avoid [əˈvɔɪd] VT evitar

await [əˈweɪt] VT esperar,
aguardar

awake [əˈweɪk] (pt **awoke**, pp
awoken) ADJ acordado ▶ VT, VI
despertar, acordar; **~ to** atento a

award [əˈwɔːd] N prêmio,
condecoração f; (Jur: damages)
sentença; (act) concessão f ▶ VT

outorgar, conceder; (damages)
determinar o pagamento de

aware [əˈwɛəʳ] ADJ: **~ of** (conscious)
consciente de; (informed)
informado de or sobre; **to become
~ of** reparar em, saber de;
awareness N consciência

away [əˈweɪ] ADV fora; (faraway)
muito longe; **two kilometres ~**
a dois quilômetros de distância;
the holiday was two weeks ~
faltavam duas semanas para as
férias; **he's ~ for a week** está
ausente uma semana; **to take ~**
levar; **to work/pedal** etc **~**
trabalhar/pedalar etc sem parar;
to fade ~ (colour) desbotar;
(enthusiasm, sound) diminuir

awe [ɔː] N temor m respeitoso

awful [ˈɔːfəl] ADJ terrível, horrível;
(quantity): **an ~ lot of** um monte
de; **awfully** ADV (very) muito

awkward [ˈɔːkwəd] ADJ (person,
movement) desajeitado; (shape)
incômodo; (problem) difícil;
(situation) embaraçoso, delicado

awoke [əˈwəuk] PT of **awake**;
awoken [əˈwəukən] PP of **awake**

axe [æks], (US) **ax** N machado ▶ VT
(project etc) abandonar; (jobs)
reduzir

axle [ˈæksl] N (Aut) eixo

B [biː] N (*Mus*) si *m*

baby ['beɪbɪ] N neném *m/f*, nenê *m/f*, bebê *m/f*; (*us inf*) querido(-a); **baby carriage** (*us*) N carrinho de bebê; **baby food** N papinha de bebê; **baby-sit** *irreg* VI tomar conta da(s) criança(s); **baby-sitter** N baby-sitter *m/f*; **baby wipe** N lenço umedecido

bachelor ['bætʃələ^r] N solteiro; **B~ of Arts** ≈ bacharel *m* em Letras; **B~ of Science** ≈ bacharel *m* em Ciências

back [bæk] N (*of person*) costas *fpl*; (*of animal*) lombo; (*of hand*) dorso; (*of car, train*) parte *f* traseira; (*of house*) fundos *mpl*; (*of chair*) encosto; (*of page*) verso; (*of book*) lombada; (*of crowd*) fundo; (*Football*) zagueiro (BR), defesa *m* (PT) ▶ VT (*candidate: also:* **~ up**) apoiar; (*horse: at races*) apostar em; (*car*) dar ré com ▶ VI (*car etc: also:* **~ up**) dar ré (BR), fazer marcha atrás (PT) ▶ CPD (*payment*) atrasado; (*Aut: seats, wheels*) de trás ▶ ADV (*not forward*) para trás; **he's ~** ele voltou; **throw the ball ~** devolva a bola; **he called ~** (*again*) chamou de novo; **he ran ~** voltou correndo; **back down** VI desistir; **back out** VI (*of promise*) voltar atrás, recuar; **back up** VT (*support*) apoiar; (*Comput*) fazer um backup de; **backache** N dor *f* nas costas; **backbone** N coluna vertebral; (*fig*) esteio; **backfire** VI (*Aut*) engasgar; (*plan*) sair pela culatra; **background** N fundo; (*of events*) antecedentes *mpl*; (*basic knowledge*) bases *fpl*; (*experience*) conhecimentos *mpl*, experiência; **family background** antecedentes *mpl* familiares; **backing** N (*fig*) apoio; **backlog** N: **backlog of work** atrasos *mpl*; **backpack** N mochila; **back pay** N salário atrasado; **backstage** ADV nos bastidores; **backstroke** N nado de costas; **backup** ADJ (*train, plane*) reserva *inv*; (*Comput*) de backup ▶ N (*support*) apoio; (*Comput: also:* **backup file**) backup *m*; **backward** ADJ (*movement*) para trás; (*person, country*) atrasado; **backwards** ADV (*move, go*) para trás; (*read a list*) às avessas; (*fall*) de costas; **backyard** N quintal *m*

bacon ['beɪkən] N toucinho, bacon *m*

bacteria [bæk'tɪərɪə] NPL bactérias *fpl*

bad [bæd] ADJ mau/má, ruim; (*child*) levado; (*mistake, injury*) grave; (*meat, food*) estragado; **his ~ leg** sua perna machucada; **to go ~** estragar-se; **bad debt** N crédito duvidoso

badge [bædʒ] N (*of school etc*) emblema *m*; (*policeman's*) crachá *m*

badger ['bædʒər] N texugo
badly ['bædlı] ADV mal;
~ **wounded** gravemente ferido;
he needs it ~ faz-lhe grande falta;
to be ~ off (for money) estar com
pouco dinheiro
badminton ['bædmɪntən] N
badminton m
bad-tempered ADJ mal
humorado; (temporary) de mau
humor
bag [bæg] N saco, bolsa; (handbag)
bolsa; (satchel, shopping bag)
sacola; (case) mala; **~s of ...** (inf:
lots of) ... de sobra; **baggage** N
bagagem f; **baggage allowance**
N franquia de bagagem; **baggy** ADJ
folgado, largo; **bagpipes** NPL gaita
de foles
bail [beɪl] N (payment) fiança;
(release) liberdade f sob fiança ▶ VT
(prisoner: grant bail to) libertar sob
fiança; (boat: also: ~ **out**) baldear a
água de; **on ~** sob fiança; **bail out**
VT (prisoner) afiançar
bait [beɪt] N isca, engodo; (for
criminal etc) atrativo, chamariz m
▶ VT iscar, cevar; (person)
apoquentar
bake [beɪk] VT cozinhar ao forno;
(Tech: clay etc) cozer ▶ VI assar;
baked beans NPL feijão m cozido
com molho de tomate; **baked
potato** N batata assada com a
casca; **baker** N padeiro(-a); **bakery**
N (for bread) padaria; (for
cakes) confeitaria; **baking** N (act)
cozimento; (batch) fornada;
baking powder N fermento em pó
balance ['bæləns] N equilíbrio;
(scales) balança; (Comm) balanço;
(remainder) resto, saldo ▶ VT
equilibrar; (budget) nivelar;
(account) fazer o balanço de;
~ **of trade/payments** balança
comercial/balanço de
pagamentos; **balanced** ADJ
(report) objetivo; (personality, diet)
equilibrado; **balance sheet** N
balanço geral
balcony ['bælkənı] N varanda;
(closed) galeria; (in theatre)
balcão m
bald [bɔːld] ADJ calvo, careca; (tyre)
careca
ball [bɔːl] N bola; (of wool, string)
novelo; (dance) baile m; **to play ~
with sb** jogar bola com alguém;
(fig) fazer o jogo de alguém
ballerina [bælə'riːnə] N bailarina
ballet ['bæleɪ] N balé m; **ballet
dancer** N bailarino(-a)
balloon [bə'luːn] N balão m
ballot ['bælət] N votação f
ballpoint ['bɔːlpɔɪnt], **ballpoint
pen** N (caneta) esferográfica
ban [bæn] N proibição f,
interdição f; (suspension, exclusion)
exclusão f ▶ VT proibir, interditar;
(exclude) excluir
banana [bə'nɑːnə] N banana
band [bænd] N orquestra; (Mil)
banda; (strip) faixa, cinta; **band
together** VI juntar-se,
associar-se
bandage ['bændɪdʒ] N atadura
(BR), ligadura (PT) ▶ VT enfaixar
B & B N ABBR = **bed and breakfast**
bang [bæŋ] N estalo; (of door)
estrondo; (of gun, exhaust)
explosão f; (blow) pancada ▶ EXCL
bum!, bumba! ▶ VT bater com
força; (door) fechar com violência
▶ VI produzir estrondo; (door)
bater; (fireworks) soltar
bangs [bæŋz] (US) NPL (fringe)
franja
banish ['bænɪʃ] VT banir

banister ['bænɪstə'] N, **banisters** ['bænɪstəz] NPL corrimão m

bank [bæŋk] N banco; (of river, lake) margem f; (of earth) rampa, ladeira ▶ VI (Aviat) ladear-se; **bank on** VT FUS contar com, apostar em; **bank account** N conta bancária; **bank card** N cartão m de garantia de cheques; **banker** N banqueiro(-a); **Bank holiday** (BRIT) N feriado nacional; **banking** N transações fpl bancárias; **banknote** N nota (bancária)

bankrupt ['bæŋkrʌpt] ADJ falido, quebrado; **to go ~** falir

bank statement N extrato bancário

banner ['bænə'] N faixa

baptism ['bæptɪzəm] N batismo

bar [bɑː'] N barra; (rod) vara; (of window etc) grade f; (fig: hindrance) obstáculo; (prohibition) impedimento; (pub) bar m; (counter: in pub) balcão m ▶ VT (road) obstruir; (person) excluir; (activity) proibir ▶ PREP: **~ none** sem exceção; **behind ~s** (prisoner) atrás das grades; **the B~** (Jur) a advocacia

barbaric [bɑː'bærɪk] ADJ bárbaro

barbecue ['bɑːbɪkjuː] N churrasco

barbed wire ['bɑːbd-] N arame m farpado

barber ['bɑːbə'] N barbeiro, cabeleireiro

bar code N código de barras

bare [bɛə'] ADJ despido; (head) descoberto; (trees, vegetation) sem vegetação; (minimum) básico ▶ VT mostrar; **barefoot** ADJ, ADV descalço; **barely** ADV apenas, mal

bargain ['bɑːgɪn] N negócio; (agreement) acordo; (good buy) pechincha ▶ VI (haggle) regatear; (negotiate): **to ~ (with sb)** pechinchar (com alguém); **into the ~** ainda por cima; **bargain for** VT FUS: **he got more than he ~ed for** ele conseguiu mais do que pediu

barge [bɑːdʒ] N barcaça; **barge in** VI irromper

bark [bɑːk] N (of tree) casca; (of dog) latido ▶ VI latir

barley ['bɑːlɪ] N cevada

barmaid ['bɑːmeɪd] N garçonete f (BR), empregada (de bar) (PT)

barman ['bɑːmən] irreg N garçom m (BR), empregado (de bar) (PT)

barn [bɑːn] N celeiro

barometer [bə'rɔmɪtə'] N barômetro

baron ['bærən] N barão m; (of press, industry) magnata m; **baroness** ['bærənɪs] N baronesa

barracks ['bærəks] NPL quartel m, caserna

barrage ['bærɑːʒ] N (Mil) fogo de barragem; (dam) barragem f; (fig): **a ~ of questions** uma saraivada de perguntas

barrel ['bærəl] N barril m; (of gun) cano

barren ['bærən] ADJ (land) árido

barricade [bærɪ'keɪd] N barricada

barrier ['bærɪə'] N barreira; (fig: to progress etc) obstáculo

barrister ['bærɪstə'] (BRIT) N advogado(-a), causídico(-a)

barrow ['bærəu] N (wheelbarrow) carrinho (de mão)

bartender ['bɑːtɛndə'] (US) N garçom m (BR), empregado (de bar) (PT)

base [beɪs] N base f ▶ VT (opinion, belief): **to ~ sth on** basear or fundamentar algo em ▶ ADJ (thoughts) sujo; **baseball** N beisebol m

basement ['beɪsmənt] N porão m

bases¹ ['beɪsɪz] NPL *of* **base**
bases² ['beɪsi:z] NPL *of* **basis**
bash [bæʃ] (*inf*) VT (*with fist*) dar soco *or* murro em; (*with object*) bater em
basic ['beɪsɪk] ADJ básico; (*facilities*) mínimo; **basically** ADV basicamente; (*really*) no fundo; **basics** NPL: **the basics** o essencial
basin ['beɪsn] N bacia; (*also:* **wash~**) pia
basis ['beɪsɪs] (*pl* **bases**) N base *f*; **on a part-time ~** num esquema de meio-expediente; **on a trial ~** em experiência
basket ['bɑːskɪt] N cesto; (*with handle*) cesta; **basketball** N basquete(bol) *m*
bass [beɪs] N (*Mus*) baixo
bastard ['bɑːstəd] N bastardo(-a); (!) filho da puta *m* (!)
bat [bæt] N (*Zool*) morcego; (*for ball games*) bastão *m*; (BRIT: *for table tennis*) raquete *f* ▶ VT: **he didn't ~ an eyelid** ele nem pestanejou
batch [bætʃ] N (*of bread*) fornada; (*of papers*) monte *m*
bath [bɑːθ] N banho; (*bathtub*) banheira ▶ VT banhar; **to have a ~** tomar banho (de banheira); *see also* **baths**
bathe [beɪð] VI banhar-se; (US: *have a bath*) tomar um banho ▶ VT (*wound*) lavar; **bathing** N banho; **bathing costume,** (US) **bathing suit** N (*woman's*) maiô *m* (BR), fato de banho (PT)
bathrobe ['bɑːθrəub] N roupão *m* de banho
bathroom ['bɑːθrum] N banheiro (BR), casa de banho (PT)
baths [bɑːθs] NPL banhos *mpl* públicos

baton ['bætən] N (*Mus*) batuta; (*Athletics*) bastão *m*; (*truncheon*) cassetete *m*
batter ['bætə^r] VT espancar; (*subj: wind, rain*) castigar ▶ N massa (mole); **battered** ['bætəd] ADJ (*hat, pan*) amassado, surrado
battery ['bætərɪ] N bateria; (*of torch*) pilha
battle ['bætl] N batalha; (*fig*) luta ▶ VI lutar; **battlefield** N campo de batalha
bay [beɪ] N (*Geo*) baía; **to hold sb at ~** manter alguém a distância
bazaar [bə'zɑː^r] N bazar *m*
BBC N ABBR (= *British Broadcasting Corporation*) companhia britânica de rádio e televisão
B.C. ADV ABBR (= *before Christ*) a.C. ▶ ABBR (CANADA) = **British Columbia**

KEYWORD

be [biː] (*pt* **was** *or* **were**, *pp* **been**) AUX VB **1** (*with present participle, forming continuous tense*) estar; **what are you doing?** o que você está fazendo (BR) *or* a fazer (PT)?; **it is raining** está chovendo (BR) *or* a chover (PT); **I've been waiting for you for hours** há horas que eu espero por você
2 (*with pp, forming passives*): **to be killed** ser morto; **the box had been opened** a caixa tinha sido aberta; **the thief was nowhere to be seen** tinha sumido o ladrão
3 (*in tag questions*): **it was fun, wasn't it?** foi divertido, não foi?; **she's back again, is she?** ela voltou novamente, é?
4 (+ *to* + *infin*): **the house is to be sold** a casa está para ser vendida; **you're to be congratulated for**

all your work você devia ser cumprimentado pelo seu trabalho; **he's not to open it** ele não pode abrir isso

▶ VB + COMPLEMENT 1 (gen): **I'm English** sou inglês; **I'm tired** estou cansado; **2 and 2 are 4** dois e dois são quatro; **be careful!** tome cuidado!; **be quiet!** fique quieto!, fique calado!; **be good!** seja bonzinho!

2 (of health) estar; **how are you?** como está?

3 (of age): **how old are you?** quantos anos você tem?; **I'm twenty (years old)** tenho vinte anos

4 (cost) ser; **how much was the meal?** quanto foi a refeição?; **that'll be £5.75, please** são £5.75, por favor

▶ VI 1 (exist, occur etc) existir, haver; **the best singer that ever was** o maior cantor de todos os tempos; **is there a God?** Deus existe?; **be that as it may ...** de qualquer forma ...; **so be it** que seja assim

2 (referring to place) estar; **I won't be here tomorrow** eu não estarei aqui amanhã; **Edinburgh is in Scotland** Edinburgo é or fica na Escócia

3 (referring to movement) ir; **where have you been?** onde você foi?; **I've been in the garden** estava no quintal

▶ IMPERS VB 1 (referring to time) ser; **it's 8 o'clock** são 8 horas; **it's the 28th of April** é 28 de abril

2 (referring to distance) ficar; **it's 10 km to the village** o lugarejo fica a 10 km de distância

3 (referring to the weather) estar; **it's too hot/cold** está quente/frio demais

4 (emphatic): **it's only me** sou eu!; **it was Maria who paid the bill** foi Maria quem pagou a conta

beach [biːtʃ] N praia ▶ VT puxar para a terra or praia, encalhar

beacon ['biːkən] N (lighthouse) farol m; (marker) baliza

bead [biːd] N (of necklace) conta; (of sweat) gota

beak [biːk] N bico

beam [biːm] N (Arch) viga; (of light) raio ▶ VI (smile) sorrir

bean [biːn] N feijão m; (of coffee) grão m; **runner/broad ~** vagem f/ fava

bear [bɛəʳ] (pt bore, pp borne) N urso ▶ VT (carry, support) arcar com; (tolerate) suportar ▶ VI: **to ~ right/ left** virar à direita/à esquerda; **bear out** VT (theory, suspicion) confirmar, corroborar; **bear up** VI aguentar, resistir

beard [bɪəd] N barba

bearing ['bɛərɪŋ] N porte m, comportamento; (connection) relação f; **bearings** NPL (also: **ball ~s**) rolimã m; **to take a ~** fazer marcação

beast [biːst] N bicho; (inf) fera

beat [biːt] (pt beat, pp beaten) N (of heart) batida; (Mus) ritmo, compasso; (of policeman) ronda ▶ VT (hit) bater em; (eggs) bater; (defeat) vencer, derrotar ▶ VI (heart) bater; **to ~ it** (inf) cair fora; **off the ~en track** fora de mão; **beat off** VT repelir; **beat up** VT (inf: person) espancar; (eggs) bater; **beating** N (thrashing) surra

beautiful ['bjuːtɪful] ADJ belo, lindo, formoso

beauty ['bjuːtɪ] N beleza; (person) beldade f, beleza

beaver ['bi:vəʳ] N castor m
because [bɪ'kɔz] CONJ porque;
~ of por causa de
beckon ['bɛkən] VT (also: **~ to**)
chamar com sinais, acenar para
become [bɪ'kʌm] (irreg: like **come**)
VI (+ n) virar, fazer-se, tornar-se;
(+ adj) tornar-se, ficar
bed [bɛd] N cama; (of flowers)
canteiro; (of coal, clay) camada,
base f; (of sea, lake) fundo; (of river)
leito; **to go to ~** ir dormir,
deitar(-se); **bed and breakfast** N
(place) pensão f; (terms) cama e
café da manhã (BR) or pequeno
almoço (PT); **bedclothes** NPL
roupa de cama; **bedding** N roupa
de cama; **bedroom** N quarto,
dormitório; **bedside** N: **at sb's
bedside** à cabeceira de alguém
▶ CPD (book, lamp) de cabeceira;
bedsit ['bɛdsɪt], **bedsitter**
['bɛdsɪtəʳ] (BRIT) N conjugado

> Um **bedsit** é um quarto
> mobiliado cujo aluguel inclui
> uso de cozinha e banheiro
> comuns. Esse sistema de
> alojamento é muito comum
> na Grã-Bretanha entre
> estudantes, jovens
> profissionais liberais etc.

bedspread ['bɛdsprɛd] N colcha
bedtime ['bɛdtaɪm] N hora de ir
para cama
bee [bi:] N abelha
beech [bi:tʃ] N faia
beef [bi:f] N carne f de vaca;
roast ~ rosbife m; **beefburger** N
hambúrguer m
been [bi:n] PP of **be**
beer [bɪəʳ] N cerveja
beetle ['bi:tl] N besouro
beetroot ['bi:tru:t] (BRIT) N
beterraba

before [bɪ'fɔːʳ] PREP (of time) antes
de; (of space) diante de ▶ CONJ
antes que ▶ ADV antes,
anteriormente; à frente, na
dianteira; **~ going** antes de ir;
the week ~ a semana anterior;
I've never seen it ~ nunca vi isso
antes; **beforehand** ADV antes
beg [bɛg] VI mendigar, pedir
esmola ▶ VT (also: **~ for**) mendigar;
to ~ sb to do sth implorar a
alguém para fazer algo; see also
pardon
began [bɪ'gæn] PT of **begin**
beggar ['bɛgəʳ] N mendigo(-a)
begin [bɪ'gɪn] (pt **began**, pp
begun) VT, VI começar, iniciar;
to ~ doing or **to do sth** começar a
fazer algo; **beginner** N
principiante m/f; **beginning** N
início, começo
behalf [bɪ'hɑːf] N: **on** or **in** (US)
~ of (as representative of) em nome
de; (for benefit of) no interesse de
behave [bɪ'heɪv] VI comportar-se;
(well: also: **~ o.s.**) comportar-se
(bem); **behaviour**, (US) **behavior**
N comportamento
behind [bɪ'haɪnd] PREP atrás de
▶ ADV atrás; (move) para trás ▶ N
traseiro; **to be ~ (schedule) with
sth** estar atrasado or com atraso
em algo; **~ the scenes** nos
bastidores
beige [beɪʒ] ADJ bege
Beijing [beɪ'ʒɪŋ] N Pequim
being ['bi:ɪŋ] N (state) existência;
(entity) ser m
belated [bɪ'leɪtɪd] ADJ atrasado
belch [bɛltʃ] VI arrotar ▶ VT (also:
~ out: smoke etc) vomitar
Belgian ['bɛldʒən] ADJ, N
belga m/f
Belgium ['bɛldʒəm] N Bélgica

b

belief [bɪˈliːf] N (opinion) opinião f; (trust, faith) fé f
believe [bɪˈliːv] VT: **to ~ sth/sb** acreditar algo/em alguém ▶ VI: **to ~ in** (God, ghosts) crer em; (method, person) acreditar em; **believer** N (Rel) crente m/f, fiel m/f
bell [bɛl] N sino; (small, doorbell) campainha
bellow [ˈbɛləʊ] VI mugir; (person) bramar
bell pepper N (esp US) pimentão m
belly [ˈbɛlɪ] N barriga, ventre m
belong [bɪˈlɔŋ] VI: **to ~ to** pertencer a; (club etc) ser sócio de; **the book ~s here** o livro fica guardado aqui; **belongings** NPL pertences mpl
beloved [bɪˈlʌvɪd] ADJ querido, amado
below [bɪˈləʊ] PREP (beneath) embaixo de; (lower than, less than) abaixo de ▶ ADV em baixo; **see ~** ver abaixo
belt [bɛlt] N cinto; (of land) faixa; (Tech) correia ▶ VT (thrash) surrar; **beltway** (US) N via circular
bemused [bɪˈmjuːzd] ADJ bestificado, estupidificado
bench [bɛntʃ] N banco; (work bench) bancada (de carpinteiro); (BRIT Pol) assento num Parlamento; **the B~** (Jur) o tribunal; (people) os magistrados, o corpo de magistrados
bend [bɛnd] (pt bent, pp bent) VT (leg, arm) dobrar; (pipe) curvar ▶ VI dobrar-se, inclinar-se ▶ N curva; (in pipe) curvatura; **bend down** VI abaixar-se; **bend over** VI debruçar-se
beneath [bɪˈniːθ] PREP abaixo de; (unworthy of) indigno de ▶ ADV em baixo

beneficial [bɛnɪˈfɪʃəl] ADJ: **~ (to)** benéfico (a)
benefit [ˈbɛnɪfɪt] N benefício, vantagem f; (money) subsídio, auxílio ▶ VT beneficiar ▶ VI: **to ~ from sth** beneficiar-se de algo
benign [bɪˈnaɪn] ADJ (person, smile) afável, bondoso; (Med) benigno
bent [bɛnt] PT, PP of bend ▶ N inclinação f ▶ ADJ: **to be ~ on** estar empenhado em
bereaved [bɪˈriːvd] NPL: **the ~** os enlutados
beret [ˈbɛreɪ] N boina
Berlin [bəːˈlɪn] N Berlim
berry [ˈbɛrɪ] N baga
berth [bəːθ] N (bed) beliche m; (cabin) cabine f; (on train) leito; (for ship) ancoradouro ▶ VI (in harbour) atracar, encostar-se; (at anchor) ancorar
beside [bɪˈsaɪd] PREP (next to) junto de, ao lado de, ao pé de; **to be ~ o.s. (with anger)** estar fora de si; **that's ~ the point** isso não tem nada a ver
besides [bɪˈsaɪdz] ADV além disso ▶ PREP (as well as) além de
best [bɛst] ADJ melhor ▶ ADV (o) melhor; **the ~ part of** (quantity) a maior parte de; **at ~** na melhor das hipóteses; **to make the ~ of sth** tirar o maior partido possível de algo; **to do one's ~** fazer o possível; **to the ~ of my knowledge** que eu saiba; **to the ~ of my ability** o melhor que eu puder; **best-before date** N validade f; **best man** N padrinho de casamento
bet [bɛt] (pt, pp bet or betted) N aposta ▶ VI: **to ~ (on)** apostar (em)
betray [bɪˈtreɪ] VT trair;

(*denounce*) delatar

better ['bɛtəʳ] ADJ, ADV melhor
▶ VT melhorar; (*go above*) superar
▶ N: **to get the ~ of sb** vencer
alguém; **you had ~ do it** é melhor
você fazer isso; **he thought ~ of it**
pensou melhor, mudou de opinião;
to get ~ melhorar; **you'd be ~ off
this way** seria melhor para você
assim

betting ['bɛtɪŋ] N jogo; **betting
shop** (BRIT) N agência de apostas

between [bɪ'twi:n] PREP no meio
de, entre ▶ ADV no meio

beverage ['bɛvərɪdʒ] N bebida

beware [bɪ'wɛəʳ] VI: **to ~ (of)**
precaver-se (de), ter cuidado
(com); **"~ of the dog"** "cuidado
com o cachorro"

bewildered [bɪ'wɪldəd] ADJ
atordoado; (*confused*) confuso

beyond [bɪ'jɔnd] PREP (*in space,
exceeding*) além de; (*exceeding*)
acima de, fora de; (*date*) mais
tarde que; (*above*) acima de ▶ ADV
além; (*in time*) mais longe, mais
adiante; **~ doubt** fora de qualquer
dúvida; **to be ~ repair** não ter
conserto

bias ['baɪəs] N parcialidade

bib [bɪb] N babadouro, babador *m*

Bible ['baɪbl] N Bíblia

bicycle ['baɪsɪkl] N bicicleta

bid [bɪd] (*pt* **bade** *or* **bid**, *pp* **bidden**
or **bid**) N oferta; (*at auction*)
lance *m*; (*attempt*) tentativa ▶ VI
fazer lance ▶ VT oferecer; **to ~ sb
good day** dar bom dia a alguém

big [bɪg] ADJ grande; (*bulky*)
volumoso; **~ brother/sister**
irmão/irmã mais velho/a

bigheaded ['bɪg'hɛdɪd] ADJ
convencido

bike [baɪk] N bicicleta

bikini [bɪ'ki:nɪ] N biquíni *m*

bilingual [baɪ'lɪŋgwəl] ADJ
bilíngue

bill [bɪl] N conta; (*invoice*) fatura;
(*Pol*) projeto de lei; (*US: banknote*)
bilhete *m*, nota; (*in restaurant*)
conta, notinha; (*notice*) cartaz *m*;
(*of bird*) bico; **to fit** *or* **fill the ~** (*fig*)
servir; **billboard** N quadro para
cartazes; **billfold** ['bɪlfəuld] (*US*) N
carteira

billiards ['bɪlɪədz] N bilhar *m*

billion ['bɪlɪən] N bilhão *m* (*BR*), mil
milhão *m* (*PT*)

bin [bɪn] N caixa; (*BRIT: also*:
dust~, litter ~) lata de lixo

bind [baɪnd] (*pt, pp* **bound**) VT atar,
amarrar; (*oblige*) obrigar; (*book*)
encadernar ▶ N (*inf*) saco

binge [bɪndʒ] (*inf*) N: **to go on a ~**
tomar uma bebedeira

bingo ['bɪŋgəu] N bingo

binoculars [bɪ'nɔkjuləz] NPL
binóculo

bio ... [baɪəu] PREFIX bio ...;
biochemistry N bioquímica;
biodiesel ['baɪəudi:zl] N biodiesel *m*;
biodiversity N biodiversidade *f*;
biofuel N biocombustível *m*;
biography N biografia; **biology** N
biologia; **biometric** ADJ biométrico

birch [bə:tʃ] N bétula

bird [bə:d] N ave *f*, pássaro; (*BRIT
inf: girl*) gatinha; **bird flu** N gripe *f*
aviária

birth [bə:θ] N nascimento; **to give
~ to** dar à luz, parir; **birth
certificate** N certidão *f* de
nascimento; **birth control** N
controle *m* de natalidade;
(*methods*) métodos *mpl*
anticoncepcionais; **birthday** N
aniversário (*BR*), dia *m* de anos (*PT*)
▶ CPD de aniversário; *see also* **happy**

biscuit ['bɪskɪt] N (BRIT) bolacha, biscoito; (US) pão m doce

bishop ['bɪʃəp] N bispo

bit [bɪt] PT of **bite** ▶ N pedaço, bocado; (of horse) freio; (Comput) bit m; **a ~ of** (a little) um pouco de; **~ by ~** pouco a pouco

bitch [bɪtʃ] N (dog) cadela, cachorra; (!) cadela (!), vagabunda (!)

bite [baɪt] (pt **bit**, pp **bitten**) VT, VI morder; (insect etc) picar ▶ N (insect bite) picada; (mouthful) bocado; **to ~ one's nails** roer as unhas; **let's have a ~ (to eat)** (inf) vamos fazer uma boquinha

bitter ['bɪtər] ADJ amargo; (wind, criticism) cortante, penetrante ▶ N (BRIT: beer) cerveja amarga

black [blæk] ADJ preto; (humour) negro ▶ N (colour) cor f preta; (person): **B~** negro(-a) ▶ VT (BRIT Industry) boicotar; **to give sb a ~ eye** esmurrar alguém e deixá-lo de olho roxo; **~ and blue** contuso, contundido; **to be in the ~** (in credit) estar com saldo credor; **blackberry** N amora(-preta) (BR), amora silvestre (PT); **blackbird** N melro; **blackboard** N quadro(-negro); **black coffee** N café m preto; **blackcurrant** N groselha negra; **blackmail** N chantagem f ▶ VT fazer chantagem a; **black market** N mercado or câmbio negro; **blackout** N blecaute m; (fainting) desmaio; (of radio signal) desvanecimento; **Black Sea** N: **the Black Sea** o mar Negro

bladder ['blædər] N bexiga

blade [bleɪd] N lâmina; (of oar, rotor) pá f; **a ~ of grass** uma folha de relva

blame [bleɪm] N culpa ▶ VT: **to ~ sb for sth** culpar alguém por algo; **to be to ~** ter a culpa

bland [blænd] ADJ (taste) brando

blank [blæŋk] ADJ em branco; (look) sem expressão ▶ N (of memory): **to go ~** dar um branco; (on form) espaço em branco; (cartridge) bala de festim

blanket ['blæŋkɪt] N cobertor m

blast [blɑːst] N (of wind) rajada; (of explosive) explosão f ▶ VT fazer voar

blatant ['bleɪtənt] ADJ descarado

blaze [bleɪz] N (fire) fogo; (in building etc) incêndio; (fig: of colour) esplendor m; (: of glory, publicity) explosão f ▶ VI (fire) arder; (guns) descarregar; (eyes) brilhar ▶ VT: **to ~ a trail** (fig) abrir (um) caminho

blazer ['bleɪzər] N casaco esportivo, blazer m

bleach [bliːtʃ] N (also: **household ~**) água sanitária ▶ VT (linen) branquear

bleak [bliːk] ADJ (countryside) desolado; (prospect) desanimador(a), sombrio; (weather) ruim

bleed [bliːd] (pt, pp **bled**) VI sangrar

blemish ['blemɪʃ] N mancha; (on reputation) mácula

blend [blend] N mistura ▶ VT misturar ▶ VI (colours etc: also: **~ in**) combinar-se, misturar-se; **blender** N liquidificador m

bless [bles] (pt, pp **blessed**) VT abençoar; **~ you!** (after sneeze) saúde!; **blessing** N bênção f; (godsend) graça, dádiva; (approval) aprovação f

blew [bluː] PT of **blow**

blind [blaɪnd] ADJ cego ▶ N (for window) persiana; (also: **Venetian ~**) veneziana ▶ VT cegar; (dazzle) deslumbrar; **the blind** NPL (blind people) os cegos; **blind alley** N beco sem saída m; **blindfold** N venda

▶ ADJ, ADV com os olhos vendados, às cegas ▶ VT vendar os olhos a

blink [blɪŋk] VI piscar

bliss [blɪs] N felicidade f

blister ['blɪstə'] N (on skin) bolha; (in paint, rubber) empola ▶ VI empolar-se

blizzard ['blɪzəd] N nevasca

bloated ['bləutɪd] ADJ (swollen) inchado; (full) empanturrado

blob [blɔb] N (drop) gota; (indistinct shape) ponto

block [blɔk] N (of wood) bloco; (of stone) laje f; (in pipes) entupimento; (of buildings) quarteirão m ▶ VT obstruir, bloquear; (progress) impedir; **~ of flats** (BRIT) prédio (de apartamentos); **mental ~** bloqueio; **blockade** [blɔ'keɪd] N bloqueio; **blockage** N obstrução f; **blockbuster** ['blɔkbʌstə'] N grande sucesso

blog ['blɔg] N blogue m ▶ VI blogar

blogger ['blɔgə'] N (person) blogueiro(-a); **blogosphere** ['blɔgəsfɪə'] N blogosfera

bloke [bləuk] (BRIT inf) N cara m (BR), gajo (PT)

blond, blonde [blɔnd] ADJ, N louro(-a)

blood [blʌd] N sangue m; **blood donor** N doador(a) m/f de sangue; **blood group** N grupo sanguíneo; **blood poisoning** N toxemia; **blood pressure** N pressão f arterial or sanguínea; **bloodshed** N matança, carnificina; **bloodshot** ADJ (eyes) injetado; **bloodstream** N corrente f sanguínea; **blood test** N exame m de sangue; **blood vessel** N vaso sanguíneo; **bloody** ADJ sangrento; (nose) ensanguentado; (BRIT !): **this bloody ...** essa droga de ..., esse maldito ...; **bloody**

strong/good forte/bom pra burro (inf)

bloom [bluːm] N flor f ▶ VI florescer

blossom ['blɔsəm] N flor f ▶ VI florescer; **to ~ into** (fig) tornar-se

blot [blɔt] N borrão m; (fig) mancha ▶ VT borrar; **blot out** VT (view) tapar; (memory) apagar

blouse [blauz] N blusa

blow [bləu] (pt **blew**, pp **blown**) N golpe m; (punch) soco ▶ VI soprar ▶ VT (subj: wind) soprar; (instrument) tocar; (fuse) queimar; **to ~ one's nose** assoar o nariz; **blow away** VT levar, arrancar ▶ VI ser levado pelo vento; **blow down** VT derrubar; **blow off** VT levar; **blow out** VT (candle) apagar; **blow over** VI passar; **blow up** VI explodir ▶ VT explodir; (tyre) encher; (Phot) ampliar; **blow-dry** N escova; **blow-out** N (of tyre) furo

blue [bluː] ADJ azul; (depressed) deprimido; **blues** N (Mus): **the ~s** o blues; **out of the ~** (fig) de estalo, inesperadamente; **bluebell** N campainha

bluff [blʌf] VI blefar ▶ N blefe m; **to call sb's ~** pagar para ver alguém

blunder ['blʌndə'] N gafe f ▶ VI cometer or fazer uma gafe

blunt [blʌnt] ADJ (knife) cego; (pencil) rombudo; (person) franco, direto

blur [bləː'] N borrão m ▶ VT (vision) embaçar

blush [blʌʃ] VI corar, ruborizar-se ▶ N rubor m, vermelhidão f

board [bɔːd] N tábua; (blackboard) quadro m; (notice board) quadro de avisos; (for chess etc) tabuleiro; (committee) junta, conselho; (in firm) diretoria, conselho administrativo; (*Naut, Aviat*): **on ~ a bordo** ▶ VT embarcar em; **full ~** (*BRIT*) pensão f completa; **half ~** (*BRIT*) meia-pensão f; **~ and lodging** casa e comida; **to go by the ~** ficar abandonado, dançar (*inf*); **board up** VT entabuar; **boarding card** N = **boarding pass**; **boarding pass** (*BRIT*) N (*Aviat, Naut*) cartão m de embarque; **boarding school** N internato

boast [bəust] VI: **to ~ (about** *or* **of)** gabar-se (de), jactar-se (de)

boat [bəut] N barco m; (*ship*) navio

bob [bɔb] VI balouçar-se; **bob up** VI aparecer, surgir

body ['bɔdɪ] N corpo m; (*corpse*) cadáver m; (*of car*) carroceria; (*fig: group*) grupo; (: *organization*) organização f; (: *quantity*) conjunto; (: *of wine*) corpo; **body-building** N musculação f; **bodyguard** N guarda-costas m inv; **bodywork** N lataria

bog [bɔg] N pântano, atoleiro ▶ VT: **to get ~ged down (in)** (*fig*) atolar-se (em)

bogus ['bəugəs] ADJ falso

boil [bɔɪl] VT ferver; (*eggs*) cozinhar ▶ VI ferver ▶ N (*Med*) furúnculo; **to come to the** (*BRIT*) *or* **a** (*US*) **~** começar a ferver; **boil down to** VT FUS (*fig*) reduzir-se a; **boil over** VI transbordar; **boiled egg** N ovo cozido; **boiled potatoes** NPL batatas fpl cozidas; **boiler** N caldeira; (*for central heating*) boiler m; **boiling point** N ponto de ebulição

bold [bəuld] ADJ corajoso; (*pej*) atrevido, insolente; (*outline, colour*) forte

Bolivia [bə'lɪvɪə] N Bolívia

bollard ['bɔləd] (*BRIT*) N (*Aut*) poste m de sinalização

bolt [bəult] N (*lock*) trinco, ferrolho; (*with nut*) parafuso, cavilha ▶ ADV: **~ upright** direito como um fuso ▶ VT (*door*) fechar a ferrolho, trancar; (*food*) engolir às pressas ▶ VI fugir; (*horse*) disparar

bomb [bɔm] N bomba ▶ VT bombardear; **bomb scare** N ameaça de bomba

bond [bɔnd] N (*binding promise*) compromisso; (*link*) vínculo, laço; (*Finance*) obrigação f; (*Comm*): **in ~** (*goods*) retido sob caução na alfândega

bone [bəun] N osso; (*of fish*) espinha ▶ VT desossar; tirar as espinhas de

bonfire ['bɔnfaɪəᵣ] N fogueira

bonnet ['bɔnɪt] N toucado; (*BRIT: of car*) capô m

bonus ['bəunəs] N (*payment*) bônus m; (*fig*) gratificação f

boo [bu:] VT vaiar ▶ EXCL ruuh!, bu!

book [buk] N livro; (*of stamps, tickets*) talão m ▶ VT reservar; (*driver*) autuar; (*football player*) mostrar o cartão amarelo a; **books** NPL (*Comm*) contas fpl, contabilidade f; **bookcase** N estante f (para livros); **booking office** (*BRIT*) N (*Rail, Theatre*) bilheteria (*BR*), bilheteira (*PT*); **book-keeping** N escrituração f, contabilidade f; **booklet** N livrinho, brochura; **bookmark** N (*for book*) marcador m de livro; (*Comput*) favorito, bookmark m; **bookshop, bookstore** N livraria

boom [bu:m] N (*noise*) barulho, estrondo; (*in sales etc*) aumento rápido ▶ VI retumbar; (*business*) tomar surto

boost [bu:st] N estímulo ▶ VT estimular

boot [bu:t] N bota; (*for football*) chuteira; (*BRIT: of car*) porta-malas m

(BR), porta-bagagem *m* (PT) ▶ VT (*Comput*) iniciar; **to ~ ...** (*in addition*) ainda por cima ...

booth [buːð] N (*at fair*) barraca; (*telephone booth, voting booth*) cabine *f*

booze [buːz] (*inf*) N bebida alcoólica

border ['bɔːdəʳ] N margem *f*; (*for flowers*) borda; (*of a country*) fronteira; (*on cloth etc*) debrum *m*, remate *m* ▶ VT (*also: ~ on*) limitar-se com; **border on** VT FUS (*fig*) chegar às raias de; **borderline** N fronteira

bore [bɔːʳ] PT *of* **bear** ▶ VT (*hole*) abrir; (*well*) cavar; (*person*) aborrecer ▶ N (*person*) chato(-a), maçante *m/f*; (*of gun*) calibre *m*; **to be ~d to tears** *or* **~d to death** *or* **~d stiff** estar muito entediado; **boredom** N tédio, aborrecimento; **boring** ADJ chato, maçante

born [bɔːn] ADJ: **to be ~** nascer

borne [bɔːn] PP *of* **bear**

borough ['bʌrə] N município

borrow ['bɔrəu] VT: **to ~ sth (from sb)** pedir algo emprestado a alguém

bosom ['buzəm] N peito

boss [bɔs] N (*employer*) patrão(-troa) *m/f* ▶ VT (*also: ~ about, ~ around*) mandar em; **bossy** ADJ mandão(-dona)

both [bəuθ] ADJ, PRON ambos(-as), os dois/as duas ▶ ADV: **~ A and B** tanto A como B; **~ of us went, we ~ went** nós dois fomos, ambos fomos

bother ['bɔðəʳ] VT (*worry*) preocupar; (*disturb*) atrapalhar ▶ VI (*also: ~ o.s.*) preocupar-se ▶ N preocupação *f*; (*nuisance*) amolação *f*, inconveniente *m*

bottle ['bɔtl] N garrafa; (*of perfume, medicine*) frasco; (*baby's*) mamadeira (BR), biberão *m* (PT) ▶ VT engarrafar; **bottle up** VT conter, refrear; **bottle bank** N depósito de vidro para reciclagem, vidrão *m* (PT); **bottle-opener** N abridor *m* (de garrafas) (BR), abre-garrafas *m inv* (PT)

bottom ['bɔtəm] N fundo; (*buttocks*) traseiro; (*of page, list*) pé *m*; (*of class*) nível *m* mais baixo ▶ ADJ (*low*) inferior, mais baixo; (*last*) último

bought [bɔːt] PT, PP *of* **buy**

boulder ['bəuldəʳ] N pedregulho, matacão *m*

bounce [bauns] VI saltar, quicar; (*cheque*) ser devolvido (*por insuficiência de fundos*) ▶ VT fazer saltar ▶ N (*rebound*) salto; **bouncer** (*inf*) N leão de chácara *m*

bound [baund] PT, PP *of* **bind** ▶ N (*leap*) pulo, salto; (*gen pl: limit*) limite *m* ▶ VI (*leap*) pular, saltar ▶ VT (*border*) demarcar ▶ ADJ: **~ by** limitado por; **to be ~ to do sth** (*obliged*) ter a obrigação de fazer algo; (*likely*) na certa ir fazer algo; **~ for** com destino a

boundary ['baundrɪ] N limite *m*, fronteira

bout [baut] N (*of malaria etc*) ataque *m*; (*of activity*) explosão *f*; (*Boxing etc*) combate *m*

bow¹ [bəu] N (*knot*) laço; (*weapon, Mus*) arco

bow² [bau] N (*of the body*) reverência; (*of the head*) inclinação *f*; (*Naut: also: ~s*) proa ▶ VI curvar-se, fazer uma reverência; (*yield*): **to ~ to** *or* **before** ceder ante, submeter-se a

bowels ['bauəlz] NPL intestinos *mpl*, tripas *fpl*; (*fig*) entranhas *fpl*

bowl [bəul] N tigela; (*ball*) bola ▶ VI (*Cricket*) arremessar a bola

bowler ['bəulə^r] N (*Cricket*) lançador *m* (da bola); (*BRIT: also:* **~ hat**) chapéu-coco *m*

bowling ['bəulɪŋ] N (*game*) boliche *m*; **bowling alley** N boliche *m*; **bowling green** N gramado (*BR*) or relvado (*PT*) para jogo de bolas

bowls [bəulz] N jogo de bolas

bow tie ['bəu-] N gravata-borboleta

box [bɔks] N caixa; (*Theatre*) camarote *m* ▶ VT encaixotar; (*Sport*) boxear contra ▶ VI (*Sport*) boxear; **boxer** N (*person*) boxeador *m*, pugilista *m*; **boxer shorts** NPL cueca samba-canção; **boxing** N (*Sport*) boxe *m*, pugilismo; **Boxing Day** (*BRIT*) N *Dia de Santo Estevão (26 de dezembro)*; **box office** N bilheteria (*BR*), bilheteira (*PT*)

boy [bɔɪ] N (*young*) menino, garoto; (*older*) moço, rapaz *m*; (*son*) filho

boycott ['bɔɪkɔt] N boicote *m*, boicotagem *f* ▶ VT boicotar

boyfriend ['bɔɪfrɛnd] N namorado

bra [brɑ:] N sutiã *m* (*BR*), soutien *m* (*PT*)

brace [breɪs] N (*on teeth*) aparelho; (*tool*) arco de pua ▶ VT retesar; **braces** NPL (*BRIT*) suspensórios *mpl*; **to ~ o.s.** (*for weight, fig*) preparar-se

bracelet ['breɪslɪt] N pulseira

bracket ['brækɪt] N (*Tech*) suporte *m*; (*group*) classe *f*, categoria; (*range*) faixa; (*also:* **round ~**) parêntese *m* ▶ VT pôr entre parênteses; (*fig*) agrupar

brag [bræg] VI gabar-se, contar vantagem

braid [breɪd] N (*trimming*) galão *m*; (*of hair*) trança

brain [breɪn] N cérebro; **brains** NPL (*Culin*) miolos *mpl*; (*intelligence*) inteligência, miolos

braise [breɪz] VT assar na panela

brake [breɪk] N freio (*BR*), travão *m* (*PT*) ▶ VT, VI frear (*BR*), travar (*PT*)

bran [bræn] N farelo

branch [brɑ:ntʃ] N ramo, galho; (*Comm*) sucursal *f*, filial *f*; **branch out** VI (*fig*) diversificar suas atividades; **to ~ out into** estender suas atividades a

brand [brænd] N marca; (*fig: type*) tipo ▶ VT (*cattle*) marcar com ferro quente; **brand-new** ADJ novo em folha, novinho

brandy ['brændɪ] N conhaque *m*

brash [bræʃ] ADJ (*forward*) descarado

brass [brɑ:s] N latão *m*; **the ~** (*Mus*) os metais; **brass band** N banda de música

brat [bræt] (*pej*) N pirralho(-a), fedelho(-a)

brave [breɪv] ADJ valente, corajoso ▶ VT (*face up to*) desafiar; **bravery** N coragem *f*, bravura

Brazil [brə'zɪl] N Brasil *m*; **Brazilian** ADJ, N brasileiro(-a)

breach [bri:tʃ] VT abrir brecha em ▶ N (*gap*) brecha; (*breaking*): **~ of contract** inadimplência (*BR*), inadimplemento (*PT*)

bread [brɛd] N pão *m*; **breadbin** (*BRIT*) N caixa de pão; **breadbox** (*US*) N caixa de pão; **breadcrumbs** NPL migalhas *fpl*; (*Culin*) farinha de rosca

breadth [brɛtθ] N largura; (*fig*) amplitude *f*

break [breɪk] (*pt* **broke**, *pp* **broken**) VT quebrar (*BR*), partir (*PT*); (*promise*) quebrar; (*law*) violar, transgredir; (*record*) bater ▶ VI

quebrar-se, partir-se; (*storm*) estourar; (*weather*) mudar; (*dawn*) amanhecer; (*story, news*) revelar ▶ N (*gap*) abertura; (*fracture*) fratura; (*rest*) descanso; (*interval*) intervalo; (*at school*) recreio; (*chance*) oportunidade *f*; **to ~ the news to sb** dar a notícia a alguém; **to ~ even** sair sem ganhar nem perder; **to ~ free** or **loose** soltar-se; **to ~ open** (*door etc*) arrombar; **break down** VT (*figures, data*) analisar ▶ VI (*machine, Aut*) enguiçar, pifar (*inf*); (*Med*) sofrer uma crise nervosa; (*person: cry*) desatar a chorar; (*talks*) fracassar; **break in** VT (*horse etc*) domar ▶ VI (*burglar*) forçar uma entrada; (*interrupt*) interromper; **break into** VT FUS (*house*) arrombar; **break off** VI (*speaker*) parar-se, deter-se; (*branch*) partir; **break out** VI (*war*) estourar; (*prisoner*) libertar-se; **to ~ out in spots/a rash** aparecer coberto de manchas/brotoejas; **break up** VI (*ship*) partir-se; (*partnership*) acabar; (*marriage*) desmanchar-se ▶ VT (*rocks*) partir; (*biscuit etc*) quebrar; (*journey*) romper; (*fight*) intervir em; **you're ~ing up** sua voz está falhando; **breakdown** N (*Aut*) enguiço, avaria; (*in communications*) interrupção *f*; (*of marriage*) fracasso, término; (*Med: also*: **nervous breakdown**) esgotamento nervoso; (*of figures*) discriminação *f*, desdobramento
breakfast ['brɛkfəst] N café *m* da manhã (BR), pequeno-almoço (PT)
break-in N roubo com arrombamento
breakthrough ['breɪkθru:] N (*fig*) avanço, novo progresso

breast [brɛst] N (*of woman*) peito, seio; (*chest, meat*) peito; **breast-feed** (*irreg: like* **feed**) VT, VI amamentar; **breaststroke** N nado de peito
breath [brɛθ] N fôlego, respiração *f*; **out of ~** ofegante, sem fôlego
breathe [bri:ð] VT, VI respirar; **breathe in** VT, VI inspirar; **breathe out** VT, VI expirar; **breathing** N respiração *f*
breathless ['brɛθlɪs] ADJ sem fôlego
breed [bri:d] (*pt, pp* **bred**) VT (*animals*) criar; (*plants*) multiplicar ▶ VI acasalar-se ▶ N raça
breeze [bri:z] N brisa, aragem *f*; **breezy** ADJ (*person*) despreocupado, animado; (*weather*) ventoso
brew [bru:] VT (*tea*) fazer; (*beer*) fermentar ▶ VI (*storm, fig*) armar-se; **brewery** N cervejaria
bribe [braɪb] N suborno ▶ VT subornar; **bribery** N suborno
brick [brɪk] N tijolo; **bricklayer** N pedreiro
bride [braɪd] N noiva; **bridegroom** N noivo; **bridesmaid** N dama de honra
bridge [brɪdʒ] N ponte *f*; (*Naut*) ponte de comando; (*Cards*) bridge *m*; (*of nose*) cavalete *m* ▶ VT transpor
bridle ['braɪdl] N cabeçada, freio
brief [bri:f] ADJ breve ▶ N (*Jur*) causa; (*task*) tarefa ▶ VT (*inform*) informar; **briefs** NPL (*for men*) cueca (BR), cuecas *fpl* (PT); (*for women*) calcinha (BR), cuecas *fpl* (PT); **briefcase** N pasta; **briefly** ADV (*glance*) rapidamente; (*say*) em poucas palavras
bright [braɪt] ADJ claro, brilhante; (*weather*) resplandecente; (*person:*

clever) inteligente; (: *lively*) alegre, animado; (*colour*) vivo; (*future*) promissor(a), favorável

brilliant ['brɪljənt] ADJ brilhante; (*inf: great*) sensacional

brim [brɪm] N borda; (*of hat*) aba

brine [braɪn] N (*Culin*) salmoura

bring [brɪŋ] (*pt, pp* **brought**) VT trazer; **bring about** VT ocasionar, produzir; **bring back** VT restabelecer; (*return*) devolver; **bring down** VT (*price*) abaixar; (*government, plane*) derrubar; **bring forward** VT adiantar; **bring off** VT (*task, plan*) levar a cabo; **bring out** VT (*object*) tirar; (*meaning*) salientar; (*new product, book*) lançar; **bring round** VT fazer voltar a si; **bring up** VT (*person*) educar, criar; (*carry up*) subir; (*question*) introduzir; (*food*) vomitar

brisk [brɪsk] ADJ vigoroso; (*tone, person*) enérgico; (*trade, business*) ativo

bristle ['brɪsl] N (*of animal*) pelo rijo; (*of beard*) pelo de barba curta; (*of brush*) cerda ▶ VI (*in anger*) encolerizar-se

Britain ['brɪtən] N (*also:* **Great ~**) Grã-Bretanha

British ['brɪtɪʃ] ADJ britânico ▶ NPL: **the ~** os britânicos; **British Isles** NPL: **the British Isles** as ilhas Britânicas

Briton ['brɪtən] N britânico(-a)

brittle ['brɪtl] ADJ quebradiço, frágil

broad [brɔːd] ADJ (*street, range*) amplo; (*shoulders, smile*) largo; (*distinction, outline*) geral; (*accent*) carregado; **in ~ daylight** em plena luz do dia; **broadband** N banda larga; **broadcast** (*pt, pp* **broadcast**) N transmissão f ▶ VT, VI transmitir; **broaden** VT alargar ▶ VI alargar-se;

to broaden one's mind abrir os horizontes; **broadly** ADV em geral; **broad-minded** ADJ tolerante, liberal

broccoli ['brɔkəlɪ] N brócolis mpl (BR), brócolos mpl (PT)

brochure ['brəʊʃjuəʳ] N folheto, brochura

broke [brəʊk] PT *of* **break** ▶ ADJ (*inf*) sem um vintém, duro; (: *company*): **to go ~** quebrar

broken ['brəʊkən] PP *of* **break** ▶ ADJ quebrado; **in ~ English** num inglês mascavado

broker ['brəʊkəʳ] N corretor(a) m/f

bronchitis [brɔŋ'kaɪtɪs] N bronquite f

bronze [brɔnz] N bronze m

brooch [brəʊtʃ] N broche m

brood [bruːd] N ninhada ▶ VI (*person*) cismar, remoer

broom [brum] N vassoura; (*Bot*) giesta-das-vassouras f

Bros. ABBR (*Comm: = brothers*) Irmãos

broth [brɔθ] N caldo

brothel ['brɔθl] N bordel m

brother ['brʌðəʳ] N irmão m; **brother-in-law** N cunhado

brought [brɔːt] PT, PP *of* **bring**

brow [brau] N (*forehead*) fronte f, testa; (*eyebrow*) sobrancelha; (*of hill*) cimo, cume m

brown [braun] ADJ marrom (BR), castanho (PT); (*hair*) castanho; (*tanned*) bronzeado, moreno ▶ N (*colour*) cor f marrom (BR) *or* castanha (PT) ▶ VT (*Culin*) dourar; **brown bread** N pão m integral; **Brownie** N (*also:* **Brownie Guide**) fadinha de bandeirante; **brown sugar** N açúcar m mascavo

browse [brauz] VI (*in shop*) dar uma olhada; **to ~ through a book** folhear um livro; **browser** N (*Comput*) browser m

bruise [bruːz] N hematoma m, contusão f ▸ VT machucar

brunette [bruːˈnɛt] N morena

brush [brʌʃ] N escova; (for painting, shaving etc) pincel m; (quarrel) bate-boca m ▸ VT varrer; (groom) escovar; (also: ~ **against**) tocar ao passar, roçar; **brush aside** VT afastar, não fazer caso de; **brush up** VT retocar, revisar

Brussels [ˈbrʌslz] N Bruxelas; **Brussels sprout** N couve-de-bruxelas f

brutal [ˈbruːtl] ADJ brutal

bubble [ˈbʌbl] N bolha (BR), borbulha (PT) ▸ VI borbulhar; **bubble bath** N banho de espuma; **bubble gum** N chiclete m (de bola) (BR), pastilha elástica (PT)

buck [bʌk] N (rabbit) macho; (deer) cervo; (US inf) dólar m ▸ VI corcovear; **to pass the ~** fazer o jogo de empurra; **buck up** VI (cheer up) animar-se, cobrar ânimo

bucket [ˈbʌkɪt] N balde m

buckle [ˈbʌkl] N fivela ▸ VT afivelar ▸ VI torcer-se, cambar-se

bud [bʌd] N broto; (of flower) botão m ▸ VI brotar, desabrochar

Buddhism [ˈbudɪzəm] N budismo

buddy [ˈbʌdɪ] (US) N camarada m, companheiro

budge [bʌdʒ] VT mover ▸ VI mexer-se

budgerigar [ˈbʌdʒərɪgɑːʳ] N periquito

budget [ˈbʌdʒɪt] N orçamento ▸ VI: **to ~ for sth** incluir algo no orçamento

budgie [ˈbʌdʒɪ] N = **budgerigar**

buff [bʌf] ADJ (colour) cor de camurça ▸ N (inf: enthusiast) aficionado(-a)

buffalo [ˈbʌfələu] (**buffalo** or pl **buffaloes**) N (BRIT) búfalo; (US: bison) bisão m

buffer [ˈbʌfəʳ] N para-choque m; (Comput) buffer m

buffet¹ [ˈbufeɪ] (BRIT) N (in station) bar m; (food) bufê m

buffet² [ˈbʌfɪt] VT fustigar

buffet car (BRIT) N vagão-restaurante m

bug [bʌg] N (esp US: insect) bicho; (fig: germ) micróbio; (spy device) microfone m oculto; escuta clandestina; (Comput: of program) erro; (: of equipment) defeito ▸ VT (inf: annoy) apoquentar, incomodar; (room) colocar microfones em; (phone) grampear

build [bɪld] (pt, pp **built**) N (of person) talhe m, estatura ▸ VT construir, edificar; **build up** VT acumular; **builder** N construtor(a) m/f, empreiteiro(-a); **building** N construção f; (residential, offices) edifício, prédio; **building society** (BRIT) N sociedade f de crédito imobiliário, financiadora

built [bɪlt] PT, PP of **build** ▸ ADJ: **~-in** (cupboard) embutido

bulb [bʌlb] N (Bot) bulbo; (Elec) lâmpada

Bulgaria [bʌlˈgɛərɪə] N Bulgária

bulge [bʌldʒ] N bojo, saliência ▸ VI inchar-se; (pocket etc) fazer bojo

bulimia [buːˈlɪmɪə] N bulimia

bulk [bʌlk] N volume m; **in ~** (Comm) a granel; **the ~ of** a maior parte de; **bulky** ADJ volumoso

bull [bul] N touro

bulldozer [ˈbuldəuzəʳ] N buldôzer m, escavadora

bullet [ˈbulɪt] N bala

bulletin [ˈbulɪtɪn] N noticiário; (journal) boletim m

bullfight ['bulfaɪt] N tourada;
bullfighter N toureiro;
bullfighting N tauromaquia

bully ['bulɪ] N fanfarrão m,
valentão m ▶ VT intimidar, tiranizar

bum [bʌm] N (inf: backside)
bumbum m; (esp US: tramp)
vagabundo(-a), vadio(-a)

bumblebee ['bʌmblbi:] N
mamangaba

bump [bʌmp] N (in car) batida;
(jolt) sacudida; (on head) galo; (on
road) elevação f ▶ VT bater contra,
dar encontrão em ▶ VI dar
sacudidas; **bump into** VT FUS
chocar-se com or contra, colidir
com; (inf: person) dar com, topar
com; **bumper** N (BRIT) para-choque
m ▶ ADJ: **bumper crop/harvest**
supersafra; **bumpy** ADJ (road)
acidentado, cheio de altos e baixos

bun [bʌn] N pão m doce (BR),
pãozinho (PT); (in hair) coque m

bunch [bʌntʃ] N (of flowers) ramo;
(of keys) molho; (of bananas, grapes)
cacho; (of people) grupo; **bunches**
NPL (in hair) cachos mpl

bundle ['bʌndl] N trouxa,
embrulho; (of sticks) feixe m; (of
papers) maço ▶ VT (also: **~ up**)
embrulhar, atar; (put): **to ~ sth/sb
into** meter or enfiar algo/alguém
correndo em

bungalow ['bʌngələu] N bangalô
m, chalé m

bunion ['bʌnjən] N joanete m

bunk [bʌŋk] N beliche m; **bunk
beds** NPL beliche m, cama-beliche f

bunker ['bʌŋkəʳ] N (coal store)
carvoeira; (Mil) abrigo, casamata;
(Golf) bunker m

buoy [bɔɪ] N boia; **buoy up** VT (fig)
animar; **buoyant** ADJ flutuante;
(person) alegre; (market) animado

burden ['bə:dn] N responsabilidade f,
fardo; (load) carga ▶ VT
sobrecarregar; (trouble): **to be a ~
to sb** ser um estorvo para alguém

bureau [bjuə'rəu] (pl **bureaux**) N
(BRIT: desk) secretária, escrivaninha;
(US: chest of drawers) cômoda; (office)
escritório, agência

bureaucracy [bjuə'rɔkrəsɪ] N
burocracia; **bureau de change**
[-də'ʃɑʒ] (pl **bureaux de change**) N
casa de câmbio

burger ['bə:gəʳ] N hambúrguer m

burglar ['bə:gləʳ] N ladrão/ladrona
m/f; **burglar alarm** N alarma de
roubo; **burglary** N roubo

burial ['bɛrɪəl] N enterro

burn [bə:n] (pt, pp **burned** or **burnt**)
VT queimar; (house) incendiar ▶ VI
queimar-se, arder; (sting) arder,
picar ▶ N queimadura; **burn down**
VT incendiar; **burning** ADJ ardente;
(hot: sand etc) abrasador(a);
(ambition) grande

burrow ['bʌrəu] N toca, lura ▶ VI
fazer uma toca, cavar; (rummage)
esquadrinhar

burst [bə:st] (pt, pp **burst**) VT
arrebentar; (banks etc) romper ▶ VI
estourar; (tyre) furar ▶ N rajada; **to
~ into flames** incendiar-se de
repente; **to ~ into tears** desatar a
chorar; **to ~ out laughing** cair na
gargalhada; **to be ~ing with**
(emotion) estar tomado de; (subj:
room, container) estar abarrotado de;
a ~ of energy/speed/enthusiasm
uma explosão de energia/
velocidade/entusiasmo; **burst into**
VT FUS (room etc) irromper em

bury ['bɛrɪ] VT enterrar; (at funeral)
sepultar; **to ~ one's head in one's
hands** cobrir o rosto com as mãos;
to ~ one's head in the sand (fig)

bancar avestruz; **to ~ the hatchet**
(*fig*) fazer as pazes
bus [bʌs] N ônibus *m inv* (BR),
autocarro (PT); **bus conductor** N
cobrador(a) *m/f* de ônibus
bush [buʃ] N arbusto, mata;
(*scrubland*) sertão *m*; **to beat
about the ~** ser evasivo
business ['bɪznɪs] N negócio;
(*trading*) comércio, negócios *mpl*;
(*firm*) empresa; (*occupation*)
profissão *f*; **to be away on ~** estar
fora a negócios; **it's my ~ to ...**
encarrego-me de ...; **it's none of
my ~** eu não tenho nada com isto;
he means ~ fala a sério; **business
class** N (*on plane*) classe *f* executiva;
businesslike ADJ eficiente,
metódico; **businessman** *irreg* N
homem *m* de negócios; **business
trip** N viagem *f* de negócios;
businesswoman *irreg* N mulher *f*
de negócios
busker ['bʌskə'] (BRIT) N artista
m/f de rua
bust [bʌst] N (*Anat*) busto ▶ ADJ
(*inf: broken*) quebrado; **to go ~** falir
busy ['bɪzɪ] ADJ (*person*) ocupado,
atarefado; (*shop, street*) animado,
movimentado; (*us Tel*) ocupado
(BR), impedido (PT) ▶ VT: **to ~ o.s.
with** ocupar-se em *or* de

(KEYWORD)

but [bʌt] CONJ **1** (*yet*) mas, porém;
he's tired but Paul isn't ele está
cansado mas Paul não; **the trip
was enjoyable but tiring** a
viagem foi agradável porém
cansativa
2 (*however*) mas; **I'd love to come,
but I'm busy** eu adoraria vir, mas
estou ocupado
3 (*showing disagreement, surprise etc*)

mas; **but that's far too
expensive!** mas isso é caro
demais!
▶ PREP (*apart from, except*) exceto,
menos; **he was/we've had
nothing but trouble** ele só deu
problema/nós só tivemos
problema; **no-one but him** só ele,
ninguém a não ser ele; **but for**
sem, se não fosse; **(I'll do)
anything but that** (eu faria)
qualquer coisa menos isso
▶ ADV (*just, only*) apenas; **had I but
known** eu eu soubesse; **I can but
try** a única coisa que eu posso
fazer é tentar; **all but finished**
quase acabado

butcher ['butʃə'] N açougueiro
(BR), homem *m* do talho (PT) ▶ VT
(*prisoners etc*) chacinar, massacrar;
(*cattle etc for meat*) abater e
carnear; **butcher's, butcher's
shop** N açougue *m* (BR), talho (PT)
butler ['bʌtlə'] N mordomo
butt [bʌt] N (*cask*) tonel *m*; (*of gun*)
coronha; (*of cigarette*) toco (BR),
ponta (PT); (BRIT *fig: target*) alvo
▶ VT (*subj: goat*) marrar; (: *person*)
dar uma cabeçada em; **butt in** VI
(*interrupt*) interromper
butter ['bʌtə'] N manteiga ▶ VT
untar com manteiga
butterfly ['bʌtəflaɪ] N borboleta;
(*Swimming: also:* **~ stroke**) nado
borboleta
buttocks ['bʌtəks] NPL nádegas
fpl
button ['bʌtn] N botão *m*; (*us:
badge*) emblema *m* ▶ VT (*also:* **~ up**)
abotoar ▶ VI ter botões
buy [baɪ] (*pt, pp* bought) VT
comprar ▶ N compra; **to ~ sb sth/
sth from sb** comprar algo para

alguém/algo a alguém; **to ~ sb a drink** pagar um drinque para alguém; **buyer** N comprador(a) *m/f*

buzz [bʌz] N zumbido; (*inf: phone call*): **to give sb a ~** dar uma ligada para alguém ▶ VI zumbir; **buzzer** N cigarra, vibrador *m*

(KEYWORD)

by [baɪ] PREP **1** (*referring to cause, agent*) por, de; **killed by lightning** morto por um raio; **a painting by Picasso** um quadro de Picasso **2** (*referring to method, manner, means*) de, com; **by bus/car/train** de ônibus/carro/trem; **to pay by cheque** pagar com cheque; **by moonlight/candlelight** sob o luar/à luz de vela; **by saving hard, he ...** economizando muito, ele ... **3** (*via, through*) por, via; **we came by Dover** viemos por *or* via Dover **4** (*close to*) perto de, ao pé de; **a holiday by the sea** férias à beira-mar; **she sat by his bed** ela sentou-se ao lado de seu leito **5** (*past*) por; **she rushed by me** ela passou por mim correndo **6** (*not later than*): **by 4 o'clock** antes das quatro; **by this time tomorrow** esta mesma hora amanhã; **by the time I got here it was too late** quando eu cheguei aqui, já era tarde demais **7** (*during*): **by daylight** durante o dia **8** (*amount*) por; **by the kilometre** por quilômetro **9** (*Math, measure*) por; **it's broader by a metre** tem um metro a mais de largura **10** (*according to*) segundo, de acordo com; **it's all right by me** por mim tudo bem **11**: **(all) by oneself** *etc*

(completamente) só, sozinho; **he did it (all) by himself** ele fez tudo sozinho **12**: **by the way** a propósito ▶ ADV **1** *see* **go, pass** *etc* **2**: **by and by** logo, mais tarde; **by and large** em geral

bye ['baɪ], **bye-bye** ['baɪ'baɪ] EXCL até logo (BR), tchau (BR), adeus (PT)

bypass ['baɪpɑːs] N via secundária, desvio; (*Med*) ponte *f* de safena ▶ VT evitar

byte [baɪt] N (*Comput*) byte *m*

C

C [siː] N (Mus) dó m
cab [kæb] N táxi m; (of truck etc) boleia; (of train) cabina de maquinista
cabaret ['kæbəreɪ] N cabaré m
cabbage ['kæbɪdʒ] N repolho (BR), couve f (PT)
cabin ['kæbɪn] N cabana; (on ship) camarote m; (on plane) cabina de passageiros; **cabin crew** N (Aviat) tripulação f
cabinet ['kæbɪnɪt] N (Pol) gabinete m; (furniture) armário; (also: **display ~**) armário com vitrina
cable ['keɪbl] N cabo; (telegram) cabograma m ▶ VT enviar cabograma para; **cable television** N televisão f a cabo
cactus ['kæktəs] (pl **cacti**) N cacto
café ['kæfeɪ] N café m
cage [keɪdʒ] N (bird cage) gaiola; (for large animals) jaula; (of lift) cabina

cagoule [kə'guːl] N casaco de náilon
Cairo ['kaɪərəu] N o Cairo
cake [keɪk] N (large) bolo; (small) doce m, bolinho; **cake of soap** N sabonete m
calculate ['kælkjuleɪt] VT calcular; (estimate) avaliar; **calculation** N cálculo; **calculator** N calculador m
calendar ['kæləndər] N calendário; **calendar month** N mês m civil; **calendar year** N ano civil
calf [kɑːf] (pl **calves**) N (of cow) bezerro, vitela; (of other animals) cria; (also: **~skin**) pele f or couro de bezerro; (Anat) barriga da perna
calibre ['kælɪbər], (US) **caliber** N (of person) capacidade f, calibre m
call [kɔːl] VT chamar; (label) qualificar, descrever; (Tel) telefonar a, ligar para; (witness) citar; (meeting, strike) convocar ▶ VI chamar; (shout) gritar; (Tel) telefonar; (visit: also: **~ in**, **~ round**) dar um pulo ▶ N (shout, announcement) chamada; (also: **telephone ~**) chamada, telefonema m; (of bird) canto; **to be ~ed** chamar-se; **on ~** de plantão; **call back** VI (return) voltar, passar de novo; (Tel) ligar de volta; **call for** VT FUS (demand) requerer, exigir; (fetch) ir buscar; **call off** VT (cancel) cancelar; **call on** VT FUS (visit) visitar; (appeal to) pedir; **call out** VI gritar, bradar; **call up** VT (Mil) chamar às fileiras; (Tel) ligar para; **call box** (BRIT) N cabine f telefônica; **call centre** (BRIT) N (Tel) central f de chamadas; **caller** N visita m/f; (Tel) chamador(a) m/f

c

callous ['kæləs] ADJ cruel, insensível

calm [kɑ:m] ADJ calmo; (*peaceful*) tranquilo; (*weather*) estável ▶ N calma ▶ VT acalmar; (*fears, grief*) abrandar; **calm down** VT acalmar, tranquilizar ▶ VI acalmar-se

calorie ['kælərɪ] N caloria

calves [kɑ:vz] NPL *of* **calf**

Cambodia [kæm'bəudjə] N Camboja

camcorder ['kæmkɔ:dər] N filmadora, máquina de filmar

came [keɪm] PT *of* **come**

camel ['kæməl] N camelo

camera ['kæmərə] N máquina fotográfica; (*Cinema, TV*) câmera; **in ~** (*Jur*) em câmara; **camera phone** N celular *m* com câmera

camouflage ['kæməflɑ:ʒ] N camuflagem *f* ▶ VT camuflar

camp [kæmp] N campo, acampamento; (*Mil*) acampamento; (*for prisoners*) campo; (*faction*) facção *f* ▶ VI acampar ▶ ADJ afeminado

campaign [kæm'peɪn] N (*Mil, Pol etc*) campanha ▶ VI fazer campanha

camper ['kæmpər] N campista *m/f*; (*vehicle*) reboque *m*

camping ['kæmpɪŋ] N camping *m* (BR), campismo (PT); **to go ~** acampar

campsite ['kæmpsaɪt] N camping *m* (BR), parque *m* de campismo (PT)

campus ['kæmpəs] N campus *m*, cidade *f* universitária

can¹ [kæn] N lata ▶ VT enlatar

(KEYWORD)

can² [kæn] (*negative* **can't** *or* **cannot**, *pt, conditional* **could**) AUX VB **1** (*be able to*) poder; **you can do it if you try** se você tentar, você consegue fazê-lo; **I'll help you all I can** ajudarei você em tudo que eu puder; **she couldn't sleep that night** ela não conseguiu dormir aquela noite; **can you hear me?** você está me ouvindo? **2** (*know how to*) saber; **I can swim** sei nadar; **can you speak Portuguese?** você fala português? **3** (*may*): **could I have a word with you?** será que eu podia falar com você? **4** (*expressing disbelief, puzzlement*): **it CAN'T be true!** não pode ser verdade!; **what CAN he want?** o que é que ele quer? **5** (*expressing possibility, suggestion etc*): **he could be in the library** ele talvez esteja na biblioteca; **they could have forgotten** eles podiam ter esquecido

Canada ['kænədə] N Canadá *m*; **Canadian** [kə'neɪdɪən] ADJ, N canadense *m/f*

canal [kə'næl] N canal *m*

canary [kə'nɛərɪ] N canário

cancel ['kænsəl] VT cancelar; (*contract*) anular; (*cross out*) riscar, invalidar; **cancellation** [kænsə'leɪʃən] N cancelamento

cancer ['kænsər] N câncer *m* (BR), cancro (PT); **C~** (*Astrology*) Câncer *m*

candidate ['kændɪdeɪt] N candidato(-a)

candle ['kændl] N vela; (*in church*) círio; **candlestick** N (*plain*) castiçal *m*; (*bigger, ornate*) candelabro, lustre *m*

candy ['kændɪ] N (*also*: **sugar ~**) açúcar *m* cristalizado; (*US*) bala (BR), rebuçado (PT)

cane [keɪn] N (*Bot*) cana; (*stick*) bengala ▶ VT (BRIT *Sch*) castigar (com bengala)

canister ['kænɪstə^r] N lata
cannabis ['kænəbɪs] N maconha
canned [kænd] ADJ (*food*) em lata, enlatado
cannon ['kænən] (*pl inv or* **cannons**) N canhão *m*
cannot ['kænɔt] = **can not**
canoe [kə'nu:] N canoa
can't [kɑ:nt] = **can not**
canteen [kæn'ti:n] N cantina; (*BRIT: of cutlery*) jogo (de talheres)
canter ['kæntə^r] VI ir a meio galope
canvas ['kænvəs] N (*material*) lona; (*for painting*) tela; (*Naut*) velas *fpl*
canvass ['kænvəs] VI (*Pol*): **to ~ for** fazer campanha por ▶ VT sondar
canyon ['kænjən] N canhão *m*, garganta, desfiladeiro
cap [kæp] N gorro; (*of pen, bottle*) tampa; (*contraceptive: also:* **Dutch ~**) diafragma *m*; (*for toy gun*) cartucho ▶ VT (*outdo*) superar; (*put limit on*) limitar
capable ['keɪpəbl] ADJ (*of sth*) capaz; (*competent*) competente, hábil
capacity [kə'pæsɪtɪ] N capacidade *f*; (*of stadium etc*) lotação *f*; (*role*) condição *f*, posição *f*
cape [keɪp] N capa; (*Geo*) cabo
caper ['keɪpə^r] N (*Culin: gen pl*) alcaparra; (*prank*) travessura
capital ['kæpɪtl] N (*also:* **~ city**) capital *f*; (*money*) capital *m*; (*also:* **~ letter**) maiúscula; **capitalism** N capitalismo; **capitalist** ADJ, N capitalista *m/f*; **capital punishment** N pena de morte

Capitol ['kæpɪtl] N *ver nota*
O Capitólio (**Capitol**) é a sede do Congresso dos Estados Unidos, localizado no monte Capitólio (*Capitol Hill*), em Washington.

Capricorn ['kæprɪkɔ:n] N Capricórnio
capsize [kæp'saɪz] VT, VI emborcar, virar
capsule ['kæpsju:l] N cápsula
captain ['kæptɪn] N capitão *m*
caption ['kæpʃən] N legenda
capture ['kæptʃə^r] VT prender, aprisionar; (*person*) capturar; (*place*) tomar; (*attention*) atrair, chamar ▶ N captura; (*of place*) tomada
car [kɑ:^r] N carro, automóvel *m*; (*Rail*) vagão *m*
caramel ['kærəməl] N (*sweet*) caramelo; (*burnt sugar*) caramelado
caravan ['kærəvæn] N reboque *m* (BR), trailer *m* (BR), rulote *f* (PT); (*in desert*) caravana
carb [kɑ:b] (*inf*) N ABBR (= *carbohydrate*) carboidrato
carbohydrate [kɑ:bəu'haɪdreɪt] N hidrato de carbono; (*food*) carboidrato
carbon ['kɑ:bən] N carbono; **carbon copy** N cópia de papel carbono; **carbon dioxide** [-daɪ'ɔksaɪd] N dióxido de carbono; **carbon footprint** N pegada de carbono; **carbon monoxide** [-mə'nɔksaɪd] N monóxido de carbono; **carbon-neutral** ADJ sem emissão de carbono; **carbon offset** N compensação *f* de emissão de carbono
carburettor [kɑ:bju'rɛtə^r], (*US*) **carburetor** N carburador *m*

card [kɑːd] N (also: **playing ~**) carta;
(visiting card, postcard etc) cartão m;
(thin cardboard) cartolina;
cardboard N cartão m, papelão m
cardigan ['kɑːdɪgən] N casaco de
lã, cardigã m
cardinal ['kɑːdɪnl] ADJ cardeal;
(Math) cardinal ▶ N (Rel) cardeal m
care [kɛəʳ] N cuidado m; (worry)
preocupação f; (charge) encargo,
custódia ▶ VI: **to ~ about** (person,
animal) preocupar-se com; (thing,
idea) ter interesse em; **~ of** (on letter)
aos cuidados de; **in sb's ~** a cargo
de alguém; **to take ~ (to do)**
cuidar-se or ter o cuidado (de fazer);
to take ~ of (person) cuidar de;
(situation) encarregar-se de; **I don't
~** não me importa; **I couldn't ~ less**
não dou a mínima; **care for** VT FUS
cuidar de; (like) gostar de
career [kə'rɪəʳ] N carreira ▶ VI (also:
~ along) correr a toda velocidade
carefree ['kɛəfriː] ADJ
despreocupado
careful ['kɛəful] ADJ (thorough)
cuidadoso; (cautious) cauteloso;
(be) ~! tenha cuidado!; **carefully**
ADV cuidadosamente;
cautelosamente
careless ['kɛəlɪs] ADJ descuidado;
(heedless) desatento
carer ['kɛərəʳ] N (professional)
acompanhante m/f; (unpaid)
cuidador(a) m/f
caretaker ['kɛəteɪkəʳ] N
zelador(a) m/f
car-ferry N barca para carros (BR),
barco de passagem (PT)
cargo ['kɑːgəʊ] (pl **cargoes**) N carga
car hire (BRIT) N aluguel m (BR) or
aluguer m (PT) de carros
Caribbean [kærɪ'biːən] N: **the ~
(Sea)** o Caribe

caring ['kɛərɪŋ] ADJ (person)
bondoso; (society) humanitário
carnation [kɑː'neɪʃən] N cravo
carnival ['kɑːnɪvəl] N carnaval m;
(US: funfair) parque m de diversões
carol ['kærəl] N: **(Christmas) ~**
cântico de Natal
car park (BRIT) N estacionamento
carpenter ['kɑːpɪntəʳ] N
carpinteiro
carpet ['kɑːpɪt] N tapete m ▶ VT
atapetar
carriage ['kærɪdʒ] N carruagem f;
(BRIT Rail) vagão m; (of goods)
transporte m; (: cost) porte m;
carriageway (BRIT) N (part of road)
pista
carrier ['kærɪəʳ] N transportador(a)
m/f; (company) empresa de
transportes, transportadora; (Med)
portador(a) m/f; **carrier bag** (BRIT)
N saco, sacola
carrot ['kærət] N cenoura
carry ['kærɪ] VT levar; (transport)
transportar; (involve:
responsibilities etc) implicar ▶ VI
(sound) projetar-se; **to get carried
away** (fig) exagerar; **carry on** VI
seguir, continuar ▶ VT prosseguir,
continuar; **carry out** VT (orders)
cumprir; (investigation) levar a cabo,
realizar
cart [kɑːt] N carroça, carreta ▶ VT
transportar (em carroça)
carton ['kɑːtən] N (box) caixa (de
papelão); (of yogurt) pote m; (of milk)
caixa; (packet) pacote m
cartoon [kɑː'tuːn] N (drawing)
desenho; (BRIT: comic strip) história
em quadrinhos (BR), banda
desenhada (PT); (film) desenho
animado
cartridge ['kɑːtrɪdʒ] N cartucho;
(of record player) cápsula

carve [kɑːv] VT (*meat*) trinchar; (*wood, stone*) cinzelar, esculpir; (*initials, design*) gravar; **carve up** VT dividir, repartir; **carving** N (*object*) escultura; (*design*) talha, entalhe m

case [keɪs] N caso; (*for spectacles etc*) estojo; (*Jur*) causa; (BRIT: *also*: **suit~**) mala; (*of wine etc*) caixa; **in ~ (of)** em caso (de); **in any ~** em todo o caso; **just in ~** *conj* se por acaso; *adv* por via das dúvidas

cash [kæʃ] N dinheiro (em espécie) ▶ VT descontar; **to pay (in) ~** pagar em dinheiro; **~ on delivery** pagamento contra entrega; **cash card** (BRIT) N cartão m de saque; **cash desk** (BRIT) N caixa; **cash dispenser** N caixa automática *or* eletrônica

cashew [kæˈʃuː] N (*also*: **~ nut**) castanha de caju

cashier [kæˈʃɪəʳ] N caixa m/f

cash point N caixa m eletrônico

cash register N caixa registradora

casino [kəˈsiːnəu] N cassino

casket [ˈkɑːskɪt] N cofre m, porta-joias m inv; (US: *coffin*) caixão m

casserole [ˈkæsərəul] N panela de ir ao forno; (*food*) ensopado (BR) no forno, guisado (PT) no forno

cassette [kæˈsɛt] N fita-cassete f; **cassette player** N toca-fitas m inv

cast [kɑːst] (*pt, pp* **cast**) VT (*throw*) lançar, atirar; (*Theatre*): **to ~ sb as Hamlet** dar a alguém o papel de Hamlet ▶ N (*Theatre*) elenco; (*also*: **plaster ~**) gesso; **to ~ one's vote** votar; **cast off** VI (*Naut*) soltar o cabo; (*Knitting*) rematar os pontos; **cast on** VI montar os pontos

caster sugar [ˈkɑːstəʳ-] (BRIT) N açúcar m branco refinado

castle [ˈkɑːsl] N castelo; (*Chess*) torre f

casual [ˈkæʒjul] ADJ (*by chance*) fortuito; (*work etc*) eventual; (*unconcerned*) despreocupado; (*clothes etc*) descontraído, informal

casualty [ˈkæʒjultɪ] N ferido(-a); (*dead*) morto(-a); (*of situation*) vítima; (*department*) pronto-socorro

cat [kæt] N gato

catalogue [ˈkætəlɔg], (US) **catalog** N catálogo ▶ VT catalogar

catarrh [kəˈtɑːʳ] N catarro

catastrophe [kəˈtæstrəfɪ] N catástrofe f

catch [kætʃ] (*pt, pp* **caught**) VT pegar (BR), apanhar (PT); (*fish*) pescar; (*arrest*) prender, deter; (*person: by surprise*) flagrar, surpreender; (*attention*) atrair; (*hear*) ouvir; (*also*: **~ up**) alcançar ▶ VI (*fire*) pegar; (*in branches etc*) ficar preso, prender-se ▶ N (*fish etc*) pesca; (*game*) manha, armadilha; (*of lock*) trinco, lingueta; **to ~ fire** pegar fogo; (*building*) incendiar-se; **to ~ sight of** avistar; **catch on** VI (*understand*) entender (BR), perceber (PT); (*grow popular*) pegar; **catch up** VI equiparar-se ▶ VT (*also*: **~ up with**) alcançar; **catching** ADJ (*Med*) contagioso

category [ˈkætɪgərɪ] N categoria

cater [ˈkeɪtəʳ] VI preparar comida; **cater for** VT FUS (*needs*) atender a; (*consumers*) satisfazer

caterpillar [ˈkætəpɪləʳ] N lagarta

cathedral [kəˈθiːdrəl] N catedral f; **Catholic** ADJ, N (*Rel*) católico(-a)

catholic [ˈkæθəlɪk] ADJ eclético

cattle [ˈkætl] NPL gado

catwalk [ˈkætwɔːk] N passarela

caught [kɔːt] PT, PP *of* **catch**

cauliflower ['kɔlɪflauər] N couve-flor f

cause [kɔːz] N causa; (*reason*) motivo, razão f ▶ VT causar, provocar

caution ['kɔːʃən] N cautela, prudência; (*warning*) aviso ▶ VT acautelar, avisar

cautious ['kɔːʃəs] ADJ cauteloso, prudente, precavido

cave [keɪv] N caverna, gruta; **cave in** VI ceder

cc ABBR (= *cubic centimetre*) cc; (*on letter etc*) = **carbon copy**

CCTV N ABBR (= *closed-circuit television*) CFTV; **CCTV camera** N câmera de segurança

CD N ABBR = **compact disc**; **CD burner, CD writer** N gravador m de CD; **CD-ROM** N ABBR (= *compact disc read-only memory*) CD-ROM m

cease [siːs] VT, VI cessar; **ceasefire** N cessar-fogo m

cedar ['siːdər] N cedro

ceiling ['siːlɪŋ] N (*also fig*) teto

celebrate ['sɛlɪbreɪt] VT celebrar ▶ VI celebrar; (*birthday, anniversary etc*) festejar; (*Rel: mass*) rezar; **celebration** [sɛlɪ'breɪʃən] N (*party*) festa

celebrity [sɪ'lɛbrɪtɪ] N celebridade f

celery ['sɛlərɪ] N aipo

cell [sɛl] N cela; (*Bio*) célula; (*Elec*) pilha, elemento; (*US: cellphone*) celular m (BR), telemóvel m (PT)

cellar ['sɛlər] N porão m; (*for wine*) adega

cellphone ['sɛlfəun] N (telefone) celular m (BR), telemóvel m (PT)

cell tower (*US*) N (*Tel*) torre f de celular

cement [sə'mɛnt] N cimento

cemetery ['sɛmɪtrɪ] N cemitério

censor ['sɛnsər] N censor(a) m/f ▶ VT censurar; **censorship** N censura

census ['sɛnsəs] N censo

cent [sɛnt] N cêntimo; *see also* **per**

centenary [sɛn'tiːnərɪ] N centenário

center ['sɛntər] (*US*) = **centre**

centigrade ['sɛntɪgreɪd] ADJ centígrado

centimetre ['sɛntɪmiːtər], (*US*) **centimeter** N centímetro

central ['sɛntrəl] ADJ central; **Central America** N América Central; **central heating** N aquecimento central

centre ['sɛntər], (*US*) **center** N centro; (*of room, circle etc*) meio ▶ VT centrar

century ['sɛntjurɪ] N século; **20th ~** século vinte

ceramic [sɪ'ræmɪk] ADJ cerâmico

cereal ['siːrɪəl] N cereal m

ceremony ['sɛrɪmənɪ] N cerimônia; (*ritual*) rito; **to stand on ~** fazer cerimônia

certain ['səːtən] ADJ (*sure*) seguro; (*person*): **a ~ Mr Smith** um certo Sr. Smith; (*particular*): **~ days/places** certos dias/lugares; (*some*): **a ~ coldness/pleasure** uma certa frieza/um certo prazer; **for ~** com certeza; **certainly** ADV certamente, com certeza; **certainty** N certeza

certificate [sə'tɪfɪkɪt] N certidão f

certify ['səːtɪfaɪ] VT certificar

cf. ABBR (= *compare*) cf

CFC N ABBR (= *chlorofluorocarbon*) CFC m

chain [tʃeɪn] N corrente f; (*of islands*) grupo; (*of mountains*) cordilheira; (*of shops*) cadeia; (*of events*) série f ▶ VT (*also*: **~ up**) acorrentar

chair [tʃɛəʳ] N cadeira; (*armchair*) poltrona; (*of university*) cátedra; (*of meeting*) presidência, mesa ▶ VT (*meeting*) presidir; **chairlift** N teleférico; **chairman** *irreg* N presidente *m*

chalk [tʃɔːk] N (*Geo*) greda; (*for writing*) giz *m*

challenge ['tʃælɪndʒ] N desafio ▶ VT desafiar; (*statement, right*) disputar, contestar; **challenging** ADJ desafiante; (*tone*) de desafio

chamber ['tʃeɪmbəʳ] N câmara; (*BRIT Jur: gen pl*) sala de audiências; **chambermaid** N arrumadeira (*BR*), empregada (*PT*); **chamber of commerce** N câmara de comércio

champagne [ʃæm'peɪn] N champanhe *m or f*

champion ['tʃæmpɪən] N campeão(-peã) *m/f*; (*of cause*) defensor(a) *m/f*; **championship** N campeonato

chance [tʃɑːns] N (*opportunity*) oportunidade, ocasião *f*; (*likelihood*) chance *f*; (*risk*) risco ▶ VT arriscar ▶ ADJ fortuito, casual; **to take a ~** arriscar-se; **by ~** por acaso; **to ~ it** arriscar-se

chancellor ['tʃɑːnsələʳ] N chanceler *m*; **C~ of the Exchequer** (*BRIT*) Ministro da Economia (Fazenda e Planejamento)

chandelier [ʃændə'lɪəʳ] N lustre *m*

change [tʃeɪndʒ] VT (*alter*) mudar; (*wheel, bulb, money*) trocar; (*replace*) substituir; (*clothes, house*) mudar de, trocar de; (*nappy*) mudar, trocar; (*transform*): **to ~ sb into** transformar alguém em ▶ VI mudar(-se); (*change clothes*) trocar-se; (*trains*) fazer baldeação (*BR*), mudar (*PT*); (*be transformed*): **to ~ into** transformar-se em ▶ N mudança; (*exchange*) troca; (*difference*) diferença; (*of clothes*) muda; (*coins*) trocado; **to ~ gear** (*Aut*) trocar de marcha; **to ~ one's mind** mudar de ideia; **for a ~** para variar; **changeable** ADJ (*weather*) instável; (*mood*) inconstante

channel ['tʃænl] N canal *m*; (*of river*) leito; (*groove*) ranhura; (*fig: medium*) meio, via ▶ VT: **to ~ (into)** canalizar (para); **the (English) C~** o Canal da Mancha

chant [tʃɑːnt] N canto; (*Rel*) cântico ▶ VT cantar; (*word, slogan*) entoar

chaos ['keɪɔs] N caos *m*

chap [tʃæp] N (*BRIT inf: man*) sujeito (*BR*), tipo (*PT*)

chapel ['tʃæpəl] N capela

chapter ['tʃæptəʳ] N capítulo

character ['kærɪktəʳ] N caráter *m*; (*in novel, film*) personagem *m/f*; (*letter*) letra; **characteristic** [kærɪktə'rɪstɪk] ADJ característico

charcoal ['tʃɑːkəul] N carvão *m* de lenha; (*Art*) carvão *m*

charge [tʃɑːdʒ] N (*Jur*) encargo, acusação *f*; (*fee*) preço, custo; (*responsibility*) encargo ▶ VT (*battery*) carregar; (*Mil*) atacar; (*customer*) cobrar dinheiro de; (*Jur*): **to ~ sb (with)** acusar alguém (de) ▶ VI precipitar-se; **charges** NPL: **bank ~s** taxas *fpl* bancárias; **to reverse the ~s** (*BRIT Tel*) ligar a cobrar; **how much do you ~?** quanto você cobra?; **to ~ an expense (up) to sb's account** pôr a despesa na conta de alguém; **to take ~ of** encarregar-se de, tomar conta de; **to be in ~ of** estar a cargo de *or* encarregado de; **charge card** N cartão *m* de crédito (*emitido por uma loja*)

charity ['tʃærɪtɪ] N caridade f; (organization) obra de caridade; (kindness) compaixão f; (money, gifts) donativo

charm [tʃɑːm] N (quality) charme m; (talisman) amuleto; (on bracelet) berloque m ▶ VT encantar, deliciar; **charming** ADJ encantador(a)

chart [tʃɑːt] N (graph) gráfico; (diagram) diagrama m; (map) carta de navegação ▶ VT traçar; **charts** NPL (hit parade) paradas fpl (de sucesso)

charter ['tʃɑːtəʳ] VT fretar ▶ N (document) carta, alvará m; **chartered accountant** (BRIT) N perito-contador/perita-contadora m/f; **charter flight** N voo charter or fretado

chase [tʃeɪs] VT perseguir; (also: ~ **away**) enxotar ▶ N perseguição f, caça

chat [tʃæt] VI (also: **have a ~**) conversar, bater papo (BR), cavaquear (PT) ▶ N conversa, bate-papo m (BR), cavaqueira (PT); **chatroom** N sala f de bate-papo; **chat show** (BRIT) N programa m de entrevistas

chatter ['tʃætəʳ] VI (person) tagarelar; (animal) emitir sons; (teeth) tiritar ▶ N tagarelice f; emissão f de sons; (of birds) chilro

chauvinist ['ʃəuvɪnɪst] N (also: **male ~**) machista m; (nationalist) chauvinista m/f

cheap [tʃiːp] ADJ barato; (poor quality) barato, de pouca qualidade; (behaviour) vulgar; (joke) de mau gosto ▶ ADV barato; **cheaply** ADV barato, por baixo preço

cheat [tʃiːt] VI trapacear; (at cards) roubar (BR), fazer batota (PT); (in exam) colar (BR), cabular (PT)

▶ N fraude f; (person) trapaceiro(-a); **to ~ sb out of sth** defraudar alguém de algo

check [tʃɛk] VT (examine) controlar; (facts) verificar; (halt) conter, impedir; (restrain) parar, refrear ▶ N controle m, inspeção f; (curb) freio; (US: bill) conta; (pattern: gen pl) xadrez m; (US) = **cheque** ▶ ADJ (pattern, cloth) xadrez inv; **check in** VI (in hotel) registrar-se; (in airport) apresentar-se ▶ VT (luggage) entregar; **check out** VI pagar a conta e sair; **check up** VI: **to ~ up on sth** verificar algo; **to ~ up on sb** investigar alguém; **checkers** (US) N (jogo de) damas fpl; **check-in, check-in desk** N check-in m; **checking account** (US) N conta corrente; **checkout** N caixa; **checkpoint** N (ponto de) controle m; **checkroom** (US) N depósito de bagagem; **checkup** N (Med) check-up m

cheek [tʃiːk] N bochecha; (impudence) folga, descaramento; **cheekbone** N maçã f do rosto; **cheeky** ADJ insolente, descarado

cheer [tʃɪəʳ] VT dar vivas a, aplaudir; (gladden) alegrar, animar ▶ VI gritar com entusiasmo ▶ N (gen pl) gritos mpl de entusiasmo; **cheers** NPL (of crowd) aplausos mpl; **~s!** saúde!; **cheer up** VI animar-se, alegrar-se ▶ VT alegrar, animar; **cheerful** ADJ alegre; **cheerio** (BRIT) EXCL tchau (BR), adeus (PT); **cheerleader** ['tʃɪəliːdəʳ] N animador(a) de torcida m/f

cheese [tʃiːz] N queijo

chef [ʃɛf] N cozinheiro-chefe/ cozinheira-chefe m/f

chemical ['kɛmɪkəl] ADJ químico ▶ N produto químico

chemist ['kɛmɪst] N (BRIT: pharmacist) farmacêutico(-a); (scientist) químico(-a); **chemistry** N química; **chemist's, chemist's shop** (BRIT) N farmácia

cheque [tʃɛk] (BRIT) N cheque m; **chequebook** N talão m (BR) or livro (PT) de cheques; **cheque card** (BRIT) N cartão m (de garantia) de cheques

cherry ['tʃɛrɪ] N cereja; (also: ~ **tree**) cerejeira

chess [tʃɛs] N xadrez m

chest [tʃɛst] N (Anat) peito; (box) caixa, cofre m

chestnut ['tʃɛsnʌt] N castanha

chest of drawers N cômoda

chew [tʃuː] VT mastigar; **chewing gum** N chiclete m (BR), pastilha elástica (PT)

chic [ʃɪk] ADJ elegante

chick [tʃɪk] N pinto; (inf: girl) broto

chicken ['tʃɪkɪn] N galinha; (food) galinha, frango; (inf: coward) covarde m/f, galinha; **chicken out** (inf) VI agalinhar-se; **chickenpox** N catapora (BR), varicela (PT)

chief [tʃiːf] N (of tribe) cacique m, morubixaba m; (of organization) chefe m/f ▶ ADJ principal; **chiefly** ADV principalmente

child [tʃaɪld] (pl **children**) N criança; (offspring) filho(-a); **childbirth** N parto; **childcare** N serviço de cuidado infantil; **childhood** N infância; **childish** ADJ infantil; **child minder** (BRIT) N cuidadora de crianças; **children** ['tʃɪldrən] NPL of **child**

Chile ['tʃɪlɪ] N Chile m

chill [tʃɪl] N frio, friagem f; (Med) resfriamento ▶ VT (Culin) semi-congelar; (person) congelar

chilli ['tʃɪlɪ], (US) **chili** N pimentão m picante

chilly ['tʃɪlɪ] ADJ frio; (person) friorento

chimpanzee [tʃɪmpæn'ziː] N chimpanzé m

chin [tʃɪn] N queixo

China ['tʃaɪnə] N China

china ['tʃaɪnə] N porcelana; (crockery) louça fina

Chinese [tʃaɪ'niːz] ADJ chinês(-esa) ▶ N INV chinês(-esa) m/f; (Ling) chinês m

chip [tʃɪp] N (gen pl: BRIT Culin) batata frita; (: US: also: **potato ~**) batatinha frita; (of wood) lasca; (of glass, stone) lasca, pedaço; (Comput: also: **micro~**) chip m ▶ VT (cup, plate) lascar; **chip in** (inf) VI interromper; (contribute) compartilhar as despesas

chiropodist [kɪ'rɔpədɪst] (BRIT) N pedicuro(-a)

chisel ['tʃɪzl] N (for wood) formão m; (for stone) cinzel m

chives [tʃaɪvz] NPL cebolinha

chocolate ['tʃɔklɪt] N chocolate m

choice [tʃɔɪs] N (selection) seleção f; (option) escolha; (preference) preferência ▶ ADJ seleto, escolhido

choir ['kwaɪəʳ] N coro

choke [tʃəuk] VI sufocar-se; (on food) engasgar ▶ VT estrangular; (block) obstruir ▶ N (Aut) afogador m (BR), ar m (PT)

cholesterol [kə'lɛstərɔl] N colesterol m

choose [tʃuːz] (pt **chose**, pp **chosen**) VT escolher; **to ~ to do** optar por fazer

chop [tʃɔp] VT (wood) cortar, talhar; (Culin: also: ~ **up**) cortar em pedaços; (meat) picar ▶ N golpe m;

(Culin) costeleta; **chops** NPL (inf: jaws) beiços mpl

chopsticks ['tʃɒpstɪks] NPL pauzinhos mpl, palitos mpl

chord [kɔːd] N (Mus) acorde m

chore [tʃɔːʳ] N tarefa; (routine task) trabalho de rotina

chorus ['kɔːrəs] N (group) coro; (song) coral m; (refrain) estribilho

chose [tʃəuz] PT of **choose**; **chosen** PP of **choose**

Christ [kraɪst] N Cristo

christen ['krɪsn] VT batizar; (nickname) apelidar

Christian ['krɪstɪən] ADJ, N cristão(-tã) m/f; **Christianity** [krɪstɪ'ænɪtɪ] N cristianismo; **Christian name** N prenome m, nome m de batismo

Christmas ['krɪsməs] N Natal m; **Happy** or **Merry ~!** Feliz Natal!; **Christmas card** N cartão m de Natal; **Christmas cracker** N ver nota

Um **Christmas cracker** é um cilindro de papelão que ao ser aberto faz estourar uma bombinha. Contém um presente surpresa e um chapéu de papel que cada convidado coloca na cabeça durante a ceia de Natal.

Christmas: Christmas Day N dia m de Natal; **Christmas Eve** N véspera de Natal; **Christmas tree** N árvore f de Natal

chronic ['krɒnɪk] ADJ crônico; (fig: drunkenness) inveterado

chubby ['tʃʌbɪ] ADJ roliço, gorducho

chuck [tʃʌk] VT jogar (BR), deitar (PT); (BRIT: also: **~ up**, **~ in**: job) largar; (: person) acabar com; **chuck out** VT (thing) jogar (BR) or deitar (PT) fora; (person) expulsar

chuckle ['tʃʌkl] VI rir

chuffed [tʃʌft] (inf) ADJ: **~ (about sth)** encantado (com algo)

chum [tʃʌm] N camarada m/f

church [tʃəːtʃ] N igreja; **churchyard** N adro, cemitério

churn [tʃəːn] N (for butter) batedeira; (also: **milk ~**) lata, vasilha; **churn out** VT produzir em série

chute [ʃuːt] N rampa; (also: **rubbish ~**) despejador m

CIA (US) N ABBR (= Central Intelligence Agency) CIA f

CID (BRIT) N ABBR = **Criminal Investigation Department**

cider ['saɪdəʳ] N sidra

cigar [sɪ'gɑːʳ] N charuto

cigarette [sɪgə'ret] N cigarro

cinema ['sɪnəmə] N cinema m

cinnamon ['sɪnəmən] N canela

circle ['səːkl] N círculo; (in cinema) balcão m ▸ VI dar voltas ▸ VT (surround) rodear, cercar; (move round) dar a volta de

circuit ['səːkɪt] N circuito; (tour, lap) volta; (track) pista

circular ['səːkjuləʳ] ADJ circular ▸ N (carta) circular f

circulate ['səːkjuleɪt] VT, VI circular; **circulation** [səːkju'leɪʃən] N circulação f; (of newspaper, book etc) tiragem f

circumstances ['səːkəmstənsɪz] NPL circunstâncias fpl; (conditions) condições fpl; (financial condition) situação f econômica

circus ['səːkəs] N circo

citizen ['sɪtɪzn] N (of country) cidadão(-dã) m/f; (of town) habitante m/f; **citizenship** N cidadania

city ['sɪtɪ] N cidade f; **the C~** centro financeiro de Londres

civic ['sɪvɪk] ADJ cívico, municipal

civil ['sɪvɪl] ADJ civil; (*polite*)
delicado, cortês; **civilian**
[sɪ'vɪlɪən] ADJ, N civil *m/f*
civilized ['sɪvɪlaɪzd] ADJ civilizado
civil servant N funcionário(-a)
público(-a)
Civil Service N administração *f*
pública
civil war N guerra civil
claim [kleɪm] VT exigir, reclamar;
(*rights etc*) reivindicar; (*responsibility*)
assumir; (*assert*): **to ~ that/to be**
afirmar que/ser ▶ VI (*for insurance*)
reclamar ▶ N reclamação *f*;
(*assertion*) afirmação *f*; (*wage claim
etc*) reivindicação *f*
clam [klæm] N molusco
clamp [klæmp] N grampo ▶ VT
prender; **clamp down on** VT FUS
reprimir
clan [klæn] N clã *m*
clap [klæp] VI bater palmas,
aplaudir
clarinet [klærɪ'nɛt] N clarinete *m*
clarity ['klærɪtɪ] N clareza
clash [klæʃ] N (*fight*) confronto;
(*disagreement*) desavença; (*of
beliefs*) divergência; (*of colours,
styles*) choque *m*; (*of dates*)
coincidência ▶ VI (*gangs, beliefs*)
chocar-se; (*disagree*) entrar em
conflito, ter uma desavença;
(*colours*) não combinar; (*dates,
events*) coincidir; (*weapons, cymbals
etc*) ressoar
clasp [klɑ:sp] N fecho; (*embrace*)
abraço ▶ VT prender; (*embrace*)
abraçar
class [klɑ:s] N classe *f*; (*lesson*)
aula; (*type*) tipo ▶ VT classificar
classic ['klæsɪk] ADJ clássico ▶ N
clássico; **classical** ADJ clássico
classmate ['klɑːsmeɪt] N colega
m/f de aula

classroom ['klɑːsrʊm] N sala de
aula
clatter ['klætəʳ] N ruído, barulho;
(*of hooves*) tropel *m* ▶ VI fazer
barulho *or* ruído
clause [klɔːz] N cláusula; (*Ling*)
oração *f*
claw [klɔː] N (*of animal*) pata; (*of
bird of prey*) garra; (*of lobster*) pinça;
claw at VT FUS arranhar; (*tear*)
rasgar
clay [kleɪ] N argila
clean [kliːn] ADJ limpo ▶ VT limpar;
(*hands, face etc*) lavar; **clean out** VT
limpar; **clean up** VT limpar, assear;
cleaner N faxineiro(-a); (*product*)
limpador *m*; **cleaner's** N (*also*: **dry
cleaner's**) tinturaria; **cleaning** N
limpeza; **clean technology** N
tecnologia limpa
clear [klɪəʳ] ADJ claro; (*footprint,
photograph*) nítido; (*obvious*)
evidente; (*glass, water*)
transparente; (*road, way*) limpo,
livre; (*conscience*) tranquilo; (*skin*)
macio ▶ VT (*space*) abrir; (*room*)
esvaziar; (*Jur: suspect*) absolver;
(*fence, wall*) saltar, transpor;
(*cheque*) compensar ▶ VI (*weather*)
abrir; (*sky*) clarear; (*fog etc*)
dissipar-se ▶ ADV: **~ of** a salvo de;
to ~ the table tirar a mesa; **clear
up** VT limpar; (*mystery*) resolver,
esclarecer; **clearance** N remoção *f*;
(*permission*) permissão *f*;
clear-cut ADJ bem definido,
nítido; **clearing** N (*in wood*)
clareira; **clearly** ADV
distintamente; (*obviously*)
claramente; (*coherently*)
coerentemente; **clearway** (*BRIT*) N
estrada onde não se pode estacionar
clench [klɛntʃ] VT apertar, cerrar;
(*teeth*) trincar

c

clerk [klɑːk, (US) kləːrk] N auxiliar m/f de escritório; (US: *sales person*) balconista m/f

clever ['klɛvəʳ] ADJ inteligente; (*deft, crafty*) hábil; (*device, arrangement*) engenhoso

click [klɪk] VT (*tongue*) estalar; (*heels*) bater; (*Comput*) clicar em ▶ VI (*make sound*) estalar; (*Comput*) clicar

client ['klaɪənt] N cliente m/f

cliff [klɪf] N penhasco

climate ['klaɪmɪt] N clima m; **climate change** N mudanças fpl climáticas

climax ['klaɪmæks] N clímax m, ponto culminante; (*sexual*) clímax

climb [klaɪm] VI subir; (*plant*) trepar; (*plane*) ganhar altitude; (*prices etc*) escalar ▶ VT (*stairs*) subir; (*tree*) trepar em; (*hill*) escalar ▶ N subida; (*of prices etc*) escalada; **climber** N alpinista m/f; (*plant*) trepadeira; **climbing** N alpinismo

clinch [klɪntʃ] VT (*deal*) fechar; (*argument*) decidir, resolver

cling [klɪŋ] (*pt, pp* **clung**) VI: **to ~ to** pegar-se a, aderir a; (*support, idea*) agarrar-se a; (*clothes*) ajustar-se a

Clingfilm® ['klɪŋfɪlm] N papel m filme

clinic ['klɪnɪk] N clínica

clip [klɪp] N (*for hair*) grampo (BR), gancho (PT); (*also:* **paper ~**) mola, clipe m; (*TV, Cinema*) clipe ▶ VT (*cut*) aparar; (*papers*) grampear

cloak [kləuk] N capa, manto ▶ VT (*fig*) encobrir; **cloakroom** N vestiário; (*BRIT: WC*) sanitários mpl (BR), lavatórios mpl (PT)

clock [klɔk] N relógio; **clock in**, **clock on** (BRIT) VI assinar o ponto na entrada; **clock off**, **clock out** (BRIT) VI assinar o ponto na saída; **clockwise** ADV em sentido horário;

clockwork N mecanismo de relógio ▶ ADJ de corda

clog [klɔg] N tamanco ▶ VT entupir ▶ VI (*also:* **~ up**) entupir-se

close [*adj, adv* kləus, *vb, n* kləuz] ADJ próximo; (*friend*) íntimo; (*examination*) minucioso; (*watch*) atento; (*contest*) apertado; (*weather*) abafado ▶ ADV perto ▶ VT fechar; (*end*) encerrar ▶ VI fechar; (*end*) concluir-se, terminar-se ▶ N (*end*) fim m, conclusão f, terminação f; **~ by, ~ at hand** perto, pertinho; **to have a ~ shave** (*fig*) livrar-se por um triz; **~ to** perto de; **close down** VI fechar definitivamente; **closed** [kləuzd] ADJ fechado

closely ['kləuslɪ] ADV (*watch*) de perto; **we are ~ related** somos parentes próximos

closet ['klɔzɪt] N (*cupboard*) armário

close-up [kləus-] N close m, close-up m

closure ['kləuʒəʳ] N fechamento

clot [klɔt] N (*gen: blood clot*) coágulo; (*inf: idiot*) imbecil m/f ▶ VI coagular-se

cloth [klɔθ] N (*material*) tecido, fazenda; (*rag*) pano

clothes [kləuðz] NPL roupa

clothing ['kləuðɪŋ] N = **clothes**

cloud [klaud] N nuvem f; **cloud computing** N computação f em nuvem; **cloudy** ADJ nublado; (*liquid*) turvo

clove [kləuv] N cravo; **clove of garlic** N dente m de alho

clown [klaun] N palhaço ▶ VI (*also:* **~ about, ~ around**) fazer palhaçadas

club [klʌb] N (*society*) clube m; (*weapon*) cacete m; (*also:* **golf ~**) taco ▶ VT esbordoar ▶ VI: **to ~ together** cotizar-se; **clubs** NPL (*Cards*) paus mpl

clue [kluː] N indício, pista; (*in crossword*) definição *f*; **I haven't a ~** não faço ideia

clumsy ['klʌmzɪ] ADJ (*person*) desajeitado; (*movement*) deselegante, mal-feito; (*attempt*) inábil

clung [klʌŋ] PT, PP *of* **cling**

cluster ['klʌstəʳ] N grupo; (*of flowers*) ramo ▶ VI agrupar-se, apinhar-se

clutch [klʌtʃ] N (*grip, grasp*) garra; (*Aut*) embreagem *f* (BR), embraiagem *f* (PT) ▶ VT empunhar, pegar em

Co. ABBR = **county**; (= *company*) Cia.

c/o ABBR (= *care of*) a/c

coach [kəutʃ] N (*bus*) ônibus *m* (BR), autocarro (PT); (*horse-drawn*) carruagem *f*, coche *m*; (*of train*) vagão *m*; (*Sport*) treinador(a) *m/f*, instrutor(a) *m/f*; (*tutor*) professor(a) *m/f* particular ▶ VT (*Sport*) treinar; (*student*) preparar, ensinar; **coach station** (BRIT) N rodoviária; **coach trip** N passeio de ônibus (BR) *or* autocarro (PT)

coal [kəul] N carvão *m*

coalition [kəuə'lɪʃən] N coalizão *f*

coarse [kɔːs] ADJ grosso, áspero; (*vulgar*) grosseiro, ordinário

coast [kəust] N costa, litoral *m* ▶ VI (*Aut*) ir em ponto morto; **coastal** ADJ costeiro; **coastguard** N (*service*) guarda costeira; (*person*) guarda-costeira *m/f*; **coastline** N litoral *m*

coat [kəut] N (*overcoat*) sobretudo; (*of animal*) pelo; (*of paint*) demão *f*, camada ▶ VT cobrir, revestir; **coat hanger** N cabide *m*; **coating** N camada

coax [kəuks] VT persuadir com meiguice

cobweb ['kɔbwɛb] N teia de aranha

cocaine [kə'keɪn] N cocaína

cock [kɔk] N (*rooster*) galo; (*male bird*) macho ▶ VT (*gun*) engatilhar; **cockerel** N frango, galo pequeno

cockney ['kɔknɪ] N londrino(-a) (*nativo dos bairros populares do leste de Londres*)

cockpit ['kɔkpɪt] N (*in aircraft*) cabina

cockroach ['kɔkrəutʃ] N barata

cocktail ['kɔkteɪl] N coquetel *m* (BR), cocktail *m* (PT)

cocoa ['kəukəu] N cacau *m*; (*drink*) chocolate *m*

coconut ['kəukənʌt] N coco

cod [kɔd] N INV bacalhau *m*

code [kəud] N cifra; (*dialling code, post code*) código; **code of practice** N deontologia

coffee ['kɔfɪ] N café *m*; **coffee bar** (BRIT) N café *m*, lanchonete *f*; **coffee bean** N grão *m* de café; **coffeepot** N cafeteira; **coffee table** N mesinha de centro

coffin ['kɔfɪn] N caixão *m*

cognitive ['kɔgnɪtɪv] ADJ cognitivo

coil [kɔɪl] N rolo; (*Elec*) bobina; (*contraceptive*) DIU *m* ▶ VT enrolar

coin [kɔɪn] N moeda ▶ VT (*word*) cunhar, criar

coincide [kəuɪn'saɪd] VI coincidir; **coincidence** [kəu'ɪnsɪdəns] N coincidência

coke [kəuk] N (*coal*) coque *m*

colander ['kɔləndəʳ] N coador *m*, passador *m*

cold [kəuld] ADJ frio ▶ N frio; (*Med*) resfriado (BR), constipação *f* (PT); **it's ~** está frio; **to be** *or* **feel ~** (*person*) estar com frio; (*object*) estar frio; **to catch ~** pegar friagem; **to catch a ~** ficar resfriado (BR), apanhar uma constipação (PT); **in ~ blood** a sangue frio; **cold sore** N herpes m labial

coleslaw ['kəʊlslɔː] N salada de repolho cru

collapse [kə'læps] VI cair, tombar; (building) desabar; (Med) desmaiar ▶ N desabamento, desmoronamento; (of government) queda; (Med) colapso

collar ['kɔlə^r] N (of shirt) colarinho; (of coat etc) gola; (for dog) coleira; (Tech) aro, colar m; **collarbone** N clavícula

colleague ['kɔliːg] N colega m/f

collect [kə'lɛkt] VT (as a hobby) colecionar; (gather) recolher; (wages, debts) cobrar; (donations, subscriptions) colher; (mail) coletar; (BRIT: call for) (ir) buscar ▶ VI (people) reunir-se ▶ ADV: **to call ~** (US Tel) ligar a cobrar; **collection** N coleção f; (of people) grupo; (of donations) arrecadação f; (of post, for charity) coleta; (of writings) coletânea; **collector** N colecionador(a) m/f; (of taxes etc) cobrador(a) m/f

college ['kɔlɪdʒ] N (of university) faculdade f; (of technology, agriculture) escola profissionalizante

Além de "universidade", **college** também se refere a um centro de educação superior para jovens que terminaram a educação obrigatória, secondary school. Alguns oferecem cursos de especialização em matérias técnicas, artísticas ou comerciais, outros oferecem disciplinas universitárias.

collide [kə'laɪd] VI: **to ~ (with)** colidir (com)

collision [kə'lɪʒən] N colisão f

Colombia [kə'lɔmbɪə] N Colômbia

colon ['kəʊlən] N (sign) dois pontos; (Med) cólon m

colonel ['kə:nl] N coronel m

colony ['kɔlənɪ] N colônia

colour ['kʌlə^r], (US) **color** N cor f ▶ VT colorir; (with crayons) colorir, pintar; (dye) tingir; (fig: account) falsear ▶ VI (blush) corar; **colours** NPL (of party, club) cores fpl; **in ~** (photograph etc) a cores; **colour in** VT (drawing) colorir; **colour-blind** ADJ daltônico; **coloured** ADJ colorido; (person) de cor; **colour film** N filme m a cores; **colourful** ADJ colorido; (account) vívido; (personality) vivo, animado; **colouring** N colorido; (complexion) tez f; (in food) colorante m; **colour television** N televisão f a cores

column ['kɔləm] N coluna; (of smoke) faixa; (of people) fila

coma ['kəʊmə] N coma m

comb [kəʊm] N pente m; (ornamental) crista ▶ VT pentear; (area) vasculhar

combat ['kɔmbæt] N combate m ▶ VT combater

combination [kɔmbɪ'neɪʃən] N combinação f; (of safe) segredo

combine [vt, vi kəm'baɪn, n 'kɔmbaɪn] VT combinar; (qualities) reunir ▶ VI combinar-se ▶ N (Econ) associação f

(KEYWORD)

come [kʌm] (pt **came**, pp **come**) VI
1 (movement towards) vir; **come with me** vem comigo; **to come running** vir correndo
2 (arrive) chegar; **she's come here to work** ela veio aqui para trabalhar; **to come home** chegar em casa

3 (*reach*): **to come to** chegar a; **the bill came to £40** a conta deu £40; **her hair came to her waist** o cabelo dela batia na cintura
4 (*occur*): **an idea came to me** uma ideia me ocorreu
5 (*be, become*) ficar; **to come loose/undone** soltar-se/desfazer-se; **I've come to like him** passei a gostar dele
come about VI suceder, acontecer
come across VT FUS (*person*) topar com; (*thing*) encontrar
come away VI (*leave*) ir-se embora; (*become detached*) desprender-se, soltar-se
come back VI (*return*) voltar
come by VT FUS (*acquire*) conseguir
come down VI (*price*) baixar; (*tree*) cair; (*building*) desmoronar-se
come forward VI apresentar-se
come from VT FUS (*subj: person*) ser de; (: *thing*) originar-se de
come in VI entrar; (*on deal etc*) participar; (*be involved*) estar envolvido
come in for VT FUS (*criticism etc*) receber
come into VT FUS (*money*) herdar; (*fashion*) ser; (*be involved*) estar envolvido em
come off VI (*button*) desprender-se, soltar-se; (*attempt*) dar certo
come on VI (*pupil, work, project*) avançar; (*lights, electricity*) ser ligado; **come on!** vamos!, vai!
come out VI (*fact*) vir à tona; (*book*) ser publicado; (*stain, sun*) sair
come round VI voltar a si
come to VI voltar a si
come up VI (*sun*) nascer; (*problem, subject*) surgir; (*event*) acontecer
come up against VT FUS (*resistance, difficulties*)

enfrentar, esbarrar em
come upon VT FUS (*find*) encontrar, achar
come up with VT FUS (*idea*) propor, sugerir; (*money*) contribuir

comedian [kə'mi:dɪən] N cômico, humorista *m*
comedy ['kɒmɪdɪ] N comédia
comfort ['kʌmfət] N (*well-being*) bem-estar *m*; (*relief*) alívio ▶ VT consolar, confortar; **comforts** NPL (*of home etc*) conforto;
comfortable ADJ confortável; (*financially*) tranquilo; (*walk, climb etc*) fácil
comic ['kɒmɪk] ADJ (*also:* **~al**) cômico ▶ N (*person*) humorista *m/f*; (BRIT: *magazine*) revista em quadrinhos (BR), revista de banda desenhada (PT), gibi *m* (BR *inf*)
comma ['kɒmə] N vírgula
command [kə'mɑ:nd] N ordem *f*, mandado; (*control*) controle *m*; (*Mil: authority*) comando; (*mastery*) domínio ▶ VT mandar; **commander** N (*Mil*) comandante *m/f*
commemorate [kə'mɛməreɪt] VT (*with monument*) comemorar; (*with celebration*) celebrar
commence [kə'mɛns] VT, VI começar, iniciar
commend [kə'mɛnd] VT elogiar, louvar; (*recommend*) recomendar
comment ['kɒmɛnt] N comentário ▶ VI comentar; **to ~ on sth** comentar algo; **"no ~"** "sem comentário"; **commentary** ['kɒməntərɪ] N comentário; **commentator** ['kɒmənteɪtər] N comentarista *m/f*
commerce ['kɒmə:s] N comércio
commercial [kə'mə:ʃəl] ADJ comercial ▶ N anúncio, comercial *m*

commission [kə'mɪʃən] N comissão f; (order for work of art etc) empreitada, encomenda ▶ VT (work of art) encomendar; **out of ~** com defeito; **commissioner** N comissário(-a)

commit [kə'mɪt] VT cometer; (money, resources) alocar; (to sb's care) entregar; **to ~ o.s. (to do)** comprometer-se (a fazer); **to ~ suicide** suicidar-se; **commitment** N compromisso; (political etc) engajamento; (undertaking) promessa

committee [kə'mɪtɪ] N comitê m

commodity [kə'mɔdɪtɪ] N mercadoria

common ['kɔmən] ADJ comum; (vulgar) ordinário, vulgar ▶ N área verde aberta ao público; **Commons** NPL (BRIT Pol): **the (House of) C~s** a Câmara dos Comuns; **to have sth in ~ (with sb)** ter algo em comum (con alguém); **commonly** ADV geralmente; **commonplace** ADJ vulgar; **common sense** N bom senso; **Commonwealth** N: **the Commonwealth** a Comunidade Britânica

communal ['kɔmjuːnl] ADJ comun

commune [n 'kɔmjuːn, vi kə'mjuːn] N (group) comuna ▶ VI: **to ~ with** comunicar-se com

communicate [kə'mjuːnɪkeɪt] VT comunicar ▶ VI: **to ~ (with)** comunicar-se (com); **communication** [kəmjuːnɪ'keɪʃən] N comunicação f; (letter, call) mensagem f

communion [kə'mjuːnɪən] N (also: **Holy C~**) comunhão f

communism ['kɔmjunɪzəm] N comunismo; **communist** ADJ, N comunista m/f

community [kə'mjuːnɪtɪ] N comunidade f; **community centre** N centro social

commute [kə'mjuːt] VI viajar diariamente ▶ VT comutar; **commuter** N viajante m/f habitual

compact [adj kəm'pækt, n 'kɔmpækt] ADJ compacto ▶ N (also: **powder ~**) estojo; **compact disc** N disco laser; **compact disc player** N som cd m

companion [kəm'pænɪən] N companheiro(-a)

company ['kʌmpənɪ] N companhia; (Comm) sociedade f, companhia; **to keep sb ~** fazer companhia a alguém

comparative [kəm'pærətɪv] ADJ (study) comparativo; (peace, safety) relativo; **comparatively** ADJ relativamente

compare [kəm'pɛər] VT comparar; **to ~ (to/with)** comparar (a/com) ▶ VI: **to ~ with** comparar-se com; **comparison** [kəm'pærɪsn] N comparação f

compartment [kəm'pɑːtmənt] N compartimento; (of wallet) divisão f

compass ['kʌmpəs] N bússola; **compasses** NPL compasso

compassion [kəm'pæʃən] N compaixão f

compatible [kəm'pætɪbl] ADJ compatível

compel [kəm'pɛl] VT obrigar

compensate ['kɔmpənseɪt] VT indenizar ▶ VI: **to ~ for** compensar; **compensation** [kɔmpən'seɪʃən] N compensação f; (damages) indenização f

compete [kəm'piːt] VI (take part) competir; (vie): **to ~ (with)** competir (com), fazer competição (com)

competent ['kɔmpɪtənt] ADJ
competente
competition [kɔmpɪ'tɪʃən] N
(*contest*) concurso; (*Econ*)
concorrência; (*rivalry*) competição f
competitive [kəm'pɛtɪtɪv] ADJ
competitivo; (*person*)
competidor(a)
competitor [kəm'pɛtɪtə^r] N (*rival*)
competidor(a) m/f; (*participant,
Econ*) concorrente m/f
complain [kəm'pleɪn] VI
queixar-se; **to ~ of** (*pain*)
queixar-se de; **complaint** N
(*objection*) objeção f; (*criticism*)
queixa; (*Med*) achaque m, doença
complement ['kɔmplɪmənt] N
complemento; (*esp ship's crew*)
tripulação f ▶ VT complementar
complete [kəm'pliːt] ADJ
completo; (*finished*) acabado ▶ VT
(*finish: building, task*) acabar; (*set,
group*) completar; (*a form*)
preencher; **completely** ADV
completamente; **completion** N
conclusão f, término; (*of contract
etc*) realização f
complex ['kɔmplɛks] ADJ
complexo ▶ N complexo; (*of
buildings*) conjunto
complexion [kəm'plɛkʃən] N (*of
face*) cor f, tez f
complicate ['kɔmplɪkeɪt] VT
complicar; **complicated** ADJ
complicado; **complication**
[kɔmplɪ'keɪʃən] N problema m;
(*Med*) complicação f
compliment [n 'kɔmplɪmənt, vt
'kɔmplɪmɛnt] N (*praise*) elogio
▶ VT elogiar; **compliments** NPL
cumprimentos mpl; **to pay sb a ~**
elogiar alguém; **complimentary**
[kɔmplɪ'mɛntərɪ] ADJ lisonjeiro;
(*free*) gratuito

comply [kəm'plaɪ] VI: **to ~ with**
cumprir com
component [kəm'pəunənt] ADJ
componente ▶ N (*part*) peça
compose [kəm'pəuz] VT compor;
to be ~d of compor-se de; **to ~
o.s.** tranquilizar-se; **composer** N
(*Mus*) compositor(a) m/f;
composition [kɔmpə'zɪʃən] N
composição f
compound ['kɔmpaund] N
(*Chem, Ling*) composto; (*enclosure*)
recinto ▶ ADJ composto
comprehensive [kɔmprɪ'hɛnsɪv]
ADJ abrangente; (*Insurance*) total;
comprehensive school (BRIT) N
escola secundária de amplo programa

> Criadas na década de 1960 pelo
> governo trabalhista da época,
> as **comprehensive schools**
> são estabelecimentos de ensino
> secundário polivalentes
> concebidos para acolher todos
> os alunos sem distinção e lhes
> oferecer oportunidades iguais,
> em oposição ao sistema seletivo
> das *grammar schools*. A maioria
> dos estudantes britânicos
> frequenta atualmente uma
> **comprehensive school**, mas
> as *grammar schools* não
> desapareceram de todo.

compress [vt kəm'prɛs, n
'kɔmprɛs] VT comprimir; (*text,
information etc*) reduzir ▶ N (*Med*)
compressa
comprise [kəm'praɪz] VT (*also:
be ~d of*) compreender, constar
de; (*constitute*) constituir
compromise ['kɔmprəmaɪz] N
meio-termo ▶ VT comprometer
▶ VI chegar a um meio-termo
compulsive [kəm'pʌlsɪv] ADJ
compulsório

compulsory [kəm'pʌlsərɪ] ADJ obrigatório; (*retirement*) compulsório

computer [kəm'pjuːtəʳ] N computador *m*; **computer game** N game *m*; **computerize** VT informatizar, computadorizar; **computer literate** ADJ capaz de lidar com um computador; **computing** N computação *f*; (*science*) informática

conceal [kən'siːl] VT ocultar; (*information*) omitir

conceited [kən'siːtɪd] ADJ vaidoso

conceive [kən'siːv] VT conceber ▶ VI conceber, engravidar

concentrate ['kɔnsəntreɪt] VI concentrar-se ▶ VT concentrar; **concentration** N concentração *f*

concept ['kɔnsɛpt] N conceito

concern [kən'səːn] N (*Comm*) empresa; (*anxiety*) preocupação *f* ▶ VT preocupar; (*involve*) envolver; (*relate to*) dizer respeito a; **to be ~ed (about)** preocupar-se (com); **concerning** PREP sobre, a respeito de, acerca de

concert ['kɔnsət] N concerto

concession [kən'sɛʃən] N concessão *f*; **tax ~** redução no imposto

conclude [kən'kluːd] VT (*finish*) acabar, concluir; (*treaty etc*) firmar; (*agreement*) chegar a; (*decide*) decidir

conclusion [kən'kluːʒən] N conclusão *f*

concrete ['kɔnkriːt] N concreto (BR), betão *m* (PT) ▶ ADJ concreto

concussion [kən'kʌʃən] N (*Med*) concussão *f* cerebral

condemn [kən'dɛm] VT denunciar; (*prisoner, building*) condenar

condensation [kɔndɛn'seɪʃən] N condensação *f*

condense [kən'dɛns] VI condensar-se ▶ VT condensar

condition [kən'dɪʃən] N condição *f*; (*Med: illness*) doença ▶ VT condicionar; **conditions** NPL (*circumstances*) circunstâncias *fpl*; **on ~ that** com a condição (de) que; **conditioner** N (*for hair*) condicionador *m*; (*for fabrics*) amaciante *m*

condom ['kɔndɔm] N preservativo, camisinha

condominium [kɔndə'mɪnɪəm] (*US*) N (*building*) edifício

condone [kən'dəun] VT admitir, aceitar

conduct [*n* 'kɔndʌkt, *vt, vi* kən'dʌkt] N conduta, comportamento ▶ VT (*research etc*) fazer; (*heat, electricity*) conduzir; (*Mus*) reger; **to ~ o.s.** comportar-se; **conducted tour** N viagem *f* organizada; **conductor** N (*of orchestra*) regente *m/f*; (*on bus*) cobrador(a) *m/f*; (*US Rail*) revisor(a) *m/f*; (*Elec*) condutor *m*

cone [kəun] N cone *m*; (*Bot*) pinha; (*for ice-cream*) casquinha

confectionery [kən'fɛkʃnərɪ] N (*sweets*) balas *fpl*; (*sweetmeats*) doces *mpl*

confer [kən'fəːʳ] VT: **to ~ on** outorgar a ▶ VI conferenciar

conference ['kɔnfərns] N congresso

confess [kən'fɛs] VT confessar ▶ VI (*admit*) admitir; **confession** N admissão *f*; (*Rel*) confissão *f*

confide [kən'faɪd] VI: **to ~ in** confiar em, fiar-se em

confidence ['kɔnfɪdns] N confiança; (*faith*) fé *f*; (*secret*) confidência; **in ~** em confidência; **confident** ADJ confiante, convicto;

(*positive*) seguro; **confidential**
[kɒnfɪ'denʃəl] ADJ confidencial
confine [kən'faɪn] VT (*shut up*)
encarcerar; (*limit*): **to ~ (to)**
confinar (a); **confined** ADJ (*space*)
reduzido
confirm [kən'fəːm] VT confirmar;
confirmation [kɒnfə'meɪʃən] N
confirmação f; (*Rel*) crisma
confiscate ['kɒnfɪskeɪt] VT
confiscar
conflict [n 'kɒnflɪkt, vi kən'flɪkt] N
(*disagreement*) divergência; (*of
interests, loyalties*) conflito;
(*fighting*) combate m ▶ VI estar em
conflito; (*opinions*) divergir
conform [kən'fɔːm] VI
conformar-se; **to ~ to** ajustar-se a,
acomodar-se a
confront [kən'frʌnt] VT (*problems*)
enfrentar; (*enemy, danger*)
defrontar-se com; **confrontation**
[kɒnfrən'teɪʃən] N confrontação f
confuse [kən'fjuːz] VT (*perplex*)
desconcertar; (*mix up*) confundir,
misturar; (*complicate*) complicar;
confused ADJ confuso; **confusing**
ADJ confuso; **confusion**
[kən'fjuːʒən] N (*mix-up*)
mal-entendido; (*perplexity*)
perplexidade f; (*disorder*) confusão f
congestion [kən'dʒestʃən] N
(*Med*) congestão f; (*traffic*)
congestionamento
congratulate [kən'grætjuleɪt]
VT parabenizar; **congratulations**
[kəngrætju'leɪʃənz] NPL
parabéns mpl
congress ['kɒŋgres] N congresso;
(*US*): **C~** Congresso

> O Congresso (**Congress**) é o
> Parlamento dos Estados
> Unidos. Consiste na *House of
> Representatives* e no Senado

> *Senate*. Os representantes e
> senadores são eleitos por
> sufrágio universal direto.
> O Congresso se reúne no
> *Capitol*, em Washington.

congressman (*US*) *irreg* N
deputado
conjure ['kʌndʒər] VI fazer
truques; **conjure up** VT (*ghost,
spirit*) fazer aparecer, invocar;
(*memories*) evocar
connect [kə'nekt] VT (*Elec, Tel*)
ligar; (*fig: associate*) associar; (*join*):
to ~ sth (to) juntar or unir algo (a)
▶ VI: **to ~ with** (*train*) conectar
com; **to be ~ed with** estar
relacionado com; **I'm trying to ~
you** (*Tel*) estou tentando
completar a ligação; **connecting
flight** N conexão f; **connection** N
ligação f; (*Elec, Rail*) conexão f; (*Tel*)
ligação f
conquer ['kɒŋkər] VT conquistar;
(*enemy*) vencer; (*feelings*) superar;
conquest ['kɒŋk] N conquista
conscience ['kɒnʃəns] N
consciência; **conscientious**
[kɒnʃɪ'enʃəs] ADJ consciencioso
conscious ['kɒnʃəs] ADJ: **~ (of)**
consciente (de); (*deliberate*)
intencional; **consciousness** N
consciência; **to lose/regain
consciousness** perder/recuperar
os sentidos
consent [kən'sent] N
consentimento ▶ VI: **to ~ to**
consentir em
consequence ['kɒnsɪkwəns] N
consequência; (*significance*): **of ~**
de importância; **consequently**
ADV por conseguinte
conservation [kɒnsə'veɪʃən] N
conservação f; (*of the environment*)
preservação f

conservative [kən'sə:vətiv] ADJ conservador(a); (cautious) moderado; (BRIT Pol): **C~** conservador(a) ▶ N (BRIT Pol) conservador(a) m/f

conservatory [kən'sə:vətrɪ] N (Mus) conservatório; (greenhouse) estufa

consider [kən'sɪdə^r] VT considerar; (take into account) levar em consideração; (study) estudar, examinar; **to ~ doing sth** pensar em fazer algo

considerable [kən'sɪdərəbl] ADJ considerável; (sum) importante

considerate [kən'sɪdərɪt] ADJ atencioso; **consideration** [kənsɪdə'reɪʃən] N consideração f; (deliberation) deliberação f; (factor) fator m

considering [kən'sɪdərɪŋ] PREP em vista de

consist [kən'sɪst] VI: **to ~ of** (comprise) consistir em

consistency [kən'sɪstənsɪ] N coerência; (thickness) consistência

consistent [kən'sɪstənt] ADJ (person) coerente, estável; (argument, idea) sólido

consolation [kɔnsə'leɪʃən] N conforto

console [vt kən'səul, n 'kɔnsəul] VT confortar ▶ N consolo

consonant ['kɔnsənənt] N consoante f

conspicuous [kən'spɪkjuəs] ADJ conspícuo

conspiracy [kən'spɪrəsɪ] N conspiração f, trama

constable ['kʌnstəbl] (BRIT) N policial m/f (BR), polícia m/f (PT); **chief ~** chefe m/f de polícia

constant ['kɔnstənt] ADJ constante

constipated ['kɔnstɪpeɪtəd] ADJ com prisão de ventre

constipation [kɔnstɪ'peɪʃən] N prisão f de ventre

constituency [kən'stɪtjuənsɪ] N (Pol) distrito eleitoral; (people) eleitorado

constitution [kɔnstɪ'tju:ʃən] N constituição f; (health) compleição f

constraint [kən'streɪnt] N coação f, pressão f; (restriction) limitação f

construct [kən'strʌkt] VT construir; **construction** N construção f; (structure) estrutura

consul ['kɔnsl] N cônsul m/f; **consulate** ['kɔnsjulɪt] N consulado

consult [kən'sʌlt] VT consultar; **consultant** N (Med) (médico(-a)) especialista m/f; (other specialist) assessor(a) m/f, consultor(a) m/f; **consulting room** (BRIT) N consultório

consume [kən'sju:m] VT (eat) comer; (drink) beber; (fire etc, Comm) consumir; **consumer** N consumidor(a) m/f

consumption [kən'sʌmpʃən] N consumo

cont. ABBR = **continued**

contact ['kɔntækt] N contato ▶ VT entrar or pôr-se em contato com; **contact lenses** NPL lentes fpl de contato

contagious [kən'teɪdʒəs] ADJ contagioso; (fig: laughter etc) contagiante

contain [kən'teɪn] VT conter; **to ~ o.s.** conter-se; **container** N recipiente m; (for shipping etc) container m, cofre m de carga

contaminate [kən'tæmɪneɪt] VT contaminar

cont'd ABBR = **continued**

contemplate ['kɔntəmpleɪt] VT
(idea) considerar; (person, painting
etc) contemplar

contemporary [kən'tɛmpərərɪ]
ADJ contemporâneo; (design etc)
moderno ▶ N contemporâneo(-a)

contempt [kən'tɛmpt] N desprezo;
contempt of court N (Jur)
desacato à autoridade do tribunal

contend [kən'tɛnd] VT (assert): **to
~ that** afirmar que ▶ VI: **to ~ with**
(struggle) lutar com; (difficulty)
enfrentar; (compete): **to ~ for**
competir por

content [adj, vt kən'tɛnt, n
'kɔntɛnt] ADJ (happy) contente;
(satisfied) satisfeito ▶ VT contentar,
satisfazer ▶ N conteúdo; (fat
content, moisture content etc)
quantidade f; **contents** NPL (of
packet, book) conteúdo;
contented ADJ contente, satisfeito

contest [n 'kɔntɛst, vt kən'tɛst] N
contenda; (competition) concurso
▶ VT (legal case) defender; (Pol) ser
candidato a; (competition)
disputar; (statement, decision)
contestar; **contestant**
[kən'tɛstənt] N competidor(a) m/f;
(in fight) adversário(-a)

context ['kɔntɛkst] N contexto

continent ['kɔntɪnənt] N
continente m; **the C~** (BRIT) o
continente europeu; **continental**
[kɔntɪ'nɛntl] ADJ continental;
continental quilt (BRIT) N
edredom m (BR), edredão m (PT)

continual [kən'tɪnjuəl] ADJ
contínuo

continue [kən'tɪnjuː] VI
prosseguir, continuar ▶ VT
continuar; (start again) recomeçar,
retomar; **continuous**
[kən'tɪnjuəs] ADJ contínuo

contour ['kɔntuəʳ] N contorno;
(also: **~ line**) curva de nível

contraceptive [kɔntrə'sɛptɪv]
ADJ anticoncepcional ▶ N
anticoncepcional m

contract [n, cpd 'kɔntrækt, vt, vi
kən'trækt] N contrato ▶ CPD
(work) de empreitada ▶ VI (become
smaller) contrair-se, encolher-se;
(Comm): **to ~ to do sth**
comprometer-se por contrato a
fazer algo ▶ VT contrair

contradict [kɔntrə'dɪkt] VT
contradizer, desmentir

contrary¹ ['kɔntrərɪ] ADJ contrário
▶ N contrário; **on the ~** muito pelo
contrário; **unless you hear to the
~** salvo aviso contrário

contrary² [kən'trɛərɪ] ADJ teimoso

contrast [n 'kɔntrɑːst, vt
kən'trɑːst] N contraste m ▶ VT
comparar; **in ~ to** or **with** em
contraste com, ao contrário de

contribute [kən'trɪbjuːt] VT
contribuir ▶ VI dar; **to ~ to** (charity)
contribuir para; (newspaper)
escrever para; (discussion)
participar de; **contribution**
[kɔntrɪ'bjuːʃən] N (donation)
doação f; (BRIT: for social security)
contribuição f; (to debate)
intervenção f; (to journal)
colaboração f; **contributor**
[kən'trɪbjutəʳ] N (to newspaper)
colaborador(a) m/f

control [kən'trəul] VT controlar;
(machinery) regular; (temper)
dominar ▶ N controle m; (of car)
direção f (BR), condução f (PT);
(check) freio, controle; **controls**
NPL (of vehicle) comandos mpl;
(on radio, television etc) controle;
to be in ~ of ter o controle de;
(in charge of) ser responsável por

controversial [kɔntrə'və:ʃl] ADJ controvertido, polêmico

controversy ['kɔntrəvə:sɪ] N controvérsia, polêmica

convenience [kən'vi:nɪəns] N (easiness) facilidade f; (suitability) conveniência; (advantage) vantagem f, conveniência; **at your ~** quando lhe convier; **all modern ~s, all mod cons** (BRIT) com todos os confortos

convenient [kən'vi:nɪənt] ADJ conveniente

convent ['kɔnvənt] N convento

convention [kən'vɛnʃən] N (custom) costume m; (agreement) convenção f; (meeting) assembleia; **conventional** ADJ convencional

conversation [kɔnvə'seɪʃən] N conversação f, conversa

convert [vt kən'və:t, n 'kɔnvə:t] VT converter ▶ N convertido(-a); **convertible** [kən'və:təbl] N conversível m

convey [kən'veɪ] VT transportar, levar; (thanks) expressar; (information) passar; **conveyor belt** N correia transportadora

convict [vt kən'vɪkt, n 'kɔnvɪkt] VT condenar ▶ N presidiário(-a); **conviction** N condenação f; (belief) convicção f; (certainty) certeza

convince [kən'vɪns] VT (assure) assegurar; (persuade) convencer; **convincing** ADJ convincente

cook [kuk] VT cozinhar; (meal) preparar ▶ VI cozinhar ▶ N cozinheiro(-a); **cookbook** N livro de receitas; **cooker** N fogão m; **cookery** N culinária; **cookery book** (BRIT) N = **cookbook**; **cookie** (US) N bolacha, biscoito; **cooking** N cozinha

cool [ku:l] ADJ fresco; (calm) calmo; (unfriendly) frio ▶ VT resfriar ▶ VI esfriar

cop [kɔp] (inf) N policial m/f (BR), polícia m/f (PT), tira m (inf)

cope [kəup] VI: **to ~ with** poder com, arcar com; (problem) estar à altura de

copper ['kɔpər] N (metal) cobre m; (BRIT inf: policeman/woman) policial m/f (BR), polícia m/f (PT); **coppers** NPL (coins) moedas fpl de pouco valor

copy ['kɔpɪ] N cópia; duplicata; (of book etc) exemplar m ▶ VT copiar; (imitate) imitar; **copyright** N direitos mpl autorais, copirraite m

coral ['kɔrəl] N coral m

cord [kɔ:d] N corda; (Elec) fio, cabo; (fabric) veludo cotelê

corduroy ['kɔ:dərɔɪ] N veludo cotelê

core [kɔ:r] N centro; (of fruit) caroço; (of problem) âmago ▶ VT descaroçar

cork [kɔ:k] N rolha; (tree) cortiça; **corkscrew** N saca-rolhas m inv

corn [kɔ:n] N (BRIT) trigo; (US: maize) milho; (on foot) calo; **~ on the cob** (Culin) espiga de milho

corned beef ['kɔ:nd-] N carne f de boi enlatada

corner ['kɔ:nər] N (outside) esquina; (inside) canto; (in road) curva; (Football etc) córner m ▶ VT (trap) encurralar; (Comm) açambarcar, monopolizar ▶ VI fazer uma curva

cornflakes ['kɔ:nfleɪks] NPL flocos mpl de milho

cornflour ['kɔ:nflauər] (BRIT) N farinha de milho, maisena®

cornstarch ['kɔ:nstɑ:tʃ] (US) N = **cornflour**

Cornwall ['kɔ:nwəl] N Cornualha

coronary ['kɔrənəri] N:
~ **(thrombosis)** trombose f
(coronária)

coronation [kɔrə'neɪʃən] N
coroação f

coroner ['kɔrənə'] N *magistrado que investiga mortes suspeitas*

corporal ['kɔ:pərl] N cabo ▶ ADJ:
~ **punishment** castigo corporal

corporate ['kɔ:pərɪt] ADJ *(finance)*
corporativo; *(action)* coletivo;
(image) da empresa

corporation [kɔ:pə'reɪʃən] N *(of town)* município, junta; *(Comm)* sociedade f

corps [kɔ:'] *(pl* **corps** [kɔ:z]) N *(Mil)*
unidade f; *(diplomatic)* corpo; **the press ~** a imprensa

corpse [kɔ:ps] N cadáver m

correct [kə'rɛkt] ADJ exato;
(proper) correto ▶ VT corrigir;
correction N correção f

correspond [kɔrɪs'pɔnd] VI *(write)*:
to ~ (with) corresponder-se (com);
(be equal to): **to ~ to** corresponder
a; *(be in accordance)*: **to ~ (with)**
corresponder (a); **correspondence**
N correspondência; **correspondent**
N correspondente m/f

corridor ['kɔrɪdɔ:'] N corredor m

corrode [kə'rəud] VT corroer
▶ VI corroer-se

corrupt [kə'rʌpt] ADJ corrupto;
(Comput) corrupto, danificado
▶ VT corromper; **corruption** N
corrupção f

Corsica ['kɔ:sɪkə] N Córsega

cosmetic [kɔz'mɛtɪk] N
cosmético ▶ ADJ *(fig)* simbólico,
superficial

cost [kɔst] *(pt, pp* **cost**) N *(price)*
preço ▶ VT custar; **costs** NPL
(Comm) custos mpl; *(Jur)* custas fpl;
at all ~s custe o que custar

co-star [kəu-] N coestrela m/f

Costa Rica ['kɔstə'ri:kə] N
Costa Rica

costly ['kɔstlɪ] ADJ caro

costume ['kɔstju:m] N traje m;
(BRIT: also: **swimming ~**: *woman's)*
maiô m *(BR)*, fato de banho *(PT)*;
(: man's) calção m *(de banho)* *(BR)*,
calções mpl de banho *(PT)*

cosy ['kəuzɪ], *(US)* **cozy** ADJ
aconchegante; *(life)* confortável

cot [kɔt] N *(BRIT)* cama *(de criança)*,
berço; *(US)* cama de lona

cottage ['kɔtɪdʒ] N casa de
campo; **cottage cheese** N queijo
tipo cottage *(BR)*, queijo creme *(PT)*

cotton ['kɔtn] N algodão m;
(thread) fio, linha; **cotton on** *(inf)*
VI: **to ~ on (to sth)** sacar *(algo)*;
cotton bud *(BRIT)* N cotonete® m;
cotton candy *(US)* N algodão m
doce; **cotton wool** *(BRIT)* N
algodão m *(hidrófilo)*

couch [kautʃ] N sofá m; *(doctor's)*
cama; *(psychiatrist's)* divã m

cough [kɔf] VI tossir ▶ N tosse f

could [kud] PT, CONDITIONAL *of*
can²

couldn't ['kudnt] = **could not**

council ['kaunsl] N conselho; **city**
or **town ~** câmara municipal;
council estate *(BRIT)* N conjunto
habitacional; **council house**
(BRIT) N casa popular; **councillor** N
vereador(a) m/f

counsellor ['kaunsələ'], *(US)*
counselor N conselheiro(-a); *(US Jur)* advogado(-a)

count [kaunt] VT contar; *(include)*
incluir ▶ VI contar ▶ N *(of votes etc)*
contagem f; *(of pollen, alcohol)* nivel
m; *(nobleman)* conde m; **count on**
VT FUS contar com; **countdown** N
contagem f regressiva

counter ['kauntə'] N (in shop) balcão m; (in post office etc) guichê m; (in games) ficha ▶ VT contrariar ▶ ADV: **~ to** ao contrário de

counterfeit ['kauntəfɪt] N falsificação f ▶ VT falsificar ▶ ADJ falso, falsificado

counterpart ['kauntəpɑːt] N (opposite number) homólogo(-a); (equivalent) equivalente m/f;

counterterrorism [kauntə'terərɪzəm] N antiterrorismo

countess ['kauntɪs] N condessa

countless ['kauntlɪs] ADJ inumerável

country ['kʌntrɪ] N país m; (nation) nação f; (native land) terra; (as opposed to town) campo; (region) região f, terra; **countryside** N campo

county ['kauntɪ] N condado

coup [kuː] N golpe m de mestre; (also: **~ d'état**) golpe (de estado)

couple ['kʌpl] N (of things, people) par m; (married couple, courting couple) casal m; **a ~ of** um par de; (a few) alguns/algumas

coupon ['kuːpɔn] N cupom m (BR), cupão m (PT); (voucher) vale m

courage ['kʌrɪdʒ] N coragem f

courier ['kurɪə'] N correio; (for tourists) guia m/f, agente m/f de turismo

course [kɔːs] N (direction) direção f; (process) desenvolvimento; (of river, Sch) curso; (of ship) rumo; (Golf) campo; (part of meal) prato; **of ~** naturalmente; (certainly) certamente; **of ~!** claro!, lógico!

court [kɔːt] N (royal) corte f; (Jur) tribunal m; (Tennis etc) quadra ▶ VT (woman) cortejar, namorar; **to take to ~** demandar, levar a julgamento

courtesy ['kəːtəsɪ] N cortesia; **(by) ~ of** com permissão de

court-house (US) N palácio de justiça

courtroom ['kɔːtrum] N sala de tribunal

courtyard ['kɔːtjɑːd] N pátio

cousin ['kʌzn] N primo(-a) m/f; **first ~** primo-irmão/prima-irmã m/f

cover ['kʌvə'] VT cobrir; (with lid) tampar; (chairs etc) revestir; (distance) percorrer; (include) abranger; (protect) abrigar; (issues) tratar ▶ N (lid) tampa; (for chair etc) capa; (for bed) cobertor m; (of book, magazine) capa; (shelter) abrigo; (Insurance) cobertura; **to take ~** abrigar-se; **under ~** (indoors) abrigado; **under separate ~** (Comm) em separado; **cover up** VI: **to ~ up for sb** cobrir alguém; **coverage** N cobertura; **cover charge** N couvert m

cover-up N encobrimento (dos fatos)

cow [kau] N vaca ▶ VT intimidar

coward ['kauəd] N covarde m/f; **cowardly** ADJ covarde

cowboy ['kaubɔɪ] N vaqueiro

cozy ['kəuzɪ] (US) ADJ = **cosy**

crab [kræb] N caranguejo

crack [kræk] N rachadura; (gap) brecha; (noise) estalo; (drug) crack m ▶ VT (nut) partir, descascar; (wall) rachar; (whip etc) estalar; (joke) soltar; (mystery) resolver; (code) decifrar ▶ ADJ (expert) de primeira classe; **crack down on** VT FUS (crime) ser linha dura com; **crack up** VI (Psych) sofrer um colapso nervoso; **cracker** N (biscuit) biscoito; (Christmas cracker) busca pé surpresa m

crackle ['krækl] vi crepitar

cradle ['kreɪdl] N berço

craft [krɑːft] N (skill) arte f; (trade) ofício; (boat) barco; **craftsman** irreg N artífice m, artesão m; **craftsmanship** N acabamento

cram [kræm] vt (fill): **to ~ sth with** encher or abarrotar algo de; (put): **to ~ sth into** enfiar algo em ▶ vi (for exams) estudar na última hora

cramp [kræmp] N (Med) cãibra; **cramped** ADJ apertado, confinado

cranberry ['krænbərɪ] N oxicoco

crane [kreɪn] N (Tech) guindaste m; (bird) grou m

crash [kræʃ] N (noise) estrondo; (of car) batida; (of plane) desastre m de avião; (Comm) falência, quebra; (Stock Exchange) craque m ▶ vt (car) bater com; (plane) jogar ▶ vi (car) bater; (plane) cair; (two cars) colidir, bater; (Comm) falir, quebrar; **crash course** N curso intensivo

crate [kreɪt] N caixote m; (for bottles) engradado

crave [kreɪv] vt, vi: **to ~ for** ansiar por

crawl [krɔːl] vi arrastar-se; (child) engatinhar; (insect) andar; (vehicle) andar a passo de tartaruga ▶ N (Swimming) crawl m

crayfish ['kreɪfɪʃ] N INV (freshwater) camarão-d'água-doce m; (saltwater) lagostim m

crayon ['kreɪən] N lápis m de cera, crayon m

craze [kreɪz] N (fashion) moda

crazy ['kreɪzɪ] ADJ louco, maluco, doido

creak [kriːk] vi ranger

cream [kriːm] N (of milk) nata; (artificial, cosmetic) creme m; (élite): **the ~ of** a fina flor de ▶ ADJ (colour) creme inv; **cream cheese** N ricota (BR), queijo creme (PT); **creamy** ADJ (colour) creme inv; (taste) cremoso

crease [kriːs] N (fold) dobra, vinco; (in trousers) vinco; (wrinkle) ruga ▶ vt (wrinkle) amassar, amarrotar ▶ vi amassar-se, amarrotar-se

create [kriːˈeɪt] vt criar; (produce) produzir

creature ['kriːtʃər] N (animal) animal m, bicho; (living thing) criatura

credit ['krɛdɪt] N crédito; (merit) mérito ▶ vt (also: **give ~ to**) acreditar; (Comm) creditar; **credits** NPL (Cinema, TV) crédito; **to ~ sb with sth** (fig) atribuir algo a alguém; **to be in ~** ter fundos; **credit card** N cartão m de crédito; **credit crunch** N contração f do crédito

creek [kriːk] N enseada; (US) riacho

creep [kriːp] (pt, pp **crept**) vi (animal) rastejar; (person) deslizar(-se)

cremate [krɪˈmeɪt] vt cremar; **crematorium** (pl **crematoria**) N crematório

crept [krɛpt] pt, pp of **creep**

crescent ['krɛsnt] N meia-lua; (street) rua semicircular

cress [krɛs] N agrião m

crest [krɛst] N (of bird) crista; (of hill) cimo, topo; (of coat of arms) timbre m

crew [kruː] N (of ship etc) tripulação f; (Cinema) equipe f

crib [krɪb] N manjedoira, presépio; (US: cot) berço ▶ vt (inf) colar

cricket ['krɪkɪt] N (insect) grilo; (game) críquete m, cricket m

crime [kraɪm] N (no pl: illegal activities) crime m; (offence) delito; (fig) pecado, maldade f; **criminal** ['krɪmɪnl] N criminoso ▶ ADJ criminal; (morally wrong) imoral

crimson ['krɪmzn] ADJ carmesim inv

cringe [krɪndʒ] VI encolher-se

cripple ['krɪpl] N aleijado(-a) ▶ VT aleijar

crisis ['kraɪsɪs] (pl **crises**) N crise f

crisp [krɪsp] ADJ fresco; (bacon etc) torrado; (manner) seco; **crisps** (BRIT) NPL batatinhas fpl fritas; **crispy** ADJ crocante

criterion [kraɪ'tɪərɪən] (pl **criteria**) N critério

critic ['krɪtɪk] N crítico(-a); **critical** ADJ crítico; (illness) grave; **to be critical of sth/sb** criticar algo/alguém; **criticism** ['krɪtɪsɪzm] N crítica; **criticize** ['krɪtɪsaɪz] VT criticar

Croatia [krəu'eɪʃə] N Croácia

crockery ['krɔkərɪ] N louça

crocodile ['krɔkədaɪl] N crocodilo

crocus ['krəukəs] N açafrão-da-primavera m

crook [kruk] N (inf: criminal) vigarista m/f; (of shepherd) cajado; **crooked** ['krukɪd] ADJ torto; (dishonest) desonesto

crop [krɔp] N (produce) colheita; (amount produced) safra; (riding crop) chicotinho ▶ VT cortar; **crop up** VI surgir

cross [krɔs] N cruz f; (hybrid) cruzamento ▶ VT cruzar; (street etc) atravessar; (thwart) contrariar ▶ ADJ zangado, mal-humorado; **cross out** VT riscar; **cross over** VI atravessar; **crossing** N (sea passage) travessia; (also: **pedestrian crossing**) faixa (para pedestres) (BR), passadeira (PT); **crossroads** N cruzamento; **crosswalk** (US) N faixa (para pedestres) (BR), passadeira (PT); **crossword** N palavras fpl cruzadas

crouch [krautʃ] VI agachar-se

crow [krəu] N (bird) corvo; (of cock) canto, cocoricó m ▶ VI (cock) cantar, cocoricar

crowd [kraud] N multidão f ▶ VT (fill) apinhar ▶ VI (gather) amontoar-se; (cram): **to ~ in** apinhar-se; **crowded** ADJ (full) lotado; (densely populated) superlotado

crown [kraun] N coroa; (of head, hill) topo ▶ VT coroar; (fig) rematar; **crown jewels** NPL joias fpl reais

crucial ['kru:ʃl] ADJ (decision) vital; (vote) decisivo

crucifix ['kru:sɪfɪks] N crucifixo

crude [kru:d] ADJ (materials) bruto; (fig: basic) tosco; (: vulgar) grosseiro

cruel ['kruəl] ADJ cruel

cruise [kru:z] N cruzeiro ▶ VI (ship) fazer um cruzeiro; (car): **to ~ at ... km/h** ir a ... km por hora

crumb [krʌm] N (of bread) migalha; (of cake) farelo

crumble ['krʌmbl] VT esfarelar ▶ VI (building) desmoronar-se; (plaster, earth) esfacelar-se; (fig) desintegrar-se

crumpet ['krʌmpɪt] N bolo leve

crumple ['krʌmpl] VT (paper) amassar; (material) amarrotar

crunch [krʌntʃ] VT (food etc) mastigar; (underfoot) esmagar ▶ N (fig): **the ~** o momento decisivo; **crunchy** ADJ crocante

crush [krʌʃ] N (crowd) aglomeração f; (love): **to have a ~ on sb** ter um rabicho por alguém; (drink): **lemon ~** limonada ▶ VT (press) esmagar;

(*squeeze*) espremer; (*paper*) amassar; (*cloth*) enrugar; (*army, opposition*) aniquilar; (*hopes*) destruir; (*person*) arrasar

crust [krʌst] N (*of bread*) casca; (*of snow, earth*) crosta

crutch [krʌtʃ] N muleta

cry [kraɪ] VI chorar; (*shout: also:* **~ out**) gritar ▶ N grito; (*of bird*) pio; (*of animal*) voz f; **cry off** VI desistir

crystal ['krɪstl] N cristal m

cub [kʌb] N filhote m; (*also:* **~ scout**) lobinho

Cuba ['kjuːbə] N Cuba

cube [kjuːb] N cubo ▶ VT (*Math*) elevar ao cubo; **cubic** ADJ cúbico

cubicle ['kjuːbɪkl] N cubículo

cuckoo ['kuku:] N cuco

cucumber ['kjuːkʌmbər] N pepino

cuddle ['kʌdl] VT abraçar ▶ VI abraçar-se

cue [kjuː] N (*Snooker*) taco; (*Theatre etc*) deixa

cuff [kʌf] N (*of shirt, coat etc*) punho; (*US: on trousers*) bainha; (*blow*) bofetada; **off the ~** de improviso

cul-de-sac ['kʌldəsæk] N beco sem saída

cull [kʌl] VT (*story, idea*) escolher, selecionar ▶ N matança seletiva

culminate ['kʌlmɪneɪt] VI: **to ~ in** terminar em

culprit ['kʌlprɪt] N culpado(-a)

cult [kʌlt] N culto

cultivate ['kʌltɪveɪt] VT cultivar

cultural ['kʌltʃərəl] ADJ cultural

culture ['kʌltʃər] N cultura

cunning ['kʌnɪŋ] N astúcia ▶ ADJ astuto, malandro; (*device, idea*) engenhoso

cup [kʌp] N xícara (BR), chávena (PT); (*prize, of bra*) taça

cupboard ['kʌbəd] N armário

curator [kjuə'reɪtər] N diretor(a) m/f

curb [kə:b] VT refrear ▶ N freio; (US) = **kerb**

curdle ['kə:dl] VI coalhar

cure [kjuər] VT curar ▶ N tratamento, cura

curfew ['kə:fjuː] N toque m de recolher

curious ['kjuərɪəs] ADJ curioso; (*nosy*) abelhudo; (*unusual*) estranho

curl [kə:l] N (*of hair*) cacho ▶ VT (*loosely*) frisar; (*tightly*) encrespar ▶ VI (*hair*) encaracolar; **curl up** VI encaracolar-se; **curler** N rolo, bobe m; **curly** ADJ cacheado, crespo

currant ['kʌrnt] N passa de corinto; (*blackcurrant, redcurrant*) groselha

currency ['kʌrnsɪ] N moeda; **to gain ~** (*fig*) consagrar-se

current ['kʌrnt] N corrente f ▶ ADJ corrente; (*present*) atual; **current account** (BRIT) N conta corrente; **current affairs** NPL atualidades fpl; **currently** ADV atualmente

curriculum [kə'rɪkjuləm] (**curriculums** *or pl* **curricula**) N programa m de estudos; **curriculum vitae** [-'viːtaɪ] N currículo

curry ['kʌrɪ] N caril m ▶ VT: **to ~ favour with** captar simpatia de

curse [kə:s] VI xingar (BR), praguejar (PT) ▶ VT (*swear at*) xingar (BR), praguejar a (PT); (*bemoan*) amaldiçoar ▶ N maldição f; (*swearword*) palavrão m (BR), baixo calão m (PT); (*problem*) castigo

cursor ['kə:sər] N (*Comput*) cursor m

curt [kə:t] ADJ seco, brusco

curtain ['kə:tn] N cortina; (*Theatre*) pano

curve [kə:v] N curva ▶ VI encurvar-se, torcer-se; (*road*) fazer (uma) curva

cushion ['kuʃən] N almofada ▶ VT amortecer

custard ['kʌstəd] N nata, creme *m*

custody ['kʌstədɪ] N custódia; **to take into ~** deter

custom ['kʌstəm] N (*tradition*) tradição *f*; (*convention*) costume *m*; (*habit*) hábito; (*Comm*) clientela; **customer** N cliente *m/f*; **customize** ['kʌstəmaɪz] VT personalizar

customs ['kʌstəmz] NPL alfândega; **customs officer** N inspetor(a) *m/f* da alfândega, aduaneiro(-a)

cut [kʌt] (*pt, pp* **cut**) VT cortar; (*reduce*) reduzir ▶ VI cortar ▶ N corte *m*; (*in spending*) redução *f*; (*of garment*) tacho; **cut down** VT (*tree*) derrubar; (*reduce*) reduzir; **cut off** VT (*piece, Tel*) cortar; (*person, village*) isolar; (*supply*) suspender; **cut out** VT (*shape*) recortar; (*activity etc*) suprimir; (*remove*) remover; **cut up** VT cortar em pedaços

cute [kju:t] ADJ bonitinho

cutlery ['kʌtlərɪ] N talheres *mpl*

cutlet ['kʌtlɪt] N costeleta

cut-price, (*US*) **cut-rate** ADJ a preço reduzido

cutting ADJ cortante ▶ N (*BRIT: from newspaper*) recorte *m*; (*from plant*) muda; **cutting-edge** ADJ (*technology, research*) de ponta

CV N ABBR = **curriculum vitae**

cyber attack ['saɪbərətæk] N ciberataque *m*

cybercafé ['saɪbəkæfeɪ] N cibercafé *m*

cyberspace ['saɪbəspeɪs] N ciberespaço

cycle ['saɪkl] N ciclo; (*bicycle*) bicicleta ▶ VI andar de bicicleta

cycling ['saɪklɪŋ] N ciclismo

cyclist ['saɪklɪst] N ciclista *m/f*

cylinder ['sɪlɪndə^r] N cilindro; (*of gas*) bujão *m*

Cyprus ['saɪprəs] N Chipre *f*

cyst [sɪst] N cisto; **cystitis** N cistite *f*

czar [zɑ:^r] N czar *m*

Czech [tʃɛk] ADJ tcheco ▶ N tcheco(-a); (*Ling*) tcheco; **Czech Republic** N: **the Czech Republic** a República Tcheca

d

D¹ [di:] N (*Mus*) ré *m*

D² (*US*) ABBR (*Pol*) = **democrat,
democratic**

dab [dæb] VT (*eyes, wound*) tocar (de
leve); (*paint, cream*) aplicar de leve

dad [dæd] (*inf*) N papai *m*

daddy ['dædɪ] N = **dad**

daffodil ['dæfədɪl] N
narciso-dos-prados *m*

daft [dɑ:ft] ADJ bobo, besta

dagger ['dægə'] N punhal *m*,
adaga

daily ['deɪlɪ] ADJ diário ▶ N (*paper*)
jornal *m*, diário ▶ ADV diariamente

dairy ['dɛərɪ] N leiteria

daisy ['deɪzɪ] N margarida

dam [dæm] N represa, barragem *f*
▶ VT represar

damage ['dæmɪdʒ] N (*harm*)
prejuízo; (*dents etc*) avaria ▶ VT
danificar; (*harm*) prejudicar;
damages NPL (*Jur*) indenização *f*
por perdas e danos

damn [dæm] VT condenar; (*curse*)
maldizer ▶ N (*inf*): **I don't give a ~**
não dou a mínima, estou me
lixando ▶ ADJ (*inf: also:* **~ed**)
danado, maldito; **~ (it)!** (*que*)
droga!

damp [dæmp] ADJ úmido ▶ N
umidade *f* ▶ VT (*also:* **~en**: *cloth,
rag*) umedecer; (*: enthusiasm etc*)
jogar água fria em

dance [dɑ:ns] N dança; (*party etc*)
baile *m* ▶ VI dançar; **dancer** N
dançarino(-a); (*professional*)
bailarino(-a); **dancing** N dança

dandelion ['dændɪlaɪən] N
dente-de-leão *m*

dandruff ['dændrəf] N caspa

Dane [deɪn] N dinamarquês(-esa)
m/f

danger ['deɪndʒə'] N perigo; (*risk*)
risco; **"~!"** (*on sign*) "perigo!"; **to be
in ~ of** correr o risco de; **in ~** em
perigo; **dangerous** ['deɪndʒərəs]
ADJ perigoso

dangle ['dæŋgl] VT balançar ▶ VI
pender balançando

Danish ['deɪnɪʃ] ADJ
dinamarquês(-esa) ▶ N (*Ling*)
dinamarquês *m*

dare [dɛə'] VT: **to ~ sb to do sth**
desafiar alguém a fazer algo ▶ VI:
to ~ (to) do sth atrever-se a fazer
algo, ousar fazer algo; **I ~ say**
(*I suppose*) acho provável que;
daring ADJ audacioso; (*bold*)
ousado ▶ N coragem *f*, destemor *m*

dark [dɑ:k] ADJ escuro;
(*complexion*) moreno ▶ N escuro;
in the ~ about (*fig*) no escuro
sobre; **after ~** depois de escurecer;
darken VT escurecer; (*colour*) fazer
mais escuro ▶ VI escurecer(-se);
darkness N escuridão *f*;
darkroom N câmara escura

darling ['dɑ:lɪŋ] ADJ, N
querido(-a)

dart [dɑːt] N dardo; (in sewing) alinhavo ▶ VI precipitar-se; **to ~ away/along** ir-se/seguir precipitadamente; **darts** N (game) jogo de dardos

dash [dæʃ] N (sign) hífen m; (: long) travessão m; (small quantity) pontinha ▶ VT arremessar; (hopes) frustrar ▶ VI precipitar-se, correr; **dash away** VI sair apressado; **dash off** VI = **dash away**

dashboard ['dæʃbɔːd] N painel m de instrumentos

data ['deɪtə] NPL dados mpl; **database** N banco de dados; **data processing** N processamento de dados

date [deɪt] N data; (with friend) encontro; (fruit) tâmara ▶ VT datar; (person) namorar; **to ~** até agora; **out of ~** desatualizado; **up to ~** moderno; **dated** ['deɪtɪd] ADJ antiquado

daughter ['dɔːtər] N filha; **daughter-in-law** (pl **daughters-in-law**) N nora

daunting ['dɔːntɪŋ] ADJ desanimador(a)

dawn [dɔːn] N alvorada, amanhecer m; (of period, situation) surgimento, início ▶ VI (day) amanhecer; (fig): **it ~ed on him that ...** começou a perceber que ...

day [deɪ] N dia m; (working day) jornada, dia útil; **the ~ before/after** a véspera/o dia seguinte; **the ~ before yesterday** anteontem; **the ~ after tomorrow** depois de amanhã; **by ~** de dia; **day-care centre** ['deɪkɛə-] N (for elderly etc) centro de convivência; (for children) creche f; **daydream** VI devanear; **daylight** N luz f (do dia); **day return** (BRIT) N bilhete m de ida

e volta no mesmo dia; **daytime** N dia m; **day-to-day** ADJ cotidiano

dazzle ['dæzl] VT (bewitch) deslumbrar; (blind) ofuscar

dead [dɛd] ADJ morto; (numb) dormente; (telephone) cortado; (Elec) sem corrente ▶ ADV completamente; (exactly) absolutamente ▶ NPL: **the ~** os mortos; **to shoot sb ~** matar alguém a tiro; **~ tired** morto de cansado; **to stop ~** estacar; **dead end** N beco sem saída; **deadline** N prazo final; **deadly** ADJ mortal, fatal; (weapon) mortífero

deaf [dɛf] ADJ surdo; **deafen** VT ensurdecer

deal [diːl] (pt, pp **dealt**) N (agreement) acordo ▶ VT (cards, blows) dar; **a good** or **great ~ (of)** bastante, muito; **deal in** VT FUS (Comm) negociar em or com; **deal with** VT FUS (people) tratar com; (problem) ocupar-se de; (subject) tratar de; **dealer** N negociante m/f; **dealings** NPL transações fpl

dean [diːn] N (Rel) decano; (Sch: BRIT) reitor(a) m/f; (: US) orientador(a) m/f de estudos

dear [dɪər] ADJ querido, caro; (expensive) caro ▶ N: **my ~** meu querido/minha querida ▶ EXCL: **~ me!** ai, meu Deus!; **D~ Sir/Madam** (in letter) Prezado Senhor/Prezada Senhora (BR), Exmo. Senhor/Exma. Senhora (PT); **D~ Mr/Mrs X** Prezado Sr. X/Prezada Sra. X; **dearly** ADV (love) ternamente; (pay) caro

death [dɛθ] N morte f; (Admin) óbito; **death penalty** N pena de morte; **death row** (US) N corredor m da morte

debate [dɪ'beɪt] N debate m ▶ VT debater

debit ['dɛbɪt] N débito ▶ VT: **to ~ a sum to sb** or **to sb's account** lançar uma quantia ao débito de alguém or à conta de alguém; see also **direct debit**; **debit card** N cartão m de débito

debt [dɛt] N dívida; (state) endividiamento; **to be in ~** ter dívidas, estar endividado

decade ['dɛkeɪd] N década

decaffeinated [dɪ'kæfɪneɪtɪd] ADJ descafeinado

decay [dɪ'keɪ] N ruína; (also: **tooth ~**) cárie f ▶ VI (rot) apodrecer-se

deceased [dɪ'siːst] N: **the ~** o falecido/a falecida

deceit [dɪ'siːt] N engano; (duplicity) fraude f

deceive [dɪ'siːv] VT enganar

December [dɪ'sɛmbər] N dezembro

decent ['diːsənt] ADJ (proper) decente; (kind, honest) honesto, amável

deception [dɪ'sɛpʃən] N engano; (deceitful act) fraude f; **deceptive** ADJ enganador(a)

decide [dɪ'saɪd] VT (person) convencer; (question, argument) resolver ▶ VI decidir; **to ~ on sth** decidir-se por algo

decimal ['dɛsɪməl] ADJ decimal ▶ N decimal m

decision [dɪ'sɪʒən] N (choice) escolha; (act of choosing) decisão f; (decisiveness) resolução f

decisive [dɪ'saɪsɪv] ADJ (action) decisivo; (person) decidido

deck [dɛk] N (Naut) convés m; (of bus): **top ~** andar m de cima; (of cards) baralho; **record/cassette ~** toca-discos m inv/toca-fitas m inv

declare [dɪ'klɛər] VT (intention) revelar; (result) divulgar; (income, at customs) declarar

decline [dɪ'klaɪn] N declínio; (lessening) diminuição f, baixa ▶ VT recusar ▶ VI diminuir

decorate ['dɛkəreɪt] VT; **decoration** [dɛkə'reɪʃən] N enfeite m; (act) decoração; (medal) condecoração f; **decorator** N (painter) pintor(a) m/f

decrease [n 'diːkriːs, vt, vi diː'kriːs] N: **~ (in)** diminuição f (de) ▶ VT reduzir ▶ VI diminuir

decree [dɪ'kriː] N decreto

decrypt [diː'krɪpt] VT (Comput, Tel) desencriptar

dedicate ['dɛdɪkeɪt] VT dedicar; **dedication** [dɛdɪ'keɪʃən] N dedicação f; (in book) dedicatória; (on radio) mensagem f

deduce [dɪ'djuːs] VT deduzir

deduct [dɪ'dʌkt] VT deduzir; **deduction** N (deducting) redução f; (amount) subtração f; (deducing) dedução f

deed [diːd] N feito; (Jur) escritura, título

deep [diːp] ADJ profundo; (voice) baixo, grave; (breath) fundo; (colour) forte, carregado ▶ ADV: **the spectators stood 20 ~** havia 20 fileiras de espectadores; **to be 4 metres ~** ter 4 metros de profundidade; **deepen** VT aprofundar ▶ VI aumentar

deer [dɪər] N INV veado, cervo

default [dɪ'fɔːlt] N (Comput) default m, padrão m; **by ~** (win) por desistência

defeat [dɪ'fiːt] N derrota; (failure) malogro ▶ VT derrotar, vencer

defect [n 'diːfɛkt, vi dɪ'fɛkt] N defeito ▶ VI: **to ~ to the enemy**

desertar para se juntar ao inimigo;
defective [dɪˈfɛktɪv] ADJ
defeituoso
defence [dɪˈfɛns], (US) **defense** N
defesa
defend [dɪˈfɛnd] VT defender; (Jur)
contestar; **defendant** N
acusado(-a); (in civil case) réu/ré
m/f; **defender** N defensor(a) m/f;
(Sport) defesa
defer [dɪˈfəːʳ] VT (postpone) adiar
defiance [dɪˈfaɪəns] N desafio;
rebeldia; **in ~ of** a despeito de
defiant [dɪˈfaɪənt] ADJ
desafiador(a)
deficiency [dɪˈfɪʃənsɪ] N (lack)
deficiência, falta; (defect) defeito
deficit [ˈdɛfɪsɪt] N déficit m
define [dɪˈfaɪn] VT definir
definite [ˈdɛfɪnɪt] ADJ (fixed)
definitivo; (clear, obvious) claro,
categórico; (certain) certo; **he was
~ about it** ele foi categórico;
definitely ADV sem dúvida
deflate [diːˈfleɪt] VT esvaziar
deflect [dɪˈflɛkt] VT desviar
defraud [dɪˈfrɔːd] VT: **to ~ sb (of
sth)** trapacear alguém (por causa
de algo)
defriend [diːˈfrɛnd] VT (on social
network) excluir (em rede social)
defrost [diːˈfrɔst] VT descongelar
defuse [diːˈfjuːz] VT tirar o estopim
or a espoleta de; (situation)
neutralizar
defy [dɪˈfaɪ] VT desafiar; (resist)
opor-se a
degree [dɪˈɡriː] N grau m; (Sch)
diploma m, título; **~ in maths**
formatura em matemática; **by ~s**
(gradually) pouco a pouco; **to some
~, to a certain ~** até certo ponto
dehydrated [diːhaɪˈdreɪtɪd] ADJ
desidratado; (milk) em pó

delay [dɪˈleɪ] VT (decision etc)
retardar, atrasar; (train, person)
atrasar ▶ VI hesitar ▶ N demora;
(postponement) adiamento; **to be
~ed** estar atrasado; **without ~** sem
demora or atraso
delegate [n ˈdɛlɪɡɪt, vt ˈdɛlɪɡeɪt] N
delegado(-a) ▶ VT (person) autorizar;
(task) delegar
delete [dɪˈliːt] VT eliminar, riscar;
(Comput) deletar, excluir
deliberate [adj dɪˈlɪbərɪt, vi
dɪˈlɪbəreɪt] ADJ (intentional)
intencional; (slow) pausado, lento
▶ VI considerar; **deliberately**
[dɪˈlɪbərɪtlɪ] ADV (on purpose) de
propósito
delicacy [ˈdɛlɪkəsɪ] N delicadeza;
(of problem) dificuldade f; (choice
food) iguaria
delicate [ˈdɛlɪkɪt] ADJ delicado;
(health) frágil
delicatessen [dɛlɪkəˈtɛsn] N
delicatessen m
delicious [dɪˈlɪʃəs] ADJ delicioso;
(food) saboroso
delight [dɪˈlaɪt] N prazer m, deleite
m; (person) encanto; (experience)
delícia ▶ VT encantar, deleitar;
to take (a) ~ in deleitar-se com;
delighted ADJ: **delighted (at or
with sth)** encantado (com algo);
delightful ADJ encantador(a),
delicioso
delinquent [dɪˈlɪŋkwənt] ADJ, N
delinquente m/f
deliver [dɪˈlɪvəʳ] VT (distribute)
distribuir; (hand over) entregar;
(message) comunicar; (speech)
proferir; (Med) partejar; **delivery** N
distribuição f; (of speaker)
enunciação f; (Med) parto; **to take
delivery of** receber
delusion [dɪˈluːʒən] N ilusão f

demand [dɪ'mɑːnd] vт exigir; (rights) reivindicar, reclamar ▶ N exigência; (claim) reivindicação f; (Econ) procura; **to be in ~** estar em demanda; **on ~** à vista; **demanding** ADJ (boss) exigente; (work) absorvente

demise [dɪ'maɪz] N falecimento

demo ['dɛməu] (inf) N ABBR (= demonstration) passeata

democracy [dɪ'mɔkrəsɪ] N democracia; **democrat** ['dɛməkræt] N democrata m/f; **democratic** [dɛmə'krætɪk] ADJ democrático

demolish [dɪ'mɔlɪʃ] vт demolir, derrubar; (argument) refutar, contestar

demonstrate ['dɛmənstreɪt] vт demonstrar ▶ vɪ: **to ~ (for/against)** manifestar-se (a favor de/contra); **demonstration** [dɛmən'streɪʃən] N (Pol) manifestação f; (: march) passeata; (proof) demonstração f; (exhibition) exibição f; **demonstrator** N manifestante m/f

demote [dɪ'məut] vт rebaixar de posto

den [dɛn] N (of animal) covil m; (of thieves) antro, esconderijo; (room) aposento privado, cantinho

denial [dɪ'naɪəl] N refutação f; (refusal) negativa

denim ['dɛnɪm] N brim m, zuarte m; **denims** NPL jeans m (BR), jeans mpl (PT)

Denmark ['dɛnmɑːk] N Dinamarca

denomination [dɪnɔmɪ'neɪʃən] N valor m, denominação f; (Rel) confissão f, seita

denounce [dɪ'nauns] vт denunciar

dense [dɛns] ADJ denso; (inf: stupid) estúpido, bronco

density ['dɛnsɪtɪ] N densidade f

dent [dɛnt] N amolgadura, depressão f ▶ vт amolgar, dentar

dental ['dɛntl] ADJ (treatment) dentário; (hygiene) dental; **dental floss** [-flɔs] N fio dental

dentist ['dɛntɪst] N dentista m/f

dentures ['dɛntʃəz] NPL dentadura

deny [dɪ'naɪ] vт negar; (refuse) recusar

deodorant [diː'əudərənt] N desodorante m (BR), desodorizante m (PT)

depart [dɪ'pɑːt] vɪ ir-se, partir; (train etc) sair; **to ~ from** (fig: differ from) afastar-se de

department [dɪ'pɑːtmənt] N (Sch) departamento; (Comm) seção f; (Pol) repartição f; **department store** N magazine m (BR), grande armazém m (PT)

departure [dɪ'pɑːtʃər] N partida, ida; (of train etc) saída; (of employee) saída; **a new ~** uma nova orientação; **departure lounge** N sala de embarque

depend [dɪ'pɛnd] vɪ: **to ~ (up)on** depender de; (rely on) contar com; **it ~s** depende; **~ing on the result ...** dependendo do resultado ...; **dependant** N dependente m/f; **dependent** ADJ: **to be dependent (on)** depender (de), ser dependente (de) ▶ N = **dependant**

depict [dɪ'pɪkt] vт (in picture) retratar, representar; (describe) descrever

deport [dɪ'pɔːt] vт deportar

deposit [dɪ'pɔzɪt] N (Comm, Geo) depósito; (Chem) sedimento;

(*of ore, oil*) jazida; (*down payment*) sinal *m* ▶ vt depositar; (*luggage*) guardar; **deposit account** N conta de depósito a prazo

depot ['dɛpəu] N (*storehouse*) depósito, armazém *m*; (*for vehicles*) garagem *f*, parque *m*; (US) estação *f*

depress [dɪ'prɛs] vt deprimir; (*press down*) apertar; **depressed** ADJ deprimido; (*area, market, trade*) em depressão; **depressing** ADJ deprimente; **depression** N depressão *f*; (*hollow*) achatamento

deprive [dɪ'praɪv] vt: **to ~ sb of** privar alguém de; **deprived** ADJ carente

depth [dɛpθ] N profundidade *f*; (*of feeling*) intensidade *f*; **in the ~s of despair** no auge do desespero; **to be out of one's ~** (BRIT: *swimmer*) estar sem pé; (*fig*) estar voando

deputy ['dɛpjuti] ADJ: **~ chairman** vice-presidente(-a) *m/f* ▶ N (*assistant*) adjunto; (*Pol: MP*) deputado(-a)

derail [dɪ'reɪl] vt: **to ~ed** descarrilhar

derelict ['dɛrɪlɪkt] ADJ abandonado

derive [dɪ'raɪv] vt: **to ~ (from)** obter *or* tirar (de) ▶ vi: **to ~ from** derivar-se de

descend [dɪ'sɛnd] vt, vi descer; **to ~ from** descer de; **to ~ to** descambar em; **descent** N descida; (*origin*) descendência

describe [dɪs'kraɪb] vt descrever; **description** [dɪs'krɪpʃən] N descrição *f*; (*sort*) classe *f*, espécie *f*

desert [n 'dɛzət, vt, vi dɪ'zə:t] N deserto ▶ vt (*place*) desertar; (*partner, family*) abandonar ▶ vi (*Mil*) desertar

deserve [dɪ'zə:v] vt merecer

design [dɪ'zaɪn] N (*sketch*) desenho, esboço; (*layout, shape*) plano, projeto; (*pattern*) desenho, padrão *m*; (*art*) design *m*; (*intention*) propósito, intenção *f* ▶ vt (*plan*) projetar

designer [dɪ'zaɪnər] N (*Art*) artista *m/f* gráfico(-a); (*Tech*) desenhista *m/f*; (*fashion designer*) estilista *m/f*

desire [dɪ'zaɪər] N anseio; (*sexual*) desejo ▶ vt querer; desejar, cobiçar

desk [dɛsk] N (*in office*) mesa, secretária; (*for pupil*) carteira *f*; (*at airport*) balcão *m*; (*in hotel*) recepção *f*; (BRIT: *in shop, restaurant*) caixa

despair [dɪs'pɛər] N desesperança ▶ vi: **to ~ of** desesperar-se de

despatch [dɪs'pætʃ] N, vt = **dispatch**

desperate ['dɛspərɪt] ADJ desesperado; (*situation*) desesperador(a); **to be ~ for sth/to do** estar louco por algo/para fazer; **desperately** ADV desesperadamente; (*very: unhappy*) terrívelmente; (: *ill*) gravemente; **desperation** [dɛspə'reɪʃən] N desespero, desesperança; **in (sheer) desperation** desesperado

despise [dɪs'paɪz] vt desprezar

despite [dɪs'paɪt] PREP apesar de, a despeito de

dessert [dɪ'zə:t] N sobremesa

destination [dɛstɪ'neɪʃən] N destino

destined ['dɛstɪnd] ADJ: **to be ~ to do sth** estar destinado a fazer algo; **~ for** com destino a

destiny ['dɛstɪnɪ] N destino

destroy [dɪs'trɔɪ] vt destruir; (*animal*) sacrificar; **destruction** N destruição *f*

detach [dɪ'tætʃ] vt separar; (unstick) desprender; **detached** ADJ (attitude) imparcial, objetivo; (house) independente, isolado

detail ['di:teɪl] N detalhe m; (trifle) bobagem f ▶ vt detalhar; **in ~** pormenorizado, em detalhe

detain [dɪ'teɪn] vt deter; (in captivity) prender; (in hospital) hospitalizar

detect [dɪ'tɛkt] vt perceber; (Med, Police) identificar; (Mil, Radar, Tech) detectar; **detection** N descoberta; **detective** N detetive m/f; **detective story** N romance m policial

detention [dɪ'tɛnʃən] N detenção f, prisão f; (Sch) castigo

deter [dɪ'tə:ʳ] vt (discourage) desanimar; (dissuade) dissuadir

detergent [dɪ'tə:dʒənt] N detergente m

deteriorate [dɪ'tɪərɪəreɪt] vi deteriorar-se

determine [dɪ'tə:mɪn] vt descobrir; (limits etc) demarcar; **determined** ADJ (person) resoluto; **determined to do** decidido a fazer

detour ['di:tuəʳ] N desvio

detract [dɪ'trækt] vi: **to ~ from** diminuir

detrimental [dɛtrɪ'mɛntl] ADJ: **~ (to)** prejudicial (a)

develop [dɪ'vɛləp] vt desenvolver; (Phot) revelar; (disease) contrair; (resources) explotar ▶ vi (advance) progredir; (evolve) evoluir; (appear) aparecer; **development** N desenvolvimento; (advance) progresso; (of land) urbanização f

device [dɪ'vaɪs] N aparelho, dispositivo

devil ['dɛvl] N diabo

devious ['di:vɪəs] ADJ (person) malandro, esperto

devise [dɪ'vaɪz] vt (plan) criar; (machine) inventar

devote [dɪ'vəut] vt: **to ~ sth to** dedicar algo a; **devoted** [dɪ'vəutɪd] ADJ (friendship) leal; (partner) fiel; **to be devoted to** estar devotado a; **the book is devoted to politics** o livro trata de política; **devotion** N devoção f; (to duty) dedicação f

devour [dɪ'vauəʳ] vt devorar

devout [dɪ'vaut] ADJ devoto

dew [dju:] N orvalho

diabetes [daɪə'bi:ti:z] N diabete f

diagnosis [daɪəg'nəusɪs] (pl **diagnoses**) N diagnóstico

diagonal [daɪ'ægənl] ADJ diagonal ▶ N diagonal f

diagram ['daɪəgræm] N diagrama m, esquema m

dial ['daɪəl] N disco ▶ vt (number) discar (BR), marcar (PT)

dial code (US) N = **dialling code**

dialect ['daɪəlɛkt] N dialeto

dialling code ['daɪəlɪŋ-] (BRIT) N código de discagem

dialling tone ['daɪəlɪŋ-] (BRIT) N sinal m de discagem (BR) or de marcar (PT)

dialogue ['daɪəlɔg], (US) **dialog** N diálogo; (conversation) conversa

diameter [daɪ'æmɪtəʳ] N diâmetro

diamond ['daɪəmənd] N diamante m; (shape) losango, rombo; **diamonds** NPL (Cards) ouros mpl

diarrhoea [daɪə'ri:ə], (US) **diarrhea** N diarreia

diary ['daɪərɪ] N (daily account) diário; (engagements book) agenda

dice [daɪs] N INV dado ▶ VT (Culin) cortar em cubos

dictate [dɪk'teɪt] VT ditar; **dictation** N ditado

dictator [dɪk'teɪtər] N ditador(a) m/f

dictionary ['dɪkʃənrɪ] N dicionário

did [dɪd] PT of **do**

didn't ['dɪdnt] = **did not**

die [daɪ] N, VI morrer; (fig: fade) murchar; **to be dying for sth/to do sth** estar louco por algo/para fazer algo; **die away** VI (sound, light) extinguir-se lentamente; **die down** VI (fire) apagar-se; (wind) abrandar; (excitement) diminuir; **die out** VI desaparecer

diesel ['diːzl] N diesel m; (also: **~ fuel, ~ oil**) óleo diesel

diet ['daɪət] N dieta; (restricted food) regime m ▶ VI (also: **be on a ~**) estar de dieta, fazer regime

differ ['dɪfər] VI (be different): **to ~ from sth** ser diferente de algo, diferenciar-se de algo; (disagree): **to ~ (about)** discordar (sobre); **difference** N diferença; (disagreement) divergência; **different** ADJ diferente; **differentiate** [dɪfə'rɛnʃɪeɪt] VI: **to differentiate (between)** distinguir (entre)

difficult ['dɪfɪkəlt] ADJ difícil; **difficulty** N dificuldade f

dig [dɪg] (pt, pp **dug**) VT cavar ▶ N (prod) pontada; (archaeological) escavação f; (remark) alfinetada; **to ~ one's nails into** cravar as unhas em; **dig into** VT FUS (savings) gastar; **dig up** VT (plant) arrancar; (information) trazer à tona

digest [vt daɪ'dʒɛst, n 'daɪdʒɛst] VT (food) digerir; (facts) assimilar ▶ N sumário; **digestion** [dɪ'dʒɛstʃən] N digestão f

digit ['dɪdʒɪt] N (Math) dígito; (finger) dedo; **digital** ADJ digital; **digital camera** N câmara digital; **digital TV** N televisão f digital

dignified ['dɪgnɪfaɪd] ADJ digno

dignity ['dɪgnɪtɪ] N dignidade f

dilemma [daɪ'lɛmə] N dilema m

dilute [daɪ'luːt] VT diluir

dim [dɪm] ADJ fraco; (outline) indistinto; (room) escuro; (inf: person) burro ▶ VT diminuir; (US Aut) baixar

dime [daɪm] (US) N (moeda de) dez centavos

dimension [dɪ'mɛnʃən] N dimensão f; (measurement) medida; (also: **~s**: scale, size) tamanho

diminish [dɪ'mɪnɪʃ] VI diminuir

din [dɪn] N zoeira

dine [daɪn] VI jantar; **diner** N comensal m/f; (US: eating place) lanchonete f

dinghy ['dɪŋgɪ] N dingue m, bote m; **rubber ~** bote de borracha

dingy ['dɪndʒɪ] ADJ (room) sombrio, lúgubre; (clothes, curtains etc) sujo

dining car ['daɪnɪŋ-] (BRIT) N (Rail) vagão-restaurante m

dining room ['daɪnɪŋ-] N sala de jantar

dinkum ['dɪŋkəm] (AUST inf) ADJ (also: **fair ~**) de verdade

dinner ['dɪnər] N (evening meal) jantar m; (lunch) almoço; (banquet) banquete m; **dinner jacket** N smoking m; **dinner party** N jantar m; **dinner time** N (midday) hora de almoçar; (evening) hora de jantar

dip [dɪp] N (slope) inclinação f; (in sea) mergulho; (Culin) pasta para servir com salgadinhos ▶ VT (in water) mergulhar; (ladle etc) meter; (BRIT Aut: lights) baixar ▶ VI descer subitamente

diploma [dɪˈpləumə] N diploma m
diplomat [ˈdɪpləmæt] N diplomata m/f
dipstick [ˈdɪpstɪk] N (Aut) vareta medidora
dire [daɪəʳ] ADJ terrível
direct [daɪˈrɛkt] ADJ direto; (route) reto; (manner) franco, sincero ▶ VT dirigir; (order): **to ~ sb to do sth** ordenar alguém para fazer algo ▶ ADV direto; **can you ~ me to ...?** pode me indicar o caminho a ...?; **direct debit** (BRIT) N (Banking) débito direto; **direction** N (way) indicação f; (TV, Radio, Cinema) direção f; **directions** NPL (instructions) instruções fpl; **directions for use** modo de usar; **directly** ADV diretamente; (at once) imediatamente; **director** N diretor(a) m/f

directory [dɪˈrɛktərɪ] N (Tel) lista (telefônica); (Comm) anuário comercial; (Comput) diretório; **directory enquiries** (BRIT), **directory assistance** N (US) (serviço de) informações fpl

dirt [dəːt] N sujeira (BR), sujidade (PT); **dirty** ADJ sujo; (joke) indecente ▶ VT sujar
disability [dɪsəˈbɪlɪtɪ] N incapacidade f
disabled [dɪsˈeɪbld] ADJ deficiente ▶ NPL: **the ~** os deficientes
disadvantage [dɪsədˈvɑːntɪdʒ] N desvantagem f; (prejudice) inconveniente m
disagree [dɪsəˈɡriː] VI (differ) diferir; (be against, think otherwise): **to ~ (with)** não concordar (com), discordar (de); **disagreeable** ADJ desagradável; **disagreement** N desacordo; (quarrel) desavença

disappear [dɪsəˈpɪəʳ] VI desaparecer, sumir; (custom etc) acabar; **disappearance** N desaparecimento, desaparição f
disappoint [dɪsəˈpɔɪnt] VT decepcionar; **disappointed** ADJ decepcionado; **disappointment** N decepção f; (cause) desapontamento
disapproval [dɪsəˈpruːvəl] N desaprovação f
disapprove [dɪsəˈpruːv] VI: **to ~ of** desaprovar
disarmament N desarmamento
disaster [dɪˈzɑːstəʳ] N (accident) desastre m; (natural) catástrofe f
disbelief [dɪsbəˈliːf] N incredulidade f
disc [dɪsk] N disco; (Comput) = **disk**
discard [dɪsˈkɑːd] VT (old things) desfazer-se de; (fig) descartar
discharge [vt dɪsˈtʃɑːdʒ, n ˈdɪstʃɑːdʒ] VT (duties) cumprir, desempenhar; (patient) dar alta a; (employee) despedir; (soldier) dar baixa em, dispensar; (defendant) pôr em liberdade; (waste etc) descarregar, despejar ▶ N (Elec) descarga; (dismissal) despedida; (of duty) desempenho; (of debt) quitação f; (from hospital) alta; (from army) baixa; (Jur) absolvição f; (Med) secreção f
discipline [ˈdɪsɪplɪn] N disciplina ▶ VT disciplinar; (punish) punir
disc jockey N (on radio) radialista m/f; (in discotheque) discotecário(-a)
disclose [dɪsˈkləuz] VT revelar
disco [ˈdɪskəu] N ABBR = **discotheque**
discomfort [dɪsˈkʌmfət] N (unease) inquietação f; (physical) desconforto

d

disconnect [dɪskə'nɛkt] VT
desligar; (*pipe, tap*) desmembrar
discontent [dɪskən'tɛnt] N
descontentamento
discontinue [dɪskən'tɪnjuː] VT
interromper; (*payments*) suspender;
"~d" (*Comm*) "fora de linha"
discotheque ['dɪskəutɛk] N
discoteca
discount [*n* 'dɪskaunt, *vt*
dɪs'kaunt] N desconto ▶ VT
descontar; (*idea*) ignorar
discourage [dɪs'kʌrɪdʒ] VT
(*dishearten*) desanimar; (*advise
against*): **to ~ sth/sb from doing**
desaconselhar algo/alguém a fazer
discover [dɪs'kʌvəʳ] VT descobrir;
(*missing person*) encontrar; (*mistake*)
achar; **discovery** N descoberta
discredit [dɪs'krɛdɪt] VT
desacreditar; (*claim*) desmerecer
discreet [dɪ'skriːt] ADJ discreto;
(*careful*) cauteloso
discrepancy [dɪ'skrɛpənsɪ] N
diferença
discretion [dɪ'skrɛʃən] N discrição
f; **at the ~ of** ao arbítrio de
discriminate [dɪ'skrɪmɪneɪt] VI:
to ~ between fazer distinção entre;
to ~ against discriminar contra;
discrimination [dɪskrɪmɪ'neɪʃən]
N (*discernment*) discernimento;
(*bias*) discriminação *f*
discuss [dɪ'skʌs] VT discutir;
(*analyse*) analisar; **discussion** N
discussão *f*; (*debate*) debate *m*
disease [dɪ'ziːz] N doença
disembark [dɪsɪm'bɑːk] VT, VI
desembarcar
disgrace [dɪs'ɡreɪs] N ignomínia;
(*shame*) desonra ▶ VT (*family*)
envergonhar; (*name, country*)
desonrar; **disgraceful** ADJ
vergonhoso; (*behaviour*) escandaloso

disgruntled [dɪs'ɡrʌntld] ADJ
descontente
disguise [dɪs'ɡaɪz] N disfarce *m*
▶ VT: **to ~ o.s. (as)** disfarçar-se (de);
in ~ disfarçado
disgust [dɪs'ɡʌst] N repugnância
▶ VT repugnar a, dar nojo em;
disgusting ADJ repugnante;
(*unacceptable*) inaceitável
dish [dɪʃ] N prato; (*serving dish*)
travessa; **to do** *or* **wash the ~es**
lavar os pratos *or* a louça; **dish out**
VT repartir; **dish up** VT servir;
dishcloth N pano de prato *or* de
louça
dishonest [dɪs'ɔnɪst] ADJ (*person*)
desonesto; (*means*) fraudulento
dishwasher ['dɪʃwɔʃəʳ] N máquina
de lavar louça *or* pratos
disillusion [dɪsɪ'luːʒən] VT desiludir
disinfectant [dɪsɪn'fɛktənt] N
desinfetante *m*
disintegrate [dɪs'ɪntɪɡreɪt] VI
desintegrar-se
disk [dɪsk] N (*Comput*) disco;
(*removable*) disquete *m*; **disk drive** N
unidade *f* de disco; **diskette**
[dɪs'kɛt] (*US*) N (*Comput*) disquete *m*
dislike [dɪs'laɪk] N desagrado ▶ VT
antipatizar com, não gostar de
dislocate ['dɪsləkeɪt] VT deslocar
disloyal [dɪs'lɔɪəl] ADJ desleal
dismal ['dɪzml] ADJ (*depressing*)
deprimente; (*very bad*) horrível
dismantle [dɪs'mæntl] VT
desmontar, desmantelar
dismay [dɪs'meɪ] N consternação *f*
▶ VT consternar
dismiss [dɪs'mɪs] VT (*worker*)
despedir; (*pupils*) dispensar;
(*soldiers*) dar baixa a; (*Jur, possibility*)
rejeitar; **dismissal** N demissão *f*
disobedient [dɪsə'biːdɪənt] ADJ
desobediente

disobey [dɪsə'beɪ] VT desobedecer a; (*rules*) transgredir

disorder [dɪs'ɔːdəʳ] N desordem f; (*rioting*) distúrbios *mpl*, tumulto; (*Med*) distúrbio

disown [dɪs'əun] VT repudiar; (*child*) rejeitar

dispatch [dɪs'pætʃ] VT (*send: parcel etc*) expedir; (: *messenger*) enviar ▶ N (*sending*) remessa; (*Press*) comunicado; (*Mil*) parte f

dispel [dɪs'pɛl] VT dissipar

dispense [dɪs'pɛns] VT (*medicine*) preparar (e vender); **dispense with** VT FUS prescindir de; **dispenser** N (*device*) distribuidor *m* automático

disperse [dɪs'pəːs] VT espalhar; (*crowd*) dispersar ▶ VI dispersar-se

display [dɪs'pleɪ] N (*in shop*) mostra; (*exhibition*) exposição f; (*Comput: information*) apresentação f visual, (: *device*) display *m*; (*of feeling*) manifestação f ▶ VT mostrar; (*ostentatiously*) ostentar

displease [dɪs'pliːz] VT (*offend*) ofender; (*annoy*) aborrecer

disposable [dɪs'pəuzəbl] ADJ descartável; (*income*) disponível

disposal [dɪs'pəuzl] N (*of rubbish*) destruição f; (*of property etc*) venda, traspasse *m*; **at sb's ~** à disposição de alguém; **disposition** [dɪspə'zɪʃən] N disposição f; (*temperament*) índole f

dispute [dɪs'pjuːt] N (*domestic*) briga; (*also*: **industrial ~**) conflito, disputa ▶ VT disputar; (*question*) questionar

disqualify [dɪs'kwɔlɪfaɪ] VT (*Sport*) desclassificar; **to ~ sb for sth/from doing sth** desqualificar alguém para algo/de fazer algo

disregard [dɪsrɪ'gɑːd] VT ignorar

disrupt [dɪs'rʌpt] VT (*plans*) desfazer; (*conversation, proceedings*) perturbar, interromper

dissect [dɪ'sɛkt] VT dissecar

dissent [dɪ'sɛnt] N dissensão f

dissertation [dɪsə'teɪʃən] N (*also: Sch*) dissertação f, tese f

dissolve [dɪ'zɔlv] VT dissolver ▶ VI dissolver-se; **to ~ in(to) tears** debulhar-se em lágrimas

distance ['dɪstns] N distância; **in the ~** ao longe

distant ['dɪstnt] ADJ distante; (*manner*) afastado, reservado

distil [dɪs'tɪl], (*US*) **distill** VT destilar; **distillery** N destilaria

distinct [dɪs'tɪŋkt] ADJ distinto; (*clear*) claro; (*unmistakable*) nítido; **as ~ from** em oposição a; **distinction** N diferença; (*honour*) honra; (*in exam*) distinção f

distinguish [dɪs'tɪŋgwɪʃ] VT (*differentiate*) diferenciar; (*identify*) identificar; **to ~ o.s.** distinguir-se; **distinguished** ADJ (*eminent*) eminente; (*in appearance*) distinto

distort [dɪs'tɔːt] VT distorcer

distract [dɪs'trækt] VT distrair; (*attention*) desviar; **distracted** ADJ distraído; (*anxious*) aturdido; **distraction** N distração f; (*confusion*) aturdimento, perplexidade f; (*amusement*) divertimento

distraught [dɪs'trɔːt] ADJ desesperado

distress [dɪs'trɛs] N angústia ▶ VT afligir; **distressing** ADJ angustiante

distribute [dɪs'trɪbjuːt] VT distribuir; (*share out*) repartir, dividir; **distribution** [dɪstrɪ'bjuːʃən] N distribuição f; (*of profits etc*) repartição f;

d

distributor N (Aut) distribuidor m; (Comm) distribuidor(a) m/f

district ['dıstrıkt] N (of country) região f; (of town) zona; (Admin) distrito; **district attorney** (US) N promotor(a) m/f público(-a)

distrust [dıs'trʌst] N desconfiança ▶ vt desconfiar de

disturb [dıs'tə:b] vt (disorganize) perturbar; (upset) incomodar; (interrupt) atrapalhar; **disturbance** N (upheaval) convulsão f; (political, violent) distúrbio; (of mind) transtorno; **disturbed** ADJ perturbado; (child) infeliz; **to be mentally/emotionally disturbed** ter problemas psicológicos/ emocionais; **disturbing** ADJ perturbador(a)

ditch [dıtʃ] N fosso; (irrigation ditch) rego ▶ vt (inf: partner) abandonar; (: car, plan etc) desfazer-se de

ditto ['dıtəu] ADV idem

dive [daıv] N (from board) salto; (underwater, of submarine) mergulho ▶ vi mergulhar; **to ~ into** (bag, drawer etc) enfiar a mão em; (shop, car etc) enfiar-se em; **diver** N mergulhador(a) m/f

diversion [daı'və:ʃən] N (BRIT Aut) desvio; (distraction, Mil) diversão f; (of funds) desvio

divert [daı'və:t] vt desviar

divide [dı'vaıd] vt (Math) dividir; (separate) separar; (share out) repartir ▶ vi dividir-se; (road) bifurcar-se; **divided highway** (US) N pista dupla

divine [dı'vaın] ADJ (also fig) divino

diving ['daıvıŋ] N salto; (underwater) mergulho; **diving board** N trampolim m

division [dı'vıʒən] N divisão f; (sharing out) repartição f;

(disagreement) discórdia; (Football) grupo

divorce [dı'vɔ:s] N divórcio ▶ vt divorciar-se de; (dissociate) dissociar; **divorced** ADJ divorciado; **divorcee** N divorciado(-a)

DIY N ABBR = **do-it-yourself**

dizzy ['dızı] ADJ tonto

DJ N ABBR = **disc jockey**

(KEYWORD)

do [du:] (pt **did**, pp **done**) AUX VB **1** (in negative constructions): **I don't understand** eu não compreendo
2 (to form questions): **didn't you know?** você não sabia?; **what do you think?** o que você acha?
3 (for emphasis, in polite expressions): **she does seem rather late** ela está muito atrasada; **do sit down/help yourself** sente-se/sirva-se; **do take care!** tome cuidado!
4 (used to avoid repeating vb): **she swims better than I do** ela nada melhor que eu; **do you agree? — yes, I do/no, I don't** você concorda? — sim, concordo/não, não concordo; **she lives in Glasgow — so do I** ela mora em Glasgow — eu também; **who broke it? — I did** quem quebrou isso? — (fui) eu
5 (in question tags): **you like him, don't you?** você gosta dele, não é?; **he laughed, didn't he?** ele riu, não foi?
▶ vt **1** (gen: carry out, perform etc) fazer; **what are you doing tonight?** o que você vai fazer hoje à noite?; **to do the washing-up/ cooking** lavar a louça/cozinhar; **to do one's teeth/nails** escovar os dentes/fazer as unhas; **to do one's hair** (comb) pentear-se; (style) fazer

um penteado; **we're doing Othello at school** (studying) nós estamos estudando Otelo na escola; (performing) nós vamos encenar Otelo na escola
2 (Aut etc): **the car was doing 190** o carro andava a 190 por hora; **we've done 200 km already** já percorremos 200 km; **he can do 190 km/h in that car** ele consegue chegar a 190 km/h naquele carro
▶ VI **1** (act, behave) fazer; **do as I do** faça como eu faço
2 (get on, fare) ir; **how do you do?** como você está indo?
3 (suit) servir; **will it do?** serve?
4 (be sufficient) bastar; **will £10 do?** £10 dá?; **that'll do** é suficiente; **that'll do!** (in annoyance) basta!, chega!; **to make do (with)** contentar-se (com)
▶ N (inf: party etc) festa; **it was rather a do** foi uma festança
do away with VT FUS (kill) matar; (law etc) abolir; (withdraw) retirar
do up VT (laces) atar; (zip) fechar; (dress, skirt) abotoar; (renovate, room, house) arrumar, renovar
do with VT FUS (be connected) ter a ver com; (need): **I could do with a drink/some help** eu bem que gostaria de tomar alguma coisa/ eu bem que precisaria de uma ajuda; **what has it got to do with you?** o que é que isso tem a ver com você?
do without VI: **if you're late for tea then you'll do without** se você chegar atrasado ficará sem almoço ▶ VT FUS passar sem

dock [dɔk] N (Naut) doca; (Jur) banco (dos réus) ▶ VI (Naut: enter dock) atracar; (Space) unir-se no espaço; **docks** NPL docas fpl
doctor ['dɔktər] N médico(-a); (PhD etc) doutor(a) m/f ▶ VT (drink etc) falsificar
document ['dɔkjumənt] N documento; **documentary** [dɔkju'mɛntərɪ] ADJ documental ▶ N documentário
dodge [dɔdʒ] N (trick) trapaça ▶ VT esquivar-se de, evitar; (tax) sonegar; (blow) furtar-se a
does [dʌz] VB see **do**
doesn't ['dʌznt] = **does not**
dog [dɔg] N cachorro, cão m ▶ VT (subj: person) seguir; (: bad luck) perseguir; **doggy bag** ['dɔgɪ-] N quentinha
do-it-yourself N sistema m faça-você-mesmo
dole [dəul] (BRIT) N (payment) subsídio de desemprego; **on the ~** desempregado; **dole out** VT distribuir
doll [dɔl] N boneca; (US inf: woman) gatinha
dollar ['dɔlər] N dólar m
dolphin ['dɔlfɪn] N golfinho
dome [dəum] N (Arch) cúpula
domestic [də'mɛstɪk] ADJ doméstico; (national) nacional
dominate ['dɔmɪneɪt] VT dominar
domino ['dɔmɪnəu] (pl **dominoes**) N peça de dominó; **dominoes** N (game) dominó m
donate [də'neɪt] VT doar
done [dʌn] PP of **do**
donkey ['dɔŋkɪ] N burro
donor ['dəunər] N doador(a) m/f; **donor card** N cartão m de doador
don't [dəunt] = **do not**
doodle ['duːdl] VI rabiscar

doom [du:m] N (*fate*) destino ▶ VT: **to be ~ed to failure** estar destinado *or* fadado ao fracasso

door [dɔ:ʳ] N porta; **doorbell** N campainha; **doorstep** N degrau *m* da porta, soleira; **doorway** N vão *m* da porta, entrada

dope [dəup] N (*inf: person*) imbecil *m/f*; (: *drugs*) maconha ▶ VT (*horse etc*) dopar

dormitory ['dɔ:mitri] N dormitório; (*US*) residência universitária

dose [dəus] N dose *f*

dot [dɔt] N ponto; (*speck*) pontinho ▶ VT: **~ted with** salpicado de; **on the ~** em ponto

dotcom [dɔt'kɔm] N empresa pontocom

double ['dʌbl] ADJ duplo ▶ ADV (*twice*): **to cost ~ (sth)** custar o dobro (de algo) ▶ N (*person*) duplo(-a) ▶ VT dobrar ▶ VI dobrar; **at the ~** (*BRIT*), **on the ~** em passo acelerado; **double bass** N contrabaixo; **double bed** N cama de casal; **double-click** VI (*Comput*) clicar duas vezes; **double-decker** [dʌbl'dɛkəʳ] N ônibus *m* (*BR*) or autocarro (*PT*) de dois andares; **double room** N quarto de casal

doubt [daut] N dúvida ▶ VT duvidar; (*suspect*) desconfiar de; **to ~ that ...** duvidar que ...; **doubtful** ADJ duvidoso; **doubtless** ADV sem dúvida

dough [dəu] N massa; **doughnut**, (*US*) **donut** N sonho (*BR*), bola de Berlim (*PT*)

dove [dʌv] N pomba

down [daun] N (*feathers*) penugem *f* ▶ ADV (*downwards*) para baixo; (*on the ground*) por terra ▶ PREP por, abaixo ▶ VT (*inf: drink*) tomar de um gole só; **~ with X!** abaixo X!; **down-and-out** N (*tramp*) vagabundo(-a); **downfall** N queda, ruína; **downhill** ADV para baixo ▶ N (*Ski: also*: **downhill race**) descida; **to go downhill** descer, ir morro abaixo; (*fig: business*) degringolar

Downing Street ['daunıŋ-] (*BRIT*) N *ver nota*

> **Downing Street** é a rua de Westminster (Londres) onde estão localizadas as residências oficiais do Primeiro-ministro (número 10) e do Ministro da Fazenda (número 11). O termo **Downing Street** é frequentemente utilizado para designar o governo britânico.

down: download ['daunləud] VT (*Comput*) baixar, fazer o download de; **downloadable** ADJ (*Comput*) baixável; **downright** ['daunrait] ADJ (*lie*) patente; (*refusal*) categórico

Down's syndrome [daunz-] N síndrome *f* de Down

down: downstairs ADV (*below*) lá em baixo; (*direction*) para baixo; **down-to-earth** ADJ prático, realista; **downtown** ADV no centro da cidade; **down under** ADV na Austrália (*or* Nova Zelândia); **downward** ['daunwəd] ADJ, ADV para baixo; **downwards** ADV = **downward**

doze [dəuz] VI dormitar; **doze off** VI cochilar

dozen ['dʌzn̩] N dúzia; **a ~ books** uma dúzia de livros; **~s of times** milhares de vezes

drab [dræb] ADJ sombrio

draft [drɑ:ft] N (*first copy*) rascunho; (*Pol: of bill*) projeto de lei; (*bank draft*) saque *m*, letra; (*US: call-up*) recrutamento ▶ vt (*plan*) esboçar; (*speech, letter*) rascunhar; *see also* **draught**

drag [dræg] vt arrastar; (*river*) dragar ▶ vi arrastar-se ▶ n (*inf*) chatice f (BR), maçada (PT); (*women's clothing*): **in ~** em travesti; **drag on** vi arrastar-se

dragon ['drægən] n dragão m

dragonfly ['drægənflaɪ] n libélula

drain [dreɪn] n bueiro; (*source of loss*) sorvedouro ▶ vt drenar; (*vegetables*) coar ▶ vi (*water*) escorrer, escoar-se; **drainage** n (*act*) drenagem f; (*system*) esgoto; **drainpipe** n cano de esgoto

drama ['drɑːmə] n (*art*) teatro; (*play, event*) drama m; **dramatic** [drə'mætɪk] adj dramático; (*theatrical*) teatral

drank [dræŋk] pt of **drink**

drape [dreɪp] vt ornar, cobrir

drastic ['dræstɪk] adj drástico

draught [drɑːft], (US) **draft** n (*of air*) corrente f; (*Naut*) calado; (*beer*) chope m; **on ~** (*beer*) de barril; **draughts** (BRIT) n (jogo de) damas fpl

draw [drɔː] (pt **drew**, pp **drawn**) vt desenhar; (*cart*) puxar; (*curtain*) fechar; (*gun*) sacar; (*attract*) atrair; (*money*) tirar; (: *from bank*) sacar ▶ vi empatar ▶ n empate m; (*lottery*) sorteio; **to ~ near** aproximar-se; **draw out** vt (*money*) sacar; **draw up** vi (*stop*) parar(-se) ▶ vt (*chair etc*) puxar; (*document*) redigir; **drawback** n inconveniente m, desvantagem f; **drawer** [drɔːʳ] n gaveta; **drawing** n desenho; **drawing pin** (BRIT) n tachinha (BR), pionés m (PT); **drawing room** n sala de visitas

drawn [drɔːn] pp of **draw**

dread [drɛd] n medo, pavor m ▶ vt temer, recear, ter medo de; **dreadful** adj terrível

dream [driːm] (pt, pp **dreamed** or **dreamt**) n sonho ▶ vt, vi sonhar

dreary ['drɪərɪ] adj (*talk, time*) monótono; (*weather*) sombrio

drench [drɛntʃ] vt encharcar

dress [drɛs] n vestido; (*no pl: clothing*) traje m ▶ vt vestir; (*wound*) fazer curativo em ▶ vi vestir-se; **to get ~ed** vestir-se; **dress up** vi vestir-se com elegância; (*in fancy dress*) fantasiar-se; **dress circle** (BRIT) n balcão m nobre; **dresser** n (BRIT: *cupboard*) aparador m; (US: *chest of drawers*) cômoda de espelho; **dressing** n (*Med*) curativo; (*Culin*) molho; **dressing gown** (BRIT) n roupão m; (*woman's*) peignoir m; **dressing room** n (*Theatre*) camarim m; (*Sport*) vestiário; **dressing table** n penteadeira (BR), toucador m (PT); **dressmaker** n costureiro(-a)

drew [druː] pt of **draw**

dribble ['drɪbl] vi (*baby*) babar ▶ vt (*ball*) driblar

dried [draɪd] adj seco; (*eggs, milk*) em pó

drier ['draɪəʳ] n = **dryer**

drift [drɪft] n (*of current etc*) força; (*of snow, sand etc*) monte m; (*meaning*) sentido ▶ vi (*boat*) derivar; (*sand, snow*) amontoar-se

drill [drɪl] n furadeira; (*bit, of dentist*) broca; (*for mining etc*) broca, furadeira; (*Mil*) exercícios mpl militares ▶ vt furar, brocar; (*Mil*) exercitar ▶ vi (*for oil*) perfurar

drink [drɪŋk] (pt **drank**, pp **drunk**) n bebida ▶ vt, vi beber; **a ~ of**

water um copo d'água; **drinker** N bebedor(a) m/f; **drinking water** N água potável

drip [drɪp] N gotejar m; (one drip) gota, pingo; (Med) gota a gota m ▶ VI gotejar, pingar

drive [draɪv] (pt **drove**, pp **driven**) N passeio (de automóvel); (journey) trajeto, percurso; (also: **~way**) entrada; (energy) energia, vigor m; (campaign) campanha; (Comput) drive m ▶ VT (car) dirigir (BR), guiar (PT); (push) empurrar; (Tech: motor) acionar; (nail): **to ~ sth into** cravar algo em ▶ VI (Aut: at controls) dirigir (BR), guiar (PT); (: travel) ir de carro; **left-/right-hand ~** direção à esquerda/direita; **to ~ sb mad** deixar alguém louco

driver ['draɪvəʳ] N motorista m/f; (Rail) maquinista m; **driver's license** (US) N carteira de motorista (BR), carta de condução (PT)

driveway ['draɪvweɪ] N entrada

driving ['draɪvɪŋ] N direção f (BR), condução f (PT); **driving instructor** N instrutor(a) m/f de autoescola (BR) or de condução (PT); **driving licence** (BRIT) N carteira de motorista (BR), carta de condução (PT); **driving test** N exame m de motorista

drizzle ['drɪzl] N chuvisco

droop [dru:p] VI pender

drop [drɔp] N (of water) gota; (lessening) diminuição f; (fall: distance) declive m ▶ VT (allow to fall) deixar cair; (voice, eyes, price) baixar; (set down from car) deixar (saltar/descer); (omit) omitir ▶ VI cair; (wind) parar; **drops** NPL (Med) gotas fpl; **drop off** VI (sleep) cochilar ▶ VT (passenger) deixar; **drop out** VI (withdraw) retirar-se; **drop-out** N

pessoa que abandona o trabalho, os estudos etc

drought [draut] N seca

drove [drəuv] PT of **drive**

drown [draun] VT afogar; (also: **~ out**: sound) encobrir ▶ VI afogar-se

drowsy ['drauzɪ] ADJ sonolento

drug [drʌg] N remédio, medicamento; (narcotic) droga ▶ VT drogar; **to be on ~s** (an addict) estar viciado em drogas; (Med) estar sob medicação; **drug addict** N toxicômano(-a); **druggist** (US) N farmacêutico(-a); **drugstore** (US) N drogaria

drum [drʌm] N tambor m; (for oil, petrol) tambor, barril m; **drums** NPL (kit) bateria; **drummer** N baterista m/f

drunk [drʌŋk] PP of **drink** ▶ ADJ bêbado ▶ N (also: **~ard**) bêbado(-a); **drunken** ADJ (laughter) de bêbado; (party) com muita bebida; (person) bêbado

dry [draɪ] ADJ seco; (day) sem chuva; (humour) irônico ▶ VT secar, enxugar; (tears) limpar ▶ VI secar; **dry up** VI secar completamente; **dry-cleaner's** N tinturaria; **dryer** N secador m; (also: **spin-dryer**) secadora

DSS (BRIT) N ABBR (= Department of Social Security) ≈ INAMPS m

DTP N ABBR (= desktop publishing) DTP m

dual ['djuəl] ADJ dual, duplo; **dual carriageway** (BRIT) N pista dupla

dubious ['dju:bɪəs] ADJ duvidoso; (reputation, company) suspeitoso

duck [dʌk] N pato ▶ VI abaixar-se repentinamente

due [dju:] ADJ (proper) devido; (expected) esperado ▶ N: **to give sb his (or her) ~** ser justo com alguém

▶ADV: **~ north** exatamente ao norte; **dues** NPL (*for club, union*) quota; (*in harbour*) direitos mpl; **in ~ course** no devido tempo; (*eventually*) no final; **~ to** devido a

duet [dju:'ɛt] N dueto

dug [dʌg] PT, PP *of* **dig**

duke [dju:k] N duque m

dull [dʌl] ADJ (*light*) sombrio; (*intelligence, wit*) lento; (*boring*) enfadonho; (*sound, pain*) surdo; (*weather, day*) nublado, carregado ▶VT (*pain, grief*) aliviar; (*mind, senses*) entorpecer

dumb [dʌm] ADJ mudo; (*pej: stupid*) estúpido

dummy ['dʌmɪ] N (*tailor's model*) manequim m; (*mock-up*) modelo; (BRIT: *for baby*) chupeta ▶ADJ falso

dump [dʌmp] N (*also*: **rubbish ~**) depósito de lixo; (*inf: place*) chiqueiro ▶VT (*put down*) depositar, descarregar; (*get rid of*) desfazer-se de

dumpling ['dʌmplɪŋ] N bolinho cozido

dungarees [dʌŋgə'ri:z] NPL macacão m (BR), fato macaco (PT)

dungeon ['dʌndʒən] N calabouço

duplex ['dju:plɛks] (US) N casa geminada; (*also*: **~ apartment**) duplex m

duplicate [n 'dju:plɪkət, vt 'dju:plɪkeɪt] N (*of document*) duplicata; (*of key*) cópia ▶VT duplicar; (*photocopy*) multigrafar; (*repeat*) reproduzir

durable ['djuərəbl] ADJ durável; (*clothes, metal*) resistente

during ['djuərɪŋ] PREP durante

dusk [dʌsk] N crepúsculo, anoitecer m

dust [dʌst] N pó m, poeira ▶VT (*furniture*) tirar o pó de; (*cake etc*):

to ~ with polvilhar com; **dustbin** N (BRIT) lata de lixo; **duster** N pano de pó; **dustman** (BRIT) *irreg* N lixeiro, gari m (BR *inf*); **dusty** ADJ empoeirado

Dutch [dʌtʃ] ADJ holandês(-esa) ▶N (*Ling*) holandês m ▶ADV: **let's go ~** (*inf*) cada um paga o seu, vamos rachar; **the Dutch** NPL (*people*) os holandeses; **Dutchman** *irreg* N holandês m; **Dutchwoman** *irreg* N holandesa

duty ['dju:tɪ] N dever m; (*tax*) taxa; **on ~** de serviço; **off ~** de folga; **duty-free** ADJ livre de impostos

duvet ['du:veɪ] (BRIT) N edredom m (BR), edredão m (PT)

DVD N ABBR (= *digital versatile or video disc*) DVD m; **DVD burner** N gravador m de DVD; **DVD player** N DVD player m; **DVD writer** N gravador m de DVD

dwarf [dwɔ:f] (*pl* **dwarves**) N anão/anã m/f ▶VT ananicar

dwindle ['dwɪndl] VI diminuir

dye [daɪ] N tintura, tinta ▶VT tingir

dynamite ['daɪnəmaɪt] N dinamite f

dyslexia [dɪs'lɛksɪə] N dislexia

E [i:] N (*Mus*) mi *m*

each [i:tʃ] ADJ cada *inv* ▶ PRON cada um(a); **~ other** um ao outro; **they hate ~ other** (eles) se odeiam

eager ['i:gər] ADJ ávido; **to be ~ to do sth** ansiar por fazer algo; **to be ~ for** ansiar por

eagle ['i:gl] N águia

ear [ɪər] N (*external*) orelha; (*inner, fig*) ouvido; (*of corn*) espiga; **earache** N dor *f* de ouvidos; **eardrum** N tímpano

earl [ə:l] N conde *m*

earlier ['ə:lɪər] ADJ mais adiantado; (*edition etc*) anterior ▶ ADV mais cedo

early ['ə:lɪ] ADV cedo; (*before time*) com antecedência ▶ ADJ (*sooner than expected*) prematuro; (*reply*) pronto; (*Christians, settlers*) primeiro; (*man*) primitivo; (*life, work*) juvenil; **in the ~ or ~ in the spring/19th century** no princípio da primavera/do século dezenove

earmark ['ɪəmɑ:k] VT: **to ~ sth for** reservar *or* destinar algo para

earn [ə:n] VT ganhar; (*Comm: interest*) render; (*praise, reward*) merecer

earnest ['ə:nɪst] ADJ (*wish*) intenso; (*manner*) sério; **in ~** a sério

earnings ['ə:nɪŋz] NPL (*personal*) vencimentos *mpl*, salário, ordenado; (*of company*) lucro

earphones NPL fones *mpl* de ouvido

earring N brinco

earth [ə:θ] N terra; (*BRIT Elec*) fio terra ▶ VT (*BRIT Elec*) ligar à terra; **earthquake** N terremoto (BR), terramoto (PT)

ease [i:z] N facilidade *f*; (*relaxed state*) sossego ▶ VT facilitar; (*pain, tension*) aliviar; (*help pass*): **to ~ sth in/out** meter/tirar algo com cuidado; **at ~!** (*Mil*) descansar!; **ease off** VI acalmar-se; (*wind*) baixar; (*rain*) moderar-se; **ease up** VI = **ease off**

easily ['i:zɪlɪ] ADV facilmente, fácil (*inf*)

east [i:st] N leste *m* ▶ ADJ (*region*) leste; (*wind*) do leste ▶ ADV para o leste; **the E~** o Oriente; (*Pol*) o leste

Easter ['i:stər] N Páscoa; **Easter egg** N ovo de Páscoa

eastern ['i:stən] ADJ do leste, oriental

easy ['i:zɪ] ADJ fácil; (*comfortable*) folgado, cômodo; (*relaxed*) natural, complacente; (*victim, prey*) desprotegido ▶ ADV: **to take it or things ~** (*not worry*) levar as coisas com calma; (*go slowly*) ir devagar; (*rest*) descansar; **easy-going** ADJ pacato, fácil

eat [i:t] (*pt* **ate**, *pp* **eaten**) VT, VI comer; **eat away** VT corroer;

eat away at VT FUS corroer;
eat into VT FUS = **eat away at**
eavesdrop ['i:vzdrɔp] VI: **to ~ (on)** escutar às escondidas
e-book ['i:buk] N livro eletrônico
e-card ['i:ka:d] N cartão m eletrônico
eccentric [ɪk'sɛntrɪk] ADJ, N excêntrico(-a)
echo ['ɛkəʊ] (pl **echoes**) N eco ▶ VT ecoar, repetir ▶ VI ressoar, repetir
eclipse [ɪ'klɪps] N eclipse m
eco-friendly [i:kəʊ'frɛndlɪ] ADJ ecológico
ecological [i:kə'lɔdʒɪkəl] ADJ ecológico
ecology [ɪ'kɔlədʒɪ] N ecologia
e-commerce N ABBR (= electronic commerce) comércio eletrônico
economic [i:kə'nɔmɪk] ADJ econômico; (business etc) rentável; **economical** ADJ econômico; **economics** N economia ▶ NPL aspectos mpl econômicos
economize [ɪ'kɔnəmaɪz] VI economizar, fazer economias
economy [ɪ'kɔnəmɪ] N economia; **economy class** N (Aviat) classe f econômica
ecstasy ['ɛkstəsɪ] N êxtase m; **ecstatic** [ɛks'tætɪk] ADJ extasiado
eczema ['ɛksɪmə] N eczema m
edge [ɛdʒ] N (of knife etc) fio; (of table, chair etc) borda; (of lake etc) margem f ▶ VT (trim) embainhar; **on ~** (fig) = **edgy**; **to ~ away from** afastar-se pouco a pouco de; **edgy** ADJ nervoso, inquieto
edible ['ɛdɪbl] ADJ comestível
Edinburgh ['ɛdɪnbərə] N Edimburgo
edit ['ɛdɪt] VT (be editor of) dirigir; (cut) cortar, redigir; (Comput, TV) editar; (Cinema) montar; **edition**

[ɪ'dɪʃən] N edição f; **editor** N redator(a) m/f; (of newspaper) diretor(a) m/f; **editorial** [ɛdɪ'tɔ:rɪəl] ADJ editorial
educate ['ɛdjukeɪt] VT educar
education [ɛdju'keɪʃən] N educação f; (schooling) ensino; (science) pedagogia; **educational** ADJ (policy, experience) educacional; (toy etc) educativo
eel [i:l] N enguia
eerie ['ɪərɪ] ADJ (strange) estranho; (mysterious) misterioso
effect [ɪ'fɛkt] N efeito ▶ VT (repairs) fazer; (savings) efetuar; **to take ~** (law) entrar em vigor; (drug) fazer efeito; **in ~** na realidade; **effective** [ɪ'fɛktɪv] ADJ eficaz; (actual) efetivo
efficiency [ɪ'fɪʃənsɪ] N eficiência
efficient [ɪ'fɪʃənt] ADJ eficiente; (machine) rentável
effort ['ɛfət] N esforço; **effortless** ADJ fácil
e.g. ADV ABBR (= exempli gratia) p. ex.
egg [ɛg] N ovo; **hard-boiled/ soft-boiled ~** ovo duro/mole; **egg on** VT incitar; **eggcup** N oveiro; **eggplant** (esp US) N beringela; **eggshell** N casca de ovo
ego ['i:gəʊ] N ego
Egypt ['i:dʒɪpt] N Egito; **Egyptian** [ɪ'dʒɪpʃən] ADJ, N egípcio(-a)
eight [eɪt] NUM oito; **eighteen** ['eɪ'ti:n] NUM dezoito; **eighteenth** NUM décimo oitavo; **eighth** [eɪtθ] NUM oitavo; **eightieth** ['eɪtɪɪθ] NUM octogésimo; **eighty** ['eɪtɪ] NUM oitenta
Eire ['ɛərə] N (República da) Irlanda
either ['aɪðəʳ] ADJ (one or other) um ou outro; (each) cada; (both) ambos ▶ PRON: **~ (of them)**

qualquer (dos dois) ▶ ADV: **no, I don't ~** eu também não ▶ CONJ: **~ yes or no** ou sim ou não

eject [ɪ'dʒɛkt] VT expulsar

elaborate [adj ɪ'læbərɪt, vt, vi ɪ'læbəreɪt] ADJ complicado ▶ VT (expand) expandir; (refine) aperfeiçoar ▶ VI: **to ~ on** acrescentar detalhes a

elastic [ɪ'læstɪk] ADJ elástico; (adaptable) flexível, adaptável ▶ N elástico; **elastic band** (BRIT) N elástico

elbow ['ɛlbəu] N cotovelo

elder ['ɛldər] ADJ mais velho ▶ N (tree) sabugueiro; (person) o/a mais velho(-a); **elderly** ADJ idoso, de idade ▶ NPL: **the elderly** as pessoas de idade, os idosos

eldest ['ɛldɪst] ADJ mais velho ▶ N o/a mais velho(-a)

elect [ɪ'lɛkt] VT eleger ▶ ADJ: **the president ~** o presidente eleito; **to ~ to do** (choose) optar por fazer; **election** N (voting) votação f; (installation) eleição f; **electorate** N eleitorado

electric [ɪ'lɛktrɪk] ADJ elétrico; **electrical** ADJ elétrico; **electric fire** N aquecedor m elétrico

electrician [ɪlɛk'trɪʃən] N eletricista m/f

electricity [ɪlɛk'trɪsɪtɪ] N eletricidade f

electrify [ɪ'lɛktrɪfaɪ] VT (fence, Rail) eletrificar; (audience) eletrizar

electronic [ɪlɛk'trɔnɪk] ADJ eletrônico; **electronic mail** N correio eletrônico; **electronics** N eletrônica

elegant ['ɛlɪgənt] ADJ (person, building) elegante; (idea) refinado

element ['ɛlɪmənt] N elemento; **elementary** [ɛlɪ'mɛntərɪ] ADJ (gen) elementar; (primitive) rudimentar; (school, education) primário; **elementary school** (US) N ver nota

Nos Estados Unidos e no Canadá, uma **elementary school** (também chamada de grade school ou grammar school nos Estados Unidos) é uma escola pública onde os alunos passam de seis a oito dos primeiros anos escolares.

elephant ['ɛlɪfənt] N elefante m

elevator ['ɛlɪveɪtər] (US) N elevador m

eleven [ɪ'lɛvn] NUM onze; **eleventh** NUM décimo-primeiro

eligible ['ɛlɪdʒəbl] ADJ elegível, apto; **to be ~ for sth** (job etc) ter qualificações para algo

elm [ɛlm] N olmo

eloquent ['ɛləkwənt] ADJ eloquente

El Salvador [ɛl'sælvədɔːr] N El Salvador

else [ɛls] ADV outro, mais; **something ~** outra coisa; **nobody ~ spoke** ninguém mais falou; **elsewhere** ADV (be) em outro lugar (BR), noutro sítio (PT); (go) para outro lugar (BR), a outro sítio (PT)

elusive [ɪ'luːsɪv] ADJ esquivo; (quality) indescritível

email ['iːmeɪl] N e-mail m, correio eletrônico ▶ VT (person) enviar um e-mail a; **email account** N conta de e-mail, conta de correio eletrônico; **email address** N e-mail m, endereço eletrônico

embark [ɪm'baːk] VI embarcar ▶ VT embarcar; **to ~ on** (fig) empreender, começar

embarrass [ɪm'bærəs] VT (politician) embaraçar; (emotionally) constranger; **embarrassed** ADJ

descomfortável; **embarrassing** ADJ embaraçoso, constrangedor(a); **embarrassment** N embaraço, constrangimento
embassy ['ɛmbəsɪ] N embaixada
embrace [ɪm'breɪs] VT abraçar, dar um abraço em; (include) abarcar, abranger ▶ VI abraçar-se ▶ N abraço
embroider [ɪm'brɔɪdə^r] VT bordar; **embroidery** N bordado
emerald ['ɛmərəld] N esmeralda
emerge [ɪ'məːdʒ] VI sair; (from sleep) acordar; (fact, idea) emergir
emergency [ɪ'məːdʒənsɪ] N emergência; **in an ~** em caso de urgência; **emergency exit** N saída de emergência; **emergency landing** N aterrissagem f forçada (BR), aterragem f forçosa (PT)
emigrate ['ɛmɪgreɪt] VI emigrar
eminent ['ɛmɪnənt] ADJ eminente
emit [ɪ'mɪt] VT (smoke) soltar; (smell) exalar; (sound) produzir
emoticon [ɪ'məutɪkən] N (Comput) emoticon m
emotion [ɪ'məuʃən] N emoção f; **emotional** ADJ (needs, exhaustion) emocional; (person) sentimental, emotivo; (scene) comovente; (tone) emocionante
emperor ['ɛmpərə^r] N imperador m
emphasis ['ɛmfəsɪs] (pl **emphases**) N ênfase f
emphasize ['ɛmfəsaɪz] VT (word, point) enfatizar, acentuar; (feature) salientar
empire ['ɛmpaɪə^r] N império
employ [ɪm'plɔɪ] VT empregar; (tool) utilizar; **employee** N empregado(-a); **employer** N empregador(a) m/f, patrão(-troa)

m/f; **employment** N (gen) emprego; (work) trabalho
empress ['ɛmprɪs] N imperatriz f
emptiness ['ɛmptɪnɪs] N vazio, vácuo
empty ['ɛmptɪ] ADJ vazio; (place) deserto; (house) desocupado; (threat) vão/vã ▶ N, VT esvaziar; (place) evacuar ▶ VI esvaziar-se; (place) ficar deserto; **empty-handed** ADJ de mãos vazias
emulsion [ɪ'mʌlʃən] N emulsão f; (also: **~ paint**) tinta plástica
enable [ɪ'neɪbl] VT: **to ~ sb to do sth** (allow) permitir que alguém faça algo; (prepare) capacitar alguém para fazer algo
enamel [ɪ'næməl] N esmalte m
enclose [ɪn'kləuz] VT (land) cercar; (with letter etc) anexar (BR), enviar junto (PT); **please find ~d** segue junto
enclosure [ɪn'kləuʒə^r] N cercado
encore [ɔŋ'kɔː^r] EXCL bis!, outra! ▶ N bis m
encounter [ɪn'kauntə^r] N encontro ▶ VT encontrar, topar com; (difficulty) enfrentar
encourage [ɪn'kʌrɪdʒ] VT (activity) encorajar; (growth) estimular; (person): **to ~ sb to do sth** animar alguém a fazer algo; **encouragement** N estímulo
encrypt [ɪn'krɪpt] VT (Comput, Tel) criptografar
encyclopaedia, encyclopedia [ɛnsaɪkləu'piːdɪə] N enciclopédia
end [ɛnd] N fim m; (of table, line, rope etc) ponta; (of street, town) final m ▶ VT acabar, terminar; (also: **bring to an ~, put an ~ to**) acabar com, pôr fim a ▶ VI terminar, acabar; **in the ~** ao fim, por fim, finalmente; **on ~** na

ponta; **to stand on ~** (*hair*) arrepiar-se; **for hours on ~** por horas a fio; **end up** vi: **to ~ up in** terminar em; (*place*) ir parar em
endanger [ɪnˈdeɪndʒəʳ] vt pôr em perigo
endearing [ɪnˈdɪərɪŋ] ADJ simpático, atrativo
endeavour [ɪnˈdevəʳ], (*US*) **endeavor** N esforço; (*attempt*) tentativa ▶ vi: **to ~ to do** esforçar-se para fazer; (*try*) tentar fazer
ending [ˈɛndɪŋ] N fim *m*, conclusão *f*; (*of book*) desenlace *m*; (*Ling*) terminação *f*
endless [ˈɛndlɪs] ADJ interminável; (*possibilities*) infinito
endorse [ɪnˈdɔːs] vt (*cheque*) endossar; (*approve*) aprovar; **endorsement** N (*BRIT: on driving licence*) descrição *f* das multas; (*approval*) aval *m*
endure [ɪnˈdjuəʳ] vt (*bear*) aguentar, suportar ▶ vi (*last*) durar
enemy [ˈɛnəmɪ] ADJ, N inimigo(-a)
energy [ˈɛnədʒɪ] N energia; **energy drink** N energético, bebida energética
enforce [ɪnˈfɔːs] vt (*Jur*) fazer cumprir
engage [ɪnˈgeɪdʒ] vt (*attention*) chamar; (*interest*) atrair; (*lawyer*) contratar; (*clutch*) engrenar ▶ vi engrenar; **to ~ in** dedicar-se a, ocupar-se com; **to ~ sb in conversation** travar conversa com alguém; **engaged** ADJ (*BRIT: phone*) ocupado (*BR*), impedido (*PT*); (: *toilet*) ocupado; (*betrothed*) noivo; **to get engaged** ficar noivo; **engaged tone** (*BRIT*) N (*Tel*) sinal *m* de ocupado (*BR*) or de impedido (*PT*); **engagement** N encontro;

(*booking*) contrato; (*to marry*) noivado; **engagement ring** N aliança de noivado
engine [ˈɛndʒɪn] N (*Aut*) motor *m*; (*Rail*) locomotiva
engineer [ɛndʒɪˈnɪəʳ] N engenheiro(-a); (*US Rail*) maquinista *m/f*; (*BRIT: for repairs*) técnico(-a); **engineering** N engenharia
England [ˈɪŋglənd] N Inglaterra
English [ˈɪŋglɪʃ] ADJ inglês(-esa) ▶ N (*Ling*) inglês *m*; **the English** NPL (*people*) os ingleses; **English Channel** N: **the English Channel** o Canal da Mancha
engraving [ɪnˈgreɪvɪŋ] N gravura
enhance [ɪnˈhɑːns] vt (*gen*) ressaltar, salientar; (*beauty*) realçar; (*position*) melhorar; (*add to*) aumentar
enjoy [ɪnˈdʒɔɪ] vt gostar de; (*health, privilege*) desfrutar de; **to ~ o.s.** divertir-se; **enjoyable** ADJ agradável; **enjoyment** N prazer *m*
enlarge [ɪnˈlɑːdʒ] vt aumentar; (*Phot*) ampliar ▶ vi: **to ~ on** (*subject*) desenvolver, estender-se sobre
enlist [ɪnˈlɪst] vt alistar; (*support*) conseguir, aliciar ▶ vi alistar-se
enormous [ɪˈnɔːməs] ADJ enorme
enough [ɪˈnʌf] ADJ: **~ time/books** tempo suficiente/livros suficientes ▶ PRON: **have you got ~?** você tem o suficiente? ▶ ADV: **big ~** suficientemente grande; **~!** basta!, chega!; **that's ~, thanks** chega, obrigado; **I've had ~ of him** estou farto dele; **which, funnily** or **oddly ~ ...** o que, por estranho que pareça ...
enquire [ɪnˈkwaɪəʳ] vt, vi = **inquire**
enrage [ɪnˈreɪdʒ] vt enfurecer, enraivecer

enrol [ɪnˈrəul], (US) **enroll** VT
inscrever; (Sch) matricular ▶ VI
inscrever-se; matricular-se;
enrolment N inscrição f; (Sch)
matrícula

ensure [ɪnˈʃuər] VT assegurar

entail [ɪnˈteɪl] VT implicar

enter [ˈɛntər] VT entrar em; (club)
ficar or fazer-se sócio de; (army)
alistar-se em; (competition)
inscrever-se em; (sb for a
competition) inscrever; (write down)
completar; (Comput) digitar ▶ VI
entrar; **enter for** VT FUS
inscrever-se em; **enter into** VT FUS
estabelecer; (plans) fazer parte de;
(debate, negotiations) entrar em;
(agreement) chegar a, firmar

enterprise [ˈɛntəpraɪz] N
empresa; (undertaking)
empreendimento; (initiative)
iniciativa; **enterprising** ADJ
empreendedor(a)

entertain [ɛntəˈteɪn] VT divertir,
entreter; (guest) receber (em casa);
(idea, plan) estudar; **entertainer** N
artista m/f; **entertaining** ADJ
divertido; **entertainment** N
(amusement) entretenimento,
diversão f; (show) espetáculo

enthusiasm [ɪnˈθuːzɪæzəm] N
entusiasmo

enthusiast [ɪnˈθuːzɪæst] N
entusiasta m/f; **enthusiastic**
[ɪnθuːzɪˈæstɪk] ADJ entusiasmado;
to be enthusiastic about
entusiasmar-se por

entire [ɪnˈtaɪər] ADJ inteiro;
entirely ADV totalmente,
completamente

entitle [ɪnˈtaɪtl] VT: **to ~ sb to sth**
dar a alguém direito a algo;
entitled [ɪnˈtaɪtld] ADJ (book etc)
intitulado; **to be entitled to sth/**

to do sth ter direito a algo/de
fazer algo

entrance [n ˈɛntrəns, vt ɪnˈtrɑːns]
N entrada; (arrival) chegada ▶ VT
encantar, fascinar; **to gain ~ to**
(university etc) ser admitido em;
entrance examination N
exame m de admissão; **entrance
fee** N joia

entrant [ˈɛntrənt] N participante
m/f; (BRIT: in exam) candidato(-a)

entrepreneur [ɔntrəprəˈnəːr] N
empresário(-a)

entrust [ɪnˈtrʌst] VT: **to ~ sth to
sb** confiar algo a alguém

entry [ˈɛntrɪ] N entrada; (in
register) registro, assentamento;
(in account) lançamento; (in
dictionary) verbete m; **"no ~"**
"entrada proibida"; (Aut)
"contramão" (BR), "entrada
proibida" (PT); **entry phone** (BRIT)
N interfone m (em apartamento)

envelope [ˈɛnvələup] N
envelope m

envious [ˈɛnvɪəs] ADJ invejoso;
(look) de inveja

environment [ɪnˈvaɪərnmənt] N
meio ambiente m; **environmental**
[ɪnvaɪərnˈmɛntl] ADJ ambiental

envisage [ɪnˈvɪzɪdʒ] VT prever

envoy [ˈɛnvɔɪ] N enviado(-a)

envy [ˈɛnvɪ] N inveja ▶ VT ter inveja
de; **to ~ sb sth** invejar alguém por
algo, cobiçar algo de alguém

epic [ˈɛpɪk] N epopeia ▶ ADJ épico

epidemic [ɛpɪˈdɛmɪk] N epidemia

epilepsy [ˈɛpɪlɛpsɪ] N epilepsia

episode [ˈɛpɪsəud] N episódio

equal [ˈiːkwl] ADJ igual; (treatment)
equitativo, equivalente ▶ N igual
m/f ▶ VT ser igual a; **to be ~ to**
(task) estar à altura de; **equality**
[iːˈkwɔlɪtɪ] N igualdade f; **equalize**

vi igualar; (*Sport*) empatar; **equally** ADV igualmente; (*share etc*) por igual

equator [ɪ'kweɪtə^r] N equador *m*

equip [ɪ'kwɪp] VT equipar; (*person*) prover, munir; **to be well ~ped** estar bem preparado *or* equipado; **equipment** N equipamento; (*machines etc*) equipamentos *mpl*, aparelhagem *f*

equivalent [ɪ'kwɪvəlnt] ADJ equivalente ▶ N equivalente *m*

era ['ɪərə] N era, época

erase [ɪ'reɪz] VT apagar; **eraser** N borracha (de apagar)

e-reader ['iːriːdə^r] N leitor *m* de livros digitais

erect [ɪ'rɛkt] ADJ (*posture*) ereto; (*tail, ears*) levantado ▶ VT erigir, levantar; (*assemble*) montar; **erection** N construção *f*; (*assembly*) montagem *f*; (*Physiol*) ereção *f*

erode [ɪ'rəud] VT (*Geo*) causar erosão em; (*confidence*) minar

erotic [ɪ'rɔtɪk] ADJ erótico

errand ['ɛrnd] N recado, mensagem *f*

erratic [ɪ'rætɪk] ADJ imprevisível

error ['ɛrə^r] N erro

erupt [ɪ'rʌpt] VI entrar em erupção; (*fig*) explodir, estourar; **eruption** N erupção *f*; (*fig*) explosão *f*

escalate ['ɛskəleɪt] VI intensificar-se

escalator ['ɛskəleɪtə^r] N escada rolante

escape [ɪ'skeɪp] N fuga, (*of gas*) escapatória ▶ VI escapar; (*flee*) fugir, evadir-se; (*leak*) vazar, escapar ▶ VT fugir de; (*elude*) escapulir de; **his name ~s me** o nome dele me foge a memória; **to ~ from** (*place*) escapar de; (*person*) escapulir de

escort [*n* 'ɛskɔːt, *vt* ɪ'skɔːt] N acompanhante *m/f*; (*Mil, Naut*)

escolta ▶ VT acompanhar

especially [ɪ'spɛʃlɪ] ADV (*above all*) sobretudo; (*particularly*) em particular

espionage ['ɛspɪɑːʒ] N espionagem *f*

essay ['ɛseɪ] N ensaio

essence ['ɛsns] N essência

essential [ɪ'sɛnʃl] ADJ (*necessary*) indispensável; (*basic*) essencial ▶ N elemento essencial

establish [ɪ'stæblɪʃ] VT estabelecer; (*facts*) verificar; (*proof*) demonstrar; (*reputation*) firmar; **establishment** N estabelecimento; **the Establishment** a classe dirigente

estate [ɪ'steɪt] N (*land*) fazenda (BR), propriedade *f* (PT); (*Jur*) herança; (*Pol*) estado; (BRIT: *also*: **housing ~**) conjunto habitacional; **estate agent** (BRIT) N corretor(a) *m/f* de imóveis (BR), agente *m/f* imobiliário(-a) (PT); **estate car** (BRIT) N perua (BR), canadiana (PT)

estimate [*n* 'ɛstɪmət, *vb* 'ɛstɪmeɪt] N (*assessment*) avaliação *f*; (*calculation*) cálculo; (*Comm*) orçamento ▶ VT estimar, avaliar, calcular

etc. ABBR (= *et cetera*) etc.

eternal [ɪ'təːnl] ADJ eterno

eternity [ɪ'təːnɪtɪ] N eternidade *f*

ethical ['ɛθɪkl] ADJ ético

ethics ['ɛθɪks] N ética ▶ NPL moral *f*

Ethiopia [iːθɪ'əupɪə] N Etiópia

ethnic ['ɛθnɪk] ADJ étnico; (*culture*) folclórico

e-ticket ['iːtɪkɪt] N bilhete *m* eletrônico

etiquette ['ɛtɪkɛt] N etiqueta

EU ABBR (= *European Union*) UE *f*

euro ['juərəu] N (*currency*) euro *m*

Europe ['juǝrǝp] N Europa;
European [juǝrǝ'piːǝn] ADJ, N
europeu(-peia); **European Union**
N: **the European Union** a União
Europeia

evacuate [ɪ'vækjueɪt] VT evacuar

evade [ɪ'veɪd] VT (*person*) evitar;
(*question, duties*) esquivar-se de;
(*tax*) sonegar

evaporate [ɪ'væpǝreɪt] VI
evaporar-se

eve [iːv] N: **on the ~ of** na véspera
de

even ['iːvn] ADJ (*level*) plano;
(*smooth*) liso; (*equal, Sport*) igual;
(*number*) par ► ADV até, mesmo;
~ if mesmo que; **~ though**
mesmo que, embora; **~ more**
ainda mais; **~ so** mesmo assim;
not ~ nem; **to get ~ with sb** ficar
quite com alguém; **even out** VI
nivelar-se

evening ['iːvnɪŋ] N (*early*) tarde f;
(*late*) noite f; (*event*) noitada; **in
the ~** à noite; **evening class** N
aula noturna

event [ɪ'vɛnt] N acontecimento;
(*Sport*) prova; **in the ~ of** no caso
de; **eventful** ADJ cheio de
acontecimentos; (*game etc*) cheio
de emoção, agitado

eventual [ɪ'vɛntʃuǝl] ADJ final;
eventually ADV finalmente; (*in
time*) por fim

ever ['ɛvǝ^r] ADV (*always*) sempre;
(*at any time*) em qualquer
momento; (*in question*): **why ~
not?** por que não, ora?; **the best ~**
o melhor que já se viu; **have you ~
seen it?** você alguma vez já viu
isto?; **better than ~** melhor que
nunca; **~ since** *adv* desde então;
conj depois que; **evergreen** N
sempre-verde f

(KEYWORD)

every ['ɛvrɪ] ADJ **1** (*each*) cada;
every one of them cada um
deles; **every shop in the town
was closed** todas as lojas da
cidade estavam fechadas
2 (*all possible*) todo(-a); **I have
every confidence in her** tenho
absoluta confiança nela; **we
wish you every success**
desejamos-lhe o maior sucesso;
**he's every bit as clever as his
brother** ele é tão inteligente
quanto o irmão
3 (*showing recurrence*) todo(-a);
**every other car had been
broken into** cada dois carros
foram arrombados; **she visits me
every other/third day** ele me
visita cada dois/três dias; **every
now and then** de vez em quando

everybody ['ɛvrɪbɔdɪ] PRON
todos, todo mundo (BR), toda a
gente (PT)

everyday ['ɛvrɪdeɪ] ADJ (*daily*)
diário; (*usual*) corrente; (*common*)
comum

everyone ['ɛvrɪwʌn] PRON =
everybody

everything ['ɛvrɪθɪŋ] PRON tudo

everywhere ['ɛvrɪwɛǝ^r] ADV (*be*)
em todo lugar (BR), em toda a
parte (PT); (*go*) a todo lugar (BR),
a toda a parte (PT); (*wherever*):
~ you go you meet ... aonde quer
que se vá, encontra-se ...

evict [ɪ'vɪkt] VT despejar

evidence ['ɛvɪdǝns] N (*proof*)
prova(s) f(pl); (*of witness*)
testemunho, depoimento;
(*indication*) sinal m; **to give ~**
testemunhar, prestar
depoimento

evident ['ɛvɪdənt] ADJ evidente;
evidently ADV evidentemente;
(*apparently*) aparentemente
evil ['i:vl] ADJ mau/má ▶ N mal *m*,
maldade *f*
evoke [ɪ'vəuk] VT evocar
evolution [i:və'lu:ʃən] N
evolução *f*; (*development*)
desenvolvimento
evolve [ɪ'vɔlv] VT desenvolver ▶ VI
desenvolver-se
exact [ɪg'zækt] ADJ exato; (*person*)
meticuloso ▶ VT: **to ~ sth (from)**
exigir algo (de); **exactly** ADV
exatamente; (*indicating agreement*)
isso mesmo
exaggerate [ɪg'zædʒəreɪt] VT, VI
exagerar; **exaggeration**
[ɪgzædʒə'reɪʃən] N exagero
exam [ɪg'zæm] N ABBR =
examination
examination [ɪgzæmɪ'neɪʃən] N
exame *m*; (*inquiry*) investigação *f*
examine [ɪg'zæmɪn] VT examinar;
(*inspect*) inspecionar; **examiner** N
examinador(a) *m/f*
example [ɪg'zɑ:mpl] N exemplo;
for ~ por exemplo
excavate ['ɛkskəveɪt] VT escavar
exceed [ɪk'si:d] VT exceder; (*number*)
ser superior a; (*speed limit*)
ultrapassar; (*limits*) ir além de;
(*powers*) exceder-se em; (*hopes*)
superar; **exceedingly** ADV
extremamente
excellent ['ɛksələnt] ADJ
excelente
except [ɪk'sɛpt] PREP (*also*: **~ for,
~ing**) exceto, a não ser ▶ VT: **to ~ sb
from** excluir alguém de; **~ if/when**
a menos que, a não ser que;
exception N exceção *f*; **to take
exception to** ressentir-se de
excerpt ['ɛksə:pt] N trecho

excess [ɪk'sɛs] N excesso; **excess
baggage** N excesso de bagagem;
excessive ADJ excessivo
exchange [ɪks'tʃeɪndʒ] N troca;
(*of teachers, students*) intercâmbio;
(*also*: **telephone ~**) estação *f*
telefônica (BR), central *f* telefónica
(PT) ▶ VT: **to ~ (for)** trocar (por);
exchange rate N (taxa de) câmbio
excite [ɪk'saɪt] VT excitar; **to get ~d**
entusiasmar-se; **excitement** N
emoções *fpl*; (*agitation*) agitação *f*;
exciting ADJ emocionante,
empolgante
exclaim [ɪk'skleɪm] VI exclamar;
exclamation [ɛksklə'meɪʃən] N
exclamação *f*; **exclamation mark**
N ponto de exclamação
exclude [ɪk'sklu:d] VT excluir
exclusive [ɪk'sklu:sɪv] ADJ exclusivo;
~ of tax sem incluir os impostos
excruciating [ɪk'skru:ʃieɪtɪŋ] ADJ
doloroso, martirizante
excursion [ɪk'skə:ʃən] N excursão *f*
excuse [*n* ɪk'skju:s, *vt* ɪk'skju:z] N
desculpa ▶ VT desculpar, perdoar;
to ~ sb from doing sth dispensar
alguém de fazer algo; **~ me!**
desculpe!; **if you will ~ me ...** com
a sua licença ...
execute ['ɛksɪkju:t] VT (*plan*)
realizar; (*order*) cumprir; (*person,
movement*) executar; **execution** N
realização *f*; (*killing*) execução *f*
executive [ɪg'zɛkjutɪv] N (*Comm,
Pol*) executivo(-a) ▶ ADJ executivo
exempt [ɪg'zɛmpt] ADJ: **~ from**
isento de ▶ VT: **to ~ sb from**
dispensar alguém de
exercise ['ɛksəsaɪz] N exercício
▶ VT exercer; (*right*) valer-se de;
(*dog*) levar para passear ▶ VI (*also*:
to take ~) fazer exercício; **exercise
book** N caderno

exert [ɪɡ'zəːt] vt exercer; **to ~ o.s.** esforçar-se, empenhar-se; **exertion** N esforço

exhale [ɛks'heɪl] vt, vi expirar

exhaust [ɪɡ'zɔːst] N (Aut: also: **~ pipe**) escape m, exaustor m; (fumes) escapamento (de gás) ▶ vt esgotar; **exhaustion** N exaustão f

exhibit [ɪɡ'zɪbɪt] N (Art) obra exposta; (Jur) objeto exposto ▶ vt (courage etc) manifestar, mostrar; (quality, emotion) demonstrar; (paintings) expor; **exhibition** [ɛksɪ'bɪʃən] N exposição f

exhilarating [ɪɡ'zɪləreɪtɪŋ] ADJ estimulante, tônico

exile ['ɛksaɪl] N exílio; (person) exilado(-a) ▶ vt desterrar, exilar

exist [ɪɡ'zɪst] vi existir; (live) viver; **existence** N existência; (life) vida; **existing** ADJ atual

exit ['ɛksɪt] N saída ▶ vi (Comput, Theatre) sair

exotic [ɪɡ'zɔtɪk] ADJ exótico

expand [ɪk'spænd] vt aumentar ▶ vi aumentar; (trade, gas etc) expandir-se; (metal) dilatar-se

expansion [ɪk'spænʃən] N (of town) desenvolvimento; (of trade) expansão f; (of population) aumento

expect [ɪk'spɛkt] vt esperar; (suppose) supor; (require) exigir ▶ vi: **to be ~ing** estar grávida; **expectation** [ɛkspɛk'teɪʃən] N esperança; (belief) expectativa

expedition [ɛkspə'dɪʃən] N expedição f

expel [ɪk'spɛl] vt expelir; (from place, school) expulsar

expense [ɪk'spɛns] N gasto, despesa; (expenditure) despesas fpl; **expenses** NPL (costs) despesas fpl; **at the ~ of** à custa de; **expense**

account N relatório de despesas

expensive [ɪk'spɛnsɪv] ADJ caro

experience [ɪk'spɪərɪəns] N experiência ▶ vt (situation) enfrentar; (feeling) sentir; **experienced** ADJ experiente

experiment [ɪk'spɛrɪmənt] N experimento, experiência ▶ vi: **to ~ (with/on)** fazer experiências (com/em)

expert ['ɛkspəːt] ADJ hábil, perito ▶ N especialista m/f; **expertise** [ɛkspəː'tiːz] N perícia

expire [ɪk'spaɪəʳ] vi expirar; (run out) vencer; **expiry** N expiração f, vencimento

explain [ɪk'spleɪn] vt explicar; (clarify) esclarecer; **explain away** vt justificar

explicit [ɪk'splɪsɪt] ADJ explícito

explode [ɪk'spləud] vi estourar, explodir

exploit [n 'ɛksplɔɪt, vt ɪk'splɔɪt] N façanha ▶ vt explorar; **exploitation** [ɛksplɔɪ'teɪʃən] N exploração f

explore [ɪk'splɔːʳ] vt explorar; (fig) examinar, pesquisar; **explorer** N explorador(a) m/f

explosion [ɪk'spləuʒən] N explosão f

explosive [ɪk'spləusɪv] ADJ explosivo ▶ N explosivo

export [vt ɛk'spɔːt, n, cpd 'ɛkspɔːt] vt exportar ▶ N exportação f ▶ cpd de exportação; **exporter** N exportador(a) m/f

expose [ɪk'spəuz] vt expor; (unmask) desmascarar; **exposed** ADJ (house etc) desabrigado

exposure [ɪk'spəuʒəʳ] N exposição f; (publicity) publicidade f; (Phot) revelação f; **to die from ~** (Med) morrer de frio

e

express [ɪkˈsprɛs] ADJ expresso, explícito; (BRIT: letter etc) urgente ▶ N rápido ▶ VT exprimir, expressar; (quantity) representar; **expression** N expressão f; **expressway** (US) N rodovia (BR), autoestrada (PT)

extend [ɪkˈstɛnd] VT (visit, street) prolongar; (building) aumentar; (offer) fazer; (hand) estender

extension [ɪkˈstɛnʃən] N (Elec) extensão f; (building) acréscimo, expansão f; (of rights) ampliação f; (Tel) ramal m (BR), extensão f (PT); (of deadline, campaign) prolongamento, prorrogação f

extensive [ɪkˈstɛnsɪv] ADJ extenso; (damage) considerável; (broad) vasto, amplo

extent [ɪkˈstɛnt] N (breadth) extensão f; (of damage etc) dimensão f; (scope) alcance m; **to some** or **to a certain ~** até certo ponto

exterior [ɛkˈstɪərɪəʳ] ADJ externo ▶ N exterior m; (appearance) aspecto

external [ɛkˈstəːnl] ADJ externo

extinct [ɪkˈstɪŋkt] ADJ extinto

extinguish [ɪkˈstɪŋgwɪʃ] VT extinguir

extra [ˈɛkstrə] ADJ adicional ▶ ADV adicionalmente ▶ N (surcharge) extra m, suplemento; (Cinema, Theatre) figurante m/f

extract [vt ɪkˈstrækt, n ˈɛkstrækt] VT tirar, extrair; (tooth) arrancar; (mineral) extrair; (money) extorquir; (promise) conseguir, obter ▶ N extrato

extradite [ˈɛkstrədaɪt] VT (from country) extraditar; (to country) obter a extradição de

extraordinary [ɪkˈstrɔːdnrɪ] ADJ extraordinário; (odd) estranho

extravagance [ɪkˈstrævəgəns] N extravagância; (no pl: spending) esbanjamento

extravagant [ɪkˈstrævəgənt] ADJ (lavish) extravagante; (wasteful) gastador(a), esbanjador(a)

extreme [ɪkˈstriːm] ADJ extremo ▶ N extremo; **extremely** ADV muito, extremamente

extrovert [ˈɛkstrəvəːt] N extrovertido(-a)

eye [aɪ] N olho; (of needle) buraco ▶ VT olhar, observar; **to keep an ~ on** vigiar, ficar de olho em; **eyebrow** N sobrancelha; **eyedrops** NPL gotas fpl para os olhos; **eyelash** N cílio; **eyelid** N pálpebra; **eyeliner** N delineador m; **eye shadow** N sombra de olhos; **eyesight** N vista, visão f

f

F [ɛf] N (*Mus*) fá *m*
fabric ['fæbrɪk] N tecido, pano
face [feɪs] N cara, rosto; (*grimace*)
careta; (*of clock*) mostrador *m*;
(*side, surface*) superfície *f*; (*of
building*) frente *f*, fachada ▶ VT
(*facts, problem*) enfrentar;
(*particular direction*) dar para;
~ down de bruços; (*card*) virado
para baixo; **to lose ~** perder o
prestígio; **to save ~** salvar as
aparências; **to make** *or* **pull a ~**
fazer careta; **in the ~ of** diante de,
à vista de; **on the ~ of it** a julgar
pelas aparências, à primeira vista;
face up to VT FUS enfrentar; **face
cloth** (*BRIT*) N pano de rosto; **face
pack** (*BRIT*) N máscara facial
facilities [fə'sɪlɪtɪz] NPL
facilidades *fpl*, instalações *fpl*;
credit ~ crediário
fact [fækt] N fato; **in ~** realmente,
na verdade
factor ['fæktə^r] N fator *m*
factory ['fæktərɪ] N fábrica

factual ['fæktjuəl] ADJ real, fatual
faculty ['fækəltɪ] N faculdade *f*;
(*US*) corpo docente
fad [fæd] (*inf*) N mania, modismo
fade [feɪd] VI desbotar; (*sound,
hope*) desvanecer-se; (*light*)
apagar-se; (*flower*) murchar
fag [fæg] (*inf*) N cigarro
fail [feɪl] VT (*candidate*) reprovar;
(*exam*) não passar em, ser
reprovado em; (*subj: leader*)
fracassar; (: *courage*) carecer;
(: *memory*) falhar ▶ VI fracassar;
(*engine, brakes, voice*) falhar; **to ~
to do sth** deixar de fazer algo;
(*be unable*) não conseguir fazer
algo; **without ~** sem falta; **failing**
N defeito ▶ PREP na *or* à falta de;
failing that senão; **failure** N
fracasso; (*mechanical etc*) falha
faint [feɪnt] ADJ fraco; (*recollection*)
vago; (*mark*) indistinto; (*smell,
trace*) leve ▶ N desmaio ▶ VI
desmaiar; **to feel ~** sentir tonteira
fair [fɛə^r] ADJ justo; (*hair*) louro;
(*complexion*) branco; (*weather*)
bom; (*good enough*) razoável;
(*sizeable*) considerável ▶ ADV: **to
play ~** fazer jogo limpo ▶ N (*also:
trade ~*) feira; (*BRIT: funfair*)
parque *m* de diversões; **fairly** ADV
(*justly*) com justiça; (*quite*)
bastante; **fair trade** N comércio
justo
fairy ['fɛərɪ] N fada
faith [feɪθ] N fé *f*; (*trust*) confiança;
(*denomination*) seita; **faithful** ADJ
fiel; (*account*) exato; **faithfully**
ADV fielmente; **yours faithfully**
(*BRIT: in letters*) atenciosamente
fake [feɪk] N (*painting etc*)
falsificação *f*; (*person*) impostor(a)
m/f ▶ ADJ falso ▶ VT fingir; (*painting
etc*) falsificar

f

falcon ['fɔːlkən] N falcão m
fall [fɔːl] (pt **fell**, pp **fallen**) N queda; (US: autumn) outono ▶ VI cair; (price) baixar; **falls** NPL (waterfall) cascata, queda d'água; **to ~ flat** cair de cara no chão; (plan) falhar; (joke) não agradar; **fall back** VI retroceder; **fall back on** VT FUS recorrer a; **fall behind** VI ficar para trás; **fall down** VI (person) cair; (building) desabar; **fall for** VT FUS (trick) cair em; (person) enamorar-se de; **fall in** VI ruir; (Mil) alinhar-se; **fall off** VI cair; (diminish) declinar, diminuir; **fall out** VI cair; (friends etc) brigar; **fall through** VI (plan, project) furar
fallout ['fɔːlaut] N chuva radioativa
false [fɔːls] ADJ falso; **false teeth** (BRIT) NPL dentadura postiça
fame [feɪm] N fama
familiar [fə'mɪlɪər] ADJ (well-known) conhecido; (tone) familiar, íntimo; **to be ~ with** (subject) estar familiarizado com
family ['fæmɪlɪ] N família
famine ['fæmɪn] N fome f
famous ['feɪməs] ADJ famoso, célebre
fan [fæn] N (hand-held) leque m; (Elec) ventilador m; (person) fã m/f ▶ VT abanar; (fire, quarrel) atiçar; **fan out** VI espalhar-se
fanatic [fə'nætɪk] N fanático(-a)
fan belt N correia do ventilador (BR) or da ventoinha (PT)
fan club N fã-clube m
fancy ['fænsɪ] N capricho; (imagination) imaginação f; (fantasy) fantasia ▶ ADJ ornamental; (luxury) luxuoso ▶ VT desejar, querer; (imagine) imaginar; (think) acreditar, achar; **to take a ~ to** tomar gosto por; **he fancies her** (inf) ele está a fim dela; **fancy dress** N fantasia

fantastic [fæn'tæstɪk] ADJ fantástico
fantasy ['fæntəsɪ] N (dream) sonho; (unreality) fantasia; (imagination) imaginação f
far [fɑːr] ADJ (distant) distante ▶ ADV (also: ~ away, ~ off) longe; **the ~ side/end** o lado de lá/a outra ponta; **~ better** muito melhor; **~ from** longe de; **by ~** de longe; **go as ~ as the farm** vá até a (BR) or à (PT) fazenda; **as ~ as I know** que eu saiba; **how ~?** até onde?; (fig) até que ponto?
farce [fɑːs] N farsa
fare [fɛər] N (on trains, buses) preço (da passagem); (in taxi: cost) tarifa; (food) comida; **half/full ~** meia/inteira passagem
Far East N: **the ~** o Extremo Oriente
farewell [fɛə'wɛl] EXCL adeus ▶ N despedida
farm [fɑːm] N fazenda (BR), quinta (PT) ▶ VT cultivar; **farmer** N fazendeiro(-a), agricultor m; **farmhouse** irreg N casa da fazenda (BR) or da quinta (PT); **farming** N agricultura; (tilling) cultura; (of animals) criação f; **farmyard** N curral m
far-reaching [-'riːtʃɪŋ] ADJ de grande alcance, abrangente
fart [fɑːt] (!) VI soltar um peido (!), peidar (!)
farther ['fɑːðər] ADV mais longe ▶ ADJ mais distante, mais afastado
farthest ['fɑːðɪst] SUPERL of **far**
fascinate ['fæsɪneɪt] VT fascinar
fashion ['fæʃən] N moda; (fashion industry) indústria da moda; (manner) maneira ▶ VT modelar, dar feitio a; **in ~** na moda; **fashionable**

ADJ da moda, elegante; **fashion show** N desfile *m* de modas

fast [fɑ:st] ADJ rápido; (*dye, colour*) firme, permanente; (*clock*): **to be ~** estar adiantado ▶ ADV rápido, rapidamente, depressa; (*stuck, held*) firmemente ▶ N jejum *m* ▶ VI jejuar; **~ asleep** dormindo profundamente

fasten ['fɑ:sn] VT fixar, prender; (*coat*) fechar; (*belt*) apertar ▶ VI prender-se, fixar-se

fast food N fast food *f*

fat [fæt] ADJ gordo; (*book*) grosso; (*wallet*) recheado; (*profit*) grande ▶ N gordura; (*lard*) banha, gordura

fatal ['feɪtl] ADJ fatal; (*injury*) mortal

fate [feɪt] N destino; (*of person*) sorte *f*

father ['fɑ:ðə'] N pai *m*; **father-in-law** N sogro

fatigue [fə'ti:g] N fadiga, cansaço

fatty ['fætɪ] ADJ (*food*) gorduroso ▶ N (*inf*) gorducho(-a)

fault [fɔ:lt] N (*blame*) culpa; (*defect*) defeito; (*Geo*) falha; (*Tennis*) falta, bola fora ▶ VT criticar; **to find ~ with** criticar, queixar-se de; **at ~** culpado; **faulty** ADJ defeituoso

favour ['feɪvə'], (*US*) **favor** N favor *m* ▶ VT favorecer; (*assist*) auxiliar; **to do sb a ~** fazer favor a alguém; **to find ~ with** cair nas boas graças de; **in ~ of** em favor de; **favourite** ['feɪvərɪt] ADJ predileto ▶ N favorito(-a)

fawn [fɔ:n] N cervo novo, cervato ▶ ADJ (*also:* **~-coloured**) castanho-claro *inv* ▶ VI: **to ~ (up)on** bajular

fax [fæks] N fax *m*, fac-símile *m* ▶ VT enviar por fax *or* fac-símile

FBI (*US*) N ABBR (= *Federal Bureau of Investigation*) FBI *m*

fear [fɪə'] N medo ▶ VT ter medo de, temer; **for ~ of** com medo de; **fearful** ADJ medonho, temível; (*cowardly*) medroso; (*awful*) terrível

feasible ['fi:zəbl] ADJ viável

feast [fi:st] N banquete *m*; (*Rel: also:* **~ day**) festa ▶ VI banquetear-se

feat [fi:t] N façanha, feito

feather ['fɛðə'] N pena, pluma

feature ['fi:tʃə'] N característica; (*article*) reportagem *f* ▶ VT (*subj: film*) apresentar ▶ VI figurar; **features** NPL (*of face*) feições *fpl*; **feature film** N longa-metragem *f*

February ['fɛbruərɪ] N fevereiro

fed [fɛd] PT, PP *de* **feed**

federal ['fɛdərəl] ADJ federal

fed up ADJ: **to be ~** estar (de saco) cheio (BR), estar farto (PT)

fee [fi:] N taxa (BR), propina (PT); (*of school*) matrícula; (*of doctor, lawyer*) honorários *mpl*

feeble ['fi:bl] ADJ fraco; (*attempt*) ineficaz

feed [fi:d] (*pt, pp* **fed**) N (*of baby*) alimento infantil; (*of animal*) ração *f*; (*on printer*) mecanismo alimentador ▶ VT alimentar; (*baby*) amamentar; (*animal*) dar de comer a; (*data, information*): **to ~ into** introduzir em; **feed on** VT FUS alimentar-se de; **feedback** ['fi:dbæk] N reação *f*

feel [fi:l] (*pt, pp* **felt**) N sensação *f*; (*sense of touch*) tato; (*impression*) impressão *f* ▶ VT tocar, apalpar; (*anger, pain etc*) sentir; (*think, believe*) achar, acreditar; **to ~ hungry/cold** estar com fome/frio (BR), ter fome/frio (PT); **to ~ lonely/better** sentir-se só/

melhor; **I don't ~ well** não estou me sentindo bem; **it ~s soft** é macio; **to ~ like** querer; **to ~ about** or **around** tatear; **feeling** N sensação f; (emotion) sentimento; (impression) impressão f

feet [fi:t] NPL of **foot**

fell [fɛl] PT of **fall** ▶ VT (tree) lançar por terra, derrubar

fellow ['fɛləu] N camarada m/f; (inf: man) cara m (BR), tipo (PT); (of learned society) membro ▶ CPD: **~ students** colegas mpl/fpl de curso; **fellowship** N amizade f; (grant) bolsa de estudo; (society) associação f

felony ['fɛlənɪ] N crime m

felt [fɛlt] PT, PP of **feel** ▶ N feltro

female ['fi:meɪl] N (pej: woman) mulher f; (Zool) fêmea ▶ ADJ fêmeo(-a); (sex, character) feminino; (vote etc) das mulheres; (child etc) do sexo feminino

feminine ['fɛmɪnɪn] ADJ feminino

feminist ['fɛmɪnɪst] N feminista m/f

fence [fɛns] N cerca ▶ VT (also: **~ in**) cercar ▶ VI esgrimir; **fencing** N (sport) esgrima

fend [fɛnd] VI: **to ~ for o.s.** defender-se, virar-se; **fend off** VT defender-se de

ferment [vi fə'mɛnt, n 'fə:mɛnt] VI fermentar ▶ N (fig) agitação f

fern [fə:n] N samambaia (BR), feto (PT)

ferocious [fə'rəuʃəs] ADJ feroz

ferret ['fɛrɪt] N furão m; **ferret out** VT (information) desenterrar, descobrir

ferry ['fɛrɪ] N (small) barco (de travessia); (large: also: **~boat**) balsa ▶ VT transportar

fertile ['fə:taɪl] ADJ fértil; (Bio) fecundo; **fertilizer** ['fə:tɪlaɪzəʳ] N adubo, fertilizante m

festival ['fɛstɪvəl] N (Rel) festa; (Art, Mus) festival m

festive ['fɛstɪv] ADJ festivo; **the ~ season** (BRIT: Christmas) a época do Natal

fetch [fɛtʃ] VT ir buscar, trazer; (sell for) alcançar

fête [feɪt] N festa

feud [fju:d] N disputa, rixa

fever ['fi:vəʳ] N febre f; **feverish** ADJ febril

few [fju:] ADJ, PRON poucos(-as); **a ~ ...** alguns/algumas ...; **fewer** ['fju:əʳ] ADJ menos; **fewest** ['fju:ɪst] ADJ o menor número de

fib [fɪb] N lorota

fickle ['fɪkl] ADJ inconstante; (weather) instável

fiction ['fɪkʃən] N ficção f; **fictional** ADJ de ficção

fiddle ['fɪdl] N (Mus) violino; (swindle) trapaça ▶ VT (BRIT: accounts) falsificar; **fiddle with** VT FUS brincar com

fidget ['fɪdʒɪt] VI estar irrequieto, mexer-se

field [fi:ld] N campo; (fig) área, esfera, especialidade f

fierce [fɪəs] ADJ feroz; (wind, attack) violento; (heat) intenso

fifteen [fɪf'ti:n] NUM quinze

fifth [fɪfθ] NUM quinto

fifty ['fɪftɪ] NUM cinquenta; **fifty-fifty** ADV: **to share** or **go fifty-fifty with sb** dividir meio a meio com alguém, rachar com alguém ▶ ADJ: **to have a fifty-fifty chance** ter 50% de chance

fig [fɪg] N figo

fight [faɪt] (pt, pp **fought**) N briga; (Mil) combate m; (struggle: against illness etc) luta ▶ VT lutar contra; (cancer, alcoholism) combater; (election) competir ▶ VI brigar, bater-se

figure [ˈfɪgəʳ] N (Drawing, Math) figura, desenho; (number, cipher) número, cifra; (outline) forma; (person) personagem m ▶ VT (esp us) imaginar ▶ VI figurar; **figure out** VT compreender

file [faɪl] N (tool) lixa; (dossier) dossiê m, pasta; (folder) pasta; (Comput) arquivo; (row) fila, coluna ▶ VT (wood, nails) lixar; (papers) arquivar; (Jur: claim) apresentar, dar entrada em ▶ VI: **to ~ in/out** entrar/sair em fila; **file sharing** N (Comput) compartilhamento de arquivos

fill [fɪl] VT encher; (vacancy) preencher; (need) satisfazer ▶ N: **to eat one's ~** encher-se or fartar-se de comer; **fill in** VT (form) preencher; (hole) tapar; (time) encher; **fill up** VT encher ▶ VI (Aut) abastecer o carro

fillet [ˈfɪlɪt] N filete m, filé m; **fillet steak** N filé m

filling [ˈfɪlɪŋ] N (Culin) recheio; (for tooth) obturação f (BR), chumbo (PT); **filling station** N posto de gasolina

film [fɪlm] N filme m; (of liquid etc) camada fina, veu m ▶ VT rodar, filmar ▶ VI filmar; **film star** N astro/estrela do cinema

filter [ˈfɪltəʳ] N filtro ▶ VT filtrar

filth [fɪlθ] N sujeira (BR), sujidade f (PT); **filthy** ADJ sujo; (language) indecente, obsceno

fin [fɪn] N barbatana

final [ˈfaɪnl] ADJ final, último; (definitive) definitivo ▶ N (Sport) final f; **finals** NPL (Sch) exames mpl finais; **finale** [fɪˈnɑːlɪ] N final m; **finalize** VT concluir, completar; **finally** ADV finalmente, por fim

finance [faɪˈnæns] N fundos mpl; (money management) finanças fpl ▶ VT financiar; **finances** NPL (personal finances) finanças; **financial** [faɪˈnænʃəl] ADJ financeiro

find [faɪnd] (pt, pp **found**) VT encontrar, achar; (discover) descobrir ▶ N achado, descoberta; **to ~ sb guilty** (Jur) declarar alguém culpado; **find out** VT descobrir; (person) desmascarar ▶ VI: **to ~ out about** (by chance) saber de; **findings** NPL (Jur) veredito, decisão f; (of report) constatações fpl

fine [faɪn] ADJ fino; (excellent) excelente ▶ ADV muito bem ▶ N (Jur) multa ▶ VT (Jur) multar; **to be ~** (person) estar bem; (weather) estar bom; **fine arts** NPL belas artes fpl

finger [ˈfɪŋgəʳ] N dedo ▶ VT manusear; **fingernail** N unha; **fingerprint** N impressão f digital; **fingertip** N ponta do dedo

finish [ˈfɪnɪʃ] N fim m; (Sport) chegada; (on wood etc) acabamento ▶ VT, VI terminar, acabar; **to ~ doing sth** terminar de fazer algo; **to ~ third** chegar no terceiro lugar; **finish off** VT terminar; (kill) liquidar; **finish up** VT acabar ▶ VI ir parar

Finland [ˈfɪnlənd] N Finlândia

Finn [fɪn] N finlandês(-esa) m/f; **Finnish** ADJ finlandês(-esa) ▶ N (Ling) finlandês m

fir [fəːʳ] N abeto

fire [ˈfaɪəʳ] N fogo; (accidental) incêndio; (gas fire, electric fire) aquecedor m ▶ VT (gun) disparar; (arrow) atirar; (interest) estimular; (dismiss) despedir ▶ VI disparar; **on ~** em chamas; **fire alarm** N alarme m de incêndio; **firearm** N arma de fogo; **fire brigade** N (corpo de)

f

bombeiros *mpl*; **fire engine** N carro de bombeiro; **fire escape** N escada de incêndio; **fire exit** N saída de emergência; **fire extinguisher** N extintor *m* de incêndio; **fireman** *irreg* N bombeiro; **fireplace** N lareira; **fire station** N posto de bombeiros; **firewall** N (*Comput*) firewall *m*; **firewood** N lenha; **fireworks** NPL fogos *mpl* de artifício

firm [fə:m] ADJ firme ▶ N firma

first [fə:st] ADJ primeiro ▶ ADV (*before others*) primeiro; (*when listing reasons etc*) em primeiro lugar ▶ N (*in race*) primeiro(-a); (*Aut*) primeira; (*BRIT Sch*) menção *f* honrosa; **at ~** no início; **~ of all** antes de tudo, antes de mais nada; **first aid** N primeiros socorros *mpl*; **first-aid kit** N estojo de primeiros socorros; **first-class** ADJ de primeira classe; **first-hand** ADJ de primeira mão; **first lady** (*US*) N primeira dama; **firstly** ADV primeiramente, em primeiro lugar; **first name** N primeiro nome *m*; **first-rate** ADJ de primeira categoria

fish [fiʃ] N INV peixe *m* ▶ VT, VI pescar; **to go ~ing** ir pescar; **fisherman** *irreg* N pescador *m*; **fishing boat** N barco de pesca; **fishing line** N linha de pesca; **fishmonger** ['fiʃmʌŋgər] N peixeiro(-a); **fishmonger's (shop)** N peixaria; **fishy** (*inf*) ADJ (*tale*) suspeito

fist [fist] N punho

fit [fit] ADJ em (boa) forma; (*suitable*) adequado, apropriado ▶ VT (*subj: clothes*) caber em; (*put in, attach*) colocar; (*equip*) equipar ▶ VI (*clothes*) servir; (*parts*) ajustar-se; (*in space, gap*) caber ▶ N (*Med*) ataque *m*; **~ to** bom para; **~ for** adequado para;

a ~ of anger/pride um acesso de raiva/orgulho; **by ~s and starts** espasmodicamente; **fit in** VI encaixar-se; (*person*) dar-se bem (com todos); **fitness** N (*Med*) saúde *f*, boa forma; **fitted kitchen** (*BRIT*) N cozinha planejada; **fitting** ADJ apropriado ▶ N (*of dress*) prova; **fittings** NPL (*in building*) instalações *fpl*, acessórios *mpl*

five [faiv] NUM cinco; **fiver** (*inf*) N (*BRIT*) nota de cinco libras; (*US*) nota de cinco dólares

fix [fiks] VT (*secure*) fixar, colocar; (*arrange*) arranjar; (*mend*) consertar; (*meal, drink*) preparar ▶ N: **to be in a ~** estar em apuros; **fix up** VT (*meeting*) marcar; **to ~ sb up with sth** arranjar algo para alguém; **fixed** ADJ (*prices, smile*) fixo; **fixture** N (*furniture*) móvel *m* fixo; (*Sport*) desafio, encontro

fizzy ['fizi] ADJ com gás, gasoso

flag [flæg] N bandeira; (*for signalling*) bandeirola; (*flagstone*) laje *f* ▶ VI acabar-se, descair; **flag down** VT: **to ~ sb down** fazer sinais a alguém para que pare

flagpole ['flægpəul] N mastro de bandeira

flair [fleər] N (*talent*) talento; (*style*) habilidade *f*

flake [fleik] N (*of rust, paint*) lasca; (*of snow, soap powder*) floco ▶ VI (*also: ~ off*) lascar, descamar-se

flamboyant [flæm'bɔiənt] ADJ (*dress*) espalhafatoso; (*person*) extravagante

flame [fleim] N chama

flammable ['flæməbl] ADJ inflamável

flan [flæn] (*BRIT*) N torta

flannel ['flænl] N (*BRIT: also: face ~*) pano de rosto; (*fabric*) flanela; **flannels** NPL calça (BR) or calças fpl (PT) de flanela

flap [flæp] N (of pocket, table) aba; (of envelope) dobra ▶ VT (arms) oscilar; (wings) bater ▶ VI (sail, flag) ondular; (inf: also: **be in a ~**) estar atarantado

flare [flɛəʳ] N fogacho, chama; (Mil) foguete m sinalizador; (in skirt etc) folga; **flare up** VI chamejar; (fig: person) encolerizar-se; (: violence) irromper

flash [flæʃ] N (of lightning) clarão m; (also: **news ~**) notícias fpl de última hora; (Phot) flash m ▶ VT piscar; (news, message) transmitir; (look, smile) brilhar ▶ VI brilhar; (light on ambulance, eyes etc) piscar; **in a ~** num instante; **to ~ by** or **past** passar como um raio; **flash drive** N (Comput) pen drive m; **flashlight** N lanterna de bolso

flat [flæt] ADJ plano; (battery) descarregado; (tyre) vazio; (beer) choco; (denial) categórico; (Mus) abemolado; (: voice) desafinado; (rate) único; (fee) fixo ▶ N (BRIT: apartment) apartamento; (Mus) bemol m; (Aut) pneu m furado; **~ out** (work) a toque de caixa; **flatten** VT (also: **flatten out**) aplanar; (demolish) arrasar

flatter ['flætəʳ] VT lisonjear; **flattering** ADJ lisonjeiro; (clothes etc) favorecedor(a)

flaunt [flɔ:nt] VT ostentar, pavonear

flavour ['fleɪvəʳ], (US) **flavor** N sabor m ▶ VT condimentar, aromatizar; **strawberry-~ed** com sabor de morango

flaw [flɔ:] N defeito; (in character) falha; **flawless** ADJ impecável

flea [fli:] N pulga

flee [fli:] (pt, pp **fled**) VT fugir de ▶ VI fugir

fleece [fli:s] N tosão m; (coat) velo; (wool) lã f ▶ VT (inf) espoliar

fleet [fli:t] N (gen, of lorries etc) frota; (of ships) esquadra

fleeting ['fli:tɪŋ] ADJ fugaz

Flemish ['flɛmɪʃ] ADJ flamengo

flesh [flɛʃ] N carne f; (of fruit) polpa

flew [flu:] PT of **fly**

flex [flɛks] N fio ▶ VT (muscles) flexionar; **flexible** ADJ flexível

flick [flɪk] N pancada leve; (with finger) peteleco, piparote m; (with whip) chicotada ▶ VT dar um peteleco, (switch) apertar; **flick through** VT FUS folhear

flicker ['flɪkəʳ] VI tremular; (eyelids) tremer

flight [flaɪt] N voo m; (escape) fuga; (of steps) lance m; **flight attendant** (US) N comissário(-a) de bordo

flimsy ['flɪmzɪ] ADJ (thin) delgado, franzino; (weak) débil; (excuse) fraco

flinch [flɪntʃ] VI encolher-se; **to ~ from sth/from doing sth** vacilar diante de algo/em fazer algo

fling [flɪŋ] (pt, pp **flung**) VT lançar

flint [flɪnt] N pederneira; (in lighter) pedra

flip-flops ['flɪpflɔps] (esp BRIT) NPL chinelo (de dedo)

flipper ['flɪpəʳ] N (of animal) nadadeira; (for swimmer) pé de pato, nadadeira

flirt [flə:t] VI flertar ▶ N namorador(a) m/f, paquerador(a) m/f

float [fləut] N boia; (in procession) carro alegórico; (sum of money) caixa ▶ VI flutuar; (swimmer) boiar

f

flock [flɔk] N rebanho; (of birds) bando ▶ VI: **to ~ to** afluir a

flood [flʌd] N enchente f, inundação f ▶ VT inundar, alagar ▶ VI (place) alagar; (people, goods): **to ~ into** inundar; **flooding** N inundação f; **floodlight** irreg N refletor m, holofote m

floor [flɔːr] N chão m; (storey) andar m; (of sea) fundo ▶ VT (fig: confuse) confundir, pasmar; **ground ~** (BRIT) or **first ~** (US) andar térreo (BR), rés-do-chão (PT); **first ~** (BRIT) or **second ~** (US) primeiro andar; **floorboard** N tábua de assoalho; **floor show** N show m

flop [flɔp] N fracasso ▶ VI fracassar; (into chair etc) cair pesadamente

floppy ['flɔpɪ] ADJ frouxo, mole ▶ N (also: **~ disk**) disquete m

florist ['flɔrɪst] N florista m/f; **florist's, florist's shop** N floricultura

flour ['flauər] N farinha

flourish ['flʌrɪʃ] VI florescer ▶ VT brandir, menear ▶ N: **with a ~** con gestos floreados

flow [fləu] N fluxo; (of river, Elec) corrente f; (of blood) circulação f ▶ VI correr; (traffic) fluir; (blood, Elec) circular; (clothes, hair) ondular

flower ['flauər] N flor f ▶ VI florescer, florir; **flower bed** N canteiro; **flowerpot** N vaso

flown [fləun] PP of **fly**

flu [fluː] N gripe f

fluctuate ['flʌktjueɪt] VI flutuar; (temperature) variar

fluent ['fluːənt] ADJ fluente; **he speaks ~ French, he's ~ in French** ele fala francês fluentemente

fluff [flʌf] N felpa, penugem f; **fluffy** ADJ macio, fofo

fluid ['fluːɪd] ADJ fluido ▶ N fluido

fluke [fluːk] (inf) N sorte f

flung [flʌŋ] PT, PP of **fling**

fluoride ['fluəraɪd] N fluoreto

flurry ['flʌrɪ] N (of snow) lufada; **~ of activity/excitement** muita atividade/animação

flush [flʌʃ] N (on face) rubor m ▶ VT lavar com água ▶ VI ruborizar-se ▶ ADJ: **~ with** rente com; **to ~ the toilet** dar descarga; **flush out** VT levantar

flute [fluːt] N flauta

flutter ['flʌtər] N agitação f; (of wings) bater m ▶ VI esvoaçar

fly [flaɪ] (pt **flew**, pp **flown**) N mosca; (on trousers: also: **flies**) braguilha ▶ VT (plane) pilotar; (passengers, cargo) transportar (de avião); (distances) percorrer ▶ VI voar; (passengers) ir de avião; (escape) fugir; (flag) hastear-se; **fly away** VI voar; **fly off** VI = **fly away**; **flying** N aviação f ▶ ADJ: **flying visit** visita de médico; **with flying colours** brilhantemente; **flying saucer** N disco voador; **flyover** (BRIT) N viaduto

foal [fəul] N potro

foam [fəum] N espuma ▶ VI espumar; **foam rubber** N espuma de borracha

focus ['fəukəs] (pl **focuses**) N foco ▶ VT enfocar ▶ VI: **to ~ on** enfocar, focalizar; **in/out of ~** em foco/fora de foco

fog [fɔg] N nevoeiro; **foggy** ADJ nevoento

foil [fɔɪl] VT frustrar ▶ N folha metálica; (also: **kitchen ~**) folha or papel m de alumínio; (complement) contraste m, complemento; (Fencing) florete m

fold [fəuld] N dobra, vinco, prega; (of skin) ruga; (Agr) redil m, curral m

▶ vt dobrar; **to ~ one's arms** cruzar os braços; **fold up** vi dobrar; (business) abrir falência ▶ vt dobrar; **folder** N pasta; **folding** ADJ dobrável

folk [fəuk] NPL gente f ▶ CPD popular, folclórico; **folks** NPL (family) família, parentes mpl; **folklore** ['fəuklɔ:ʳ] N folclore m

follow ['fɔləu] vt seguir ▶ vi seguir; (result) resultar; **I don't quite ~ you** não consigo acompanhar o seu raciocínio; **to ~ suit** fazer o mesmo; **follow up** vt (letter) responder a; (offer) levar adiante; (case) acompanhar; **follower** N seguidor(a) m/f; **following** ADJ seguinte ▶ N adeptos mpl

fond [fɔnd] ADJ carinhoso; (hopes) absurdo, descabido; **to be ~ of** gostar de

food [fu:d] N comida; **food mixer** N batedeira; **food poisoning** N intoxicação f alimentar; **food processor** N multiprocessador m de cozinha

fool [fu:l] N tolo(-a); (Culin) puré m de frutas com creme ▶ vt enganar ▶ vi (gen: fool around) brincar; **foolish** ADJ burro; (careless) imprudente; **foolproof** ADJ infalível

foot [fut] (pl **feet**) N pé m; (of animal) pata; (measure) pé (304 mm; 12 inches) ▶ vt (bill) pagar; **on ~** a pé; **footage** N (Cinema: length) ≈ metragem f; (: material) sequências fpl; **football** N bola; (game: BRIT) futebol m; (: US) futebol norte-americano; **footballer** N, **football player** N jogador m de futebol; **footbridge** N passarela; **foothold** N apoio

para o pé; **footing** N (fig) posição f; **to lose one's footing** escorregar; **footnote** N nota ao pé da página, nota de rodapé; **footpath** N caminho, atalho; **footprint** N pegada; **footstep** N passo; **footwear** N calçados mpl

(KEYWORD)

for [fɔ:ʳ] PREP **1** (indicating destination, direction) para; **he went for the paper** foi pegar o jornal; **is this for me?** é para mim?; **it's time for lunch** é hora de almoçar
2 (indicating purpose) para; **what's it for?** para quê serve?; **to pray for peace** orar pela paz
3 (on behalf of, representing) por; **he works for the government/a local firm** ele trabalha para o governo/uma firma local; **G for George** G de George
4 (because of) por; **for this reason** por esta razão; **for fear of being criticized** com medo de ser criticado
5 (with regard to) para; **it's cold for July** está frio para julho
6 (in exchange for) por; **it was sold for £5** foi vendido por £5
7 (in favour of) a favor de; **are you for or against us?** você está a favor de ou contra nós?; **I'm all for it** concordo plenamente, tem todo o meu apoio; **vote for X** vote em X
8 (referring to distance): **there are road works for 5 km** há obras na estrada por 5 quilômetros; **we walked for miles** andamos quilômetros
9 (referring to time): **she will be away for a month** ela ficará fora um mês; **I have known her**

for years eu a conheço há anos; **can you do it for tomorrow?** você pode fazer isso para amanhã? **10** (*with infinite clause*): **it is not for me to decide** não cabe a mim decidir; **it would be best for you to leave** seria melhor que você fosse embora; **there is still time for you to do it** ainda há tempo para você fazer isso; **for this to be possible ...** para que isso seja possível ...

11 (*in spite of*) apesar de ▶ CONJ (*since, as: rather formal*) pois, porque

forbid [fəˈbɪd] (*pt* **forbad(e)**, *pp* **forbidden**) VT proibir; **to ~ sb to do sth** proibir alguém de fazer algo

force [fɔːs] N força ▶ VT forçar; **the Forces** (BRIT) NPL as Forças Armadas; **in ~** em vigor; **forceful** ADJ enérgico, vigoroso

ford [fɔːd] N vau *m*

fore [fɔːʳ] N: **to come to the ~** salientar-se

forearm [ˈfɔːrɑːm] N antebraço

forecast [ˈfɔːkɑːst] (*irreg: like* **cast**) N previsão *f*; (*also:* **weather ~**) previsão do tempo ▶ VT prognosticar, prever

forefinger [ˈfɔːfɪŋgəʳ] N (dedo) indicador *m*

foreground [ˈfɔːgraund] N primeiro plano

forehead [ˈfɔrɪd] N testa

foreign [ˈfɔrɪn] ADJ estrangeiro; (*trade*) exterior; **foreigner** N estrangeiro(-a); **foreign exchange** N câmbio; **Foreign Office** (BRIT) N Ministério das Relações Exteriores

foreman [ˈfɔːmən] *irreg* N capataz *m*; (*in construction*) contramestre *m*; primeiro jurado

foremost [ˈfɔːməust] ADJ principal ▶ ADV: **first and ~** antes de mais nada

forensic [fəˈrɛnsɪk] ADJ forense; **~ medicine** medicina legal

foresee [fɔːˈsiː] (*irreg: like* **see**) VT prever; **foreseeable** ADJ previsível

forest [ˈfɔrɪst] N floresta

forestry [ˈfɔrɪstrɪ] N silvicultura

forever [fəˈrɛvəʳ] ADV para sempre

foreword [ˈfɔːwəːd] N prefácio

forfeit [ˈfɔːfɪt] VT perder (direito a)

forgave [fəˈgeɪv] PT *of* **forgive**

forge [fɔːdʒ] N ferraria ▶ VT falsificar; (*metal*) forjar; **forge ahead** VI avançar constantemente; **forger** N falsificador(a) *m/f*; **forgery** N falsificação *f*

forget [fəˈgɛt] (*pt* **forgot**, *pp* **forgotten**) VT, VI esquecer; **forgetful** ADJ esquecido

forgive [fəˈgɪv] (*pt* **forgave**, *pp* **forgiven**) VT perdoar; **to ~ sb for sth** perdoar algo a alguém, perdoar alguém de algo

forgot [fəˈgɔt] PT *of* **forget**

forgotten [fəˈgɔtn] PP *of* **forget**

fork [fɔːk] N (*for eating*) garfo; (*for gardening*) forquilha; (*of roads etc*) bifurcação *f* ▶ VI bifurcar-se; **fork out** (*inf*) VT (*pay*) desembolsar, morrer em

forlorn [fəˈlɔːn] ADJ desolado; (*attempt*) desesperado; (*hope*) último

form [fɔːm] N forma; (*type*) tipo; (*Sch*) série *f*; (*questionnaire*) formulário ▶ VT formar; (*organization*) criar; **to ~ a queue** (BRIT) fazer fila; **in top ~** em plena forma

formal [ˈfɔːməl] ADJ (*offer, receipt*) oficial; (*person etc*) cerimonioso; (*occasion, education*) formal;

(*dress*) a rigor (BR), de cerimônia
(*PT*); (*garden*) simétrico

format ['fɔːmæt] N formato ▶ VT
(*Comput*) formatar

former ['fɔːmə^r] ADJ anterior;
(*earlier*) antigo; **the ~ ...the latter
...** aquele ... este ...; **formerly** ADV
anteriormente

formidable ['fɔːmɪdəbl] ADJ
terrível, temível

formula ['fɔːmjulə] (*pl* **formulas**
or **formulae**) N fórmula

fort [fɔːt] N forte m

fortify ['fɔːtɪfaɪ] VT (*city*) fortificar;
(*person*) fortalecer

fortnight ['fɔːtnaɪt] (BRIT) N
quinzena, quinze dias mpl;
fortnightly ADJ quinzenal ▶ ADV
quinzenalmente

fortunate ['fɔːtʃənɪt] ADJ (*event*)
feliz; (*person*): **to be ~** ter sorte; **it
is ~ that ...** é uma sorte que ...;
fortunately ADV felizmente

fortune ['fɔːtʃən] N sorte f;
(*wealth*) fortuna; **fortune-teller** N
adivinho(-a)

forty ['fɔːtɪ] NUM quarenta

forward ['fɔːwəd] ADJ (*movement*)
para a frente; (*position*) avançado;
(*not shy*) imodesto, presunçoso ▶ N
(*Sport*) atacante m ▶ VT (*letter*)
remeter; (*goods, parcel*) expedir;
(*career*) promover; (*plans*) ativar;
to move ~ avançar; **~ planning**
planejamento para o futuro;
forwards ADV para a frente;
forward slash N barra

foster ['fɔstə^r] VT tutelar; (*activity*)
promover; **foster child** *irreg* N
tutelado(-a)

fought [fɔːt] PT, PP de **fight**

foul [faul] ADJ horrível; (*language*)
obsceno ▶ N (*Sport*) falta ▶ VT
sujar; **foul play** N (*Jur*) crime m

found [faund] PT, PP *of* **find** ▶ VT
(*establish*) fundar; **foundation**
[faun'deɪʃən] N (*act*) fundação f;
(*base*) base f; (*also*: **foundation
cream**) creme m base;
foundations NPL (*of building*)
alicerces mpl

founder ['faundə^r] N fundador(a)
m/f ▶ VI naufragar

fountain ['fauntɪn] N chafariz m;
fountain pen N caneta-tinteiro f

four [fɔː^r] NUM quatro; **on all ~s**
de quatro; **four-by-four** [fɔbaɪ'fɔ^r]
N 4x4 m (*quatro por quatro*);
four-letter word N palavrão m;
fourteen NUM catorze; *see also*
five; **fourth** NUM quarto

fowl [faul] N ave f (doméstica)

fox [fɔks] N raposa ▶ VT deixar
perplexo

foyer ['fɔɪeɪ] N saguão m

fraction ['frækʃən] N fração f

fracture ['fræktʃə^r] N fratura ▶ VT
fraturar

fragile ['frædʒaɪl] ADJ frágil

fragment ['frægmənt] N
fragmento

frail [freɪl] ADJ (*person*) fraco;
(*structure*) frágil

frame [freɪm] N (*of building*)
estrutura; (*body*) corpo; (*of picture,
door*) moldura; (*of spectacles: also:*
~s) armação f, aro ▶ VT (*picture*)
emoldurar; **framework** N
armação f

France [frɑːns] N França

frank [fræŋk] ADJ franco ▶ VT
(*letter*) franquear; **frankly** ADV
francamente; (*candidly*)
abertamente

frantic ['fræntɪk] ADJ frenético;
(*person*) fora de si

fraud [frɔːd] N fraude f; (*person*)
impostor(a) m/f

fraught [frɔːt] ADJ tenso; **~ with** repleto de
fray [freɪ] N combate m, luta ▶ VI esfiapar-se; **tempers were ~ed** estavam com os nervos em frangalhos
freak [friːk] N (person) anormal m/f; (event) anomalia
freckle ['frɛkl] N sarda
free [friː] ADJ livre; (seat) desocupado; (costing nothing) gratis, gratuito ▶ VT pôr em liberdade; (jammed object) soltar; **~ (of charge)** grátis, de graça; **freedom** N liberdade f; **freelance** ADJ freelance; **freely** ADV livremente; **free-range** N (egg) caseiro; **freeway** (US) N via expressa; **free will** N livre arbítrio; **of one's own free will** por sua própria vontade
freeze [friːz] (pt **froze**, pp **frozen**) VI gelar(-se), congelar-se ▶ VT congelar ▶ N geada; (on arms, wages) congelamento; **freezer** N congelador m, freezer m (BR); **freezing** ADJ: **freezing (cold)** (weather) glacial; (water) gelado; **3 degrees below freezing** 3 graus abaixo de zero; **freezing point** N ponto de congelamento
freight [freɪt] N (goods) carga; (money charged) frete m; **freight train** (US) N trem m de carga
French [frɛntʃ] ADJ francês (-esa) ▶ N (Ling) francês m; **the French** NPL os franceses; **French bean** (BRIT) N feijão m comum; **French fried potatoes** NPL batatas fpl fritas; **Frenchman** irreg N francês m; **Frenchwoman** irreg N francesa
frenzy ['frɛnzɪ] N frenesi m
frequent [adj 'friːkwənt, vt frɪ'kwɛnt] ADJ frequente ▶ VT frequentar; **frequently** ADV

frequentemente, a miúdo
fresh [frɛʃ] ADJ fresco; (new) novo; (cheeky) atrevido; **freshen** VI (wind, air) tornar-se mais forte; **freshen up** VI (person) lavar-se, refrescar-se; **freshly** ADV recentemente, há pouco
fret [frɛt] VI afligir-se
friction ['frɪkʃən] N fricção f; (between people) atrito
Friday ['fraɪdɪ] N sexta-feira f
fridge [frɪdʒ] N geladeira (BR), frigorífico (PT)
fried [fraɪd] ADJ frito; **~ egg** ovo estrelado or frito
friend [frɛnd] N amigo(-a) ▶ VT (on social network) adicionar como amigo; **friendly** ADJ simpático ▶ N (also: **friendly match**) amistoso; **friendship** N amizade f
fries [fraɪz] (esp US) NPL = **French fried potatoes**
fright [fraɪt] N terror m; (scare) pavor m; **to take ~** assustar-se; **frighten** VT assustar; **frightened** ADJ: **to be frightened of** ter medo de; **frightening** ADJ assustador(a); **frightful** ADJ terrível, horrível
frill [frɪl] N babado
fringe [frɪndʒ] N franja; (on shawl etc) beira, orla; (edge: of forest etc) margem f
fritter ['frɪtər] N bolinho frito; **fritter away** VT desperdiçar
frivolous ['frɪvələs] ADJ frívolo; (activity) fútil
fro [frəʊ] ADJ see **to**
frock [frɔk] N vestido
frog [frɔg] N rã f; **frogman** irreg N homem-rã m

(KEYWORD)

from [frɔm] PREP **1** (indicating starting place) de; **where do you come from?** de onde você é?; **we**

flew from London to Glasgow fomos de avião de Londres para Glasgow; **to escape from sth/sb** escapar de algo/alguém

2 (*indicating origin etc*) de; **a letter/telephone call from my sister** uma carta/um telefonema da minha irmã; **tell him from me that ...** diga a ele que da minha parte ...; **to drink from the bottle** beber na garrafa

3 (*indicating time*): **from one o'clock to** *or* **until** *or* **till two** da uma hora até às duas; **from January (on)** a partir de janeiro

4 (*indicating distance*) de; **we're still a long way from home** ainda estamos muito longe de casa

5 (*indicating price, number etc*) de; **prices range from £10 to £50** os preços vão de £10 a £50

6 (*indicating difference*) de; **he can't tell red from green** ele não pode diferenciar vermelho do verde

7 (*because of/on the basis of*): **from what he says** pelo que ele diz; **to act from conviction** agir por convicção; **weak from hunger** fraco de fome

front [frʌnt] N frente *f*; (*of vehicle*) parte *f* dianteira; (*of house*) fachada; (*also:* **sea ~**) orla marítima ▶ ADJ da frente; **in ~ (of)** em frente (de); **front door** N porta principal; **frontier** ['frʌntɪəʳ] N fronteira; **front page** N primeira página

frost [frɔst] N geada; (*also:* **hoar~**) gelo; **frostbite** N ulceração *f* produzida pelo frio; **frosty** ADJ (*window*) coberto de geada; (*welcome*) glacial

froth [frɔθ] N espuma

frown [fraun] VI franzir as sobrancelhas, amarrar a cara

froze [frəuz] PT *of* **freeze**

frozen ['frəuzn] PP *of* **freeze**

fruit [fru:t] N INV fruta; (*fig*) fruto; **fruit juice** N suco (BR) *or* sumo (PT) de frutas; **fruit machine** (BRIT) N caça-níqueis *m inv* (BR), máquina de jogo (PT); **fruit salad** N salada de frutas

frustrate [frʌs'treɪt] VT frustrar

fry [fraɪ] (*pt, pp* **fried**) VT fritar; *see also* **small**; **frying pan** N frigideira

fudge [fʌdʒ] N (*Culin*) ≈ doce *m* de leite

fuel [fjuəl] N (*gen, for heating*) combustível *m*; (*for propelling*) carburante *m*; **fuel tank** N depósito de combustível

fulfil [ful'fɪl], (US) **fulfill** VT (*function*) cumprir; (*condition*) satisfazer; (*wish, desire*) realizar

full [ful] ADJ cheio; (*use, volume*) máximo; (*complete*) completo; (*information*) detalhado; (*price*) integral; (*skirt*) folgado ▶ ADV: **~ well** perfeitamente; **I'm ~ (up)** estou satisfeito; **~ employment** pleno emprego; **a ~ two hours** duas horas completas; **at ~ speed** a toda a velocidade; **in ~** integralmente; **full stop** N ponto (final); **full-time** ADJ (*work*) de tempo completo *or* integral; **fully** ADV completamente; (*at least*) pelo menos

fumble ['fʌmbl] VI atrapalhar-se; **fumble with** VT FUS atrapalhar-se com

fume [fju:m] VI fumegar; (*be angry*) estar com raiva; **fumes** NPL gases *mpl*

fun [fʌn] N divertimento; **to have ~** divertir-se; **for ~** de brincadeira;

to make ~ of fazer troça de, zombar de

function ['fʌŋkʃən] N função f; (reception, dinner) recepção f ▶ VI funcionar

fund [fʌnd] N fundo; (source, store) fonte f; **funds** NPL (money) fundos mpl

fundamental [fʌndə'mɛntl] ADJ fundamental

funeral ['fju:nərəl] N (burial) enterro

funfair ['fʌnfɛəʳ] (BRIT) N parque m de diversões

fungus ['fʌŋɡəs] (pl **fungi**) N fungo; (mould) bolor m, mofo

funnel ['fʌnl] N funil m; (of ship) chaminé f

funny ['fʌnɪ] ADJ engraçado, divertido; (strange) esquisito, estranho

fur [fəːʳ] N pele f; (BRIT: in kettle etc) depósito, crosta

furious ['fjuərɪəs] ADJ furioso; (effort) incrível

furnish ['fəːnɪʃ] VT mobiliar (BR), mobilar (PT); (supply): **to ~ sb with sth** fornecer algo a alguém; **furnishings** NPL mobília

furniture ['fəːnɪtʃəʳ] N mobília, móveis mpl; **piece of ~** móvel m

furry ['fəːrɪ] ADJ peludo

further ['fəːðəʳ] ADJ novo, adicional ▶ ADV mais longe; (more) mais; (moreover) além disso ▶ VT promover; **further education** (BRIT) N educação f superior; **furthermore** ADV além disso

furthest ['fəːðɪst] SUPERL of **far**

fury ['fjuərɪ] N fúria

fuse [fju:z] N fusível m; (for bomb etc) espoleta, mecha ▶ VT fundir; (fig) unir ▶ VI (metal) fundir-se; unir-se; **to ~ the lights** (BRIT Elec) queimar as luzes; **fuse box** N caixa de fusíveis

fuss [fʌs] N estardalhaço; (complaining) escândalo; **to make a ~** criar caso; **to make a ~ of sb** paparicar alguém; **fussy** ADJ (person) exigente; (dress, style) espalhafatoso

future ['fju:tʃəʳ] ADJ futuro ▶ N futuro; **in (the) ~** no futuro

fuze [fju:z] (US) = **fuse**

fuzzy ['fʌzɪ] ADJ (Phot) indistinto; (hair) frisado, encrespado

g

G [dʒiː] N (*Mus*) sol *m*

gadget ['gædʒɪt] N aparelho, engenhoca

Gaelic ['geɪlɪk] ADJ gaélico(-a) ▶ N (*Ling*) gaélico

gag [gæg] N (*on mouth*) mordaça; (*joke*) piada ▶ VT amordaçar

gain [geɪn] N ganho; (*profit*) lucro ▶ VT ganhar ▶ VI (*watch*) adiantar-se; (*benefit*): **to ~ from sth** tirar proveito de algo; **to ~ on sb** aproximar-se de alguém; **to ~ 3lbs (in weight)** engordar 3 libras

gal. ABBR = **gallon**

gale [geɪl] N ventania; **~ force 10** vento de força 10

gallery ['gælərɪ] N (*in theatre etc*) galeria; (*also*: **art ~**: *public*) museu *m*; (: *private*) galeria (de arte)

gallon ['gæln] N galão *m* (*Brit* = 4.5 *litros*, *US* = 3.8 *litros*)

gallop ['gæləp] N galope *m* ▶ VI galopar

gallstone ['gɔːlstəun] N cálculo biliar

gamble ['gæmbl] N risco ▶ VT, VI jogar, arriscar; **gambler** N jogador(a) *m/f*; **gambling** N jogo

game [geɪm] N jogo; (*match*) partida; (*Tennis*) jogada; (*strategy*) plano, esquema *m*; (*Hunting*) caça ▶ ADJ (*willing*): **to be ~ for anything** topar qualquer parada; **big ~** caça grossa; **games console** [geɪmz-] N console *m* de videogames (BR), consola de videojogos (PT); **game show** N game show *m*; **gaming** ['geɪmɪŋ] N (*with video games*) jogos *mpl* de computador

gang [gæŋ] N bando, grupo; (*of criminals*) gangue *f*; (*of workmen*) turma ▶ VI: **to ~ up on sb** conspirar contra alguém

gangster ['gæŋstər] N gângster *m*, bandido

gap [gæp] N brecha, fenda; (*in trees, traffic*) abertura; (*in time*) intervalo; (*difference*): **~ (between)** diferença (entre)

gape [geɪp] VI (*person*) estar or ficar boquiaberto; (*hole*) abrir-se

garage ['gærɑːʒ] N garagem *f*; (*for car repairs*) oficina (mecânica)

garbage ['gɑːbɪdʒ] N (US) lixo; (*inf: nonsense*) disparates *mpl*; **garbage can** (US) N lata de lixo; **garbage collector** (US) N lixeiro(-a)

garden ['gɑːdn] N jardim *m*; **gardens** NPL (*public park*) jardim público, parque *m*; **gardener** N jardineiro(-a); **gardening** N jardinagem *f*

garlic ['gɑːlɪk] N alho

garment ['gɑːmənt] N peça de roupa

garrison ['gærɪsn] N guarnição *f*

gas [gæs] N gás m; (US: *gasoline*) gasolina ▶ VT asfixiar com gás; **gas cooker** (BRIT) N fogão m a gás; **gas cylinder** N bujão m de gás; **gas fire** (BRIT) N aquecedor m a gás

gasket ['gæskɪt] N (Aut) junta, gaxeta

gasoline ['gæsəliːn] (US) N gasolina

gasp [gɑːsp] N arfada ▶ VI arfar; **gasp out** VT dizer com voz entrecortada

gas station (US) N posto de gasolina

gastric ['gæstrɪk] ADJ gástrico; **gastric band** N (Med) banda gástrica

gate [geɪt] N portão m; **gate-crash** ['geɪtkræʃ] (BRIT) VT entrar de penetra em; **gated community** ['geɪtɪd-] N condomínio fechado; **gateway** N portão m, passagem f

gather ['gæðə^r] VT colher; (*assemble*) reunir; (*Sewing*) franzir; (*understand*) compreender ▶ VI reunir-se; **to ~ speed** acelerar(-se); **gathering** N reunião f, assembleia

gauge [geɪdʒ] N (*instrument*) medidor m ▶ VT (*fig: sb's capabilities, character*) avaliar

gave [geɪv] PT of **give**

gay [geɪ] ADJ (*homosexual*) gay; (*old-fashioned: cheerful*) alegre; (*colour*) vistoso; (*music*) vivo

gaze [geɪz] N olhar m fixo ▶ VI: **to ~ at sth** fitar algo

GB ABBR = **Great Britain**

gear [gɪə^r] N equipamento; (*Tech*) engrenagem f; (*Aut*) velocidade f, marcha (BR), mudança (PT) ▶ VT (*fig: adapt*): **to ~ sth to** preparar algo para; **top** (BRIT) or **high** (US)**/low ~** quinta/primeira (marcha); **in ~** engrenado

geese [giːs] NPL of **goose**

gel [dʒɛl] N gel m

gem [dʒɛm] N joia, gema

Gemini ['dʒɛmɪnaɪ] N Gêminis m, Gêmeos mpl

gender ['dʒɛndə^r] N gênero

general ['dʒɛnərl] N general m ▶ ADJ geral; **in ~** em geral; **general anaesthetic** N anestesia geral; **generally** ADV geralmente; **general practitioner** N clínico(-a) geral

generate ['dʒɛnəreɪt] VT gerar; **generator** N gerador m

generous ['dʒɛnərəs] ADJ generoso; (*measure etc*) abundante

genetically [dʒɪ'nɛtɪklɪ] ADV: **~ modified** (*food etc*) transgênico

Geneva [dʒɪ'niːvə] N Genebra

genitals ['dʒɛnɪtlz] NPL órgãos mpl genitais

genius ['dʒiːnɪəs] N gênio

genome ['dʒiːnəum] N genoma m

gentle ['dʒɛntl] ADJ (*touch, breeze*) leve, suave; (*landscape*) suave; (*animal*) manso

gentleman ['dʒɛntlmən] *irreg* N senhor m; (*referring to social position*) fidalgo; (*well-bred man*) cavalheiro

gently ['dʒɛntlɪ] ADV suavemente

gents [dʒɛnts] N banheiro de homens (BR), casa de banho dos homens (PT)

genuine ['dʒɛnjuɪn] ADJ autêntico; (*person*) sincero

geography [dʒɪ'ɔgrəfɪ] N geografia

geology [dʒɪ'ɔlədʒɪ] N geologia

geometry [dʒɪ'ɔmətrɪ] N geometria

geranium [dʒɪ'reɪnjəm] N gerânio

geriatric [dʒɛrɪ'ætrɪk] ADJ geriátrico

germ [dʒəːm] N micróbio, bacilo

German ['dʒəːmən] ADJ alemão(-mã) ▶ N alemão(-mã) m/f;

(*Ling*) alemão *m*; **German measles** N rubéola
Germany ['dʒɜ:mənɪ] N Alemanha
gesture ['dʒɛstjəʳ] N gesto

(KEYWORD)

get [gɛt] (*pt*, *pp* **got**, (*US*) *pp* **gotten**) VI 1 (*become*, *be*) ficar, tornar-se; **to get old/tired/cold** envelhecer/cansar-se/resfriar-se; **to get annoyed/bored** aborrecer-se/amuar-se; **to get drunk** embebedar-se; **to get dirty** sujar-se; **to get killed/married** ser morto/casar-se; **when do I get paid?** quando eu recebo?, quando eu vou ser pago?; **it's getting late** está ficando tarde 2 (*go*): **to get to/from** ir para/de; **to get home** chegar em casa 3 (*begin*) começar a; **to get to know sb** começar a conhecer alguém; **let's get going** *or* **started** vamos lá!
▶ MODAL AUX VB: **you've got to do it** você tem que fazê-lo
▶ VT 1: **to get sth done** (*do*) fazer algo; (*have done*) mandar fazer algo; **to get one's hair cut** cortar o cabelo; **to get the car going** *or* **to go** fazer o carro andar; **to get sb to do sth** convencer alguém a fazer algo; **to get sth/sb ready** preparar algo/arrumar alguém 2 (*obtain*) ter; (*find*) achar; (*fetch*) buscar; **to get sth for sb** arranjar algo para alguém; (*fetch*) ir buscar algo para alguém; **get me Mr Harris, please** (*Tel*) pode chamar o Sr Harris, por favor; **can I get you a drink?** você está servido? 3 (*receive: present, letter*) receber;

(*acquire: reputation, prize*) ganhar 4 (*catch*) agarrar; (*hit: target etc*) pegar; **to get sb by the arm/throat** agarrar alguém pelo braço/pela garganta; **get him!** pega ele! 5 (*take, move*) levar; **to get sth to sb** levar algo para alguém; **I can't get it in/out/through** não consigo enfiá-lo/tirá-lo/passá-lo; **do you think we'll get it through the door?** você acha que conseguiremos passar isto na porta? 6 (*plane, bus etc*) pegar, tomar; **where do I get the train to Birmingham?** onde eu pego o trem para Birmingham? 7 (*understand*) entender; (*hear*) ouvir; **I've got it** entendi; **I don't get your meaning** não entendo o que você quer dizer 8 (*have, possess*): **to have got** ter

get about VI (*news*) espalhar-se
get along VI (*agree*) entender-se; (*depart*) ir embora; (*manage*) = **get by**
get around = **get round**
get at VT FUS (*attack, criticize*) atacar; (*reach*) alcançar; **what are you getting at?** o que você está querendo dizer?
get away VI (*leave*) partir; (*escape*) escapar
get away with VT FUS conseguir fazer impunemente
get back VI (*return*) regressar, voltar ▶ VT receber de volta, recobrar
get by VI (*pass*) passar; (*manage*) virar-se
get down VI descer ▶ VT FUS abaixar ▶ VT (*object*) abaixar, descer; (*depress: person*) deprimir

g

get down to VT FUS (*work*) pôr-se a (fazer)

get in VI entrar; (*train*) chegar; (*arrive home*) voltar para casa

get into VT FUS entrar em; (*vehicle*) subir em; (*clothes*) pôr, vestir, enfiar; **to get into bed/a rage** meter-se na cama/ficar com raiva

get off VI (*from train etc*) saltar (BR), descer (PT); (*depart*) sair; (*escape*) escapar ▶ VT (*remove: clothes, stain*) tirar; (*send off*) mandar ▶ VT FUS (*train, bus*) saltar de (BR), sair de (PT)

get on VI (*at exam etc*): **how are you getting on?** como vai?; (*agree*): **to get on (with)** entender-se (com) ▶ VT FUS (*train etc*) subir em (BR), subir para (PT); (*horse*) montar em

get out VI (*of place, vehicle*) sair ▶ VT (*take out*) tirar

get out of VT FUS (*duty etc*) escapar de

get over VT FUS (*illness*) restabelecer-se de

get round VT FUS rodear; (*fig: person*) convencer

get through VI (*Tel*) completar a ligação

get through to VT FUS (*Tel*) comunicar-se com

get together VI (*people*) reunir-se ▶ VT reunir

get up VI levantar-se ▶ VT FUS levantar

get up to VT FUS (*reach*) chegar a; (*BRIT: prank etc*) fazer

getaway ['gɛtəweɪ] N fuga, escape *m*

ghastly ['gɑːstlɪ] ADJ horrível; (*building*) medonho; (*appearance*) horripilante; (*pale*) pálido

ghost [gəʊst] N fantasma *m*

giant ['dʒaɪənt] N gigante *m* ▶ ADJ gigantesco, gigante

gift [gɪft] N presente *m*, dádiva; (*ability*) dom *m*, talento; **gifted** ADJ bem-dotado; **gift shop**, (US) **gift store** N loja de presentes

gigabyte ['gɪgəbaɪt] N gigabyte *m*

gigantic [dʒaɪ'gæntɪk] ADJ gigantesco

giggle ['gɪgl] VI dar risadinha boba

gills [gɪlz] NPL (*of fish*) guelras *fpl*, brânquias *fpl*

gilt [gɪlt] ADJ dourado ▶ N dourado

gimmick ['gɪmɪk] N truque *m or* macete *m* (publicitário)

gin [dʒɪn] N gim *m*, genebra

ginger ['dʒɪndʒə^r] N gengibre *m*

gipsy ['dʒɪpsɪ] N cigano

giraffe [dʒɪ'rɑːf] N girafa

girl [gəːl] N (*small*) menina (BR), rapariga (PT); (*young woman*) jovem *f*, moça; (*daughter*) filha; **girlfriend** N (*of girl*) amiga; (*of boy*) namorada; **Girl Guide** (BRIT) N bandeirante *f*

gist [dʒɪst] N essencial *m*

(KEYWORD)

give [gɪv] (*pt* **gave**, *pp* **given**) VT
1 (*hand over*) dar; **to give sb sth, give sth to sb** dar algo a alguém
2 (*used with n to replace a vb*): **to give a cry/sigh/push** *etc* dar um grito/suspiro/empurrão *etc*; **to give a speech/a lecture** fazer um discurso/uma palestra
3 (*tell, deliver: news, advice, message etc*) dar; **to give the right/wrong answer** dar a resposta certa/errada
4 (*supply, provide: opportunity, surprise, job etc*) dar; (*bestow: title, honour, right*) conceder; **the sun gives warmth and light** o sol fornece calor e luz

5 (*dedicate: time, one's life/attention*) dedicar; **she gave it all her attention** ela dedicou toda sua atenção a isto

6 (*organize*): **to give a party/dinner** *etc* dar uma festa/jantar *etc*

▶ vi **1** (*also*: **give way**: *break, collapse*) dar folga; **his legs gave beneath him** suas pernas bambearam; **the roof/floor gave as I stepped on it** o telhado/chão desabou quando eu pisei nele **2** (*stretch: fabric*) dar de si

give away vt (*money, opportunity*) dar; (*secret, information*) revelar

give back vt devolver

give in vi (*yield*) ceder ▶ vt (*essay etc*) entregar

give off vt (*heat, smoke*) soltar

give out vt (*distribute*) distribuir; (*make known*) divulgar

give up vi (*surrender*) desistir, dar-se por vencido ▶ vt (*job, boyfriend, habit*) renunciar a; (*idea, hope*) abandonar; **to give up smoking** deixar de fumar; **to give o.s. up** entregar-se

give way vi (*yield*) ceder; (*break, collapse: rope*) arrebentar; (: *ladder*) quebrar; (BRIT *Aut*) dar a preferência (BR), dar prioridade (PT)

glacier ['glæsɪəʳ] N glaciar *m*, geleira

glad [glæd] ADJ contente

gladly ['glædlɪ] ADV com muito prazer

glamorous ['glæmərəs] ADJ encantador(a), glamouroso

glamour ['glæməʳ] N encanto, glamour *m*

glance [glɑːns] N relance *m*, vista de olhos ▶ vi: **to ~ at** olhar (de relance); **glance off** vt FUS (*bullet*) ricochetear de

gland [glænd] N glândula

glare [glɛəʳ] N (*of anger*) olhar *m* furioso; (*of light*) luminosidade *f*; (*of publicity*) foco ▶ vi brilhar; **to ~ at** olhar furiosamente para; **glaring** ADJ (*mistake*) notório

glass [glɑːs] N vidro, cristal *m*; (*for drinking*) copo; **glasses** NPL (*spectacles*) óculos *mpl*

glaze [gleɪz] vt (*door*) envidraçar; (*pottery*) vitrificar ▶ N verniz *m*

gleam [gliːm] vi brilhar

glide [glaɪd] vi deslizar; (*Aviat: birds*) planar; **glider** N (*Aviat*) planador *m*

glimmer ['glɪməʳ] N luz *f* trêmula; (*of interest, hope*) lampejo

glimpse [glɪmps] N vista rápida, vislumbre *m* ▶ vt vislumbrar, ver de relance

glint [glɪnt] vi cintilar

glisten ['glɪsn] vi brilhar

glitter ['glɪtəʳ] vi reluzir, brilhar

global ['gləubl] ADJ mundial; **globalization** [gləubəlaɪˈzeɪʃən] N globalização *f*; **global warming** N aquecimento global

globe [gləub] N globo, esfera

gloom [gluːm] N escuridão *f*; (*sadness*) tristeza; **gloomy** ADJ escuro; (*sad*) triste

glorious ['glɔːrɪəs] ADJ (*weather*) magnífico; (*future*) glorioso

glory ['glɔːrɪ] N glória

gloss [glɔs] N (*shine*) brilho; (*also*: **~ paint**) pintura brilhante, esmalte *m*; **gloss over** vt FUS encobrir

glossary ['glɔsərɪ] N glossário

glossy ['glɔsɪ] ADJ lustroso

glove [glʌv] N luva

glow [gləu] vi (*shine*) brilhar; (*fire*) arder

glucose ['glu:kəus] N glicose f
glue [glu:] N cola ▶ VT colar
GM ADJ ABBR (= *genetically modified*)
geneticamente modificado; **GM
crop** N plantação f geneticamente
modificada; **GM foods** NPL
alimentos *mpl* geneticamente
modificados
gnaw [nɔ:] VT roer

(KEYWORD)

go [gəu] (*pt* **went**, *pp* **gone**, *pl* **goes**)
VI **1** (*travel, move*) viajar; **a car
went by** um carro passou; **he has
gone to Aberdeen** ele foi para
Aberdeen
2 (*depart*) sair, ir embora
3 (*attend*) ir; **she went to
university in Rio** ela fez
universidade no Rio; **he goes to
the local church** ele frequenta a
igreja local
4 (*take part in an activity*) ir; **to go for
a walk** ir passear
5 (*work*) funcionar; **the bell went
just then** a campainha acabou de
tocar
6 (*become*): **to go pale/mouldy**
ficar pálido/mofado
7 (*be sold*): **to go for £10** ser vendido
por £10
8 (*fit, suit*): **to go with** acompanhar,
combinar com
9 (*be about, intend to*): **he's going
to do it** ele vai fazê-lo; **are you
going to come?** você vem?
10 (*time*) passar
11 (*event, activity*) ser; **how did it go?**
como foi?
12 (*be given*): **the job is to go to
someone else** o emprego vai ser
dado para outra pessoa
13 (*break*) romper-se; **the fuse went**
o fusível queimou; **the leg of the
chair went** a perna da cadeira
quebrou
14 (*be placed*): **where does this cup
go?** onde é que põe esta xícara?;
the milk goes in the fridge pode
guardar o leite na geladeira
▶ N **1** (*try*): **to have a go (at)** tentar
2 (*turn*) vez f
3 (*move*): **to be on the go** ter muito
para fazer
go about VI (*also*: **go around**:
rumour) espalhar-se ▶ VT FUS: **how
do I go about this?** como é que eu
faço isto?
go ahead VI (*make progress*)
progredir; (*get going*) ir em frente
go along VI ir ▶ VT FUS ladear; **to go
along with** concordar com
go away VI (*leave*) ir-se, ir embora
go back VI (*return*) voltar; (*go again*)
ir de novo
go back on VT FUS (*promise*) faltar
com
go by VI (*years, time*) passar ▶ VT FUS
(*book, rule*) guiar-se por
go down VI (*descend*) descer, baixar;
(*ship*) afundar; (*sun*) pôr-se ▶ VT FUS
(*stairs, ladder*) descer
go for VT FUS (*fetch*) ir buscar; (*like*)
gostar de; (*attack*) atacar
go in VI (*enter*) entrar
go in for VT FUS (*competition*)
inscrever-se em; (*like*) gostar de
go into VT FUS (*enter*) entrar em;
(*investigate*) investigar; (*embark on*)
embarcar em
go off VI (*leave*) ir-se; (*food*)
estragar, apodrecer; (*bomb, gun*)
explodir; (*event*) realizar-se ▶ VT FUS
(*person, place, food etc*) deixar de
gostar de
go on VI (*continue*) seguir, continuar;
(*happen*) acontecer, ocorrer
go out VI sair (*for entertainment*):

are you going out tonight? você vai sair hoje à noite?; (couple): **they went out for 3 years** eles namoraram durante 3 anos; (fire, light) apagar-se
go over VI (ship) soçobrar ▶ VT FUS (check) revisar
go round VI (news, rumour) circular
go through VT FUS (town etc) atravessar; (search through) vasculhar; (examine) percorrer de cabo a rabo
go up VI (ascend) subir; (price, level) aumentar
go without VT FUS passar sem

go-ahead ADJ empreendedor(a) ▶ N luz f verde
goal [gəul] N meta, alvo; (Sport) gol m (BR), golo (PT); **goalkeeper** N goleiro(-a) (BR), guarda-redes m/f inv (PT)
goat [gəut] N cabra
gobble ['gɔbl] VT (also: **~ down, ~ up**) engolir rapidamente, devorar
god [gɔd] N deus m; **G~** Deus; **godchild** irreg N afilhado(-a); **goddess** N deusa; **godfather** N padrinho; **godmother** N madrinha
goggles ['gɔglz] NPL óculos mpl de proteção
going ['gəuɪŋ] N (conditions) estado do terreno ▶ ADJ: **the ~ rate** tarifa corrente or em vigor
gold [gəuld] N ouro ▶ ADJ de ouro; **golden** ADJ (made of gold) de ouro; (gold in colour) dourado; **goldfish** N INV peixe-dourado m; **gold-plated** ADJ plaquê inv
golf [gɔlf] N golfe m; **golf ball** N bola de golfe; (on typewriter) esfera; **golf club** N clube m de golfe; (stick) taco; **golf course** N campo de golfe; **golfer** N jogador(a) m/f de golfe, golfista m/f
gone [gɔn] PP of **go**
gong [gɔŋ] N gongo
good [gud] ADJ bom/boa; (kind) bom, bondoso; (well-behaved) educado ▶ N bem m; **goods** NPL (Comm) mercadorias fpl; **~!** bom!; **to be ~ at** ser bom em; **to be ~ for** servir para; **it's ~ for you** faz-lhe bem; **a ~ deal (of)** muito; **a ~ many** muitos; **to make ~** reparar; **it's no ~ complaining** não adianta se queixar; **for ~** para sempre, definitivamente; **~ morning/afternoon!** bom dia/boa tarde!; **~ evening!** boa noite!; **~ night!** boa noite!; **goodbye** EXCL até logo (BR), adeus (PT); **to say goodbye** despedir-se; **Good Friday** N Sexta-Feira Santa; **good-looking** ADJ bonito; **good-natured** ADJ (person) de bom gênio; (pet) de boa índole; **goodwill** N boa vontade f
Google® ['gu:gəl] VT, VI pesquisar no Google®
goose [gu:s] (pl **geese**) N ganso
gooseberry ['guzbərɪ] N groselha; **to play ~** (BRIT) ficar de vela
gorge [gɔ:dʒ] N desfiladeiro ▶ VT: **to ~ o.s. (on)** empanturrar-se (de)
gorgeous ['gɔ:dʒəs] ADJ magnífico, maravilhoso; (person) lindo
gorilla [gə'rɪlə] N gorila m
gosh [gɔʃ] (inf) EXCL puxa
gospel ['gɔspl] N evangelho
gossip ['gɔsɪp] N (scandal) fofocas fpl (BR), mexericos mpl (PT); (chat) conversa; (scandalmonger) fofoqueiro(-a) (BR), mexeriqueiro(-a) (PT) ▶ VI (chat) bater (um) papo (BR), cavaquear (PT)

got [gɔt] PT, PP *of* **get**

gotten ['gɔtn] (US) PP *of* **get**

govern ['gʌvən] VT governar; (*event*) controlar

government ['gʌvnmənt] N governo

governor ['gʌvənəʳ] N governador(a) *m/f*; (*of school, hospital, jail*) diretor(a) *m/f*

gown [gaun] N vestido; (*of teacher, judge*) toga

GP N ABBR (*Med*) = **general practitioner**

GPS N ABBR (= *global positioning system*) GPS *m*

grab [græb] VT agarrar ▶ VI: **to ~ at** tentar agarrar

grace [greis] N (*Rel*) graça; (*gracefulness*) elegância, fineza ▶ VT (*honour*) honrar; (*adorn*) adornar; **5 days' ~** um prazo de 5 dias; **graceful** ADJ elegante, gracioso; **gracious** ['greiʃəs] ADJ gracioso, afável

grade [greid] N (*quality*) classe *f*, qualidade *f*; (*degree*) grau *m*; (US: *Sch*) série *f*, classe ▶ VT classificar; **grade crossing** (US) N passagem *f* de nível; **grade school** (US) N escola primária

gradient ['greidiənt] N declive *m*

gradual ['grædjuəl] ADJ gradual, gradativo; **gradually** ADV gradualmente, gradativamente, pouco a pouco

graduate [N 'grædjuit, VI 'grædjueit] N graduado, licenciado; (US) diplomado do colégio ▶ VI formar-se, licenciar-se; **graduation** [grædju'eiʃən] N formatura

graffiti [grə'fi:ti] N, NPL pichações *fpl*

graft [grɑ:ft] N (*Agr, Med*) enxerto; (BRIT *inf*) trabalho pesado; (*bribery*) suborno ▶ VT enxertar

grain [grein] N grão *m*; (*no pl: cereals*) cereais *mpl*; (*in wood*) veio, fibra

gram [græm] N grama *m*

grammar ['græməʳ] N gramática; **grammar school** N (BRIT) ≈ liceo

gramme [græm] N = **gram**

gran [græn] (BRIT *inf*) N vó *f*

grand [grænd] ADJ grandioso; (*inf: wonderful*) ótimo; **granddad** N vovô *m*; **granddaughter** N neta; **grandfather** N avô *m*; **grandma** ['grænmɑ:] N avó *f*, vovó *f*; **grandmother** N avó *f*; **grandpa** ['grænpɑ:] N = **granddad**; **grandparents** NPL avós *mpl*; **grand piano** N piano de cauda; **grandson** N neto

granite ['grænit] N granito

granny ['græni] (*inf*) N avó *f*, vovó *f*

grant [grɑ:nt] VT (*concede*) conceder; (*a request etc*) anuir a; (*admit*) admitir ▶ N (*Sch*) bolsa; (*Admin*) subvenção *f*, subsídio; **to take sth for ~ed** dar algo por certo

grape [greip] N uva

grapefruit ['greipfru:t] N toranja, grapefruit *m* (BR)

graph [grɑ:f] N gráfico; **graphic** ['græfik] ADJ gráfico; **graphics** N (*art*) artes *fpl* gráficas ▶ NPL (*drawings*) desenhos *mpl*

grasp [grɑ:sp] VT agarrar, segurar; (*understand*) compreender, entender ▶ N mão *f*; (*understanding*) compreensão *f*

grass [grɑ:s] N grama (BR), relva (PT); **grasshopper** N gafanhoto

grate [greit] N (*fireplace*) lareira ▶ VI ranger ▶ VT (*Culin*) ralar

grateful ['greitful] ADJ agradecido, grato

grater ['greɪtəʳ] N ralador *m*

gratitude ['grætɪtjuːd] N agradecimento

grave [greɪv] N cova, sepultura ▶ ADJ sério; (*mistake*) grave

gravestone ['greɪvstəun] N lápide *f*

graveyard ['greɪvjɑːd] N cemitério

gravity ['grævɪtɪ] N (*Phys*) gravidade *f*; (*seriousness*) seriedade *f*, gravidade *f*

gravy ['greɪvɪ] N molho (de carne)

gray [greɪ] (*US*) ADJ = **grey**

graze [greɪz] VI pastar ▶ VT (*touch lightly*) roçar; (*scrape*) raspar ▶ N (*Med*) esfoladura, arranhadura

grease [griːs] N (*fat*) gordura; (*lubricant*) graxa, lubrificante *m* ▶ VT (*dish*) untar; (*brakes etc*) lubrificar, engraxar; **greasy** ADJ gordurento, gorduroso; (*skin, hair*) oleoso

great [greɪt] ADJ grande; (*inf*) genial; (*pain, heat*) forte; (*important*) importante; **Great Britain** N Grã-Bretanha

> A Grã-Bretanha, **Great Britain** ou **Britain** em inglês, designa a maior das ilhas britânicas e, portanto, engloba a Escócia e o País de Gales. Junto com a Irlanda, a ilha de Man e as ilhas Anglo-normandas, a Grã-Bretanha forma as ilhas Britânicas, ou *British Isles*. Reino Unido, em inglês *United Kingdom* ou *UK*, é o nome oficial da entidade política que compreende a Grã-Bretanha e a Irlanda do Norte.

great: great-grandfather N bisavô *m*; **great-grandmother** N bisavó *f*; **greatly** ADV imensamente, muito

Greece [griːs] N Grécia

greed [griːd] N (*also:* **~iness**) avidez *f*, cobiça; **greedy** ADJ avarento; (*for food*) guloso

Greek [griːk] ADJ grego ▶ N grego(-a); (*Ling*) grego

green [griːn] ADJ verde; (*inexperienced*) inexperiente, ingênuo ▶ N verde *m*; (*stretch of grass*) gramado (BR), relvado (PT); (*on golf course*) green *m*; **greens** NPL (*vegetables*) verduras *fpl*; **greenhouse** N estufa; **greenhouse effect** N: **the greenhouse effect** o efeito estufa; **greenhouse gas** N gás *m* de efeito estufa

Greenland ['griːnlənd] N Groenlândia

green tax N imposto ecológico

greet [griːt] VT acolher; (*news*) receber; **greeting** N acolhimento; **greeting card, greetings card** N cartão *m* comemorativo

grew [gruː] PT *of* **grow**

grey [greɪ], (*US*) **gray** ADJ cinzento; (*dismal*) sombrio; **grey-haired** ADJ grisalho; **greyhound** N galgo; **grey vote** N voto dos idosos

grid [grɪd] N grade *f*; (*Elec*) rede *f*; **gridlock** N (*traffic jam*) paralisia do trânsito

grief [griːf] N dor *f*, pesar *m*

grievance ['griːvəns] N motivo de queixa, agravo

grieve [griːv] VI sofrer ▶ VT dar pena a, afligir; **to ~ for** chorar por

grill [grɪl] N (*on cooker*) grelha; (*also:* **mixed ~**) prato de grelhados ▶ VT (BRIT) grelhar; (*question*) interrogar cerradamente

grille [grɪl] N grade *f*; (*Aut*) grelha

grim [grɪm] ADJ desagradável; (*unattractive*) feio; (*stern*) severo

grime [graɪm] N sujeira (BR), sujidade f (PT)

grin [grɪn] N sorriso largo ▶ VI: **to ~ (at)** dar um sorriso largo (para)

grind [graɪnd] (*pt, pp* **ground**) VT triturar; (*coffee, pepper etc*) moer; (*make sharp*) afiar; (*US: meat*) picar ▶ N (*work*) trabalho (repetitivo e maçante)

grip [grɪp] N (*of hands*) aperto; (*handle*) punho; (*of tyre, shoe*) aderência; (*holdall*) valise f ▶ VT agarrar; (*attention*) prender; **to come** *or* **get to ~s with** arcar com

gripping ['grɪpɪŋ] ADJ absorvente, emocionante

grit [grɪt] N areia, grão m de areia; (*courage*) coragem f ▶ VT (*road*) pôr areia em; **to ~ one's teeth** cerrar os dentes

groan [grəun] N gemido ▶ VI gemer

grocer ['grəusər] N dono(-a) de mercearia; **grocer's, grocer's shop** N mercearia; **grocery** N mercearia; **groceries** NPL comestíveis mpl

groin [grɔɪn] N virilha

groom [gru:m] N cavalariço; (*also*: **bride~**) noivo ▶ VT (*horse*) tratar; (*fig*): **to ~ sb for sth** preparar alguém para algo; **well-~ed** bem-posto

groove [gru:v] N ranhura, entalhe m

grope [grəup] VI: **to ~ for** procurar às cegas

gross [grəus] ADJ (*flagrant*) grave; (*vulgar*) vulgar; (*: building*) de mau-gosto; (*Comm*) bruto

ground [graund] PT, PP *of* **grind** ▶ N terra, chão m; (*Sport*) campo; (*land*) terreno; (*reason: gen pl*) motivo, razão f; (*US: also*: **~ wire**) (ligação f à) terra, fio-terra m ▶ VT (*plane*) manter em terra; (*US Elec*) ligar à terra; **grounds** NPL (*of coffee etc*) borra; (*gardens etc*) jardins mpl, parque m; **on the ~** no chão; **to the ~** por terra; **groundsheet** (BRIT) N capa impermeável; **groundwork** N base f, preparação f

group [gru:p] N grupo; (*also*: **pop ~**) conjunto ▶ VT (*also*: **~ together**) agrupar ▶ VI (*also*: **~ together**) agrupar-se

grouse [graus] N INV (*bird*) tetraz m, galo-silvestre m ▶ VI (*complain*) queixar-se, resmungar

grovel ['grɔvl] VI: **to ~ (before)** abaixar-se (diante de)

grow [grəu] (*pt* **grew**, *pp* **grown**) VI crescer; (*increase*) aumentar; (*develop*): **to ~ (out of/from)** originar-se (de) ▶ VT plantar, cultivar; (*beard*) deixar crescer; **to ~ rich/weak** enriquecer(-se)/ enfraquecer-se; **grow up** VI crescer, fazer-se homem/mulher

growl [graul] VI rosnar

grown [grəun] PP *of* **grow**

grown-up N adulto(-a), pessoa mais velha

growth [grəuθ] N crescimento; (*increase*) aumento; (*Med*) abcesso, tumor m

grub [grʌb] N larva, lagarta; (*inf: food*) comida, rango (BR)

grubby ['grʌbɪ] ADJ encardido

grudge [grʌdʒ] N motivo de rancor ▶ VT: **to ~ sb sth** dar algo a alguém de má vontade, invejar algo a alguém; **to bear sb a ~ for sth** guardar rancor de alguém por algo

gruelling ['gruəlɪŋ], (US) **grueling** ADJ duro, árduo

gruesome ['gru:səm] ADJ horrível

grumble ['grʌmbl] vı resmungar, bufar

grumpy ['grʌmpı] adj rabugento

grunt [grʌnt] vı grunhir

guarantee [gærən'ti:] n garantia ▶ vt garantir

guard [gɑ:d] n guarda; (one person) guarda m; (brit Rail) guarda-freio; (on machine) dispositivo de segurança; (also: **fire~**) guarda-fogo ▶ vt (protect): **to ~ (against)** proteger (contra); (prisoner) vigiar; **to be on one's ~** estar prevenido; **guard against** vt fus prevenir-se contra; **guardian** n protetor(a) m/f; (of minor) tutor(a) m/f

Guatemala [gwɔtə'mɑ:lə] n Guatemala

guerrilla [gə'rılə] n guerrilheiro(-a)

guess [gɛs] vt, vı (estimate) avaliar, conjeturar; (correct answer) adivinhar; (us) achar, supor ▶ n suposição f, conjetura; **to take** or **have a ~** adivinhar, chutar (inf)

guest [gɛst] n convidado(-a); (in hotel) hóspede m/f

guidance ['gaıdəns] n conselhos mpl

guide [gaıd] n (person) guia m/f; (book, fig) guia m; (brit: also: **girl ~**) escoteira ▶ vt guiar; **guidebook** n guia m; **guide dog** n cão m de guia; **guided tour** n visita guiada; **guidelines** npl (advice) orientação f

guilt [gılt] n culpa; **guilty** adj culpado

guinea pig ['gınıpıg] n porquinho-da-Índia m, cobaia; (fig) cobaia

guitar [gı'tɑ:ʳ] n violão m

gulf [gʌlf] n golfo; (abyss: also fig) abismo

gull [gʌl] n gaivota

gulp [gʌlp] vı engolir em seco ▶ vt (also: **~ down**) engolir

gum [gʌm] n (Anat) gengiva; (glue) goma; (also: **~ drop**) bala de goma; (also: **chewing-~**) chiclete m (br), pastilha elástica (pt) ▶ vt colar

gun [gʌn] n (gen) arma (de fogo); (revolver) revólver m; (small) pistola; (rifle) espingarda; (cannon) canhão m; **gunfire** n tiroteio; **gunman** irreg n pistoleiro; **gunpoint** n: **at gunpoint** sob a ameaça de uma arma; **gunpowder** n pólvora; **gunshot** n tiro (de arma de fogo)

gust [gʌst] n (of wind) rajada

gut [gʌt] n intestino, tripa; **guts** npl (Anat) entranhas fpl; (inf: courage) coragem f, raça (inf)

gutter ['gʌtəʳ] n (of roof) calha; (in street) sarjeta

guy [gaı] n (also: **~rope**) corda; (inf: man) cara m (br), tipo (pt); **Guy Fawkes' Night** n ver nota

> A **Guy Fawkes' Night**, também chamada de bonfire night, é a ocasião em que se comemora o fracasso da conspiração (a Gunpowder Plot) contra James I e o Parlamento, em 5 de novembro de 1605. Um dos conspiradores, Guy Fawkes, foi surpreendido no porão do Parlamento quando estava prestes a atear fogo a explosivos. Todo ano, no dia 5 de novembro, as crianças preparam antecipadamente um boneco de Guy Fawkes e pedem às pessoas que passam na rua a penny for the Guy (uma moedinha para o Guy), com o qual compram fogos de artifício.

gym [dʒɪm] N (also: **gymnasium**) ginásio; (also: **gymnastics**) ginástica

gymnast ['dʒɪmnæst] N ginasta m/f

gymnastics [dʒɪm'næstɪks] N ginástica

gynaecologist [gaɪnɪ'kɔlədʒɪst], (US) **gynecologist** N ginecologista m/f

gypsy ['dʒɪpsɪ] N = **gipsy**

haberdashery ['hæbə'dæʃərɪ] (BRIT) N armarinho

habit ['hæbɪt] N hábito, costume m; (addiction) vício; (Rel) hábito

hack [hæk] VT (cut) cortar; (chop) talhar ▶ N (pej: writer) escrevinhador(a) m/f; **hacker** N (Comput) hacker m

had [hæd] PT, PP of **have**

haddock ['hædək] (**haddocks** or pl **haddock**) N hadoque m (BR), eglefim m (PT)

hadn't ['hædnt] = **had not**

haemorrhage ['hɛmərɪdʒ], (US) **hemorrhage** N hemorragia

haemorrhoids ['hɛmərɔɪdz], (US) **hemorrhoids** NPL hemorróidas fpl

haggle ['hægl] VI pechinchar, regatear

hail [heɪl] N granizo; (of objects) chuva; (of criticism) torrente f ▶ VT (greet) cumprimentar, saudar; (call) chamar ▶ VI chover granizo; **hailstone** N pedra de granizo

hair [hɛəʳ] N (*of human*) cabelo; (*of animal, on legs*) pelo; **to do one's ~** pentear-se; **hairbrush** N escova de cabelo; **haircut** N corte *m* de cabelo; **hairdo** N penteado; **hairdresser** N cabeleireiro(-a); **hairdresser's** N cabeleireiro; **hair dryer** N secador *m* de cabelo; **hair gel** N gel *m* para o cabelo; **hair spray** N laquê *m* (*br*), laca (*pt*); **hairstyle** N penteado; **hairy** ADJ cabeludo, peludo; (*inf: situation*) perigoso

hake [heɪk] (*pl* **hakes** or **hake**) N abrótea

half [hɑːf] (*pl* **halves**) N metade *f* ▶ ADJ meio ▶ ADV meio, pela metade; **~ a pound** meia libra; **two and a ~** dois e meio; **~ a dozen** meia-dúzia; **to cut sth in ~** cortar algo ao meio; **half-hearted** ADJ irresoluto, indiferente; **half-hour** N meia hora; **half-price** ADJ, ADV pela metade do preço; **half term** (*brit*) N (*Sch*) dias de folga *no meio do semestre*; **half-time** N meio tempo; **halfway** ADV a meio caminho; (*in time*) no meio

hall [hɔːl] N (*for concerts*) sala; (*entrance way*) hall *m*, entrada

hallmark ['hɔːlmɑːk] N (*also fig*) marca

hall of residence (*brit*) (*pl* **halls of residence**) N residência universitária

Hallowe'en ['hæləʊ'iːn] N Dia *m* das Bruxas (*31 de outubro*)

Segundo a tradição, **Hallowe'en** é a noite dos fantasmas e dos bruxos. Na Escócia e nos Estados Unidos, sobretudo (bem menos na Inglaterra), as crianças, para festejar o **Hallowe'en**, se fantasiam e batem de porta em porta pedindo prendas (chocolates, maçãs etc).

hallway ['hɔːlweɪ] N hall *m*, entrada

halo ['heɪləʊ] N (*of saint etc*) auréola

halt [hɔːlt] N parada (*br*), paragem *f* (*pt*) ▶ VI parar ▶ VT deter; (*process*) interromper

halve [hɑːv] VT (*divide*) dividir ao meio; (*reduce by half*) reduzir à metade

halves [hɑːvz] NPL *of* **half**

ham [hæm] N presunto, fiambre *m* (*pt*)

hamburger ['hæmbəːgəʳ] N hambúrguer *m*

hammer ['hæməʳ] N martelo ▶ VT martelar ▶ VI (*on door*) bater insistentemente

hammock ['hæmək] N rede *f*

hamper ['hæmpəʳ] VT dificultar, atrapalhar ▶ N cesto

hamster ['hæmstəʳ] N hamster *m*

hand [hænd] N mão *f*; (*of clock*) ponteiro; (*writing*) letra; (*of cards*) cartas *fpl*; (*worker*) trabalhador *m* ▶ VT dar, passar; **to give** or **lend sb a ~** dar uma mãozinha a alguém, dar uma ajuda a alguém; **at ~** à mão, disponível; **in ~** livre; (*situation*) sob controle; **to be on ~** (*person*) estar disponível; (*emergency services*) estar num estado de prontidão; **on the one ~ ..., on the other ~ ...** por um lado ..., por outro (lado) ...; **hand in** VT entregar; **hand out** VT distribuir; **hand over** VT entregar; (*powers etc*) transmitir; **handbag** N bolsa; **handbook** N manual *m*; **handbrake** N freio (*br*) or travão *m* (*pt*) de mão; **handcuffs** NPL

h

algemas *fpl*; **handful** N punhado;
(*of people*) grupo
handicap ['hændɪkæp] N (*Med*)
incapacidade *f*; (*disadvantage*)
desvantagem *f*; (*Sport*) handicap *m*
▶ VT prejudicar; **mentally/
physically ~ped** deficiente
mental/físico
handkerchief ['hæŋkətʃɪf] N lenço
handle ['hændl] N (*of door etc*)
maçaneta; (*of cup etc*) asa; (*of knife
etc*) cabo; (*for winding*) manivela
▶ VT manusear; (*deal with*) tratar de;
(*treat: people*) lidar com; **"~ with
care"** "cuidado — frágil"; **to fly off
the ~** perder as estribeiras;
handlebar N, **handlebars**
['hɑːndlbɑːz] NPL guidom *m* (BR),
guidão *m* (PT)
handmade ['hændmeɪd] ADJ feito
a mão
handout ['hændaut] N (*money,
food*) doação *f*; (*leaflet*) folheto;
(*at lecture*) apostila
hands-free kit ['hændzfriː-] N
viva-voz *m*
handsome ['hænsəm] ADJ bonito;
(*building*) elegante; (*profit*)
considerável
handwriting ['hændraɪtɪŋ] N
letra, caligrafia
handy ['hændɪ] ADJ (*close at hand*) à
mão; (*useful*) útil; (*skilful*)
habilidoso, hábil
hang [hæŋ] (*pt, pp* **hung**) VT
pendurar; (*criminal: pt, pp* **hanged**)
enforcar ▶ VI estar pendurado; (*hair,
drapery*) cair ▶ N (*inf*) **to get the ~ of
(doing) sth** pegar o jeito de (fazer)
algo; **hang about** VI vadiar,
vagabundear; **hang around** VI =
hang about; **hang on** VI (*wait*)
esperar; **hang up** VT (*coat*) pendurar
▶ VI (*Tel*) desligar; **to ~ up on sb**

bater o telefone na cara de alguém
hanger ['hæŋəʳ] N cabide *m*
hang-gliding N voo livre
hangover ['hæŋəuvəʳ] N ressaca
happen ['hæpən] VI acontecer;
as it ~s ... acontece que ...
happily ['hæpɪlɪ] ADV (*luckily*)
felizmente; (*cheerfully*) alegremente
happiness ['hæpɪnɪs] N felicidade *f*
happy ['hæpɪ] ADJ feliz; (*cheerful*)
contente; **to be ~ (with)** estar
contente (com); **to be ~ to do**
(*willing*) estar disposto a fazer;
~ birthday! feliz aniversário
harass ['hærəs] VT importunar;
harassment N perseguição *f*
harbour ['hɑːbəʳ], (US) **harbor** N
porto ▶ VT (*hope etc*) abrigar; (*hide*)
esconder
hard [hɑːd] ADJ duro; (*difficult*)
difícil; (*work*) árduo; (*person*) severo,
cruel; (*facts*) verdadeiro ▶ ADV (*work*)
muito, diligentemente; (*think, try*)
seriamente; **to look ~ at** olhar
firme *or* fixamente para; **no ~
feelings!** sem ressentimentos!; **to
be ~ of hearing** ser surdo; **to be ~
done by** ser tratado injustamente;
hardback N livro de capa dura;
hard disk N (*Comput*) disco rígido;
hard drive N (*Comput*) disco rígido;
harden VT endurecer; (*steel*)
temperar; (*fig*) tornar insensível ▶ VI
endurecer-se
hardly ['hɑːdlɪ] ADV (*scarcely*)
apenas; (*no sooner*) mal; **~ ever**
quase nunca
hardship ['hɑːdʃɪp] N privação *f*
hardware ['hɑːdwɛəʳ] N ferragens
fpl; (*Comput*) hardware *m*
hard-working ADJ trabalhador(a);
(*student*) aplicado
hardy ['hɑːdɪ] ADJ forte; (*plant*)
resistente

hare [hɛəʳ] N lebre f
harm [hɑːm] N mal m; (*damage*)
dano ▸ VT (*person*) fazer mal a,
prejudicar; (*thing*) danificar; **out
of ~'s way** a salvo; **harmful** ADJ
prejudicial, nocivo; **harmless** ADJ
inofensivo
harmony ['hɑːmənɪ] N harmonia
harness ['hɑːnɪs] N (*for horse*)
arreios *mpl*; (*for child*) correia;
(*safety harness*) correia de
segurança ▸ VT (*horse*) arrear, pôr
arreios em; (*resources*) aproveitar
harp [hɑːp] N harpa ▸ VI: **to ~ on
about** bater sempre na mesma
tecla sobre
harsh [hɑːʃ] ADJ (*life*) duro
harvest ['hɑːvɪst] N colheita ▸ VT
colher
has [hæz] VB *see* **have**
hash [hæʃ] N (*symbol*) sustenido;
hashtag ['hæʃtæg] N (*on Twitter*)
hashtag *f*
hasn't ['hæznt] = **has not**
hassle ['hæsl] (*inf*) N complicação *f*
haste [heɪst] N pressa; **hasten**
['heɪsn] VT acelerar ▸ VI: **to
hasten to do sth** apressar-se em
fazer algo; **hastily** ADV depressa;
hasty ADJ apressado; (*rash*)
precipitado
hat [hæt] N chapéu *m*
hatch [hætʃ] N (*Naut: also:* **~way**)
escotilha; (*also:* **service ~**)
comunicação *f* entre a cozinha e a
sala de jantar ▸ VI sair do ovo,
chocar
hate [heɪt] VT odiar, detestar ▸ N
ódio; **hatred** ['heɪtrɪd] N ódio
haul [hɔːl] VT puxar ▸ N (*of fish*)
redada; (*of stolen goods etc*)
pilhagem *f*, presa
haunt [hɔːnt] VT (*subj: ghost*)
assombrar; (: *problem, memory*)

perseguir ▸ N reduto; (*haunted
house*) casa mal-assombrada

(KEYWORD)

have [hæv] (*pt, pp* **had**) AUX VB
1 (*gen*) ter; **to have arrived/
gone/eaten/slept** ter chegado/
ido/comido/dormido; **he has
been kind/promoted** ele foi
bondoso/promovido; **having
finished** *or* **when he had
finished, he left** quando ele
terminou, foi embora
2 (*in tag questions*): **you've done it,
haven't you?** você fez isto, não
foi?; **he hasn't done it, has he?**
ele não fez isto, fez?
3 (*in short questions and answers*):
**you've made a mistake — no I
haven't/so I have** você fez um
erro — não, eu não fiz/sim, eu fiz;
**I've been there before, have
you?** eu já estive lá, e você?
▸ MODAL AUX VB (*be obliged*): **to
have (got) to do sth** ter que fazer
algo; **I haven't got** *or* **I don't have
to wear glasses** eu não preciso
usar óculos
▸ VT 1 (*possess*) ter; **he has (got)
blue eyes/dark hair** ele tem
olhos azuis/cabelo escuro
2 (*referring to meals etc*): **to have
breakfast** tomar café (BR), tomar
o pequeno almoço (PT); **to have
lunch/dinner** almoçar/jantar; **to
have a drink/a cigarette** tomar
um drinque/fumar um cigarro
3 (*receive, obtain etc*): **may I have
your address?** pode me dar seu
endereço?; **you can have it for
5 pounds** você pode levá-lo por
5 libras; **to have a baby** dar à luz
(BR), ter um nenê *or* bebê (PT)
4 (*maintain, allow*): **he will have it**

that he is right ele vai insistir que ele está certo; **I won't have it/this nonsense!** não vou aguentar isso/este absurdo!; **we can't have that** não podemos permitir isto
5: **to have sth done** mandar fazer algo; **to have one's hair cut** ir cortar o cabelo; **to have sb do sth** mandar alguém fazer algo
6 (*experience, suffer*): **to have a cold/flu** estar resfriado (BR) or constipado (PT)/com gripe; **she had her bag stolen/her arm broken** ela teve sua bolsa roubada/ela quebrou o braço; **to have an operation** fazer uma operação
7 (+ *n: take, hold etc*): **to have a swim/walk/bath/rest** ir nadar/passear/tomar um banho/descansar; **let's have a look** vamos dar uma olhada; **to have a party** fazer uma festa
8 (*inf: dupe*): **he's been had** ele comprou gato por lebre
have out VT: **to have it out with sb** (*settle a problem*) explicar-se com alguém

haven ['heɪvn] N porto; (*fig*) abrigo, refúgio
haven't ['hævnt] = **have not**
havoc ['hævək] N destruição f; **to play ~ with** (*fig*) estragar
hawk [hɔːk] N falcão m
hay [heɪ] N feno; **hay fever** N febre f do feno; **haystack** N palheiro
hazard ['hæzəd] N perigo, risco ▶ VT aventurar, arriscar; **hazard warning lights** NPL (*Aut*) pisca-alerta m
haze [heɪz] N névoa
hazelnut ['heɪzlnʌt] N avelã f
hazy ['heɪzɪ] ADJ nublado; (*idea*) confuso

he [hiː] PRON ele; **he who ...** quem ..., aquele que ...
head [hɛd] N cabeça; (*of table*) cabeceira; (*of queue*) frente f; (*of organization*) chefe m/f; (*of school*) diretor(a) m/f ▶ VT (*list*) encabeçar; (*group*) liderar; **~s or tails** cara ou coroa; **~ first** de cabeça; **~ over heels** de pernas para o ar; **~ over heels in love** apaixonadíssimo; **to ~ the ball** cabecear a bola; **head for** VT FUS dirigir-se a; (*disaster*) estar procurando; **headache** N dor f de cabeça; **heading** N título, cabeçalho; **headlamp** (BRIT) N = **headlight**; **headlight** N farol m; **headline** N manchete f; **head office** N matriz f; **headphones** NPL fones mpl de ouvido; **headquarters** NPL sede f; (*Mil*) quartel m general; **headroom** N (*in car*) espaço (para a cabeça); (*under bridge*) vão m livre; **headscarf** irreg N lenço de cabeça
heal [hiːl] VT curar ▶ VI cicatrizar
health [hɛlθ] N saúde f; **good ~!** saúde!; **health care** N assistência médica; **healthy** ADJ (*person*) saudável; (*air, walk*) sadio; (*economy*) próspero, forte
heap [hiːp] N pilha, montão m ▶ VT (*plate*) encher; **~s (of)** (*inf*) um monte (de)
hear [hɪəʳ] (*pt, pp heard*) VT ouvir; (*listen to*) escutar; (*news*) saber; **to ~ about** ouvir falar de; **to ~ from sb** ter notícias de alguém; **hearing** N (*sense*) audição f; (*Jur*) audiência; **hearing aid** N aparelho para a surdez
hearse [həːs] N carro fúnebre
heart [hɑːt] N coração m; (*of problem, city*) centro; **hearts** NPL (*Cards*) copas fpl; **to lose/take ~**

perder o ânimo/criar coragem;
at ~ no fundo; **by ~** (*learn, know*)
de cor; **heart attack** N ataque m
de coração; **heartbeat** N batida
do coração; **heartbroken** ADJ: **to
be heartbroken** estar
inconsolável; **heartburn** N azia

hearty ['hɑːtɪ] ADJ (*person*)
energético; (*laugh*) animado;
(*appetite*) bom/boa; (*welcome*)
sincero; (*dislike*) absoluto

heat [hiːt] N calor m; (*excitement*)
ardor m; (*Sport: also:* **qualifying ~**)
(*prova*) eliminatória ▶ VT
esquentar; (*room, house*) aquecer;
heat up VI aquecer-se, esquentar
▶ VT esquentar; **heated** ADJ
aquecido; (*fig*) acalorado; **heater**
N aquecedor m

heather ['hɛðə] N urze f

heating ['hiːtɪŋ] N aquecimento,
calefação f

heaven ['hɛvn] N céu m, paraíso;
heavenly ADJ celestial; (*Rel*) divino

heavily ['hɛvɪlɪ] ADV
pesadamente; (*drink, smoke*)
excessivamente; (*sleep, depend*)
profundamente

heavy ['hɛvɪ] ADJ pesado; (*work*)
duro; (*responsibility*) grande; (*rain,
meal*) forte; (*drinker, smoker*)
inveterado; (*weather*) carregado

Hebrew ['hiːbruː] ADJ hebreu/
hebreia ▶ N (*Ling*) hebraico

Hebrides ['hɛbrɪdiːz] NPL: **the ~**
as (ilhas) Hébridas

hectic ['hɛktɪk] ADJ agitado

he'd [hiːd] **= he would; = he had**

hedge [hɛdʒ] N cerca viva, sebe f
▶ VI dar evasivas ▶ VT: **to ~ one's
bets** (*fig*) resguardar-se

hedgehog ['hɛdʒhɔg] N ouriço

heed [hiːd] VT (*also:* **take ~ of**)
prestar atenção a

heel [hiːl] N (*of shoe*) salto; (*of foot*)
calcanhar m ▶ VT (*shoe*) pôr salto
em

hefty ['hɛftɪ] ADJ (*person*) robusto;
(*parcel*) pesado; (*profit*) alto

height [haɪt] N (*of person*)
estatura; (*of building, tree*) altura;
(*of plane*) altitude f; (*high ground*)
monte m; (*fig: of power*) auge m;
(*: of luxury*) máximo; (*: of stupidity*)
cúmulo; **heighten** VT elevar; (*fig*)
aumentar

heir [ɛə] N herdeiro; **heiress** N
herdeira

held [hɛld] PT, PP *of* **hold**

helicopter ['hɛlɪkɔptə] N
helicóptero

hell [hɛl] N inferno; **~!** (*inf*) droga!

he'll [hiːl] **= he will; = he shall**

hello [hə'ləu] EXCL oi! (*BR*), olá!
(*PT*); (*surprise*) ora essa!

helmet ['hɛlmɪt] N capacete m

help [hɛlp] N ajuda; (*charwoman*)
faxineira ▶ VT ajudar; **~!** socorro!;
~ yourself sirva-se; **he can't ~ it**
não tem culpa; **help desk** N
atendimento telefônico; **helper** N
ajudante m/f; **helpful** ADJ
prestativo; (*advice*) útil; **helping** N
porção f; **helpless** ADJ (*incapable*)
incapaz; (*defenceless*) indefeso;
helpline N disque-ajuda m (*BR*),
linha de apoio (*PT*)

hem [hɛm] N bainha ▶ VT
embainhar; **hem in** VT cercar,
encurralar

hemorrhage ['hɛmərɪdʒ] (*US*) N
= haemorrhage

hemorrhoids ['hɛmərɔɪdz] (*US*)
NPL **= haemorrhoids**

hen [hɛn] N galinha; (*female bird*)
fêmea

hence [hɛns] ADV daí, portanto;
2 years ~ daqui a 2 anos

her [hə:ʳ] PRON (*direct*) a; (*indirect*)
lhe; (*stressed, after prep*) ela ▶ ADJ
seu/sua, dela; *see also* **me, my**

herb [hə:b] N erva

herd [hə:d] N rebanho

here [hɪəʳ] ADV aqui; (*at this point*)
nesse ponto; **~!** (*present*) presente!;
~ is/are aqui está/estão; **~ he/she
is!** aqui está ele/ela!

heritage ['hɛrɪtɪdʒ] N patrimônio

hernia ['hə:nɪə] N hérnia

hero ['hɪərəu] (*pl* **heroes**) N herói *m*;
(*of book, film*) protagonista *m*

heroin ['hɛrəuɪn] N heroína

heroine ['hɛrəuɪn] N heroína;
(*of book, film*) protagonista

heron ['hɛrən] N garça

herring ['hɛrɪŋ] (*pl* **herrings** *or*
herring) N arenque *m*

hers [hə:z] PRON (o) seu/(a) sua,
(o/a) dela; *see also* **mine¹**

herself [hə:'sɛlf] PRON (*reflexive*) se;
(*emphatic*) ela mesma; (*after prep*) si
(mesma); *see also* **oneself**

he's [hi:z] = **he is**; = **he has**

hesitant ['hɛzɪtənt] ADJ hesitante,
indeciso

hesitate ['hɛzɪteɪt] VI hesitar;
hesitation [hɛzɪ'teɪʃən] N
hesitação *f*, indecisão *f*

heterosexual ['hɛtərəu'sɛksjuəl]
ADJ heterossexual

heyday ['heɪdeɪ] N: **the ~ of** o auge
or apogeu de

hi [haɪ] EXCL oi!

hibernate ['haɪbəneɪt] VI hibernar

hiccup ['hɪkʌp] VI soluçar ▶ NPL: **~s**
soluço; **to have (the) ~s** estar com
soluço

hide [haɪd] (*pt* **hid**, *pp* **hidden**) N
(*skin*) pele *f* ▶ VT esconder, ocultar;
(*view*) obscurecer ▶ VI: **to ~ (from
sb)** esconder-se *or* ocultar-se (de
alguém)

hideous ['hɪdɪəs] ADJ horrível

hiding ['haɪdɪŋ] N (*beating*) surra;
to be in ~ (*concealed*) estar
escondido

hi-fi ['haɪfaɪ] N alta-fidelidade *f*;
(*system*) som *m* ▶ ADJ de
alta-fidelidade

high [haɪ] ADJ alto; (*number*) grande;
(*price*) alto, elevado; (*wind*) forte;
(*voice*) agudo; (*opinion*) ótimo;
(*principles*) nobre ▶ ADV alto, a
grande altura; **it is 20 m ~** tem
20 m de altura; **~ in the air** nas
alturas; **highchair** N cadeira alta
(para criança); **higher education** N
ensino superior; **high jump** N
(*Sport*) salto em altura; **highlands**
NPL: **the Highlands** (*in Scotland*)
a Alta Escócia; **highlight** N (*fig*)
ponto alto; (*in hair*) mecha ▶ VT
realçar, ressaltar; **highly** ADV:
highly paid muito bem pago;
to speak highly of falar
elogiosamente de; **high-rise** ADJ
alto; **high school** N (*BRIT*) escola
secundária; (*US*) científico

> Uma **high school** é um
> estabelecimento de ensino
> secundário. Nos Estados
> Unidos, existem uma *Junior High
> School*, que equivale
> aproximadamente aos dois
> últimos anos do primeiro grau,
> e a *Senior High School*, que
> corresponde ao segundo grau.
> Na Grã-Bretanha, esse termo às
> vezes é utilizado para as escolas
> secundárias.

high street (*BRIT*) N rua principal

highway (*US*) N estrada; (*main road*)
rodovia

hijack ['haɪdʒæk] VT sequestrar;
hijacker N sequestrador(a) *m/f* (de
avião)

hike [haɪk] vi caminhar ▶ N caminhada, excursão f a pé; **hiker** N caminhante m/f, andarilho(-a)

hilarious [hɪˈlɛərɪəs] ADJ hilariante

hill [hɪl] N colina; (high) montanha; (slope) ladeira, rampa; **hillside** N vertente f; **hilly** ADJ montanhoso

him [hɪm] PRON (direct) o; (indirect) lhe; (stressed, after prep) ele; see also **me**; **himself** PRON (reflexive) se; (emphatic) ele mesmo; (after prep) si (mesmo); see also **oneself**

hinder [ˈhɪndər] vt retardar

hindsight [ˈhaɪndsaɪt] N: **with (the benefit of) ~** em retrospecto

Hindu [ˈhɪnduː] ADJ hindu

hinge [hɪndʒ] N dobradiça ▶ vi (fig): **to ~ on** depender de

hint [hɪnt] N (suggestion) indireta; (advice) dica; (sign) sinal m ▶ vt: **to ~ that** insinuar que ▶ vi: **to ~ at** fazer alusão a

hip [hɪp] N quadril m

hippopotamus [hɪpəˈpotəməs] (pl **hippopotamuses** or **hippopotami**) N hipopótamo

hire [ˈhaɪər] vt (BRIT: car, equipment) alugar; (worker) contratar ▶ N aluguel m; **for ~** aluga-se; (taxi) livre; **hire purchase** (BRIT) N compra a prazo

his [hɪz] PRON (o) seu/(a) sua, (o/a) dele ▶ ADJ seu/sua, dele; see also **my, mine¹**

hiss [hɪs] vi (snake, fat) assoviar; (gas) silvar; (boo) vaiar

historic [hɪˈstɔrɪk], **historical** [hɪˈstɔrɪkl] ADJ histórico

history [ˈhɪstərɪ] N história

hit [hɪt] (pt, pp **hit**) vt bater em; (target) acertar, alcançar; (car) bater em, colidir com; (fig: affect) atingir ▶ N golpe m; (success) sucesso; (internet visit) visita; **to ~ it off with sb** dar-se bem com alguém

hitch [hɪtʃ] vt (fasten) atar, amarrar; (also: ~ up) levantar ▶ N (difficulty) dificuldade f; **to ~ a lift** pegar carona (BR), arranjar uma boleia (PT)

hitch-hike vi pegar carona (BR), andar à boleia (PT); **hitch-hiker** N carona m/f (BR), viajante m/f à boleia (PT)

hi-tech ADJ tecnologicamente avançado ▶ N alta tecnologia

HIV ABBR: **~-negative/-positive** HIV negativo/positivo

hive [haɪv] N colmeia; **hive off** (inf) vt transferir

hoard [hɔːd] N provisão f; (of money) tesouro ▶ vt acumular

hoarse [hɔːs] ADJ rouco

hoax [həuks] N trote m

hob [hɔb] N parte de cima do fogão

hobble [ˈhɔbl] vi coxear

hobby [ˈhɔbɪ] N hobby m, passatempo predileto

hobo [ˈhəubəu] (US) N vagabundo

hockey [ˈhɔkɪ] N hóquei m

hog [hɔg] N porco ▶ vt (fig) monopolizar; **to go the whole ~** ir até o fim

hoist [hɔɪst] vt içar

hold [həuld] (pt, pp **held**) vt segurar; (contain) conter; (have) ter; (meeting) realizar; (detain) deter; (consider): **to ~ sb responsible (for sth)** responsabilizar alguém (por algo) ▶ vi (withstand pressure) resistir; (be valid) ser válido ▶ N (fig) influência, domínio; (of ship) porão m; (of plane) compartimento para cargo; **~ the line!** (Tel) não desligue!; **to ~ one's own** (fig) virar-se, sair-se

h

bem; **to catch** or **get (a) ~ of** agarrar, pegar; **hold back** VT reter; (secret) manter, guardar; **hold down** VT (person) segurar; (job) manter; **hold off** VT (enemy) afastar, repelir; **hold on** VI agarrar-se; (wait) esperar; **~ on!** espera aí!; (Tel) não desligue!; **hold on to** VT FUS agarrar-se a; (keep) guardar, ficar com; **hold out** VT estender ▸ VI (resist) resistir; **hold up** VT (raise) levantar; (support) apoiar; (delay) atrasar; (rob) assaltar; **holdall** (BRIT) N bolsa de viagem; **holder** N (of ticket) portador(a) m/f; (of record) detentor(a) m/f; (of office, title etc) titular m/f; **hold-up** N (robbery) assalto; (delay) demora; (BRIT: in traffic) engarrafamento

hole [həul] N buraco; (small, in sock etc) furo ▸ VT esburacar

holiday ['hɔlədɪ] N (BRIT: vacation) férias fpl; (day off) dia m de folga; (public holiday) feriado; **to be on ~** estar de férias; **holiday camp** (BRIT) N colônia de férias; **holiday-maker** (BRIT) N pessoa (que está) de férias; **holiday resort** N local m de férias

Holland ['hɔlənd] N Holanda

hollow ['hɔləu] ADJ oco, vazio; (cheeks) côncavo; (eyes) fundo; (sound) surdo; (laugh, claim) falso ▸ N (in ground) cavidade f, depressão f ▸ VT: **to ~ out** escavar

holly ['hɔlɪ] N azevinho

holy ['həulɪ] ADJ sagrado; (person) santo; bento

home [həum] N casa, lar m; (country) pátria; (institution) asilo ▸ CPD caseiro, doméstico; (Econ, Pol) nacional, interno; (Sport: team) de casa; (: game) no próprio campo ▸ ADV (direction) para casa; (right in: nail etc) até o fundo; **at ~** em casa;

make yourself at ~ fique à vontade; **home address** N endereço residencial; **homeland** N terra (natal); **homeless** ADJ sem casa, desabrigado; **homely** ADJ (simple) simples inv; **home-made** ADJ caseiro; **Home Office** (BRIT) N Ministério do Interior; **home page** N (Comput) página inicial; **Home Secretary** (BRIT) N Ministro(a) do Interior; **homesick** ADJ: **to be homesick** estar com saudades (do lar); **home town** N cidade f natal; **homework** N dever m de casa

homoeopathic [həumɪə'pæθɪk], (US) **homeopathic** ADJ homeopático

homosexual [hɔməu'sɛksjuəl] ADJ, N homossexual m/f

Honduras [hɔn'djuərəs] N Honduras m (no article)

honest ['ɔnɪst] ADJ (truthful) franco; (trustworthy) honesto; (sincere) sincero; **honestly** ADV honestamente; **honesty** N honestidade f, sinceridade f

honey ['hʌnɪ] N mel m; **honeymoon** N lua-de-mel f; (trip) viagem f de lua-de-mel

honorary ['ɔnərərɪ] ADJ (unpaid) não remunerado; (duty, title) honorário

honour ['ɔnər], (US) **honor** VT honrar ▸ N honra; **honourable** ADJ honrado

hood [hud] N capuz m; (of cooker) tampa; (BRIT Aut) capota; (US Aut) capô m

hoof [hu:f] (pl **hooves**) N casco, pata

hook [huk] N gancho; (on dress) colchete m; (for fishing) anzol m ▸ VT prender com gancho (or colchete); (fish) fisgar

hooligan ['huːlɪgən] N
desordeiro(-a), bagunceiro(-a)
hoop [huːp] N arco
hooray [huː'reɪ] EXCL = **hurrah**
hoot [huːt] VI (Aut) buzinar; (siren)
tocar; (owl) piar
hooves [huːvz] NPL of **hoof**
hop [hɔp] VI saltar, pular; (on one
foot) pular num pé só
hope [həup] VI esperar ▶ N
esperança; **I ~ so/not** espero que
sim/não; **hopeful** ADJ (person)
otimista, esperançoso; (situation)
promissor; **hopefully** ADV
esperançosamente; **hopefully,
they'll come back** é de esperar or
esperamos que voltem; **hopeless**
ADJ desesperado, irremediável;
(useless) inútil
horizon [hə'raɪzn] N horizonte m;
horizontal [hɔrɪ'zɔntl] ADJ
horizontal
horn [hɔːn] N corno, chifre m;
(material) chifre; (Mus) trompa;
(Aut) buzina
horoscope ['hɔrəskəup] N
horóscopo
horrendous [hə'rɛndəs] ADJ
horrendo
horrible ['hɔrɪbl] ADJ horrível;
(terrifying) terrível
horrid ['hɔrɪd] ADJ horrível
horror ['hɔrəʳ] N horror m; **horror
film** N filme m de terror
horse [hɔːs] N cavalo;
horseback: on horseback ADJ,
ADV a cavalo; **horse chestnut** N
castanha-da-índia;
horsepower N cavalo-vapor m;
horse-racing N corridas fpl de
cavalo, turfe m
hose [həuz] N (also: **~pipe**)
mangueira
hospital ['hɔspɪtl] N hospital m

hospitality [hɔspɪ'tælɪtɪ] N
hospitalidade f
host [həust] N anfitrião m; (TV,
Radio) apresentador(a) m/f; (Rel)
hóstia; (large number): **a ~ of** uma
multidão de
hostage ['hɔstɪdʒ] N refém m/f
hostel ['hɔstl] N albergue m,
abrigo; (also: **youth ~**) albergue da
juventude
hostess ['həustɪs] N anfitriã f;
(BRIT: air hostess) aeromoça (BR),
hospedeira de bordo (PT); (TV,
Radio) apresentadora
hostile ['hɔstaɪl] ADJ hostil
hostility [hɔ'stɪlɪtɪ] N hostilidade f
hot [hɔt] ADJ quente; (as opposed to
only warm) muito quente; (spicy)
picante; (fierce) ardente; **to be ~**
(person) estar com calor; (thing,
weather) estar quente; **hot dog** N
cachorro-quente m
hotel [həu'tɛl] N hotel m
hotspot ['hɔtspɔt] N (Comput:
also: **wireless ~**) hotspot m (local
público com acesso à Internet sem fio)
hound [haund] VT acossar,
perseguir ▶ N cão m de caça,
sabujo
hour ['auəʳ] N hora; **hourly** ADJ de
hora em hora; (rate) por hora
house [n haus, vt hauz] N (gen,
firm) casa; (Pol) câmara; (Theatre)
assistência, lotação f ▶ VT (person)
alojar; (collection) abrigar; **on the
~** (fig) por conta da casa;
household N família; (house) casa;
housekeeper N governanta;
housekeeping N (work) trabalhos
mpl domésticos; (money) economia
doméstica; **housewife** irreg N
dona de casa; **housework** N
trabalhos mpl domésticos;
housing N (provision) alojamento;

(*houses*) residências *fpl*; **housing development** N conjunto residencial; **housing estate** (*BRIT*) N = **housing development**
hover ['hɔvəʳ] VI pairar; **hovercraft** N aerobarco

(KEYWORD)

how [hau] ADV **1** (*in what way*) como; **how was the film?** que tal o filme?; **how are you?** como vai? **2** (*to what degree*) quanto; **how much milk/many people?** quanto de leite/quantas pessoas?; **how long have you been here?** há quanto tempo você está aqui?; **how old are you?** quantos anos você tem?; **how tall is he?** qual é a altura dele?; **how lovely/awful!** que ótimo/terrível!

however [hau'ɛvəʳ] ADV de qualquer modo; (+ *adj*) por mais … que; (*in questions*) como ▶ CONJ no entanto, contudo
howl [haul] VI uivar
H.P. (*BRIT*) N ABBR = **hire purchase**
h.p. ABBR (*Aut*: = *horsepower*) CV
HQ N ABBR (= *headquarters*) QG *m*
HTML N ABBR (= *Hypertext Mark-up Language*) HTML *f*
huddle ['hʌdl] VI: **to ~ together** aconchegar-se
huff [hʌf] N: **in a ~** com raiva
hug [hʌg] VT abraçar; (*thing*) agarrar, prender
huge [hju:dʒ] ADJ enorme, imenso
hull [hʌl] N (*of ship*) casco
hum [hʌm] VT cantarolar ▶ VI cantarolar; (*insect, machine etc*) zumbir
human ['hju:mən] ADJ humano ▶ N (*also*: **~ being**) ser *m* humano
humane [hju:'meɪn] ADJ humano

humanitarian [hju:mænɪ'tɛərɪən] ADJ humanitário
humanity [hju:'mænɪtɪ] N humanidade *f*
human rights NPL direitos *mpl* humanos
humble ['hʌmbl] ADJ humilde ▶ VT humilhar
humid ['hju:mɪd] ADJ úmido
humiliate [hju:'mɪlɪeɪt] VT humilhar
humorous ['hju:mərəs] ADJ humorístico; (*person*) engraçado
humour ['hju:məʳ], (*US*) **humor** N humorismo, senso de humor; (*mood*) humor *m* ▶ VT fazer a vontade de
hump [hʌmp] N (*in ground*) elevação *f*; (*camel's*) corcova, giba; (*deformity*) corcunda
hunch [hʌntʃ] N (*premonition*) pressentimento, palpite *m*
hundred ['hʌndrəd] NUM cem; (*before lower numbers*) cento; **~s of people** centenas de pessoas; **hundredth** NUM centésimo
hung [hʌŋ] PT, PP of **hang**
Hungary ['hʌŋgərɪ] N Hungria
hunger ['hʌŋgəʳ] N fome *f* ▶ VI: **to ~ for** (*desire*) desejar ardentemente
hungry ['hʌŋgrɪ] ADJ faminto, esfomeado; (*keen*): **~ for** (*fig*) ávido de, ansioso por; **to be ~** estar com fome
hunt [hʌnt] VT buscar, perseguir; (*Sport*) caçar ▶ VI caçar ▶ N caça, caçada; **hunter** N caçador(a) *m/f*; **hunting** N caça
hurdle ['hə:dl] N (*Sport*) barreira; (*fig*) obstáculo
hurl [hə:l] VT arremessar, lançar; (*abuse*) gritar
hurrah [hu'rɑ:] EXCL oba!, viva!

hurray [hu'reɪ] EXCL = **hurrah**
hurricane ['hʌrɪkən] N furacão m
hurry ['hʌrɪ] N pressa ▶ VI (also:
~ **up**) apressar-se ▶ VT (also: ~ **up**:
person) apressar; (: work) acelerar;
to be in a ~ estar com pressa
hurt [həːt] (pt, pp **hurt**) VT
machucar; (injure) ferir; (fig)
magoar ▶ VI doer
husband ['hʌzbənd] N marido,
esposo
hush [hʌʃ] N silêncio, quietude f
▶ VT silenciar, fazer calar; ~**!**
silêncio!, psiu!; **hush up** VT abafar,
encobrir
husky ['hʌskɪ] ADJ rouco ▶ N cão m
esquimó
hut [hʌt] N cabana, choupana;
(shed) alpendre m
hyacinth ['haɪəsɪnθ] N jacinto
hydrofoil ['haɪdrəfɔɪl] N
hidrofoil m, aliscafo
hydrogen ['haɪdrədʒən] N
hidrogênio
hygiene ['haɪdʒiːn] N higiene f
hymn [hɪm] N hino
hype [haɪp] (inf) N tititi m, falatório
hyperlink ['haɪpəlɪŋk] N
hiperlink m
hypermarket ['haɪpəmɑːkɪt]
(BRIT) N hipermercado
hyphen ['haɪfn] N hífen m
hypnotize ['hɪpnətaɪz] VT
hipnotizar
hypocrite ['hɪpəkrɪt] N hipócrita
m/f; **hypocritical** ADJ hipócrita
hysterical [hɪ'stɛrɪkl] ADJ
histérico; (funny) hilariante;
hysterics NPL (nervous) crise f
histérica; (laughter) ataque m de
riso; **to be in** or **have hysterics**
ter uma crise histérica

I [aɪ] PRON eu ▶ ABBR (= island, isle) I
ice [aɪs] N gelo; (ice cream) sorvete
m ▶ VT (cake) cobrir com glacê ▶ VI
(also: ~ **over**, ~ **up**) gelar; **iceberg**
N iceberg m; **ice cream** N sorvete
m (BR), gelado (PT); **ice cube** N
pedra de gelo; **ice hockey** N
hóquei m sobre o gelo
Iceland ['aɪslənd] N Islândia
ice lolly (BRIT) N picolé m
ice rink N pista de gelo, rinque m
icing ['aɪsɪŋ] N (Culin) glacê m;
icing sugar (BRIT) N açúcar m glacê
icon ['aɪkɒn] N (gen, Comput)
ícone m
ICT N ABBR (= Information and
Communication(s) Technology) TIC f
icy ['aɪsɪ] ADJ gelado
I'd [aɪd] = **I would**; = **I had**
idea [aɪ'dɪə] N ideia
ideal [aɪ'dɪəl] N ideal m ▶ ADJ ideal
identical [aɪ'dɛntɪkl] ADJ idêntico
identification [aɪdɛntɪfɪ'keɪʃən]
N identificação f; **means of ~**
documentos pessoais

identify [aɪ'dɛntɪfaɪ] VT identificar
identity [aɪ'dɛntɪtɪ] N identidade f;
identity card N carteira de
identidade; **identity theft** N roubo
de identidade
idiom ['ɪdɪəm] N expressão f
idiomática; (*style of speaking*) idioma
m, linguagem f
idiot ['ɪdɪət] N idiota m/f
idle ['aɪdl] ADJ ocioso; (*lazy*)
preguiçoso; (*unemployed*)
desempregado; (*pointless*) inútil,
vão/vã ▶ VI (*machine*) funcionar com
a transmissão desligada; **idle away**
VT: **to ~ away the time** perder or
desperdiçar tempo
idol ['aɪdl] N ídolo
i.e. ABBR (= *id est*) i.e., isto é

(KEYWORD)

if [ɪf] CONJ **1** (*conditional use*) se;
if necessary se necessário; **if I
were you** se eu fôsse você
2 (*whenever*) quando
3 (*although*): **(even) if** mesmo que
4 (*whether*) se
5: **if so/not** sendo assim/do
contrário; **if only** se pelo menos;
see also **as**

ignition [ɪg'nɪʃən] N (*Aut*) ignição f;
to switch on/off the ~ ligar/
desligar o motor
ignorant ['ɪgnərənt] ADJ ignorante;
to be ~ of ignorar
ignore [ɪg'nɔːʳ] VT (*person*) não fazer
caso de; (*fact*) não levar em
consideração, ignorar
ill [ɪl] ADJ doente; (*harmful: effects*)
nocivo ▶ N mal m ▶ ADV: **to speak/
think ~ of sb** falar/pensar mal de
alguém; **to take** or **be taken ~** ficar
doente
I'll [aɪl] = **I will**; = **I shall**

illegal [ɪ'liːgl] ADJ ilegal
illegible [ɪ'lɛdʒɪbl] ADJ ilegível
illegitimate [ɪlɪ'dʒɪtɪmət] ADJ
ilegítimo
illiterate [ɪ'lɪtərət] ADJ analfabeto
illness ['ɪlnɪs] N doença
illuminate [ɪ'luːmɪneɪt] VT
iluminar, clarear
illusion [ɪ'luːʒən] N ilusão f
illustrate ['ɪləstreɪt] VT ilustrar;
(*point*) exemplificar; **illustration**
[ɪlə'streɪʃən] N ilustração f;
(*example*) exemplo; (*explanation*)
esclarecimento
I'm [aɪm] = **I am**
image ['ɪmɪdʒ] N imagem f
imaginary [ɪ'mædʒɪnərɪ] ADJ
imaginário
imagination [ɪmædʒɪ'neɪʃən] N
imaginação f; (*inventiveness*)
inventividade f
imagine [ɪ'mædʒɪn] VT imaginar
imbalance [ɪm'bæləns] N
desigualdade f
imitate ['ɪmɪteɪt] VT imitar;
imitation [ɪmɪ'teɪʃən] N imitação f;
(*copy*) cópia; (*mimicry*) mímica
immaculate [ɪ'mækjulət] ADJ
impecável; (*Rel*) imaculado
immature [ɪmə'tjuəʳ] ADJ imaturo;
(*fruit*) verde
immediate [ɪ'miːdɪət] ADJ imediato;
(*pressing*) urgente, premente;
(*neighbourhood, family*) próximo;
immediately ADV imediatamente;
immediately next to bem junto a
immense [ɪ'mɛns] ADJ imenso;
(*importance*) enorme
immerse [ɪ'məːs] VT submergir;
to be ~d in (*fig*) estar absorto em
immigrant ['ɪmɪgrənt] N
imigrante m/f
immigration [ɪmɪ'greɪʃən] N
imigração f

imminent ['ɪmɪnənt] ADJ
iminente

immoral [ɪ'mɔrl] ADJ imoral

immortal [ɪ'mɔːtl] ADJ imortal

immune [ɪ'mjuːn] ADJ: **~ to**
imune a, imunizado contra;
immune system N sistema *m*
imunológico

impact ['ɪmpækt] N impacto (BR),
impacte *m* (PT)

impair [ɪm'pɛəʳ] VT prejudicar

impartial [ɪm'pɑːʃl] ADJ imparcial

impatience [ɪm'peɪʃəns] N
impaciência

impatient [ɪm'peɪʃənt] ADJ
impaciente; **to get** or **grow ~**
impacientar-se

impeccable [ɪm'pɛkəbl] ADJ
impecável

impending [ɪm'pɛndɪŋ] ADJ
iminente, próximo

imperative [ɪm'pɛrətɪv] ADJ (*tone*)
imperioso, obrigatório; (*necessary*)
indispensável ▶ N (*Ling*) imperativo

imperfect [ɪm'pə:fɪkt] ADJ
imperfeito; (*goods etc*) defeituoso
▶ N (*Ling*: *also*: **~ tense**) imperfeito

imperial [ɪm'pɪərɪəl] ADJ imperial

impersonal [ɪm'pə:sənl] ADJ
impessoal

impersonate [ɪm'pə:səneɪt] VT
fazer-se passar por, personificar;
(*Theatre*) imitar

implement [*n* 'ɪmplɪmənt, *vt*
'ɪmplɪmɛnt] N instrumento,
ferramenta; (*for cooking*) utensílio
▶ VT efetivar

implicit [ɪm'plɪsɪt] ADJ implícito;
(*complete*) absoluto

imply [ɪm'plaɪ] VT (*mean*)
significar; (*hint*) dar a entender que

impolite [ɪmpə'laɪt] ADJ
indelicado, mal-educado

import [*vt* ɪm'pɔ:t, *n, cpd* 'ɪmpɔ:t]

VT importar ▶ N importação *f*;
(*article*) mercadoria importada

importance [ɪm'pɔ:təns] N
importância

important [ɪm'pɔ:tənt] ADJ
importante; **it's not ~** não tem
importância, não importa

impose [ɪm'pəuz] VT impor ▶ VI:
to ~ on sb abusar de alguém;
imposing ADJ imponente

impossible [ɪm'pɔsɪbl] ADJ
impossível; (*situation*) inviável;
(*person*) insuportável

impotent ['ɪmpətənt] ADJ
impotente

impoverished [ɪm'pɔvərɪʃt] ADJ
empobrecido; (*land*) esgotado

impractical [ɪm'præktɪkl] ADJ
pouco prático

impress [ɪm'prɛs] VT
impressionar; (*mark*) imprimir;
to ~ sth on sb inculcar algo em
alguém

impression [ɪm'prɛʃən] N
impressão *f*; **to be under the ~
that** estar com a impressão de que

impressive [ɪm'prɛsɪv] ADJ
impressionante

imprison [ɪm'prɪzn] VT encarcerar

improbable [ɪm'prɔbəbl] ADJ
improvável; (*story*) inverossímil
(BR), inverosímil (PT)

improper [ɪm'prɔpəʳ] ADJ
(*unsuitable*) impróprio; (*dishonest*)
desonesto

improve [ɪm'pruːv] VT melhorar
▶ VI melhorar; (*pupils*) progredir;
improvement N melhora;
progresso

improvise ['ɪmprəvaɪz] VT, VI
improvisar

impulse ['ɪmpʌls] N impulso,
ímpeto; (*Elec*) impulso; **to act on
~** agir sem pensar or num impulso

(KEYWORD)

in [ɪn] PREP **1** (*indicating place, position*) em; **in the house/garden** na casa/no jardim; **I have the money in my hand** estou com o dinheiro na mão; **in here/there** aqui dentro/lá dentro
2 (*with place names: of town, country, region*) em; **in London** em Londres; **in England/Japan/Canada/the United States** na Inglaterra/no Japão/no Canadá/nos Estados Unidos; **in Rio** no Rio
3 (*indicating time: during*) em; **in spring/autumn** na primavera/no outono; **in 1988** em 1988; **in May** em maio; **I'll see you in July** até julho; **in the morning** de manhã; **at 4 o'clock in the afternoon** às 4 da tarde
4 (*indicating time: in the space of*) em; **I did it in 3 hours/days** fiz isto em 3 horas/dias; **in 2 weeks, in 2 weeks' time** daqui a 2 semanas
5 (*indicating manner etc*): **in a loud/soft voice** em voz alta/numa voz suave; **written in pencil/ink** escrito a lápis/à caneta; **in English/Portuguese** em inglês/português; **the boy in the blue shirt** o menino de camisa azul
6 (*indicating circumstances*): **in the sun** ao *or* sob o sol; **in the rain** na chuva; **a rise in prices** um aumento nos preços
7 (*indicating mood, state*): **in tears** aos prantos; **in anger/despair** com raiva/desesperado; **in good condition** em boas condições
8 (*with ratios, numbers*): **1 in 10** 1 em 10, 1 em cada 10; **20 pence in the pound** vinte pênis numa libra; **they lined up in twos** eles se alinharam dois a dois
9 (*referring to people, works*) em
10 (*indicating profession etc*): **to be in teaching/publishing** ser professor/trabalhar numa editora
11 (*after superl*): **the best pupil in the class** o melhor aluno da classe; **the biggest/smallest in Europe** o maior/menor na Europa
12 (*with present participle*): **in saying this** ao dizer isto
▶ ADV: **to be in** (*person: at home*) estar em casa; (: *at work*) estar no trabalho; (*fashion*) estar na moda; (*ship, plane, train*): **it's in** chegou; **is he in?** ele está?; **to ask sb in** convidar alguém para entrar; **to run/limp** *etc* **in** entrar correndo/mancando *etc*
▶ N: **the ins and outs** (*of proposal, situation etc*) os cantos e recantos, os pormenores

in. ABBR = **inch**
inability [ɪnə'bɪlɪtɪ] N: **~ (to do)** incapacidade *f* (de fazer)
inaccurate [ɪn'ækjurət] ADJ inexato, impreciso
inadequate [ɪn'ædɪkwət] ADJ insuficiente; (*person*) impróprio
inadvertently [ɪnəd'və:tntlɪ] ADV inadvertidamente, sem querer
inappropriate [ɪnə'prəuprɪət] ADJ inadequado; (*word, expression*) impróprio
inbox ['ɪnbɔks] N (*Comput*) caixa de entrada; (*US: for papers*) cesta para correspondência de entrada
incapable [ɪn'keɪpəbl] ADJ incapaz
incense [*n* 'ɪnsɛns, *vt* ɪn'sɛns] N incenso ▶ VT (*anger*) exasperar, enraivecer
incentive [ɪn'sɛntɪv] N incentivo
inch [ɪntʃ] N polegada (= 25 mm; 12 in a foot); **to be within an ~ of** estar a

um passo de; **he didn't give an ~**
ele não cedeu nem um milímetro;
inch forward VI avançar palmo a
palmo

incident ['ɪnsɪdnt] N incidente *m*,
evento

inclination [ɪnklɪ'neɪʃən] N
(*tendency*) tendência; (*disposition*)
inclinação *f*

incline [*n* 'ɪnklaɪn, *vt, vi* ɪn'klaɪn] N
inclinação *f*, ladeira ▶ VT curvar,
inclinar ▶ VI inclinar-se; **to be ~d
to** tender a, ser propenso a

include [ɪn'klu:d] VT incluir

including [ɪn'klu:dɪŋ] PREP
inclusive

inclusive [ɪn'klu:sɪv] ADJ incluído,
incluso; **~ of** incluindo

income ['ɪŋkʌm] N (*earnings*)
renda, rendimentos *mpl*;
(*unearned*) renda; **income tax** N
imposto de renda (BR), imposto
complementar (PT)

incoming ['ɪnkʌmɪŋ] ADJ (*flight,
passenger*) de chegada; (*mail*) de
entrada; (*government, tenant*) novo

incompetent [ɪn'kɔmpɪtənt] ADJ
incompetente

incomplete [ɪnkəm'pli:t] ADJ
incompleto; (*unfinished*) por
terminar

inconsistent [ɪnkən'sɪstnt] ADJ
inconsistente; **~ with**
incompatível com

inconvenience [ɪnkən'vi:njəns]
N (*quality*) inconveniência;
(*problem*) inconveniente *m* ▶ VT
incomodar

inconvenient [ɪnkən'vi:njənt]
ADJ inconveniente, incômodo;
(*time, place*) inoportuno

incorporate [ɪn'kɔ:pəreɪt] VT
incorporar; (*contain*) compreender

incorrect [ɪnkə'rɛkt] ADJ incorreto

increase [*n* 'ɪnkri:s, *vi, vt* ɪn'kri:s]
N aumento ▶ VI, VT aumentar

incredible [ɪn'krɛdɪbl] ADJ
inacreditável; (*enormous*) incrível

incur [ɪn'kə:ʳ] VT incorrer em;
(*expenses*) contrair

indecent [ɪn'di:snt] ADJ indecente

indeed [ɪn'di:d] ADV de fato;
(*certainly*) certamente;
(*furthermore*) aliás; **yes ~!** claro que
sim!

indefinitely [ɪn'dɛfɪnɪtlɪ] ADV
indefinidamente

independence [ɪndɪ'pɛndns] N
independência; **Independence
Day** N *ver nota*

O dia da Independência
Independence Day é a festa
nacional dos Estados Unidos.
Todo dia 4 de julho os
americanos comemoram a
adoção, em 1776, da declaração
de Independência escrita por
Thomas Jefferson que
proclamava a separação das 13
colônias americanas da
Grã-Bretanha.

independent [ɪndɪ'pɛndnt] ADJ
independente; (*inquiry*) imparcial

index ['ɪndɛks] N (*pl* **indexes**) (*in
book*) índice *m*; (*in library etc*)
catálogo; (*pl* **indices**) (*ratio, sign*)
índice *m*, expoente *m*

India ['ɪndɪə] N Índia; **Indian** ADJ, N
(*from India*) indiano(-a); (*American,
Brazilian*) índio(-a)

indicate ['ɪndɪkeɪt] VT (*show*)
sugerir; (*point to*) indicar;
indication [ɪndɪ'keɪʃən] N indício,
sinal *m*; **indicative** [ɪn'dɪkətɪv] ADJ
indicativo ▶ N (*Ling*) indicativo; **to
be indicative of sth** ser
sintomático de algo; **indicator** N
indicador *m*; (*Aut*) pisca-pisca *m*

indices ['ɪndɪsi:z] NPL *of* **index**
indifferent [ɪn'dɪfrənt] ADJ
indiferente; *(quality)* medíocre
indigenous [ɪn'dɪdʒɪnəs] ADJ
indígena, nativo
indigestion [ɪndɪ'dʒɛstʃən] N
indigestão *f*
indignant [ɪn'dɪgnənt] ADJ: **to be
~ about sth/with sb** estar
indignado com algo/alguém,
indignar-se de algo/alguém
indirect [ɪndɪ'rɛkt] ADJ indireto
individual [ɪndɪ'vɪdjuəl] N
indivíduo ▶ ADJ individual; *(personal)*
pessoal; *(characteristic)* particular
Indonesia [ɪndə'ni:zɪə] N
Indonésia
indoor ['ɪndɔːʳ] ADJ *(inner)* interno,
interior; *(inside)* dentro de casa;
(swimming pool) coberto; *(games,
sport)* de salão; **indoors** ADV em
lugar fechado
induce [ɪn'dju:s] VT *(Med)* induzir;
(bring about) causar, produzir
indulge [ɪn'dʌldʒ] VT *(desire)*
satisfazer; *(whim)* condescender
com; *(person)* comprazer; *(child)*
fazer a vontade de ▶ VI: **to ~ in**
entregar-se a, satisfazer-se com;
indulgent ADJ indulgente
industrial [ɪn'dʌstrɪəl] ADJ industrial
industry ['ɪndəstrɪ] N indústria;
(diligence) aplicação *f*, diligência
inefficient [ɪnɪ'fɪʃənt] ADJ
ineficiente
inequality [ɪnɪ'kwɔlɪtɪ] N
desigualdade *f*
inevitable [ɪn'ɛvɪtəbl] ADJ
inevitável; **inevitably** ADV
inevitavelmente
inexpensive [ɪnɪk'spɛnsɪv] ADJ
barato, econômico
inexperienced [ɪnɪk'spɪərɪənst]
ADJ inexperiente

infamous ['ɪnfəməs] ADJ infame,
abominável
infant ['ɪnfənt] N *(baby)* bebê *m*;
(young child) criança
infant school (BRIT) N pré-escola
infect [ɪn'fɛkt] VT *(person)*
contagiar; *(food)* contaminar;
infection N infecção *f*; **infectious**
ADJ contagioso; *(fig)* infeccioso
infer [ɪn'fəːʳ] VT deduzir, inferir
inferior [ɪn'fɪərɪəʳ] ADJ inferior;
(goods) de qualidade inferior ▶ N
inferior *m/f*; *(in rank)* subalterno(-a)
infertile [ɪn'fəːtaɪl] ADJ infértil;
(person, animal) estéril
infinite ['ɪnfɪnɪt] ADJ infinito
infirmary [ɪn'fəːmərɪ] N
enfermaria, hospital *m*
inflamed [ɪn'fleɪmd] ADJ inflamado
inflammation [ɪnflə'meɪʃən] N
inflamação *f*
inflatable [ɪn'fleɪtəbl] ADJ inflável
inflate [ɪn'fleɪt] VT *(tyre, balloon)*
inflar, encher; *(price)* inflar;
inflation N *(Econ)* inflação *f*
inflict [ɪn'flɪkt] VT: **to ~ sth on sb**
infligir algo em alguém
influence ['ɪnfluəns] N influência
▶ VT influir em, influenciar; **under
the ~ of alcohol** sob o efeito do
álcool; **influential** [ɪnflu'ɛnʃl] ADJ
influente
influenza [ɪnflu'ɛnzə] N gripe *f*
inform [ɪn'fɔːm] VT: **to ~ sb of sth**
informar alguém de algo ▶ VI: **to ~
on sb** delatar alguém
informal [ɪn'fɔːml] ADJ informal;
(visit, discussion) extraoficial
information [ɪnfə'meɪʃən] N
informação *f*, informações *fpl*;
(knowledge) conhecimento; **a piece
of ~** uma informação
informative [ɪn'fɔːmətɪv] ADJ
informativo

infuriating [ɪnˈfjuərɪeɪtɪŋ] ADJ de dar raiva, enfurecedor(a)

ingenious [ɪnˈdʒiːnjəs] ADJ engenhoso

ingredient [ɪnˈgriːdɪənt] N ingrediente m; (of situation) fator m

inhabit [ɪnˈhæbɪt] VT habitar; **inhabitant** N habitante m/f

inhale [ɪnˈheɪl] VT inalar ▶ VI (in smoking) tragar; **inhaler** [ɪnˈheɪləʳ] N inalador m

inherent [ɪnˈhɪərənt] ADJ: ~ **in** or **to** inerente a

inherit [ɪnˈhɛrɪt] VT herdar; **inheritance** N herança

inhibit [ɪnˈhɪbɪt] VT inibir; **inhibition** [ɪnhɪˈbɪʃən] N inibição f

initial [ɪˈnɪʃl] ADJ inicial ▶ N inicial f ▶ VT marcar com iniciais; **initials** NPL (of name) iniciais fpl; **initially** ADV inicialmente, no início

initiate [ɪˈnɪʃɪeɪt] VT (start) iniciar, começar; (person) iniciar; **to ~ sb into a secret** revelar um segredo a alguém; **to ~ proceedings against sb** (Jur) abrir um processo contra alguém

initiative [ɪˈnɪʃətɪv] N iniciativa

inject [ɪnˈdʒɛkt] VT (liquid, fig: money) injetar; (person) dar uma injeção em; **injection** N injeção f

injure [ˈɪndʒəʳ] VT ferir; (reputation etc) prejudicar; (offend) ofender; **injured** ADJ ferido; (feelings) ofendido, magoado; **injury** N ferida

injustice [ɪnˈdʒʌstɪs] N injustiça

ink [ɪŋk] N tinta

inland [adj ˈɪnlənd, adv ɪnˈlænd] ADJ interior, interno ▶ ADV para o interior; **Inland Revenue** (BRIT) N ≈ fisco, ≈ receita federal (BR)

inmate [ˈɪnmeɪt] N (in prison) presidiário(-a); (in asylum) internado(-a)

inn [ɪn] N hospedaria, taberna

inner [ˈɪnəʳ] ADJ (place) interno; (feeling) interior; **inner city** N aglomeração f urbana, metrópole f

innocent [ˈɪnəsnt] ADJ inocente

in-patient N paciente m/f interno(-a)

input [ˈɪnput] N entrada; (resources) investimento

inquest [ˈɪnkwɛst] N inquérito judicial

inquire [ɪnˈkwaɪəʳ] VI pedir informação ▶ VT perguntar; **inquire into** VT FUS investigar, indagar; **inquiry** N pergunta; (Jur) investigação f, inquérito

ins. ABBR = **inches**

insane [ɪnˈseɪn] ADJ louco, doido; (Med) demente, insano; **insanity** [ɪnˈsænɪtɪ] N loucura; (Med) insanidade f, demência

inscrutable [ɪnˈskruːtəbl] ADJ inescrutável, impenetrável

insect [ˈɪnsɛkt] N inseto

insecure [ɪnsɪˈkjuəʳ] ADJ inseguro

insensitive [ɪnˈsɛnsɪtɪv] ADJ insensível

insert [ɪnˈsəːt] VT (between things) intercalar; (into sth) introduzir, inserir

inside [ˈɪnˈsaɪd] N interior m ▶ ADJ interior, interno ▶ ADV (be) dentro; (go) para dentro ▶ PREP dentro de; (of time): ~ **10 minutes** em menos de 10 minutos; **insides** NPL (inf) entranhas fpl; **inside out** ADV às avessas; (know) muito bem; **to turn sth inside out** virar algo pelo avesso

insight [ˈɪnsaɪt] N insight m

insignificant [ɪnsɪɡˈnɪfɪknt] ADJ insignificante

insincere [ɪnsɪnˈsɪəʳ] ADJ insincero

insist [ɪn'sɪst] vɪ insistir; **to ~ on doing** insistir em fazer; **to ~ that** insistir que; (claim) cismar que; **insistent** ADJ insistente, pertinaz; (continual) persistente

insomnia [ɪn'sɔmnɪə] N insônia

inspect [ɪn'spɛkt] vT inspecionar; (building) vistoriar; (BRIT: tickets) fiscalizar; (troops) passar revista em; **inspection** N inspeção f; (of building) vistoria; (BRIT: of tickets) fiscalização f; **inspector** N inspetor(a) m/f; (BRIT: on buses, trains) fiscal m

inspire [ɪn'spaɪər] vT inspirar

install [ɪn'stɔːl] vT instalar; (official) nomear; **installation** [ɪnstə'leɪʃən] N instalação f

installment [ɪn'stɔːlmənt] (US) N = **instalment**

instalment [ɪn'stɔːlmənt] N (of money) prestação f; (of story) fascículo; (of TV serial etc) capítulo; **in ~s** (pay) a prestações; (receive) em várias vezes

instance ['ɪnstəns] N exemplo; **for ~** por exemplo; **in the first ~** em primeiro lugar

instant ['ɪnstənt] N instante m, momento ▶ ADJ imediato; (coffee) instantâneo; **instantly** ADV imediatamente; **instant message** N mensagem f instantânea; **instant messaging** N sistema m de mensagens instantâneas

instead [ɪn'stɛd] ADV em vez disso; **~ of** em vez de, em lugar de

instinct ['ɪnstɪŋkt] N instinto

institute ['ɪnstɪtjuːt] N instituto; (professional body) associação f ▶ vT (inquiry) começar, iniciar; (proceedings) instituir, estabelecer

institution [ɪnstɪ'tjuːʃən] N instituição f; (organization) instituto; (Med: home) asilo; (asylum) manicômio; (custom) costume m

instruct [ɪn'strʌkt] vT: **to ~ sb in sth** instruir alguém em or sobre algo; **to ~ sb to do sth** dar instruções a alguém para fazer algo; **instruction** N (teaching) instrução f; **instructions** NPL ordens fpl; **instructions (for use)** modo de usar; **instructor** N instrutor(a) m/f

instrument ['ɪnstrumənt] N instrumento

insufficient [ɪnsə'fɪʃənt] ADJ insuficiente

insulate ['ɪnsjuleɪt] vT isolar; (protect) segregar; **insulation** [ɪnsju'leɪʃən] N isolamento

insulin ['ɪnsjulɪn] N insulina

insult [n 'ɪnsʌlt, vt ɪn'sʌlt] N ofensa ▶ vT insultar, ofender

insurance [ɪn'ʃuərəns] N seguro; **fire/life ~** seguro contra incêndio/de vida

insure [ɪn'ʃuər] vT segurar

intact [ɪn'tækt] ADJ intacto, íntegro; (unharmed) ileso, são e salvo

intake ['ɪnteɪk] N (of food) quantidade f ingerida; (BRIT Sch): **an ~ of 200 a year** 200 matriculados por ano

integral ['ɪntɪgrəl] ADJ (part) integrante, essencial

integrate ['ɪntɪgreɪt] vT integrar ▶ vɪ integrar-se

intellect ['ɪntəlɛkt] N intelecto; **intellectual** [ɪntə'lɛktjuəl] ADJ, N intelectual m/f

intelligence [ɪn'tɛlɪdʒəns] N inteligência; (Mil etc) informações fpl

intelligent [ɪn'tɛlɪdʒənt] ADJ inteligente

intend [ɪn'tɛnd] VT (*gift etc*): **to ~ sth for** destinar algo a; **to ~ to do sth** tencionar or pretender fazer algo; (*plan*) planejar fazer algo

intense [ɪn'tɛns] ADJ intenso; (*person*) muito emotivo

intensive [ɪn'tɛnsɪv] ADJ intensivo; **intensive care unit** N unidade *f* de tratamento intensivo

intent [ɪn'tɛnt] N intenção *f* ▶ ADJ: **to be ~ on doing sth** estar resolvido a fazer algo; **to all ~s and purposes** para todos os efeitos

intention [ɪn'tɛnʃən] N intenção *f*, propósito; **intentional** ADJ intencional, propositado

interact [ɪntər'ækt] VI interagir; **interactive** [ɪntər'æktɪv] ADJ interativo

interchange ['ɪntətʃeɪndʒ] N intercâmbio; (*exchange*) troca, permuta; (*on motorway*) trevo

intercourse ['ɪntəkɔːs] N: **sexual ~** relações *fpl* sexuais

interest ['ɪntrɪst] N interesse *m*; (*Comm: sum of money*) juros *mpl*; (: *in company*) participação *f* ▶ VT interessar; **to be ~ed in** interessar-se por, estar interessado em; **interesting** ADJ interessante

interface ['ɪntəfeɪs] N (*Comput*) interface *f*

interfere [ɪntə'fɪər] VI: **to ~ in** interferir or intrometer-se em; **to ~ with** (*objects*) mexer em; (*hinder*) impedir; (*plans*) interferir em

interference [ɪntə'fɪərəns] N intromissão *f*; (*Radio, TV*) interferência

interior [ɪn'tɪərɪər] N interior *m* ▶ ADJ interno; (*ministry*) do interior

intermediate [ɪntə'miːdɪət] ADJ intermediário

intermission [ɪntə'mɪʃən] N intervalo

intern [*vt* ɪn'tə:n, *n* 'ɪntə:n] VT internar ▶ N (*US: in hospital*) médico interno/médica interna; (*on work placement*) estagiário(-a)

internal [ɪn'tə:nl] ADJ interno

international [ɪntə'næʃənl] ADJ internacional ▶ N (*BRIT Sport: game*) jogo internacional

Internet ['ɪntənɛt] N: **the ~** a Internet; **Internet café** N cibercafé *m*; **Internet Service Provider** N provedor de acesso à Internet; **Internet user** N internauta *m/f*

interpret [ɪn'tə:prɪt] VT interpretar; (*translate*) traduzir ▶ VI interpretar; **interpreter** N intérprete *m/f*

interrogate [ɪn'tɛrəugeɪt] VT interrogar; **interrogation** [ɪntɛrə'geɪʃən] N interrogatório

interrupt [ɪntə'rʌpt] VT, VI interromper; **interruption** N interrupção *f*

interval ['ɪntəvl] N intervalo

intervene [ɪntə'viːn] VI intervir; (*event*) ocorrer; (*time*) decorrer

interview ['ɪntəvjuː] N entrevista ▶ VT entrevistar; **interviewer** N entrevistador(a) *m/f*

intimate [*adj* 'ɪntɪmət, *vt* 'ɪntɪmeɪt] ADJ íntimo; (*knowledge*) profundo ▶ VT insinuar, sugerir

(KEYWORD)

into ['ɪntu] PREP
1 (*indicating motion or direction*) em; **come into the house/garden** venha para dentro/o jardim; **research into cancer** pesquisa sobre o câncer; **he worked late**

into the night ele trabalhou até altas horas

2 (*indicating change of condition, result*): **she burst into tears** ela desatou a chorar; **he was shocked into silence** ele ficou mudo de choque; **into 3 pieces/French** em 3 pedaços/para o francês

intolerant [ɪn'tɔlərənt] ADJ: **~ (of)** intolerante (com *or* para com)

intranet ['ɪntrənet] N intranet *f*

intricate ['ɪntrɪkət] ADJ complexo, complicado

intrigue [ɪn'triːg] N intriga ▶ VT intrigar; **intriguing** ADJ intrigante

introduce [ɪntrə'djuːs] VT introduzir; **to ~ sb (to sb)** apresentar alguém (a alguém); **to ~ sb to** (*pastime, technique*) iniciar alguém em; **introduction** N introdução *f*; (*of person*) apresentação *f*; **introductory** ADJ introdutório

intrude [ɪn'truːd] VI: **to ~ (on** *or* **into)** intrometer-se (em); **intruder** N intruso(-a)

inundate ['ɪnʌndeɪt] VT: **to ~ with** inundar de

invade [ɪn'veɪd] VT invadir

invalid [n 'ɪnvəlɪd, adj ɪn'vælɪd] N inválido(-a) ▶ ADJ inválido, nulo

invaluable [ɪn'væljuəbl] ADJ valioso, inestimável

invariably [ɪn'veərɪəblɪ] ADV invariavelmente

invent [ɪn'vent] VT inventar; **invention** N invenção *f*; (*inventiveness*) engenho; (*lie*) ficção *f*, mentira; **inventor** N inventor(a) *m/f*

inventory ['ɪnvəntrɪ] N inventário, relação *f*

invest [ɪn'vest] VT investir ▶ VI: **to ~ in** investir em; (*acquire*) comprar

investigate [ɪn'vestɪgeɪt] VT investigar; **investigation** [ɪnvestɪ'geɪʃən] N investigação *f*

investment [ɪn'vestmənt] N investimento

invisible [ɪn'vɪzɪbl] ADJ invisível

invitation [ɪnvɪ'teɪʃən] N convite *m*

invite [ɪn'vaɪt] VT convidar; (*opinions etc*) solicitar; **inviting** ADJ convidativo

invoice ['ɪnvɔɪs] N fatura ▶ VT faturar

involve [ɪn'vɔlv] VT (*entail*) implicar; (*require*) exigir; **to ~ sb (in)** envolver alguém (em); **involved** ADJ (*complex*) complexo; **to be/get involved in sth** estar/ficar envolvido em algo; **involvement** N envolvimento

inward ['ɪnwəd] ADJ (*movement*) interior, interno; (*thought, feeling*) íntimo ▶ ADV para dentro; **inwards** ADV para dentro

iPod® ['aɪpɔd] N iPod® *m*

IQ N ABBR (= *intelligence quotient*) QI *m*

IRA N ABBR (= *Irish Republican Army*) IRA *m*

Iran [ɪ'rɑːn] N Irã *m* (BR), Irão *m* (PT)

Iraq [ɪ'rɑːk] N Iraque *m*

Ireland ['aɪələnd] N Irlanda

iris ['aɪrɪs] (*pl* **irises**) N íris *f*

Irish ['aɪrɪʃ] ADJ irlandês(-esa); **the Irish** NPL os irlandeses; **Irishman** *irreg* N irlandês *m*; **Irish Sea** N: **the Irish Sea** o mar da Irlanda; **Irishwoman** *irreg* N irlandesa

iron ['aɪən] N ferro; (*for clothes*) ferro de passar roupa ▶ ADJ de ferro ▶ VT (*clothes*) passar; **iron out** VT (*problem*) resolver

ironic [aɪ'rɔnɪk], **ironical** [aɪ'rɔnɪkl] ADJ irônico

ironing ['aɪənɪŋ] N (*activity*) passar roupa; (*clothes*) roupa passada;

ironing board N tábua de passar roupa

irony ['aɪrənɪ] N ironia

irrational [ɪ'ræʃənl] ADJ irracional

irregular [ɪ'regjʊləʳ] ADJ irregular; (surface) desigual

irrelevant [ɪ'reləvənt] ADJ irrelevante

irresistible [ɪrɪ'zɪstɪbl] ADJ irresistível

irresponsible [ɪrɪ'spɒnsɪbl] ADJ irresponsável

irrigation [ɪrɪ'geɪʃən] N irrigação f

irritate ['ɪrɪteɪt] VT irritar; **irritating** ADJ irritante; **irritation** [ɪrɪ'teɪʃən] N irritação f

is [ɪz] VB see **be**

Islam ['ɪzlɑːm] N islamismo

island ['aɪlənd] N ilha; **islander** N ilhéu/ilhoa m/f

isle [aɪl] N ilhota, ilha

isn't ['ɪznt] = **is not**

ISP N ABBR (= Internet Service Provider) ISP m

Israel ['ɪzreɪl] N Israel; **Israeli** [ɪz'reɪlɪ] ADJ, N israelense m/f

issue ['ɪsjuː] N questão f, tema m; (of book) edição f; (of stamps) emissão f ▶ VT (rations, equipment) distribuir; (orders) dar; **at ~** em debate; **to take ~ with sb (over sth)** discordar de alguém (sobre algo); **to make an ~ of sth** criar caso com algo

(KEYWORD)

it [ɪt] PRON **1** (specific: subject) ele/ela; (: direct object) o/a; (: indirect object) lhe; **it's on the table** está em cima da mesa; **I can't find it** não consigo achá-lo; **give it to me** dê-mo; **about/from it** sobre/de isto; **did you go to it?** (party, concert etc) você foi?

2 (impers) isto, isso; (after prep) ele, ela; **it's raining** está chovendo (BR) or a chover (PT); **it's six o'clock/the 10th of August** são seis horas/hoje é (dia) 10 de agosto; **who is it? — it's me** quem é? — sou eu

Italian [ɪ'tæljən] ADJ italiano ▶ N italiano(-a); (Ling) italiano

italics [ɪ'tælɪks] NPL itálico

Italy ['ɪtəlɪ] N Itália

itch [ɪtʃ] N comichão f, coceira ▶ VI (person) estar com or sentir comichão or coceira; (part of body) comichar, coçar; **I'm ~ing to do something** estou louco para fazer algo; **itchy** ADJ que coça; **to be itchy** (person) estar com or sentir comichão or coceira; (part of body) comichar, coçar

it'd ['ɪtd] = **it would**; = **it had**

item ['aɪtəm] N item m; (on agenda) assunto; (in programme) número; (also: **news ~**) notícia

itinerary [aɪ'tɪnərərɪ] N itinerário

it'll ['ɪtl] = **it will**; = **it shall**

its [ɪts] ADJ seu/sua, dele/dela ▶ PRON o seu/a sua, o dele/a dela

it's [ɪts] = **it is**; = **it has**

itself [ɪt'self] PRON (reflexive) si mesmo(-a); (emphatic) ele mesmo/ela mesma

ITV (BRIT) N ABBR (= Independent Television) canal de televisão comercial

I've [aɪv] = **I have**

ivory ['aɪvərɪ] N marfim m

ivy ['aɪvɪ] N hera

J

jab [dʒæb] VT cutucar ▶ N cotovelada, murro; (*Med: inf*) injeção *f*; **to ~ sth into sth** cravar algo num algo

jack [dʒæk] N (*Aut*) macaco; (*Cards*) valete *m*; **jack up** VT (*Aut*) levantar com macaco

jacket ['dʒækɪt] N jaqueta, casaco curto; (*of boiler etc*) forro; (*of book*) sobrecapa

jackpot ['dʒækpɔt] N bolada, sorte *f* grande

jagged ['dʒægɪd] ADJ dentado, denteado

jail [dʒeɪl] N prisão *f*, cadeia ▶ VT encarcerar

jam [dʒæm] N geleia; (*also:* **traffic ~**) engarrafamento; (*inf*) apuro ▶ VT obstruir, atravancar; (*mechanism*) emperrar; (*Radio*) bloquear, interferir ▶ VI (*mechanism, drawer etc*) emperrar; **to ~ sth into sth** forçar algo dentro de algo

Jamaica [dʒə'meɪkə] N Jamaica

janitor ['dʒænɪtər] N zelador *m*

January ['dʒænjuərɪ] N janeiro

Japan [dʒə'pæn] N Japão *m*; **Japanese** [dʒæpə'niːz] ADJ japonês(-esa) ▶ N INV japonês(-esa) *m/f*; (*Ling*) japonês *m*

jar [dʒɑːr] N jarro ▶ VI (*sound*) ranger, chiar; (*colours*) destoar

jargon ['dʒɑːgən] N jargão *m*

javelin ['dʒævlɪn] N dardo de arremesso

jaw [dʒɔː] N mandíbula, maxilar *m*

jazz [dʒæz] N jazz *m*; **jazz up** VT animar, avivar

jealous ['dʒɛləs] ADJ ciumento; **jealousy** N ciúmes *mpl*

jeans [dʒiːnz] NPL jeans *m* (*BR*), jeans *mpl* (*PT*)

jelly ['dʒɛlɪ] N (*jam*) geleia; **jellyfish** ['dʒɛlɪfɪʃ] N INV água-viva

jerk [dʒəːk] N solavanco, sacudida; (*wrench*) puxão *m*; (*inf: idiot*) babaca *m* ▶ VT sacudir ▶ VI dar um solavanco

jersey ['dʒəːzɪ] N suéter *m* (*BR*), camisola (*PT*); (*fabric*) jérsei *m*, malha

Jesus ['dʒiːzəs] N Jesus *m* (Cristo)

jet [dʒɛt] N (*of gas, liquid*) jato *m*; (*Aviat*) (avião *m* a) jato; (*stone*) azeviche *m*; **jet lag** N cansaço devido à diferença de fuso horário

jetty ['dʒɛtɪ] N quebra-mar *m*, cais *m*

Jew [dʒuː] N judeu(-dia) *m/f*

jewel ['dʒuːəl] N joia; **jeweller**, (*US*) **jeweler** N joalheiro(-a); **jewellery**, (*US*) **jewelry** N joias *fpl*, pedrarias *fpl*

Jewish ['dʒuːɪʃ] ADJ judeu/judia

jigsaw ['dʒɪgsɔː] N (*also:* **~ puzzle**) quebra-cabeça *m*

job [dʒɔb] N trabalho; (*task*) tarefa; (*duty*) dever *m*; (*post*) emprego; **it's not my ~** não faz parte das minhas funções; **it's a good ~ that ...** ainda bem que ...; **just the ~!** justo o que queria!; **jobless** ADJ desempregado

jockey ['dʒɔkɪ] N jóquei m ▶ VI: **to ~ for position** manobrar para conseguir uma posição

jog [dʒɔg] VT empurrar, sacudir ▶ VI fazer jogging or cooper ▶ VI ir levando; **jog along** VI ir levando; **jogging** N jogging m

john [dʒɔn] (US inf) N trono m (inf) (no banheiro)

join [dʒɔɪn] VT (things) juntar, unir; (queue) entrar em; (become member of) associar-se a; (meet) encontrar-se com; (accompany) juntar-se a ▶ VI (roads, rivers) confluir ▶ N junção f; **join in** VI participar ▶ VT FUS participar em; **join up** VI unir-se; (Mil) alistar-se

joint [dʒɔɪnt] N (Tech) junta, união f; (wood) encaixe m; (Anat) articulação f; (BRIT Culin) quarto; (inf: place) espelunca; (: marijuana cigarette) baseado ▶ ADJ comum; (combined) conjunto; (committee) misto

joke [dʒəuk] N piada; (also: **practical ~**) brincadeira, peça ▶ VI brincar; **to play a ~ on** pregar uma peça em; **joker** N (Cards) curingão m

jolly ['dʒɔlɪ] ADJ (merry) alegre; (enjoyable) divertido ▶ ADV (BRIT inf) muito, extremamente

jolt [dʒəult] N (shake) sacudida, solavanco; (shock) susto ▶ VT sacudir; (emotionally) abalar

Jordan ['dʒɔːdən] N Jordânia; (river) Jordão m

journal ['dʒəːnl] N jornal m; (magazine) revista; (diary) diário; **journalism** N jornalismo; **journalist** N jornalista m/f

journey ['dʒəːnɪ] N viagem f; (distance covered) trajeto

joy [dʒɔɪ] N alegria

judge [dʒʌdʒ] N juiz/juíza m/f; (in competition) árbitro; (fig: expert) especialista m/f, conhecedor(a) m/f ▶ VT julgar; (competition) arbitrar; (estimate) avaliar; (consider) considerar

judo ['dʒuːdəu] N judô m

jug [dʒʌg] N jarro

juggle ['dʒʌgl] VI fazer malabarismos; **juggler** N malabarista m/f

juice [dʒuːs] N suco (BR), sumo (PT); **juicy** ADJ suculento

July [dʒuːˈlaɪ] N julho

jumble ['dʒʌmbl] N confusão f, mixórdia ▶ VT (also: **~ up**: mix up) misturar; **jumble sale** (BRIT) N bazar m

As **jumble sales** têm lugar dentro de igrejas, salões de festa e escolas, onde são vendidos diversos tipos de mercadorias, em geral baratas e sobretudo de segunda mão, a fim de coletar dinheiro para uma obra de caridade, uma escola ou uma igreja.

jump [dʒʌmp] VI saltar, pular; (start) sobressaltar-se; (increase) disparar ▶ VT pular, saltar ▶ N pulo, salto; (increase) alta; (fence) obstáculo; **to ~ the queue** (BRIT) furar a fila (BR), pôr-se à frente (PT)

jumper ['dʒʌmpəʳ] N (BRIT: pullover) suéter m (BR), camisola (PT); (US: pinafore dress) avental m; **jumper cables** (US) NPL = **jump leads**

jump leads, (US) **jumper cables** NPL cabos mpl para ligar a bateria

Jun. ABBR = **junior**

junction ['dʒʌŋkʃən] (BRIT) N (of roads) cruzamento; (Rail) entroncamento

June [dʒuːn] N junho

jungle ['dʒʌŋgl] N selva, mato

junior ['dʒuːnɪəʳ] ADJ (in age) mais novo or moço; (position) subalterno ▶ N jovem m/f

junk [dʒʌŋk] N (cheap goods) tranqueira, velharias fpl; (rubbish) lixo; **junk food** N comida pronta de baixo valor nutritivo; **junk mail** N correspondência não-solicitada

jury ['dʒuərɪ] N júri m

just [dʒʌst] ADJ justo ▶ ADV (exactly) justamente, exatamente; (only) apenas, somente; **he's ~ done it/left** ele acabou (BR) or acaba (PT) de fazê-lo/ir; **~ right** perfeito; **~ two o'clock** duas (horas) em ponto; **she's ~ as clever as you** ela é tão inteligente como você; **~ as well that ...** ainda bem que ...; **~ as he was leaving** no momento em que ele saía; **~ before/enough** justo antes/o suficiente; **~ here** bem aqui; **he ~ missed** falhou por pouco; **~ listen** escute aqui!

justice ['dʒʌstɪs] N justiça; (US: judge) juiz/juíza m/f; **to do ~ to** (fig) apreciar devidamente

justify ['dʒʌstɪfaɪ] VT justificar

jut [dʒʌt] VI (also: **~ out**) sobressair

juvenile ['dʒuːvənaɪl] ADJ juvenil; (court) de menores; (books) para adolescentes ▶ N menor m/f de idade

K ABBR (= kilobyte) K ▶ N ABBR (= one thousand) mil

kangaroo [kæŋgə'ruː] N canguru m

karate [kə'rɑːtɪ] N karatê m

kebab [kə'bæb] N churrasquinho, espetinho

keen [kiːn] ADJ (interest, desire) grande, vivo; (eye, intelligence) penetrante; (competition) acirrado, intenso; (edge) afiado; (eager) entusiasmado; **to be ~ to do or on doing sth** sentir muita vontade de fazer algo; **to be ~ on sth/sb** gostar de algo/alguém

keep [kiːp] (pt, pp **kept**) VT ficar com; (house etc) cuidar; (detain) deter; (shop etc) tomar conta de; (preserve) conservar; (family etc) manter; (promise) cumprir; (chickens, bees etc) criar; (prevent): **to ~ sb from doing sth** impedir alguém de fazer algo ▶ VI (food) conservar-se; (remain) ficar ▶ N (of castle) torre f de menagem; (food etc): **to earn one's ~** ganhar a vida;

(*inf*): **for ~s** para sempre; **to ~ doing sth** continuar fazendo algo; **to ~ sb happy** manter alguém satisfeito; **to ~ a place tidy** manter um lugar limpo; **keep on** vi: **to ~ on doing** continuar fazendo; **keep out** vt impedir de entrar; **"~ out"** "entrada proibida"; **keep up** vt manter ▶ vi não atrasar-se, acompanhar; **to ~ up with** (*pace*) acompanhar; (*level*) manter-se ao nível de; **keeper** N guarda m, guardião(-diã) m/f
kennel ['kɛnl] N casa de cachorro; **kennels** N (*establishment*) canil m
kept [kɛpt] PT, PP *of* **keep**
kerb [kə:b] (BRIT) N meio-fio (BR), borda do passeio (PT)
kettle ['kɛtl] N chaleira
key [ki:] N chave f; (*Mus*) clave f; (*of piano, typewriter*) tecla ▶ CPD (*issue etc*) chave ▶ vt (*also*: **~ in**) digitar; **keyboard** N teclado; **keyhole** N buraco da fechadura; **keyring** N chaveiro
khaki ['kɑ:kɪ] ADJ cáqui
kick [kɪk] vt dar um pontapé em; (*ball*) chutar; (*inf: habit*) conseguir superar ▶ vi (*horse*) dar coices ▶ N (*from person*) pontapé m; (*from animal*) coice m, patada; (*to ball*) chute m; (*inf: thrill*): **he does it for ~s** faz isso para curtir; **kick off** vi (*Sport*) dar o chute inicial
kid [kɪd] N (*inf: child*) criança; (*animal*) cabrito; (*leather*) pelica ▶ vi (*inf*) brincar
kidnap ['kɪdnæp] vt sequestrar
kidney ['kɪdnɪ] N rim m
kill [kɪl] vt matar; (*murder*) assassinar ▶ N ato de matar; **killer** N assassino(-a); **killing** N assassinato; **to make a killing** (*inf*) faturar uma boa nota

kiln [kɪln] N forno
kilo ['ki:ləu] N quilo; **kilobyte** N kilobyte m; **kilogram**, **kilogramme** N quilograma m; **kilometre**, (US) **kilometer** N quilômetro; **kilowatt** N quilowatt m
kilt [kɪlt] N saiote m escocês
kin [kɪn] N *see* **next-of-kin**
kind [kaɪnd] ADJ (*friendly*) gentil; (*generous*) generoso; (*good*) bom/boa, bondoso, amável ▶ N espécie f, classe f; (*species*) gênero; **in ~** (*Comm*) em espécie
kindergarten ['kɪndəgɑ:tn] N jardim m de infância
kindly ['kaɪndlɪ] ADJ (*good*) bom/boa, bondoso; (*gentle*) gentil, carinhoso ▶ ADV bondosamente, amavelmente; **will you ~ ...** você pode fazer o favor de ...
kindness ['kaɪndnɪs] N bondade f, gentileza
king [kɪŋ] N rei m; **kingdom** N reino; **kingfisher** N martim-pescador m
kiosk ['ki:ɔsk] N banca (BR), quiosque m (PT); (BRIT: *also:* **telephone ~**) cabine f
kipper ['kɪpəʳ] N tipo de arenque defumado
kiss [kɪs] N beijo ▶ vt beijar; **to ~ (each other)** beijar-se; **kiss of life** (BRIT) N respiração f boca-a-boca
kit [kɪt] N (*for sport etc*) kit m; (*equipment*) equipamento; (*set of tools etc*) caixa de ferramentas; (*for assembly*) kit m para montar
kitchen ['kɪtʃɪn] N cozinha
kite [kaɪt] N (*toy*) papagaio, pipa
kitten ['kɪtn] N gatinho
kitty ['kɪtɪ] N fundo comum, vaquinha
km ABBR (= *kilometre*) km

knack [næk] N: **there's a ~ (to it)**
tem um jeito

knee [ni:] N joelho; **kneecap** N
rótula

kneel [ni:l] (pt, pp **knelt**) VI (also: **~
down**) ajoelhar-se

knew [nju:] PT of **know**

knickers ['nɪkəz] (BRIT) NPL
calcinha (BR), cuecas fpl (PT)

knife [naɪf] (pl **knives**) N faca ▶ VT
esfaquear

knight [naɪt] N cavaleiro; (Chess)
cavalo

knit [nɪt] VT tricotar; (brows) franzir
▶ VI tricotar (BR), fazer malha (PT);
(bones) consolidar-se; **knitting** N
ato de tricotar, tricô (BR), malha
(PT); **knitting needle** N agulha de
tricô (BR) or de malha (PT);
knitwear N roupa de malha

knives [naɪvz] NPL of **knife**

knob [nɔb] N (of door) maçaneta;
(of stick) castão m; (on radio, TV etc)
botão m

knock [nɔk] VT bater em; (bump
into) colidir com; (inf) criticar,
malhar ▶ N pancada, golpe m;
(on door) batida ▶ VI: **to ~ at** or **on
the door** bater à porta; **knock
down** VT derrubar; (pedestrian)
atropelar; **knock off** VI (inf: finish)
terminar ▶ VT (inf: steal) abafar;
(from price): **to ~ off £10** dar um
desconto de £10; **knock out** VT pôr
nocaute, nocautear; (defeat)
eliminar; **knock over** VT derrubar;
(pedestrian) atropelar

knot [nɔt] N nó m ▶ VT dar nó em

know [nəu] (pt **knew**, pp **known**) VT
saber; (person, author, place)
conhecer ▶ VI: **to ~ about** or **of sth**
saber de algo; **to ~ how to swim**
saber nadar; **know-how** N
know-how m, experiência;

knowingly ADV (purposely) de
propósito; (spitefully)
maliciosamente

knowledge ['nɔlɪdʒ] N
conhecimento; (range of learning)
saber m, conhecimentos mpl;
knowledgeable ADJ entendido,
versado

known [nəun] PP of **know**

knuckle ['nʌkl] N nó m

Koran [kɔ'rɑːn] N: **the ~** o Alcorão

Korea [kə'rɪə] N Coreia

kosher ['kəuʃər] ADJ kosher inv

Kosovo ['kɒsəvəu] N Kosovo m

L ABBR (BRIT Aut: = *learner*) (condutor(a) *m/f*) aprendiz *m/f*

lab [læb] N ABBR = **laboratory**

label ['leɪbl] N etiqueta, rótulo ▶ VT etiquetar, rotular

labor ['leɪbər] (US) = **labour**

laboratory [lə'bɔrətərɪ] N laboratório

labour ['leɪbər], (US) **labor** N trabalho; (*work force*) mão-de-obra *f*; (*Med*): **to be in ~** estar em trabalho de parto ▶ VI: **to ~ (at)** trabalhar (em) ▶ VT insistir em; **the L~ Party** (BRIT) o Partido Trabalhista; **labourer** N operário; **farm labourer** trabalhador *m* rural, peão *m*

lace [leɪs] N renda; (*of shoe etc*) cadarço ▶ VT (*shoe*) amarrar

lack [læk] N falta ▶ VT (*money, confidence*) faltar; (*intelligence*) carecer de; **through** or **for ~ of** por falta de; **to be ~ing** faltar; **to be ~ing in** carecer de

lacquer ['lækər] N laca; (*hair*) fixador *m*

lad [læd] N menino, rapaz *m*, moço

ladder ['lædər] N escada *f* de mão; (BRIT: *in tights*) defeito (em forma de escada)

ladle ['leɪdl] N concha (de sopa)

lady ['leɪdɪ] N senhora; (*distinguished, noble*) dama; (*in address*): **ladies and gentlemen, ...** senhoras e senhores, ...; **young ~** senhorita; **"ladies' (toilets)"** "senhoras"; **ladybird**, (US) **ladybug** N joaninha

lag [læg] N atraso, retardamento ▶ VI (*also*: **~ behind**) ficar para trás ▶ VT (*pipes*) revestir com isolante térmico

lager ['lɑːgər] N *cerveja leve e clara*

lagoon [lə'guːn] N lagoa

laid [leɪd] PT, PP of **lay**

lain [leɪn] PP of **lie**

lake [leɪk] N lago

lamb [læm] N cordeiro

lame [leɪm] ADJ coxo, manco; (*excuse, argument*) pouco convincente, fraco

lament [lə'mɛnt] N lamento, queixa ▶ VT lamentar-se de

lamp [læmp] N lâmpada; **lamppost** (BRIT) N poste *m*; **lampshade** N abajur *m*, quebra-luz *m*

land [lænd] N terra; (*country*) país *m*; (*piece of land*) terreno; (*estate*) terras *fpl*, propriedades *fpl* ▶ VI (*from ship*) desembarcar; (*Aviat*) pousar, aterrissar (BR), aterrar (PT); (*fig: arrive unexpectedly*) cair, terminar ▶ VT desembarcar; **to ~ sb with sth** (*inf*) sobrecarregar alguém com algo; **land up** VI: **to ~ up in/at** ir parar em; **landfill site** ['lændfɪl-] N aterro sanitário; **landing** N (*Aviat*) pouso, aterrissagem *f* (BR), aterragem *f* (PT); (*of staircase*) patamar m; **landlady** N senhoria; (of pub) dona, proprietária; **landline** N telefone m fixo; **landlord** N senhorio, locador m; (of pub etc) dono, proprietário; **landmark** N lugar m conhecido; (fig) marco; **landowner** N latifundiário(-a)

landscape ['lændskeɪp] N paisagem f

landslide ['lændslaɪd] N (Geo) desmoronamento, desabamento; (fig: Pol) vitória esmagadora

lane [leɪn] N caminho, estrada estreita; (Aut) pista; (in race) raia

language ['læŋgwɪdʒ] N língua; (way one speaks, Comput, style) linguagem f; **bad ~** palavrões mpl; **language laboratory** N laboratório de línguas; **language school** N escola de línguas

lantern ['læntn] N lanterna

lap [læp] N (of track) volta; (of person) colo ▶ VT (also: **~ up**) lamber ▶ VI (waves) marulhar; **lap up** VT (fig) receber com sofreguidão

lapel [lə'pɛl] N lapela

lapse [læps] N lapso; (bad behaviour) deslize m ▶ VI (law) prescrever; **to ~ into bad habits** adquirir maus hábitos

laptop ['læptɔp], **laptop computer** N laptop m

lard [lɑːd] N banha de porco

larder ['lɑːdəʳ] N despensa

large [lɑːdʒ] ADJ grande; **at ~** (free) em liberdade; (generally) em geral; **largely** ADV em grande parte; (introducing reason) principalmente; **large-scale** ADJ (map) em grande escala; (fig) importante, de grande alcance

lark [lɑːk] N (bird) cotovia; (joke) brincadeira, peça; **lark about** VI divertir-se, brincar

laryngitis [lærɪn'dʒaɪtɪs] N laringite f

laser ['leɪzəʳ] N laser m; **laser printer** N impressora a laser

lash [læʃ] N (blow) chicotada; (also: **eye~**) pestana, cílio ▶ VT chicotear, açoitar; (subj: rain, wind) castigar; (tie) atar; **lash out** VI: **to ~ out (at sb)** atacar (alguém) violentamente; **to ~ out at** or **against sb** (criticize) atacar alguém verbalmente

lass [læs] (BRIT) N moça

last [lɑːst] ADJ último; (final) derradeiro ▶ ADV em último lugar ▶ VI durar; (continue) continuar; **~ week** na semana passada; **~ night** ontem à noite; **at ~** finalmente; **~ but one** penúltimo; **lastly** ADV por fim, por último; (finally) finalmente; **last-minute** ADJ de última hora

latch [lætʃ] N trinco, fecho, tranca

late [leɪt] ADJ (not on time) atrasado; (far on in day etc) tardio; (former) antigo, ex-, anterior; (dead) falecido ▶ ADV tarde; (behind time, schedule) atrasado; **of ~** recentemente; **in ~ May** no final de maio; **latecomer** N retardatário(-a); **lately** ADV ultimamente; **later** ADJ (date etc) posterior; (version etc) mais recente ▶ ADV mais tarde, depois; **later on** mais tarde; **latest** ADJ último; **at the latest** no mais tardar

lather ['lɑːðəʳ] N espuma (de sabão) ▶ VT ensaboar

Latin ['lætɪn] N (Ling) latim m ▶ ADJ latino; **Latin America** N América Latina; **Latin American** ADJ, N latino-americano(-a)

latitude ['lætɪtjuːd] N latitude f

latter ['lætəʳ] ADJ último; (of two) segundo ▶ N: **the ~** o último, este

laugh [lɑːf] N riso, risada ▶ VI rir, dar risada (or gargalhada); **(to do sth) for a ~** (fazer algo) só de curtição; **laugh at** VT FUS rir de; **laugh off** VT disfarçar sorrindo; **laughter** N riso, risada

launch [lɔːntʃ] N (boat) lancha; (Comm, of rocket etc) lançamento ▶ VT lançar; **launch into** VT FUS lançar-se a

laundry ['lɔːndrɪ] N lavanderia; (clothes) roupa para lavar

lava ['lɑːvə] N lava

lavatory ['lævətərɪ] N privada (BR), casa de banho (PT)

lavender ['lævəndəʳ] N lavanda

lavish ['lævɪʃ] ADJ (amount) generoso; (person): **~ with** pródigo em, generoso com ▶ VT: **to ~ sth on sb** encher or cobrir alguém de algo

law [lɔː] N lei f; (rule) regra; (Sch) direito; **lawful** ADJ legal, lícito

lawn [lɔːn] N gramado (BR), relvado (PT); **lawnmower** N cortador m de grama (BR) or de relva (PT)

lawsuit ['lɔːsuːt] N ação f judicial, processo

lawyer ['lɔːjəʳ] N advogado(-a); (for sales, wills etc) notário(-a), tabelião(-liã) m/f

lax [læks] ADJ (discipline) relaxado; (person) negligente

laxative ['læksətɪv] N laxante m

lay [leɪ] (pt, pp **laid**) PT of **lie** ▶ ADJ leigo ▶ VT colocar; (eggs, table) pôr; **lay aside** VT pôr de lado; **lay by** VT = **lay aside**; **lay down** VT depositar; (rules etc) impor, estabelecer; **to ~ down the law** (pej) impor regras; **to ~ down one's life** sacrificar voluntariamente a vida; **lay off** VT (workers) demitir; **lay on** VT (meal, entertainment) prover; **lay out** VT (spread out) dispor em ordem; **lay-by** (BRIT) N acostamento

layer ['leɪəʳ] N camada

layman ['leɪmən] irreg N leigo

layout ['leɪaut] N (of garden, building) desenho; (of piece of writing) leiaute m

lazy ['leɪzɪ] ADJ preguiçoso; (movement) lento

lb. ABBR (weight) = **pound**

lead¹ [liːd] N (front position) dianteira; (Sport) liderança; (fig) vantagem f; (clue) pista; (Elec) fio; (for dog) correia; (in play, film) papel m principal ▶ VT levar; (be leader of) chefiar; (start, guide: activity) encabeçar ▶ VI encabeçar; **to be in the ~** (Sport: in race) estar na frente; (: in match) estar ganhando; **to ~ the way** assumir a direção; **lead away** VT levar; **lead back** VT levar de volta; **lead on** VT (tease) provocar; **lead to** VT FUS levar a, conduzir a; **lead up to** VT FUS conduzir a

lead² [lɛd] N chumbo; (in pencil) grafite f

leader ['liːdəʳ] N líder m/f; **leadership** N liderança; (quality) poder m de liderança

lead-free [lɛd-] ADJ sem chumbo

leading ['liːdɪŋ] ADJ principal; (role) de destaque; (first, front) primeiro, dianteiro

lead singer [liːd-] N cantor(a) m/f

leaf [liːf] (pl **leaves**) N folha ▶ VI: **to ~ through** (book) folhear; **to turn over a new ~** mudar de vida, partir para outra (inf)

leaflet ['liːflɪt] N folheto

league [liːg] N liga; **to be in ~ with** estar de comum acordo com

leak [liːk] N (*of liquid, gas*) escape *m*, vazamento; (*hole*) buraco, rombo; (*in roof*) goteira; (*fig: of information*) vazamento ▶ VI (*ship*) fazer água; (*shoe*) deixar entrar água; (*roof*) gotejar; (*pipe, container, liquid*) vazar; (*gas*) escapar ▶ VT (*news*) vazar

lean [liːn] (*pt, pp* **leaned** *or* **leant**) ADJ magro ▶ VT: **to ~ sth on** encostar *or* apoiar algo em ▶ VI inclinar-se; **to ~ against** encostar-se *or* apoiar-se contra; **to ~ on** encostar-se *or* apoiar-se em; **lean back** VI inclinar-se para trás; **lean forward** VI inclinar-se para frente; **lean out** VI: **to ~ out (of)** inclinar-se para fora (de); **lean over** VI debruçar-se ▶ VT FUS debruçar-se sobre

leap [liːp] (*pt, pp* **leaped** *or* **leapt**) N salto, pulo ▶ VI saltar; **leap year** N ano bissexto

learn [ləːn] (*pt, pp* **learned** *or* **learnt**) VT aprender; (*by heart*) decorar ▶ VI aprender; **to ~ about sth** (*hear, read*) saber de algo; **learner** N principiante *m/f*; (BRIT: *also*: **learner driver**) aprendiz *m/f* de motorista

lease [liːs] N arrendamento ▶ VT arrendar

leash [liːʃ] N correia

least [liːst] ADJ: **the ~** (+ *n*) o/a menor; (*smallest amount of*) a menor quantidade de ▶ ADV: **the ~** (+ *adj*) o/a menos; **at ~** pelo menos; **not in the ~** de maneira nenhuma

leather [ˈlɛðəʳ] N couro

leave [liːv] (*pt, pp* **left**) VT deixar; (*go away from*) abandonar ▶ VI ir-se, sair; (*train*) sair ▶ N licença; **to ~ sth to sb** deixar algo para alguém; **to**

be left sobrar; **leave behind** VT deixar para trás; (*forget*) esquecer; **leave out** VT omitir

leaves [liːvz] NPL *of* **leaf**

Lebanon [ˈlɛbənən] N Líbano

lecture [ˈlɛktʃəʳ] N conferência, palestra; (*Sch*) aula ▶ VI dar aulas, lecionar ▶ VT (*scold*) passar um sermão em; **lecturer** N (BRIT: *at university*) professor(a) *m/f*

led [lɛd] PT, PP *of* **lead¹**

ledge [lɛdʒ] N (*of window*) peitoril *m*; (*of mountain*) saliência, proeminência

leek [liːk] N alho-poró *m*

left [lɛft] PT, PP *of* **leave** ▶ ADJ esquerdo ▶ N esquerda ▶ ADV à esquerda; **on the ~** à esquerda; **to the ~** para a esquerda; **the L~** (*Pol*) a Esquerda; **left-handed** ADJ canhoto; **left-luggage**, (BRIT) **left-luggage office** N depósito de bagagem

left-wing ADJ (*Pol*) de esquerda, esquerdista

leg [lɛg] N perna; (*of animal*) pata; (*Culin: of meat*) perna; (*of journey*) etapa; **1st/2nd ~** (*Sport*) primeiro/ segundo turno

legacy [ˈlɛgəsɪ] N legado; (*fig*) herança

legal [ˈliːgl] ADJ legal

legend [ˈlɛdʒənd] N lenda; (*person*) mito

leggings [ˈlɛgɪnz] NPL legging *f*

legislation [lɛdʒɪsˈleɪʃən] N legislação *f*

legitimate [lɪˈdʒɪtɪmət] ADJ legítimo

leisure [ˈlɛʒəʳ] N lazer *m*; **at ~** desocupado, livre

lemon [ˈlɛmən] N limão(-galego) *m*; **lemonade** [lɛməˈneɪd] N limonada; **lemon tea** N chá *m* de limão

lend [lɛnd] (*pt, pp* **lent**) VT: **to ~ sth to sb** emprestar algo a alguém

length [lɛŋθ] N comprimento, extensão *f*; (*amount of time*) duração *f*; **at ~** (*at last*) finalmente, afinal; (*lengthily*) por extenso; **lengthen** VT encompridar, alongar ▶ VI encompridar-se; **lengthways** ADV longitudinalmente, ao comprido; **lengthy** ADJ comprido, longo; (*meeting*) prolongado

lens [lɛnz] N (*of spectacles*) lente *f*; (*of camera*) objetiva

Lent [lɛnt] N Quaresma

lent [lɛnt] PT, PP *of* **lend**

lentil ['lɛntl] N lentilha

Leo ['liːəu] N Leão *m*

leotard ['liːətɑːd] N collant *m*

lesbian ['lɛzbɪən] N lésbica

less [lɛs] ADJ, PRON, ADV menos ▶ PREP: **~ tax/10% discount** menos imposto/10% de desconto; **~ than ever** menos do que nunca; **~ and ~** cada vez menos; **the ~ he works ...** quanto menos trabalha ...

lessen ['lɛsn] VI diminuir, minguar ▶ VT diminuir, reduzir

lesser ['lɛsə^r] ADJ menor; **to a ~ extent** *or* **degree** nem tanto

lesson ['lɛsn] N aula; (*example, warning*) lição *f*; **to teach sb a ~** (*fig*) dar uma lição em alguém

let [lɛt] (*pt, pp* **let**) VT (*allow*) deixar; (BRIT: *lease*) alugar; **to ~ sb know sth** avisar alguém de algo; **~'s go!** vamos!; **"to ~"** "aluga-se"; **let down** VT (*tyre*) esvaziar; (*disappoint*) desapontar; **let go** VT, VI soltar; **let in** VT deixar entrar; (*visitor etc*) fazer entrar; **let off** VT (*culprit*) perdoar; (*firework etc*) soltar; **let on** VI revelar; **let out** VT deixar sair; (*scream*) soltar; **let up** VI cessar, afrouxar

lethal ['liːθl] ADJ letal

letter ['lɛtə^r] N (*of alphabet*) letra; (*correspondence*) carta; **letterbox** (BRIT) N caixa do correio

lettuce ['lɛtɪs] N alface *f*

leukaemia [luːˈkiːmɪə], (US) **leukemia** N leucemia

level ['lɛvl] ADJ (*flat*) plano ▶ ADV no mesmo nível ▶ N nível *m*; (*height*) altura ▶ VT aplanar; **"A" ~s** *npl* (BRIT) ≈ vestibular *m*; **"O" ~s** *npl* (BRIT) *provas prestadas no final do ensino fundamental*; **to be ~ with** estar no mesmo nível que; **on the ~** em nível; (*fig: honest*) sincero; **level off** VI (*prices etc*) estabilizar-se; **level out** VI, VT = **level off**; **level crossing** (BRIT) N passagem *f* de nível

lever ['liːvə^r] N alavanca; (*fig*) estratagema *m*; **leverage** N força de uma alavanca; (*fig: influence*) influência

liability [laɪəˈbɪlətɪ] N responsabilidade *f*; (*handicap*) desvantagem *f*; **liabilities** NPL (*Comm*) exigibilidades *fpl*, obrigações *fpl*

liable ['laɪəbl] ADJ (*subject*): **~ to** sujeito a; (*responsible*): **~ for** responsável por; (*likely*): **~ to do** capaz de fazer

liaise [liːˈeɪz] VI: **to ~ (with)** cooperar (com)

liar ['laɪə^r] N mentiroso(-a)

libel ['laɪbl] N difamação *f* ▶ VT caluniar, difamar

liberal ['lɪbərl] ADJ liberal; (*generous*) generoso

liberation N liberação *f*, libertação *f*

liberty ['lɪbətɪ] N liberdade *f*; (*criminal*): **to be at ~** estar livre; **to be at ~ to do** ser livre de fazer

Libra ['li:brə] N Libra, Balança
librarian [laɪ'brɛərɪən] N
bibliotecário(-a)
library ['laɪbrərɪ] N biblioteca
Libya ['lɪbɪə] N Líbia
licence ['laɪsns], (US) **license** N
(gen, Comm) licença; (Aut) carta de
motorista (BR), carta de condução (PT)
license ['laɪsns] N (US) = **licence**
▶ VT autorizar, dar licença a; **licensed**
ADJ (car) autorizado oficialmente;
(for alcohol) autorizado para vender
bebidas alcoólicas; **license plate**
(US) N (Aut) placa (de identificação)
(do carro)
lick [lɪk] VT lamber; (inf: defeat)
arrasar, surrar; **to ~ one's lips** (also
fig) lamber os beiços
lid [lɪd] N tampa; (eyelid) pálpebra
lie [laɪ] VI (pt **lay**, pp **lain**) (act)
deitar-se; (state) estar deitado;
(object: be situated) estar,
encontrar-se; (fig: problem, cause)
residir; (in race, league) ocupar;
(pt, pt **lied**) (tell lies) mentir ▶ N
mentira; **to ~ low** (fig) esconder-se;
lie about VI (things) estar
espalhado; (people) vadiar; **lie
around** VI = **lie about**; **lie-in** (BRIT)
N: **to have a lie-in** dormir até tarde
lieutenant [lɛf'tɛnənt, (US)
lu:'tɛnənt] N (Mil) tenente m
life [laɪf] (pl **lives**) N vida; **to come
to ~** animar-se; **lifeboat** N barco
salva-vidas; **lifeguard** N salva-vidas
m/f; **life jacket** N colete m
salva-vidas; **lifelike** ADJ natural;
(realistic) realista; **life preserver**
(US) N = **life jacket**; **life sentence** N
pena de prisão perpétua; **lifetime** N
vida
lift [lɪft] VT levantar ▶ VI (fog)
dispersar-se, dissipar-se ▶ N (BRIT:
elevator) elevador m; **to give sb a ~**

(BRIT) dar uma carona para alguém
(BR), dar uma boleia a alguém (PT);
lift-off N decolagem f
light [laɪt] (pt, pp **lit**) N luz f; (Aut:
headlight) farol m; (: rear light) luz
traseira; (for cigarette etc): **have you
got a ~?** tem fogo? ▶ VT acender;
(room) iluminar ▶ ADJ (colour, room)
claro; (not heavy, also fig) leve; (rain,
traffic) fraco; (movement, action)
delicado; **lights** NPL (Aut) sinal m de
trânsito; **to come to ~** vir à tona;
in the ~ of à luz de; **light up** VI
iluminar-se ▶ VT iluminar; **light
bulb** N lâmpada; **lighten** VT tornar
mais leve; **lighter** N (also: **cigarette
lighter**) isqueiro, acendedor m;
light-hearted ADJ alegre,
despreocupado; **lighthouse** N farol
m; **lighting** N iluminação f; **lightly**
ADV ligeiramente; **to get off lightly**
conseguir se safar, livrar a cara (inf)
lightning ['laɪtnɪŋ] N relâmpago,
raio
lightweight ['laɪtweɪt] ADJ (suit)
leve; (Boxing) peso-leve
like [laɪk] VT gostar de ▶ PREP como;
(such as) tal qual ▶ ADJ parecido,
semelhante ▶ N: **the ~** coisas fpl
parecidas; **his ~s and dislikes** seus
gostos e aversões; **I would ~, I'd ~**
(eu) gostaria de; **to be** or **look ~ sb/
sth** parecer-se com alguém/algo,
parecer alguém/algo; **do it ~ this**
faça isso assim; **it is nothing ~ ...**
não se parece nada com ...; **likeable**
ADJ simpático, agradável
likelihood ['laɪklɪhud] N
probabilidade f
likely ['laɪklɪ] ADJ provável; **he's ~
to leave** é provável que ele se vá;
not ~! (inf) nem morto!
likewise ['laɪkwaɪz] ADV
igualmente; **to do ~** fazer o mesmo

liking ['laɪkɪŋ] N afeição f, simpatia; **to be to sb's ~** ser ao gosto de alguém

lilac ['laɪlək] N lilás m

lily ['lɪlɪ] N lírio, açucena

limb [lɪm] N membro

limbo ['lɪmbəu] N: **to be in ~** (fig) viver na expectativa

lime [laɪm] N (tree) limeira; (fruit) limão m; (also: **~ juice**) suco (BR) or sumo (PT) de limão; (Geo) cal f

limelight ['laɪmlaɪt] N: **to be in the ~** ser o centro das atenções

limestone ['laɪmstəun] N pedra calcária

limit ['lɪmɪt] N limite m ▶ VT limitar; **limited** ADJ limitado; **to be limited to** limitar-se a

limp [lɪmp] N: **to have a ~** mancar, ser coxo ▶ VI mancar ▶ ADJ frouxo

line [laɪn] N linha; (rope) corda; (wire) fio; (row) fila, fileira; (on face) ruga ▶ VT (road, room) encarreirar; (container, clothing): **to ~ sth (with)** forrar algo (de); **to ~ the streets** ladear as ruas; **in ~ with** de acordo com; **line up** VI enfileirar-se ▶ VT enfileirar; (set up, have ready) preparar, arranjar

linen ['lɪnɪn] N artigos de cama e mesa; (cloth) linho

liner ['laɪnə'] N navio de linha regular; (also: **bin ~**) saco para lata de lixo

linger ['lɪŋgə'] VI demorar-se, retardar-se; (smell, tradition) persistir

lining ['laɪnɪŋ] N forro; (Anat) parede f

link [lɪŋk] N (of a chain) elo; (connection) conexão f ▶ VT vincular, unir; (associate): **to ~**

with or **to** unir a; **links** NPL (Golf) campo de golfe; **link up** VT acoplar ▶ VI unir-se

lion ['laɪən] N leão m; **lioness** N leoa

lip [lɪp] N lábio; **lipread** irreg VI ler os lábios; **lip salve** N pomada para os lábios; **lipstick** N batom m

liqueur [lɪ'kjuə'] N licor m

liquid ['lɪkwɪd] ADJ líquido ▶ N líquido

liquor ['lɪkə'] N licor m, bebida alcoólica; **liquor store** (US) N loja que vende bebidas alcoólicas

Lisbon ['lɪzbən] N Lisboa

lisp [lɪsp] N ceceio ▶ VI cecear, falar com a língua presa

list [lɪst] N lista ▶ VT (write down) fazer uma lista or relação de; (enumerate) enumerar

listen ['lɪsn] VI escutar, ouvir; **to ~ to** escutar; **listener** N ouvinte m/f

lit [lɪt] PT, PP of **light**

liter ['liːtə'] (US) N = **litre**

literacy ['lɪtərəsɪ] N capacidade f de ler e escrever, alfabetização f

literal ['lɪtərl] ADJ literal

literary ['lɪtərərɪ] ADJ literário

literate ['lɪtərət] ADJ alfabetizado, instruído; (educated) culto, letrado

literature ['lɪtərɪtʃə'] N literatura; (brochures etc) folhetos mpl

litre ['liːtə'], (US) **liter** N litro

litter ['lɪtə'] N (rubbish) lixo; (young animals) ninhada; **litter bin** (BRIT) N lata de lixo

little ['lɪtl] ADJ (small) pequeno; (not much) pouco ▶ ADV pouco; **a ~** um pouco (de); **~ house** casinha; **for a ~ while** por um instante; **as ~ as possible** o menos possível; **~ by ~** pouco a pouco

live [*vi, vt* lɪv, *adj* laɪv] vɪ viver; (*reside*) morar ▶ ADJ vivo; (*wire*) eletrizado; (*broadcast*) ao vivo; (*shell*) carregado; **~ ammunition** munição de guerra; **live down** vт redimir; **live on** vт FUS viver de, alimentar-se de; **to ~ on £50 a week** viver com £50 por semana; **live together** vɪ viver juntos; **live up to** vт FUS (*fulfil*) cumprir

livelihood ['laɪvlɪhud] N meio de vida, subsistência

lively ['laɪvlɪ] ADJ vivo

liven up ['laɪvn-] vт animar ▶ vɪ animar-se

liver ['lɪvəʳ] N fígado

lives [laɪvz] NPL *of* **life**

living ['lɪvɪŋ] ADJ vivo ▶ N: **to earn** or **make a ~** ganhar a vida; **living room** N sala de estar; **living will** N testamento em vida

lizard ['lɪzəd] N lagarto

load [ləud] N carga; (*weight*) peso ▶ vт (*gen, Comput*) carregar; **a ~ of, ~s of** (*fig*) um monte de, uma porção de; **loaded** ADJ (*question, word*) intencionado; (*inf: rich*) cheio da nota; (*vehicle*): **to be loaded with** estar carregado de

loaf [ləuf] (*pl* **loaves**) N pão-de-forma *m*

loan [ləun] N empréstimo ▶ vт emprestar; **on ~** emprestado

loathe [ləuð] vт detestar, odiar

loaves [ləuvz] NPL *of* **loaf**

lobby ['lɔbɪ] N vestíbulo, saguão *m*; (*Pol: pressure group*) grupo de pressão, lobby *m* ▶ vт pressionar

lobster ['lɔbstəʳ] N lagostim *m*; (*large*) lagosta

local ['ləukl] ADJ local ▶ N (*pub*) bar *m* (local); **the locals** NPL (*local inhabitants*) os moradores locais; **local anaesthetic** N anestesia local

locate [ləu'keɪt] vт (*find*) localizar, situar; (*situate*): **to be ~d in** estar localizado em

location [ləu'keɪʃən] N local *m*, posição *f*; **on ~** (*Cinema*) em externas

loch [lɔx] N lago

lock [lɔk] N (*of door, box*) fechadura; (*of canal*) eclusa; (*of hair*) anel *m*, mecha ▶ vт (*with key*) trancar ▶ vɪ (*door etc*) fechar-se à chave; (*wheels*) travar-se; **lock in** vт trancar dentro; **lock out** vт trancar do lado de fora; **lock up** vт (*criminal, mental patient*) prender; (*house*) trancar ▶ vɪ fechar tudo

locker ['lɔkəʳ] N compartimento com chave; **locker-room** (*us*) N (*Sport*) vestiário

locksmith ['lɔksmɪθ] N serralheiro(-a)

lodge [lɔdʒ] N casa do guarda, guarita; (*hunting lodge*) pavilhão *m* de caça ▶ vɪ (*person*): **to ~ (with)** alojar-se (na casa de) ▶ vт (*complaint*) apresentar; **lodger** N inquilino(-a), hóspede *m/f*

loft [lɔft] N sótão *m*

log [lɔg] N (*of wood*) tora; (*book*) = **logbook** ▶ vт registrar; **logbook** N (*Naut*) diário de bordo; (*Aviat*) diário de voo; (*of car*) documentação *f* (do carro)

logic ['lɔdʒɪk] N lógica; **logical** ADJ lógico

login ['lɔgɪn] N (*Comput*) login *m*

LOL (*inf*) ABBR (= *laugh out loud*) rs, LOL

lollipop ['lɔlɪpɔp] N pirulito (BR), chupa-chupa *m* (PT); **lollipop lady** (BRIT) N mulher que ajuda as crianças a atravessarem a rua; **lollipop man** (BRIT) N homem que ajuda as crianças a atravessarem a rua

Lollipop men/ladies são as pessoas que ajudam as crianças a atravessar a rua nas proximidades das escolas na hora da entrada e da saída. São facilmente localizados graças a suas longas capas brancas e à placa redonda com a qual pedem aos motoristas que parem. São chamados assim por causa da forma circular da placa, que lembra um pirulito (lollipop).

lolly ['lɔlɪ] (inf) N (ice) picolé m; (lollipop) pirulito

London ['lʌndən] N Londres; **Londoner** N londrino(-a)

lone [ləun] ADJ (person) solitário; (thing) único

loneliness ['ləunlɪnɪs] N solidão f, isolamento

lonely ['ləunlɪ] ADJ (person) só; (place, childhood) solitário, isolado

long [lɔŋ] ADJ longo; (road, hair, table) comprido ▶ ADV muito tempo ▶ VI: **to ~ for sth** ansiar or suspirar por algo; **how ~ is the street?** qual é a extensão da rua?; **how ~ is the lesson?** quanto dura a lição?; **all night ~** a noite inteira; **he no ~er comes** ele não vem mais; **~ before/after** muito antes/depois; **before ~** (+ future) dentro de pouco; (+ past) pouco tempo depois; **at ~ last** por fim, no final; **so** or **as ~ as** contanto que; **long-distance** ADJ (travel) de longa distância; (call) interurbano; **longing** N desejo, anseio

longitude ['lɔŋɡɪtjuːd] N longitude f;

long: long jump N salto em distância; **long-sighted** ADJ presbita; **long-standing** ADJ de muito tempo; **long-term** ADJ a longo prazo

loo [luː] (BRIT inf) N banheiro (BR), casa de banho (PT)

look [luk] VI olhar; (seem) parecer; (building etc): **to ~ south/(out) onto the sea** dar para o sul/o mar ▶ N olhar m; (glance) olhada, vista de olhos; (appearance) aparência, aspecto; **looks** NPL (good looks) físico, aparência; **~ (here)!** (annoyance) escuta aqui!; **~!** (surprise) olha!; **look after** VT FUS cuidar de; (deal with) lidar com; **look at** VT FUS olhar (para); (read quickly) ler rapidamente; (consider) considerar; **look back** VI: **to ~ back on** (remember) recordar, rever; **look down on** VT FUS (fig) desdenhar, desprezar; **look for** VT FUS procurar; **look forward to** VT FUS aguardar com prazer, ansiar por; (in letter): **we ~ forward to hearing from you** no aguardo de suas notícias; **look into** VT FUS investigar; **look on** VI assistir; **look out** VI (beware): **to ~ out (for)** tomar cuidado (com); **look out for** VT FUS (await) esperar; **look round** VI virar a cabeça, voltar-se; **look through** VT FUS (papers, book) examinar; **look to** VT FUS (rely on) contar com; **look up** VI levantar os olhos; (improve) melhorar ▶ VT (word) procurar

loop [luːp] N laço ▶ VT: **to ~ sth round sth** prender algo em torno de algo

loose [luːs] ADJ solto; (not tight) frouxo ▶ N: **to be on the ~** estar solto; **loosely** ADV frouxamente, folgadamente; **loosen** VT (free) soltar; (slacken) afrouxar

loot [luːt] N saque m, despojo ▶ VT saquear, pilhar

lord [lɔːd] N senhor m; **L~ Smith** Lord Smith; **the L~** (Rel) o Senhor; **good L~!** Deus meu!; **the (House of) L~s** (BRIT) a Câmara dos Lordes

lorry ['lɔrɪ] (BRIT) N caminhão m (BR), camião m (PT); **lorry driver** (BRIT) N caminhoneiro (BR), camionista m/f (PT)

lose [luːz] (pt, pp **lost**) VT, VI perder; **to ~ (time)** (clock) atrasar-se; **loser** N perdedor(a) m/f; (inf: failure) derrotado(-a), fracassado(-a)

loss [lɔs] N perda; (Comm): **to make a ~** sair com prejuízo; **heavy ~es** (Mil) grandes perdas; **to be at a ~** estar perplexo

lost [lɔst] PT, PP of **lose** ▶ ADJ perdido; **~ and found** (US) (seção f de) perdidos e achados mpl; **lost property** (BRIT) N (objetos mpl) perdidos e achados mpl

lot [lɔt] N (set of things) porção f; (at auctions) lote m; **the ~** tudo, todos(-as); **a ~** muito, bastante; **a ~ of, ~s of** muito(s); **I read a ~** leio bastante; **to draw ~s** tirar à sorte

lotion ['ləʊʃən] N loção f

lottery ['lɔtərɪ] N loteria

loud [laʊd] ADJ (voice) alto; (shout) forte; (noise) barulhento; (support, condemnation) veemente; (gaudy) berrante ▶ ADV alto; **out ~** em voz alta; **loudly** ADV ruidosamente; (aloud) em voz alta; **loudspeaker** N alto-falante m

lounge [laʊndʒ] N sala de estar f; (of airport) salão m; (BRIT: also: **~ bar**) bar m social ▶ VI recostar-se, espreguiçar-se; **lounge about, lounge around** VI ficar à-toa

lousy ['laʊzɪ] (inf) ADJ ruim, péssimo; (ill): **to feel ~** sentir-se mal

love [lʌv] N amor m ▶ VT amar; (like a lot) adorar; **to ~ to do** adorar fazer; **~ (from) Anne** (on letter) um abraço or um beijo, Anne; **I ~ you** eu te amo; **I ~ coffee** adoro o café; **"15 ~"** (Tennis) "15 a zero"; **to be in ~ with** estar apaixonado por; **to fall in ~ with** apaixonar-se por; **to make ~** fazer amor; **love affair** N aventura (amorosa), caso f de amor); **love life** N vida sentimental

lovely ['lʌvlɪ] ADJ (delightful) encantador(a), delicioso; (beautiful) lindo, belo; (holiday, surprise) muito agradável, maravilhoso

lover ['lʌvər] N amante m/f

loving ['lʌvɪŋ] ADJ carinhoso, afetuoso; (actions) dedicado

low [ləʊ] ADJ baixo; (depressed) deprimido; (ill) doente ▶ ADV baixo ▶ N (Meteorology) área de baixa pressão; **to be ~ on** (supplies) ter pouco; **to reach a new** or **an all-time ~** cair para o seu nível mais baixo; **low-alcohol** ADJ de baixo teor alcoólico; **low-calorie** ADJ de baixo teor calórico; **low-carb** (inf) ADJ (diet, meal) com baixo carboidrato; **lower** ADJ mais baixo; (less important) inferior ▶ VT abaixar; (reduce) reduzir, diminuir; **low-fat** ADJ magro

loyal ['lɔɪəl] ADJ leal; **loyalty** N lealdade f

loyalty card (BRIT) N cartão m de fidelidade

L-plates ['ɛlpleɪts] (BRIT) NPL placas fpl de aprendiz de motorista

As **L-plates** são placas quadradas com um "L" vermelho que são colocadas na parte de trás do carro para mostrar que a pessoa ao volante ainda não tem carteira de motorista. Até a obtenção da carteira, o motorista aprendiz possui uma permissão provisória e não tem direito de dirigir sem um motorista qualificado ao lado. Os motoristas aprendizes não podem dirigir em estradas mesmo que estejam acompanhados.

Ltd (BRIT) ABBR (= *limited (liability) company*) SA

luck [lʌk] N sorte *f*; **bad ~** azar *m*; **good ~!** boa sorte!; **bad** or **hard** or **tough ~!** que azar!; **luckily** ADV por sorte, felizmente; **lucky** ADJ (*person*) sortudo; (*situation*) afortunado; (*object*) de sorte

ludicrous ['lu:dɪkrəs] ADJ ridículo

luggage ['lʌgɪdʒ] N bagagem *f*; **luggage rack** N porta-bagagem *m*, bagageiro

lukewarm ['lu:kwɔ:m] ADJ morno, tépido; (*fig*) indiferente

lull [lʌl] N pausa, interrupção *f* ▶ VT: **to ~ sb to sleep** acalentar alguém; **to be ~ed into a false sense of security** ser acalmado com uma falsa sensação de segurança

lullaby ['lʌləbaɪ] N canção *f* de ninar

lumber ['lʌmbə^r] N (*junk*) trastes *mpl* velhos; (*wood*) madeira serrada, tábua ▶ VT: **to ~ sb with sth/sb** empurrar algo/alguém para cima de alguém

luminous ['lu:mɪnəs] ADJ luminoso

lump [lʌmp] N torrão *m*; (*fragment*) pedaço; (*on body*) galo, caroço; (*also*: **sugar ~**) cubo de açúcar ▶ VT: **to ~ together** amontoar; **lump sum** N montante *m* único; **lumpy** ADJ encaroçado

lunatic ['lu:nətɪk] ADJ louco(-a)

lunch [lʌntʃ] N almoço; **lunch break, lunch hour** N hora do almoço

lung [lʌŋ] N pulmão *m*

lure [luə^r] N isca ▶ VT atrair, seduzir

lurk [lə:k] VI (*hide*) esconder-se; (*wait*) estar à espreita

lush [lʌʃ] ADJ exuberante

lust [lʌst] N luxúria; (*greed*) cobiça; **lust after** VT FUS cobiçar; **lust for** VT FUS = **lust after**

Luxembourg ['lʌksəmbə:g] N Luxemburgo

luxurious [lʌg'zjuərɪəs] ADJ luxuoso

luxury ['lʌkʃərɪ] N luxo ▶ CPD de luxo

lying ['laɪɪŋ] N mentira(s) *f(pl)* ▶ ADJ mentiroso, falso

lyrics ['lɪrɪks] NPL (*of song*) letra

M.A. ABBR (*Sch*) = **Master of Arts**
mac [mæk] (*BRIT*) N capa impermeável
macaroni [mækə'rəunɪ] N macarrão *m*
machine [mə'ʃiːn] N máquina ▶ VT (*dress etc*) costurar à máquina; (*Tech*) usinar; **machine gun** N metralhadora; **machinery** N maquinaria; (*fig*) máquina
mackerel ['mækrl] N INV cavala
mackintosh ['mækɪntɔʃ] (*BRIT*) N capa impermeável
mad [mæd] ADJ louco; (*foolish*) tolo; (*angry*) furioso, brabo; (*keen*): **to be ~ about** ser louco por
madam ['mædəm] N senhora, madame *f*
made [meɪd] PT, PP *of* **make**; **made-to-measure** (*BRIT*) ADJ feito sob medida; **made-up** ['meɪdʌp] ADJ (*story*) inventado
madly ['mædlɪ] ADV loucamente; **~ in love** louco de amor
madman ['mædmən] *irreg* N louco

madness ['mædnɪs] N loucura; (*foolishness*) tolice *f*
magazine [mægə'ziːn] N (*Press*) revista; (*Radio, TV*) programa *m* de atualidades
maggot ['mægət] N larva de inseto
magic ['mædʒɪk] N magia, mágica ▶ ADJ mágico; **magical** ADJ mágico; **magician** [mə'dʒɪʃən] N mago(-a); (*entertainer*) mágico(-a)
magistrate ['mædʒɪstreɪt] N magistrado(-a), juiz/juíza *m/f*
magnet ['mægnɪt] N ímã *m*; **magnetic** [mæg'nɛtɪk] ADJ magnético
magnificent [mæg'nɪfɪsnt] ADJ magnífico
magnify ['mægnɪfaɪ] VT aumentar; **magnifying glass** N lupa, lente *f* de aumento
magpie ['mægpaɪ] N pega
mahogany [mə'hɔgənɪ] N mogno, acaju *m*
maid [meɪd] N empregada; **old ~** (*pej*) solteirona
maiden name ['meɪdn-] N nome *m* de solteira
mail [meɪl] N correio; (*letters*) cartas *fpl* ▶ VT pôr no correio; **mailbox** N (*US*) caixa do correio; **mailing list** N lista de clientes, mailing list *m*
main [meɪn] ADJ principal ▶ N (*pipe*) cano *or* esgoto principal; **the mains** NPL (*Elec, gas, water*) a rede; **in the ~** na maior parte; **mainland** N: **the mainland** o continente; **mainly** ADV principalmente; **main road** N estrada principal; **mainstream** N corrente *f* principal
maintain [meɪn'teɪn] VT manter; (*keep up*) conservar (em bom estado); (*affirm*) sustentar, afirmar; **maintenance** ['meɪntənəns] N

manutenção f; (*alimony*) alimentos mpl, pensão f alimentícia

maize [meɪz] N milho

majesty ['mædʒɪstɪ] N majestade f

major ['meɪdʒər] N (*Mil*) major m
▶ ADJ (*main*) principal; (*considerable*) importante; (*Mus*) maior

Majorca [mə'jɔːkə] N Maiorca

majority [mə'dʒɔrɪtɪ] N maioria

make [meɪk] (*pt*, *pp* **made**) VT fazer; (*manufacture*) fabricar, produzir; (*cause to be*): **to ~ sb sad** entristecer alguém, fazer alguém ficar triste; (*force*): **to ~ sb do sth** fazer com que alguém faça algo; (*equal*): **2 and 2 ~ 4** dois e dois são quatro ▶ N marca; **to ~ a profit/ loss** ter um lucro/uma perda; **to ~ it** (*arrive*) chegar; (*succeed*) ter sucesso; **what time do you ~ it?** que horas você tem?; **to ~ do with** contentar-se com; **make for** VT FUS (*place*) dirigir-se a; **make out** VT (*decipher*) decifrar; (*understand*) compreender; (*see*) divisar, avistar; **make up** VT (*constitute*) constituir; (*invent*) inventar; (*parcel*) embrulhar ▶ VI reconciliar-se; (*with cosmetics*) maquiar-se (BR), maquilhar-se (PT); **make up for** VT FUS compensar; **maker** N (*of film, programme*) criador m; (*manufacturer*) fabricante m/f; **makeshift** ADJ provisório; **make-up** N maquilagem f (BR), maquilhagem f (PT)

malaria [mə'lɛərɪə] N malária

Malaysia [mə'leɪzɪə] N Malaísia (BR), Malásia (PT)

male [meɪl] N macho ▶ ADJ masculino; (*child etc*) do sexo masculino

malignant [mə'lɪgnənt] ADJ (*Med*) maligno

mall [mɔːl] N (*also*: **shopping ~**) shopping m

mallet ['mælɪt] N maço, marreta

malt [mɔːlt] N malte m

Malta ['mɔːltə] N Malta

malware ['mælwɛər] N (*Comput*) software m malicioso

mammal ['mæml] N mamífero

mammoth ['mæməθ] N mamute m ▶ ADJ gigantesco, imenso

man [mæn] (*pl* **men**) N homem m ▶ VT (*Naut*) tripular; (*Mil*) guarnecer; (*machine*) operar; **an old ~** um velho; **~ and wife** marido e mulher

manage ['mænɪdʒ] VI arranjar-se, virar-se ▶ VT (*be in charge of*) dirigir, administrar; (*business*) gerenciar; (*ship, person*) controlar; **manageable** ADJ manejável; (*task etc*) viável; **management** N administração f, direção f, gerência; **manager** N gerente m/f; (*Sport*) técnico(-a); **manageress** N gerente f; **managerial** [mænə'dʒɪə:rɪəl] ADJ administrativo, gerencial; **managing director** N diretor(a) m/f, diretor-gerente/ diretora-gerente m/f

mandarin ['mændərɪn] N (*also*: **~ orange**) tangerina; (*person*) mandarim m

mandatory ['mændətərɪ] ADJ obrigatório

mane [meɪn] N (*of horse*) crina; (*of lion*) juba

maneuver [mə'nuːvər] (*US*) = **manoeuvre**

mango ['mæŋgəu] (*pl* **mangoes**) N manga

manhole ['mænhəul] N poço de inspeção

m

manhood ['mænhud] N (age)
idade f adulta; (masculinity)
virilidade f

mania ['meɪnɪə] N mania; **maniac**
['meɪnɪæk] N maníaco(-a); (fig)
louco(-a)

manic ['mænɪk] ADJ maníaco

manicure ['mænɪkjuəʳ] N
manicure f (BR), manicura (PT)

manifest ['mænɪfɛst] VT
manifestar, mostrar ▶ ADJ
manifesto, evidente

manipulate [mə'nɪpjuleɪt] VT
manipular

mankind [mæn'kaɪnd] N
humanidade f, raça humana

man-made ADJ sintético, artificial

manner ['mænəʳ] N modo,
maneira; (behaviour) conduta,
comportamento; **manners** NPL
(conduct) boas maneiras fpl,
educação f; **bad ~s** falta de
educação; **all ~ of** todo tipo de; **all
~ of things** todos os tipos de coisa

manoeuvre [mə'nu:vəʳ], (US)
maneuver VT manobrar;
(manipulate) manipular ▶ VI
manobrar ▶ N manobra

manpower ['mænpauəʳ] N
potencial m humano, mão-de-obra f

mansion ['mænʃən] N mansão f,
palacete m

manslaughter ['mænslɔ:təʳ] N
homicídio involuntário

mantelpiece ['mæntlpi:s] N
consolo da lareira

manual ['mænjuəl] ADJ manual
▶ N manual m

manufacture [mænju'fæktʃəʳ] VT
manufaturar, fabricar ▶ N
fabricação f; **manufacturer** N
fabricante m/f

manure [mə'njuəʳ] N estrume m,
adubo

manuscript ['mænjuskrɪpt] N
manuscrito

many ['mɛnɪ] ADJ, PRON
muitos(-as); **a great ~**
muitíssimos; **~ a time** muitas vezes

map [mæp] N mapa m; **map out** VT
traçar

maple ['meɪpl] N bordo

mar [mɑ:ʳ] VT estragar

marathon ['mærəθən] N
maratona

marble ['mɑ:bl] N mármore m; (toy)
bola de gude

March [mɑ:tʃ] N março

march [mɑ:tʃ] VI marchar;
(demonstrators) desfilar ▶ N marcha,
passeata

mare [mɛəʳ] N égua

margarine [mɑ:dʒə'ri:n] N
margarina

margin ['mɑ:dʒɪn] N margem f;
marginal ADJ marginal; **marginal
seat** (Pol) cadeira ganha por
pequena maioria

marigold ['mærɪgəuld] N
malmequer m

marijuana [mærɪ'wɑ:nə] N
maconha

marine [mə'ri:n] ADJ marinho;
(engineer) naval ▶ N fuzileiro naval

marital ['mærɪtl] ADJ matrimonial,
marital; **~ status** estado civil

marjoram ['mɑ:dʒərəm] N
manjerona

mark [mɑ:k] N marca, sinal m;
(imprint) impressão f; (stain)
mancha; (BRIT Sch) nota; (currency)
marco ▶ VT marcar; (stain)
manchar; (indicate) indicar;
(commemorate) comemorar; (BRIT
Sch) dar nota em; (: correct) corrigir;
to ~ time marcar passo; **marker** N
(sign) marcador m, marca;
(bookmark) marcador

market ['mɑ:kɪt] N mercado ▶ VT (Comm) comercializar; **marketing** N marketing m; **marketplace** N mercado; **market research** N pesquisa de mercado

marmalade ['mɑ:məleɪd] N geleia de laranja

maroon [mə'ru:n] VT: **to be ~ed** ficar abandonado (numa ilha) ▶ ADJ vinho inv

marquee [mɑ:'ki:] N toldo, tenda

marriage ['mærɪdʒ] N casamento

married ['mærɪd] ADJ casado; (life, love) conjugal

marrow ['mærəu] N medula; (vegetable) abóbora

marry ['mærɪ] VT casar(-se) com; (subj: father, priest etc) casar, unir ▶ VI (also: **get married**) casar(-se)

Mars [mɑ:z] N Marte m

marsh [mɑ:ʃ] N pântano; (salt marsh) marisma

marshal ['mɑ:ʃl] N (Mil: also: **field ~**) marechal m; (at sports meeting etc) oficial m ▶ VT (thoughts, support) organizar; (soldiers) formar

martyr ['mɑ:tər] N mártir m/f

marvel ['mɑ:vl] N maravilha ▶ VI: **to ~ (at)** maravilhar-se (de or com); **marvellous**, (US) **marvelous** ADJ maravilhoso

Marxist ['mɑ:ksɪst] ADJ, N marxista m/f

mascara [mæs'kɑ:rə] N rímel m

masculine ['mæskjulɪn] ADJ masculino

mash [mæʃ] VT (Culin) fazer um purê de; (crush) amassar

mask [mɑ:sk] N máscara ▶ VT (face) encobrir; (feelings) esconder, ocultar

mason ['meɪsn] N (also: **stone ~**) pedreiro(-a); (also: **free~**) maçom m; **masonry** N alvenaria

mass [mæs] N quantidade f; (people) multidão f; (Phys) massa; (Rel) missa; (great quantity) montão m ▶ CPD de massa ▶ VI reunir-se; (Mil) concentrar-se; **the masses** NPL (ordinary people) as massas; **~es of** (inf) montes de

massacre ['mæsəkər] N massacre m, carnificina

massage ['mæsɑ:ʒ] N massagem f

massive ['mæsɪv] ADJ (large) enorme; (support) massivo

mass media NPL meios mpl de comunicação de massa, mídia

mast [mɑ:st] N (Naut) mastro m; (Radio etc) antena

master ['mɑ:stər] N mestre m; (fig: of situation) dono; (in secondary school) professor m; (title for boys): **M~ X** o menino X ▶ VT controlar; (learn) conhecer a fundo; **mastermind** N (fig) cabeça ▶ VT dirigir, planejar; **masterpiece** N obra-prima

mat [mæt] N esteira; (also: **door~**) capacho; (also: **table ~**) descanso

match [mætʃ] N fósforo; (game) jogo, partida; (equal) igual m/f ▶ VT (also: **~ up**) casar, emparelhar; (go well with) combinar com; (equal) igualar; (correspond to) corresponder a ▶ VI combinar; **to be a good ~** (couple) formar um bom casal; **matchbox** N caixa de fósforos; **matching** ADJ que combina (com)

mate [meɪt] N (inf) colega m/f; (assistant) ajudante m/f; (animal) macho/fêmea; (in merchant navy) imediato ▶ VI acasalar-se

material [mə'tɪərɪəl] N (substance) matéria; (equipment) material m; (cloth) pano, tecido;

(*data*) dados *mpl* ▶ ADJ material;
materials NPL (*equipment*) material
maternal [mə'tə:nl] ADJ maternal
maternity [mə'tə:nɪtɪ] N
maternidade *f*
mathematical [mæθə'mætɪkl]
ADJ matemático
mathematics [mæθə'mætɪks] N
matemática
maths [mæθs], (US) **math** N
matemática
matron ['meɪtrən] N (*in hospital*)
enfermeira-chefe *f*; (*in school*)
inspetora
matter ['mætə'] N questão *f*,
assunto; (*Phys*) matéria; (*substance*)
substância; (*reading matter etc*)
material *m*; (*Med: pus*) pus *m* ▶ VI
importar; **matters** NPL (*affairs*)
questões *fpl*; **it doesn't ~** não
importa; (*I don't mind*) tanto faz;
what's the ~? o que (é que) há?,
qual é o problema?; **no ~ what**
aconteça o que acontecer; **as a ~ of**
course por rotina; **as a ~ of fact** na
realidade, de fato
mattress ['mætrɪs] N colchão *m*
mature [mə'tjuə'] ADJ maduro;
(*cheese, wine*) amadurecido ▶ VI
amadurecer
maul [mɔ:l] VT machucar, maltratar
mauve [məuv] ADJ cor de malva *inv*
maximum ['mæksɪməm] (*pl*
maxima *or* **maximums**) ADJ
máximo ▶ N máximo
May [meɪ] N maio
may [meɪ] (*conditional* **might**) AUX
VB (*indicating possibility*): **he ~ come**
pode ser que ele venha, é capaz de
vir; (*be allowed to*): **~ I smoke?** posso
fumar?; (*wishes*): **~ God bless you!**
que Deus lhe abençoe
maybe ['meɪbi:] ADV talvez; **~ not**
talvez não

mayhem ['meɪhɛm] N caos *m*
mayonnaise [meɪə'neɪz] N
maionese *f*
mayor [mɛə'] N prefeito (BR),
presidente *m* do município (PT);
mayoress N prefeita (BR),
presidenta do município (PT)
maze [meɪz] N labirinto

(KEYWORD)

me [mi:] PRON **1** (*direct*) me; **he**
heard me ele me ouviu; **it's me**
sou eu
2 (*indirect*) me; **he gave me the**
money ele me deu o dinheiro; **give**
it to me dá isso para mim
3 (*stressed, after prep*) mim; **with me**
comigo; **without me** sem mim

meadow ['mɛdəu] N prado, campina
meagre ['mi:gə'], (US) **meager** ADJ
escasso
meal [mi:l] N refeição *f*; (*flour*)
farinha; **mealtime** N hora da
refeição
mean [mi:n] (*pt, pp* **meant**) ADJ
(*with money*) sovina, avarento,
pão-duro *inv* (BR); (*unkind*)
mesquinho; (*shabby*) malcuidado,
dilapidado; (*average*) médio ▶ VT
(*signify*) significar, querer dizer;
(*refer to*): **I thought you ~t her** eu
pensei que você estivesse se
referindo a ela; (*intend*): **to ~ to do**
sth pretender *or* tencionar fazer
algo ▶ N meio, meio termo; **means**
NPL (*way, money*) meio; **by ~s of** por
meio de, mediante; **by all ~s!** claro
que sim!, pois não; **do you ~ it?**
você está falando sério?
meaning ['mi:nɪŋ] N sentido,
significado; **meaningful** ADJ
significativo; (*relationship*) sério;
meaningless ADJ sem sentido

meant [mɛnt] PT, PP *of* **mean**

meantime ['miːntaɪm] ADV (*also:* **in the ~**) entretanto, enquanto isso

meanwhile ['miːnwaɪl] ADV = **meantime**

measles ['miːzlz] N sarampo

measure ['mɛʒəʳ] VT, VI medir ▶ N medida; (*also:* **tape ~**) fita métrica

measurement ['mɛʒəmənt] N medida; **measurements** NPL (*size*) medidas *fpl*

meat [miːt] N carne *f*; **cold ~s** (*BRIT*) frios; **meatball** N almôndega

Mecca ['mɛkə] N Meca; (*fig*): **a ~ (for)** a meca (de)

mechanic [mɪ'kænɪk] N mecânico; **mechanical** ADJ mecânico

mechanism ['mɛkənɪzəm] N mecanismo

medal ['mɛdl] N medalha

meddle ['mɛdl] VI: **to ~ in** meter-se em, intrometer-se em; **to ~ with sth** mexer em algo

media ['miːdɪə] NPL meios *mpl* de comunicação, mídia

mediaeval [mɛdɪ'iːvl] ADJ = **medieval**

mediate ['miːdɪeɪt] VI mediar

medical ['mɛdɪkl] ADJ médico ▶ N (*examination*) exame *m* médico

medication [mɛdɪ'keɪʃən] N medicação *f*

medicine ['mɛdsɪn] N medicina; (*drug*) remédio, medicamento

medieval [mɛdɪ'iːvl] ADJ medieval

mediocre [miːdɪ'əukəʳ] ADJ medíocre

meditate ['mɛdɪteɪt] VI meditar

Mediterranean [mɛdɪtə'reɪnɪən] ADJ mediterrâneo; **the ~ (Sea)** o (mar) Mediterrâneo

medium ['miːdɪəm] (*pl* **media** *or* **mediums**) ADJ médio ▶ N (*means*) meio; (*pl* **mediums**: *person*) médium *m/f*

meek [miːk] ADJ manso, dócil

meet [miːt] (*pt, pp* **met**) VT encontrar; (*accidentally*) topar com, dar de cara com; (*by arrangement*) encontrar-se com, ir ao encontro de; (*for the first time*) conhecer; (*go and fetch*) ir buscar; (*opponent, problem*) enfrentar; (*obligations*) cumprir; (*need*) satisfazer ▶ VI encontrar-se; (*for talks*) reunir-se; (*join*) unir-se; (*get to know*) conhecer-se; **meet with** VT FUS reunir-se com; (*difficulty*) encontrar; **meeting** N encontro; (*session: of club, Comm*) reunião *f*; (*assembly*) assembleia, (*Sport*) corrida

megabyte ['mɛgəbaɪt] N (*Comput*) megabyte *m*

megaphone ['mɛgəfəun] N megafone *m*

megapixel ['mɛgəpɪksl] N megapixel *m*

melancholy ['mɛlənkəlɪ] N melancolia ▶ ADJ melancólico

melody ['mɛlədɪ] N melodia

melon ['mɛlən] N melão *m*

melt [mɛlt] VI (*metal*) fundir-se; (*snow*) derreter ▶ VT derreter; **melt down** VT fundir

member ['mɛmbəʳ] N membro(-a); (*of club*) sócio(-a); (*Anat*) membro; **M~ of Parliament** (*BRIT*) deputado(-a); **membership** N (*state*) adesão *f*; (*members*) número de sócios; **membership card** N carteira de sócio

memento [mə'mɛntəu] N lembrança

memo ['mɛməu] N memorando, nota

memorandum [mɛmə'rændəm] (*pl* **memoranda**) N memorando

memorial [mɪ'mɔːrɪəl] N monumento comemorativo ▶ ADJ comemorativo; **Memorial Day** (US) N *ver nota*

Memorial Day é um feriado nos Estados Unidos, a última segunda-feira de maio na maior parte dos estados, em memória aos soldados americanos mortos em combate.

memorize ['mɛməraɪz] VT decorar, aprender de cor

memory ['mɛmərɪ] N memória; (*recollection*) lembrança; **memory stick** N (*Comput: flash pen*) pen drive *m*; (*card*) cartão *m* de memória

men [mɛn] NPL *of* **man**

menace ['mɛnəs] N ameaça; (*nuisance*) droga ▶ VT ameaçar

mend [mɛnd] VT consertar, reparar; (*darn*) remendar ▶ N: **to be on the ~** estar melhorando

meningitis [mɛnɪn'dʒaɪtɪs] N meningite *f*

menopause ['mɛnəupɔːz] N menopausa

menstruation [mɛnstru'eɪʃən] N menstruação *f*

mental ['mɛntl] ADJ mental; **mentality** [mɛn'tælɪtɪ] N mentalidade *f*

mention ['mɛnʃən] N menção *f* ▶ VT (*speak of*) falar de; **don't ~ it!** não tem de quê!, de nada!

menu ['mɛnjuː] N (*set menu, Comput*) menu *m*; (*printed*) cardápio (BR), ementa (PT)

MEP N ABBR (= *Member of the European Parliament*) deputado(-a)

mercenary ['məːsɪnərɪ] ADJ mercenário ▶ N mercenário

merchandise ['məːtʃəndaɪz] N mercadorias *fpl*

merchant ['məːtʃənt] N comerciante *m/f*

merciless ['məːsɪlɪs] ADJ desumano, inclemente

mercury ['məːkjurɪ] N mercúrio

mercy ['məːsɪ] N piedade *f*; (*Rel*) misericórdia; **at the ~ of** à mercê de

mere [mɪər] ADJ mero, simples *inv*; **merely** ADV simplesmente, somente, apenas

merge [məːdʒ] VT unir ▶ VI unir-se; (*Comm*) fundir-se; **merger** N fusão *f*

meringue [mə'ræŋ] N suspiro, merengue *m*

merit ['mɛrɪt] N mérito; (*advantage*) vantagem *f* ▶ VT merecer

mermaid ['məːmeɪd] N sereia

merry ['mɛrɪ] ADJ alegre; **M~ Christmas!** Feliz Natal!; **merry-go-round** N carrossel *m*

mesh [mɛʃ] N malha

mess [mɛs] N confusão *f*; (*in room*) bagunça; (*Mil*) rancho; **to be in a ~** ser uma bagunça, estar numa bagunça; **mess about** (*inf*) VI perder tempo; (*pass the time*) vadiar; **mess about with** (*inf*) VT FUS mexer com; **mess around** (*inf*) VI = **mess about**; **mess up** VT (*spoil*) estragar; (*dirty*) sujar

message ['mɛsɪdʒ] N recado, mensagem *f* ▶ VT enviar uma mensagem para; **message board** N (*on internet*) fórum *m* de discussão

messenger ['mɛsɪndʒər] N mensageiro(-a)

messy ['mɛsɪ] ADJ (*dirty*) sujo; (*untidy*) desarrumado

met [mɛt] PT, PP *of* **meet**

metal ['mɛtl] N metal *m*

meteorology [mi:tɪəˈrɔlədʒɪ] N
meteorologia
meter [ˈmiːtəʳ] N (instrument)
medidor m; (also: **parking ~**)
parcômetro; (US: unit) = **metre**
method [ˈmɛθəd] N método;
methodical [mɪˈθɔdɪkl] ADJ
metódico
metre [ˈmiːtəʳ], (US) **meter** N metro
metric [ˈmɛtrɪk] ADJ métrico
metropolitan [mɛtrəˈpɔlɪtən]
ADJ metropolitano
Mexico [ˈmɛksɪkəu] N México
mice [maɪs] NPL of **mouse**
micro... [maɪkrəu] PREFIX
micro; **microblog** [ˈmaɪkrəublɔg]
N microblog(ue) m; **microchip** N
microchip m; **microphone** N
microfone m; **microscope** N
microscópio; **microwave** N
(also: **microwave oven**)
micro-ondas m inv
mid [mɪd] ADJ: **in ~ May** em
meados de maio; **in ~ afternoon**
no meio da tarde; **in ~ air** em
pleno ar; **midday** N meio-dia m
middle [ˈmɪdl] N meio; (waist)
cintura ▶ ADJ meio; (quantity, size)
médio, mediano; **middle-aged**
ADJ de meia-idade; **Middle Ages**
NPL: **the Middle Ages** a Idade
Média; **Middle East** N: **the**
Middle East o Oriente Médio;
middle name N segundo nome m
midge [mɪdʒ] N mosquito
midget [ˈmɪdʒɪt] N anão(-anã) m/f
midnight [ˈmɪdnaɪt] N meia-noite f
midst [mɪdst] N: **in the ~ of** no
meio de, entre
midsummer [mɪdˈsʌməʳ] N:
a ~ day um dia em pleno verão
midway [mɪdˈweɪ] ADJ, ADV:
~ (between) no meio do caminho
(entre)

midweek [mɪdˈwiːk] ADV no meio
da semana
midwife [ˈmɪdwaɪf] (pl **midwives**)
N parteira
might [maɪt] VB see **may** ▶ N
poder m, força; **mighty** ADJ
poderoso, forte
migraine [ˈmiːgreɪn] N
enxaqueca
migrant [ˈmaɪgrənt] ADJ
migratório; (worker) emigrante
migrate [maɪˈgreɪt] VI emigrar;
(birds) arribar
mike [maɪk] N ABBR =
microphone
mild [maɪld] ADJ (character)
pacífico; (climate) temperado;
(taste) suave; (illness) leve,
benigno; (interest) pequeno
mile [maɪl] N milha (1609 m);
mileage N número de milhas;
(Aut) ≈ quilometragem f;
milestone [ˈmaɪlstəun] N marco
miliário
military [ˈmɪlɪtərɪ] ADJ militar
milk [mɪlk] N leite m ▶ VT (cow)
ordenhar; (fig) explorar, chupar;
milk chocolate N chocolate m de
leite; **milkman** irreg N leiteiro;
milky ADJ leitoso
mill [mɪl] N (windmill etc) moinho;
(coffee mill) moedor m de café;
(factory) moinho, engenho ▶ VT
moer ▶ VI (also: **~ about**)
aglomerar-se, remoinhar
millimetre, (US) **millimeter**
[ˈmɪlɪmiːtəʳ] N milímetro
million [ˈmɪljən] N milhão m;
a ~ times um milhão de vezes;
millionaire N milionário(-a);
millionth NUM milionésimo
mime [maɪm] N mimo; (actor)
mímico(-a), comediante m/f ▶ VT
imitar ▶ VI fazer mímica

m

mimic ['mɪmɪk] N mímico(-a), imitador(a) m/f ▶ VT imitar, parodiar

min. ABBR (= minute, minimum) min

mince [mɪns] VT moer ▶ VI (in walking) andar com afetação ▶ N (BRIT Culin) carne f moída; **mincemeat** N recheio de sebo e frutas picadas; (US: meat) carne f moída; **mince pie** N pastel com recheio de sebo e frutas picadas

mind [maɪnd] N mente f; (intellect) intelecto; (opinion): **to my ~** a meu ver; (sanity): **to be out of one's ~** estar fora de si ▶ VT (attend to, look after) tomar conta de, cuidar de; (be careful of) ter cuidado com; (object to): **I don't ~ the noise** o barulho não me incomoda; **it is on my ~** não me sai da cabeça; **to keep** or **bear sth in ~** levar algo em consideração, não esquecer-se de algo; **to make up one's ~** decidir-se; **I don't ~** (it doesn't worry me) eu nem ligo; (it's all the same to me) para mim tanto faz; **~ you, ...** se bem que ...; **never ~!** não faz mal, não importa!; (don't worry) não se preocupe!; **"~ the step"** "cuidado com o degrau"; **mindless** ADJ (violence, crime) insensato; (job) monótono

mine¹ [maɪn] PRON o meu/a minha; **a friend of ~** um amigo meu

mine² [maɪn] N mina ▶ VT (coal) extrair, explorar; (ship, beach) minar

miner ['maɪnər] N mineiro

mineral ['mɪnərəl] ADJ mineral ▶ N mineral m; **minerals** NPL (BRIT: soft drinks) refrigerantes mpl; **mineral water** N água mineral

mingle ['mɪŋgl] VI: **to ~ with** misturar-se com

miniature ['mɪnətʃər] ADJ em miniatura ▶ N miniatura

minibus ['mɪnɪbʌs] N micro-ônibus m

minimal ['mɪnɪml] ADJ mínimo

minimum ['mɪnɪməm] (pl **minima**) ADJ mínimo ▶ N mínimo

mining ['maɪnɪŋ] N exploração f de minas

miniskirt ['mɪnɪskəːt] N minissaia

minister ['mɪnɪstər] N (BRIT Pol) ministro(-a); (Rel) pastor m ▶ VI: **to ~ to sb** prestar assistência a alguém; **to ~ to sb's needs** atender às necessidades de alguém

ministry ['mɪnɪstrɪ] N (BRIT Pol) ministério; (Rel): **to go into the ~** ingressar no sacerdócio

minor ['maɪnər] ADJ menor; (unimportant) de pouca importância; (Mus) menor ▶ N (Jur) menor m/f de idade

minority [maɪ'nɔrɪtɪ] N minoria

mint [mɪnt] N (plant) hortelã f; (sweet) bala de hortelã ▶ VT (coins) cunhar; **the (Royal) M~** (BRIT) or **the (US) M~** (US) ≈ a Casa da Moeda; **in ~ condition** em perfeito estado

minus ['maɪnəs] N (also: **~ sign**) sinal m de subtração ▶ PREP menos

minute¹ [maɪ'njuːt] ADJ miúdo, diminuto; (search) minucioso

minute² ['mɪnɪt] N minuto; **minutes** NPL (of meeting) atas fpl; **at the last ~** no último momento

miracle ['mɪrəkl] N milagre m

mirage ['mɪraːʒ] N miragem f

mirror ['mɪrər] N espelho; (in car) retrovisor m

misbehave [mɪsbɪ'heɪv] VI comportar-se mal

miscarriage ['mɪskærɪdʒ] N (Med) aborto (espontâneo); (failure): **~ of justice** erro judicial

miscellaneous [mɪsɪˈleɪnɪəs] ADJ (*items, expenses*) diverso; (*selection*) variado

mischief [ˈmɪstʃɪf] N (*naughtiness*) travessura; (*fun*) diabrura; (*maliciousness*) malícia; **mischievous** [ˈmɪstʃɪvəs] ADJ (*naughty*) travesso; (*playful*) traquino

misconception [mɪskənˈsɛpʃən] N concepção ferrada, conceito errado

misconduct [mɪsˈkɔndʌkt] N comportamento impróprio; **professional ~** má conduta profissional

miser [ˈmaɪzəʳ] N avaro(-a), sovina m/f

miserable [ˈmɪzərəbl] ADJ triste; (*wretched*) miserável; (*weather, person*) deprimente; (*contemptible: offer*) desprezível; (: *failure*) humilhante

misery [ˈmɪzərɪ] N (*unhappiness*) tristeza; (*wretchedness*) miséria

misfortune [mɪsˈfɔːtʃən] N desgraça, infortúnio

misguided [mɪsˈgaɪdɪd] ADJ enganado

mishap [ˈmɪshæp] N desgraça, contratempo

misinterpret [mɪsɪnˈtəːprɪt] VT interpretar mal

misjudge [mɪsˈdʒʌdʒ] VT fazer um juízo errado de, julgar mal

mislay [mɪsˈleɪ] *irreg* VT extraviar, perder

mislead [mɪsˈliːd] *irreg* VT induzir em erro, enganar; **misleading** ADJ enganoso, errôneo

misplace [mɪsˈpleɪs] VT extraviar, perder

misprint [ˈmɪsprɪnt] N erro tipográfico

Miss [mɪs] N Senhorita (BR), a menina (PT)

miss [mɪs] VT (*train, class, opportunity*) perder; (*fail to hit*) errar, não acertar em; (*fail to see*): **you can't ~ it** e impossível não ver; (*regret the absence of*): **I ~ him** sinto a falta dele ▶ VI falhar ▶ N (*shot*) tiro perdido *or* errado; **miss out** (BRIT) VT omitir

missile [ˈmɪsaɪl] N míssil m; (*object thrown*) projétil m

missing [ˈmɪsɪn] ADJ (*pupil*) ausente; (*thing*) perdido; (*removed*) que está faltando; (*Mil*) desaparecido; **to be ~** estar desaparecido; **to go ~** desaparecer

mission [ˈmɪʃən] N missão f; (*official representatives*) delegação f

mist [mɪst] N (*light*) neblina; (*heavy*) névoa; (*at sea*) bruma ▶ VI (*eyes: also:* **~ over**) enevoar-se; (BRIT: *also:* **~ over, ~ up**: *windows*) embaçar

mistake [mɪsˈteɪk] *irreg* N erro, engano ▶ VT entender *or* interpretar mal; **by ~** por engano; **to make a ~** fazer um erro; **to ~ A for B** confundir A com B; **mistaken** PP *of* **mistake** ▶ ADJ errado; **to be mistaken** enganar-se, equivocar-se

mister [ˈmɪstəʳ] (*inf*) N senhor m; *see* **Mr**

mistletoe [ˈmɪsltəu] N visco

mistook [mɪsˈtuk] PT *of* **mistake**

mistress [ˈmɪstrɪs] N (*lover*) amante f; (*of house*) dona (da casa); (BRIT: *in school*) professora, mestra; (*of situation*) dona; *see* **Mrs**

mistrust [mɪsˈtrʌst] VT desconfiar de

misty [ˈmɪstɪ] ADJ (*day*) nublado; (*glasses etc*) embaçado

m

misunderstand [mɪsʌndə'stænd]
irreg vt, vi entender *or* interpretar
mal; **misunderstanding** N
mal-entendido; (*disagreement*)
desentendimento

misuse [*n* mɪs'juːs, *vt* mɪs'juːz] N
uso impróprio; (*of power*) abuso;
(*of funds*) desvio ▶ vt abusar de;
desviar

mix [mɪks] vt misturar; (*combine*)
combinar ▶ vi (*people*) entrosar-se
▶ N mistura; (*combination*)
combinação f; **mix up** vt (*confuse:
things*) misturar; (: *people*)
confundir; **mixed** ADJ misto;
mixed-up ADJ confuso; **mixer** N
(*for food*) batedeira; (*person*) pessoa
sociável; **mixture** N mistura; (*Med*)
preparado; **mix-up** N trapalhada,
confusão f

mm ABBR (= *millimetre*) mm

moan [məun] N gemido ▶ vi
gemer; (*inf: complain*): **to ~ (about)**
queixar-se (de), bufar (sobre) (*inf*)

moat [məut] N fosso

mob [mɔb] N multidão f ▶ vt cercar

mobile ['məubaɪl] ADJ móvel ▶ N
móvel *m*; **mobile phone** N telefone
m celular (*BR*), telemóvel *m* (*PT*)

mock [mɔk] vt ridicularizar; (*laugh
at*) zombar de, gozar de ▶ ADJ falso,
fingido; (*exam, battle*) simulado;
mockery N zombaria; **to make a
mockery of sth** ridicularizar algo

mode [məud] N modo; (*of transport*)
meio

model ['mɔdl] N modelo; (*Arch*)
maqueta; (*person: for fashion, Art*)
modelo *m/f* ▶ ADJ exemplar ▶ vt
modelar; **to ~ o.s. on** mirar-se em
▶ vi servir de modelo; (*in fashion*)
trabalhar como modelo

modem ['məudɛm] N modem *m*

moderate [*adj, n* 'mɔdərət, *vi, vt*
'mɔdəreɪt] ADJ, N moderado(-a) ▶ vi
moderar-se, acalmar-se ▶ vt moderar

modern ['mɔdən] ADJ moderno;
modernize vt modernizar,
atualizar

modest ['mɔdɪst] ADJ modesto;
modesty N modéstia

modify ['mɔdɪfaɪ] vt modificar

moist [mɔɪst] ADJ úmido (*BR*),
húmido (*PT*), molhado; **moisture** N
umidade f (*BR*), humidade f (*PT*);
moisturizer N creme *m* hidratante

mole [məul] N (*animal*) toupeira;
(*spot*) sinal *m*, lunar *m*; (*fig*)
espião(-piã) *m/f*

molest [məu'lɛst] vt molestar;
(*attack sexually*) atacar sexualmente

molten ['məultən] ADJ fundido;
(*lava*) liquefeito

mom [mɔm] (*US*) N = **mum**

moment ['məumənt] N momento;
at the ~ neste momento;
momentary ADJ momentâneo;
momentous [məu'mɛntəs] ADJ
importantíssimo

momentum [məu'mɛntəm] N
momento; (*fig*) ímpeto; **to
gather ~** ganhar ímpeto

mommy ['mɔmɪ] (*US*) N = **mummy**

Monaco ['mɔnəkəu] N Mônaco (*no
article*)

monarch ['mɔnək] N monarca *m/f*;
monarchy N monarquia

monastery ['mɔnəstərɪ] N
mosteiro, convento

Monday ['mʌndɪ] N segunda-feira

monetary ['mʌnɪtərɪ] ADJ
monetário

money ['mʌnɪ] N dinheiro;
(*currency*) moeda; **to make ~**
ganhar dinheiro; **money order** N
vale *m* (postal)

mongrel ['mʌŋgrəl] N (*dog*)
vira-lata *m*

monitor ['mɒnɪtəʳ] N (*Comput*) monitor *m* ▶ VT (*heartbeat, pulse*) controlar; (*broadcasts, progress*) monitorar

monk [mʌŋk] N monge *m*

monkey ['mʌŋkɪ] N macaco

monopoly [mə'nɒpəlɪ] N monopólio

monotonous [mə'nɒtənəs] ADJ monótono

monsoon [mɒn'suːn] N monção *f*

monster ['mɒnstəʳ] N monstro

month [mʌnθ] N mês *m*; **monthly** ADJ mensal ▶ ADV mensalmente

monument ['mɒnjumənt] N monumento

mood [muːd] N humor *m*; (*of crowd*) atmosfera; **to be in a good/bad ~** estar de bom/mau humor; **moody** ADJ (*variable*) caprichoso, de veneta; (*sullen*) rabugento

moon [muːn] N lua; **moonlight** N luar *m* ▶ VI ter dois empregos, ter um bico

moor [muəʳ] N charneca ▶ VT (*ship*) amarrar ▶ VI fundear, atracar

moose [muːs] N INV alce *m*

mop [mɒp] N esfregão *m*; (*for dishes*) esponja com cabeça; (*of hair*) grenha ▶ VT esfregar; **mop up** VT limpar

mope [məup] VI estar *or* andar deprimido *or* desanimado

moped ['məupɛd] N moto *f* pequena (BR), motorizada (PT)

moral ['mɒrl] ADJ moral ▶ N moral *f*; **morals** NPL (*principles*) moralidade *f*, costumes *mpl*

morale [mɒ'rɑːl] N moral *f*, estado de espírito

morality [mə'rælɪtɪ] N moralidade *f*; (*correctness*) retidão *f*, probidade *f*

more [mɔːʳ] ADJ **1** (*greater in number etc*) mais; **more people/work/ letters than we expected** mais pessoas/trabalho/cartas do que esperávamos

2 (*additional*) mais; **do you want (some) more tea?** você quer mais chá?; **I have no** *or* **I don't have any more money** não tenho mais dinheiro

▶ PRON **1** (*greater amount*) mais; **more than 10** mais de 10; **it cost more than we expected** custou mais do que esperávamos

2 (*further or additional amount*) mais; **is there any more?** tem ainda mais?; **there's no more** não tem mais

▶ ADV mais; **more dangerous/ difficult** *etc* **than** mais perigoso/ difícil *etc* do que; **more easily/ economically/quickly (than)** mais fácil/econômico/rápido (do que); **more and more** cada vez mais; **more or less** mais ou menos; **more than ever** mais do que nunca

m

moreover [mɔː'rəuvəʳ] ADV além do mais, além disso

morning ['mɔːnɪŋ] N manhã *f*; (*early morning*) madrugada ▶ CPD da manhã; **in the ~** de manhã; **7 o'clock in the ~** (as) 7 da manhã; **morning sickness** N náusea matinal

Morocco [mə'rɒkəu] N Marrocos *m*

moron ['mɔːrɒn] (*inf*) N débil mental *m/f*, idiota *m/f*

Morse [mɔːs] N (*also:* **~ code**) código Morse

mortar ['mɔːtəʳ] N (*cannon*) morteiro; (*Constr*) argamassa; (*dish*) pilão *m*, almofariz *m*

mortgage ['mɔːgɪdʒ] N hipoteca
▶ VT hipotecar
mortuary ['mɔːtjuərɪ] N
necrotério
mosaic [məʊˈzeɪɪk] N mosaico
Moscow ['mɒskəʊ] N Moscou (BR),
Moscovo (PT)
Moslem ['mɒzləm] ADJ, N =
Muslim
mosque [mɒsk] N mesquita
mosquito [mɒsˈkiːtəʊ] (pl
mosquitoes) N mosquito
moss [mɒs] N musgo

(KEYWORD)

most [məʊst] ADJ 1 (almost all:
people, things etc) a maior parte de,
a maioria de; **most people** a
maioria das pessoas
2 (largest, greatest: interest) máximo
(money): **who has (the) most
money?** quem é que tem mais
dinheiro?; **he derived the most
pleasure from her visit** ele teve o
maior prazer em recebê-la
▶ PRON (greatest quantity, number) a
maior parte, a maioria; **most of it/
them** a maioria dele/deles; **most
of the money** a maior parte do
dinheiro; **do the most you can**
faça o máximo que você puder;
I saw the most vi mais; **to make
the most of sth** aproveitar algo ao
máximo; **at the (very) most**
quando muito, no máximo
▶ ADV (+ vb, adj, adv) o mais; **the
most intelligent/expensive** etc
o mais inteligente/caro etc; (very:
polite, interesting etc) muito; **a most
interesting book** um livro
interessantíssimo

mostly ['məʊstlɪ] ADV
principalmente, na maior parte

MOT (BRIT) N ABBR = **Ministry of
Transport**; **the ~ (test)** vistoria
anual dos veículos automotores
motel [məʊˈtɛl] N motel m
moth [mɒθ] N mariposa; (clothes
moth) traça
mother ['mʌðəʳ] N mãe f ▶ ADJ
materno (care for) ▶ VT cuidar de
(como uma mãe); **motherhood** N
maternidade f; **mother-in-law** N
sogra; **mother-of-pearl** N
madrepérola; **mother-to-be** N
futura mamãe f; **mother tongue** N
língua materna
motion ['məʊʃən] N movimento;
(gesture) gesto, sinal m; (at meeting)
moção f ▶ VT, VI: **to ~ (to) sb to do
sth** fazer sinal a alguém para que
faça algo; **motionless** ADJ imóvel;
motion picture N filme m
(cinematográfico)
motive ['məʊtɪv] N motivo
motor ['məʊtəʳ] N motor m; (BRIT
inf: vehicle) carro, automóvel m
▶ CPD (industry) de automóvel;
motorbike N moto(cicleta) f,
motoca (inf); **motorboat** N barco a
motor; **motorcar** (BRIT) N carro,
automóvel m; **motorcycle** N
motocicleta; **motorist** N motorista
m/f; **motor racing** (BRIT) N corrida
de carros, automobilismo;
motorway (BRIT) N rodovia (BR),
autoestrada (PT)
motto ['mɒtəʊ] (pl **mottoes**) N
lema m
mound [maʊnd] N (of earth)
monte m; (of blankets, leaves etc)
pilha, montanha
mount [maʊnt] N monte m ▶ VT
(horse etc) montar em, subir a;
(stairs) subir; (exhibition) montar;
(picture) emoldurar ▶ VI (increase)
aumentar; **mount up** VI aumentar

mountain ['mauntɪn] N
montanha ▶ CPD de montanha;
mountain bike N mountain bike f;
mountaineer [mauntɪ'nɪəʳ] N
alpinista m/f, montanhista m/f;
mountaineering N alpinismo;
mountainous ADJ montanhoso

mourn [mɔːn] VT chorar, lamentar
▶ VI: **to ~ for** chorar or lamentar a
morte de; **mourning** N luto; **(to
be) in mourning** (estar) de luto

mouse [maus] (pl **mice**) N
camundongo (BR), rato (PT);
(Comput) mouse m; **mouse mat,
mouse pad** N (Comput) mouse
pad m

mousse [muːs] N musse f; (for
hair) mousse f

moustache [məs'taːʃ], (US)
mustache N bigode m

mouth [mauθ] N boca; (of cave,
hole) entrada; (of river)
desembocadura; **mouthful** N
bocado; **mouth organ** N gaita;
mouthwash N colutório

move [muːv] N movimento;
(in game) lance m, jogada; (: turn
to play) turno, vez f; (of house, job)
mudança ▶ VT (change position of)
mudar; (in game) jogar;
(emotionally) comover; (Pol:
resolution etc) propor ▶ VI mexer-se,
mover-se; (traffic) circular; (also:
~ house) mudar-se; (develop:
situation) desenvolver; **to ~ sb to
do sth** convencer alguém a fazer
algo; **to get a ~ on** apressar-se;
move about VI (fidget) mexer-se;
(travel) deslocar-se; **move along** VI
avançar; **move around** VI = **move
about**; **move away** VI afastar-se;
move back VI voltar; **move
forward** VI avançar; **move in** VI
(to a house) instalar-se (numa casa);

move on VI ir andando; **move
out** VI sair (de uma casa); **move
over** VI afastar-se; **move up** VI
ser promovido

movement ['muːvmənt] N
movimento; (gesture) gesto; (of
goods) transporte m; (in attitude,
policy) mudança

movie ['muːvɪ] N filme m; **to go
to the ~s** ir ao cinema

moving ['muːvɪŋ] ADJ (emotional)
comovente; (that moves) móvel

mow [məu] (pt **mowed**, pp
mowed or **mown**) VT (grass)
cortar; (corn) ceifar; **mow down**
VT (massacre) chacinar; **mower** N
ceifeira; (also: **lawnmower**)
cortador m de grama (BR) or de
relva (PT)

Mozambique [məuzəm'biːk] N
Moçambique m (no article)

MP N ABBR = **Member of
Parliament**

MP3 player N tocador m de MP3

mph ABBR = **miles per hour**

Mr ['mɪstəʳ], (US) **Mr.** N: **Mr Smith**
(o) Sr. Smith

Mrs ['mɪsɪz], (US) **Mrs.** N: **~ Smith**
(a) Sra. Smith

Ms [mɪz], (US) **Ms.** N (= Miss or
Mrs): **Ms X** (a) Sa X

> **Ms** é um título utilizado em lugar
> de Mrs (senhora) ou de Miss
> (senhorita) para evitar a distinção
> tradicional entre mulheres
> casadas e solteiras. É aceito,
> portanto, como o equivalente
> de Mr (senhor) para os homens.
> Muitas vezes reprovado por ter
> surgido como manifestação
> de um feminismo exacerbado,
> é uma forma de tratamento
> muito comum hoje em dia.

MSc N ABBR = **Master of Science**

much [mʌtʃ] ADJ muito; **how much money/time do you need?** quanto dinheiro/tempo você precisa?; **he's done so much work for the charity** ele trabalhou muito para a obra de caridade; **as much as** tanto como
▶ PRON muito; **much has been gained from our discussions** nossas discussões foram muito proveitosas; **how much does it cost? — too much** quanto custa isso? — caro demais
▶ ADV **1** (greatly, a great deal) muito; **thank you very much** muito obrigado(-a); **we are very much looking forward to your visit** estamos aguardando a sua visita com muito ansiedade; **he is very much the gentleman/politician** ele é muito cavalheiro/político; **as much as** tanto como; **as much as you** tanto quanto você
2 (by far) de longe; **I'm much better now** estou bem melhor agora
3 (almost) quase; **how are you feeling? — much the same** como você está (se sentindo)? — do mesmo jeito

muck [mʌk] N (dirt) sujeira (BR), sujidade f (PT); **muck about** (inf) VI fazer besteiras; **muck around** VI = **muck about**; **muck up** (inf) VT estragar
mud [mʌd] N lama
muddle ['mʌdl] N confusão f, bagunça; (mix-up) trapalhada ▶ VT (also: **~ up**: person, story) confundir; (: things) misturar; **muddle through** VI virar-se
muddy ['mʌdɪ] ADJ (road) lamacento

mudguard ['mʌdgɑːd] N para-lama m
muesli ['mjuːzlɪ] N muesli m
muffin ['mʌfɪn] N bolinho redondo e chato
mug [mʌg] N (cup) caneca; (for beer) caneco, canecão; (inf: face) careta; (: fool) bobo(-a) ▶ VT (assault) assaltar; **mugging** N assalto
muggy ['mʌgɪ] ADJ abafado
mule [mjuːl] N mula
multimedia [mʌltɪ'miːdɪə] ADJ multimídia
multiple ['mʌltɪpl] ADJ múltiplo
▶ N múltiplo; **multiple sclerosis** [-sklɪ'rəʊsɪs] N esclerose f múltipla
multiply ['mʌltɪplaɪ] VT multiplicar ▶ VI multiplicar-se
multistorey ['mʌltɪ'stɔːrɪ] (BRIT) ADJ de vários andares
mum [mʌm] N (BRIT inf) mamãe f ▶ ADJ: **to keep ~** ficar calado
mumble ['mʌmbl] VT, VI resmungar, murmurar
mummy ['mʌmɪ] N (BRIT: mother) mamãe f; (embalmed) múmia
mumps [mʌmps] N caxumba
municipal [mjuː'nɪsɪpl] ADJ municipal
murder ['məːdəʳ] N assassinato ▶ VT assassinar; **murderer** N assassino
murky ['məːkɪ] ADJ escuro; (water) turvo
murmur ['məːməʳ] N murmúrio ▶ VT, VI murmurar
muscle ['mʌsl] N músculo; (fig: strength) força (muscular); **muscle in** VI imiscuir-se, impor-se; **muscular** ['mʌskjʊləʳ] ADJ muscular; (person) musculoso
museum [mjuː'zɪəm] N museu m
mushroom ['mʌʃrʊm] N cogumelo

▶ vi crescer da noite para o dia, pipocar

music ['mju:zɪk] N música; **musical** ADJ musical; (*harmonious*) melodioso ▶ N musical m; **musician** [mju:'zɪʃən] N músico(-a)

Muslim ['mʌzlɪm] ADJ, N muçulmano(-a)

mussel ['mʌsl] N mexilhão m

must [mʌst] AUX VB (*obligation*): **I ~ do it** tenho que or devo fazer isso; (*probability*): **he ~ be there by now** ele já deve estar lá; (*suggestion, invitation*): **you ~ come and see me soon** você tem que vir me ver em breve; (*indicating sth unwelcome*): **why ~ he behave so badly?** por que ele tem que se comportar tão mal? ▶ N necessidade f; **it's a ~** é imprescindível

mustache ['mʌstæʃ] (*US*) N = **moustache**

mustard ['mʌstəd] N mostarda

mustn't ['mʌsnt] = **must not**

mute [mju:t] ADJ, N mudo(-a)

mutiny ['mju:tɪnɪ] N motim m, rebelião f

mutter ['mʌtər] VT, VI resmungar, murmurar

mutton ['mʌtn] N carne f de carneiro

mutual ['mju:tʃuəl] ADJ mútuo; (*shared*) comum

muzzle ['mʌzl] N (*of animal*) focinho; (*guard: for dog*) focinheira; (*of gun*) boca ▶ VT pôr focinheira em

my [maɪ] ADJ meu/minha; **this is my house/car/brother** esta é a minha casa/meu carro/meu irmão; **I've washed my hair/ cut my finger** lavei meu cabelo/ cortei meu dedo

myself [maɪ'sɛlf] PRON (*reflexive*) me; (*emphatic*) eu mesmo; (*after prep*) mim mesmo; *see also* **oneself**

mysterious [mɪs'tɪərɪəs] ADJ misterioso

mystery ['mɪstərɪ] N mistério

mystify ['mɪstɪfaɪ] VT mistificar

myth [mɪθ] N mito; **mythology** [mɪ'θɒlədʒɪ] N mitologia

m

n

nag [næg] vt ralhar, apoquentar
nail [neɪl] n (*human*) unha; (*metal*) prego ▶ vt pregar; **to ~ sb down to a date/price** conseguir que alguém se defina sobre a data/o preço; **nailbrush** n escova de unhas; **nailfile** n lixa de unhas; **nail polish** n esmalte *m* (BR) or verniz *m* (PT) de unhas; **nail polish remover** n removedor *m* de esmalte (BR) or verniz (PT); **nail scissors** NPL tesourinha de unhas; **nail varnish** (BRIT) n = **nail polish**
naïve [naɪˈiːv] ADJ ingênuo
naked [ˈneɪkɪd] ADJ nu(a)
name [neɪm] n nome *m*; (*surname*) sobrenome *m*; (*reputation*) reputação *f*, fama ▶ vt (*child*) pôr nome em; (*criminal*) apontar; (*price*) fixar; (*date*) marcar; **what's your ~?** qual é o seu nome?, como (você) se chama?; **by ~** de nome; **in the ~ of** em nome de; **namely** ADV a saber, isto é

nanny [ˈnænɪ] n babá *f*
nap [næp] n (*sleep*) soneca ▶ vi: **to be caught ~ping** ser pego de surpresa
napkin [ˈnæpkɪn] n (*also*: **table ~**) guardanapo
nappy [ˈnæpɪ] (BRIT) n fralda
narrative [ˈnærətɪv] n narrativa
narrow [ˈnærəu] ADJ estreito; (*fig: majority*) pequeno; (: *ideas*) tacanho ▶ vi (*road*) estreitar-se; (*difference*) diminuir; **to have a ~ escape** escapar por um triz; **to ~ sth down to** restringir or reduzir algo a; **narrowly** ADV (*miss*) por pouco; **narrow-minded** ADJ de visão limitada, bitolado
nasty [ˈnɑːstɪ] ADJ (*unpleasant: remark*) desagradável; (: *person*) mau, ruim; (*malicious*) maldoso; (*rude*) grosseiro, obsceno; (*taste, smell*) repugnante, asqueroso; (*wound, disease etc*) grave, sério
nation [ˈneɪʃən] n nação *f*
national [ˈnæʃənl] ADJ, n nacional *m/f*; **national anthem** n hino nacional; **National Health Service** (BRIT) n *serviço nacional de saúde*; **nationality** [næʃəˈnælɪtɪ] n nacionalidade *f*; **nationalize** vt nacionalizar; **national park** n parque *m* nacional; **National Trust** (BRIT) n *ver nota*

O **National Trust** é uma instituição independente, sem fins lucrativos, cuja missão é proteger e valorizar os monumentos e a paisagem da Grã-Bretanha devido a seu interesse histórico ou beleza natural.

nationwide [ˈneɪʃənwaɪd] ADJ de âmbito or a nível nacional ▶ ADV em todo o país

native ['neɪtɪv] N natural m/f, nativo(-a); (in colonies) indígena m/f, nativo(-a) ▶ ADJ (indigenous) indígena; (of one's birth) natal; (language) materno; (innate) inato, natural; **a ~ speaker of Portuguese** uma pessoa de língua (materna) portuguesa

NATO ['neɪtəu] N ABBR (= North Atlantic Treaty Organization) OTAN f

natural ['nætʃrəl] ADJ natural; **naturally** ADV naturalmente; (of course) claro, evidentemente

nature ['neɪtʃəʳ] N natureza; (character) caráter m, índole f

naughty ['nɔːtɪ] ADJ travesso, levado

nausea ['nɔːsɪə] N náusea

naval ['neɪvl] ADJ naval

nave [neɪv] N nave f

navel ['neɪvl] N umbigo

navigate ['nævɪgeɪt] VI navegar; (Aut) ler o mapa; **navigation** [nævɪ'geɪʃən] N (action) navegação f; (science) náutica

navy ['neɪvɪ] N marinha (de guerra)

Nazi ['nɑːtsɪ] N nazista m/f (BR), nazi m/f (PT)

NB ABBR (= nota bene) NB

near [nɪəʳ] ADJ (place) vizinho; (time) próximo; (relation) íntimo ▶ ADV perto ▶ PREP (also: **~ to**: space) perto de; (: time) perto de, quase ▶ VT aproximar-se de; **nearby** [nɪə'baɪ] ADJ próximo, vizinho ▶ ADV à mão, perto; **nearly** ADV quase; **I nearly fell** quase que caí; **near-sighted** ADJ míope

neat [niːt] ADJ (place) arrumado, em ordem; (person) asseado, arrumado; (work) caprichado; (plan) engenhoso, bem bolado; (spirits) puro; **neatly** ADV

caprichosamente, com capricho; (skilfully) habilmente

necessarily ['nɛsɪsrɪlɪ] ADV necessariamente

necessary ['nɛsɪsrɪ] ADJ necessário

necessity [nɪ'sɛsɪtɪ] N (thing needed) necessidade f, requisito; (compelling circumstances) necessidade; **necessities** NPL (essentials) artigos mpl de primeira necessidade

neck [nɛk] N (Anat) pescoço; (of garment) gola; (of bottle) gargalo ▶ VI (inf) ficar de agarramento; **~ and ~** emparelhados

necklace ['nɛklɪs] N colar m

necktie ['nɛktaɪ] N (esp US) N gravata

need [niːd] N (lack) falta, carência; (necessity) necessidade f; (thing needed) requisito, necessidade ▶ VT precisar de; **I ~ to do it** preciso fazê-lo

needle ['niːdl] N agulha ▶ VT (inf) provocar, alfinetar

needless ['niːdlɪs] ADJ inútil, desnecessário; **~ to say ...** desnecessário dizer que ...

needlework ['niːdlwəːk] N costura

needn't ['niːdnt] = **need not**

needy ['niːdɪ] ADJ necessitado, carente

negative ['nɛgətɪv] ADJ negativo ▶ N (Phot) negativo; (Ling) negativa

neglect [nɪ'glɛkt] VT (one's duty) negligenciar, não cumprir com; (child) descuidar, esquecer-se de ▶ N (of child) descuido, desatenção f; (of house etc) abandono; (of duty) negligência

negotiate [nɪ'gəuʃɪeɪt] VI negociar ▶ VT (treaty, transaction) negociar; (*obstacle*) contornar; (*bend in road*) fazer; **negotiation** [nɪɡəʊʃɪ'eɪʃən] N negociação f

neighbour ['neɪbər], (*US*) **neighbor** N vizinho(-a); **neighbourhood** N (*place*) vizinhança, bairro; (*people*) vizinhos *mpl*; **neighbouring** ADJ vizinho

neither ['naɪðər] CONJ: **I didn't move and ~ did he** não me movi nem ele ▸ ADJ, PRON nenhum (dos dois), nem um nem outro ▸ ADV: **~ good nor bad** nem bom nem mau; **~ story is true** nenhuma das estórias é verdade

neon ['niːɔn] N neônio, néon *m*

nephew ['nɛvjuː] N sobrinho

nerve [nəːv] N (*Anat*) nervo; (*courage*) coragem f; (*impudence*) descaramento, atrevimento; **to have a fit of ~s** ter uma crise nervosa

nervous ['nəːvəs] ADJ (*Anat*) nervoso; (*anxious*) apreensivo; (*timid*) tímido, acanhado; **nervous breakdown** N esgotamento nervoso

nest [nɛst] VI aninhar-se ▸ N (*of bird*) ninho; (*of wasp*) vespeiro

net [nɛt] N rede f; (*fabric*) filó *m* ▸ ADJ (*Comm*) líquido ▸ VT pegar na rede; (*money: subj: person*) faturar; (: *deal, sale*) render; **the Net** (*Internet*) a Rede; **netball** N espécie de basquetebol

Netherlands ['nɛðələndz] NPL: **the ~** os Países Baixos

nett [nɛt] ADJ = **net**

nettle ['nɛtl] N urtiga

network ['nɛtwəːk] N rede f; **there's no ~ coverage here** (*Tel*) aqui não tem cobertura

neurotic [njuə'rɔtɪk] ADJ, N neurótico(-a)

neuter ['njuːtər] ADJ neutro ▸ VT (*cat etc*) castrar, capar

neutral ['njuːtrəl] ADJ neutro ▸ N (*Aut*) ponto morto

never ['nɛvər] ADV nunca; *see also* **mind**; **never-ending** ADJ sem fim, interminável; **nevertheless** ADV todavia, contudo

new [njuː] ADJ novo; **New Age** N esoterismo; **newborn** ADJ recém-nascido; **newcomer** N recém-chegado(-a), novato(-a); **newly** ADV recém, novamente

news [njuːz] N notícias *fpl*; (*Radio, TV*) noticiário; **a piece of ~** uma notícia; **newsagent** (*BRIT*) N jornaleiro(-a); **newscaster** N locutor(a) *m/f*; **newsletter** N boletim *m* informativo; **newspaper** N jornal *m*; **newsreader** N = **newscaster**

newt [njuːt] N tritão *m*

New Year N ano novo; **New Year's Day** N dia *m* de ano novo; **New Year's Eve** N véspera de ano novo

New Zealand [-'ziːlənd] N Nova Zelândia; **New Zealander** N neozelandês(-esa) *m/f*

next [nɛkst] ADJ (*in space*) próximo, vizinho; (*in time*) seguinte, próximo ▸ ADV depois; depois, logo; **~ time** na próxima vez; **~ year** o ano que vem; **~ to** ao lado de; **~ to nothing** quase nada; **next door** ADV na casa do lado ▸ ADJ vizinho; **next-of-kin** N parentes *mpl* mais próximos

NHS (*BRIT*) N ABBR = **National Health Service**

nibble ['nɪbl] VT mordiscar, beliscar

Nicaragua [nɪkə'ræɡjuə] N Nicarágua

nice [naɪs] ADJ (*likeable*) simpático; (*kind*) amável, atencioso; (*pleasant*) agradável; (*attractive*) bonito;

nicely ADV agradavelmente, bem
nick [nɪk] N (wound) corte m; (cut, indentation) entalhe m, incisão f
▶ VT (inf: steal) furtar; **in the ~ of time** na hora H, em cima da hora
nickel ['nɪkl] N níquel m; (US) moeda de 5 centavos
nickname ['nɪkneɪm] N apelido (BR), alcunha (PT) ▶ VT apelidar de (BR), alcunhar de (PT)
niece [ni:s] N sobrinha
Nigeria [naɪ'dʒɪərɪə] N Nigéria
night [naɪt] N noite f; **at** or **by ~** à or de noite; **the ~ before last** anteontem à noite; **nightclub** N boate f; **nightlife** ['naɪtlaɪf] N vida noturna; **nightly** ['naɪtlɪ] ADJ noturno, de noite ▶ ADV todas as noites, cada noite; **nightmare** ['naɪtmɛəʳ] N pesadelo; **night-time** N noite f
nil [nɪl] N nada; (BRIT Sport) zero
nine [naɪn] NUM nove; **nineteen** [naɪn'ti:n] NUM dezenove (BR), dezanove (PT); **nineteenth** [naɪn'ti:nθ] NUM décimo nono; **ninetieth** ['naɪntiɪθ] NUM nonagésimo; **ninety** ['naɪntɪ] NUM noventa; **ninth** [naɪnθ] NUM nono
nip [nɪp] VT (pinch) beliscar; (bite) morder
nipple ['nɪpl] N (Anat) bico do seio, mamilo
nitrogen ['naɪtrədʒən] N nitrogênio

(KEYWORD)

no [nəu] (pl **noes**) ADV (opposite of "yes") não; **are you coming? — no (I'm not)** você vem? — não (não vou)
▶ ADJ (not any) nenhum(a), não ... algum(a); **I have no more**

money/time/books não tenho mais dinheiro/tempo/livros;
"no entry" "entrada proibida";
"no smoking" "é proibido fumar"
▶ N não m, negativa

nobility [nəu'bɪlɪtɪ] N nobreza
noble ['nəubl] ADJ (person) nobre; (title) de nobreza
nobody ['nəubədɪ] PRON ninguém
no-brainer [nəu'breɪnəʳ] (inf) N:
it's a ~ isso é meio óbvio
nod [nɔd] VI (greeting) cumprimentar com a cabeça; (in agreement) acenar (que sim) com a cabeça; (doze) cochilar, dormitar
▶ VT: **to ~ one's head** inclinar a cabeça ▶ N inclinação f da cabeça;
nod off VI cochilar
noise [nɔɪz] N barulho; **noisy** ADJ barulhento
nominate ['nɔmɪneɪt] VT (propose) propor; (appoint) nomear;
nominee [nɔmɪ'ni:] N pessoa nomeada, candidato(-a)
none [nʌn] PRON (person) ninguém; (thing) nenhum(a), nada; **~ of you** nenhum de vocês;
I've ~ left não tenho mais
nonetheless [nʌnðə'lɛs] ADV no entanto, apesar disso, contudo
non-fiction [nɔn-] N literatura de não-ficção
nonsense ['nɔnsəns] N disparate m, besteira, absurdo; **~!** bobagem!, que nada!
non-smoker N não-fumante m/f
non-stick ADJ tefal ®, não-aderente
noodles ['nu:dlz] NPL talharim m
noon [nu:n] N meio-dia m
no-one PRON = **nobody**
nor [nɔ:ʳ] CONJ = **neither** ▶ ADV see **neither**

n

norm [nɔːm] N (*convention*) norma;
(*requirement*) regra
normal ['nɔːml] ADJ normal
north [nɔːθ] N norte *m* ▶ ADJ do
norte, setentrional ▶ ADV ao *or* para
o norte; **North America** N América
do Norte; **north-east** N nordeste
m; **northern** ['nɔːðən] ADJ do norte,
setentrional; **Northern Ireland** N
Irlanda do Norte; **North Pole** N:
the North Pole o Pólo Norte;
North Sea N: **the North Sea** o
Mar do Norte; **north-west** N
noroeste *m*
Norway ['nɔːweɪ] N Noruega;
Norwegian [nɔːˈwiːdʒən] ADJ
norueguês(-esa) ▶ N
norueguês(-esa) *m/f*; (*Ling*)
norueguês *m*
nose [nəuz] N (*Anat*) nariz *m*; (*Zool*)
focinho; (*sense of smell: of person*)
olfato; (: *of animal*) faro; **nose about**
VI bisbilhotar; **nose around** VI =
nose about; **nosebleed** N
hemorragia nasal; **nosey** (*inf*) ADJ
= **nosy**
nostalgia [nɔsˈtældʒɪə] N
nostalgia
nostril ['nɔstrɪl] N narina
nosy ['nəuzɪ] (*inf*) ADJ intrometido,
abelhudo
not [nɔt] ADV não; **he is ~** *or* **isn't**
here ele não está aqui; **it's too**
late, isn't it? é muito tarde, não?;
he asked me ~ to do it ele me
pediu para não fazer isto; **~ yet/**
now ainda/agora não; *see also* **all,**
only
notably ['nəutəblɪ] ADV
(*particularly*) particularmente;
(*markedly*) notavelmente
notch [nɔtʃ] N (*in wood*) entalhe *m*;
(*in blade*) corte *m*
note [nəut] N (*Mus, banknote*) nota;

(*letter*) nota, bilhete *m*; (*record*) nota,
anotação *f*; (*tone*) tom *m* ▶ VT
(*observe*) observar, reparar em;
(*also:* **~ down**) anotar, tomar nota
de; **notebook** N caderno; **notepad**
N bloco de anotações; **notepaper** N
papel *m* de carta
nothing ['nʌθɪŋ] N nada; (*zero*)
zero; **he does ~** ele não faz nada;
~ new/much nada de novo/de
mais; **for ~** de graça, grátis; (*in vain*)
à toa, por nada
notice ['nəutɪs] N (*sign*) aviso,
anúncio; (*warning*) aviso; (*of leaving*
or losing job) aviso prévio ▶ VT
reparar em, notar; **at short ~** de
repente, em cima da hora; **until**
further ~ até nova ordem; **to hand**
in *or* **give one's ~** demitir, pedir a
demissão; **to take ~ of** prestar
atenção a, fazer caso de; **to bring**
sth to sb's ~ levar algo ao
conhecimento de alguém;
noticeable ADJ evidente, visível;
notice board (BRIT) N quadro de
avisos
notify ['nəutɪfaɪ] VT: **to ~ sb of sth**
avisar alguém de algo
notion ['nəuʃən] N noção *f*, ideia
nought [nɔːt] N zero
noun [naun] N substantivo
nourish ['nʌrɪʃ] VT nutrir,
alimentar; (*fig*) fomentar, alentar;
nourishment N alimento,
nutrimento
novel ['nɔvl] N romance *m* ▶ ADJ
novo, recente; **novelist** N
romancista *m/f*; **novelty** N
novidade *f*
November [nəuˈvɛmbəʳ] N
novembro
now [nau] ADV agora; (*these days*)
atualmente, hoje em dia ▶ CONJ:
~ (that) agora que; **right ~** agora

mesmo; **by ~** já; **just ~** agora; **~ and then, ~ and again** de vez em quando; **from ~ on** de agora em diante; **nowadays** ADV hoje em dia

nowhere ['nəuwɛəʳ] ADV (go) a lugar nenhum; (be) em nenhum lugar

nozzle ['nɔzl] N bocal m

nuclear ['nju:klɪəʳ] ADJ nuclear

nucleus ['nju:klɪəs] (pl **nuclei**) N núcleo

nude [nju:d] ADJ nu(a) ▶ N (Art) nu m; **in the ~** nu, pelado

nudge [nʌdʒ] VT acotovelar, cutucar (BR)

nudist ['nju:dɪst] N nudista m/f

nuisance ['nju:sns] N amolação f, aborrecimento; (person) chato; **what a ~!** que saco! (BR), que chatice! (PT)

numb [nʌm] ADJ dormente; **~ with cold** duro de frio; **~ with fear** paralisado de medo

number ['nʌmbəʳ] N número; (numeral) algarismo ▶ VT (pages etc) numerar; (amount to) montar a; **a ~ of** vários, muitos; **to be ~ed among** figurar entre; **they were ten in ~** eram em número de dez; **number plate** (BRIT) N placa (do carro)

numerous ['nju:mərəs] ADJ numeroso

nun [nʌn] N freira

nurse [nə:s] N enfermeiro(-a); (also: **~maid**) ama-seca, babá f ▶ VT (patient) cuidar de, tratar de

nursery ['nə:sərɪ] N (institution) creche f; (room) quarto das crianças; (for plants) viveiro; **nursery rhyme** N poesia infantil; **nursery school** N escola maternal

nursing ['nə:sɪŋ] N (profession)

enfermagem f; (care) cuidado, assistência; **nursing home** N sanatório, clínica de repouso

nut [nʌt] N (Tech) porca; (Bot) noz f

nutmeg ['nʌtmɛg] N noz-moscada

nutritious [nju:'trɪʃəs] ADJ nutritivo

nuts [nʌts] (inf) ADJ: **he's ~** ele é doido

nylon ['naɪlɔn] N náilon m (BR), nylon m (PT) ▶ ADJ de náilon or nylon

n

O

oak [əuk] N carvalho ▶ ADJ de carvalho

OAP (BRIT) N ABBR = **old-age pensioner**

oar [ɔːʳ] N remo

oasis [əu'eɪsɪs] (pl **oases**) N oásis m inv

oath [əuθ] N juramento; (swear word) palavrão m

oatmeal ['əutmiːl] N farinha or mingau m de aveia

oats [əuts] N aveia

obedient [ə'biːdɪənt] ADJ obediente

obey [ə'beɪ] VT obedecer a; (instructions, regulations) cumprir

obituary [ə'bɪtjuərɪ] N necrológio

object [n 'ɔbdʒɪkt, vi əb'dʒɛkt] N objeto; (purpose) objetivo ▶ VI: **to ~ to** (attitude) desaprovar, objetar a; (proposal) opor-se a; **I ~!** protesto!; **he ~ed that ...** ele objetou que ...; **expense is no ~** o preço não é problema; **objection** [əb'dʒɛkʃən] N objeção f; **I have no objection to ...** não

tenho nada contra ...; **objective** N objetivo

obligation [ɔblɪ'geɪʃən] N obrigação f; **without ~** sem compromisso

obligatory [ə'blɪgətərɪ] ADJ obrigatório

oblige [ə'blaɪdʒ] VT (do a favour for) obsequiar, fazer um favor a; (force) obrigar, forçar; **to be ~d to sb for doing sth** ficar agradecido por alguém fazer algo

oblong ['ɔblɔŋ] ADJ oblongo, retangular ▶ N retângulo

obnoxious [əb'nɔkʃəs] ADJ odioso, detestável; (smell) enjoativo

oboe ['əubəu] N oboé m

obscene [əb'siːn] ADJ obsceno

obscure [əb'skjuəʳ] ADJ obscuro, desconhecido; (difficult to understand) pouco claro ▶ VT ocultar, escurecer; (hide: sun etc) esconder

observant [əb'zəːvnt] ADJ observador(a)

observation [ɔbzə'veɪʃən] N observação f; (Med) exame m

observatory [əb'zəːvətrɪ] N observatório

observe [əb'zəːv] VT observar; (rule) cumprir; **observer** N observador(a) m/f

obsess [əb'sɛs] VT obsedar, obcecar

obsolete ['ɔbsəliːt] ADJ obsoleto

obstacle ['ɔbstəkl] N obstáculo; (hindrance) estorvo, impedimento

obstinate ['ɔbstɪnɪt] ADJ obstinado

obstruct [əb'strʌkt] VT obstruir; (hinder) estorvar

obtain [əb'teɪn] VT obter; (achieve) conseguir

obvious ['ɔbvɪəs] ADJ óbvio; **obviously** ADV evidentemente;

obviously not! (é)claro que não!
occasion [ə'keɪʒən] N ocasião f;
(*event*) acontecimento;
  occasional ADJ de vez em quando;
  occasionally ADV de vez em
  quando
occupation [ɔkju'peɪʃən] N
ocupação f; (*job*) profissão f
occupy ['ɔkjupaɪ] VT ocupar;
(*house*) morar em; **to ~ o.s. in
doing** ocupar-se de fazer
occur [ə'kəːʳ] VI ocorrer;
(*phenomenon*) acontecer; **to ~ to
sb** ocorrer a alguém; **occurrence**
N ocorrência, acontecimento;
(*existence*) existência
ocean ['əuʃən] N oceano
o'clock [ə'klɔk] ADV: **it is 5 ~** são
cinco horas
October [ɔk'təubəʳ] N outubro
octopus ['ɔktəpəs] N polvo
odd [ɔd] ADJ (*strange*) estranho,
esquisito; (*number*) ímpar; (*sock
etc*) desemparelhado; **60-~** 60 e
tantos; **at ~ times** às vezes, de vez
em quando; **to be the ~ one out**
ficar sobrando, ser a exceção;
  oddly ADV curiosamente; *see also*
  enough; **odds** NPL (*in betting*)
pontos mpl de vantagem; **it
makes no odds** dá no mesmo;
at odds brigados(-as), de mal
odour ['əudəʳ], (*US*) **odor** N odor m,
cheiro; (*unpleasant*) fedor m

KEYWORD

of [ɔv, əv] PREP 1 (*gen*) de; **a friend
of ours** um amigo nosso; **a boy
of 10** um menino de 10 anos; **that
was very kind of you** foi muito
gentil da sua parte
2 (*expressing quantity, amount, dates
etc*) de; **how much of this do you
need?** de quanto você precisa?;

3 of them 3 deles; **3 of us went**
3 de nós foram; **the 5th of July**
dia 5 de julho
3 (*from, out of*) de; **made of wood**
feito de madeira

KEYWORD

off [ɔf] ADV 1 (*distance, time*): **it's a
long way off** fica bem longe; **the
game is 3 days off** o jogo é daqui
a 3 dias
2 (*departure*): **I'm off** estou de
partida; **to go off to Paris/Italy**
ir para Paris/a Itália; **I must be off**
devo ir-me
3 (*removal*): **to take off one's hat/
coat/clothes** tirar o chapéu/o
casaco/a roupa; **the button
came off** o botão caiu; **10% off**
(*Comm*) 10% de abatimento or
desconto
4 (*not at work*): **to have a day off**
tirar um dia de folga; (: *sick*): **to be
off sick** estar ausente por motivo
de saúde
▶ ADJ 1 (*not turned on: machine,
water, gas*) desligado; (: *light*)
apagado; (: *tap*) fechado
2 (*cancelled*) cancelado
3 (*not fresh: food*) passado; (: *milk*)
talhado, anulado
4: **on the off chance** (*just in case*)
ao acaso; **today I had an off day**
(*not as good as usual*) hoje não foi o
meu dia
▶ PREP 1 (*indicating motion, removal,
etc*) de; **the button came off my
coat** o botão do meu casaco caiu
2 (*distant from*) de; **5 km off (the
road)** a 5 km (da estrada); **off the
coast** em frente à costa
3: **to be off meat** (*no longer eat it*)
não comer mais carne; (*no longer
like it*) enjoar de carne

offence [əˈfɛns], (US) **offense** N
(crime) delito; **to take ~ at**
ofender-se com, melindrar-se com
offend [əˈfɛnd] VT ofender;
offender N delinquente m/f
offensive [əˈfɛnsɪv] ADJ (weapon,
remark) ofensivo; (smell etc)
repugnante ▶ N (Mil) ofensiva
offer [ˈɔfəʳ] N oferta; (proposal)
proposta ▶ VT oferecer;
(opportunity) proporcionar; **"on ~"**
(Comm) "em oferta"
office [ˈɔfɪs] N (place) escritório;
(room) gabinete m; (position) cargo,
função f; **to take ~** tomar posse;
doctor's ~ (US) consultório; **office
block**, (US) **office building** N
conjunto de escritórios
officer [ˈɔfɪsəʳ] N (Mil etc) oficial m/f;
(of organization) diretor(a) m/f; (also:
police ~) agente m/f policial or de
polícia
office worker N empregado(-a) or
funcionário(-a) de escritório
official [əˈfɪʃl] ADJ oficial ▶ N
oficial m/f; (civil servant)
funcionário(-a) público(-a)
off-licence (BRIT) N loja de bebidas
alcoólicas

> Uma loja **off-licence** vende
> bebidas alcóolicas (para viagem)
> nos horários em que os pubs
> estão fechados. Nesses
> estabelecimentos também se
> pode comprar bebidas
> não-alcoólicas, cigarros,
> batatas fritas, balas,
> chocolates etc.

offline ADJ, ADV (Comput) off-line
off-peak ADJ (heating etc) de período
de pouco consumo; (ticket, train) de
período de pouco movimento
off-putting (BRIT) ADJ
desconcertante

off-season ADJ, ADV fora de estação
or temporada
offset [ˈɔfsɛt] irreg VT compensar,
contrabalançar
offshore [ɔfˈʃɔːʳ] ADJ (breeze) de
terra; (fishing) costeiro; **~ oilfield**
campo petrolífero ao largo
offside [ɔfˈsaɪd] ADJ (Sport)
impedido; (Aut) do lado do
motorista
offspring [ˈɔfsprɪŋ] N
descendência, prole f
often [ˈɔfn] ADV muitas vezes,
frequentemente; **how ~ do you
go?** com que frequência você vai?
oil [ɔɪl] N (Culin) azeite m; (petroleum)
petróleo; (for heating) óleo ▶ VT
(machine) lubrificar; **oil painting** N
pintura a óleo; **oil rig** N torre f de
perfuração; **oil slick** N mancha
de óleo; **oil tanker** N (ship)
petroleiro; (truck) carro-tanque m
de petróleo; **oil well** N poço
petrolífero; **oily** ADJ oleoso;
(food) gorduroso
ointment [ˈɔɪntmənt] N pomada
O.K. [ˈəuˈkeɪ] EXCL está bem, está
bom, tá (bem or bom) (inf) ▶ ADJ
bom; (correct) certo ▶ VT aprovar
old [əuld] ADJ velho; (former) antigo,
anterior; **how ~ are you?** quantos
anos você tem?; **he's 10 years ~** ele
tem 10 anos; **~er brother** irmão
mais velho; **old age** N velhice f;
old-age pensioner (BRIT) N
aposentado(-a) (BR), reformado(-a)
(PT); **old-fashioned** ADJ fora de
moda; (person) antiquado; (values)
obsoleto, retrógrado
olive [ˈɔlɪv] N (fruit) azeitona; (tree)
oliveira ▶ ADJ (also: **~-green**)
verde-oliva inv; **olive oil** N azeite m
de oliva
Olympic [əuˈlɪmpɪk] ADJ olímpico

omelette, (US) **omelet** ['ɔmlɪt] N
omelete f
omen ['əumən] N presságio,
agouro
OMG (inf) ABBR (= Oh my God!) OMG
ominous ['ɔmɪnəs] ADJ
preocupante
omit [əu'mɪt] VT omitir

(KEYWORD)

on [ɔn] PREP **1** (indicating position)
sobre, em (cima de); **on the wall**
na parede; **on the left** à esquerda
2 (indicating means, method,
condition etc): **on foot** a pé; **on the
train/plane** no trem/avião; **on
the telephone/radio** no
telefone/rádio; **on television** na
televisão; **to be on drugs**
(addicted) ser viciado em drogas;
(Med) estar sob medicação; **to be
on holiday/business** estar de
férias/a negócio
3 (referring to time): **on Friday** na
sexta-feira; **a week on Friday**
sem ser esta sexta-feira, a outra;
on arrival ao chegar; **on seeing
this** ao ver isto
4 (about, concerning) sobre
▶ ADV **1** (referring to dress): **to have
one's coat on** estar de casaco;
what's she got on? o que ela está
usando?; **she put her boots on**
ela calçou as botas; **he put his
gloves/hat on** ele colocou as
luvas/o chapéu
2: **screw the lid on tightly**
atarraxar bem a tampa
3 (further, continuously): **to walk/
drive on** continuar andando/
dirigindo; **to go on** continuar (em
frente); **to read on** continuar a ler
▶ ADJ **1** (functioning, in operation:
machine) em funcionamento;

(: light) aceso; (: radio) ligado;
(: tap) aberto; (: brakes: of car etc):
to be on estar freado; (meeting):
is the meeting still on? (in
progress) a reunião ainda está
sendo realizada?; (not cancelled)
ainda vai haver reunião?; **there's
a good film on at the cinema**
tem um bom filme passando no
cinema
2: **that's not on!** (inf: of behaviour)
isso não se faz!

once [wʌns] ADV uma vez;
(formerly) outrora ▶ CONJ depois
que; **~ he had left/it was done**
depois que ele saiu/foi feito; **at ~**
imediatamente; (simultaneously)
de uma vez, ao mesmo tempo;
~ more mais uma vez; **~ and for
all** uma vez por todas; **~ upon a
time** era uma vez
oncoming ['ɔnkʌmɪŋ] ADJ (traffic)
que vem de frente

(KEYWORD)

one [wʌn] NUM um(a); **one
hundred and fifty** cento e
cinquenta; **one by one** um por
um
▶ ADJ **1** (sole) único; **the one book
which ...** o único livro que ...
2 (same) mesmo; **they came in
the one car** eles vieram no
mesmo carro
▶ PRON **1** um(a); **this one** este/
esta; **that one** esse/essa, aquele/
aquela; **I've already got one/
a red one** eu já tenho um/um
vermelho
2: **one another** um ao outro;
**do you two ever see one
another?** vocês dois se veem de
vez em quando?

3 (*impers*): **one never knows** nunca se sabe; **to cut one's finger** cortar o dedo; **one needs to eat** é preciso comer

oneself [wʌn'sɛlf] PRON (*reflexive*) se; (*after prep, emphatic*) si (mesmo(-a)); **by ~** sozinho(-a); **to hurt ~** ferir-se; **to keep sth for ~** guardar algo para si mesmo; **to talk to ~** falar consigo mesmo

one-sided ADJ parcial

one-way ADJ (*street, traffic*) de mão única (BR), de sentido único (PT)

ongoing ['ɔngəuɪŋ] ADJ (*project*) em andamento; (*situation*) existente

onion ['ʌnjən] N cebola

online ADJ, ADV (*Comput*) on-line, online

onlooker ['ɔnlukəʳ] N espectador(a) *m/f*

only ['əunlɪ] ADV somente, apenas ▶ ADJ único, só ▶ CONJ só que, porém; **an ~ child** um filho único; **not ~ ... but also ...** não só ... mas também ...

onset ['ɔnsɛt] N começo

onto ['ɔntu] PREP = **on to**

onward ['ɔnwəd], **onwards** ['ɔnwədz] ADV (*move*) para diante, para a frente; **from this time ~(s)** de (ag)ora em diante

ooze [u:z] VI ressumar, filtrar-se

opaque [əu'peɪk] ADJ opaco, fosco

open ['əupn] ADJ aberto; (*car*) descoberto; (*road*) livre; (*fig: frank*) aberto, franco; (*meeting*) aberto, sem restrições ▶ VT abrir ▶ VI abrir(-se); (*book etc*) começar; **in the ~ (air)** ao ar livre; **open on to** VT FUS (*subj: room, door*) dar para; **open up** VT abrir; (*blocked road*) desobstruir ▶ VI (*Comm*) abrir; **opening** ADJ de abertura ▶ N

abertura; (*start*) início; (*opportunity*) oportunidade *f*; **openly** ADV abertamente; **open-minded** ADJ aberto, imparcial; **open-necked** ADJ aberto no colo; **open-plan** ADJ sem paredes divisórias; **Open University** (BRIT) N *ver nota*

Fundada em 1969, a **Open University** oferece um tipo de ensino que compreende cursos (alguns blocos da programação da TV e do rádio são reservados para esse fim), deveres que são enviados pelo aluno ao diretor ou diretora de estudos e uma estada obrigatória em uma universidade de verão. É preciso cumprir um certo número de unidades ao longo de um período determinado e obter a média em um certo número delas para receber o diploma almejado.

opera ['ɔpərə] N ópera

operate ['ɔpəreɪt] VT fazer funcionar, pôr em funcionamento ▶ VI funcionar; (*Med*): **to ~ on sb** operar alguém

operation [ɔpə'reɪʃən] N operação *f*; (*of machine*) funcionamento; **to be in ~** (*system*) estar em vigor

operator ['ɔpəreɪtəʳ] N (*of machine*) operador(a) *m/f*, manipulador(a) *m/f*; (*Tel*) telefonista *m/f*

opinion [ə'pɪnɪən] N opinião *f*; **in my ~** na minha opinião, a meu ver

opponent [ə'pəunənt] N oponente *m/f*; (*Mil, Sport*) adversário(-a)

opportunity [ɔpə'tju:nɪtɪ] N oportunidade *f*; **to take the ~ of doing** aproveitar a oportunidade para fazer

oppose [ə'pəuz] VT opor-se a; **to be ~d to sth** opor-se a algo, estar contra algo; **as ~d to** em oposição a

opposite ['ɔpəzɪt] ADJ oposto; (*house etc*) em frente ▶ ADV (lá) em frente ▶ PREP em frente de, defronte de ▶ N oposto, contrário

opposition [ɔpə'zɪʃən] N oposição f

opt [ɔpt] VI: **to ~ for** optar por; **to ~ to do** optar por fazer; **opt out** VI: **to ~ out of doing sth** optar por não fazer algo

optician [ɔp'tɪʃən] N oculista m/f

optimist ['ɔptɪmɪst] N otimista m/f; **optimistic** [ɔptɪ'mɪstɪk] ADJ otimista

option ['ɔpʃən] N opção f; **optional** ADJ opcional, facultativo

or [ɔːʳ] CONJ ou; (*with negative*): **he hasn't seen or heard anything** ele não viu nem ouviu nada; **or else** senão

oral ['ɔːrəl] ADJ oral ▶ N prova f oral

orange ['ɔrɪndʒ] N (*fruit*) laranja ▶ ADJ cor de laranja *inv*, alaranjado

orbit ['ɔːbɪt] N órbita ▶ VT orbitar

orchard ['ɔːtʃəd] N pomar m

orchestra ['ɔːkɪstrə] N orquestra; (*US: seating*) plateia

orchid ['ɔːkɪd] N orquídea

ordeal [ɔː'diːl] N experiência penosa, provação f

order ['ɔːdəʳ] N ordem f; (*Comm*) encomenda ▶ VT (*also:* **put in ~**) pôr em ordem, arrumar; (*in restaurant*) pedir; (*Comm*) encomendar; (*command*) mandar, ordenar; **in (working) ~** em bom estado; **in ~ to do/that** para fazer/que (+ *sub*); **good ~** bom estado; **on ~** (*Comm*) encomendado; **out of ~** com defeito, enguiçado; **order form** N

impresso para encomendas; **orderly** N (*Mil*) ordenança m; (*Med*) servente m/f ▶ ADJ (*room*) arrumado, ordenado; (*person*) metódico

ordinary ['ɔːdnrɪ] ADJ comum, usual; (*pej*) ordinário, medíocre; **out of the ~** fora do comum, extraordinário

ore [ɔːʳ] N minério

organ ['ɔːgən] N órgão m; **organic** [ɔː'gænɪk] ADJ orgânico

organization [ɔːgənaɪ'zeɪʃən] N organização f

organize ['ɔːgənaɪz] VT organizar

orgasm ['ɔːgæzəm] N orgasmo

origin ['ɔrɪdʒɪn] N origem f

original [ə'rɪdʒɪnl] ADJ original ▶ N original m

originate [ə'rɪdʒɪneɪt] VI: **to ~ from** originar-se de, surgir de; **to ~ in** ter origem em

Orkney ['ɔːknɪ] N (*also:* **the ~ Islands, the ~s**) as ilhas Órcadas

ornament ['ɔːnəmənt] N ornamento; (*on dress*) enfeite m; **ornamental** [ɔːnə'mɛntl] ADJ decorativo, ornamental

ornate [ɔː'neɪt] ADJ enfeitado, requintado

orphan ['ɔːfn] N órfão/órfã m/f

orthopaedic [ɔːθə'piːdɪk], (*US*) **orthopedic** ADJ ortopédico

ostrich ['ɔstrɪtʃ] N avestruz m/f

other ['ʌðəʳ] ADJ outro ▶ PRON: **the ~ (one)** o outro/a outra ▶ ADV (*usually in negatives*): **~ than** (*apart from*) além de; (*anything but*) exceto; **~s** (*other people*) outros; **otherwise** ADV (*in a different way*) de outra maneira; (*apart from that*) além disso ▶ CONJ (*if not*) senão

otter ['ɔtəʳ] N lontra

ouch [autʃ] EXCL ai!

o

ought [ɔːt] (*pt* **ought**) AUX VB: **I ~ to do it** eu deveria fazê-lo; **he ~ to win** (*probability*) ele deve ganhar

ounce [auns] N onça (= 28.35g)

our ['auə'] ADJ nosso; *see also* **my**; **ours** PRON (o) nosso/(a) nossa *etc*; *see also* **mine¹**; **ourselves** [auə'sɛlvz] PRON PL (*reflexive, after prep*) nós; (*emphatic*) nós mesmos(-as); *see also* **oneself**

oust [aust] VT expulsar

(KEYWORD)

out [aut] ADV **1** (*not in*) fora; **(to stand) out in the rain/snow** (estar em pé) na chuva/neve; **out loud** em voz alta
2 (*not at home, absent*) fora (de casa); **Mr Green is out at the moment** Sr. Green não está no momento; **to have a day/night out** passar o dia fora/sair à noite
3 (*indicating distance*): **the boat was 10 km out** o barco estava a 10 km da costa
4 (*Sport*): **the ball is/has gone out** a bola caiu fora; **out!** (*Tennis etc*) fora!
▶ ADJ **1**: **to be out** (*unconscious*) estar inconsciente; (*out of game*) estar fora; (*out of fashion*) estar fora de moda
2 (*have appeared: news, secret*) do conhecimento público; **the flowers are out** as flores desabrocharam
3 (*extinguished: light, fire*) apagado; **before the week was out** (*finished*) antes da semana acabar
4: **to be out to do sth** (*intend*) pretender fazer algo; **to be out in one's calculations** (*wrong*) enganar-se nos cálculos
▶ **out of** PREP **1** (*outside, beyond*) fora de; **to go out of the house** sair da casa; **to look out of the window** olhar pela janela
2 (*cause, motive*) por
3 (*origin*): **to drink sth out of a cup** beber algo na xícara
4 (*from among*): **1 out of every 3 smokers** 1 entre 3 fumantes
5 (*without*) sem; **to be out of milk/ sugar/petrol** *etc* não ter leite/ açúcar/gasolina *etc*

outback ['autbæk] N (*in Australia*): **the ~** o interior; **outbox** ['autbɒks] N (*Comput*) caixa de saída; (*US: for papers*) cesta de saída

outbreak ['autbreɪk] N (*of war*) deflagração *f*; (*of disease*) surto; (*of violence etc*) explosão *f*

outburst ['autbɜːst] N explosão *f*

outcast ['autkɑːst] N pária *m/f*

outcome ['autkʌm] N resultado

outcry ['autkraɪ] N clamor *m* (de protesto)

outdated [aut'deɪtɪd] ADJ antiquado, fora de moda

outdoor [aut'dɔː'] ADJ ao ar livre; (*clothes*) de sair; **outdoors** ADV ao ar livre

outer ['autə'] ADJ exterior, externo; **outer space** N espaço (exterior)

outfit ['autfɪt] N roupa, traje *m*

outgoing ['autɡəuɪŋ] ADJ de saída; (*character*) extrovertido, sociável; **outgoings** (BRIT) NPL despesas *fpl*

outing ['autɪŋ] N excursão *f*

outlaw ['autlɔː] N fora-da-lei *m/f*
▶ VT (*person*) declarar fora da lei; (*practice*) declarar ilegal

outlay ['autleɪ] N despesas *fpl*

outlet ['autlɛt] N saída, escape *m*; (*of pipe*) desague *m*, escoadouro; (*US Elec*) tomada; (*also*: **retail ~**) posto de venda

outline ['autlaɪn] N (*shape*) contorno, perfil *m*; (*of plan*) traçado;

(*sketch*) esboço, linhas *fpl* gerais
▶ vт (*theory, plan*) traçar, delinear

outlook ['autluk] N (*attitude*)
ponto de vista; (*fig: prospects*)
perspectiva; (: *for weather*)
previsão *f*

outnumber [aut'nʌmbə^r] vт
exceder em número

out-of-date ADJ (*passport, ticket*)
sem validade; (*clothes*) fora de
moda

out-of-the-way ADJ remoto,
afastado

outpatient ['autpeɪʃənt] N
paciente *m/f* externo(-a) *or* de
ambulatório

outpost ['autpəust] N posto
avançado

output ['autput] N (volume *m* de)
produção *f*; (*Comput*) saída ▶ vт
(*Comput*) dar saída em

outrage ['autreɪdʒ] N escândalo;
(*atrocity*) atrocidade *f* ▶ vт ultrajar;
outrageous [aut'reɪdʒəs] ADJ
ultrajante, escandaloso

outright [*adv* aut'raɪt, *adj* 'autraɪt]
ADV (*kill, win*) completamente;
(*ask, refuse*) abertamente ▶ ADJ
completo; franco

outset ['autsɛt] N início, princípio

outside [aut'saɪd] N exterior *m*
▶ ADJ exterior, externo ▶ ADV (lá)
fora ▶ PREP fora de; (*beyond*) além
(dos limites) de; **at the ~** (*fig*) no
máximo; **outsider** N (*stranger*)
estranho(-a), forasteiro(-a)

outsize ['autsaɪz] ADJ (*clothes*) de
tamanho extra-grande *or* especial

outskirts ['autskə:ts] NPL
arredores *mpl*, subúrbios *mpl*

outspoken [aut'spəukən] ADJ
franco, sem rodeios

outstanding [aut'stændɪŋ] ADJ
excepcional; (*work, debt*) pendente

outward ['autwəd] ADJ externo;
(*journey*) de ida; **outwards** (*esp*
BRIT) ADV para fora

outweigh [aut'weɪ] vт ter mais
valor do que

oval ['əuvl] ADJ ovalado ▶ N oval *m*;
Oval Office N *ver nota*

> O Salão Oval (**Oval Office**) é
> o escritório particular do
> presidente dos Estados Unidos
> na Casa Branca, assim
> chamado devido a sua forma
> oval. Por extensão, o termo se
> refere à presidência em si.

ovary ['əuvəri] N ovário

oven ['ʌvn] N forno

(KEYWORD)

over ['əuvə^r] ADV 1 (*across: walk,
jump, fly etc*) por cima; **to cross
over to the other side of the
road** atravessar para o outro lado
da rua; **over here** por aqui, cá;
over there por ali, lá; **to ask sb
over** (*to one's home*) convidar
alguém

2: **to fall over** cair; **to knock
over** derrubar; **to turn over** virar;
to bend over curvar-se,
debruçar-se

3 (*finished*): **to be over** estar
acabado

4 (*excessively: clever, rich, fat etc*)
muito, demais; **she's not over
intelligent** ela não é superdotada

5 (*remaining: money, food etc*): **there
are 3 over** tem 3 sobrando/
sobraram 3

6: **all over** (*everywhere*) por todos
os lados; **over and over (again)**
repetidamente

▶ PREP 1 (*on top of*) sobre; (*above*)
acima de

2 (*on the other side of*) no outro

lado de; **he jumped over the wall** ele pulou o muro
3 (*more than*) mais de; **over and above** além de
4 (*during*) durante

overall [*n, adj* əuvərɔːl, *adv* əuvərˈɔːl] ADJ (*length*) total; (*study*) global ▶ ADV (*view*) globalmente; (*measure, paint*) totalmente;
overalls NPL macacão *m* (BR), (fato) macaco (PT)

overboard [ˈəuvəbɔːd] ADV (*Naut*) ao mar

overcast [ˈəuvəkɑːst] ADJ nublado, fechado

overcharge [əuvəˈtʃɑːdʒ] VT: **to ~ sb** cobrar em excesso a alguém

overcoat [ˈəuvəkəut] N sobretudo

overcome [əuvəˈkʌm] *irreg* VT vencer, dominar; (*difficulty*) superar

overcrowded [əuvəˈkraudɪd] ADJ superlotado

overdo [əuvəˈduː] *irreg* VT exagerar; (*overcook*) cozinhar demais; **to ~ it** (*work too hard*) exceder-se

overdose [ˈəuvədəus] N overdose *f*, dose *f* excessiva

overdraft [ˈəuvədrɑːft] N saldo negativo

overdrawn [əuvəˈdrɔːn] ADJ (*account*) sem fundos, a descoberto

overdue [əuvəˈdjuː] ADJ atrasado; (*change*) tardio

overestimate [əuvərˈɛstɪmeɪt] VT sobrestimar

overflow [*vi* əuvəˈfləu, *n* ˈəuvəfləu] VI transbordar ▶ N (*also:* **~ pipe**) tubo de descarga, ladrão *m*

overgrown [əuvəˈgrəun] ADJ (*garden*) coberto de vegetação

overhaul [*vt* əuvəˈhɔːl, *n* ˈəuvəhɔːl] VT revisar ▶ N revisão *f*

overhead [*adv* əuvəˈhɛd, *adj, n* ˈəuvəhɛd] ADV por cima, em cima; (*in the sky*) no céu ▶ ADJ (*lighting*) superior; (*railway*) suspenso ▶ N (*US*) = **overheads**; **overheads** NPL (*expenses*) despesas *fpl* gerais

overhear [əuvəˈhɪər] *irreg* VT ouvir por acaso

overheat [əuvəˈhiːt] VI (*engine*) aquecer demais

overland [ˈəuvəlænd] ADJ, ADV por terra

overlap [əuvəˈlæp] VI (*edges*) sobrepor-se em parte; (*fig*) coincidir

overload [əuvəˈləud] VT sobrecarregar

overlook [əuvəˈluk] VT (*have view on*) dar para; (*miss*) omitir; (*forgive*) fazer vista grossa a

overnight [*adv* əuvəˈnaɪt, *adj* ˈəuvənaɪt] ADV durante a noite; (*fig*) da noite para o dia ▶ ADJ de uma (*or* de) noite; **to stay ~** passar a noite, pernoitar

overpass [ˈəuvəpɑːs] (*esp US*) N viaduto

overpower [əuvəˈpauər] VT dominar, subjugar; (*fig*) assolar

overrule [əuvəˈruːl] VT (*decision*) anular; (*claim*) indeferir

overrun [əuvəˈrʌn] *irreg* VT (*country etc*) invadir; (*time limit*) ultrapassar, exceder

overseas [əuvəˈsiːz] ADV (*abroad*) no estrangeiro, no exterior ▶ ADJ (*trade*) exterior; (*visitor*) estrangeiro

overshadow [əuvəˈʃædəu] VT ofuscar

oversight [ˈəuvəsaɪt] N descuido

oversleep [əuvəˈsliːp] *irreg* VI dormir além da hora

overt [əuˈvəːt] ADJ aberto, indissimulado

overtake [əuvə'teɪk] *irreg* VT
ultrapassar

overthrow [əuvə'θrəu] *irreg* VT
(*government*) derrubar

overtime ['əuvətaɪm] N horas *fpl*
extras

overturn [əuvə'təːn] VT virar;
(*system*) derrubar; (*decision*) anular
▶ VI capotar

overweight [əuvə'weɪt] ADJ
acima do peso

overwhelm [əuvə'wɛlm] VT
esmagar, assolar; **overwhelming**
ADJ (*victory, defeat*) esmagador(a);
(*heat*) sufocante; (*desire*) irresistível

owe [əu] VT: **to ~ sb sth, to ~ sth
to sb** dever algo a alguém; **owing
to** PREP devido a, por causa de

owl [aul] N coruja

own [əun] ADJ próprio ▶ VT possuir,
ter; **a room of my ~** meu próprio
quarto; **to get one's ~ back** ir à
forra; **on one's ~** sozinho; **own
up** VI: **to ~ up to sth** confessar
algo; **owner** N dono(-a),
proprietário(-a); **ownership** N
posse *f*

ox [ɔks] (*pl* **oxen**) N boi *m*

oxygen ['ɔksɪdʒən] N oxigênio

oyster ['ɔɪstər] N ostra

oz. ABBR = **ounce**

ozone ['əuzəun] N ozônio

P

p [piː] ABBR (= *page*) p; (BRIT) =
penny, pence

p.a. ABBR (= *per annum*) por ano

pace [peɪs] N passo; (*speed*)
velocidade *f* ▶ VI: **to ~ up and
down** andar de um lado para o
outro; **to keep ~ with**
acompanhar o passo de;
pacemaker N (*Med*) marcapasso *m*

Pacific [pə'sɪfɪk] N: **the ~ (Ocean)**
o (Oceano) Pacífico

pack [pæk] N pacote *m*, embrulho;
(*of hounds*) matilha; (*of thieves etc*)
bando, quadrilha; (*of cards*)
baralho; (*backpack*) mochila ▶ VT
encher; (*in suitcase etc*) arrumar
(na mala); (*cram*): **to ~ into**
entupir de, entulhar com ▶ VI: **to ~
(one's bags)** fazer as malas; **~ it
in!** para com isso!; **pack off** VT
(*person*) despedir

package ['pækɪdʒ] N pacote *m*;
(*bulky*) embrulho, fardo; (*also:
~ deal*) pacote; **package tour**
(BRIT) N excursão *f* organizada

packed lunch [pækt-] (BRIT) N merenda

packet ['pækɪt] N pacote m; (of cigarettes) maço; (of washing powder etc) caixa

packing ['pækɪŋ] N embalagem f; (act) empacotamento

pad [pæd] N (of paper) bloco; (to prevent friction) acolchoado; (inf: home) casa ▶ VT acolchoar, enchumaçar

paddle ['pædl] N remo curto; (US: for table tennis) raquete f ▶ VT remar ▶ VI patinhar; **paddling pool** (BRIT) N lago de recreação

paddock ['pædək] N cercado; (at race course) paddock m

padlock ['pædlɔk] N cadeado

paedophile, (US) **pedophile** ['pi:dəufaɪl] N pedófilo(-a)

page [peɪdʒ] N página; (also: ~ **boy**) mensageiro ▶ VT mandar chamar

pager ['peɪdʒəʳ] N bip m

paid [peɪd] PT, PP of **pay** ▶ ADJ (work) remunerado; (holiday) pago; (official) assalariado; **to put ~ to** (BRIT) acabar com

pain [peɪn] N dor f; **to be in ~** sofrer or sentir dor; **to take ~s to do sth** dar-se ao trabalho de fazer algo; **painful** ADJ doloroso; (laborious) penoso; (unpleasant) desagradável; **painkiller** N analgésico; **painstaking** ['peɪnzteɪkɪŋ] ADJ (work) esmerado; (person) meticuloso

paint [peɪnt] N pintura ▶ VT pintar; **paintbrush** N (artist's) pincel m; (decorator's) broxa; **painter** N pintor(a) m/f; **painting** N pintura; (picture) tela, quadro

pair [pɛəʳ] N par m; **a ~ of scissors** uma tesoura; **a ~ of trousers** uma calça (BR), umas calças (PT)

pajamas [pɪ'dʒɑːməz] (US) NPL pijama m

Pakistan [pɑːkɪ'stɑːn] N Paquistão m; **Pakistani** ADJ, N paquistanês(-esa) m/f

pal [pæl] (inf) N camarada m/f, colega m/f

palace ['pæləs] N palácio

pale [peɪl] ADJ pálido; (colour) claro; (light) fraco ▶ VI empalidecer ▶ N: **to be beyond the ~** passar dos limites

Palestine ['pælɪstaɪn] N Palestina; **Palestinian** [pælɪs'tɪnɪən] ADJ, N palestino(-a)

palm [pɑːm] N (hand, leaf) palma; (also: ~ **tree**) palmeira ▶ VT: **to ~ sth off on sb** (inf) impingir algo a alguém

pamper ['pæmpəʳ] VT paparicar, mimar

pamphlet ['pæmflət] N panfleto

pan [pæn] N (also: **sauce~**) panela (BR), caçarola (PT); (also: **frying ~**) frigideira

Panama ['pænəmɑː] N Panamá m

pancake ['pænkeɪk] N panqueca

panda ['pændə] N panda m/f

pandemic [pæn'dɛmɪk] N pandemia

pane [peɪn] N vidraça, vidro

panel ['pænl] N (of wood, Radio, TV) painel m

panic ['pænɪk] N pânico ▶ VI entrar em pânico

pansy ['pænzɪ] N (Bot) amor-perfeito; (inf, pej) bicha (BR), maricas m (PT)

pant [pænt] VI arquejar, ofegar

panther ['pænθəʳ] N pantera

panties ['pæntɪz] NPL calcinha (BR), cuecas fpl (PT)

pantomime ['pæntəmaɪm] (BRIT) N pantomima

Uma **pantomime**, também chamada simplesmente de *panto*, é um gênero de comédia em que o personagem principal em geral é um rapaz e na qual há sempre uma *dame*, isto é, uma mulher idosa representada por um homem, e um vilão. Na maior parte das vezes, a história é baseada em um conto de fadas, como "A gata borralheira" ou "O gato de botas", e a plateia é encorajada a participar prevenindo os heróis dos perigos que estão por vir. Esse tipo de espetáculo, voltado sobretudo para as crianças, visa também ao público adulto por meio de diversas brincadeiras que fazem alusão aos fatos atuais.

pants [pænts] NPL (BRIT: *underwear: woman's*) calcinha (BR), cuecas *fpl* (PT); (: *man's*) cueca (BR), cuecas (PT); (US: *trousers*) calça (BR), calças *fpl* (PT)

paper ['peɪpəʳ] N papel *m*; (*also:* **news~**) jornal *m*; (*also:* **wall~**) papel de parede; (*study, article*) artigo, dissertação *f*; (*exam*) exame *m*, prova ▶ ADJ de papel ▶ VT (*room*) revestir (com papel de parede); **papers** NPL (*also:* **identity ~s**) documentos *mpl*; **paperback** N livro de capa mole; **paper bag** N saco de papel; **paper clip** N clipe *m*; **paperwork** N trabalho burocrático; (*pej*) papelada

par [pɑːʳ] N paridade *f*, igualdade *f*; (*Golf*) média *f*; **on a ~ with** em pé de igualdade com

parachute ['pærəʃuːt] N para-quedas *m inv*

parade [pə'reɪd] N desfile *m* ▶ VT (*show off*) exibir ▶ VI (*Mil*) passar revista

paradise ['pærədaɪs] N paraíso

paraffin ['pærəfɪn] (BRIT) N: **~ (oil)** querosene *m*

paragraph ['pærəgrɑːf] N parágrafo

Paraguay ['pærəgwaɪ] N Paraguai *m*

parallel ['pærəlɛl] ADJ (*lines etc*) paralelo; (*fig*) correspondente ▶ N paralela; correspondência

paralysis [pə'rælɪsɪs] (*pl* **paralyses**) N paralisia

paranoid ['pærənɔɪd] ADJ paranoico

parcel ['pɑːsl] N pacote *m* ▶ VT (*also:* **~ up**) embrulhar, empacotar

pardon ['pɑːdn] N (*Jur*) indulto ▶ VT perdoar; **~ me!, I beg your ~** (*apologizing*) desculpe(-me); (**I beg your**) **~?** (BRIT), **~ me?** (US) (*not hearing*) como?, como disse?

parent ['pɛərənt] N (*father*) pai *m*; (*mother*) mãe *f*; **parents** NPL (*mother and father*) pais *mpl*

Paris ['pærɪs] N Paris

parish ['pærɪʃ] N paróquia, freguesia

park [pɑːk] N parque *m* ▶ VT, VI estacionar; **park and ride** N *esquema de transporte feito parcialmente com carro, que em seguida é estacionado para o uso de transporte público*

parking ['pɑːkɪŋ] N estacionamento; **"no ~"** "estacionamento proibido"; **parking lot** (US) N (parque *m* de) estacionamento; **parking meter** N parquímetro; **parking ticket** N multa por estacionamento proibido

parliament ['pɑːləmənt] (BRIT) N parlamento

parole [pə'rəʊl] N: **on ~** em liberdade condicional, sob promessa

parrot ['pærət] N papagaio

parsley ['pɑːslɪ] N salsa

parsnip ['pɑːsnɪp] N cherivia, pastinaga

parson ['pɑːsn] N padre m, clérigo; (in Church of England) pastor m

part [pɑːt] N parte f; (of machine) peça; (Theatre etc) papel m; (of serial) capítulo; (US: in hair) risca, repartido ▶ ADV = **partly** ▶ VT dividir; (hair) repartir ▶ VI (people) separar-se; (crowd) dispersar-se; **to take ~ in** participar de, tomar parte em; **to take sb's ~** defender alguém; **for my ~** pela minha parte; **for the most ~** na maior parte; **to take sth in good ~** não se ofender com algo; **part with** VT FUS ceder, entregar; (money) pagar

partial ['pɑːʃl] ADJ parcial; **to be ~ to** gostar de, ser apreciador(a) de

participate [pɑː'tɪsɪpeɪt] VI: **to ~ in** participar de

particle ['pɑːtɪkl] N partícula; (of dust) grão m

particular [pə'tɪkjulər] ADJ (special) especial; (specific) específico; (fussy) exigente, minucioso; **in ~** em particular; **particularly** ADV em particular, especialmente; **particulars** NPL detalhes mpl; (personal details) dados mpl pessoais

parting ['pɑːtɪŋ] N (act) separação f; (farewell) despedida; (BRIT: in hair) risca, repartido ▶ ADJ de despedida; **~ shot** (fig) flecha de parto

partition [pɑː'tɪʃən] N (Pol) divisão f; (wall) tabique m, divisória

partly ['pɑːtlɪ] ADV em parte

partner ['pɑːtnər] N (Comm) sócio(-a); (Sport) parceiro(-a); (at dance) par m; (spouse) cônjuge m/f; **partnership** N associação f, parceria; (Comm) sociedade f

partridge ['pɑːtrɪdʒ] N perdiz f

part-time ADJ, ADV de meio expediente

party ['pɑːtɪ] N (Pol) partido; (celebration) festa; (group) grupo; (Jur) parte f interessada, litigante m/f ▶ CPD (Pol) do partido, partidário

pass [pɑːs] VT passar; (exam) passar em; (place) passar por; (overtake, surpass) ultrapassar; (approve) aprovar ▶ VI passar; (Sch) ser aprovado, passar ▶ N (permit) passe m; (membership card) carteira; (in mountains) desfiladeiro; (Sport) passe m; (Sch): **to get a ~ in** ser aprovado em; **to make a ~ at sb** tomar liberdade com alguém; **pass away** VI falecer; **pass by** VI passar ▶ VT passar por cima de; **pass for** VT FUS passar por; **pass on** VT (news, illness) transmitir; (object) passar para; **pass out** VI desmaiar; **pass up** VT deixar passar; **passable** ADJ (road) transitável; (work) aceitável

passage ['pæsɪdʒ] N (also: **~way**: indoors) corredor m; (: outdoors) passagem f; (Anat) via; (act of passing) trânsito; (in book) trecho; (by boat) travessia; (Mechanics, Med) conduto

passenger ['pæsɪndʒər] N passageiro(-a)

passer-by ['pɑːsər-] (pl **passers-by**) N transeunte m/f

passion ['pæʃən] N paixão f; **passionate** ADJ apaixonado; **passion fruit** N maracujá m

passive ['pæsɪv] ADJ passivo

passport ['pɑːspɔːt] N passaporte m

password ['pɑːswəːd] N senha

past [pɑːst] PREP (drive, walk etc: in front of) por; (: beyond) mais além de; (later than) depois de ▶ ADJ passado; (president etc) ex-, anterior ▶ N passado; **he's ~ forty** ele tem mais de quarenta anos; **ten/quarter ~ four** quatro e dez/ quinze; **for the ~ few/3 days** nos últimos/3 dias

pasta ['pæstə] N massa

paste [peɪst] N pasta; (glue) grude m, cola ▶ VT grudar; **tomato ~** massa de tomate

pasteurized ['pæstəraɪzd] ADJ pasteurizado

pastime ['pɑːstaɪm] N passatempo

pastry ['peɪstrɪ] N massa; (cake) bolo

pasture ['pɑːstʃəʳ] N pasto

pasty [n 'pæstɪ, adj 'peɪstɪ] N empadão m de carne ▶ ADJ (complexion) pálido

pat [pæt] VT dar palmadinhas em; (dog etc) fazer festa em

patch [pætʃ] N retalho; (eye patch) tapa-olho m; (area) aréa pequena; (mend) remendo ▶ VT remendar; **(to go through) a bad ~** (passar por) um mau pedaço; **patch up** VT consertar provisoriamente; (quarrel) resolver; **patchy** ADJ (colour) desigual; (information) incompleto

pâté ['pæteɪ] N patê m

patent ['peɪtnt] N patente f ▶ VT patentear ▶ ADJ patente, evidente

paternal [pə'təːnl] ADJ paternal; (relation) paterno

path [pɑːθ] N caminho; (trail, track) trilha, senda; (trajectory) trajetória

pathetic [pə'θetɪk] ADJ (pitiful) patético, digno de pena; (very bad) péssimo

pathway ['pɑːθweɪ] N caminho, trilha

patience ['peɪʃns] N paciência

patient ['peɪʃnt] ADJ, N paciente m/f

patio ['pætɪəu] N pátio

patrol [pə'trəul] N patrulha ▶ VT patrulhar; **patrol car** N carro de patrulha

patron ['peɪtrən] N (customer) cliente m/f, freguês(-esa) m/f; (of charity) benfeitor(a) m/f; **~ of the arts** mecenas m

pattern ['pætən] N (Sewing) molde m; (design) desenho

pause [pɔːz] N pausa ▶ VI fazer uma pausa

pave [peɪv] VT pavimentar; **to ~ the way for** preparar o terreno para

pavement ['peɪvmənt] N (BRIT) calçada (BR), passeio (PT)

pavilion [pə'vɪlɪən] N (Sport) barraca

paving ['peɪvɪŋ] N pavimento, calçamento

paw [pɔː] N pata; (of cat) garra

pawn [pɔːn] N (Chess) peão m; (fig) títere m ▶ VT empenhar; **pawnbroker** N agiota m/f

pay [peɪ] (pt, pp **paid**) N salário; (of manual worker) paga ▶ VT pagar; (debt) liquidar, saldar; (visit) fazer ▶ VI valer a pena, render; **to ~ attention (to)** prestar atenção (a); **to ~ one's respects to sb** fazer uma visita de cortesia a alguém; **pay back** VT (money) devolver; (person) pagar; **pay for** VT FUS pagar a; (fig) recompensar; **pay in** VT depositar; **pay off** VT

P

(*debts*) saldar, liquidar; (*creditor*) pagar, reembolsar ▶ vi (*plan, patience*) valer a pena; **pay up** vt pagar; **payable** ADJ pagável; (*cheque*): **payable to** nominal em favor de; **payment** N pagamento; **monthly payment** pagamento mensal; **pay packet** (BRIT) N envelope m de pagamento; **pay phone** N telefone m público; **payroll** N folha de pagamento; **pay television** N televisão f por assinatura

PC N ABBR (= *personal computer*) PC m

PDA N ABBR (= *personal digital assistant*) PDA m (*assistente digital pessoal*)

pea [piː] N ervilha

peace [piːs] N paz f; (*calm*) tranquilidade f, quietude f; **peaceful** ADJ (*person*) tranquilo, pacífico; (*place, time*) tranquilo, sossegado

peach [piːtʃ] N pêssego

peacock [ˈpiːkɔk] N pavão m

peak [piːk] N (*of mountain: top*) cume m; (*of cap*) pala, viseira; (*fig*) apogeu m

peanut [ˈpiːnʌt] N amendoim m; **peanut butter** N manteiga de amendoim

pear [pɛər] N pera

pearl [pəːl] N pérola

peasant [ˈpɛznt] N camponês(-esa) m/f

peat [piːt] N turfa

pebble [ˈpɛbl] N seixo, calhau m

peck [pɛk] vt (*also:* ~ **at**) bicar, dar bicadas em ▶ N bicada; (*kiss*) beijoca; **peckish** (BRIT *inf*) ADJ: **I feel peckish** estou a fim de comer alguma coisa

peculiar [pɪˈkjuːlɪər] ADJ (*strange*) estranho, esquisito; ~ **to** (*belonging to*) próprio de

pedal [ˈpɛdl] N pedal m ▶ vi pedalar

pedestrian [pɪˈdɛstrɪən] N pedestre m/f (BR), peão m (PT) ▶ ADJ (*fig*) prosaico; **pedestrian crossing** (BRIT) N passagem f para pedestres (BR), passadeira (PT)

pedigree [ˈpɛdɪɡriː] N raça; (*fig*) genealogia ▶ CPD (*animal*) de raça

pedophile [ˈpiːdəfaɪl] (US) N = **paedophile**

pee [piː] (*inf*) vi fazer xixi, mijar

peek [piːk] vi: **to ~ at** espiar, espreitar

peel [piːl] N casca ▶ vt descascar ▶ vi (*paint, skin*) descascar; (*wallpaper*) desprender-se

peep [piːp] N (BRIT: *look*) espiadela; (*sound*) pio ▶ vi espreitar; **peep out** (BRIT) vi mostrar-se, surgir

peer [pɪər] vi: **to ~ at** perscrutar, fitar ▶ N (*noble*) par m/f; (*equal*) igual m/f; (*contemporary*) contemporâneo(-a)

peg [pɛɡ] N (*for coat etc*) cabide m; (BRIT: *also*: **clothes ~**) pregador m

pelican [ˈpɛlɪkən] N pelicano

pelt [pɛlt] vt: **to ~ sb with sth** atirar algo em alguém ▶ vi (*rain: also*: ~ **down**) chover a cântaros; (*inf: run*) correr ▶ N pele f (não curtida)

pelvis [ˈpɛlvɪs] N pelvis f, bacia

pen [pɛn] N caneta; (*for sheep etc*) redil m, cercado

penalty [ˈpɛnltɪ] N pena, penalidade f; (*fine*) multa; (*Sport*) punição f

pence [pɛns] (BRIT) NPL of **penny**

pencil [ˈpɛnsl] N lápis m; **pencil case** N lapiseira, porta-lápis m inv; **pencil sharpener** N apontador m (de lápis) (BR), apara-lápis m inv (PT)

pendant [ˈpɛndnt] N pingente m

pending [ˈpɛndɪŋ] PREP até ▶ ADJ pendente

penetrate ['pɛnɪtreɪt] VT
penetrar

penfriend ['pɛnfrɛnd] (BRIT) N
amigo(-a) por correspondência

penguin ['pɛŋgwɪn] N pinguim m

peninsula [pə'nɪnsjulə] N
península

penis ['piːnɪs] N pênis m

penitentiary [pɛnɪ'tɛnʃərɪ] (US)
N penitenciária, presídio

penknife ['pɛnnaɪf] irreg N
canivete m

penniless ['pɛnɪlɪs] ADJ sem
dinheiro, sem um tostão

penny ['pɛnɪ] (pl **pennies**, BRIT
pence) N pêni m; (US) cêntimo

penpal ['pɛnpæl] N amigo(-a) por
correspondência

pension ['pɛnʃən] N pensão f;
(old-age pension) aposentadoria;
pensioner (BRIT) N aposentado(-a)
(BR), reformado(-a) (PT)

Pentagon ['pɛntəgən] N: **the ~**
o Pentágono

> O Pentágono (**Pentagon**) é o
> nome dado aos escritórios do
> Ministério da Defesa
> americano, localizados em
> Arlington, no estado da
> Virgínia, por causa da forma
> pentagonal do edifício onde se
> encontram. Por extensão, o
> termo é utilizado também para
> se referir ao ministério.

penthouse ['pɛnthaus] N
cobertura

people ['piːpl] NPL gente f, pessoas
fpl; (inhabitants) habitantes mpl/fpl;
(citizens) povo; (Pol): **the ~** o povo
▶ N (nation, race) povo; **several ~
came** vieram várias pessoas;
~ say that ... dizem que ...

pepper ['pɛpər] N pimenta;
(vegetable) pimentão m ▶ VT

apimentar; (fig): **to ~ with**
salpicar de; **peppermint** N (sweet)
bala de hortelã

per [pəːr] PREP por

perceive [pə'siːv] VT perceber;
(notice) notar; (realize)
compreender

per cent N por cento

percentage [pə'sɛntɪdʒ] N
porcentagem f, percentagem f

perch [pəːtʃ] (pl **perches**) N (for
bird) poleiro; (fish) perca ▶ VI:
to ~ (on) (bird) empoleirar-se (em);
(person) encarapitar-se (em)

perfect [adj, n 'pəːfɪkt, vt pə'fɛkt]
ADJ perfeito; (utter) completo ▶ N
(also: **~ tense**) perfeito ▶ VT
aperfeiçoar; **perfectly** ADV
perfeitamente

perform [pə'fɔːm] VT (carry out)
realizar, fazer; (piece of music)
interpretar ▶ VI (well, badly)
interpretar; **performance** N
desempenho; (of play, by artist)
atuação f; (of car) performance f;
performer N (actor) artista m/f,
ator/atriz m/f; (Mus) intérprete
m/f

perfume ['pəːfjuːm] N perfume m

perhaps [pə'hæps] ADV talvez

perimeter [pə'rɪmɪtər] N
perímetro

period ['pɪərɪəd] N período; (Sch)
aula; (US: full stop) ponto final;
(Med) menstruação f, regra ▶ ADJ
(costume, furniture) da época

perish ['pɛrɪʃ] VI perecer; (decay)
deteriorar-se

perjury ['pəːdʒərɪ] N (Jur) perjúrio,
falso testemunho

perk [pəːk] (inf) N mordomia,
regalia; **perk up** VI (cheer up)
animar-se

perm [pəːm] N permanente f

permanent ['pə:mənənt] ADJ permanente

permission [pə'mɪʃən] N permissão f; (authorization) autorização f

permit [n 'pə:mɪt, vt pə'mɪt] N licença; (to enter) passe m ▶ VT permitir; (authorize) autorizar

perplex [pə'plɛks] VT deixar perplexo

persecute ['pə:sɪkju:t] VT perseguir

persevere [pə:sɪ'vɪər] VI perseverar

Persian ['pə:ʃən] ADJ persa ▶ N (Ling) persa m; **the (~) Gulf** o golfo Pérsico

persist [pə'sɪst] VI: **to ~ (in doing sth)** persistir (em fazer algo); **persistent** [pə'sɪstənt] ADJ persistente; (determined) teimoso

person ['pə:sn] N pessoa; **in ~** em pessoa; **personal** ADJ pessoal; (private) particular; (visit) em pessoa, pessoal; **personal assistant** N secretário(-a) particular; **personal computer** N computador m pessoal; **personality** [pə:sə'nælɪtɪ] N personalidade f; **personal organizer** N agenda

personnel [pə:sə'nɛl] N pessoal m

perspective [pə'spɛktɪv] N perspectiva

perspiration [pə:spɪ'reɪʃən] N transpiração f

persuade [pə'sweɪd] VT: **to ~ sb to do sth** persuadir alguém a fazer algo

Peru [pə'ru:] N Peru m

pervert [n 'pə:və:t, vt pə'və:t] N pervertido(-a) ▶ VT perverter, corromper; (truth) distorcer

pessimist ['pɛsɪmɪst] N pessimista m/f; **pessimistic** [pɛsɪ'mɪstɪk] ADJ pessimista

pest [pɛst] N (animal) praga; (fig) peste f

pester ['pɛstər] VT incomodar

pet [pɛt] N animal m de estimação ▶ CPD predileto ▶ VT acariciar ▶ VI (inf) acariciar-se; **teacher's ~** (favourite) preferido(-a) do professor

petal ['pɛtl] N pétala

petite [pə'ti:t] ADJ delicado, mignon

petition [pə'tɪʃən] N petição f; (list of signatures) abaixo-assinado

petrified ['pɛtrɪfaɪd] ADJ (fig) petrificado, paralisado

petrol ['pɛtrəl] (BRIT) N gasolina; **two/four-star ~** gasolina comum/ premium

petroleum [pə'trəʊlɪəm] N petróleo

petrol: petrol pump (BRIT) N bomba de gasolina; **petrol station** (BRIT) N posto (BR) or bomba (PT) de gasolina; **petrol tank** (BRIT) N tanque m de gasolina

petticoat ['pɛtɪkəʊt] N anágua

petty ['pɛtɪ] ADJ (mean) mesquinho; (unimportant) insignificante

pew [pju:] N banco (de igreja)

pewter ['pju:tər] N peltre m

phantom ['fæntəm] N fantasma m

pharmacy ['fɑ:məsɪ] N farmácia

phase [feɪz] N fase f ▶ VT: **to ~ in/ out** introduzir/retirar por etapas

PhD N ABBR = **Doctor of Philosophy** ≈ doutorado

pheasant ['fɛznt] N faisão m

phenomenon [fə'nɔmɪnən] (pl **phenomena**) N fenômeno

philosophical [fɪlə'sɔfɪkl] ADJ filosófico; (fig) calmo, sereno

philosophy [fɪ'lɔsəfɪ] N filosofia

phishing ['fɪʃɪŋ] N phishing m; **~ attack** golpe m de phishing

phobia ['fəʊbjə] N fobia

phone [fəʊn] N telefone m ▶ VT telefonar para, ligar para; **to be on**

the ~ ter telefone; (*be calling*) estar no telefone; **phone back** VT, VI ligar de volta; **phone up** VT telefonar para ▶ VI telefonar; **phone book** N lista telefônica; **phone box** (BRIT) N cabine f telefônica; **phone call** N telefonema m, ligação f; **phone card** N cartão m telefônico; **phone number** N número de telefone

phonetics [fə'nɛtɪks] N fonética

phoney ['fəunɪ] ADJ falso; (*person*) fingido

photo ['fəutəu] N foto f

photo... ['fəutəu] PREFIX foto...; **photocopier** N fotocopiadora f; **photocopy** N fotocópia, xerox ® m ▶ VT fotocopiar, xerocar

photograph ['fəutəgrɑːf] N fotografia ▶ VT fotografar; **photographer** [fə'tɔgrəfər] N fotógrafo(-a); **photography** [fə'tɔgrəfɪ] N fotografia

phrase [freɪz] N frase f ▶ VT expressar; **phrase book** N livro de expressões idiomáticas (para turistas)

physical ['fɪzɪkl] ADJ físico

physician [fɪ'zɪʃən] N médico(-a)

physics ['fɪzɪks] N física

physiotherapy [fɪzɪəu'θɛrəpɪ] N fisioterapia

physique [fɪ'ziːk] N físico

pianist ['piːənɪst] N pianista m/f

piano [pɪ'ænəu] N piano

pick [pɪk] N (*also:* **~axe**) picareta ▶ VT (*select*) escolher, selecionar; (*gather*) colher; (*remove*) tirar; (*lock*) forçar; **take your ~** escolha o que quiser; **the ~ of** o melhor de; **to ~ one's nose** colocar o dedo no nariz; **to ~ one's teeth** palitar os dentes; **to ~ a quarrel** *or* **a fight with sb** comprar uma briga com

alguém; **pick at** VT FUS (*food*) beliscar; **pick on** VT FUS (*person: criticize*) criticar; (: *treat badly*) azucrinar, aporrinhar; **pick out** VT escolher; (*distinguish*) distinguir; **pick up** VI (*improve*) melhorar ▶ VT (*from floor, Aut*) apanhar; (*Police*) prender; (*collect*) buscar; (*for sexual encounter*) paquerar; (*learn*) aprender; (*Radio, TV, Tel*) pegar; **to ~ up speed** acelerar; **to ~ o.s. up** levantar-se

pickle ['pɪkl] N (*also:* **~s**: *as condiment*) picles mpl; (*fig: mess*) apuro ▶ VT (*in vinegar*) conservar em vinagre; (*in salt*) conservar em sal e água

pickpocket ['pɪkpɔkɪt] N batedor(a) m/f de carteira (BR), carteirista m/f (PT)

picnic ['pɪknɪk] N piquenique m

picture ['pɪktʃər] N quadro; (*painting*) pintura; (*drawing*) desenho; (*etching*) água-forte f; (*photograph*) foto(grafia) f; (*TV*) imagem f; (*film*) filme m; (*fig: description*) descrição f; (: *situation*) conjuntura ▶ VT imaginar-se; **the pictures** NPL (BRIT *inf*) o cinema; **picture messaging** N serviço de mensagens multimídia

pie [paɪ] N (*vegetable*) pastelão m; (*fruit*) torta; (*meat*) empadão m

piece [piːs] N pedaço, (*portion*) fatia; (*item*): **a ~ of clothing/ furniture/advice** uma roupa/um móvel/um conselho ▶ VT: **to ~ together** juntar; **to take to ~s** desmontar

pie chart N gráfico de setores

pier [pɪər] N cais m; (*jetty*) embarcadouro, molhe m

pierce [pɪəs] VT furar, perfurar

pig [pɪg] N porco; (*fig*)

porcalhão(-lhona) *m/f*; *(pej: unkind person)* grosseiro(-a); *(: greedy person)* ganancioso(-a)
pigeon ['pɪdʒən] N pombo
piggy bank ['pɪgɪ-] N cofre em forma de porquinho
pigsty ['pɪgstaɪ] N chiqueiro
pigtail ['pɪgteɪl] N rabo-de-cavalo, trança
pike [paɪk] *(pl* **pike** *or* **pikes)** N *(fish)* lúcio
pilchard ['pɪltʃəd] N sardinha
pile [paɪl] N *(heap)* monte *m*; *(of carpet)* pelo; *(of cloth)* lado felpudo ▶VT *(also: ~ up)* empilhar ▶VI *(also: ~ up: objects)* empilhar-se; *(: problems, work)* acumular-se; **pile into** VT FUS *(car)* apinhar-se
piles [paɪlz] NPL hemorróidas *fpl*
pile-up N *(Aut)* engavetamento
pilgrim ['pɪlgrɪm] N peregrino(-a)
pill [pɪl] N pílula; **the ~** a pílula
pillar ['pɪlə'] N pilar *m*; **pillar box** *(BRIT)* N caixa coletora (do correio) *(BR)*, marco do correio *(PT)*
pillow ['pɪləu] N travesseiro *(BR)*, almofada *(PT)*; **pillowcase** N fronha
pilot ['paɪlət] N piloto(-a) ▶CPD *(scheme etc)* piloto *inv* ▶VT pilotar; **pilot light** N piloto
pimple ['pɪmpl] N espinha
PIN N ABBR *(= personal identification number)* senha
pin [pɪn] N alfinete *m* ▶VT alfinetar; **~s and needles** comichão *f*, sensação *f* de formigamento; **to ~ sth on sb** *(fig)* culpar alguém de algo; **pin down** VT *(fig)*: **to ~ sb down** conseguir que alguém se defina *or* tome atitude
pinafore ['pɪnəfɔ:'] N *(also: ~ dress)* avental *m*
pinch [pɪntʃ] N *(of salt etc)* pitada ▶VT beliscar; *(inf: steal)* afanar; **at a ~** em último caso

pine [paɪn] N pinho ▶VI: **to ~ for** ansiar por; **pine away** VI consumir-se, definhar
pineapple ['paɪnæpl] N abacaxi *m* *(BR)*, ananás *m* *(PT)*
pink [pɪŋk] ADJ cor de rosa *inv* ▶N *(colour)* cor *f* de rosa; *(Bot)* cravo, cravina
pinpoint ['pɪnpɔɪnt] VT *(discover)* descobrir; *(explain)* identificar; *(locate)* localizar com precisão
pint [paɪnt] N quartilho *(Brit = 568cc, US = 473cc)*
pioneer [paɪə'nɪə'] N pioneiro(-a)
pious ['paɪəs] ADJ pio, devoto
pip [pɪp] N *(seed)* caroço, semente *f*; **the pips** NPL *(BRIT: time signal on radio)* ≈ o toque de seis segundos
pipe [paɪp] N cano; *(for smoking)* cachimbo ▶VT canalizar, encanar; **pipes** NPL *(also: bag~s)* gaita de foles; **pipe down** *(inf)* VI calar o bico, meter a viola no saco; **pipeline** N *(for oil)* oleoduto; *(for gas)* gaseoduto
pirate ['paɪərət] N pirata *m* ▶VT piratear
Pisces ['paɪsi:z] N Pisces *m*, Peixes *mpl*
piss [pɪs] *(!)* VI mijar; **pissed** *(!)* ADJ *(drunk)* bêbado, de porre
pistol ['pɪstl] N pistola
piston ['pɪstən] N pistão *m*, êmbolo
pit [pɪt] N cova, fossa; *(quarry, hole in surface of sth)* buraco; *(also: coal ~)* mina de carvão ▶VT: **to ~ one's wits against sb** competir em conhecimento *or* inteligência contra alguém; **pits** NPL *(Aut)* box *m*
pitch [pɪtʃ] N *(Mus)* tom *m*; *(fig: degree)* intensidade *f*; *(BRIT Sport)* campo; *(tar)* piche *m*, breu *m* ▶VT *(throw)* arremessar, lançar; *(tent)* armar ▶VI *(fall forwards)* cair (para

frente); **pitch-black** ADJ escuro como o breu

pitfall ['pɪtfɔːl] N perigo (imprevisto), armadilha

pitiful ['pɪtɪful] ADJ comovente, tocante

pity ['pɪtɪ] N compaixão *f*, piedade *f* ▶ VT ter pena de, compadecer-se de

pixel ['pɪksl] N pixel *m*

pizza ['piːtsə] N pizza

placard ['plækɑːd] N placar *m*; (*in march etc*) cartaz *m*

place [pleɪs] N lugar *m*; (*rank, position*) posição *f*; (*post*) posto; (*role*) papel *m*; (*home*): **at/to his ~** na/para a casa dele ▶ VT pôr, colocar; (*identify*) identificar, situar; **to take ~** realizar-se; (*occur*) ocorrer; **out of ~** (*not suitable*) fora de lugar, deslocado; **in the first ~** em primeiro lugar; **to change ~s with sb** trocar de lugar com alguém; **to be ~d** (*in race, exam*) classificar-se

plague [pleɪg] N (*Med*) peste *f*; (*fig*) praga ▶ VT atormentar, importunar

plaice [pleɪs] N INV solha

plain [pleɪn] ADJ (*unpatterned*) liso; (*clear*) claro, evidente; (*simple*) simples *inv*, despretensioso; (*not handsome*) sem atrativos ▶ ADV claramente, com franqueza ▶ N planície *f*, campina; **plain chocolate** N chocolate *m* amargo; **plainly** ADV claramente, obviamente; (*hear, see*) facilmente; (*state*) francamente

plaintiff ['pleɪntɪf] N querelante *m/f*, queixoso(-a)

plait [plæt] N trança, dobra

plan [plæn] N plano; (*scheme*) projeto; (*schedule*) programa *m* ▶ VT planejar (BR), planear (PT)

▶ VI fazer planos; **to ~ to do** pretender fazer

plane [pleɪn] N (*Aviat*) avião *m*; (*also:* **~ tree**) plátano; (*fig: level*) nível *m*; (*tool*) plaina; (*Math*) plano

planet ['plænɪt] N planeta *m*

plank [plæŋk] N tábua

planning ['plænɪŋ] N planejamento (BR), planeamento (PT); **family ~** planejamento *or* planeamento familiar

plant [plɑːnt] N planta; (*machinery*) maquinaria; (*factory*) usina, fábrica ▶ VT plantar; (*field*) semear; (*bomb*) colocar, pôr

plaster ['plɑːstəʳ] N (*for walls*) reboco; (*also:* **~ of Paris**) gesso; (BRIT: *also:* **sticking ~**) esparadrapo, band-aid *m* ▶ VT rebocar; (*cover*): **to ~ with** encher *or* cobrir de

plastic ['plæstɪk] N plástico ▶ ADJ de plástico; **plastic bag** N sacola de plástico; **plastic surgery** N cirurgia plástica

plate [pleɪt] N prato; (*on door, Phot, dental*) chapa; (*in book*) gravura; **gold/silver ~** placa de ouro/prata

plateau ['plætəu] N (*pl* **plateaus** *or* **plateaux**) planalto

platform ['plætfɔːm] N (*Rail*) plataforma (BR), cais *m* (PT); (*at meeting*) tribuna; (*raised structure: for landing etc*) plataforma; (BRIT: *of bus*) plataforma; (*Pol*) programa *m* partidário

platinum ['plætɪnəm] N platina

plausible ['plɔːzɪbl] ADJ plausível; (*person*) convincente

play [pleɪ] N (*Theatre*) obra, peça ▶ VT jogar; (*team, opponent*) jogar contra; (*instrument, music, record*) tocar ▶ VI (*music*) tocar; (*frolic*) brincar; **to ~ safe** não se arriscar,

p

não correr riscos; **play down** VT minimizar; **play up** VI (*person*) dar trabalho; (*TV, car*) estar com defeito; **player** N jogador(a) *m/f*; (*Theatre*) ator/atriz *m/f*; (*Mus*) músico(-a); **playful** ADJ brincalhão(-lhona); **playground** N (*in park*) playground *m*; (*in school*) pátio de recreio; **playgroup** N *espécie de jardim de infância*; **playing card** N carta de baralho; **playing field** N campo de esportes (BR) or jogos (PT); **playtime** N (*Sch*) recreio; **playwright** N dramaturgo(-a)

plea [pli:] N (*request*) apelo, petição *f*; (*Jur*) defesa

plead [pli:d] VT (*Jur*) defender, advogar; (*give as excuse*) alegar ▶ VI (*Jur*) declarar-se; (*beg*) **to ~ with sb** suplicar or rogar a alguém

pleasant ['plɛznt] ADJ agradável; (*person*) simpático

please [pli:z] EXCL por favor ▶ VT agradar a, dar prazer a ▶ VI agradar, dar prazer; (*think fit*): **do as you ~** faça o que or como quiser; **~ yourself!** (*inf*) como você quiser!, você que sabe!; **pleased** ADJ: **pleased (with)** satisfeito (com); **pleased to meet you** prazer (em conhecê-lo)

pleasure ['plɛʒəʳ] N prazer *m*; **"it's a ~"** "não tem de quê"

pleat [pli:t] N prega

pledge [plɛdʒ] N (*promise*) promessa ▶ VT prometer; **to ~ support for sb** empenhar-se a apoiar alguém

plentiful ['plɛntɪful] ADJ abundante

plenty ['plɛntɪ] N: **~ of** (*food, money*) bastante; (*jobs, people*) muitos(-as)

pliers ['plaɪəz] NPL alicate *m*

plod [plɔd] VI caminhar pesadamente; (*fig*) trabalhar laboriosamente

plonk [plɔŋk] (*inf*) N (BRIT: *wine*) zurrapa ▶ VT: **to ~ sth down** deixar cair algo (pesadamente)

plot [plɔt] N (*scheme*) conspiração *f*, complô *m*; (*of story, play*) enredo, trama; (*of land*) lote *m* ▶ VT (*conspire*) tramar, planejar (BR), planear (PT); (*Aviat, Naut, Math*) plotar ▶ VI conspirar; **a vegetable ~** (BRIT) uma horta

plough [plau], (US) **plow** N arado ▶ VT arar; **to ~ money into** investir dinheiro em; **plough through** VT FUS abrir caminho por; **ploughman's lunch** (BRIT) N lanche de pão, queijo e picles

ploy [plɔɪ] N estratagema *m*

pls ABBR (= *please*) por favor

pluck [plʌk] VT (*fruit*) colher; (*musical instrument*) dedilhar; (*bird*) depenar ▶ N coragem *f*, puxão *m*; **to ~ one's eyebrows** fazer as sobrancelhas; **to ~ up courage** criar coragem

plug [plʌg] N (*Elec*) tomada (BR), ficha (PT); (*in sink*) tampa; (*Aut: also*: **spark(ing) ~**) vela (de ignição) ▶ VT (*hole*) tapar; (*inf: advertise*) fazer propaganda de; **plug in** VT (*Elec*) ligar; **plug-in** N (*Comput*) plug-in *m*

plum [plʌm] N (*fruit*) ameixa ▶ CPD (*inf*): **a ~ job** um emprego joia

plumber ['plʌməʳ] N bombeiro(-a) (BR), encanador(a) *m/f* (BR), canalizador(a) *m/f* (PT)

plumbing ['plʌmɪŋ] N (*trade*) ofício de encanador; (*piping*) encanamento

plummet ['plʌmɪt] VI: **to ~ (down)** (*bird, aircraft*) cair rapidamente; (*price*) baixar rapidamente

plump [plʌmp] ADJ roliço, rechonchudo ▶ VI: **to ~ for**

(*inf: choose*) escolher, optar por;
plump up VT (*cushion*) afofar

plunge [plʌndʒ] N (*dive*) salto;
(*fig*) queda ▶ VT (*hand, knife*) enfiar,
meter ▶ VI (*fall, fig*) cair; (*dive*)
mergulhar; **to take the ~** topar a
parada

plural ['pluərl] ADJ plural ▶ N
plural *m*

plus [plʌs] N (*also:* **~ sign**) sinal *m*
de adição ▶ PREP mais; **ten/**
twenty ~ dez/vinte e tantos;
plus-one ['plʌs'wʌn] (*inf*) N
acompanhante *m/f*

ply [plaɪ] N (*of wool*) fio ▶ VT (*a*
trade) exercer ▶ VI (*ship*) ir e vir;
to ~ sb with drink/questions
bombardear alguém com bebidas/
perguntas; **plywood** N madeira
compensada

p.m. ADV ABBR (= *post meridiem*) da
tarde, da noite

PMT N ABBR (= *premenstrual tension*)
TPM *f*, tensão *f* pré-menstrual

pneumatic drill [njuːˈmætɪk
drɪl] N perfuratriz *f*

poach [pəʊtʃ] VT (*cook: fish*)
escaldar; (*: eggs*) fazer pochê (BR),
escalfar (PT); (*steal*) furtar ▶ VI
caçar (*or* pescar) em propriedade
alheia

pocket ['pɔkɪt] N bolso; (*fig: small*
area) pedaço ▶ VT meter no bolso;
(*steal*) embolsar; **to be out of ~**
(BRIT) ter prejuízo; **pocketbook**
(US) N carteira; **pocket money** N
dinheiro para despesas miúdas;
(*for child*) mesada

pod [pɔd] N vagem *f*

podcast ['pɔdkɑːst] N podcast *m*;
podcasting N podcasting *m*

podiatrist [pɔˈdiːətrɪst] (US) N
pedicuro(-a)

poem ['pəʊɪm] N poema *m*

poet ['pəʊɪt] N poeta/poetisa *m/f*;
poetic [pəʊˈɛtɪk] ADJ poético;
poetry ['pəʊɪtrɪ] N poesia

point [pɔɪnt] N ponto; (*of needle,*
knife etc) ponta; (*purpose*)
finalidade *f*; (*significant part*) ponto
principal; (*position, place*) lugar *m*,
posição *f*; (*moment*) momento;
(*stage*) estágio; (*Elec:* **power**
~) tomada; (*also:* **decimal ~**): **2 ~ 3**
(2.3) dois vírgula três ▶ VT
mostrar; (*gun etc*): **to ~ sth at sb**
apontar algo para alguém ▶ VI
apontar; **points** NPL (*Aut*)
platinado, contato; (*Rail*) agulhas
fpl; **to ~ at** apontar para; **to be on**
the ~ of doing sth estar prestes a
or a ponto de fazer algo; **to make**
a ~ of fazer questão de, insistir em;
to get the ~ perceber; **to miss**
the ~ compreender mal; **to come**
to the ~ ir ao assunto; **there's no**
~ (in doing) não há razão (para
fazer); **~ of view** ponto de vista;
point out VT (*in debate etc*)
ressaltar; **point to** VT FUS (*fig*)
indicar; **point-blank** ADV
categoricamente; (*also:* **at**
point-blank range) à
queima-roupa; **pointed** ADJ (*stick*
etc) pontudo; (*remark*) mordaz;
pointer N (*on chart*) indicador *m*;
(*on machine*) ponteiro; (*fig*) dica;
pointless ADJ (*useless*) inútil;
(*senseless*) sem sentido

poison ['pɔɪzn] N veneno ▶ VT
envenenar; **poisonous** ADJ
venenoso; (*fumes etc*) tóxico

poke [pəʊk] VT cutucar; (*put*):
to ~ sth in(to) enfiar *or* meter algo
em; **poke about** VI escarafunchar,
espionar

poker ['pəʊkəʳ] N atiçador *m* (de
brasas); (*Cards*) pôquer *m*

Poland ['pəulənd] N Polônia
polar ['pəulə^r] ADJ polar; **polar bear**
N urso polar
Pole [pəul] N polonês(-esa) *m/f*
pole [pəul] N vara; (*Geo*) polo;
(*telegraph pole*) poste *m*; (*flagpole*)
mastro; **pole bean** (*US*) N
feijão-trepador *m*; **pole vault** N
salto com vara
police [pə'liːs] N polícia ▶ VT
policiar; **police car** N rádio-
patrulha *f*; **policeman** *irreg* N
policial *m* (*BR*), polícia *m* (*PT*); **police
station** N delegacia (de polícia) (*BR*),
esquadra (*PT*); **policewoman** *irreg*
N policial *f* (feminina) (*BR*), mulher *f*
polícia (*PT*)
policy ['pɔlisi] N política; (*also:*
insurance ~) apólice *f*
polio ['pəuliəu] N polio(mielite) *f*
Polish ['pəuliʃ] ADJ polonês(-esa)
▶ N (*Ling*) polonês *m*
polish ['pɔliʃ] N (*for shoes*) graxa;
(*for floor*) cera (para encerar); (*shine*)
brilho; (*fig*) refinamento, requinte *m*
▶ VT (*shoes*) engraxar; (*make shiny*)
lustrar, dar brilho a; **polish off** VT
(*work*) dar os arremates a; (*food*)
raspar
polite [pə'lait] ADJ educado;
politeness N gentileza, cortesia
political [pə'litikl] ADJ político
politician [pɔli'tiʃən] N político(-a)
politics ['pɔlitiks] N, NPL política
poll [pəul] N (*votes*) votação *f*; (*also:*
opinion ~) pesquisa, sondagem *f*
▶ VT (*votes*) receber, obter
pollen ['pɔlən] N pólen *m*
pollute [pə'luːt] VT poluir;
pollution N poluição *f*
polyester [pɔli'ɛstə^r] N poliéster *m*
polystyrene [pɔli'stairiːn] N
isopor® *m*
polythene ['pɔliθiːn] N politeno

pomegranate ['pɔmigrænit] N
romã *f*
pond [pɔnd] N (*natural*) lago
pequeno; (*artificial*) tanque *m*
ponder ['pɔndə^r] VT, VI ponderar,
meditar (sobre)
pony ['pəuni] N pônei *m*; **ponytail**
N rabo-de-cavalo; **pony trekking**
(*BRIT*) N excursão *f* em pônei
poodle ['puːdl] N cão-d'água *m*
pool [puːl] N (*puddle*) poça, charco;
(*pond*) lago; (*also:* **swimming ~**)
piscina; (*fig: of light*) feixe *m*; (: *of
liquid*) poça; (*Sport*) sinuca ▶ VT
juntar; **pools** NPL (*football pools*)
loteria esportiva (*BR*), totobola (*PT*);
typing (*BRIT*) or **secretary** (*US*) **~**
seção *f* de datilografia
poor [puə^r] ADJ pobre; (*bad*) inferior,
mau ▶ NPL: **the ~** os pobres; **~ in**
(*resources etc*) deficiente em; **poorly**
ADJ adoentado, indisposto ▶ ADV
mal
pop [pɔp] N (*sound*) estalo, estouro;
(*Mus*) pop *m*; (*US inf: father*) papai *m*;
(*inf: fizzy drink*) bebida gasosa ▶ VT:
to ~ sth into/onto *etc* (*put*) pôr algo
em/sobre *etc* ▶ VI estourar; (*cork*)
saltar; **pop in** VI dar por um pulo; **pop
out** VI dar uma saída; **pop up** VI
surgir, aparecer inesperadamente;
popcorn N pipoca
pope [pəup] N papa *m*
poplar ['pɔplə^r] N álamo, choupo
poppy ['pɔpi] N papoula
popular ['pɔpjulə^r] ADJ popular;
(*person*) querido
population [pɔpju'leiʃən] N
população *f*
porcelain ['pɔːslin] N porcelana
porch [pɔːtʃ] N pórtico; (*US:
verandah*) varanda
pore [pɔː^r] N poro ▶ VI: **to ~ over**
examinar minuciosamente

pork [pɔ:k] N carne f de porco

pornography [pɔ:'nɔgrəfɪ] N pornografia

porridge ['pɔrɪdʒ] N mingau m (de aveia)

port [pɔ:t] N (harbour) porto; (Naut: left side) bombordo; (wine) vinho do Porto; **~ of call** porto de escala

portable ['pɔ:təbl] ADJ portátil

porter ['pɔ:tə^r] N (for luggage) carregador m; (doorkeeper) porteiro

portfolio [pɔ:t'fəulɪəu] N (case) pasta; (Pol) pasta ministerial; (Finance) carteira de ações ou títulos; (of artist) pasta, portfólio

portion ['pɔ:ʃən] N porção f, quinhão m; (of food) ração f

portrait ['pɔ:treɪt] N retrato

portray [pɔ:'treɪ] VT retratar; (act) interpretar

Portugal ['pɔ:tjugl] N Portugal m (no article)

Portuguese [pɔ:tju'gi:z] ADJ português(-esa) ▶ N INV português(-esa) m/f; (Ling) português m

pose [pəuz] N postura, pose f ▶ VI (pretend): **to ~ as** fazer-se passar por ▶ VT (question) fazer; (problem) causar; **to ~ for** (painting) posar para

posh [pɔʃ] (inf) ADJ fino, chique; (upper-class) de classe alta

position [pə'zɪʃən] N posição f; (job) cargo; (situation) situação f ▶ VT colocar, situar

positive ['pɔzɪtɪv] ADJ positivo; (certain) certo; (definite) definitivo

possess [pə'zɛs] VT possuir; **possession** N posse f, possessão f; **possessions** NPL (belongings) pertences mpl; **to take**

possession of sth tomar posse de algo

possibility [pɔsɪ'bɪlɪtɪ] N possibilidade f; (of sth happening) probabilidade f

possible ['pɔsɪbl] ADJ possível; **possibly** ADV pode ser, talvez; (surprise): **what could they possibly want with me?** o que eles podem querer comigo?; (emphasizing effort): **they did everything they possibly could** eles fizeram tudo o que podiam; **I cannot possibly go** não posso ir de jeito nenhum

post [pəust] N (BRIT: mail) correio; (job) cargo, posto; (pole) poste m; (on internet) post m; (Mil) nomeação f ▶ VT (BRIT: send by post) pôr no correio; (on internet) postar; (BRIT: appoint): **to ~ to** destinar a; **postage** N porte m, franquia; **postal order** N vale m postal; **postbox** (BRIT) N caixa de correio; **postcard** N cartão m postal; **postcode** (BRIT) N código postal, ≈ CEP m (BR)

poster ['pəustə^r] N cartaz m; (as decoration) pôster m

postman ['pəustmən] irreg N carteiro

postmark ['pəustmɑ:k] N carimbo do correio

post office N (building) agência do correio, correio; (organization) ≈ Empresa Nacional dos Correios e Telégrafos (BR), ≈ Correios, Telégrafos e Telefones (PT)

postpone [pəs'pəun] VT adiar

posture ['pɔstʃə^r] N postura; (fig) atitude f

pot [pɔt] N (for cooking) panela; (for flowers) vaso; (container) pote m; (teapot) bule m; (inf: marijuana) maconha ▶ VT (*plant*) plantar em vaso; **to go to ~** (*inf*) arruinar-se, degringolar

potato [pə'teɪtəu] (*pl* **potatoes**) N batata; **potato peeler** N descascador *m* de batatas

potent ['pəutnt] ADJ poderoso; (*drink*) forte; (*man*) potente

potential [pə'tɛnʃl] ADJ potencial ▶ N potencial *m*

pothole ['pɔthəul] N (*in road*) buraco; (*BRIT: underground*) caldeirão *m*, cova

potter ['pɔtə'] N (*artistic*) ceramista *m/f*; (*artisan*) oleiro(-a) ▶ VI (*BRIT*): **to ~ around, ~ about** ocupar-se com pequenos trabalhos; **pottery** N cerâmica; (*factory*) olaria

potty ['pɔtɪ] ADJ (*inf: mad*) maluco, doido ▶ N penico

pouch [pautʃ] N (*Zool*) bolsa; (*for tobacco*) tabaqueira

poultry ['pəultrɪ] N aves *fpl* domésticas; (*meat*) carne *f* de aves domésticas

pounce [pauns] VI: **to ~ on** lançar-se sobre; (*person*) agarrar em; (*fig: mistake etc*) apontar

pound [paund] N libra (*weight = 453g, 16 ounces; money = 100 pence*) ▶ VT (*beat*) socar, esmurrar; (*crush*) triturar ▶ VI (*heart*) bater

pour [pɔː'] VT despejar; (*drink*) servir ▶ VI correr, jorrar; **pour away** VT esvaziar, decantar; **pour in** VI (*people*) entrar numa enxurrada; (*information*) chegar numa enxurrada; **pour off** VT esvaziar, decantar; **pour out** VI (*people*) sair aos borbotões ▶ VT (*drink*) servir; (*fig*) extravasar; **pouring** ['pɔːrɪŋ] ADJ: **pouring rain** chuva torrencial

pout [paut] VI fazer beicinho *or* biquinho

poverty ['pɔvətɪ] N pobreza, miséria

powder ['paudə'] N pó *m*; (*face powder*) pó-de-arroz *m* ▶ VT (*face*) empoar, passar pó em; **powdered milk** N leite *m* em pó

power ['pauə'] N poder *m*; (*of explosion, engine*) força, potência; (*ability, Pol*) poder; (*electricity*) força; **to be in ~** estar no poder; **power cut** (*BRIT*) N corte *m* de energia, blecaute *m* (*BR*); **powerful** ADJ poderoso; (*engine*) potente; (*body*) vigoroso; (*blow*) violento; (*argument*) convincente; (*emotion*) intenso; **powerless** ADJ impotente; **power point** (*BRIT*) N tomada; **power station** N central *f* elétrica

PR N ABBR = **public relations**

practical ['præktɪkl] ADJ prático; **practical joke** N brincadeira, peça

practice ['præktɪs] N (*habit, Rel*) costume *m*, hábito; (*exercise*) prática; (*of profession*) exercício; (*training*) treinamento; (*Med*) consultório; (*Jur*) escritório ▶ VT, VI (*US*) = **practise**; **in ~** na prática; **out of ~** destreinado

practise ['præktɪs], (*US*) **practice** VT praticar; (*profession*) exercer; (*sport*) treinar ▶ VI (*doctor*) ter consultório; (*lawyer*) ter escritório; (*train*) treinar, praticar

practitioner [præk'tɪʃənə'] N (*Med*) médico(-a)

prairie ['prɛərɪ] N campina, pradaria

praise [preɪz] N louvor *m*; (*admiration*) elogio ▶ VT elogiar, louvar

pram [præm] (*BRIT*) N carrinho de bebê

prank [præŋk] N travessura, peça

prawn [prɔːn] N pitu *m*; (*small*) camarão *m*

pray [preɪ] VI: **to ~ for/that** rezar por/para que; **prayer** [preə^r] N (*activity*) reza; (*words*) oração *f*, prece *f*

preach [priːtʃ] VT pregar ▶ VI pregar; (*pej*) catequizar

precede [prɪˈsiːd] VT preceder

precedent [ˈprɛsɪdənt] N precedente *m*

preceding [prɪˈsiːdɪŋ] ADJ anterior

precinct [ˈpriːsɪŋkt] N (*US: district*) distrito policial; **precincts** NPL (*of large building*) arredores *mpl*; **pedestrian ~** (BRIT) zona para pedestres (BR) *or* peões (PT); **shopping ~** (BRIT) zona comercial

precious [ˈprɛʃəs] ADJ precioso

precise [prɪˈsaɪs] ADJ exato, preciso; (*plans*) detalhado

predecessor [ˈpriːdɪsɛsə^r] N predecessor(a) *m/f*, antepassado(-a)

predicament [prɪˈdɪkəmənt] N situação *f* difícil, apuro

predict [prɪˈdɪkt] VT prever, predizer, prognosticar; **predictable** ADJ previsível

predominantly [prɪˈdɔmɪnəntlɪ] ADV predominantemente; na maioria

preface [ˈprɛfəs] N prefácio

prefect [ˈpriːfɛkt] N (BRIT Sch) monitor(a) *m/f*, tutor(a) *m/f*; (*in Brazil*) prefeito(-a)

prefer [prɪˈfəː^r] VT preferir; **preferably** [ˈprɛfrəblɪ] ADV de preferência

prefix [ˈpriːfɪks] N prefixo

pregnancy [ˈprɛgnənsɪ] N gravidez *f*; (*animal*) prenhez *f*

pregnant [ˈprɛgnənt] ADJ grávida; (*animal*) prenha

prehistoric [priːhɪsˈtɔrɪk] ADJ pré-histórico

prejudice [ˈprɛdʒudɪs] N preconceito; **prejudiced** ADJ (*person*) preconceituoso

premature [ˈprɛmətʃuə^r] ADJ prematuro

première [ˈprɛmɪɛə^r] N estreia

premium [ˈpriːmɪəm] N prêmio; **to be at a ~** ser caro

premonition [prɛməˈnɪʃən] N presságio, pressentimento

preoccupied [priːˈɔkjupaɪd] ADJ (*worried*) preocupado

prepaid [priːˈpeɪd] ADJ com porte pago

preparation [prɛpəˈreɪʃən] N preparação *f*; **preparations** NPL (*arrangements*) preparativos *mpl*

prepare [prɪˈpɛə^r] VT preparar ▶ VI: **to ~ for** preparar-se *or* aprontar-se para; **~d to** disposto a; **~d for** pronto para

preposition [prɛpəˈzɪʃən] N preposição *f*

prerequisite [priːˈrɛkwɪzɪt] N pré-requisito, condição *f* prévia

prescribe [prɪˈskraɪb] VT prescrever; (*Med*) receitar

prescription [prɪˈskrɪpʃən] N receita

presence [ˈprɛzns] N presença; (*spirit*) espectro

present [*adj, n* ˈprɛznt, *vt* prɪˈzɛnt] ADJ presente; (*current*) atual ▶ N presente *m*; (*actuality*): **the ~** o presente ▶ VT (*give*) entregar algo a alguém; (*describe*) descrever; **at ~** no momento, agora; **to give sb a ~** presentear alguém; **presentation** [prɛznˈteɪʃən] N apresentação *f*; (*ceremony*) entrega; (*of plan etc*) exposição *f*; **present-day** ADJ atual, de hoje;

P

presenter N apresentador(a) m/f;
presently ADV (*soon after*) logo
depois; (*soon*) logo, em breve; (*now*)
atualmente
preservative [prɪ'zə:vətɪv] N
conservante m
preserve [prɪ'zə:v] VT (*situation*)
conservar, manter; (*building,
manuscript*) preservar; (*food*) pôr em
conserva ▶ N (*often pl: jam*) geleia;
(: *fruit*) compota, conserva
president ['prɛzɪdənt] N
presidente(-a) m/f; **presidential**
[prɛzɪ'dɛnʃl] ADJ presidencial
press [prɛs] N (*printer's*) imprensa,
prelo; (*newspapers*) imprensa;
(*of switch*) pressão f ▶ VT apertar;
(*clothes: iron*) passar; (*put pressure
on: person*) pressionar; (*insist*): **to ~
sth on sb** insistir para que alguém
aceite algo ▶ VI (*squeeze*) apertar;
(*pressurize*): **to ~ for** pressionar por;
we are ~ed for time/money
estamos com pouco tempo/
dinheiro; **press on** VI continuar;
pressing ADJ urgente; **press stud**
(BRIT) N botão m de pressão;
press-up (BRIT) N flexão f
pressure ['prɛʃəʳ] N pressão f; **to
put ~ on sb (to do sth)** pressionar
alguém (a fazer algo); **pressure
cooker** N panela de pressão
prestige [prɛs'ti:ʒ] N prestígio
presume [prɪ'zju:m] VT supor
pretence [prɪ'tɛns], (US) **pretense**
N pretensão f; **under false ~s** por
meios fraudulentos
pretend [prɪ'tɛnd] VT, VI fingir
pretense [prɪ'tɛns] (US) N =
pretence
pretty ['prɪtɪ] ADJ bonito ▶ ADV
(*quite*) bastante
prevail [prɪ'veɪl] VI triunfar;
(*be current*) imperar

prevalent ['prɛvələnt] ADJ
(*common*) predominante
prevent [prɪ'vɛnt] VT impedir
preview ['pri:vju:] N pré-estreia
previous ['pri:vɪəs] ADJ (*earlier*)
anterior; **previously** ADV (*before*)
previamente; (*in the past*)
anteriormente
prey [preɪ] N presa ▶ VI: **to ~ on**
(*feed on*) alimentar-se de; **it was
~ing on his mind** preocupava-o,
atormentava-o
price [praɪs] N preço ▶ VT fixar o
preço de; **priceless** ADJ inestimável;
(*inf: amusing*) impagável
prick [prɪk] N picada ▶ VT picar;
(*make hole in*) furar; **to ~ up one's
ears** aguçar os ouvidos
pride [praɪd] N orgulho; (*pej*)
soberba ▶ VT: **to ~ o.s. on** orgulhar-
se de
priest [pri:st] N (*Christian*) padre m;
(*non-Christian*) sacerdote m
primarily ['praɪmərɪlɪ] ADV
principalmente
primary ['praɪmərɪ] ADJ primário;
(*first in importance*) principal ▶ N
(*US: election*) eleição f primária;
primary school (BRIT) N escola
primária

As **primary schools** da
Grã-Bretanha acolhem crianças
de 5 a 11 anos. Assinalam o início
do ciclo escolar obrigatório e são
compostas de duas partes: a
pré-escola (*infant school*) e o
primário (*junior school*).

prime [praɪm] ADJ primeiro,
principal; (*excellent*) de primeira
▶ VT (*wood*) imprimar; (*fig*) preparar
▶ N: **in the ~ of life** na primavera da
vida; **~ example** exemplo típico;
prime minister N primeiro-
ministro/primeira-ministra

primitive ['prɪmɪtɪv] ADJ
primitivo; (crude) rudimentar
primrose ['prɪmrəuz] N prímula,
primavera
prince [prɪns] N príncipe m
princess [prɪn'sɛs] N princesa
principal ['prɪnsɪpl] ADJ principal
▶ N (of school, college) diretor(a) m/f
principle ['prɪnsɪpl] N princípio;
in ~ em princípio; **on ~** por
princípio
print [prɪnt] N (letters) letra de
forma; (fabric) estampado; (Art)
estampa, gravura; (Phot) cópia;
(footprint) pegada; (fingerprint)
impressão f digital ▶ VT imprimir;
(write in capitals) escrever em letra
de imprensa; **out of ~** esgotado;
printer N (person) impressor(a)
m/f; (firm) gráfica; (machine)
impressora; **printout** N (Comput)
cópia impressa
prior ['praɪər] ADJ anterior, prévio;
(more important) prioritário; **~ to
doing** antes de fazer
priority [praɪ'ɔrɪtɪ] N
prioridade f
prison ['prɪzn] N prisão f ▶ CPD
carcerário; **prisoner** N (in prison)
preso(-a), presidiário(-a); (under
arrest) detido(-a)
privacy ['praɪvəsɪ] N isolamento,
solidão f
private ['praɪvɪt] ADJ privado;
(personal) particular; (confidential)
confidencial, reservado; (personal:
belongings) pessoal; (: thoughts,
plans) secreto, íntimo; (place)
isolado; (quiet: person) reservado;
(intimate) íntimo ▶ N soldado raso;
"~" (on envelope) "confidencial";
(on door) "privativo"; **in ~** em
particular; **privatize** VT privatizar
privilege ['prɪvɪlɪdʒ] N privilégio

prize [praɪz] N prêmio ▶ ADJ de
primeira classe ▶ VT valorizar;
prizewinner N premiado(-a) f
pro [prəu] N (Sport) profissional m/f
▶ PREP a favor de; **the ~s and cons**
os prós e os contras
probability [prɔbə'bɪlɪtɪ] N
probabilidade f
probable ['prɔbəbl] ADJ provável;
(plausible) verossímil
probation [prə'beɪʃən] N: **on ~**
(employee) em estágio probatório;
(Jur) em liberdade condicional
probe [prəub] N (Med, Space)
sonda; (enquiry) pesquisa ▶ VT
investigar, esquadrinhar
problem ['prɔbləm] N problema m
procedure [prə'siːdʒər] N
procedimento; (method) método,
processo
proceed [prə'siːd] VI (do
afterwards): **to ~ to do sth** passar a
fazer algo; (continue): **to ~ (with)**
continuar or prosseguir (com);
(activity, event) continuar; (go) ir em
direção a, dirigir-se a;
proceedings NPL evento,
acontecimento; **proceeds**
['prəusiːdz] NPL produto,
proventos mpl
process ['prəusɛs] N processo ▶ VT
processar; **procession** [prə'sɛʃən]
N desfile m, procissão f; **funeral
procession** cortejo fúnebre
proclaim [prə'kleɪm] VT anunciar
prod [prɔd] VT empurrar; (with
finger, stick) cutucar ▶ N empurrão
m; cotovelada; espetada
produce [n 'prɔdjuːs, vt prə'djuːs]
N (Agr) produtos mpl agrícolas
▶ VT produzir; (cause) provocar;
(evidence, argument) apresentar,
mostrar; (show) apresentar, exibir;
(Theatre) pôr em cena or em cartaz;

producer N (*Theatre*) diretor(a) *m/f*; (*Agr, Cinema, of record*) produtor(a) *m/f*; (*country*) produtor *m*

product ['prɔdʌkt] N produto

production [prə'dʌkʃən] N produção *f*; (*of electricity*) geração *f*; (*Theatre*) encenação *f*

profession [prə'fɛʃən] N profissão *f*; (*people*) classe *f*; **professional** N profissional *m/f* ▶ ADJ profissional; (*work*) de profissional

professor [prə'fɛsər] N (*BRIT*) catedrático(-a); (*US, CANADA*) professor(a) *m/f*

profile ['prəufaıl] N perfil *m*

profit ['prɔfıt] N (*Comm*) lucro ▶ VI: **to ~ by** or **from** (*benefit*) aproveitar-se de, tirar proveito de; **profitable** ADJ (*Econ*) lucrativo, rendoso

profound [prə'faund] ADJ profundo

programme ['prəugræm], (*US or COMPUT*) **program** N programa *m* ▶ VT programar; **programming**, **programing** N programação *f*

progress [*n* 'prəugrɛs, *vi* prə'grɛs] N progresso ▶ VI progredir, avançar; **in ~** em andamento; **progressive** [prə'grɛsıv] ADJ progressivo; (*person*) progressista

prohibit [prə'hıbıt] VT proibir

project [*n* 'prɔdʒɛkt, *vt, vi* prə'dʒɛkt] N projeto; (*Sch: research*) pesquisa ▶ VT projetar; (*figure*) estimar ▶ VI (*stick out*) ressaltar, sobressair

projection [prə'dʒɛkʃən] N projeção *f*; (*overhang*) saliência

projector [prə'dʒɛktər] N projetor *m*

prolong [prə'lɔŋ] VT prolongar

prom [prɔm] N ABBR = **promenade**, **promenade concert**; (*US: ball*) baile *m* de estudantes

promenade [prɔmə'nɑ:d] N (*by sea*) passeio (à orla marítima); **promenade concert** (*BRIT*) N concerto (de música clássica)

> Na Grã-Bretanha, um **promenade concert** (ou **prom**) é um concerto de música clássica, assim chamado porque originalmente o público não ficava sentado, mas de pé ou caminhando. Hoje em dia, uma parte do público permanece de pé, mas há também lugares sentados (mais caros). Os **Proms** mais conhecidos são os londrinos. A última sessão (*the Last Night of the Proms*) é um acontecimento carregado de emoção, quando são executadas árias tradicionais e patrióticas. Nos Estados Unidos e no Canadá, o **prom**, ou **promenade**, é um baile organizado pelas escolas secundárias.

prominent ['prɔmınənt] ADJ (*standing out*) proeminente; (*important*) eminente, notório

promise ['prɔmıs] N promessa; (*hope*) esperança ▶ VT, VI prometer; **promising** ADJ promissor(a), prometedor(a)

promote [prə'məut] VT promover; (*product*) promover, fazer propaganda de; **promotion** N promoção *f*

prompt [prɔmpt] ADJ pronto, rápido ▶ ADV (*exactly*) em ponto, pontualmente ▶ N (*Comput*) sinal *m* de orientação, prompt *m* ▶ VT (*urge*) incitar, impelir; (*cause*) provocar, ocasionar; **to ~ sb to do sth** induzir alguém a fazer algo; **promptly** ADV imediatamente; (*exactly*) pontualmente

prone [prəun] ADJ (lying) de bruços; **~ to** propenso a, predisposto a

pronoun ['prəunaun] N pronome m

pronounce [prə'nauns] VT pronunciar; (verdict, opinion) declarar

pronunciation [prənʌnsɪ'eɪʃən] N pronúncia

proof [pru:f] N prova ▶ ADJ: **~ against** à prova de

prop [prɔp] N suporte m, escora; (fig) amparo, apoio ▶ VT (also: **~ up**) apoiar, escorar; (lean): **to ~ sth against** apoiar algo contra

propaganda [prɔpə'gændə] N propaganda

proper ['prɔpər] ADJ (correct) correto; (socially acceptable) respeitável, digno; (authentic) genuíno, autêntico; (referring to place): **the village ~** a cidadezinha propriamente dita; **properly** ADV (eat, study) bem; (behave) decentemente

property ['prɔpəti] N propriedade f; (goods) posses fpl, bens mpl; (buildings) imóveis mpl

prophet ['prɔfit] N profeta m/f

proportion [prə'pɔ:ʃən] N proporção f; **proportional** ADJ proporcional

proposal [prə'pəuzl] N proposta; (of marriage) pedido

propose [prə'pəuz] VT propor; (toast) erguer ▶ VI propor casamento; **to ~ to do** propor-se fazer

proposition [prɔpə'zɪʃən] N proposta, proposição f; (offer) oferta

proprietor [prə'praɪətər] N proprietário(-a), dono(-a)

prose [prəuz] N prosa

prosecute ['prɔsɪkju:t] VT processar; **prosecution** [prɔsɪ'kju:ʃən] N acusação f; (accusing side) autor m da demanda

prospect [n 'prɔspɛkt, vt, vi prə'spɛkt] N (chance) probabilidade f; (outlook, potential) perspectiva ▶ VI: **to ~ (for)** prospectar (por); **prospects** NPL (for work etc) perspectivas fpl

prospectus [prə'spɛktəs] N prospecto, programa m

prostitute ['prɔstɪtju:t] N prostituta; **male ~** prostituto

protect [prə'tɛkt] VT proteger; **protection** N proteção f; **protective** ADJ protetor(a)

protein ['prəuti:n] N proteína

protest [n 'prəutɛst, vi, vt prə'tɛst] N protesto ▶ VI protestar ▶ VT insistir

Protestant ['prɔtɪstənt] ADJ, N protestante m/f

protester [prə'tɛstər] N manifestante m/f

proud [praud] ADJ orgulhoso; (pej) vaidoso, soberbo

prove [pru:v] VT comprovar ▶ VI: **to ~ (to be) correct** etc vir a ser correto etc; **to ~ o.s.** mostrar seu valor

proverb ['prɔvə:b] N provérbio

provide [prə'vaɪd] VT fornecer, proporcionar; **to ~ sb with sth** fornecer alguém de algo, fornecer algo a alguém; **provide for** VT FUS (person) prover à subsistência de

providing [prə'vaɪdɪŋ] CONJ: **~ (that)** contanto que (+ sub)

province ['prɔvɪns] N província; (fig) esfera; **provincial** [prə'vɪnʃəl] ADJ provincial; (pej) provinciano

provision [prə'vɪʒən] N (*supplying*) abastecimento; (*in contract*) cláusula, condição f; **provisions** N PL (*food*) mantimentos *mpl*; **provisional** ADJ provisório, interino; (*agreement, licence*) provisório

provocative [prə'vɒkətɪv] ADJ provocante; (*sexually*) excitante

provoke [prə'vəuk] VT provocar; (*cause*) causar

prowl [praul] VI (*also:* **~ about, ~ around**) rondar, andar à espreita ▶ N: **on the ~** de ronda, rondando

proxy ['prɒksɪ] N: **by ~** por procuração

prudent ['pru:dənt] ADJ prudente

prune [pru:n] N ameixa seca ▶ VT podar

pry [praɪ] VI: **to ~ (into)** intrometer-se (em)

PS N ABBR (= *postscript*) PS *m*

pseudonym ['sju:dənɪm] N pseudônimo

psychiatrist [saɪ'kaɪətrɪst] N psiquiatra *m/f*

psychic ['saɪkɪk] ADJ psíquico; (*also:* **~al**: *person*) sensível a forças psíquicas

psychologist [saɪ'kɒlədʒɪst] N psicólogo(-a)

psychology [saɪ'kɒlədʒɪ] N psicologia

PTO ABBR (= *please turn over*) v.v., vire

pub [pʌb] N ABBR (= *public house*) pub *m*, bar *m*, botequim *m*

> Um **pub** geralmente consiste em duas salas: uma (*the lounge*) é bastante confortável, com poltronas e bancos estofados, enquanto a outra ("*the public bar*") é simplesmente um bar onde a consumação é em geral mais barata. O ("*the public bar*") é muitas vezes também um salão de jogos, dos quais os mais comuns são os dardos, dominó e bilhar. Atualmente muitos pubs servem refeições, sobretudo na hora do almoço, e essa é a única hora em que a entrada de crianças é permitida, desde que estejam acompanhadas por adultos. Em geral os pubs funcionam das 11 às 23 horas, mas isso pode variar de acordo com sua permissão de funcionamento; alguns pubs fecham à tarde.

public ['pʌblɪk] ADJ público ▶ N público; **in ~** em público; **to make ~** tornar público; **public convenience** (BRIT) N banheiro público; **public holiday** N feriado; **public house** (BRIT) N pub *m*, bar *m*, taberna

publicity [pʌb'lɪsɪtɪ] N publicidade f

publicize ['pʌblɪsaɪz] VT divulgar

public: public relations N relações *fpl* públicas; **public school** (BRIT) escola particular; (US) escola pública; **public transport**, (US) **public transportation** N transporte *m* coletivo

publish ['pʌblɪʃ] VT publicar; **publisher** N editor(a) *m/f*; (*company*) editora; **publishing** N a indústria editorial

pudding ['pudɪŋ] N (BRIT: *dessert*) sobremesa; (*cake*) pudim *m*, doce *m*; **black** (BRIT) or **blood** (US) **~** morcela

puddle ['pʌdl] N poça

puff [pʌf] N sopro; (*of cigarette*) baforada; (*of air, smoke*) lufada ▶ VT: **to ~ one's pipe** tirar baforadas do cachimbo ▶ VI (*pant*) arquejar; **puff out** VT (*cheeks*) encher; **puff pastry**, (US) **puff paste** N massa folhada

pull [pul] N (*tug*): **to give sth a ~** dar um puxão em algo ▶ VT puxar; (*trigger*) apertar; (*curtain, blind*) fechar ▶ VI puxar, dar um puxão; **to ~ to pieces** picar em pedacinhos; **to ~ one's punches** não usar toda a força; **to ~ one's weight** fazer a sua parte; **to ~ o.s. together** recompor-se; **to ~ sb's leg** (*fig*) brincar com alguém, sacanear alguém (*inf*); **pull apart** VT (*break*) romper; **pull down** VT (*building*) demolir, derrubar; **pull in** VI (*Aut: at the kerb*) encostar; (*Rail*) chegar (na plataforma); **pull off** VT tirar; (*fig: deal etc*) acertar; **pull out** VI (*Aut: from kerb*) sair; (*Rail*) partir ▶ VT tirar, arrancar; **pull over** VI (*Aut*) encostar; **pull through** VI (*Med*) sobreviver; **pull up** VI (*stop*) deter-se, parar ▶ VT levantar; (*uproot*) desarraigar, arrancar
pulley ['puli] N roldana
pullover ['puləuvəʳ] N pulôver m
pulp [pʌlp] N (*of fruit*) polpa
pulse [pʌls] N (*Anat*) pulso; (*of music, engine*) cadência; (*Bot*) legume m
pump [pʌmp] N bomba; (*shoe*) sapatilha (de dança) ▶ VT bombear; **pump up** VT encher
pumpkin ['pʌmpkɪn] N abóbora
pun [pʌn] N jogo de palavras, trocadilho
punch [pʌntʃ] N (*blow*) soco, murro; (*tool*) punção m; (*drink*) ponche m ▶ VT (*hit*): **to ~ sb/sth** esmurrar *or* socar alguém/algo
punctual ['pʌŋktjuəl] ADJ pontual
punish ['pʌnɪʃ] VT punir, castigar; **punishment** N castigo, punição f
punk [pʌŋk] N (*also: ~ rocker*) punk m/f; (*also: ~ rock*) punk m; (*US inf: hoodlum*) pinta-brava m

pupil ['pjuːpl] N aluno(-a); (*of eye*) pupila
puppet ['pʌpɪt] N marionete f, títere m; (*fig*) fantoche m
puppy ['pʌpɪ] N cachorrinho (BR), cachorro (PT)
purchase ['pəːtʃɪs] N compra ▶ VT comprar
pure [pjuəʳ] ADJ puro
purple ['pəːpl] ADJ roxo, purpúreo
purpose ['pəːpəs] N propósito, objetivo; **on ~** de propósito
purse [pəːs] N (BRIT) carteira; (US) bolsa ▶ VT enrugar, franzir
pursue [pə'sjuː] VT perseguir; (*fig: activity*) exercer; (*: interest, plan*) dedicar-se a; (*: result*) lutar por
pursuit [pə'sjuːt] N perseguição f; (*fig*) busca
push [puʃ] N empurrão m; (*of button*) aperto ▶ VT empurrar; (*button*) apertar; (*promote*) promover ▶ VI empurrar; (*press*) apertar; (*fig*): **to ~ for** reivindicar; **push aside** VT afastar com a mão; **push off** (*inf*) VI dar o fora; **push on** VI prosseguir; **push through** VI abrir caminho ▶ VT (*measure*) forçar a aceitação de; **push up** VT forçar a alta de; **pushchair** (BRIT) N carrinho; **pusher** N (*also: **drug pusher**) traficante m/f; **push-up** (US) N flexão f
put [put] (*pt, pp* **put**) VT pôr, colocar; (*put into*) meter; (*person: in institution etc*) internar; (*say*) dizer, expressar; (*case*) expor; (*question*) fazer; (*estimate*) avaliar, calcular; (*write, type etc*) colocar; **put about** VT (*rumour*) espalhar; **put across** VT (*ideas*) comunicar; **put away** VT guardar; **put back** VT (*replace*) repor; (*postpone*) adiar; (*delay*) atrasar; **put by** VT

(*money etc*) poupar, pôr de lado;
put down VT pôr em; (*animal*)
sacrificar; (*in writing*) anotar,
inscrever; (*revolt etc*) sufocar;
(*attribute*): **to ~ sth down to**
atribuir algo a; **put forward** VT
apresentar, propor; **put in** VT
(*application, complaint*) apresentar;
(*time, effort*) investir, gastar; **put off**
VT adiar, protelar; (*discourage*)
desanimar; **put on** VT (*clothes,
make-up, dinner*) pôr; (*light*) acender;
(*play*) encenar; (*weight*) ganhar;
(*brake*) aplicar; (*record, video, kettle*)
ligar; (*accent, manner*) assumir; **put
out** VT (*take out*) colocar fora; (*fire,
cigarette, light*) apagar; (*one's hand*)
estender; (*inf: person*): **to be ~ out**
estar aborrecido; **put through** VT
(*call*) transferir; (*plan*) aprovar; **put
up** VT (*raise*) levantar, erguer; (*hang*)
prender; (*build*) construir, edificar;
(*tent*) armar; (*increase*) aumentar;
(*accommodate*) hospedar; **put up
with** VT FUS suportar, aguentar
puzzle ['pʌzl] N charada; (*jigsaw*)
quebra-cabeça *m*; (*also:* **crossword ~**)
palavras cruzadas *fpl*; (*mystery*)
mistério ▶ VT desconcertar,
confundir ▶ VI: **to ~ over sth** tentar
entender algo; **puzzling** ADJ
intrigante, confuso
pyjamas [pɪ'dʒɑːməz], (US)
pajamas NPL pijama *m or f*
pylon ['paɪlən] N pilono, poste *m*,
torre *f*
pyramid ['pɪrəmɪd] N pirâmide *f*
Pyrenees [pɪrə'niːz] NPL: **the ~**
os Pirineus

q

quack [kwæk] N grasnido; (*pej:
doctor*) curandeiro(-a),
charlatão(-tã) *m/f*
quaint [kweɪnt] ADJ (*ideas*)
curioso, esquisito; (*village etc*)
pitoresco
quake [kweɪk] VI (*with fear*) tremer
▶ N ABBR = **earthquake**
qualification [kwɔlɪfɪ'keɪʃən] N
(*skill, quality*) qualificação *f*;
(*reservation*) restrição *f*, ressalva;
(*modification*) modificação *f*;
(*often pl: degree, training*) título,
qualificação
qualified ['kwɔlɪfaɪd] ADJ (*trained*)
habilitado, qualificado;
(*professionally*) diplomado; (*fit*): **~ to**
apto para, capaz de; (*limited*)
limitado
qualify ['kwɔlɪfaɪ] VT (*modify*)
modificar ▶ VI: **to ~ (for)** reunir os
requisitos (para)
quality ['kwɔlɪtɪ] N qualidade *f*;
quality (news)papers (BRIT) NPL
ver nota

Os **quality (news)papers** (ou **quality press**) englobam os jornais "sérios", diários ou semanais, em oposição aos jornais populares (**tabloid press**). Esses jornais visam a um público que procura informações detalhadas sobre uma grande variedade de assuntos e que está disposto a dedicar um bom tempo à leitura. Geralmente os *quality newspapers* são publicados em formato grande.

quantify ['kwɔntɪfaɪ] VT quantificar

quantity ['kwɔntɪtɪ] N quantidade f

quarantine ['kwɔrntiːn] N quarentena

quarrel ['kwɔrl] N (*argument*) discussão f ▶ VI: **to ~ (with)** brigar (com)

quarry ['kwɔrɪ] N (*for stone*) pedreira; (*animal*) presa, caça

quart [kwɔːt] N quarto de galão (1.136 l)

quarter ['kwɔːtər] N quarto, quarta parte f; (*of year*) trimestre m; (*district*) bairro; (*US: 25 cents*) (moeda de) 25 centavos mpl de dólar ▶ VT dividir em quatro; (*Mil: lodge*) aquartelar; **quarters** NPL (*Mil*) quartel m; (*living quarters*) alojamento; **a ~ of an hour** um quarto de hora; **quarter final** N quarta de final; **quarterly** ADJ trimestral ▶ ADV trimestralmente

quay [kiː] N (*also*: **~side**) cais m

queasy ['kwiːzɪ] ADJ (*sickly*) enjoado

queen [kwiːn] N rainha; (*also*: **~ bee**) abelha-mestra, rainha; (*Cards etc*) dama

queer [kwɪər] ADJ (*odd*) esquisito, estranho ▶ N (*inf: homosexual*) bicha m (BR), maricas m inv (PT)

quench [kwɛntʃ] VT: **to ~ one's thirst** matar a sede

query ['kwɪərɪ] N pergunta ▶ VT questionar

quest [kwɛst] N busca

question ['kwɛstʃən] N pergunta; (*doubt*) dúvida; (*issue, in test*) questão f ▶ VT (*doubt*) duvidar; (*interrogate*) interrogar, inquirir; **beyond ~** sem dúvida; **out of the ~** fora de cogitação, impossível; **questionable** ADJ discutível; (*doubtful*) duvidoso; **question mark** N ponto de interrogação; **questionnaire** [kwɛstʃə'nɛər] N questionário

queue [kjuː] (BRIT) N fila (BR), bicha (PT) ▶ VI (*also*: **~ up**) fazer fila (BR) or bicha (PT)

quick [kwɪk] ADJ rápido; (*agile*) ágil; (*mind*) sagaz, despachado ▶ N: **to cut sb to the ~** ferir alguém; **be ~!** ande depressa!, vai rápido!; **quickly** ADV rapidamente, depressa

quid [kwɪd] (BRIT inf) N INV libra

quiet ['kwaɪət] ADJ (*voice, music*) baixo; (*peaceful: place*) tranquilo; (*calm: person*) calmo; (*not noisy: place*) silencioso; (*not talkative: person*) calado; (*silent*) silencioso; (*ceremony*) discreto ▶ N (*peacefulness*) sossego; (*silence*) quietude f ▶ VT, VI (US) = **quieten**; **quieten, quieten down** VI (*grow calm*) acalmar-se; (*grow silent*) calar-se ▶ VT tranquilizar; fazer calar; **quietly** ADV silenciosamente; (*talk*) baixo

quilt [kwɪlt] N acolchoado, colcha; (BRIT: *also* **continental ~**) edredom m (BR), edredão m (PT)

quit [kwɪt] (pt, pp **quit** or **quitted**)
vт (smoking etc) parar; (job) deixar;
(premises) desocupar ▶ vı desistir;
(resign) pedir demissão

quite [kwaɪt] ADV (rather) bastante;
(entirely) completamente,
totalmente; **that's not ~ big
enough** não é suficientemente
grande; **~ a few of them** um bom
número deles; **~ (so)!** exatamente!,
isso mesmo!

quiver ['kwɪvəʳ] vı estremecer

quiz [kwɪz] N concurso (de cultura
geral) ▶ vт interrogar

quota ['kwəutə] N cota, quota

quotation [kwəu'teɪʃən] N citação
f; (estimate) orçamento; **quotation
marks** NPL aspas fpl

quote [kwəut] N citação f;
(estimate) orçamento ▶ vт citar;
(price) propor; (figure, example) citar,
dar; **quotes** NPL aspas fpl

rabbi ['ræbaɪ] N rabino

rabbit ['ræbɪt] N coelho

rabies ['reɪbiːz] N raiva

RAC (BRIT) N ABBR (= Royal Automobile
Club) ≈ TCB m (BR), ≈ ACP m (PT)

race [reɪs] N corrida; (species) raça
▶ vт (horse) fazer correr ▶ vı
(compete) competir; (run) correr;
(pulse) bater rapidamente; **race car**
(US) N = **racing car**; **racecourse** N
hipódromo; **racehorse** N cavalo de
corridas; **racetrack** N pista de
corridas; (for cars) autódromo

racing ['reɪsɪŋ] N corrida; **racing
car** (BRIT) N carro de corrida; **racing
driver** (BRIT) N piloto(-a) de corrida

racism ['reɪsɪzəm] N racismo;
racist (pej) ADJ, N racista m/f

rack [ræk] N (also: **luggage ~**)
bagageiro; (shelf) estante f; (also:
roof ~) xalmas fpl, porta-bagagem
m; (also: **dish ~**) secador m de prato
▶ vт: **~ed by** (pain, anxiety) tomado
por; **to ~ one's brains** quebrar a
cabeça

racket ['rækɪt] N (for tennis) raquete f (BR), raqueta (PT); (noise) barulheira, zoeira; (swindle) negócio ilegal, fraude f

racquet ['rækɪt] N raquete f (BR), raqueta (PT)

radiation [reɪdɪ'eɪʃən] N radiação f

radiator ['reɪdɪeɪtəʳ] N radiador m

radical ['rædɪkl] ADJ radical

radio ['reɪdɪəu] N rádio ▶ VT: **to ~ sb** comunicar-se por rádio com alguém

radio... [reɪdɪəu] PREFIX radio...; **radioactive** ['reɪdɪəu'æktɪv] ADJ radioativo; **radio station** N emissora, estação f de rádio

radish ['rædɪʃ] N rabanete m

raffle ['ræfl] N rifa

raft [rɑːft] N balsa

rag [ræg] N trapo; (torn cloth) farrapo; (pej: newspaper) jornaleco; (University) atividades estudantis beneficentes; **rags** NPL (torn clothes) trapos mpl, farrapos mpl

rage [reɪdʒ] N (fury) raiva, furor m ▶ VI (person) estar furioso; (storm) assolar; (debate) continuar calorosamente; **it's all the ~** é a última moda

ragged ['rægɪd] ADJ (edge) irregular, desigual; (clothes) puído, gasto; (appearance) esfarrapado, andrajoso

raid [reɪd] N (Mil) incursão f; (criminal) assalto; (attack) ataque m; (by police) batida ▶ VT invadir, atacar; assaltar; atacar; fazer uma batida em

rail [reɪl] N (on stair) corrimão m; (on bridge, balcony) parapeito, anteparo; (of ship) amurada; **rails** NPL (for train) trilhos mpl; **by ~** de trem (BR), por caminho de ferro

(PT); **railing** N, **railings** NPL grade f; **railroad** (US) N = **railway**; **railway** N estrada (BR) or caminho (PT) de ferro; **railway line** (BRIT) N linha de trem (BR) or de comboio (PT); **railway station** (BRIT) N estação f ferroviária (BR) or de caminho de ferro (PT)

rain [reɪn] N chuva ▶ VI chover; **it's ~ing** está chovendo (BR), está a chover (PT); **rainbow** N arco-íris m inv; **raincoat** N impermeável m, capa de chuva; **raindrop** N gota de chuva; **rainfall** N chuva; (measurement) pluviosidade f; **rainforest** N floresta tropical; **rainy** ADJ chuvoso; **a rainy day** um dia de chuva

raise [reɪz] N aumento ▶ VT levantar; (salary, production) aumentar; (morale, standards) melhorar; (doubts) suscitar, despertar; (cattle, family) criar; (crop) cultivar, plantar; (army) recrutar, alistar; (funds) angariar; (loan) levantar, obter; **to ~ one's voice** levantar a voz

raisin ['reɪzn] N passa, uva seca

rake [reɪk] N ancinho ▶ VT (garden) revolver or limpar com o ancinho; (with machine gun) varrer

rally ['rælɪ] N (Pol etc) comício; (Aut) rally m, rali m; (Tennis) rebatida ▶ VT reunir ▶ VI reorganizar-se; (sick person, stock exchange) recuperar-se; **rally round** VT FUS dar apoio a

RAM [ræm] N ABBR (Comput: = random access memory) RAM f

ram [ræm] N carneiro ▶ VT (push) cravar; (crash into) colidir com

ramble ['ræmbl] N caminhada, excursão f a pé ▶ VI caminhar; (talk: also: **~ on**) divagar; **rambler**

N caminhante m/f; (Bot) roseira trepadeira; **rambling** ADJ (speech) desconexo, incoerente; (house) cheio de recantos; (plant) rastejante

ramp [ræmp] N (incline) rampa; **on/ off ~** (US Aut) entrada (para a rodovia)/saída da rodovia

rampage [ræm'peɪdʒ] N: **to be on the ~** alvoroçar-se

ran [ræn] PT of **run**

ranch [rɑːntʃ] N rancho, fazenda, estância

random ['rændəm] ADJ ao acaso, casual, fortuito; (Comput, Math) aleatório ▶ N: **at ~** a esmo, aleatoriamente

rang [ræŋ] PT of **ring**

range [reɪndʒ] N (of mountains) cadeia, cordilheira; (of missile) alcance m; (of voice) extensão f; (series) série f; (of products) gama, sortimento; (Mil: also: **shooting ~**) estande m; (also: **kitchen ~**) fogão m ▶ VT (place) colocar; (arrange) arrumar, ordenar ▶ VI: **to ~ over** (extend) estender-se por; **to ~ from ... to ...** variar de ... a ..., oscilar entre ... e ...

rank [ræŋk] N (row) fila, fileira; (Mil) posto; (status) categoria, posição f; (BRIT: also: **taxi ~**) ponto de táxi ▶ VI: **to ~ among** figurar entre ▶ ADJ fétido, malcheiroso; **the ~ and file** (fig) a gente comum

ransom ['rænsəm] N resgate m; **to hold sb to ~** (fig) encostar alguém contra a parede

rant [rænt] VI arengar

rap [ræp] N, VT bater de leve; (also: **~ music**) rap m

rape [reɪp] N estupro; (Bot) colza ▶ VT violentar, estuprar

rapid ['ræpɪd] ADJ rápido

rapids ['ræpɪdz] NPL (Geo) cachoeira

rapist ['reɪpɪst] N estuprador m

rapport [ræ'pɔːʳ] N harmonia, afinidade f

rare [rɛəʳ] ADJ raro; (Culin: steak) mal passado

rascal ['rɑːskl] N maroto, malandro

rash [ræʃ] ADJ impetuoso, precipitado ▶ N (Med) exantema m, erupção f cutânea; (of events) série f, torrente f

rasher ['ræʃəʳ] N fatia fina

raspberry ['rɑːzbərɪ] N framboesa

rat [ræt] N rato (BR), ratazana (PT)

rate [reɪt] N (ratio) razão f; (price) preço, taxa; (: of hotel) diária; (of interest, change) taxa; (speed) velocidade f ▶ VT (value) taxar; (estimate) avaliar; **rates** NPL (BRIT) imposto predial e territorial; (fees) pagamento; **to ~ sb/sth as** considerar algo/alguém como

rather ['rɑːðəʳ] ADV (somewhat) um tanto, meio; (to some extent) até certo ponto; (more accurately): **or ~** ou melhor; **it's ~ expensive** (quite) é meio caro; (too) é caro demais; **there's ~ a lot** há bastante or muito; **I would** or **I'd ~ go** preferiria or preferia ir; **or ~** ou melhor

ratio ['reɪʃɪəʊ] N razão f, proporção f

ration ['ræʃən] N ração f ▶ VT racionar; **rations** NPL (Mil) mantimentos mpl, víveres mpl

rational ['ræʃənl] ADJ lógico; (person) sensato, razoável

rat race N: **the ~** a competição acirrada na vida moderna

rattle ['rætl] N (of door) batida; (of train etc) chocalhada; (of coins) chocalhar m; (object: for baby) chocalho ▶ VI (small objects) tamborilar; (vehicle): **to ~ along** mover-se ruidosamente ▶ VT sacudir, fazer bater; (unnerve) perturbar

rave [reɪv] vi (*in anger*) encolerizar-se; (*Med*) delirar; (*with enthusiasm*): **to ~ about** vibrar com

raven ['reɪvən] N corvo

ravine [rə'viːn] N ravina, barranco

raw [rɔː] ADJ (*uncooked*) cru(a); (*not processed*) bruto; (*sore*) vivo; (*inexperienced*) inexperiente, novato; (*weather*) muito frio

ray [reɪ] N raio; **~ of hope** fio de esperança

razor ['reɪzə^r] N (*open*) navalha; (*safety razor*) aparelho de barbear; (*electric*) aparelho de barbear elétrico; **razor blade** N gilete m (BR), lâmina de barbear (PT)

Rd ABBR = **road**

re [riː] PREP referente a

reach [riːtʃ] N alcance m; (*of river etc*) extensão f ▶ vt alcançar; (*arrive at: place*) chegar em; (*: agreement, conclusion*) chegar a; (*by telephone*) conseguir falar com ▶ vi (*stretch out*) esticar-se; **within ~** ao alcance (da mão); **out of** or **beyond ~** fora de alcance; **reach out** vt (*hand*) esticar ▶ vi: **to ~ out for sth** estender or esticar a mão para pegar (em) algo

react [riː'ækt] vi reagir; **reaction** N reação f; **reactions** NPL (*reflexes*) reflexos mpl

reactor [riː'æktə^r] N (*also*: **nuclear ~**) reator m nuclear

read [riːd] (*pt, pp* **read** [rɛd]) vi ler ▶ vt ler; (*understand*) compreender; (*study*) estudar; **read out** vt ler em voz alta; **reader** N leitor(a) m/f; (*book*) livro de leituras; (*BRIT: at university*) professor(a) m/f adjunto(-a)

readily ['rɛdɪlɪ] ADV (*willingly*) de boa vontade; (*easily*) facilmente; (*quickly*) sem demora, prontamente

reading ['riːdɪŋ] N leitura; (*on instrument*) indicação f, registro (BR), registo (PT)

ready ['rɛdɪ] ADJ pronto, preparado; (*willing*) disposto; (*available*) disponível ▶ N: **at the ~** (*Mil*) pronto para atirar; **to get ~** vi preparar-se; vt preparar; **ready-made** ADJ (já) feito; (*clothes*) pronto

real [rɪəl] ADJ real; (*genuine*) verdadeiro, autêntico; **in ~ terms** em termos reais; **real estate** N bens mpl imobiliários or de raiz; **realistic** [rɪə'lɪstɪk] ADJ realista

reality [riː'ælɪtɪ] N realidade f; **reality TV** N reality TV f

realization [rɪəlaɪ'zeɪʃən] N (*fulfilment*) realização f; (*understanding*) compreensão f; (*Comm*) conversão f em dinheiro, realização

realize ['rɪəlaɪz] vt (*understand*) perceber; (*fulfil, Comm*) realizar

really ['rɪəlɪ] ADV (*for emphasis*) realmente; (*actually*): **what ~ happened?** o que aconteceu na verdade?; **~?** (*interest*) é mesmo?; (*surprise*) verdade!; **~!** (*annoyance*) realmente!

realm [rɛlm] N reino; (*fig*) esfera, domínio

realtor ['rɪəltə^r] (US) N corretor(a) m/f de imóveis (BR), agente m/f imobiliário(-a) (PT)

reappear [riːə'pɪə^r] vi reaparecer

rear [rɪə^r] ADJ traseiro, de trás ▶ N traseira ▶ vt criar ▶ vi (*also*: **~ up**) empinar-se

reason ['riːzn] N (*cause*) razão f; (*ability to think*) raciocínio; (*sense*) bom-senso ▶ vi: **to ~ with sb** argumentar com alguém, persuadir alguém; **it stands to ~**

that é razoável or lógico que;
  reasonable ADJ (fair) razoável;
  (sensible) sensato; **reasonably** ADV
  razoavelmente; (sensibly)
  sensatamente; **reasoning** N
  raciocínio
reassurance [riːəˈʃuərəns] N
  garantia
reassure [riːəˈʃuəʳ] VT tranquilizar;
  to ~ sb of reafirmar a confiança de
  alguém acerca de
rebate [ˈriːbeɪt] N devolução f
rebel [n ˈrɛbl, vi rɪˈbɛl] N rebelde m/f
  ▶ VI rebelar-se; **rebellious**
  [rɪˈbɛljəs] ADJ insurreto; (behaviour)
  rebelde
recall [rɪˈkɔːl] VT (remember)
  recordar, lembrar; (parliament)
  reunir de volta; (ambassador etc)
  chamar de volta ▶ N (memory)
  recordação f, lembrança; (of
  ambassador etc) chamada
  (de volta)
receipt [rɪˈsiːt] N recibo; (act of
  receiving) recebimento (BR),
  receção f (PT); **receipts** NPL (Comm)
  receitas fpl
receive [rɪˈsiːv] VT receber; (guest)
  acolher; (wound, criticism) sofrer;
  receiver N (Tel) fone m (BR),
  auscultador m (PT); (Radio, TV)
  receptor m; (of stolen goods)
  receptador(a) m/f; (Comm)
  curador(a) m/f síndico(-a) de massa
  falida
recent [ˈriːsnt] ADJ recente;
  recently ADV recentemente;
  (in recent times) ultimamente
reception [rɪˈsɛpʃən] N recepção f;
  (welcome) acolhida; **reception desk**
  N (mesa de) recepção f;
  receptionist N recepcionista m/f
recession [rɪˈsɛʃən] N recessão f
recipe [ˈrɛsɪpɪ] N receita

recipient [rɪˈsɪpɪənt] N recipiente
  m/f, recebedor(a) m/f; (of letter)
  destinatário(-a)
recite [rɪˈsaɪt] VT recitar
reckless [ˈrɛkləs] ADJ (driver)
  imprudente; (speed) imprudente,
  excessivo; (spending) irresponsável
reckon [ˈrɛkən] VT (calculate)
  calcular, contar; (think): **I ~ that ...**
  acho que ...; **reckon on** VT FUS
  contar com
reclaim [rɪˈkleɪm] VT (demand back)
  reivindicar; (waste materials)
  reaproveitar
recline [rɪˈklaɪn] VI reclinar-se
recognition [rɛkəgˈnɪʃən] N
  reconhecimento
recognize [ˈrɛkəgnaɪz] VT
  reconhecer
recommend [rɛkəˈmɛnd] VT
  recomendar
reconcile [ˈrɛkənsaɪl] VT
  reconciliar; (two facts) conciliar,
  harmonizar; **to ~ o.s. to sth**
  resignar-se a or conformar-se com
  algo
reconsider [riːkənˈsɪdəʳ] VT
  reconsiderar
reconstruct [riːkənˈstrʌkt] VT
  reconstruir; (event) reconstituir
record [n, adj ˈrɛkɔːd, vt rɪˈkɔːd] N
  (Mus) disco; (of meeting etc) ata,
  minuta; (Comput, of attendance)
  registro (BR), registo (PT); (written)
  história; (also: **criminal ~**)
  antecedentes mpl; (Sport) recorde m
  ▶ VT (write down) anotar;
  (temperature, speed) registrar (BR),
  registar (PT); (Mus: song etc) gravar
  ▶ ADJ: **in ~ time** num tempo
  recorde; **off the ~** adj confidencial;
  adv confidencialmente; **recorder** N
  (Mus) flauta; **recording** N (Mus)
  gravação f; **record player** N

toca-discos *m inv* (BR), gira-discos *m inv* (PT)

recover [rɪ'kʌvəʳ] VT recuperar ▶ VI (*from illness*) recuperar-se; (*from shock*) refazer-se; **recovery** N recuperação *f*; (*Med*) recuperação, melhora

recreation [rɛkrɪ'eɪʃən] N recreio; **recreational drug** N droga recreacional

recruit [rɪ'kru:t] N recruta *m/f*; (*in company*) novato(-a) ▶ VT recrutar

rectangle ['rɛktæŋgl] N retângulo

rector ['rɛktəʳ] N (*Rel*) pároco

recur [rɪ'kə:ʳ] VI repetir-se, ocorrer outra vez; (*symptoms*) reaparecer

recyclable [rɪ:'saɪkləbl] ADJ reciclável; **recycle** VT reciclar; **recycling** N reciclagem *f*

red [rɛd] N vermelho; (*Pol: pej*) vermelho(-a) ▶ ADJ vermelho; (*hair*) ruivo; (*wine*) tinto; **to be in the ~** não ter fundos; **Red Cross** N Cruz *f* Vermelha

redeem [rɪ'di:m] VT (*Rel*) redimir; (*sth in pawn*) tirar do prego; (*loan, fig: situation*) salvar

red: red-haired ADJ ruivo; **redhead** ['rɛdhɛd] N ruivo(-a); **red-hot** ADJ incandescente; **red-light district** N zona (de meretrício)

reduce [rɪ'dju:s] VT reduzir; (*lower*) rebaixar; **"~ speed now"** (*Aut*) "diminua a velocidade"; **to ~ sb to** (*silence, begging*) levar alguém a; (*tears*) reduzir alguém a; **reduction** [rɪ'dʌkʃən] N redução *f*; (*of price*) abatimento

redundancy [rɪ'dʌndənsɪ] N (BRIT: *dismissal*) demissão *f*; (*unemployment*) desemprego

redundant [rɪ'dʌndnt] ADJ (BRIT: *worker*) desempregado; (*detail, object*) redundante, supérfluo; **to be made ~** ficar desempregado *or* sem trabalho

reed [ri:d] N (*Bot*) junco; (*Mus: of clarinet etc*) palheta

reef [ri:f] N (*at sea*) recife *m*

reel [ri:l] N carretel *m*, bobina; (*of film*) rolo, filme *m*; (*on fishing-rod*) carretilha; (*dance*) dança típica da Escócia ▶ VI (*sway*) cambalear, oscilar; **reel in** VT puxar enrolando a linha

ref [rɛf] (*inf*) N ABBR = **referee**

refectory [rɪ'fɛktərɪ] N refeitório

refer [rɪ'fə:ʳ] VT (*matter, problem*): **to ~ sth to** submeter algo à apreciação de; (*person, patient*): **to ~ sb to** encaminhar alguém a ▶ VI: **to ~ to** referir-se *or* aludir a; (*consult*) recorrer a

referee [rɛfə'ri:] N árbitro(-a); (BRIT: *for job application*) referência ▶ VT apitar

reference ['rɛfrəns] N referência; (*mention*) menção *f*; **with ~ to** com relação a; (*Comm: in letter*) com referência a; **"please quote this ~"** (*Comm*) "queira citar esta referência"

refill [*vt* ri:'fɪl, *n* 'ri:fɪl] VT reencher; (*lighter etc*) reabastecer ▶ N (*for pen*) carga nova

refine [rɪ'faɪn] VT refinar; **refined** ADJ refinado, culto

reflect [rɪ'flɛkt] VT refletir ▶ VI (*think*) refletir, meditar; **it ~s badly/well on him** isso repercute mal/bem para ele; **reflection** N reflexo; (*thought, act*) reflexão *f*; (*criticism*): **reflection on** crítica de; **on reflection** pensando bem

reflex ['ri:flɛks] ADJ, N reflexo

reform [rɪ'fɔ:m] N reforma ▶ VT reformar

refrain [rɪ'freɪn] vɪ: **to ~ from doing** abster-se de fazer ▶ N estribilho, refrão *m*

refresh [rɪ'frɛʃ] vt refrescar; **refreshing** ADJ refrescante; (*sleep*) repousante

refreshment [rɪ'frɛʃmənt] N (*eating*): **for some ~** para comer alguma coisa; **refreshments** NPL comes e bebes *mpl*

refrigerator [rɪ'frɪdʒəreɪtəʳ] N refrigerador *m*, geladeira (BR), frigorífico (PT)

refuel [ri:'fjuəl] vɪ reabastecer

refuge ['rɛfjuːdʒ] N refúgio; **to take ~ in** refugiar-se em

refugee [rɛfju'dʒiː] N refugiado(-a)

refund [n 'riːfʌnd, vt rɪ'fʌnd] N reembolso ▶ vt devolver, reembolsar

refurbish [riː'fəːbɪʃ] vt renovar

refusal [rɪ'fjuːzəl] N recusa, negativa; **first ~** primeira opção

refuse¹ [rɪ'fjuːz] vt recusar; (*order*) recusar-se a ▶ vɪ recusar-se, negar-se; (*horse*) recusar-se a pular a cerca

refuse² ['rɛfjuːs] N refugo, lixo

regain [rɪ'geɪn] vt recuperar, recobrar

regard [rɪ'gɑːd] N (*gaze*) olhar *m* firme; (*attention*) atenção *f*; (*esteem*) estima, consideração *f* ▶ vt (*consider*) considerar; **to give one's ~s to** dar lembranças a; **"with kindest ~s"** "cordialmente"; **as ~s, with ~ to** com relação a, com respeito a, quanto a; **regarding** PREP com relação a; **regardless** ADV apesar de tudo; **regardless of** apesar de

regiment ['rɛdʒɪmənt] N regimento

region ['riːdʒən] N região *f*; **in the ~ of** (*fig*) por volta de, ao redor de; **regional** ADJ regional

register ['rɛdʒɪstəʳ] N registro (BR), registo (PT); (*Sch*) chamada ▶ vt registrar (BR), registar (PT); (*subj: instrument*) marcar, indicar ▶ vɪ (*at hotel*) registrar-se (BR), registar-se (PT); (*for work*) candidatar-se; (*as student*) inscrever-se; (*make impression*) causar impressão; **registered** ADJ (*letter, parcel*) registrado (BR), registado (PT)

registrar ['rɛdʒɪstrɑːʳ] N oficial *m/f* de registro (BR) or registo (PT), escrivão(-vã) *m/f*; (*in college*) funcionário(-a) administrativo(-a) sênior; (*in hospital*) médico(-a) sênior

registration [rɛdʒɪs'treɪʃən] N (*act*) registro (BR), registo (PT); (*Aut: also: ~ number*) número da placa

regret [rɪ'grɛt] N desgosto, pesar *m* ▶ vt lamentar; (*repent of*) arrepender-se de

regular ['rɛgjuləʳ] ADJ regular; (*frequent*) frequente; (*usual*) habitual; (*soldier*) de linha ▶ N habitual *m/f*; **regularly** ADV regularmente; (*shaped*) simetricamente; (*often*) frequentemente

regulate ['rɛgjuleɪt] vt (*speed*) regular; (*spending*) controlar; (*Tech*) regular, ajustar; **regulation** [rɛgju'leɪʃən] N (*rule*) regra, regulamento; (*adjustment*) ajuste *m*

rehearsal [rɪ'həːsəl] N ensaio

rehearse [rɪ'həːs] vt ensaiar

reign [reɪn] N reinado; (*fig*) domínio ▶ vɪ reinar; imperar

reimburse [riːɪm'bəːs] vt reembolsar

rein [reɪn] N (*for horse*) rédea

reindeer ['reɪndɪəʳ] N INV rena

reinforce [riːɪn'fɔːs] vt reforçar

reinstate [ri:ɪn'steɪt] VT (worker) readmitir; (tax, law) reintroduzir

reject [n 'ri:dʒɛkt, vt rɪ'dʒɛkt] N (Comm) artigo defeituoso ▶ VT rejeitar; (offer of help) recusar; (goods) refugar; **rejection** N rejeição f; (of offer of help) recusa

rejoice [rɪ'dʒɔɪs] VI: **to ~ at** or **over** regozijar-se or alegrar-se de

relate [rɪ'leɪt] VT (tell) contar, relatar; (connect): **to ~ sth to** relacionar algo com ▶ VI: **to ~ to** relacionar-se com; **~d to** ligado a, relacionado a

relation [rɪ'leɪʃən] N (person) parente m/f; (link) relação f; **relations** NPL (dealings) relações fpl; (relatives) parentes mpl; **relationship** N relacionamento; (between two things) relação f; (also: **family relationship**) parentesco

relative ['rɛlətɪv] N parente m/f ▶ ADJ relativo; **relatively** ADV relativamente

relax [rɪ'læks] VI (unwind) descontrair-se; (muscle) relaxar-se ▶ VT (grip) afrouxar; (control) relaxar; (mind, person) descansar; **relaxation** [ri:læk'seɪʃən] N (rest) descanso; (of muscle, control) relaxamento; (of grip) afrouxamento; (recreation) lazer m; **relaxed** ADJ relaxado; (tranquil) descontraído

relay ['ri:leɪ] N (race) (corrida de) revezamento ▶ VT (message) retransmitir

release [rɪ'li:s] N (from prison) libertação f; (from obligation) liberação f; (of gas) escape m; (of water) despejo; (of film, book etc) lançamento ▶ VT (prisoner) pôr em liberdade; (book, film) lançar; (report, news) publicar; (gas etc)

soltar; (free: from wreckage etc) soltar; (Tech: catch, spring etc) desengatar, desapertar

relegate ['rɛləgeɪt] VT relegar; (Sport): **to be ~d** ser rebaixado

relent [rɪ'lɛnt] VI (yield) ceder; **relentless** ADJ (unceasing) contínuo; (determined) implacável

relevant ['rɛləvənt] ADJ pertinente; **~ to** relacionado com

reliable [rɪ'laɪəbl] ADJ (person, firm) de confiança, confiável, sério; (method, machine) seguro; (news) fidedigno

relic ['rɛlɪk] N (Rel) relíquia; (of the past) vestígio

relief [rɪ'li:f] N alívio; (help, supplies) ajuda, socorro; (Art, Geo) relevo

relieve [rɪ'li:v] VT (pain, fear) aliviar; (bring help to) ajudar, socorrer; (take over from: gen) substituir, revezar; (: guard) render; **to ~ sb of sth** (load) tirar algo de alguém; (duties) destituir alguém de algo; **to ~ o.s.** fazer as necessidades

religion [rɪ'lɪdʒən] N religião f; **religious** ADJ religioso

relish ['rɛlɪʃ] N (Culin) condimento, tempero; (enjoyment) entusiasmo ▶ VT (food etc) saborear; (thought) ver com satisfação

reluctant [rɪ'lʌktənt] ADJ relutante; **reluctantly** ADV relutantemente, de má vontade

rely on [rɪ'laɪ-] VT FUS confiar em, contar com; (be dependent on) depender de

remain [rɪ'meɪn] VI (survive) sobreviver; (stay) ficar, permanecer; (be left) sobrar; (continue) continuar; **remainder** N resto, restante m; **remaining** ADJ restante; **remains** NPL (of body) restos mpl; (of meal) sobras fpl; (of building) ruínas fpl

remand [rɪˈmɑːnd] N: **on ~** sob prisão preventiva ▶ VT: **to be ~ed in custody** continuar sob prisão preventiva, manter sob custódia

remark [rɪˈmɑːk] N observação f, comentário ▶ VT comentar; **remarkable** ADJ (outstanding) extraordinário

remarry [riːˈmærɪ] VI casar-se de novo

remedy [ˈrɛmədɪ] N: **~ (for)** remédio (contra or a) ▶ VT remediar

remember [rɪˈmɛmbəʳ] VT lembrar-se de, lembrar; (bear in mind) ter em mente; (send greetings): **~ me to her** dê lembranças a ela

remembrance [rɪˈmɛmbrəns] N (memory) memória; (souvenir) lembrança, recordação f; **Remembrance Sunday** N ver nota

Remembrance Sunday ou **Remembrance Day** é o domingo mais próximo do dia 11 de novembro, dia em que a Primeira Guerra Mundial terminou oficialmente e no qual se homenageia as vítimas das duas guerras mundiais. Nessa ocasião são observados dois minutos de silêncio às 11 horas, horário da assinatura do armistício com a Alemanha em 1918. Nos dias anteriores, papoulas de papel são vendidas por associações de caridade e a renda é revertida aos ex-combatentes e suas famílias.

remind [rɪˈmaɪnd] VT: **to ~ sb to do sth** lembrar a alguém que tem de fazer algo; **to ~ sb of sth** lembrar algo a alguém, lembrar alguém de

algo; **reminder** N lembrança; (letter) carta de advertência

remnant [ˈrɛmnənt] N resto; (of cloth) retalho; **remnants** NPL (Comm) retalhos mpl

remorse [rɪˈmɔːs] N remorso

remote [rɪˈməut] ADJ remoto; (person) reservado, afastado; **remote control** N controle m remoto; **remotely** ADV remotamente; (slightly) levemente

removal [rɪˈmuːvəl] N (taking away) remoção f; (BRIT: from house) mudança; (from office: sacking) afastamento, demissão f; (Med) extração f; **removal van** (BRIT) N caminhão m (BR) or camião m (PT) de mudanças

remove [rɪˈmuːv] VT tirar, retirar; (clothing) tirar; (stain) remover; (employee) afastar, demitir; (name from list, obstacle) eliminar, remover; (doubt, abuse) afastar; (Med) extrair, extirpar

render [ˈrɛndəʳ] VT (thanks) trazer; (service) prestar; (make) fazer, tornar

rendezvous [ˈrɔndɪvuː] N encontro; (place) ponto de encontro

renew [rɪˈnjuː] VT retomar, recomeçar; (loan etc) prorrogar; (negotiations, acquaintance) reatar

renovate [ˈrɛnəveɪt] VT renovar; (house, room) reformar

rent [rɛnt] N aluguel m (BR), aluguer m (PT) ▶ VT (also: **~ out**) alugar; **rental** N (for television, car) aluguel m (BR), aluguer m (PT)

rep [rɛp] N ABBR (Comm) = **representative**

repair [rɪˈpɛəʳ] N reparação f, conserto ▶ VT consertar; **in good/ bad ~** em bom/mau estado; **repair kit** N caixa de ferramentas

repay [ri:'pei] *irreg* VT (*money*) reembolsar, restituir; (*person*) pagar de volta; (*debt*) saldar, liquidar; (*sb's efforts*) corresponder, retribuir; (*favour*) retribuir; **repayment** N reembolso; (*of debt*) pagamento

repeat [ri'pi:t] N (*Radio, TV*) repetição *f* ▶ VT repetir; (*Comm: order*) renovar ▶ VI repetir-se

repetitive [ri'petitiv] ADJ repetitivo

replace [ri'pleis] VT (*put back*) repor, devolver; (*take the place of*) substituir; **replacement** N (*substitution*) substituição *f*; (*substitute*) substituto(-a)

replay ['ri:plei] N (*of match*) partida decisiva; (*TV: also:* **action ~**) replay *m*

replica ['replikə] N réplica, cópia, reprodução *f*

reply [ri'plai] N resposta ▶ VI responder

report [ri'pɔ:t] N relatório; (*Press etc*) reportagem *f*; (*BRIT: also:* **school ~**) boletim *m* escolar; (*of gun*) estampido, detonação *f* ▶ VT informar sobre; (*Press etc*) fazer uma reportagem sobre; (*bring to notice*) comunicar, anunciar ▶ VI (*make a report*): **to ~ (on)** apresentar um relatório (sobre); (*present o.s.*): **to ~ (to sb)** apresentar-se (a alguém); (*be responsible to*): **to ~ to sb** obedecer as ordens de alguém; **report card** (US, SCOTLAND) N boletim *m* escolar; **reportedly** ADV: **she is reportedly living in Spain** dizem que ela mora na Espanha; **reporter** N repórter *m/f*

represent [repri'zent] VT representar; (*constitute*) constituir; (*Comm*) ser representante de; **representation** [reprizen'teiʃən] N representação *f*; (*picture, statue*) representação, retrato; (*petition*) petição *f*; **representations** NPL (*protest*) reclamação *f*, protesto; **representative** [repri'zentətiv] N representante *m/f*; (US Pol) deputado(-a) ▶ ADJ: **representative (of)** representativo (de)

repress [ri'pres] VT reprimir; **repression** N repressão *f*

reproduce [ri:prə'dju:s] VT reproduzir ▶ VI reproduzir-se

reptile ['reptail] N réptil *m*

republic [ri'pʌblik] N república; **republican** ADJ, N republicano(-a); (US Pol): **Republican** membro(-a) do Partido Republicano

reputable ['repjutəbl] ADJ (*make etc*) bem conceituado, de confiança; (*person*) honrado, respeitável

reputation [repju'teiʃən] N reputação *f*

request [ri'kwest] N pedido; (*formal*) petição *f* ▶ VT: **to ~ sth of** *or* **from sb** pedir algo a alguém; (*formally*) solicitar algo a alguém; **request stop** (BRIT) N (*for bus*) parada não obrigatória

require [ri'kwaiə^r] VT (*need: subj: person*) precisar de, necessitar; (*: thing, situation*) requerer, exigir; (*want*) pedir; (*order*): **to ~ sb to do sth/sth of sb** exigir que alguém faça algo/algo de alguém; **requirement** N (*need*) necessidade *f*; (*want*) pedido

rescue ['reskju:] N salvamento, resgate *m* ▶ VT: **to ~ (from)** resgatar (de); (*save, fig*) salvar (de)

research [rɪ'sə:tʃ] N pesquisa ▶ VT pesquisar

resemblance [rɪ'zɛmbləns] N semelhança

resemble [rɪ'zɛmbl] VT parecer-se com

resent [rɪ'zɛnt] VT (attitude) ressentir-se de; (person) estar ressentido com; **resentful** ADJ ressentido

reservation [rɛzə'veɪʃən] N reserva

reserve [rɪ'zə:v] N reserva; (Sport) suplente m/f, reserva m/f (BR) ▶ VT reservar; **reserves** NPL (Mil) (tropas fpl da) reserva; (Comm) reserva; **in ~** de reserva; **reserved** ADJ reservado

residence ['rezɪdəns] N residência; (formal: home) domicílio; **residence permit** (BRIT) N autorização f de residência

resident ['rezɪdənt] N (of country, town) habitante m/f; (in hotel) hóspede m/f ▶ ADJ (population) permanente; (doctor) interno, residente; **residential** [rezɪ'dɛnʃəl] ADJ residencial

residue ['rezɪdju:] N resto

resign [rɪ'zaɪn] VT renunciar a, demitir-se de ▶ VI: **to ~ (from)** demitir-se (de); **to ~ o.s. to** resignar-se a; **resignation** [rezɪg'neɪʃən] N demissão f; (state of mind) resignação f

resist [rɪ'zɪst] VT resistir a

resolution [rezə'lu:ʃən] N resolução f; (of problem) solução f

resolve [rɪ'zɔlv] N resolução f ▶ VT resolver ▶ VI: **to ~ to do** resolver-se a fazer

resort [rɪ'zɔ:t] N local m turístico, estação f de veraneio; (recourse) recurso ▶ VI: **to ~ to** recorrer a; **in the last ~** em último caso, em última instância

resource [rɪ'sɔ:s] N (raw material) recurso natural; **resources** NPL (coal, money, energy) recursos mpl; **resourceful** ADJ engenhoso, habilidoso

respect [rɪs'pɛkt] N respeito ▶ VT respeitar; **respects** NPL (greetings) cumprimentos mpl; **respectable** ADJ respeitável; (large) considerável; (result, player) razoável; **respectful** ADJ respeitoso

respond [rɪs'pɔnd] VI (answer) responder; (react) reagir; **response** N resposta; (reaction) reação f

responsibility [rɪspɔnsɪ'bɪlɪtɪ] N responsabilidade f; (duty) dever m

responsible [rɪs'pɔnsɪbl] ADJ sério, responsável; (job) de responsabilidade; (liable): **~ (for)** responsável (por)

responsive [rɪs'pɔnsɪv] ADJ receptivo

rest [rest] N descanso, repouso; (pause) pausa, intervalo; (support) apoio; (remainder) resto; (Mus) pausa ▶ VI descansar; (stop) parar; (be supported): **to ~ on** apoiar-se em ▶ VT descansar; (lean): **to ~ sth on/ against** apoiar algo em or sobre/ contra; **the ~ of them** os outros; **it ~s with him to do it** cabe a ele fazê-lo

restaurant ['restərɔn] N restaurante m; **restaurant car** (BRIT) N vagão-restaurante m

restless ['restlɪs] ADJ desassossegado, irrequieto

restore [rɪ'stɔ:r] VT (building, order) restaurar; (sth stolen) restituir; (peace, health) restabelecer

restrain [rɪs'treɪn] VT (feeling) reprimir; (growth, inflation) refrear; (person): **to ~ (from doing)** impedir (de fazer); **restraint** N (restriction)

restrição f; (*moderation*)
moderação f, comedimento;
(*of style*) sobriedade f
restrict [rɪs'trɪkt] vт restringir,
limitar; (*people, animals*) confinar;
(*activities*) limitar; **restriction** N
restrição f, limitação f
rest room (*us*) N banheiro (*br*),
lavabo (*pt*)
result [rɪ'zʌlt] N resultado ▶ vi: **to
~ in** resultar em; **as a ~ of** como
resultado *or* consequência de
resume [rɪ'zju:m] vт (*work,
journey*) retomar, recomeçar ▶ vi
recomeçar
résumé ['reɪzju:meɪ] N (*summary*)
resumo; (*us: curriculum vitae*)
curriculum vitae m, currículo
resuscitate [rɪ'sʌsɪteɪt] vт (*Med*)
ressuscitar, reanimar
retail ['ri:teɪl] ADJ a varejo (*br*),
a retalho (*pt*) ▶ ADV a varejo (*br*),
a retalho (*pt*); **retailer** N varejista
m/f (*br*), retalhista m/f (*pt*)
retain [rɪ'teɪn] vт (*keep*) reter,
conservar
retire [rɪ'taɪər] vi aposentar-se;
(*withdraw*) retirar-se; (*go to bed*)
deitar-se; **retired** ADJ aposentado
(*br*), reformado (*pt*); **retirement**
N aposentadoria (*br*), reforma (*pt*)
retort [rɪ'tɔ:t] vi replicar, retrucar
retreat [rɪ'tri:t] N (*place*) retiro;
(*act*) retirada ▶ vi retirar-se
retrieve [rɪ'tri:v] vт (*sth lost*)
reaver, recuperar; (*situation,
honour*) salvar; (*error, loss*) reparar
retrospect ['retrəspekt] N: **in ~**
retrospectivamente, em
retrospecto; **retrospective**
[retrə'spektɪv] ADJ retrospectivo;
(*law*) retroativo
return [rɪ'tə:n] N regresso, volta;
(*of sth stolen etc*) devolução f;

(*Finance: from land, shares*)
rendimento ▶ CPD (*journey*) de
volta; (*brit: ticket*) de ida e volta;
(*match*) de revanche ▶ vi voltar,
regressar; (*symptoms etc*) voltar;
(*regain*): **to ~ to** (*consciousness*)
recobrar; (*power*) retornar a ▶ vт
devolver; (*favour, love etc*) retribuir;
(*verdict*) proferir, anunciar; (*Pol:
candidate*) eleger; **returns** NPL
(*Comm*) receita; **in ~ (for)** em troca
(de); **many happy ~s (of the
day)!** parabéns!; **by ~ (of post)**
por volta do correio
retweet [ri:'twi:t] N (*on Twitter*)
retweet m
reunion [ri:'ju:nɪən] N (*family*)
reunião f; (*two people, class*)
reencontro
reunite [ri:ju:'naɪt] vт reunir;
(*reconcile*) reconciliar
revamp ['ri:'væmp] vт dar um
jeito em
reveal [rɪ'vi:l] vт revelar; (*make
visible*) mostrar; **revealing** ADJ
revelador(a)
revel ['revl] vi: **to ~ in sth/in
doing sth** deleitar-se com algo/
em fazer algo
revenge [rɪ'vendʒ] N vingança,
desforra; **to take ~ on** vingar-se de
revenue ['revənju:] N receita,
renda
reversal [rɪ'və:sl] N (*of order*)
reversão f; (*of direction*) mudança
em sentido contrário; (*of decision*)
revogação f; (*of roles*) inversão f
reverse [rɪ'və:s] N (*opposite*)
contrário; (*back: of cloth*) avesso;
(*: of coin*) reverso; (*: of paper*) dorso;
(*Aut: also*: **~ gear**) marcha à ré (*br*),
marcha atrás (*pt*); (*setback*) revés
m, derrota ▶ ADJ (*order*) inverso,
oposto; (*direction*) contrário;

(*process*) inverso ▶ VT inverter; (*position*) mudar; (*process, decision*) revogar; (*car*) dar ré com ▶ VI (BRIT Aut) dar (marcha à) ré (BR), fazer marcha atrás (PT); **reverse-charge call** (BRIT) N (Tel) ligação f a cobrar

revert [rɪ'vəːt] VI: **to ~ to** voltar a; (*Jur*) reverter a

review [rɪ'vjuː] N (*magazine, Mil*) revista; (*of book, film*) crítica, resenha; (*examination*) recapitulação f, exame m ▶ VT rever, examinar; (*Mil*) passar em revista; (*book, film*) fazer a crítica or resenha de

revise [rɪ'vaɪz] VT (*manuscript*) corrigir; (*opinion, procedure*) alterar; (*price*) revisar; **revision** [rɪ'vɪʒən] N correção f; (*for exam*) revisão f

revival [rɪ'vaɪvəl] N (*recovery*) restabelecimento; (*of interest*) renascença, renascimento; (*Theatre*) reestreia; (*of faith*) despertar m

revive [rɪ'vaɪv] VT (*person*) reanimar, ressuscitar; (*economy*) recuperar; (*custom*) restabelecer, restaurar; (*hope, courage*) despertar; (*play*) reapresentar ▶ VI (*person: from faint*) voltar a si, recuperar os sentidos; (: *from ill-health*) recuperar-se; (*activity, economy*) reativar-se; (*hope, interest*) renascer

revolt [rɪ'vəult] N revolta, rebelião f, insurreição f ▶ VI revoltar-se ▶ VT causar aversão a, repugnar; **revolting** ADJ revoltante, repulsivo

revolution [rɛvə'luːʃən] N revolução f; (*of wheel, earth*) rotação f

revolve [rɪ'vɔlv] VI girar

revolver [rɪ'vɔlvəʳ] N revólver m

reward [rɪ'wɔːd] N recompensa ▶ VT: **to ~ (for)** recompensar or premiar (por); **rewarding** ADJ (*fig*) gratificante, compensador(a)

rewind [riː'waɪnd] *irreg* VT (*tape*) voltar para trás

rewritable [riː'raɪtəbl] ADJ regravável

rheumatism ['ruːmətɪzəm] N reumatismo

rhinoceros [raɪ'nɔsərəs] N rinoceronte m

rhubarb ['ruːbɑːb] N ruibarbo

rhyme [raɪm] N rima; (*verse*) verso(s) m(pl) rimado(s), poesia

rhythm ['rɪðm] N ritmo

rib [rɪb] N (*Anat*) costela ▶ VT (*mock*) zombar de, encarnar em

ribbon ['rɪbən] N fita; **in ~s** (*torn*) em tirinhas, esfarrapado

rice [raɪs] N arroz m; **rice pudding** N arroz m doce

rich [rɪtʃ] ADJ rico; (*clothes*) valioso; (*soil*) fértil; (*food*) suculento, forte; (*colour*) intenso; (*voice*) suave, cheio ▶ NPL: **the ~** os ricos; **riches** NPL (*wealth*) riquezas fpl

rid [rɪd] (*pt, pp* **rid**) VT: **to ~ sb of sth** livrar alguém de algo; **to get ~ of** livrar-se de; (*sth no longer required*) desfazer-se de

riddle ['rɪdl] N (*conundrum*) adivinhação f; (*mystery*) enigma m, charada ▶ VT: **to be ~d with** estar cheio de

ride [raɪd] (*pt* **rode**, *pp* **ridden**) N (*gen*) passeio; (*on horse*) passeio a cavalo; (*distance covered*) percurso, trajeto ▶ VI (*as sport*) montar; (*go somewhere: on horse, bicycle*) ir (a cavalo, de bicicleta); (*journey: on bicycle, motorcycle, bus*) viajar ▶ VT (*a horse*) montar a; (*bicycle, motorcycle*) andar de; (*distance*) percorrer; **to ~ at anchor** (*Naut*) estar ancorado; **to take sb for a ~** (*fig*) enganar alguém; **rider** N (*on horse: male*) cavaleiro; (: *female*) amazona; (*on bicycle*) ciclista *m/f*; (*on motorcycle*) motociclista *m/f*

ridge [rɪdʒ] N (*of hill*) cume *m*, topo; (*of roof*) cumeeira; (*wrinkle*) ruga

ridicule ['rɪdɪkjuːl] N escárnio, zombaria, mofa ▶ VT ridicularizar, zombar de; **ridiculous** ADJ ridículo

riding ['raɪdɪŋ] N equitação *f*

rife [raɪf] ADJ: **to be ~** ser comum; **to be ~ with** estar repleto de, abundar em

rifle ['raɪfl] N rifle *m*, fuzil *m* ▶ VT saquear; **rifle through** VT FUS vasculhar

rift [rɪft] N fenda, fratura; (*in clouds*) brecha; (*fig: between friends*) desentendimento; (: *in party*) rompimento, divergência

rig [rɪg] N (*also*: **oil ~**) torre *f* de perfuração ▶ VT adulterar *or* falsificar os resultados de; **rig out** (BRIT) VT: **to ~ out as/in** ataviar *or* vestir como/com; **rig up** VT instalar, montar, improvisar

right [raɪt] ADJ certo, correto; (*suitable*) adequado, conveniente; (: *decision*) certo; (*just*) justo; (*morally good*) bom; (*not left*) direito ▶ N direito; (*not left*) direita ▶ ADV bem, corretamente; (*fairly*) adequadamente, justamente; (*not on the left*) à direita; (*exactly*): **~ now** agora mesmo ▶ VT colocar em pé; (*correct*) corrigir, indireitar ▶ EXCL bom!; **to be ~** (*person*) ter razão; (*answer, clock*) estar certo; **by ~s** por direito; **on the ~** à direita; **to be in the ~** ter razão; **~ away** imediatamente, logo, já; **~ in the middle** bem no meio; **rightful** ADJ (*heir*) legítimo; (*place*) justo, legítimo; **right-handed** ADJ destro; **rightly** ADV (*with reason*) com razão; **right of way** N

prioridade *f* de passagem; (*Aut*) preferência; **right-wing** ADJ de direita

rigid ['rɪdʒɪd] ADJ rígido; (*principle*) inflexível

rim [rɪm] N borda, beira; (*of spectacles, wheel*) aro

rind [raɪnd] N (*of bacon*) pele *f*; (*of lemon etc*) casca; (*of cheese*) crosta, casca

ring [rɪŋ] (*pt* **rang**, *pp* **rung**) N (*of metal*) aro; (*on finger*) anel *m*; (*of people, objects*) círculo, grupo; (*for boxing*) ringue *m*; (*of circus*) pista, picadeiro; (*bullring*) picadeiro, arena; (*of light, smoke*) círculo; (*sound: of small bell*) toque *m*; (: *of large bell*) badalada, repique *m* ▶ VI (*on telephone*) telefonar; (*bell*) tocar; (*also*: **~ out**) soar; (*ears*) zumbir ▶ VT (BRIT *Tel*) telefonar a, ligar para; (*bell etc*) badalar; (*doorbell*) tocar; **to give sb a ~** (BRIT *Tel*) dar uma ligada *or* ligar para alguém; **ring back** (BRIT) VI (*Tel*) telefonar *or* ligar de volta ▶ VT telefonar *or* ligar de volta para; **ring off** (BRIT) VI (*Tel*) desligar; **ring up** (BRIT) VT (*Tel*) telefonar a, ligar para; **ring-fence** VT (*money, tax*) restringir (o uso de alguma verba); **ringing tone** (BRIT) N (*Tel*) sinal *m* de chamada; **ringleader** N cabeça *m/f*, cérebro; **ring road** (BRIT) N estrada periférica *or* perimetral; **ringtone** N (*on cellphone*) toque *m*

rink [rɪŋk] N (*also*: **ice ~**) pista de patinação, rinque *m*

rinse [rɪns] N enxaguada ▶ VT enxaguar; (*also*: **~ out**: *mouth*) bochechar

riot ['raɪət] N distúrbio, motim *m*, desordem *f*; (*of colour*) festival *m*, profusão f ▶ VI provocar distúrbios, amotinar-se; **to run ~** desenfrear-se

rip [rɪp] N rasgão m ▶ VT rasgar ▶ VI rasgar-se

ripe [raɪp] ADJ maduro

ripple ['rɪpl] N ondulação f, encrespação f; (of laughter etc) onda ▶ VI encrespar-se

rise [raɪz] (pt **rose**, pp **risen**) N elevação f, ladeira; (hill) colina, rampa; (increase: BRIT: in wages) aumento; (: in prices, temperature) subida; (to power etc) ascensão f ▶ VI levantar-se, erguer-se; (prices, waters) subir; (sun) nascer; (from bed etc) levantar(-se); (sound, voice) aumentar, erguer-se; (also: **~ up**: building) erguer-se; (: rebel) sublevar-se; (in rank) ascender, subir; **to give ~ to** ocasionar, dar origem a; **to ~ to the occasion** mostrar-se à altura da situação; **rising** ADJ (increasing: prices) em alta; (: number) crescente, cada vez maior; (tide) montante; (sun, moon) nascente

risk [rɪsk] N risco, perigo; (Insurance) risco ▶ VT pôr em risco; (chance) arriscar, aventurar; **to take** or **run the ~ of doing** correr o risco de fazer; **at ~** em perigo; **at one's own ~** por sua própria conta e risco; **risky** ADJ perigoso

rite [raɪt] N rito; **last ~s** últimos sacramentos

ritual ['rɪtjuəl] ADJ ritual ▶ N ritual m; (of initiation) rito

rival ['raɪvl] ADJ, N rival m/f; (in business) concorrente m/f ▶ VT competir com; **rivalry** N rivalidade f

river ['rɪvər] N rio ▶ CPD (port, traffic) fluvial; **up/down ~** rio acima/abaixo; **riverbank** N margem f (do rio)

road [rəud] N via; (motorway etc) estrada (de rodagem); (in town) rua ▶ CPD rodoviário; **road accident** N acidente m de trânsito; **roadblock** N barricada; **road map** N mapa m rodoviário; **road rage** N conduta agressiva dos motoristas no trânsito; **roadside** N beira da estrada; **road sign** N placa de sinalização; **roadworks** ['rəudwə:ks] NPL obras fpl de estrada

roam [rəum] VI vagar, perambular, errar

roar [rɔːʳ] N (of animal) rugido, urro; (of crowd) bramido; (of vehicle, storm) estrondo; (of laughter) barulho ▶ VI (animal, engine) rugir; (person, crowd) bradar; **to ~ with laughter** dar gargalhadas

roast [rəust] N carne f assada, assado ▶ VT assar; (coffee) torrar; **roast beef** N rosbife m

rob [rɔb] VT roubar; (bank) assaltar; **to ~ sb of sth** roubar algo de alguém; (fig: deprive) despojar alguém de algo; **robber** N ladrão/ladra m/f; **robbery** N roubo

robe [rəub] N toga, beca; (also: **bath ~**) roupão m (de banho)

robin ['rɔbɪn] N pisco-de-peito-ruivo (BR), pintarroxo (PT)

robot ['rəubɔt] N robô m

robust [rəu'bʌst] ADJ robusto, forte; (appetite) sadio; (economy) forte

rock [rɔk] N rocha; (boulder) penhasco, rochedo; (US: small stone) cascalho; (BRIT: sweet) pirulito ▶ VT (swing gently: cradle) balançar, oscilar; (: child) embalar, acalentar; (shake) sacudir ▶ VI (object) balançar-se; (person) embalar-se; **on the ~s** (drink) com gelo; (marriage etc) arruinado, em dificuldades; **rock and roll** N rock-and-roll m

rocket ['rɔkɪt] N foguete m

rocky ['rɔkɪ] ADJ rochoso; bambo, instável; (marriage etc) instável

rod [rɔd] N vara, varinha; (also: **fishing ~**) vara de pescar

rode [rəud] PT of **ride**

rodent ['rəudnt] N roedor m

rogue [rəug] N velhaco, maroto

role [rəul] N papel m; **role model** N modelo

roll [rəul] N rolo; (of banknotes) maço; (also: **bread ~**) pãozinho; (register) rol m, lista; (of drums etc) rufar m ▶ VT rolar; (also: **~ up**: string) enrolar; (: sleeves) arregaçar; (cigarette) enrolar; (eyes) virar; (also: **~ out**: pastry) esticar; (lawn, road etc) aplanar ▶ VI rolar; (drum) rufar; (vehicle: also: **~ along**) rodar; (ship) balançar, jogar; **roll about** VI ficar rolando; **roll around** VI = **roll about**; **roll by** VI (time) passar; **roll in** VI (mail, cash) chegar em grande quantidade; **roll over** VI dar uma volta; **roll up** VI (inf) pintar, chegar, aparecer ▶ VT (carpet etc) enrolar; **roller** N (in machine) rolo, cilindro; (wheel) roda, roldana; (for lawn, road) rolo compressor; (for hair) rolo; **roller coaster** N montanha-russa; **roller skates** NPL patins mpl de roda

rolling pin N rolo de pastel

ROM [rɔm] N ABBR (Comput: = read-only memory) ROM f

Roman ['rəumən] ADJ, N romano(-a); **Roman Catholic** ADJ, N católico(-a) (romano(-a))

romance [rə'mæns] N aventura amorosa, romance m; (book etc) história de amor; (charm) romantismo

Romania [ruː'meɪnɪə] N Romênia; **Romanian** ADJ romeno ▶ N romeno(-a); (Ling) romeno

romantic [rə'mæntɪk] ADJ romântico

Rome [rəum] N Roma

roof [ruːf] N (of house) telhado; (of car) capota, teto ▶ VT telhar, cobrir com telhas; **the ~ of the mouth** o céu da boca; **roof rack** N (Aut) bagageiro

rook [ruk] N (bird) gralha; (Chess) torre f

room [ruːm] N (in house) quarto, aposento; (also: **bed~**) quarto, dormitório; (in school etc) sala; (space) espaço, lugar m; (scope: for improvement etc) espaço; **rooms** NPL (lodging) alojamento; **"~s to let"** (BRIT), **"~s for rent"** (US) "alugam-se quartos or apartamentos"; **roommate** N companheiro(-a) de quarto; **room service** N serviço de quarto; **roomy** ADJ espaçoso; (garment) folgado

rooster ['ruːstəʳ] N galo

root [ruːt] N raiz f; (fig) origem f ▶ VI enraizar, arraigar; **roots** NPL (family origins) raízes fpl; **root about** VI (fig): **to ~ about in** (drawer) vasculhar; (house) esquadrinhar; **root for** VT FUS torcer por; **root out** VT extirpar

rope [rəup] N corda; (Naut) cabo ▶ VT (tie) amarrar; (climbers: also: **~ together**) amarrar or atar com uma corda; (area: also: **~ off**) isolar; **to know the ~s** (fig) estar por dentro (do assunto); **rope in** VT (fig): **to ~ sb in** persuadir alguém a tomar parte

rose [rəuz] PT of **rise** ▶ N rosa; (also: **~bush**) roseira; (on watering can) crivo

rosé ['rəuzeɪ] N rosado, rosé m

rosemary ['rəuzmərɪ] N alecrim m

rosy ['rəuzɪ] ADJ rosado, rosáceo; (*cheeks*) rosado; (*situation*) cor-de-rosa *inv*; **a ~ future** um futuro promissor

rot [rɒt] N (*decay*) putrefação *f*, podridão *f*; (*fig: pej*) besteira ▶ VT, VI apodrecer

rota ['rəutə] N lista de tarefas, escala de serviço

rotate [rəu'teɪt] VT fazer girar, dar voltas em ▶ VI girar, dar voltas

rotten ['rɒtn] ADJ podre; (*wood*) carcomido; (*fig*) corrupto; (*inf: bad*) péssimo; **to feel ~** (*ill*) sentir-se podre

rough [rʌf] ADJ (*skin, surface*) áspero; (*terrain*) acidentado; (*road*) desigual; (*voice*) áspero, rouco; (*weather*) tempestuoso; (*treatment*) brutal, mau/má; (*sea*) agitado; (*district*) violento; (*plan*) preliminar; (*work, cloth*) grosseiro; (*guess*) aproximado ▶ N (*Golf*): **in the ~** na grama crescida; **to sleep ~** (*BRIT*) dormir na rua; **roughly** ADV bruscamente; (*make*) toscamente; (*approximately*) aproximadamente

roulette [ruːˈlɛt] N roleta

round [raund] ADJ redondo ▶ N (*BRIT: of toast*) rodela; (*of policeman*) ronda; (*of milkman*) trajeto; (*of doctor*) visitas *fpl*; (*game: of cards, golf, in competition*) partida; (*of ammunition*) cartucho; (*Boxing*) round *e m*, assalto; (*of talks*) ciclo ▶ VT virar, dobrar ▶ PREP (*surrounding*): **~ his neck/the table** em volta de seu pescoço/ao redor da mesa; (*in a circular movement*): **to go ~ the world** dar a volta ao mundo; (*in various directions*): **to move ~ a house** mover-se por uma casa; (*approximately*): **~ about** aproximadamente ▶ ADV: **all ~** por todos os lados; **the long way ~**

o caminho mais comprido; **all the year ~** durante todo o ano; **it's just ~ the corner** (*fig*) está pertinho; **~ the clock** ininterrupto; **to go ~ the back** passar por detrás; **to go ~ a house** visitar uma casa; **enough to go ~** suficiente para todos; **a ~ of applause** uma salva de palmas; **a ~ of drinks** uma rodada de bebidas; **~ of sandwiches** sanduíche *m* (*BR*), sandes *f inv* (*PT*); **round off** VT terminar, completar; **round up** VT (*cattle*) encurralar; (*people*) reunir; (*price, figure*) arredondar; **roundabout** N (*BRIT: Aut*) rotatória; (*: at fair*) carrossel *m* ▶ ADJ indireto; **round trip** N viagem *f* de ida e volta

rouse [rauz] VT (*wake up*) despertar, acordar; (*stir up*) suscitar

route [ruːt] N caminho, rota; (*of bus*) trajeto; (*of shipping*) rumo, rota; (*of procession*) rota

routine [ruːˈtiːn] ADJ (*work*) rotineiro; (*procedure*) de rotina ▶ N rotina; (*Theatre*) número

row¹ [rəu] N (*line*) fila, fileira; (*in theatre, boat*) fileira; (*Knitting*) carreira, fileira ▶ VI, VT remar; **in a ~** (*fig*) a fio, seguido

row² [rau] N barulho, balbúrdia; (*dispute*) discussão *f*, briga; (*scolding*) repreensão *f* ▶ VI brigar; **to have a ~** ter uma briga

rowboat ['rəubəut] (*US*) N barco a remo

rowing ['rəuɪŋ] N remo; **rowing boat** (*BRIT*) N barco a remo

royal ['rɔɪəl] ADJ real

Royal Academy (*BRIT*) N *ver nota*

A **Royal Academy**, ou **Royal Academy of Arts**, fundada em 1768 por George III para desenvolver a pintura, a escultura e a arquitetura, situa-se em Burlington House, Piccadilly. A cada verão há uma exposição de obras de artistas contemporâneos. A **Royal Academy** também oferece cursos de pintura, escultura e arquitetura.

royalty N família real, realeza; (*payment: to author*) direitos *mpl* autorais

rpm ABBR (= *revolutions per minute*) rpm

rub [rʌb] VT (*part of body*) esfregar; (*object*) friccionar ▶ N: **to give sth a ~** dar uma esfregada em algo; **to ~ sb up** (BRIT) *or* **~ sb** (US) **the wrong way** irritar alguém; **rub off** VI sair esfregando; **rub off on** VT FUS transmitir-se para, influir sobre; **rub out** VT apagar

rubber ['rʌbəʳ] N borracha; (BRIT: *eraser*) borracha; **rubber band** N elástico, tira elástica

rubbish ['rʌbɪʃ] N (*waste*) refugo; (*from household, in street*) lixo; (*junk*) coisas *fpl* sem valor; (*fig: pej: nonsense*) disparates *mpl*, asneiras *fpl*; **rubbish bin** (BRIT) N lata de lixo; **rubbish dump** N (*in town*) depósito (de lixo)

rubble ['rʌbl] N (*debris*) entulho; (*Constr*) escombros *mpl*

ruby ['ruːbɪ] N rubi *m*

rucksack ['rʌksæk] N mochila

rudder ['rʌdəʳ] N leme *m*; (*of plane*) leme de direção

rude [ruːd] ADJ (*person*) grosso, mal-educado; (*word, manners*) grosseiro; (*shocking*) obsceno, chocante

rug [rʌg] N tapete *m*; (BRIT: *for knees*) manta (de viagem)

rugby ['rʌgbɪ] N (*also: ~ football*) rúgbi *m* (BR), râguebi *m* (PT)

rugged ['rʌgɪd] ADJ (*landscape*) acidentado, irregular; (*features*) marcado; (*character*) severo, austero

ruin ['ruːɪn] N ruína; (*of plans*) destruição f; (*downfall*) queda; (*bankruptcy*) bancarrota ▶ VT destruir; (*future, person*) arruinar; (*spoil*) estragar; **ruins** NPL (*of building*) ruínas *fpl*

rule [ruːl] N (*norm*) regra; (*regulation*) regulamento; (*government*) governo, domínio; (*ruler*) régua ▶ VT governar ▶ VI governar; (*monarch*) reger; (*Jur*): **to ~ in favour of/against** decidir oficialmente a favor de/contra; **as a ~** por via de regra, geralmente; **rule out** VT excluir; **ruler** N (*sovereign*) soberano(-a); (*for measuring*) régua; **ruling** ADJ (*party*) dominante; (*class*) dirigente ▶ N (*Jur*) parecer *m*, decisão f

rum [rʌm] N rum *m*

rumble ['rʌmbl] N ruído surdo, barulho; (*of thunder*) estrondo, ribombo ▶ VI ribombar, ressoar; (*stomach*) roncar; (*pipe*) fazer barulho; (*thunder*) ribombar

rumour ['ruːməʳ], (US) **rumor** N rumor *m*, boato ▶ VT: **it is ~ed that ...** corre o boato de que ...

rump steak [rʌmp-] N alcatra

run [rʌn] (*pt* **ran**, *pp* **run**) N corrida; (*in car*) passeio (de carro); (*distance travelled*) trajeto, percurso; (*journey*) viagem f; (*series*) série f; (*Theatre*) temporada; (*Ski*) pista; (*in stockings*) fio puxado ▶ VT (*race*) correr; (*operate: business*) dirigir; (: *competition, course*) organizar; (: *hotel, house*) administrar; (*water*) deixar correr; (*bath*) encher; (*Press: feature*) publicar; (*Comput*) rodar;

r

(*hand, finger*) passar ▶ VI correr; (*work: machine*) funcionar; (*bus, train: operate*) circular; (: *travel*) ir; (*continue: play*) continuar em cartaz; (: *contract*) ser válido; (*river, bath*) fluir, correr; (*colours, washing*) desbotar; (*in election*) candidatar-se; (*nose*) escorrer; **there was a ~ on** houve muita procura de; **in the long ~** no final das contas, mais cedo ou mais tarde; **on the ~** em fuga, foragido; **run about** VI correr por todos os lados; **run across** VT FUS encontrar por acaso, topar com, dar com; **run around** VI = **run about**; **run away** VI fugir; **run down** VT (*Aut*) atropelar; (*production*) reduzir; (*criticize*) criticar; **to be ~ down** estar enfraquecido *or* exausto; **run in** (*BRIT*) VT (*car*) rodar; **run into** VT FUS (*meet: person*) dar com, topar com; (: *trouble*) esbarrar em; (*collide with*) bater em; **run off** VI fugir; **run out** VI (*person*) sair correndo; (*liquid*) escorrer, esgotar-se; (*lease, passport*) caducar, vencer; (*money*) acabar; **run out of** VT FUS ficar sem; **run over** VT (*Aut*) atropelar ▶ VT FUS (*revise*) recapitular; **run through** VT FUS (*instructions*) recapitular; **run up** VT (*debt*) acumular ▶ VI: **to ~ up against** esbarrar em; **runaway** ADJ (*horse*) desembestado; (*truck*) desgovernado; (*person*) fugitivo

rung [rʌŋ] PP *of* **ring** ▶ N (*of ladder*) degrau *m*

runner ['rʌnər] N (*in race*) corredor(a) *m/f*; (: *horse*) corredor *m*; (*on sledge*) patim *m*, lâmina; (*for drawer*) corrediça; **runner bean** (*BRIT*) N (*Bot*) vagem *f* (*BR*), feijão *m* verde (*PT*); **runner-up** N segundo(-a) colocado(-a)

running ['rʌnɪŋ] N (*sport, race*) corrida; (*of business*) direção *f* ▶ ADJ (*water*) corrente; (*commentary*) contínuo, seguido; **6 days ~** 6 dias seguidos *or* consecutivos; **to be in/ out of the ~ for sth** disputar algo/ estar fora da disputa por algo

runny ['rʌnɪ] ADJ aguado; (*egg*) mole; **to have a ~ nose** estar com coriza, estar com o nariz escorrendo

run-up N: **~ to sth** (*election etc*) período que antecede algo; **during** *or* **in the ~ to** nas vésperas de

runway ['rʌnweɪ] N (*Aviat*) pista (de decolagem *or* de pouso)

rupture ['rʌptʃər] N (*Med*) hérnia

rural ['ruərl] ADJ rural

rush [rʌʃ] N (*hurry*) pressa; (*Comm*) grande procura *or* demanda; (*Bot*) junco; (*current*) torrente *f*; (*of emotion*) ímpeto ▶ VT apressar ▶ VI apressar-se, precipitar-se; **rush hour** N rush *m* (*BR*), hora de ponta (*PT*)

Russia ['rʌʃə] N Rússia; **Russian** ADJ russo ▶ N russo(-a); (*Ling*) russo

rust [rʌst] N ferrugem *f* ▶ VI enferrujar

rusty ['rʌstɪ] ADJ enferrujado

ruthless ['ruːθlɪs] ADJ implacável, sem piedade

rye [raɪ] N centeio

S

Sabbath ['sæbəθ] N (Christian) domingo; (Jewish) sábado

sabotage ['sæbətɑ:ʒ] N sabotagem f ▶ VT sabotar

saccharin, saccharine ['sækərɪn] N sacarina

sachet ['sæʃeɪ] N sachê m

sack [sæk] N (bag) saco, saca ▶ VT (dismiss) despedir; (plunder) saquear; **to get the ~** ser demitido

sacred ['seɪkrɪd] ADJ sagrado

sacrifice ['sækrɪfaɪs] N sacrifício ▶ VT sacrificar

sad [sæd] ADJ triste; (deplorable) deplorável, triste

saddle ['sædl] N sela; (of cycle) selim m ▶ VT selar; **to ~ sb with sth** (inf: task, bill) pôr algo nas costas de alguém; (: responsibility) sobrecarregar alguém com algo

sadistic [sə'dɪstɪk] ADJ sádico

sadly ['sædlɪ] ADV tristemente; (regrettably) infelizmente; (mistaken, neglected) gravemente; **~ lacking (in)** muito carente (de)

sadness ['sædnɪs] N tristeza

safe [seɪf] ADJ seguro; (out of danger) fora de perigo; (unharmed) ileso, incólume ▶ N cofre m, caixa-forte f; **~ from** protegido de; **~ and sound** são e salvo; **(just) to be on the ~ side** por via das dúvidas; **safely** ADV com segurança, a salvo; (without mishap) sem perigo

safety ['seɪftɪ] N segurança; **safety belt** N cinto de segurança; **safety pin** N alfinete m de segurança

sag [sæg] VI (breasts) cair; (roof) afundar; (hem) desmanchar

sage [seɪdʒ] N salva; (man) sábio

Sagittarius [sædʒɪ'tɛərɪəs] N Sagitário

Sahara [sə'hɑːrə] N: **the ~ (Desert)** o Saara

said [sɛd] PT, PP of say

sail [seɪl] N (on boat) vela; (trip): **to go for a ~** dar um passeio de barco a vela ▶ VT (boat) governar ▶ VI (travel: ship) navegar, velejar; (: passenger) ir de barco; (Sport) velejar; (set off) zarpar; **they ~ed into Rio de Janeiro** entraram no porto do Rio de Janeiro; **sail through** VT FUS (fig) fazer com facilidade; **sailboat** (US) N barco a vela; **sailing** N (Sport) navegação f a vela, vela; **to go sailing** ir velejar

sailor ['seɪlər] N marinheiro, marujo

saint [seɪnt] N santo(-a)

sake [seɪk] N: **for the ~ of** por (causa de), em consideração a; **for sb's/sth's ~** pelo bem de alguém/algo

salad ['sæləd] N salada; **salad cream** (BRIT) N maionese f; **salad dressing** N tempero or molho da salada

S

salami [sə'lɑːmɪ] N salame m
salary ['sælərɪ] N salário
sale [seɪl] N venda; (at reduced prices) liquidação f, saldo; (auction) leilão m; **sales** NPL (total amount sold) vendas fpl; **"for ~"** "vende-se"; **on ~** à venda; **on ~ or return** em consignação; **sales assistant**, (US) **sales clerk** N vendedor(a) m/f
salmon ['sæmən] N INV salmão m
salon ['sælɔn] N (hairdressing salon) salão m (de cabeleireiro); (beauty salon) salão (de beleza)
saloon [sə'luːn] N (US) bar m, botequim m; (BRIT Aut) sedã m; (ship's lounge) salão m
salt [sɔːlt] N sal m ▶ VT salgar; **saltwater** ADJ de água salgada; **salty** ADJ salgado
salute [sə'luːt] N (greeting) saudação f; (of guns) salva; (Mil) continência ▶ VT saudar; (Mil) fazer continência a
salvage ['sælvɪdʒ] N (saving) salvamento, recuperação f; (things saved) salvados mpl ▶ VT salvar
same [seɪm] ADJ mesmo ▶ PRON: **the ~** o mesmo/a mesma; **the ~ book as** o mesmo livro que; **all** or **just the ~** apesar de tudo, mesmo assim; **the ~ to you!** igualmente!
sample ['sɑːmpl] N amostra ▶ VT (food, wine) provar, experimentar
sanction ['sæŋkʃən] N sanção f ▶ VT sancionar
sanctuary ['sæŋktjuərɪ] N (holy place) santuário; (refuge) refúgio, asilo; (for animals) reserva
sand [sænd] N areia; (beach: also: **~s**) praia ▶ VT (also: **~ down**) lixar
sandal ['sændl] N sandália
sand: sandbox ['sændbɔks] (US) N (for children) caixa de areia; **sand castle** N castelo de areia;

sandpaper ['sændpeɪpər] N lixa; **sandpit** ['sændpɪt] (BRIT) N (for children) caixa de areia; **sandstone** ['sændstəun] N arenito, grés m
sandwich ['sændwɪtʃ] N sanduíche m (BR), sandes f inv (PT) ▶ VT: **~ed between** encaixado entre
sandy ['sændɪ] ADJ arenoso; (colour) vermelho amarelado
sane [seɪn] ADJ são/sã do juízo; (sensible) ajuizado, sensato
sang [sæŋ] PT of **sing**
sanity ['sænɪtɪ] N sanidade f, equilíbrio mental; (common sense) juízo, sensatez f
sank [sæŋk] PT of **sink**
Santa Claus [sæntə'klɔːz] N Papai Noel m
sap [sæp] N (of plants) seiva ▶ VT (strength) esgotar, minar
sapphire ['sæfaɪər] N safira
sarcasm ['sɑːkæzm] N sarcasmo
sardine [sɑː'diːn] N sardinha
Sardinia [sɑː'dɪnɪə] N Sardenha
sat [sæt] PT, PP of **sit**
satchel ['sætʃl] N sacola
satellite ['sætəlaɪt] N satélite m; **satellite dish** N antena parabólica; **satellite television** N televisão f via satélite
satin ['sætɪn] N cetim m ▶ ADJ acetinado
satire ['sætaɪər] N sátira
satisfaction [sætɪs'fækʃən] N satisfação f; (refund, apology etc) compensação f; **satisfactory** ADJ satisfatório
satisfy ['sætɪsfaɪ] VT satisfazer; (convince) convencer, persuadir
Saturday ['sætədɪ] N sábado
sauce [sɔːs] N molho; (sweet) calda; **saucepan** N panela (BR), caçarola (PT)
saucer ['sɔːsər] N pires m inv

Saudi ['saudɪ] ADJ, N (also:
~ **Arabia**) Arábia Saudita;
(also: ~ **Arabian**) saudita m/f
sauna ['sɔːnə] N sauna
sausage ['sɔsɪdʒ] N salsicha,
linguiça; (cold meat) frios mpl;
sausage roll N folheado de
salsicha
savage ['sævɪdʒ] ADJ (cruel, fierce)
cruel, feroz; (primitive) selvagem
▶ N selvagem m/f
save [seɪv] VT (rescue, Comput)
salvar; (money) poupar,
economizar; (time) ganhar; (Sport)
impedir; (avoid: trouble) evitar;
(keep: seat) guardar ▶ VI (also: ~ **up**)
poupar ▶ N (Sport) salvamento
▶ PREP salvo, exceto
saw [sɔː] (pt **sawed**, pp **sawed** or
sawn) PT of **see** ▶ N (tool) serra
▶ VT serrar; **sawdust** N serragem f,
pó m de serra
saxophone ['sæksəfəun] N
saxofone m
say [seɪ] (pt, pp **said**) N: **to have
one's ~** exprimir sua opinião,
vender seu peixe (inf) ▶ VT dizer,
falar; **to have** or **some ~ in sth**
opinar sobre algo, ter que ver com
algo; **could you ~ that again?**
poderia repetir?; **that is to ~** ou
seja; **saying** N ditado, provérbio
scab [skæb] N casca, crosta (de
ferida); (pej) fura-greve m/f inv
scald [skɔːld] N escaldadura ▶ VT
escaldar, queimar
scale [skeɪl] N escala; (of fish)
escama; (of salaries, fees etc) tabela
▶ VT (mountain) escalar; **scales** NPL
(for weighing) balança; **~ of
charges** tarifa, lista de preços;
scale down VT reduzir
scallop ['skɔləp] N (Zool) vieira,
venera; (Sewing) barra, arremate m

scalp [skælp] N couro cabeludo
▶ VT escalpar
scam [skæm] (inf) N maracutaia,
falcatrua
scampi ['skæmpɪ] NPL camarões
mpl fritos
scan [skæn] VT (examine)
esquadrinhar, perscrutar; (glance
at quickly) passar uma vista de
olhos por; (TV, Radar) explorar
▶ N (Med) exame m
scandal ['skændl] N escândalo;
(gossip) fofocas fpl; (fig: disgrace)
vergonha
Scandinavian [skændɪ'neɪvɪən]
ADJ, N escandinavo(-a)
scanner ['skænə'] N (Med, Comput)
scanner m
scapegoat ['skeɪpgəut] N bode m
expiatório
scar [skɑː] N cicatriz f ▶ VT marcar
(com uma cicatriz)
scarce [skɛəs] ADJ escasso, raro;
to make o.s. ~ (inf) dar o fora, cair
fora; **scarcely** ADV mal, quase não;
(barely) apenas
scare [skɛə'] N susto; (panic)
pânico ▶ VT assustar; **to ~ sb stiff**
deixar alguém morrendo de medo;
bomb ~ alarme de bomba; **scare
away** VT espantar; **scare off** VT =
scare away; **scarecrow** N
espantalho; **scared** ADJ: **to be
scared** estar assustado or com
medo
scarf [skɑːf] (pl **scarfs** or **scarves**)
N cachecol m; (square) lenço (de
cabeça)
scarlet ['skɑːlɪt] ADJ escarlate
scary ['skɛərɪ] (inf) ADJ
assustador(a)
scatter ['skætə'] VT espalhar;
(put to flight) dispersar ▶ VI
espalhar-se

s

scene [si:n] N (*Theatre, fig*) cena; (*of crime, accident*) cenário; (*sight*) vista, panorama m; (*fuss*) escândalo; **scenery** ['si:nərɪ] N (*Theatre*) cenário; (*landscape*) paisagem f; **scenic** ADJ pitoresco

scent [sɛnt] N perfume m; (*smell*) aroma; (*track, fig*) pista, rastro

schedule [(BRIT) 'ʃɛdju:l, (US) 'skɛdju:l] N (*of trains*) horário; (*of events*) programa m; (*list*) lista ▶ VT (*timetable*) planejar; (*visit*) marcar (a hora de); **on ~** na hora, sem atraso; **to be ahead of/behind ~** estar adiantado/atrasado

scheme [ski:m] N (*plan, plot*) maquinação f; (*pension scheme etc*) projeto; (*arrangement*) arranjo ▶ VI conspirar

scholar ['skɔlər] N aluno(-a), estudante m/f; (*learned person*) sábio(-a), erudito(-a); **scholarship** N erudição f; (*grant*) bolsa de estudos

school [sku:l] N escola; (*secondary school*) colégio; (*US: university*) universidade f ▶ CPD escolar; **schoolboy** N aluno; **schoolchildren** NPL alunos mpl; **schoolgirl** N aluna; **schoolteacher** N professor(a) m/f

science ['saɪəns] N ciência; **science fiction** N ficção f científica; **scientific** [saɪən'tɪfɪk] ADJ científico; **scientist** N cientista m/f

scissors ['sɪzəz] NPL tesoura; **a pair of ~** uma tesoura

scold [skəuld] VT ralhar

scone [skɔn] N *bolinho de trigo*

scoop [sku:p] N colherona; (*for flour etc*) pá f; (*Press*) furo (jornalístico); **scoop out** VT escavar; **scoop up** VT recolher

scooter ['sku:tər] N (*also*: **motor ~**) lambreta; (*toy*) patinete m

scope [skəup] N liberdade f de ação; (*of plan, undertaking*) âmbito; (*of person*) competência; (*opportunity*) oportunidade f

score [skɔːr] N (*points etc*) escore m, contagem f; (*Mus*) partitura; (*twenty*) vintena ▶ VT (*goal, point*) fazer; (*mark*) marcar, entalhar; (*success*) alcançar ▶ VI (*in game*) marcar; (*Football*) marcar or fazer um gol; (*keep score*) marcar o escore; **on that ~** a esse respeito, por esse motivo; **~s of** (*fig*) um monte de; **to ~ 6 out of 10** tirar nota 6 num total de 10; **score out** VT riscar; **scoreboard** N marcador m, placar m

scorn [skɔːn] N desprezo ▶ VT desprezar, rejeitar

Scorpio ['skɔːpɪəu] N Escorpião m

Scot [skɔt] N escocês(-esa) m/f

Scotch [skɔtʃ] N uísque m (BR) or whisky m (PT) escocês

Scotland ['skɔtlənd] N Escócia; **Scots** ADJ escocês(-esa); **Scotsman** irreg N escocês m; **Scotswoman** irreg N escocesa; **Scottish** ADJ escocês(-esa)

scout [skaut] N (*Mil*) explorador m, batedor m; (*also*: **boy ~**) escoteiro; **girl ~** (*US*) escoteira; **scout around** VI explorar

scowl [skaul] VI franzir a testa; **to ~ at sb** olhar de cara feia para alguém

scramble ['skræmbl] N (*climb*) escalada (difícil); (*struggle*) luta ▶ VI: **to ~ out/through** conseguir sair com dificuldade; **to ~ for** lutar por; **scrambled eggs** NPL ovos mpl mexidos

scrap [skræp] N (*of paper*) pedacinho; (*of material*) fragmento; (*fig: of truth*) mínimo; (*fight*) rixa, luta; (*also*: **~ iron**) ferro velho, sucata ▶ VT sucatar, jogar no ferro

velho; (*fig*) descartar, abolir ▶ vi
brigar; **scraps** NPL (*leftovers*)
sobras *fpl*, restos *mpl*; **scrapbook**
N álbum *m* de recortes

scrape [skreɪp] N (*fig*): **to get into
a ~** meter-se numa enrascada ▶ vt
raspar; (*also*: **~ against**: *hand, car*)
arranhar, roçar ▶ vi: **to ~ through**
(*in exam*) passar raspando; **scrape
together** vt (*money*) juntar com
dificuldade

scrap paper N papel *m* de
rascunho

scratch [skrætʃ] N arranhão *m*;
(*from claw*) arranhadura ▶ cpd:
~ team time *m* improvisado,
escrete *m* ▶ vt (*rub*) coçar; (*with
claw, nail*) arranhar, unhar;
(*damage*) arranhar ▶ vi coçar(-se);
to start from ~ partir do zero;
to be up to ~ estar à altura (das
circunstâncias)

scream [skri:m] N grito ▶ vi gritar

screen [skri:n] N (*Cinema, TV,
Comput*) tela (BR), ecrã *m* (PT);
(*movable*) biombo; (*fig*) cortina
▶ vt (*conceal*) esconder, tapar;
(*from the wind etc*) proteger; (*film*)
projetar; (*candidates etc, Med*)
examinar; **screenplay** N roteiro;
screensaver ['skri:nseɪvəʳ] N
protetor *m* de tela; **screenshot** N
(*Comput*) captura de tela

screw [skru:] N parafuso ▶ vt
aparafusar; (*also*: **~ in**) apertar,
atarraxar; **screw up** vt (*paper etc*)
amassar; **to ~ up one's eyes**
franzir os olhos; **screwdriver** N
chave *f* de fenda *or* de parafuso

scribble ['skrɪbl] N garrancho
▶ vt escrevinhar ▶ vi rabiscar

script [skrɪpt] N (*Cinema etc*)
roteiro, script *m*; (*writing*) escrita,
caligrafia

scroll [skrəul] N rolo de
pergaminho

scrub [skrʌb] N mato, cerrado ▶ vt
esfregar; (*inf*) cancelar, eliminar

scruffy ['skrʌfɪ] ADJ desmazelado

scrutiny ['skru:tɪnɪ] N escrutínio,
exame *m* cuidadoso

sculptor ['skʌlptəʳ] N escultor(a)
m/f

sculpture ['skʌlptʃəʳ] N escultura

scum [skʌm] N (*on liquid*) espuma;
(*pej: people*) ralé *f*, gentinha

scurry ['skʌrɪ] vi sair correndo;
scurry off vi sair correndo, dar
no pé

sea [si:] N mar *m* ▶ cpd do mar,
marino; **on the ~** (*boat*) no mar;
(*town*) junto ao mar; **to go by ~**
viajar por mar; **out to sea** *or* **at ~** em
alto mar; **to be all at ~** (*fig*) estar
confuso *or* desorientado; **seafood**
N mariscos *mpl*; **seagull** N gaivota

seal [si:l] N (*animal*) foca; (*stamp*)
selo ▶ vt fechar; **seal off** vt fechar

sea level N nível *m* do mar

seam [si:m] N costura; (*where
edges meet*) junta; (*of coal*) veio,
filão *m*

search [sə:tʃ] N busca, procura;
(*Comput*) busca; (*inspection*) exame
m, investigação *f* ▶ vt (*look in*)
procurar em; (*examine*) examinar;
(*person, place*) revistar ▶ vi: **to ~ for**
procurar; **in ~ of** à procura de;
search through vt fus dar busca
em; **search engine** N (*on Internet*)
site *m* de busca; **search party** N
equipe *f* de salvamento

sea: seashore N praia, beira-mar *f*,
litoral *m*; **seasick** ADJ: **to be** *or* **get
seasick** enjoar; **seaside** N praia;
seaside resort N balneário

season ['si:zn] N (*of year*) estação *f*;
(*sporting etc*) temporada; (*of films*

etc) série *f* ▶ vt (*food*) temperar;
to be in/out of ~ (*fruit*) estar na
época/fora de época; **season
ticket** N bilhete *m* de temporada
seat [siːt] N (*in bus, train: place*)
assento; (*chair*) cadeira; (*Pol*)
lugar *m*, cadeira; (*buttocks*)
traseiro, nádegas *fpl*; (*of trousers*)
fundilhos *mpl* ▶ vt sentar; (*have
room for*) ter capacidade para; **to be
~ed** estar sentado; **seat belt** N
cinto de segurança
sea water N água do mar
seaweed ['siːwiːd] N alga marinha
sec. ABBR (= *second*) seg.
secluded [sɪ'kluːdɪd] ADJ (*place*)
afastado; (*life*) solitário
second¹ [sɪ'kɒnd] (BRIT) VT
(*employee*) transferir
temporariamente
second² ['sɛkənd] ADJ segundo
▶ ADV (*in race etc*) em segundo lugar
▶ N segundo; (*Aut: also:* **~ gear**)
segunda; (*Comm*) artigo defeituoso;
(BRIT *Sch: degree*) uma qualificação boa
mas sem distinção ▶ vt (*motion*)
apoiar, secundar; **secondary** ADJ
secundário; **secondary school** N
escola secundária, colégio

> Na Grã-Bretanha, uma
> **secondary school** é um
> estabelecimento de ensino para
> alunos de 11 a 18 anos, alguns dos
> quais interrompem os estudos
> aos 16 anos.

second: second-class ADV em
segunda classe; **secondhand** ADJ
de (BR) *or* em (PT) segunda mão,
usado; **second hand** N (*on clock*)
ponteiro de segundos; **secondly**
ADV em segundo lugar;
second-rate ADJ de segunda
categoria; **second thoughts** NPL,
(US) **second thought**: **to have**

**second thoughts (about doing
sth)** pensar duas vezes (antes de
fazer algo); **on second thoughts**
pensando bem
secrecy ['siːkrəsɪ] N sigilo
secret ['siːkrɪt] ADJ secreto ▶ N
segredo
secretary ['sɛkrətərɪ] N
secretário(-a); (BRIT *Pol*): **S~ of
State** Ministro(-a) de Estado
secretive ['siːkrətɪv] ADJ sigiloso,
reservado
section ['sɛkʃən] N seção *f*; (*part*)
parte *f*, porção *f*; (*of document*)
parágrafo, artigo; (*of opinion*) setor
m; **cross-~** corte *m* transversal
sector ['sɛktəʳ] N setor *m*
secular ['sɛkjuləʳ] ADJ (*priest*)
secular; (*music, society*) leigo
secure [sɪ'kjuəʳ] ADJ (*safe*) seguro;
(*firmly fixed*) firme, rígido ▶ vt (*fix*)
prender; (*get*) conseguir, obter;
security N segurança; (*for loan*)
fiança, garantia; **security guard** N
segurança *m/f*
sedate [sɪ'deɪt] ADJ calmo ▶ vt
sedar, tratar com calmantes;
sedative N calmante *m*, sedativo
seduce [sɪ'djuːs] vt seduzir;
seductive ADJ sedutor(a)
see [siː] (*pt* **saw**, *pp* **seen**) vt ver;
(*understand*) entender; (*accompany*):
to ~ sb to the door acompanhar *or*
levar alguém até a porta ▶ vi ver;
(*find out*) achar ▶ N sé *f*, sede *f*; **to ~
that** (*ensure*) assegurar que; **~ you
soon/later/tomorrow!** até logo/
mais tarde/amanhã!; **see about** vt
FUS tratar de; **see off** vt despedir-se
de; **see through** vt FUS enxergar
através de ▶ vt levar a cabo; **see to**
vt FUS providenciar
seed [siːd] N semente *f*; (*sperm*)
esperma *m*; (*fig: gen pl*) germe *m*;

(*Tennis*) pré-selecionado(-a); **to go to ~** produzir sementes; (*fig*) deteriorar-se

seeing ['si:ɪŋ] CONJ: **~ (that)** visto (que), considerando (que)

seek [si:k] (*pt, pp* **sought**) VT procurar; (*post*) solicitar

seem [si:m] VI parecer; **there ~s to be ...** parece que há ...

seen [si:n] PP *of* **see**

seesaw ['si:sɔ:] N gangorra, balanço

segment ['sɛgmənt] N segmento; (*of orange*) gomo

seize [si:z] VT agarrar, pegar; (*power, hostage*) apoderar-se de, confiscar; (*territory*) tomar posse de; (*opportunity*) aproveitar; **seize on** VT FUS valer-se de; **seize up** VI (*Tech*) gripar; **seize upon** VT FUS = **seize on**; **seizure** N (*Med*) ataque *m*, acesso; (*Jur, of power*) confisco, embargo

seldom ['sɛldəm] ADV raramente

select [sɪ'lɛkt] ADJ seleto, fino ▶ VT escolher, selecionar; (*Sport*) selecionar, escalar; **selection** N seleção *f*, escolha; (*Comm*) sortimento

self [sɛlf] (*pl* **selves**) PRON *see* **herself, himself, itself, myself, oneself, ourselves, themselves, yourself** ▶ N: **the ~** o eu; **self-assured** ADJ seguro de si; **self-catering** (BRIT) ADJ (*flat*) com cozinha; (*holiday*) em casa alugada; **self-centred**, (US) **self-centered** ADJ egocêntrico; **self-confidence** N autoconfiança, confiança em si; **self-conscious** ADJ inibido, constrangido; **self-control** N autocontrole *m*, autodomínio; **self-defence**, (US) **self-defense** N legítima defesa,

autodefesa; **in self-defence** em legítima defesa; **self-employed** ADJ autônomo; **self-harm** N autoimolação *f*; **self-interest** N egoísmo; **selfish** ADJ egoísta; **self-pity** N pena de si mesmo; **self-respect** N amor *m* próprio; **self-service** ADJ de autosserviço

sell [sɛl] (*pt, pp* **sold**) VT vender; (*fig*): **to ~ sb an idea** convencer alguém de uma ideia ▶ VI vender-se; **to ~ at** *or* **for £10** vender a *or* por £10; **sell off** VT liquidar; **sell out** VI vender todo o estoque ▶ VT: **the tickets are all sold out** todos os ingressos já foram vendidos; **sell-by date** N vencimento; **seller** N vendedor(a) *m/f*

selves [sɛlvz] PL *of* **self**

semi... [sɛmɪ] PREFIX semi..., meio...; **semicircle** N semicírculo; **semidetached, semidetached house** (BRIT) N (*casa*) geminada

seminar ['sɛmɪnɑ:ʳ] N seminário

senate ['sɛnɪt] N senado; **senator** N senador(a) *m/f*

send [sɛnd] (*pt, pp* **sent**) VT mandar, enviar; (*dispatch*) expedir, remeter; (*transmit*) transmitir; **send away** VT (*letter, goods*) expedir, mandar; (*unwelcome visitor*) mandar embora; **send away for** VT FUS encomendar, pedir pelo correio; **send back** VT devolver, mandar de volta; **send for** VT FUS mandar buscar; (*by post*) pedir pelo correio, encomendar; **send off** VT (*goods*) despachar, expedir; (BRIT Sport: *player*) expulsar; **send on** VT (BRIT: *letter*) remeter; (*luggage etc: in advance*) mandar com antecedência; **send out** VT (*invitation*) distribuir;

(*signal*) emitir; **send up** VT (*person, price*) fazer subir; (BRIT: *parody*) parodiar; **sender** N remetente *m/f*; **send-off** N: **a good send-off** uma boa despedida

senior ['si:nɪəʳ] ADJ (*older*) mais velho *or* idoso; (*on staff*) mais antigo; (*of higher rank*) superior; **senior citizen** N idoso(-a)

sensation [sɛn'seɪʃən] N sensação *f*; **sensational** ADJ sensacional; (*headlines, result*) sensacionalista

sense [sɛns] N sentido; (*feeling*) sensação *f*; (*good sense*) bom senso ▶ VT sentir, perceber; **it makes ~** faz sentido; **senseless** ADJ insensato, estúpido; (*unconscious*) sem sentidos, inconsciente; **sensible** ADJ sensato, de bom senso; (*reasonable: price*) razoável; (: *advice, decision*) sensato

sensitive ['sɛnsɪtɪv] ADJ sensível; (*fig: touchy*) suscetível

sensual ['sɛnsjuəl] ADJ sensual

sensuous ['sɛnsjuəs] ADJ sensual

sent [sɛnt] PT, PP *of* **send**

sentence ['sɛntəns] N (*Ling*) frase *f*, oração *f*; (*Jur*) sentença ▶ VT: **to ~ sb to death/to 5 years** condenar alguém à morte/a 5 anos de prisão

sentiment ['sɛntɪmənt] N sentimento; (*opinion: also pl*) opinião *f*; **sentimental** [sɛntɪ'mɛntl] ADJ sentimental

separate [*adj* 'sɛprɪt, *vt, vi* 'sɛpəreɪt] ADJ separado; (*distinct*) diferente ▶ VT separar; (*part*) dividir ▶ VI separar-se; **separately** ADV separadamente

September [sɛp'tɛmbəʳ] N setembro

septic ['sɛptɪk] ADJ sético; (*wound*) infeccionado

sequel ['si:kwl] N consequência, resultado; (*of film, story*) continuação *f*

sequence ['si:kwəns] N série *f*, sequência; (*Cinema*) série

sequin ['si:kwɪn] N lantejoula, paetê *m*

sergeant ['sɑ:dʒənt] N sargento

serial ['sɪərɪəl] N seriado; **serial killer** N assassino(-a) em série, serial killer *m/f*; **serial number** N número de série

series ['sɪərɪz] N INV série *f*

serious ['sɪərɪəs] ADJ sério; (*matter*) importante; (*illness*) grave; **seriously** ADV a sério, com seriedade; (*hurt*) gravemente

sermon ['sə:mən] N sermão *m*

servant ['sə:vənt] N empregado(-a); (*fig*) servidor(a) *m/f*

serve [sə:v] VT servir; (*customer*) atender; (*subj: train*) passar por; (*apprenticeship*) fazer; (*prison term*) cumprir ▶ VI (*at table*) servir-se; (*Tennis*) sacar; (*be useful*): **to ~ as/ for/to do** servir como/para/para fazer ▶ N (*Tennis*) saque *m*; **it ~s him right** é bem feito para ele; **serve out** VT (*food*) servir; **serve up** VT = **serve out**; **server** ['sə:vəʳ] N (*Comput*) servidor *m*

service ['sə:vɪs] N serviço; (*Rel*) culto; (*Aut*) revisão *f*; (*Tennis*) saque *m*; (*also*: **dinner ~**) aparelho de jantar ▶ VT (*car, washing machine*) fazer a revisão de, revisar; **the Services** NPL (*army, navy etc*) as Forças Armadas; **to be of ~ to sb** ser útil a alguém; **service area** N (*on motorway*) posto de gasolina com bar, restaurante etc; **service charge** (BRIT) N serviço; **serviceman** *irreg* N militar *m*; **service station** N posto de gasolina (BR), estação *f* de serviço (PT)

serviette [sə:vɪˈɛt] (BRIT) N guardanapo

session [ˈsɛʃən] N sessão f; **to be in ~** estar reunido em sessão

set [sɛt] (pt, pp **set**) N (collection of things) jogo; (radio set, TV set) aparelho; (of utensils) bateria de cozinha; (of cutlery) talher m; (of books) coleção f; (group of people) grupo; (Tennis) set m; (Theatre, Cinema) cenário; (Hairdressing) penteado; (Math) conjunto ▶ ADJ fixo; (ready) pronto ▶ VT pôr, colocar; (table) pôr; (price) fixar; (rules etc) estabelecer, decidir; (record) estabelecer; (time) marcar; (adjust) ajustar; (task, exam) passar ▶ VI (sun) pôr-se; (jam, jelly, concrete) endurecer, solidificar-se; **to be ~ on doing sth** estar decidido a fazer algo; **to ~ to music** musicar, pôr música em; **to ~ on fire** botar fogo em, incendiar; **to ~ free** libertar; **to ~ sth going** pôr algo em movimento; **set about** VT FUS começar com; **set aside** VT deixar de lado; **set back** VT (cost): **it ~ me back £50** custou £50; (in time): **to ~ sb back (by)** atrasar alguém (em); **set off** VI partir, ir indo ▶ VT (bomb) fazer explodir; (alarm) disparar; (chain of events) iniciar; (show up well) ressaltar; **set out** VI partir ▶ VT (arrange) colocar, dispor; (state) expor, explicar; **to ~ out to do sth** pretender fazer algo; **set up** VT fundar, estabelecer; **setback** N revés m, contratempo; **set menu** N refeição f a preço fixo

settee [sɛˈtiː] N sofá m

setting [ˈsɛtɪŋ] N (background) cenário; (position) posição f; (of sun) pôr(do sol) m; (of jewel) engaste m

settle [ˈsɛtl] VT (argument, matter) resolver, esclarecer; (accounts) ajustar, liquidar; (Med: calm) acalmar, tranquilizar ▶ VI (dust etc) assentar; (calm down: children) acalmar-se; (also: **~ down**) instalar-se, estabilizar-se; **to ~ for sth** concordar em aceitar algo; **to ~ on sth** optar por algo; **settle in** VI instalar-se; **settle up** VI: **to ~ up with sb** ajustar as contas com alguém; **settlement** N (payment) liquidação f; (agreement) acordo, convênio; (village etc) povoado, povoação f

setup [ˈsɛtʌp] N (organization) organização f; (situation) situação f

seven [ˈsɛvn] NUM sete; **seventeen** [ˈsɛvnˈtiːn] NUM dezessete; **seventeenth** [sɛvnˈtiːnθ] NUM décimo sétimo; **seventh** [ˈsɛvnθ] NUM sétimo; **seventieth** [ˈsɛvntɪɪθ] NUM septuagésimo; **seventy** [ˈsɛvntɪ] NUM setenta

sever [ˈsɛvər] VT cortar; (relations) romper

several [ˈsɛvərl] ADJ, PRON vários(-as); **~ of us** vários de nós

severe [sɪˈvɪər] ADJ severo; (serious) grave; (hard) duro; (pain) intenso; (dress) austero

sew [səu] (pt **sewed**, pp **sewn**) VT coser, costurar; **sew up** VT coser, costurar

sewage [ˈsuːɪdʒ] N detritos mpl

sewer [ˈsuːər] N (cano do) esgoto, bueiro

sewing [ˈsəuɪŋ] N costura; **sewing machine** N máquina de costura

sewn [səun] PP of **sew**

sex [sɛks] N sexo; **sexist** ADJ sexista

s

sexual ['sɛksjuəl] ADJ sexual;
sexuality [sɛksju'ælɪtɪ] N
sexualidade f
sexy ['sɛksɪ] ADJ sexy
shabby ['ʃæbɪ] ADJ (person)
esfarrapado, maltrapilho; (clothes)
usado, surrado; (behaviour) indigno
shack [ʃæk] N choupana, barraca
shade [ʃeɪd] N sombra; (for lamp)
quebra-luz m; (of colour) tom m,
tonalidade f; (small quantity): **a ~
(more/too big)** um pouquinho
(mais/grande) ▶ VT dar sombra a;
(eyes) sombrear; **in the ~** à sombra
shadow ['ʃædəu] N sombra ▶ VT
(follow) seguir de perto (sem ser
visto)
shady ['ʃeɪdɪ] ADJ à sombra; (fig:
dishonest: person) suspeito,
duvidoso; (: deal) desonesto
shaft [ʃɑ:ft] N (of arrow, spear) haste
f; (Aut, Tech) eixo, manivela; (of mine,
of lift) poço; (of light) raio
shake [ʃeɪk] (pt shook, pp shaken)
VT sacudir; (building, confidence)
abalar; (surprise) surpreender ▶ VI
tremer; **to ~ hands with sb**
apertar a mão de alguém; **to ~
one's head** (in refusal etc) dizer não
com a cabeça; (in dismay) sacudir a
cabeça; **shake off** VT sacudir; (fig)
livrar-se de; **shake up** VT sacudir;
(fig) reorganizar; **shaky** ADJ (hand,
voice) trêmulo; (table) instável;
(building) abalado
shall [ʃæl] AUX VB: **I ~ go** irei; **~ I
open the door?** posso abrir a
porta?; **I'll get some, ~ I?** eu vou
pegar algum, está bem?
shallow ['ʃæləu] ADJ raso;
(breathing) fraco; (fig) superficial
sham [ʃæm] N fraude f, fingimento
▶ VT fingir, simular
shambles ['ʃæmblz] N confusão f

shame [ʃeɪm] N vergonha ▶ VT
envergonhar; **it is a ~ (that/to do)**
é (uma) pena (que/fazer); **what a ~!**
que pena!; **shameful** ADJ
vergonhoso; **shameless** ADJ sem
vergonha, descarado
shampoo [ʃæm'pu:] N xampu m
(BR), champô m (PT) ▶ VT lavar o
cabelo (com xampu or champô)
shandy ['ʃændɪ] N mistura de cerveja
com refresco gaseificado
shan't [ʃɑ:nt] = **shall not**
shape [ʃeɪp] N forma ▶ VT (form)
moldar; (sb's ideas) formar; (sb's life)
definir, determinar; **to take ~**
tomar forma; **shape up** VI (events)
desenrolar-se; (person) tomar jeito
share [ʃɛəʳ] N parte f; (contribution)
cota; (Comm) ação f ▶ VT dividir;
(have in common) compartilhar;
share out VI distribuir;
shareholder N acionista m/f
shark [ʃɑ:k] N tubarão m
sharp [ʃɑ:p] ADJ (razor, knife) afiado;
(point, features) pontiagudo;
(outline) definido, bem marcado;
(pain, voice) agudo; (taste) acre;
(Mus) desafinado; (contrast)
marcado; (quick-witted) perspicaz;
(dishonest) desonesto ▶ N (Mus)
sustenido ▶ ADV: **at 2 o'clock ~** às
2 (horas) em ponto; **sharpen** VT
afiar; (pencil) apontar, fazer a ponta
de; (fig) aguçar; **sharpener** N (also:
pencil sharpener) apontador m
(BR), apara-lápis m inv (PT); **sharply**
ADV (abruptly) bruscamente; (clearly)
claramente; (harshly) severamente
shatter ['ʃætəʳ] VT despedaçar,
estilhaçar; (fig: ruin) destruir,
acabar com; (: upset) arrasar ▶ VI
despedaçar-se, estilhaçar-se
shave [ʃeɪv] VT barbear, fazer a
barba de ▶ VI fazer a barba,

barbear-se ▶N: **to have a ~** fazer a barba; **shaver** N barbeador *m*; **electric shaver** barbeador elétrico; **shaving cream** N creme *m* de barbear; **shaving foam** N espuma de barbear

shawl [ʃɔːl] N xale *m*

she [ʃiː] PRON ela ▶PREFIX: **~-elephant** *etc* elefante *etc* fêmea

sheath [ʃiːθ] N bainha; (*contraceptive*) camisa-de-vênus *f*, camisinha

shed [ʃɛd] (*pt, pp* **shed**) N alpendre *m*, galpão *m* ▶VT (*skin*) mudar; (*load, leaves, fur*) perder; (*tears, blood*) derramar; (*workers*) despedir

she'd [ʃiːd] = **she had;** = **she would**

sheep [ʃiːp] N INV ovelha; **sheepdog** N cão *m* pastor; **sheepskin** N pele *f* de carneiro, pelego

sheer [ʃɪəʳ] ADJ (*utter*) puro, completo; (*steep*) íngreme, empinado; (*almost transparent*) fino, translúcido ▶ADV a pique

sheet [ʃiːt] N (*on bed*) lençol *m*; (*of paper*) folha; (*of glass, metal*) lâmina, chapa; (*of ice*) camada

sheik, sheikh [ʃeɪk] N xeque *m*

shelf [ʃelf] (*pl* **shelves**) N prateleira

shell [ʃɛl] N (*on beach*) concha; (*of egg, nut etc*) casca; (*explosive*) obus *m*; (*of building*) armação *f*, esqueleto ▶VT (*peas*) descascar; (*Mil*) bombardear

she'll [ʃiːl] = **she will;** = **she shall**

shellfish [ˈʃɛlfɪʃ] N INV crustáceo; (*as food*) frutos *mpl* do mar, mariscos *mpl*

shelter [ˈʃɛltəʳ] N (*building*) abrigo; (*protection*) refúgio ▶VT (*protect*) proteger; (*give lodging to*) abrigar ▶VI abrigar-se, refugiar-se

shepherd [ˈʃepəd] N pastor *m* ▶VT guiar, conduzir; **shepherd's pie** (*BRIT*) N empadão *m* de carne e batata

sheriff [ˈʃerɪf] (*US*) N xerife *m*

sherry [ˈʃerɪ] N (*vinho de*) Xerez *m*

she's [ʃiːz] = **she is;** = **she has**

Shetland [ˈʃetlənd] N (*also:* **the ~s, the ~ Isles**) as ilhas Shetland

shield [ʃiːld] N escudo, (*Sport*) escudo, brasão *m*; (*protection*) proteção *f* ▶VT: **to ~ (from)** proteger (contra)

shift [ʃɪft] N mudança; (*of work*) turno; (*of workers*) turma ▶VT transferir; (*remove*) tirar ▶VI mudar

shin [ʃɪn] N canela (da perna)

shine [ʃaɪn] (*pt, pp* **shone**) N brilho, lustre *m* ▶VI brilhar ▶VT (*shoes: pt, pp* **shined**) lustrar; **to ~ a torch on sth** apontar uma lanterna para algo

shingles [ˈʃɪŋɡlz] N (*Med*) herpes-zoster *m*

shiny [ˈʃaɪnɪ] ADJ brilhante, lustroso

ship [ʃɪp] N barco ▶VT (*goods*) embarcar; (*send*) transportar or mandar (por via marítima); **shipment** N carregamento; **shipping** N (*ships*) navios *mpl*; (*cargo*) transporte *m* de mercadorias (por via marítima); (*traffic*) navegação *f*; **shipwreck** N (*event*) malogro; (*ship*) naufrágio ▶VT: **to be shipwrecked** naufragar; **shipyard** N estaleiro

shirt [ʃəːt] N (*man's*) camisa; (*woman's*) blusa; **in ~ sleeves** em manga de camisa

shit [ʃɪt] (*!*) EXCL merda (*!*)

shiver [ˈʃɪvəʳ] N tremor *m*, arrepio ▶VI tremer, estremecer, tiritar

s

shock [ʃɔk] N (*impact*) choque m; (*Elec*) descarga; (*emotional*) comoção f, abalo; (*start*) susto, sobressalto; (*Med*) trauma m ▶ VT dar um susto em, chocar; (*offend*) escandalizar; **shocking** ADJ chocante, lamentável; (*outrageous*) revoltante, chocante

shoe [ʃuː] (*pt, pp* **shod**) N sapato; (*for horse*) ferradura ▶ VT (*horse*) ferrar; **shoelace** N cadarço, cordão m (de sapato); **shoe polish** N graxa de sapato; **shoeshop** N sapataria

shone [ʃɔn] PT, PP *of* **shine**

shook [ʃuk] PT *of* **shake**

shoot [ʃuːt] (*pt, pp* **shot**) N (*on branch, seedling*) broto ▶ VT disparar; (*kill*) matar à bala, balear; (*wound*) ferir à bala, balear; (*execute*) fuzilar; (*film*) filmar, rodar ▶ VI: **to ~ (at)** atirar (em); (*Football*) chutar; **shoot down** VT (*plane*) derrubar, abater; **shoot in** VI entrar correndo; **shoot out** VI sair correndo; **shoot up** VI (*fig*) subir vertiginosamente

shop [ʃɔp] N loja; (*workshop*) oficina ▶ VI (*also:* **go ~ping**) ir fazer compras; **shop assistant** (*BRIT*) N vendedor(a) m/f; **shopkeeper** N lojista m/f; **shoplifting** N furto (em lojas); **shopping** N (*goods*) compras fpl; **shopping bag** N bolsa (de compras); **shopping cart** (*US*) N carrinho de compras; **shopping centre**, (*US*) **shopping center** N shopping (center) m; **shopping mall** N shopping m; **shopping trolley** (*BRIT*) N carrinho de compras; **shop window** N vitrine f (*BR*), montra (*PT*)

shore [ʃɔːʳ] N (*of sea*) costa, praia; (*of lake*) margem f ▶ VT: **to ~ (up)** reforçar, escorar; **on ~** em terra

short [ʃɔːt] ADJ curto; (*in time*) breve, de curta duração; (*person*) baixo; (*curt*) seco, brusco; (*insufficient*) insuficiente, em falta; **to be ~ of sth** estar em falta de algo; **in ~** em resumo; **~ of doing …** a não ser fazer …; **everything ~ of …** tudo a não ser …; **it is ~ for** é a abreviatura de; **to cut ~** (*speech, visit*) encurtar; **to fall ~ of** não ser à altura de; **to run ~ of sth** ficar sem algo; **to stop ~** parar de repente; **to stop ~ of** chegar quase a; **shortage** N escassez f, falta; **shortbread** N biscoito amanteigado; **shortcoming** N defeito, imperfeição f, falha; **shortcrust pastry**, (*BRIT*) **short pastry** N massa amanteigada; **shortcut** N atalho; **shorten** VT encurtar; (*visit*) abreviar; **shorthand** (*BRIT*) N estenografia; **shortly** ADV em breve, dentro em pouco; **shorts** NPL: **(a pair of) shorts** um calção (*BR*), um short (*BR*), uns calções (*PT*); **short-sighted** (*BRIT*) ADJ míope; (*fig*) imprevidente; **short story** N conto; **short-tempered** ADJ irritadiço; **short-term** ADJ a curto prazo

shot [ʃɔt] PT, PP *of* **shoot** ▶ N (*of gun*) tiro; (*pellets*) chumbo; (*try, Football*) tentativa; (*injection*) injeção f; (*Phot*) fotografia; **to be a good/bad ~** (*person*) ter boa/má pontaria; **like a ~** como um relâmpago, de repente; **shotgun** N espingarda

should [ʃud] AUX VB: **I ~ go now** devo ir embora agora; **he ~ be there now** ele já deve ter chegado; **I ~ go if I were you** se eu fosse você eu iria; **I ~ like to** eu gostaria de

shoulder [ˈʃəuldəʳ] N ombro ▶ VT (*fig*) arcar com; **shoulder blade** N omoplata m

shouldn't ['ʃudnt] = **should not**

shout [ʃaut] N grito ▶ VT gritar ▶ VI (*also*: ~ **out**) gritar, berrar; **shout down** VT fazer calar com gritos

shove [ʃʌv] VT empurrar; (*inf*: *put*): **to ~ sth in** botar algo em; **shove off** VI (*inf*) dar o fora

shovel ['ʃʌvl] N pá f; (*mechanical*) escavadeira ▶ VT cavar com pá

show [ʃəu] (*pt* **showed**, *pp* **shown**) N (*of emotion*) demonstração f; (*semblance*) aparência; (*exhibition*) exibição f; (*Theatre*) espetáculo, representação f; (*Cinema*) sessão f ▶ VT mostrar; (*courage etc*) demonstrar, dar prova de; (*exhibit*) exibir, expor; (*depict*) ilustrar; (*film*) exibir ▶ VI mostrar-se; (*appear*) aparecer; **to be on ~** estar em exposição; **show in** VT mandar entrar; **show off** VI (*pej*) mostrar-se, exibir-se ▶ VT (*display*) exibir, mostrar; **show out** VT levar até a porta; **show up** VI (*stand out*) destacar-se; (*inf*: *turn up*) aparecer, pintar ▶ VT descobrir; **show business** N o mundo do espetáculo

shower ['ʃauər] N (*rain*) pancada de chuva; (*of stones etc*) chuva, enxurrada; (*also*: ~ **bath**) chuveiro ▶ VI tomar banho (de chuveiro) ▶ VT: **to ~ sb with** (*gifts etc*) cumular alguém de; **to have** or **take a ~** tomar banho (de chuveiro)

showing ['ʃəuɪŋ] N (*of film*) projeção f, exibição f

show jumping [-'dʒʌmpɪŋ] N hipismo

shown [ʃəun] PP *of* **show**

show-off (*inf*) N (*person*) exibicionista m/f, faroleiro(-a)

showpiece ['ʃəupi:s] N (*of exhibition etc*) obra mais importante

showroom ['ʃəurum] N sala de exposição

shrank [ʃræŋk] PT *of* **shrink**

shred [ʃrɛd] N (*gen pl*) tira, pedaço ▶ VT rasgar em tiras, retalhar; (*Culin*) desfiar, picar

shrewd [ʃru:d] ADJ perspicaz

shriek [ʃri:k] N grito ▶ VI gritar, berrar

shrimp [ʃrɪmp] N camarão m

shrine [ʃraɪn] N santuário

shrink [ʃrɪŋk] (*pt* **shrank**, *pp* **shrunk**) VI encolher; (*be reduced*) reduzir-se; (*also*: ~ **away**) encolher-se ▶ VT (*cloth*) fazer encolher ▶ N (*inf*, *pej*) psicanalista m/f; **to ~ from doing sth** não se atrever a fazer algo

shrivel ['ʃrɪvl] VT (*also*: ~ **up**: *dry*) secar; (: *crease*) enrugar ▶ VI secar-se; enrugar-se, murchar

Shrove Tuesday [ʃrəuv-] N terça-feira gorda

shrub [ʃrʌb] N arbusto

shrug [ʃrʌg] N encolhimento dos ombros ▶ VT, VI: **to ~ (one's shoulders)** encolher os ombros, dar de ombros (BR); **shrug off** VT negar a importância de

shrunk [ʃrʌŋk] PP *of* **shrink**

shudder ['ʃʌdər] N estremecimento, tremor m ▶ VI estremecer, tremer de medo

shuffle ['ʃʌfl] VT (*cards*) embaralhar ▶ VI: **to ~ (one's feet)** arrastar os pés

shun [ʃʌn] VT evitar, afastar-se de

shut [ʃʌt] (*pt*, *pp* **shut**) VT fechar ▶ VI fechar(-se); **shut down** VT, VI fechar; **shut off** VT cortar, interromper; **shut up** VI (*inf*: *keep* *quiet)* calar-se, calar a boca ▶ VT *(close)* fechar; *(silence)* calar; **shutter** N veneziana; *(Phot)* obturador *m*

shuttle ['ʃʌtl] N *(plane: also:* **~ service)** ponte f aérea; *(space shuttle)* ônibus *m* espacial

shuttlecock ['ʃʌtlkɔk] N peteca

shy [ʃaɪ] ADJ tímido; *(reserved)* reservado

sick [sɪk] ADJ *(ill)* doente; *(nauseated)* enjoado; *(humour)* negro; *(vomiting):* **to be ~** vomitar; **to feel ~** estar enjoado; **to be ~ of** *(fig)* estar cheio *or* farto de; **sickening** ADJ *(fig)* repugnante; **sick leave** N licença por doença; **sickly** ADJ doentio; *(causing nausea)* nauseante; **sickness** N doença, indisposição f; *(vomiting)* náusea, enjoo

side [saɪd] N lado; *(of body)* flanco; *(of lake)* margem f; *(aspect)* aspecto; *(team)* time *m* (BR), equipa (PT); *(of hill)* declive *m* ▶ CPD *(door, entrance)* lateral ▶ VI: **to ~ with sb** tomar o partido de alguém; **by the ~ of** ao lado de; **~ by ~** lado a lado, juntos; **from ~ to ~** para lá e para cá; **to take ~s with** pôr-se ao lado de; **sideboard** N aparador *m*; **sideboards** NPL (BRIT) = **sideburns**; **sideburns** NPL suíças fpl, costeletas fpl; **side effect** N efeito colateral; **sidelight** N *(Aut)* luz f lateral; **side order** N acompanhamento; **sidetrack** VT *(fig)* desviar (do seu propósito); **sidewalk** (US) N calçada; **sideways** ADV de lado

siege [siːdʒ] N sítio, assédio

sieve [sɪv] N peneira ▶ VT peneirar

sift [sɪft] VT peneirar; *(fig)* esquadrinhar, analisar minuciosamente

sigh [saɪ] N suspiro ▶ VI suspirar

sight [saɪt] N *(faculty)* vista, visão f; *(spectacle)* espetáculo; *(on gun)* mira ▶ VT avistar; **in ~** à vista; **on ~** *(shoot)* no local; **out of ~** longe dos olhos; **sightseeing** N turismo; **to go sightseeing** fazer turismo, passear

sign [saɪn] N *(with hand)* sinal *m*, aceno; *(indication)* indício; *(notice)* letreiro, tabuleta; *(written, of zodiac)* signo ▶ VT assinar; **to ~ sth over to sb** assinar a transferência de algo para alguém; **sign on** VI *(Mil)* alistar-se; (BRIT: *as unemployed)* cadastrar-se para receber auxílio-desemprego; *(for course)* inscrever-se ▶ VT *(Mil)* alistar; *(employee)* efetivar; **sign up** VI *(Mil)* alistar-se; *(for course)* inscrever-se ▶ VT recrutar

signal ['sɪɡnl] N sinal *m*, aviso ▶ VI *(also: Aut)* sinalizar, dar sinal ▶ VT *(person)* fazer sinais para; *(message)* transmitir

signature ['sɪɡnətʃəʳ] N assinatura

significance [sɪɡ'nɪfɪkəns] N importância; **significant** ADJ significativo; *(important)* importante

sign language N mímica, linguagem f através de sinais

silence ['saɪləns] N silêncio ▶ VT silenciar, impor silêncio a

silent ['saɪlənt] ADJ silencioso; *(not speaking)* calado; *(film)* mudo; **to keep** *or* **remain ~** manter-se em silêncio

silhouette [sɪluː'ɛt] N silhueta

silicon chip ['sɪlɪkən tʃɪp] N placa *or* chip *m* de silício

silk [sɪlk] N seda ▶ ADJ de seda

silly ['sɪlɪ] ADJ *(person)* bobo, idiota, imbecil; *(idea)* absurdo, ridículo

silver ['sɪlvə^r] N prata; (money) moedas fpl; (also: **~ware**) prataria ▶ ADJ de prata; **silver-plated** ADJ prateado, banhado a prata

SIM card ['sɪm-] N (Tel) cartão m SIM, chip m

similar ['sɪmɪlə^r] ADJ: **~ to** parecido com, semelhante a

simmer ['sɪmə^r] VI cozer em fogo lento, ferver lentamente

simple ['sɪmpl] ADJ simples inv; (foolish) ingênuo; **simply** ADV de maneira simples; (merely) simplesmente

simultaneous [sɪməl'teɪnɪəs] ADJ simultâneo

sin [sɪn] N pecado ▶ VI pecar

since [sɪns] ADV desde então, depois ▶ PREP desde ▶ CONJ (time) desde que; (because) porque, visto que, já que; **~ then** desde então; **(ever) ~ I arrived** desde que eu cheguei

sincere [sɪn'sɪə^r] ADJ sincero; **sincerely** ADV: **yours sincerely** (BRIT), **sincerely yours** (US) (at end of letter) atenciosamente

sing [sɪŋ] (pt **sang**, pp **sung**) VT, VI cantar

Singapore [sɪŋgə'pɔː^r] N Cingapura (no article)

singer ['sɪŋə^r] N cantor(a) m/f

singing ['sɪŋɪŋ] N canto; (songs) canções fpl

single ['sɪŋgl] ADJ único, só; (unmarried) solteiro; (not double) simples inv ▶ N (BRIT: also: **~ ticket**) passagem f de ida; (record) compacto; **single out** VT (choose) escolher; (distinguish) distinguir; **single file** N: **in single file** em fila indiana; **single-handed** ADV sem ajuda, sozinho; **single-minded** ADJ determinado; **single room** N quarto individual

singular ['sɪŋgjulə^r] ADJ (odd) esquisito; (outstanding) extraordinário, excepcional; (Ling) singular ▶ N (Ling) singular m

sinister ['sɪnɪstə^r] ADJ sinistro

sink [sɪŋk] (pt **sank**, pp **sunk**) N pia ▶ VT (ship) afundar; (foundations) escavar ▶ VI afundar-se; (heart) partir; (spirits) ficar deprimido; (also: **~ back, ~ down**) cair or mergulhar gradativamente; **to ~ sth into** enterrar algo em; **sink in** VI (fig) penetrar

sinus ['saɪnəs] N (Anat) seio (paranasal)

sip [sɪp] N gole m ▶ VT sorver, beberricar

sir [sə^r] N senhor m; **S~ John Smith** Sir John Smith; **yes, ~** sim, senhor

siren ['saɪərn] N sirena

sirloin ['sə:lɔɪn] N lombo de vaca

sister ['sɪstə^r] N irmã f; (BRIT: nurse) enfermeira-chefe f; (nun) freira; **sister-in-law** N cunhada

sit [sɪt] (pt, pp **sat**) VI sentar-se; (be sitting) estar sentado; (assembly) reunir-se; (for painter) posar ▶ VT (exam) prestar; **sit down** VI sentar-se; **sit on** VT FUS assistir a; **sit up** VI (after lying) levantar-se; (straight) endireitar-se; (not go to bed) aguardar acordado, velar

sitcom ['sɪtkɔm] N ABBR (= situation comedy) comédia de costumes

site [saɪt] N local m, sítio; (also: **building ~**) lote m (de terreno) ▶ VT situar, localizar

sitting ['sɪtɪŋ] N (in canteen) turno; **sitting room** N sala de estar

situation [sɪtju'eɪʃən] N situação f; (job) posição f; (location) local m; **"~s vacant/wanted"**

S

(BRIT) "empregos oferecem-se/procuraram"

six [sɪks] NUM seis; **sixteen** NUM dezesseis; **sixteenth** [sɪks'tiːnθ] NUM décimo sexto; **sixth** NUM sexto; **sixtieth** ['sɪkstɪɪθ] NUM sexagésimo; **sixty** NUM sessenta

size [saɪz] N tamanho; (extent) extensão f; (of clothing) tamanho, medida; (of shoes) número; **size up** VT avaliar, formar uma opinião sobre; **sizeable** ADJ considerável, importante

sizzle ['sɪzl] VI chiar

skate [skeɪt] N patim m; (fish: pl inv) arraia ▶ VI patinar; **skateboard** N skate m, patim-tábua m; **skating** N patinação f; **skating rink** N rinque m de patinação

skeleton ['skɛlɪtn] N esqueleto; (Tech) armação f; (outline) esquema m, esboço

sketch [skɛtʃ] N (drawing) desenho; (outline) esboço, croqui m; (Theatre) quadro, esquete m ▶ VT desenhar, esboçar; (ideas: also: **~ out**) esboçar

skewer ['skjuːər] N espetinho

ski [skiː] N esqui m ▶ VI esquiar; **ski boot** N bota de esquiar

skid [skɪd] N derrapagem f ▶ VI deslizar; (Aut) derrapar

skier ['skiːər] N esquiador(a) m/f

skiing ['skiːɪŋ] N esqui m

skilful ['skɪlful], (US) **skillful** ADJ habilidoso, jeitoso

ski lift N ski lift m

skill [skɪl] N habilidade f, perícia; (for work) técnica; **skilled** ADJ hábil, perito; (worker) especializado, qualificado

skim [skɪm] VT (milk) desnatar; (glide over) roçar ▶ VI: **to ~ through** (book) folhear; **skimmed milk** N leite m desnatado

skin [skɪn] N pele f; (of fruit, vegetable) casca ▶ VT (fruit etc) descascar; (animal) tirar a pele de; **skinny** ADJ magro, descarnado

skip [skɪp] N salto, pulo; (BRIT: container) balde m ▶ VI saltar; (with rope) pular corda ▶ VT (pass over) omitir, saltar; (miss) deixar de

skipper ['skɪpər] N capitão m

skipping rope ['skɪpɪŋ-] (BRIT) N corda (de pular)

skirt [skəːt] N saia ▶ VT orlar, circundar; **skirting board** (BRIT) N rodapé m

skull [skʌl] N caveira; (Anat) crânio

skunk [skʌŋk] N gambá m

sky [skaɪ] N céu m; **skyscraper** N arranha-céu m

slab [slæb] N (stone) bloco; (flat) laje f; (of cake) fatia grossa

slack [slæk] ADJ (loose) frouxo; (slow) lerdo; (careless) descuidoso, desmazelado; **slacks** NPL (trousers) calça (BR), calças fpl (PT)

slain [sleɪn] PP of **slay**

slam [slæm] VT (door) bater or fechar (com violência); (throw) atirar violentamente; (criticize) malhar, criticar ▶ VI fechar-se (com violência)

slander ['slɑːndər] N calúnia, difamação f

slang [slæŋ] N gíria; (jargon) jargão m

slant [slɑːnt] N declive m, inclinação f; (fig) ponto de vista

slap [slæp] N tapa m or f ▶ VT dar um(a) tapa em; (paint etc): **to ~ sth on sth** passar algo em algo descuidadamente ▶ ADV diretamente, exatamente

slash [slæʃ] VT cortar, talhar; (fig: prices) cortar

slate [sleɪt] N ardósia ▶ VT (fig: criticize) criticar duramente, arrasar

slaughter ['slɔ:tə^r] N (of animals) matança; (of people) carnificina ▶ VT abater; matar, massacrar; **slaughterhouse** N matadouro

slave [sleɪv] N escravo(-a) ▶ VI (also: **~ away**) trabalhar como escravo; **slavery** N escravidão f

slay [sleɪ] (pt **slew**, pp **slain**) VT (literary) matar

sleazy ['sli:zɪ] ADJ sórdido

sledge [slɛdʒ] N trenó m

sleek [sli:k] ADJ (hair, fur) macio, lustroso; (car, boat) aerodinâmico

sleep [sli:p] (pt, pp **slept**) N sono ▶ VI dormir; **to go to ~** dormir, adormecer; **sleep around** VI ser promíscuo sexualmente; **sleep in** VI (oversleep) dormir demais; **sleeper** N (Rail: train) vagão-leitos m (BR), carruagem-camas (PT); **sleeping bag** N saco de dormir; **sleeping car** N vagão-leitos m (BR), carruagem-camas f (PT); **sleeping pill** N pílula para dormir; **sleepy** ADJ sonolento; (fig) morto

sleet [sli:t] N chuva com neve or granizo

sleeve [sli:v] N manga; (of record) capa

sleigh [sleɪ] N trenó m

slender ['slɛndə^r] ADJ esbelto, delgado; (means) escasso, insuficiente

slept [slɛpt] PT, PP of **sleep**

slew [slu:] PT of **slay**

slice [slaɪs] N (of meat, bread) fatia; (of lemon) rodela; (utensil) pá f or espátula de bolo ▶ VT cortar em fatias

slick [slɪk] ADJ (skilful) jeitoso, ágil, engenhoso; (clever) esperto, astuto ▶ N (also: **oil ~**) mancha de óleo

slide [slaɪd] (pt, pp **slid**) N deslizamento, escorregão m; (in playground) escorregador m; (Phot) slide m; (BRIT: also: **hair ~**) passador m ▶ VT deslizar ▶ VI escorregar; **slide show** N apresentação f de slides; **sliding** ADJ (door) corrediço

slight [slaɪt] ADJ (slim) fraco, franzino; (frail) delicado; (error, pain, increase) pequeno; (trivial) insignificante ▶ N desfeita, desconsideração f; **not in the ~est** em absoluto, de maneira alguma; **slightly** ADV ligeiramente, um pouco

slim [slɪm] ADJ esbelto, delgado; (chance) pequeno ▶ VI emagrecer

slimming N emagrecimento

sling [slɪŋ] (pt, pp **slung**) N (Med) tipoia; (for baby) bebêbag m; (weapon) estilingue m, funda ▶ VT atirar, arremessar, lançar

slip [slɪp] N (fall) escorregão m; (mistake) erro, lapso; (underskirt) combinação f; (of paper) tira ▶ VT deslizar ▶ VI (slide) deslizar; (lose balance) escorregar; (decline) decair; (move smoothly): **to ~ into/ out of** entrar furtivamente em/ sair furtivamente de; **to ~ sth on/ off** enfiar/tirar algo; **to give sb the ~** esguerar-se de alguém; **a ~ of the tongue** um lapso da língua; **slip away** VI escapulir; **slip in** VT meter ▶ VI (errors) surgir; **slip out** VI (go out) sair (um momento); **slip up** VI cometer um erro

slipper ['slɪpə^r] N chinelo

slippery ['slɪpərɪ] ADJ escorregadio

slip-up N equívoco, mancada

slit [slɪt] (pt, pp **slit**) N fenda; (cut) corte m ▶ VT (cut) rachar, cortar; (open) abrir

S

slog [slɒg] (BRIT) VI mourejar ▶ N:
it was a ~ deu um trabalho louco
slogan ['sləugən] N lema m,
slogan m
slope [sləup] N ladeira; (side of
mountain) encosta, vertente f;
(ski slope) pista; (slant) inclinação f,
declive m ▶ VI: **to ~ down** estar em
declive; **to ~ up** inclinar-se;
sloping ADJ inclinado, em declive;
(handwriting) torto
sloppy ['slɒpɪ] ADJ (work)
descuidado; (appearance) relaxado
slot [slɒt] N (in machine) fenda ▶ VT:
to ~ into encaixar em
slow [sləu] ADJ lento; (not clever)
bronco, de raciocínio lento; (watch):
to be ~ atrasar ▶ ADV lentamente,
devagar ▶ VT, VI ir (mais) devagar;
"~" (road sign) "devagar"; **slowly** ADV
lentamente, devagar; **slow motion**
N: **in slow motion** em câmara lenta
slug [slʌg] N lesma; **sluggish** ADJ
vagaroso; (business) lento
slum [slʌm] N (area) favela; (house)
cortiço, barraco
slump [slʌmp] N (economic)
depressão f; (Comm) baixa, queda
▶ VI (person) cair; (prices) baixar
repentinamente
slung [slʌŋ] PT, PP of **sling**
slur [slə:ʳ] N calúnia ▶ VT pronunciar
indistintamente
slush [slʌʃ] N neve f meio derretida
sly [slaɪ] ADJ (person) astuto; (smile,
remark) malicioso, velhaco
smack [smæk] N palmada ▶ VT
bater; (child) dar uma palmada em;
(on face) dar um tabefe em ▶ VI:
to ~ of cheirar a, saber a
small [smɔ:l] ADJ pequeno; **small
change** N trocado
smart [smɑ:t] ADJ elegante;
(clever) inteligente, astuto;

(quick) vivo, esperto ▶ VI sofrer;
SMART Board® N quadro
interativo; **smart phone** N
smartphone m
smash [smæʃ] N (also: **~-up**)
colisão f, choque m; (smash hit)
sucesso de bilheteira ▶ VT (break)
escangalhar, despedaçar; (car etc)
bater com; (Sport: record) quebrar
▶ VI despedaçar-se; (against wall etc)
espatifar-se; **smashing** (inf) ADJ
excelente
smear [smɪəʳ] N mancha, nódoa;
(Med) esfregaço ▶ VT untar; (to make
dirty) lambuzar
smell [smɛl] (pt, pp **smelt** or
smelled) N cheiro; (sense) olfato
▶ VT cheirar ▶ VI (food etc) cheirar;
(pej) cheirar mal; **to ~ of** cheirar a;
smelly (pej) ADJ fedorento,
malcheiroso
smile [smaɪl] N sorriso ▶ VI sorrir
smirk [smə:k] (pej) N sorriso falso or
afetado
smog [smɒg] N nevoeiro com
fumaça (BR) or fumo (PT)
smoke [sməuk] N fumaça (BR),
fumo (PT) ▶ VI fumar; (chimney)
fumegar ▶ VT (cigarettes) fumar;
smoked ADJ (bacon) defumado;
(glass) fumée; **smoker** N (person)
fumante m/f; (Rail) vagão m para
fumantes; **smoking** N: **"no
smoking"** (sign) "proibido fumar";
he's given up smoking ele deixou
de fumar; **smoky** ADJ enfumaçado;
(taste) defumado
smooth [smu:ð] ADJ liso, macio;
(sauce) cremoso; (sea) tranquilo,
calmo; (flavour, movement) suave
▶ VT (also: **~ out**) alisar; (: difficulties)
aplainar
smother ['smʌðəʳ] VT (fire) abafar;
(person) sufocar; (emotions) reprimir

SMS N ABBR (= *short message service*) SMS *m*

smudge [smʌdʒ] N mancha ▶ VT manchar, sujar

smug [smʌg] (*pej*) ADJ convencido

smuggle ['smʌgl] VT contrabandear; **smuggling** N contrabando

snack [snæk] N lanche *m* (BR), merenda (PT); **snack bar** N lanchonete *f* (BR), snackbar *m* (PT)

snag [snæg] N dificuldade *f*, obstáculo

snail [sneɪl] N caracol *m*

snake [sneɪk] N cobra

snap [snæp] N (*sound*) estalo; (*photograph*) foto *f* ▶ ADJ repentino ▶ VT quebrar; (*fingers, whip*) estalar ▶ VI quebrar; (*fig: person*) retrucar asperamente; **to ~ shut** fechar com um estalo; **snap at** VT FUS (*subj: dog*) tentar morder; **snap off** VT (*break*) partir; **snap up** VT arrebatar, comprar rapidamente; **snapshot** N foto *f* (instantânea)

snarl [snɑːl] VI grunhir

snatch [snætʃ] N (*small piece*) trecho ▶ VT agarrar; (*fig: look*) roubar

sneak [sniːk] (*pt* **sneaked**) VI: **to ~ in/out** entrar/sair furtivamente ▶ N (*inf*) dedo-duro; **to ~ up on sb** chegar de mansinho perto de alguém; **sneakers** NPL tênis *m* (BR), sapatos *mpl* de treino (PT)

sneer [snɪəʳ] VI rir-se com desdém; (*mock*): **to ~ at** zombar de, desprezar

sneeze [sniːz] N espirro ▶ VI espirrar

sniff [snɪf] N fungada; (*of dog*) farejada; (*of person*) fungadela ▶ VI fungar ▶ VT fungar, farejar; (*glue, drug*) cheirar

snigger ['snɪgəʳ] VI rir-se com dissimulação

snip [snɪp] N tesourada; (BRIT *inf*) pechincha ▶ VT cortar com tesoura

sniper ['snaɪpəʳ] N franco-atirador(a) *m/f*

snob [snɔb] N esnobe *m/f*

snooker ['snuːkəʳ] N sinuca

snoop [snuːp] VI: **to ~ about** bisbilhotar

snooze [snuːz] N soneca ▶ VI tirar uma soneca, dormitar

snore [snɔːʳ] VI roncar ▶ N ronco

snorkel ['snɔːkl] N tubo snorkel

snort [snɔːt] N bufo, bufido ▶ VI bufar

snow [snəu] N neve *f* ▶ VI nevar; **snowball** N bola de neve ▶ VI (*fig*) aumentar (como bola de neve); **snowboarding** ['snəubɔːdɪŋ] N snowboard *m*; **snowdrift** N monte *m* de neve (formado pelo vento); **snowman** *irreg* N boneco de neve; **snowplough**, (US) **snowplow** N máquina limpa-neve, removedor *m* de neve; **snowstorm** N nevasca, tempestade *f* de neve

snub [snʌb] VT desdenhar, menosprezar ▶ N repulsa

snug [snʌg] ADJ (*sheltered*) abrigado, protegido; (*fitted*) justo, cômodo

(KEYWORD)

so [səu] ADV **1** (*thus, likewise*) assim, deste modo; **so saying he walked away** falou isto e foi embora; **if so** se for assim, se assim é; **I didn't do it — you did so** não fiz isso — você fez!; **so do I, so am I** *etc* eu também; **so it is!** é verdade!; **I hope/think so** espero/acho que sim; **so far** até aqui

2 (*in comparisons etc: to such a degree*) tão; **so big/quickly (that)**

tão grande/rápido (que)
3: **so much** (adj, adv) tanto; **I've got so much work** tenho tanto trabalho; **so many** tantos(-as); **there are so many people to see** tem tanta gente para ver
4 (phrases): **10 or so** uns 10; **so long!** (inf: goodbye) tchau!
▶ CONJ **1** (expressing purpose): **so as to do** para fazer; **we hurried so as not to be late** nós nos apressamos para não chegarmos atrasados; **so (that)** para que, a fim de que
2 (result) de modo que; **he didn't arrive so I left** como ele não chegou, eu fui embora; **so i was right after all** então eu estava certo no final das contas

soak [səuk] VT embeber, ensopar; (put in water) pôr de molho ▶ VI estar de molho, impregnar-se; **soak in** VI infiltrar; **soak up** VT absorver
soap [səup] N sabão m; **soap opera** N novela; **soap powder** N sabão m em pó
soar [sɔːʳ] VI (on wings) elevar-se em voo; (rocket, temperature) subir; (building etc) levantar-se; (price, production) disparar
sob [sɔb] N soluço ▶ VI soluçar
sober ['səubəʳ] ADJ (serious) sério; (not drunk) sóbrio; (colour, style) discreto; **sober up** VI ficar sóbrio
so-called [-'kɔːld] ADJ chamado
soccer ['sɔkəʳ] N futebol m
social ['səuʃl] ADJ social ▶ N reunião f social; **socialism** N socialismo; **socialist** ADJ, N socialista m/f; **socialize** VI: **to socialize (with)** socializar (com); **social media** NPL mídias fpl sociais (BR), meios mpl de comunicação social (PT); **social networking** [-'nɛtwəːkɪŋ] N redes

fpl sociais; **social networking site** N rede f social; **social security** (BRIT) N previdência social; **social work** N assistência social, serviço social; **social worker** N assistente m/f social
society [sə'saɪətɪ] N sociedade f; (club) associação f; (also: **high ~**) alta sociedade
sociology [səusɪ'ɔlədʒɪ] N sociologia
sock [sɔk] N meia (BR), peúga (PT)
socket ['sɔkɪt] N bocal m, encaixe m; (BRIT Elec) tomada
soda ['səudə] N (Chem) soda; (also: **~ water**) água com gás; (US: also: **~ pop**) soda
sofa ['səufə] N sofá m
soft [sɔft] ADJ mole; (voice, music, light) suave; (kind) meigo, bondoso; **soft drink** N refrigerante m; **soften** VT amolecer, amaciar; (effect) abrandar; (expression) suavizar ▶ VI amolecer-se; (voice, expression) suavizar-se; **softly** ADV suavemente; (gently) delicadamente; **software** N software m
soggy ['sɔgɪ] ADJ ensopado, encharcado
soil [sɔɪl] N terra, solo; (territory) território ▶ VT sujar, manchar
solar ['səuləʳ] ADJ solar; **solar panel** N painel m solar; **solar power** N energia solar
sold [səuld] PT, PP of **sell** ▶ ADJ: **~ out** (Comm) esgotado
soldier ['səuldʒəʳ] N soldado; (army man) militar m
sole [səul] N (of foot, shoe) sola; (fish: pl inv) solha, linguado ▶ ADJ único
solicitor [sə'lɪsɪtəʳ] (BRIT) N (for wills etc) tabelião(-lioa) m/f; (in court) ≈ advogado(-a)

solid ['sɔlɪd] ADJ sólido; (*gold etc*) maciço; (*person*) sério ▶ N sólido; **solids** NPL (*food*) comida sólida

solitary ['sɔlɪtərɪ] ADJ solitário, só; (*walk*) só; (*isolated*) isolado, retirado; (*single*) único

solo ['səuləu] N, ADV solo; **soloist** N solista *m/f*

solution [sə'lu:ʃən] N solução *f*

solve [sɔlv] VT resolver, solucionar

solvent ['sɔlvənt] ADJ (*Comm*) solvente ▶ N (*Chem*) solvente *m*

(KEYWORD)

some [sʌm] ADJ 1 (*a certain number or amount*): **some tea/water/ biscuits** um pouco de chá/água/ uns biscoitos; **some children came** algumas crianças vieram
2 (*certain: in contrasts*) algum(a); **some people say that ...** algumas pessoas dizem que ...
3 (*unspecified*) um pouco de; **some woman was asking for you** uma mulher estava perguntando por você; **some day** um dia
▶ PRON 1 (*a certain number*) alguns/ algumas; **I've got some** (*books etc*) tenho alguns; **some went for a taxi and some walked** alguns foram pegar um táxi e outros foram andando
2 (*a certain amount*) um pouco; **I've got some** (*milk, money etc*) tenho um pouco
▶ ADV: **some 10 people** umas 10 pessoas

somebody ['sʌmbədɪ] PRON = **someone**

somehow ['sʌmhau] ADV de alguma maneira; (*for some reason*) por uma razão ou outra

someone ['sʌmwʌn] PRON alguém

someplace ['sʌmpleɪs] (*US*) ADV = **somewhere**

something ['sʌmθɪŋ] PRON alguma coisa, algo (BR)

sometime ['sʌmtaɪm] ADV (*in future*) algum dia, em outra oportunidade; (*in past*): **~ last month** durante o mês passado

sometimes ['sʌmtaɪmz] ADV às vezes, de vez em quando

somewhat ['sʌmwɔt] ADV um tanto

somewhere ['sʌmwɛər] ADV (*be*) em algum lugar; (*go*) para algum lugar; **~ else** (*be*) em outro lugar; (*go*) para outro lugar

son [sʌn] N filho

song [sɔŋ] N canção *f*; (*of bird*) canto

son-in-law ['sʌnɪnlɔ:] N genro

soon [su:n] ADV logo, brevemente; (*a short time after*) logo após; (*early*) cedo; **~ afterwards** pouco depois; *see also* **as**; **sooner** ADV antes, mais cedo; (*preference*): **I would sooner do that** preferia fazer isso; **sooner or later** mais cedo ou mais tarde

soothe [su:ð] VT acalmar, sossegar; (*pain*) aliviar, suavizar

soprano [sə'prɑ:nəu] N soprano *m/f*

sore [sɔ:ʳ] ADJ dolorido ▶ N chaga, ferida

sorrow ['sɔrəu] N tristeza, mágoa, dor *f*; **sorrows** NPL (*causes of grief*) tristezas *fpl*

sorry ['sɔrɪ] ADJ (*regretful*) arrependido; (*condition, excuse*) lamentável; **~!** desculpe!, perdão!, sinto muito!; **to feel ~ for sb** sentir pena de alguém

S

sort [sɔːt] N tipo ▶ VT (*also:* **~ out**: *papers*) classificar; (: *problems*) solucionar, resolver

SOS N ABBR (= *save our souls*) S.O.S. *m*

so-so ADV mais ou menos, regular

sought [sɔːt] PT, PP *of* **seek**

soul [səul] N alma; (*person*) criatura

sound [saund] ADJ (*healthy*) saudável, sadio; (*safe, not damaged*) sólido, completo; (*secure*) seguro; (*reliable*) confiável; (*sensible*) sensato ▶ ADV: **~ asleep** dormindo profundamente ▶ N (*noise*) som *m*, ruído, barulho; (*volume: on TV etc*) volume *m*; (*Geo*) estreito, braço (de mar) ▶ VT (*alarm*) soar ▶ VI soar, tocar; (*fig: seem*) parecer; **to ~ like** parecer; **sound out** VI sondar; **soundtrack** N trilha sonora

soup [suːp] N sopa; **in the ~** (*fig*) numa encrenca

sour ['sauər] ADJ azedo, ácido; (*milk*) talhado; (*fig*) mal-humorado, rabugento; **it's ~ grapes!** (*fig*) é despeito!

source [sɔːs] N fonte *f*

south [sauθ] N sul *m* ▶ ADJ do sul, meridional ▶ ADV ao *or* para o sul; **South Africa** N África do Sul; **South African** ADJ, N sul-africano(-a); **South America** N América do Sul; **South American** ADJ, N sul-americano(-a); **south-east** N sudeste *m*; **southern** ['sʌðən] ADJ (*to the south*) para o sul, em direção do sul; (*from the south*) do sul, sulista; **the southern hemisphere** o Hemisfério Sul; **South Pole** N Pólo Sul; **southward, southwards** ADV para o sul; **south-west** N sudoeste *m*

souvenir [suːvə'nɪər] N lembrança

sovereign ['sɔvrɪn] N soberano(-a)

sow¹ [sau] N porca

sow² [səu] (*pt* **sowed**, *pp* **sown**) VT semear; (*fig: spread*) disseminar, espalhar

soya ['sɔɪə], (*US*) **soy** [sɔɪ] N soja; **soya bean**, (*US*) **soybean** N semente *f* de soja; **soya sauce**, (*US*) **soy sauce** N molho de soja

spa [spɑː] N (*town*) estância hidro-mineral; (*US: also:* **health ~**) estância balnear

space [speɪs] N (*gen*) espaço; (*room*) lugar *m* ▶ CPD espacial ▶ VT (*also:* **~ out**) espaçar; **spacecraft** N nave *f* espacial; **spaceship** N =**spacecraft**; **spacious** ['speɪʃəs] ADJ espaçoso

spade [speɪd] N pá *f*; **spades** NPL (*Cards*) espadas *fpl*

Spain [speɪn] N Espanha

spam ['spæm] N (*junk email*) spam *m*

span [spæn] N (*also:* **wing~**) envergadura; (*of arch*) vão *m*; (*in time*) lapso, espaço ▶ VT estender-se sobre, atravessar; (*fig*) abarcar

Spaniard ['spænjəd] N espanhol(a) *m/f*

Spanish ['spænɪʃ] ADJ espanhol(a) ▶ N (*Ling*) espanhol *m*, castelhano; **the Spanish** NPL os espanhóis

spanner ['spænər] N (*BRIT*) chave *f* inglesa

spare [spɛər] ADJ vago, desocupado; (*surplus*) de sobra, a mais ▶ N = **spare part** ▶ VT dispensar, passar sem; (*make available*) dispor de; (*refrain from hurting*) perdoar, poupar; **to ~** de sobra; **spare part** N peça sobressalente; **spare time** N tempo livre; **spare wheel** N estepe *m*

spark [spɑːk] N chispa, faísca; (*fig*) centelha

sparkle ['spɑːkl] N cintilação *f*, brilho ▶ VI (*shine*) brilhar, faiscar;

sparkling ADJ (mineral water) gasoso; (wine) espumante; (conversation) animado; (performance) brilhante

sparrow ['spærəu] N pardal m

sparse [spɑːs] ADJ escasso; (hair) ralo

spasm ['spæzəm] N (Med) espasmo

spat [spæt] PT, PP of **spit**

speak [spiːk] (pt **spoke**, pp **spoken**) VT (language) falar; (truth) dizer ▶ VI falar; (make a speech) discursar; **~ up!** fale alto!; **speaker** N (in public) orador(a) m/f; (also: **loudspeaker**) alto-falante m; (Pol): **the Speaker** o Presidente da Câmara

spear [spɪər] N lança ▶ VT lancear, arpoar

special ['spɛʃl] ADJ especial; (edition etc) extra; (delivery) rápido; **specialist** N especialista m/f; **speciality** [spɛʃɪˈælɪtɪ] N especialidade f; **specialize** VI: **to specialize (in)** especializar-se (em); **specially** ADV especialmente; **specialty** ['spɛʃəltɪ] (esp US) N = **speciality**

species ['spiːʃiːz] N INV espécie f

specific [spəˈsɪfɪk] ADJ específico

specimen ['spɛsɪmən] N espécime m, amostra; (for testing, Med) espécime

speck [spɛk] N mancha, pinta

spectacle ['spɛktəkl] N espetáculo; **spectacles** NPL (glasses) óculos mpl; **spectacular** [spɛkˈtækjulər] ADJ espetacular ▶ N (Cinema etc) superprodução f

spectator [spɛkˈteɪtər] N espectador(a) m/f

spectrum ['spɛktrəm] (pl **spectra**) N espectro

sped [spɛd] PT, PP of **speed**

speech [spiːtʃ] N (faculty, Theatre) fala; (formal talk) discurso; **speechless** ADJ estupefato, emudecido

speed [spiːd] (pt, pp **sped**) N velocidade f; (rate) rapidez f; (haste) pressa; (promptness) prontidão f; **at full** or **top ~** a toda a velocidade; **speed up** (pt, pp **speeded up**) VT, VI acelerar; **speedboat** N lancha; **speed camera** N radar m de velocidade; **speeding** N (Aut) excesso de velocidade; **speed limit** N limite m de velocidade, velocidade f máxima; **speedometer** [spɪˈdɒmɪtər] N velocímetro; **speedy** ADJ veloz, rápido; (prompt) pronto, imediato

spell [spɛl] (pt, pp **spelled** or **spelt**) N (also: **magic ~**) encanto, feitiço; (period of time) período, temporada ▶ VT (also: **~ out**) soletrar; (fig) pressagiar, ser sinal de; **to cast a ~ on sb** enfeitiçar alguém; **he can't ~** não sabe escrever bem, comete erros de ortografia; **spellchecker** ['spɛltʃɛkər] N (Comput) corretor m ortográfico

spend [spɛnd] (pt, pp **spent**) VT (money) gastar; (time) passar

sperm [spəːm] N esperma

sphere [sfɪər] N esfera

spice [spaɪs] N especiaria ▶ VT condimentar

spicy ['spaɪsɪ] ADJ condimentado

spider ['spaɪdər] N aranha

spike [spaɪk] N (point) ponta, espigão m; (Bot) espiga

spill [spɪl] (pt, pp **spilt** or **spilled**) VT entornar, derramar ▶ VI derramar-se; **spill over** VI transbordar

S

spin [spɪn] (pt, pp **spun**) N (Aviat) parafuso; (trip in car) volta or passeio de carro; (ball): **to put ~ on** fazer rolar ▶ VT (wool etc) fiar, tecer ▶ VI girar, rodar; (make thread) tecer; **spin out** VT prolongar; (money) fazer render

spinach ['spɪnɪtʃ] N espinafre m

spinal cord ['spaɪnl kɔːd] N espinha dorsal

spin doctor (inf) N marqueteiro(-a)

spin-dryer (BRIT) N secadora

spine [spaɪn] N espinha dorsal; (thorn) espinho

spiral ['spaɪərl] N espiral f ▶ VI (prices) disparar

spire ['spaɪər] N flecha, agulha

spirit ['spɪrɪt] N (soul) alma; (ghost) fantasma m; (courage) coragem f, ânimo; (frame of mind) estado de espírito; (sense) sentido; **spirits** NPL (drink) álcool m; **in good ~s** alegre, de bom humor; **spiritual** ADJ espiritual ▶ N (also: **Negro spiritual**) canto religioso dos negros

spit [spɪt] (pt, pp **spat**) N (for roasting) espeto; (saliva) saliva ▶ VI cuspir; (sound) escarrar; (rain) chuviscar

spite [spaɪt] N rancor m, ressentimento ▶ VT contrariar; **in ~ of** apesar de, a despeito de; **spiteful** ADJ maldoso, malévolo

splash [splæʃ] N (sound) borrifo, respingo; (of colour) mancha ▶ VT: **to ~ (with)** salpicar (de) ▶ VI (also: **~ about**) borrifar, respingar

splendid ['splendɪd] ADJ esplêndido; (impressive) impressionante

splinter ['splɪntər] N (of wood, glass) lasca; (in finger) farpa ▶ VI lascar-se, estilhaçar-se, despedaçar-se

split [splɪt] (pt, pp **split**) N fenda, brecha; (fig: division) rompimento;

(: difference) diferença; (Pol) divisão f ▶ VT partir, fender; (party, work) dividir; (profits) repartir ▶ VI (divide) dividir-se, repartir-se; **split up** VI (couple) separar-se, acabar; (meeting) terminar

spoil [spɔɪl] (pt, pp **spoilt** or **spoiled**) VT (damage) danificar; (mar) estragar, arruinar; (child) mimar

spoke [spəʊk] PT of **speak** ▶ N raio

spoken ['spəʊkn] PP of **speak**

spokesman ['spəʊksmən] irreg N porta-voz m

spokeswoman ['spəʊkswʊmən] irreg N porta-voz f

sponge [spʌndʒ] N esponja; (cake) pão de ló m ▶ VT lavar com esponja ▶ VI: **to ~ on sb** viver às custas de alguém; **sponge bag** (BRIT) N bolsa de toalete

sponsor ['spɒnsər] N patrocinador(a) m/f ▶ VT patrocinar; apadrinhar; fiar; (applicant, proposal) apoiar, defender; **sponsorship** N patrocínio

spontaneous [spɒn'teɪnɪəs] ADJ espontâneo

spooky ['spuːkɪ] (inf) ADJ arrepiante

spoon [spuːn] N colher f; **spoonful** N colherada

sport [spɔːt] N esporte m (BR), desporto (PT); (person) bom perdedor/boa perdedora m/f ▶ VT (wear) exibir; **sport jacket** (US) N = **sports jacket**; **sports car** N carro esporte (BR), carro de sport (PT); **sports drink** N isotônico; **sports jacket** (BRIT) N casaco esportivo (BR) or desportivo (PT); **sportsman** irreg N esportista m (BR), desportista m (PT); **sportswear** N roupa esportiva (BR) or desportiva (PT) or esporte; **sportswoman** irreg N esportista (BR), desportista (PT);

sporty ADJ esportivo (BR), desportivo (PT)

spot [spɔt] N (mark) marca; (place) lugar m, local m; (dot: on pattern) mancha, ponto; (on skin) espinha; (Radio, TV) hora; (small amount): **a ~ of** um pouquinho de ▶ VT notar; **on the ~** na hora; (there) ali mesmo; (in difficulty) em apuros; **spotless** ADJ sem mancha, imaculado; **spotlight** N holofote m, refletor m

spouse [spauz] N cônjuge m/f

sprain [spreɪn] N distensão f, torcedura ▶ VT torcer

sprang [spræŋ] PT of **spring**

sprawl [sprɔːl] VI esparramar-se

spray [spreɪ] N borrifo; (container) spray m, atomizador m; (garden spray) vaporizador m; (of flowers) ramalhete m ▶ VT pulverizar; (crops) borrifar, regar

spread [sprɛd] (pt, pp **spread**) N extensão f; (distribution) expansão f, difusão f; (Culin) pasta; (inf: food) banquete m ▶ VT espalhar; (butter) untar, passar; (wings, sails) abrir, desdobrar; (workload, wealth) distribuir; (scatter) disseminar ▶ VI (news, stain) espalhar-se; (disease) alastrar-se; **spread out** VI dispersar-se; **spreadsheet** N (Comput) planilha

spree [spriː] N: **to go on a ~** cair na farra

spring [sprɪŋ] (pt **sprang**, pp **sprung**) N salto, pulo; (coiled metal) mola; (season) primavera; (of water) fonte f; **spring up** VI aparecer de repente

sprinkle ['sprɪŋkl] VT (liquid) salpicar; (salt, sugar) borrifar; **to ~ water on, ~ with water** salpicar de água

sprint [sprɪnt] N corrida de pequena distância ▶ VI correr a toda velocidade

sprung [sprʌŋ] PP of **spring**

spun [spʌn] PT, PP of **spin**

spur [spəːʳ] N espora; (fig) estímulo ▶ VT (also: ~ **on**) incitar, estimular; **on the ~ of the moment** de improviso, de repente

spurt [spəːt] N (of energy) acesso; (of blood etc) jorro ▶ VI jorrar

spy [spaɪ] N espião/espiã m/f ▶ VI: **to ~ on** espiar, espionar ▶ VT enxergar, avistar; **spyware** ['spaɪwɛəʳ] N (Comput) spyware m, software m espião

sq. ABBR (Math etc) = **square**

squabble ['skwɔbl] VI brigar, discutir

squad [skwɔd] N (Mil, Police) pelotão m, esquadra; (Football) seleção f

squadron ['skwɔdrən] N (Mil) esquadrão m; (Aviat) esquadrilha; (Naut) esquadra

squander ['skwɔndəʳ] VT esbanjar, dissipar; (chances) desperdiçar

square [skwɛəʳ] N quadrado; (in town) praça; (inf: person) quadrado(-a), careta m/f ▶ ADJ quadrado; (inf: ideas, tastes) careta, antiquado ▶ VT (arrange) ajustar, acertar; (Math) elevar ao quadrado; (reconcile) conciliar; **all ~** igual, quite; **a ~ meal** uma refeição substancial; **2 metres ~** um quadrado de dois metros de lado; **2 ~ metres** 2 metros quadrados

squash [skwɔʃ] N (BRIT: drink): **lemon/orange ~** limonada/laranjada concentrada; (Sport) squash m; (US: vegetable) abóbora ▶ VT esmagar

squat [skwɔt] ADJ atarracado ▶ VI (*also:* **~ down**) agachar-se, acocorar-se; **squatter** N posseiro(-a)

squeak [skwiːk] VI (*door*) ranger; (*mouse*) guinchar

squeal [skwiːl] VI guinchar, gritar agudamente

squeeze [skwiːz] N (*gen, of hand*) aperto; (*Econ*) arrocho ▶ VT comprimir, socar; (*hand, arm*) apertar; **squeeze out** VT espremer; (*fig*) extorquir

squid [skwɪd] (*pl* **squids** *or* **squid**) N lula

squint [skwɪnt] VI olhar *or* ser vesgo ▶ N (*Med*) estrabismo

squirm [skwəːm] VI retorcer-se

squirrel ['skwɪrəl] N esquilo

squirt [skwəːt] VI, VT jorrar, esguichar

Sr ABBR = **senior**

St ABBR (= *saint*) S.; = **street**

stab [stæb] N (*with knife etc*) punhalada; (*of pain*) pontada; (*inf: try*): **to have a ~ at (doing) sth** tentar (fazer) algo ▶ VT apunhalar

stable ['steɪbl] ADJ estável ▶ N estábulo, cavalariça

stack [stæk] N montão *m*, pilha ▶ VT amontoar, empilhar

stadium ['steɪdɪəm] (*pl* **stadia** *or* **stadiums**) N estádio

staff [stɑːf] N (*work force*) pessoal *m*, quadro; (*BRIT Sch: also:* **teaching ~**) corpo docente ▶ VT prover de pessoal

stag [stæg] N veado, cervo

stage [steɪdʒ] N palco, cena; (*point*) etapa, fase *f*; (*platform*) plataforma, estrado; (*profession*): **the ~** o palco, o teatro ▶ VT pôr em cena, representar; (*demonstration*) montar, organizar; **in ~s** por etapas

stagger ['stægəʳ] VI cambalear ▶ VT (*amaze*) surpreender, chocar; (*hours, holidays*) escalonar; **staggering** ADJ (*amazing*) surpreendente, chocante

stain [steɪn] N mancha; (*colouring*) tinta, tintura ▶ VT manchar; (*wood*) tingir

stair [stɛəʳ] N (*step*) degrau *m*; **stairs** NPL (*flight of steps*) escada; **staircase** N escadaria, escada; **stairway** N = **staircase**

stake [steɪk] N estaca, poste *m*; (*Comm: interest*) interesse *m*, participação *f*; (*Betting: gen pl*) aposta ▶ VT apostar; (*claim*) reivindicar; **to be at ~** estar em jogo

stale [steɪl] ADJ (*bread*) dormido; (*food*) estragado; (*air*) viciado; (*smell*) mofado; (*beer*) velho

stalk [stɔːk] N talo, haste *f* ▶ VT caçar de tocaia; **to ~ in/out** entrar/ sair silenciosamente; **to ~ off** andar com arrogância

stall [stɔːl] N (*BRIT: in market*) barraca; (*in stable*) baia ▶ VT (*Aut*) fazer morrer; (*fig: delay*) impedir, atrasar ▶ VI morrer; esquivar-se, ganhar tempo; **stalls** NPL (*BRIT: in cinema, theatre*) plateia

stamina ['stæmɪnə] N resistência

stammer ['stæməʳ] N gagueira ▶ VI gaguejar, balbuciar

stamp [stæmp] N selo; (*rubber stamp*) carimbo, timbre *m*; (*mark, also fig*) marca, impressão *f* ▶ VI (*also:* **~ one's foot**) bater com o pé ▶ VT (*letter*) selar; (*mark*) marcar; (*with rubber stamp*) carimbar

stampede [stæm'piːd] N debandada, estouro (da boiada)

stance [stæns] N postura, posição *f*

stand [stænd] (*pt, pp* **stood**) N posição *f*, postura; (*for taxis*) ponto;

(also: **hall ~**) pedestal m; (also: **music ~**) estante f; (Sport) tribuna, palanque m; (stall) barraca ▶ VI (be) estar, encontrar-se; (be on foot) estar em pé; (rise) levantar-se; (remain: decision, offer) estar de pé; (in election) candidatar-se ▶ VT (place) pôr, colocar; (tolerate, withstand) aguentar, suportar; (cost) pagar; **to make a ~** resistir; (fig) ater-se a um princípio; **to ~ for parliament** (BRIT) apresentar-se como candidato ao parlamento; **stand by** VI estar a postos ▶ VT FUS (opinion) aferrar-se a; (person) ficar ao lado de; **stand down** VI retirar-se; **stand for** VT FUS (signify) significar; (represent) representar; (tolerate) tolerar, permitir; **stand in for** VT FUS substituir; **stand out** VI (be prominent) destacar-se; **stand up** VI levantar-se; **stand up for** VT FUS defender; **stand up to** VT FUS enfrentar

standard ['stændəd] N padrão m, critério; (flag) estandarte m; (level) nível m ▶ ADJ padronizado, regular, normal; **standards** NPL (morals) valores mpl morais; **standard of living** N padrão m de vida (BR), nível m de vida (PT)

stand-by ADJ de reserva ▶ N: **to be on ~** estar de sobreaviso or de prontidão; **stand-by ticket** N bilhete m de stand-by

standing ['stændɪŋ] ADJ (on foot) em pé; (permanent) permanente ▶ N posição f, reputação f; **of many years' ~** de muitos anos

standpoint ['stændpɔɪnt] N ponto de vista

standstill ['stændstɪl] N: **at a ~** paralisado, parado; **to come to**

a ~ (car) parar; (factory, traffic) ficar paralisado

stank [stæŋk] PT of **stink**

staple ['steɪpl] N (for papers) grampo ▶ ADJ (food etc) básico ▶ VT grampear

star [stɑːʳ] N estrela; (celebrity) astro/estrela ▶ VI: **to ~ in** ser a estrela em, estrelar ▶ VT (Cinema) ser estrelado por; **the stars** NPL (horoscope) o horóscopo

starboard ['stɑːbəd] N estibordo

starch [stɑːtʃ] N (in food) amido, fécula; (for clothes) goma

stardom ['stɑːdəm] N estrelato

stare [stɛəʳ] N olhar m fixo ▶ VI: **to ~ at** olhar fixamente, fitar

stark [stɑːk] ADJ severo, áspero ▶ ADV: **~ naked** completamente nu, em pelo

start [stɑːt] N princípio, começo; (departure) partida; (sudden movement) sobressalto, susto; (advantage) vantagem f ▶ VT começar, iniciar; (cause) causar; (found) fundar; (engine) ligar ▶ VI começar, iniciar; (with fright) sobressaltar-se, assustar-se; (train etc) sair; **start off** VI começar, principiar; (leave) sair, pôr-se a caminho; **start up** VI começar; (car) pegar, pôr-se em marcha ▶ VT começar; (car) ligar; **starter** N (Aut) arranque m; (Sport: official) juiz/juíza m/f da partida; **starting point** N ponto de partida

startle ['stɑːtl] VT assustar, aterrar; **startling** ADJ surpreendente

starvation [stɑːˈveɪʃən] N fome f

starve ['stɑːv] VI passar fome; (to death) morrer de fome ▶ VT fazer passar fome; (fig): **to ~ (of)** privar (de)

state [steɪt] N estado ▶ VT afirmar, declarar; **the States** NPL (*Geo*) os Estados Unidos; **to be in a ~** estar agitado; **statement** N declaração f; **statesman** *irreg* N estadista *m*

static ['stætɪk] N (*Radio, TV*) interferência ▶ ADJ estático

station ['steɪʃən] N estação f; (*Police*) delegacia; (*Radio*) emissora ▶ VT colocar

stationary ['steɪʃnərɪ] ADJ estacionário

station wagon (*US*) N perua (*BR*), canadiana (*PT*)

statistic [stə'tɪstɪk] N estatística; **statistics** [stə'tɪstɪks] N (*science*) estatística

statue ['stætjuː] N estátua

status ['steɪtəs] N posição f; (*official classification*) categoria; (*importance*) status *m*

staunch [stɔːntʃ] ADJ fiel

stay [steɪ] N estadia, estada ▶ VI ficar; (*as guest*) hospedar-se; (*spend some time*) demorar-se; **to ~ put** não se mexer; **to ~ the night** pernoitar; **stay behind** VI ficar atrás; **stay in** VI ficar em casa; **stay on** VI ficar; **stay out** VI ficar fora de casa; **stay up** VI (*at night*) velar, ficar acordado

steadily ['stɛdɪlɪ] ADV (*firmly*) firmemente; (*unceasingly*) sem parar, constantemente; (*walk*) regularmente

steady ['stɛdɪ] ADJ (*job, boyfriend*) constante; (*speed*) fixo; (*regular*) regular; (*person, character*) sensato; (*calm*) calmo, sereno ▶ VT (*stabilize*) estabilizar; (*nerves*) acalmar

steak [steɪk] N filé *m*; (*beef*) bife *m*

steal [stiːl] (*pt* **stole**, *pp* **stolen**) VT roubar ▶ VI mover-se furtivamente

steam [stiːm] N vapor *m* ▶ VT (*Culin*) cozinhar no vapor ▶ VI fumegar; **steamy** ADJ vaporoso; (*room*) cheio de vapor, úmido (*BR*), húmido (*PT*); (*heat, atmosphere*) vaporoso

steel [stiːl] N aço ▶ ADJ de aço

steep [stiːp] ADJ íngreme; (*increase*) acentuado; (*price*) exorbitante ▶ VT (*food*) colocar de molho; (*cloth*) ensopar, encharcar

steeple ['stiːpl] N campanário, torre f

steer [stɪə^r] VT (*person*) guiar; (*vehicle*) dirigir ▶ VI conduzir; **steering** N (*Aut*) direção f; **steering wheel** N volante *m*

stem [stɛm] N (*of plant*) caule *m*, haste f; (*of glass*) pé *m* ▶ VT deter, reter; (*blood*) estancar; **stem from** VT FUS originar-se de

step [stɛp] N passo, (*stair*) degrau *m* ▶ VI: **to ~ forward** dar um passo a frente/atrás; **steps** NPL (*BRIT*) = **stepladder**; **to be in ~ (with)** (*fig*) manter a paridade (com); **to be out of ~ (with)** (*fig*) estar em disparidade (com); **step down** VI (*fig*) renunciar; **step on** VT FUS pisar; **step up** VT aumentar; **stepbrother** N meio-irmão *m*; **stepdaughter** N enteada; **stepfather** N padrasto; **stepladder** (*BRIT*) N escada portátil *or* de abrir; **stepmother** N madrasta; **stepsister** N meia-irmã f; **stepson** N enteado

stereo ['stɛrɪəu] N estéreo; (*record player*) (aparelho de) som *m* ▶ ADJ (*also*: **~phonic**) estereofônico

sterile ['stɛraɪl] ADJ esterelizado; (*barren*) estéril; **sterilize** ['stɛrɪlaɪz] VT esterilizar

sterling ['stəːlɪŋ] ADJ esterlino; (*silver*) de lei ▶ N (*currency*) libra esterlina; **one pound ~** uma libra esterlina

stern [stə:n] ADJ severo, austero
▶ N (Naut) popa, ré f

stew [stju:] N guisado, ensopado
▶ VT guisar, ensopar; (fruit) cozinhar

steward ['stju:əd] N (Aviat)
comissário de bordo; **stewardess**
N aeromoça (BR), hospedeira de
bordo (PT)

stick [stɪk] (pt, pp **stuck**) N pau m;
(as weapon) cacete m; (walking
stick) bengala, cajado ▶ VT (glue)
colar; (inf: put) meter; (: tolerate)
aguentar, suportar; (thrust): **to ~
sth into** cravar or enfiar algo em
▶ VI (become attached) colar-se; (be
unmoveable) emperrar; (in mind etc)
gravar-se; **stick out** VI estar
saliente, projetar-se; **stick up** VI
estar saliente, projetar-se; **stick
up for** VT FUS defender; **sticker** N
adesivo; **sticking plaster** N
esparadrapo

sticky ['stɪkɪ] ADJ pegajoso; (label)
adesivo; (fig) delicado

stiff [stɪf] ADJ (strong) forte; (hard)
duro; (difficult) difícil; (moving with
difficulty: person) teso; (: door, zip)
empenado; (formal) formal ▶ ADV
(bored, worried) extremamente

stigma ['stɪɡmə] N estigma m

stiletto [stɪ'letəu] (BRIT) N (also:
~ heel) salto alto e fino

still [stɪl] ADJ parado ▶ ADV (up to
this time) ainda; (even, yet) ainda;
(nonetheless) entretanto, contudo

stimulate ['stɪmjuleɪt] VT
estimular

stimulus ['stɪmjuləs] (pl **stimuli**)
N estímulo, incentivo

sting [stɪŋ] (pt, pp **stung**) N
(wound) picada; (pain) ardência;
(of insect) ferrão m ▶ VT arguilhar
▶ VI (insect, animal) picar; (eyes,
ointment) queimar

stink [stɪŋk] (pt **stank**, pp **stunk**)
N fedor m, catinga ▶ VI feder,
cheirar mal

stir [stə:ʳ] N (fig) comoção f,
rebuliço ▶ VT mexer; (fig)
comover ▶ VI mover-se,
remexer-se; **stir up** VT excitar;
(trouble) provocar

stitch [stɪtʃ] N (Sewing, Knitting,
Med) ponto; (pain) pontada ▶ VT
costurar; (Med) dar pontos em,
suturar

stock [stɔk] N suprimento;
(Comm: reserves) estoque m,
provisão f; (: selection) sortimento;
(Agr) gado; (Culin) caldo; (lineage)
estirpe f, linhagem f; (Finance)
valores mpl, títulos mpl ▶ ADJ
(reply etc) de sempre, costumeiro
▶ VT ter em estoque, estocar; **in ~**
em estoque; **out of ~** esgotado;
to take ~ of (fig) fazer um balanço
de; **~s and shares** valores e títulos
mobiliários; **stock up** VI: **to ~ up
(with)** abastecer-se (de);
stockbroker N corretor(a) m/f de
valores; **stock cube** (BRIT) N cubo
de caldo; **stock exchange** N Bolsa
de Valores

stocking ['stɔkɪŋ] N meia

stock market (BRIT) N Bolsa,
mercado de valores

stole [stəul] PT of **steal** ▶ N estola

stolen ['stəuln] PP of **steal**

stomach ['stʌmək] N (Anat)
estômago; (belly) barriga, ventre m
▶ VT suportar, tolerar

stone [stəun] N pedra; (pebble)
pedrinha; (in fruit) caroço; (Med)
pedra, cálculo; (BRIT: weight) =
6.348kg; 14 pounds ▶ ADJ de pedra
▶ VT apedrejar; (fruit) tirar o(s)
caroço(s) de

stood [stud] PT, PP of **stand**

S

stool [stu:l] N tamborete m, banco
stoop [stu:p] VI (also: **have a ~**) ser
corcunda; (also: **~ down**)
debruçar-se, curvar-se
stop [stɔp] N parada, interrupção f;
(for bus etc) parada (BR), ponto (BR),
paragem f (PT); (also: **full ~**) ponto
▶ VT parar, deter; (break off)
interromper; (pay, cheque) sustar,
suspender; (also: **put a ~ to**)
impedir ▶ VI parar, deter-se; (watch,
noise) parar; (end) acabar; **to ~
doing sth** deixar de fazer algo;
stop dead VI parar de repente; **stop
off** VI dar uma parada; **stop up** VT
tapar; **stopover** N parada rápida;
(Aviat) escala
storage ['stɔːrɪdʒ] N armazenagem f
store [stɔːʳ] N (in stock) suprimento;
(depot) armazém m; (reserve)
estoque m; (BRIT: large shop) loja de
departamentos; (US: shop) loja ▶ VT
armazenar; **stores** NPL (provisions)
víveres mpl, provisões fpl; **who
knows what is in ~ for us?** quem
sabe o que nos espera?; **store up** VT
acumular
storey ['stɔːrɪ], (US) **story** N
andar m
storm [stɔːm] N tempestade f; (fig)
tumulto ▶ VI (fig) enfurecer-se ▶ VT
tomar de assalto, assaltar; **stormy**
ADJ tempestuoso
story ['stɔːrɪ] N história, estória;
(lie) mentira; (US) = **storey**
stout [staut] ADJ sólido, forte; (fat)
gordo, corpulento; (resolute)
decidido, resoluto ▶ N cerveja preta
stove [stəuv] N (for cooking) fogão
m; (for heating) estufa, fogareiro
straight [streɪt] ADJ reto, (back)
esticado; (hair) liso; (honest)
honesto; (simple) simples inv ▶ ADV
reto; (drink) puro; **to put** or **get**

sth ~ esclarecer algo; **~ away, ~ off**
(at once) imediatamente;
straighten VT arrumar; **to
straighten things out** arrumar as
coisas; **straighten out** VT
endireitar; (fig) esclarecer;
straightforward ADJ (simple)
simples inv, direto; (honest)
honesto, franco
strain [streɪn] N tensão f; (Tech)
esforço; (Med: back strain) distensão f;
(: tension) luxação f; (breed) raça,
estirpe f ▶ VT forçar, torcer, distender;
(stretch) puxar, estirar; (Culin) coar;
strains NPL (Mus) acordes mpl;
strained ADJ distendido; (laugh)
forçado; (relations) tenso; **strainer**
N coador m; (sieve) peneira
strait [streɪt] N estreito; **straits**
NPL: **to be in dire ~s** estar em
apuros
strand [strænd] N (of thread, hair)
fio; (of rope) tira; **stranded** ADJ
preso
strange [streɪndʒ] ADJ (not known)
desconhecido; (odd) estranho,
esquisito; **strangely** ADV
estranhamente; **stranger** N
desconhecido(-a); (from another
area) forasteiro(-a)
strangle ['stræŋgl] VT estrangular;
(fig) sufocar
strap [stræp] N correia; (of slip,
dress) alça
strategic [strə'tiːdʒɪk] ADJ
estratégico
strategy ['strætɪdʒɪ] N estratégia
straw [strɔː] N palha; (drinking
straw) canudo; **that's the last ~!**
essa foi a última gota!
strawberry ['strɔːbərɪ] N morango
stray [streɪ] ADJ (animal) extraviado;
(bullet) perdido; (scattered)
espalhado ▶ VI perder-se

streak [striːk] N listra, traço; (*in hair*) mecha ▶ VT listrar ▶ VI: **to ~ past** passar como um raio

stream [striːm] N riacho, córrego; (*of people, vehicles*) fluxo; (*of smoke*) rastro; (*of questions etc*) torrente f ▶ VT (*Sch*) classificar ▶ VI correr, fluir; **to ~ in/out** entrar/sair em massa

street [striːt] N rua; **streetcar** (*US*) N bonde m (BR), eléctrico (PT); **street plan** N mapa m

strength [strɛŋθ] N força; (*of girder, knot etc*) firmeza, resistência; (*fig*) poder m; **strengthen** VT fortificar; (*fig*) fortalecer

strenuous ['strɛnjuəs] ADJ enérgico; (*determined*) tenaz

stress [strɛs] N pressão f; (*mental strain*) tensão f, stress m; (*emphasis*) ênfase f; (*Tech*) tensão ▶ VT realçar, dar ênfase a; (*syllable*) acentuar; **stressed** ADJ (*tense*) estressado; (*syllable*) tônico

stretch [strɛtʃ] N (*of sand etc*) trecho, extensão f ▶ VI espreguiçar-se; (*extend*): **to ~ to** or **as far as** estender-se até ▶ VT estirar, esticar; (*fig: subj: job, task*) exigir o máximo de; **stretch out** VI esticar-se ▶ VT (*arm etc*) esticar; (*spread*) estirar

stretcher ['strɛtʃər] N maca, padiola

strict [strɪkt] ADJ (*person*) severo, rigoroso; (*meaning*) exato, estrito

stride [straɪd] (*pt* **strode**, *pp* **stridden**) N passo largo ▶ VI andar a passos largos

strike [straɪk] (*pt, pp* **struck**) N greve f; (*of oil etc*) descoberta; (*attack*) ataque m ▶ VT bater em; (*oil etc*) descobrir; (*deal*) fechar, acertar; (*fig*): **the thought** or **it ~s me that ...** me ocorre que ...; ▶ VI estar em greve; (*attack: soldiers, illness*) atacar; (: *disaster*) assolar; (*clock*) bater; **on ~** em greve; **to ~ a match** acender um fósforo; **strike down** VT derrubar; **strike up** VT (*Mus*) começar a tocar; (*conversation, friendship*) travar; **striker** N grevista m/f; (*Sport*) atacante m/f; **striking** ADJ impressionante

string [strɪŋ] (*pt, pp* **strung**) N (*cord*) barbante m (BR), cordel m (PT); (*of beads*) cordão m; (*of onions*) réstia; (*Mus*) corda ▶ VT: **to ~ out** esticar; **the strings** NPL (*Mus*) os instrumentos de corda; **to ~ together** (*words*) unir; (*ideas*) concatenar; **to get a job by pulling ~s** (*fig*) usar pistolão

strip [strɪp] N tira; (*of land*) faixa; (*of metal*) lâmina, tira ▶ VT despir ▶ VI despir-se

stripe [straɪp] N listra, (*Mil*) galão m; **striped** ADJ listrado, com listras

strive [straɪv] (*pt* **strove**, *pp* **striven**) VI: **to ~ for sth/to do sth** esforçar-se por or batalhar para algo/para fazer algo

strode [strəʊd] PT *of* **stride**

stroke [strəʊk] N (*blow*) golpe m; (*Med*) derrame m cerebral; (*of paintbrush*) pincelada; (*Swimming: style*) nado ▶ VT acariciar, afagar; **at a ~** de repente, de golpe

stroll [strəʊl] N volta, passeio ▶ VI passear, dar uma volta; **stroller** (*US*) N carrinho (de criança)

strong [strɒŋ] ADJ forte; (*imagination*) fértil; (*personality*) forte, dominante; (*nerves*) de aço; **they are 50 ~** são 50 pessoas; **stronghold** N fortaleza; (*fig*) baluarte m; **strongly** ADV firmemente; (*push, defend*) vigorosamente; (*believe*) profundamente

strove [strəuv] PT *of* **strive**

struck [strʌk] PT, PP *of* **strike**

structure ['strʌktʃər] N estrutura; (*building*) construção f

struggle ['strʌgl] N luta, contenda ▶ VI (*fight*) lutar; (*try hard*) batalhar

strung [strʌŋ] PT, PP *of* **string**

stub [stʌb] N (*of ticket etc*) canhoto; (*of cigarette*) toco, ponta; **to ~ one's toe** dar uma topada; **stub out** VT apagar

stubble ['stʌbl] N restolho; (*on chin*) barba por fazer

stubborn ['stʌbən] ADJ teimoso, cabeçudo, obstinado

stuck [stʌk] PT, PP *of* **stick** ▶ ADJ (*jammed*) emperrado

stud [stʌd] N (*shirt stud*) botão m; (*earring*) tarraxa, rosca; (*of boot*) cravo; (*also:* **~ farm**) fazenda de cavalos; (*also:* **~ horse**) garanhão m ▶ VT (*fig*) salpicado de

student ['stju:dənt] N estudante m/f ▶ ADJ estudantil; **student driver** (*US*) N aprendiz m/f

studio ['stju:dɪəu] N estúdio; (*sculptor's*) ateliê m

study ['stʌdɪ] N estudo; (*room*) sala de leitura *or* estudo ▶ VT estudar; (*examine*) examinar, investigar ▶ VI estudar; **studies** NPL (*subjects*) estudos mpl, matérias fpl

stuff [stʌf] N (*substance*) troço; (*things*) troços mpl, coisas fpl ▶ VT (*Culin*) rechear; (*animals*) empalhar; (*inf: push*) enfiar; **~ed toy** brinquedo de pelúcia; **stuffing** N recheio; **stuffy** ADJ (*room*) abafado, mal ventilado; (*person*) rabujento, melindroso

stumble ['stʌmbl] VI tropeçar; **to ~ across** *or* **on** (*fig*) topar com

stump [stʌmp] N (*of tree*) toco; (*of limb*) coto ▶ VT: **to be ~ed** ficar perplexo

stun [stʌn] VT (*subj: blow*) aturdir; (*: news*) pasmar

stung [stʌŋ] PT, PP *of* **sting**

stunk [stʌŋk] PP *of* **stink**

stunning ['stʌnɪŋ] ADJ (*news*) atordoante; (*appearance*) maravilhoso

stunt [stʌnt] N façanha sensacional; (*publicity stunt*) truque m publicitário

stupid ['stju:pɪd] ADJ estúpido, idiota

sturdy ['stə:dɪ] ADJ (*person*) robusto, firme; (*thing*) sólido

stutter ['stʌtər] N gagueira, gaguez f ▶ VI gaguejar

style [staɪl] N estilo; (*elegance*) elegância; **stylish** ADJ elegante, chique

subconscious [sʌb'kɔnʃəs] ADJ do subconsciente

subject [n 'sʌbdʒɪkt, vt səb'dʒɛkt] N (*of king*) súdito(-a); (*theme*) assunto; (*Sch*) matéria; (*Ling*) sujeito ▶ VT: **to ~ sb to sth** submeter alguém a algo; **to be ~ to** estar sujeito a; **subjective** [səb'dʒɛktɪv] ADJ subjetivo; **subject matter** N assunto; (*content*) conteúdo

submarine ['sʌbməri:n] N submarino

submission [səb'mɪʃən] N submissão f; (*to committee*) petição f; (*of plan*) apresentação f, exposição f

submit [səb'mɪt] VT submeter ▶ VI submeter-se

subordinate [sə'bɔ:dɪnət] ADJ, N subordinado(-a)

subscribe [səb'skraɪb] VI subscrever; **to ~ to** (*opinion*) concordar com; (*fund*) contribuir para; (*newspaper*) assinar;

subscription [səb'skrɪpʃən] N
assinatura

subsequent ['sʌbsɪkwənt] ADJ
subsequente, posterior;
subsequently ADV
posteriormente, depois

subside [səb'saɪd] VI (feeling, wind)
acalmar-se; (flood) baixar

subsidiary [səb'sɪdɪərɪ] ADJ
secundário ▶ N (also: ~ **company**)
subsidiária

subsidize ['sʌbsɪdaɪz] VT subsidiar

subsidy ['sʌbsɪdɪ] N subsídio

substance ['sʌbstəns] N
substância

substantial [səb'stænʃl] ADJ
(solid) sólido; (reward, meal)
substancial

substitute ['sʌbstɪtjuːt] N
substituto(-a); (person) suplente
m/f ▶ VT: **to ~ A for B** substituir B
por A

subtitled ['sʌbtaɪtld] ADJ (film)
legendado

subtle ['sʌtl] ADJ sutil

subtract [səb'trækt] VT subtrair,
deduzir

suburb ['sʌbəːb] N subúrbio;
suburban [sə'bəːbən] ADJ
suburbano; (train etc) de subúrbio

subway ['sʌbweɪ] N (BRIT)
passagem f subterrânea; (US)
metrô m (BR), metro(-politano) (PT)

succeed [sək'siːd] VI (person) ser
bem sucedido, ter êxito; (plan) sair
bem ▶ VT suceder a; **to ~ in doing**
conseguir fazer

success [sək'sɛs] N êxito; (hit,
person) sucesso; **successful** ADJ
(venture) bem sucedido; (writer) de
sucesso, bem sucedido; **to be
successful (in doing)** conseguir
(fazer); **successfully** ADV com
sucesso, com êxito

succession [sək'sɛʃən] N
sucessão f, série f; (to throne)
sucessão

such [sʌtʃ] ADJ tal, semelhante;
(of that kind: singular): **~ a book** um
livro parecido, tal livro; (: plural):
~ books tais livros; (so much):
~ courage tanta coragem ▶ ADV
tão; **~ a long trip** uma viagem tão
longa; **~ a lot of** tanto; **~ as** tal
como; **as ~** como tal;
such-and-such ADJ tal e qual

suck [sʌk] VT chupar; (breast)
mamar

sudden ['sʌdn] ADJ (rapid)
repentino, súbito; (unexpected)
imprevisto; **all of a ~**
inesperadamente; **suddenly** ADV
inesperadamente

sudoku [su'dəuku:] N sudoku m

sue [su:] VT processar

suede [sweɪd] N camurça

suffer ['sʌfə'] VT sofrer; (bear)
aguentar, suportar ▶ VI sofrer,
padecer; **to ~ from** sofrer de, estar
com; **suffering** N sofrimento

sufficient [sə'fɪʃənt] ADJ
suficiente, bastante

suffocate ['sʌfəkeɪt] VI
sufocar(-se), asfixiar(-se)

sugar ['ʃugə'] N açúcar m ▶ VT pôr
açúcar em, açucarar

suggest [sə'dʒɛst] VT sugerir;
(indicate) indicar; **suggestion** N
sugestão f; (indication) indicação f

suicide ['suɪsaɪd] N suicídio; (person)
suicida m/f; see also **commit**;
suicide attack N ataque m suicida,
atentado suicida; **suicide bomber**
N homem-bomba m,
mulher-bomba f; **suicide
bombing** N ataque m suicida

suit [su:t] N (man's) terno (BR), fato
(PT); (woman's) conjunto;

S

(*Jur*) processo; (*Cards*) naipe *m* ▶ VT convir a; (*clothes*) ficar bem a; (*adapt*): **to ~ sth to** adaptar *or* acomodar algo a; **they are well ~ed** fazem um bom par; **suitable** ADJ conveniente; (*appropriate*) apropriado

suitcase ['su:tkeɪs] N mala

suite [swi:t] N (*of rooms*) conjunto de salas; (*Mus*) suite *f*; **a three-piece ~** um conjunto estofado (sofá e duas poltronas)

sulfur ['sʌlfər] (*US*) = **sulphur**

sulk [sʌlk] VI ficar emburrado, fazer beicinho *or* biquinho (*inf*)

sulphur ['sʌlfər], (*US*) **sulfur** N enxofre *m*

sultana [sʌl'tɑ:nə] N passa branca

sum [sʌm] N soma; (*calculation*) cálculo; **sum up** VT, VI resumir

summarize ['sʌməraɪz] VT resumir

summary ['sʌməri] N resumo

summer ['sʌmər] N verão *m* ▶ ADJ de verão; **in (the) ~** no verão; **summertime** N (*season*) verão *m*

summit ['sʌmɪt] N topo, cume *m*; (*also*: **~ conference**) (conferência de) cúpula

summon ['sʌmən] VT (*person*) mandar chamar; (*meeting*) convocar; (*Jur: witness*) convocar; **summon up** VT concentrar

sun [sʌn] N sol *m*; **sunbathe** VI tomar sol; **sunblock** N bloqueador *m* solar; **sunburn** N queimadura do sol

Sunday ['sʌndɪ] N domingo

sunflower ['sʌnflauər] N girassol *m*

sung [sʌŋ] PP *of* **sing**

sunglasses ['sʌnglɑ:sɪz] NPL óculos *mpl* de sol

sunk [sʌŋk] PP *of* **sink**

sun: sunlight N (luz *f* do) sol *m*; **sunny** ADJ cheio de sol; (*day*) ensolarado, de sol; **sunrise** N nascer *m* do sol; **sun roof** N (*Aut*) teto solar; **sunscreen** N protetor *m* solar; **sunset** N pôr *m* do sol; **sunshade** N para-sol *m*; **sunshine** N (luz *f* do) sol *m*; **sunstroke** N insolação *f*; **suntan** N bronzeado; **suntan lotion** N loção *f* de bronzear

super ['su:pər] (*inf*) ADJ bacana (*BR*), muito giro (*PT*)

superb [su:'pə:b] ADJ excelente

superintendent [su:pərɪn'tɛndənt] N superintendente *m/f*; (*Police*) chefe *m/f* de polícia

superior [su'pɪərɪər] ADJ superior; (*smug*) desdenhoso ▶ N superior *m*

supermarket ['su:pəmɑ:kɪt] N supermercado

supernatural [su:pə'nætʃərəl] ADJ sobrenatural ▶ N: **the ~** o sobrenatural

superpower ['su:pəpauər] N (*Pol*) superpotência

superstitious [su:pə'stɪʃəs] ADJ supersticioso

supervise ['su:pəvaɪz] VT supervisar, supervisionar; **supervision** [su:pə'vɪʒən] N supervisão *f*; **supervisor** N supervisor(a) *m/f*; (*academic*) orientador(a) *m/f*

supper ['sʌpər] N jantar *m*; (*late evening*) ceia

supple ['sʌpl] ADJ flexível

supplement [n 'sʌplɪmənt, vt sʌplɪ'mɛnt] N suplemento ▶ VT suprir, completar

supplier [sə'plaɪər] N abastecedor(a) *m/f*, fornecedor(a) *m/f*

supply [sə'plaɪ] VT (*provide*): **to ~ sth (to sb)** fornecer algo (a alguém); (*equip*): **to ~ (with)** suprir (de) ▶ N fornecimento, provisão *f*;

(*stock*) estoque *m*; (*supplying*) abastecimento

support [sə'pɔːt] N (*moral, financial etc*) apoio; (*Tech*) suporte *m* ▶ VT apoiar; (*financially*) manter; (*Tech: hold up*) sustentar; (*theory etc*) defender; **supporter** N (*Pol etc*) partidário(-a); (*Sport*) torcedor(a) *m/f*

suppose [sə'pəuz] VT supor; (*imagine*) imaginar; (*duty*): **to be ~d to do sth** dever fazer algo; **supposedly** [sə'pəuzɪdlɪ] ADV supostamente, pretensamente; **supposing** CONJ caso, supondo-se que

suppress [sə'prɛs] VT (*information*) suprimir; (*feelings, revolt*) reprimir; (*yawn*) conter

supreme [su'priːm] ADJ supremo

surcharge ['səːtʃɑːdʒ] N sobretaxa

sure [ʃuəʳ] ADJ seguro; (*definite*) certo; (*aim*) certeiro; **to make ~ of sth/that** assegurar-se de algo/que; **~!** (*of course*) claro que sim!; **~ enough** efetivamente; **surely** ADV (*certainly: US: also:* **sure**) certamente

surf [səːf] N (*waves*) ondas *fpl*, arrebentação *f*

surface ['səːfɪs] N superfície *f* ▶ VT (*road*) revestir ▶ VI vir à superfície *or* à tona; (*fig: news, feeling*) vir à tona

surfboard ['səːfbɔːd] N prancha de surfe

surfer ['səːfəʳ] N surfista *m/f*; (*on the Internet*) internauta *m/f*

surfing ['səːfɪŋ] N surfe *m*

surge [səːdʒ] N onda ▶ VI (*sea*) encapelar-se; (*people, vehicles*) precipitar-se; (*feeling*) aumentar repentinamente

surgeon ['səːdʒən] N cirurgião(-giã) *m/f*

surgery ['səːdʒərɪ] N cirurgia; (BRIT: *room*) consultório; (*also:* **~ hours**) horas *fpl* de consulta

surname ['səːneɪm] N sobrenome *m* (BR), apelido (PT)

surplus ['səːpləs] N excedente *m*; (*Comm*) superávit *m* ▶ ADJ excedente, de sobra

surprise [sə'praɪz] N surpresa ▶ VT surpreender; **surprising** ADJ surpreendente

surrender [sə'rɛndəʳ] N rendição *f*, entrega ▶ VI render-se, entregar-se

surround [sə'raund] VT circundar, rodear; (*Mil etc*) cercar; **surrounding** ADJ circundante, adjacente; **surroundings** NPL arredores *mpl*, cercanias *fpl*

surveillance [səː'veɪləns] N vigilância

survey [*n* 'səːveɪ, *vt* səː'veɪ] N inspeção *f*; (*of habits etc*) pesquisa; (*of house*) inspeção *f*; (*of land*) levantamento ▶ VT observar, contemplar; (*land*) fazer um levantamento de; **surveyor** N (*of land*) agrimensor(a) *m/f*; (*of building*) inspetor(a) *m/f*

survival [sə'vaɪvl] N sobrevivência; (*relic*) remanescente *m*

survive [sə'vaɪv] VI sobreviver; (*custom etc*) perdurar ▶ VT sobreviver a; **survivor** N sobrevivente *m/f*

suspect [*adj, n* 'sʌspɛkt, *vt* səs'pɛkt] ADJ, N suspeito(-a) ▶ VT suspeitar, desconfiar

suspend [səs'pɛnd] VT suspender; **suspenders** NPL (BRIT) ligas *fpl*; (US) suspensórios *mpl*

suspense [səs'pɛns] N incerteza, ansiedade *f*; (*in film etc*) suspense *m*;

to keep sb in ~ manter alguém em suspense *or* na expectativa
suspension [səsˈpɛnʃən] N suspensão *f*; (*of driving licence*) cassação *f*
suspicion [səsˈpɪʃən] N suspeita; **suspicious** ADJ (*suspecting*) suspeitoso; (*causing suspicion*) suspeito
sustain [səsˈteɪn] VT sustentar; (*suffer*) sofrer; **sustainable** ADJ sustentável
SUV N ABBR (= *sports utility vehicle*) SUV *m*
swallow [ˈswɔləu] N (*bird*) andorinha ▶ VT engolir, tragar; (*fig: story*) engolir; (*pride*) pôr de lado; (*one's words*) retirar; **swallow up** VT (*savings etc*) consumir
swam [swæm] PT *of* **swim**
swamp [swɔmp] N pântano, brejo ▶ VT atolar, inundar; (*fig*) assoberbar
swan [swɔn] N cisne *m*
swap [swɔp] N troca, permuta ▶ VT: **to ~ (for)** trocar (por); (*replace (with)*) substituir (por)
swarm [swɔːm] N (*of bees*) enxame *m*; (*of people*) multidão *f* ▶ VI enxamear; aglomerar-se; (*place*): **to be ~ing with** estar apinhado de
sway [sweɪ] VI balançar-se, oscilar ▶ VT (*influence*) influenciar
swear [swɛəʳ] (*pt* **swore**, *pp* **sworn**) VI (*curse*) xingar ▶ VT (*promise*) jurar; **swearword** N palavrão *m*
sweat [swɛt] N suor *m* ▶ VI suar
sweater N suéter *m or f* (BR), camisola (PT)
sweaty ADJ suado
Swede [swiːd] N sueco(-a)
swede [swiːd] N *tipo de nabo*
Sweden [ˈswiːdən] N Suécia; **Swedish** ADJ sueco ▶ N (*Ling*) sueco

sweep [swiːp] (*pt, pp* **swept**) N (*act*) varredura; (*also*: **chimney ~**) limpador *m* de chaminés ▶ VT varrer; (*with arm*) empurrar; (*subj: current*) arrastar; (: *fashion, craze*) espalhar-se por ▶ VI varrer; **sweep away** VT varrer; **sweep past** VI passar rapidamente; **sweep up** VI varrer
sweet [swiːt] N (*candy*) bala (BR), rebuçado (PT); (BRIT: *pudding*) sobremesa ▶ ADJ doce; (*fig: air*) fresco; (: *water, smell*) doce; (: *sound*) suave; (: *baby, kitten*) bonitinho; (*kind*) meigo; **sweetheart** N namorado(-a)
swell [swɛl] (*pt* **swelled**, *pp* **swollen** *or* **swelled**) N (*of sea*) vaga, onda ▶ ADJ (*us inf: excellent*) bacana ▶ VI (*increase*) aumentar; (*get stronger*) intensificar-se; (*also*: **~ up**) inchar(-se); **swelling** N (*Med*) inchação *f*
swept [swɛpt] PT, PP *of* **sweep**
swerve [swəːv] VI desviar-se
swift [swɪft] N (*bird*) andorinhão *m* ▶ ADJ rápido
swim [swɪm] (*pt* **swam**, *pp* **swum**) N: **to go for a ~** ir nadar ▶ VI nadar; (*head, room*) rodar ▶ VT atravessar a nado; (*distance*) percorrer (a nado); **swimmer** N nadador(a) *m/f*; **swimming** N natação *f*; **swimming costume** (BRIT) N (*woman's*) maiô *m* (BR), fato de banho (PT); (*man's*) calção *m* de banho (BR), calções *mpl* de banho (PT); **swimming pool** N piscina; **swimming trunks** NPL sunga (BR), calções *mpl* de banho (PT); **swimsuit** N maiô *m* (BR), fato de banho (PT)
swine flu [ˈswaɪn-] N gripe *f* suína
swing [swɪŋ] (*pt, pp* **swung**) N (*in playground*) balanço; (*movement*)

balanceio, oscilação f; (*change: in opinion*) mudança; virada; (*rhythm*) ritmo ▶ VT balançar; (*also*: **~ round**) girar, rodar ▶ VI oscilar; (*on swing*) balançar; (*also*: **~ round**) voltar-se bruscamente; **to be in full ~** estar a todo vapor

swirl [swə:l] VI redemoinhar

Swiss [swɪs] ADJ, N INV suíço(-a)

switch [swɪtʃ] N (*for light, radio etc*) interruptor m; (*change*) mudança ▶ VT (*change*) trocar; **switch off** VT apagar; (*engine*) desligar; **switch on** VT acender; ligar; **switchboard** N (*Tel*) mesa telefônica

Switzerland ['swɪtsələnd] N Suíça

swollen ['swəulən] PP *of* **swell**

swoop [swu:p] N (*by police etc*) batida ▶ VI (*also*: **~ down**) precipitar-se, cair

swop [swɔp] N, VT = **swap**

sword [sɔ:d] N espada

swore [swɔ:ʳ] PT *of* **swear**

sworn [swɔ:n] PP *of* **swear** ▶ ADJ (*statement*) sob juramento; (*enemy*) declarado

swum [swʌm] PP *of* **swim**

swung [swʌŋ] PT, PP *of* **swing**

syllable ['sɪləbl] N sílaba

syllabus ['sɪləbəs] N programa m de estudos

symbol ['sɪmbl] N símbolo

sympathetic [sɪmpə'θɛtɪk] ADJ (*understanding*) compreensivo; (*likeable*) agradável; (*supportive*): **~ to(wards)** solidário com

sympathize ['sɪmpəθaɪz] VI: **to ~ with** (*person*) compadecer-se de; (*sb's feelings*) compreender; (*cause*) simpatizar com

sympathy ['sɪmpəθɪ] N compaixão f; **sympathies** NPL (*tendencies*) simpatia; **in ~ with**

em acordo com; (*strike*) em solidariedade com; **with our deepest ~** com nossos mais profundos pêsames

symphony ['sɪmfənɪ] N sinfonia

symptom ['sɪmptəm] N sintoma m; (*sign*) indício

syndicate ['sɪndɪkɪt] N sindicato; (*of newspapers*) cadeia

synthetic [sɪn'θɛtɪk] ADJ sintético

Syria ['sɪrɪə] N Síria

syringe [sɪ'rɪndʒ] N seringa

syrup ['sɪrəp] N xarope m; (*also*: **golden ~**) melaço

system ['sɪstəm] N sistema m; (*method*) método; (*Anat*) organismo; **systematic** [sɪstə'mætɪk] ADJ sistemático

S

t

dia que contenham um certo toque de escândalo; veja **quality (news)papers**.

tack [tæk] N (*nail*) tachinha, percevejo ▶ VT prender com tachinha; (*stitch*) alinhavar ▶ VI virar de bordo

tackle ['tækl] N (*gear*) equipamento; (*also*: **fishing ~**) apetrechos *mpl*; (*for lifting*) guincho; (*Football*) ato de tirar a bola de adversário ▶ VT (*difficulty*) atacar; (*challenge: person*) desafiar; (*grapple with*) atracar-se com; (*Football*) tirar a bola de

tacky ['tækɪ] ADJ pegajoso, grudento; (*inf: tasteless*) cafona

tact [tækt] N tato, diplomacia; **tactful** ADJ diplomático

tactics ['tæktɪks] N, NPL tática

tactless ['tæktlɪs] ADJ sem diplomacia

tab [tæb] N lingueta, aba; (*label*) etiqueta; **to keep ~s on** (*fig*) vigiar

table ['teɪbl] N mesa ▶ VT (*motion etc*) apresentar; **to lay** *or* **set the ~** pôr a mesa; **~ of contents** índice *m*, sumário; **tablecloth** N toalha de mesa; **tablespoon** N colher *f* de sopa; (*also*: **tablespoonful**: *as measurement*) colherada

tablet ['tæblɪt] N (*Med*) comprimido; (*also*: **~ computer**) tablet *m*; (*of stone*) lápide *f*

table tennis N pingue-pongue *m*, tênis *m* de mesa

tabloid ['tæblɔɪd] N tabloide *m*; **tabloid press** N *ver nota*

tag [tæg] N (*label*) etiqueta; **tag along** VI seguir

tail [teɪl] N rabo; (*of bird, comet, plane*) cauda; (*of shirt, coat*) aba ▶ VT (*follow*) seguir bem de perto; *see also* **head**; **tail away** VI diminuir gradualmente; **tail off** VI diminuir gradualmente

tailor ['teɪlə'] N alfaiate *m*

take [teɪk] (*pt* **took**, *pp* **taken**) VT tomar; (*photo, holiday*) tirar; (*grab*) pegar (em); (*prize*) ganhar; (*effort, courage*) requerer, exigir; (*tolerate*) aguentar; (*accompany, bring, carry: person*) acompanhar, trazer; (*: thing*) trazer, carregar; (*exam*) fazer; (*passengers etc*): **it ~s 50 people** cabem 50 pessoas; **to ~ sth from** (*drawer etc*) tirar algo de; (*person*) pegar algo de; **I ~ it that ...** suponho que ...; **take after** VT FUS parecer-se com; **take apart** VT desmontar; **take away** VT (*extract*)

> O termo **tabloid press** refere-se aos jornais populares de formato meio jornal que apresentam muitas fotografias e adotam um estilo bastante conciso. O público-alvo desses jornais é composto por leitores que se interessam pelos fatos do

tirar; (*carry off*) levar; (*subtract*) subtrair; **take back** VT (*return*) devolver; (*one's words*) retirar; **take down** VT (*building*) demolir; (*dismantle*) desmontar; (*letter etc*) tomar por escrito; **take in** VT (*deceive*) enganar; (*understand*) compreender; (*include*) abranger; (*lodger*) receber; **take off** VI (*Aviat*) decolar; (*go away*) ir-se ▶ VT (*remove*) tirar; **take on** VT (*work*) empreender; (*employee*) empregar; (*opponent*) desafiar; **take out** VT tirar; (*extract*) extrair; (*invite*) acompanhar; **take over** VT (*business*) assumir; (*country*) tomar posse de ▶ VI: **to ~ over from sb** suceder a alguém; **take to** VT FUS (*person*) simpatizar com; (*activity*) afeiçoar-se a; **to ~ to doing sth** criar o hábito de fazer algo; **take up** VT (*dress*) encurtar; (*time, space*) ocupar; (*hobby etc*) dedicar-se a; (*offer, challenge*) aceitar; **to ~ sb up on a suggestion/offer** aceitar a oferta/sugestão de alguém sobre algo; **takeaway** (BRIT) ADJ (*food*) para levar; **takeoff** N (*Aviat*) decolagem f; **takeover** N (*Comm*) aquisição f de controle; **takings** NPL (*Comm*) receita, renda

talc [tælk] N (also: **talcum powder**) talco

tale [teɪl] N (*story*) conto; (*account*) narrativa; **to tell ~s** (*fig: lie*) dizer mentiras

talent ['tælənt] N talento; **talented** ADJ talentoso

talk [tɔːk] N conversa, fala; (*gossip*) mexerico, fofocas fpl; (*conversation*) conversa, conversação f ▶ VI falar; **talks** NPL (*Pol etc*) negociações fpl; **to ~ about** falar sobre; **to ~ sb into doing sth** convencer alguém

a fazer algo; **to ~ sb out of doing sth** dissuadir alguém de fazer algo; **to ~ shop** falar sobre negócios/questões profissionais; **talk over** VT discutir

tall [tɔːl] ADJ alto; **to be 6 feet ~** medir 6 pés, ter 6 pés de altura

tame [teɪm] ADJ domesticado; (*fig: story, style*) sem graça, insípido

tamper ['tæmpə'] VI: **to ~ with** mexer em

tampon ['tæmpɔn] N tampão m

tan [tæn] N (also: **sun~**) bronzeado ▶ VI bronzear-se ▶ ADJ (*colour*) bronzeado, marrom claro

tangerine [tændʒə'riːn] N tangerina, mexerica

tangle ['tæŋgl] N emaranhado; **to get in(to) a ~** meter-se num rolo

tank [tæŋk] N depósito, tanque m; (*for fish*) aquário; (*Mil*) tanque m

tanker ['tæŋkə'] N (*ship*) navio-tanque m; (*truck*) caminhão-tanque m

tantrum ['tæntrəm] N chilique m, acesso (de raiva)

tap [tæp] N (*on sink etc*) torneira; (*gentle blow*) palmadinha; (*gas tap*) chave f ▶ VT dar palmadinha em, bater de leve; (*resources*) utilizar, explorar; (*telephone*) grampear; **on ~** disponível

tape [teɪp] N fita; (also: **magnetic ~**) fita magnética; (*sticky tape*) fita adesiva ▶ VT (*record*) gravar (em fita); (*stick with tape*) colar; **tape measure** N fita métrica, trena

tar [tɑː'] N alcatrão m

target ['tɑːgɪt] N alvo

tariff ['tærɪf] N tarifa

tarmac ['tɑːmæk] N (BRIT: *on road*) macadame m; (*Aviat*) pista

tarpaulin [tɑː'pɔːlɪn] N lona alcatroada

tart [tɑːt] N (Culin) torta; (BRIT inf, pej: woman) piranha ▶ ADJ (flavour) ácido, azedo; **tart up** (inf) VT arrumar, dar um jeito em; **to ~ o.s. up** arrumar-se; (pej) empetecar-se

tartan ['tɑːtn] N pano escocês axadrezado, tartan m ▶ ADJ axadrezado

tartar ['tɑːtəʳ] N (on teeth) tártaro

taste [teɪst] N gosto; (also: **after~**) gosto residual; (sample, fig) amostra, ideia ▶ VT provar; (test) experimentar ▶ VI: **to ~ of** or **like** ter gosto or sabor de; **you can ~ the garlic (in it)** sente-se o gosto de alho; **in good/bad ~** de bom/mau gosto; **tasteful** ADJ de bom gosto; **tasteless** ADJ insípido, insosso; (remark) de mau gosto; **tasty** ADJ saboroso, delicioso

tatters ['tætəz] NPL: **in ~** (clothes) em farrapos; (papers etc) em pedaços

tattoo [tə'tuː] N tatuagem f; (spectacle) espetáculo militar ▶ VT tatuar

taught [tɔːt] PT, PP of **teach**

taunt [tɔːnt] N zombaria, escárnio ▶ VT zombar de, mofar de

Taurus ['tɔːrəs] N Touro

taut [tɔːt] ADJ esticado

tax [tæks] N imposto ▶ VT tributar; (fig: test) sobrecarregar; (: patience) esgotar; **tax-free** ADJ isento de impostos

taxi ['tæksɪ] N táxi m ▶ VI (Aviat) taxiar; **taxi driver** N motorista m/f de táxi; **taxi rank** (BRIT) N ponto de táxi; **taxi stand** N ponto de táxi

tax: tax payer N contribuinte m/f; **tax return** N declaração f de rendimentos

TB ABBR of **tuberculosis**

tea [tiː] N chá m; (BRIT: meal) refeição f à noite; **high ~** (BRIT) ajantarado; **tea bag** N saquinho (BR) or carteira (PT) de chá; **tea break** (BRIT) N pausa (para o chá)

teach [tiːtʃ] (pt, pp **taught**) VT: **to ~ sb sth, ~ sth to sb** ensinar algo a alguém; (in school) lecionar ▶ VI ensinar; (be a teacher) lecionar; **teacher** N professor(a) m/f; **teaching** N ensino; (as profession) magistério

teacup ['tiːkʌp] N xícara (BR) or chávena (PT) de chá

team [tiːm] N (Sport) time m (BR), equipa f (PT); (group) equipe f (BR), equipa (PT); (of animals) parelha

teapot ['tiːpɔt] N bule m de chá

tear¹ [tɪəʳ] N lágrima; **in ~s** chorando, em lágrimas

tear² [tɛəʳ] (pt **tore**, pp **torn**) N rasgão m ▶ VT rasgar ▶ VI rasgar-se; **tear along** VI (rush) precipitar-se; **tear up** VT rasgar

tearful ['tɪəful] ADJ choroso

tear gas N gás m lacrimogênio

tearoom ['tiːruːm] N salão m de chá

tease [tiːz] VT implicar com

teaspoon ['tiːspuːn] N colher f de chá; (also: **~ful**: as measurement) (conteúdo de) colher de chá

teatime ['tiːtaɪm] N hora do chá

tea towel (BRIT) N pano de prato

technical ['tɛknɪkl] ADJ técnico

technician [tɛk'nɪʃn] N técnico(-a)

technique [tɛk'niːk] N técnica

technology [tɛk'nɔlədʒɪ] N tecnologia

teddy ['tɛdɪ], **teddy bear** N ursinho de pelúcia

tedious ['tiːdɪəs] ADJ maçante, chato

teenage ['tiːneɪdʒ] ADJ (fashions etc) de or para adolescentes; **teenager** N adolescente m/f, jovem m/f

teens [ti:nz] NPL: **to be in one's ~**
estar entre os 13 e 19 anos, estar na
adolescência

teeth [ti:θ] NPL of **tooth**

teetotal ['ti:'təutl] ADJ abstêmio

teleconferencing
['telɪkɔnfərənsɪŋ] N
teleconferência f

telegram ['telɪgræm] N
telegrama m

telephone ['telɪfəun] N telefone m
▶ VT (person) telefonar para;
(message) telefonar; **to be on the ~**
(BRIT), **to have a ~** (subscriber) ter
telefone; **to be on the ~** (be
speaking) estar falando no telefone;
telephone booth, (BRIT)
telephone box N cabine f
telefônica; **telephone call** N
telefonema m; **telephone
directory** N lista telefônica,
catálogo (BR); **telephone number**
N (número de) telefone m

telesales ['telɪseɪlz] NPL
televendas fpl

telescope ['telɪskəup] N telescópio

television ['telɪvɪʒən] N
televisão f; **on ~** na televisão

tell [tel] (pt, pp **told**) VT dizer;
(relate: story) contar; (distinguish):
to ~ sth from distinguir algo de
▶ VI (have effect) ter efeito; (talk):
to ~ (of) falar (de or em); **to ~ sb
to do sth** dizer para alguém fazer
algo; **tell off** VT repreender

telly ['telɪ] (BRIT inf) N ABBR =
television

temp [temp] (BRIT inf) N
temporário(-a) ▶ VI trabalhar
como temporário(-a)

temper ['tempə'] N (nature)
temperamento; (mood) humor m;
(fit of anger) cólera ▶ VT (moderate)
moderar; **to be in a ~** estar de

mau humor; **to lose one's ~**
perder a paciência or a calma,
ficar zangado

temperament ['temprəmənt] N
temperamento; **temperamental**
[temprə'mentl] ADJ
temperamental

temperature ['temprətʃə'] N
temperatura; **to have** or **run a ~**
ter febre

temple ['templ] N (building)
templo; (Anat) têmpora

temporary ['tempərərɪ] ADJ
temporário; (passing) transitório

tempt [tempt] VT tentar;
tempting ['temptɪŋ] ADJ
tentador(a)

ten [ten] NUM dez; see also **five**

tenant ['tenənt] N inquilino(-a),
locatário(-a)

tend [tend] VT (sick etc) cuidar de
▶ VI: **to ~ to do sth** tender a fazer
algo

tendency ['tendənsɪ] N tendência

tender ['tendə'] ADJ terno; (age)
tenro; (sore) sensível, dolorido;
(meat) macio ▶ N (Comm: offer)
oferta, proposta; (money): **legal ~**
moeda corrente or legal ▶ VT
oferecer; **to ~ one's resignation**
pedir demissão

tennis ['tenɪs] N tênis m; **tennis
ball** N bola de tênis; **tennis court**
N quadra de tênis; **tennis player** N
jogador(a) m/f de tênis; **tennis
racket** N raquete f de tênis

tenor ['tenə'] N (Mus) tenor m

tense [tens] ADJ tenso; (muscle)
rígido, teso ▶ N (Ling) tempo

tension ['tenʃən] N tensão f

tent [tent] N tenda, barraca

tentative ['tentətɪv] ADJ
provisório, tentativo; (person)
hesitante, indeciso

t

tenth [tɛnθ] NUM décimo
tent peg N estaca
tent pole N pau *m*
tepid ['tɛpɪd] ADJ tépido, morno
term [təːm] N (*word, expression*)
termo, expressão *f*; (*period*) período;
(*Sch*) trimestre *m* ▶ VT denominar;
terms NPL (*conditions*) condições *fpl*;
(*Comm*) cláusulas *fpl*, termos *mpl*;
in the short/long ~ a curto/longo
prazo; **to be on good ~s with sb**
dar-se bem com alguém; **to come
to ~s with** aceitar
terminal ['təːmɪnl] ADJ incurável
▶ N (*Elec*) borne *m*; (BRIT: *also*: **air ~**)
terminal *m*; (*for oil, ore etc, also:
Comput*) terminal *m*; (BRIT: *also:*
coach ~) estação *f* rodoviária
terminate ['təːmɪneɪt] VT
terminar; **to ~ a pregnancy** fazer
um aborto
terminus ['təːmɪnəs] (*pl* **termini**) N
terminal *m*
terrace ['tɛrəs] N terraço; (BRIT:
row of houses) lance *m* de casas; **the
terraces** NPL (BRIT *Sport*) a
arquibancada (BR), a geral (PT);
terraced ADJ (*house*) ladeado por
outras casas; (*garden*) em dois níveis
terrain [tɛ'reɪn] N terreno
terrible ['tɛrɪbl] ADJ terrível,
horroroso; (*conditions*) precário;
(*inf: awful*) terrível; **terribly** ADV
terrivelmente; (*very badly*)
pessimamente
terrific [tə'rɪfɪk] ADJ terrível,
magnífico; (*wonderful*) maravilhoso,
sensacional
terrify ['tɛrɪfaɪ] VT apavorar
territory ['tɛrɪtərɪ] N território
terror ['tɛrəʳ] N terror *m*; **terrorist**
N terrorista *m/f*
test [tɛst] N (*trial, check*) prova,
ensaio; (*of courage etc, Chem*) prova;

(*Med*) exame *m*; (*exam*) teste *m*,
prova; (*also:* **driving ~**) exame de
motorista ▶ VT testar, pôr à prova
testicle ['tɛstɪkl] N testículo
testify ['tɛstɪfaɪ] VI (*Jur*) depor,
testemunhar; **to ~ to sth** atestar
algo; testemunhar algo
testimony ['tɛstɪmənɪ] N (*Jur*)
testemunho, depoimento; **to be
(a) ~ to** ser uma prova de
test match N (*Cricket, Rugby*) jogo
internacional
test tube N proveta, tubo de ensaio
tetanus ['tɛtənəs] N tétano
text [tɛkst] N texto; (*also:* **~ message**)
mensagem *f* de texto, torpedo (*inf*)
▶ VT mandar uma mensagem de
texto *or* (*inf*) um torpedo para;
textbook N livro didático; (*Sch*) livro
escolar; **text message** N
mensagem *f* de texto, torpedo (*inf*)
texture ['tɛkstʃəʳ] N textura
Thailand ['taɪlænd] N Tailândia
Thames [tɛmz] N: **the ~** o Tâmisa
(BR), o Tamisa (PT)
than [ðæn, ðən] CONJ (*in
comparisons*) do que; **more ~ 10**
mais de 10; **I have more/less ~ you**
tenho mais/menos do que você;
she has more apples ~ pears ela
tem mais maçãs do que peras; **she
is older ~ you think** ela é mais
velha do que você pensa
thank [θæŋk] VT agradecer; **~ you
(very much)** muito obrigado(-a);
thanks NPL agradecimentos *mpl*
▶ EXCL obrigado(-a)!
Thanksgiving ['θæŋksgɪvɪŋ],
Thanksgiving Day N Dia *m* de
Ação de Graças

> O feriado de Ação de graças
> (**Thanksgiving Day**) nos
> Estados Unidos, quarta
> quinta-feira do mês de

novembro, é o dia em que se comemora a boa colheita feita pelos peregrinos originários da Grã-Bretanha em 1621; tradicionalmente, é um dia em que se agradece a Deus e se organiza um grande banquete. Uma festa semelhante é celebrada no Canadá na segunda segunda-feira de outubro.

(KEYWORD)

that [ðæt, ðət] (pl **those**) ADJ (demonstrative) esse/essa; (more remote) aquele/aquela; **that man/woman/book** aquele homem/aquela mulher/aquele livro; **that one** esse/essa
▶ PRON 1 (demonstrative) esse/essa, aquele/aquela; (neuter) isso, aquilo; **who's/what's that?** quem é?/o que é isso?; **is that you?** é você?; **I prefer this to that** eu prefiro isto a aquilo; **that's what he said** foi isso o que ele disse; **that is (to say)** isto é, quer dizer
2 (relative, direct: thing, person) que; (: person) quem; (relative, indirect: thing, person) o/a qual sg, os/as quais pl; (: person) quem; **the book (that) I read** o livro que eu li; **the box (that) I put it in** a caixa na qual eu o coloquei; **the man (that) I spoke to** o homem com quem or o qual falei
3 (relative, of time): **on the day that he came** no dia em que ele veio
▶ CONJ que; **she suggested that I phone you** ela sugeriu que eu telefonasse para você
▶ ADV (demonstrative): **I can't work that much** não posso trabalhar tanto; **I didn't realize it was that**

bad não pensei que fôsse tão ruim; **that high** dessa altura, até essa altura

thatched [θætʃt] ADJ (roof) de sapê; **~ cottage** chalé m com telhado de sapê or de colmo
thaw [θɔː] N degelo ▶ VI (ice) derreter-se; (food) descongelar-se ▶ VT (food) descongelar

(KEYWORD)

the [ðiː, ðə] DEF ART 1 (gen: singular) o/a; (: plural) os/as; **the books/children are in the library** os livros/as crianças estão na biblioteca; **she put it on the table** ela colocou-o na mesa; **he took it from the drawer** ele tirou isto da gaveta; **to play the piano/violin** tocar piano/violino; **I'm going to the cinema** vou ao cinema
2 (+ adj to form n): **the rich and the poor** os ricos e os pobres; **to attempt the impossible** tentar o impossível
3 (in titles): **Richard the Second** Ricardo II; **Peter the Great** Pedro o Grande
4 (in comparisons): **the more he works, the more he earns** quanto mais ele trabalha, mais ele ganha

theatre ['θɪətər], (US) **theater** N teatro; (Med: also: **operating ~**) sala de operação
theft [θɛft] N roubo
their [ðɛər] ADJ seu/sua, deles/delas; **theirs** PRON (o) seu/(a) sua
them [ðɛm, ðəm] PRON (direct) os/as; (indirect) lhes; (stressed, after prep) a eles/a elas

theme [θi:m] N tema *m*; **theme park** N *parque de diversões em torno de um único tema*

themselves [ðəm'sɛlvz] PRON (*subject*) eles mesmos/elas mesmas; se; (*after prep*) si (*mesmos/as*)

then [ðɛn] ADV (*at that time*) então; (*next*) em seguida; (*later*) logo, depois; (*and also*) além disso ▶ CONJ (*therefore*) então, nesse caso, portanto ▶ ADJ: **the ~ president** o então presidente; **by ~** (*past*) até então; (*future*) até lá; **from ~ on** a partir de então

theology [θɪ'ɔlədʒɪ] N teologia

theory ['θɪərɪ] N teoria; **in ~** em teoria, teoricamente

therapy ['θɛrəpɪ] N terapia

(KEYWORD)

there [ðɛəʳ] ADV **1**: **there is, there are** há, tem; **there are 3 of them** são três; **there is no-one here/no bread left** não tem ninguém aqui/ não tem mais pão; **there has been an accident** houve um acidente **2** (*referring to place*) aí, ali, lá; **put it in/on/up/down there** põe isto lá dentro/cima/em cima/embaixo; **I want that book there** quero aquele livro lá; **there he is!** lá está ele! **3**: **there, there!** (*esp to child*) calma!

thereabouts ['ðɛərəbauts] ADV por aí; (*amount*) aproximadamente

thereafter [ðɛər'ɑ:ftəʳ] ADV depois disso

thereby ['ðɛəbaɪ] ADV assim, deste modo

therefore ['ðɛəfɔ:] ADV portanto

there's [ðɛəz] = **there is**; = **there has**

thermal ['θə:ml] ADJ térmico

thermometer [θə'mɔmɪtəʳ] N termômetro

thermostat ['θə:məustæt] N termostato

these [ði:z] PL ADJ, PRON estes/ estas

thesis ['θi:sɪs] (*pl* **theses**) N tese *f*

they [ðeɪ] PRON PL eles/elas; **~ say that ...** (*it is said that*) diz-se que ..., dizem que ...; **they'd = they had**; = **they would**; **they'll = they shall**; = **they will**; **they've = they have**

thick [θɪk] ADJ espesso; (*mud, fog, forest*) denso; (*sauce*) grosso; (*stupid*) burro ▶ N: **in the ~ of the battle** em plena batalha; **it's 20 cm ~** tem 20 cm de espessura; **thicken** VI (*fog*) adensar-se; (*plot etc*) complicar-se ▶ VT engrossar; **thickness** N espessura, grossura

thief [θi:f] (*pl* **thieves**) N ladrão/ ladra *m/f*

thigh [θaɪ] N coxa

thin [θɪn] ADJ magro; (*slice, line, book*) fino; (*light*) leve; (*hair*) ralo; (*crowd*) pequeno; (*soup, sauce*) aguado ▶ VT (*also:* **~ down**) diluir

thing [θɪŋ] N coisa; (*object*) negócio; (*matter*) assunto, negócio; (*mania*) mania; **things** N PL (*belongings*) pertences *mpl*; **to have a ~ about sb/sth** ser vidrado em alguém/ algo; **the best ~ would be to ...** o melhor seria ...; **how are ~s?** como vai?, tudo bem?; **she's got a ~ about ...** ela detesta ...; **poor ~!** coitadinho(-a)!

think [θɪŋk] (*pt, pp* **thought**) VI pensar; (*believe*) achar ▶ VT pensar, achar; (*imagine*) imaginar; **what did you ~ of them?** o que você achou deles?; **to ~ about sth/sb** pensar em algo/alguém; **I'll ~ about it** vou pensar sobre isso;

to ~ of doing sth pensar em fazer algo; **I ~ so/not** acho que sim/não; **to ~ well of sb** fazer bom juízo de alguém; **think over** vt refletir sobre, meditar sobre; **think up** vt inventar, bolar

third [θə:d] ADJ terceiro ▶ N terceiro(-a); (fraction) terço; (Aut) terceira; (Sch: degree) terceira categoria; **thirdly** ADV em terceiro lugar; **third party insurance** N seguro contra terceiros; **Third World** N: **the Third World** o Terceiro Mundo

thirst [θə:st] N sede f; **thirsty** ADJ (person) sedento, com sede; (work) que dá sede; **to be thirsty** estar com sede

thirteen ['θə:'ti:n] NUM treze

thirty ['θə:tɪ] NUM trinta

(KEYWORD)

this [ðɪs] (pl **these**) ADJ (demonstrative) este/esta; **this man/woman/book** este homem/esta mulher/este livro; **these people/children/records** estas pessoas/crianças/estes discos; **this one** este aqui ▶ PRON (demonstrative) este/esta; (neuter) isto; **who/what is this?** quem é esse?/o que é isso?; **this is where I live** é aqui que eu moro; **this is Mr Brown** este é o Sr Brown; (on phone) aqui é o Sr Brown ▶ ADV (demonstrative): **this high** desta altura; **this long** deste comprimento; **we can't stop now we've gone this far** não podemos parar agora que fomos tão longe

thistle ['θɪsl] N cardo

thorn [θɔ:n] N espinho

thorough ['θʌrə] ADJ (search) minucioso; (knowledge, research, person) metódico, profundo; **thoroughly** ADV minuciosamente; (search) profundamente; (wash) completamente; (very) muito

those [ðəuz] PRON PL, ADJ esses/essas

though [ðəu] CONJ embora, se bem que ▶ ADV no entanto

thought [θɔ:t] PT, PP of **think** ▶ N pensamento; (idea) ideia; (opinion) opinião f; (reflection) reflexão f; **thoughtful** ADJ pensativo; (serious) sério; (considerate) atencioso; **thoughtless** ADJ desatencioso; (words, person) inconsequente

thousand ['θauzənd] NUM mil; **two ~** dois mil; **~s (of)** milhares mpl (de); **thousandth** ADJ milésimo

thrash [θræʃ] vt surrar, malhar; (defeat) derrotar; **thrash about** vi debater-se; **thrash out** vt discutir exaustivamente

thread [θrɛd] N fio, linha; (of screw) rosca ▶ vt (needle) enfiar

threat [θrɛt] N ameaça; **threaten** vi ameaçar ▶ vt: **to threaten sb with sth/to do** ameaçar alguém com algo/de fazer

three [θri:] NUM três; **three-dimensional** ADJ tridimensional, em três dimensões; **three-piece suit** N terno (3 peças) (BR), fato de 3 peças (PT)

threshold ['θrɛʃhəuld] N limiar m

threw [θru:] PT of **throw**

thrill [θrɪl] N emoção f; (shudder) estremecimento ▶ vt emocionar, vibrar; **to be ~ed** (with gift etc) estar emocionado; **thriller** N romance *m or* filme *m* de suspense; **thrilling** ADJ emocionante

throat [θrəʊt] N garganta; **to have a sore ~** estar com dor de garganta

throb [θrɔb] N (*of heart*) batida; (*of engine*) vibração *f*; (*of pain*) latejo ▶ VI (*heart*) bater, palpitar; (*pain*) dar pontadas; (*engine*) vibrar

throne [θrəʊn] N trono

through [θruː] PREP por, através de; (*time*) durante; (*by means of*) por meio de, por intermédio de; (*owing to*) devido a ▶ ADJ (*ticket, train*) direto ▶ ADV através; **to put sb ~ to sb** (*Tel*) ligar alguém com alguém; **to be ~** (*Tel*) estar na linha; (*have finished*) acabar; **"no ~ road"** "rua sem saída"; **I'm halfway ~ the book** estou na metade do livro; **throughout** PREP (*place*) por todo(-a); (*time*) durante todo(-a) ▶ ADV por *or* em todas as partes

throw [θrəʊ] (*pt* **threw**, *pp* **thrown**) N arremesso, tiro; (*Sport*) lançamento ▶ VT jogar, atirar; (*Sport*) lançar; (*rider*) derrubar; (*fig*) desconcertar; **to ~ a party** dar uma festa; **throw away** VT (*dispose of*) jogar fora; (*waste*) desperdiçar; **throw off** VT desfazer-se de; (*habit, cold*) livrar-se; **throw out** VT expulsar; (*rubbish*) jogar fora; (*idea*) rejeitar; **throw up** VI vomitar, botar para fora

thru [θruː] (*us*) PREP, ADJ, ADV = **through**

thrush [θrʌʃ] N (*Zool*) tordo

thrust [θrʌst] (*pt, pp* **thrust**) N impulso; (*Tech*) empuxo ▶ VT empurrar

thud [θʌd] N baque *m*, som *m* surdo

thug [θʌɡ] N facínora *m/f*

thumb [θʌm] N (*Anat*) polegar *m*; **to ~ a lift** pegar carona (BR),

arranjar uma boleia (PT); **thumb through** VT FUS folhear; **thumbtack** (*us*) N percevejo, tachinha

thump [θʌmp] N murro, pancada; (*sound*) baque *m* ▶ VT dar um murro em ▶ VI bater

thunder ['θʌndər] N trovão *m* ▶ VI trovejar; (*train etc*): **to ~ past** passar como um raio; **thunderstorm** N tempestade *f* com trovoada, temporal *m*

Thursday ['θəːzdɪ] N quinta-feira

thyme [taɪm] N tomilho

tick [tɪk] N (*of clock*) tique-taque *m*; (*mark*) tique *m*, marca; (*Zool*) carrapato; (BRIT *inf*): **in a ~** num instante ▶ VI fazer tique-taque ▶ VT marcar, ticar; **tick off** VT assinalar, ticar; (*person*) dar uma bronca em; **tick over** (BRIT) VI (*engine*) funcionar em marcha lenta; (*fig*) ir indo

ticket ['tɪkɪt] N (*for bus, plane*) passagem *f*; (*for theatre, raffle*) bilhete *m*; (*for cinema*) entrada; (*in shop: on goods*) etiqueta; (*for library*) cartão *m*; (*also*: **parking ~**: *fine*) multa; **to get a (parking) ~** (*Aut*) ganhar uma multa (por estacionamento ilegal); **ticket barrier** (BRIT) N (*Rail*) catraca de embarque/desembarque; **ticket collector** N revisor(a) *m/f*; **ticket office** N bilheteria (BR), bilheteira (PT)

tickle ['tɪkl] VT fazer cócegas em ▶ VI fazer cócegas; **ticklish** ADJ coceguento; (*problem*) delicado

tide [taɪd] N maré *f*; (*fig*) curso; **high/low ~** maré alta/baixa; **the ~ of public opinion** a corrente da opinião pública; **tide over** VT ajudar num período difícil

tidy ['taɪdɪ] ADJ (*room*) arrumado; (*dress, work*) limpo; (*person*) bem arrumado ▶ vt (*also:* **~ up**) pôr em ordem, arrumar

tie [taɪ] N (*string etc*) fita, corda; (BRIT: *also:* **neck~**) gravata; (*fig: link*) vínculo, laço; (*Sport: draw*) empate m ▶ vt amarrar ▶ vi (*Sport*) empatar; **to ~ in a bow** dar um laço em; **to ~ a knot in sth** dar um nó em algo; **tie down** vt amarrar; (*fig: restrict*) limitar, restringir; (*: to date, price etc*) obrigar; **tie up** vt embrulhar; (*dog*) prender; (*boat, prisoner etc*) amarrar; (*arrangements*) concluir; **to be ~d up** estar ocupado

tier [tɪər] N fileira; (*of cake*) camada

tiger ['taɪgər] N tigre m

tight [taɪt] ADJ (*rope*) esticado, firme; (*money*) escasso; (*clothes, shoes*) justo; (*bend*) fechado; rigoroso; (*inf: drunk*) bêbado ▶ ADV (*squeeze*) bem forte; (*shut*) hermeticamente; **tighten** vt (*rope*) esticar; (*screw, grip*) apertar; (*security*) aumentar ▶ vi esticar-se; apertar-se; **tightly** ADV firmemente

tile [taɪl] N (*on roof*) telha; (*on floor*) ladrilho; (*on wall*) azulejo, ladrilho

till [tɪl] N caixa (registradora) ▶ vt (*land*) cultivar ▶ PREP, CONJ = **until**

tilt [tɪlt] vt inclinar ▶ vi inclinar-se

timber ['tɪmbər] N (*material*) madeira; (*trees*) mata, floresta

time [taɪm] N tempo; (*epoch: often pl*) época; (*by clock*) hora; (*moment*) momento; (*occasion*) vez f; (*Mus*) compasso ▶ vt calcular *or* medir o tempo de; (*visit etc*) escolher o momento para; **a long ~** muito tempo; **4 at a ~** quatro de uma vez; **for the ~ being** por enquanto; **from ~ to ~** de vez em quando; **at ~s** às vezes; **in ~** (*soon enough*) a tempo; (*after some time*) com o tempo; (*Mus*) no compasso; **in a week's ~** dentro de uma semana; **in no ~** num abrir e fechar de olhos; **any ~** a qualquer hora; **on ~** na hora; **5 ~s 5 is 25** 5 vezes 5 são 25; **what ~ is it?** que horas são?; **to have a good ~** divertir-se; **timely** ADJ oportuno; **timetable** N horário; **time zone** N fuso horário

timid ['tɪmɪd] ADJ tímido

timing ['taɪmɪŋ] N escolha do momento; (*Sport*) cronometragem f; **the ~ of his resignation** o momento que escolheu para se demitir

tin [tɪn] N estanho; (*also:* **~ plate**) folha-de-flandres f; (BRIT: *can*) lata

tingle ['tɪŋgl] vi formigar

tinned [tɪnd] (BRIT) ADJ (*food*) em lata, em conserva

tin opener (BRIT) N abridor m de latas (BR), abre-latas m inv (PT)

tinsel ['tɪnsl] N ouropel m

tint [tɪnt] N matiz m; (*for hair*) tintura, tinta; **tinted** ADJ (*hair*) pintado; (*spectacles, glass*) fumê inv

tiny ['taɪnɪ] ADJ pequenininho, minúsculo

tip [tɪp] N ponta; (*gratuity*) gorjeta; (BRIT: *for rubbish*) depósito; (*advice*) dica ▶ vt dar uma gorjeta a; (*tilt*) inclinar; (*overturn: also:* **~ over**) virar, emborcar; (*empty: also:* **~ out**) esvaziar, entornar

tiptoe ['tɪptəʊ] N: **on ~** na ponta dos pés

tire ['taɪər] N (US) = **tyre** ▶ vt cansar ▶ vi cansar-se; (*become bored*) chatear-se; **tired** ADJ cansado; **to be tired of sth** estar farto *or* cheio de algo; **tiring** ADJ cansativo

tissue ['tɪʃuː] N tecido; *(paper handkerchief)* lenço de papel; **tissue paper** N papel *m* de seda
tit [tɪt] N *(bird)* passarinho; **to give ~ for tat** pagar na mesma moeda
title ['taɪtl] N título
TM N ABBR = **trademark**

(KEYWORD)

to [tuː, tə] PREP **1** *(direction)* a, para; *(towards)* para; **to go to France/London/school/the station** ir à França/a Londres/ao colégio/à estação; **to go to Lígia's/the doctor's** ir à casa da Lígia/ao médico; **the road to Edinburgh** a estrada para Edinburgo; **to the left/right** à esquerda/direita
2 *(as far as)* até; **to count to 10** contar até 10; **from 40 to 50 people** de 40 a 50 pessoas
3 *(with expressions of time)*: **a quarter to 5** quinze para as 5 (BR), 5 menos um quarto (PT)
4 *(for, or)* de, para; **the key to the front door** a chave da porta da frente; **a letter to his wife** uma carta para a sua mulher
5 *(expressing indirect object)*: **to give sth to sb** dar algo a alguém; **to talk to sb** falar com alguém; **I sold it to a friend** vendi isto para um amigo; **to cause damage to sth** causar danos em algo
6 *(in relation to)* para; **3 goals to 2** 3 a 2; **8 apples to the kilo** 8 maçãs por quilo
7 *(purpose, result)* para; **to come to sb's aid** prestar ajuda a alguém; **to sentence sb to death** condenar alguém à morte; **to my surprise** para minha surpresa
▶ WITH VB **1** *(simple infin)*: **to go/eat** ir/comer
2 *(following another vb)*: **to want/try to do** querer/tentar fazer; **to start to do** começar a fazer
3 *(with vb omitted)*: **I don't want to** eu não quero; **you ought to** você deve
4 *(purpose, result)* para
5 *(equivalent to relative clause)* para, a; **I have things to do** eu tenho coisas para fazer; **the main thing is to try** o principal é tentar
6 *(after adj etc)* para; **ready to go** pronto para ir; **too old/young to ...** muito velho/jovem para ...
▶ ADV: **pull/push the door to** puxar/empurrar a porta

toad [təud] N sapo
toadstool ['təudstuːl] N chapéu-de-cobra *m*, cogumelo venenoso
toast [təust] N *(Culin)* torradas *fpl*; *(drink, speech)* brinde *m* ▶ VT torrar; *(drink to)* brindar; **toaster** N torradeira
tobacco [tə'bækəu] N tabaco, fumo (BR)
today [tə'deɪ] ADV, N hoje *m*
toddler ['tɔdlər] N criança que começa a andar
toe [təu] N dedo do pé; *(of shoe)* bico ▶ VT: **to ~ the line** *(fig)* conformar-se, cumprir as obrigações
toffee ['tɔfɪ] N puxa-puxa *m* (BR), caramelo (PT)
together [tə'gɛðər] ADV juntos; *(at same time)* ao mesmo tempo; **~ with** junto com
toilet ['tɔɪlət] N privada, vaso sanitário; *(BRIT: lavatory)* banheiro (BR), casa de banho (PT) ▶ CPD de toalete; **toilet paper** N papel *m* higiênico; **toiletries** NPL artigos *mpl*

de toalete; **toilet roll** N rolo de papel higiênico

token ['təukən] N (*sign*) sinal *m*, símbolo, prova; (*souvenir*) lembrança; (*substitute coin*) ficha ▶ CPD simbólico; **book/record ~** (BRIT) vale para comprar livros/discos

told [təuld] PT, PP *of* **tell**

tolerant ['tɔlərənt] ADJ: **~ of** tolerante com

tolerate ['tɔləreit] VT suportar; (*Med, Tech*) tolerar

toll [təul] N (*of casualties*) número de baixas; (*tax, charge*) pedágio (BR), portagem *f* (PT) ▶ VI dobrar, tanger

tomato [tə'mɑːtəu] (*pl* **tomatoes**) N tomate *m*

tomb [tuːm] N tumba

tombstone ['tuːmstəun] N lápide *f*

tomorrow [tə'mɔrəu] ADV, N amanhã *m*; **the day after ~** depois de amanhã; **~ morning** amanhã de manhã

ton [tʌn] N tonelada; **~s of** (*inf*) um monte de

tone [təun] N tom *m* ▶ VI harmonizar; **tone down** VT (*colour, criticism*) suavizar; (*sound*) baixar; (*Mus*) entoar; **tone up** VT (*muscles*) tonificar

tongs [tɔŋz] NPL (*for coal*) tenaz *f*; (*for hair*) ferros *mpl* de frisar cabelo

tongue [tʌŋ] N língua; **~ in cheek** ironicamente

tonic ['tɔnik] N (*Med*) tônico; (*also:* **~ water**) (água) tônica

tonight [tə'nait] ADV, N esta noite, hoje à noite

tonsil ['tɔnsəl] N amígdala; **tonsillitis** [tɔnsi'laitis] N amigdalite *f*

too [tuː] ADV (*excessively*) demais; muito; (*also*) também; **~ much** (*adv*) demais; (*adj*) demasiado; **~ many** demasiados(-as)

took [tuk] PT *of* **take**

tool [tuːl] N ferramenta

tooth [tuːθ] (*pl* **teeth**) N (*Anat, Tech*) dente *m*; (*molar*) molar *m*; **toothache** N dor *f* de dente; **to have toothache** estar com dor de dente; **toothbrush** N escova de dentes; **toothpaste** N pasta de dentes, creme *m* dental; **toothpick** N palito

top [tɔp] N (*of mountain*) cume *m*, cimo; (*of tree*) topo; (*of head*) cocuruto; (*of cupboard, table*) superfície *f*, topo; (*of box, jar, bottle*) tampa; (*of ladder, page*) topo; (*toy*) pião *m*; (*blouse etc*) top *m*, blusa ▶ ADJ (*highest: shelf, step*) mais alto; (: *marks*) máximo; (*in rank*) principal, superior ▶ VT exceder; (*be first in*) estar à cabeça de; **on ~ of** sobre, em cima de; (*in addition to*) além de; **from ~ to toe** (BRIT) da cabeça aos pés; **from ~ to bottom** de cima abaixo; **top up**, (*US*) **top off** VT completar; (*mobile phone*) recarregar; **top floor** N último andar *m*

topic ['tɔpik] N tópico, assunto; **topical** ADJ atual

topless ['tɔplis] ADJ (*bather etc*) topless *inv*, sem a parte superior do biquíni

topple ['tɔpl] VT derrubar ▶ VI cair para frente

top-up card N cartão de recarga (para celular)

torch [tɔːtʃ] N (BRIT) lanterna

tore [tɔːʳ] PT *of* **tear²**

torment [*n* 'tɔːmɛnt, *vt* tɔː'mɛnt] N tormento, suplício ▶ VT

t

atormentar; (*fig: annoy*) chatear, aborrecer

torn [tɔ:n] PP *of* **tear²**

tornado [tɔ:'neɪdəu] (*pl* **tornadoes**) N tornado

torrent ['tɔrənt] N torrente *f*

tortoise ['tɔ:təs] N tartaruga

torture ['tɔ:tʃə'] N tortura ▶ VT torturar; (*fig*) atormentar

Tory ['tɔ:rɪ] (BRIT) ADJ, N (*Pol*) conservador(a) *m/f*

toss [tɔs] VT atirar, arremessar; (*head*) lançar para trás ▶ VI: **to ~ and turn in bed** virar de um lado para o outro na cama; **to ~ a coin** tirar cara ou coroa; **to ~ up for sth** (BRIT) jogar cara ou coroa por algo

total ['təutl] ADJ total ▶ N total *m*, soma ▶ VT (*add up*) somar; (*amount to*) montar a

touch [tʌtʃ] N (*sense*) toque *m*; (*contact*) contato ▶ VT tocar (em); (*tamper with*) mexer com; (*make contact with*) fazer contato com; (*emotionally*) comover; **a ~ of** (*fig*) um traço de; **to get in ~ with sb** entrar em contato com alguém; **to lose ~** perder o contato; **touch on** VT FUS (*topic*) tocar em, fazer menção de; **touch up** VT (*paint*) retocar; **touchdown** N aterrissagem *f* (BR), aterragem *f* (PT); (*on sea*) amerissagem *f* (BR), amaragem *f* (PT); (*US Football*) touchdown *m* (*colocação da bola no chão atrás da linha de gol*); **touching** ADJ comovedor(a); **touch screen** N (*Comput*) touch screen *m*, ecrã táctil (PT)

tough [tʌf] ADJ duro; (*difficult*) difícil; (*resistant*) resistente; (*person: physically*) forte; (: *mentally*) tenaz; (*firm*) firme, inflexível

tour ['tuə'] N viagem *f*, excursão *f*; (*also:* **package ~**) excursão

organizada; (*of town, museum*) visita; (*by artist*) turnê *f* ▶ VT (*country, city*) excursionar por; (*factory*) visitar

tourism ['tuərɪzm] N turismo

tourist ['tuərɪst] N turista *m/f* ▶ CPD turístico; **tourist office** (*in country*) escritório de turismo; (*in embassy etc*) departamento de turismo

tournament ['tuənəmənt] N torneio

tow [təu] VT rebocar; **"on ~"** (BRIT), **"in ~"** (US) (*Aut*) "rebocado"

toward [tə'wɔ:d], **towards** [tə'wɔ:dz] PREP em direção a; (*of attitude*) para com; (*of purpose*) para; **~(s) noon/the end of the year** perto do meio-dia/do fim do ano

towel ['tauəl] N toalha; **towelling** N (*fabric*) tecido para toalhas

tower ['tauə'] N torre *f*; **tower block** (BRIT) N prédio alto, espigão *m*, cortiço (BR)

town [taun] N cidade *f*; **to go to ~** ir à cidade; (*fig*) fazer com entusiasmo, mandar brasa (BR); **town centre** N centro (da cidade); **town hall** N prefeitura (BR), concelho (PT)

toy [tɔɪ] N brinquedo; **toy with** VT FUS brincar com; (*idea*) contemplar

trace [treɪs] N (*sign*) sinal *m*; (*small amount*) traço ▶ VT (*draw*) traçar, esboçar; (*follow*) seguir a pista de; (*locate*) encontrar

track [træk] N (*mark*) pegada, vestígio; (*path: gen*) caminho, vereda; (: *of bullet etc*) trajetória; (: *of suspect, animal*) pista, rasto; (*Rail*) trilhos (BR), carris *mpl* (PT); (*on tape*) trilha; (*Sport*) pista; (*on record*) faixa ▶ VT seguir a pista de; **to keep ~ of** não perder de vista; (*fig*) manter-se informado sobre; **track down** vt (*prey*) seguir a pista de; (*sth lost*) procurar e encontrar

tractor ['træktə'] N trator *m*

trade [treɪd] N comércio; (*skill, job*) ofício ▶ vi negociar, comerciar ▶ vt: **to ~ sth (for sth)** trocar algo (por algo); **trade in** vt dar como parte do pagamento; **trademark** N marca registrada; **trader** N comerciante *m/f*; **tradesman** *irreg* N lojista *m*; **trade union** N sindicato

tradition [trə'dɪʃən] N tradição *f*; **traditional** ADJ tradicional

traffic ['træfɪk] N trânsito; (*air traffic etc*) tráfego; (*illegal*) tráfico ▶ vi: **to ~ in** (*pej: liquor, drugs*) traficar com, fazer tráfico com; **traffic circle** (*US*) N rotatória; **traffic jam** N engarrafamento, congestionamento; **traffic lights** NPL sinal *m* luminoso; **traffic warden** N guarda *m/f* de trânsito

tragedy ['trædʒədɪ] N tragédia

tragic ['trædʒɪk] ADJ trágico

trail [treɪl] N (*tracks*) rasto, pista; (*path*) caminho, trilha; (*of smoke, dust*) rasto ▶ vt (*drag*) arrastar; (*follow*) seguir a pista de ▶ vi arrastar-se; (*hang loosely*) pender; (*in game, contest*) ficar para trás; **trail behind** vi atrasar-se; **trailer** N (*Aut*) reboque *m*; (*US: caravan*) trailer *m* (BR), rulote *f* (PT); (*Cinema*) trailer

train [treɪn] N trem *m* (BR), comboio (PT); (*of dress*) cauda ▶ vt formar; (*teach skills to*) instruir; (*Sport*) treinar; (*dog*) adestrar, amestrar; (*point: gun etc*): **to ~ on** apontar para ▶ vi (*learn a skill*) instruir-se; (*Sport*) treinar; (*be educated*) ser treinado; **to lose one's ~ of thought** perder o fio;

trainee [treɪ'niː] N estagiário(-a);

trainer N (*Sport*) treinador(a) *m/f*; (*of animals*) adestrador(a) *m/f*;

trainers NPL (*shoes*) tênis *m*;

training N instrução *f*; (*Sport, for occupation*) treinamento; (*professional*) formação

trait [treɪt] N traço

traitor ['treɪtə'] N traidor(a) *m/f*

tram [træm] (BRIT) N (*also*: **~car**) bonde *m* (BR), eléctrico (PT)

tramp [træmp] N (*person*) vagabundo(-a); (*inf, pej: woman*) piranha ▶ vi caminhar pesadamente

trample ['træmpl] vt: **to ~ (underfoot)** calcar aos pés

trampoline ['træmpəliːn] N trampolim *m*

tranquil ['træŋkwɪl] ADJ tranquilo; **tranquillizer** N (*Med*) tranquilizante *m*

transfer [*n* 'trænsfə', *vt* træns'fə:'] N transferência; (*picture, design*) decalcomania ▶ vt transferir; **to ~ the charges** (*BRIT Tel*) ligar a cobrar

transform [træns'fɔːm] vt transformar

transfusion [træns'fjuːʒən] N (*also*: **blood ~**) transfusão *f* (de sangue)

transit ['trænzɪt] N: **in ~** em trânsito, de passagem

translate [trænz'leɪt] vt traduzir; **translation** N tradução *f*; **translator** N tradutor(a) *m/f*

transmission [trænz'mɪʃən] N transmissão *f*

transmit [trænz'mɪt] vt transmitir

transparent [træns'pærnt] ADJ transparente

t

transplant [vt træns'plɑ:nt, n 'trænsplɑ:nt] vt transplantar ▶ N (Med) transplante m

transport [n 'trænspɔ:t, vt træns'pɔ:t] N transporte m ▶ vt transportar; (carry) acarretar; **transportation** [trænspɔ:'teɪʃən] N transporte m

trap [træp] N (snare) armadilha, cilada; (trick) cilada; (carriage) aranha, charrete f ▶ vt (animal, person) pegar numa armadilha; (immobilize) bloquear; **to be ~ped** (in bad marriage, fire) estar preso(-a)

trash [træʃ] N (US: rubbish) lixo; **trash can** (US) N lata de lixo

trauma ['trɔ:mə] N trauma m

travel ['trævl] N viagem f ▶ vi viajar; (sound) propagar-se; (news) levar; (wine): **this wine ~s well** este vinho não sofre alteração ao ser transportado ▶ vt percorrer; **travels** NPL (journeys) viagens fpl; **travel agent** N agente m/f de viagens; **traveller**, (US) **traveler** N viajante m/f; (Comm) caixeiro(-a) viajante; **traveller's cheque**, (US) **traveler's check** N cheque m de viagem; **travelling**, (US) **traveling** N as viagens, viajar m ▶ ADJ (circus, exhibition) itinerante; (salesman) viajante ▶ CPD de viagem; **travel sickness** N enjoo

tray [treɪ] N bandeja; (on desk) cesta

treacherous ['tretʃərəs] ADJ traiçoeiro; (ground, tide) perigoso

treacle ['tri:kl] N melado

tread [tred] (pt **trod**, pp **trodden**) N (step) passo, pisada; (sound) passada; (of stair) piso; (of tyre) banda de rodagem ▶ vi pisar; **tread on** vt FUS pisar (em)

treasure ['treʒər] N tesouro; (person) joia ▶ vt (value) apreciar, estimar; **treasures** NPL (art treasures etc) preciosidades fpl

treasurer ['treʒərər] N tesoureiro(-a)

treasury ['treʒərɪ] N tesouraria

treat [tri:t] N regalo, deleite m ▶ vt tratar; **to ~ sb to sth** convidar alguém para algo

treatment ['tri:tmənt] N tratamento

treaty ['tri:tɪ] N tratado, acordo

treble ['trebl] ADJ tríplice ▶ vt triplicar ▶ vi triplicar(-se)

tree [tri:] N árvore f

trek [trek] N (long journey) jornada; (walk) caminhada

tremble ['trembl] vi tremer

tremendous [trɪ'mendəs] ADJ tremendo; (enormous) enorme; (excellent) sensacional, fantástico

trench [trentʃ] N trincheira

trend [trend] N (tendency) tendência; (of events) curso; (fashion) modismo, tendência; (on social network: also: **~ing topic**) trending topic m ▶ vi (on social network) ser compartilhado no Twitter até virar trending topic; **trendy** ADJ (idea) de acordo com a tendência atual; (clothes) da última moda

trespass ['trespəs] vi: **to ~ on** invadir; **"no ~ing"** "entrada proibida"

trial ['traɪəl] N (Jur) processo; (test: of machine etc) prova, teste m; **trials** NPL (unpleasant experiences) dissabores mpl; **by ~ and error** por tentativas; **to be on ~** ser julgado; **trial period** N período de experiência

triangle ['traɪæŋgl] N (Math, Mus) triângulo

tribe [traɪb] N tribo f

tribunal [traɪ'bjuːnl] N tribunal m

tribute ['trɪbjuːt] N homenagem f;
to pay ~ to prestar homenagem a,
homenagear

trick [trɪk] N truque m; (joke) peça,
brincadeira; (skill, knack)
habilidade f; (Cards) vaza ▶ VT
enganar; **to play a ~ on sb** pregar
uma peça em alguém; **that
should do the ~** (inf) isso deveria
dar resultado

trickle ['trɪkl] N (of water etc) fio
(de água) ▶ VI gotejar, pingar

tricky ['trɪkɪ] ADJ difícil,
complicado

trifle ['traɪfl] N bobagem f,
besteira; (Culin) tipo de bolo com
fruta e creme ▶ ADV: **a ~ long** um
pouquinho longo

trigger ['trɪɡər] N (of gun) gatilho;
trigger off VT desencadear

trim [trɪm] ADJ (figure) elegante;
(house) arrumado; (garden) bem
cuidado ▶ N (haircut etc) aparada;
(on car) estofamento ▶ VT aparar,
cortar; (decorate): **to ~ (with)**
enfeitar (com); (Naut: sail) ajustar

trip [trɪp] N viagem f; (outing)
excursão f; (stumble) tropeção m
▶ VI tropeçar; (go lightly) andar
com passos ligeiros; **on a ~** de
viagem; **trip up** VI tropeçar ▶ VT
passar uma rasteira em

triple ['trɪpl] ADJ triplo, tríplice;
triplets NPL trigêmeos(-as) mpl/fpl

tripod ['traɪpɔd] N tripé m

triumph ['traɪʌmf] N (satisfaction)
satisfação f; (great achievement)
triunfo ▶ VI: **to ~ (over)** triunfar
(sobre)

trivial ['trɪvɪəl] ADJ insignificante;
(commonplace) trivial

trod [trɔd] PT of **tread**; **trodden** PP
of **tread**

troll [trɔl, trəʊl] (inf: Comput) N
troll m ▶ VI trollar

trolley ['trɔlɪ] N carrinho; (table on
wheels) mesa volante

trombone [trɔm'bəʊn] N
trombone m

troop [truːp] N bando, grupo ▶ VI:
to ~ in/out entrar/sair em bando;
troops NPL (Mil) tropas fpl; **~ing the
colour** (BRIT) saudação da bandeira

trophy ['trəʊfɪ] N troféu m

tropic ['trɔpɪk] N trópico; **tropical**
ADJ tropical

trot [trɔt] N trote m; (fast pace)
passo rápido ▶ VI trotar; (person)
andar rapidamente; **on the ~**
(fig: inf) a fio

trouble ['trʌbl] N problema(s)
m(pl), dificuldade(s) f(pl); (worry)
preocupação f; (bother, effort)
incômodo, trabalho; (Pol)
distúrbios mpl; (Med): **stomach ~**
etc problemas mpl gástricos etc
▶ VT perturbar; (worry) preocupar,
incomodar ▶ VI: **to ~ to do sth**
incomodar-se or preocupar-se de
fazer algo; **troubles** NPL (Pol etc)
distúrbios mpl; **to be in ~** estar
num aperto; (ship, climber etc) estar
em dificuldade; **what's the ~?**
qual é o problema?; **troubled** ADJ
preocupado; (epoch, life) agitado;
troublemaker N criador(a)-de-
casos m/f; (child) encrenqueiro(-a);
troublesome ADJ importuno;
(child, cough) incômodo

trough [trɔf] N (also: **drinking ~**)
bebedouro, cocho; (also: **feeding ~**)
gamela; (depression) depressão f

trousers ['traʊzəz] NPL calça (BR),
calças fpl (PT)

trout [traʊt] N INV truta

truant ['truənt] (BRIT) N: **to play ~**
matar aula (BR), fazer gazeta (PT)

t

truce [truːs] N trégua, armistício
truck [trʌk] N caminhão *m* (BR), camião *m* (PT); (*Rail*) vagão *m*; **truck driver** N caminhoneiro(-a)(BR), camionista *m/f* (PT)
true [truː] ADJ verdadeiro; (*accurate*) exato; (*genuine*) autêntico; (*faithful*) fiel, leal; **to come ~** realizar-se, tornar-se realidade
truly ['truːlɪ] ADV realmente; (*truthfully*) verdadeiramente; (*faithfully*) fielmente; **yours ~** (*in letter*) atenciosamente
trumpet ['trʌmpɪt] N trombeta
trunk [trʌŋk] N tronco; (*of elephant*) tromba; (*case*) baú *m*; (*us Aut*) mala (BR), porta-bagagens *m* (PT); **trunks** NPL (*also*: **swimming ~s**) sunga (BR), calções *mpl* de banho (PT)
trust [trʌst] N confiança; (*responsibility*) responsibilidade *f*; (*Jur*) fideicomisso ▶ VT (*rely on*) confiar em; (*entrust*): **to ~ sth to sb** confiar algo a alguém; (*hope*): **to ~ (that)** esperar que; **to take sth on ~** aceitar algo sem verificação prévia; **trusted** ADJ de confiança; **trustworthy** ADJ digno de confiança
truth [truːθ] N verdade *f*; **truthful** ADJ (*person*) sincero, honesto
try [traɪ] N tentativa; (*Rugby*) ensaio ▶ VT (*Jur*) julgar; (*test: sth new*) provar, pôr à prova; (*strain*) cansar ▶ VI tentar; **to have a ~** fazer uma tentativa; **to ~ to do sth** tentar fazer algo; **try on** VT (*clothes*) experimentar, provar; **trying** ADJ exasperante
T-shirt N camiseta (BR), T-shirt *f* (PT)
tub [tʌb] N tina; (*bath*) banheira
tube [tjuːb] N tubo; (*pipe*) cano; (BRIT: *underground*) metrô *m* (BR), metro(-politano) (PT); (*for tyre*) câmara-de-ar *f*

tuberculosis [tjubəːkjuˈləusɪs] N tuberculose *f*
tuck [tʌk] VT (*put*) enfiar, meter; **tuck away** VT esconder; **to be ~ed away** estar escondido; **tuck in** VT enfiar para dentro; (*child*) aconchegar ▶ VI (*eat*) comer com apetite; **tuck up** VT (*child*) aconchegar
Tuesday ['tjuːzdɪ] N terça-feira
tug [tʌg] N (*ship*) rebocador *m* ▶ VT puxar
tuition [tjuːˈɪʃən] N ensino; (*private tuition*) aulas *fpl* particulares; (*us: fees*) taxas *fpl* escolares
tulip ['tjuːlɪp] N tulipa
tumble ['tʌmbl] N (*fall*) queda ▶ VI cair, tombar; **to ~ to sth** (*inf*) sacar algo
tumbler ['tʌmblər] N copo
tummy ['tʌmɪ] (*inf*) N (*belly*) barriga; (*stomach*) estômago
tumour ['tjuːmər], (*us*) **tumor** N tumor *m*
tuna ['tjuːnə] N INV (*also*: **~ fish**) atum *m*
tune [tjuːn] N melodia ▶ VT (*Mus*) afinar; (*Radio, TV*) sintonizar; (*Aut*) regular; **to be in/out of ~** (*instrument*) estar afinado/desafinado; (*singer*) cantar afinado/desafinar; **to be in/out of ~ with** (*fig*) harmonizar-se com/destoar de; **tune in** VI (*Radio, TV*): **to ~ in (to)** sintonizar (com); **tune up** VI (*musician*) afinar (seu instrumento)
tunic ['tjuːnɪk] N túnica
Tunisia [tjuːˈnɪzɪə] N Tunísia
tunnel ['tʌnl] N túnel *m*; (*in mine*) galeria ▶ VI abrir um túnel (*or* uma galeria)
turbulence ['təːbjuləns] N (*Aviat*) turbulência

turf [tə:f] N torrão *m* ▶ VT relvar, gramar; **turf out** (*inf*) VT (*person*) pôr no olho da rua

Turk [tə:k] N turco(-a)

Turkey ['tə:kɪ] N Turquia

turkey ['tə:kɪ] N peru(a) *m/f*

Turkish ['tə:kɪʃ] ADJ turco(-a) ▶ N (*Ling*) turco

turmoil ['tə:mɔɪl] N tumulto, distúrbio, agitação *f*; **in ~** agitado, tumultuado

turn [tə:n] N volta, turno; (*in road*) curva; (*of mind, events*) propensão *f*, tendência; (*Theatre*) número; (*Med*) choque *m* ▶ VT dar volta a, fazer girar; (*collar*) virar; (*change*): **to ~ sth into** converter algo em ▶ VI virar; (*person: look back*) voltar-se; (*reverse direction*) mudar de direção; (*milk*) azedar; (*become*) tornar-se, virar; **to ~ nasty** engrossar; **to ~ forty** fazer quarenta anos; **a good ~** um favor; **it gave me quite a ~** me deu um susto enorme; **"no left ~"** (*Aut*) "proibido virar à esquerda"; **it's your ~** é a sua vez; **in ~** por sua vez; **to take ~s (at)** revezar (em); **turn away** VI virar a cabeça ▶ VT (*business, applicants*) recusar; **turn back** VI voltar atrás ▶ VT voltar para trás; (*clock*) atrasar; **turn down** VT (*refuse*) recusar; (*reduce*) baixar; (*fold*) dobrar, virar para baixo; **turn in** VI (*inf: go to bed*) ir dormir ▶ VT (*fold*) dobrar para dentro; **turn off** VI (*from road*) virar, sair do caminho ▶ VT (*light, radio etc*) apagar; (*engine*) desligar; **turn on** VT (*light*) acender; (*engine, radio*) ligar; (*tap*) abrir; **turn out** VT (*light, gas*) apagar; (*produce*) produzir ▶ VI (*troops*) ser mobilizado; **to ~ out to be ...** revelar-se (ser) ..., resultar (ser) ..., vir a ser ...; **turn over** VI

(*person*) virar-se ▶ VT (*object*) virar; **turn round** VI voltar-se, virar-se; **turn up** VI (*person*) aparecer, pintar; (*lost object*) aparecer ▶ VT (*collar*) subir; (*volume, radio etc*) aumentar; **turning** N (*in road*) via lateral

turnip ['tə:nɪp] N nabo

turnout ['tə:naut] N assistência; (*in election*) comparecimento às urnas

turnover ['tə:nəuvəʳ] N (*Comm: amount of money*) volume *m* de negócios; (: *of goods*) movimento; (*of staff*) rotatividade *f*

turn-up (BRIT) N (*on trousers*) volta, dobra

turquoise ['tə:kwɔɪz] N (*stone*) turquesa ▶ ADJ azul-turquesa *inv*

turtle ['tə:tl] N tartaruga, cágado

tusk [tʌsk] N defesa (de elefante)

tutor ['tju:təʳ] N professor(a) *m/f*; (*private tutor*) professor(a) *m/f* particular; **tutorial** [tju:'tɔ:rɪəl] N (*Sch*) seminário

tuxedo [tʌk'si:dəu] (US) N smoking *m*

TV N ABBR (= *television*) TV *f*

tweed [twi:d] N tweed *m*, pano grosso de lã

tweet [twi:t] (*on Twitter*) N tweet *m* ▶ VT, VI tuitar

tweezers ['twi:zəz] NPL pinça (pequena)

twelfth [twɛlfθ] NUM décimo segundo

twelve [twɛlv] NUM doze; **at ~ (o'clock)** (*midday*) ao meio-dia; (*midnight*) à meia-noite

twentieth ['twɛntɪɪθ] NUM vigésimo

twenty ['twɛntɪ] NUM vinte

twice [twaɪs] ADV duas vezes; **~ as much** duas vezes mais

twig [twɪg] N graveto, varinha ▶ vɪ (inf) sacar

twilight ['twaɪlaɪt] N crepúsculo, meia-luz f

twin [twɪn] ADJ gêmeo(-a); (beds) separado ▶ N gêmeo(-a) ▶ vt irmanar; **twin-bedded room** N quarto com duas camas

twinkle ['twɪŋkl] vɪ cintilar; (eyes) pestanejar

twist [twɪst] N torção f; (in road, coil) curva; (in wire, flex) virada; (in story) mudança imprevista ▶ vt torcer, retorcer; (ankle) torcer; (weave) entrelaçar; (roll around) enrolar; (fig) deturpar ▶ vɪ serpentear

twit [twɪt] (inf) N idiota m/f, bobo(-a)

twitch [twɪtʃ] N puxão m; (nervous) tique m nervoso ▶ vɪ contrair-se

two [tuː] NUM dois; **to put ~ and ~ together** (fig) tirar conclusões; **two-way** ADJ: **two-way traffic** trânsito em mão dupla

type [taɪp] N (category) tipo, espécie f; (model) modelo; (Typ) tipo, letra ▶ vt (letter etc) datilografar, bater (à máquina); **typewriter** N máquina de escrever

typhoid ['taɪfɔɪd] N febre f tifoide

typical ['tɪpɪkl] ADJ típico

typing ['taɪpɪŋ] N datilografia

typist ['taɪpɪst] N datilógrafo(-a) m/f

tyre ['taɪəʳ], (US) **tire** N pneu m

u

UFO ['juːfəu] N ABBR (= unidentified flying object) óvni m

Uganda [juːˈgændə] N Uganda (no article)

ugly ['ʌglɪ] ADJ feio; (dangerous) perigoso

UK N ABBR = **United Kingdom**

ulcer ['ʌlsəʳ] N úlcera; **mouth ~** afta

ultimate ['ʌltɪmət] ADJ último, final; (authority) máximo; **ultimately** ADV (in the end) no final, por último; (fundamentally) no fundo

ultrasound ['ʌltrəsaund] N (Med) ultrassom m

umbrella [ʌmˈbrɛlə] N guarda-chuva m; (for sun) guarda-sol m, barraca (da praia)

umpire ['ʌmpaɪəʳ] N árbitro ▶ vt arbitrar

UN N ABBR (= United Nations) ONU f

unable [ʌnˈeɪbl] ADJ: **to be ~ to do sth** não poder fazer algo

unanimous [juːˈnænɪməs] ADJ unânime

unarmed [ʌn'ɑːmd] ADJ (*without a weapon*) desarmado; (*defenceless*) indefeso

unattended [ʌnə'tɛndɪd] ADJ (*car, luggage*) abandonado

unattractive [ʌnə'træktɪv] ADJ sem atrativos; (*building, appearance, idea*) pouco atraente

unavoidable [ʌnə'vɔɪdəbl] ADJ inevitável

unaware [ʌnə'wɛəʳ] ADJ: **to be ~ of** ignorar, não perceber

unawares [ʌnə'wɛəz] ADV improvisadamente, de surpresa

unbearable [ʌn'bɛərəbl] ADJ insuportável

unbeatable [ʌn'biːtəbl] ADJ (*team*) invencível; (*price*) sem igual

unbelievable [ʌnbɪ'liːvəbl] ADJ inacreditável; (*amazing*) incrível

unborn [ʌn'bɔːn] ADJ por nascer

unbutton [ʌn'bʌtn] VT desabotoar

uncalled-for [ʌn'kɔːld-] ADJ desnecessário, gratuito

uncanny [ʌn'kænɪ] ADJ estranho; (*knack*) excepcional

uncertain [ʌn'səːtn] ADJ incerto; (*character*) indeciso; (*unsure*): **~ about** inseguro sobre; **in no ~ terms** em termos precisos; **uncertainty** N incerteza; (*also pl: doubts*) dúvidas *fpl*

uncle ['ʌŋkl] N tio

uncomfortable [ʌn'kʌmfətəbl] ADJ incômodo; (*uneasy*) pouco à vontade; (*situation*) desagradável

uncommon [ʌn'kɔmən] ADJ raro, incomum, excepcional

unconditional [ʌnkən'dɪʃənl] ADJ incondicional

unconscious [ʌn'kɔnʃəs] ADJ sem sentidos, desacordado; (*unaware*): **~ of** inconsciente de

▶ N: **the ~** o inconsciente

uncontrollable [ʌnkən'trəuləbl] ADJ (*temper*) ingovernável; (*child, animal, laughter*) incontrolável

unconventional [ʌnkən'vɛnʃənl] ADJ inconvencional

uncover [ʌn'kʌvəʳ] VT descobrir; (*take lid off*) destapar, destampar

undecided [ʌndɪ'saɪdɪd] ADJ indeciso; (*question*) não respondido, pendente

under ['ʌndəʳ] PREP embaixo de (BR), debaixo de (PT); (*fig*) sob; (*less than*) menos de; (*according to*) segundo, de acordo com ▶ ADV embaixo; (*movement*) por baixo; **~ there** ali embaixo; **~ repair** em conserto; **undercover** ADJ secreto, clandestino; **underdog** N o mais fraco; **underdone** ADJ (*Culin*) mal passado; **underestimate** VT subestimar; **undergo** *irreg* VT sofrer; (*test*) passar por; (*operation, treatment*) ser submetido a; **undergraduate** N universitário(-a); **underground** N (BRIT) metrô *m* (BR), metro(-politano) (PT); (*Pol*) organização *f* clandestina ▶ ADJ subterrâneo; (*fig*) clandestino ▶ ADV (*work*) embaixo da terra; (*fig*) na clandestinidade; **undergrowth** N vegetação *f* rasteira; **underline** VT sublinhar; **undermine** VT minar, solapar; **underneath** ADV embaixo, debaixo, por baixo ▶ PREP embaixo de (BR), debaixo de (PT); **underpaid** ADJ mal pago; **underpants** (BRIT) NPL cueca (BR), cuecas *fpl* (PT); **underpass** (BRIT) N passagem *f* inferior; **underprivileged** ADJ menos favorecido

u

understand [ʌndə'stænd] *irreg* VT entender, compreender ▶ VI: **to ~ that** acreditar que;
understandable ADJ compreensível; **understanding** ADJ compreensivo ▶ N compreensão *f*; (*knowledge*) entendimento; (*agreement*) acordo

understatement [ʌndə'steɪtmənt] N (*quality*) subestimação *f*; (*euphemism*) eufemismo; **it's an ~ to say that ...** é uma subestimação dizer que ...

understood [ʌndə'stud] PT, PP *of* **understand** ▶ ADJ entendido; (*implied*) subentendido, implícito

undertake [ʌndə'teɪk] (*irreg: like* **take**) VT incumbir-se de, encarregar-se de; **to ~ to do sth** comprometer-se a fazer algo

undertaking ['ʌndəteɪkɪŋ] N empreendimento; (*promise*) promessa

underwater [ʌndə'wɔːtəʳ] ADV sob a água ▶ ADJ subaquático

underwear ['ʌndəwɛəʳ] N roupa de baixo

underworld ['ʌndəwəːld] N (*of crime*) submundo

undo [ʌn'duː] (*irreg: like* **do**) VT (*unfasten*) desatar; (*spoil*) desmanchar

undress [ʌn'drɛs] VI despir-se, tirar a roupa

unearth [ʌn'əːθ] VT desenterrar; (*fig*) revelar

uneasy [ʌn'iːzɪ] ADJ (*person*) preocupado; (*feeling*) incômodo; (*peace, truce*) desconfortável

uneducated [ʌn'ɛdjukeɪtɪd] ADJ inculto, sem instrução, não escolarizado

unemployed [ʌnɪm'plɔɪd] ADJ desempregado ▶ NPL: **the ~** os desempregados

unemployment [ʌnɪm'plɔɪmənt] N desemprego

uneven [ʌn'iːvn] ADJ desigual; (*road etc*) irregular, acidentado

unexpected [ʌnɪk'spɛktɪd] ADJ inesperado; **unexpectedly** [ʌnɪk'spɛktɪdlɪ] ADV inesperadamente

unfair [ʌn'fɛəʳ] ADJ: **~ (to)** injusto (com); **it's ~ that ...** não é justo que ...

unfaithful [ʌn'feɪθful] ADJ infiel

unfamiliar [ʌnfə'mɪlɪəʳ] ADJ pouco familiar, desconhecido; **to be ~ with sth** não estar familiarizado com algo

unfashionable [ʌn'fæʃnəbl] ADJ fora da moda

unfasten [ʌn'fɑːsn] VT desatar; (*open*) abrir

unfavourable [ʌn'feɪvərəbl], (*US*) **unfavorable** ADJ desfavorável

unfinished [ʌn'fɪnɪʃt] ADJ incompleto, inacabado

unfit [ʌn'fɪt] ADJ sem preparo físico; (*incompetent*) incompetente, incapaz; **~ for work** inapto para trabalhar

unfold [ʌn'fəuld] VT desdobrar ▶ VI (*story, situation*) desdobrar-se

unfortunate [ʌn'fɔːtʃənət] ADJ infeliz; (*event, remark*) inoportuno

unfriend [ʌn'frɛnd] VT excluir (em rede social)

unfriendly [ʌn'frɛndlɪ] ADJ antipático

unhappiness [ʌn'hæpɪnɪs] N infelicidade *f*

unhappy [ʌn'hæpɪ] ADJ triste; (*unfortunate*) desventurado; (*childhood*) infeliz; (*dissatisfied*): **~ with** descontente com, insatisfeito com

unhealthy [ʌn'hɛlθɪ] ADJ insalubre; (*person*) doentio; (*fig*) anormal

unheard-of [ʌn'hə:d-] ADJ insólito

unhurt [ʌn'hə:t] ADJ ileso

uniform ['ju:nɪfɔ:m] N uniforme *m* ▶ ADJ uniforme

uninhabited [ʌnɪn'hæbɪtɪd] ADJ inabitado

uninstall ['ʌnɪnstɔ:l] VT (*Comput*) desinstalar

unintentional [ʌnɪn'tɛnʃənəl] ADJ involuntário, não intencional

union ['ju:njən] N união *f*; (*also*: **trade ~**) sindicato (de trabalhadores) ▶ CPD sindical; **Union Jack** N bandeira britânica

unique [ju:'ni:k] ADJ único, sem igual

unit ['ju:nɪt] N unidade *f*; (*of furniture etc*) seção *f*; (*team, squad*) equipe *f*; **kitchen ~** armário de cozinha

unite [ju:'naɪt] VT unir ▶ VI unir-se; **united** ADJ unido; (*effort*) conjunto; **United Kingdom** N Reino Unido; **United Nations, United Nations Organization** N (Organização *f* das) Nações *fpl* Unidas; **United States, United States of America** N Estados Unidos *mpl* (da América)

universal [ju:nɪ'və:sl] ADJ universal

universe ['ju:nɪvə:s] N universo

university [ju:nɪ'və:sɪtɪ] N universidade *f*

unjust [ʌn'dʒʌst] ADJ injusto

unkind [ʌn'kaɪnd] ADJ maldoso; (*comment etc*) cruel

unknown [ʌn'nəun] ADJ desconhecido

unlawful [ʌn'lɔ:ful] ADJ ilegal

unleaded [ʌn'lɛdɪd] ADJ (*petrol, fuel*) sem chumbo

unleash [ʌn'li:ʃ] VT (*fig*) desencadear

unless [ʌn'lɛs] CONJ a menos que, a não ser que; **~ he comes** a menos que ele venha

unlike [ʌn'laɪk] ADJ diferente ▶ PREP diferente de, ao contrário de

unlikely [ʌn'laɪklɪ] ADJ (*not likely*) improvável; (*unexpected*) inesperado

unlisted [ʌn'lɪstɪd] ADJ (*Us Tel*): **an ~ number** um número que não consta na lista telefônica

unload [ʌn'ləud] VT descarregar

unlock [ʌn'lɔk] VT destrancar

unlucky [ʌn'lʌkɪ] ADJ infeliz; (*object, number*) de mau agouro; **to be ~** ser azarado, ter azar

unmarried [ʌn'mærɪd] ADJ solteiro

unmistakable, unmistakeable [ʌnmɪs'teɪkəbl] ADJ inconfundível

unnatural [ʌn'nætʃrəl] ADJ antinatural, artificial; (*manner*) afetado; (*habit*) depravado

unnecessary [ʌn'nɛsəsərɪ] ADJ desnecessário, inútil

UNO ['ju:nəu] N ABBR (= *United Nations Organization*) ONU *f*

unofficial [ʌnə'fɪʃl] ADJ não-oficial, informal; (*strike*) desautorizado

unpack [ʌn'pæk] VI desembrulhar ▶ VT desfazer

unpleasant [ʌn'plɛznt] ADJ desagradável; (*person, manner*) antipático

unplug [ʌn'plʌg] VT desligar

unpopular [ʌn'pɔpjuləʳ] ADJ impopular

unprecedented [ʌn'prɛsɪdəntɪd] ADJ sem precedentes

unpredictable [ʌnprɪ'dɪktəbl] ADJ imprevisível

u

unravel [ʌnˈrævl] VT
desemaranhar; (*mystery*) desvendar

unreal [ʌnˈrɪəl] ADJ irreal, ilusório;
(*extraordinary*) extraordinário

unrealistic [ʌnrɪəˈlɪstɪk] ADJ pouco
realista

unreasonable [ʌnˈriːznəbl] ADJ
insensato; (*demand*) absurdo

unrelated [ʌnrɪˈleɪtɪd] ADJ sem
relação; (*family*) sem parentesco

unreliable [ʌnrɪˈlaɪəbl] ADJ (*person*)
indigno de confiança; (*machine*)
incerto, perigoso

unrest [ʌnˈrɛst] N inquietação *f*,
desassossego; (*Pol*) distúrbios *mpl*

unroll [ʌnˈrəʊl] VT desenrolar

unruly [ʌnˈruːlɪ] ADJ indisciplinado;
(*hair*) desalinhado

unsafe [ʌnˈseɪf] ADJ perigoso

unsatisfactory [ʌnsætɪsˈfæktərɪ]
ADJ insatisfatório

unscrew [ʌnˈskruː] VT
desparafusar

unsettled [ʌnˈsɛtld] ADJ (*weather*)
instável; (*person*) inquieto

unsightly [ʌnˈsaɪtlɪ] ADJ feio,
disforme

unskilled [ʌnˈskɪld] ADJ
não-especializado

unstable [ʌnˈsteɪbl] ADJ em falso;
(*government, mentally*) instável

unsteady [ʌnˈstɛdɪ] ADJ (*hand,
person*) trêmulo; (*ladder*) instável

unsuccessful [ʌnsəkˈsɛsful] ADJ
(*attempt*) frustrado, vão/vã; (*writer,
proposal*) sem êxito; **to be ~** (*in
attempting sth*) ser mal sucedido, não
conseguir; (*application*) ser recusado

unsuitable [ʌnˈsuːtəbl] ADJ
inadequado; (*time, moment*)
inconveniente

unsure [ʌnˈʃuəʳ] ADJ inseguro,
incerto; **to be ~ of o.s.** não ser
seguro de si

untidy [ʌnˈtaɪdɪ] ADJ (*room*)
desarrumado, desleixado;
(*appearance*) desmazelado,
desalinhado

untie [ʌnˈtaɪ] VT desatar, desfazer;
(*dog, prisoner*) soltar

until [ənˈtɪl] PREP até ▶ CONJ até
que; **~ he comes** até que ele venha;
~ now até agora; **~ then** até então

unused¹ [ʌnˈjuːzd] ADJ novo, sem
uso

unused² [ʌnˈjuːst] ADJ: **to be ~ to
sth/to doing sth** não estar
acostumado com algo/a fazer algo

unusual [ʌnˈjuːʒuəl] ADJ (*strange*)
estranho; (*rare*) incomum;
(*exceptional*) extraordinário

unveil [ʌnˈveɪl] VT desvelar,
descobrir

unwanted [ʌnˈwɒntɪd] ADJ não
desejado, indesejável

unwell [ʌnˈwɛl] ADJ: **to be ~** estar
doente; **to feel ~** estar indisposto

unwilling [ʌnˈwɪlɪŋ] ADJ: **to be ~
to do sth** relutar em fazer algo,
não querer fazer algo

unwind [ʌnˈwaɪnd] *irreg* VT
desenrolar ▶ VI (*relax*) relaxar-se

unwise [ʌnˈwaɪz] ADJ imprudente

unwrap [ʌnˈræp] VT desembrulhar

⸻KEYWORD⸻

up [ʌp] PREP: **to go/be up sth** subir
algo/estar em cima de algo; **we
climbed/walked up the hill** nós
subimos/andamos até em cima da
colina; **they live further up the
street** eles moram mais adiante
nesta rua

▶ ADV **1** (*upwards, higher*) em cima,
para cima; **up in the sky/the
mountains** lá no céu/nas
montanhas; **up there** lá em cima;
up above em cima

2: **to be up** (*out of bed*) estar de pé; (*prices, level*) estar elevado; (*building, tent*) estar erguido

3: **up to** (*as far as*) até; **up to now** até agora

4: **to be up to** (*depending on*): **it is up to you** você é quem sabe, você decide

5: **to be up to** (*equal to*) estar à altura de; **he's not up to it** (*job, task etc*) ele não é capaz de fazê-lo; **his work is not up to the required standard** seu trabalho não atende aos padrões exigidos

6: **to be up to** (*inf: be doing*) estar fazendo (*BR*) *or* a fazer (*PT*); **what is he up to?** o que ele está querendo?, o que ele está tramando?

▶ N: **ups and downs** altos *mpl* e baixos

upbringing ['ʌpbrɪŋɪŋ] N educação *f*, criação *f*

update [ʌp'deɪt] VT atualizar, pôr em dia

upgrade [ʌp'greɪd] VT (*person*) promover; (*job*) melhorar; (*house*) reformar

upheaval [ʌp'hiːvl] N transtorno; (*unrest*) convulsão *f*

uphill [ʌp'hɪl] ADJ ladeira acima; (*fig: task*) trabalhoso, árduo ▶ ADV: **to go ~** ir morro acima

upload ['ʌpləʊd] VT (*Comput*) fazer upload, transferir

upon [ə'pɔn] PREP sobre

upper ['ʌpəʳ] ADJ superior, de cima ▶ N (*of shoe*) gáspea, parte *f* superior; **upper-class** ADJ de classe alta

upright ['ʌpraɪt] ADJ vertical; (*straight*) reto; (*fig*) honesto

uprising ['ʌpraɪzɪŋ] N revolta, rebelião *f*, sublevação *f*

uproar ['ʌprɔːʳ] N tumulto, algazarra

upset [n 'ʌpsɛt, vt, adj ʌp'sɛt] (*irreg: like* **set**) N (*to plan etc*) revés *m*, reviravolta; (*stomach upset*) indisposição *f* ▶ VT (*glass etc*) virar; (*plan*) perturbar; (*person: annoy*) aborrecer ▶ ADJ aflito; (*stomach*) indisposto

upside down ['ʌpsaɪd-] ADV de cabeça para baixo; **to turn a place ~** (*fig*) deixar um lugar de cabeça para baixo

upstairs [ʌp'stɛəz] ADV (*be*) em cima; (*go*) lá em cima ▶ ADJ (*room*) de cima ▶ N andar *m* de cima

up-to-date ADJ (*person*) moderno, atualizado; (*information*) atualizado

upward ['ʌpwəd] ADJ ascendente, para cima ▶ ADV para cima

upwards ['ʌpwədz] ADV = **upward**

urban ['əːbən] ADJ urbano, da cidade

urge [əːdʒ] N desejo ▶ VT: **to ~ sb to do sth** incitar alguém a fazer algo

urgent ['əːdʒənt] ADJ urgente; (*tone, plea*) insistente

urinal [ju'raɪnl] (*BRIT*) N (*vessel*) urinol *m*; (*building*) mictório

urine ['juərɪn] N urina

URL ABBR (= *uniform resource locator*) URL *m*

Uruguay ['juərəgwaɪ] N Uruguai *m*

US N ABBR (= *United States*) EUA *mpl*

us [ʌs] PRON nos; (*after prep*) nós; *see also* **me**

USA N ABBR (= *United States (of America)*) EUA *mpl*

USB ABBR (*Comput*) (= *universal serial bus*) USB *m*; **USB stick** N (*Comput*) pen drive *m*

u

use [*n* juːs, *vt* juːz] N uso, emprego; (*usefulness*) utilidade *f* ▶ VT usar, utilizar; (*phrase*) empregar; **in ~** em uso; **out of ~** fora de uso; **to be of ~** ser útil; **it's no ~** (*pointless*) é inútil; (*not useful*) não serve; **to be ~d to** estar acostumado a; **she ~d to do it** ela costumava fazê-lo; **use up** VT esgotar, consumir; (*money*) gastar; **used** [juːzd] ADJ usado; **useful** ['juːsful] ADJ útil; **useless** ['juːslɪs] ADJ inútil; (*person*) incapaz; **user** ['juːzər] N usuário(-a) (BR), utente *m/f* (PT); **user-friendly** ADJ de fácil utilização

USP N ABBR (= *unique selling proposition*) *proposta única de valor*

usual ['juːʒuəl] ADJ usual, habitual; **as ~** como de hábito, como sempre; **usually** ['juːʒuəlɪ] ADV normalmente

utensil [juːˈtɛnsl] N utensílio

utmost ['ʌtməust] ADJ maior ▶ N: **to do one's ~** fazer todo o possível

utter ['ʌtər] ADJ total ▶ VT (*sounds*) emitir; (*words*) proferir, pronunciar; **utterly** ADV completamente, totalmente

U-turn N retorno

V

vacancy ['veɪkənsɪ] N (BRIT: *job*) vaga; (*room*) quarto livre

vacant ['veɪkənt] ADJ desocupado, livre; (*expression*) distraído

vacate [vəˈkeɪt] VT (*house*) desocupar; (*job*) deixar

vacation [vəˈkeɪʃən] (*esp* US) N férias *fpl*

vacuum ['vækjum] N vácuo *m*; **vacuum cleaner** N aspirador *m* de pó

vagina [vəˈdʒaɪnə] N vagina

vague [veɪɡ] ADJ vago; (*blurred: memory*) fraco

vain [veɪn] ADJ vaidoso; (*useless*) vão/vã, inútil; **in ~** em vão

valentine ['væləntaɪn] N (*also:* **~ card**) cartão *m* do Dia dos Namorados; (*person*) namorado

valid ['vælɪd] ADJ válido

valley ['vælɪ] N vale *m*

valuable ['væljuəbl] ADJ (*jewel*) de valor; (*time*) valioso; (*help*) precioso; **valuables** NPL objetos *mpl* de valor

value ['væljuː] N valor *m*;

(*importance*) importância ▶ VT (*fix price of*) avaliar; (*appreciate*) valorizar, estimar; **values** NPL (*principles*) valores mpl

valve [vælv] N válvula

van [væn] N (*Aut*) camionete f (BR), camioneta (PT)

vandal ['vændl] N vândalo(-a); **vandalize** VT destruir, depredar

vanilla [və'nɪlə] N baunilha

vanish ['vænɪʃ] VI desaparecer, sumir

vanity ['vænɪtɪ] N vaidade f

vapour ['veɪpəʳ], (US) **vapor** N vapor m

variety [və'raɪətɪ] N variedade f, diversidade f; (*type, quantity*) variedade

various ['vɛərɪəs] ADJ vários(-as), diversos(-as); (*several*) vários(-as)

varnish ['vɑːnɪʃ] N verniz m; (*nail varnish*) esmalte m ▶ VT envernizar; (*nails*) pintar (com esmalte)

vary ['vɛərɪ] VT mudar ▶ VI variar; (*become different*): **to ~ with** or **according to** variar de acordo com

vase [vɑːz] N vaso

vast [vɑːst] ADJ enorme

VAT [væt] (BRIT) N ABBR (= *value added tax*) ≈ ICM m (BR), IVA m (PT)

vault [vɔːlt] N (*of roof*) abóbada; (*tomb*) sepulcro; (*in bank*) caixa-forte f ▶ VT (*also:* **~ over**) saltar (por cima de)

veal [viːl] N carne f de vitela

vegan ['viːgən] N vegetalista m/f

vegetable ['vɛdʒtəbl] N (*Bot*) vegetal m; (*edible plant*) legume m, hortaliça ▶ ADJ vegetal

vegetarian [vɛdʒɪ'tɛərɪən] ADJ, N vegetariano(-a)

vehicle ['viːɪkl] N veículo

veil [veɪl] N véu m ▶ VT velar

vein [veɪn] N veia; (*of ore etc*) filão m; (*on leaf*) nervura

velvet ['vɛlvɪt] N veludo ▶ ADJ aveludado

vending machine ['vɛndɪŋ-] N vendedor m automático

Venezuela [vɛnɛ'zweɪlə] N Venezuela

vengeance ['vɛndʒəns] N vingança; **with a ~** (*fig*) para valer

venison ['vɛnɪsn] N carne f de veado

venom ['vɛnəm] N veneno; (*bitterness*) malevolência

vent [vɛnt] N (*opening, in jacket*) abertura; (*also:* **air ~**) respiradouro ▶ VT (*fig: feelings*) desabafar, descarregar

venture ['vɛntʃəʳ] N empreendimento ▶ VT (*opinion*) arriscar ▶ VI arriscar-se; **business ~** empreendimento comercial

venue ['vɛnjuː] N local m

verb [vəːb] N verbo

verdict ['vəːdɪkt] N veredicto, decisão f; (*fig*) opinião f, parecer m

verge [vəːdʒ] N beira, margem f; (*on road*) acostamento (BR), berma (PT); **"soft ~s"** (BRIT Aut) "acostamento mole"; **to be on the ~ of doing sth** estar a ponto or à beira de fazer algo; **verge on** VT FUS beirar em

versatile ['vəːsətaɪl] ADJ (*person*) versátil; (*machine, tool etc*) polivalente

verse [vəːs] N verso, poesia; (*stanza*) estrofe f; (*in bible*) versículo

version ['vəːʃən] N versão f

versus ['vəːsəs] PREP contra, versus

vertical ['vəːtɪkl] ADJ vertical

very ['vɛrɪ] ADV muito ▶ ADJ: **the ~ book which** o mesmo livro que;

the ~ last o último (de todos), bem o último; **at the ~ least** no mínimo; **~ much** muitíssimo

vessel ['vɛsl] N (Naut) navio, barco; (container) vaso, vasilha

vest [vɛst] N (BRIT) camiseta (BR), camisola interior (PT); (US: waistcoat) colete m

vet [vɛt] N ABBR (= veterinary surgeon) veterinário(-a) ▶ VT examinar

veteran ['vɛtərn] N (also: **war ~**) veterano de guerra

veto ['vi:təu] (pl **vetoes**) N veto ▶ VT vetar

via ['vaɪə] PREP por, via

vibrate [vaɪ'breɪt] VI vibrar

vicar ['vɪkəʳ] N vigário

vice [vaɪs] N (evil) vício; (Tech) torno mecânico

vice- [vaɪs] PREFIX vice-

vice versa ['vaɪsɪ'vəːsə] ADV vice-versa

vicinity [vɪ'sɪnɪtɪ] N proximidade f; **in the ~ of** nas proximidades de

vicious ['vɪʃəs] ADJ violento; (cruel) cruel

victim ['vɪktɪm] N vítima f

victor ['vɪktəʳ] N vencedor(a) m/f

Victorian [vɪk'tɔːrɪən] ADJ vitoriano

victory ['vɪktərɪ] N vitória

video ['vɪdɪəu] N (video film) vídeo; (also: **~ cassette**) videocassete m; (also: **~ cassette recorder**) videocassete m; **video camera** N filmadora; **videophone** N videofone m

Vienna [vɪ'ɛnə] N Viena

Vietnam ['vjɛt'næm] N Vietnã m (BR), Vietname m (PT); **Vietnamese** [vjɛtnə'miːz] ADJ vietnamita ▶ N INV vietnamita m/f; (Ling) vietnamita m

view [vjuː] N vista; (outlook) perspectiva; (opinion) opinião f,

parecer m ▶ VT olhar; **in full ~ (of)** à plena vista (de); **in my ~** na minha opinião; **in ~ of the weather/the fact that** em vista do tempo/do fato de que; **viewer** N telespectador(a) m/f; **viewpoint** N ponto de vista; (place) lugar m

vigorous ['vɪgərəs] ADJ vigoroso; (plant) vigoso

vile [vaɪl] ADJ vil, infame; (smell) repugnante, repulsivo; (temper) violento

villa ['vɪlə] N (country house) casa de campo; (suburban house) vila, quinta

village ['vɪlɪdʒ] N aldeia, povoado; **villager** N aldeão/aldeã m/f

villain ['vɪlən] N (scoundrel) patife m; (BRIT: in novel etc) vilão m; (criminal) marginal m/f

vine [vaɪn] N planta trepadeira

vinegar ['vɪnɪgəʳ] N vinagre m

vineyard ['vɪnjɑːd] N vinha, vinhedo

vintage ['vɪntɪdʒ] N vindima; (year) safra, colheita ▶ CPD (comedy) de época; (performance) clássico; **the 1970 ~** a safra de 1970

viola [vɪ'əulə] N viola

violate ['vaɪəleɪt] VT violar

violence ['vaɪələns] N violência; (strength) força

violent ['vaɪələnt] ADJ violento; (intense) intenso

violet ['vaɪələt] ADJ violeta ▶ N violeta

violin [vaɪə'lɪn] N violino

VIP N ABBR (= very important person) VIP m/f

viral ['vaɪərəl] ADJ (Med) viral; **to go ~** (Comput) propagar-se rapidamente

virgin ['vəːdʒɪn] N virgem m/f ▶ ADJ virgem

Virgo ['vəːgəu] N Virgem f

virtually ['və:tjuəlɪ] ADV
praticamente

virtual reality ['və:tjuəl-] N
(*Comput*) realidade *f* virtual

virtue ['və:tju:] N virtude *f*;
(*advantage*) vantagem *f*; **by ~ of**
em virtude de

virus ['vaɪərəs] N vírus *m*

visa ['vi:zə] N visto

visible ['vɪzəbl] ADJ visível

vision ['vɪʒən] N (*sight*) vista,
visão *f*; (*foresight, in dream*) visão *f*

visit ['vɪzɪt] N visita ▶ VT (*person:*
US: also: **~ with**) visitar, fazer uma
visita a; (*place*) ir a, ir conhecer;
visiting hours NPL horário de
visita; **visitor** N visitante *m/f*;
(*to a house*) visita; (*tourist*)
turista *m/f*

visual ['vɪzjuəl] ADJ visual;
visualize VT visualizar

vital ['vaɪtl] ADJ essencial,
indispensável; (*important*) de
importância vital; (*crucial*) crucial;
(*person*) vivo; (*of life*) vital

vitamin ['vɪtəmɪn] N vitamina

vivid ['vɪvɪd] ADJ (*account*) vívido;
(*light*) claro, brilhante;
(*imagination, colour*) vivo

V-neck N (*also:* **~ jumper, ~**
pullover) suéter *f* com decote em V

vocabulary [vəu'kæbjulərɪ] N
vocabulário

vocal ['vəukl] ADJ vocal; (*noisy*)
clamoroso; (*articulate*) claro,
eloquente

vodka ['vɔdkə] N vodca

vogue [vəug] N voga, moda; **to be**
in ~ estar na moda

voice [vɔɪs] N voz *f* ▶ VT expressar;
voice mail N (*system*) correio *m* de
voz; (*device*) caixa *f* postal

void [vɔɪd] N vazio; (*hole*) oco ▶ ADJ
nulo; (*empty*): **~ of** destituido de

volatile ['vɔlətaɪl] ADJ volátil;
(*situation, person*) imprevisível

volcano [vɔl'keɪnəu] (*pl*
volcanoes) N vulcão *m*

volt [vəult] N volt *m*

volume ['vɔljuːm] N volume *m*;
(*of tank*) capacidade *f*

voluntarily ['vɔləntrɪlɪ] ADV
livremente, voluntariamente

voluntary ['vɔləntərɪ] ADJ
voluntário; (*unpaid*) (a título)
gratuito

volunteer [vɔlən'tɪər] N
voluntário(-a) ▶ VT oferecer
voluntariamente ▶ VI (*Mil*)
alistar-se voluntariamente; **to ~**
to do oferecer-se voluntariamente
para fazer

vomit ['vɔmɪt] N vômito ▶ VT, VI
vomitar

vote [vəut] N voto; (*votes cast*)
votação *f*; (*right to vote*) direito de
votar ▶ VT: **to be ~d chairman** *etc*
ser eleito presidente *etc*; (*propose*):
to ~ that propor que; (*in election*)
votar ▶ VI votar; **voter** N votante
m/f, eleitor(a) *m/f*

voucher ['vautʃər] N (*with petrol*
etc) vale *m*; (*gift voucher*) vale *m*
para presente

vow [vau] N voto ▶ VT: **to ~ to do/**
that prometer solenemente fazer/
que

vowel ['vauəl] N vogal *f*

voyage ['vɔɪɪdʒ] N viagem *f*

vulgar ['vʌlgər] ADJ grosseiro,
ordinário; (*in bad taste*) vulgar,
baixo

vulture ['vʌltʃər] N abutre *m*,
urubu *m*

v

W

wade [weɪd] vɪ: **to ~ through** andar em; (*fig: a book*) ler com dificuldade

wafer ['weɪfə^r] N (*biscuit*) bolacha

waffle ['wɔfl] N (*Culin*) waffle *m*; (*empty talk*) lengalenga ▶ vɪ encher linguiça

wag [wæg] vт (*tail*) sacudir; (*finger*) menear ▶ vɪ abanar

wage [weɪdʒ] N (*also:* **~s**) salário, ordenado ▶ vт: **to ~ war** empreender *or* fazer guerra

waggon, wagon ['wægən] N (*horse-drawn*) carroça; (*BRIT Rail*) vagão *m*

wail [weɪl] N lamento, gemido ▶ vɪ lamentar-se, gemer; (*siren*) tocar

waist [weɪst] N cintura; **waistcoat** N colete *m*

wait [weɪt] N espera ▶ vɪ esperar; **I can't ~ to** (*fig*) estou morrendo de vontade; **to ~ for sb/sth** esperar por alguém/algo; **wait behind** vɪ ficar para trás; **wait on** vт fus

servir; **waiter** N garçom *m* (*BR*), empregado (*PT*); **waiting list** N lista de espera; **waiting room** N sala de espera; **waitress** N garçonete *f* (*BR*), empregada (*PT*)

waive [weɪv] vт abrir mão de

wake [weɪk] (*pt* **woke**, *pp* **woken**) vт (*also:* **~ up**) acordar ▶ vɪ acordar ▶ N (*for dead person*) velório; (*Naut*) esteira

Wales [weɪlz] N País *m* de Gales

walk [wɔːk] N passeio; (*hike*) excursão *f* a pé, caminhada; (*gait*) passo, modo de andar; (*in park etc*) alameda, passeio ▶ vɪ andar; (*for pleasure, exercise*) passear ▶ vт (*distance*) percorrer a pé, andar; (*dog*) levar para passear; **it's 10 minutes' ~ from here** daqui são 10 minutos a pé; **people from all ~s of life** pessoas de todos os níveis; **walk out** vɪ sair; (*audience*) retirar-se; (*strike*) entrar em greve; **walk out on** vт fus abandonar; **walkie-talkie** ['wɔːkɪ'tɔːkɪ] N transmissor-receptor *m* portátil, walkie-talkie *m*; **walking** N o andar; **walking shoes** NPL sapatos *mpl* de caminhada; **walking stick** N bengala; **walkway** N passeio, passadiço

wall [wɔːl] N parede *f*; (*exterior*) muro; (*city wall etc*) muralha

wallet ['wɔlɪt] N carteira

wallpaper ['wɔːlpeɪpə^r] N papel *m* de parede ▶ vт colocar papel de parede em

walnut ['wɔːlnʌt] N noz *f*; (*tree, wood*) nogueira

walrus ['wɔːlrəs] (*pl* **walrus** *or* **walruses**) N morsa

waltz [wɔːlts] N valsa ▶ vɪ valsar

wand [wɔnd] N (*also:* **magic ~**) varinha de condão

wander ['wɔndə^r] vi (person) vagar, perambular; (thoughts) divagar ▶ vt perambular

want [wɔnt] vt querer; (demand) exigir; (need) precisar de, necessitar; **wanted** ADJ (criminal etc) procurado (pela polícia); **"cook wanted"** (in advertisement) "precisa-se cozinheiro"

war [wɔ:^r] N guerra; **to make ~ (on)** fazer guerra (contra)

ward [wɔ:d] N (in hospital) ala; (Pol) distrito eleitoral; (Jur: child) tutelado(-a), pupilo(-a); **ward off** vt desviar, aparar; (attack) repelir

warden ['wɔ:dn] N (BRIT: of institution) diretor(a) m/f; (of park, game reserve) administrador(a) m/f; (BRIT: also: **traffic ~**) guarda m/f

wardrobe ['wɔ:drəub] N guarda-roupa m

warehouse ['wɛəhaus] N armazém m, depósito

warfare ['wɔ:fɛə^r] N guerra, combate m

warhead ['wɔ:hɛd] N ogiva

warm [wɔ:m] ADJ quente; (thanks, welcome) caloroso; **it's ~** está quente; **I'm ~** = estou com calor; **warm up** vi esquentar ▶ vt esquentar; **warmly** ADV calorosamente; **warmth** N calor m; (friendliness) calor humano

warn [wɔ:n] vt prevenir, avisar; **to ~ sb that/of/(not) to do** prevenir alguém de que/de/para (não) fazer

warning ['wɔ:nɪŋ] N advertência; (in writing) aviso; (signal) sinal m

warrant ['wɔrnt] N (voucher) comprovante m; (Jur: to arrest) mandado de prisão; (: to search) mandado de busca; **warranty** N garantia

warrior ['wɔrɪə^r] N guerreiro(-a)

Warsaw ['wɔ:sɔ:] N Varsóvia

warship ['wɔ:ʃɪp] N navio de guerra

wart [wɔ:t] N verruga

wartime ['wɔ:taɪm] N: **in ~** em tempo de guerra

wary ['wɛərɪ] ADJ cauteloso, precavido

was [wɔz] PT of **be**

wash [wɔʃ] vt lavar ▶ vi lavar-se; (sea etc): **to ~ over/against sth** bater/chocar-se contra algo ▶ N (clothes etc) lavagem f; (of ship) esteira; **to have a ~** lavar-se; **wash away** vt (stain) tirar ao lavar; (subj: river etc) levar, arrastar; **wash off** vt tirar lavando ▶ vi sair ao lavar; **wash up** vi (BRIT) lavar a louça; (US) lavar-se; **washbasin** N pia (BR), lavatório (PT); **washing** (BRIT) N (dirty) roupa suja; (clean) roupa lavada; **washing machine** N máquina de lavar roupa, lavadora; **washing powder** (BRIT) N sabão m em pó; **washing-up** N: **to do the washing-up** lavar a louça; **washing-up liquid** N detergente m; **washroom** (US) N banheiro (BR), casa de banho (PT)

wasn't ['wɔznt] = **was not**

wasp [wɔsp] N vespa

waste [weɪst] N desperdício, esbanjamento; (of time) perda; (also: **household ~**) detritos mpl domésticos; (rubbish) lixo ▶ ADJ (material) de refugo; (left over) de sobra; (land) baldio ▶ vt (squander) esbanjar, desperdiçar; (time, opportunity) perder; **wastes** NPL ermos mpl; **to lay ~** devastar; **waste away** vi definhar

watch [wɔtʃ] N (clock) relógio; (also: **wrist~**) relógio de pulso;

W

(*act of watching*) vigia; (*guard: Mil*) sentinela; (*Naut: spell of duty*) quarto ▶ vt (*look at*) observar, olhar; (*programme, match*) assistir a; (*television*) ver; (*spy on, guard*) vigiar; (*be careful of*) tomar cuidado com ▶ vi ver, olhar; (*keep guard*) montar guarda; **watch out** vi ter cuidado; **watchdog** N cão m de guarda; (*fig*) vigia m/f

water ['wɔ:tər] N água ▶ vt (*plant*) regar ▶ vi (*eyes*) lacrimejar; (*mouth*) salivar; **in British ~s** nas águas territoriais britânicas; **water down** vt (*milk*) aguar; (*fig*) diluir; **watercolour**, (*us*) **watercolor** N aquarela; **waterfall** N cascata, cachoeira; **watering can** N regador m; **watermelon** N melancia; **waterproof** ADJ impermeável; **water-skiing** N esqui m aquático

watt [wɔt] N watt m

wave [weɪv] N onda; (*of hand*) aceno, sinal m; (*in hair*) onda, ondulação f ▶ vi acenar com a mão; (*flag, grass, branches*) tremular ▶ vt (*hand*) acenar; (*handkerchief*) acenar com; (*weapon*) brandir; **wavelength** N comprimento de onda; **to be on the same wavelength as** ter os mesmos gostos e atitudes que

waver ['weɪvər] vi vacilar; (*voice, eyes, love*) hesitar

wavy ['weɪvɪ] ADJ (*hair*) ondulado; (*line*) ondulante

wax [wæks] N cera ▶ vt encerar; (*car*) polir ▶ vi (*moon*) crescer

way [weɪ] N caminho; (*distance*) percurso; (*direction*) direção f, sentido; (*manner*) maneira, modo; (*habit*) costume m; **which ~? — this ~** por onde? — por aqui; **on the ~ (to)**

a caminho (de); **to be on one's ~** estar a caminho; **to be in the ~** atrapalhar; **to go out of one's ~ to do sth** dar-se ao trabalho de fazer algo; **to lose one's ~** perder-se; **to be under ~** estar em andamento; **in a ~** de certo modo, até certo ponto; **in some ~s** a certos respeitos; **by the ~** a propósito; **"~ in"** (*brit*) "entrada"; **"~ out"** (*brit*) "saída"; **the ~ back** o caminho de volta; **"give ~"** (*brit Aut*) "dê a preferência"; **no ~!** (*inf*) de jeito nenhum!

WC ['dʌblju:'si:] N ABBR (= *water closet*) privada

we [wi:] PRON PL nós

weak [wi:k] ADJ fraco, débil; (*morally, currency*) fraco; (*excuse*) pouco convincente; (*tea*) aguado, ralo; **weaken** vi enfraquecer(-se); (*give way*) ceder; (*influence, power*) diminuir ▶ vt enfraquecer; **weakness** N fraqueza; (*fault*) ponto fraco; **to have a weakness for** ter uma queda por

wealth [wɛlθ] N riqueza; (*of details*) abundância; **wealthy** ADJ rico, abastado; (*country*) rico

weapon ['wɛpən] N arma; **~s of mass destruction** armas de destruição em massa

wear [wɛər] (*pt* **wore**, *pp* **worn**) N (*use*) uso; (*deterioration through use*) desgaste m; (*clothing*): **baby/ sports ~** roupa infantil/de esporte ▶ vt (*clothes*) usar; (*shoes*) usar, calçar; (*put on*) vestir; (*damage: through use*) desgastar ▶ vi (*last*) durar; (*rub through etc*) gastar-se; **town/evening ~** traje m de passeio/de gala; **wear away** vt gastar ▶ vi desgastar-se; **wear down** vt gastar; (*strength*) esgotar;

wear off vi (*pain etc*) passar; **wear out** vt desgastar; (*person, strength*) esgotar

weary ['wɪərɪ] adj cansado; (*dispirited*) deprimido ▶ vi: **to ~ of** cansar-se de

weasel ['wiːzl] n (*Zool*) doninha

weather ['wɛðəʳ] n tempo ▶ vt (*storm, crisis*) resistir a; **under the ~** (*fig: ill*) doente; **weather forecast** n previsão f do tempo

weave [wiːv] (*pt, pp* **wove** or **woven**) vt tecer

web [wɛb] n (*of spider*) teia; (*on foot*) membrana; (*network*) rede f; **the (World Wide) W~** a (World Wide) Web; **web address** n endereço web; **webcam** ['wɛbkæm] n webcam f; **webinar** ['wɛbɪnɑːʳ] n seminário online, webinar m; **weblog** n weblog m; **webmail** n (serviço m de) webmail m; **web page** n página (da) web; **website** n site m, website m

wed [wɛd] (*pt, pp* **wedded**) vt casar ▶ vi casar-se

we'd [wiːd] = **we had**; = **we would**

wedding ['wɛdɪŋ] n casamento, núpcias fpl; **wedding dress** n vestido de noiva; **wedding ring** n anel m or aliança de casamento

wedge [wɛdʒ] n (*of wood etc*) cunha, calço; (*of cake*) fatia ▶ vt (*pack tightly*) apinhar; (*door*) pôr calço em

Wednesday ['wɛdnzdɪ] n quarta-feira

wee [wiː] (SCOTLAND) adj pequeno, pequenino

weed [wiːd] n erva daninha ▶ vt capinar; **weedkiller** n herbicida m

week [wiːk] n semana; **a ~ today** daqui a uma semana; **a ~ on Tuesday** sem ser essa terça-feira, a outra; **every other ~** uma semana sim, uma semana não; **weekday** n dia m de semana; (*Comm*) dia útil; **weekend** n fim m de semana; **weekly** adv semanalmente ▶ adj semanal ▶ n semanário

weep [wiːp] (*pt, pp* **wept**) vi (*person*) chorar

weigh [weɪ] vt, vi pesar; **to ~ anchor** levantar ferro; **weigh down** vt sobrecarregar; (*fig: with worry*) deprimir, acabrunhar; **weigh up** vt ponderar, avaliar

weight [weɪt] n peso; **to lose/put on ~** emagrecer/engordar

weird [wɪəd] adj esquisito, estranho

welcome ['wɛlkəm] adj bem-vindo ▶ n acolhimento, recepção f ▶ vt dar as boas-vindas a; (*be glad of*) saudar; **you're ~** (*after thanks*) de nada

weld [wɛld] n solda ▶ vt soldar, unir

welfare ['wɛlfɛəʳ] n bem-estar m; (*social aid*) assistência social; **welfare state** n país auto-financiador da sua assistência social

well [wɛl] n poço ▶ adv bem ▶ adj: **to be ~** estar bem (de saúde) ▶ excl bem!, então!; **as ~** também; **as ~ as** assim como; **~ done!** muito bem!; **get ~ soon!** melhoras!; **to do ~** ir or sair-se bem; (*business*) ir bem; **well up** vi brotar

we'll [wiːl] = **we will**; = **we shall**

well: well-behaved [-bɪ'heɪvd] adj bem comportado; **well-built** adj robusto; (*house*) bem construído; **well-dressed** [-drɛst] adj bem vestido

W

wellingtons [ˈwɛlɪŋtənz] N (also: **wellington boots**) botas de borracha até os joelhos

well-known ADJ conhecido

well-off ADJ próspero, rico

Welsh [wɛlʃ] ADJ galês/galesa ▶ N (Ling) galês m; **the Welsh** NPL (people) os galeses; **Welshman** irreg N galês m; **Welshwoman** irreg N galesa

went [wɛnt] PT of **go**

wept [wɛpt] PT, PP of **weep**

were [wəːʳ] PT of **be**

we're [wɪəʳ] = **we are**

weren't [wəːnt] = **were not**

west [wɛst] N oeste m ▶ ADJ ocidental, do oeste ▶ ADV para o oeste or ao oeste; **the W~** (Pol) o Oeste, o Ocidente; **western** ADJ ocidental ▶ N (Cinema) western m, bangue-bangue (BR inf); **West Indian** ADJ, N antilhano(-a); **West Indies** NPL Antilhas fpl

wet [wɛt] ADJ molhado; (damp) úmido; (wet through) encharcado; (rainy) chuvoso ▶ N (BRIT Pol) político de tendência moderada; **to get ~** molhar-se; **"~ paint"** "tinta fresca"; **wetsuit** N roupa de mergulho

we've [wiːv] = **we have**

whale [weɪl] N (Zool) baleia

wharf [wɔːf] (pl **wharves**) N cais m inv

(KEYWORD)

what [wɔt] ADJ **1** (in direct/indirect questions) que, qual; **what size is it?** que tamanho é este?; **what colour/ shape is it?** qual é a cor/o formato?; **he asked me what books I needed** ele me perguntou de quais os livros eu precisava
2 (in exclamations) quê!, como!; **what a mess!** que bagunça!

▶ PRON **1** (interrogative) que, o que; **what are you doing?** o que é que você está fazendo?; **what is it called?** como se chama?; **what about me?** e eu?; **what about doing …?** que tal fazer …?
2 (relative) o que; **I saw what you did/was on the table** eu vi o que você fez/estava na mesa; **he asked me what she had said** ele me perguntou o que ela tinha dito
▶ EXCL (disbelieving): **what, no coffee?** ué, não tem café?

whatever [wɔtˈɛvəʳ] ADJ: **~ book you choose** qualquer livro que você escolha ▶ PRON: **do ~ is necessary/ you want** faça tudo o que for preciso/o que você quiser; **~ happens** aconteça o que acontecer; **no reason ~** or **whatsoever** nenhuma razão seja qual for or em absoluto; **nothing ~** nada em absoluto

whatsoever [wɔtsəuˈɛvəʳ] ADJ = **whatever**

wheat [wiːt] N trigo

wheel [wiːl] N roda; (also: **steering ~**) volante m; (Naut) roda do leme ▶ VT (pram etc) empurrar ▶ VI (birds) dar voltas; (also: **~ round**) girar, dar voltas, virar-se; **wheelbarrow** N carrinho de mão; **wheelchair** N cadeira de rodas; **wheel clamp** N (Aut) grampo com que se imobiliza carros estacionados ilegalmente

wheeze [wiːz] VI respirar ruidosamente

(KEYWORD)

when [wɛn] ADV quando
▶ CONJ **1** (at, during, after the time that) quando; **when you've read it, tell me what you think** depois

que você tiver lido isto, diga-me o que acha; **that was when I needed you** foi quando eu precisei de você 2 (*on, at which*) quando, em que; **on the day when I met him** no dia em que o conheci; **one day when it was raining** um dia quando estava chovendo 3 (*whereas*) ao passo que; **you said I was wrong when in fact I was right** você disse que eu estava errado quando, na verdade, eu estava certo

whenever [wɛn'ɛvəʳ] CONJ quando, quando quer que; (*every time that*) sempre que ▶ ADV quando você quiser

where [wɛəʳ] ADV onde ▶ CONJ onde, aonde; **this is ~ ...** aqui é onde ...; **whereabouts** ['wɛərəbauts] ADV (por) onde ▶ N: **nobody knows his whereabouts** ninguém sabe o seu paradeiro; **whereas** [wɛər'æz] CONJ uma vez que, ao passo que; **whereby** ADV (*formal*) pelo qual (*or* pela qual *etc*); **wherever** [wɛər'ɛvəʳ] CONJ onde quer que ▶ ADV (*interrogative*) onde?
whether ['wɛðəʳ] CONJ se; **I don't know ~ to accept or not** não sei se aceito ou não; **~ you go or not** quer você vá quer não; **it's doubtful ~ ...** não é certo que ...

(KEYWORD)

which [wɪtʃ] ADJ **1** (*interrogative*) que, qual; **which picture do you want?** que quadro você quer?; **which books are yours?** quais são os seus livros?; **which one?** qual?

2: **in which case** em cujo caso; **by which time** momento em que

▶ PRON **1** (*interrogative*) qual; **which (of these) are yours?** quais (destes) são seus? **2** (*relative*) que, o que, o qual *etc*; **the apple which you ate** a maçã que você comeu; **the chair on which you are sitting** a cadeira na qual você está sentado; **he said he knew, which is true** ele disse que sabia, o que é verdade; **after which** depois do que

whichever [wɪtʃ'ɛvəʳ] ADJ: **take ~ book you prefer** pegue o livro que preferir; **~ book you take** qualquer livro que você pegue
while [waɪl] N tempo, momento ▶ CONJ enquanto, ao mesmo tempo que; (*as long as*) contanto que; (*although*) embora; **for a ~** durante algum tempo; **while away** VT (*time*) encher
whim [wɪm] N capricho, veneta
whine [waɪn] N (*of pain*) gemido; (*of engine, siren*) zunido ▶ VI gemer; zunir; (*fig*) lamuriar-se
whip [wɪp] N açoite m; (*for riding*) chicote m; (*Pol*) líder m/f da bancada ▶ VT chicotear; (*snatch*) apanhar de repente; (*cream, eggs*) bater; (*move quickly*): **to ~ sth out/off/away** *etc* arrancar algo; **whipped cream** [wɪpt-] N creme m chantilly
whirl [wəːl] VT fazer girar ▶ VI (*dancers*) rodopiar; (*leaves, water etc*) redemoinhar
whisk [wɪsk] N (*Culin*) batedeira ▶ VT bater; **to ~ sb away** *or* **off** levar alguém rapidamente
whiskers ['wɪskəz] NPL (*of animal*) bigodes mpl; (*of man*) suíças fpl
whisky ['wɪskɪ], (US, IRELAND) **whiskey** N uísque m (BR), whisky m (PT)

W

whisper ['wɪspər] N sussurro, murmúrio ▶ VT, VI sussurrar
whistle ['wɪsl] N (sound) assobio; (object) apito ▶ VT, VI assobiar
white [waɪt] ADJ branco; (pale) pálido ▶ N branco; (of egg) clara; **whiteboard** N quadro branco; **interactive whiteboard** quadro interativo; **white coffee** N café m com leite; **White House** N ver nota

> A Casa Branca (**White House**) é um grande edifício branco situado em Washington D.C. onde reside o presidente dos Estados Unidos. Por extensão, o termo se refere também ao poder executivo americano.

whitewash ['waɪtwɔʃ] N (paint) cal f ▶ VT caiar; (fig) encobrir
whiting ['waɪtɪŋ] N INV pescada-marlonga
Whitsun ['wɪtsn] N Pentecostes m
whizz [wɪz] VI: **to ~ past** or **by** passar a toda velocidade

KEYWORD

who [hu:] PRON **1** (interrogative) quem?; **who is it?** quem é?
2 (relative) que, o qual etc, quem; **my cousin, who lives in New York** meu primo que mora em Nova Iorque; **the man/woman who spoke to me** o homem/a mulher que falou comigo

whole [həul] ADJ (complete) todo, inteiro; (not broken) intacto ▶ N (all): **the ~ of the time** o tempo todo; (entire unit) conjunto; **on the ~**, **as a ~** como um todo, no conjunto; **wholemeal** (BRIT) ADJ integral; **wholesale** N venda por atacado ▶ ADJ por atacado; (destruction) em grande escala ▶ ADV por atacado;

wholewheat ADJ = **wholemeal**;
wholly ['həulɪ] ADV totalmente, completamente

KEYWORD

whom [hu:m] PRON **1** (interrogative) quem?; **to whom did you give it?** para quem você deu isto?
2 (relative) que, quem; **the man whom I saw/to whom I spoke** o homem que eu vi/com quem eu falei

whore [hɔːr] (inf, pej) N puta

KEYWORD

whose [hu:z] ADJ **1** (possessive, interrogative): **whose book is this?**, **whose is this book?** de quem é este livro?; **I don't know whose it is** eu não sei de quem é isto
2 (possessive, relative): **the man whose son you rescued** o homem cujo filho você salvou; **the woman whose car was stolen** a mulher de quem o carro foi roubado
▶ PRON de quem

KEYWORD

why [waɪ] ADV por que (BR), porque (PT); (at end of sentence) por quê (BR), porquê (PT)
▶ CONJ por que; **that's not why I'm here** não é por isso que estou aqui; **the reason why** a razão por que
▶ EXCL (expressing surprise, shock, annoyance) ora essa!; (explaining) bem!; **why, it's you!** ora, é você!

wicked ['wɪkɪd] ADJ perverso; (smile) malicioso
wicket ['wɪkɪt] N (Cricket) arco

wide [waɪd] ADJ largo; (*area, publicity, knowledge*) amplo ▶ ADV: **to open ~** abrir totalmente; **to shoot ~** atirar longe do alvo; **widely** ADV extremamente; (*travelled, spaced*) muito; (*believed, known*) amplamente; **widen** VT alargar; (*one's experience*) aumentar ▶ VI alargar-se; **wide open** ADJ (*eyes*) arregalado; (*door*) escancarado; **widespread** ADJ (*belief etc*) difundido, comum
widget ['wɪdʒɪt] N (*Comput*) widget *m*
widow ['wɪdəu] N viúva; **widower** N viúvo
width [wɪdθ] N largura
wield [wi:ld] VT (*sword*) brandir, empunhar; (*power*) exercer
wife [waɪf] (*pl* **wives**) N mulher *f*, esposa
Wi-Fi ['waɪfaɪ] N Wi-Fi *m*
wig [wɪg] N peruca
wild [waɪld] ADJ (*animal*) selvagem; (*plant*) silvestre; (*rough*) violento, furioso; (*idea*) disparatado, extravagante; (*person*) insensato; **wilderness** ['wɪldənɪs] N ermo; **wildlife** N animais *mpl* (e plantas *fpl*) selvagens; **wildly** ADV (*behave*) freneticamente; (*hit, guess*) irrefletidamente; (*happy*) extremamente

(KEYWORD)

will [wɪl] (*pt, pp* **willed**) AUX VB
1 (*forming future tense*): **I will finish it tomorrow** vou acabar isto amanhã; **I will have finished it by tomorrow** até amanhã eu terei terminado isto; **will you do it? — yes I will/no I won't** você vai fazer isto? — sim, vou/não eu não vou
2 (*in conjectures, predictions*): **he will**

come ele virá; **he will** or **he'll be there by now** nesta altura ele está lá; **that will be the postman** deve ser o carteiro; **this medicine will/won't help you** este remédio vai/não vai fazer efeito em você
3 (*in commands, requests, offers*): **will you be quiet!** fique quieto, por favor!; **will you come?** você vem?; **will you help me?** você pode me ajudar?; **will you have a cup of tea?** você vai querer uma xícara de chá or um chá?; **I won't put up with it** eu não vou tolerar isto
▶ VT: **to will sb to do sth** desejar que alguém faça algo; **he willed himself to go on** reuniu grande força de vontade para continuar ▶ N (*volition*) vontade *f*; (*testament*) testamento

willing ['wɪlɪŋ] ADJ disposto, pronto; (*enthusiastic*) entusiasmado; **willingly** ADV de bom grado, de boa vontade
willow ['wɪləu] N salgueiro
willpower ['wɪlpauər] N força de vontade
wilt [wɪlt] VI (*flower*) murchar; (*plant*) morrer
win [wɪn] (*pt, pp* **won**) N vitória ▶ VT ganhar, vencer; (*obtain*) conseguir, obter; (*support*) alcançar ▶ VI ganhar; **win over** VT conquistar; **win round** (BRIT) VT = **win over**
wince [wɪns] VI encolher-se, estremecer
wind¹ [wɪnd] N vento; (*Med*) gases *mpl*, flatulência; (*breath*) fôlego ▶ VT deixar sem fôlego
wind² [waɪnd] (*pt, pp* **wound**) VT enrolar, bobinar; (*wrap*) envolver;

W

(*clock, toy*) dar corda a ▶ vi (*road, river*) serpentear; **wind up** vt (*clock*) dar corda em; (*debate*) rematar, concluir

windfall ['wɪndfɔːl] N golpe m de sorte

wind farm N parque m eólico

winding ['waɪndɪŋ] ADJ (*road*) sinuoso, tortuoso; (*staircase*) de caracol, em espiral

windmill ['wɪndmɪl] N moinho de vento

window ['wɪndəu] N janela; (*in shop etc*) vitrine f (BR), montra (PT); **window box** N jardineira (no peitoril da janela); **window cleaner** N limpador(a) m/f de janelas; **window-shopping** N: **to go window-shopping** ir ver vitrines

windscreen ['wɪndskriːn] (BRIT) N para-brisa m; **windscreen wiper** (BRIT) N limpador m de para-brisa

windshield ['wɪndʃiːld] (US) N = **windscreen**

wind turbine ['wɪndtəːbaɪn] N turbina eólica

windy ['wɪndɪ] ADJ com muito vento, batido pelo vento; **it's ~** está ventando (BR), faz vento (PT)

wine [waɪn] N vinho; **wine bar** N bar m para degustação de vinhos; **wine glass** N cálice m (de vinho); **wine list** N lista de vinhos

wing [wɪŋ] N asa; (*of building*) ala; (*Aut*) aleta, para-lamas m inv; **wings** NPL (*Theatre*) bastidores mpl

wink [wɪŋk] N piscadela ▶ vi piscar o olho; (*light etc*) piscar

winner ['wɪnər] N vencedor(a) m/f

winning ['wɪnɪŋ] ADJ (*team*) vencedor(a); (*goal*) decisivo; (*smile*) sedutor(a)

winter ['wɪntər] N inverno; **winter sports** NPL esportes mpl (BR) or desportos mpl (PT) de inverno

wipe [waɪp] N: **to give sth a ~** limpar algo com um pano ▶ vt limpar; (*rub*) esfregar; (*erase: tape*) apagar; **wipe off** vt remover esfregando; **wipe out** vt (*debt*) liquidar; (*memory*) apagar; (*destroy*) exterminar; **wipe up** vt limpar

wire ['waɪər] N arame m; (*Elec*) fio (elétrico); (*telegram*) telegrama m ▶ vt (*house*) instalar a rede elétrica em; (*also*: **~ up**) conectar; (*telegram*) telegrafar para

wireless ['waɪəlɪs] ADJ sem fio (BR), sem fios (PT)

wiring ['waɪərɪŋ] N instalação f elétrica

wisdom ['wɪzdəm] N prudência; (*of action, remark*) bom-senso, sabedoria; **wisdom tooth** irreg N dente m do siso

wise [waɪz] ADJ prudente; (*action, remark*) sensato

wish [wɪʃ] N desejo ▶ vt (*want*) querer; **best ~es** (*on birthday etc*) parabéns mpl, felicidades fpl; **with best ~es** (*in letter*) cumprimentos; **to ~ sb goodbye** despedir-se de alguém; **he ~ed me well** me desejou boa sorte; **to ~ to do/sb to do sth** querer fazer/que alguém faça algo; **to ~ for** desejar

wistful ['wɪstful] ADJ melancólico

wit [wɪt] N (*wittiness*) presença de espírito, engenho; (*intelligence*: also: **~s**) entendimento; (*person*) espirituoso(-a)

witch [wɪtʃ] N bruxa

(KEYWORD)

with [wɪð, wɪθ] PREP **1** (*accompanying, in the company of*) com; **I was with him** eu estava com ele; **to stay overnight with friends** dormir na casa de amigos; **we'll take the**

children with us vamos levar as crianças conosco; **I'll be with you in a minute** vou vê-lo num minuto; **I'm with you** (I understand) compreendo; **to be with it** (inf) estar por dentro; (: aware) estar a par da situação; (: up-to-date) estar atualizado com

2 (descriptive) com, de; **a room with a view** um quarto com vista; **the man with the grey hat/blue eyes** o homem do chapéu cinza/de olhos azuis

3 (indicating manner, means, cause) com, de; **with tears in her eyes** com os olhos cheios de lágrimas; **to fill sth with water** encher algo de água

withdraw [wɪð'drɔ:] irreg vt tirar, remover; (offer) retirar ▶ vi retirar-se; **to ~ money (from the bank)** retirar dinheiro (do banco); **withdrawal** N retirada; **withdrawal symptoms** NPL síndrome f de abstinência; **withdrawn** ADJ (person) reservado, introvertido

wither ['wɪðər] vi murchar

withhold [wɪð'həuld] (irreg: like **hold**) vt (money) reter; (permission) negar; (information) esconder

within [wɪð'ɪn] PREP dentro de ▶ ADV dentro; **~ reach** ao alcance da mão; **~ sight** à vista; **~ the week** antes do fim da semana; **~ a mile of** a uma milha de

without [wɪð'aut] PREP sem; **~ anybody knowing** sem ninguém saber; **to go** or **do ~ sth** passar sem algo

withstand [wɪð'stænd] (irreg: like **stand**) vt resistir a

witness ['wɪtnɪs] N testemunha ▶ vt testemunhar, presenciar;

(document) legalizar; **to bear ~ to sth** (fig) testemunhar algo

witty ['wɪtɪ] ADJ espirituoso

wives [waɪvz] NPL of **wife**

wizard ['wɪzəd] N feiticeiro, mago

wk ABBR = **week**

wobble ['wɔbl] vi oscilar; (chair) balançar

woe [wəu] N dor f, mágoa

woke [wəuk] PT of **wake; woken** PP of **wake**

wolf [wulf] (pl **wolves**) N lobo

woman ['wumən] (pl **women**) N mulher f; **~ doctor** médica

womb [wu:m] N (Anat) matriz f, útero

women ['wɪmɪn] NPL of **woman**

won [wʌn] PT, PP of **win**

wonder ['wʌndər] N maravilha, prodígio; (feeling) espanto ▶ vi: **to ~ whether/why** perguntar-se a si mesmo se/por quê; **to ~ at** admirar-se de; **to ~ about** pensar sobre or em; **it's no ~ that** não é de admirar que; **wonderful** ADJ maravilhoso; (miraculous) impressionante

won't [wəunt] = **will not**

wood [wud] N (timber) madeira; (forest) floresta, bosque m; **wooden** ADJ de madeira; (fig) inexpressivo; **woodwind** N (Mus) instrumentos mpl de sopro de madeira; **woodwork** N carpintaria

wool [wul] N lã f; **to pull the ~ over sb's eyes** (fig) enganar alguém, vender a alguém gato por lebre; **woollen** ADJ de lã; **woolly**, (US) **wooly** ADJ de lã; (fig) confuso

word [wə:d] N palavra; (news) notícia ▶ vt redigir; **in other ~s** em outras palavras, ou seja; **to break/keep one's ~** faltar à palavra/cumprir a promessa;

w

to have ~s with sb discutir com alguém; **wording** N fraseado; **word processing** N processamento de textos; **word processor** N processador *m* de textos

wore [wɔːʳ] PT *of* **wear**

work [wəːk] N trabalho; (*job*) emprego, trabalho; (*Art, Literature*) obra ▶ VI trabalhar; (*mechanism*) funcionar; (*medicine etc*) surtir efeito, ser eficaz ▶ VT (*clay*) moldar; (*wood etc*) talhar; (*mine etc*) explorar; (*machine*) fazer trabalhar, manejar; (*effect, miracle*) causar; **to ~ loose** (*part*) soltar-se; (*knot*) afrouxar-se; **work on** VT FUS trabalhar em, dedicar-se a; (*principle*) basear-se em; **work out** VI dar certo, surtir efeito ▶ VT (*problem*) resolver; (*plan*) elaborar, formular; **it ~s out at £100** dá £100; **worker** N trabalhador(a) *m/f*, operário(-a); **working class** N proletariado, classe *f* operária ▶ ADJ: **working-class** do proletariado, da classe operária; **workman** *irreg* N operário, trabalhador *m*; **worksheet** N (*with exercises*) folha de exercícios; **workshop** N oficina; (*practical session*) aula prática

world [wəːld] N mundo ▶ CPD mundial; **to think the ~ of sb** (*fig*) ter alguém em alto conceito

worm [wəːm] N (*also:* **earth~**) minhoca, lombriga

worn [wɔːn] PP *of* **wear** ▶ ADJ gasto; **worn-out** ADJ (*object*) gasto; (*person*) esgotado, exausto

worry ['wʌrɪ] N preocupação *f* ▶ VT preocupar, inquietar ▶ VI preocupar-se, afligir-se

worse [wəːs] ADJ, ADV pior ▶ N o pior; **a change for the ~** uma mudança para pior, uma piora;

worsen VT, VI piorar; **worse off** ADJ com menos dinheiro; (*fig*): **you'll be worse off this way** assim você ficará pior que nunca

worship ['wəːʃɪp] N adoração *f* ▶ VT adorar, venerar; (*person, thing*) adorar; **Your W~** (BRIT: *to mayor*) vossa Excelência; (: *to judge*) senhor Juiz

worst [wəːst] ADJ (o/a) pior ▶ ADV pior ▶ N o pior; **at ~** na pior das hipóteses

worth [wəːθ] N valor *m*, mérito ▶ ADJ: **to be ~** valer; **it's ~ it** vale a pena; **to be ~ one's while (to do)** valer a pena (fazer); **worthless** ADJ (*person*) imprestável; (*thing*) inútil; **worthwhile** ADJ (*activity*) que vale a pena; (*cause*) de mérito, louvável

worthy ['wəːðɪ] ADJ (*person*) merecedor(a), respeitável; (*motive*) justo; **~ of** digno de

(KEYWORD)

would [wud] AUX VB **1** (*conditional tense*): **if you asked him, he would do it** se você pedisse, ele faria isto; **if you had asked him, he would have done it** se você tivesse pedido, ele teria feito isto
2 (*in offers, invitations, requests*): **would you like a biscuit?** você quer um biscoito?; **would you ask him to come in?** pode pedir a ele para entrar?; **would you close the door, please?** quer fechar a porta por favor?
3 (*in indirect speech*): **I said I would do it** eu disse que eu faria isto
4 (*emphatic*): **you WOULD say that, wouldn't you?** é lógico que você vai dizer isso
5 (*insistence*): **she wouldn't behave** não houve jeito dela se comportar

6 (*conjecture*): **it would have been midnight** devia ser meia-noite; **it would seem so** parece que sim **7** (*indicating habit*): **he would go on Mondays** costumava ir nas segundas-feiras

wouldn't ['wʊdnt] = **would not**
wound¹ [waʊnd] PT, PP *of* **wind²**
wound² [wuːnd] N ferida ▶ VT ferir
wove [wəʊv] PT *of* **weave**; **woven** PP *of* **weave**
wrap [ræp] N (*stole*) xale *m*; (*cape*) capa ▶ VT (*cover*) envolver; (*also*: **~ up**) embrulhar; **wrapper** N invólucro; (BRIT: *of book*) capa; **wrapping paper** N papel *m* de embrulho; (*fancy*) papel de presente
wreath [riːθ] N coroa
wreck [rɛk] N (*of vehicle*) destroços *mpl*; (*ship*) restos *mpl* do naufrágio; (*pej: person*) caco ▶ VT destruir, danificar; (*fig*) arruinar, arrasar; **wreckage** N (*of car, plane*) destroços *mpl*; (*of ship*) restos *mpl*; (*of building*) escombros *mpl*
wren [rɛn] N (*Zool*) carriça
wrench [rɛntʃ] N (*Tech*) chave *f* inglesa; (*tug*) puxão *m*; (*fig*) separação *f* penosa ▶ VT torcer com força; **to ~ sth from sb** arrancar algo de alguém
wrestle ['rɛsl] VI: **to ~ (with sb)** lutar (com or contra alguém); **wrestler** N lutador *m*; **wrestling** N luta (livre)
wretched ['rɛtʃɪd] ADJ desventurado, infeliz; (*inf*) maldito
wriggle ['rɪɡl] VI (*also*: **~ about**) retorcer-se, contorcer-se
wring [rɪŋ] (*pt, pp* **wrung**) VT (*clothes, neck*) torcer; (*hands*) apertar; (*fig*): **to ~ sth out of sb**

arrancar algo de alguém
wrinkle ['rɪŋkl] N (*on skin*) ruga; (*on paper*) prega ▶ VT franzir ▶ VI enrugar-se
wrist [rɪst] N pulso
write [raɪt] (*pt* **wrote**, *pp* **written**) VT escrever; (*cheque, prescription*) passar ▶ VI escrever; **to ~ to sb** escrever para alguém; **write down** VT (*note*) anotar; (*put on paper*) pôr no papel; **write off** VT cancelar; **write out** VT escrever por extenso; (*cheque etc*) passar; **write up** VT redigir; **write-off** N perda total; **writer** N escritor(a) *m/f*
writing ['raɪtɪŋ] N escrita; (*handwriting*) caligrafia, letra; (*of author*) obra; **in ~** por escrito
wrong [rɒŋ] ADJ (*bad*) errado, mau; (*unfair*) injusto; (*incorrect*) errado, equivocado; (*inappropriate*) impróprio ▶ ADV mal, errado ▶ N injustiça ▶ VT ser injusto com; **you are ~ to do it** você se engana ao fazê-lo; **you are ~ about that, you've got it ~** você está enganado sobre isso; **to be in the ~** não ter razão; **what's ~?** o que é que há?; **to go ~** (*person*) desencaminhar-se; (*plan*) dar errado; (*machine*) sofrer uma avaria; **wrongly** ADV errado
wrote [rəʊt] PT *of* **write**
wrung [rʌŋ] PT, PP *of* **wring**
WWW N ABBR = **World Wide Web**; **the ~** a WWW

W

Xmas [ˈɛksməs] N ABBR
  = **Christmas**
X-ray [ɛksˈreɪ] N radiografia ▶ VT
  radiografar, tirar uma chapa de

yacht [jɔt] N iate *m*; **yachting** N
  iatismo
yard [jɑːd] N pátio, quintal *m*;
  (*measure*) jarda (*914 mm; 3 feet*)
yarn [jɑːn] N fio; (*tale*) história
  inverossímil
yawn [jɔːn] N bocejo ▶ VI bocejar
yeah [jɛə] (*inf*) ADV é
year [jɪəʳ] N ano; **to be 8 ~s old** ter
  8 anos; **an eight-~-old child** uma
  criança de oito anos (de idade);
  yearly ADJ anual ▶ ADV anualmente
yearn [jəːn] VI: **to ~ to do/for sth**
  ansiar fazer/por algo
yeast [jiːst] N levedura, fermento
yell [jɛl] N grito, berro ▶ VI gritar,
  berrar
yellow [ˈjɛləu] ADJ amarelo;
  Yellow Pages® NPL (*Tel*) Páginas
  Amarelas *fpl*
yes [jɛs] ADV, N sim *m*
yesterday [ˈjɛstədɪ] ADV, N ontem *m*
yet [jɛt] ADV ainda ▶ CONJ porém, no
  entanto; **the best ~** o melhor até
  agora; **as ~** até agora, ainda

yew [ju:] N teixo
yield [ji:ld] N (*Agr*) colheita;
(*Comm*) rendimento ▶ VT produzir;
(*profit*) render; (*surrender*) ceder
▶ VI render-se, ceder; (*US Aut*) ceder
yoghurt, yogurt ['jəugət] N
iogurte *m*
yolk [jəuk] N gema (do ovo)

(KEYWORD)

you [ju:] PRON 1 (*subj: singular*) tu,
você; (: *plural*) vós, vocês; **you
French enjoy your food** vocês
franceses gostam de comer; **you
and I will go** nós iremos
2 (*direct object: singular*) te, o/a;
(: *plural*) vos, os/as; (*indirect object:
singular*) te, lhe; (: *plural*) vos, lhes;
I know you eu lhe conheço;
I gave it to you dei isto para você
3 (*stressed*) você; **I told YOU to do
it** eu disse para você fazer isto
4 (*after prep, in comparisons:
singular*) ti, você; (: *plural*) vós,
vocês; (*polite form: singular*) o
senhor/a senhora; (: *plural*) os
senhores/as senhoras; **it's for
you** é para você; **with you**
contigo, com você; convosco,
com vocês; com o senhor *etc*
5 (*impers: one*): **you never know**
nunca se sabe; **apples do you
good** as maçãs fazem bem à saúde

you'd [ju:d] = **you had;** = **you
would**
you'll [ju:l] = **you will;** = **you shall**
young [jʌŋ] ADJ jovem ▶ NPL (*of
animal*) filhotes *mpl*, crias *fpl*;
(*people*): **the ~** a juventude, os
jovens; **younger** ADJ mais novo
your [jɔ:ʳ] ADJ teu/tua, seu/sua;
(*plural*) vosso, seu/sua; (*formal*) do
senhor/da senhora; *see also* **my**

you're [juəʳ] = **you are**
yours [jɔːz] PRON teu/tua, seu/
sua; (*plural*) vosso, seu/sua;
(*formal*) do senhor/da senhora;
~ sincerely or **faithfully**
atenciosamente; *see also* **mine¹**
yourself [jɔːˈsɛlf] PRON (*emphatic*)
tu mesmo, você mesmo; (*object,
reflexive*) te, se; (*after prep*) ti
mesmo, si mesmo; (*formal*) o
senhor mesmo/a senhora mesma;
yourselves PRON vós mesmos,
vocês mesmos; (*object, reflexive*)
vos, se; (*after prep*) vós mesmos,
vôces mesmos; (*formal*) os
senhores mesmos/as senhoras
mesmas; *see also* **oneself**
youth [ju:θ] N mocidade *f*,
juventude *f*; (*young man*) jovem *m*;
youth club N associação *f* de
juventude; **youthful** ADJ juvenil;
youth hostel N albergue *m* da
juventude
you've [ju:v] = **you have**

Y

Z

zebra ['ziːbrə] N zebra; **zebra crossing** (BRIT) N faixa (para pedestres) (BR), passadeira (PT)

zero ['zɪərəu] N zero

zest [zɛst] N vivacidade f, entusiasmo; (of lemon etc) zesto

zigzag ['zɪgzæg] N ziguezague m ▶ VI ziguezaguear

zinc [zɪŋk] N zinco

zip [zɪp] N (also: **~ fastener**) fecho ecler (BR) or éclair (PT) ▶ VT (also: **~ up**) fechar o fecho ecler de, subir o fecho ecler de; **zip code** (US) N código postal; **zip file** N arquivo zipado; **zipper** (US) N = **zip**

zit [zɪt] (inf) N espinha

zodiac ['zəudɪæk] N zodíaco

zone [zəun] N zona

zoo [zuː] N (jardim m) zoológico

zoom [zuːm] VI: **to ~ past** passar zunindo; **zoom lens** N zoom m, zum m

zucchini [zuːˈkiːnɪ] (US) NPL abobrinha

Portuguese
in Action

Inglês
em Ação

Contents   Índice

Correspondência

▶ Carta pessoal

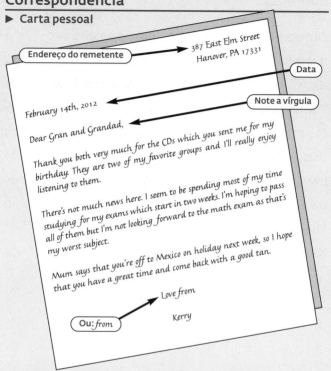

Endereço do remetente

387 East Elm Street
Hanover, PA 17331

Data

February 14th, 2012

Note a vírgula

Dear Gran and Grandad,

Thank you both very much for the CDs which you sent me for my birthday. They are two of my favorite groups and I'll really enjoy listening to them.

There's not much news here. I seem to be spending most of my time studying for my exams which start in two weeks. I'm hoping to pass all of them but I'm not looking forward to the math exam as that's my worst subject.

Mum says that you're off to Mexico on holiday next week, so I hope that you have a great time and come back with a good tan.

Love from

Kerry

Ou: from

A introdução numa carta pessoal

Thank you for your letter.	*Obrigado/da por sua carta.*
It was lovely to hear from you.	*Foi ótimo/Adorei receber notícias suas.*
I'm sorry I didn't write earlier.	*Desculpe por eu não ter te escrito mais cedo.*

A despedida numa carta pessoal

Write soon!	*Escreva em breve!*
Give my love to Vanessa.	*Mande um beijo para a Vanessa.*
Samuel sends his best wishes.	*Samuel manda lembranças/abraços.*

Correspondence

▶ **Personal letter**

Rio de Janeiro, 5 de junho de 2012 ← **Place & Date**

Queridos vovó e vovô,

Muito obrigado pelos CDs que vocês me enviaram de presente de aniversário. São dois dos minhas bandas favoritas, e estou gostando muito de escutá-los.

Não há muitas novidades por aqui. Tenho passado a maior parte do tempo estudando para os meus exames, que começam daqui a duas semanas. Espero ser aprovada em todos, mas não estou muito animada com o exame de matemática porque é a matéria em que sou mais fraca.

Mamãe me falou que vocês vão de férias para Fortaleza na semana que vem. Espero que se divirtam bastante e voltem com um belo bronzeado.

Com um beijo da

Mônica.

Starting a personal letter

Obrigado/da por sua carta. — *Thank you for your letter.*

Foi ótimo/Adorei receber notícias suas. — *It was lovely to hear from you.*

Desculpe por eu não ter te escrito mais cedo. — *I'm sorry I didn't write earlier.*

Ending a personal letter

Escreva em breve! — *Write soon!*

Mande um beijo para a Vanessa. — *Give my love to Vanessa.*

Samuel manda lembranças/abraços. — *Samuel sends his best wishes.*

5

7933 Countryside Lane
Niwot, CO 80503

March 29th, 2012

Mrs. Elaine Harris, Manager
Mountain View Retreat
PO Box 58
Estes Park, CO 80517

Dear Mrs Harris,

My sister stayed with you last year and has highly
recommended your guest house.

I would like to reserve a room for one week from August
18th–24th of this year. I would be obliged if you would let
me know how much this would be for two adults and two
children, and whether you have rooms free on those dates.

I hope to hear from you soon,

Yours sincerely,

Correspondence

▶ Letters

Rosalinda Pereira
Rua Barreto, 109
Curitiba, PR
CEP 80000-999

29 de março de 2012

Sra. Eliana Gomes
Gerente
Pousada Acalanto
Mauá

Prezada Sra. Gomes,

Minha irmã hospedou-se em sua pousada no ano passado e a recomendou muito.

Gostaria de fazer a reserva de um quarto por uma semana, de 18 a 24 de agosto deste ano. Agradeceria se pudesse me informar quanto sairia para dois adultos e duas crianças, e se há vaga nessas datas.

No aguardo de um contato seu em breve,

Atenciosamente,

Miss C Sauterelle
Rua Porto Gomes, 262
Catete – 22475-120
Rio de Janeiro, RJ

April 13th, 2012

Mrs Akien Fields
Funky Fashions
610 1st Ave
New York, NY 10003

Dear Mrs Fields,

I am anxious to find a job in New York during my summer holiday from University and wish to gain experience in the fashion industry. I would be obliged if you could offer me work in any capacity. I can supply references from former employers, if you would like them.

Yours sincerely,

Correspondence

▶ Letters

Ms Eileen Ross
85 Rush Lane
Triptown
Lancs
LC4 2DT
UK

13 de abril de 2012

Srta. Cristina Santos
Rua Porto Gomes, 262
Catete, Rio de Janeiro, RJ
CEP 22475-120

Prezada Srta. Santos,

Quero muito trabalhar no Brasil durante o período de minhas férias universitárias e adquirir experiência na indústria da moda. Ficaria grata por uma posição na empresa, qualquer que fosse. Posso fornecer cartas de referência de empregadores anteriores, se desejar.

Atenciosamente,

Correspondência

▶ Cartas

Sra. Maria Antônia Gonçalves
Avenida 20 de Março, apto. 302,
Goiânia, GO
CEP 74000-310

March 2nd, 2012

Mr. Brian Goodman
Human Resources Manager
DTL Thompson Co.
30 Brownwood Street
Houston, TX 77020

Dear Mr. Goodman,

I am 19 years old and a student of English at São Paulo University. I would like to work in Houston in order to perfect my English. I would be grateful if you would let me know if your agency could offer me work for a period of about ten months from Easter.

Yours in anticipation,

Maria Antônia Gonçalves

Correspondence

▶ Letters

129 Strathmore Ave
Edinburgh
EH11 2AD

2 de março de 2012

Sr. Carlos Mota
Rua dos Andradas, 29,
Centro, Rio de Janeiro, RJ
CEP 22475-000

Prezado Sr. Mota,

Tenho 19 anos e sou estudante de graduação em Português
na Universidade de Edimburgo. Gostaria de trabalhar no
Brasil para aperfeiçoar meu português. Gostaria de saber se
a sua agência poderia me arrumar trabalho por um
período de dez meses, a partir da Páscoa.

Atenciosamente,

Jessica Lister

Correspondência

▶ Carta de apresentação

Rosalind Williamson
11 North Street
Barnton
BN7 2BT

Human Resources Dept.
J. M. Kenyon, Inc.
580 Main Street
Clifton, NJ 97503

February 20th, 2012

Dear Sir or Madam,

With reference to your advertisement in today's Herald,
I wish to apply for the post of Human Resources Manager.

I enclose my resume. Please do not hesitate to contact me
if you require any further details.

Yours faithfully,
Rosalind Williamson

Enc: resume with two references.

Correspondence

▶ Covering letter

Rosalinda Pereira
Rua Norte 204
apto 201
São Paulo – SP

20 de fevereiro de 2012

Dept. de Recursos Humanos
Kenyon Ltda.
Rua da Graça, 25
São Paulo - SP

Prezado Senhor/Senhora,

Gostaria de me candidatar à posição de Gerente de
Recursos Humanos, conforme vaga anunciada no jornal
O Globo nesta data.

Envio meu currículo e coloco-me à disposição para fornecer
informações adicionais, caso deseje.

Cordialmente,
Rosalinda Pereira

Em anexo: CV e duas cartas de referência.

▶ Résumé

760 Shallot Circle
Lafayette, CO 80026

720 384 5923
markbates@aol.com

Mark Bates

Objective
A senior sales management position in a Fortune 500 company

Experience
Arbor Sheetrock Longmont, CO
2007–2012
National Sales Manager
- Increased sales from $50 million to $100 million.
- Doubled sales per representative from $5 million to $10 million.
- Suggested new products that increased earnings by 23%.

Fleet and Wardell Durango, CO
2004–2007
District Sales Manager
- Increased regional sales from $25 million to $350 million.
- Managed 250 sales representatives in 10 Western states.
- Implemented training course for new recruits — speeding profitability.

Ojaz Farm Products Las Cruces, NM
2000–2004
Senior Sales Representative
- Expanded sales team from 50 to 100 representatives.
- Tripled division revenues for each sales associate.
- Expanded sales to include mass market accounts.

Pecan Growers Cooperative Hatch, NM
1995–2000
Sales Representative
- Expanded territorial sales by 400%.
- Received company's highest sales award four years in a row.
- Developed Excellence In Sales training course.

Education
New Mexico State University Albuquerque, NM
1991–1995
- B.A., Business Administration

Interests
birdwatching, running, gardening, carpentry, hunting

References
Provided upon request

Correspondence

▶ Curriculum vitae

CURRÍCULO

Nome: Rosalinda PEREJRA

Endereço: Rua Norte 204, apto 201, São Paulo – SP

Telefone: (11) 4762 3081

Data de Nascimento: 6/5/1985

Estado Civil: Solteira

Nacionalidade: Brasileira

Qualificações: Certificado de Conclusão do Ensino Médio (2003)
Licenciatura em italiano e francês,
USP, São Paulo (2007)

Cargo atual: Assistente de RH, Companhia Metaldom
S/A, São Paulo, SP (desde fevereiro de 2009)

Cargo anterior: Novembro 2007 – Janeiro 2009:
Estagiária na área de RH,
Companhia Metaldom S/A
Outubro 2003 – Junho 2007:
Estudante, USP

Habilidades, Interesses e Experiência
Fluência em italiano e francês;
bom conhecimento de alemão;
conhecimento rudimentar de russo;
proprietária de veículo, carteira de motorista
(sem pontuação); hipismo e iatismo.

Referências:
Sra. Alice Amaral, Gerente de Recursos Humanos, Companhia
Metaldom S/A, São Paulo, SP
Dr I.O. Sono, Departamento de Italiano, USP, São Paulo, SP

Correspondência

▶ Correio eletrônico/e-mail

Em inglês, pronuncia-se o endereço eletrônico assim:
'eli dot ward at mymail dot com'

New Message

To:	eli.ward@mymail.com
From:	gordon@onemo.net
Subject:	concert next week
cc:	jeremy@bit.com
bcc:	

Attachment   **Send**

Hi guys

I've just bought the new album by Rockstar, and it's brilliant!
I've got two spare tickets to a concert they're giving in
Chicago next Wednesday evening, so I hope you can both
make it.

See you soon!

New message	Nova mensagem
To	Para
From	De
Subject	Assunto
cc	Cc
bcc	Cco
Attachment	Anexo
Send	Enviar

Correspondence

▶ Email

To give your email address to someone in Portuguese, say:
'isabel ponto costa arroba globanet ponto com ponto b r'

Nova Mensagem

De:	isabel.costa@globanet.com.br
Para:	su@oneri.com
Assunto:	concerto
Cc:	paulolmuniz@folig.com
Cco:	

Anexo	Enviar

Olá!

Como foi o fim de semana? Sobraram duas entradas para o show de amanhã, de uns amigos que não vão poder ir. Se interessar a você, ou se conhecer alguém que queira ir, me avise assim que puder.

Abraços,

Nova mensagem	New message
Para	To
De	From
Assunto	Subject
Cc	cc
Cco	bcc
Anexo	Attachment
Enviar	Send

The telephone

O telefone

▶ When your number answers

- Hello! Could I speak to Susana, please?
- Could you ask him/her to call me back, please?
- I'll call back later.

▶ Answering the telephone

- Hello! It's Marcos speaking.
- Speaking.
- Who's speaking?

▶ When the switchboard answers

- Who shall I say is calling?
- I'm putting you through.
- Please hold.
- Would you like to leave a message?

▶ Problems

- I don't have a signal.
- My battery's low.
- I can't hear you.
- Sorry, I dialled the wrong number.
- This is a very bad line.

- You're breaking up.

▶ Ao telefonar para alguém

- Alô! Posso falar com a Susana, por favor?
- Você podia pedir a ele/ela para retornar minha ligação?
- Volto a ligar mais tarde.

▶ Ao atender o telefone

- Alô! Aqui é o Marcos.
- É ele/ela.
- Com quem falo?

▶ Quando a/o telefonista atende

- Quem gostaria de falar?
- Vou transferir a ligação.
- Aguarde, por favor.
- Gostaria de deixar um recado?

▶ Problemas

- Estou sem sinal.
- Estou quase sem bateria.
- Não estou escutando.
- Desculpe, foi engano.

- A ligação está muito ruim.
- A ligação está cortando.

18

False friends   # Falsos amigos

English ≠ *Portuguese*

actual ≠ *atual*

The film is based on actual events. → O filme se baseia em eventos reais.

O filme se baseia em eventos atuais. → The film is based on current events.

agenda ≠ *agenda*

I've drawn up an agenda for the meeting. → Preparei uma pauta para a reunião.

Perdi minha agenda. → I lost my calendar (BRIT diary).

beef ≠ *bife*

Did you buy beef or pork? → Você comprou carne de vaca ou porco?

bife com batatas fritas → steak and fries (BRIT chips)

deception ≠ *decepção*

Katie continued to keep up the deception. → Katie continuou mantendo (BR)/ a manter (PT) a ilusão.

Ontem tive uma grande decepção. → Yesterday I had a big disappointment.

exit ≠ *êxito*

"Exit" (sign) → "Saída" (placa)

Seu filme obteve grande êxito. → Her film was a huge success.

19

False friends   Falsos amigos

expert ≠ *esperto*

She's an **expert** in marine biology. → Ela é **especialista** em biologia marinha.

Meu irmão é muito **esperto**. → My brother is very **smart**.

fabric ≠ *fábrica*

five metres of **fabric** → cinco metros de **tecido**

Ela trabalha em uma **fábrica**. → She works in a **factory**.

intend ≠ *entender*

I didn't **intend** to hurt her feelings. → Eu não **pretendia** ferir seus sentimentos.

Não **entendi** a pergunta. → I didn't **understand** the question.

large ≠ *largo*

a **large** house → uma casa **grande**

A estrada é bastante **larga**. → The road is very **wide**.

library ≠ *livraria*

the public **library** → a **biblioteca** pública

Esta é minha **livraria** preferida. → This is my favourite **bookstore** (BRIT **bookshop**).

False friends
Falsos amigos

location ≠ locação

The location is still to be decided.	→ O local ainda precisa ser decidido.
A empresa lida com locação de apartamentos.	→ The company deals with apartment rentals.

lunch ≠ lanche

Let's have lunch at one.	→ Vamos almoçar à uma da tarde.
Vamos fazer um lanche mais tarde.	→ Let's have a snack later.

notice ≠ notícia

There's a notice on the board about the trip.	→ Há um aviso no quadro sobre a viagem.
Recebi boas notícias.	→ I got some good news.

parent ≠ parente

My parents are Scottish.	→ Meus pais são escoceses.
Meus parentes vieram me visitar.	→ My relatives came to visit me.

pretend ≠ pretender

He was just pretending to be ill.	→ Ele só estava fingindo que estava doente.
Pretendo terminar o trabalho hoje.	→ I intend to finish the job today.

False friends

push ≠ *puxar*

Push the door to open it.	→ Empurre a porta para abri-la.
O assaltante quase puxou o gatilho.	→ The robber almost pulled the trigger.

record ≠ *recordar*

They've just recorded a new album.	→ Eles acabaram de gravar um novo álbum.
Eu me recordo dessa pessoa.	→ I remember this person.

retired ≠ *retirado*

Is your dad retired yet?	→ Seu pai já é aposentado?
O computador deve ser retirado da caixa com cuidado.	→ The computer must be removed from the box carefully.

sensible ≠ *sensível*

Be sensible!	→ Seja sensato!
Ela é uma pessoa muito sensível.	→ She is a very sensitive person.

sympathetic ≠ *simpático*

She's a sympathetic listener.	→ Ela é uma ouvinte muito compassiva.
Meu amigo é muito simpático.	→ My friend is very nice.

Useful phrases

Frases úteis

Greetings

Hello!
Goodbye!
Bye!
Good morning.
Good afternoon.
Good evening.
Good night.
Welcome!
How are you?
I'm fine, thank you.
Pleased to meet you.
How's life?
See you tomorrow!
See you later!
Good luck!
Congratulations!
Have fun!
Cheers!
Bless you!

Take care!
Enjoy your meal!
Happy Birthday!
Merry Christmas!
Happy New Year!

On the telephone

Hello?
Who's speaking?
It's Laura speaking.
Could I speak to ..., please?
My phone number is ...
My cell number (BRIT mobile number) is ...

Saudações

Oi! *(BR)*, Olá! *(PT)*
Adeus!
Tchau!
Bom dia.
Boa tarde.
Boa noite. *(para saudar)*
Boa noite. *(para despedir-se)*
Bem-vindo!
Como está?
Bem, obrigado.
Prazer em conhecê-lo.
Tudo bem?
Até amanhã!
Até logo!
Boa sorte!
Parabéns!/Felicidades!
Divirta-se!
Saúde! *(brinde)*
Saúde! *(ao espirrar) (BR)*,
 Santinho! *(PT)*

Cuide-se!
Bom apetite!
Parabéns!
Feliz Natal!
Feliz Ano Novo!

Ao telefone

Alô? *(BR)*, Estou? *(PT)*
Quem fala?
Aqui fala a Laura.
Posso falar com ...?
O meu (número de) telefone é ...
O meu número de celular *(BR)*
or telemóvel *(PT)* é ...

It's busy (*BRIT* engaged).	Está ocupado.
There's no reply.	Ninguém atende.
Do you speak Portuguese/English?	Fala português/inglês?
Please hold the line.	Não desligue, por favor.
Could you put me through to extension 3395?	Eu gostaria de falar com o ramal 3395?
Would you like to leave a message?	Quer deixar recado?
Could you tell him that I called?	Pode dizer que eu liguei?
I'll call back later.	Volto a ligar mais tarde.
I'm afraid you have the wrong number.	Acho que você ligou para o número errado.

Letter writing

Cartas

Dear Sir/Madam	Exmo(-a). Senhor(a)
Yours faithfully	Atenciosamente
Dear Mr. Fontes	Caro Sr. Fontes
Yours sincerely	Atenciosamente
Best wishes	Cordialmente
Kind regards	Cumprimentos
Dear Carlota	Cara Carlota
All the best	Um abraço
With love from ...	Um beijo
Please find enclosed ...	Envio anexo ...
Thank you for your letter.	Obrigado(-a) pela sua carta.

Email

Correio eletrônico

Do you have email?	Você tem e-mail/correio eletrônico?
What's your email address?	Qual é o seu endereço de e-mail/correio eletrônico?
My email address is ...	Meu endereço de e-mail/correio eletrônico é ...
emma@coolmail.com	emma@coolmail.com
= *"emma at coolmail dot com"*	= *"emma arroba coolmail ponto com"*

Verbos irregulares em inglês

PRESENT	PT	PP	PRESENT	PT	PP
arise	arose	arisen	fight	fought	fought
awake	awoke	awoken	find	found	found
be (am, is, are; being)	was, were	been	fling	flung	flung
			fly	flew	flown
bear	bore	born(e)	forbid	forbad(e)	forbidden
beat	beat	beaten	forecast	forecast	forecast
begin	began	begun	forget	forgot	forgotten
bend	bent	bent	forgive	forgave	forgiven
bet	bet, betted	bet, betted	freeze	froze	frozen
			get	got	got, (US) gotten
bid (at auction)	bid	bid			
bind	bound	bound	give	gave	given
bite	bit	bitten	go (goes)	went	gone
bleed	bled	bled	grind	ground	ground
blow	blew	blown	grow	grew	grown
break	broke	broken	hang	hung	hung
breed	bred	bred	hang (execute)	hanged	hanged
bring	brought	brought	have	had	had
build	built	built	hear	heard	heard
burn	burnt, burned	burnt, burned	hide	hid	hidden
			hit	hit	hit
burst	burst	burst	hold	held	held
buy	bought	bought	hurt	hurt	hurt
can	could	(been able)	keep	kept	kept
cast	cast	cast	kneel	knelt, kneeled	knelt, kneeled
catch	caught	caught			
choose	chose	chosen	know	knew	known
cling	clung	clung	lay	laid	laid
come	came	come	lead	led	led
cost	cost	cost	lean	leant, leaned	leant, leaned
creep	crept	crept			
cut	cut	cut	leap	leapt, leaped	leapt, leaped
deal	dealt	dealt	learn	learnt, learned	learnt, learned
dig	dug	dug			
do (does)	did	done			
draw	drew	drawn	leave	left	left
dream	dreamed, dreamt	dreamed, dreamt	lend	lent	lent
			let	let	let
drink	drank	drunk	lie (lying)	lay	lain
drive	drove	driven	light	lit, lighted	lit, lighted
eat	ate	eaten			
fall	fell	fallen	lose	lost	lost
feed	fed	fed	make	made	made
feel	felt	felt	may	might	–

Verbos irregulares em inglês

PRESENT	PT	PP	PRESENT	PT	PP
mean	meant	meant	speak	spoke	spoken
meet	met	met	speed	sped,	sped,
mistake	mistook	mistaken		speeded	speeded
mow	mowed	mown,	spell	spelt,	spelt,
		mowed		spelled	spelled
must	(had to)	(had to)	spend	spent	spent
pay	paid	paid	spill	spilt,	spilt,
put	put	put		spilled	spilled
quit	quit,	quit,	spin	spun	spun
	quitted	quitted	spit	spat	spat
read	read	read	spoil	spoiled,	spoiled,
rid	rid	rid		spoilt	spoilt
ride	rode	ridden	spread	spread	spread
ring	rang	rung	spring	sprang	sprung
rise	rose	risen	stand	stood	stood
run	ran	run	steal	stole	stolen
saw	sawed	sawed,	stick	stuck	stuck
		sawn	sting	stung	stung
say	said	said	stink	stank	stunk
see	saw	seen	stride	strode	stridden
sell	sold	sold	strike	struck	struck
send	sent	sent	swear	swore	sworn
set	set	set	sweep	swept	swept
sew	sewed	sewn	swell	swelled	swollen,
shake	shook	shaken			swelled
shear	sheared	shorn,	swim	swam	swum
		sheared	swing	swung	swung
shed	shed	shed	take	took	taken
shine	shone	shone	teach	taught	taught
shoot	shot	shot	tear	tore	torn
show	showed	shown	tell	told	told
shrink	shrank	shrunk	think	thought	thought
shut	shut	shut	throw	threw	thrown
sing	sang	sung	thrust	thrust	thrust
sink	sank	sunk	tread	trod	trodden
sit	sat	sat	wake	woke,	woken,
sleep	slept	slept		waked	waked
slide	slid	slid	wear	wore	worn
sling	slung	slung	weave	wove	woven
slit	slit	slit	weep	wept	wept
smell	smelt,	smelt,	win	won	won
	smelled	smelled	wind	wound	wound
sow	sowed	sown,	wring	wrung	wrung
		sowed	write	wrote	written

Portuguese verb forms

1 Gerund. 2 Imperative. 3 Present. 4 Imperfect. 5 Preterite. 6 Future.
7 Present subjunctive. 8 Imperfect subjunctive. 9 Future subjunctive.
10 Past participle. 11 Pluperfect. 12 Personal infinitive.

etc indicates that the irregular root is used for all persons of the tense,
e.g. ouvir 7 ouça ouça, ouças, ouça, ouçamos, ouçais, ouçam.

abrir 10 aberto
acudir 2 acode 3 acudo, acodes,
  acode, acodem
aderir 3 adiro 7 adira
advertir 3 advirto 7 advirta *etc*
agir 3 ajo 7 aja *etc*
agradecer 3 agradeço 7 agradeça *etc*
agredir 2 agride 3 agrido, agrides,
  agride, agridem 7 agrida *etc*
AMAR 1 amando 2 ama, amai
  3 amo, amas, ama, amamos, amais,
  amam 4 amava, amavas, amava,
  amávamos, amáveis, amavam
  5 amei, amaste, amou, amamos
  (*PT*: amámos), amastes, amaram
  6 amarei, amarás, amará,
  amaremos, amareis, amarão
  7 ame, ames, ame, amemos, ameis,
  amem 8 amasse, amasses, amasse,
  amássemos, amásseis, amassem
  9 amar, amares, amar, amarmos,
  amardes, amarem 10 amado
  11 amara, amaras, amara,
  amáramos, amáreis, amaram
  12 amar, amares, amar, amarmos,
  amardes, amarem
ameaçar 5 ameacei 7 ameace *etc*
ansiar 2 anseia 3 anseio, anseias,
  anseia, anseiam 7 anseie *etc*
arrancar 7 arranque *etc*
arruinar 2 arruína 3 arruíno, arruínas,
  arruína, arruínam 7 arruíne *etc*
  arruínes, arruíne, arruínem
atribuir 3 atribuo, atribuis, atribui,

atribuímos, atribuís, atribuem
bulir 2 bole 3 bulo, boles, bole,
  bolem
caber 3 caibo 5 coube *etc* 7 caiba *etc*
  8 coubesse *etc* 9 couber *etc*
cair 2 cai 3 caio, cais, cai, caímos,
  caís, caem 4 caía *etc* 5 caí, caíste
  7 caia *etc* 8 caísse *etc*
cobrir 3 cubro 7 cubra *etc* 10 coberto
compelir 3 compilo 7 compila *etc*
crer 2 crê 3 creio, crês, crê, cremos,
  credes, creem 5 cri, creste, creu,
  cremos, crestes, creram 7 creia *etc*
cuspir 2 cospe 3 cuspo, cospes, cospe,
  cospem
dar 2 dá 3 dou, dás, dá, damos, dais,
  dão 5 dei, deste, deu, demos,
  destes, deram 7 dê, dês, dê, demos,
  deis, deem 8 desse *etc* 9 der *etc*
  11 dera *etc*
deduzir 2 deduz 3 deduzo, deduzes,
  deduz
denegrir 2 denigre 3 denigro,
  denigres, denigre, denigrem
  7 denigre *etc*
despir 3 dispo 7 dispa *etc*
dizer 2 diz (dize) 3 digo, dizes, diz,
  dizemos, dizeis, dizem 5 disse *etc*
  6 direi *etc* 7 diga *etc* 8 dissesse *etc*
  9 disser *etc* 10 dito
doer 2 dói 3 doo, dóis, dói
dormir 3 durmo 7 durma *etc*
emergir 3 emirjo 7 emirja *etc*
escrever 10 escrito

27

Portuguese verb forms

ESTAR 2 está 3 estou, estás, está,
estamos, estais, estão 4 estava *etc*
5 estive, estiveste, esteve,
estivemos, estivestes, estiveram
7 esteja *etc* 8 estivesse *etc*
9 estiver *etc* 11 estivera *etc*
extorquir 3 exturco 7 exturca *etc*
FAZER 3 faço 5 fiz, fizeste, fez,
fizemos, fizestes, fizeram 6 farei *etc*
7 faça *etc* 8 fizesse *etc* 9 fizer *etc*
10 feito 11 fizera *etc*
ferir 3 firo 7 fira *etc*
fluir 3 fluo, fluis, flui, fluímos, fluís,
fluem
fugir 2 foge 3 fujo, foges, foge, fogem
7 fuja *etc*
ganhar 10 ganho
gastar 10 gasto
gerir 3 giro 7 gira *etc*
haver 2 há 3 hei, hás, há, havemos,
haveis, hão 4 havia *etc* 5 houve,
houveste, houve, houvemos,
houvestes, houveram 7 haja *etc*
8 houvesse *etc* 9 houver *etc*
11 houvera *etc*
ir 1 indo 2 vai 3 vou, vais, vai, vamos,
ides, vão 4 ia *etc* 5 fui, foste, foi,
fomos, fostes, foram 7 vá, vás, vá,
vamos, vades, vão 8 fosse, fosses,
fosse, fôssemos, fôsseis, fossem
9 for *etc* 10 ido 11 fora *etc*
ler 2 lê 3 leio, lês, lê, lemos, ledes,
leem 5 li, leste, leu, lemos, lestes,
leram 7 leia *etc*
medir 3 meço, 7 meça *etc*
mentir 3 minto 7 minta *etc*
ouvir 3 ouço 7 ouça *etc*
pagar 10 pago
parir 3 pairo 7 paira *etc*
pecar 7 peque *etc*

pedir 3 peço 7 peça *etc*
perder 3 perco 7 perca *etc*
poder 3 posso 5 pude, pudeste, pôde,
pudemos, pudestes, puderam
7 possa *etc* 8 pudesse *etc* 9 puder *etc*
11 pudera *etc*
polir 2 pule 3 pulo, pules, pule,
pulem 7 pula *etc*
pôr 1 pondo 2 põe 3 ponho, pões, põe,
pomos, pondes, põem 4 punha *etc*
5 pus, puseste, pôs, pusemos,
pusestes, puseram 6 porei *etc*
7 ponha *etc* 8 pusesse *etc* 9 puser *etc*
10 posto 11 pusera *etc*
preferir 3 prefiro 7 prefire *etc*
prevenir 2 previne 3 previno,
prevines, previne, previnem
7 previna *etc*
prover 2 provê 3 provejo, provês,
provê, provemos, provedes,
proveem 5 provi, proveste, proveu,
provemos, provestes, proveram
7 proveja *etc* 8 provesse *etc* 9 prover
etc
querer 3 quero, queres, quer 5 quis,
quiseste, quis, quisemos, quisestes,
quiseram 7 queira *etc* 8 quisesse *etc*
9 quiser *etc* 11 quisera *etc*
refletir 3 reflito 7 reflita *etc*
repetir 3 repito 7 repita *etc*
requerer 3 requeiro, requeres, requer
7 requeira *etc*
reunir 2 reúne 3 reúno, reúnes,
reúne, reúnem 7 reúna *etc*
rir 2 ri 3 rio, ris, ri, rimos, rides,
ridem 5 ri, riste, riu, rimos, ristes,
riram 7 ria *etc*
saber 3 sei, sabes, sabe, sabemos,
sabeis, sabem 5 soube, soubeste,
soube, soubemos, soubestes,

Portuguese verb forms

souberam 7 saiba *etc* 8 soubesse *etc*
9 souber *etc* 11 soubera *etc*
seguir 3 sigo 7 siga *etc*
sentir 3 sinto 7 sinta *etc*
ser 2 sê 3 sou, és, é, somos, sois, são
4 era *etc* 5 fui, foste, foi, fomos,
fostes, foram 7 seja *etc* 8 fosse *etc*
9 for *etc* 11 fora *etc*
servir 3 sirvo 7 sirva *etc*
subir 2 sobe 3 subo, sobes, sobe, sobem
suster 2 sustém 3 sustenho, sustens,
sustém, sustendes, sustêm
5 sustive, sustiveste, susteve,
sustivemos, sustivestes,
sustiveram 7 sustenha *etc*
ter 2 tem 3 tenho, tens, tem, temos,
tendes, têm 4 tinha *etc* 5 tive,
tiveste, teve, tivemos, tivestes,
tiveram 6 terei *etc* 7 tenha *etc*
8 tivesse *etc* 9 tiver *etc* 11 tivera *etc*
torcer 3 torço 7 torça *etc*
tossir 3 tusso 7 tussa *etc*
trair 2 trai 3 traio, trais, trai,
traímos, traís, traem 7 traia *etc*
trazer 2 (traze) traz 3 trago, trazes,
traz, 5 trouxe, trouxeste, trouxe,
trouxemos, trouxestes, trouxeram
6 trarei *etc* 7 traga *etc* 8 trouxesse *etc*
9 trouxer *etc* 11 trouxera *etc*
UNIR 1 unindo 2 une, uni 3 uno,
unes, une, unimos, unis, unem
4 unia, unias, uníamos, uníeis,
uniam 5 uni, uniste, uniu, unimos,
unistes, uniram 6 unirei, unirás,
unirá, uniremos, unireis, unirão

7 una, unas, una, unamos, unais,
unam 8 unisse, unisses, unisse,
uníssemos, unísseis, unissem
9 unir, unires, unir, unirmos,
unirdes, unirem 10 unido 11 unira,
uniras, unira, uníramos, uníreis,
uniram 12 unir, unires, unir,
unirmos, unirdes, unirem
valer 3 valho 7 valha *etc*
ver 2 vê 3 vejo, vês, vê, vemos, vedes,
veem 4 via *etc* 5 vi, viste, viu, vimos,
vistes, viram 7 veja *etc* 8 visse *etc*
9 vir *etc* 10 visto 11 vira
vir 1 vindo, 2 vem 3 venho, vens,
vem, vimos, vindes, vêm 4 vinha *etc*
5 vim, vieste, veio, viemos, viestes,
vieram 7 venha *etc* 8 viesse *etc* 9 vier
etc 10 vindo 11 viera *etc*
VIVER 1 vivendo 2 vive, vivei 3 vivo,
vives, vive, vivemos, viveis, vivem
4 vivia, vivias, vivia, vivíamos,
vivíeis, viviam 5 vivi, viveste,
viveu, vivemos, vivestes, viveram
6 viverei, viverás, viverá,
viveremos, vivereis, viverão 7 viva,
vivas, viva, vivamos, vivais, vivam
8 vivesse, vivesses, vivesse,
vivêssemos, vivêsseis, vivessem
9 viver, viveres, viver, vivermos,
viverdes, viverem 10 vivido
11 vivera, viveras, vivera,
vivêramos, vivêreis, viveram
12 viver, viveres, viver, vivermos,
viverdes, viverem

Dates   Datas

Days of the week

Monday
Tuesday
Wednesday
Thursday
Friday
Saturday
Sunday

Dias da semana

segunda(-feira)
terça(-feira)
quarta(-feira)
quinta(-feira)
sexta(-feira)
sábado
domingo

Months

January
February
March
April
May
June
July
August
September
October
November
December

Meses

janeiro
fevereiro
março
abril
maio
junho
julho
agosto
setembro
outubro
novembro
dezembro

Useful vocabulary

What day is it today?
Today is the 28th.
When?
today
tomorrow
yesterday
this morning/afternoon
in two weeks *ou* a fortnight
in a week's time
last/next month

Vocabulário útil

Que dia é hoje?
Hoje é dia 28.
Quando?
hoje
amanhã
ontem
hoje de manhã/à tarde
em duas semanas
daqui a uma semana
mês passado/que vem

The time

As horas

What time is it?

Que horas são?

É uma e quinze.
É uma e um quarto (PT).

It's a quarter past one.
It's one fifteen. (BRIT)

É meio-dia /É meia-noite.

It's noon (BRIT midday).
/It's midnight.

São três e meia.

It's three-thirty.
It's half past three. (BRIT)

Faltam dez para as duas.
São duas menos dez (PT).

It's ten to two.

São nove (horas) da
manhã /da noite.

It's nine o'clock in the
morning/at night.

Faltam vinte para as oito.
São oito menos vinte (PT).

It's twenty to eight.

31

Numbers   Números

Cardinal numbers   Números cardinais

one	1	um (uma)
two	2	dois (duas)
three	3	três
four	4	quatro
five	5	cinco
six	6	seis
seven	7	sete
eight	8	oito
nine	9	nove
ten	10	dez
eleven	11	onze
twelve	12	doze
thirteen	13	treze
fourteen	14	catorze
fifteen	15	quinze
sixteen	16	dezesseis (BR), dezasseis (PT)
seventeen	17	dezessete (BR), dezassete (PT)
eighteen	18	dezoito
nineteen	19	dezenove (BR), dezanove (PT)
twenty	20	vinte
twenty-one	21	vinte e um (uma)
thirty	30	trinta
forty	40	quarenta
fifty	50	cinquenta
sixty	60	sessenta
seventy	70	setenta
eighty	80	oitenta
ninety	90	noventa
a hundred	100	cem
a hundred and one	101	cento e um (uma)
two hundred	200	duzentos(-as)
three hundred	300	trezentos(-as)
five hundred	500	quinhentos(-as)
a thousand	1.000/1,000	mil
a million	1.000.000/1,000,000	um milhão

Numbers   Números

Fractions etc   ## Frações etc

zero point five	0,5/0.5	zero vírgula cinco
three point four	3,4/3.4	três vírgula quatro
ten percent (BRIT per cent)	10%	dez por cento
a hundred percent (BRIT per cent)	100%	cem por cento

Ordinal numbers   ## Números ordinais

first	$1°$/1st	primeiro
second	$2°$/2nd	segundo
third	$3°$/3rd	terceiro
fourth	$4°$/4th	quarto
fifth	$5°$/5th	quinto
sixth	$6°$/6th	sexto
seventh	$7°$/7th	sétimo
eighth	$8°$/8th	oitavo
ninth	$9°$/9th	nono
tenth	$10°$/10th	décimo
eleventh	$11°$/11th	décimo primeiro
twentieth	$20°$/20th	vigésimo
thirtieth	$30°$/30th	trigésimo
fortieth	$40°$/40th	quadragésimo
fiftieth	$50°$/50th	quinquagésimo
hundredth	$100°$/100th	centésimo
hundred-and-first	$101°$/101st	centésimo primeiro
thousandth	$1000°$/1000th	milésimo

Português – Inglês

Portuguese – English

a

over 100 km/h
8 (*depois de certos verbos*):
começou a nevar it started
snowing *ou* to snow; **passar a
fazer** to become
9 (+ *infin*): **ao vê-lo, reconheci-o
imediatamente** when I saw him,
I recognized him immediately; **ele
ficou muito nervoso ao falar
com o professor** he became very
nervous while he was talking to
the teacher
10 (PT: + *infin, gerúndio*): **a correr**
running; **estou a trabalhar** I'm
working

à [a] = **a + a**; *ver* **a**
(a) ABR (= *assinado*) signed
aba ['aba] F (*de chapéu*) brim; (*de
casaco*) tail; (*de montanha*) foot
abacate [aba'katʃi] M avocado
(pear)
abacaxi [abaka'ʃi] (BR) M
pineapple
abafado, -a [aba'fadu, a] ADJ (*ar*)
stuffy; (*tempo*) humid, close;
(*ocupado*) (extremely) busy;
(*angustiado*) anxious
abaixar [abaj'ʃar] VT to lower;
(*luz, som*) to turn down;
abaixar-se VR to stoop
abaixo [a'bajʃu] ADV down ▶ PREP:
~ de below; **~ o governo!** down
with the government!; **morro ~**
downhill; **rio ~** downstream;
mais ~ further down; **~ e acima**
up and down; **~ assinado**
undersigned; **abaixo-assinado**
[-asi'nadu] (*pl* **-s**) M petition
abalado, -a [aba'ladu, a] ADJ
unstable, unsteady; (*fig*) shaken
abalar [aba'lar] VT to shake; (*fig:
comover*) to affect ▶ VI to shake;
abalar-se VR to be moved

a [a] ART DEF the; *ver tb* **o**
▶ PRON (*ela*) her; (*você*) you; (*coisa*)
it; *ver tb* **o**
▶ PREP (*a + o(s) = ao(s); a + a(s) = à(s);
a + aquele/a(s) = àquele/a(s)*)
1 (*direção*) to; **à direita/esquerda**
to *ou* on the right/left
2 (*distância*): **está a 15 km daqui**
it's 15 km from here
3 (*posição*): **ao lado de** beside, at
the side of
4 (*tempo*) at; **a que horas?** at what
time?; **às 5 horas** at 5 o'clock; **à
noite** at night; **aos 15 anos** at 15
years of age
5 (*maneira*): **à francesa** in the
French way; **a cavalo/pé** on
horseback/foot
6 (*meio, instrumento*): **à força** by
force; **a mão** by hand; **a lápis** in
pencil; **fogão a gás** gas stove
7 (*razão*): **a R$10 o quilo** at R$10
a kilo; **a mais de 100 km/h** at

abalo [a'balu] M (*comoção*) shock; (*ação*) shaking; **~ sísmico** earth tremor

abanar [aba'nar] VT to shake; (*rabo*) to wag; (*com leque*) to fan

abandonar [abãdo'nar] VT to leave; (*ideia*) to reject; (*esperança*) to give up; (*descuidar*) to neglect

abarrotado, -a [abaho'tadu, a] ADJ (*gaveta*) crammed full; (*lugar*) packed

abastecer [abaste'ser] VT to supply; (*motor*) to fuel; (*Auto*) to fill up; (*Aer*) to refuel; **abastecer-se** VR: **~-se de** to stock up with

abastecimento [abastesi'mẽtu] M supply; (*comestíveis*) provisions *pl*; (*ato*) supplying; **abastecimentos** MPL (*suprimentos*) supplies

abater [aba'ter] VT (*gado*) to slaughter; (*preço*) to reduce; (*desalentar*) to upset; **abatido, -a** [aba'tʃidu, a] ADJ depressed, downcast; **abatimento** [abatʃi'mẽtu] M (*fraqueza*) weakness; (*de preço*) reduction; (*prostração*) depression; **fazer um abatimento em** to give a discount on

abdômen [ab'domẽ] M abdomen

á-bê-cê [abe'se] M alphabet

abecedário [abese'darju] M alphabet, ABC

abelha [a'beʎa] F bee

abelhudo, -a [abe'ʎudu, a] ADJ nosy

abençoar [abẽ'swar] VT to bless

aberto, -a [a'bɛrtu, a] PP *de* **abrir** ▶ ADJ open; (*céu*) clear; (*sinal*) green; (*torneira*) on

abestalhado, -a [abesta'ʎadu, a] ADJ stupid

abismado, -a [abiz'madu, a] ADJ astonished

ABL ABR F = **Academia Brasileira de Letras**

abnegado, -a [abne'gadu, a] ADJ self-sacrificing

abnegar [abne'gar] VT to renounce

abóbada [a'bɔbada] F vault; (*telhado*) arched roof

abobalhado, -a [aboba'ʎadu, a] ADJ (*criança*) simple

abóbora [a'bɔbora] F pumpkin

abobrinha [abo'briɲa] F courgette (BRIT), zucchini (US)

abolir [abo'lir] VT to abolish

aborrecer [abohe'ser] VT (*chatear*) to annoy; (*maçar*) to bore; **aborrecer-se** VR to get upset; to get bored; **aborrecido, -a** [abohe'sidu, a] ADJ boring; (*chateado*) annoyed; **aborrecimento** [abohesi'mẽtu] M boredom; (*chateação*) annoyance

abortar [abor'tar] VI (*Med*) to have a miscarriage; (: *de propósito*) to have an abortion; **aborto** [a'bortu] M miscarriage; (*forçado*) abortion; **fazer/ter um aborto** to have an abortion/a miscarriage

abotoadura [abotwa'dura] F cufflink

abotoar [abo'twar] VT to button up ▶ VI (*Bot*) to bud

abraçar [abra'sar] VT to hug; (*causa*) to embrace; **abraçar-se** VR to embrace; **ele abraçou-se a mim** he embraced me; **abraço** [a'brasu] M embrace, hug; **com um abraço** (*em carta*) with best wishes

abre-garrafas ['abri-] (PT) M INV bottle opener

abre-latas ['abri-] (PT) M INV tin (BRIT) *ou* can opener

abreviar [abre'vjar] VT to abbreviate; (*texto*) to abridge; **abreviatura** [abrevja'tura] F abbreviation

abridor [abri'dor] (BR) M: **~ (de**

lata) tin (BRIT) *ou* can opener; **~ de garrafa** bottle opener

abrigar [abri'gar] VT to shelter; (*proteger*) to protect; **abrigar-se** VR to take shelter

abrigo [a'brigu] M shelter, cover; **~ antiaéreo** air-raid shelter; **~ antinuclear** fall-out shelter

abril [a'briw] M April

On 25 April (**25 de abril**) 1974 in Portugal, the MAF (Armed Forces Movement) instigated the bloodless revolution that was to topple the 48-year-old dictatorship presided over until 1968 by António de Oliveira Salazar. The red carnation has come to symbolize the coup, as it is said that the Armed Forces took to the streets with carnations in the barrels of their rifles. 25 April is now a public holiday in Portugal.

abrir [a'brir] VT to open; (*fechadura*) to unlock; (*vestuário*) to unfasten; (*torneira*) to turn on; (*buraco, exceção*) to make ▶ VI to open; (*sinal*) to go green; **abrir-se** VR: **~-se com alguém** to confide in sb

abrupto, -a [a'bruptu, a] ADJ abrupt; (*repentino*) sudden

absolutamente [absoluta'mētʃi] ADV absolutely; (*em resposta*) absolutely not, not at all

absoluto, -a [abso'lutu, a] ADJ absolute; **em ~** absolutely not, not at all

absorto, -a [ab'sortu, a] PP *de* **absorver** ▶ ADJ absorbed, engrossed

absorvente [absor'vētʃi] ADJ (*papel etc*) absorbent; (*livro etc*) absorbing

absorver [absor'ver] VT to absorb; **absorver-se** VR: **~-se em** to concentrate on

abstêmio, -a [abs'temju, a] ADJ abstemious; (*álcool*) teetotal ▶ M/F abstainer; teetotaller (BRIT), teetotaler (US)

abster-se [ab'stersi] (*irreg: como* **ter**) VR: **~ de** to abstain *ou* refrain from

abstinência [abstʃi'nēsja] F abstinence; (*jejum*) fasting

abstrato, -a [abs'tratu, a] ADJ abstract

absurdo, -a [abi'surdu, a] ADJ absurd ▶ M nonsense

abundante [abũ'dãtʃi] ADJ abundant; **abundar** [abũ'dar] VI to abound

abusar [abu'zar] VI to go too far; **~ de** to abuse

abuso [a'buzu] M abuse; (*Jur*) indecent assault

a.C. ABR (= *antes de Cristo*) B.C.

a/c ABR (= *aos cuidados de*) Attn:

acabado, -a [aka'badu, a] ADJ finished; (*esgotado*) worn out

acabamento [akaba'mētu] M finish

acabar [aka'bar] VT to finish, complete; (*consumir*) to use up; (*rematar*) to finish off ▶ VI to finish, end; **acabar-se** VR to be over; (*prazo*) to expire; (*esgotar-se*) to run out; **~ com** to put an end to; **~ de chegar** to have just arrived; **~ por fazer** to end up (by) doing; **acabou-se!** it's all over!; (*basta!*) that's enough!

academia [akade'mia] F academy; **Academia Brasileira de Letras** *see note*

Founded in 1896 in Rio de Janeiro, on the initiative of the author Machado de Assis, the

Academia Brasileira de Letras, or ABL, aims to preserve and develop the Portuguese language and Brazilian literature. Machado de Assis was its president until 1908. It is made up of forty life members known as the *imortais*. The Academia's activities include publication of reference books, promotion of literary prizes, and running a library, museum and archive.

acadêmico, -a [aka'demiku, a] ADJ, M/F academic

açafrão [asa'frãw] M saffron

acalmar [akaw'mar] VT to calm ▶ VI (*vento etc*) to abate; **acalmar-se** VR to calm down

acampamento [akãpa'mẽtu] M camping; (*Mil*) camp, encampment

acampar [akã'par] VI to camp

acanhado, -a [aka'ɲadu, a] ADJ shy

acanhamento [akaɲa'mẽtu] M shyness

acanhar-se [aka'ɲarsi] VR to be shy

ação [a'sãw] (*pl* **-ões**) F action; (*ato*) act, deed; (*Mil*) battle; (*enredo*) plot; (*Jur*) lawsuit; (*Com*) share; **~ ordinária/preferencial** (*Com*) ordinary/preference share

acarajé [akara'ʒɛ] M (*Culin*) beans fried in palm oil

acarretar [akahe'tar] VT to result in, bring about

acaso [a'kazu] M chance; **ao ~** at random; **por ~** by chance

acatar [aka'tar] VT to respect; (*lei*) to obey

aceitação [asejta'sãw] F acceptance; (*aprovação*) approval

aceitar [asej'tar] VT to accept; (*aprovar*) to approve; **aceitável** [asej'tavew] (*pl* **-eis**) ADJ acceptable; **aceito, -a** [a'sejtu, a] PP *de* **aceitar**

acelerador [aselera'dor] M accelerator

acelerar [asele'rar] VT, VI to accelerate; **~ o passo** to go faster

acenar [ase'nar] VI (*com a mão*) to wave; (*com a cabeça*) to nod

acender [asẽ'der] VT (*cigarro, fogo*) to light; (*luz*) to switch on; (*fig*) to excite, inflame

acento [a'sẽtu] M accent; (*de intensidade*) stress; **acentuar** [asẽ'twar] VT to accent; (*salientar*) to stress, emphasize

acepção [asep'sãw] (*pl* **-ões**) F (*de uma palavra*) sense

acerca [a'serka] ADV: **~ de** about, concerning

acertado, -a [aser'tadu, a] ADJ right, correct; (*sensato*) sensible

acertar [aser'tar] VT (*ajustar*) to put right; (*relógio*) to set; (*alvo*) to hit; (*acordo*) to reach; (*pergunta*) to get right ▶ VI to get it right, be right; **~ o caminho** to find the right way; **~ com** to hit upon

aceso, -a [a'sezu, a] PP *de* **acender** ▶ ADJ (*luz, gás, TV*) on; (*fogo*) alight; (*excitado*) excited; (*furioso*) furious

acessar [ase'sar] VT (*Comput*) to access

acessível [ase'sivew] (*pl* **-eis**) ADJ accessible; (*pessoa*) approachable; (*preço*) reasonable, affordable

acesso [a'sɛsu] M access; (*Med*) fit, attack

acessório, -a [ase'sɔrju, a] ADJ (*máquina, equipamento*) backup ▶ M accessory

achado [a'ʃadu] M find, discovery; (*pechincha*) bargain; (*sorte*) godsend

achar [a'ʃar] VT (*descobrir*) to find; (*pensar*) to think; **achar-se** VR to think (that) one is; (*encontrar-se*) to be; **~ de fazer** (*resolver*) to decide to do; **o que é que você acha disso?** what do you think of it?; **acho que sim** I think so

achatar [aʃa'tar] vt to squash, flatten

acidentado, -a [asidẽ'tadu, a] ADJ (*terreno*) rough; (*estrada*) bumpy; (*viagem*) eventful; (*vida*) difficult ▶ M/F injured person

acidental [asidẽ'taw] (*pl* -**ais**) ADJ accidental

acidente [asi'dẽtʃi] M accident; **por ~** by accident; **~ de trânsito** road accident

acidez [asi'dez] F acidity

ácido, -a ['asidu, a] ADJ acid; (*azedo*) sour ▶ M acid

acima [a'sima] ADV above; (*para cima*) up ▶ PREP: **~ de** above; (*além de*) beyond; **mais ~** higher up; **rio ~** up river; **passar rua ~** to go up the street; **~ de 1000** more than 1000

acionar [asjo'nar] vt to set in motion; (*máquina*) to operate; (*Jur*) to sue

acionista [asjo'nista] M/F shareholder

acirrado, -a [asi'hadu, a] ADJ (*luta, competição*) tough

acirrar [asi'har] vt to incite, stir up

aclamar [akla'mar] vt to acclaim; (*aplaudir*) to applaud

aço ['asu] M steel

acocorar-se [akoko'rarsi] VR to squat, crouch

acode [a'kɔdʒi] VB *ver* **acudir**

ações [a'sõjs] FPL *de* **ação**

acolá [ako'la] ADV over there

acolchoado [akow'ʃwadu] M quilt

acolhedor, a [akoʎe'dor(a)] ADJ welcoming; (*hospitaleiro*) hospitable

acolher [ako'ʎer] vt to welcome; (*abrigar*) to shelter; (*aceitar*) to accept; **acolher-se** VR to shelter; **acolhida** [ako'ʎida] F (*recepção*) reception, welcome; (*refúgio*) refuge; **acolhimento** [akoʎi'mẽtu] M = **acolhida**

acomodação [akomoda'sãw] (*pl* -**ões**) F accommodation; (*arranjo*) arrangement; (*adaptação*) adaptation

acomodar [akomo'dar] vt to accommodate; (*arrumar*) to arrange; (*adaptar*) to adapt

acompanhamento [akõpaɲa'mẽtu] M attendance; (*cortejo*) procession; (*Mús*) accompaniment; (*Culin*) side dish

acompanhante [akõpa'ɲatʃi] M/F companion; (*Mús*) accompanist; (*de idoso, doente*) carer (BRIT), caregiver (US)

acompanhar [akõpa'ɲar] vt to accompany

aconchegante [akõʃe'gãtʃi] ADJ cosy (BRIT), cozy (US)

aconselhar [akõse'ʎar] vt to advise; **aconselhar-se** VR: **~-se com** to consult

acontecer [akõte'ser] vi to happen; **acontecimento** [akõtesi'mẽtu] M event

acordar [akor'dar] vt to wake (up); (*concordar*) to agree (on) ▶ vi to wake up

acorde [a'kɔrdʒi] M chord

acordo [a'kordu] M agreement; **"de ~!"** "agreed!"; **de ~ com** (*pessoa*) in agreement with; (*conforme*) in accordance with; **estar de ~** to agree

Açores [a'soris] MPL: **os ~** the Ázores; **açoriano, -a** [aso'rjanu, a] ADJ, M/F Azorean

acossar [ako'sar] VT (*perseguir*) to pursue; (*atormentar*) to harass

acostamento [akosta'mẽtu] M hard shoulder (BRIT), berm (US)

acostumado, -a [akostu'madu, a] ADJ usual, customary; **estar ~ a algo** to be used to sth

acostumar [akostu'mar] VT to accustom; **acostumar-se** VR: **~-se a** to get used to

açougue [a'sogi] M butcher's (shop); **açougueiro** [aso'gejru] M butcher

acovardar-se [akovar'darsi] VR (*desanimar*) to lose courage; (*amedrontar-se*) to flinch, cower

acreditado, -a [akredʒi'tadu, a] ADJ accredited

acreditar [akredʒi'tar] VT to believe; (*Com*) to credit; (*afiançar*) to guarantee ▶ VI: **~ em** to believe in

acrescentar [akresẽ'tar] VT to add

açúcar [a'sukar] M sugar; **açucareiro** [asuka'rejru] M sugar bowl

açude [a'sudʒi] M dam

acudir [aku'dʒir] VT (*ir em socorro*) to help, assist ▶ VI (*responder*) to reply, respond; **~ a** to come to the aid of

acumular [akumu'lar] VT to accumulate; (*reunir*) to collect; (*funções*) to combine

acusação [akuza'sãw] (*pl* **-ões**) F accusation, charge; (*Jur*) prosecution

acusar [aku'zar] VT to accuse; (*revelar*) to reveal; (*culpar*) to blame; **~ o recebimento de** to acknowledge receipt of

acústico, -a [a'kustʃiku, a] ADJ acoustic

adaptar [adap'tar] VT to adapt; (*acomodar*) to fit; **adaptar-se** VR: **~-se a** to adapt to

adega [a'dɛga] F cellar

ademais [adʒi'majs] ADV besides, moreover

adentro [a'dẽtru] ADV inside, in; **mata ~** into the woods

adequado, -a [ade'kwadu, a] ADJ appropriate

adereço [ade'resu] M adornment; **adereços** MPL (*Teatro*) stage props

aderente [ade'rẽtʃi] ADJ adhesive, sticky ▶ M/F supporter

aderir [ade'rir] VI to adhere

adesão [ade'zãw] F adhesion; (*patrocínio*) support

adesivo, -a [ade'zivu, a] ADJ adhesive, sticky ▶ M adhesive tape; (*Med*) sticking plaster

adestrar [ades'trar] VT to train; (*cavalo*) to break in

adeus [a'dews] EXCL goodbye!

adiantado, -a [adʒjã'tadu, a] ADJ advanced; (*relógio*) fast; **chegar ~** to arrive ahead of time; **pagar ~** to pay in advance

adiantamento [adʒjãta'mẽtu] M progress; (*dinheiro*) advance (payment)

adiantar [adʒjã'tar] VT (*dinheiro, salário*) to advance; (*relógio*) to put forward; **não adianta reclamar/insistir** there's no point *ou* it's no use complaining/insisting

adiante [a'dʒjãtʃi] ADV (*na frente*) in front; (*para a frente*) forward; **mais ~** further on; (*no futuro*) later on

adiar [a'dʒjar] VT to postpone, put off; (*sessão*) to adjourn

adição [adʒi'sãw] (*pl* **-ões**) F addition; (*Mat*) sum; **adicionar** [adʒisjo'nar] VT to add

adido, -a [a'dʒidu, a] M/F attaché

adiro [a'diru] VB *ver* **aderir**

adivinhar [adʒivi'ɲar] VT to guess; (*ler a sorte*) to foretell ▶ VI to guess;

~ o pensamento de alguém
to read sb's mind; **adivinho, -a**
[adʒiˈviɲu, a] M/F fortune-teller
adjetivo [adʒeˈtʃivu] M adjective
adjudicar [adʒudʒiˈkar] VT to
award, grant
administração
[adʒiministraˈsãw] (pl **-ões**) F
administration; (direção)
management; (comissão) board
administrador, a
[adʒiministraˈdor(a)] M/F
administrator; (diretor) director;
(gerente) manager
administrar [adʒiminisˈtrar] VT
to administer, manage; (governar)
to govern
admiração [adʒimiraˈsãw] F
wonder; (estima) admiration;
ponto de ~ (PT) exclamation mark
admirado, -a [adʒimiˈradu, a]
ADJ astonished, surprised
admirar [adʒimiˈrar] VT to
admire; **admirar-se** VR: **~-se de**
to be astonished ou surprised at;
admirável [adʒimiˈravew] (pl
-eis) ADJ amazing
admissão [adʒimiˈsãw] (pl **-ões**) F
admission; (consentimento para
entrar) admittance; (de escola)
intake
admitir [adʒimiˈtʃir] VT to admit;
(permitir) to allow; (funcionário) to
take on
adoção [adoˈsãw] F adoption
adoçar [adoˈsar] VT to sweeten
adoecer [adoeˈser] VI to fall ill
▶ VT to make ill; **~ de** ou **com** to fall
ill with
adoidado, -a [adojˈdadu, a] ADJ
crazy
adolescente [adoleˈsẽtʃi] ADJ,
M/F adolescent
adorar [adoˈrar] VT to adore;

(venerar) to worship
adormecer [adormeˈser] VI to fall
asleep; (entorpecer-se) to go numb;
adormecido, -a [adormeˈsidu, a]
ADJ sleeping ▶ M/F sleeper
adorno [aˈdornu] M adornment
adotar [adoˈtar] VT to adopt;
adotivo, -a [adoˈtʃivu, a] ADJ (filho)
adopted
adquirir [adʒikiˈrir] VT to acquire
Adriático, -a [aˈdrjatʃiku, a] ADJ:
o (mar) ~ the Adriatic (Sea)
adro [ˈadru] M (church) forecourt;
(em volta da igreja) churchyard
adulação [adulaˈsãw] F flattery
adulterar [aduwteˈrar] VT to
adulterate; (contas) to falsify
▶ VI to commit adultery
adultério [aduwˈtɛrju] M
adultery
adulto, -a [aˈduwtu, a] ADJ, M/F
adult
advento [adˈvẽtu] M advent; **o A~**
Advent
advérbio [adʒˈvɛrbju] M adverb
adverso, -a [adʒiˈvɛrsu, a] ADJ
adverse; (oposto): **~ a** opposed to
advertência [adʒiverˈtẽsja] F
warning
advertir [adʒiverˈtʃir] VT to warn;
(repreender) to reprimand; (chamar
a atenção a) to draw attention to
advogado, -a [adʒivoˈgadu, a]
M/F lawyer
advogar [adʒivoˈgar] VT to
advocate; (Jur) to plead ▶ VI to
practise (BRIT) ou practice (US) law
aéreo, -a [aˈɛrju, a] ADJ air atr
aerobarco [aeroˈbarku] M jetfoil
aeromoço, -a [aeroˈmosu, a] (BR)
M/F flight attendant
aeronáutica [aeroˈnawtʃika] F
air force; (ciência) aeronautics sg
aeronave [aeroˈnavi] F aircraft

aeroporto [aero'portu] M airport

aerossol [aero'sɔw] (pl **-óis**) M
aerosol

afã [a'fã] M (entusiasmo)
enthusiasm; (diligência) diligence;
(ânsia) eagerness; (esforço) effort

afagar [afa'gar] VT to caress;
(cabelo) to stroke

afastado, -a [afas'tadu, a] ADJ
(distante) remote; (isolado)
secluded; **manter-se ~** to keep
to o.s.

afastamento [afasta'mẽtu] M
removal; (distância) distance; (de
pessoal) lay-off

afastar [afas'tar] VT to remove;
(separar) to separate; (ideia) to put
out of one's mind; (pessoal) to lay
off; **afastar-se** VR to move away

afável [a'favew] (pl **-eis**) ADJ friendly

afazeres [afa'zeris] MPL business
sg; (dever) duties, tasks;
~ domésticos household chores

afeição [afej'sãw] F affection,
fondness; (dedicação) devotion;
afeiçoado, -a [afej'swadu, a] ADJ:
afeiçoado a (amoroso) fond of;
(devotado) devoted to; **afeiçoar-se**
[afej'swarsi] VR: **afeiçoar-se a** to
take a liking to

afeito, -a [a'fejtu, a] ADJ: **~ a**
accustomed to, used to

aferrado, -a [afe'hadu, a] ADJ
obstinate, stubborn

afetar [afe'tar] VT to affect; (fingir)
to feign

afetivo, -a [afe'tʃivu, a] ADJ
affectionate; (problema) emotional

afeto [a'fɛtu] M affection;
afetuoso, -a [afe'twozu, ɔza] ADJ
affectionate

afiado, -a [a'fjadu, a] ADJ sharp;
(pessoa) well-trained

afiar [a'fjar] VT to sharpen

aficionado, -a [afisjo'nadu, a]
M/F enthusiast

afilhado, -a [afi'ʎadu, a] M/F
godson/goddaughter

afim [a'fĩ] (pl **-ns**) ADJ (semelhante)
similar; (consanguíneo) related
▶ M/F relative, relation

afinado, -a [afi'nadu, a] ADJ in tune

afinal [afi'naw] ADV at last, finally;
~ (de contas) after all

afinar [afi'nar] VT (Mús) to tune

afinco [a'fĩku] M tenacity,
persistence

afins [a'fĩs] PL de **afim**

afirmação [afirma'sãw] (pl **-ões**) F
affirmation; (declaração) statement

afirmar [afir'mar] VT, VI to affirm,
assert; (declarar) to declare

afirmativo, -a [afirma'tʃivu, a]
ADJ affirmative

afixar [afik'sar] VT (cartazes) to
stick, post

aflição [afli'sãw] F affliction;
(ansiedade) anxiety; (angústia)
anguish

afligir [afli'ʒir] VT to distress;
(atormentar) to torment; (inquietar)
to worry; **afligir-se** VR: **~-se com**
to worry about; **aflito, -a** [a'flitu,
a] PP de **afligir** ▶ ADJ distressed,
anxious

afluência [a'flwẽsja] F affluence;
(corrente copiosa) flow; (de pessoas)
stream; **afluente** [a'flwẽtʃi] ADJ
copious; (rico) affluent ▶ M tributary

afobação [afoba'sãw] F fluster;
(ansiedade) panic

afobado, -a [afo'badu, a] ADJ
flustered; (ansioso) panicky, nervous

afobar [afo'bar] VT to fluster;
(deixar ansioso) to make nervous ou
panicky ▶ VI to get flustered; to
panic, get nervous; **afobar-se** VR to
get flustered

afogar [afoˈgar] vt to drown ▶ vi (*Auto*) to flood; **afogar-se** vr to drown

afoito, -a [aˈfojtu, a] adj bold, daring

afortunado, -a [afortuˈnadu, a] adj fortunate, lucky

África [ˈafrika] f: **a ~** Africa; **a ~ do Sul** South Africa; **africano, -a** [afriˈkanu, a] adj, m/f African

afro-brasileiro, -a [ˈafru-] (*pl* -s) adj Afro-Brazilian

afronta [aˈfrõta] f insult, affront; **afrontar** [afrõˈtar] vt to insult; (*ofender*) to offend

afrouxar [afroˈʃar] vt (*desapertar*) to slacken; (*soltar*) to loosen ▶ vi to come loose

afta [ˈafta] f (mouth) ulcer

afugentar [afuʒẽˈtar] vt to drive away, put to flight

afundar [afũˈdar] vt to sink; (*cavidade*) to deepen; **afundar-se** vr to sink

agachar-se [agaˈʃarsi] vr (*acaçapar-se*) to crouch, squat; (*curvar-se*) to stoop

agarrar [agaˈhar] vt to seize, grasp; **agarrar-se** vr: **~-se a** to cling to, hold on to

agasalhar [agazaˈʎar] vt to dress warmly, wrap up; **agasalhar-se** vr to wrap o.s. up

agasalho [agaˈzaʎu] m (*casaco*) coat; (*suéter*) sweater

ágeis [ˈaʒejs] pl de **ágil**

agência [aˈʒẽsja] f agency; (*escritório*) office; **~ de correio** (br) post office; **~ de viagens** travel agency

agenda [aˈʒẽda] f diary; **~ eletrônica** personal organizer

agente [aˈʒẽtʃi] m/f agent; (*de polícia*) policeman/woman

ágil [ˈaʒiw] (*pl* -eis) adj agile

agir [aˈʒir] vi to act

agitação [aʒitaˈsãw] (*pl* -ões) f agitation; (*perturbação*) disturbance; (*inquietação*) restlessness

agitado, -a [aʒiˈtadu, a] adj agitated, disturbed; (*inquieto*) restless

agitar [aʒiˈtar] vt to agitate, disturb; (*sacudir*) to shake; (*cauda*) to wag; (*mexer*) to stir; **agitar-se** vr to get upset; (*mar*) to get rough

aglomeração [aglomeraˈsãw] (*pl* -ões) f gathering; (*multidão*) crowd

aglomerar [aglomeˈrar] vt to heap up, pile up; **aglomerar-se** vr (*multidão*) to crowd together

agonia [agoˈnia] f agony, anguish; (*ânsia da morte*) death throes pl; **agonizante** [agoniˈzãtʃi] adj dying ▶ m/f dying person; **agonizar** [agoniˈzar] vi to be dying; (*afligir-se*) to agonize

agora [aˈgɔra] adv now; **~ mesmo** right now; (*há pouco*) a moment ago; **até ~** so far, up to now; **por ~** for now

agosto [aˈgostu] m August

agouro [aˈgoru] m omen

agraciar [agraˈsjar] vt to decorate

agradar [agraˈdar] vt to please; (*fazer agrados a*) to be nice to ▶ vi to be pleasing; (*satisfazer*) to go down well

agradável [agraˈdavew] (*pl* -eis) adj pleasant

agradecer [agradeˈser] vt: **~ algo a alguém, ~ a alguém por algo** to thank sb for sth; **agradecido, -a** [agradeˈsidu, a] adj grateful; **mal agradecido** ungrateful;

agradecimento [agradesi'mẽtu] M gratitude; **agradecimentos** MPL (*gratidão*) thanks

agrado [a'gradu] M: **fazer um ~ a alguém** (*afagar*) to be affectionate with sb; (*ser agradável*) to be nice to sb

agrário, -a [a'grarju, a] ADJ agrarian; **reforma agrária** land reform

agravante [agra'vãtʃi] ADJ aggravating ▶ F aggravating circumstance

agravar [agra'var] VT to aggravate, make worse; **agravar-se** VR (*piorar*) to get worse

agredir [agre'dʒir] VT to attack; (*insultar*) to insult

agregar [agre'gar] VT (*juntar*) to collect; (*acrescentar*) to add

agressão [agre'sãw] (*pl* -**ões**) F aggression; (*ataque*) attack; (*assalto*) assault

agressivo, -a [agre'sivu, a] ADJ aggressive

agressões [agre'sõjs] FPL *de* **agressão**

agreste [a'grɛstʃi] ADJ rural, rustic; (*terreno*) wild

agrião [a'grjãw] M watercress

agrícola [a'grikola] ADJ agricultural

agricultor [agrikuw'tor] M farmer

agricultura [agrikuw'tura] F agriculture, farming

agrido [a'gridu] VB *ver* **agredir**

agridoce [agri'dosi] ADJ bittersweet

agronegócio [agrone'gɔsju] M agribusiness

agronomia [agrono'mia] F agronomy

agropecuária [agrope'kwarja] F farming, agriculture

agrupar [agru'par] VT to group;

agrupar-se VR to group together

agrura [a'grura] F bitterness

água ['agwa] F water; **águas** FPL (*mar*) waters; (*chuvas*) rain *sg*; (*maré*) tides; **~ abaixo/acima** downstream/upstream; **dar ~ na boca** (*comida*) to be mouthwatering; **estar na ~** (*bêbado*) to be drunk; **fazer ~** (*Náut*) to leak; **~ benta** holy water; **~ corrente** running water; **~ de coco** coconut water; **~ doce** fresh water; **~ dura/leve** hard/soft water; **~ mineral** mineral water; **~ oxigenada** peroxide; **~ salgada** salt water; **~ sanitária** household bleach

água-de-colônia (*pl* **águas-de-colônia**) F eau-de-cologne

aguado, -a [a'gwadu, a] ADJ watery

aguardar [agwar'dar] VT to wait for; (*contar com*) to expect ▶ VI to wait

aguardente [agwar'dẽtʃi] M spirit (BRIT), liquor (US)

aguçado, -a [agu'sadu, a] ADJ pointed; (*espírito, sentidos*) acute

agudo, -a [a'gudu, a] ADJ sharp; shrill; (*intenso*) acute

aguentar [agwẽ'tar] VT (*muro etc*) to hold up; (*dor, injustiças*) to stand, put up with; (*peso*) to withstand ▶ VI to last; **aguentar-se** VR to remain, hold on; **~ fazer algo** to manage to do sth; **não ~ de** not to be able to stand

águia ['agja] F eagle; (*fig*) genius

agulha [a'guʎa] F (*de coser, tricô*) needle; (*Náut*) compass; (*Ferro*) points *pl* (BRIT), switch (US); **trabalho de ~** needlework

ai [aj] EXCL (*suspiro*) oh!; (*de dor*) ouch! ▶ M (*suspiro*) sigh; (*gemido*) groan; **ai de mim** poor me!

aí [a'i] ADV there; (*então*) then; **por aí** (*em lugar indeterminado*) somewhere over there, thereabouts; **espera aí!** wait!, hang on a minute!; **está aí!** (*col*) right!; **e aí?** and then what?

AIDS ['ajdʒs] F AIDS

ainda [a'ĩda] ADV still; (*mesmo*) even; **~ agora** just now; **~ assim** even so, nevertheless; **~ bem** just as well; **~ por cima** on top of all that, in addition; **~ não** not yet; **~ que** even if; **maior ~** even bigger

aipo ['ajpu] M celery

ajeitar [aʒej'tar] VT (*adaptar*) to fit, adjust; (*arranjar*) to arrange; **ajeitar-se** VR to adapt

ajo ['aʒu] VB *ver* **agir**

ajoelhar [aʒweʎar] VI to kneel (down); **ajoelhar-se** VR to kneel down

ajuda [a'ʒuda] F help; (*subsídio*) grant, subsidy; **dar ~ a alguém** to lend *ou* give sb a hand; **~ de custo** allowance; **ajudante** [aʒu'dãtʃi] M/F assistant, helper; (*Mil*) adjutant

ajudar [aʒu'dar] VT to help

ajuizado, -a [aʒwi'zadu, a] ADJ (*sensato*) sensible; (*sábio*) wise; (*prudente*) discreet

ajuntamento [aʒũta'mẽtu] M gathering

ajustagem [aʒus'taʒẽ] (BR) (*pl* **-ns**) F (*Tec*) adjustment

ajustamento [aʒusta'mẽtu] M adjustment; (*de contas*) settlement

ajustar [aʒus'tar] VT to adjust; (*conta, disputa*) to settle; (*acomodar*) to fit; (*roupa*) to take in; (*preço*) to agree on; **ajustar-se** VR: **~-se a** to conform to; (*adaptar-se*) to adapt to

ajuste [a'ʒustʃi] M (*acordo*) agreement; (*de contas*) settlement; (*adaptação*) adjustment

ala ['ala] F (*fileira*) row; (*passagem*) aisle; (*de edifício, exército, ave*) wing

alagar [ala'gar] VT, VI to flood

alameda [ala'meda] F (*avenida*) avenue; (*arvoredo*) grove

alarde [a'lardʒi] M ostentation; (*jactância*) boasting; **fazer ~ de** to boast about; **alardear** [alar'dʒjar] VT to show off; (*gabar-se de*) to boast of ▶ VI to boast; **alardear-se** VR to boast

alargar [alar'gar] VT to extend; (*fazer mais largo*) to widen, broaden; (*afrouxar*) to loosen, slacken

alarma [a'larma] F alarm; (*susto*) panic; (*tumulto*) tumult; (*vozearia*) outcry; **dar o sinal de ~** to raise the alarm; **~ de roubo** burglar alarm; **alarmante** [alar'mãtʃi] ADJ alarming; **alarmar** [alar'mar] VT to alarm; **alarmar-se** VR to be alarmed

alarme [a'larmi] M = **alarma**

alastrar [alas'trar] VT to scatter; (*disseminar*) to spread; **alastrar-se** VR (*epidemia, rumor*) to spread

alavanca [ala'vãka] F lever; (*pé de cabra*) crowbar; **~ de mudanças** gear lever

albergue [aw'bɛrgi] M (*estalagem*) inn; (*refúgio*) hospice, shelter; **~ noturno** hotel; **~ para jovens** youth hostel

álbum ['awbũ] (*pl* **-ns**) M album; **~ de recortes** scrapbook

alça ['awsa] F strap; (*asa*) handle; (*de fusil*) sight

alcachofra [awka'ʃofra] F artichoke

alcançar [awkã'sar] VT to reach; (*estender*) to hand, pass; (*obter*) to obtain, get; (*atingir*) to attain; (*compreender*) to understand; (*desfalcar*): **~ uma firma em $1 milhão** to embezzle $1 million from a firm

alcance [aw'kãsi] M reach; (*competência*) power; (*compreensão*) understanding; (*de tiro, visão*) range; **ao ~ de** within reach *ou* range of; **ao ~ da voz** within earshot; **de grande ~** far-reaching; **fora do ~ da mão** out of reach; **fora do ~ de alguém** beyond sb's grasp

alcaparra [awka'paha] F caper

alcatrão [awka'trãw] M tar

álcool ['awkɔw] M alcohol; **alcoólatra** [aw'kɔlatra] M/F alcoholic; **alcoólico, -a** [aw'kɔliku, a] ADJ, M/F alcoholic

Alcorão [awko'rãw] M Koran

alcova [aw'kova] F bedroom

alcunha [aw'kuɲa] F nickname

aldeão, -deã [aw'dʒjãw, jã] (*pl -ões/-s*) M/F villager

aldeia [aw'deja] F village

aldeões [aw'dʒjõjs] MPL *de* **aldeão**

alecrim [ale'krĩ] M rosemary

alegar [ale'gar] VT to allege; (*Jur*) to plead

alegoria [alego'ria] F allegory

alegórico, -a [ale'gɔriku, a] ADJ allegorical; **carro ~** float

alegrar [ale'grar] VT to cheer (up), gladden; (*ambiente*) to brighten up; (*animar*) to liven (up); **alegrar-se** VR to cheer up

alegre [a'lɛgri] ADJ cheerful; (*contente*) happy, glad; (*cores*) bright; (*embriagado*) merry, tight; **alegria** [ale'gria] F joy, happiness

aleijado, -a [alej'ʒadu, a] ADJ crippled ▶ M/F cripple

aleijar [alej'ʒar] VT to maim

além [a'lẽj] ADV (*lá ao longe*) over there; (*mais adiante*) further on ▶ M: **o ~** the hereafter ▶ PREP: **~ de** beyond; (*no outro lado de*) on the other side of; (*para mais de*) over; (*ademais de*) apart from, besides; **~ disso** moreover; **mais ~** further

alemã [ale'mã] F *de* **alemão**

alemães [ale'mãjs] MPL *de* **alemão**

Alemanha [ale'mãɲa] F: **a ~** Germany

alemão, -mã [ale'mãw, 'mã] (*pl -ães/-s*) ADJ, M/F German ▶ M (*Ling*) German

alento [a'lẽtu] M (*fôlego*) breath; (*ânimo*) courage; **dar ~** to encourage; **tomar ~** to draw breath

alergia [aler'ʒia] F: **~ (a)** allergy (to); (*fig*) aversion (to); **alérgico, -a** [a'lɛrʒiku, a] ADJ: **alérgico (a)** allergic (to)

alerta [a'lɛrta] ADJ alert ▶ ADV on the alert ▶ M alert

alfabetizar [awfabetʃi'zar] VT to teach to read and write; **alfabetizar-se** VR to learn to read and write

alfabeto [awfa'bɛtu] M alphabet

alface [aw'fasi] F lettuce

alfaiate [awfa'jatʃi] M tailor

alfândega [aw'fãdʒiga] F customs *pl*, customs house; **alfandegário, -a** [awfãde'garju, a] M/F customs officer

alfazema [awfa'zɛma] F lavender

alfinete [awfi'netʃi] M pin; **~ de segurança** safety pin

alga ['awga] F seaweed

Algarve [aw'garvi] M: **o ~** the Algarve

algazarra [awga'zaha] F uproar, racket

álgebra ['awʒebra] F algebra

algemas [aw'ʒemas] FPL handcuffs

algo ['awgu] ADV somewhat, rather ▶ PRON something; (*qualquer coisa*) anything

algodão [awgo'dãw] M cotton; **~ (hidrófilo)** cotton wool (BRIT), absorbent cotton (US)

alguém [aw'gẽj] PRON someone, somebody; (*em frases interrogativas ou negativas*) anyone, anybody

algum, a [aw'gũ, 'guma] ADJ some; (*em frases interrogativas ou negativas*) any ▶ PRON one; (*no plural*) some; (*negativa*): **de modo ~** in no way; **coisa ~a** nothing; **~ dia** one day; **~ tempo** for a while; **~a coisa** something; **~a vez** sometime

alheio, -a [a'ʎeju, a] ADJ (*de outra pessoa*) someone else's; (*de outras pessoas*) other people's; (*estranho*) alien; (*estrangeiro*) foreign; (*impróprio*) irrelevant

alho ['aʎu] M garlic

ali [a'li] ADV there; **até ~** up to there; **por ~** around there; (*direção*) that way; **~ por** (*tempo*) round about; **de ~ por diante** from then on; **~ dentro** in there

aliado, -a [a'ljadu, a] ADJ allied ▶ M/F ally

aliança [a'ljãsa] F alliance; (*anel*) wedding ring

aliar [a'ljar] VT to ally; **aliar-se** VR to form an alliance

aliás [a'ljajs] ADV (*a propósito*) as a matter of fact; (*ou seja*) rather, that is; (*contudo*) nevertheless; (*diga-se de passagem*) incidentally

álibi ['alibi] M alibi

alicate [ali'katʃi] M pliers *pl*; **~ de unhas** nail clippers *pl*

alienação [aljena'sãw] F alienation; (*de bens*) transfer (of property); **~ mental** insanity

alienado, -a [alje'nadu, a] ADJ alienated; (*demente*) insane; (*bens*) transferred ▶ M/F lunatic

alienar [alje'nar] VT (*bens*) to transfer; (*afastar*) to alienate

alimentação [alimẽta'sãw] F (*alimentos*) food; (*ação*) feeding; (*nutrição*) nourishment; (*Elet*) supply

alimentar [alimẽ'tar] VT to feed; (*fig*) to nurture ▶ ADJ (*produto*) food *atr*; (*hábitos*) eating *atr*; **alimentar-se** VR: **~-se de** to feed on

alimento [ali'mẽtu] M food; (*nutrição*) nourishment

alisar [ali'zar] VT to smooth; (*cabelo*) to straighten; (*acariciar*) to stroke

aliviar [ali'vjar] VT to relieve

alívio [a'livju] M relief

alma ['awma] F soul; (*entusiasmo*) enthusiasm; (*caráter*) character

almejar [awme'ʒar] VT to long for, yearn for

almirante [awmi'rãtʃi] M admiral

almoçar [awmo'sar] VI to have lunch ▶ VT: **~ peixe** to have fish for lunch

almoço [aw'mosu] M lunch; **pequeno ~** (PT) breakfast

almofada [awmo'fada] F cushion; (PT: *travesseiro*) pillow

almoxarifado [awmoʃari'fadu] M storeroom

alô [a'lo] (BR) EXCL (*Tel*) hello!

alocar [alo'kar] VT to allocate

alojamento [aloʒa'mẽtu] M accommodation (BRIT), accommodations *pl* (US); (*habitação*) housing

alojar [alo'ʒar] VT to lodge; (*Mil*) to billet; **alojar-se** VR to stay

alongar [alõ'gar] VT to lengthen; (*prazo*) to extend; (*prolongar*) to prolong; (*braço*) to stretch out; **alongar-se** VR (*sobre um assunto*) to dwell

aloprado, -a [alo'pradu, a] (*col*) ADJ nutty

alpendre [aw'pēdri] M (*telheiro*) shed; (*pórtico*) porch

Alpes ['awpis] MPL: **os ~** the Alps

alpinismo [awpi'nizmu] M mountaineering, climbing; **alpinista** [awpi'nista] M/F mountaineer, climber

alta ['awta] F (*de preços*) rise; (*de hospital*) discharge

altar [aw'tar] M altar

alterado, -a [awte'radu, a] ADJ bad-tempered, irritated

alterar [awte'rar] VT to alter; (*falsificar*) to falsify; **alterar-se** VR (*mudar-se*) to change; (*enfurecer-se*) to lose one's temper

alternar [awter'nar] VT, VI to alternate; **alternar-se** VR to alternate; (*por turnos*) to take turns

alternativa [awterna'tʃiva] F alternative

alternativo, -a [awterna'tʃivu, a] ADJ alternative; (*Elet*) alternating

alteza [aw'teza] F highness

altitude [awtʃi'tudʒi] F altitude

alto, -a ['awtu, a] ADJ high; (*pessoa*) tall; (*som*) loud; (*Geo*) upper ▶ ADV (*falar*) loudly, loud; (*voar*) high ▶ EXCL halt! ▶ M top, summit; **do ~** from above; **por ~** superficially; **alta fidelidade** high fidelity, hi-fi; **alta noite** dead of night

alto-falante (*pl* **-s**) M loudspeaker

altura [aw'tura] F height; (*momento*) point, juncture; (*altitude*) altitude; (*de um som*) pitch; **em que ~ da Rio Branco fica a livraria?** whereabouts in Rio Branco is the bookshop?; **nesta ~** at this

juncture; **estar à ~ de** (*ser capaz de*) to be up to; **ter 1.80 metros de ~** to be 1.80 metres (BRIT) *ou* meters (US) tall

alucinado, -a [alusi'nadu, a] ADJ crazy

alugar [alu'gar] VT (*tomar de aluguel*) to rent, hire; (*dar de aluguel*) to let, rent out; **alugar-se** VR to let; **aluguel** [alu'gɛw] (*pl* **-éis**) (BR) M rent; (*ação*) renting; **aluguel de carro** car hire (BRIT) *ou* rental (US); **aluguer** [alu'gɛr] (PT) M = **aluguel**

alumínio [alu'minju] M aluminium (BRIT), aluminum (US)

aluno, -a [a'lunu, a] M/F pupil, student

alvejar [awve'ʒar] VT (*tomar como alvo*) to aim at; (*branquear*) bleach

alvenaria [awvena'ria] F masonry; **de ~** brick *atr*, brick-built

alvéolo [aw'vɛolu] M cavity

alvo, -a ['awvu, a] ADJ white ▶ M target

alvorada [awvo'rada] F dawn

alvorecer [awvore'ser] VI to dawn

alvoroço [awvo'rosu] M commotion; (*entusiasmo*) enthusiasm

amabilidade [amabili'dadʒi] F kindness; (*simpatia*) friendliness

amaciante [ama'sjãtʃi] M: **~ (de roupa)** fabric conditioner

amaciar [ama'sjar] VT (*tornar macio*) to soften; (*carro*) to run in

amado, -a [a'madu, a] M/F beloved, sweetheart

amador, a [ama'dor(a)] ADJ, M/F amateur

amadurecer [amadure'ser] VT, VI (*frutos*) to ripen; (*fig*) to mature

âmago ['amagu] M (*centro*) heart, core; (*medula*) pith; (*essência*) essence

amalgamar [amawga'mar] VT
to amalgamate; (*combinar*) to fuse
(BRIT), fuze (US), blend

amalucado, -a [amalu'kadu, a]
ADJ crazy, whacky

amamentar [amamẽ'tar] VT, VI
to breast-feed

amanhã [ama'ɲã] ADV, M tomorrow

amanhecer [amaɲe'ser] VI
(*alvorecer*) to dawn; (*encontrar-se
pela manhã*): **amanhecemos em
Paris** we were in Paris at daybreak
▶ M dawn; **ao ~** at daybreak

amansar [amã'sar] VT (*animais*) to
tame; (*cavalos*) to break in;
(*aplacar*) to placate

amante [a'mãtʃi] M/F lover

amar [a'mar] VT to love; **eu te
amo** I love you

amarelo, -a [ama'rɛlu, a] ADJ
yellow ▶ M yellow

amargar [amar'gar] VT to make
bitter; (*fig*) to embitter

amargo, -a [a'margu, a] ADJ
bitter; **amargura** [amar'gura] F
bitterness

amarrar [ama'har] VT to tie (up);
(*Náut*) to moor; **~ a cara** to frown,
scowl

amarrotar [amaho'tar] VT to
crease

amassar [ama'sar] VT (*pão*) to
knead; (*misturar*) to mix; (*papel*) to
screw up; (*roupa*) to crease; (*carro*)
to dent

amável [a'mavew] (*pl* -**eis**) ADJ
kind

Amazonas [ama'zɔnas] M: **o ~**
the Amazon

Amazônia [ama'zonja] F: **a ~** the
Amazon region

> **Amazônia** is the region formed
> by the basin of the river Amazon
> (the river with the largest

volume of water in the world)
and its tributaries. With a total
area of almost 7 million square
kilometres, it stretches from
the Atlantic to the Andes. Most
of **Amazônia** is in Brazilian
territory, although it also
extends into Peru, Colombia,
Venezuela and Bolivia. It
contains the richest biodiversity
and largest area of tropical
rainforest in the world.

ambição [ambi'sãw] (*pl* -**ões**) F
ambition; **ambicionar**
[ãbisjo'nar] VT to aspire to;
ambicioso, -a [ãbi'sjozu, ɔza] ADJ
ambitious

ambidestro, -a [ãbi'destru, a]
ADJ ambidextrous

ambientar [ãbjẽ'tar] VT (*filme etc*)
to set; (*adaptar*): **~ alguém a algo**
to get sb used to sth;
ambientar-se VR to fit in

ambiente [ã'bjẽtʃi] M
atmosphere; (*meio, Comput*)
environment; **meio ~**
environment; **temperatura ~**
room temperature

ambíguo, -a [ã'bigwu, a] ADJ
ambiguous

âmbito ['ãbitu] M extent; (*campo
de ação*) scope, range

ambos, ambas ['ãbus, as] ADJ PL
both

ambulância [ãbu'lãsja] F
ambulance

ambulante [ãbu'lãtʃi] ADJ
walking; (*errante*) wandering;
(*biblioteca*) mobile

ambulatório [ãbula'tɔrju] M
outpatient department

ameaça [ame'asa] F threat; **~ de
bomba** bomb scare; **ameaçar**
[amea'sar] VT to threaten

amedrontar [amedrõ'tar] vt to scare, intimidate; **amedrontar-se** vr to be frightened

ameixa [a'mejʃa] f plum; (*passa*) prune

amém [a'mẽj] excl amen!

amêndoa [a'mẽdwa] f almond; **amendoeira** [amẽ'dwejra] f almond tree

amendoim [amẽdo'ĩ] (*pl* **-ns**) m peanut

amenidade [ameni'dadʒi] f wellbeing; **amenidades** fpl (*assuntos superficiais*) small talk *sg*

amenizar [ameni'zar] vt (*abrandar*) to soften; (*tornar agradável*) to make pleasant; (*facilitar*) to ease

ameno, -a [a'mɛnu, a] adj pleasant; (*clima*) mild

América [a'mɛrika] f: **a ~** America; **a ~ do Norte/do Sul** North/South America; **a ~ Central/Latina** Central/Latin America; **americano, -a** [ameri'kanu, a] adj, m/f American

amestrar [ames'trar] vt to train

amianto [a'mjãtu] m asbestos

amido [a'midu] m starch

amigável [ami'gavew] (*pl* **-eis**) adj amicable

amígdala [a'migdala] f tonsil; **amigdalite** [amigda'litʃi] f tonsillitis

amigo, -a [a'migu, a] adj friendly ▶ m/f friend; **ser ~ de** to be friends with

amistoso, -a [amis'tozu, ɔza] adj friendly, cordial ▶ m (*jogo*) friendly

amiúde [a'mjudʒi] adv often, frequently

amizade [ami'zadʒi] f (*relação*) friendship; (*simpatia*) friendliness

amnistia [amnis'tia] (*pt*) f = **anistia**

amolação [amola'sãw] (*pl* **-ões**) f bother, annoyance

amolar [amo'lar] vt to sharpen; (*aborrecer*) to annoy, bother ▶ vi to be annoying

amolecer [amole'ser] vt to soften ▶ vi to soften; (*abrandar-se*) to relent

amônia [a'monja] f ammonia

amoníaco [amo'niaku] m ammonia

amontoar [amõ'twar] vt to pile up, accumulate; **~ riquezas** to amass a fortune

amor [a'mor] m love; **por ~ de** for the sake of; **fazer ~** to make love

amora [a'mɔra] f (*amora-preta*) blackberry; **~ silvestre** blackberry

amordaçar [amorda'sar] vt to gag

amoroso, -a [amo'rozu, ɔza] adj loving, affectionate

amor-perfeito (*pl* **amores-perfeitos**) m pansy

amortização [amortʃiza'sãw] f payment in instalments (*brit*) *ou* installments (*us*)

amortizar [amortʃi'zar] vt to pay in instalments (*brit*) *ou* installments (*us*)

amostra [a'mɔstra] f sample

amparar [ãpa'rar] vt to support; (*ajudar*) to assist; **amparar-se** vr: **~-se em/contra** to lean on/against

amparo [ã'paru] m support; (*auxílio*) help, assistance

ampliação [amplja'sãw] (*pl* **-ões**) f enlargement; (*extensão*) extension

ampliar [ã'pljar] vt to enlarge; (*conhecimento*) to broaden

amplificador [ãplifika'dor] m amplifier

amplificar [ãplifi'kar] vt to amplify

amplitude [ãpli'tudʒi] f (*espaço*) spaciousness; (*fig: extensão*) extent

amplo, -a ['ãplu, a] ADJ (sala) spacious; (conhecimento, sentido) broad; (possibilidade) ample

amputar [ãpu'tar] VT to amputate

Amsterdã [amister'dã] (BR) N Amsterdam

Amsterdão [amister'dãw] (PT) N = **Amsterdã**

amuado, -a [a'mwadu, a] ADJ sulky

anã [a'nã] F de **anão**

anais [a'najs] MPL annals

analfabeto, -a [anawfa'bɛtu, a] ADJ, M/F illiterate

analgésico, -a [anaw'ʒɛziku, a] ADJ analgesic ▶ M painkiller

analisar [anali'zar] VT to analyse; **análise** [a'nalizi] F analysis; **analista** [ana'lista] M/F analyst

ananás [ana'nas] (pl **ananases**) M (BR) variety of pineapple; (PT) pineapple

anão, anã [a'nãw, a'nã] (pl **-ões/-s**) M/F dwarf

anarquia [anar'kia] F anarchy; **anarquista** [anar'kista] M/F anarchist

anatomia [anato'mia] F anatomy

anca ['ãka] F (de pessoa) hip; (de animal) rump

ancião, anciã [ã'sjãw, ã'sjã] (pl **-ões/-s**) ADJ old ▶ M/F old man/woman; (de uma tribo) elder

anciões [a'sjõjs] MPL de **ancião**

âncora ['ãkora] F anchor; **ancorar** [ãko'rar] VT, VI to anchor

andaime [ã'dajmi] M (Arq) scaffolding

andamento [ãda'mẽtu] M (progresso) progress; (rumo) course; (Mús) tempo; **em ~** in progress

andar [ã'dar] VI to walk; (máquina) to work; (progredir) to progress; (estar): **ela anda triste** she's been sad lately ▶ M gait; (pavimento) floor, storey (BRIT), story (US); **anda!** hurry up!; **~ a cavalo** to ride; **~ de trem/avião/bicicleta** to travel by train/to fly/to ride a bike

Andes ['ãdʒis] MPL: **os ~** the Andes

andorinha [ãdo'riɲa] F (pássaro) swallow

anedota [ane'dɔta] F anecdote

anel [a'nɛw] (pl **-éis**) M ring; (elo) link; (de cabelo) curl; **~ de casamento** wedding ring

anestesia [aneste'zia] F anaesthesia (BRIT), anesthesia (US); (anestésico) anaesthetic (BRIT), anesthetic (US)

anexar [anek'sar] VT to annex; (juntar) to attach; (documento) to enclose; **anexo, -a** [a'nɛksu, a] ADJ attached ▶ M annexe; (em carta) enclosure; (em e-mail) attachment; **segue em anexo** please find enclosed

anfitrião, -triã [ãfi'trjãw, 'trjã] (pl **-ões/-s**) M/F host/hostess

angina [ã'ʒina] F: **~ do peito** angina (pectoris)

Angola [ã'gɔla] F Angola

angu [ã'gu] M corn-meal purée

ângulo ['ãgulu] M angle; (canto) corner

angústia [ã'gustʃja] F anguish, distress

animado, -a [ani'madu, a] ADJ lively; (alegre) cheerful; **~ com** enthusiastic about

animador, a [anima'dor(a)] ADJ encouraging ▶ M/F (BR TV) presenter; (de festa) entertainer; **~(a) de torcida** cheerleader

animal [ani'maw] (pl **-ais**) ADJ, M

animal; **~ de estimação** pet (animal)

animar [ani'mar] vт to liven up; (encorajar) to encourage; **animar-se** vʀ to cheer up; (festa etc) to liven up; **~-se a** to bring o.s. to

ânimo ['animu] м (coragem) courage; **~!** cheer up!; **perder o ~** to lose heart; **recobrar o ~** to pluck up courage; (alegrar-se) to cheer up

aninhar [ani'ɲar] vт to nestle; **aninhar-se** vʀ to nestle

anis [a'nis] м aniseed

anistia [anis'tʃia] ꜰ amnesty

aniversário [aniver'sarju] м anniversary; (de nascimento) birthday; (: festa) birthday party

anjo ['aʒu] м angel; **~ da guarda** guardian angel

ano ['anu] м year; **Feliz A~ Novo!** Happy New Year!; **o ~ que vem** next year; **por ~** per annum; **fazer ~s** to have a birthday; **ter dez ~s** to be ten (years old); **dia de ~s** (PT) birthday; **~ letivo** academic year; (da escola) school year

anões [a'nõjs] MPL de **anão**

anoitecer [anojte'ser] vɪ to grow dark ▶ м nightfall

anomalia [anoma'lia] ꜰ anomaly

anônimo, -a [a'nonimu, a] ADJ anonymous

anoraque [ano'raki] м anorak

anormal [anor'maw] (pl **-ais**) ADJ abnormal; (excepcional) handicapped; **anormalidade** [anormali'dadʒi] ꜰ abnormality

anotação [anota'sãw] (pl **-ões**) ꜰ annotation; (nota) note

anotar [ano'tar] vт (tomar nota) to note down; (esclarecer) to annotate

anseio [ã'seju] vʙ ver **ansiar**

ânsia ['ãsja] ꜰ anxiety; (desejo): **~ (de)** longing (for); **ter ~s (de**

vômito) to feel sick

ansiar [ã'sjar] vɪ: **~ por** (desejar) to yearn for; **~ por fazer** to long to do

ansiedade [ãsje'dadʒi] ꜰ anxiety; (desejo) eagerness

ansioso, -a [ã'sjozu, ɔza] ADJ anxious; (desejoso) eager

antártico, -a [ã'tartʃiku, a] ADJ antarctic ▶ м: **o A~** the Antarctic

ante ['ãtʃi] PREP (na presença de) before; (em vista de) in view of, faced with

antecedência [ãtese'dẽsja] ꜰ: **com ~** in advance; **3 dias de ~** three days' notice

antecedente [ãtese'dẽtʃi] ADJ preceding ▶ м antecedent; **antecedentes** MPL (registro) record sg; (passado) background sg

anteceder [ãtese'der] vт to precede

antecipação [ãtesipa'sãw] ꜰ anticipation; **com um mês de ~** a month in advance; **~ de pagamento** advance (payment)

antecipadamente [ãtesipada'mẽtʃi] ADV in advance, beforehand

antecipado, -a [ãtesi'padu, a] ADJ (pagamento) (in) advance

antecipar [ãtesi'par] vт to anticipate, forestall; (adiantar) to bring forward

antemão [ante'mãw] ADV: **de ~** beforehand

antena [ã'tɛna] ꜰ (Bio) antenna, feeler; (Rádio, TV) aerial

anteontem [ãtʃi'õtẽ] ADV the day before yesterday

antepassado [ãtʃipa'sadu] м ancestor

anterior [ãte'rjor] ADJ previous; (antigo) former; (de posição) front

antes ['ãtʃis] ADV before;

(*antigamente*) formerly; (*ao contrário*) rather ▶ PREP: **~ de** before; **o quanto ~** as soon as possible; **~ de partir** before leaving; **~ de tudo** above all; **~ que** before

anti- [ãtʃi] PREFIXO anti-

antiácido, -a [ã'tʃjasidu, a] ADJ, M antacid

antibiótico, -a [ãtʃi'bjɔtʃiku, a] ADJ, M antibiotic

anticaspa [ãtʃi'kaspa] ADJ INV anti-dandruff

anticlímax [ãtʃi'klimaks] M anticlimax

anticoncepcional [ãtʃikõsepsjo'naw] (*pl* **-ais**) ADJ, M contraceptive

antidepressivo, -a [ãtʃidepre'sivu, a] ADJ, M anti-depressant

antigamente [ãtʃiga'mẽtʃi] ADV formerly; (*no passado*) in the past

antiglobalização [ãtʃiglobaliza'sãw] F antiglobalization

antigo, -a [ã'tʃigu, a] ADJ old; (*histórico*) ancient; (*de estilo*) antique; (*chefe etc*) former

antiguidade [ãtʃigwi'dadʒi] F antiquity, ancient times *pl*; (*de emprego*) seniority; **antiguidades** FPL (*monumentos*) ancient monuments; (*artigos*) antiques

anti-horário, -a ADJ anticlockwise

antilhano, -a [ãtʃi'ʎanu, a] ADJ, M/F West Indian

Antilhas [ã'tʃiʎas] FPL: **as ~** the West Indies

antipatia [ãtʃipa'tʃia] F dislike; **antipático, -a** [ãtʃi'patʃiku, a] ADJ unpleasant, unfriendly

antipatizar [ãtʃipatʃi'zar] VI:

~ com alguém to dislike sb

antiquado, -a [ãtʃi'kwadu, a] ADJ antiquated; (*fora de moda*) out of date, old-fashioned

antiquário, -a [ãtʃi'kwarju, a] M/F antique dealer ▶ M (*loja*) antique shop

antissemita ADJ anti-Semitic

antisséptico, -a ADJ, M antiseptic

antissocial (*pl* **-ais**) ADJ antisocial

antivírus [ãtʃi'virus] M INV (*Comput*) antivirus

antologia [ãtolo'ʒia] F anthology

anual [a'nwaw] (*pl* **-ais**) ADJ annual, yearly

anulação [anula'sãw] (*pl* **-ões**) F cancellation; (*de contrato, casamento*) annulment

anular [anu'lar] VT to cancel; (*contrato*) to annul; (*efeito*) to cancel out ▶ M ring finger

anunciante [anũ'sjãtʃi] M (*Com*) advertiser

anunciar [anũ'sjar] VT to announce; (*Com*) to advertise

anúncio [a'nũsju] M announcement; (*Com*) advertisement; (*cartaz*) notice; **~s classificados** small *ou* classified ads

ânus ['anus] M INV anus

anzol [ã'zɔw] (*pl* **-óis**) M fish-hook

ao [aw] = **a + o**; *ver* **a**

aonde [a'õdʒi] ADV where; **~ quer que** wherever

aos [aws] = **a + os**; *ver* **a**

Ap. ABR = **apartamento**

apagado, -a [apa'gadu, a] ADJ (*fogo*) out; (*luz elétrica*) off

apagão [apa'gãw] (*pl* **-ões**) M power cut (BRIT), power outage (US)

apagar [apa'gar] VT to put out; (*luz elétrica*) to switch off; (*vela*) to blow out; (*com borracha*) to rub out, erase; **apagar-se** VR to go out

apaixonado, -a [apajʃo'nadu, a]

ADJ (*discurso*) impassioned; (*pessoa*): **ele está ~ por ela** he is in love with her; **ele é ~ por tênis** he's mad about tennis

apaixonar-se [apajʃo'narsi] VR: **~ por** to fall in love with

apalpar [apaw'par] VT to touch, feel; (*Med*) to examine

apanhado [apa'ɲadu] M (*de flores*) bunch; (*resumo*) summary

apanhar [apa'ɲar] VT to catch; (*algo à mão, do chão*) to pick up; (*ir buscar, surra, táxi*) to get; (*flores, frutas*) to pick; (*agarrar*) to grab ▶ VI to get a beating; **~ sol/chuva** to sunbathe/get soaked

aparador [apara'dor] M sideboard

apara-lápis [apara'lapis] (*PT*) M INV pencil sharpener

aparar [apa'rar] VT (*cabelo*) to trim; (*lápis*) to sharpen; (*algo arremessado*) to catch

aparato [apa'ratu] M pomp; (*coleção*) array

aparecer [apare'ser] VI to appear; (*apresentar-se*) to turn up; (*ser publicado*) to be published; **~ em casa de alguém** to call on sb; **aparecimento** [aparesi'mẽtu] M appearance; (*publicação*) publication

aparelho [apa'reʎu] M apparatus; (*equipamento*) equipment; (*Pesca*) tackle; (*máquina*) machine; (*BR: fone*) telephone; **~ de barbear** electric shaver; **~ de chá** tea set; **~ de rádio/TV** radio/TV set; **~ doméstico** domestic appliance

aparência [apa'rẽsja] F appearance; **na ~** apparently; **sob a ~ de** under the guise of; **ter ~ de** to look like, seem

aparentar [aparẽ'tar] VT (*fingir*) to feign; (*parecer*) to give the appearance of

aparente [apa'rẽtʃi] ADJ apparent

aparição [apari'sãw] (*pl* -**ões**) F (*visão*) apparition; (*fantasma*) ghost

apartamento [aparta'mẽtu] M apartment, flat (*BRIT*)

apartar [apar'tar] VT to separate; **apartar-se** VR to separate

apatia [apa'tʃia] F apathy

apático, -a [a'patʃiku, a] ADJ apathetic

apavorado, -a [apavo'radu, a] ADJ terrified

apavorante [apavo'rãtʃi] ADJ terrifying

apavorar [apavo'rar] VT to terrify ▶ VI to be terrifying; **apavorar-se** VR to be terrified

apear-se [a'pjarsi] VR: **~ de** (*cavalo*) to dismount from

apegado, -a [ape'gadu, a] ADJ: **ser ~** (*gostar de*) to be attached to

apegar-se [ape'garsi] VR: **~ a** (*afeiçoar-se*) to become attached to

apego [a'pegu] M (*afeição*) attachment

apelar [ape'lar] VI to appeal; **~ da sentença** (*Jur*) to appeal against the sentence; **~ para** to appeal to; **~ para a ignorância/violência** to resort to abuse/violence

apelido [ape'lidu] M (*PT: nome de família*) surname; (*BR: alcunha*) nickname

apelo [a'pelu] M appeal

apenas [a'pɛnas] ADV only

apendicite [apẽdʒi'sitʃi] F appendicitis

aperfeiçoar [aperfej'swar] VT to perfect; (*melhorar*) to improve

apertado, -a [aper'tadu, a] ADJ tight; (*estreito*) narrow; (*sem dinheiro*) hard-up; (*vida*) hard

apertar [aper'tar] VT (*agarrar*) to hold tight; (*roupa*) to take in;

(*esponja*) to squeeze; (*botão*) to press; (*despesas*) to limit; (*vigilância*) to step up; (*coração*) to break; (*fig: pessoa*) to put pressure on ▶ VI (*sapatos*) to pinch; (*chuva, frio*) to get worse; (*estrada*) to narrow; **~ em** (*insistir*) to insist on; **~ a mão de alguém** to shake hands with sb

aperto [a'pertu] M (*pressão*) pressure; (*situação difícil*) spot of bother, jam; **um ~ de mãos** a handshake

apesar [ape'zar] PREP: **~ de** in spite of, despite; **~ disso** nevertheless; **~ de que** even though

apetecer [apete'ser] VI (*comida*) to be appetizing

apetite [ape't∫it∫i] M appetite; **bom ~!** enjoy your meal!

apetrechos [ape'tre∫us] MPL gear *sg*; (*Pesca*) tackle *sg*

apinhado, -a [api'ɲadu, a] ADJ crowded

apitar [api'tar] VI to whistle; **apito** [a'pitu] M whistle

aplacar [apla'kar] VT to placate ▶ VI to calm down; **aplacar-se** VR to calm down

aplaudir [aplaw'dʒir] VT to applaud

aplauso [a'plawzu] M applause; (*apoio*) support; (*elogio*) praise; (*aprovação*) approval

aplicação [aplika'sãw] (*pl* **-ões**) F application; (*esforço*) effort; (*da lei*) enforcement; (*de dinheiro*) investment; (PT *Comput*) application, app (*col*)

aplicado, -a [apli'kadu, a] ADJ hard-working

aplicar [apli'kar] VT to apply; (*lei*) to enforce; (*dinheiro*) to invest;

aplicar-se VR: **~-se a** to devote o.s. to

aplicativo [aplika't∫ivu] M (BR *Comput*) application, app (*col*)

apoderar-se [apode'rarsi] VR: **~ de** to seize, take possession of

apodrecer [apodre'ser] VT to rot; (*dente*) to decay ▶ VI to rot; to decay

apogeu [apo'ʒew] M (*fig*) height, peak

apoiar [apo'jar] VT to support; (*basear*) to base; (*moção*) to second; **apoiar-se** VR: **~-se em** to rest on

apoio [a'poju] M support; (*financeiro*) backing

apólice [a'pɔlisi] F (*certificado*) policy, certificate; (*ação*) share, bond; **~ de seguro** insurance policy

apontamento [apõta'mẽtu] M (*nota*) note

apontar [apõ'tar] VT (*fusil*) to aim; (*erro*) to point out; (*com o dedo*) to point at ou to; (*razão*) to put forward ▶ VI to begin to appear; (*brotar*) to sprout; (*com o dedo*) to point; **~ para** to point to; (*com arma*) to aim at

após [a'pɔjs] PREP after

aposentado, -a [apozẽ'tadu, a] ADJ retired ▶ M/F retired person, pensioner; **ser ~** to be retired; **aposentadoria** [apozẽtado'ria] F retirement; (*dinheiro*) pension

aposentar [apozẽ'tar] VT to retire; **aposentar-se** VR to retire

aposento [apo'zẽtu] M room

apossar-se [apo'sarsi] VR: **~ de** to take possession of, seize

apostar [apos'tar] VT to bet ▶ VI: **~ em** to bet on

apóstrofo [a'pɔstrofu] M apostrophe

apreciar [apre'sjar] VT to appreciate; (*gostar de*) to enjoy

apreço [a'presu] M esteem, regard; (*consideração*) consideration; **em ~** in question

apreender [aprjẽ'der] VT to apprehend; (*tomar*) to seize; (*entender*) to grasp

apreensão [aprjẽ'sãw] (*pl* **-ões**) F (*percepção*) perception; (*tomada*) seizure; (*receio*) apprehension

apreensivo, -a [aprjẽ'sivu, a] ADJ apprehensive

apreensões [aprjẽ'sõjs] FPL *de* **apreensão**

apregoar [apre'gwar] VT to proclaim, announce; (*mercadorias*) to cry

aprender [aprẽ'der] VT, VI to learn; **~ a ler** to learn to read; **~ de cor** to learn by heart

aprendizagem [aprẽdʒi'zaʒẽ] F (*num ofício*) apprenticeship; (*numa profissão*) training; (*escolar*) learning

apresentação [aprezẽta'sãw] (*pl* **-ões**) F presentation; (*de peça, filme*) performance; (*de pessoas*) introduction; (*porte pessoal*) appearance

apresentador, a [aprezẽta'dor(a)] M/F presenter

apresentar [aprezẽ'tar] VT to present; (*pessoas*) to introduce; **apresentar-se** VR to introduce o.s.; (*problema*) to present itself; (*à polícia etc*) to report; **quero ~-lhe ...** may I introduce you to ...

apressado, -a [apre'sadu, a] ADJ hurried, hasty; **estar ~** to be in a hurry

apressar [apre'sar] VT to hurry; **apressar-se** VR to hurry (up)

aprisionar [aprizjo'nar] VT (*cativar*) to capture; (*encarcerar*) to imprison

aprontar [aprõ'tar] VT to get ready, prepare; **aprontar-se** VR to get ready

apropriado, -a [apro'prjadu, a] ADJ appropriate, suitable

aprovado, -a [apro'vadu, a] ADJ approved; **ser ~ num exame** to pass an exam

aprovar [apro'var] VT to approve of; (*exame*) to pass ▶ VI to make the grade

aproveitador, a [aprovejta'dor(a)] M/F opportunist

aproveitamento [aprovejta'mẽtu] M use, utilization; (*nos estudos*) progress

aproveitar [aprovej'tar] VT to take advantage of; (*utilizar*) to use; (*oportunidade*) to take ▶ VI to make the most of it; (PT) to be of use; **aproveite!** enjoy yourself!

aproximação [aprosima'sãw] (*pl* **-ões**) F approximation; (*chegada*) approach; (*proximidade*) nearness

aproximar [aprosi'mar] VT to bring near; (*aliar*) to bring together; **aproximar-se** VR: **~-se de** (*acercar-se*) to approach

aptidão [aptʃi'dãw] F aptitude; (*jeito*) knack; **~ física** physical fitness

apto, -a ['aptu, a] ADJ apt; (*capaz*) capable

apto. ABR = **apartamento**

apunhalar [apuɲa'lar] VT to stab

apurado, -a [apu'radu, a] ADJ refined

apurar [apu'rar] VT to perfect; (*averiguar*) to investigate; (*dinheiro*) to raise, get; (*votos*) to count; **apurar-se** VR to dress up

aquarela [akwa'rɛla] F watercolour (BRIT), watercolor (US)

aquário [a'kwarju] M aquarium;

A~ (*Astrologia*) Aquarius

aquático, -a [a'kwatʃiku, a] ADJ aquatic, water *atr*

aquecer [ake'ser] VT to heat ▶ VI to heat up; **aquecer-se** VR to heat up; **aquecido, -a** [ake'sidu, a] ADJ heated; **aquecimento** [akesi'mẽtu] M heating; **aquecimento central** central heating; **aquecimento global** global warming

aquele, -ela [a'keli, ɛla] ADJ (*sg*) that; (*pl*) those ▶ PRON (*sg*) that one; (*pl*) those (ones)

àquele, -ela [a'keli, ɛla] = **a + aquele, -ela**

aquém [a'kẽj] ADV on this side; **~ de** on this side of

aqui [a'ki] ADV here; **eis ~** here is/ are; **~ mesmo** right here; **até ~** up to here; **por ~** hereabouts; (*nesta direção*) this way

aquilo [a'kilu] PRON that; **~ que** what

àquilo [a'kilu] = **a + aquilo**

aquisição [akizi'sãw] (*pl* **-ões**) F acquisition

ar [ar] M air; (*aspecto*) look; (*brisa*) breeze; (PT *Auto*) choke; **ares** MPL (*atitude*) airs; (*clima*) climate *sg*; **ao ar livre** in the open air; **no ar** (*TV, Rádio*) on air; (*fig: planos*) up in the air; **dar-se ares** to put on airs

árabe ['arabi] ADJ, M/F Arab ▶ M (*Ling*) Arabic

Arábia [a'rabja] F: **a ~ Saudita** Saudi Arabia

arame [a'rami] M wire

aranha [a'raɲa] F spider

arara [a'rara] F macaw

arbitragem [arbi'traʒẽ] F arbitration

arbitrar [arbi'trar] VT to arbitrate; (*Esporte*) to referee

arbitrário, -a [arbi'trarju, a] ADJ arbitrary

arbítrio [ar'bitrju] M decision; **ao ~ de** at the discretion of

árbitro ['arbitru] M (*juiz*) arbiter; (*Jur*) arbitrator; (*Futebol*) referee; (*Tênis*) umpire

arbusto [ar'bustu] M shrub, bush

arca ['arka] F chest, trunk; **~ de Noé** Noah's Ark

arcar [ar'kar] VT: **~ com** (*responsabilidades*) to shoulder; (*despesas*) to handle; (*consequencias*) to take

arcebispo [arse'bispu] M archbishop

arco ['arku] M (*Arq*) arch; (*Mil, Mús*) bow; (*Elet, Mat*) arc

arco-íris (*pl* **arcos-íris**) M rainbow

ar-condicionado (*pl* **ares-condicionados**) M (*aparelho*) air conditioner; (*sistema*) air conditioning

arder [ar'der] VI to burn; (*pele, olhos*) to sting; **~ de raiva** to seethe (with rage)

ardiloso, -a [ardʒi'lozu, ɔza] ADJ cunning

ardor [ar'dor] M ardour (BRIT), ardor (US); **ardoroso, -a** [ardo'rozu, ɔza] ADJ ardent

árduo, -a ['ardwu, a] ADJ arduous; (*difícil*) hard, difficult

área ['arja] F area; (*Esporte*) penalty area; (*fig*) field; **~ (de serviço)** balcony (*for hanging washing etc*)

areia [a'reja] F sand; **~ movediça** quicksand

arejar [are'ʒar] VT to air ▶ VI to get some air; (*descansar*) to have a breather; **arejar-se** VR to get some air; to have a break

arena [a'rɛna] F arena; (*de circo*) ring

Argélia [ar'ʒɛlja] F: **a ~** Algeria
Argentina [arʒē'tʃina] F: **a ~** Argentina
argila [ar'ʒila] F clay
argola [ar'gɔla] F ring; **argolas** FPL (*brincos*) hooped earrings; **~ (de porta)** door-knocker
argumentação [argumēta'sãw] F line of argument
argumentar [argumē'tar] VT, VI to argue
argumento [argu'mētu] M argument; (*de obra*) theme
aridez [ari'deʒ] F dryness; (*esterilidade*) barrenness; (*falta de interesse*) dullness
árido, -a ['aridu, a] ADJ arid, dry; (*estéril*) barren; (*maçante*) dull
Áries ['aris] F Aries
aritmética [aritʃ'mɛtʃika] F arithmetic
arma ['arma] F weapon; **armas** FPL (*nucleares etc*) arms; (*brasão*) coat sg of arms; **passar pelas ~s** to shoot, execute; **~ convencional/nuclear** conventional/nuclear weapon; **~s de destruição em massa** weapons of mass destruction; **~ de fogo** firearm
armação [arma'sãw] (*pl* **-ões**) F (*armadura*) frame; (*Pesca*) tackle; (*Náut*) rigging; (*de óculos*) frames pl
armado, -a [ar'madu, a] ADJ armed
armar [ar'mar] VT to arm; (*montar*) to assemble; (*barraca*) to pitch; (*um aparelho*) to set up; (*armadilha*) to set; (*Náut*) to fit out; **armar-se** VR to arm o.s.; **~ uma briga com** to pick a quarrel with
armarinho [arma'riɲu] M haberdashery (BRIT), notions pl (US)
armário [ar'marju] M cupboard; (*de roupa*) wardrobe
armazém [arma'zēj] (*pl* **-ns**) M (*depósito*) warehouse; (*loja*) grocery store; **armazenar** [armaze'nar] VT to store; (*provisões*) to stock
aro ['aru] M (*argola*) ring; (*de óculos, roda*) rim; (*de porta*) frame
aroma [a'roma] M aroma; **aromático, -a** [aro'matʃiku, a] ADJ (*comida*) aromatic; (*perfume*) fragrant
arpão [ar'pãw] (*pl* **-ões**) M harpoon
arqueiro, -a [ar'kejru, a] M/F archer; (*goleiro*) goalkeeper
arqueologia [arkjolo'ʒia] F archaeology (BRIT), archeology (US); **arqueólogo, -a** [ar'kjɔlogu, a] M/F archaeologist (BRIT), archeologist (US)
arquiteto, -a [arki'tɛtu, a] M/F architect; **arquitetónico, -a** [arkite'toniku, a] ADJ architectural; **arquitetura** [arkite'tura] F architecture
arquivar [arki'var] VT to file; (*projeto*) to shelve
arquivo [ar'kivu] M (*ger, Comput*) file; (*lugar*) archive; (*de empresa*) files pl; (*móvel*) filing cabinet; **~ zipado** (*Comput*) zip file
arraial [aha'jaw] (*pl* **-ais**) M (PT: *festa*) fair
arrancada [ahã'kada] F (*puxão*) jerk; **dar uma ~** (*em carro*) to pull away (suddenly)
arrancar [ahã'kar] VT to pull out; (*botão etc*) to pull off; (*arrebatar*) to snatch (away); (*fig: confissão*) to extract ▶ VI to start (off); **arrancar-se** VR to leave; (*fugir*) to run off
arranha-céu [a'haɲa-] (*pl* **-s**) M skyscraper
arranhão [aha'ɲãw] (*pl* **-ões**) M scratch
arranhar [aha'ɲar] VT to scratch
arranjar [ahã'ʒar] VT to arrange;

(*emprego etc*) to get, find; (*doença*) to get, catch; (*questão*) to settle; **arranjar-se** VR to manage; (*conseguir emprego*) to get a job; **~-se sem** to do without

arranjo [a'hãʒu] M arrangement

arrasar [aha'zar] VT to devastate; (*demolir*) to demolish; (*estragar*) to ruin; **arrasar-se** VR to be devastated; (*destruir-se*) to destroy o.s.; (*arruinar-se*) to lose everything

arrastão [ahas'tãw] (*pl* **-ões**) M tug; (*rede*) dragnet

arrastar [ahas'tar] VT to drag; (*atrair*) to draw ▶ VI to trail; **arrastar-se** VR to crawl; (*tempo*) to drag; (*processo*) to drag on

arrebatado, -a [aheba'tadu, a] ADJ rash, impetuous

arrebatar [aheba'tar] VT to snatch (away); (*levar*) to carry off; (*enlevar*) to entrance; (*enfurecer*) to enrage; **arrebatar-se** VR to be entranced

arrebentado, -a [ahebẽ'tadu, a] ADJ broken; (*estafado*) worn out

arrebentar [ahebẽ'tar] VT to break; (*porta*) to break down; (*corda*) to snap ▶ VI to break; to snap; (*guerra*) to break out

arrebitado, -a [ahebi'tadu, a] ADJ turned-up; (*nariz*) snub

arrecadar [aheka'dar] VT (*impostos etc*) to collect

arredondado, -a [ahedõ'dadu, a] ADJ round, rounded

arredondar [ahedõ'dar] VT to round (off); (*conta*) to round up

arredores [ahe'dɔris] MPL suburbs; (*cercanias*) outskirts

arrefecer [ahefe'ser] VT to cool; (*febre*) to lower; (*desanimar*) to discourage ▶ VI to cool (off); to get discouraged

arregaçar [ahega'sar] VT to roll up

arregalado, -a [ahega'ladu, a] ADJ (*olhos*) wide

arregalar [ahega'lar] VT: **~ os olhos** to stare in amazement

arrematar [ahema'tar] VT (*dizer concluindo*) to conclude; (*comprar*) to buy by auction; (*vender*) to sell by auction; (*Costura*) to finish off

arremessar [aheme'sar] VT to throw, hurl; **arremesso** [ahe'mesu] M throw

arremeter [aheme'ter] VI to lunge; **~ contra** (*acometer*) to attack, assail

arrendar [ahẽ'dar] VT to lease

arrepender-se [ahepẽ'dersi] VR to repent; (*mudar de opinião*) to change one's mind; **~ de** to regret, be sorry for; **arrependido, -a** [ahepẽ'dʒidu, a] ADJ (*pessoa*) sorry; **arrependimento** [ahepẽdʒi'mẽtu] M regret; (*Rel, de crime*) repentance

arrepiar [ahe'pjar] VT (*amedrontar*) to horrify; (*cabelo*) to cause to stand on end; **arrepiar-se** VR to shiver; (*cabelo*) to stand on end; **(ser) de ~ os cabelos** (to be) hair-raising

arrepio [ahe'piu] M shiver; (*de frio*) chill; **isso me dá ~s** it gives me the creeps

arriar [a'hjar] VT to lower; (*depor*) to lay down ▶ VI to drop; (*vergar*) to sag; (*desistir*) to give up; (*fig*) to collapse

arriscado, -a [ahis'kadu, a] ADJ risky; (*audacioso*) daring

arriscar [ahis'kar] VT to risk; (*pôr em perigo*) to endanger, jeopardize; **arriscar-se** VR to take a risk; **~-se a fazer** to risk doing

arrogante [aho'gãtʃi] ADJ arrogant

arrojado, -a [aho'ʒadu, a] ADJ (*design*) bold; (*temerário*) rash; (*ousado*) daring

arrolar [aho'lar] VT to list

arrombar [ahõ'bar] VT (*porta*) to break down; (*cofre*) to crack

arrotar [aho'tar] VI to belch ▶ VT (*alardear*) to boast of

arroz [a'hoz] M rice; **~ doce** rice pudding

arruinar [ahwi'nar] VT to ruin; (*destruir*) to destroy; **arruinar-se** VR to be ruined; (*perder a saúde*) to ruin one's health

arrumação [ahuma'sãw] F arrangement; (*de um quarto etc*) tidying up; (*de malas*) packing

arrumadeira [ahuma'dejra] F cleaning lady; (*num hotel*) chambermaid

arrumar [ahu'mar] VT to put in order, arrange; (*quarto etc*) to tidy up; (*malas*) to pack; (*emprego*) to get; (*vestir*) to dress up; (*desculpa*) to make up, find; (*vida*) to sort out; **arrumar-se** VR (*aprontar-se*) to get dressed, get ready; (*na vida*) to sort o.s. out; (*virar-se*) to manage

arte ['artʃi] F art; (*habilidade*) skill; (*ofício*) trade, craft

artefato [artʃi'fatu], (PT) **artefacto** M (manufactured) article

artéria [ar'tɛrja] F (*Anat*) artery

artesão, -sã [arte'zãw, zã] (*pl* **-s/-s**) M/F artisan, craftsman/woman

ártico, -a ['artʃiku, a] ADJ Arctic ▶ M: **o Á~** the Arctic

artificial [artʃifi'sjaw] (*pl* **-ais**) ADJ artificial

artifício [artʃi'fisju] M stratagem, trick

artigo [ar'tʃigu] M article; (*Com*) item; **artigos** MPL (*produtos*) goods

artista [ar'tʃista] M/F artist; **artístico, -a** [ar'tʃistʃiku, a] ADJ artistic

artrite [ar'tritʃi] F (*Med*) arthritis

árvore ['arvori] F tree; (*Tec*) shaft; **~ de Natal** Christmas tree

as [as] ART DEF *ver* **a**

ás [ajs] M ace

às [as] = **a + as**; *ver* **a**

asa ['aza] F wing; (*de xícara etc*) handle

ascendência [asẽ'dẽsja] F (*antepassados*) ancestry; (*domínio*) ascendancy, sway; **ascendente** [asẽ'dẽtʃi] ADJ rising, upward

ascender [asẽ'der] VI to rise, ascend

ascensão [asẽ'sãw] (*pl* **-ões**) F ascent; (*Rel*): **dia da A~** Ascension Day

asco ['asku] M loathing, revulsion; **dar ~ a** to revolt, disgust

asfalto [as'fawtu] M asphalt

asfixia [asfik'sia] F asphyxia, suffocation

Ásia ['azja] F: **a ~** Asia

asiático, -a [a'zjatʃiku, a] ADJ, M/F Asian

asilo [a'zilu] M (*refúgio*) refuge; (*estabelecimento*) home; **~ político** political asylum

asma ['azma] F asthma

asneira [az'nejra] F (*tolice*) stupidity; (*ato, dito*) stupid thing

asno ['aznu] M donkey; (*fig*) ass

aspas ['aspas] FPL inverted commas

aspecto [as'pɛktu] M aspect; (*aparência*) look, appearance; (*característica*) feature; (*ponto de vista*) point of view

aspereza [aspe'reza] F roughness; (*severidade*) harshness; (*rudeza*) rudeness

áspero, -a ['asperu, a] ADJ rough; (*severo*) harsh; (*rude*) rude

aspiração [aspira'sãw] (*pl* **-ões**) F aspiration; (*inalação*) inhalation

aspirador [aspira'dor] M: **~ (de pó)** vacuum cleaner; **passar o ~ (em)** to vacuum

aspirante [aspi'rãtʃi] ADJ aspiring ▶ M/F candidate

aspirar [aspi'rar] VT to breathe in; (*bombear*) to suck up ▶ VI to breathe; (*soprar*) to blow; (*desejar*): **~ a algo** to aspire to sth

aspirina [aspi'rina] F aspirin

asqueroso, -a [aske'rozu, ɔza] ADJ disgusting, revolting

assado, -a [a'sadu, a] ADJ roasted; (*Culin*) roast ▶ M roast; **carne assada** roast beef

assaltante [asaw'tãtʃi] M/F assailant; (*de banco*) robber; (*de casa*) burglar; (*na rua*) mugger

assaltar [asaw'tar] VT to attack; (*casa*) to break into; (*banco*) to rob; (*pessoa na rua*) to mug; **assalto** [a'sawtu] M attack, raid; (*a um banco etc*) robbery; (*a uma casa*) burglary, break-in; (*a uma pessoa na rua*) mugging; (*Boxe*) round

assar [a'sar] VT to roast; (*na grelha*) to grill

assassinar [asasi'nar] VT to murder, kill; (*Pol*) to assassinate; **assassinato** [asasi'natu] M murder, killing; (*Pol*) assassination; **assassino, -a** [asa'sinu, a] M/F murderer; (*Pol*) assassin; **assassino em série** serial killer

assaz [a'saz] ADV (*suficientemente*) sufficiently; (*muito*) rather

assediar [ase'dʒjar] VT (*sitiar*) to besiege; (*importunar*) to pester; **assédio** [a'sɛdʒu] M siege; (*insistência*) insistence

assegurar [asegu'rar] VT to secure; (*garantir*) to ensure; (*afirmar*) to assure; **assegurar-se** VR: **~-se de** to make sure of

asseio [a'seju] M cleanliness

assembleia [asẽ'blɛja] F assembly; (*reunião*) meeting; **~ geral (ordinária)** annual general meeting

assentar [asẽ'tar] VT (*fazer sentar*) to seat; (*colocar*) to place; (*estabelecer*) to establish; (*decidir*) to decide upon ▶ VI (*pó etc*) to settle; **assentar-se** VR to sit down; **~ em** *ou* **a** (*roupa*) to suit

assentir [asẽ'tʃir] VI: **~ (em)** to consent *ou* agree (to)

assento [a'sẽtu] M seat; (*base*) base

assíduo, -a [a'sidwu, a] ADJ (*aluno*) who attends regularly; (*diligente*) assiduous; (*constante*) constant; **ser ~ num lugar** to be a regular visitor to a place

assim [a'sĩ] ADV (*deste modo*) like this, in this way, thus; (*portanto*) therefore; (*igualmente*) likewise; **~ ~** so-so; **~ mesmo** in any case; **e ~ por diante** and so on; **~ como** as well as; **como ~?** how do you mean?; **~ que** (*logo que*) as soon as

assimilar [asimi'lar] VT to assimilate; (*apreender*) to take in; (*assemelhar*) to compare

assinante [asi'nãtʃi] M/F (*de jornal etc*) subscriber

assinar [asi'nar] VT to sign

assinatura [asina'tura] F (*nome*) signature; (*de jornal etc*) subscription; (*Teatro*) season ticket

assinto [a'sĩtu] VB *ver* **assentir**

assistência [asis'tẽsja] F (*presença*) presence; (*público*) audience; (*auxílio*) aid; **~ médica**

medical aid; **~ social** social work

assistente [asis'tētʃi] ADJ assistant ▶ M/F spectator, onlooker; (*ajudante*) assistant; **~ social** social worker

assistir [asis'tʃir] VT, VI: **~ (a)** (*Med*) to attend (to); **~ a** to assist; (*TV, filme, jogo*) to watch; (*reunião*) to attend

assoar [aso'ar] VT: **~ o nariz** to blow one's nose; **assoar-se** VR (*PT*) to blow one's nose

assobiar [aso'bjar] VI to whistle

assobio [aso'biu] M whistle

associação [asosja'sāw] (*pl* -**ões**) F association; (*organização*) society; (*parceria*) partnership

associado, -a [aso'sjadu, a] ADJ associate ▶ M/F associate, member; (*Com*) associate; (*sócio*) partner

associar [aso'sjar] VT to associate; **associar-se** VR: **~-se a** to associate with

assombração [asōbra'sāw] (*pl* -**ões**) F ghost

assombro [a'sōbru] M amazement, astonishment; (*maravilha*) marvel; **assombroso, -a** [asō'brozu, ɔza] ADJ astonishing, amazing

assoviar [aso'vjar] VT = **assobiar**

assovio [aso'viu] M = **assobio**

assumir [asu'mir] VT to assume, take on; (*reconhecer*) to accept

assunto [a'sūtu] M subject, matter; (*enredo*) plot

assustador, a [asusta'dor(a)] ADJ (*alarmante*) startling; (*amedrontador*) frightening

assustar [asus'tar] VT to frighten, startle; **assustar-se** VR to be frightened

asteca [as'tɛka] ADJ, M/F Aztec

astral [as'traw] (*pl* -**ais**) M mood; **bom ~** good vibe; **alto ~** upbeat mood; **baixo ~** gloom; **estar de baixo ~** to be feeling glum

astrologia [astrolo'ʒia] F astrology

astronauta [astro'nawta] M/F astronaut

astronave [astro'navi] F spaceship

astronomia [astrono'mia] F astronomy

astúcia [as'tusja] F cunning

ata ['ata] F (*de reunião*) minutes *pl*

atacado, -a [ata'kadu, a] ADJ (*col: pessoa*) in a bad mood ▶ M: **por ~** wholesale

atacante [ata'kātʃi] ADJ attacking ▶ M/F attacker, assailant ▶ M (*Futebol*) forward

atacar [ata'kar] VT to attack; (*problema etc*) to tackle

atado, -a [a'tadu, a] ADJ (*desajeitado*) clumsy, awkward; (*perplexo*) puzzled

atalho [a'taʎu] M (*caminho*) short cut

ataque [a'taki] M attack; **~ aéreo** air raid; **~ suicida** suicide attack

atar [a'tar] VT to tie (up), fasten; **não ~ nem desatar** (*pessoa*) to waver; (*negócio*) to be in the air

atarefado, -a [atare'fadu, a] ADJ busy

atarracado, -a [ataha'kadu, a] ADJ stocky

até [a'tɛ] PREP (*PT: + a: lugar*) up to, as far as; (*tempo etc*) until, till ▶ ADV (*tb:* **~ mesmo**) even; **~ certo ponto** to a certain extent; **~ em cima** to the top; **~ já** see you soon; **~ logo** bye!; **~ onde** as far as; **~ que** until; **~ que enfim!** at last!

atear [ate'ar] VT (*fogo*) to kindle; (*fig*) to incite, inflame; **atear-se** VR to blaze; (*paixões*) to flare up

ateia [a'tɛja] F *de* **ateu**

atemorizar [atemori'zar] VT to frighten; (*intimidar*) to intimidate

Atenas [a'tenas] N Athens

atenção [atẽ'sãw] (*pl* **-ões**) F attention; (*cortesia*) courtesy; (*bondade*) kindness; **~!** be careful!; **chamar a ~** to attract attention; **atencioso, -a** [atẽ'sjozu, ɔza] ADJ considerate

atender [atẽ'der] VT: **~ (a)** to attend to; (*receber*) to receive; (*deferir*) to grant; (*telefone etc*) to answer; (*paciente*) to see ▶ VI to answer; (*dar atenção*) to pay attention; **atendimento** [atẽdʒi'mẽtu] M service; (*recepção*) reception; **horário de atendimento** opening hours; (*em consultório*) surgery (BRIT) *ou* office (US) hours

atentado [atẽ'tadu] M attack; (*crime*) crime; (*contra a vida de alguém*) attempt on sb's life; **~ suicida** suicide attack

atento, -a [a'tẽtu, a] ADJ attentive; **estar ~ a** to be aware *ou* mindful of

atenuante [ate'nwãtʃi] ADJ extenuating ▶ M extenuating circumstance

atenuar [ate'nwar] VT to reduce, lessen

aterragem [ate'haʒẽj] (PT) (*pl* **-ns**) F (*Aer*) landing

aterrar [ate'har] VI (PT Aer) to land

aterrissagem [atehi'saʒẽ] (BR) (*pl* **-ns**) F (*Aer*) landing

aterrissar [atehi'sar] (BR) VI (*Aer*) to land

aterro [a'tehu] M: **~ sanitário** landfill (site)

aterrorizante [atehori'zãtʃi] ADJ terrifying

aterrorizar [atehori'zar] VT to terrorize

atestado, -a [ates'tadu, a] ADJ certified ▶ M certificate; (*prova*) proof; (*Jur*) testimony

ateu, ateia [a'tew, a'tɛja] ADJ, M/F atheist

atinar [atʃi'nar] VT (*acertar*) to guess correctly ▶ VI: **~ com** (*solução*) to find; **~ em** to notice; **~ a fazer algo** to succeed in doing sth

atingir [atʃi'ʒir] VT to reach; (*acertar*) to hit; (*afetar*) to affect; (*objetivo*) to achieve; (*compreender*) to grasp

atirador, a [atʃira'dor(a)] M/F marksman/woman; **~ de tocaia** sniper

atirar [atʃi'rar] VT to throw, fling ▶ VI (*arma*) to shoot; **atirar-se** VR: **~-se a** to hurl o.s. at

atitude [atʃi'tudʒi] F attitude; (*postura*) posture

atividade [atʃivi'dadʒi] F activity

ativo, -a [a'tʃivu, a] ADJ active ▶ M (*Com*) assets *pl*

atlântico, -a [at'lãtʃiku, a] ADJ Atlantic ▶ M: **o (Oceano) A~** the Atlantic (Ocean)

atlas ['atlas] M INV atlas

atleta [at'lɛta] M/F athlete; **atlético, -a** [at'lɛtʃiku, a] ADJ athletic; **atletismo** [atle'tʃizmu] M athletics *sg*

atmosfera [atmos'fɛra] F atmosphere

ato ['atu] M act, action; (*cerimônia*) ceremony; (*Teatro*) act; **em ~ contínuo** straight after; **no ~** on the spot; **no mesmo ~** at the same time

atômico, -a [a'tomiku, a] ADJ atomic

átomo ['atomu] M atom

atônito, -a [a'tonitu, a] ADJ astonished, amazed

ator [a'tor] M actor

atordoado, -a [ator'dwadu, a] ADJ
dazed

atordoar [ator'dwar] VT to daze,
stun

atormentar [atormẽ'tar] VT to
torment

atração [atra'sãw] (pl **-ões**) F
attraction

atracar [atra'kar] VT, VI (Náut) to
moor; **atracar-se** VR to grapple

atrações [atra'sõjs] FPL de **atração**

atraente [atra'ẽtʃi] ADJ attractive

atrair [atra'ir] VT to attract;
(fascinar) to fascinate

atrapalhar [atrapa'ʎar] VT to
confuse; (perturbar) to disturb;
(dificultar) to hinder ▶ VI to be a
nuisance

atrás [a'trajs] ADV behind; (no
fundo) at the back ▶ PREP: **~ de**
behind; (no tempo) after; **dois
meses ~** two months ago

atrasado, -a [atra'zadu, a] ADJ
late; (país etc) backward; (relógio
etc) slow; (pagamento) overdue;
atrasados [atra'zadus] MPL (Com)
arrears

atrasar [atra'zar] VT to delay;
(progresso, desenvolvimento) to hold
back; (relógio) to put back;
(pagamento) to be late with ▶ VI
(relógio etc) to be slow; (avião,
pessoa) to be late; **atrasar-se** VR to
be late; (num trabalho) to fall behind;
(num pagamento) to get into arrears

atraso [a'trazu] M delay; (de país
etc) backwardness; **atrasos** MPL
(Com) arrears; **com 20 minutos de
~** 20 minutes late

atrativo, -a [atra'tʃivu, a] ADJ
attractive ▶ M attraction;
(incentivo) incentive; **atrativos** MPL
(encantos) charms

através [atra'vɛs] ADV across; **~ de**
across; (pelo centro de) through

atravessar [atrave'sar] VT to cross;
(pôr ao través) to put ou lay across;
(traspassar) to pass through

atrever-se [atre'versi] VR: **~ a** to
dare to; **atrevido, -a** [atre'vidu, a]
ADJ cheeky; (corajoso) bold;
atrevimento [atrevi'mẽtu] M
(ousadia) boldness; (insolência)
cheek

atribuir [atri'bwir] VT: **~ algo a** to
attribute sth to; (prêmios, regalias) to
confer sth on

atributo [atri'butu] M attribute

átrio ['atrju] M hall; (pátio)
courtyard

atrito [a'tritu] M (fricção) friction;
(desentendimento) disagreement

atriz [a'triz] F actress

atropelamento [atropela'mẽtu]
M (de pedestre) accident involving a
pedestrian

atropelar [atrope'lar] VT to knock
down, run over; (empurrar) to jostle

atuação [atwa'sãw] (pl **-ões**) F
acting; (de ator etc) performance

atual [a'twaw] (pl **-ais**) ADJ current;
(pessoa, carro) modern; **atualidade**
[atwali'dadʒi] F present (time);
atualidades FPL (notícias) news sg;
atualizar [atwali'zar] VT to update;
atualmente [atwaw'mẽtʃi] ADV at
present, currently; (hoje em dia)
nowadays

atuante [a'twãtʃi] ADJ active

atuar [a'twar] VI to act; **~ para** to
contribute to; **~ sobre** to influence

atum [a'tũ] (pl **-ns**) M tuna (fish)

aturdido, -a [atur'dʒidu, a] ADJ
stunned; (com barulho) deafened;
(com confusão, movimento)
bewildered

audácia [aw'dasja] F boldness;

audição [awdʒi'sãw] (pl **-ões**) F audition

audiência [aw'dʒjēsja] F audience; (de tribunal) session, hearing

auditar [awdʒi'tar] VT to audit

auditor, a [awdʒi'tor(a)] M/F auditor; (juiz) judge; (ouvinte) listener

auditoria [awdʒito'ria] F: **fazer a ~ de** to audit

auditório [awdʒi'tɔrju] M audience; (recinto) auditorium

auge ['awʒi] M height, peak

aula ['awla] F (PT: sala) classroom; (lição) lesson, class; **dar ~** to teach

aumentar [awmē'tar] VT to increase; (salários, preços) to raise; (sala, casa) to expand, extend; (suj: lente) to magnify; (acrescentar) to add ▶ VI to increase; (preço, salário) to rise, go up

aumento [aw'mētu] M increase; (de preços) rise; (ampliação) enlargement; (crescimento) growth

ausência [aw'zēsja] F absence

ausentar-se [awzē'tarsi] VR (ir-se) to go away; (afastar-se) to stay away

ausente [aw'zētʃi] ADJ absent

austral [aws'traw] (pl **-ais**) ADJ southern

Austrália [aws'tralja] F: **a ~** Australia; **australiano, -a** [awstra'ljanu, a] ADJ, M/F Australian

Áustria ['awstrja] F: **a ~** Austria; **austríaco, -a** [aws'triaku, a] ADJ, M/F Austrian

autêntico, -a [aw'tētʃiku, a] ADJ authentic; (pessoa) genuine; (verdadeiro) true, real

auto ['awtu] M car; **autos** MPL (Jur: processo) legal proceedings; (documentos) legal papers

autobiografia [awtobjogra'fia] F autobiography

autobronzeador [awtobrõza'dor] ADJ self-tanning

autocarro [awto'kahu] (PT) M bus

autodefesa [awtode'feza] F self-defence (BRIT), self-defense (US)

autódromo [aw'tɔdromu] M race track

autoestrada [awtois'trada] F motorway (BRIT), expressway (US)

autografar [awtogra'far] VT to autograph

autógrafo [aw'tɔgrafu] M autograph

automático, -a [awto'matʃiku, a] ADJ automatic

automobilismo [awtomobi'lizmu] M motoring; (Esporte) motor car racing

automóvel [awto'mɔvew] (pl **-eis**) M motor car (BRIT), automobile (US)

autonomia [awtono'mia] F autonomy

autor, a [aw'tor(a)] M/F author; (de um crime) perpetrator; (Jur) plaintiff

autoral [awto'raw] (pl **-ais**) ADJ: **direitos autorais** copyright sg

autoridade [awtori'dadʒi] F authority

autorização [awtoriza'sãw] (pl **-ões**) F permission, authorization; **dar ~ a alguém para** to authorize sb to

autorizar [awtori'zar] VT to authorize

autosserviço [awtoser'visu] M self-service

auxiliar [awsi'ljar] ADJ auxiliary
▶ M/F assistant ▶ VT to help;
auxílio [aw'silju] M help,
assistance

Av. ABR (= *avenida*) Ave.

aval [a'vaw] (*pl* -**ais**) M guarantee

avalancha [ava'lãʃa] F avalanche

avaliar [ava'ljar] VT to value; to
assess

avançado, -a [avã'sadu, a] ADJ
advanced; (*ideias, pessoa*)
progressive

avançar [avã'sar] VT to move
forward ▶ VI to advance; **avanço**
[a'vãsu] M advancement;
(*progresso*) progress

avaria [ava'ria] F (*Tec*) breakdown;
avariado, -a [ava'rjadu, a] ADJ
(*máquina*) out of order; (*carro*)
broken down; **avariar** [ava'rjar] VT
to damage ▶ VI to suffer damage;
(*Tec*) to break down

ave ['avi] F bird

aveia [a'veja] F oats *pl*

avelã [ave'lã] F hazelnut

avenida [ave'nida] F avenue

avental [avẽ'taw] (*pl* -**ais**) M apron;
(*vestido*) pinafore dress (BRIT),
jumper (US)

averiguar [averi'gwar] VT to
investigate; (*verificar*) to verify

avermelhado, -a [averme'ʎadu,
a] ADJ reddish

avesso, -a [a'vesu, a] ADJ (*lado*)
opposite, reverse ▶ M wrong side,
reverse; **ao ~** inside out; **às
avessas** (*inverso*) upside down;
(*oposto*) the wrong way round

avestruz [aves'truz] M ostrich

aviação [avja'sãw] F aviation,
flying

aviador, a [avja'dor(a)] M/F
aviator, airman/woman

avião [a'vjãw] (*pl* -**ões**) M
aeroplane; **~ a jato** jet

ávido, -a ['avidu, a] ADJ greedy;
(*desejoso*) eager

aviões [a'vjõjs] MPL *de* **avião**

avisar [avi'zar] VT to warn;
(*informar*) to tell, let know; **aviso**
[a'vizu] M (*comunicação*) notice

avistar [avis'tar] VT to catch sight
of

avô, avó [a'vo, a'vɔ] M/F
grandfather/mother; **avós** MPL
grandparents

avulso, -a [a'vuwsu, a] ADJ
separate, detached

axila [ak'sila] F armpit

azar [a'zar] M bad luck; **~!** too bad!,
bad luck!; **estar com ~, ter ~** to be
unlucky; **azarento, -a** [aza'rẽtu, a]
ADJ unlucky

azedar [aze'dar] VT to turn sour ▶ VI
to turn sour; (*leite*) to go off; **azedo,
-a** [a'zedu, a] ADJ sour; (*leite*) off;
(*fig*) grumpy

azeite [a'zejtʃi] M oil; (*de oliva*) olive
oil

azeitona [azej'tɔna] F olive

azia [a'zia] F heartburn

azougue [a'zogi] M (*Quím*) mercury

azul [a'zuw] (*pl* -**uis**) ADJ blue

azulejo [azu'leʒu] M (glazed) tile

azul-marinho ADJ INV navy blue

azul-turquesa ADJ INV turquoise

b

baba ['baba] F dribble

babá [ba'ba] F nanny

babado [ba'badu] M frill; (col) piece of gossip

babador [baba'dor] M bib

babar [ba'bar] VI to dribble; **babar-se** VR to dribble

baby-sitter ['bejbisiter] (pl **-s**) M/F baby-sitter

bacalhau [baka'ʎaw] M (dried) cod

bacana [ba'kana] (col) ADJ great

bacharel [baʃa'rɛw] (pl **-éis**) M graduate

bacia [ba'sia] F basin; (Anat) pelvis

backup [ba'kapi] (pl **-s**) M (Comput) back-up; **fazer um ~ de** to back up

bactéria [bak'tɛrja] F germ, bacterium; **bactérias** MPL bacteria pl

badalar [bada'lar] VT, VI to ring

baderna [ba'dɛrna] F commotion

bafo ['bafu] M (bad) breath

bagaço [ba'gasu] M (de frutos) pulp; (PT: cachaça) brandy; **estar/ficar um ~** (fig: pessoa) to be/get run down

bagageiro [baga'ʒejru] M (Auto) roof rack; (PT) porter

bagagem [ba'gaʒẽ] F luggage; (fig) baggage; **recebimento de ~** (Aer) baggage reclaim

bagulho [ba'guʎu] M (objeto) piece of junk

bagunça [ba'gũsa] F mess, shambles sg; **bagunçado, -a** [bagũ'sadu, a] ADJ messy; **bagunçar** [bagũ'sar] VT to mess up; **bagunceiro, -a** [bagũ'sejru, a] ADJ messy

baía [ba'ia] F bay

bailado [baj'ladu] M dance; (balé) ballet

bailarino, -a [bajla'rinu, a] M/F ballet dancer

baile ['bajli] M dance; (formal) ball; **~ à fantasia** fancy-dress ball

bainha [ba'iɲa] F (de arma) sheath; (de costura) hem

bairro ['bajhu] M district

baixa ['bajʃa] F decrease; (de preço) reduction, fall; drop; (em combate) casualty; (do serviço) discharge

baixar [baj'ʃar] VT to lower; (ordem) to issue; (lei) to pass; (Comput) to download ▶ VI to go (ou come) down; (temperatura, preço) to drop, fall

baixinho [baj'ʃiɲu] ADV (falar) softly, quietly; (em segredo) secretly

baixo, -a ['bajʃu, a] ADJ low; (pessoa) short, small; (rio) shallow; (linguagem) common; (olhos) lowered; (atitude) mean; (metal) base ▶ ADV low; (em posição baixa) low down; (falar) softly ▶ M (Mús) bass; **em ~** below; (em casa) downstairs; **em voz baixa** in a quiet voice; **para ~** down, downwards; (*em casa*) downstairs; **por ~ de** under, underneath

bala ['bala] F bullet; (BR: *doce*) sweet

balança [ba'lãsa] F scales *pl*; **B~** (*Astrologia*) Libra; **~ comercial** balance of trade; **~ de pagamentos** balance of payments

balançar [balã'sar] VT to swing; (*pesar*) to weigh (up) ▶ VI to swing; (*carro, avião*) to shake; (*em cadeira*) to rock; **balançar-se** VR to swing; **balanço** [ba'lãsu] M (*movimento*) swinging; (*brinquedo*) swing; (*de carro, avião*) shaking; (*Com: registro*) balance (sheet); (: *verificação*) audit; **fazer um balanço de** (*fig*) to take stock of

balão [ba'lãw] (*pl* **-ões**) M balloon

balbúrdia [baw'burdʒja] F uproar, bedlam

balcão [baw'kãw] (*pl* **-ões**) M balcony; (*de loja*) counter; (*Teatro*) circle; **balconista** [bawko'nista] M/F shop assistant

balde ['bawdʒi] M bucket, pail

balé [ba'lɛ] M ballet

baleia [ba'leja] F whale

baliza [ba'liza] F (*estaca*) post; (*boia*) buoy; (*luminosa*) beacon; (*Esporte*) goal

balneário [baw'njarju] M bathing resort

balões [ba'lõjs] MPL *de* **balão**

baloiço [ba'lojsu] (PT) M (*de criança*) swing; (*ação*) swinging

balsa ['bawsa] F raft; (*barca*) ferry

bamba ['bãba] ADJ, M/F expert

bambo, -a ['bãbu, a] ADJ slack, loose

banana [ba'nana] F banana; **bananeira** [bana'nejra] F banana tree

banca ['bãka] F bench; (*escritório*) office; (*em jogo*) bank; **~ (de**

jornais) newsstand; **bancada** [bã'kada] F (*banco, Pol*) bench; (*de cozinha*) worktop

bancar [bã'kar] VT to finance ▶ VI (*fingir*): **~ que** to pretend that; **bancário, -a** [bã'karju, a] ADJ bank *atr* ▶ M/F bank employee

bancarrota [bãka'hota] F bankruptcy; **ir à ~** to go bankrupt

banco ['bãku] M (*assento*) bench; (*Com*) bank; **~ de areia** sandbank; **~ de dados** (*Comput*) database

banda ['bãda] F band; (*lado*) side; (*cinto*) sash; **de ~** sideways; **pôr de ~** to put aside; **~ desenhada** (PT) cartoon; **~ larga** (*Tel*) broadband

bandeira [bã'dejra] F flag; (*estandarte, fig*) banner; **bandeirinha** [bãdej'riɲa] M (*Esporte*) linesman

bandeja [bã'deʒa] F tray

bandido [bã'dʒidu] M bandit

bando ['bãdu] M band; (*grupo*) group; (*de malfeitores*) gang; (*de ovelhas*) flock; (*de gado*) herd; (*de livros etc*) pile

banha ['baɲa] F fat; (*de porco*) lard

banhar [ba'ɲar] VT to wet; (*mergulhar*) to dip; (*lavar*) to wash; **banhar-se** VR to bathe

banheira [ba'ɲejra] F bath

banheiro [ba'ɲejru] M bathroom

banho ['baɲu] M bath; (*mergulho*) dip; **tomar ~** to have a bath; (*de chuveiro*) to have a shower; **~ de chuveiro** shower; **~ de sol** sunbathing

banir [ba'nir] VT to banish

banqueiro, -a [bã'kejru, a] M/F banker

banquete [bã'ketʃi] M banquet

bar [bar] M bar

baralho [ba'raʎu] M pack of cards

barata [ba'rata] F cockroach

barateiro, -a [bara'tejru, a] ADJ
cheap

barato, -a [ba'ratu, a] ADJ cheap
▶ ADV cheaply

barba ['barba] F beard; **fazer a ~**
to shave

bárbaro, -a ['barbaru, a] ADJ
barbaric; (*dor, calor*) terrible;
(*maravilhoso*) great

barbeador [barbja'dor] M razor;
(*tb: ~ elétrico*) shaver

barbear [bar'bjar] VT to shave;
barbear-se VR to shave;
barbearia [barbja'ria] F barber's
(shop)

barbeiro [bar'bejru] M barber;
(*loja*) barber's

barca ['barka] F barge; (*de
travessia*) ferry

barco ['barku] M boat; **~ a motor**
motorboat; **~ a remo** rowing
boat; **~ a vela** sailing boat

barganha [bar'gaɲa] F bargain;
barganhar [barga'ɲar] VT, VI to
negotiate

barman [bar'mã] (*pl* **-men**) M
barman

barra ['baha] F bar; (*faixa*) strip;
(*traço*) stroke; (*alavanca*) lever; (*em
endereço web*) forward slash

barraca [ba'haka] F (*tenda*) tent;
(*de feira*) stall; (*de madeira*) hut; (*de
praia*) sunshade; **barracão**
[baha'kãw] (*pl* **-ões**) M shed;
barraco [ba'haku] M shack,
shanty; (*col: confusão*) scene

barragem [ba'haʒẽ] (*pl* **-ns**) F
dam; (*impedimento*) barrier

barrar [ba'har] VT to bar

barreira [ba'hejra] F barrier;
(*cerca*) fence; (*Esporte*) hurdle

barricada [bahi'kada] F barricade

barriga [ba'higa] F belly; **estar de
~** to be pregnant; **~ da perna** calf;

barrigudo, -a [bahi'gudu, a] ADJ
paunchy, pot-bellied

barril [ba'hiw] (*pl* **-is**) M barrel,
cask

barro ['bahu] M clay; (*lama*) mud

barulhento, -a [baru'ʎẽtu, a] ADJ
noisy

barulho [ba'ruʎu] M (*ruído*) noise;
(*tumulto*) din

base ['bazi] F base; (*fig*) basis; **sem
~** groundless; **com ~ em** based
on; **na ~ de** by means of

basear [ba'zjar] VT to base;
basear-se VR: **~-se em** to be
based on

básico, -a ['baziku, a] ADJ basic

basquete [bas'kɛtʃi] M
= **basquetebol**

basquetebol [baskete'bɔw] M
basketball

basta ['basta] M: **dar um ~ em** to
call a halt to

bastante [bas'tãtʃi] ADJ (*suficiente*)
enough; (*muito*) quite a lot (of)
▶ ADV enough; a lot

bastão [bas'tãw] (*pl* **-ões**) M stick

bastar [bas'tar] VI to be enough,
be sufficient; **bastar-se** VR to be
self-sufficient; **basta!** (that's)
enough!; **~ para** to be enough to

bastardo, -a [bas'tardu, a] ADJ,
M/F bastard

bastões [bas'tõjs] MPL *de* **bastão**

bata ['bata] F (*de mulher*) smock;
(*de médico*) overall

batalha [ba'taʎa] F battle;
batalhador, a [bataʎa'dor(a)] ADJ
struggling ▶ M/F fighter;
batalhão [bata'ʎãw] (*pl* **-ões**) M
battalion; **batalhar** [bata'ʎar] VI
to battle, fight; (*esforçar-se*) to
make an effort, try hard ▶ VT
(*emprego*) to go after

batata [ba'tata] F potato; **~ doce**

sweet potato; **~ frita** chips pl (BRIT), French fries pl; (de pacote) crisps pl (BRIT), (potato) chips pl (US)

bate-boca ['batʃi-] (pl **-s**) M row, quarrel

batedeira [bate'dejra] F beater; (de manteiga) churn; **~ elétrica** mixer

batente [ba'tẽtʃi] M doorpost

bate-papo ['batʃi-] (pl **-s**) (BR) M chat

bater [ba'ter] VT to beat; to strike; (pé) to stamp; (foto) to take; (porta) to slam; (asas) to flap; (recorde) to break; (roupa) to wear all the time ▶ VI to slam; (sino) to ring; (janela) to bang; (coração) to beat; (sol) to beat down; **bater-se** VR: **~-se para fazer/por** to fight to do/for; **~ (à porta)** to knock (at the door); **~ à maquina** to type; **~ em** to hit; **~ com o carro** to crash one's car; **~ com a cabeça** to bang one's head; **~ com o pé (em)** to kick

bateria [bate'ria] F battery; (Mús) drums pl; **~ de cozinha** kitchen utensils pl; **baterista** [bate'rista] M/F drummer

batida [ba'tʃida] F beat; (da porta) slam; (à porta) knock; (da polícia) raid; (Auto) crash; (bebida) cocktail of cachaça, fruit and sugar

batido, -a [ba'tʃidu, a] ADJ beaten; (roupa) worn ▶ M: **~ de leite** (PT) milk shake

batina [ba'tʃina] F (Rel) cassock

batismo [ba'tʃiʒmu] M baptism, christening

batizar [batʃi'zar] VT to baptize, christen

batom [ba'tõ] (pl **-ns**) M lipstick

batucada [batu'kada] F dance percussion group

batucar [batu'kar] VT, VI to drum

baú [ba'u] M trunk

baunilha [baw'niʎa] F vanilla

bazar [ba'zar] M bazaar; (loja) shop

bêbado, -a ['bebadu, a] ADJ, M/F drunk

bebê [be'be] M baby

bebedeira [bebe'dejra] F drunkenness; **tomar uma ~** to get drunk

bêbedo, -a ['bebedu, a] ADJ, M/F =**bêbado**

bebedouro [bebe'douru] M drinking fountain

beber [be'ber] VT to drink; (absorver) to soak up ▶ VI to drink; **bebida** [be'bida] F drink

beça ['bɛsa] (col) F: **à ~** (com vb) a lot; (com n) a lot of

beco ['beku] M alley, lane; **~ sem saída** cul-de-sac

bege ['bɛʒi] ADJ INV beige

beija-flor [bejʒa'flɔr] (pl **-es**) M hummingbird

beijar [bej'ʒar] VT to kiss; **beijar-se** VR to kiss (one another); **beijo** ['bejʒu] M kiss; **dar beijos em alguém** to kiss sb

beira ['bejra] F edge; (de rio) bank; (orla) border; **à ~ de** on the edge of; (ao lado de) beside, by; (fig) on the verge of; **~ do telhado** eaves pl; **beira-mar** F seaside

belas-artes FPL FINE arts

beldade [bew'dadʒi] F beauty

beleza [be'leza] F beauty; **que ~!** how lovely!

belga ['bɛwga] ADJ, M/F Belgian

Bélgica ['bɛwʒika] F: **a ~** Belgium

beliche [be'liʃi] M bunk

beliscão [belis'kãw] (pl **-ões**) M pinch; **beliscar** [belis'kar] VT to pinch, nip; (comida) to nibble

Belize [be'lizi] M Belize

belo, -a ['bɛlu, a] ADJ beautiful

PALAVRA-CHAVE

bem [bẽj] ADV **1** (*de maneira satisfatória, correta etc*) well; **trabalha/come bem** she works/eats well; **respondeu bem** he answered correctly; **me sinto/não me sinto bem** I feel fine/I don't feel very well; **tudo bem? — tudo bem** how's it going? — fine **2** (*valor intensivo*) very; **um quarto bem quente** a nice warm room; **bem se vê que ...** it's clear that ... **3** (*bastante*) quite, fairly; **a casa é bem grande** the house is quite big **4** (*exatamente*): **bem ali** right there; **não é bem assim** it's not quite like that **5** (*estar bem*): **estou muito bem aqui** I feel very happy here; **está bem!** vou fazê-lo oh all right, I'll do it! **6** (*de bom grado*): **eu bem que iria mas ...** I'd gladly go but ... **7** (*cheirar*) good, nice
▶ M **1** (*bem-estar*) good; **estou dizendo isso para o seu bem** I'm telling you for your own good; **o bem e o mal** good and evil **2** (*posses*): **bens** goods, property *sg*; **bens de consumo** consumer goods; **bens de família** family possessions; **bens móveis/imóveis** moveable property *sg*/real estate *sg*
▶ EXCL **1** (*aprovação*): **bem!** OK!; **muito bem!** well done! **2** (*desaprovação*): **bem feito!** it serves you right!
▶ ADJ INV (*tom depreciativo*): **gente bem** posh people
▶ CONJ **1**: **nem bem** as soon as, no sooner than; **nem bem ela chegou começou a dar ordens** as soon as she arrived she started to give orders, no sooner had she arrived than she started to give orders **2**: **se bem que** though; **gostaria de ir se bem que não tenho dinheiro** I'd like to go even though I've got no money **3**: **bem como** as well as; **o livro bem como a peça foram escritos por ele** the book as well as the play was written by him

bem-conceituado, -a [-kõsej'twadu, a] ADJ highly regarded
bem-disposto, -a [-dʒis'postu, 'pɔsta] ADJ well, in good form
bem-me-quer (*pl* -**es**) M daisy
bem-vindo, -a ADJ welcome
bênção ['bẽsãw] (*pl* -**s**) F blessing
beneficência [benefi'sẽsja] F kindness; (*caridade*) charity
beneficiar [benefi'sjar] VT to benefit; (*melhorar*) to improve; **beneficiar-se** VR to benefit
benefício [bene'fisju] M benefit, profit; (*favor*) favour (BRIT), favor (US); **em ~ de** in aid of; **benéfico, -a** [be'nɛfiku, a] ADJ beneficial; (*generoso*) generous
bengala [bẽ'gala] F walking stick
benigno, -a [be'nignu, a] ADJ kind; (*agradável*) pleasant; (*Med*) benign
bens [bẽjs] MPL *de* **bem**
bento, -a ['bẽtu, a] PP *de* **benzer**
▶ ADJ blessed; (*água*) holy
benzer [bẽ'zer] VT to bless; **benzer-se** VR to cross o.s.
berço ['bersu] M cradle; (*cama*) cot; (*origem*) birthplace
Berlim [ber'lĩ] N Berlin
berma ['berma] (*PT*) F hard shoulder (BRIT), berm (US)

berrar [be'har] vi to bellow; (*criança*) to bawl; **berreiro** [be'hejru] m: **abrir o berreiro** to burst out crying; **berro** ['bɛhu] m yell

besta ['bɛsta] ADJ stupid; (*convencido*) full of oneself; **~ de carga** beast of burden; **besteira** [bes'tejra] F foolishness; **dizer besteiras** to talk nonsense; **fazer uma besteira** to do something silly; **bestial** [bes'tʃjaw] (*pl* **-ais**) ADJ bestial; (*repugnante*) repulsive

best-seller [bɛst'sɛler] (*pl* **-s**) m best seller

betão [be'tãw] (PT) m concrete

beterraba [bete'haba] F beetroot

bexiga [be'ʃiga] F bladder

bezerro, -a [be'zehu, a] m/F calf

BI ABR m *see note*

> All Portuguese citizens are required to carry an identity card, known as the **BI** or *bilhete de identidade*. The photocard, which gives the holder's name, date of birth, marital status, height and a fingerprint, can be used instead of a passport for travel within the European Union. Failure to produce a valid identity card when stopped by the police can result in a fine.

Bíblia ['biblja] F Bible

bibliografia [bibljogra'fia] F bibliography

biblioteca [bibljo'tɛka] F library; (*estante*) bookcase; **bibliotecário, -a** [bibljote'karju, a] m/F librarian

bica ['bika] F tap; (PT) black coffee, expresso

bicha ['biʃa] F (*lombriga*) worm; (PT: *fila*) queue

bicho ['biʃu] m animal; (*inseto*) insect, bug

bicicleta [bisi'klɛta] F bicycle; (*col*) bike; **andar de ~** to cycle

bico ['biku] m (*de ave*) beak; (*ponta*) point; (*de chaleira*) spout; (*boca*) mouth; (*de pena*) nib; (*do peito*) nipple; (*de gás*) jet; (*col: emprego*) casual job; (*chupeta*) dummy; **calar o ~** to shut up

bidê [bi'de] m bidet

bife ['bifi] m (beef) steak; **~ a cavalo** steak with fried eggs; **~ à milanesa** beef escalope; **~ de panela** beef stew

bifurcação [bifurka'sãw] (*pl* **-ões**) F fork

bifurcar-se [bifur'karsi] VR to fork, divide

bigode [bi'gɔdʒi] m moustache

bijuteria [biʒute'ria] F (costume) jewellery (BRIT) *ou* jewelry (US)

bilhão [bi'ʎãw] (*pl* **-ões**) m billion

bilhar [bi'ʎar] m (*jogo*) billiards *sg*

bilhete [bi'ʎetʃi] m ticket; (*cartinha*) note; **~ eletrônico** e-ticket; **~ de ida** single (BRIT) *ou* one-way ticket; **~ de ida e volta** return (BRIT) *ou* round-trip (US) ticket; **bilheteira** [biʎe'tejra] (PT) F ticket office; (*Teatro*) box office; **bilheteiro, -a** [biʎe'tejru, a] m/F ticket seller; **bilheteria** [biʎete'ria] F ticket office

bilhões [bi'ʎõjs] MPL *de* **bilhão**

bilíngue [bi'lĩgwi] ADJ bilingual

binóculo [bi'nɔkulu] m binoculars *pl*; (*para teatro*) opera glasses *pl*

biocombustível [bjokõbus'tʃivew] (*pl* **-eis**) m biofuel

biodiesel [bjo'dʒizew] m biodiesel

biodiversidade [bjodʒiversi'dadʒi] F biodiversity

biografia [bjogra'fia] F biography

biologia [bjolo'ʒia] F biology

biombo ['bjõbu] m screen

bioterrorismo [bjoteho'rizmu] M bioterrorism

bip [bip] N pager

biquíni [bi'kini] M bikini

birita [bi'rita] (col) F drink

biruta [bi'ruta] ADJ crazy ▶ F windsock

bis [bis] EXCL encore!

bisavô, -vó [biza'vo, vɔ] M/F great-grandfather/great-grandmother; **bisavós** [biza'vɔs] MPL great-grandparents

biscate [bis'katʃi] M odd job

biscoito [bis'kojtu] M biscuit (BRIT), cookie (US)

bispo ['bispu] M bishop

bissexto, -a [bi'sestu, a] ADJ: **ano ~** leap year

bit ['bitʃi] M (Comput) bit

bizarro, -a [bi'zahu, a] ADJ bizarre

blasfemar [blasfe'mar] VT to curse ▶ VI to blaspheme; **blasfêmia** [blas'femja] F blasphemy

blazer ['blejzer] (pl -s) M blazer

blecaute [ble'kawtʃi] M power cut

blindado, -a [blĩ'dadu, a] ADJ armoured (BRIT), armored (US)

blitz [blits] F police road block

bloco ['blɔku] M block; (Pol) bloc; (de escrever) writing pad; **~ de carnaval** carnival troupe

blog ['blɔgi] M blog; **blogar** [blo'gar] VI to blog; **blogosfera** [blɔgos'fɛra] F blogosphere; **blogue** ['blɔgi] M blog; **blogueiro, -a** [blo'gejru, a] M/F blogger

bloqueador [blokja'dor] M: **~ solar** sunblock

bloquear [blo'kjar] VT to blockade; (obstruir) to block; **bloqueio** [blo'keju] M (Mil) blockade; (obstrução) blockage

blusa ['bluza] F (de mulher) blouse; (de homem) shirt; **~ de lã** jumper; **blusão** [blu'zãw] (pl -ões) M jacket

boa ['boa] ADJ F de **bom** ▶ F boa constrictor

boate ['bwatʃi] F nightclub

boato ['bwatu] M rumour (BRIT), rumor (US)

bobagem [bo'baʒẽ] (pl -ns) F silliness, nonsense; (dito, ato) silly thing

bobo, -a ['bobu, a] ADJ silly, daft ▶ M/F fool ▶ M (de corte) jester; **fazer-se de ~** to act the fool

bobó [bo'bɔ] M beans, palm oil and manioc

boca ['boka] F mouth; (entrada) entrance; (de fogão) ring; **de ~ aberta** amazed; **bater ~** to argue

bocadinho [boka'dʒiɲu] M: **um ~** (pouco tempo) a little while; (pouquinho) a little bit

bocado [bo'kadu] M mouthful, bite; (pedaço) piece, bit; **um ~ de tempo** quite sometime

boçal [bo'saw] (pl -ais) ADJ ignorant; (grosseiro) uncouth

bocejar [bose'ʒar] VI to yawn; **bocejo** [bo'seʒu] M yawn

bochecha [bo'ʃeʃa] F cheek; **bochecho** [bo'ʃeʃu] M mouthwash

boda ['boda] F wedding; **bodas** FPL (aniversário de casamento) wedding anniversary sg

bode ['bɔdʒi] M goat; **~ expiatório** scapegoat

bofetada [bofe'tada] F slap

bofetão [bofe'tãw] (pl -ões) M punch

boi [boj] M ox

boia ['bɔja] F buoy; (col) grub; (de braço) armband, water wing

boiar [bo'jar] VT, VI to float

boi-bumbá [-bũ'ba] N see note

The **boi-bumbá**, or *bumba-meu-boi*, is a traditional folk dance from north-eastern Brazil, which brings together human, animal and mythological characters in a theatrical performance. The ox, which the dance is named after, is played by a dancer wearing an iron frame covered in pieces of colourful fabric. Eventually the beast is "killed" and its meat is symbolically shared out before it comes back to life in the finale.

boicotar [bojko'tar] VT to boycott; **boicote** [boj'kɔtʃi] M boycott

bola ['bɔla] F ball; **dar ~ para** (*flertar*) to flirt with; **ela não dá a menor ~ (para isso)** she couldn't care less (about it); **não ser certo da ~** (*col*) not to be right in the head

bolacha [bo'laʃa] F biscuit (BRIT), cookie (US); (*col: bofetada*) wallop; (*para chope*) beer mat

boleia [bo'leja] F (*de caminhão*) cab; (PT: *carona*) lift; **dar uma ~ a alguém** (PT) to give sb a lift

boletim [bole'tʃĩ] (*pl* -**ns**) M report; (*publicação*) newsletter; **~ meteorológico** weather forecast

bolha ['boʎa] F (*na pele*) blister; (*de ar, sabão*) bubble

boliche [bo'liʃi] M bowling, skittles *sg*

bolinho [bo'liɲu] M: **~ de carne** meat ball; **~ de arroz/bacalhau** rice/dry cod cake

Bolívia [bo'livja] F: **a ~** Bolivia

bolo ['bolu] M cake; (*monte: de gente*) bunch; (: *de papéis*) bundle; **dar o ~ em alguém** to stand sb up; **vai dar ~** (*col*) there's going to be trouble

bolor [bo'lor] M mould (BRIT), mold

(US); (*nas plantas*) mildew; (*bafio*) mustiness

bolota [bo'lɔta] F acorn

bolsa ['bowsa] F bag; (*Com: tb:* **~ de valores**) stock exchange; **~ (de estudos)** scholarship

bolso ['bowsu] M pocket; **de ~** pocket *atr*

⟨PALAVRA-CHAVE⟩

bom, boa [bõ, 'boa] (*pl* **bons/boas**) ADJ 1 (*ótimo*) good; **é um livro bom** *ou* **um bom livro** it's a good book; **a comida está boa** the food is delicious; **o tempo está bom** the weather's fine; **ele foi muito bom comigo** he was very nice *ou* kind to me

2 (*apropriado*): **ser bom para** to be good for; **acho bom você não ir** I think it's better if you don't go

3 (*irônico*): **um bom quarto de hora** a good quarter of an hour; **que bom motorista você é!** a fine *ou* some driver you are!; **seria bom que ...!** a fine thing it would be if ...!; **essa é boa!** what a cheek!

4 (*saudação*): **bom dia!** good morning!; **boa tarde!** good afternoon!; **boa noite!** good evening!; (*ao deitar-se*) good night!; **tudo bom?** how's it going?

5 (*outras frases*): **está bom?** OK?
▶ EXCL: **bom!** all right!; **bom, ...** right, ...

bomba ['bõba] F bomb; (*Tec*) pump; (*fig*) bombshell; **~ atômica/ relógio/de fumaça** atomic/time/ smoke bomb; **~ de gasolina** petrol (BRIT) *ou* gas (US) pump; **~ de incêndio** fire extinguisher

bombardear [bõbar'dʒjar] VT to bomb; (*fig*) to bombard;

bombardeio [bõbar'deju] M bombing, bombardment; **bombardeio suicida** suicide bombing

bombeiro [bõ'bejru] M fireman; (BR: *encanador*) plumber; **o corpo de ~s** fire brigade

bombom [bõ'bõ] (*pl* **-ns**) M chocolate

bondade [bõ'dadʒi] F goodness, kindness; **tenha a ~ de vir** would you please come

bonde ['bõdʒi] (BR) M tram

bondoso, -a [bõ'dozu, ɔza] ADJ kind, good

boné [bo'nɛ] M cap

boneca [bo'nɛka] F doll

boneco [bo'neku] M dummy

bonito, -a [bo'nitu, a] ADJ pretty; (*gesto, dia*) nice ▶ M (*peixe*) tuna (fish), tunny

bônus ['bonus] M INV bonus

boquiaberto, -a [bokja'bɛrtu, a] ADJ dumbfounded, astonished

borboleta [borbo'leta] F butterfly; (BR: *roleta*) turnstile

borbotão [borbo'tãw] (*pl* **-ões**) M gush, spurt; **sair aos borbotões** to gush out

borbulhar [borbu'ʎar] VI to bubble

borda ['bɔrda] F edge; (*do rio*) bank; **à ~ de** on the edge of

bordado [bor'dadu] M embroidery

bordar [bor'dar] VT to embroider

bordo ['bɔrdu] M (*de navio*) side; **a ~** on board

borra ['bɔha] F dregs *pl*

borracha [bo'haʃa] F rubber; **borracheiro** [boha'ʃejru] M tyre (BRIT) *ou* tire (US) specialist

borrão [bo'hãw] (*pl* **-ões**) M (*rascunho*) rough draft; (*mancha*) blot

borrifar [bohi'far] VT to sprinkle; **borrifo** [bo'hifu] M spray

borrões [bo'hõjs] MPL *de* **borrão**

bosque ['bɔski] M wood, forest

bossa ['bɔsa] F charm; (*inchaço*) swelling; **Bossa nova** (*Mús*) *see note*

> **Bossa nova** is a type of music invented by young, middle-class inhabitants of Rio de Janeiro at the end of the 1950s. It has an obvious jazz influence, an unusual, rhythmic beat and lyrics praising beauty and love. **Bossa nova** became known around the world through the work of the conductor and composer Antônio Carlos Jobim, whose compositions, working with the poet Vinícius de Morais, include the famous song "The Girl from Ipanema".

bota ['bɔta] F boot; **~s de borracha** wellingtons

botânica [bo'tanika] F botany

botão [bo'tãw] (*pl* **-ões**) M button; (*flor*) bud

botar [bo'tar] VT to put; (*roupa, sapatos*) to put on; (*mesa*) to set; (*defeito*) to find; (*ovos*) to lay

bote ['bɔtʃi] M boat; (*com arma*) thrust; (*salto*) spring

botequim [botʃi'kĩ] (*pl* **-ns**) M bar

botija [bo'tʃiʒa] F (earthenware) jug

botões [bo'tõjs] MPL *de* **botão**

boxe ['bɔksi] M boxing

brabo, -a ['brabu, a] ADJ fierce; (*zangado*) angry; (*ruim*) bad; (*calor*) unbearable

braçada [bra'sada] F armful; (*Natação*) stroke

bracelete [brase'letʃi] M bracelet

braço ['brasu] M arm; **de ~s cruzados** with arms folded; (*fig*) without lifting a finger; **de ~ dado** arm-in-arm

bradar [bra'dar] VT, VI to shout, yell; **brado** ['bradu] M shout, yell

braguilha [bra'giʎa] F flies *pl*

branco, -a ['brãku, a] ADJ white ▸ M/F white man/woman ▸ M (*espaço*) blank; **em ~** blank; **noite em ~** sleepless night; **brancura** [brã'kura] F whiteness

brando, -a ['brãdu, a] ADJ gentle; (*mole*) soft

brasão [bra'zãw] (*pl* -**ões**) M coat of arms

braseiro [bra'zejru] M brazier

Brasil [bra'ziw] M: **o ~** Brazil; **brasileiro, -a** [brazi'lejru, a] ADJ, M/F Brazilian

Brasília [bra'zilja] N Brasília

brasões [bra'zõjs] MPL *de* **brasão**

bravata [bra'vata] F bravado, boasting

bravio, -a [bra'viu, a] ADJ (*selvagem*) wild; (*feroz*) ferocious

bravo, -a ['bravu, a] ADJ brave; (*furioso*) angry; (*mar*) rough ▸ M brave man; **~!** bravo!; **bravura** [bra'vura] F courage, bravery

brecar [bre'kar] VT (*carro*) to stop; (*reprimir*) to curb ▸ VI to brake

breu [brew] M tar, pitch

breve ['brɛvi] ADJ short; (*conciso, rápido*) brief ▸ ADV soon; **em ~** soon, shortly; **até ~** see you soon

bridge ['bridʒi] M bridge

briga ['briga] F fight; (*verbal*) quarrel

brigada [bri'gada] F brigade

brigão, -gona [bri'gãw, ɔna] (*pl* -**ões/-s**) ADJ quarrelsome ▸ M/F troublemaker

brigar [bri'gar] VI to fight; (*altercar*) to quarrel

brigões [bri'gõjs] MPL *de* **brigão**

brigona [bri'gona] F *de* **brigão**

brilhante [bri'ʎãtʃi] ADJ brilliant ▸ M diamond

brilhar [bri'ʎar] VI to shine

brincadeira [brĩka'dejra] F fun; (*gracejo*) joke; (*de criança*) game; **deixe de ~s!** stop fooling!; **de ~** for fun

brincalhão, -lhona [brĩka'ʎãw, ɔna] (*pl* -**ões/-s**) ADJ playful ▸ M/F joker, teaser

brincar [brĩ'kar] VI to play; (*gracejar*) to joke; **estou brincando** I'm only kidding; **~ de soldados** to play (at) soldiers; **~ com alguém** to tease sb

brinco ['brĩku] M (*joia*) earring

brindar [brĩ'dar] VT to drink to; (*presentear*) to give a present to; **brinde** ['brĩdʒi] M toast; (*presente*) free gift

brinquedo [brĩ'kedu] M toy

brio ['briu] M self-respect, dignity

brisa ['briza] F breeze

britânico, -a [bri'taniku, a] ADJ British ▸ M/F Briton

broche ['brɔʃi] M brooch

brochura [bro'ʃura] F (*livro*) paperback; (*folheto*) brochure, pamphlet

brócolis ['brɔkolis] MPL broccoli *sg*

bronca ['brõka] (*col*) F telling off; **dar uma ~ em** to tell off; **levar uma ~** to get told off

bronco, -a ['brõku, a] ADJ (*rude*) coarse; (*burro*) thick

bronquite [brõ'kitʃi] F bronchitis

bronze ['brõzi] M bronze; **bronzear** [brõ'zjar] VT to tan; **bronzear-se** VR to get a tan

broto ['brotu] M bud; (*fig*) youngster

broxa ['brɔʃa] F (large) paint brush

bruços ['brusus] MPL: **de ~** face down

bruma ['bruma] F mist, haze

brusco, -a ['brusku, a] ADJ brusque; (*súbito*) sudden

brutal [bru'taw] (*pl* **-ais**) ADJ brutal

bruto, -a ['brutu, a] ADJ brutish; (*grosseiro*) coarse; (*móvel*) heavy; (*petróleo*) crude; (*peso, Com*) gross ▶ M brute; **em ~** raw, unworked

bruxa ['bruʃa] F witch; **bruxaria** [bruʃa'ria] F witchcraft

Bruxelas [bru'ʃelas] N Brussels

bruxo ['bruʃu] M wizard

budismo [bu'dʒizmu] M Buddhism

bufar [bu'far] VI to puff, pant; (*com raiva*) to snort; (*reclamar*) to moan, grumble

bufê [bu'fe] M sideboard; (*comida*) buffet

buffer ['bafer] (*pl* **-s**) M (*Comput*) buffer

bula ['bula] F (*Med*) directions *pl* for use

bule ['buli] M (*de chá*) teapot; (*de café*) coffeepot

Bulgária [buw'garja] F: **a ~** Bulgaria; **búlgaro, -a** ['buwgaru, a] ADJ, M/F Bulgarian ▶ M (*Ling*) Bulgarian

bulimia [buli'mia] F bulimia

bunda ['bũda] (*col*) F bottom, backside

buquê [bu'ke] M bouquet

buraco [bu'raku] M hole; (*de agulha*) eye; **ser um ~** to be tough; **~ da fechadura** keyhole

burguês, -guesa [bur'ges, 'geza] ADJ middle-class, bourgeois; **burguesia** [burge'zia] F middle class, bourgeoisie

burocracia [burokra'sia] F bureaucracy

burro, -a ['buhu, a] ADJ stupid ▶ M/F (*Zool*) donkey; (*pessoa*) fool, idiot; **pra ~** (*col*) a lot; (*com adj*) really; **~ de carga** (*fig*) hard worker

busca ['buska] F search; **em ~ de** in search of; **dar ~ a** to search for

buscador [buska'dor] M search engine

buscar [bus'kar] VT to fetch; (*procurar*) to look *ou* search for; **ir ~** to fetch, go for; **mandar ~** to send for

bússola ['busola] F compass

busto ['bustu] M bust

buzina [bu'zina] F horn; **buzinar** [buzi'nar] VI to sound one's horn, toot the horn ▶ VT to hoot

búzio ['buzju] M conch

b

C

hair; (*postiça*) wig; **cabeleireiro, -a** [kabelej'rejru, a] M/F hairdresser

cabelo [ka'belu] M hair; **cortar/fazer o ~** to have one's hair cut/done; **cabeludo, -a** [kabe'ludu, a] ADJ hairy

caber [ka'ber] VI: **~ (em)** to fit; (*ser compatível*) to be appropriate (in); **~ a** (*em partilha*) to fall to; **cabe a alguém fazer** it is up to sb to do; **não cabe aqui fazer comentários** this is not the time or place to comment

cabide [ka'bidʒi] M (coat) hanger; (*móvel*) hat stand; (*fixo à parede*) coat rack

cabine [ka'bini] F cabin; (*em loja*) fitting room; **~ do piloto** (*Aer*) cockpit; **~ telefônica** telephone box (BRIT) *ou* booth

cabo ['kabu] M (*extremidade*) end; (*de faca, vassoura etc*) handle; (*corda*) rope; (*elétrico etc*) cable; (*Geo*) cape; (*Mil*) corporal; **ao ~ de** at the end of; **de ~ a rabo** from beginning to end; **levar a ~** to carry out; **dar ~ de** to do away with

caboclo, -a [ka'boklu, a] (BR) M/F mestizo

cabra ['kabra] F goat

cabreiro, -a [ka'brejru, a] (*col*) ADJ suspicious

cabrito [ka'britu] M kid

caça ['kasa] F hunting; (*busca*) hunt; (*animal*) quarry, game ▶ M (*Aer*) fighter (plane); **caçador, a** [kasa'dor(a)] M/F hunter

cação [ka'sãw] (*pl* -**ões**) M shark

caçar [ka'sar] VT to hunt; (*com espingarda*) to shoot; (*procurar*) to seek ▶ VI to hunt, go hunting

caçarola [kasa'rɔla] F (sauce)pan

cacau [ka'kaw] M cocoa; (*Bot*) cacao

cá [ka] ADV here; **de cá** on this side; **para cá** here, over here; **para lá e para cá** back and forth; **de lá para cá** since then

caatinga [ka'tʃīga] (BR) F scrub(-land)

cabana [ka'bana] F hut

cabeça [ka'besa] F head; (*inteligência*) brain; (*de uma lista*) top ▶ M/F leader; **de ~** off the top of one's head; (*calcular*) in one's head; **de ~ para baixo** upside down; **por ~** per person, per head; **cabeçada** [kabe'sada] F (*pancada com cabeça*) butt; (*Futebol*) header; (*asneira*) blunder; **cabeçalho** [kabe'saʎu] M (*de livro*) title page; (*de página, capítulo*) heading

cabeceira [kabe'sejra] F (*de cama*) head

cabeçudo, -a [kabe'sudu, a] ADJ with a big head; (*teimoso*) headstrong

cabeleira [kabe'lejra] F head of

cacetada [kase'tada] F blow (with a stick)

cachaça [ka'ʃasa] F (white) rum

cachaceiro, -a [kaʃa'sejru, a] ADJ drunk ▶ M/F drunkard

cachê [ka'ʃe] M fee

cachecol [kaʃe'kɔw] (pl **-óis**) M scarf

cachimbo [ka'ʃĩbu] M pipe

cacho ['kaʃu] M bunch; (de cabelo) curl; (longo) ringlet

cachoeira [kaʃo'wejra] F waterfall

cachorra [ka'ʃoha] F bitch, (female) puppy

cachorrinho, -a [kaʃo'hiɲu, a] M/F puppy

cachorro [ka'ʃohu] M dog, puppy; **cachorro-quente** (pl **cachorros-quentes**) M hot dog

cacique [ka'siki] M (Indian) chief; (mandachuva) local boss

caco ['kaku] M bit, fragment; (pessoa velha) old relic

caçoar [ka'swar] VT, VI to mock

cacoete [ka'kwetʃi] M twitch, tic

cacto ['kaktu] M cactus

cada ['kada] ADJ INV each; (todo) every; **~ um** each one; **~ semana** each week; **a ~ 3 horas** every 3 hours; **~ vez mais** more and more

cadastrar [kadas'trar] VT to register; **cadastrar-se** VR to register

cadastro [ka'dastru] M register; (ato) registration; (de criminosos) criminal record

cadáver [ka'daver] M corpse, (dead) body

cadê [ka'de] (col) ADV: **~ ...?** where's/where are ...?, what's happened to ...?

cadeado [ka'dʒjadu] M padlock

cadeia [ka'deja] F chain; (prisão) prison; (rede) network

cadeira [ka'dejra] F chair; (disciplina) subject; (Teatro) stall; (função) post; **cadeiras** FPL (Anat) hips; **~ de balanço** rocking chair; **~ de rodas** wheelchair

cadela [ka'dɛla] F (cão) bitch

caderneta [kader'neta] F notebook; **~ de poupança** savings account

caderno [ka'dɛrnu] M exercise book; (de notas) notebook; (de jornal) section

caducar [kadu'kar] VI to lapse, expire; **caduco, -a** [ka'duku, a] ADJ invalid, expired; (senil) senile; (Bot) deciduous

cães [kãjs] MPL de **cão**

cafajeste [kafa'ʒɛstʃi] (col) ADJ roguish; (vulgar) vulgar, coarse ▶ M/F rogue; rough customer

café [ka'fɛ] M coffee; (estabelecimento) café; **~ com leite** white coffee (BRIT), coffee with cream (US); **~ preto** black coffee; **~ da manhã** (BR) breakfast

cafeteira [kafe'tejra] F coffeepot; (máquina) percolator; **cafezal** [kafe'zaw] (pl **-ais**) M coffee plantation; **cafezinho** [kafe'ziɲu] M small black coffee

cagada [ka'gada] (!) F shit (!)

cágado ['kagadu] M turtle

cagar [ka'gar] (!) VI to (have a) shit (!)

caguetar [kagwe'tar] VT to inform on; **caguete** [ka'gwetʃi] M informer

caiba ['kajba] VB ver **caber**

cãibra ['kãjbra] F (Med) cramp

caída [ka'ida] F = **queda**

caído, -a [ka'idu, a] ADJ dejected; (derrubado) fallen; (pendente) droopy; **~ por** (apaixonado) in love with

câimbra ['kãjbra] F = **cãibra**

caipirinha [kajpi'riɲa] F *cocktail of cachaça, lemon and sugar*

cair [ka'ir] VI to fall; **~ bem/mal** (*roupa*) to fit well/badly; (*col: pessoa*) to look good/bad; **~ em si** to come to one's senses; **ao ~ da noite** at nightfall; **essa comida me caiu mal** that food did not agree with me

Cairo ['kajru] M: **o ~** Cairo

cais [kajs] M (*Náut*) quay; (*PT Ferro*) platform

caixa ['kajʃa] F box; (*cofre*) safe; (*de uma loja*) cash desk ▶ M/F (*pessoa*) cashier; **~ automática** ou **eletrônico** cash machine; **pequena ~** petty cash; **~ de correio** letter box; **~ de mudanças** (*BR*) ou **de velocidades** gear box; **~ econômica** savings bank; **~ postal** P.O. box; **~ registradora** cash register; **caixa-forte** (*pl* **caixas-fortes**) F vault

caixão [kaj'ʃãw] (*pl* -**ões**) M (*ataúde*) coffin; (*caixa grande*) large box

caixeiro-viajante, caixeira-viajante (*pl* **caixeiros-viajantes/ caixeiras-viajantes**) M/F commercial traveller (*BRIT*) ou traveler (*US*)

caixilho [kaj'ʃiʎu] M (*moldura*) frame

caixões [kaj'ʃõjs] MPL *de* **caixão**

caixote [kaj'ʃɔtʃi] M packing case; **~ do lixo** (*PT*) dustbin (*BRIT*), garbage can (*US*)

caju [ka'ʒu] M cashew fruit

cal [kaw] F lime; (*na água*) chalk; (*para caiar*) whitewash

calabouço [kala'bosu] M dungeon

calado, -a [ka'ladu, a] ADJ quiet

calafrio [kala'friu] M shiver; **ter ~s** to shiver

calamidade [kalami'dadʒi] F calamity, disaster

calão [ka'lãw] M: **(baixo) ~** slang

calar [ka'lar] VT (*não dizer*) to keep quiet about; (*impor silêncio a*) to silence ▶ VI to go quiet; (*manter-se calado*) to keep quiet; **calar-se** VR to go quiet; to keep quiet; **cala a boca!** shut up!

calça ['kawsa] F (*tb*: **~s**) trousers *pl* (*BRIT*), pants *pl* (*US*)

calçada [kaw'sada] F (*PT*: *rua*) roadway; (*BR*: *passeio*) pavement (*BRIT*), sidewalk (*US*)

calçadão [kawsa'dãw] (*pl* -**ões**) M pedestrian precinct (*BRIT*), pedestrian zone (*US*)

calçado, -a [kaw'sadu, a] ADJ (*rua*) paved ▶ M shoe; **calçados** MPL (*para os pés*) footwear *sg*

calçadões [kawsa'dõjs] MPL *de* **calçadão**

calçamento [kawsa'mẽtu] M paving

calcanhar [kawka'ɲar] M (*Anat*) heel

calção [kaw'sãw] (*pl* -**ões**) M shorts *pl*; **~ de banho** swimming trunks *pl*

calcar [kaw'kar] VT to tread on; (*espezinhar*) to trample (on)

calçar [kaw'sar] VT (*sapatos, luvas*) to put on; (*pavimentar*) to pave; **calçar-se** VR to put on one's shoes; **ela calça (número) 28** she takes size 28 (in shoes)

calcário, -a [kaw'karju, a] ADJ (*água*) hard ▶ M limestone

calcinha [kaw'siɲa] F panties *pl*

calço ['kawsu] M wedge

calções [kaw'sõjs] MPL *de* **calção**

calculador [kawkula'dor] M = **calculadora**

calculadora [kawkula'dora] F calculator

calcular [kawku'lar] VT to calculate; (*imaginar*) to imagine; **~ que** to reckon that

cálculo ['kawkulu] M calculation; (*Mat*) calculus; (*Med*) stone

calda ['kawda] F (*de doce*) syrup; **caldas** FPL (*águas termais*) hot springs

caldeirada [kawdej'rada] (*PT*) F (*guisado*) fish stew

caldo ['kawdu] M broth; (*de fruta*) juice; **~ de carne/galinha** beef/chicken stock; **~ verde** potato and cabbage broth

calendário [kalẽ'darju] M calendar

calhar [ka'ʎar] VI: **calhou viajarmos no mesmo avião** we happened to travel on the same plane; **calhou que** it so happened that; **~ a** (*cair bem*) to suit; **se ~** (*PT*) perhaps, maybe

calibre [ka'libri] M (*de cano*) calibre (*BRIT*), caliber (*US*)

cálice ['kalisi] M wine glass; (*Rel*) chalice

calista [ka'lista] M/F chiropodist (*BRIT*), podiatrist (*US*)

calma ['kawma] F calm

calmante [kaw'mãtʃi] ADJ soothing ▶ M (*Med*) tranquilliser

calmo, -a ['kawmu, a] ADJ calm

calo ['kalu] M callus; (*no pé*) corn

calor [ka'lor] M heat; (*fig*) warmth; **está** *ou* **faz ~** it is hot; **estar com ~** to be hot

calorento, -a [kalo'rẽtu, a] ADJ (*pessoa*) sensitive to heat; (*lugar*) hot

caloria [kalo'ria] F calorie

caloroso, -a [kalo'rozu, ɔza] ADJ warm; (*entusiástico*) enthusiastic

calouro, -a [ka'loru, a] M/F (*Educ*) fresher (*BRIT*), freshman (*US*)

calúnia [ka'lunja] F slander

calvo, -a ['kawvu, a] ADJ bald

cama ['kama] F bed; **~ de casal** double bed; **~ de solteiro** single bed; **de ~** (*doente*) ill (in bed)

camada [ka'mada] F layer; (*de tinta*) coat

câmara ['kamara] F chamber; (*PT Foto*) camera; **~ de ar** inner tube; **~ municipal** (*BR*) town council; (*PT*) town hall

camarão [kama'rãw] (*pl* **-ões**) M shrimp; (*graúdo*) prawn

camarões [kama'rõjs] MPL *de* **camarão**

camarote [kama'rɔtʃi] M (*Náut*) cabin; (*Teatro*) box

cambaleante [kãba'ljãtʃi] ADJ unsteady (on one's feet)

cambalhota [kãba'ʎɔta] F somersault

câmbio ['kãbju] M (*dinheiro etc*) exchange; (*preço de câmbio*) rate of exchange; **~ livre** free trade; **~ oficial/paralelo** official/black market

cambista [kã'bista] M money changer

Camboja [kã'bɔja] M: **o ~** Cambodia

camelo [ka'melu] M camel

câmera ['kamera] (*BR*) F camera; **em ~ lenta** in slow motion; **~ de segurança** security camera, CCTV camera; **~ digital** digital camera

camião [ka'mjãw] (*pl* **-ões**) (*PT*) M lorry (*BRIT*), truck (*US*)

caminhada [kami'ɲada] F walk

caminhão [kami'ɲãw] (*pl* **-ões**) (*BR*) M lorry (*BRIT*), truck (*US*)

caminhar [kami'ɲar] VI to walk; (*processo*) to get under way; (*negócios*) to progress

caminho [ka'miɲu] M way;

(*vereda*) road, path; **~ de ferro** (PT) railway (BRIT), railroad (US); **a ~** on the way, en route; **cortar ~** to take a short cut; **pôr-se a ~** to set off

caminhões [kami'ɲõjs] MPL de **caminhão**

caminhoneiro, -a [kamiɲo'nejru, a] M/F lorry driver (BRIT), truck driver (US)

camiões [ka'mjõjs] MPL de **camião**

camioneta [kamjo'neta] (PT) F (*para passageiros*) coach; (*comercial*) van

camionista [kamjo'nista] (PT) M/F lorry driver (BRIT), truck driver (US)

camisa [ka'miza] F shirt; **~ de dormir** nightshirt; **~ de força** straitjacket; **~ esporte/polo/social** sports/polo/dress shirt

camiseta [kami'zɛta] (BR) F T-shirt; (*interior*) vest

camisinha [kami'ziɲa] (col) F condom

camisola [kami'zɔla] F (BR) nightdress; (PT: *pulôver*) sweater; **~ interior** (PT) vest

campainha [kampa'iɲa] F bell

campanário [kãpa'narju] M church tower, steeple

campeão, -peã [kã'pjãw, 'pjã] (pl **-ões/-s**) M/F champion;

campeonato [kãpjo'natu] M championship

campestre [kã'pɛstri] ADJ rural, rustic

camping ['kãpĩŋ] (BR) (pl **-s**) M camping; (*lugar*) campsite

campismo [kã'pizmu] M camping; **parque de ~** campsite

campista [kã'pista] M/F camper

campo [kãpu] M field; (*fora da cidade*) countryside; (*Esporte*) ground; (*acampamento*) camp; (*Tênis*) court

camponês, -esa [kãpo'nes, eza] M/F countryman/woman; (*agricultor*) farmer

campus ['kãpus] M INV campus

camuflagem [kamu'flaʒẽ] F camouflage

camundongo [kamũ'dõgu] (BR) M mouse

camurça [ka'mursa] F suede

cana ['kana] F cane; (col: *cadeia*) nick; (*de açúcar*) sugar cane

Canadá [kana'da] M: **o ~** Canada;

canadense [kana'dẽsi] ADJ, M/F Canadian

canal [ka'naw] (pl **-ais**) M channel; (*de navegação*) canal; (*Anat*) duct

canalização [kanaliza'sãw] F plumbing

canalizador, a [kanaliza'dor(a)] (PT) M/F plumber

canário [ka'narju] M canary

canastra [ka'nastra] F (big) basket

canção [kã'sãw] (pl **-ões**) F song; **~ de ninar** lullaby

cancela [kã'sɛla] F gate

cancelamento [kãsela'mẽtu] M cancellation

cancelar [kãse'lar] VT to cancel; (*riscar*) to cross out

câncer ['kãser] M cancer; **C~** (*Astrologia*) Cancer

canções [kã'sõjs] FPL de **canção**

cancro ['kãkru] (PT) M cancer

candelabro [kãde'labru] M candlestick; (*lustre*) chandelier

candidato, -a [kãdʒi'datu, a] M/F candidate; (*a cargo*) applicant

cândido, -a ['kãdʒidu, a] ADJ naive; (*inocente*) innocent

candomblé [kãdõ'blɛ] M see note

Candomblé is Brazil's most influential Afro-Brazilian religion. Practised mainly in Bahia, it mixes catholicism with

Yoruba traditions. According to **candomblé**, believers become possessed by spirits and thus become an instrument of communication between divine and mortal forces. **Candomblé** ceremonies are great spectacles of African rhythm and dance held in *terreiros*.

caneca [ka'nɛka] F mug

canela [ka'nɛla] F cinnamon; (*Anat*) shin

caneta [ka'neta] F pen; **~ esferográfica** ballpoint pen; **~ pilot** felt-tip pen

cangaceiro [kãga'sejru] (*BR*) M bandit

canguru [kãgu'ru] M kangaroo

canhão [ka'ɲãw] (*pl* **-ões**) M cannon; (*Geo*) canyon

canhoto, -a [ka'ɲotu, a] ADJ left-handed ▶ M/F left-handed person ▶ M (*de cheque*) stub

canibal [kani'baw] (*pl* **-ais**) M/F cannibal

canil [ka'niw] (*pl* **-is**) M kennel

canja ['kãʒa] F chicken broth; (*col*) cinch, pushover

canjica [kã'ʒika] F maize porridge

cano ['kanu] M pipe; (*tubo*) tube; (*de arma de fogo*) barrel; (*de bota*) top; **~ de esgoto** sewer

canoa [ka'noa] F canoe

cansaço [kã'sasu] M tiredness

cansado, -a [kã'sadu, a] ADJ tired

cansar [kã'sar] VT to tire; (*entediar*) to bore ▶ VI to get tired; **cansar-se** VR to get tired; **cansativo, -a** [kãsa'tʃivu, a] ADJ tiring; (*tedioso*) tedious

cantar [kã'tar] VT, VI to sing ▶ M song

canteiro [kã'tejru] M stonemason; (*de flores*) flower bed

cantiga [kã'tʃiga] F ballad; **~ de ninar** lullaby

cantil [kã'tʃiw] (*pl* **-is**) M canteen

cantina [kã'tʃina] F canteen

cantis [kã'tʃis] MPL *de* **cantil**

canto ['kãtu] M corner; (*lugar*) place; (*canção*) song

cantor, a [kã'tor(a)] M/F singer

cão [kãw] (*pl* **cães**) M dog

caolho, -a [ka'oʎu, a] ADJ cross-eyed

caos ['kaos] M chaos

capa ['kapa] F cape; (*cobertura*) cover; **livro de ~ dura/mole** hardback/paperback (book)

capacete [kapa'setʃi] M helmet

capacidade [kapasi'dadʒi] F capacity; (*aptidão*) ability, competence

capaz [ka'paz] ADJ able, capable; **ser ~ de** to be able to (*ou* capable of); **sou ~ de ...** (*talvez*) I might ...; **é ~ de chover hoje** it might rain today

capela [ka'pɛla] F chapel

capim [ka'pĩ] M grass

capitães [kapi'tãjs] MPL *de* **capitão**

capital [kapi'taw] (*pl* **-ais**) ADJ, M capital ▶ F (*cidade*) capital; **~ (em) ações** (*Com*) share capital

capitalismo [kapita'lizmu] M capitalism; **capitalista** [kapita'lista] M/F capitalist

capitalizar [kapitali'zar] VT to capitalize on; (*Com*) to capitalize

capitão [kapi'tãw] (*pl* **-ães**) M captain

capítulo [ka'pitulu] M chapter

capô [ka'po] M (*Auto*) bonnet (*BRIT*), hood (*US*)

capoeira [ka'pwejra] F (*PT*) hencoop

Capoeira is a fusion of martial arts and dance which originated among African slaves in colonial Brazil. It is danced in a circle to the sound of the *berimbau*, a percussion instrument of African origin. Opposed by the Brazilian authorities until the beginning of the twentieth century, today **capoeira** is regarded as a national sport.

capota [ka'pɔta] F (*Auto*) hood, top

capotar [kapo'tar] VI to overturn

capricho [ka'priʃu] M whim, caprice; (*teimosia*) obstinacy; (*apuro*) care; **caprichoso, -a** [kapri'ʃozu, ɔza] ADJ capricious; (*com apuro*) meticulous

Capricórnio [kapri'kɔrnju] M Capricorn

cápsula ['kapsula] F capsule

captar [kap'tar] VT (*atrair*) to win; (*Rádio*) to pick up

captura [kap'tura] F capture; **~ de tela** (*Comput*) screenshot; **capturar** [kaptu'rar] VT to capture

capuz [ka'puz] M hood

cáqui ['kaki] ADJ khaki

cara ['kara] F face; (*aspecto*) appearance ▶ M (*col*) guy; **~ ou coroa?** heads or tails?; **de ~** straightaway; **dar de ~ com** to bump into; **ser a ~ de** (*col*) to be the spitting image of; **ter ~ de** to look (like)

caracol [kara'kɔw] (*pl* -óis) M snail; (*de cabelo*) curl; **escada em ~** spiral staircase

caracteres [karak'tɛris] MPL *de* **caráter**

característica [karakte'ristʃika] F characteristic, feature

característico, -a [karakte'ristʃiku, a] ADJ characteristic

cara de pau F cheek ▶ ADJ INV brazen

caramelo [kara'mɛlu] M caramel; (*bala*) toffee

caranguejo [karã'geʒu] M crab

caratê [kara'te] M karate

caráter [ka'rater] (*pl* **caracteres**) M character

caravana [kara'vana] F caravan

carboidrato [karboi'dratu] M carbohydrate

cardápio [kar'dapju] (BR) M menu

cardeal [kar'dʒjaw] (*pl* -ais) ADJ, M cardinal

cardigã [kardʒi'gã] M cardigan

careca [ka'rɛka] ADJ bald

carecer [kare'ser] VI: **~ de** to lack; (*precisar*) to need

carência [ka'rẽsja] F lack; (*necessidade*) need; (*privação*) deprivation; **carente** [ka'rẽtʃi] ADJ wanting; (*pessoa*) needy, deprived

carga ['karga] F load; (*de navio, avião*) cargo; (*ato de carregar*) loading; (*Elet*) charge; (*fig: peso*) burden; (*Mil*) attack, charge

cargo ['kargu] M responsibility; (*função*) post; **a ~ de** in charge of; **ter a ~** to be in charge of; **tomar a ~** to take charge of

Caribe [ka'ribi] M: **o ~** the Caribbean (Sea)

caridade [kari'dadʒi] F charity; **obra de ~** charity

cárie ['kari] F tooth decay

carimbar [karĩ'bar] VT to stamp; (*no correio*) to postmark

carimbo [ka'rĩbu] M stamp; (*postal*) postmark

carinho [ka'riɲu] M affection, fondness; (*carícia*) caress; **fazer ~** to caress; **com ~** affectionately; (*com cuidado*) with care; **carinhoso, -a** [kari'ɲozu, ɔza] ADJ affectionate

carioca [ka'rjɔka] ADJ of Rio de Janeiro ▶ M/F native of Rio de Janeiro ▶ M (*café*) type of weak coffee

carnal [kar'naw] (*pl* -**ais**) ADJ carnal; **primo ~** first cousin

carnaval [karna'vaw] (*pl* -**ais**) M carnival

> In Brazil, **Carnaval** is the popular festival held each year in the four days before Lent. It is celebrated in very different ways in different parts of the country. In Rio de Janeiro, for example, the big attraction is the parades of the *escolas de samba*, in Salvador the *trios elétricos*, in Recife the *frevo* and, in Olinda, the giant figures, such as the *Homen da meia-noite* and *Mulher do meio-dia*. In Portugal, **Carnaval** is celebrated on Shrove Tuesday, with street parties and processions taking place throughout the country.

carne ['karni] F flesh; (*Culin*) meat; **em ~ e osso** in the flesh

carnê [kar'ne] M (*para compras*) payment book

carneiro [kar'nejru] M sheep; (*macho*) ram; **perna/costeleta de ~** leg of lamb/lamb chop

carnificina [karnifi'sina] F slaughter

caro, -a ['karu, a] ADJ dear; **cobrar/pagar ~** to charge a lot/pay dearly

carochinha [karo'ʃiɲa] F: **conto da ~** fairy tale

caroço [ka'rosu] M (*de frutos*) stone; (*endurecimento*) lump

carona [ka'rɔna] F lift; **viajar de ~** to hitchhike; **pegar uma ~** to get a lift

carpete [kar'pɛtʃi] M (fitted) carpet

carpinteiro [karpĩ'tejru] M carpenter

carrapato [kaha'patu] M (*inseto*) tick

carrasco [ka'hasku] M executioner; (*fig*) tyrant

carregado, -a [kahe'gadu, a] ADJ loaded; (*semblante*) sullen; (*céu*) dark; (*ambiente*) tense

carregador [kahega'dor] M porter

carregamento [kahega'mẽtu] M (*ação*) loading; (*carga*) load, cargo

carregar [kahe'gar] VT to load; (*levar*) to carry; (*bateria*) to charge; (PT: *apertar*) to press; (*levar para longe*) to take away ▶ VI: **~ em** to overdo; (*pôr enfase*) to bring out

carreira [ka'hejra] F run, running; (*profissão*) career; (*Turfe*) race; (*Náut*) slipway; (*fileira*) row; **às ~s** in a hurry

carretel [kahe'tɛw] (*pl* -**éis**) M spool, reel

carrinho [ka'hiɲu] M trolley; (*brinquedo*) toy car; **~ (de criança)** pram; **~ de mão** wheelbarrow; **~ de compras** shopping trolley (BRIT), shopping cart (US)

carro ['kaho] M car; (*de bois*) cart; (*de mão*) barrow; (*de máquina de escrever*) carriage; **~ de corrida** racing car; **~ de passeio** saloon car; **~ de praça** cab; **~ de bombeiro** fire engine; **~ de esporte** sports car

carroça [ka'hɔsa] F cart, wagon

carroçeria [kahose'ria] F (*Auto*) bodywork

carro-chefe (*pl* **carros-chefe(s)**) M (*de desfile*) main float; (*fig*) flagship, centrepiece (BRIT), centerpiece (US)

carrossel [kaho'sɛw] (pl -éis) M merry-go-round

carruagem [ka'hwaʒẽ] (pl -ns) F carriage, coach

carta ['karta] F letter; (de jogar) card; (mapa) chart; **~ aérea** airmail letter; **~ registrada** registered letter; **~ de condução** (PT) driving licence (BRIT), driver's license (US); **dar as ~s** to deal

cartão [kar'tãw] (pl -ões) M card; (PT: material) cardboard; **~ de crédito** credit card; **~ de débito** debit card; **~ de memória** memory card; **~ de recarga** (para celular) top-up card; **~ telefônico** phone card; **cartão-postal** (pl **cartões-postais**) M postcard; (lugar turístico) sight

cartaz [kar'taz] M poster, bill (US); **(estar) em ~** (Teatro, Cinema) (to be) showing

carteira [kar'tejra] F desk; (para dinheiro) wallet; (de ações) portfolio; **~ de identidade** identity card; **~ de motorista** driving licence (BRIT), driver's license (US)

carteiro [kar'tejru] M postman (BRIT), mailman (US)

cartões [kar'tõjs] MPL de **cartão**

cartola [kar'tola] F top hat

cartolina [karto'lina] F card

cartório [kar'tɔrju] M registry office

cartucho [kar'tuʃu] M cartridge; (saco de papel) packet

cartum [kar'tũ] (pl -ns) M cartoon

carvalho [kar'vaʎu] M oak

carvão [kar'vãw] (pl -ões) M coal; (de madeira) charcoal

casa ['kaza] F house; (lar) home; (Com) firm; (Mat: decimal) place; **em/para ~** (at) home/home; **~ de saúde** hospital; **~ da moeda** mint;

~ de banho (PT) bathroom; **~ e comida** board and lodging; **~ de câmbio** bureau de change; **~ de cômodos** tenement; **~ de repouso** old people's home (BRIT), retirement home (US); **~ popular** ≈ council house

casacão [kaza'kãw] (pl -ões) M overcoat

casaco [ka'zaku] M coat; (paletó) jacket

casacões [kaza'kõjs] MPL de **casacão**

casado, -a [ka'zadu, a] ADJ married

casal [ka'zaw] (pl -ais) M couple

casamento [kaza'mẽtu] M marriage; (boda) wedding

casar [ka'zar] VT to marry; (combinar) to match (up); **casar-se** VR to get married; (harmonizar-se) to combine well

casarão [kaza'rãw] (pl -ões) M mansion

casca ['kaska] F (de árvore) bark; (de banana) skin; (de ferida) scab; (de laranja) peel; (de nozes, ovos) shell; (de milho etc) husk; (de pão) crust

cascata [kas'kata] F waterfall

casco ['kasku] M skull; (de animal) hoof; (de navio) hull; (para bebidas) empty bottle; (de tartaruga) shell

caseiro, -a [ka'zejru, a] ADJ home-made; (pessoa, vida) domestic ▶ M/F housekeeper

caso ['kazu] M case; (tb: **~ amoroso**) affair; (estória) story ▶ CONJ in case, if; **no ~** in case (of); **em todo ~** in any case; **neste ~** in that case; **~ necessário** if necessary; **criar ~** to cause trouble; **não fazer ~ de** to ignore; **~ de emergência** emergency

caspa ['kaspa] F dandruff

casquinha [kas'kiɲa] F (de sorvete)

cone; (*pele*) skin
cassar [ka'sar] VT (*direitos, licença*) to cancel, withhold; (*políticos*) to ban
cassete [ka'sɛtʃi] M cassette
cassino [ka'sinu] M casino
castanha [kas'taɲa] F chestnut; **~ de caju** cashew nut; **castanha-do-pará** [-pa'ra] (*pl* **castanhas-do-pará**) F Brazil nut
castanheiro [kasta'ɲejru] M chestnut tree
castanho, -a [kas'taɲu, a] ADJ brown
castelo [kas'tɛlu] M castle
castiçal [kastʃi'saw] (*pl* **-ais**) M candlestick
castiço, -a [kas'tʃisu, a] ADJ pure
castidade [kastʃi'dadʒi] F chastity
castigar [kastʃi'gar] VT to punish; **castigo** [kas'tʃigu] M punishment; (*fig: mortificação*) pain
casto, -a ['kastu, a] ADJ chaste
casual [ka'zwaw] (*pl* **-ais**) ADJ chance *atr*, accidental; (*fortuito*) fortuitous; **casualidade** [kazwali'dadʒi] F chance; (*acidente*) accident
cata ['kata] F: **à ~ de** in search of
catalizador, a [kataliza'dor(a)] ADJ catalytic ▶ M catalyst
catalogar [katalo'gar] VT to catalogue (BRIT), catalog (US)
catálogo [ka'talogu] M catalogue (BRIT), catalog (US); **~ (telefônico)** telephone directory
catapora [kata'pɔra] (BR) F chickenpox
catar [ka'tar] VT to pick (up); (*procurar*) to look for, search for; (*recolher*) to collect, gather
catarata [kata'rata] F waterfall; (*Med*) cataract

catarro [ka'tahu] M catarrh
catástrofe [ka'tastrofi] F catastrophe
cata-vento M weathercock
catedral [kate'draw] (*pl* **-ais**) F cathedral
categoria [katego'ria] F category; (*social*) rank; (*qualidade*) quality; **de alta ~** first-rate
cativar [katʃi'var] VT to enslave; (*fascinar*) to captivate; (*atrair*) to charm
cativeiro [katʃi'vejru] M captivity; (*escravidão*) slavery; (*cadeia*) prison
católico, -a [ka'tɔliku, a] ADJ, M/F Catholic
catorze [ka'torzi] NUM fourteen
catraca [ka'traka] F turnstile; **~ de embarque/desembarque** (*em estação*) ticket barrier
caução [kaw'sãw] (*pl* **-ões**) F security, guarantee; (*Jur*) bail; **sob ~** on bail
caule ['kauli] M stalk, stem
causa ['kawza] F cause; (*motivo*) motive, reason; (*Jur*) lawsuit, case; **por ~ de** because of; **causador, a** [kawza'dor(a)] ADJ which caused ▶ M cause, bring about; **causar** [kaw'zar] VT to cause, bring about
cautela [kaw'tɛla] F caution; (*senha*) ticket; **~ (de penhor)** pawn ticket; **cauteloso, -a** [kawte'lozu, ɔza] ADJ cautious, wary
cavado, -a [ka'vadu, a] ADJ (*olhos*) sunken; (*roupa*) low-cut
cavala [ka'vala] F mackerel
cavaleiro [kava'lejru] M rider, horseman; (*medieval*) knight
cavalheiro, -a [kava'ʎejru, a] ADJ courteous, gallant ▶ M gentleman
cavalo [ka'valu] M horse; (*Xadrez*) knight; **a ~** on horseback;

50 ~s(-vapor), 50 ~s de força 50 horsepower; **~ de corrida** racehorse

cavaquinho [kava'kiɲu] M small guitar

cavar [ka'var] VT to dig; (esforçar-se para obter) to try to get ▶ VI to dig; (fig) to delve; (animal) to burrow

cave ['kavi] (PT) F wine cellar

caveira [ka'vejra] F skull

cavidade [kavi'dadʒi] F cavity

caxumba [ka'ʃũba] F mumps sg

CD ABR M CD

cê [se] (col) PRON = **você**

cear [sjar] VT to have for supper ▶ VI to dine

cebola [se'bola] F onion; **cebolinha** [sebo'liɲa] F spring onion

ceder [se'der] VT to give up; (dar) to hand over; (emprestar) to lend ▶ VI to give in, yield; (porta etc) to give (way)

cedilha [se'dʒiʎa] F cedilla

cedo ['sedu] ADV early; (em breve) soon

cedro ['sɛdru] M cedar

cédula ['sedula] F banknote; (eleitoral) ballot paper

CEE ABR F (= Comunidade Econômica Europeia) EEC

cegar [se'gar] VT to blind; (ofuscar) to dazzle ▶ VI to be dazzling

cego, -a ['sɛgu, a] ADJ blind; (total) complete, total; (tesoura) blunt ▶ M/F blind man/woman; **às cegas** blindly

ceia ['seja] F supper

cela ['sɛla] F cell

celebração [selebra'sãw] (pl **-ões**) F celebration

celebrar [sele'brar] VT to celebrate; (exaltar) to praise; (acordo) to seal

celebridade [selebri'dadʒi] F celebrity

celeiro [se'lejru] M granary; (depósito) barn

celeste [se'lɛstʃi] ADJ celestial, heavenly

celibatário, -a [seliba'tarju, a] ADJ unmarried, single ▶ M/F bachelor/spinster

celofane [selo'fani] M cellophane; **papel ~** cling film

célula ['sɛlula] F (Bio, Elet) cell; **celular** [selu'lar] ADJ cellular ▶ N: **(telefone) celular** mobile (phone) (BRIT), cellphone (US); **celular com câmera** camera phone

cem [sẽ] NUM hundred

cemitério [semi'tɛrju] M cemetery, graveyard

cena ['sɛna] F scene; (palco) stage

cenário [se'narju] M scenery; (Cinema) scenario; (de um acontecimento) setting

cenoura [se'nora] F carrot

censo ['sẽsu] M census

censor, a [sẽ'sor(a)] M/F censor

censura [sẽ'sura] F censorship; (reprovação) censure, criticism; **censurar** [sẽsu'rar] VT to censure; (filme, livro etc) to censor

centavo [sẽ'tavu] M cent; **estar sem um ~** to be penniless

centeio [sẽ'teju] M rye

centelha [sẽ'teʎa] F spark

centena [sẽ'tɛna] F hundred; **às ~s** in hundreds

centenário, -a [sẽte'narju, a] ADJ centenary ▶ M centenary

centígrado [sẽ'tʃigradu] M centigrade

centímetro [sẽ'tʃimetru] M centimetre (BRIT), centimeter (US)

cento ['sẽtu] M: **~ e um** one hundred and one; **por ~** per cent

centopeia [sẽto'peja] F centipede

central [sẽ'traw] (pl **-ais**) ADJ

central ► F (*de polícia etc*) head office; **~ elétrica** (electric) power station; **~ telefônica** telephone exchange; **centralizar** [sẽtrali'zar] VT to centralize

centrar [sẽ'trar] VT to centre (BRIT), center (US)

centro ['sẽtru] M centre (BRIT), center (US); (*de uma cidade*) town centre; **centroavante** [sẽtroa'vãtʃi] M (*Futebol*) centre forward

CEP ['sɛpi] (BR) ABR M (= *Código de Endereçamento Postal*) postcode (BRIT), zip code (US)

cera ['sera] F wax

cerâmica [se'ramika] F pottery

cerca ['serka] F fence ► PREP: **~ de** (*aproximadamente*) around, about; **~ viva** hedge

cercado, -a [ser'kadu, a] ADJ surrounded ► M enclosure; (*para animais*) pen; (*para crianças*) playpen

cercanias [serka'nias] FPL outskirts; (*vizinhança*) neighbourhood *sg* (BRIT), neighborhood *sg* (US)

cerco ['serku] M siege; **pôr ~ a** to besiege

cereal [se'rjaw] (*pl* -**ais**) M cereal

cérebro ['sɛrebru] M brain; (*fig*) brains *pl*

cereja [se'reʒa] F cherry

cerimônia [seri'monja] F ceremony

cerração [seha'sãw] F fog

cerrado, -a [se'hadu, a] ADJ shut, closed; (*denso*) thick ► M scrub(land)

certeza [ser'teza] F certainty; **com ~** certainly, surely; (*provavelmente*) probably; **ter ~ de** to be certain *ou* sure of; **ter ~ de que** to be sure that

certidão [sertʃi'dãw] (*pl* -**ões**) F certificate

certificado [sertʃifi'kadu] M certificate

certificar [sertʃifi'kar] VT to certify; (*assegurar*) to assure; **certificar-se** VR: **~-se de** to make sure of

certo, -a ['sɛrtu, a] ADJ certain, sure; (*exato, direito*) right; (*um, algum*) a certain ► ADV correctly; **na certa** certainly; **ao ~** for certain; **está ~** okay, all right

cerveja [ser'veʒa] F beer; **cervejaria** [serveʒa'ria] F (*fábrica*) brewery; (*bar*) bar, public house

cervical [servi'kaw] (*pl* -**ais**) ADJ cervical

cessação [sesa'sãw] F halting, ceasing

cessão [se'sãw] (*pl* -**ões**) F surrender

cessar [se'sar] VI to cease, stop; **sem ~** continually; **cessar-fogo** M INV cease-fire

cessões [se'sõjs] FPL *de* **cessão**

cesta ['sesta] F basket; **~ básica** food parcel

cesto ['sestu] M basket; (*com tampa*) hamper

cético, -a ['sɛtʃiku, a] M/F sceptic (BRIT), skeptic (US)

cetim [se'tʃĩ] M satin

céu [sɛw] M sky; (*Rel*) heaven; (*da boca*) roof

cevada [se'vada] F barley

CFTV ABR M (= *circuito fechado de TV*) CCTV

chá [ʃa] M tea

chácara ['ʃakara] F farm; (*casa de campo*) country house

chacina [ʃa'sina] F slaughter; **chacinar** [ʃasi'nar] VT (*matar*) to slaughter

chacota [ʃaˈkɔta] F mockery

chafariz [ʃafaˈriz] M fountain

chalé [ʃaˈlɛ] M chalet

chaleira [ʃaˈlejra] F kettle; (*bajulador*) crawler, toady

chama [ˈʃama] F flame

chamada [ʃaˈmada] F call; (*Mil*) roll call; (*Educ*) register; (*no jornal*) headline; **dar uma ~ em alguém** to tell sb off

chamar [ʃaˈmar] VT to call; (*convidar*) to invite; (*atenção*) to attract ▶ VI to call; (*telefone*) to ring; **chamar-se** VR to be called; **chamo-me João** my name is John; **~ alguém de idiota/Dudu** to call sb an idiot/Dudu; **mandar ~** to summon, send for

chamariz [ʃamaˈriz] M decoy

chamativo, -a [ʃamaˈtʃivu, a] ADJ showy, flashy

chaminé [ʃamiˈnɛ] F chimney; (*de navio*) funnel

champanha [ʃãˈpaɲa] M *ou* F champagne

champanhe [ʃãˈpaɲi] M *ou* F = **champanha**

champu [ʃãˈpu] (*PT*) M shampoo

chance [ˈʃãsi] F chance

chantagear [ʃãtaˈʒjar] VT to blackmail

chantagem [ʃãˈtaʒẽ] F blackmail

chão [ʃãw] (*pl* **chãos**) M ground; (*terra*) soil; (*piso*) floor

chapa [ˈʃapa] F (*placa*) plate; (*eleitoral*) list; **~ de matrícula** (*PT Auto*) number (*BRIT*) *ou* license (*US*) plate; **oi, meu ~!** hi, mate!

chapéu [ʃaˈpɛw] M hat

charco [ˈʃarku] M marsh, bog

charme [ˈʃarmi] M charm; **fazer ~** to be nice, use one's charm; **charmoso, -a** [ʃarˈmozu, ɔza] ADJ charming

charrete [ʃaˈhɛtʃi] F cart

charuto [ʃaˈrutu] M cigar

chassi [ʃaˈsi] M (*Auto, Elet*) chassis

chata [ˈʃata] F barge; *ver tb* **chato**

chateação [ʃatʃjaˈsãw] (*pl* **-ões**) F bother, hassle; (*maçada*) bore

chatear [ʃaˈtʃjar] VT to bother, upset; (*importunar*) to pester; (*entediar*) to bore; (*irritar*) to annoy ▶ VI to be upsetting; to be boring; to be annoying; **chatear-se** VR to get upset; to get bored; to get annoyed

chatice [ʃaˈtʃisi] F nuisance

chato, -a [ˈʃatu, a] ADJ flat; (*tedioso*) boring; (*irritante*) annoying; (*que fica mal*) rude ▶ M/F bore; (*quem irrita*) pain

chauvinista [ʃawviˈnista] ADJ chauvinistic ▶ M/F chauvinist

chavão [ʃaˈvãw] (*pl* **-ões**) M cliché

chave [ˈʃavi] F key; (*Elet*) switch; **~ de porcas** spanner; **~ inglesa** (monkey) wrench; **~ de fenda** screwdriver

chávena [ˈʃavena] (*PT*) F cup

checar [ʃeˈkar] VT to check

check-up [tʃeˈkapi] (*pl* **-s**) M check-up

chefe [ˈʃɛfi] M/F head, chief; (*patrão*) boss; **~ de estação** stationmaster; **chefia** [ʃeˈfia] F leadership; (*direção*) management; (*repartição*) headquarters *sg*; **chefiar** [ʃeˈfjar] VT to lead

chegada [ʃeˈgada] F arrival

chegado, -a [ʃeˈgadu, a] ADJ near; (*íntimo*) close

chegar [ʃeˈgar] VT to bring near ▶ VI to arrive; (*ser suficiente*) to be enough; **chegar-se** VR: **~-se a** to approach; **chega!** that's enough!; **~ a** (*atingir*) to reach; (*conseguir*) to manage to

cheio, -a ['ʃeju, a] ADJ full; (*repleto*) full up; (*col: farto*) fed up

cheirar [ʃej'rar] VT, VI to smell; **~ a** to smell of; **cheiro** ['ʃejru] M smell; **ter cheiro de** to smell of; **cheiroso, -a** [ʃej'rozu, ɔza] ADJ: **ser** *ou* **estar cheiroso** to smell nice

cheque ['ʃɛki] M cheque (BRIT), check (US); **~ de viagem** traveller's cheque (BRIT), traveler's check (US)

chiar [ʃjar] VI to squeak; (*porta*) to creak; (*vapor*) to hiss; (*col: reclamar*) to grumble

chiclete [ʃi'klɛtʃi] M chewing gum

chicória [ʃi'kɔrja] F chicory

chicote [ʃi'kɔtʃi] M whip

chifre ['ʃifri] M horn

Chile ['ʃili] M: **o ~** Chile

chimarrão [ʃima'hãw] (*pl* **-ões**) M *mate tea without sugar taken from a pipe-like cup*

chimpanzé [ʃĩpã'zɛ] M chimpanzee

China ['ʃina] F: **a ~** China

chinelo [ʃi'nɛlu] M slipper; **~ (de dedo)** flip-flop

chinês, -esa [ʃi'nes, eza] ADJ, M/F Chinese ▶ M (*Ling*) Chinese

chip ['ʃipi] M (*Comput*) chip

Chipre ['ʃipri] F Cyprus

chique ['ʃiki] ADJ stylish, chic

chocalho [ʃo'kaʎu] M (*Mús, brinquedo*) rattle; (*para animais*) bell

chocante [ʃo'kãtʃi] ADJ shocking; (*col*) amazing

chocar [ʃo'kar] VT to hatch, incubate; (*ofender*) to shock, offend ▶ VI to shock; **chocar-se** VR to crash, collide; to be shocked

chocho, -a ['ʃoʃu, a] ADJ hollow, empty; (*fraco*) weak; (*sem graça*) dull

chocolate [ʃoko'latʃi] M chocolate

chofer [ʃo'fer] M driver

chope ['ʃopi] M draught beer

choque¹ ['ʃɔki] M shock; (*colisão*) collision; (*impacto*) impact; (*conflito*) clash

choque² ['ʃɔki] VB *ver* **chocar**

choramingar [ʃoramĩ'gar] VI to whine, whimper

chorão, -rona [ʃo'rãw, rɔna] (*pl* **-ões/-s**) ADJ tearful ▶ M/F crybaby ▶ M (*Bot*) weeping willow

chorar [ʃo'rar] VT, VI to weep, cry

chorinho [ʃo'riɲu] M *type of Brazilian music*

choro ['ʃoru] M crying; (*Mús*) *type of Brazilian music*

choupana [ʃo'pana] F shack, hut

chouriço [ʃo'risu] M (*BR*) black pudding; (*PT*) spicy sausage

chover [ʃo'ver] VI to rain; **~ a cântaros** to rain cats and dogs

chulé [ʃu'lɛ] M foot odour (BRIT) *ou* odor (US)

chulo, -a ['ʃulu, a] ADJ vulgar

chumbo ['ʃũbu] M lead; (*de caça*) gunshot; (*PT: de dente*) filling; **sem ~** (*gasolina*) unleaded

chupar [ʃu'par] VT to suck

chupeta [ʃu'peta] F dummy (BRIT), pacifier (US)

churrasco [ʃu'hasku] M barbecue; **churrasqueira** [ʃuhas'kejra] F barbecue

churrasquinho [ʃuhas'kiɲu] M kebab

chutar [ʃu'tar] VT to kick; (*col: adivinhar*) to guess at; (: *dar o fora em*) to dump ▶ VI to kick; to guess; (*col: mentir*) to lie

chute ['ʃutʃi] M kick; (*col: mentira*) lie; **dar o ~ em alguém** (*col*) to give sb the boot

chuteira [ʃu'tejra] F football boot

chuva ['ʃuva] F rain; **chuveiro** [ʃu'vejru] M shower

chuviscar [ʃuvis'kar] VI to drizzle; **chuvisco** [ʃu'visku] M drizzle

chuvoso, -a [ʃu'vozu, ɔza] ADJ rainy

Cia. ABR (= *companhia*) Co

cibercafé [siberka'fɛ] M cybercafé

ciberespaço [siberis'pasu] M cyberspace

cicatriz [sika'triz] F scar; **cicatrizar** [sikatri'zar] VI to heal; (*rosto*) to scar

cicerone [sise'rɔni] M tourist guide

ciclismo [si'klizmu] M cycling

ciclista [si'klista] M/F cyclist

ciclo ['siklu] M cycle

ciclovia [siklo'via] F cycle path

cidadã [sida'dã] F *de* **cidadão**

cidadania [sidada'nia] F citizenship

cidadão, cidadã [sida'dãw] (*pl* **-s/-s**) M/F citizen

cidade [si'dadʒi] F town; (*grande*) city

ciência ['sjẽsja] F science

ciente ['sjẽtʃi] ADJ aware

científico, -a [sjẽ'tʃifiku, a] ADJ scientific

cientista [sjẽ'tʃista] M/F scientist

cifra ['sifra] F cipher; (*algarismo*) number, figure; (*total*) sum

cigano, -a [si'ganu, a] ADJ, M/F gypsy

cigarra [si'gaha] F cicada; (*Elet*) buzzer

cigarrilha [siga'hiʎa] F cheroot

cigarro [si'gahu] M cigarette

cilada [si'lada] F ambush; (*armadilha*) trap; (*embuste*) trick

cilindro [si'lĩdru] M cylinder; (*rolo*) roller

cima ['sima] F: **de ~ para baixo** from top to bottom; **para ~** up; **em ~ de** on, on top of; **por ~ de** over; **de ~** from above; **lá em ~** up there; (*em casa*) upstairs; **ainda por ~** on top of that

cimento [si'mẽtu] M cement; (*fig*) foundation

cimo ['simu] M top, summit

cinco ['sĩku] NUM five

cineasta [sine'asta] M/F film maker

cinema [si'nɛma] F cinema

Cingapura [sĩga'pura] F Singapore

cinquenta [sĩ'kwẽta] NUM fifty

cinta ['sĩta] F sash; (*de mulher*) girdle

cinto ['sĩtu] M belt; **~ de segurança** safety belt; (*Auto*) seat belt

cintura [sĩ'tura] F waist; (*linha*) waistline

cinza ['sĩza] ADJ INV grey (BRIT), gray (US) ▶ F ash, ashes *pl*

cinzeiro [sĩ'zejru] M ashtray

cinzento, -a [sĩ'zẽtu, a] ADJ grey (BRIT), gray (US) ▶

cio [siu] M: **no ~** on heat, in season

cipreste [si'prɛstʃi] M cypress (tree)

cipriota [si'prjɔta] ADJ, M/F Cypriot

circo ['sirku] M circus

circuito [sir'kwitu] M circuit

circulação [sirkula'sãw] F circulation

circular [sirku'lar] ADJ circular ▶ F (*carta*) circular ▶ VI to circulate; (*girar, andar*) to go round ▶ VT to circulate; (*estar em volta de*) to surround; (*percorrer em roda*) to go round

círculo ['sirkulu] M circle

circundar [sirkũ'dar] VT to surround

circunferência [sirkũfe'rẽsja] F circumference

circunflexo, -a [sirkũ'flɛksu, a] ADJ circumflex ▶ M circumflex (accent)

circunstância [sirkũ'stãsja] F

circumstance; **~s atenuantes** mitigating circumstances

cirurgia [sirur'ʒia] F surgery; **~ plástica/estética** plastic/cosmetic surgery

cirurgião, -giã [sirur'ʒjãw, 'ʒjã] (pl **-ões/-s**) M/F surgeon

cisco ['sisku] M speck

cismado, -a [siz'madu, a] ADJ with fixed ideas

cismar [siz'mar] VI (pensar): **~ em** to brood over; (antipatizar): **~ com** to take a dislike to ▶ VT: **~ que** to be convinced that; **~ de** ou **em fazer** (meter na cabeça) to get into one's head to do; (insistir) to insist on doing

cisne ['sizni] M swan

cisterna [sis'tɛrna] F cistern, tank

citação [sita'sãw] (pl **-ões**) F quotation; (Jur) summons sg

citar [si'tar] VT to quote; (Jur) to summon

ciúme ['sjumi] M jealousy; **ter ~s de** to be jealous of; **ciumento, -a** [sju'mẽtu, a] ADJ jealous

cívico, -a ['siviku, a] ADJ civic

civil [si'viw] (pl **-is**) ADJ civil ▶ M/F civilian; **civilidade** [sivili'dadʒi] F politeness

civilização [siviliza'sãw] (pl **-ões**) F civilization

civis [si'vis] PL de **civil**

clamar [kla'mar] VT to clamour (BRIT) ou clamor (US) for ▶ VI to cry out, clamo(u)r

clamor [kla'mor] M outcry, uproar

clandestino, -a [klãdes'tʃinu, a] ADJ clandestine; (ilegal) underground

clara ['klara] F egg white

clarão [kla'rãw] (pl **-ões**) M (cintilação) flash; (claridade) gleam

clarear [kla'rjar] VI (dia) to dawn; (tempo) to clear up, brighten up ▶ VT to clarify

claridade [klari'dadʒi] F brightness

clarim [kla'rĩ] (pl **-ns**) M bugle

clarinete [klari'netʃi] M clarinet

clarins [kla'rĩs] MPL de **clarim**

claro, -a ['klaru, a] ADJ clear; (luminoso) bright; (cor) light; (evidente) clear, evident ▶ M (na escrita) space; (clareira) clearing ▶ ADV clearly; **~!** of course!; **~ que sim!/não!** of course!/of course not!; **às claras** openly

classe ['klasi] F class; **~ econômica/executiva** economy/business class

clássico, -a ['klasiku, a] ADJ classical; (fig) classic; (habitual) usual ▶ M classic

classificação [klasifika'sãw] (pl **-ões**) F classification; (Esporte) place, placing

classificado, -a [klasifi'kadu, a] ADJ (em exame) successful; (anúncio) classified; (Esporte) placed ▶ M classified ad

classificar [klasifi'kar] VT to classify; **classificar-se** VR: **~-se de algo** to call o.s. sth, describe o.s. as sth

cláusula ['klawzula] F clause

clausura [klaw'zura] F enclosure

clavícula [kla'vikula] F collar bone

clemência [kle'mẽsja] F mercy

clero ['klɛru] M clergy

clicar [kli'kar] VI (Comput) to click; **~ duas vezes em** to double-click on

cliente ['kljẽtʃi] M client; customer; (de médico) patient; **clientela** [kljẽ'tɛla] F clientele; (de loja) customers pl

clima ['klima] M climate

clímax ['klimaks] M INV climax

clipe ['klipi] M clip; (*para papéis*) paper clip

clique ['kliki] M (*Comput*) click

cloro ['klɔru] M chlorine

close ['klɔzi] M close-up

clube ['klubi] M club

coadjuvante [koadʒu'vãtʃi] ADJ supporting ▶ M/F (*num crime*) accomplice; (*Teatro, Cinema*) co-star

coador [koa'dor] M strainer; (*de café*) filter bag; (*para legumes*) colander

coalhada [koa'ʎada] F curd

coalizão [koali'zãw] (*pl* **-ões**) F coalition

coar [ko'ar] VT (*líquido*) to strain

coberta [ko'bɛrta] F cover, covering; (*Náut*) deck

cobertor [kober'tor] M blanket

cobertura [kober'tura] F covering; (*telhado*) roof; (*apartamento*) penthouse; (*TV, Rádio, Jornalismo*) coverage; (*Seguros*) cover; (*Tel*) network coverage; **aqui não tem ~** there's no network coverage here

cobiça [ko'bisa] F greed

cobra ['kɔbra] F snake

cobrador, a [kobra'dor(a)] M/F collector; (*em transporte*) conductor; **~ de ônibus** bus conductor

cobrança [ko'brãsa] F collection; (*ato de cobrar*) charging

cobrar [ko'brar] VT to collect; (*preço*) to charge

cobre ['kɔbri] M copper; **cobres** MPL (*dinheiro*) money *sg*

cobrir [ko'brir] VT to cover

cocada [ko'kada] F coconut sweet

cocaína [koka'ina] F cocaine

coçar [ko'sar] VT to scratch ▶ VI to itch; **coçar-se** VR to scratch o.s.

cócegas ['kɔsegas] FPL: **fazer ~ em** to tickle; **tenho ~ nos pés** I have tickly feet; **sentir ~** to be ticklish

coceira [ko'sejra] F itch; (*qualidade*) itchiness

cochichar [koʃi'ʃar] VI to whisper; **cochicho** [ko'ʃiʃu] M whispering

cochilar [koʃi'lar] VI to snooze, doze; **cochilo** [ko'ʃilu] M nap

coco ['koku] M coconut

cócoras ['kɔkoras] FPL: **de ~** squatting; **ficar de ~** to squat (down)

código ['kɔdʒigu] M code; **~ de barras** bar code

coelho [ko'eʎu] M rabbit

coerente [koe'rẽtʃi] ADJ coherent; (*consequente*) consistent

cofre ['kɔfri] M safe; (*caixa*) strongbox; **os ~s públicos** public funds

cogitar [koʒi'tar] VT, VI to contemplate

cognitivo, -a [kogni'tʃivu, a] ADJ cognitive

cogumelo [kogu'mɛlu] M mushroom; **~ venenoso** toadstool

coice ['kojsi] M kick; (*de arma*) recoil; **dar ~s em** to kick

coincidência [koĩsi'dẽsja] F coincidence

coincidir [koĩsi'dʒir] VI to coincide; (*concordar*) to agree

coisa ['kojza] F thing; (*assunto*) matter; **~ de** about

coitado, -a [koj'tadu, a] ADJ poor, wretched

cola ['kɔla] F glue

colaborador, a [kolabora'dor(a)] M/F collaborator; (*em jornal*) contributor

colaborar [kolabo'rar] VI to collaborate; (*ajudar*) to help; (*escrever artigos etc*) to contribute

colante [ko'lãtʃi] ADJ (*roupa*) skin-tight

colapso [ko'lapsu] M collapse;
~ **cardíaco** heart failure

colar [ko'lar] VT to stick, glue; (BR:
copiar) to crib ▶ VI to stick; to cheat
▶ M necklace

colarinho [kola'riɲu] M collar

colarinho-branco (*pl*
colarinhos-brancos) M
white-collar worker

colcha ['kowʃa] F bedspread

colchão [kow'ʃãw] (*pl* **-ões**) M
mattress

colchete [kow'ʃetʃi] M clasp,
fastening; (*parêntese*) square
bracket; ~ **de gancho** hook and
eye; ~ **de pressão** press stud,
popper

colchões [kow'ʃõjs] MPL *de*
colchão

coleção [kole'sãw] (*pl* **coleções**) F
collection; **colecionador, a**
[kolesjona'dor(a)] M/F collector;
colecionar [kolesjo'nar] VT to
collect

colega [ko'lɛga] M/F colleague;
(*de escola*) classmate

colegial [kole'ʒjaw] (*pl* **-ais**) M/F
schoolboy/girl

colégio [ko'lɛʒu] M school

coleira [ko'lejra] F collar

cólera ['kɔlera] F anger ▶ M *ou* F
(*Med*) cholera

colesterol [koleste'rɔw] M
cholesterol

colete [ko'letʃi] M waistcoat
(BRIT), vest (US); ~ **salva-vidas** life
jacket (BRIT), life preserver (US)

coletivo, -a [kole'tʃivu, a] ADJ
collective; (*transportes*) public
▶ M bus

colheita [ko'ʎejta] F harvest

colher [ko'ʎer] VT to gather, pick;
(*dados*) to gather ▶ F spoon; ~ **de
chá/sopa** teaspoon/tablespoon

colidir [koli'dʒir] VI: ~ **com**
to collide with, crash into

coligação [koliga'sãw] (*pl* **-ões**) F
coalition

colina [ko'lina] F hill

colisão [koli'zãw] (*pl* **-ões**) F
collision

collant [ko'lã] (*pl* **-s**) M tights *pl*
(BRIT), pantyhose (US); (*blusa*)
leotard

colmeia [kow'meja] F beehive

colo ['kɔlu] M neck; (*regaço*) lap

colocar [kolo'kar] VT to put, place;
(*empregar*) to find a job for, place;
(*Com*) to market; (*pneus, tapetes*) to
fit; (*questão, ideia*) to put forward

Colômbia [ko'lõbja] F: **a ~**
Colombia

colônia [ko'lonja] F colony;
(*perfume*) cologne; **colonial**
[kolo'njaw] (*pl* **-ais**) ADJ colonial

colonizador, a [koloniza'dor(a)]
M/F colonist, settler

coloquial [kolo'kjaw] (*pl* **-ais**) ADJ
colloquial

colóquio [ko'lɔkju] M conversation;
(*congresso*) conference

colorido, -a [kolo'ridu, a] ADJ
colourful (BRIT), colorful (US)
▶ M colouring (BRIT), coloring (US)

colorir [kolo'rir] VT to colour
(BRIT), color (US)

coluna [ko'luna] F column; (*pilar*)
pillar; ~ **dorsal** *ou* **vertebral**
spine; **colunável** [kolu'navew]
(*pl* **-eis**) ADJ famous ▶ M/F
celebrity; **colunista** [kolu'nista]
M/F columnist

com [kõ] PREP with; **estar ~ fome**
to be hungry; ~ **cuidado** carefully;
estar ~ dinheiro/câncer to have
some money on one/have cancer

coma ['kɔma] F coma

comandante [komã'dãtʃi] M

commander; (*Mil*) commandant;
(*Náut*) captain
comandar [komã'dar] VT to
command
comando [ko'mãdu] M command
combate [kõ'batʃi] M combat;
combater [kõba'ter] VT to fight;
(*opor-se a*) to oppose ▶ VI to fight;
combater-se VR to fight
combinação [kõbina'sãw] (*pl
-ões*) F combination; (*Quím*)
compound; (*acordo*) arrangement;
(*plano*) scheme; (*roupa*) slip
combinar [kõbi'nar] VT to
combine; (*jantar etc*) to arrange;
(*fuga etc*) to plan ▶ VI (*roupas etc*) to
go together; **combinar-se** VR to
combine; (*pessoas*) to get on well
together; **~ com** (*harmonizar-se*) to
go with; **~ de fazer** to arrange to
do; **combinado!** agreed!
comboio [kõ'boju] M (*PT*) train; (*de
navios, carros*) convoy
combustível [kõbus'tʃivew] M fuel
começar [kome'sar] VT, VI to begin,
start; **~ a fazer** to begin *ou* start to
do
começo [ko'mesu] M beginning,
start
comédia [ko'mɛdʒja] F comedy
comemorar [komemo'rar] VT to
commemorate, celebrate
comentar [komẽ'tar] VT to
comment on; (*maliciosamente*) to
make comments about
comentário [komẽ'tarju] M
comment, remark; (*análise*)
commentary
comer [ko'mer] VT to eat; (*Damas,
Xadrez*) to take, capture ▶ VI to eat;
dar de ~ a to feed
comercial [komer'sjaw] (*pl -ais*)
ADJ commercial; (*relativo ao negócio*)
business *atr* ▶ M commercial

comercializar [komersjali'zar] VT
to market
comerciante [komer'sjãtʃi] M/F
trader
comércio [ko'mɛrsju] M
commerce; (*tráfico*) trade; (*negócio*)
business; (*lojas*) shops *pl*;
~ eletrônico e-commerce; **~ justo**
fair trade
comes ['kɔmis] MPL: **~ e bebes**
food and drink
comestíveis [komes'tʃiveis] MPL
foodstuffs, food *sg*
comestível [komes'tʃivew] (*pl -eis*)
ADJ edible
cometer [kome'ter] VT to commit
comício [ko'misju] M (*Pol*) rally,
meeting; (*assembleia*) assembly
cômico, -a ['komiku, a] ADJ
comic(al) ▶ M comedian; (*de teatro*)
actor
comida [ko'mida] F (*alimento*) food;
(*refeição*) meal; **~ pronta** ready
meal (*BRIT*), TV dinner (*US*)
comigo [ko'migu] PRON with me
comilão, -lona [komi'lãw, lɔna]
(*pl -ões/-s*) ADJ greedy ▶ M/F
glutton
comiserar [komize'rar] VT to move
to pity; **comiserar-se** VR: **~-se (de)**
to sympathize (with)
comissão [komi'sãw] (*pl -ões*) F
commission; (*comitê*) committee
comissário [komi'sarju] M
commissioner; (*Com*) agent; **~ de
bordo** (*Aer*) steward; (*Náut*) purser
comissões [komi'sõjs] FPL *de*
comissão
comitê [komi'te] M committee

(PALAVRA-CHAVE)

como ['kɔmu] ADV **1** (*modo*) as; **ela
fez como eu pedi** she did as I
asked; **como se** as if; **como quiser**

as you wish; **seja como for** be that as it may

2 (*assim como*) like; **ela tem olhos azuis como o pai** she has blue eyes like her father's; **ela trabalha numa loja, como a mãe** she works in a shop, as does her mother

3 (*de que maneira*) how; **como?** pardon?; **como!** what!; **como assim?** what do you mean?; **como não!** of course!

▶ CONJ (*porque*) as, since; **como estava tarde ele dormiu aqui** since it was late he slept here

comoção [komo'sãw] (*pl* **-ões**) F distress; (*revolta*) commotion

cômoda ['komoda] F chest of drawers (BRIT), bureau (US)

comodidade [komodʒi'dadʒi] F comfort; (*conveniência*) convenience

comodismo [komo'dʒizmu] M complacency

cômodo, -a ['komodu, a] ADJ comfortable; (*conveniente*) convenient ▶ M room

comovente [komo'vẽtʃi] ADJ moving, touching

comover [komo'ver] VT to move ▶ VI to be moving; **comover-se** VR to be moved

compacto, -a [kõ'paktu, a] ADJ compact; (*espesso*) thick; (*sólido*) solid ▶ M (*disco*) single

compadecer-se [kõpade'sersi] VR: **~ de** to pity

compadre [kõ'padri] M (*col: companheiro*) buddy, pal

compaixão [kõpaj'ʃãw] M compassion; (*misericórdia*) mercy

companheiro, -a [kõpa'ɲejru, a] M/F companion; (*colega*) friend;

(*col*) buddy, mate

companhia [kõpa'ɲia] F company

comparação [kõpara'sãw] (*pl* **-ões**) F comparison

comparar [kõpa'rar] VT to compare; **~ com** to compare with; **~ a** to liken to

comparecer [kõpare'ser] VI to appear, make an appearance; **~ a uma reunião** to attend a meeting

comparsa [kõ'parsa] M/F (*Teatro*) extra; (*cúmplice*) accomplice

compartilhar [kõpartʃi'ʎar] VT to share ▶ VI: **~ de** to share in, participate in

compartimento [kõpartʃi'mẽtu] M compartment; (*aposento*) room

compasso [kõ'pasu] M (*instrumento*) pair of compasses; (*Mús*) time; (*ritmo*) beat

compatível [kõpa'tʃivew] (*pl* **-eis**) ADJ compatible

compensar [kõpẽ'sar] VT to make up for, compensate for; (*equilibrar*) to offset; (*cheque*) to clear

competência [kõpe'tẽsja] F competence, ability; (*responsabilidade*) responsibility; **competente** [kõpe'tẽtʃi] ADJ competent; (*apropriado*) appropriate; (*responsável*) responsible

competição [kõpetʃi'sãw] (*pl* **-ões**) F competition

competidor, a [kõpetʃi'dor(a)] M/F competitor

competir [kõpe'tʃir] VI to compete; **~ a alguém** to be sb's responsibility; (*caber*) to be up to sb

competitivo, -a [kõpetʃi'tʃivu, a] ADJ competitive

compito [kõ'pitu] VB *ver* **competir**

complementar [kõplemē'tar] ADJ complementary ▶ VT to supplement

complemento [kõple'mētu] M complement

completamente [kõpleta'mētʃi] ADV completely, quite

completar [kõple'tar] VT to complete; to fill up; **~ dez anos** to be ten

completo, -a [kõ'plɛtu, a] ADJ complete; (cheio) full (up); **por ~** completely

complexo, -a [kõ'plɛksu, a] ADJ complex ▶ M complex

complicação [kõplika'sãw] (pl -ões) F complication

complicado, -a [kõpli'kadu, a] ADJ complicated

complicar [kõpli'kar] VT to complicate

complô [kõ'plo] M plot, conspiracy

componente [kõpo'nētʃi] ADJ, M component

compor [kõ'por] (irreg: como **pôr**) VT to compose; (discurso, livro) to write; (arranjar) to arrange ▶ VI to compose; **compor-se** VR (controlar-se) to compose o.s.; **~-se de** to consist of

comportamento [kõporta'mētu] M behaviour (BRIT), behavior (US)

comportar [kõpor'tar] VT to put up with; **comportar-se** VR (portar-se) to behave; **~-se mal** to misbehave, behave badly

composição [kõpozi'sãw] (pl -ões) F composition; (Tip) typesetting

compositor, a [kõpozi'tor(a)] M/F composer; (Tip) typesetter

compota [kõ'pɔta] F fruit in syrup

compra ['kõpra] F purchase; **fazer ~s** to go shopping; **comprador, a** [kõpra'dor(a)] M/F buyer, purchaser

comprar [kõ'prar] VT to buy

compreender [kõprjen'der] VT to understand; (constar de) to comprise, consist of, be composed of; (abranger) to cover

compreensão [kõprjẽ'sãw] F understanding, comprehension; **compreensivo, -a** [kõprjẽ'sivu, a] ADJ understanding

compressa [kõ'prɛsa] F compress

comprido, -a [kõ'pridu, a] ADJ long; (alto) tall; **ao ~** lengthways

comprimento [kõpri'mētu] M length

comprimido, -a [kõpri'midu, a] ADJ compressed ▶ M pill; tablet

comprimir [kõpri'mir] VT to compress

comprometer [kõprome'ter] VT to compromise; (envolver) to involve; (arriscar) to jeopardize; (empenhar) to pledge; **comprometer-se** VR: **~-se a** to undertake to, promise to

compromisso [kõpro'misu] M promise; (obrigação) commitment; (hora marcada) appointment; (acordo) agreement

comprovante [kõpro'vãtʃi] M receipt; **~ de residência** proof of address

comprovar [kõpro'var] VT to prove; (confirmar) to confirm

compulsivo, -a [kõpuw'sivu, a] ADJ compulsive

compulsório, -a [kõpuw'sɔrju, a] ADJ compulsory

computação [kõputa'sãw] F computer science, computing; **~ em nuvem** cloud computing

computador [kõputa'dor] M computer

computar [kõpu'tar] VT (calcular) to calculate; (contar) to count

comum [ko'mũ] (pl -ns) ADJ

ordinary, common; (*habitual*) usual; **em ~** in common

comungar [komũ'gar] vı to take communion

comunhão [komu'ɲãw] (*pl* **-ões**) F communion

comunicação [komunika'sãw] (*pl* **-ões**) F communication; (*mensagem*) message; (*acesso*) access

comunicado [komuni'kadu] M notice

comunicar [komuni'kar] vt, vı to communicate; **comunicar-se** vr to communicate; **~-se com** (*entrar em contato*) to get in touch with

comunidade [komuni'dadʒi] F community; **C~ (Econômica) Europeia** European (Economic) Community

comunismo [komu'nizmu] M communism; **comunista** [komu'nista] ADJ, M/F communist

comuns [ko'mũs] PL *de* **comum**

conceber [kõse'ber] vt, vı to conceive

conceder [kõse'der] vt to allow; (*outorgar*) to grant; (*dar*) to give ▶ vı: **~ em** to agree to

conceito [kõ'sejtu] M concept, idea; (*fama*) reputation; (*opinião*) opinion; **conceituado, -a** [kõsej'twadu, a] ADJ well thought of, highly regarded

concentração [kõsẽtra'sãw] (*pl* **-ões**) F concentration

concepção [kõsep'sãw] (*pl* **-ões**) F (*geração*) conception; (*noção*) idea, concept; (*opinião*) opinion

concerto [kõ'sertu] M concert

concessão [kõse'sãw] (*pl* **-ões**) F concession; (*permissão*) permission

concha ['kõʃa] F shell; (*para líquidos*) ladle

conchavo [kõ'ʃavu] M conspiracy

conciliar [kõsi'ljar] vt to reconcile

concluir [kõ'klwir] vt, vı to conclude

conclusão [kõklu'zãw] (*pl* **-ões**) F end; (*dedução*) conclusion

conclusões [kõklu'zõjs] FPL *de* **conclusão**

concordância [kõkor'dãsja] F agreement

concordar [kõkor'dar] vı, vt to agree

concorrência [kõko'hẽsja] F competition; (*a um cargo*) application

concorrente [kõko'hẽtʃi] M/F contestant; (*candidato*) candidate

concorrer [kõko'her] vı to compete; **~ a** to apply for

concretizar [kõkretʃi'zar] vt to make real; **concretizar-se** vr (*sonho*) to come true; (*ambições*) to be realized

concreto, -a [kõ'krɛtu, a] ADJ concrete ▶ M concrete

concurso [kõ'kursu] M contest; (*exame*) competition

conde ['kõdʒi] M count

condenar [kõde'nar] vt to condemn; (*Jur: sentenciar*) to sentence; (: *declarar culpado*) to convict

condensar [kõdẽ'sar] vt to condense; **condensar-se** vr to condense

condessa [kõ'desa] F countess

condimento [kõdʒi'mẽtu] M seasoning

condomínio [kõdo'minju] M condominium; **~ fechado** gated community

condução [kõdu'sãw] F driving; (*transporte*) transport; (*ônibus*) bus

condutor, a [kõdu'tor(a)] M/F (*de*

veículo) driver ▶ M (*Elet*) conductor

conduzir [kõdu'zir] VT (*levar*) to lead; (*Fís*) to conduct; **conduzir-se** VR to behave; **~ a** to lead to

cone ['kɔni] M cone

conectar [konek'tar] VT to connect

conexão [konek'sãw] (*pl* **-ões**) F connection; (*voo*) connecting flight

confecção [kõfek'sãw] (*pl* **-ões**) F making; (*de um boletim*) production; (*roupa*) ready-to-wear clothes *pl*; (*negócio*) business selling ready-to-wear clothes

confeccionar [kõfeksjo'nar] VT to make; (*fabricar*) to manufacture

confecções [kõfek'sõjs] FPL *de* **confecção**

confeitaria [kõfejta'ria] F patisserie

conferência [kõfe'rẽsja] F conference; (*discurso*) lecture

conferir [kõfe'rir] VT to check; (*comparar*) to compare; (*outorgar*) to grant ▶ VI to tally

confessar [kõfe'sar] VT, VI to confess; **confessar-se** VR to confess

confiança [kõ'fjãsa] F confidence; (*fé*) trust; **de ~** reliable; **ter ~ em alguém** to trust sb

confiar [kõ'fjar] VT to entrust; (*segredo*) to confide ▶ VI: **~ em** to trust; (*ter fé*) to have faith in

confiável [kõ'fjavew] (*pl* **-eis**) ADJ reliable

confidência [kõfi'dẽsja] F secret; **em ~** in confidence; **confidencial** [kõfidẽ'sjaw] (*pl* **-ais**) ADJ confidential

confirmação [kõfirma'sãw] (*pl* **-ões**) F confirmation

confirmar [kõfir'mar] VT to confirm

confiro [kõ'firu] VB *ver* **conferir**

confissão [kõfi'sãw] (*pl* **-ões**) F confession

conformar [kõfor'mar] VT to form ▶ VI: **~ com** to conform to; **conformar-se** VR: **~-se com** to resign o.s. to; (*acomodar-se*) to conform to

conforme [kõ'fɔrmi] PREP according to; (*dependendo de*) depending on ▶ CONJ (*logo que*) as soon as; (*como*) as, according to what; (*à medida que*) as; **você vai? — ~** are you going? — it depends

conformidade [kõformi'dadʒi] F agreement; **em ~ com** in accordance with

confortar [kõfor'tar] VT to comfort, console

confortável [kõfor'tavew] (*pl* **-eis**) ADJ comfortable

conforto [kõ'fortu] M comfort

confrontar [kõfrõ'tar] VT to confront; (*comparar*) to compare

confronto [kõ'frõtu] M confrontation; (*comparação*) comparison

confusão [kõfu'zãw] (*pl* **-ões**) F confusion; (*tumulto*) uproar; (*problemas*) trouble

confuso, -a [kõ'fuzu, a] ADJ confused; (*problema*) confusing

confusões [kõfu'zõjs] FPL *de* **confusão**

congelador [kõʒela'dor] M freezer, deep freeze

congelamento [kõʒela'mẽtu] M freezing; (*Econ*) freeze

congelar [kõʒe'lar] VT to freeze; **congelar-se** VR to freeze

congestão [kõʒes'tãw] F congestion; **congestionado, -a** [kõʒestʃjo'nadu, a] ADJ congested; (*olhos*) bloodshot; (*rosto*) flushed; **congestionamento** [kõʒestʃjona'mẽtu] M congestion; **um congestionamento (de**

tráfego) a traffic jam

congestionar [kõʒestʃjo'nar] vt
to congest; **congestionar-se** vr
(rosto) to go red

congressista [kõgre'sista] m/f
congressman/woman

congresso [kõ'grɛsu] m congress,
conference

conhaque [ko'ɲaki] m cognac,
brandy

conhecedor, a [koɲese'dor(a)]
adj knowing ▶ m/f connoisseur,
expert

conhecer [koɲe'ser] vt to know;
(travar conhecimento com) to meet;
(descobrir) to discover;
conhecer-se vr to meet; (ter
conhecimento) to know each other

conhecido, -a [koɲe'sidu, a] adj
known; (célebre) well-known
▶ m/f acquaintance

conhecimento [koɲesi'mẽtu] m
knowledge; (ideia) idea;
(conhecido) acquaintance; (Com)
bill of lading; **conhecimentos** mpl
(informações) knowledge sg; **levar
ao ~ de alguém** to bring to sb's
notice

conjugado [kõʒu'gadu] m studio

cônjuge ['kõʒuʒi] m spouse

conjunção [kõʒũ'sãw] (pl **-ões**) f
union; (Ling) conjunction

conjuntivo [kõʒũ'tʃivu] (pt) m
(Ling) subjunctive

conosco [ko'nosku] pron with us

conquista [kõ'kista] f conquest;
conquistador, a [kõkista'dor(a)]
adj conquering ▶ m conqueror;
conquistar [kõkis'tar] vt to
conquer; (alcançar) to achieve;
(ganhar) to win

consciência [kõ'sjẽsja] f
conscience; (percepção)
awareness; (senso de
responsabilidade) conscientiousness

consciente [kõ'sjẽtʃi] adj
conscious

conseguinte [kõse'gĩtʃi] adj:
por ~ consequently

conseguir [kõse'gir] vt to get,
obtain; **~ fazer** to manage to do,
succeed in doing

conselho [kõ'seʎu] m piece of
advice; (corporação) council;
conselhos mpl (advertência) advice
sg; **~ de guerra** court martial;
C~ de ministros (Pol) Cabinet

consentimento [kõsẽtʃi'mẽtu]
m consent

consentir [kõsẽ'tʃir] vt to allow,
permit; (aprovar) to agree to ▶ vi:
~ em to agree to

consequência [kõse'kwẽsja] f
consequence; **por ~** consequently

consertar [kõser'tar] vt to mend,
repair; (remediar) to put right;
conserto [kõ'sertu] m repair

conserva [kõ'serva] f pickle;
em ~ pickled

conservação [kõserva'sãw] f
conservation; (de vida, alimentos)
preservation

conservador, a [kõserva'dor(a)]
adj conservative ▶ m/f (Pol)
conservative

conservante [kõser'vãtʃi] m
preservative

conservar [kõser'var] vt to
preserve, maintain; (reter, manter)
to keep, retain; **conservar-se** vr
to keep

conservatório [kõserva'tɔrju] m
conservatory

consideração [kõsidera'sãw] (pl
-ões) f consideration; (estima)
respect, esteem; **levar em ~** to
take into account

considerar [kõside'rar] vt to

consider; (*prezar*) to respect ▶ vi to consider

considerável [kõside'ravew] (*pl* **-eis**) ADJ considerable

consigo¹ [kõ'sigu] PRON (*m*) with him; (*f*) with her; (*pl*) with them; (*com você*) with you

consigo² VB *ver* **conseguir**

consinto [kõ'sĩtu] VB *ver* **consentir**

consistente [kõsis'tẽtʃi] ADJ solid; (*espesso*) thick

consistir [kõsis'tʃir] VI: ~ **em** to be made up of, consist of

consoante [kõso'ãtʃi] F consonant ▶ PREP according to ▶ CONJ: ~ **prometera** as he had promised

consolação [kõsola'sãw] (*pl* **-ões**) F consolation

consolar [kõso'lar] VT to console

console [kõ'sɔli], **consola** [kõ'sɔla] F (*Comput*) console

consolidar [kõsoli'dar] VT to consolidate; (*fratura*) to knit ▶ vi to become solid; to knit together

consolo [kõ'solu] M consolation

consome [kõ'somi] VB *ver* **consumir**

consórcio [kõ'sɔrsju] M (*união*) partnership; (*Com*) consortium

conspiração [kõspira'sãw] (*pl* **-ões**) F plot, conspiracy

conspirar [kõspi'rar] VT, VI to plot

constante [kõs'tãtʃi] ADJ constant

constar [kõs'tar] VI to be in; **ao que me consta** as far as I know

constatar [kõsta'tar] VT to establish; (*notar*) to notice; (*evidenciar*) to show up

consternado, -a [kõster'nadu, a] ADJ depressed; (*desolado*) distressed

constipação [kõstʃipa'sãw] (*pl* **-ões**) F (*PT*) cold

constipado, -a [kõstʃi'padu, a] (*PT*) ADJ: **estar ~** to have a cold

constituição [kõstʃitwi'sãw] (*pl* **-ões**) F constitution

constituinte [kõstʃi'twĩtʃi] M/F (*deputado*) member ▶ F: **a C~** the Constituent Assembly

constituir [kõstʃi'twir] VT to constitute; (*formar*) to form; (*estabelecer*) to establish; (*nomear*) to appoint

constrangimento [kõstrãʒi'mẽtu] M constraint; (*acanhamento*) embarrassment

construção [kõstru'sãw] (*pl* **-ões**) F building, construction

construir [kõs'trwir] VT to build, construct

construtivo, -a [kõstru'tʃivu, a] ADJ constructive

construtor, a [kõstru'tor(a)] M/F builder

cônsul ['kõsuw] (*pl* **cônsules**) M consul; **consulado** [kõsu'ladu] M consulate

consulta [kõ'suwta] F consultation; **livro de ~** reference book; **horário de ~** surgery hours *pl* (*BRIT*), office hours *pl* (*US*); **consultar** [kõsuw'tar] VT to consult; **consultor, a** [kõsuw'tor(a)] M/F consultant

consultório [kõsuw'tɔrju] M surgery

consumidor, a [kõsumi'dor(a)] ADJ consumer *atr* ▶ M/F consumer

consumir [kõsu'mir] VT to consume; (*gastar*) to use up; **consumir-se** VR to waste away

consumo [kõ'sumu] M consumption; **artigos de ~** consumer goods

conta ['kõta] F count; (*em restaurante*) bill; (*fatura*) invoice; (*bancária*) account; (*de colar*) bead; **contas** FPL (*Com*) accounts; **levar**

ou **ter em ~** to take into account; **tomar ~ de** to take care of; (*dominar*) to take hold of; **afinal de ~s** after all; **dar-se ~ de** to realize; (*notar*) to notice; **~ corrente** current account; **~ de e-mail** *ou* **de correio eletrônico** email account

contabilista [kõtabi'lista] (PT) M/F accountant

contabilizar [kõtabili'zar] VT to write up, book

contacto [kõ'tatu] (PT) M = **contato**

contador, a [kõta'dor(a)] M/F (*Com*) accountant ▶ M (*Tec: medidor*) meter

contagiante [kõta'ʒjãtʃi] ADJ (*alegria*) contagious

contagiar [kõta'ʒjar] VT to infect

contágio [kõ'taʒju] M infection

contagioso, -a [kõta'ʒjozu, ɔza] ADJ (*doença*) contagious

contaminar [kõtami'nar] VT to contaminate

contanto que [kõ'tãtu ki] CONJ provided that

conta-quilómetros (PT) M INV speedometer

contar [kõ'tar] VT to count; (*narrar*) to tell; (*pretender*) to intend ▶ VI to count; **~ com** to count on; (*esperar*) to expect; **~ em fazer** to count on doing, expect to do

contatar [kõta'tar] VT to contact; **contato** [kõ'tatu] M contact; **entrar em contato com** to get in touch with, contact

contemplar [kõtē'plar] VT to contemplate; (*olhar*) to gaze at

contemplativo, -a [kõtēpla'tʃivu, a] ADJ (*pessoa*) thoughtful

contemporâneo, -a

[kõtēpo'ranju, a] ADJ, M/F contemporary

contentamento [kõtēta'mētu] M (*felicidade*) happiness; (*satisfação*) contentment

contente [kõ'tētʃi] ADJ happy; (*satisfeito*) pleased, satisfied

contento [kõ'tētu] M: **a ~** satisfactorily

conter [kõ'ter] (*irreg: como* **ter**) VT to contain, hold; (*refrear*) to restrain, hold back; (*gastos*) to curb

contestação [kõtesta'sãw] (*pl* **-ões**) F challenge; (*negação*) denial

contestar [kõtes'tar] VT to dispute, contest; (*impugnar*) to challenge

conteúdo [kõte'udu] M contents *pl*; (*de um texto*) content

contexto [kõ'testu] M context

contigo [kõ'tʃigu] PRON with you

contíguo, -a [kõ'tʃigwu, a] ADJ: **~ a** next to

continental [kõtʃinē'taw] (*pl* **-ais**) ADJ continental

continente [kõtʃi'nētʃi] M continent

continuação [kõtʃinwa'sãw] F continuation

continuar [kõtʃi'nwar] VT, VI to continue; **~ falando** *ou* **a falar** to go on talking; **ela continua doente** she is still sick

continuidade [kõtʃinwi'dadʒi] F continuity

conto ['kõtu] M story, tale; (PT: *dinheiro*) 1000 escudos

contorcer [kõtor'ser] VT to twist; **contorcer-se** VR to writhe

contornar [kõtor'nar] VT (*rodear*) to go round; (*ladear*) to skirt; (*fig: problema*) to get round

contorno [kõ'tornu] M outline; (*da terra*) contour; (*do rosto*) profile

contra ['kõtra] PREP against ► M:
os prós e os ~s the pros and cons;
dar o ~ (a) to be opposed (to)

contra-ataque M counterattack

contrabandear [kõtrabã'dʒjar] VT
to smuggle; **contrabandista**
[kõtrabã'dʒista] M/F smuggler;
contrabando [kõtra'bãdu] M
smuggling; (artigos) contraband

contraceptivo, -a [kõtrasep'tʃivu,
a] ADJ contraceptive ► M
contraceptive

contracheque [kõtra'ʃɛki] M pay
slip (BRIT), check stub (US)

contradição [kõtradʒi'sãw] (pl
-ões) F contradiction

contraditório, -a [kõtradʒi'tɔrju,
a] ADJ contradictory

contradizer [kõtradʒi'zer] (irreg:
como **dizer**) VT to contradict

contragosto [kõtra'gostu] M: **a ~**
against one's will, unwillingly

contrair [kõtra'ir] VT to contract;
(hábito) to form

contramão [kõtra'mãw] ADJ
one-way ► F: **na ~** the wrong way
down a one-way street

contraproducente
[kõtraprodu'sẽtʃi] ADJ
counterproductive

contrário, -a [kõ'trarju, a] ADJ
(oposto) opposite; (pessoa) opposed;
(desfavorável) unfavourable (BRIT),
unfavorable (US), adverse ► M
opposite; **do ~** otherwise; **pelo** ou
ao ~ on the contrary; **ao ~** the
other way round

contrassenso M nonsense

contrastar [kõtras'tar] VT to
contrast; **contraste** [kõ'trastʃi] M
contrast

contratação [kõtrata'sãw] F (de
pessoal) employment

contratar [kõtra'tar] VT (serviços)
to contract; (pessoal) to employ,
take on

contratempo [kõtra'tẽpu] M
setback; (aborrecimento) upset;
(dificuldade) difficulty

contrato [kõ'tratu] M contract;
(acordo) agreement

contribuição [kõtribwi'sãw] (pl
-ões) F contribution; (imposto) tax

contribuinte [kõtri'bwĩtʃi] M/F
contributor; (que paga impostos)
taxpayer

contribuir [kõtri'bwir] VT to
contribute ► VI to contribute;
(pagar impostos) to pay taxes

controlar [kõtro'lar] VT to control

controle [kõ'trɔli] M control;
~ remoto remote control; **~ de
crédito** (Com) credit control; **~ de
qualidade** (Com) quality control

controvérsia [kõtro'vɛrsja] F
controversy; (discussão) debate;
controverso, -a [kõtro'vɛrsu, a]
ADJ controversial

contudo [kõ'tudu] CONJ
nevertheless, however

contumaz [kõtu'majz] ADJ
obstinate, stubborn

contusão [kõtu'zãw] (pl -ões) F
bruise

convenção [kõvẽ'sãw] (pl -ões) F
convention; (acordo) agreement

convencer [kõvẽ'ser] VT to
convince; (persuadir) to persuade;
convencer-se VR: **~-se de** to be
convinced about; **convencido, -a**
[kõvẽ'sidu, a] ADJ convinced; (col:
imodesto) conceited, smug

convencional [kõvẽsjo'naw] (pl
-ais) ADJ conventional

convenções [kõvẽ'sõjs] FPL de
convenção

conveniência [kõve'njẽsja] F
convenience

conveniente [kõve'njẽtʃi] ADJ convenient, suitable; (*vantajoso*) advantageous

convênio [kõ'venju] M (*reunião*) convention; (*acordo*) agreement

convento [kõ'vẽtu] M convent

conversa [kõ'vɛrsa] F conversation; **~ fiada** idle talk; (*promessa falsa*) hot air

conversão [kõver'sãw] (*pl* **-ões**) F conversion

conversar [kõver'sar] VI to talk; to chat

conversões [kõver'sõjs] FPL *de* **conversão**

converter [kõver'ter] VT to convert

convés [kõ'vɛs] (*pl* **-eses**) M (*Náut*) deck

convexo, -a [kõ'vɛksu, a] ADJ convex

convicção [kõvik'sãw] (*pl* **-ões**) F conviction

convidado, -a [kõvi'dadu, a] M/F guest

convidar [kõvi'dar] VT to invite

convincente [kõvĩ'sẽtʃi] ADJ convincing

convir [kõ'vir] (*irreg: como* **vir**) VI to suit, be convenient; (*ficar bem*) to be appropriate; (*concordar*) to agree; **convém fazer isso o mais rápido possível** we must do this as soon as possible

convite [kõ'vitʃi] M invitation

convivência [kõvi'vẽsja] F living together; (*familiaridade*) familiarity, intimacy

conviver [kõvi'ver] VI: **~ com** (*viver em comum*) to live with; (*ter familiaridade*) to get on with; **convívio** [kõ'vivju] M living together; (*familiaridade*) familiarity

convocar [kõvo'kar] VT to

summon, call upon; (*reunião, eleições*) to call; (*para o serviço militar*) to call up

convosco [kõ'vosku] ADV with you

convulsão [kõvuw'sãw] (*pl* **-ões**) F convulsion

cooper ['kuper] M jogging; **fazer ~** to go jogging *ou* running

cooperação [koopera'sãw] F cooperation

cooperar [koope'rar] VI to cooperate

coordenada [koorde'nada] F coordinate

copa ['kɔpa] F (*de árvore*) top; (*torneio*) cup; **copas** FPL (*Cartas*) hearts

cópia ['kɔpja] F copy; **tirar ~ de** to copy; **copiadora** [kopja'dora] F duplicating machine

copiar [ko'pjar] VT to copy

copo ['kɔpu] M glass

coque ['kɔki] M (*penteado*) bun

coqueiro [ko'kejru] M (*Bot*) coconut palm

coquetel [koke'tɛw] (*pl* **-éis**) M cocktail; (*festa*) cocktail party

cor¹ [kɔr] M: **de ~** by heart

cor² [kor] F colour (BRIT), color (US); **de ~** colo(u)red

coração [kora'sãw] (*pl* **-ões**) M heart; **de bom ~** kind-hearted; **de todo o ~** wholeheartedly

corado, -a [ko'radu, a] ADJ ruddy

coragem [ko'raʒẽ] F courage; (*atrevimento*) nerve

corais [ko'rajs] MPL *de* **coral**

corajoso, -a [kora'ʒozu, ɔza] ADJ courageous

coral [ko'raw] (*pl* **-ais**) M (*Mús*) choir; (*Zool*) coral

corar [ko'rar] VT (*roupa*) to bleach (in the sun) ▶ VI to blush; (*tornar-se* *branco*) to bleach

corda ['kɔrda] F rope, line; (*Mús*) string; (*varal*) clothes line; (*de relógio*) spring; **dar ~ em** to wind up; **~s vocais** vocal chords

cordão [kor'dãw] (*pl* **-ões**) M string, twine; (*joia*) chain; (*no carnaval*) group; (*Elet*) lead; (*fileira*) row

cordeiro [kor'dejru] M lamb

cordel [kor'dɛw] (*pl* **-éis**) M string; **literatura de ~** pamphlet literature

cor-de-rosa ADJ INV pink

cordões [kor'dõjs] MPL *de* **cordão**

coreano, -a [ko'rjanu, a] ADJ Korean ▶ M/F Korean ▶ M (*Ling*) Korean

Coreia [ko'rɛja] F: **a ~** Korea

coreto [ko'retu] M bandstand

córner ['kɔrner] M (*Futebol*) corner

coro ['koru] M chorus; (*conjunto de cantores*) choir

coroa [ko'roa] F crown; (*de flores*) garland ▶ M/F (*BR col*) old timer

coroar [koro'ar] VT to crown; (*premiar*) to reward

coronel [koro'nɛw] (*pl* **-éis**) M colonel; (*político*) local political boss

corpo ['kɔrpu] M body; (*aparência física*) figure; (*: de homem*) build; (*de vestido*) bodice; (*Mil*) corps *sg*; **de ~ e alma** (*fig*) wholeheartedly; **~ diplomático** diplomatic corps *sg*

corpulento, -a [korpu'lẽtu, a] ADJ stout

correção [kohe'sãw] (*pl* **-ões**) F correction; (*exatidão*) correctness; **casa de ~** reformatory

corre-corre [kɔhi'kɔhi] (*pl* **-s**) M (*pressa*) scramble; (*de muitas pessoas*) stampede

corredor, a [kohe'dor(a)] M/F runner ▶ M corridor; (*em avião etc*) aisle; (*cavalo*) racehorse

correia [ko'heja] F strap; (*de*

máquina) belt; (*para cachorro*) leash

correio [ko'heju] M mail, post; (*local*) post office; (*carteiro*) postman (BRIT), mailman (US); **~ aéreo** air mail; **pôr no ~** to post; **~ eletrônico** email; **~ de voz** voice mail

corrente [ko'hẽtʃi] ADJ (*atual*) current; (*águas*) running; (*comum*) usual, common ▶ F current; (*cadeia, joia*) chain; **~ de ar** draught (BRIT), draft (US); **correnteza** [kohẽ'teza] F (*de ar*) draught (BRIT), draft (US); (*de rio*) current

correr [ko'her] VT to run; (*viajar por*) to travel across ▶ VI to run; (*em carro*) to drive fast, speed; (*o tempo*) to elapse; (*boato*) to go round; (*atuar com rapidez*) to rush; **correria** [kohe'ria] F rush

correspondência [kohespõ'dẽsja] F correspondence; **correspondente** [kohespõ'dẽtʃi] ADJ corresponding ▶ M correspondent

corresponder [kohespõ'der] VI: **~ a** to correspond to; (*ser igual*) to match (up to); **corresponder-se** VR: **~-se com** to correspond with

correto, -a [ko'hɛtu, a] ADJ correct; (*conduta*) right; (*pessoa*) straight, honest

corretor, a [kohe'tor(a)] M/F broker; **~ de fundos** *ou* **de bolsa** stockbroker; **~ de imóveis** estate agent (BRIT), realtor (US); **~ ortográfico** spellchecker

corrida [ko'hida] F running; (*certame*) race; (*de taxi*) fare; **~ de cavalos** horse race

corrido, -a [ko'hidu, a] ADJ quick; (*expulso*) driven out ▶ ADV quickly

corrigir [kohi'ʒir] VT to correct

corriqueiro, -a [kohi'kejru, a] ADJ

common; (*problema*) trivial
corromper [kohõ'per] vт to
corrupt; (*subornar*) to bribe;
corromper-se vʀ to be corrupted
corrosão [koho'zãw] ꜰ corrosion;
(*fig*) erosion
corrosivo, -a [koho'zivu, a] ᴀᴅᴊ
corrosive
corrupção [kohup'sãw] ꜰ
corruption
corrupto, -a [ko'huptu, a] ᴀᴅᴊ
corrupt
Córsega ['kɔrsega] ꜰ: **a ~** Corsica
cortada [kor'tada] ꜰ: **dar uma ~
em alguém** (*fig*) to cut sb short
cortante [kor'tãtʃi] ᴀᴅᴊ cutting
cortar [kor'tar] vт to cut;
(*eliminar*) to cut out; (*água, telefone
etc*) to cut off; (*efeito*) to stop ▶ vι
to cut; (*encurtar caminho*) to take a
short cut; **~ o cabelo** (*no
cabeleireiro*) to have one's hair cut;
~ a palavra de alguém to
interrupt sb
corte¹ ['kɔrtʃi] м cut; (*de luz*)
power cut; **sem ~** (*tesoura etc*)
blunt; **~ de cabelo** haircut
corte² ['kɔrtʃi] ꜰ court; **cortes** ꜰᴘʟ
(*ᴘᴛ*) parliament *sg*
cortejo [kor'teʒu] м procession
cortesia [korte'zia] ꜰ politeness;
(*de empresa*) free offer
cortiça [kor'tʃisa] ꜰ cork
cortiço [kor'tʃisu] м slum
tenement
cortina [kor'tʃina] ꜰ curtain
coruja [ko'ruʒa] ꜰ owl
corvo ['korvu] м crow
coser [ko'zer] vт, vι to sew
cosmético, -a [koz'metʃiku, a]
ᴀᴅᴊ, м cosmetic
cospe ['kɔspi] vʙ *ver* **cuspir**
costa ['kɔsta] ꜰ coast; **costas** ꜰᴘʟ
(*dorso*) back *sg*; **dar as ~s a** to turn

one's back on
Costa Rica ꜰ: **a ~** Costa Rica
costela [kos'tɛla] ꜰ rib
costeleta [koste'leta] ꜰ chop,
cutlet; **costeletas** ꜰᴘʟ (*suíças*)
side-whiskers
costumar [kostu'mar] vт
(*habituar*) to accustom ▶ vι: **ele
costuma chegar às 6.00** he
usually arrives at 6.00;
costumava dizer ... he used to
say ...
costume [kos'tumi] м custom,
habit; (*traje*) costume; **costumes**
мᴘʟ (*comportamento*) behaviour *sg*
(*ʙʀɪᴛ*), behavior *sg* (*us*); (*conduta*)
conduct *sg*; (*de um povo*) customs;
de ~ usual; **como de ~** as usual
costura [kos'tura] ꜰ sewing;
(*sutura*) seam; **costurar**
[kostu'rar] vт, vι to sew;
costureira [kostu'rejra] ꜰ
dressmaker
cota ['kɔta] ꜰ quota, share
cotação [kota'sãw] (*pl* **-ões**) ꜰ
(*de preços*) list, quotation; (*Bolsa*)
price; (*consideração*) esteem;
~ bancária bank rate
cotado, -a [ko'tadu, a] ᴀᴅᴊ (*Com:
ação*) quoted; (*bem-conceituado*)
well thought of; (*num concurso*)
fancied
cotar [ko'tar] vт (*ações*) to quote;
~ algo em to value sth at
cotejar [kote'ʒar] vт to compare
cotidiano, -a [kotʃi'dʒanu, a] ᴀᴅᴊ
daily, everyday ▶ м: **o ~** daily life
cotonete® [koto'nɛtʃi] м cotton
bud (*ʙʀɪᴛ*)
cotovelada [kotove'lada] ꜰ
shove; (*cutucada*) nudge
cotovelo [koto'velu] м (*Anat*)
elbow; (*curva*) bend; **falar pelos
~s** to talk non-stop

coube ['kobi] vb *ver* **caber**

couro ['koru] м leather; (*de um animal*) hide

couve ['kovi] ϝ spring greens *pl*; **couve-flor** (*pl* **couves-flor(es)**) ϝ cauliflower

couvert [ku'vεr] м cover charge

cova ['kɔva] ϝ pit; (*caverna*) cavern; (*sepultura*) grave

covarde [ko'vardʒi] ADJ cowardly ▶ м/ϝ coward; **covardia** [kovar'dʒia] ϝ cowardice

covil [ko'viw] (*pl* -**is**) м den, lair

covis [ko'vis] MPL *de* **covil**

coxa ['koʃa] ϝ thigh

coxear [ko'ʃjar] vı to limp

coxia [ko'ʃia] ϝ aisle, gangway

coxo, -a ['koʃu, a] ADJ lame

cozer [ko'zer] vт, vı to cook

cozido [ko'zidu] м stew

cozinha [ko'ziɲa] ϝ kitchen; (*arte*) cookery; **~ planejada** fitted kitchen

cozinhar [kozi'ɲar] vт, vı to cook

cozinheiro, -a [kozi'ɲejru, a] м/ϝ cook

CP ABR = **Caminhos de Ferro Portugueses**

CPF (BR) ABR м (= *Cadastro de Pessoa Física*) identification number

CPLP ABR ϝ *see note*

The **CPLP** o the *Comunidade de Países de Língua Portuguesa* was set up in 1996 to establish economic and diplomatic links between all countries where the official language is Portuguese. The members are Brazil, Portugal, Angola, Mozambique, Guinea-Bissau, Cape Verde and São Tomé e Príncipe. Portuguese is spoken by around 170 million people around the world today.

crachá [kra'ʃa] м badge

crânio ['kranju] м skull

craque ['kraki] м/ϝ ace, expert

crasso, -a ['krasu, a] ADJ crass

cratera [kra'tεra] ϝ crater

cravar [kra'var] vт (*prego etc*) to drive (in); (*com os olhos*) to stare at; **cravar-se** vʀ to penetrate

cravo ['kravu] м carnation; (*Mús*) harpsichord; (*especiaria*) clove; (*na pele*) blackhead; (*prego*) nail

creche ['krεʃi] ϝ crèche, day-care centre

credenciais [kredē'sjajs] FPL credentials

creditar [kredʒi'tar] vт to guarantee; (*Com*) to credit; **~ algo a alguém** to credit sb with sth; (*garantir*) to assure sb of sth

crédito ['krεdʒitu] м credit; **digno de ~** reliable

creme ['kremi] ADJ INV cream ▶ м cream; (*Culin: doce*) custard; **~ dental** toothpaste; **cremoso, -a** [kre'mozu, ɔza] ADJ creamy

crença ['krēsa] ϝ belief

crente ['krētʃi] м/ϝ believer

crepúsculo [kre'puskulu] м dusk, twilight

crer [krer] vт, vı to believe; **crer-se** vʀ to believe o.s. to be; **~ em** to believe in; **creio que sim** I think so

crescer [kre'ser] vı to grow; **crescimento** [kresi'mētu] м growth

crespo, -a ['krespu, a] ADJ (*cabelo*) curly

cretinice [kretʃi'nisi] ϝ stupidity; (*ato, dito*) stupid thing

cretino [kre'tʃinu] м cretin, imbecile

cria ['kria] ϝ (*animal: sg*) baby animal; (: *pl*) young *pl*

criação [krja'sāw] (*pl* -**ões**) ϝ creation; (*de animais*) raising, breeding; (*educação*) upbringing; (*animais domésticos*) livestock pl; **filho de ~** adopted child

criado, -a ['krjadu, a] M/F servant

criador, a [krja'dor(a)] M/F creator; **~ de gado** cattle breeder

criança ['krjãsa] ADJ childish ▶ F child; **criançada** [krjã'sada] F: **a criançada** the kids

criar [krjar] VT to create; (*crianças*) to bring up; (*animais*) to raise; (*amamentar*) to suckle, nurse; (*planta*) to grow; **criar-se** VR: **~-se (com)** to grow up (with); **~ caso** to make trouble

criatura [kria'tura] F creature; (*indivíduo*) individual

crime ['krimi] M crime; **criminal** [krimi'naw] (*pl* **-ais**) ADJ criminal; **criminalidade** [kriminali'dadʒi] F crime; **criminoso, -a** [krimi'nozu, ɔza] ADJ, M/F criminal

crina ['krina] F mane

crioulo, -a ['krjolu, a] ADJ creole ▶ M/F creole; (BR: *negro*) Black (person)

criptografar [kriptogra'far] VT *Comput* to encrypt

crise ['krizi] F crisis; (*escassez*) shortage; (*Med*) attack, fit

crista ['krista] F (*de serra, onda*) crest; (*de galo*) cock's comb

cristal [kris'taw] (*pl* **-ais**) M crystal; (*vidro*) glass; **cristais** MPL (*copos*) glassware sg; **cristalino, -a** [krista'linu, a] ADJ crystal-clear

cristão, -tã [kris'tãw, 'tã] (*pl* **-s/-s**) ADJ, M/F Christian

cristianismo [kristʃja'nizmu] M Christianity

Cristo ['kristu] M Christ

critério [kri'tɛrju] M criterion; (*juízo*) discretion, judgement;

criterioso, -a [krite'rjozu, ɔza] ADJ thoughtful, careful

crítica ['kritʃika] F criticism; *ver tb* **crítico**

criticar [kritʃi'kar] VT to criticize; (*um livro*) to review

crítico, -a ['kritʃiku, a] ADJ critical ▶ M/F critic

crivar [kri'var] VT (*com balas etc*) to riddle

crivo ['krivu] M sieve

crocante [kro'kãtʃi] ADJ (*pão, alface*) crispy; (*nozes, chocolate*) crunchy

crônica ['kronika] F chronicle; (*coluna de jornal*) newspaper column; (*texto jornalístico*) feature; (*conto*) short story

crônico, -a ['kroniku, a] ADJ chronic

cronológico, -a [krono'lɔʒiku, a] ADJ chronological

croquete [kro'kɛtʃi] M croquette

cru, a [kru, 'krua] ADJ raw; (*não refinado*) crude

crucial [kru'sjaw] (*pl* **-ais**) ADJ crucial

crucificar [krusifi'kar] VT to crucify

crucifixo [krusi'fiksu] M crucifix

cruel [kru'ɛw] (*pl* **-éis**) ADJ cruel; **crueldade** [kruew'dadʒi] F cruelty

cruz [kruz] F cross; **C~ Vermelha** Red Cross

cruzado, -a [kru'zadu, a] ADJ crossed ▶ M (*moeda*) cruzado

cruzamento [kruza'mẽtu] M crossroads

cruzar [kru'zar] VT to cross ▶ VI (*Náut*) to cruise; (*pessoas*) to pass each other by; **~ com** to meet

cruzeiro [kru'zejru] M (*cruz*) (monumental) cross; (*moeda*) cruzeiro; (*viagem de navio*) cruise

cu [ku] (!) M arse (!); **vai tomar no cu** fuck off (!)

Cuba ['kuba] F Cuba

cubro ['kubru] VB *ver* **cobrir**

cuca ['kuka] (*col*) F head; **fundir a ~** (*quebrar a cabeça*) to rack one's brain; (*baratinar*) to boggle the mind; (*perturbar*) to drive crazy

cuco ['kuku] M cuckoo

cueca ['kwɛka] F (BR) underpants *pl*; **cuecas** FPL (PT) underpants *pl*; (*para mulheres*) panties *pl*

cuíca ['kwika] F kind of musical instrument

cuidado [kwi'dadu] M care; **aos ~s de** in the care of; **ter ~** to be careful; **~!** watch out!, be careful!; **tomar ~ (de)** to be careful (of); **cuidadoso, -a** [kwida'dozu, ɔza] ADJ careful

cuidar [kwi'dar] VI: **~ de** to take care of, look after; **cuidar-se** VR to look after o.s.

cujo, -a ['kuʒu, a] PRON (*de quem*) whose; (*de que*) of which

culinária [kuli'narja] F cookery

culpa ['kuwpa] F fault; (*Jur*) guilt; **ter ~ de** to be to blame for; **por ~ de** because of; **culpado, -a** [kuw'padu, a] ADJ guilty ▶ M/F culprit; **culpar** [kuw'par] VT to blame; (*acusar*) to accuse; **culpar-se** VR to take the blame; **culpável** [kuw'pavew] (*pl* -**eis**) ADJ guilty

cultivar [kuwtʃi'var] VT to cultivate; (*plantas*) to grow; **cultivo** [kuw'tʃivu] M cultivation

culto, -a ['kuwtu, a] ADJ cultured ▶ M (*homenagem*) worship; (*religião*) cult

cultura [kuw'tura] F culture; (*da terra*) cultivation; **cultural** [kuwtu'raw] (*pl* **culturais**) ADJ cultural

cume ['kumi] M top, summit; (*fig*) climax

cúmplice ['kũplisi] M/F accomplice

cumprimentar [kũprimẽ'tar] VT to greet; (*dar parabéns*) to congratulate

cumprimento [kũpri'mẽtu] M fulfilment; (*saudação*) greeting; (*elogio*) compliment; **cumprimentos** MPL (*saudações*) best wishes; **~ de uma lei/ordem** compliance with a law/an order

cumprir [kũ'prir] VT (*desempenhar*) to carry out; (*promessa*) to keep; (*lei*) to obey; (*pena*) to serve ▶ VI to be necessary; **~ a palavra** to keep one's word; **fazer ~** to enforce

cúmulo ['kumulu] M height; **é o ~!** that's the limit!

cunha ['kuɲa] F wedge

cunhado, -a [ku'ɲadu, a] M/F brother-in-law/sister-in-law

cunho ['kuɲu] M (*marca*) hallmark; (*caráter*) nature

cupim [ku'pĩ] (*pl* -**ns**) M termite

cupins [ku'pĩs] MPL *de* **cupim**

cúpula ['kupula] F dome; (*de abajur*) shade; (*de partido etc*) leadership; **(reunião de) ~** summit (meeting)

cura ['kura] F cure; (*tratamento*) treatment; (*de carnes etc*) curing, preservation ▶ M priest

curar [ku'rar] VT (*doença*) to cure; (*ferida*) to treat; **curar-se** VR to get well

curativo [kura'tʃivu] M dressing

curiosidade [kurjozi'dadʒi] F curiosity; (*objeto raro*) curio

curioso, -a [ku'rjozu, ɔza] ADJ curious ▶ M/F snooper, inquisitive person; **curiosos** MPL (*espectadores*) onlookers

curral [ku'haw] (pl **-ais**) M pen, enclosure

currículo [ku'hikulu] M (curriculum) curriculum vitae

cursar [kur'sar] VT (aulas, escola) to attend; (cursos) to follow; **ele está cursando História** he's studying ou doing history

curso ['kursu] M course; (direção) direction; **em ~** (ano etc) current; (processo) in progress

cursor [kur'sor] M (Comput) cursor

curtição [kurtʃi'sāw] F fun

curtir [kur'tʃir] VT (couro) to tan; (tornar rijo) to toughen up; (padecer) to suffer, endure; (col) to enjoy

curto, -a ['kurtu, a] ADJ short ▶ M (Elet) short (circuit); **curto-circuito** (pl **curtos-circuitos**) M short circuit

curva ['kurva] F curve; (de estrada, rio) bend; **~ fechada** hairpin bend

curvo, -a ['kurvu, a] ADJ curved; (estrada) winding

cuscuz [kus'kuz] M couscous

cuspe ['kuspi] M spit, spittle

cuspir [kus'pir] VT, VI to spit

custa ['kusta] F: **à ~ de** at the expense of; **custas** FPL (Jur) costs

custar [kus'tar] VI to cost; **~ a fazer** to have trouble doing; (demorar) to take a long time to do

custo ['kustu] M cost; **a ~** with difficulty; **a todo ~** at all costs

cutelo [ku'telu] M cleaver

cutícula [ku'tʃikula] F cuticle

cutucar [kutu'kar] VT (com o dedo) to prod, poke; (com o cotovelo) to nudge

d

D ABR = **Dona**; (= direito) r; (= deve) d

d/ ABR = **dia**

da [da] = **de** + **a**

dá [da] VB ver **dar**

dactilografar [datilogra'far] (PT) = **datilografar** etc

dado, -a ['dadu, a] ADJ given; (sociável) sociable ▶ M (em jogo) die; (fato) fact; **dados** MPL dice; (fatos, Comput) data sg; **~ que** supposing that; (uma vez que) given that

daí [da'ji] ADV (= de + aí) (desse lugar) from there; (desse momento) from then; **~ a um mês** a month later

dali [da'li] ADV = **de** + **ali**

daltônico, -a [daw'toniku, a] ADJ colour-blind (BRIT), color-blind (US)

dama ['dama] F lady; (Xadrez, Cartas) queen; **damas** FPL (jogo) draughts (BRIT), checkers (US); **~ de honra** bridesmaid

damasco [da'masku] M apricot

danado, -a [da'nadu, a] ADJ damned; (zangado) furious;

(*menino*) mischievous

dança ['dãsa] F dance; **dançar** [dã'sar] vi to dance

danificar [danifi'kar] vt to damage

dano ['danu] m (*tb*: **~s**) damage; harm; (*a uma pessoa*) injury

dantes ['dãtʃis] ADV before, formerly

daquele, -a [da'kele, 'kɛla] = **de + aquele**

daqui [da'ki] ADV (= **de + aqui**) (*deste lugar*) from here; **~ a pouco** soon, in a little while; **~ a uma semana** a week from now; **~ em diante** from now on

daquilo [da'kilu] = **de + aquilo**

(PALAVRA-CHAVE)

dar [dar] vt 1 (*ger*) to give; (*festa*) to hold; (*problemas*) to cause; **dar algo a alguém** to give sb sth, give sth to sb; **dar de beber a alguém** to give sb a drink; **dar aula de francês** to teach French

2 (*produzir: fruta etc*) to produce

3 (*notícias no jornal*) to publish

4 (*cartas*) to deal

5 (+ *n, perífrase de vb*): **me dá medo/pena** it frightens/upsets me

▶ vi 1: **dar com** (*coisa*) to find; (*pessoa*) to meet

2: **dar em** (*bater*) to hit; (*resultar*) to lead to; (*lugar*) to come to

3: **dá no mesmo** it's all the same

4: **dar de si** (*sapatos etc*) to stretch, give

5: **dar para** (*impess: ser possível*) to be able to; **dá para trocar dinheiro aqui?** can I change money here?; **vai dar para eu ir amanhã** I'll be able to go tomorrow; **dá para você vir amanhã? — não, amanhã não vai dar** can you come tomorrow?

— no, I can't

6 (*ser suficiente*): **dar para/para fazer** to be enough for/to do; **dá para todo mundo?** is there enough for everyone?

dar-se vr 1 (*sair-se*): **dar-se bem/mal** to do well/badly

2: **dar-se (com alguém)** to be acquainted (with sb); **dar-se bem (com alguém)** to get on well (with sb)

3: **dar-se por vencido** to give up

das [das] = **de + as**

data ['data] F date; (*época*) time; **datar** [da'tar] vt to date ▶ vi: **datar de** to date from

datilografar [datʃilogra'far] vt to type; **datilografia** [datʃilogra'fia] F typing; **datilógrafo, -a** [datʃi'lɔgrafu, a] m/f typist (BRIT), stenographer (US)

d.C. ABR (= *depois de Cristo*) A.D.

DDD ABR F (= *discagem direta a distância*) direct long-distance dialling ▶ ABR M (*código*) dialling code (BRIT), area code (US)

DDI ABR F (= *discagem direta internacional*) IDD ▶ ABR M (*código de país*) country code

(PALAVRA-CHAVE)

de [dʒi] (*de + o(s)/a(s) = do(s)/da(s); + ele(s)/a(s) = dele(s)/a(s); + esse(s)/a(s) = desse(s)/a(s); + isso = disso; + este(s)/a(s) = deste(s)/a(s); + isto = disto; + aquele(s)/a(s) = daquele(s)/a(s); + aquilo = daquilo*) PREP 1 (*posse*) of; **a casa de João/da irmã** João's/my sister's house; **é dele** it's his; **um romance de** a novel by

2 (*origem, distância, com números*) from; **sou de São Paulo** I'm from

São Paulo; **de 8 a 20** from 8 to 20; **sair do cinema** to leave the cinema; **de dois em dois** two by two, two at a time

3 (*valor descritivo*): **um copo de vinho** a glass of wine; **um homem de cabelo comprido** a man with long hair; **o infeliz do homem** (*col*) the poor man; **um bilhete de avião** an air ticket; **uma criança de três anos** a three-year-old (child); **uma máquina de costurar** a sewing machine; **aulas de inglês** English lessons; **feito de madeira** made of wood; **vestido de branco** dressed in white

4 (*modo*): **de trem/avião** by train/plane; **de lado** sideways

5 (*hora, tempo*): **às 8 da manhã** at 8 o'clock in the morning; **de dia/noite** by day/night; **de hoje a oito dias** a week from now; **de dois em dois dias** every other day

6 (*comparações*): **mais/menos de cem pessoas** more/less than a hundred people; **é o mais caro da loja** it's the most expensive in the shop; **ela é mais bonita do que sua irmã** she's prettier than her sister; **gastei mais do que pretendia** I spent more than I intended

7 (*causa*): **estou morto de calor** I'm boiling hot; **ela morreu de câncer** she died of cancer

8 (*adj + de + infin*): **fácil de entender** easy to understand

dê [de] VB *ver* **dar**

debaixo [de'bajʃu] ADV below, underneath ▶ PREP: **~ de** under, beneath

debate [de'batʃi] M discussion, debate; (*disputa*) argument; **debater** [deba'teɾ] VT to debate; (*discutir*) to discuss; **debater-se** VR to struggle

débil ['debiw] (*pl* **-eis**) ADJ weak, feeble ▶ M: **~ mental** mentally handicapped person; **debilidade** [debili'dadʒi] F weakness; **debilidade mental** mental handicap; **debilitar** [debili'taɾ] VT to weaken; **debilitar-se** VR to become weak, weaken; **debiloide** [debi'lɔjdʒi] (*col*) ADJ idiotic ▶ M/F idiot

debitar [debi'taɾ] VT: **~ $40 à** *ou* **na conta de alguém** to debit $40 to sb's account; **débito** ['dɛbitu] M debit

debochado, -a [debo'ʃadu, a] ADJ (*pessoa*) sardonic; (*jeito, tom*) mocking

década ['dɛkada] F decade

decadência [deka'dẽsja] F decadence

decair [deka'iɾ] VI to decline

decente [de'sẽtʃi] ADJ decent; (*apropriado*) proper; (*honrado*) honourable (BRIT), honorable (US); (*trabalho*) neat; **decentemente** [desẽtʃi'mẽtʃi] ADV decently; (*apropriadamente*) properly; (*honradamente*) honourably (BRIT), honorably (US)

decepção [desep'sãw] (*pl* **-ões**) F disappointment; **decepcionar** [desepsjo'naɾ] VT to disappoint; (*desiludir*) to disillusion; **decepcionar-se** VR to be disappointed; to be disillusioned

decidir [desi'dʒiɾ] VT to decide; (*solucionar*) to resolve; **decidir-se** VR: **~-se a** to make up one's mind to; **~-se por** to decide on, go for

decifrar [desi'fraɾ] VT to decipher;

(*futuro*) to foretell; (*compreender*) to understand

decimal [desi'maw] (*pl* **-ais**) ADJ, M decimal

décimo, -a ['dɛsimu, a] ADJ tenth ▶ M tenth; *ver tb* **quinto**

decisão [desi'zãw] (*pl* **-ões**) F decision; **decisivo, -a** [desi'zivu, a] ADJ (*fator*) decisive; (*jogo*) deciding

declaração [deklara'sãw] (*pl* **-ões**) F declaration; (*depoimento*) statement

declarado, -a [dekla'radu, a] ADJ (*intenção*) declared; (*opinião*) professed; (*inimigo*) sworn; (*alcoólatra*) self-confessed; (*cristão etc*) avowed

declarar [dekla'rar] VT to declare; (*confessar*) to confess

declinar [dekli'nar] VT to decline ▶ VI (*sol*) to go down; (*terreno*) to slope down; **declínio** [de'klinju] M decline

declive [de'klivi] M slope, incline

decolagem [deko'laʒẽ] (*pl* **-ns**) F (*Aer*) take-off

decolar [deko'lar] VI (*Aer*) to take off

decompor [dekõ'por] (*irreg: como* **pôr**) VT to analyse; (*apodrecer*) to rot; **decompor-se** VR to rot, decompose

decomposição [dekõpozi'sãw] (*pl* **-ões**) F decomposition; (*análise*) dissection

decorar [deko'rar] VT to decorate; (*aprender*) to learn by heart; **decorativo, -a** [dekora'tʃivu, a] ADJ decorative

decoro [de'koru] M decency; (*dignidade*) decorum

decorrente [deko'hẽtʃi] ADJ: **~ de** resulting from

decorrer [deko'her] VI (*tempo*) to

pass; (*acontecer*) to take place, happen ▶ M: **no ~ de** in the course of; **~ de** to result from

decrescer [dekre'ser] VI to decrease, diminish

decretar [dekre'tar] VT to decree, order; **decreto** [de'krɛtu] M decree, order; **decreto-lei** (*pl* **decretos-leis**) M act, law

dedetizar [dedetʃi'zar] VT to spray with insecticide

dedicação [dedʒika'sãw] F dedication; (*devotamento*) devotion

dedicar [dedʒi'kar] VT to dedicate; (*tempo, atenção*) to devote; **dedicar-se** VR: **~-se a** to devote o.s. to; **dedicatória** [dedʒika'tɔrja] F (*de obra*) dedication

dedo ['dedu] M finger; (*do pé*) toe; **~ anular** ring finger; **~ indicador** index finger; **~ mínimo** *ou* **mindinho** little finger

dedução [dedu'sãw] (*pl* **-ões**) F deduction

deduzir [dedu'zir] VT (*concluir*): **~ (de)** to deduce (from), infer (from); (*quantia*) to deduct

defasagem [defa'zaʒẽ] (*pl* **-ns**) F discrepancy

defeito [de'fejtu] M defect, flaw; **pôr ~s em** to find fault with; **com ~** broken, out of order; **para ninguém botar ~** (*col*) perfect; **defeituoso, -a** [defej'twozu, ɔza] ADJ defective, faulty

defender [defẽ'der] VT to defend; **defender-se** VR to stand up for o.s.; (*numa língua*) to get by

defensiva [defẽ'siva] F: **estar** *ou* **ficar na ~** to be on the defensive

defensor, a [defẽ'sor(a)] M/F defender; (*Jur*) defending counsel

defesa [de'feza] F defence (*BRIT*), defense (*US*); (*Jur*) counsel for the defence ▶ M (*Futebol*) back

deficiente [defi'sjẽtʃi] ADJ (*imperfeito*) defective; (*carente*): **~ (em)** deficient (in)

déficit ['dɛfisitʃi] (*pl* **-s**) M deficit

definição [defini'sãw] (*pl* **-ões**) F definition

definir [defi'nir] VT to define; **definir-se** VR to make a decision; (*explicar-se*) to make one's position clear; **~-se a favor de/contra algo** to come out in favo(u)r of/against sth

definitivamente [definitʃiva'mẽtʃi] ADV definitively; (*permanentemente*) for good; (*sem dúvida*) definitely

definitivo, -a [defini'tʃivu, a] ADJ final, definitive; (*permanente*) permanent; (*resposta, data*) definite

defronte [de'frõtʃi] ADV opposite ▶ PREP: **~ de** opposite

defumar [defu'mar] VT (*presunto*) to smoke; (*perfumar*) to perfume

defunto, -a [de'fũtu, a] ADJ dead ▶ M/F dead person

degelar [deʒe'lar] VT to thaw; (*geladeira*) to defrost ▶ VI to thaw out; to defrost

degradar [degra'dar] VT to degrade, debase; **degradar-se** VR to demean o.s.

degrau [de'graw] M step; (*de escada de mão*) rung

degustação [degusta'sãw] (*pl* **-ões**) F tasting, sampling; (*saborear*) savouring (BRIT), savoring (US)

degustar [degus'tar] VT (*provar*) to taste; (*saborear*) to savour (BRIT), savor (US)

dei [dej] VB *ver* **dar**

deitada [dej'tada] (*col*) F: **dar**

uma ~ to have a lie-down

deitado, -a [dej'tadu, a] ADJ (*estendido*) lying down; (*na cama*) in bed

deitar [dej'tar] VT to lay down; (*na cama*) to put to bed; (*colocar*) to put, place; (*lançar*) to cast; (PT: *líquido*) to pour; **deitar-se** VR to lie down; to go to bed; **~ sangue** (PT) to bleed; **~ abaixo** to knock down, flatten; **~ a fazer algo** to start doing sth; **~ uma carta** (PT) to post a letter; **~ fora** (PT) to throw away *ou* out; **~ e rolar** (*col*) to do as one likes

deixa ['dejʃa] F clue, hint; (*Teatro*) cue; (*chance*) chance

deixar [dej'ʃar] VT to leave; (*abandonar*) to abandon; (*permitir*) to let, allow ▶ VI: **~ de** (*parar*) to stop; (*não fazer*) to fail to; **não posso ~ de ir** I must go; **~ cair** to drop; **~ alguém louco** to drive sb crazy *ou* mad; **~ alguém cansado/nervoso** *etc* to make sb tired/nervous *etc*; **deixa disso!** (*col*) come off it!; **deixa para lá!** (*col*) forget it!

dela ['dɛla] = **de** + **ela**

delatar [dela'tar] VT (*pessoa*) to inform on; (*abusos*) to reveal; (*à polícia*) to report; **delator, a** [dela'tor(a)] M/F informer

dele ['deli] = **de** + **ele**

delegacia [delega'sia] F office; **~ de polícia** police station

delegado, -a [dele'gadu, a] M/F delegate, representative; **~ de polícia** police chief

delegar [dele'gar] VT to delegate

deleitar [delej'tar] VT to delight; **deleitar-se** VR: **~-se com** to delight in

delgado, -a [dew'gadu, a] ADJ

thin; (*esbelto*) slim; (*fino*) fine

deliberação [delibera'sãw] (*pl* **-ões**) F deliberation; (*decisão*) decision

deliberar [delibe'rar] VT to decide, resolve ▶ VI to deliberate

delicadeza [delika'deza] F delicacy; (*cortesia*) kindness

delicado, -a [deli'kadu, a] ADJ delicate; (*frágil*) fragile; (*cortês*) polite; (*sensível*) sensitive

delícia [de'lisja] F delight; (*prazer*) pleasure; **que ~!** how lovely!;

deliciar [deli'sjar] VT to delight; **deliciar-se** VR: **deliciar-se com algo** to take delight in sth

delicioso, -a [deli'sjozu, ɔza] ADJ lovely; (*comida, bebida*) delicious

delinear [deli'njar] VT to outline

delinquente [delĩ'kwẽtʃi] ADJ, M/F delinquent, criminal

delirar [deli'rar] VI (*com febre*) to be delirious; (*de ódio, prazer*) to go mad, go wild

delírio [de'lirju] M (*Med*) delirium; (*êxtase*) ecstasy; (*excitação*) excitement

delito [de'litu] M (*crime*) crime; (*falta*) offence (BRIT), offense (US)

demais [dʒi'majs] ADV (*em demasia*) too much; (*muitíssimo*) a lot, very much ▶ PRON: **os/as ~** the rest (of them); **já é ~!** this is too much!; **é bom ~** it's really good; **foi ~** (*col: bacana*) it was great

demanda [de'mãda] F lawsuit; (*disputa*) claim; (*requisição*) request; (*Econ*) demand; **em ~ de** in search of; **demandar** [demã'dar] VT (*Jur*) to sue; (*exigir, reclamar*) to demand

demasia [dema'zia] F excess, surplus; (*imoderação*) lack of moderation; **em ~** (*dinheiro, comida etc*) too much; (*cartas, problemas etc*) too many

demasiadamente [demazjada'mẽtʃi] ADV too much; (*com adj*) too

demasiado, -a [dema'zjadu, a] ADJ too much; (*pl*) too many ▶ ADV too much; (*com adj*) too

demitir [demi'tʃir] VT to dismiss; (*col*) to sack, fire; **demitir-se** VR to resign

democracia [demokra'sia] F democracy

democrático, -a [demo'kratʃiku, a] ADJ democratic

demolir [demo'lir] VT to demolish, knock down; (*fig*) to destroy

demonstração [demõstra'sãw] (*pl* **-ões**) F demonstration; (*de amizade*) show, display; (*prova*) proof

demonstrar [demõs'trar] VT to demonstrate; (*provar*) to prove; (*amizade etc*) to show

demora [de'mɔra] F delay; (*parada*) stop; **sem ~** at once, without delay; **qual é a ~ disso?** how long will this take?; **demorado, -a** [demo'radu, a] ADJ slow; **demorar** [demo'rar] VT to delay, slow down ▶ VI (*permanecer*) to stay; (*tardar a vir*) to be late; (*conserto*) to take (a long) time; **demorar-se** VR to stay for a long time, linger; **demorar a chegar** to be a long time coming; **vai demorar muito?** will it take long?; **não vou demorar** I won't be long

dendê [dẽ'de] M (*Culin: óleo*) palm oil; (*Bot*) oil palm

dengoso, -a [dẽ'gozu, ɔza] ADJ coy; (*criança: choraminguento*): **ser ~** to be a crybaby

dengue ['dẽgi] F (*Med*) dengue

denominar [denomi'nar] VT: **~ algo/alguém ...** to call sth/sb ...; **denominar-se** VR to be called; (*a si mesmo*) to call o.s.

denotar [deno'tar] vt (*indicar*) to show, indicate; (*significar*) to signify

densidade [dẽsi'dadʒi] F density

denso, -a ['dẽsu, a] ADJ dense; (*espesso*) thick; (*compacto*) compact

dentada [dẽ'tada] F bite

dentadura [dẽta'dura] F teeth *pl*, set of teeth; (*artificial*) dentures *pl*

dente ['dẽtʃi] M tooth; (*de animal*) fang; (*de elefante*) tusk; (*de alho*) clove; **falar entre os ~s** to mutter, mumble; **~ de leite/do siso** milk/wisdom tooth; **~s postiços** false teeth

dentista [dẽ'tʃista] M/F dentist

dentre [dẽtri] PREP (*from*) among

dentro ['dẽtru] ADV inside ▶ PREP: **~ de** inside; (*tempo*) (with)in; **de ~ para fora** inside out; **dar uma ~** (*col*) to get it right; **aí ~** in there; **por ~** on the inside; **estar por ~** (*col: fig*) to be in the know

denúncia [de'nũsja] F denunciation; (*acusação*) accusation; (*de roubo*) report; **denunciar** [denũ'sjar] vt (*acusar*) to denounce; (*delatar*) to inform on; (*revelar*) to reveal

deparar [depa'rar] vt to reveal; (*fazer aparecer*) to present ▶ vI: **~ com** to come across, meet; **deparar-se** vR: **~-se com** to come across, meet

departamento [departa'mẽtu] M department

dependência [depẽ'dẽsja] F dependence; (*edificação*) annexe (BRIT), annex (US); (*colonial*) dependency; (*cômodo*) room

dependente [depẽ'dẽtʃi] M/F dependant

depender [depẽ'der] vI: **~ de** to depend on

depilar [depi'lar] vt to wax; **depilatório** [depila'tɔrju] M hair-remover

deplorável [deplo'ravew] (*pl* **-eis**) ADJ deplorable; (*lamentável*) regrettable

depoimento [depoj'mẽtu] M testimony, evidence; (*na polícia*) statement

depois [de'pojs] ADV afterwards ▶ PREP: **~ de** after; **~ de comer** after eating; **~ que** after

depor [de'por] (*irreg: como* **pôr**) vt (*pôr*) to place; (*indicar*) to indicate; (*rei*) to depose; (*governo*) to overthrow ▶ vI (*Jur*) to testify, give evidence; (*na polícia*) to give a statement

depositar [depozi'tar] vt to deposit; (*voto*) to cast; (*colocar*) to place

depósito [de'pɔzitu] M deposit; (*armazém*) warehouse, depot; (*de lixo*) dump; (*reservatório*) tank; **~ de bagagens** left-luggage office (BRIT), checkroom (US)

depreciação [depresja'sãw] F depreciation

depredar [depre'dar] vt to wreck

depressa [dʒi'prɛsa] ADV fast, quickly; **vamos ~** let's get a move on!

depressão [depre'sãw] (*pl* **-ões**) F depression

deprimente [depri'mẽtʃi] ADJ depressing

deprimido, -a [depri'midu, a] ADJ depressed

deprimir [depri'mir] vt to depress; **deprimir-se** vR to get depressed

deputado, -a [depu'tadu, a] M/F deputy; (*agente*) agent; (*Pol*)

≈ Member of Parliament (BRIT), ≈ Representative (US)

der [der] VB ver **dar**

deriva [de'riva] F drift; **ir à ~** to drift; **ficar à ~** to be adrift

derivar [deri'var] VT to divert; (*Ling*) to derive ▶ VI to drift; **derivar-se** VR to be derived; (*ir à deriva*) to drift; (*provir*) **~(-se) (de)** to derive *ou* be derived (from)

derradeiro, -a [deha'dejru, a] ADJ last, final

derramamento [dehama'mētu] M spilling; (*de sangue, lágrimas*) shedding

derramar [deha'mar] VT to spill; (*entornar*) to pour; (*sangue, lágrimas*) to shed; **derramar-se** VR to pour out

derrame [de'hami] M haemorrhage (BRIT), hemorrhage (US)

derrapar [deha'par] VI to skid

derreter [dehe'ter] VT to melt; **derreter-se** VR to melt; (*coisa congelada*) to thaw; (*enternecer-se*) to be touched

derrota [de'hɔta] F defeat, rout; (*Náut*) route; **derrotar** [deho'tar] VT (*vencer*) to defeat; (*em jogo*) to beat

derrubar [dehu'bar] VT to knock down; (*governo*) to bring down; (*suj: doença*) to lay low; (*col: prejudicar*) to put down

desabafar [dʒizaba'far] VT (*sentimentos*) to give vent to ▶ VI: **~ (com)** to unburden o.s. (to); **desabafar-se** VR: **~-se (com)** to unburden o.s. (to); **desabafo** [dʒiza'bafu] M confession

desabamento [dʒizaba'mētu] M collapse

desabar [dʒiza'bar] VI (*edifício,*

ponte) to collapse; (*chuva*) to pour down; (*tempestade*) to break

desabitado, -a [dʒizabi'tadu, a] ADJ uninhabited

desabotoar [dʒizabo'twar] VT to unbutton

desabrigado, -a [dʒizabri'gadu, a] ADJ (*sem casa*) homeless; (*exposto*) exposed

desabrochar [dʒizabro'ʃar] VI (*flores, fig*) to blossom

desacatar [dʒizaka'tar] VT (*desrespeitar*) to have *ou* show no respect for; (*afrontar*) to defy; (*desprezar*) to scorn; **desacato** [dʒiza'katu] M disrespect; (*desprezo*) disregard

desaconselhar [dʒizakõse'ʎar] VT: **~ algo (a alguém)** to advise (sb) against sth

desacordado, -a [dʒizakor'dadu, a] ADJ unconscious

desacordo [dʒiza'kordu] M disagreement; (*desarmonia*) discord

desacostumado, -a [dʒizakostumadu, a] ADJ: **~ (a)** unaccustomed (to)

desacreditar [dʒizakredʒi'tar] VT to discredit; **desacreditar-se** VR to lose one's reputation

desafiador, a [dʒizafja'dor(a)] ADJ challenging; (*pessoa*) defiant ▶ M/F challenger

desafiar [dʒiza'fjar] VT to challenge; (*afrontar*) to defy

desafinado, -a [dʒizafi'nadu, a] ADJ out of tune

desafio [dʒiza'fiu] M challenge; (PT Esporte) match, game

desaforado, -a [dʒizafo'radu, a] ADJ rude, insolent

desaforo [dʒiza'foru] M insolence, abuse

desafortunado, -a

[dʒizafortu'nadu, a] ADJ unfortunate, unlucky

desagradar [dʒizagra'dar] VT to displease ▶ VI: **~ a alguém** to displease sb; **desagradável** [dʒizagra'davew] (pl **-eis**) ADJ unpleasant; **desagrado** [dʒiza'gradu] M displeasure

desaguar [dʒiza'gwar] VT to drain ▶ VI: **~ (em)** to flow ou empty (into)

desajeitado, -a [dʒizaʒej'tadu, a] ADJ clumsy, awkward

desalentado, -a [dʒizalē'tadu, a] ADJ disheartened

desalentar [dʒizalē'tar] VT to discourage; (deprimir) to depress; **desalento** [dʒiza'lētu] M discouragement

desalmado, -a [dʒizaw'madu, a] ADJ cruel, inhuman

desalojar [dʒizalo'ʒar] VT (expulsar) to oust; **desalojar-se** VR to move out

desamarrar [dʒizama'har] VT to untie ▶ VI (Náut) to cast off

desamor [dʒiza'mor] M dislike

desamparado, -a [dʒizãpa'radu, a] ADJ abandoned; (sem apoio) helpless

desanimação [dʒizanima'sãw] F dejection

desanimado, -a [dʒizani'madu, a] ADJ (pessoa) fed up, dispirited; (festa) dull; **ser ~** (pessoa) to be apathetic

desanuviar [dʒizanu'vjar] VT (céu) to clear; **desanuviar-se** VR to clear; (fig) to stop; **~ alguém** to put sb's mind at rest

desaparafusar [dʒizaparafu'zar] VT to unscrew

desaparecer [dʒizapare'ser] VI to disappear, vanish; **desaparecido,**

-a [dʒizapare'sidu, a] ADJ lost, missing ▶ M/F missing person; **desaparecimento** [dʒizaparesi'mētu] M disappearance; (falecimento) death

desapego [dʒiza'pegu] M indifference, detachment

desapercebido, -a [dʒizaperse'bidu, a] ADJ unnoticed

desapertar [dʒizaper'tar] VT to loosen; (livrar) to free

desapontamento [dʒizapõta'mētu] M disappointment

desapontar [dʒizapõ'tar] VT to disappoint

desapropriar [dʒizapro'prjar] VT (bens) to expropriate; (pessoa) to dispossess

desaprovar [dʒizapro'var] VT to disapprove of; (censurar) to object to

desarmamento [dʒizarma'mētu] M disarmament

desarmar [dʒizar'mar] VT to disarm; (desmontar) to dismantle; (bomba) to defuse

desarmonia [dʒizarmo'nia] F discord

desarranjo [dʒiza'hãʒu] M disorder; (enguiço) breakdown; (diarreia) diarrhoea (BRIT), diarrhea (US)

desarrumado, -a [dʒizahu'madu, a] ADJ untidy, messy

desarrumar [dʒizahu'mar] VT to mess up; (mala) to unpack

desassossego [dʒizaso'segu] M (inquietação) disquiet; (perturbação) restlessness

desastrado, -a [dʒizas'tradu, a] ADJ clumsy

desastre [dʒi'zastri] M disaster;

(*acidente*) accident; (*de avião*) crash

desatar [dʒiza'tar] VT (*nó*) to undo, untie ▶ VI: **~ a fazer** to begin to do; **~ a chorar** to burst into tears; **~ a rir** to burst out laughing

desatento, -a [dʒiza'tētu, a] ADJ inattentive

desatinado, -a [dʒizatʃi'nadu, a] ADJ crazy, wild ▶ M/F lunatic

desatino [dʒiza'tʃinu] M madness; (*ato*) folly

desativar [dʒizatʃi'var] VT (*firma, usina*) to shut down; (*veículos*) to withdraw from service; (*bomba*) to deactivate, defuse

desatualizado, -a [dʒizatwali'zadu, a] ADJ out of date; (*pessoa*) out of touch

desavença [dʒiza'vēsa] F (*briga*) quarrel; (*discórdia*) disagreement; **em ~** at loggerheads

desavergonhado, -a [dʒizavergo'ɲadu, a] ADJ shameless

desavisado, -a [dʒizavi'zadu, a] ADJ careless

desbastar [dʒizbas'tar] VT (*cabelo, plantas*) to thin (out); (*vegetação*) to trim

desbocado, -a [dʒizbo'kadu, a] ADJ foul-mouthed

desbotar [dʒizbo'tar] VT to discolour (BRIT), discolor (US) ▶ VI to fade

desbragadamente [dʒizbragada'mētʃi] ADV (*beber*) to excess; (*mentir*) blatantly

desbravar [dʒizbra'var] VT (*terras desconhecidas*) to explore

descabelar [dʒiskabe'lar] VT: **~ alguém** to mess up sb's hair; **descabelar-se** VR to get one's hair messed up

descabido, -a [dʒiska'bidu, a] ADJ improper; (*inoportuno*) inappropriate

descafeinado [dʒiskafej'nadu] ADJ decaffeinated ▶ N decaf

descalçar [dʒiskaw'sar] VT (*sapatos*) to take off; **descalçar-se** VR to take off one's shoes

descalço, -a [dʒis'kawsu, a] ADJ barefoot

descansado, -a [dʒiskã'sadu, a] ADJ calm, quiet; (*vagaroso*) slow; **fique ~** don't worry; **pode ficar ~ que ...** you can rest assured that ...

descansar [dʒiskã'sar] VT to rest; (*apoiar*) to lean ▶ VI to rest; to lean; **descanso** [dʒis'kãsu] M rest; (*folga*) break; (*para prato*) mat

descarregamento [dʒiskahega'mētu] M (*de carga*) unloading; (*Elet*) discharge

descarregar [dʒiskahe'gar] VT (*carga*) to unload; (*Elet*) to discharge; (*aliviar*) to relieve; (*raiva*) to vent, give vent to; (*arma*) to fire ▶ VI to unload; (*bateria*) to run out; **~ a raiva em alguém** to take it out on sb

descartar [dʒiskar'tar] VT to discard; **descartar-se** VR: **~-se de** to get rid of; **descartável** [dʒiskar'tavew] (*pl* **-eis**) ADJ disposable

descascar [dʒiskas'kar] VT (*fruta*) to peel; (*ervilhas*) to shell ▶ VI (*depois do sol*) to peel; (*cobra*) to shed its skin

descaso [dʒis'kazu] M disregard

descendência [desē'dēsja] F descendants *pl*, offspring *pl*

descendente [desē'dētʃi] ADJ descending, going down ▶ M/F descendant

descer [de'ser] VT (*escada*) to go (*ou* come) down; (*bagagem*) to take down ▶ VI (*saltar*) to get off; (*baixar*) to go (*ou* come) down; **descida** [de'sida] F descent; (*declive*) slope;

(*abaixamento*) fall, drop

desclassificar [dʒisklasifi'kar]
vt to disqualify; (*desacreditar*) to
discredit

descoberta [dʒisko'bɛrta] F
discovery; (*invenção*) invention

descoberto, -a [dʒisko'bɛrtu, a]
PP *de* **descobrir** ▶ ADJ bare, naked;
(*exposto*) exposed ▶ M overdraft; **a
~** openly; **conta a ~** overdrawn
account; **pôr** *ou* **sacar a ~** (*conta*)
to overdraw

descobridor, a [dʒiskobri'dor(a)]
M/F discoverer; (*explorador*)
explorer

descobrimento
[dʒiskobri'mẽtu] M discovery;
Descobrimentos MPL *see note*

Mainly due to the seafaring
expertise of Henry the
Navigator, Portugal enjoyed a
period of unrivalled overseas
expansion during the 15th
century. He organized and
financed several voyages to
Africa, which eventually led
to the rounding of the Cape
of Good Hope in 1488 by
Bartolomeu Dias. In 1497,
Vasco da Gama became the
first European to travel by sea
to India, where he established
a lucrative spice trade, and a
few years later, in 1500, Pedro
Álvares Cabral reached Brazil,
which he claimed for Portugal.
Brazil remained under
Portuguese rule until 1822.

descobrir [dʒisko'brir] vt to
discover; (*tirar a cobertura de*) to
uncover; (*panela*) to take the lid
off; (*averiguar*) to find out; (*enigma*)
to solve

descolar [dʒisko'lar] vt to unstick

▶ vi: **a criança não descola da
mãe** the child won't leave its
mother's side

descolorante [dʒiskolo'rãtʃi] M
bleach

descolorir [dʒiskolo'rir] vt to
discolour (BRIT), discolor (US);
(*cabelo*) to bleach ▶ vi to fade

descompostura
[dʒiskõpos'tura] F (*repreensão*)
dressing-down; (*insulto*) abuse;
passar uma ~ em alguém to give
sb a dressing-down; to hurl abuse
at sb

desconcentrar [dʒiskõsẽ'trar]
vt to distract; **desconcentrar-se**
vr to lose one's concentration

desconfiado, -a [dʒiskõ'fjadu, a]
ADJ suspicious, distrustful ▶ M/F
suspicious person

desconfiança [dʒiskõ'fjãsa] F
suspicion, distrust

desconfiar [dʒiskõ'fjar] vi to be
suspicious; **~ de alguém** (*não ter
confiança em*) to distrust sb;
(*suspeitar*) to suspect sb; **~ que ...**
to have the feeling that ...

desconfortável
[dʒiskõfor'tavew] (*pl* **-eis**) ADJ
uncomfortable

desconforto [dʒiskõ'fortu] M
discomfort

desconhecer [dʒiskoɲe'ser] vt
(*ignorar*) not to know; (*não
reconhecer*) not to recognize; (*um
benefício*) not to acknowledge; (*não
admitir*) not to accept;
desconhecido, -a [dʒiskoɲe'sidu,
a] ADJ unknown ▶ M/F stranger;
desconhecimento
[dʒiskoɲesi'mẽtu] M ignorance

desconsolado, -a
[dʒiskõso'ladu, a] ADJ miserable,
disconsolate

descontar [dʒiskõ'tar] vt to deduct; (*não levar em conta*) to discount; (*não fazer caso de*) to make light of

descontentamento [dʒiskõtēta'mētu] m discontent; (*desprazer*) displeasure

desconto [dʒis'kõtu] m discount; **com ~** at a discount; **dar um ~ (para)** (*fig*) to make allowances (for)

descontraído, -a [dʒiskõtra'idu, a] ADJ casual, relaxed

descontrair [dʒiskõtra'ir] vt to relax; **descontrair-se** VR to relax

descontrolar-se [dʒiskõtro'larsi] VR (*situação*) to get out of control; (*pessoa*) to lose one's self-control

desconversar [dʒiskõver'sar] vi to change the subject

descortesia [dʒiskorte'zia] f rudeness, impoliteness

descoser [dʒisko'zer] vt (*descosturar*) to unstitch; (*rasgar*) to rip apart; **descoser-se** VR to come apart at the seams

descrença [dʒis'krēsa] f disbelief, incredulity

descrente [dʒis'krētʃi] ADJ sceptical (BRIT), skeptical (US) ▶ M/F sceptic (BRIT), skeptic (US)

descrever [dʒiskre'ver] vt to describe

descrição [dʒiskri'sãw] (*pl* -ões) f description

descriptografar [dʒiskrɪptografa'far] vt *Comput* to decrypt

descritivo, -a [dʒiskri'tʃivu, a] ADJ descriptive

descrito, -a [dʒis'kritu, a] pp *de* **descrever**

descubro [dʒis'kubru] vb *ver* **descobrir**

descuidar [dʒiskwi'dar] vt to neglect ▶ vi: **~ de** to neglect, disregard; **descuido** [dʒis'kwidu] m carelessness; (*negligência*) neglect; (*erro*) oversight, slip; **por descuido** inadvertently

desculpa [dʒis'kuwpa] f excuse; (*perdão*) pardon; **pedir ~s a alguém por ou de algo** to apologize to sb for sth; **desculpar** [dʒiskuw'par] vt to excuse; (*perdoar*) to pardon, forgive; **desculpar-se** VR to apologize; **desculpar algo a alguém** to forgive sb for sth; **desculpe!** (I'm) sorry, I beg your pardon; **desculpável** [dʒiskuw'pavew] (*pl* -eis) ADJ forgivable

⌐(**PALAVRA-CHAVE**)

desde ['dezdʒi] PREP **1** (*lugar*): **desde ... até ...** from ... to ...; **andamos desde a praia até o restaurante** we walked from the beach to the restaurant
2 (*tempo, + adv, n*): **desde então** from then on, ever since; **desde já** (*de agora*) from now on; (*imediatamente*) at once, right now; **desde o casamento** since the wedding
3 (*tempo, + vb*) since; for; **conhecemo-nos desde 1978/há 20 anos** we've known each other since 1978/for 20 years; **não o vejo desde 1983** I haven't seen him since 1983
4 (*variedade*): **desde os mais baratos até os mais luxuosos** from the cheapest to the most luxurious
▶ CONJ: **desde que** since; **desde que comecei a trabalhar não o vi mais** I haven't seen him since I started work; **não saiu de casa**

desde que chegou he hasn't been out since he arrived

desdizer [dʒizdʒi'zer] (*irreg: como* **dizer**) VT to contradict; **desdizer-se** VR to go back on one's word

desdobrar [dʒizdo'brar] VT (*abrir*) to unfold; (*esforços*) to increase, redouble; (*tropas*) to deploy; (*bandeira*) to unfurl; (*dividir em grupos*) to split up; **desdobrar-se** VR (*empenhar-se*) to work hard, make a big effort

desejar [dese'ʒar] VT to want, desire

desejo [de'zeʒu] M wish, desire; **desejoso, -a** [deze'ʒozu, ɔza] ADJ: **desejoso de algo** wishing for sth; **desejoso de fazer** keen to do

desembaraçar [dʒizẽbara'sar] VT (*livrar*) to free; (*cabelo*) to untangle; **desembaraçar-se** VR (*desinibir-se*) to lose one's inhibitions; **~-se de** to get rid of

desembaraço [dʒizẽba'rasu] M liveliness; (*facilidade*) ease; (*confiança*) self-assurance

desembarcar [dʒizẽbar'kar] VT (*carga*) to unload; (*passageiros*) to let off ▶ VI to disembark; **desembarque** [dʒizẽ'barki] M landing, disembarkation; **"desembarque"** (*no aeroporto*) "arrivals"

desembolsar [dʒizẽbow'sar] VT to spend

desembrulhar [dʒizẽbru'ʎar] VT to unwrap

desempacotar [dʒizẽpako'tar] VT to unpack

desempatar [dʒizẽpa'tar] VT to decide ▶ VI to decide the match (*ou* race *etc*); **desempate** [dʒizẽ'patʃi]

M: **partida de desempate** (*jogo*) play-off, decider

desempenhar [dʒizẽpe'ɲar] VT (*cumprir*) to carry out, fulfil (BRIT), fulfill (US); (*papel*) to play; **desempenho** [dʒizẽ'peɲu] M performance; (*de obrigações etc*) fulfilment (BRIT), fulfillment (US)

desempregado, -a [dʒizẽpre'gadu, a] ADJ unemployed ▶ M/F unemployed person

desempregar-se [dʒizẽpre'garsi] VR to lose one's job

desemprego [dʒizẽ'pregu] M unemployment

desencadear [dʒizẽka'dʒjar] VT to unleash; (*despertar*) to provoke, trigger off ▶ VI (*chuva*) to pour; **desencadear-se** VR to break loose; (*tempestade*) to break

desencaixar [dʒizẽkaj'ʃar] VT to put out of joint; (*deslocar*) to dislodge; **desencaixar-se** VR to become dislodged

desencaixotar [dʒizẽkajʃo'tar] VT to unpack

desencarregar-se [dʒizẽkahe'garsi] VR (*de obrigação*) to discharge o.s.

desencontrar [dʒizẽkõ'trar] VT to keep apart; **desencontrar-se** VR (*não se encontrar*) to miss each other; (*perder-se um do outro*) to lose each other; **~-se de** to miss; to get separated from

desencorajar [dʒizẽkora'ʒar] VT to discourage

desencostar [dʒizẽkos'tar] VT to move away; **desencostar-se** VR: **~-se de** to move away from

desencriptar [dʒizẽkrip'tar] VT (*Comput, Tel*) to decrypt

desenfreado, -a [dʒizẽ'frjadu, a] ADJ wild

desenganado, -a [dʒizẽga'nadu, a] ADJ incurable; (desiludido) disillusioned

desenganar [dʒizẽga'nar] VT: **~ alguém** to disillusion sb; (de falsas crenças) to open sb's eyes; (doente) to give up hope of curing; **desenganar-se** VR to become disillusioned; (sair de erro) to realize the truth; **desengano** [dʒizẽ'ganu] M disillusionment; (desapontamento) disappointment

desengonçado, -a [dʒizẽgõ'sadu, a] ADJ (malseguro) rickety; (pessoa) ungainly

desenhar [deze'nar] VT to draw; (Tec) to design; **desenhar-se** VR (destacar-se) to stand out; (figurar-se) to take shape; **desenhista** [deze'niʃta] M/F (Tec) designer

desenho [de'zɛnu] M drawing; (modelo) design; (esboço) sketch; (plano) plan; **~ animado** cartoon

desenlace [dʒizẽ'lasi] M outcome

desenrolar [dʒizẽho'lar] VT to unroll; (narrativa) to develop; **desenrolar-se** VR to unfold

desentender [dʒizẽtẽ'der] VT to misunderstand; **desentender-se** VR: **~-se com** to have a disagreement with; **desentendido, -a** [dʒizẽtẽ'dʒidu, a] ADJ: **fazer-se de desentendido** to pretend not to understand; **desentendimento** [dʒizẽtẽdʒi'mẽtu] M misunderstanding

desenterrar [dʒizẽte'har] VT (cadáver) to exhume; (tesouro) to dig up; (descobrir) to bring to light

desentupir [dʒizẽtu'pir] VT to unblock

desenvoltura [dʒizẽvow'tura] F self-confidence

desenvolver [dʒizẽvow'ver] VT to develop; **desenvolver-se** VR to develop; **desenvolvimento** [dʒizẽvowvi'mẽtu] M development; (crescimento) growth; **país em desenvolvimento** developing country

deserção [dezer'sãw] F desertion

desertar [deser'tar] VT to desert, abandon ▶ VI to desert; **deserto, -a** [de'zɛrtu, a] ADJ deserted ▶ M desert; **desertor, a** [dezer'tor(a)] M/F deserter

desesperado, -a [dʒizespe'radu, a] ADJ desperate; (furioso) furious

desesperador, a [dʒizespera'dor(a)] ADJ desperate; (enfurecedor) maddening

desesperança [dʒizespe'rãsa] F despair

desesperar [dʒizespe'rar] VT to drive to despair; (enfurecer) to infuriate; **desesperar-se** VR to despair; (enfurecer-se) to become infuriated; **desespero** [dʒizes'peru] M despair, desperation; (raiva) fury

desestimular [dʒizestʃimu'lar] VT to discourage

desfalcar [dʒisfaw'kar] VT (dinheiro) to embezzle; (reduzir): **~ (de)** to reduce (by); **o jogo está desfalcado** the game is incomplete

desfalecer [dʒisfale'ser] (enfraquecer) to weaken ▶ VI (enfraquecer) to weaken; (desmaiar) to faint

desfalque [dʒis'fawki] M (de dinheiro) embezzlement; (diminuição) reduction

desfavorável [dʒisfavo'ravew] (pl **-eis**) ADJ unfavourable (BRIT), unfavorable (US)

desfazer [dʒisfa'zer] (*irreg: como* **fazer**) VT (*costura*) to undo; (*dúvidas*) to dispel; (*agravo*) to redress; (*grupo*) to break up; (*contrato*) to dissolve; (*noivado*) to break off ▶ VI: **~ de alguém** to belittle sb; **desfazer-se** VR to vanish; (*tecido*) to come to pieces; (*grupo*) to break up; (*vaso*) to break; **~-se de** (*livrar-se*) to get rid of; **~-se em lágrimas/gentilezas** to burst into tears/go out of one's way to please

desfecho [dʒis'feʃu] M ending, outcome

desfeito, -a [dʒis'fejtu, a] ADJ undone; (*cama*) unmade; (*contrato*) broken

desfilar [dʒisfi'lar] VI to parade; **desfile** [dʒis'fili] M parade, procession

desforra [dʒis'fɔha] F revenge; (*reparação*) redress; **tirar ~** to get even

desfrutar [dʒisfru'tar] VT to enjoy ▶ VI: **~ de** to enjoy

desgarrado, -a [dʒizga'hadu, a] ADJ stray; (*navio*) off course

desgastante [dʒizgas'tãtʃi] ADJ (*fig*) stressful

desgrudar [dʒizgru'dar] VT to unstick ▶ VI: **~ de** to tear o.s. away from; **~ algo de algo** to take sth off sth

desidratar [dʒizidra'tar] VT to dehydrate

design [dʒi'zãjn] M design

designar [dezig'nar] VT to designate; (*nomear*) to name, appoint; (*dia, data*) to fix

desigual [dezi'gwaw] (*pl* **-ais**) ADJ unequal; (*terreno*) uneven; **desigualdade** [dʒizigwaw'dadʒi] F inequality

desiludir [dʒizilu'dʒir] VT to disillusion; (*causar decepção a*) to disappoint; **desiludir-se** VR to lose one's illusions

desimpedido, -a [dʒizĩpe'dʒidu, a] ADJ free

desinfetante [dʒizĩfe'tãtʃi] ADJ, M disinfectant

desinfetar [dʒizĩfe'tar] VT to disinfect

desinstalar [dʒizĩsta'lar] VT (*Comput*) to uninstall

desintegração [dʒizĩtegra'sãw] F disintegration, break-up

desintegrar [dʒizĩte'grar] VT to separate; **desintegrar-se** VR to disintegrate, fall to pieces

desistir [dezis'tʃir] VI to give up; **~ de fumar** to stop smoking; **ele ia, mas no final desistiu** he was going, but in the end he gave up the idea *ou* he decided not to

desjejum [dʒizʒe'ʒũ] M breakfast

deslavado, -a [dʒizla'vadu, a] ADJ (*pessoa, atitude*) shameless; (*mentira*) blatant

desleal [dʒizle'aw] (*pl* **-ais**) ADJ disloyal

desleixo [dʒiz'lejʃu] M sloppiness

desligado, -a [dʒizli'gadu, a] ADJ (*eletricidade*) off; (*pessoa*) absent-minded; **estar ~** to be miles away

desligar [dʒizli'gar] VT (*Tec*) to disconnect; (*luz, TV, motor*) to switch off; (*telefone*) to hang up; **desligar-se** VR: **~-se de algo** (*afastar-se*) to leave sth; (*problemas etc*) to turn one's back on sth; **não desligue** (*Tel*) hold the line

deslizar [dʒizli'zar] VI to slide; (*por acidente*) to slip; (*passar de leve*) to glide; **deslize** [dʒiz'lizi] M lapse; (*escorregadela*) slip

deslocado, -a [dʒizlo'kadu, a] ADJ (*membro*) dislocated; (*desambientado*) out of place

deslumbramento [dʒizlũbra'mẽtu] M dazzle; (*fascinação*) fascination

deslumbrante [dʒizlũ'brãtʃi] ADJ dazzling; (*casa, festa*) amazing

deslumbrar [dʒizlũ'brar] VT to dazzle; (*maravilhar*) to amaze; (*fascinar*) to fascinate ▶ VI to be dazzling; to be amazing; **deslumbrar-se** VR: **~-se com** to be fascinated by

desmaiado, -a [dʒizma'jadu, a] ADJ unconscious; (*cor*) pale

desmaiar [dʒizma'jar] VI to faint; **desmaio** [dʒiz'maju] M faint

desmanchar [dʒizman'ʃar] VT (*costura*) to undo; (*contrato*) to break; (*noivado*) to break off; (*penteado*) to mess up; **desmanchar-se** VR (*costura*) to come undone

desmarcar [dʒizmar'kar] VT (*compromisso*) to cancel

desmascarar [dʒizmaska'rar] VT to unmask

desmazelado, -a [dʒizmaze'ladu, a] ADJ slovenly, untidy

desmedido, -a [dʒizme'dʒidu, a] ADJ excessive

desmentido [dʒizmẽ'tʃidu] M (*negação*) denial; (*contradição*) contradiction

desmentir [dʒizmẽ'tʃir] VT (*contradizer*) to contradict; (*negar*) to deny

desmiolado, -a [dʒizmjo'ladu, a] ADJ brainless; (*esquecido*) forgetful

desmoronamento [dʒizmorona'mẽtu] M collapse

desmoronar [dʒizmoro'nar] VT to knock down ▶ VI to collapse

desnatado, -a [dʒizna'tadu, a] ADJ (*leite*) skimmed

desnaturado, -a [dʒiznatu'radu, a] ADJ inhumane ▶ M/F monster

desnecessário, -a [dʒiznese'sarju, a] ADJ unnecessary

desnutrição [dʒiznutri'sãw] F malnutrition

desobedecer [dʒizobede'ser] VT to disobey; **desobediência** [dʒizobe'dʒjẽsja] F disobedience; **desobediente** [dʒizobe'dʒjẽtʃi] ADJ disobedient

desobstruir [dʒizobis'trwir] VT to unblock

desocupado, -a [dʒizoku'padu, a] ADJ (*casa*) empty, vacant; (*disponível*) free; (*sem trabalho*) unemployed

desocupar [dʒizoku'par] VT (*casa*) to vacate; (*liberar*) to free

desodorante [dʒizodo'rãtʃi], (PT) **desodorizante** [dʒizodori'zãtʃi] M deodorant

desolação [dezola'sãw] F (*consternação*) grief; (*de um lugar*) desolation; **desolado, -a** [dezo'ladu, a] ADJ distressed; (*lugar*) desolate

desonesto, -a [dezo'nɛstu, a] ADJ dishonest

desordem [dʒi'zordẽ] F disorder, confusion; **em ~** (*casa*) untidy

desorganizar [dʒizorgani'zar] VT to disorganize; (*dissolver*) to break up; **desorganizar-se** VR to become disorganized; to break up

desorientação [dʒizorjẽta'sãw] F bewilderment, confusion

desorientar [dʒizorjẽ'tar] VT (*desnortear*) to throw off course; (*perturbar*) to confuse; (*desvairar*) to unhinge; **desorientar-se** VR to lose one's way; to get confused; to go mad

desovar [dʒizo'var] vт to lay; (*peixe*) to spawn

despachado, -a [dʒispa'ʃadu, a] ADJ (*pessoa*) efficient

despachar [dʒispa'ʃar] vт to dispatch, send off; (*atender, resolver*) to deal with; (*despedir*) to sack; **despachar-se** vʀ to hurry (up); **despacho** [dʒis'paʃu] м dispatch; (*de negócios*) handling; (*nota em requerimento*) ruling; (*reunião*) consultation; (*macumba*) witchcraft

despeço [dʒis'pɛsu] vʙ *ver* **despedir**

despedaçar [dʒispeda'sar] vт (*quebrar*) to smash; (*rasgar*) to tear apart; **despedaçar-se** vʀ to smash; to tear

despedida [dʒispe'dʒida] ꜰ farewell; (*de trabalhador*) dismissal

despedir [dʒispe'dʒir] vт (*de emprego*) to dismiss, sack; **despedir-se** vʀ: **~-se (de)** to say goodbye (to)

despeitado, -a [dʒispej'tadu, a] ADJ spiteful; (*ressentido*) resentful

despeito [dʒis'pejtu] м spite; **a ~ de** in spite of, despite

despejar [dʒispe'ʒar] vт (*água*) to pour; (*esvaziar*) to empty; (*inquilino*) to evict; **despejo** [dʒis'peʒu] м eviction; **quarto de despejo** junk room

despencar [dʒispẽ'kar] vɪ to fall down, tumble down

despentear [dʒispẽ'tʃjar] vт (*cabelo: sem querer*) to mess up; (: *de propósito*) to let down; **despentear-se** vʀ to mess one's hair up; to let one's hair down

despercebido, -a [dʒisperse'bidu, a] ADJ unnoticed

desperdiçar [dʒisperdʒi'sar] vт to waste; (*dinheiro*) to squander; **desperdício** [dʒisper'dʒisju] м waste

despertador [dʒisperta'dor] м (*tb:* **relógio ~**) alarm clock

despertar [dʒisper'tar] vт to wake; (*suspeitas, interesse*) to arouse; (*reminiscências*) to revive; (*apetite*) to whet ▶ vɪ to wake up ▶ м awakening; **desperto, -a** [dʒis'pɛrtu, a] ADJ awake

despesa [dʒis'peza] ꜰ expense; **despesas** ꜰPL (*de uma empresa*) expenses, costs; **~s gerais** (*Com*) overheads

despido, -a [dʒis'pidu, a] ADJ naked, bare; (*livre*) free

despir [dʒis'pir] vт (*roupa*) to take off; (*pessoa*) to undress; (*despojar*) to strip; **despir-se** vʀ to undress

despojar [dʒispo'ʒar] vт (*casas*) to loot, sack; (*pessoas*) to rob

despontar [dʒispõ'tar] vɪ to emerge; (*sol*) to come out; (: *ao amanhecer*) to come up; **ao ~ do dia** at daybreak

desporto [dʒis'portu] м sport

desprender [dʒisprẽ'der] vт to loosen; (*desatar*) to unfasten; (*emitir*) to emit; **desprender-se** vʀ (*botão*) to come off; (*cheiro*) to be given off

desprezar [dʒispre'zar] vт to despise, disdain; (*não dar importância a*) to disregard, ignore; **desprezível** [dʒispre'zivew] (*pl* **-eis**) ADJ despicable; **desprezo** [dʒis'prezu] м scorn, contempt; **dar ao desprezo** to ignore

desproporcional [dʒisproporsjo'naw] ADJ disproportionate

despropósito [dʒispro'pɔzitu] м nonsense

desprovido, -a [dʒispro'vidu, a] ADJ deprived; **~ de** without

desqualificar [dʒiskwalifi'kar] VT (*Esporte etc*) to disqualify; (*tornar indigno*) to disgrace, lower

desregrado, -a [dʒizhe'gradu, a] ADJ disorderly, unruly; (*devasso*) immoderate

desrespeito [dʒizhe'spejtu] M disrespect

desse¹, -a ['desi, a] = **de + esse**, **~ a**

desse² VB *ver* **dar**

destacar [dʒista'kar] VT (*Mil*) to detail; (*separar*) to detach; (*enfatizar*) to emphasize ▶ VI to stand out; **destacar-se** VR to stand out; (*pessoa*) to be outstanding

destampar [dʒistã'par] VT to take the lid off

destapar [dʒista'par] VT to uncover

destaque [dʒis'taki] M distinction; (*pessoa, coisa*) highlight

deste ['destʃi, a] = **de + este**, **~ a**

destemido, -a [deste'midu, a] ADJ fearless, intrepid

destilar [destʃi'lar] VT to distil (BRIT), distill (US)

destinação [destʃina'sãw] (*pl* **-ões**) F destination

destinar [destʃi'nar] VT to destine; (*dinheiro*): **~ (para)** to set aside (for); **destinar-se** VR: **~-se a** to be intended for; (*carta*) to be addressed to

destinatário, -a [destʃina'tarju, a] M/F addressee

destino [des'tʃinu] M destiny, fate; (*lugar*) destination; **com ~ a** bound for

destituir [destʃi'twir] VT to dismiss; **~ de** (*privar de*) to deprive of

destrancar [dʒistrã'kar] VT to unlock

destratar [dʒistra'tar] VT to abuse, insult

destreza [des'treza] F skill; (*agilidade*) dexterity

destro, -a ['destru, a] ADJ skilful (BRIT), skillful (US); (*ágil*) agile; (*não canhoto*) right-handed

destrocar [dʒistro'kar] VT to give back, return

destroçar [dʒistro'sar] VT to destroy; (*quebrar*) to smash, break; **destroços** [dʒis'trɔsus] MPL wreckage *sg*

destruição [dʒistrwi'sãw] F destruction

destruir [dʒis'trwir] VT to destroy

desvairado, -a [dʒizvaj'radu, a] ADJ (*louco*) crazy, demented; (*desorientado*) bewildered

desvalorizar [dʒizvalori'zar] VT to devalue

desvantagem [dʒizvã'taʒẽ] (*pl* **-ns**) F disadvantage

desvão [dʒiz'vãw] (*pl* **-s**) M loft

desventura [dʒizvẽ'tura] F misfortune; (*infelicidade*) unhappiness

desvio [dʒiz'viu] M diversion, detour; (*curva*) bend; (*fig*) deviation; (*de dinheiro*) embezzlement

detalhadamente [detaʎada'metʃi] ADV in detail

detalhado, -a [detaʎadu, a] ADJ detailed

detalhe [de'taʎi] M detail

detectar [detek'tar] VT to detect

detector [detek'tor] M detector

detenção [detẽ'sãw] (*pl* **-ões**) F detention

deter [de'ter] (*irreg: como* **ter**) VT to stop; (*prender*) to arrest, detain; (*reter*) to keep; (*conter: riso*) to contain; **deter-se** VR to stop; (*ficar*) to stay; (*conter-se*) to restrain o.s.

detergente [deter'ʒẽtʃi] M detergent

deteriorar [deterjo'rar] VT to spoil, damage; **deteriorar-se** VR to deteriorate; (*relações*) to worsen

determinação [determina'sãw] F determination; (*decisão*) decision; (*ordem*) order

determinado, -a [determi'nadu, a] ADJ determined; (*certo*) certain, given

determinar [determi'nar] VT to determine; (*decretar*) to order; (*resolver*) to decide (on); (*causar*) to cause

detestar [detes'tar] VT to hate; **detestável** [detes'tavew] (*pl* -eis) ADJ horrible, hateful

detetive [dete'tʃivi] M/F detective

detido, -a [de'tʃidu, a] ADJ (*preso*) under arrest; (*minucioso*) thorough ▶ M/F person under arrest, prisoner

detonação [detona'sãw] (*pl* -ões) F explosion

detonar [deto'nar] VI, VT to detonate

detrás [de'trajs] ADV behind ▶ PREP: **~ de** behind

detrimento [detri'mẽtu] M: **em ~ de** to the detriment of

detrito [de'tritu] M debris *sg*; (*de comida*) remains *pl*; (*resíduo*) dregs *pl*

deturpação [deturpa'sãw] F corruption; (*de palavras*) distortion

deturpar [detur'par] VT to corrupt; (*desfigurar*) to disfigure; (*palavras*) to twist

deu [dew] VB *ver* **dar**

deus, a [dews, 'dewza] M/F god/ goddess; **D~ me livre!** God forbid!; **graças a D~** thank goodness; **meu D~!** good Lord!

devagar [dʒiva'gar] ADV slowly

devaneio [deva'neju] M daydream

devassa [de'vasa] F investigation, inquiry

devassidão [devasi'dãw] F debauchery

devasso, -a [de'vasu, a] ADJ dissolute

deve ['dɛvi] M debit

dever [de'ver] M duty ▶ VT to owe ▶ VI (*suposição*): **deve (de) estar doente** he must be ill; (*obrigação*): **devo partir às oito** I must go at eight; **você devia ir ao médico** you should go to the doctor; **que devo fazer?** what shall I do?

devido, -a [de'vidu, a] ADJ (*maneira*) proper; (*respeito*) due; **~ a** due to, owing to; **no ~ tempo** in due course

devoção [devo'sãw] F devotion

devolução [devolu'sãw] F devolution; (*restituição*) return; (*reembolso*) refund; **~ de impostos** tax rebate

devolver [devow'ver] VT to give back, return; (*Com*) to refund

devorar [devo'rar] VT to devour; (*destruir*) to destroy

devotar [devo'tar] VT to devote

dez [dɛz] NUM ten

dezanove [deza'nɔvə] (PT) NUM = **dezenove**

dezasseis [deza'sejs] (PT) NUM = **dezesseis**

dezassete [deza'setə] (PT) NUM = **dezessete**

dezembro [de'zẽbru] M December

dezena [de'zena] F: **uma ~** ten

dezenove [deze'nɔvi] NUM nineteen

dezesseis [deze'sejs] NUM sixteen

dezessete [dezi'setʃi] NUM
seventeen

dezoito [dʒi'zojtu] NUM eighteen

dia ['dʒia] M day; (claridade)
daylight; **~ a ~** day by day; **~ santo**
holy day; **~ útil** weekday; **estar** ou
andar em ~ (com) to be up to date
(with); **de ~** in the daytime, by day;
mais ~ menos ~ sooner or later;
~ sim, ~ não every other day; **no ~
seguinte** the next day; **bom ~**
good morning; **um ~ desses** one of
these days; **~s a fio** days on end;
~ cheio/morto busy/quiet ou slow
day; **todo santo ~** (col) every single
day, day after day; **recebo por ~** I'm
paid by the day; **um bebê de ~s** a
newborn baby; **ele está com os ~s
contados** his days are numbered;
dia a dia M daily life, everyday life

diabete, diabetes [dʒja'bɛtʃi(s)] F
diabetes sg; **diabético, -a**
[dʒja'bɛtʃiku, a] ADJ, M/F diabetic

diabo ['dʒjabu] M devil; **que ~!** (col)
damn it!

diabrura [dʒja'brura] F prank;
diabruras FPL (travessura) mischief
sg

diagnóstico [dʒjag'nɔstʃiku] M
diagnosis

diagonal [dʒjago'naw] (pl -ais) ADJ,
F diagonal

diagrama [dʒja'grama] M diagram

dialeto [dʒja'lɛtu] M dialect

dialogar [dʒjalo'gar] VI: **~ (com
alguém)** to talk (to sb); (Pol) to have
ou hold talks (with sb)

diálogo ['dʒjalogu] M dialogue;
(conversa) talk, conversation

diamante [dʒja'mãtʃi] M diamond

diâmetro ['dʒjametru] M diameter

diante ['dʒjãtʃi] PREP: **~ de** before;
(na frente de) in front of; (problemas
etc) in the face of; **e assim por ~**
and so on; **para ~** forward

dianteira [dʒjã'tejra] F front,
vanguard; **tomar a ~** to get ahead

dianteiro, -a [dʒjã'tejru, a] ADJ
front

diapositivo [dʒjapozi'tʃivu] M
(Foto) slide

diária ['dʒjarja] F (de hotel) daily rate

diário, -a ['dʒjarju, a] ADJ daily ▶ M
diary; (jornal) (daily) newspaper;
~ de bordo (Aer) logbook

diarreia [dʒja'hɛja] F diarrhoea
(BRIT), diarrhea (US)

dica ['dʒika] (col) F hint

dicionário [dʒisjo'narju] M
dictionary

dieta ['dʒjɛta] F diet; **fazer ~** to go
on a diet

diferença [dʒife'rẽsa] F difference;
ela tem uma ~ comigo she's got
something against me

diferenciar [dʒiferẽ'sjar] VT to
differentiate

diferente [dʒife'rẽtʃi] ADJ different;
estar ~ com alguém to be at odds
with sb

difícil [dʒi'fisiw] (pl -eis) ADJ
difficult; (improvável) unlikely; **o ~ é
...** the difficult thing is ...; **acho ~
ela aceitar nossa proposta** I think
it's unlikely she will accept our
proposal; **dificilmente**
[dʒifisiw'mẽtʃi] ADV with difficulty;
(mal) hardly; (raramente) hardly ever

dificuldade [dʒifikuw'dadʒi] F
difficulty; **em ~s** in trouble

dificultar [dʒifikuw'tar] VT to
make difficult; (complicar) to
complicate

difundir [dʒifũ'dʒir] VT to diffuse;
to spread

digerir [dʒiʒe'rir] VT, VI to digest

digestão [dʒiʒes'tãw] F digestion

digital [dʒiʒi'taw] (pl -ais) ADJ:

impressão ~ fingerprint

digitar [dʒiʒi'tar] vt (Comput: dados) to key (in)

dígito ['dʒiʒitu] m digit

dignidade [dʒigni'dadʒi] f dignity

digno, -a ['dʒignu, a] ADJ (merecedor) worthy; (nobre) dignified

digo ['dʒigu] vb ver **dizer**

dilatar [dʒila'tar] vt to dilate, expand; (prolongar) to prolong; (retardar) to delay

dilema [dʒi'lema] m dilemma

diluir [dʒi'lwir] vt to dilute

dilúvio [dʒi'luvju] m flood

dimensão [dʒimē'sāw] (pl **-ões**) f dimension; **dimensões** FPL (medidas) measurements

diminuição [dʒiminwi'sāw] f reduction

diminuir [dʒimi'nwir] vt to reduce; (som) to turn down; (interesse) to lessen ▶ vi to lessen, diminish; (preço) to go down; (dor) to wear off; (barulho) to die down

diminutivo, -a [dʒiminu'tʃivu, a] ADJ diminutive ▶ m (Ling) diminutive

Dinamarca [dʒina'marka] f Denmark; **dinamarquês, -quesa** [dʒinamar'kes, 'keza] ADJ Danish ▶ m/f Dane ▶ m (Ling) Danish

dinâmico, -a [dʒi'namiku, a] ADJ dynamic

dínamo ['dʒinamu] m dynamo

dinheirão [dʒiɲej'rāw] m: **um ~** loads pl of money

dinheiro [dʒi'ɲejru] m money; **~ à vista** cash for paying in cash; **~ em caixa** money in the till; **~ em espécie** cash

dinossauro [dʒino'sawru] m dinosaur

diploma [dʒip'lɔma] m diploma

diplomacia [dʒiploma'sia] f diplomacy; (fig) tact

diplomata [dʒiplo'mata] m/f diplomat; **diplomático, -a** [dʒiplo'matʃiku, a] ADJ diplomatic

dique ['dʒiki] m dam; (Geo) dyke

direção [dʒire'sāw] (pl **-ões**) f direction; (endereço) address; (Auto) steering; (administração) management; (comando) leadership; (diretoria) board of directors; **em ~ a** towards

direi [dʒi'rej] vb ver **dizer**

direita [dʒi'rejta] f (mão) right hand; (lado) right-hand side; (Pol) right wing; **à ~** on the right

direito, -a [dʒi'rejtu, a] ADJ (lado) right-hand; (mão) right; (honesto) honest; (devido) proper; (justo) right, just ▶ m right; (Jur) law ▶ ADV straight; (bem) right; (de maneira certa) properly; **direitos** MPL (humanos) rights; (alfandegários) duty sg

direto, -a [dʒi'rɛtu, a] ADJ direct ▶ ADV straight; **transmissão direta** (TV) live broadcast

diretor, a [dʒire'tor(a)] ADJ directing, guiding ▶ m/f director; (de jornal) editor; (de escola) head teacher; **diretoria** [dʒireto'ria] f (Com) management

dirigente [dʒiri'ʒētʃi] m/f (de país, partido) leader; (diretor) director; (gerente) manager

dirigir [dʒiri'ʒir] vt to direct; (Com) to manage; (veículo) to drive ▶ vi to drive; **dirigir-se** vr: **~-se a** (falar com) to speak to; (ir, recorrer) to go to; (esforços) to be directed towards

discagem [dʒis'kaʒē] f (Tel) dialling

discar [dʒis'kar] vт to dial

disciplina [dʒisi'plina] ϝ discipline; **disciplinar** [dʒisipli'nar] vт to discipline

discípulo, -a [dʒi'sipulu, a] м/ϝ disciple; (*aluno*) pupil

disco ['dʒisku] м disc; (*Comput*) disk; (*Mús*) record; (*de telefone*) dial; **~ rígido** (*Comput*) hard drive, hard disk; **~ do sistema** system disk; **~ voador** flying saucer

discordar [dʒiskor'dar] vι: **~ de alguém em algo** to disagree with sb on sth

discórdia [dʒis'kɔrdʒja] ϝ discord, strife

discoteca [dʒisko'tɛka] ϝ discotheque, disco (*col*)

discrepância [dʒiskre'pãsja] ϝ discrepancy; (*desacordo*) disagreement; **discrepante** [dʒiskre'pãtʃi] ADJ conflicting

discreto, -a [dʒis'krɛtu, a] ADJ discreet; (*modesto*) modest; (*prudente*) shrewd; (*roupa*) plain; **discrição** [dʒiskri'sãw] ϝ discretion

discriminação [dʒiskrimina'sãw] ϝ discrimination

discriminar [dʒiskrimi'nar] vт to distinguish ▶ vι: **~ entre** to discriminate between

discurso [dʒis'kursu] м speech

discussão [dʒisku'sãw] (*pl* -**ões**) ϝ discussion; (*contenda*) argument

discutir [dʒisku'tʃir] vт to discuss ▶ vι: **~ (sobre algo)** to talk (about sth); (*contender*) to argue (about sth)

disenteria [dʒizẽte'ria] ϝ dysentery

disfarçar [dʒisfar'sar] vт to disguise ▶ vι to pretend; **disfarçar-se** vʀ: **~-se em** *ou* **de algo** to disguise o.s. as sth; **disfarce** [dʒis'farsi] м disguise;

(*máscara*) mask

dislexia [dʒizlek'sia] ϝ dyslexia

disparar [dʒispa'rar] vт to shoot, fire ▶ vι to fire; (*arma*) to go off; (*correr*) to shoot off, bolt

disparatado, -a [dʒispara'tadu, a] ADJ silly, absurd

disparate [dʒispa'ratʃi] м nonsense, rubbish

disparidade [dʒispari'dadʒi] ϝ disparity

dispensar [dʒispẽ'sar] vт to excuse; (*prescindir de*) to do without; (*conferir*) to grant; **dispensável** [dʒispẽ'savew] (*pl* -**eis**) ADJ expendable

dispersar [dʒisper'sar] vт, vι to disperse; **disperso, -a** [dʒis'pɛrsu, a] ADJ scattered

displicência [dʒispli'sẽsja] (ʙʀ) ϝ negligence, carelessness; **displicente** [dʒispli'sẽtʃi] ADJ careless

dispo ['dʒispu] vʙ *ver* **despir**

disponível [dʒispo'nivew] (*pl* -**eis**) ADJ available

dispor [dʒis'por] (*irreg: como* **pôr**) vт to arrange ▶ vι: **~ de** to have the use of; (*ter*) to have, own; (*pessoas*) to have at one's disposal; **dispor-se** vʀ: **~-se a** (*estar pronto a*) to be prepared to, be willing to; (*decidir*) to decide to; **~ sobre** to talk about; **disponha!** feel free!

disposição [dʒispozi'sãw] (*pl* -**ões**) ϝ arrangement; (*humor*) disposition; (*inclinação*) inclination; **à sua ~** at your disposal

dispositivo [dʒispozi'tʃivu] м gadget, device; (*determinação de lei*) provision

disputa [dʒis'puta] ϝ dispute, argument; (*competição*) contest; **disputar** [dʒispu'tar] vт to dispute;

(*concorrer a*) to compete for; (*lutar por*) to fight over ▶ vɪ to quarrel, argue; to compete; **disputar uma corrida** to run a race

disquete [dʒis'ketʃi] м (*Comput*) diskette

disse ['dʒisi] vʙ *ver* **dizer**

disseminar [dʒisemi'nar] vт to disseminate; (*espalhar*) to spread

dissertar [dʒiser'tar] vɪ to speak

dissidência [dʒisi'dẽsja] ꜰ (*cisão*) difference of opinion

disso ['dʒisu] = **de + isso**

dissolução [dʒisolu'sãw] ꜰ (*libertinagem*) debauchery; (*de casamento*) dissolution

dissolver [dʒisow'ver] vт to dissolve; (*dispersar*) to disperse; (*motim*) to break up

dissuadir [dʒiswa'dʒir] vт to dissuade; **~ alguém de fazer algo** to talk sb out of doing sth, dissuade sb from doing sth

distância [dʒis'tãsja] ꜰ distance; **a 3 quilômetros de ~** 3 kilometres (ʙʀɪᴛ) *ou* kilometers (ᴜꜱ) away

distanciar [dʒistã'sjar] vт to distance, set apart; (*colocar por intervalos*) to space out; **distanciar-se** vʀ to move away; (*fig*) to distance o.s.

distante [dʒis'tãtʃi] ᴀᴅᴊ distant

distender [dʒistẽ'der] vт to expand; (*estirar*) to stretch; (*dilatar*) to distend; (*músculo*) to pull; **distender-se** vʀ to expand; to distend

distinção [dʒistʃĩ'sãw] (*pl* **-ões**) ꜰ distinction; **fazer ~** to make a distinction

distinguir [dʒistʃĩ'gir] vт to distinguish; (*avistar, ouvir*) to make out; **distinguir-se** vʀ to stand out

distinto, -a [dʒis'tʃĩtu, a] ᴀᴅᴊ

different; (*eminente*) distinguished; (*claro*) distinct; (*refinado*) refined

disto ['dʒistu] = **de + isto**

distorcer [dʒistor'ser] vт to distort

distração [dʒistra'sãw] (*pl* **-ões**) ꜰ (*alheamento*) absent-mindedness; (*divertimento*) pastime; (*descuido*) oversight

distraído, -a [dʒistra'idu, a] ᴀᴅᴊ absent-minded; (*não atento*) inattentive

distrair [dʒistra'ir] vт to distract; (*divertir*) to amuse

distribuição [dʒistribwi'sãw] ꜰ distribution; (*de cartas*) delivery

distribuidor, a [dʒistribwi'dor(a)] м/ꜰ distributor ▶ м (*Auto*) distributor ▶ ꜰ (*Com*) distribution company, distributor

distribuir [dʒistri'bwir] vт to distribute; (*repartir*) to share out; (*cartas*) to deliver

distrito [dʒis'tritu] м district; (*delegacia*) police station; **~ eleitoral** constituency; **~ federal** federal area

distúrbio [dʒis'turbju] м disturbance

ditado [dʒi'tadu] м dictation; (*provérbio*) saying

ditador [dʒita'dor] м dictator; **ditadura** [dʒita'dura] ꜰ dictatorship

ditar [dʒi'tar] vт to dictate; (*impor*) to impose

dito, -a ['dʒitu, a] ᴘᴘ *de* **dizer**; **~ e feito** no sooner said than done

diurno, -a ['dʒjurnu, a] ᴀᴅᴊ daytime *atr*

divã [dʒi'vã] м couch, divan

divergir [dʒiver'ʒir] vɪ to diverge; (*discordar*): **~ (de alguém)** to disagree (with sb)

diversão [dʒiver'sãw] (pl **-ões**) F
amusement; (passatempo) pastime

diverso, -a [dʒi'vɛrsu, a] ADJ
different; (pl) various

diversões [diver'sõjs] FPL de
diversão

diversos [dʒi'vɛrsus] MPL sundries

divertido, -a [dʒiver'tʃidu, a] ADJ
amusing, funny

divertimento [dʒivertʃi'mẽtu] M
amusement, entertainment

divertir [dʒiver'tʃir] VT to amuse,
entertain; **divertir-se** VR to enjoy
o.s., have a good time

dívida ['dʒivida] F debt; **contrair
~s** to run into debt; **~ externa**
foreign debt

dividir [dʒivi'dʒir] VT to divide;
(despesas, lucro, comida etc) to share;
(separar) to separate ▶ VI (Mat) to
divide; **dividir-se** VR to divide, split
up

divino, -a [dʒi'vinu, a] ADJ divine
▶ M Holy Ghost

divirjo [dʒi'virʒu] VB ver **divergir**

divisa [dʒi'viza] F emblem; (frase)
slogan; (fronteira) border; (Mil)
stripe; **divisas** FPL (câmbio) foreign
exchange sg

divisão [dʒivi'zãw] (pl **-ões**) F
division; (discórdia) split; (partilha)
sharing

divisões [dʒivi'zõjs] FPL de **divisão**

divisória [dʒivi'zɔrja] F partition

divorciado, -a [dʒivor'sjadu, a]
ADJ divorced ▶ M/F divorcé(e)

divorciar [dʒivor'sjar] VT to
divorce; **divorciar-se** VR to get
divorced; **divórcio** [dʒi'vɔrsju] M
divorce

divulgar [dʒivuw'gar] VT (notícias)
to spread; (segredo) to divulge;
(produto) to market; (livro) to

publish; **divulgar-se** VR to leak out

dizer [dʒi'zer] VT to say ▶ M saying;
dizer-se VR to claim to be; **diz-se** ou
dizem que ... it is said that ...;
~ algo a alguém to tell sb sth;
(falar) to say sth to sb; **~ a alguém
que ...** to tell sb that ...; **o que você
diz da minha sugestão?** what do
you think of my suggestion?;
querer ~ to mean; **quer ~** that is to
say; **digo** (ou seja) I mean; **não
diga!** you don't say!; **por assim ~**
so to speak; **até ~ chega** as much
as possible

do [du] = **de + o**

doação [doa'sãw] (pl **-ões**) F
donation

doador, a [doa'dor(a)] M/F donor

doar [do'ar] VT to donate, give

dobra ['dɔbra] F fold; (prega) pleat;
(de calças) turn-up

dobradiça [dobra'dʒisa] F hinge

dobradinha [dobra'dʒiɲa] F (Culin)
tripe stew

dobrar [do'brar] VT to double;
(papel) to fold; (joelho) to bend;
(esquina) to turn, go round; (fazer
ceder): **~ alguém** to talk sb round
▶ VI to double; (sino) to toll; (vergar)
to bend; **dobrar-se** VR to double
(up)

dobro ['dobru] M double

doce ['dosi] ADJ sweet; (terno)
gentle ▶ M sweet

dóceis ['dɔsejs] ADJ PL de **dócil**

dócil ['dɔsiw] (pl **-eis**) ADJ docile

documentação [dokumẽta'sãw]
F documentation; (documentos)
papers pl

documentário, -a
[dokumẽ'tarju, a] ADJ, M
documentary

documento [doku'mẽtu] M
document

doçura [do'sura] F sweetness; (*brandura*) gentleness

doença [do'ẽsa] F illness

doente [do'ẽtʃi] ADJ ill, sick ▶ M/F sick person; (*cliente*) patient

doentio, -a [doẽ'tʃiu, a] ADJ (*pessoa*) sickly; (*clima*) unhealthy; (*curiosidade*) morbid

doer [do'er] VI to hurt, ache; **~ a alguém** (*pesar*) to grieve sb

doido, -a ['dojdu, a] ADJ mad, crazy ▶ M/F madman/woman

doído, -a [do'idu, a] ADJ painful; (*moralmente*) hurt; (*que causa dor*) painful

dois, duas [dojs, 'duas] NUM two; **conversa a ~** tête-à-tête

dólar ['dɔlar] M dollar; **~ oficial** dollar at the official rate; **~ turismo** dollar at the special tourist rate; **doleiro, -a** [do'lejru, a] M/F (black market) dollar dealer

dolorido, -a [dolo'ridu, a] ADJ painful, sore

dom [dõ] M gift; (*aptidão*) knack

domar [do'mar] VT to tame

doméstica [do'mɛstʃika] F maid

domesticar [domestʃi'kar] VT to domesticate; (*povo*) to tame

doméstico, -a [do'mɛstʃiku, a] ADJ domestic; (*vida*) home *atr*

domicílio [domi'silju] M home, residence; **"entregamos a ~"** "we deliver"

dominador, a [domina'dor(a)] ADJ (*pessoa*) domineering; (*olhar*) imposing ▶ M/F ruler

dominar [domi'nar] VT to dominate; (*reprimir*) to overcome ▶ VI to dominate; **dominar-se** VR to control o.s.

domingo [do'mĩgu] M Sunday

domínio [do'minju] M power; (*dominação*) control; (*território*) domain; (*esfera*) sphere; **~ próprio** self-control

dona ['dɔna] F owner; (*col: mulher*) lady; **~ de casa** housewife; **D~ Lígia** Lígia; **D~ Luísa Souza** Mrs Luísa Souza

donde ['dõdə] (PT) ADV from where; (*daí*) thus

dono ['donu] M owner

dopar [do'par] VT (*cavalo*) to dope

dor [dor] F ache; (*aguda*) pain; (*fig*) grief, sorrow; **~ de cabeça** headache; **~ de dentes** toothache; **~ de estômago** stomachache

dormente [dor'mẽtʃi] ADJ numb ▶ M (*Ferro*) sleeper

dormir [dor'mir] VI to sleep; **~ fora** to spend the night away

dormitório [dormi'tɔrju] M bedroom; (*coletivo*) dormitory

dorso ['dorsu] M back

dos [dus] = **de + os**

dosagem [do'zaʒẽ] M dosage

dose ['dɔzi] F dose

dossiê [do'sje] M dossier, file

dotado, -a [do'tadu, a] ADJ gifted; **~ de** endowed with

dotar [do'tar] VT to endow

dou [do] VB *ver* **dar**

dourado, -a [do'radu, a] ADJ golden; (*com camada de ouro*) gilt ▶ M gilt

doutor, a [do'tor(a)] M/F doctor; **D~** (*forma de tratamento*) Sir; **D~ Eduardo Souza** Mr Eduardo Souza

doutrina [do'trina] F doctrine

doze ['dozi] NUM twelve

Dr. ABR (= *Doutor*) Dr

Dra. ABR (= *Doutora*) Dr

dragão [dra'gãw] (*pl* -**ões**) M dragon

dragões [dra'gõjs] MPL *de* **dragão**

drama ['drama] M drama;
dramático, -a [dra'matʃiku, a] ADJ
dramatic; **dramatizar**
[dramatʃi'zar] VT, VI to dramatize

drástico, -a ['drastʃiku, a] ADJ
drastic

dreno ['drɛnu] M drain

driblar [dri'blar] VT (*Futebol*) to
dribble

drinque ['drĩki] M drink

droga ['drɔga] F drug; (*fig*) rubbish;
drogado, -a [dro'gadu, a] M/F drug
addict; **drogar** [dro'gar] VT to drug;
drogar-se VR to take drugs

drogaria [droga'ria] F chemist's
shop (*BRIT*), drugstore (*US*)

duas ['duas] F *de* **dois**

ducha ['duʃa] F shower

dueto ['dwetu] M duet

duna ['duna] F dune

dupla ['dupla] F pair; (*Esporte*):
~ masculina/feminina/mista
men's/women's/mixed doubles

duplicar [dupli'kar] VT to duplicate
▶ VI to double; **duplicata**
[dupli'kata] F duplicate; (*título*)
trade note, bill

duplo, -a ['duplu, a] ADJ, M double

duque ['duki] M duke

duração [dura'sãw] F duration;
de pouca ~ short-lived

durante [du'rãtʃi] PREP during;
~ uma hora for an hour

durar [du'rar] VI to last

durável [du'ravew] (*pl* **-eis**) ADJ
lasting

durex® [du'rɛks] ADJ: **fita ~**
adhesive tape, Sellotape® (*BRIT*),
Scotch tape® (*US*)

durmo ['durmu] VB *ver* **dormir**

duro, -a ['duru, a] ADJ hard; (*severo*)
harsh; (*resistente, fig*) tough; **estar
~** (*col*) to be broke

dúvida ['duvida] F doubt; **sem ~**
undoubtedly, without a doubt;
duvidar [duvi'dar] VT to doubt ▶ VI
to have one's doubts; **duvidar de
alguém/algo** to doubt sb/sth;
duvidar que ... to doubt that ...;
duvido! I doubt it!; **duvidoso, -a**
[duvi'dozu, ɔza] ADJ doubtful;
(*suspeito*) dubious

duzentos, -as [du'zẽtus, as] NUM
two hundred

dúzia ['duzja] F dozen; **meia ~** half
a dozen

DVD ABR M (= *disco digital versátil*)
DVD

dz. ABR = **dúzia**

e [i] CONJ and; **e a bagagem?** what about the luggage?

é [ɛ] VB *ver* **ser**

eclipse [e'klipsi] M eclipse

eco ['ɛku] M echo; **ter ~** to catch on; **ecoar** [e'kwar] VT to echo ▶ VI (*ressoar*) to echo

ecologia [ekolo'ʒia] F ecology

ecológico, -a [eko'lɔʒiku, a] ADJ ecological, eco-friendly

economia [ekono'mia] F economy; (*ciência*) economics *sg*; **economias** FPL (*poupanças*) savings; **fazer ~ (de)** to economize (with)

econômico, -a [eko'nomiku, a] ADJ economical; (*pessoa*) thrifty; (*Com*) economic

economizar [ekonomi'zar] VT (*gastar com economia*) to economize on; (*poupar*) to save (up) ▶ VI to economize; to save up

ecrã, écran ['ɛkrã] (PT) M screen; **~ tactil** touch screen

edição [edʒi'sãw] (*pl* **-ões**) F publication; (*conjunto de exemplares*) edition; (*TV, Cinema*) editing

edifício [edʒi'fisju] M building; **~ garagem** multistorey car park (BRIT), multistory parking lot (US)

Edimburgo [edʒĩ'burgu] N Edinburgh

editar [edʒi'tar] VT to publish; (*Comput etc*) to edit

editor, a [edʒi'tor(a)] ADJ publishing *atr* ▶ M/F publisher; (*redator*) editor ▶ F publishing company; **casa ~a** publishing house

editoração [edʒitora'sãw] F: **~ eletrônica** desktop publishing; **editorial** [edʒitor'jaw] (*pl* **-ais**) ADJ publishing *atr* ▶ M editorial

edredão [ədrə'dãw] (*pl* **-ões**) (PT) M = **edredom**

edredom [edre'dõ] (*pl* **-ns**) M eiderdown

educação [eduka'sãw] F education; (*criação*) upbringing; (*de animais*) training; (*maneiras*) good manners *pl*; **educacional** [edukasjo'naw] (*pl* **-ais**) ADJ education *atr*

educar [edu'kar] VT to educate; (*criar*) to bring up; (*animal*) to train

efeito [e'fejtu] M effect; **fazer ~** to work; **levar a ~** to put into effect; **com ~** indeed

efeminado, -a [efemi'nadu, a] ADJ effeminate

efervescente [eferve'sẽtʃi] ADJ fizzy

efetivamente [efetʃiva'mẽtʃi] ADV effectively; (*realmente*) really, in fact

efetivo, -a [efe'tʃivu, a] ADJ effective; (*real*) actual, real; (*cargo, funcionário*) permanent

efetuar [efe'twar] VT to carry out; (*soma*) to do, perform

eficaz [efi'kaz] ADJ (*pessoa*) efficient; (*tratamento*) effective

eficiência [efi'sjēsja] F efficiency; **eficiente** [efi'sjētʃi] ADJ efficient

egípcio, -a [e'ʒipsju, a] ADJ, M/F Egyptian

Egito [e'ʒitu] M: **o ~** Egypt

egoísmo [ego'izmu] M selfishness, egoism; **egoísta** [ego'ista] ADJ selfish, egoistic ▶ M/F egoist

égua ['ɛgwa] F mare

ei [ej] EXCL hey!

ei-lo = **eis + o**

eis [ejs] ADV (*sg*) here is; (*pl*) here are; **~ aí** there is; there are

ejacular [eʒaku'lar] VT (*sêmen*) to ejaculate; (*líquido*) to spurt ▶ VI to ejaculate

ela ['ɛla] PRON (*pessoa*) she; (*coisa*) it; (*com prep*) her; it; **elas** FPL they; (*com prep*) them; **~s por ~s** (*col*) tit for tat

elaboração [elabora'sāw] (*pl* **-ões**) F (*de uma teoria*) working out; (*preparo*) preparation

elaborar [elabo'rar] VT to prepare; (*fazer*) to make

elástico, -a [e'lastʃiku, a] ADJ elastic; (*flexível*) flexible; (*colchão*) springy ▶ M elastic band

ele ['elɪ] PRON he; (*coisa*) it; (*com prep*) him; it; **eles** MPL they; (*com prep*) them

elefante, -ta [ele'fātʃi, ta] M/F elephant

elegante [ele'gātʃi] ADJ elegant; (*da moda*) fashionable

eleger [ele'ʒer] VT to elect; (*escolher*) to choose

eleição [elej'sāw] (*pl* **-ões**) F election; (*escolha*) choice

eleito, -a [e'lejtu, a] PP *de* **eleger**

▶ ADJ elected; (*escolhido*) chosen

eleitor, a [elej'tor(a)] M/F voter

elejo [e'leʒu] VB *ver* **eleger**

elementar [elemē'tar] ADJ elementary; (*fundamental*) basic, fundamental

elemento [ele'mētu] M element; (*parte*) component; (*recurso*) means; (*informação*) grounds *pl*; **elementos** MPL (*rudimentos*) rudiments

elenco [e'lēku] M list; (*de atores*) cast

eletricidade [eletrisi'dadʒi] F electricity

eletricista [eletri'sista] M/F electrician

elétrico, -a [e'lɛtriku, a] ADJ electric; (*fig: agitado*) worked up ▶ M tram (BRIT), streetcar (US)

eletrificar [eletrifi'kar] VT to electrify

eletrizar [eletri'zar] VT to electrify; (*fig*) to thrill

eletro... [eletru] PREFIXO electro...; **eletrocutar** [eletroku'tar] VT to electrocute; **eletrodo** [ele'trodu], (PT) **elétrodo** [e'letrodu] M electrode; **eletrodomésticos** [eletrodo'mɛstʃikus] (BR) MPL (electrical) household appliances

eletrônica [ele'tronika] F electronics *sg*

eletrônico, -a [ele'troniku, a] ADJ electronic

elevação [eleva'sāw] (*pl* **-ões**) F (*Arq*) elevation; (*aumento*) rise; (*ato*) raising; (*altura*) height; (*promoção*) promotion; (*ponto elevado*) bump

elevador [eleva'dor] M lift (BRIT), elevator (US)

elevar [ele'var] VT to lift up; (*voz, preço*) to raise; (*exaltar*) to exalt; (*promover*) to promote; **elevar-se** VR to rise

eliminar [elimi'nar] vt to remove; (*suprimir*) to delete; (*possibilidade*) to rule out; (*Med, banir*) to expel; (*Esporte*) to eliminate; **eliminatória** [elimina'tɔrja] F (*Esporte*) heat, preliminary round; (*exame*) test

elite [e'litʃi] F elite

elogiar [elo'ʒjar] vt to praise; **elogio** [elo'ʒiu] M praise; (*cumprimento*) compliment

El Salvador [ew-] N El Salvador

(PALAVRA-CHAVE)

em [ẽ] (*em + o(s)/a(s) = no(s)/na(s); + ele(s)/a(s) = nele(s)/a(s); + esse(s)/a(s) = nesse(s)/a(s); + isso = nisso; + este(s)/a(s) = neste(s)/a(s); + isto = nisto; + aquele(s)/a(s) = naquele(s)/a(s); + aquilo = naquilo*) PREP **1** (*posição*) in; (: *sobre*) on; **está na gaveta/no bolso** it's in the drawer/pocket; **está na mesa/no chão** it's on the table/floor

2 (*lugar*) in; (: *casa, escritório etc*) at; (: *andar, meio de transporte*) on; **no Brasil/em São Paulo** in Brazil/São Paulo; **em casa/no dentista** at home/the dentist; **no avião** on the plane; **no quinto andar** on the fifth floor

3 (*ação*) into; **ela entrou na sala de aula** she went into the classroom; **colocar algo na bolsa** to put sth into one's bag

4 (*tempo*) in; on; **em 1962/3 semanas** in 1962/3 weeks; **no inverno** in the winter; **em janeiro, no mês de janeiro** in January; **nessa ocasião/altura** on that occasion/at that time; **em breve** soon

5 (*diferença*): **reduzir/aumentar em 20%** to reduce/increase by 20%

6 (*modo*): **escrito em inglês** written in English

7 (*após vb que indica gastar etc*) on; **a metade do seu salário vai em comida** he spends half his salary on food

8 (*tema, ocupação*): **especialista no assunto** expert on the subject; **ele trabalha na construção civil** he works in the building industry

emagrecer [imagre'ser] vt to make thin ▶ vi to grow thin; (*mediante regime*) to slim; **emagrecimento** [imagresi'mẽtu] M (*mediante regime*) slimming

e-mail [i'mew] M email; **mandar um ~ para alguém** to email sb; **mandar algo por ~** to email sth

emaranhado, -a [imara'ɲadu, a] ADJ tangled ▶ M tangle

embaixada [ẽbaj'ʃada] F embassy

embaixador, a [ẽbajʃa'dor(a)] M/F ambassador

embaixatriz [ẽbajʃa'triz] F ambassador; (*mulher de embaixador*) ambassador's wife

embaixo [ẽ'bajʃu] ADV below, underneath ▶ PREP: **~ de** under, underneath; **(lá) ~** (*em andar inferior*) downstairs

embalagem [ẽba'laʒẽ] F packing; (*de produto: caixa etc*) packaging

embalar [ẽba'lar] vt to pack; (*balançar*) to rock

embaraçar [ẽbara'sar] vt to hinder; (*complicar*) to complicate; (*encabular*) to embarrass; (*confundir*) to confuse; (*obstruir*) to block; **embaraçar-se** vr to become embarrassed

embaraço [ēba'rasu] M hindrance; (*cábula*) embarrassment; **embaraçoso, -a** [ēbara'sozu, ɔza] ADJ embarrassing

embarcação [ēbarka'sãw] (*pl* **-ões**) F vessel

embarcar [ēbar'kar] VT to embark, put on board; (*mercadorias*) to ship, stow ▶ VI to go on board, embark

embarque [ē'barkı] M (*de pessoas*) boarding, embarkation; (*de mercadorias*) shipment

embebedar [ēbebe'dar] VT to make drunk ▶ VI: **o vinho embebeda** wine makes you drunk; **embebedar-se** VR to get drunk

emblema [ē'blɛma] M emblem; (*na roupa*) badge

êmbolo [ˈēbolu] M piston

embolsar [ēbow'sar] VT to pocket; (*herança etc*) to come into

embora [ē'bɔra] CONJ though, although ▶ EXCL even so; **ir(-se) ~** to go away

emboscada [ēbos'kada] F ambush

embriagar [ēbrja'gar] VT to make drunk, intoxicate; **embriagar-se** VR to get drunk; **embriaguez** [ēbrja'gez] F drunkenness; (*fig*) rapture

embrião [e'brjãw] (*pl* **-ões**) M embryo

embromar [ēbro'mar] VT (*adiar*) to put off; (*enganar*) to cheat ▶ VI (*prometer e não cumprir*) to make empty promises, be all talk (and no action); (*protelar*) to stall; (*falar em rodeios*) to beat about the bush

embrulhar [ēbru'ʎar] VT (*pacote*) to wrap; (*enrolar*) to roll up; (*confundir*) to muddle up; (*enganar*) to cheat; (*estômago*) to upset; **embrulhar-se** VR to get into a muddle

embrulho [ē'bruʎu] M package, parcel; (*confusão*) mix-up

emburrar [ēbu'har] VI to sulk

embutido, -a [ēbu'tʃidu, a] ADJ (*armário*) built-in, fitted

emenda [e'mēda] F correction; (*Jur*) amendment; (*de uma pessoa*) improvement; (*ligação*) join; (*sambladura*) joint; (*Costura*) seam

emendar [emē'dar] VT to correct; (*reparar*) to mend; (*injustiças*) to make amends for; (*Jur*) to amend; (*ajuntar*) to put together; **emendar-se** VR to mend one's ways

ementa [e'mēta] (PT) F menu

emergência [imer'ʒēsja] F emergence; (*crise*) emergency

emigrado, -a [emi'gradu, a] ADJ emigrant

emigrante [emi'grãtʃi] M/F emigrant

emigrar [emi'grar] VI to emigrate; (*aves*) to migrate

eminência [emi'nēsja] F eminence; (*altura*) height; **eminente** [emi'nētʃi] ADJ eminent, distinguished; (*Geo*) high

emissão [emi'sãw] (*pl* **-ões**) F emission; (*Rádio*) broadcast; (*de moeda, ações*) issue; **emissões de carbono** carbon emissions

emissor, a [emi'sor(a)] ADJ (*de moeda-papel*) issuing ▶ M (*Rádio*) transmitter ▶ F (*estação*) broadcasting station; (*empresa*) broadcasting company

emitir [emi'tʃir] VT (*som*) to give out; (*cheiro*) to give off; (*moeda, ações*) to issue; (*Rádio*) to broadcast; (*opinião*) to express ▶ VI (*emitir moeda*) to print money

emoção [emo'sãw] (*pl* **-ões**) F emotion; (*excitação*) excitement; **emocional** [imosjo'naw] (*pl* **-ais**) ADJ emotional; **emocionante**

[imosjo'nãtʃi] ADJ moving; (*excitante*) exciting; **emocionar** [imosjo'nar] VT to move; (*perturbar*) to upset; (*excitar*) to excite, thrill ▶ VI to be exciting; (*comover*) to be moving; **emocionar-se** VR to get emotional

emotivo, -a [emo'tʃivu, a] ADJ emotional

empacotar [ẽpako'tar] VT to pack, wrap up

empada [ẽ'pada] F pie

empadão [ẽpa'dãw] (*pl* -**ões**) M pie

empalidecer [ẽpalide'ser] VI to turn pale

empanturrar [ẽpãtu'har] VT: ~ **alguém de algo** to stuff sb full of sth

empatar [ẽpa'tar] VT to hinder; (*dinheiro*) to tie up; (*no jogo*) to draw; (*tempo*) to take up ▶ VI (*no jogo*): ~ **(com)** to draw (with); **empate** [ẽ'patʃi] M draw; (*numa corrida etc*) tie; (*Xadrez*) stalemate; (*em negociações*) deadlock

empecilho [ẽpe'siʎu] M obstacle; (*col*) snag

empenhar [ẽpe'ɲar] VT (*objeto*) to pawn; (*palavra*) to pledge; (*empregar*) to exert; (*compelir*) to oblige; **empenhar-se** VR: ~-**se em fazer** to strive to do, do one's utmost to do; **empenho** [ẽ'peɲu] M pawning; (*palavra*) pledge; (*insistência*): **empenho (em)** commitment (to)

empilhar [ẽpi'ʎar] VT to pile up

empinado, -a [ẽpi'nadu, a] ADJ upright; (*cavalo*) rearing; (*colina*) steep

empinar [ẽpi'nar] VT to raise, uplift

empobrecer [ẽpobre'ser] VT to impoverish ▶ VI to become poor; **empobrecimento** [ẽpobresi'mẽtu] M impoverishment

empolgação [ẽpowga'sãw] F excitement; (*entusiasmo*) enthusiasm

empolgante [ẽpow'gãtʃi] ADJ exciting

empolgar [ẽpow'gar] VT to stimulate, fill with enthusiasm; (*prender a atenção de*): ~ **alguém** to keep sb riveted

empossar [ẽpo'sar] VT to appoint

empreendedor, a [ẽprjẽde'dor(a)] ADJ enterprising ▶ M/F entrepreneur

empreender [ẽprjẽ'der] VT to undertake; **empreendimento** [ẽprjẽdʒi'mẽtu] M undertaking

empregada [ẽpre'gada] F (BR: *doméstica*) maid; (PT: *de restaurante*) waitress; *ver tb* **empregado**

empregado, -a [ẽpre'gadu, a] M/F employee; (*em escritório*) clerk ▶ M (PT: *de restaurante*) waiter

empregador, a [ẽprega'dor(a)] M/F employer

empregar [ẽpre'gar] VT (*pessoa*) to employ; (*coisa*) to use; **empregar-se** VR to get a job

emprego [ẽ'pregu] M job; (*uso*) use

empreiteiro [ẽprej'tejru] M contractor

empresa [ẽ'preza] F undertaking; (*Com*) enterprise, firm; ~ **pontocom** dotcom; **empresário, -a** [ẽpre'zarju, a] M/F businessman/woman; (*de cantor, boxeador etc*) manager

emprestado, -a [ẽpres'tadu, a] ADJ on loan; **pedir** ~ to borrow; **tomar algo** ~ to borrow sth

emprestar [ẽpres'tar] vt to lend; **empréstimo** [ẽ'prɛstʃimu] м loan

empunhar [ẽpu'ɲar] vt to grasp, seize

empurrão [ẽpu'hãw] (pl **-ões**) м push, shove; **aos empurrões** jostling

empurrar [ẽpu'har] vt to push

empurrões [ẽpu'hõjs] мpl de **empurrão**

emudecer [emude'ser] vt to silence ▶ vi to fall silent, go quiet

enamorado, -a [enamo'radu, a] adj enchanted; (apaixonado) in love

encabulado, -a [ẽkabu'ladu, a] adj shy

encadernação [ẽkaderna'sãw] (pl **-ões**) f (de livro) binding

encadernado, -a [ẽkader'nadu, a] adj bound; (de capa dura) hardback

encadernar [ẽkader'nar] vt to bind

encaixar [ẽkaj'ʃar] vt (colocar) to fit in; (inserir) to insert ▶ vi to fit; **encaixe** [ẽ'kajʃi] м (ato) fitting; (ranhura) groove; (buraco) socket

encalço [ẽ'kawsu] м pursuit; **ir no ~ de** to pursue

encaminhar [ẽkami'ɲar] vt to direct; (no bom caminho) to put on the right path; (processo) to set in motion; **encaminhar-se** vr: **~-se para/a** to set out for/to

encanar [ẽka'nar] vt to channel

encantado, -a [ẽkã'tadu, a] adj delighted; (castelo etc) enchanted; (fascinado): **~ (por alguém/algo)** smitten (with sb/sth)

encantamento [ẽkãta'mẽtu] м (magia) spell; (fascinação) charm

encanto [ẽ'kãtu] м delight; (fascinação) charm

encarar [ẽka'rar] vt to face; (olhar) to look at; (considerar) to consider

encargo [ẽ'kargu] м responsibility; (ocupação) job, assignment; (oneroso) burden

encarnação [ẽkarna'sãw] (pl **-ões**) f incarnation

encarnado, -a [ẽkar'nadu, a] adj red, scarlet

encarnar [ẽkar'nar] vt to embody, personify; (Teatro) to play

encarregado, -a [ẽkahe'gadu, a] adj: **~ de** in charge of ▶ м/f person in charge ▶ м (de operários) foreman

encarregar [ẽkahe'gar] vt: **~ alguém de algo** to put sb in charge of sth; **encarregar-se** vr: **~-se de fazer** to undertake to do

encenação [ẽsena'sãw] (pl **-ões**) f (de peça) staging, putting on; (produção) production; (fingimento) play-acting; (atitude fingida) put-on

encerar [ẽse'rar] vt to wax

encerramento [ẽseha'mẽtu] м close, end

encerrar [ẽse'har] vt to shut in, lock up; (conter) to contain; (concluir) to close

encharcar [ẽʃar'kar] vt to flood; (ensopar) to soak, drench; **encharcar-se** vr to get soaked ou drenched

enchente [ẽ'ʃẽtʃi] f flood

encher [ẽ'ʃer] vt to fill (up); (balão) to blow up; (tempo) to fill, take up ▶ vi (col) to be annoying; **encher-se** vr to fill up; **~-se (de)** (col) to get fed up (with); **enchimento** [ẽʃi'mẽtu] м filling

enciclopédia [ẽsiklo'pɛdʒja] f encyclopedia, encyclopaedia (brit)

encoberto, -a [ẽko'bɛrtu, a] pp de **encobrir** ▶ adj concealed; (tempo) overcast

encobrir [ẽko'brir] vt to conceal, hide

encolher [ẽko'ʎer] VT (*pernas*) to draw up; (*os ombros*) to shrug; (*roupa*) to shrink ▶ VI to shrink; **encolher-se** VR (*de frio*) to huddle

encomenda [ẽko'mẽda] F order; **feito de ~** made to order, custom-made; **encomendar** [ẽkomẽ'dar] VT: **encomendar algo a alguém** to order sth from sb

encontrar [ẽkõ'trar] VT to find; (*inesperadamente*) to come across, meet; (*dar com*) to bump into ▶ VI: **~ com** to bump into; **encontrar-se** VR (*achar-se*) to be; (*ter encontro*): **~-se (com alguém)** to meet (sb)

encontro [ẽ'kõtru] M (*de pessoas*) meeting; (*Mil*) encounter; **~ marcado** appointment; **ir/vir ao ~ de** to go/come and meet; (*aspirações*) to meet, fulfil (BRIT), fulfill (US)

encorajar [ẽkora'ʒar] VT to encourage

encosta [ẽ'kɔsta] F slope

encostar [ẽkos'tar] VT (*cabeça*) to put down; (*carro*) to park; (*pôr de lado*) to put to one side; (*pôr junto*) to put side by side; (*porta*) to leave ajar ▶ VI to pull in; **encostar-se** VR: **~-se em** to lean against; (*deitar-se*) to lie down on; **~ em** to lean against; **~ a mão em** (*bater*) to hit

encosto [ẽ'kostu] M (*arrimo*) support; (*de cadeira*) back

encrencar [ẽkrẽ'kar] (*col*) VT (*situação*) to complicate; (*pessoa*) to get into trouble ▶ VI to get complicated; (*carro*) to break down; **encrencar-se** VR to get complicated; to get into trouble

encriptar [ẽkrip'tar] VT (*Comput, Tel*) to encrypt

encruzilhada [ẽkruzi'ʎada] F crossroads *sg*

encurtar [ẽkur'tar] VT to shorten

endereçar [ẽdere'sar] VT (*carta*) to address; (*encaminhar*) to direct

endereço [ẽde'resu] M address; **~ de e-mail** email address; **~ web** web address

endiabrado, -a [ẽdʒja'bradu, a] ADJ devilish; (*travesso*) mischievous

endinheirado, -a [ẽdʒiɲeʼradu, a] ADJ rich, wealthy

endireitar [ẽdʒirej'tar] VT (*objeto*) to straighten; (*retificar*) to put right; **endireitar-se** VR to straighten up

endividar [ẽdʒivi'dar] VT to put into debt; **endividar-se** VR to run into debt

endossar [ẽdo'sar] VT to endorse

endurecer [ẽdure'ser] VT, VI to harden

energético, -a [ener'ʒɛtʃiku, a] ADJ energy *atr* ▶ M energy source; (*tb*: **bebida energética**) energy drink

energia [ener'ʒia] F energy, drive; (*Tec*) power, energy; **~ solar** solar power; **enérgico, -a** [e'nɛrʒiku, a] ADJ energetic, vigorous

enervante [ener'vãtʃi] ADJ annoying

enevoado, -a [ene'vwadu, a] ADJ misty, hazy

enfado [ẽ'fadu] M annoyance

ênfase ['ẽfazi] F emphasis, stress

enfastiado, -a [ẽfas'tʃjadu, a] ADJ bored

enfático, -a [ẽ'fatʃiku, a] ADJ emphatic

enfatizar [ẽfatʃi'zar] VT to emphasize

enfeitar [ẽfej'tar] VT to decorate; **enfeitar-se** VR to dress up;

enfeite [ẽ'fejtʃi] M decoration

enfermeiro, -a [ẽfer'mejru, a] M/F nurse

enfermidade [ẽfermi'dadʒi] F illness

enfermo, -a [ẽ'fermu, a] ADJ ill, sick ▶ M/F sick person, patient

enferrujar [ẽfehu'ʒar] VT to rust, corrode ▶ VI to go rusty

enfiar [ẽ'fjar] VT (meter) to put; (agulha) to thread; (vestir) to slip on; **enfiar-se** VR: **~-se em** to slip into

enfim [ẽ'fĩ] ADV finally, at last; (em suma) in short; **até que ~!** at last!

enfoque [ẽ'fɔki] M approach

enforcar [ẽfor'kar] VT to hang; (trabalho, aulas) to skip; **enforcar-se** VR to hang o.s.

enfraquecer [ẽfrake'ser] VT to weaken ▶ VI to grow weak

enfrentar [ẽfrẽ'tar] VT to face; (confrontar) to confront; (problemas) to face up to

enfurecer [ẽfure'ser] VT to infuriate; **enfurecer-se** VR to get furious

enganado, -a [ẽga'nadu, a] ADJ mistaken; (traído) deceived

enganar [ẽga'nar] VT to deceive; (desonrar) to seduce; (cônjuge) to be unfaithful to; (fome) to stave off; **enganar-se** VR to be wrong, be mistaken; (iludir-se) to deceive o.s.

engano [ẽ'gãnu] M mistake; (ilusão) deception; (logro) trick; **é ~** (Tel) I've (ou you've) got the wrong number

engarrafamento [ẽgahafa'mẽtu] M bottling; (de trânsito) traffic jam

engarrafar [ẽgaha'far] VT to bottle; (trânsito) to block

engasgar [ẽgaz'gar] VT to choke ▶ VI to choke; (máquina) to splutter; **engasgar-se** VR to choke

engatinhar [ẽgatʃi'nar] VI to crawl

engenharia [ẽʒena'ria] F engineering; **engenheiro, -a** [ẽʒe'nejru, a] M/F engineer

engenhoso, -a [ẽʒe'nozu, ɔza] ADJ clever, ingenious

engessar [ẽʒe'sar] VT (perna) to put in plaster; (parede) to plaster

englobar [ẽglo'bar] VT to include

engodo [ẽ'godu] M bait

engolir [ẽgo'lir] VT to swallow

engordar [ẽgor'dar] VT to fatten ▶ VI to put on weight

engraçado, -a [ẽgra'sadu, a] ADJ funny, amusing

engradado [ẽgra'dadu] M crate

engraxador [ẽgraʃa'dor] (PT) M shoe shiner

engraxar [ẽgra'ʃar] VT to polish

engrenagem [ẽgre'naʒẽ] (pl **-ns**) F (Auto) gear

engrenar [ẽgre'nar] VT to put into gear; (fig: conversa) to strike up ▶ VI: **~ com alguém** to get on with sb

engrossar [ẽgro'sar] VT (sopa) to thicken; (aumentar) to swell; (voz) to raise ▶ VI to thicken; to swell; to rise; (col: pessoa, conversa) to turn nasty

enguia [ẽ'gia] F eel

enguiçar [ẽgi'sar] VI (máquina) to break down ▶ VT to cause to break down; **enguiço** [ẽ'gisu] M snag; (desarranjo) breakdown

enigma [e'nigma] M enigma; (mistério) mystery

enjeitado, -a [ẽʒej'tadu, a] M/F foundling, waif

enjoado, -a [ẽ'ʒwadu, a] ADJ sick; (enfastiado) bored; (enfadonho) boring; (mal-humorado) in a bad mood

enjoar [ẽ'ʒwar] VT to make sick; (enfastiar) to bore ▶ VI (pessoa) to be sick; (*remédio, comida*) to cause nausea; **enjoar-se** VR: **~-se de** to get sick of

enjoo [ẽ'ʒou] M sickness; (*em carro*) travel sickness; (*em navio*) seasickness; (*aborrecimento*) boredom

enlatado, -a [ẽla'tadu, a] ADJ tinned (BRIT), canned ► M (*pej: filme*) foreign import; **enlatados** MPL (*comida*) tinned (BRIT) *ou* canned foods

enlouquecer [ẽloke'ser] VT to drive mad ► VI to go mad

enlutado, -a [ẽlu'tadu, a] ADJ in mourning

enorme [e'nɔrmi] ADJ enormous, huge; **enormidade** [enormi'dadʒi] F enormity; **uma enormidade (de)** (*col*) a hell of a lot (of)

enquanto [ẽ'kwãtu] CONJ while; (*considerado como*) as; **~ isso** meanwhile; **por ~** for the time being; **~ ele não vem** until he comes; **~ que** whereas

enquete [ẽ'kɛtʃi] F survey

enraivecer [ẽhajve'ser] VT to enrage

enredo [ẽ'hedu] M (*de uma obra*) plot; (*intriga*) intrigue

enriquecer [ẽhike'ser] VT to make rich; (*fig*) to enrich ► VI to get rich; **enriquecer-se** VR to get rich

enrolar [ẽho'lar] VT to roll up; (*agasalhar*) to wrap up; (*col: enganar*) to con ► VI (*col*) to waffle; **enrolar-se** VR to roll up; to wrap up; (*col: confundir-se*) to get mixed *ou* muddled up

enroscar [ẽhos'kar] VT (*torcer*) to twist, wind (round); **enroscar-se** VR to coil up

enrugar [ẽhu'gar] VT (*pele*) to

wrinkle; (*testa*) to furrow; (*tecido*) to crease ► VI (*pele, mãos*) to go wrinkly; (*pessoa*) to get wrinkles

ensaiar [ẽsa'jar] VT to test, try out; (*treinar*) to practise (BRIT), practice (US); (*Teatro*) to rehearse

ensaio [ẽ'saju] M test; (*tentativa*) attempt; (*treino*) practice; (*Teatro*) rehearsal; (*literário*) essay

enseada [ẽ'sjada] F inlet, cove; (*baía*) bay

ensejo [ẽ'seʒu] M chance, opportunity

ensinamento [ẽsina'mẽtu] M teaching; (*exemplo*) lesson

ensinar [ẽsi'nar] VT, VI to teach

ensino [ẽ'sinu] M teaching, tuition; (*educação*) education; **~ fundamental** primary education; **~ médio** secondary education

ensopado, -a [ẽso'padu, a] ADJ soaked ► M stew

ensurdecer [ẽsurde'ser] VT to deafen ► VI to go deaf

entalar [ẽta'lar] VT to wedge, jam; (*encher*): **ela me entalou de comida** she stuffed me full of food

entalhar [ẽta'ʎar] VT to carve; **entalhe** [ẽ'taʎi] M groove, notch

entanto [ẽ'tãtu] ADV: **no ~** yet, however

então [ẽ'tãw] ADV then; **até ~** up to that time; **desde ~** ever since; **e ~?** well then?; **para ~** so that; **pois ~** in that case; **~, você vai ou não?** so, are you going or not?

entardecer [ẽtarde'ser] VI to get late ► M sunset

ente ['ẽtʃi] M being

enteado, -a [ẽ'tʃjadu, a] M/F stepson/stepdaughter

entediar [ẽte'dʒjar] VT to bore; **entediar-se** VR to get bored

entender [ẽtẽ'der] VT to understand; (*pensar*) to think; (*ouvir*) to hear; **entender-se** VR to understand one another; **dar a ~** to imply; **no meu ~** in my opinion; **~ de música** to know about music; **~ de fazer** to decide to do; **~-se por** to be meant by; **~-se com alguém** to get along with sb; (*dialogar*) to sort things out with sb

entendimento [ẽtẽdʒi'mẽtu] M understanding

enterrar [ẽte'har] VT to bury; (*faca*) to plunge; (*lever à ruina*) to ruin; (*assunto*) to close

enterro [ẽ'tehu] M burial; (*funeral*) funeral

entidade [ẽtʃi'dadʒi] F (*ser*) being; (*corporação*) body; (*coisa que existe*) entity

entornar [ẽtor'nar] VT to spill; (*fig: copo*) to drink ▶ VI to drink a lot

entorpecente [ẽtorpe'sẽtʃi] M narcotic

entorpecimento [ẽtorpesi'mẽtu] M numbness; (*torpor*) lethargy

entorse [ẽ'tɔrsi] F sprain

entortar [ẽtor'tar] VT (*curvar*) to bend; (*empenar*) to warp; **~ os olhos** to squint

entrada [ẽ'trada] F (*ato*) entry; (*lugar*) entrance; (*Tec*) inlet; (*de casa*) doorway; (*começo*) beginning; (*bilhete*) ticket; (*Culin*) starter, entrée; (*Comput*) input; (*pagamento inicial*) down payment; (*corredor de casa*) hall; **entradas** FPL (*no cabelo*) receding hairline; **~ gratuita** admission free; **"~ proibida"** "no entry", "no admittance"; **meia ~** half-price ticket

entra e sai ['ẽtrai'saj] M comings and goings *pl*

entranhado, -a [ẽtra'ɲadu, a] ADJ deep-rooted

entranhas [ẽ'traɲas] FPL bowels, entrails; (*sentimentos*) feelings; (*centro*) heart *sg*

entrar [ẽ'trar] VI to go (*ou* come) in, enter; **~ com** (*Comput: dados etc*) to enter; **eu entrei com £100** I put in £100; **~ de férias/licença** to start one's holiday (BRIT) *ou* vacation (US)/leave; **~ em** to go (*ou* come) into, enter; (*assunto*) to get onto; (*comida, bebida*) to start in on

entrave [ẽ'travi] M (*fig*) impediment

entre ['ẽtri] PREP (*dois*) between; (*mais de dois*) among(st); **~ si** amongst themselves

entreaberto, -a [ẽtrja'bɛrtu, a] ADJ half-open; (*porta*) ajar

entrega [ẽ'trega] F (*de mercadorias*) delivery; (*a alguém*) handing over; (*rendição*) surrender; **~ rápida** special delivery

entregar [ẽtre'gar] VT to hand over; (*mercadorias*) to deliver; (*confiar*) to entrust; (*devolver*) to return; **entregar-se** VR (*render-se*) to give o.s. up; (*dedicar-se*) to devote o.s.

entregue [ẽ'tregi] PP *de* **entregar**

entrelinha [ẽtre'liɲa] F line space; **ler nas ~s** to read between the lines

entreolhar-se [ẽtrio'ʎarsi] VR to exchange glances

entretanto [ẽtri'tãtu] CONJ however

entretenimento [ẽtriteni'mẽtu] M entertainment; (*distração*) pastime

entreter [ẽtri'ter] (*irreg: como* **ter**) VT to entertain, amuse; (*ocupar*) to occupy; (*manter*) to keep up; (*esperanças*) to cherish; **entreter-se** VR to amuse o.s.; to occupy o.s.

entrevista [ẽtre'vista] F interview;

~ coletiva (à imprensa) press conference; **entrevistar** [ẽtrevis'tar] VT to interview; **entrevistar-se** VR to have an interview

entristecer [ẽtriste'ser] VT to sadden, grieve ▶ VI to feel sad; **entristecer-se** VR to feel sad

entroncamento [ẽtrõka'mẽtu] M junction

entrudo [ẽ'trudu] (PT) M carnival; (Rel) Shrovetide

entulhar [ẽtu'ʎar] VT to cram full; (suj: multidão) to pack

entupido, -a [ẽtu'pidu, a] ADJ blocked; **estar ~** (col: congestionado) to have a blocked-up nose; (de comida) to be fit to burst, be full up

entupimento [ẽtupi'mẽtu] M blockage

entupir [ẽtu'pir] VT to block, clog; **entupir-se** VR to become blocked; (de comida) to stuff o.s.

entusiasmar [ẽtuzjaz'mar] VT to fill with enthusiasm; (animar) to excite; **entusiasmar-se** VR to get excited

entusiasmo [ẽtu'zjazmu] M enthusiasm; (júbilo) excitement

entusiasta [ẽtu'zjasta] ADJ enthusiastic ▶ M/F enthusiast

enumerar [enume'rar] VT to enumerate; (com números) to number

envelhecer [ẽveʎe'ser] VT to age ▶ VI to grow old, age

envelope [ẽve'lɔpi] M envelope

envenenamento [ẽvenena'mẽtu] M poisoning; **~ do sangue** blood poisoning

envenenar [ẽvene'nar] VT to poison; (fig) to corrupt; (: declaração, palavras) to distort,

twist; (tornar amargo) to sour ▶ VI to be poisonous; **envenenar-se** VR to poison o.s.

envergonhado, -a [ẽvergo'ɲadu, a] ADJ ashamed; (tímido) shy

envergonhar [ẽvergo'ɲar] VT to shame; (degradar) to disgrace; **envergonhar-se** VR to be ashamed

enviado, -a [ẽ'vjadu, a] M/F envoy, messenger

enviar [ẽ'vjar] VT to send

envio [ẽ'viu] M sending; (expedição) dispatch; (remessa) remittance; (de mercadorias) consignment

enviuvar [ẽvju'var] VI to be widowed

envolver [ẽvow'ver] VT to wrap (up); (cobrir) to cover; (comprometer, acarretar) to involve; (nos braços) to embrace; **envolver-se** VR (intrometer-se) to become involved; (cobrir-se) to wrap o.s. up; **envolvimento** [ẽvowvi'mẽtu] M involvement

enxada [ẽ'ʃada] F hoe

enxaguar [ẽʃa'gwar] VT to rinse

enxame [ẽ'ʃami] M swarm

enxaqueca [ẽʃa'keka] F migraine

enxergar [ẽʃer'gar] VT (avistar) to catch sight of; (divisar) to make out; (notar) to observe, see

enxofre [ẽ'ʃofri] M sulphur (BRIT), sulfur (US)

enxotar [ẽʃo'tar] VT to drive out

enxoval [ẽʃo'vaw] (pl -ais) M (de noiva) trousseau; (de recém-nascido) layette

enxugar [ẽʃu'gar] VT to dry; (fig: texto) to tidy up

enxurrada [ẽʃu'hada] F (de água) torrent; (fig) spate

enxuto, -a [ẽ'ʃutu, a] ADJ dry; (*corpo*) shapely; (*bonito*) good-looking

épico, -a ['ɛpiku, a] ADJ epic ▶ M epic poet

epidemia [epide'mia] F epidemic

epilepsia [epile'psia] F epilepsy

episódio [epi'zɔdʒu] M episode

época ['ɛpoka] F time, period; (*da história*) age, epoch; **naquela ~** at that time; **fazer ~** to be epoch-making

equação [ekwa'sãw] (*pl* **-ões**) F equation

Equador [ekwa'dor] M: **o ~** Ecuador

equador [ekwa'dor] M equator

equilibrar [ekili'brar] VT to balance; **equilibrar-se** VR to balance; **equilíbrio** [eki'librju] M balance

equipa [e'kipa] (PT) F team

equipamento [ekipa'mẽtu] M equipment, kit

equipar [eki'par] VT (*navio*) to fit out; (*prover*) to equip

equipe [e'kipi] (BR) F team

equitação [ekita'sãw] F (*ato*) riding; (*arte*) horsemanship

equivalente [ekiva'lẽtʃi] ADJ, M equivalent

equivaler [ekiva'ler] VI: **~ a** to be the same as, equal

equivocado, -a [ekivo'kadu, a] ADJ mistaken, wrong

equivocar-se [ekivo'karsi] VR to make a mistake, be wrong

era¹ ['ɛra] F era, age

era² VB *ver* **ser**

erário [e'rarju] M exchequer

ereto, -a [e'rɛtu, a] ADJ upright, erect

erguer [er'ger] VT to raise, lift; (*edificar*) to build, erect; **erguer-se** VR to rise; (*pessoa*) to stand up

eriçar [eri'sar] VT: **~ o cabelo de alguém** to make sb's hair stand on end; **eriçar-se** VR to bristle; (*cabelos*) to stand on end

erigir [eri'ʒir] VT to erect

erosão [ero'zãw] F erosion

erótico, -a [e'rɔtʃiku, a] ADJ erotic

errado, -a [e'hadu, a] ADJ wrong; **dar ~** to go wrong

errar [e'har] VT (*alvo*) to miss; (*conta*) to get wrong ▶ VI to wander, roam; (*enganar-se*) to be wrong, make a mistake; **~ o caminho** to lose one's way

erro ['ehu] M mistake; **salvo ~** unless I am mistaken; **~ de imprensa** misprint

errôneo, -a [e'honju, a] ADJ wrong, mistaken; (*falso*) false, untrue

erva ['ɛrva] F herb; **~ daninha** weed; (*col: dinheiro*) dosh; (: *maconha*) dope

erva-mate (*pl* **ervas-mate(s)**) F mate

ervilha [er'viʎa] F pea

esbanjar [izbã'ʒar] VT to squander, waste

esbarrar [izba'har] VI: **~ em** to bump into; (*obstáculo, problema*) to come up against

esbelto, -a [iz'bɛwtu, a] ADJ slim, slender

esboçar [izbo'sar] VT to sketch; (*delinear*) to outline; (*plano*) to draw up; **esboço** [iz'bosu] M sketch; (*primeira versão*) draft; (*fig: resumo*) outline

esbofetear [izbofe'tʃjar] VT to slap, hit

esburacar [izbura'kar] VT to make holes (*ou* a hole) in

esc (PT) ABR = **escudo**

escabroso, -a [iska'brozu, ɔza] ADJ

(*difícil*) tough; (*indecoroso*) indecent

escada [is'kada] F (*dentro da casa*) staircase, stairs *pl*; (*fora da casa*) steps *pl*; (*de mão*) ladder; **~ de incêndio** fire escape; **~ rolante** escalator; **escadaria** [iskada'ria] F staircase

escala [is'kala] F scale; (*Náut*) port of call; (*parada*) stop; **fazer ~ em** to call at; **sem ~** non-stop

escalada [iska'lada] F (*de guerra*) escalation

escalão [eska'lãw] (*pl* -**ões**) M step; (*Mil*) echelon

escalar [iska'lar] VT (*montanha*) to climb; (*muro*) to scale; (*designar*) to select

escaldar [iskaw'dar] VT to scald; **escaldar-se** VR to scald o.s.

escalões [ɛska'lõjs] MPL *de* **escalão**

escama [is'kama] F (*de peixe*) scale; (*de pele*) flake

escancarado, -a [iskãka'radu, a] ADJ wide open

escandalizar [iskãdali'zar] VT to shock; **escandalizar-se** VR to be shocked; (*ofender-se*) to be offended

escândalo [is'kãdalu] M scandal; (*indignação*) outrage; **fazer ou dar um ~** to make a scene; **escandaloso, -a** [iskãda'lozu, ɔza] ADJ shocking, scandalous

Escandinávia [iskãdʒi'navja] F: **a ~** Scandinavia; **escandinavo, -a** [iskãdʒi'navu, a] ADJ, M/F Scandinavian

escangalhar [iskãga'ʎar] VT to break, smash (up); **escangalhar-se** VR: **~-se de rir** to split one's sides laughing

escapar [iska'par] VI: **~ a** *ou* **de** to escape from; (*fugir*) to run away

from; **escapar-se** VR to run away, flee; **deixar ~** (*uma oportunidade*) to miss; (*palavras*) to blurt out; **~ de boa** (*col*) to have a close shave

escapatória [iskapa'tɔrja] F way out; (*desculpa*) excuse

escape [is'kapi] M (*de gás*) leak; (*Auto*) exhaust

escapulir [iskapu'lir] VI: **~ (de)** to get away (from); (*suj: coisa*) to slip (from)

escarrar [iska'har] VT to spit, cough up ▶ VI to spit

escarro [is'kahu] M phlegm, spit

escassear [iska'sjar] VT to skimp on ▶ VI to become scarce

escassez [iska'sez] F (*falta*) shortage

escavar [iska'var] VT to excavate

esclarecer [isklare'ser] VT (*situação*) to explain; (*mistério*) to clear up, explain; **esclarecer-se** VR: **~-se (sobre algo)** to find out (about) sth; **esclarecimento** [isklaresi'mẽtu] M explanation; (*informação*) information

escoadouro [iskoa'doru] M drain; (*cano*) drainpipe

escocês, -esa [isko'ses, seza] ADJ Scottish, Scots ▶ M/F Scot, Scotsman/woman

Escócia [is'kɔsja] F Scotland

escola [is'kɔla] F school; **~ de línguas** language school; **~ naval** naval college; **~ primária/ secundária** primary (BRIT) *ou* elementary (US) /secondary (BRIT) *ou* high (US) school; **~ particular/ pública** private/state (BRIT) *ou* public (US) school; **~ superior** college

> **Escolas de samba** are musical and recreational associations made up, among others, of

samba dancers, percussionists and carnival dancers. Although they exist throughout Brazil, the most famous schools are in Rio de Janeiro. The schools in Rio rehearse all year long for the **carnaval**, when they parade along the *Sambódromo*, a purpose-built avenue flanked by stands for spectators, and compete for the samba school championship. Characterised by their extravagance, the biggest schools have up to 4,000 members and are one of Brazil's major tourist attractions.

escolar [isko'lar] ADJ school atr ▶ M/F schoolboy/girl

escolha [is'koʎa] F choice

escolher [isko'ʎer] VT to choose, select

escolho [is'koʎu] M (recife) reef; (rocha) rock

escolta [is'kɔwta] F escort; **escoltar** [iskow'tar] VT to escort

escombros [is'kõbrus] MPL ruins, debris sg

esconde-esconde [iskõdʒis'kõdʒi] M hide-and-seek

esconder [iskõ'der] VT to hide, conceal; **esconder-se** VR to hide

escondidas [iskõ'dʒidas] FPL: **às ~** secretly

escopo [is'kopu] M aim, purpose

escorar [isko'rar] VT to prop (up); (amparar) to support; (esperar de espreita) to lie in wait for ▶ VI to lie in wait; **escorar-se** VR: **~-se em** (fundamentar-se) to go by; (amparar-se) to live off

escore [is'kɔri] M score

escoriação [iskorja'sãw] (pl **-ões**) F abrasion, scratch

escorpião [iskorpi'ãw] (pl **-ões**) M

scorpion; **E~** (Astrologia) Scorpio

escorrega [isko'hɛga] F slide; **escorregadela** [iskohega'dɛla] F slip; **escorregadio, -a** [iskohega'dʒiu, a] ADJ slippery; **escorregão** [iskohe'gãw] (pl **-ões**) M slip; (fig) slip(-up); **escorregar** [iskohe'gar] VI to slip; (errar) to slip up

escorrer [isko'her] VT to drain (off); (verter) to pour out ▶ VI (pingar) to drip; (correr em fio) to trickle

escoteiro [isko'tejru] M scout

escova [is'kova] F brush; (penteado) blow-dry; **~ de dentes** toothbrush; **~ progressiva** keratin straightening; **escovar** [isko'var] VT to brush

escravatura [iskrava'tura] F (tráfico) slave trade; (escravidão) slavery

escravidão [iskravi'dãw] F slavery

escravizar [iskravi'zar] VT to enslave; (cativar) to captivate

escravo, -a [is'kravu, a] ADJ captive ▶ M/F slave

escrever [iskre'ver] VT, VI to write; **escrever-se** VR to write to each other; **~ à máquina** to type

escrita [es'krita] F writing; (pessoal) handwriting

escrito, -a [es'kritu, a] PP de **escrever** ▶ ADJ written ▶ M piece of writing; **~ à mão** handwritten; **dar por ~** to put in writing

escritor, a [iskri'tor(a)] M/F writer; (autor) author

escritório [iskri'tɔrju] M office; (em casa) study

escritura [iskri'tura] F (Jur) deed; (na compra de imóveis) ≈ exchange of contracts; **as Sagradas E~s** the Scriptures

escrivã [iskri'vã] F de **escrivão**

escrivaninha [iskriva'niɲa] F writing desk

escrivão, -vã [iskri'vãw, vã] (pl **-ões/-s**) M/F registrar, recorder

escrupuloso, -a [iskrupu'lozu, ɔza] ADJ scrupulous; (cuidadoso) careful

escudo [is'kudu] M shield; (moeda) escudo

esculhambado, -a [iskuʎã'badu, a] (!) ADJ shabby, slovenly; (estragado) knackered

esculhambar [iskuʎã'bar] (!) VT to mess up, fuck up (!); **~ alguém** (criticar) to give sb stick; (descompor) to give sb a bollocking (!)

esculpir [iskuw'pir] VT to carve, sculpt; (gravar) to engrave

escultor, a [iskuw'tor(a)] M/F sculptor

escultura [iskuw'tura] F sculpture

escuras [is'kuras] FPL: **às ~** in the dark

escurecer [iskure'ser] VT to darken ▸ VI to get dark; **ao ~** at dusk

escuridão [iskuri'dãw] F (trevas) darkness

escuro, -a [is'kuru, a] ADJ dark; (dia) overcast; (pessoa) swarthy ▸ M dark

escuso, -a [is'kuzu, a] ADJ shady

escuta [is'kuta] F listening; **à ~** listening out; **ficar na ~** to stand by

escutar [isku'tar] VT to listen to; (sem prestar atenção) to hear ▸ VI to listen; to hear

esfacelar [isfase'lar] VT to destroy

esfaquear [isfaki'ar] VT to stab

esfarrapado, -a [isfaha'padu, a] ADJ (roupa) ragged, tattered; (desculpa) lame

esfera [is'fɛra] F sphere; (globo) globe

esfolar [isfo'lar] VT to skin; (arranhar) to graze; (cobrar demais a) to overcharge, fleece

esfomeado, -a [isfo'mjadu, a] ADJ famished, starving

esforçado, -a [isfor'sadu, a] ADJ committed, dedicated

esforçar-se [isfor'sarsi] VR: **~ para** to try hard to, strive to

esforço [is'forsu] M effort

esfregar [isfre'gar] VT to rub; (com água) to scrub

esfriar [is'frjar] VT to cool, chill ▸ VI to get cold; (fig) to cool off

esganar [izga'nar] VT to strangle, choke

esgotado, -a [izgo'tadu, a] ADJ exhausted; (consumido) used up; (livros) out of print; **os ingressos estão ~s** the tickets are sold out

esgotamento [izgota'mẽtu] M exhaustion

esgotar [izgo'tar] VT to drain, empty; (recursos) to use up; (pessoa, assunto) to exhaust; **esgotar-se** VR to become exhausted; (mercadorias, edição) to be sold out; (recursos) to run out

esgoto [iz'gotu] M drain; (público) sewer

esgrima [iz'grima] F (Esporte) fencing

esgueirar-se [izgej'rarsi] VR to slip away, sneak off

esguelha [iz'geʎa] F slant; **olhar alguém de ~** to look at sb out of the corner of one's eye

esguio, -a [ez'giu, a] ADJ slender

esmagador, a [izmaga'dor(a)] ADJ crushing; (provas) irrefutable; (maioria) overwhelming

esmalte [iz'mawtʃi] M enamel;

(*de unhas*) nail polish

esmeralda [izme'rawda] F emerald

esmerar-se [izme'rarsi] VR: **~ em** to take great care to

esmigalhar [izmiga'ʎar] VT to crumble; (*despedaçar*) to shatter; (*esmagar*) to crush; **esmigalhar-se** VR to crumble; (*vaso*) to smash, shatter

esmo ['ezmu] M: **a ~** at random; **falar a ~** to prattle

esmola [iz'mɔla] F alms *pl*; **pedir ~s** to beg

esmurrar [izmu'har] VT to punch

esoterismo [ezote'rizmu] M New Age

espacial [ispa'sjaw] (*pl* **-ais**) ADJ space *atr*; **nave ~** spaceship

espaço [is'pasu] M space; (*tempo*) period; **~ para 3 pessoas** room for 3 people; **a ~s** from time to time; **espaçoso, -a** [ispa'sozu, ɔza] ADJ spacious, roomy

espada [is'pada] F sword; **espadas** FPL (*Cartas*) spades

espadarte [ispa'dartʃi] M swordfish

espairecer [ispajre'ser] VT to amuse, entertain ▶ VI to relax; **espairecer-se** VR to relax

espaldar [ispaw'dar] M (chair) back

espalhafato [ispaʎa'fatu] M din, commotion

espalhar [ispa'ʎar] VT to scatter; (*boato, medo*) to spread; (*luz*) to shed; **espalhar-se** VR to spread; (*refestelar-se*) to lounge

espanador [ispana'dor] M duster

espancar [ispã'kar] VT to beat up

Espanha [is'paɲa] F: **a ~** Spain; **espanhol, a** [ispa'ɲɔw, ɔla] (*pl* **-óis/-s**) ADJ Spanish ▶ M/F Spaniard

▶ M (*Ling*) Spanish; **os espanhóis** MPL the Spanish

espantado, -a [ispã'tadu, a] ADJ astonished

espantalho [ispã'taʎu] M scarecrow

espantar [ispã'tar] VT to frighten; (*admirar*) to amaze, astonish; (*afugentar*) to frighten away ▶ VI to be amazing; **espantar-se** VR to be amazed; (*assustar-se*) to be frightened

espanto [is'pãtu] M fright, fear; (*admiração*) amazement; **espantoso, -a** [ispã'tozu, ɔza] ADJ amazing

esparadrapo [ispara'drapu] M (sticking) plaster (BRIT), bandaid® (US)

esparramar [ispaha'mar] VT to splash; (*espalhar*) to scatter

esparso, -a [is'parsu, a] ADJ scattered; (*solto*) loose

espasmo [is'pazmu] M spasm, convulsion

espatifar [ispatʃi'far] VT to smash; **espatifar-se** VR to smash; (*avião*) to crash

especial [ispe'sjaw] (*pl* **-ais**) ADJ special; **em ~** especially; **especialidade** [ispesjali'dadʒi] F speciality (BRIT), specialty (US); (*ramo de atividades*) specialization; **especialista** [ispesja'lista] M/F specialist; (*perito*) expert; **especializar-se** [ispesjali'zarsi] VR: **especializar-se (em)** to specialize (in)

espécie [is'pɛsi] F (*Bio*) species; (*tipo*) sort, kind; **causar ~** to be surprising; **pagar em ~** to pay in cash

especificar [ispesifi'kar] VT to specify; **específico, -a** [ispe'sifiku, a] ADJ specific

espécime [is'pɛsimi] M specimen

espécimen [is'pɛsimẽ] (pl **-s**) M = **espécime**

espectador, a [ispekta'dor(a)] M/F onlooker; (TV) viewer; (Esporte) spectator; (Teatro) member of the audience; **espectadores** MPL audience sg

especular [ispeku'lar] VI: **~ (sobre)** to speculate (on)

espelho [is'peʎu] M mirror; (fig) model; **~ retrovisor** (Auto) rear-view mirror

espera [is'pɛra] F (demora) wait; (expectativa) expectation; **à ~ de** waiting for; **à minha ~** waiting for me

esperança [ispe'rãsa] F hope; (expectativa) expectation; **dar ~s a alguém** to get sb's hopes up; **esperançoso, -a** [isperã'sozu, ɔza] ADJ hopeful

esperar [ispe'rar] VT to wait for; (desejar) to hope for; (contar com, bebê) to expect ▶ VI to wait; to hope; to expect

esperma [is'pɛrma] M sperm

espertalhão, -lhona [isperta'ʎãw, ʎɔna] (pl **-ões/-s**) ADJ crafty, shrewd

esperteza [isper'teza] F cleverness; (astúcia) cunning

esperto, -a [is'pɛrtu, a] ADJ clever; (espertalhão) crafty

espetacular [ispetaku'lar] ADJ spectacular

espetáculo [ispe'takulu] M (Teatro) show; (vista) sight; (cena ridícula) spectacle; **dar ~** to make a spectacle of o.s.

espetar [ispe'tar] VT (carne) to put on a spit; (cravar) to stick; **espetar-se** VR to prick o.s.; **~ algo em algo** to pin sth to sth

espeto [is'petu] M spit; (pau) pointed stick; **ser um ~** (ser difícil) to be awkward

espevitado, -a [ispevi'tadu, a] ADJ (fig: vivo) lively

espiã [is'pjã] F de **espião**

espiada [is'pjada] F: **dar uma ~** to have a look

espião, -piã [is'pjãw, 'pjã] (pl **-ões/-s**) M/F spy

espiar [is'pjar] VT to spy on; (uma ocasião) to watch out for; (olhar) to watch ▶ VI to spy; (olhar) to peer

espiga [is'piga] F (de milho) ear

espinafre [ispi'nafri] M spinach

espingarda [ispī'garda] F shotgun, rifle

espinha [is'pina] F (de peixe) bone; (na pele) spot, zit (col); (coluna vertebral) spine

espinho [is'pinu] M thorn; (de animal) spine; (fig: dificuldade) snag; **espinhoso, -a** [ispi'nozu, ɔza] ADJ (planta) prickly, thorny; (fig: difícil) difficult; (: problema) thorny

espiões [is'pjõjs] MPL de **espião**

espionar [ispjo'nar] VT to spy on ▶ VI to spy, snoop

espírito [is'piritu] M spirit; (pensamento) mind; **~ esportivo** sense of humo(u)r; **E~ Santo** Holy Spirit

espiritual [ispiri'twaw] (pl **-ais**) ADJ spiritual

espirituoso, -a [ispiri'twozu, ɔza] ADJ witty

espirrar [ispi'har] VI to sneeze; (jorrar) to spurt out ▶ VT (água) to spurt; **espirro** [is'pihu] M sneeze

esplêndido, -a [is'plẽdʒidu, a] ADJ splendid

esplendor [isplẽ'dor] M splendour (BRIT), splendor (US)

esponja [is'põʒa] F sponge

espontâneo, -a [ispõ'tanju, a] ADJ spontaneous; (*pessoa*) straightforward

esporádico, -a [ispo'radʒiku, a] ADJ sporadic

esporte [is'pɔrtʃi] (BR) M sport; **esportista** [ispor'tʃista] ADJ sporting ▶ M/F sportsman/woman; **esportivo, -a** [ispor'tʃivu, a] ADJ sporting

esposa [is'poza] F wife

esposo [is'pozu] M husband

espreguiçadeira [ispregisa'dejra] F deck chair; (*com lugar para as pernas*) lounger

espreguiçar-se [ispregi'sarsi] VR to stretch

espreita [is'prejta] F: **ficar à ~** to keep watch

espreitar [isprej'tar] VT to spy on; (*observar*) to observe, watch

espremer [ispre'mer] VT (*fruta*) to squeeze; (*roupa molhada*) to wring out; (*pessoas*) to squash; **espremer-se** VR (*multidão*) to be squashed together; (*uma pessoa*) to squash up

espuma [is'puma] F foam; (*de cerveja*) froth, head; (*de sabão*) lather; (*de ondas*) surf; **~ de borracha** foam rubber; **espumante** [ispu'mãtʃi] ADJ frothy, foamy; (*vinho*) sparkling

esq. ABR (= *esquerdo*) l.; = **esquina**

esquadra [is'kwadra] F (*Náut*) fleet; (PT: *da polícia*) police station

esquadrão [iskwa'drãw] (*pl* -**ões**) M squadron

esquadrilha [iskwa'driʎa] F squadron

esquadrões [iskwa'drõjs] MPL *de* **esquadrão**

esquartejar [iskwarte'ʒar] VT to quarter

esquecer [iske'ser] VT, VI to forget; **esquecer-se** VR: **~-se de** to forget; **esquecido, -a** [iske'sidu, a] ADJ forgotten; (*pessoa*) forgetful

esqueleto [iske'letu] M skeleton; (*arcabouço*) framework

esquema [is'kɛma] M outline; (*plano*) scheme; (*diagrama*) diagram, plan

esquentar [iskē'tar] VT to heat (up), warm (up); (*fig: irritar*) to annoy ▶ VI to warm up; (*casaco*) to be warm; **esquentar-se** VR to get annoyed

esquerda [is'kerda] F (*tb Pol*) left; **à ~** on the left

esquerdista [isker'dʒista] ADJ left-wing ▶ M/F left-winger

esquerdo, -a [is'kerdu, a] ADJ left

esqui [is'ki] M (*patim*) ski; (*esporte*) skiing; **~ aquático** water skiing; **fazer ~** to go skiing; **esquiar** [is'kjar] VI to ski

esquilo [is'kilu] M squirrel

esquina [is'kina] F corner

esquisito, -a [iski'zitu, a] ADJ strange, odd

esquivar-se [iski'varsi] VR: **~ de** to escape from, get away from; (*deveres*) to get out of

esquivo, -a [is'kivu, a] ADJ aloof, standoffish

essa ['ɛsa] PRON: **~ é/foi boa** that is/was a good one; **~ não, sem ~** come off it!; **vamos nessa** let's go!; **ainda mais ~!** that's all I need!; **corta ~!** cut it out!; **por ~s e outras** for these and other reasons; **~ de fazer ...** this business of doing ...

esse ['esi] ADJ (*sg*) that; (*pl*) those; (BR: *este*: *sg*) this; (: *pl*) these ▶ PRON (*sg*) that one; (*pl*) those (ones); (BR: *este*: *sg*) this one; (: *pl*) these (ones)

essência [e'sẽsja] F essence;

essencial [esẽ'sjaw] (pl **-ais**) ADJ essential; (*principal*) main ▶ M: **o essencial** the main thing

esta ['ɛsta] F *de* **este²**

estabelecer [istabele'ser] VT to establish; (*fundar*) to set up

estabelecimento [istabelesi'mẽtu] M establishment; (*casa comercial*) business

estábulo [is'tabulu] M cow-shed

estaca [is'taka] F post, stake; (*de barraca*) peg

estação [ista'sãw] (pl **-ões**) F station; (*do ano*) season; **~ de águas** spa; **~ balneária** seaside resort; **~ emissora** broadcasting station

estacionamento [istasjona'mẽtu] M (*ato*) parking; (*lugar*) car park (BRIT), parking lot (US)

estacionar [istasjo'nar] VT to park ▶ VI to park; (*não mover*) to remain stationary

estacionário, -a [istasjo'narju, a] ADJ (*veículo*) stationary; (*Com*) slack

estações [ista'sõjs] FPL *de* **estação**

estada [is'tada] F stay

estadia [ista'dʒia] F = **estada**

estádio [is'tadʒu] M stadium

estadista [ista'dʒista] M/F statesman/woman

estado [i'stadu] M state; **E~s Unidos (da América)** United States (of America); **~ civil** marital status; **~ de espírito** state of mind; **~ maior** staff; **estadual** [ista'dwaw] (pl **-ais**) ADJ state atr

estafa [is'tafa] F fatigue; (*esgotamento*) nervous exhaustion

estagiário, -a [ista'ʒjarju, a] M/F (*empregado*) trainee; (*estudante*) intern; (*professor*) student teacher; (*médico*) junior doctor

estágio [is'taʒu] M (*aprendizado: de empregado*) traineeship; (: *de estudante*) internship; (*fase*) stage

estagnado, -a [istag'nadu, a] ADJ stagnant

estalar [ista'lar] VT to break; (*os dedos*) to snap ▶ VI to split, crack; (*crepitar*) to crackle

estalido [ista'lidu] M pop

estalo [is'talu] M (*de chicote*) crack; (*dos dedos*) snap; (*dos lábios*) smack; (*de foguete*) bang; **~ de trovão** thunderclap; **de ~** suddenly

estampa [is'tãpa] F (*figura impressa*) print; (*ilustração*) picture

estampado, -a [istã'padu, a] ADJ printed ▶ M (*tecido*) print; (*num tecido*) pattern

estampar [istã'par] VT to print; (*marcar*) to stamp

estancar [istã'kar] VT to staunch; (*fazer cessar*) to stop; **estancar-se** VR to stop

estância [is'tãsja] F ranch, farm

estandarte [istã'dartʃi] M standard, banner

estanho [is'taɲu] M (*metal*) tin

estante [is'tãtʃi] F bookcase; (*suporte*) stand

PALAVRA-CHAVE

estar [is'tar] VI **1** (*lugar*) to be; (*em casa*) to be in; (*no telefone*): **a Lúcia está? — não, ela não está** is Lúcia there? — no, she's not in **2** (*estado*) to be; **estar doente** to be ill; **estar bem** (*de saúde*) to be well; (*financeiramente*) to be well off; **estar calor/frio** to be hot/cold; **estar com fome/sede/medo** to be hungry/thirsty/afraid **3** (*ação contínua*): **estar fazendo**

(BR) *ou* **a fazer** (PT) to be doing
4 (+ *pp, como adj*): **estar sentado/cansado** to be sitting down/tired
5 (+ *pp, uso passivo*): **está condenado à morte** he's been condemned to death; **o livro está emprestado** the book's been borrowed
6: **estar de férias/licença** to be on holiday (BRIT) *ou* vacation (US)/leave; **ela estava de chapéu** she had a hat on, she was wearing a hat
7: **estar para fazer** to be about to do; **ele está para chegar a qualquer momento** he'll be here any minute; **não estar para conversas** not to be in the mood for talking
8: **estar por fazer** to be still to be done
9: **estar sem dinheiro** to have no money; **estar sem dormir** not to have slept; **estou sem dormir há três dias** I haven't slept for three days; **está sem terminar** it isn't finished yet
10 (*frases*): **tá (bem)** (col) OK; **estar bem com** to be on good terms with

estardalhaço [istarda'ʎasu] M fuss; (*ostentação*) ostentation
estas ['ɛstas] FPL *de* **este²**
estatal [ista'taw] (pl **-ais**) ADJ nationalized, state-owned ▶ F state-owned company
estático, -a [is'tatʃiku, a] ADJ static
estatística [ista'tʃistʃika] F statistic; (*ciência*) statistics *sg*
estatizar [istatʃi'zar] VT to nationalize
estátua [is'tatwa] F statue
estatura [ista'tura] F stature
estável [is'tavew] (pl **-eis**) ADJ stable

este¹ ['ɛstʃi] M east ▶ ADJ INV (*região*) eastern; (*vento, direção*) easterly
este², esta [estʃi, 'ɛsta] ADJ (*sg*) this; (pl) these ▶ PRON this one; (pl) these; (*a quem/que se referiu por último*) the latter; **esta noite** (*noite passada*) last night; (*noite de hoje*) tonight
esteira [is'tejra] F mat; (*de navio*) wake; (*rumo*) path
esteja [is'teʒa] VB *ver* **estar**
estelionato [isteljo'natu] M fraud
estender [istẽ'der] VT to extend; (*mapa*) to spread out; (*pernas*) to stretch; (*massa*) to roll out; (*conversa*) to draw out; (*corda*) to pull tight; (*roupa molhada*) to hang out; **estender-se** VR to lie down; (*fila, terreno*) to stretch, extend; **~-se sobre algo** to dwell on sth, expand on sth; **~ a mão** to hold out one's hand
estéreis [is'tɛrejs] ADJ PL *de* **estéril**
estereo... [isterju] PREFIXO stereo...; **estereofônico, -a** [isterjo'foniku, a] ADJ stereo(phonic); **estereótipo** [iste'rjɔtʃipu] M stereotype
estéril [is'tɛriw] (pl **-eis**) ADJ sterile; (*terra*) infertile; (*fig*) futile; **esterilizar** [isterili'zar] VT to sterilize
esteve [is'tevi] VB *ver* **estar**
esticar [istʃi'kar] VT to stretch; **esticar-se** VR to stretch out
estigma [is'tʃigima] M mark, scar; (*fig*) stigma
estilhaçar [istʃiʎa'sar] VT to splinter; (*despedaçar*) to shatter; **estilhaçar-se** VR to shatter; **estilhaço** [istʃi'ʎasu] M fragment; (*de pedra*) chip; (*de madeira, metal*) splinter
estilo [is'tʃilu] M style; (*Tec*) stylus;

~ de vida way of life

estima [is'tʃima] F esteem; (*afeto*) affection

estimação [istʃima'sãw] F: **... de ~** favourite (BRIT) ..., favorite (US) ...

estimado, -a [istʃi'madu, a] ADJ respected; (*em cartas*): **E~ Senhor** Dear Sir

estimar [istʃi'mar] VT to appreciate; (*avaliar*) to value; (*ter estima a*) to have a high regard for; (*calcular aproximadamente*) to estimate

estimativa [istʃima'tʃiva] F estimate

estimulante [istʃimu'lãtʃi] ADJ stimulating ▶ M stimulant

estimular [istʃimu'lar] VT to stimulate; (*incentivar*) to encourage; **estímulo** [is'tʃimulu] M stimulus; (*ânimo*) encouragement

estipular [istʃipu'lar] VT to stipulate

estirar [istʃi'rar] VT to stretch (out); **estirar-se** VR to stretch

estive [is'tʃivi] VB ver **estar**

estocada [isto'kada] F stab, thrust

estocar [isto'kar] VT to stock

estofo [is'tofu] M (*tecido*) material; (*para acolchoar*) padding, stuffing

estojo [is'toʒu] M case; **~ de ferramentas** tool kit; **~ de unhas** manicure set

estômago [is'tomagu] M stomach; **ter ~ para (fazer) algo** to be up to (doing) sth

estontear [istõ'tʃjar] VT to stun, daze

estoque [is'tɔki] M (Com) stock

estourado, -a [isto'radu, a] ADJ (*temperamental*) explosive; (*col: cansado*) knackered, worn out

estourar [isto'rar] VI to explode; (*pneu*) to burst; (*escândalo*) to blow up; (*guerra*) to break out; (BR: *chegar*) to turn up, arrive; **~ (com alguém)** (*zangar-se*) to blow up (at sb)

estouro [is'toru] M explosion; **dar o ~** (fig: *zangar-se*) to blow up, blow one's top

estrábico, -a [is'trabiku, a] ADJ cross-eyed

estraçalhar [istrasa'ʎar] VT (*livro, objeto*) to pull to pieces; (*pessoa*) to tear to pieces

estrada [is'trada] F road; **~ de ferro** (BR) railway (BRIT), railroad (US); **~ principal** main road (BRIT), state highway (US)

estrado [is'tradu] M (*tablado*) platform; (*de cama*) base

estragado, -a [istra'gadu, a] ADJ ruined; (*fruta*) rotten; (*muito mimado*) spoiled, spoilt (BRIT)

estraga-prazeres [istraga-] M/F INV spoilsport

estragar [istra'gar] VT to spoil; (*arruinar*) to ruin, wreck; (*desperdiçar*) to waste; (*saúde*) to damage; (*mimar*) to spoil; **estrago** [is'tragu] M destruction; (*desperdício*) waste; (*dano*) damage; **os estragos da guerra** the ravages of war

estrangeiro, -a [istrã'ʒejru, a] ADJ foreign ▶ M/F foreigner; **no ~** abroad

estrangular [istrãgu'lar] VT to strangle

estranhar [istra'ɲar] VT to be surprised at; (*achar estranho*): **~ algo** to find sth strange; **estranhei o clima** the climate did not agree with me; **não é de se ~** it's not surprising

estranho, -a [iʃ'traɲu, a] ADJ
strange, odd; (*influências*) outside
▶ M/F (*desconhecido*) stranger; (*de fora*) outsider

estratégia [iʃtra'tɛʒa] F strategy

estrear [iʃ'trjar] VT (*vestido*) to wear
for the first time; (*peça de teatro*) to
perform for the first time; (*veículo*)
to use for the first time; (*filme*) to
show for the first time, première;
(*iniciar*): **~ uma carreira** to embark
on *ou* begin a career ▶ VI (*ator,
jogador*) to make one's first
appearance; (*filme, peça*) to open

estrebaria [iʃtreba'ria] F stable

estreia [iʃ'treja] F (*de artista*) debut;
(*de uma peça*) first night; (*de um filme*)
première, opening

estreitar [iʃtrej'tar] VT to narrow;
(*roupa*) to take in; (*abraçar*) to hug;
(*laços de amizade*) to strengthen ▶ VI
(*estrada*) to narrow

estreito, -a [iʃ'trejtu, a] ADJ
narrow; (*saia*) straight; (*vínculo,
relação*) close; (*medida*) strict ▶ M
strait

estrela [iʃ'trela] F star; **~ cadente**
falling star; **estrelado, -a**
[iʃtre'ladu, a] ADJ (*céu*) starry; (*ovo*)
fried

estremecer [iʃtreme'ser] VT to
shake; (*amizade*) to strain; (*fazer
tremer*): **~ alguém** to make sb
shudder ▶ VI to shake; (*tremer*) to
tremble; (*horrorizar-se*) to shudder;
(*amizade*) to be strained

estremecimento
[iʃtremesi'mẽtu] M shaking,
trembling; (*tremor*) tremor; (*numa
amizade*) tension

estresse [iʃ'tresi] M stress

estribeira [iʃtri'bejra] F: **perder
as ~s** (*col*) to fly off the handle, lose
one's temper

estridente [iʃtri'dẽtʃi] ADJ shrill,
piercing

estrofe [iʃ'trɔfi] F stanza

estrondo [iʃ'trõdu] M (*de trovão*)
rumble; (*de armas*) din

estrutura [iʃtru'tura] F structure;
(*armação*) framework; (*de edifício*)
fabric

estudante [iʃtu'dãtʃi] M/F
student; **estudantil** [iʃtudã'tʃiw]
(*pl* **-is**) ADJ student *atr*

estudar [iʃtu'dar] VT, VI to study

estúdio [iʃ'tudʒu] M studio

estudo [iʃ'tudu] M study

estufa [iʃ'tufa] F (*fogão*) stove; (*de
plantas*) greenhouse; (*de fogão*) plate
warmer; **efeito ~** greenhouse
effect

estufado [iʃtu'fadu] (*PT*) M stew

estupefato, -a [iʃtupe'fatu, a],
(*PT*) **estupefacto** ADJ
dumbfounded

estupendo, -a [iʃtu'pẽdu, a] ADJ
wonderful; (*col*) terrific

estupidez [iʃtupi'deʒ] F stupidity;
(*ato, dito*) stupid thing; (*grosseria*)
rudeness

estúpido, -a [iʃ'tupidu, a] ADJ
stupid; (*grosseiro*) rude, churlish
▶ M/F idiot; (*grosseiro*) oaf

estuprar [iʃtu'prar] VT to rape;
estupro [iʃ'tupru] M rape

esvaziar [izva'zjar] VT to empty;
esvaziar-se VR to empty

etapa [e'tapa] F stage

etc. ABR (= *et cetera*) etc

eternidade [eterni'dadʒi] F
eternity

ética ['ɛtʃika] F ethics *pl*

ético, -a ['ɛtʃiku, a] ADJ ethical

Etiópia [e'tʃjɔpja] F: **a ~** Ethiopia

etiqueta [etʃi'keta] F etiquette;
(*rótulo, em roupa*) label; (*que se
amarra*) tag

étnico, -a ['ɛtʃniku, a] ADJ ethnic

etos ['ɛtus] M INV ethos

eu [ew] PRON I ▸ M self; **sou eu** it's me

EUA ABR MPL (= *Estados Unidos da América*) USA

eucaristia [ewkaris'tʃia] F Holy Communion

euro ['ewru] M (*moeda*) euro

Europa [ew'rɔpa] F: **a ~** Europe; **europeu, -peia** [ewro'peu, 'pɐja] ADJ, M/F European

evacuar [eva'kwar] VT to evacuate; (*sair de*) to leave; (*Med*) to discharge ▸ VI to defecate

evadir [eva'dʒir] VT to evade; **evadir-se** VR to escape

evangelho [evã'ʒeʎu] M gospel

evaporar [evapo'rar] VT, VI to evaporate; **evaporar-se** VR to evaporate; (*desaparecer*) to vanish

evasão [eva'zãw] (*pl* **-ões**) F escape, flight; (*fig*) evasion

evasiva [eva'ziva] F excuse

evasivo, -a [eva'zivu, a] ADJ evasive

evasões [eva'zõjs] FPL *de* **evasão**

evento [e'vẽtu] M event; (*eventualidade*) eventuality

eventual [evẽ'tuaw] (*pl* **-ais**) ADJ fortuitous, accidental; **eventualidade** [evẽtwali'dadʒi] F eventuality

evidência [evi'dẽsja] F evidence, proof; **evidenciar** [evidẽ'sjar] VT to prove; (*mostrar*) to show; **evidenciar-se** VR to be evident, be obvious

evidente [evi'dẽtʃi] ADJ obvious, evident

evitar [evi'tar] VT to avoid; **~ de fazer algo** to avoid doing sth

evocar [evo'kar] VT to evoke; (*espíritos*) to invoke

evolução [evolu'sãw] (*pl* **-ões**) F development; (*Mil*) manoeuvre (BRIT), maneuver (US); (*movimento*) movement; (*Bio*) evolution

evoluir [evo'lwir] VI to evolve; **~ para** to evolve into

Ex.a ABR = **excelência**

exagerar [ezaʒe'rar] VT to exaggerate ▸ VI to exaggerate; (*agir com exagero*) to overdo it; **exagero** [eza'ʒeru] M exaggeration

exalar [eza'lar] VT (*odor*) to give off

exaltado, -a [ezaw'tadu, a] ADJ fanatical; (*apaixonado*) overexcited

exaltar [ezaw'tar] VT (*elevar: pessoa, virtude*) to exalt; (*louvar*) to praise; (*excitar*) to excite; (*irritar*) to annoy; **exaltar-se** VR (*irritar-se*) to get worked up; (*arrebatar-se*) to get carried away

exame [e'zami] M (*Educ*) examination, exam; (*Med etc*) examination; **fazer um ~** (*Educ*) to take an exam; (*Med*) to have an examination

examinar [ezami'nar] VT to examine

exatidão [ezatʃi'dãw] F accuracy; (*perfeição*) correctness

exato, -a [e'zatu, a] ADJ right, correct; (*preciso*) exact; **~!** exactly!

exaustão [ezaw'stãw] F exhaustion; **exausto, -a** [e'zawstu, a] ADJ exhausted

exaustor [ezaw'stor] M extractor fan

exceção [ese'sãw] (*pl* **-ões**) F exception; **com ~ de** with the exception of; **abrir ~** to make an exception

excecional (PT) ADJ = **excepcional**

excedente [ese'dẽtʃi] ADJ excess; (*Com*) surplus ▸ M (*Com*) surplus

exceder [ese'der] VT to exceed; (*superar*) to surpass; **exceder-se** VR (*cometer excessos*) to go too far; (*cansar-se*) to overdo things

excelência [ese'lēsja] F excellence; **por ~** par excellence; **Vossa E~** Your Excellency; **excelente** [ese'lētʃi] ADJ excellent

excêntrico, -a [e'sētriku, a] ADJ, M/F eccentric

excepcional [esepsjo'naw] (*pl* **-ais**) ADJ exceptional; (*especial*) special; (*Med*) handicapped

excesso [e'sɛsu] M excess; (*Com*) surplus

exceto [e'sɛtu] PREP except (for), apart from

excitação [esita'sāw] F excitement

excitado, -a [esi'tadu, a] ADJ excited; (*estimulado*) aroused

excitante [esi'tātʃi] ADJ exciting

exclamação [isklama'sāw] (*pl* **-ões**) F exclamation

exclamar [iskla'mar] VI to exclaim

excluir [is'klwir] VT to exclude, leave out; (*eliminar*) to rule out; (*ser incompatível com*) to preclude; **exclusão** [isklu'zāw] F exclusion; **exclusivo, -a** [isklu'zivu, a] ADJ exclusive

excursão [iskur'sāw] (*pl* **-ões**) F outing; excursion; **~ a pé** hike; **excursionista** [iskursjo'nista] M/F tourist; (*para o dia*) day-tripper; (*a pé*) hiker

execução [ezeku'sāw] (*pl* **-ões**) F execution; (*de música*) performance

executar [ezeku'tar] VT to execute; (*Mús*) to perform; (*plano*) to carry out; (*papel teatral*) to play

executivo, -a [ezeku'tʃivu, a] ADJ, M/F executive

exemplar [ezē'plar] ADJ exemplary ▶ M model, example; (*Bio*) specimen; (*livro*) copy; (*peça*) piece

exemplo [e'zēplu] M example; **por ~** for example

exercer [ezer'ser] VT to exercise; (*influência, pressão*) to exert; (*função*) to perform; (*profissão*) to practise (BRIT), practice (US); (*obrigações*) to carry out

exercício [ezer'sisju] M exercise; (*de medicina*) practice; (*Mil*) drill; (*Com*) financial year

exercitar [ezersi'tar] VT (*profissão*) to practise (BRIT), practice (US); (*direitos, músculos*) to exercise; (*adestrar*) to train

exército [e'zɛrsitu] M army

exibição [ezibi'sāw] (*pl* **-ões**) F show, display; (*de filme*) showing

exibir [ezi'bir] VT to show, display; (*alardear*) to show off; (*filme*) to show, screen; **exibir-se** VR to show off; (*indecentemente*) to expose o.s.

exigência [ezi'ʒēsja] F demand; (*o necessário*) requirement; **exigente** [ezi'ʒētʃi] ADJ demanding

exigir [ezi'ʒir] VT to demand

exíguo, -a [e'zigwu, a] ADJ (*diminuto*) small; (*escasso*) scanty

exilado, -a [ezi'ladu, a] M/F exile

exilar [ezi'lar] VT to exile; **exilar-se** VR to go into exile; **exílio** [e'zilju] M exile; (*forçado*) deportation

existência [ezis'tēsja] F existence; (*vida*) life

existir [ezis'tʃir] VI to exist; **existe/ existem ...** (*há*) there is/are ...

êxito ['ezitu] M result; (*sucesso*) success; (*música, filme etc*) hit; **ter ~ (em)** to succeed (in), be successful (in)

Exmo, -a (*pl* **-s/-s**) ABR (= *Excelentíssimo*) Dear

êxodo ['ezodu] M exodus

exorcista [ezor'sista] M/F exorcist

exótico, -a [e'zɔtʃiku, a] ADJ exotic

expandir [ispã'dʒir] VT to expand; (espalhar) to spread; **expandir-se** VR to expand; **~-se com alguém** to be frank with sb

expansão [ispã'sãw] F expansion, spread; (de alegria) effusiveness

expansivo, -a [ispã'sivu, a] ADJ (pessoa) outgoing

expeça [is'pɛsa] VB ver **expedir**

expectativa [ispekta'tʃiva] F expectation

expedição [ispedʒi'sãw] (pl -ões) F (viagem) expedition; (de mercadorias) despatch; (por navio) shipment; (de passaporte etc) issue

expediente [ispe'dʒiẽtʃi] M means; (serviço) working day; (correspondência) correspondence ▶ ADJ expedient; **~ bancário** banking hours pl; **~ do escritório** office hours pl

expedir [ispe'dʒir] VT to send, despatch; (bilhete, passaporte, decreto) to issue

expelir [ispe'lir] VT to expel; (sangue) to spit

experiência [ispe'rjẽsja] F experience; (prova) experiment, test; **em ~** on trial

experimentar [isperimẽ'tar] VT (comida) to taste; (vestido) to try on; (pôr à prova) to try out, test; (conhecer pela experiência) to experience; (sofrer) to suffer, undergo; **experimento** [isperi'mẽtu] M experiment

expilo [is'pilu] VB ver **expelir**

expirar [ispi'rar] VT to exhale, breathe out ▶ VI to die; (terminar) to end

explicação [isplika'sãw] (pl -ões) F explanation

explicar [ispli'kar] VT, VI to explain; **explicar-se** VR to explain o.s.

explícito, -a [is'plisitu, a] ADJ explicit, clear

explodir [isplo'dʒir] VT, VI to explode

exploração [isplora'sãw] F exploration; (abuso) exploitation; (de uma mina) running

explorador, a [isplora'dor(a)] M/F explorer; (de outros) exploiter

explorar [isplo'rar] VT (região) to explore; (mina) to work, run; (ferida) to probe; (trabalhadores etc) to exploit

explosão [isplo'zãw] (pl -ões) F explosion; (fig) outburst; **explosivo, -a** [isplo'zivu, a] ADJ explosive; (pessoa) hot-headed ▶ M explosive

expor [is'por] (irreg: como **pôr**) VT to expose; (a vida) to risk; (teoria) to explain; (revelar) to reveal; (mercadorias) to display; (quadros) to exhibit; **expor-se** VR to expose o.s.

exportação [isporta'sãw] F (ato) export(ing); (mercadorias) exports pl

exportador, a [isporta'dor(a)] ADJ exporting ▶ M/F exporter

exportar [ispor'tar] VT to export

exposição [ispozi'sãw] (pl -ões) F exhibition; (explicação) explanation; (declaração) statement; (narração) account; (Foto) exposure

exposto, -a [is'postu, 'pɔsta] ADJ (lugar) exposed; (quadro, mercadoria) on show ou display ▶ M: **o acima ~** the above

expressão [ispre'sãw] (pl -ões) F expression

expressar [ispre'sar] VT to express;

expressivo, -a [ispre'sivu, a] ADJ expressive; (*pessoa*) demonstrative

expresso, -a [is'prɛsu, a] PP *de* **exprimir** ▶ ADJ definite, clear; (*trem, ordem, carta*) express ▶ M express

expressões [ispre'sõjs] FPL *de* **expressão**

exprimir [ispri'mir] VT to express

expulsão [ispul'sãw] (*pl* -**ões**) F expulsion; (*Esporte*) sending off

expulsar [ispuw'sar] VT to expel; (*de uma festa, clube etc*) to throw out; (*inimigo*) to drive out; (*estrangeiro*) to expel, deport; (*jogador*) to send off

expulso, -a [is'puwsu, a] PP *de* **expulsar**

expulsões [ispul'sõjs] FPL *de* **expulsão**

êxtase ['estazi] M ecstasy

extenso, -a [is'tẽsu, a] ADJ extensive; (*comprido*) long; (*artigo*) full, comprehensive; **por ~** in full

extenuante [iste'nwãtʃi] ADJ exhausting; (*debilitante*) debilitating

exterior [iste'rjor] ADJ (*de fora*) outside, exterior; (*aparência*) outward; (*comércio*) foreign ▶ M (*da casa*) outside; (*aspecto*) outward appearance; **do ~** (*do estrangeiro*) from abroad; **no ~** abroad

exterminar [istermi'nar] VT (*inimigo*) to wipe out, exterminate; (*acabar com*) to do away with

externo, -a [is'tɛrnu, a] ADJ external; (*aparente*) outward; **aluno ~** day pupil

extinguir [istʃĩ'gir] VT (*fogo*) to put out, extinguish; (*um povo*) to wipe out; **extinguir-se** VR (*fogo, luz*) to go out; (*Bio*) to become extinct

extinto, -a [is'tʃĩtu, a] ADJ (*fogo*) extinguished; (*língua*) dead; (*animal, vulcão*) extinct; (*associação etc*) defunct; **extintor** [istʃĩ'tor] M

(fire) extinguisher

extorsão [istor'sãw] F extortion

extra ['ɛstra] ADJ extra ▶ M/F extra person; (*Teatro*) extra

extração [istra'sãw] (*pl* -**ões**) F extraction; (*de loteria*) draw

extrair [istra'jir] VT to extract, take out

extraordinário, -a [istraordʒi'narju, a] ADJ extraordinary; (*despesa*) extra; (*reunião*) special

extrato [is'tratu] M extract; (*resumo*) summary; **~ (bancário)** (bank) statement

extravagância [istrava'gãsja] F extravagance; **extravagante** [istrava'gãtʃi] ADJ extravagant; (*roupa*) outlandish; (*conduta*) wild

extravasar [istrava'zar] VI to overflow

extraviado, -a [istra'vjadu, a] ADJ lost, missing

extraviar [istra'vjar] VT to mislay; (*pessoa*) to lead astray; (*dinheiro*) to embezzle; **extraviar-se** VR to get lost; **extravio** [istra'viu] M loss; (*roubo*) embezzlement; (*fig*) deviation

extremado, -a [istre'madu, a] ADJ extreme

extremidade [istremi'dadʒi] F extremity; (*do dedo*) tip; (*ponta*) end; (*beira*) edge

extremo, -a [is'trɛmu, a] ADJ extreme ▶ M extreme; **ao ~** extremely

extrovertido, -a [estrover'tʃidu, a] ADJ extrovert, outgoing ▶ M/F extrovert

exultante [ezuw'tãtʃi] ADJ jubilant, exultant

f

fã [fã] (col) M/F fan

fábrica ['fabrika] F factory; **~ de cerveja** brewery; **a preço de ~** wholesale

fabricação [fabrika'sāw] F manufacture; **~ em série** mass production

fabuloso, -a [fabu'lozu, ɔza] ADJ fabulous

faca ['faka] F knife; **facada** [fa'kada] F stab, cut

façanha [fa'saɲa] F exploit, deed

facção [fak'sāw] (pl **-ões**) F faction

face ['fasi] F face; (bochecha) cheek; **em ~ de** in view of; **fazer ~ a** to face up to

fáceis ['fasejs] ADJ PL de **fácil**

faceta [fa'seta] F facet

fachada [fa'ʃada] F façade, front

fácil ['fasiw] (pl **-eis**) ADJ easy; (temperamento, pessoa) easy-going ▶ ADV easily; **facilidade** [fasili'dadʒi] F ease; (jeito) facility; **facilidades** FPL (recursos) facilities; **ter facilidade para algo** to have a talent ou a facility for sth

facilitar [fasili'tar] VT to facilitate, make easy; (fornecer): **~ algo a alguém** to provide sb with sth

fã-clube [fã'klubi] (pl **-s**) M fan club

faço ['fasu] VB ver **fazer**

facto ['faktu] (PT) M = **fato**

factual [fak'twaw] (pl **-ais**) ADJ factual

faculdade [fakuw'dadʒi] F faculty; (poder) power

facultativo, -a [fakuwta'tʃivu, a] ADJ optional ▶ M/F doctor

fadado, -a [fa'dadu, a] ADJ destined

fadiga [fa'dʒiga] F fatigue

fadista [fa'dʒista] M/F "fado" singer ▶ M (PT) ruffian

fado ['fadu] M fate; (canção) traditional song of Portugal

> The best-known musical form in Portugal is the melancholic **fado**, which is traditionally sung by a soloist (known as a *fadista*) accompanied by the Portuguese *guitarra*. There are two main types of **fado**: Coimbra **fado** is traditionally sung by men, and is considered to be more cerebral than the **fado** from Lisbon, which is sung by both men and women. The theme is nearly always one of deep nostalgia known as *saudade*, and the harsh reality of life.

faia ['faja] F beech (tree)

faisão [faj'zāw] (pl **-ões**) M pheasant

faísca [fa'iska] F spark; (brilho) flash

faisões [faj'zõjs] MPL de **faisão**

faixa ['fajʃa] F (cinto, Judô) belt;

(*tira*) strip; (*área*) zone; (*Auto: pista*) lane; (BR: *para pedestres*) zebra crossing (BRIT), crosswalk (US); (*Med*) bandage; (*num disco*) track

fala ['fala] F speech; **chamar às ~s** to call to account; **sem ~** speechless

falante [fa'lãtʃi] ADJ talkative

falar [fa'lar] VT (*língua*) to speak; (*besteira etc*) to talk; (*dizer*) to say; (*verdade, mentira*) to tell ▶ VI to speak; **~ algo a alguém** to tell sb sth; **~ de** *ou* **em algo** to talk about sth; **~ com alguém** to talk to sb; **por ~ em** speaking of; **sem ~ em** not to mention; **falou!, 'tá falado!** (*col*) OK!

falcão [faw'kãw] (*pl* -**ões**) M falcon

falcatrua [fawka'trua] F (*col*) scam

falecer [fale'ser] VI to die; **falecimento** [falesi'mẽtu] M death

falência [fa'lẽsja] F bankruptcy; **abrir ~** to declare o.s. bankrupt; **ir à ~** to go bankrupt; **levar à ~** to bankrupt

falésia [fa'lɛzja] F cliff

falha ['faʎa] F fault; (*lacuna*) omission; (*de caráter*) flaw

falhar [fa'ʎar] VI to fail; (*não acertar*) to miss; (*errar*) to be wrong; **sua voz está falhando** you're breaking up

falho, -a ['faʎu, a] ADJ faulty; (*deficiente*) wanting

falido, -a [fa'lidu, a] ADJ, M/F bankrupt

falir [fa'lir] VI to fail; (*Com*) to go bankrupt

falsário, -a [faw'sarju, a] M/F forger

falsidade [fawsi'dadʒi] F falsehood; (*fingimento*) pretence (BRIT), pretense (US)

falsificar [fawsifi'kar] VT (*forjar*) to forge; (*falsear*) to falsify; (*adulterar*) to adulterate; (*desvirtuar*) to misrepresent

falso, -a ['fawsu, a] ADJ false; (*fraudulento*) dishonest; (*errôneo*) wrong; (*joia, moeda, quadro*) fake; **pisar em ~** to blunder

falta ['fawta] F (*carência*) lack; (*ausência*) absence; (*defeito, culpa*) fault; (*Futebol*) foul; **por** *ou* **na ~ de** for lack of; **sem ~** without fail; **fazer ~** to be lacking, be needed; **sentir ~ de alguém/algo** to miss sb/sth; **ter ~ de** to lack, be in need of

faltar [faw'tar] VI to be lacking, be wanting; (*pessoa*) to be absent; (*falhar*) to fail; **~ ao trabalho** to be absent from work; **~ à palavra** to break one's word; **falta pouco para ...** it won't be long until ...

fama ['fama] F (*renome*) fame; (*reputação*) reputation

família [fa'milja] F family

familiar [fami'ljar] ADJ (*da família*) family *atr*; (*conhecido*) familiar ▶ M/F relation, relative; **familiaridade** [familjari'dadʒi] F familiarity; (*sem-cerimônia*) informality

famoso, -a [fa'mozu, ɔza] ADJ famous

fanático, -a [fa'natʃiku, a] ADJ fanatical ▶ M/F fanatic

fantasia [fãta'zia] F fantasy; (*imaginação*) imagination; (*capricho*) fancy; (*traje*) fancy dress

fantasiar [fãta'zjar] VT to imagine ▶ VI to daydream; **fantasiar-se** VR to dress up (in fancy dress)

fantasma [fã'tazma] M ghost; (*alucinação*) illusion

fantástico, -a [fã'tastʃiku, a] ADJ fantastic; (*ilusório*) imaginary; (*incrível*) unbelievable

fantoche [fã'tɔʃi] M puppet

farda ['farda] F uniform

farei [fa'rej] VB ver **fazer**

farinha [fa'riɲa] F: **~ (de mesa)** (manioc) flour; **~ de rosca** breadcrumbs pl; **~ de trigo** plain flour

farmacêutico, -a [farma'sewtʃiku, a] ADJ pharmaceutical ▶ M/F pharmacist, chemist (BRIT)

farmácia [far'masja] F pharmacy, chemist's (shop) (BRIT)

faro ['faru] M sense of smell; (fig) flair

farofa [fa'rɔfa] F (Culin) side dish based on manioc flour

farol [fa'rɔw] (pl **-óis**) M lighthouse; (Auto) headlight; **~ alto** (Auto) full (BRIT) ou high (US) beam; **~ baixo** dipped headlights pl (BRIT), dimmed beam (US)

farra ['faha] F binge, spree

farrapo [fa'hapu] M rag

farsa ['farsa] F farce; **farsante** [far'sãtʃi] M/F joker

fartar [far'tar] VT to satiate; (encher) to fill up; **fartar-se** VR to gorge o.s.

farto, -a ['fartu, a] ADJ full, satiated; (abundante) plentiful; (aborrecido) fed up

fartura [far'tura] F abundance

fascinante [fasi'nãtʃi] ADJ fascinating

fascinar [fasi'nar] VT to fascinate; (encantar) to charm; **fascínio** [fa'sinju] M fascination

fase ['fazi] F phase

fashion ['fɛʃjõ] (col) ADJ trendy

fatal [fa'taw] (pl **-ais**) ADJ (mortal) fatal; (inevitável) fateful; **fatalidade** [fatali'dadʒi] F fate; (desgraça) disaster

fatia [fa'tʃia] F slice

fatigante [fatʃi'gãtʃi] ADJ tiring; (aborrecido) tiresome

fatigar [fatʃi'gar] VT to tire; (aborrecer) to bore; **fatigar-se** VR to get tired

Fátima ['fatima] F see note

> **Fátima**, situated in central Portugal, is known worldwide as a site of pilgrimage for Catholics. It is said that, in 1917, the Virgin Mary appeared six times to three shepherd children (os três pastorinhos). Millions of pilgrims visit Fátima every year.

fato ['fatu] M fact; (acontecimento) event; (PT: traje) suit; **~ de banho** (PT) swimming costume (BRIT), bathing suit (US); **de ~** in fact, really

fator [fa'tor] M factor

fatura [fa'tura] F bill, invoice; **faturar** [fatu'rar] VT to invoice; (dinheiro) to make ▶ VI (col: ganhar dinheiro): **faturar (alto)** to rake it in

fava ['fava] F broad bean; **mandar alguém às ~s** to send sb packing

favela [fa'vela] F slum

favor [fa'vor] M favour (BRIT), favor (US); **a ~ de** in favo(u)r of; **por ~** please; **se faz ~** (PT) please; **faça ou faz o ~ de ...** would you be so good as to ..., kindly ...; **favorável** [favo'ravew] (pl **-eis**) ADJ: **favorável (a)** favourable (BRIT) ou favorable (US) (to); **favorecer** [favore'ser] VT to favour (BRIT), favor (US); (beneficiar) to benefit; (suj: vestido) to suit; (: retrato) to flatter; **favorito, -a** [favo'ritu, a] ADJ, M/F (tb Comput) favourite (BRIT), favorite (US)

fax [faks] M fax; **enviar por ~** to fax

faxina [fa'ʃina] F: **fazer ~** to clean up; **faxineiro, -a** [faʃi'nejru, a] M/F cleaner

fazenda [fa'zẽda] F farm; (*de café*) plantation; (*de gado*) ranch; (*pano*) cloth, fabric; (*Econ*) treasury; **fazendeiro** [fazẽ'dejru] M farmer; (*de café*) plantation-owner; (*de gado*) rancher, ranch-owner

(PALAVRA-CHAVE)

fazer [fa'zer] VT
1 (*fabricar, produzir*) to make; (*construir*) to build; (*pergunta*) to ask; (*poema, música*) to write; **fazer um filme/ruído** to make a film/noise
2 (*executar*) to do; **o que você está fazendo?** what are you doing?; **fazer a comida** to do the cooking; **fazer o papel de** (*Teatro*) to play
3 (*estudos, alguns esportes*) to do; **fazer medicina/direito** to do *ou* study medicine/law; **fazer ioga/ginástica** to do yoga/keep-fit
4 (*transformar, tornar*) **sair o fará sentir melhor** going out will make him feel better; **sua partida fará o trabalho mais difícil** his departure will make work more difficult
5 (*como sustituto de vb*): **ele bebeu e eu fiz o mesmo** he drank and I did likewise
6: **ele faz anos hoje** it's his birthday today; **fiz 30 anos ontem** I was 30 yesterday
▶ VI 1 (*portar-se*) to act, behave; **fazer bem/mal** to do the right/wrong thing; **não fiz por mal** I didn't mean it; **faz como quem não sabe** act as if you don't know anything
2: **fazer com que alguém faça algo** to make sb do sth

▶ VB IMPESS 1: **faz calor/frio** it's hot/cold
2 (*tempo*): **faz um ano** a year ago; **faz dois anos que ele se formou** it's two years since he graduated; **faz três meses que ele está aqui** he's been here for three months
3: **não faz mal** never mind; **tanto faz** it's all the same

fazer-se VR 1: **fazer-se de desentendido** to pretend not to understand
2: **faz-se com ovos e leite** it's made with eggs and milk; **isso não se faz** that's not done

fé [fɛ] F faith; (*crença*) belief; (*confiança*) trust; **de boa/má fé** in good/bad faith

febre ['fɛbri] F fever; (*fig*) excitement; **~ do feno** hay fever; **febril** [fe'briw] (*pl* **-is**) ADJ feverish

fechado, -a [fe'ʃadu, a] ADJ shut, closed; (*pessoa*) reserved; (*sinal*) red; (*luz, torneira*) off; (*tempo*) overcast; (*cara*) stern

fechadura [feʃa'dura] F (*de porta*) lock

fechar [fe'ʃar] VT to close, shut; (*concluir*) to finish, conclude; (*luz, torneira*) to turn off; (*rua*) to close off; (*ferida*) to close up; (*bar, loja*) to close down ▶ VI to close (up), shut; to close down; (*tempo*) to cloud over; **fechar-se** VR to close, shut; (*pessoa*) to withdraw; **~ à chave** to lock

fecho ['feʃu] M fastening; (*trinco*) latch; (*término*) close; **~ ecler** zip fastener (*BRIT*), zipper (*US*)

fécula ['fɛkula] F starch

feder [fe'der] VI to stink

federação [federa'sãw] (*pl* **-ões**) F federation

federal [fede'raw] (*pl* **-ais**) ADJ federal; (*col: grande*) huge

fedor [fe'dor] M stench

feijão [fej'ʒãw] (*pl* **-ões**) M bean(s) (*pl*); (*preto*) black bean(s) (*pl*); **feijoada** [fej'ʒwada] F (*Culin*) meat, rice and black beans

feio, -a [feju, a] ADJ ugly; (*situação*) grim; (*atitude*) bad; (*tempo*) horrible ▶ ADV (*perder*) badly

feira [fejra] F fair; (*mercado*) market

feiticeira [fejtʃi'sejra] F witch

feiticeiro, -a [fejtʃi'sejru, a] ADJ bewitching, enchanting ▶ M wizard

feitiço [fej'tʃisu] M charm, spell

feitio [fej'tʃiu] M shape, pattern; (*caráter*) nature, manner; (*Tec*) workmanship

feito, -a [fejtu, a] PP *de* **fazer** ▶ ADJ finished, ready ▶ M act, deed; (*façanha*) feat ▶ CONJ like; **~ a mão** hand-made; **homem ~** grown man

feiura [fe'jura] F ugliness

felicidade [felisi'dadʒi] F happiness; (*sorte*) good luck; (*êxito*) success; **felicidades** FPL (*congratulações*) congratulations

felicitações [felisita'sõjs] FPL congratulations, best wishes

feliz [fe'liz] ADJ happy; (*afortunado*) lucky; **felizmente** [feliz'mẽtʃi] ADV fortunately

feltro [fewtru] M felt

fêmea [femja] F female

feminino, -a [femi'ninu, a] ADJ feminine; (*sexo*) female; (*equipe, roupa*) women's ▶ M (*Ling*) feminine

feminista [femi'nista] ADJ, M/F feminist

feno [fenu] M hay

fenomenal [fenome'naw] (*pl* **-ais**) ADJ phenomenal; (*espantoso*) amazing; (*pessoa*) brilliant

fenômeno [fe'nomenu] M phenomenon

fera [fɛra] F wild animal

feriado [fe'rjadu] M (public) holiday (BRIT), vacation (US)

férias [fɛrjas] FPL holiday(s) (BRIT), vacation *sg* (US); **de ~** on holiday (BRIT) *ou* vacation (US); **tirar ~** to have *ou* take a holiday (BRIT) *ou* vacation (US)

ferida [fe'rida] F wound, injury; *ver tb* **ferido**

ferido, -a [fe'ridu, a] ADJ injured; (*em batalha*) wounded; (*magoado*) hurt ▶ M/F casualty

ferimento [feri'mẽtu] M injury; (*em batalha*) wound

ferir [fe'rir] VT to injure; (*tb fig*) to hurt; (*em batalha*) to wound; (*ofender*) to offend

fermentar [fermẽ'tar] VI to ferment

fermento [fer'mẽtu] M yeast; **~ em pó** baking powder

feroz [fe'roz] ADJ fierce, ferocious; (*cruel*) cruel

ferragem [fe'haʒẽ] (*pl* **-ns**) F (*peças*) hardware; (*guarnição*) metalwork; **loja de ferragens** ironmonger's (BRIT), hardware store (US)

ferramenta [feha'mẽta] F tool; (*caixa de ferramentas*) tool kit

ferrão [fe'hãw] (*pl* **-ões**) M goad; (*de inseto*) sting

ferrenho, -a [fe'heɲu, a] ADJ (*vontade*) iron

ferro [fɛhu] M iron; **ferros** MPL (*algemas*) shackles, chains; **~ batido** wrought iron; **~ de**

passar iron; **~ fundido** cast iron;
~ ondulado corrugated iron
ferrões [fe'hõjs] MPL de **ferrão**
ferrolho [fe'hoʎu] M (trinco) bolt
ferrovia [feho'via] F railway (BRIT),
railroad (US); **ferroviário, -a**
[feho'vjarju, a] ADJ railway atr
(BRIT), railroad atr (US) ▶ M/F railway
ou railroad worker
ferrugem [fe'huʒẽ] F rust
fértil ['fɛrtʃiw] (pl **-eis**) ADJ fertile;
fertilizante [fertʃili'zãtʃi] M
fertilizer; **fertilizar** [fertʃili'zar] VT
to fertilize
ferver [fer'ver] VT, VI to boil; **~ de
raiva/indignação** to seethe with
rage/indignation; **~ em fogo baixo**
(Culin) to simmer
fervilhar [fervi'ʎar] VI to simmer;
(com atividade) to hum; (pulular):
~ de to swarm with
fervor [fer'vor] M fervour (BRIT),
fervor (US)
festa ['fɛsta] F (reunião) party;
(conjunto de ceremônias) festival;
festas FPL (carícia) embrace; **boas
~s** Merry Christmas and a Happy
New Year; **dia de ~** public holiday
festejar [feste'ʒar] VT to celebrate;
(acolher) to welcome, greet; **festejo**
[fes'teʒu] M festivity; (ato)
celebration
festival [festʃi'vaw] (pl **-ais**) M
festival
festividade [festʃivi'dadʒi] F
festivity
festivo, -a [fes'tʃivu, a] ADJ festive
fetiche [fe'tʃiʃi] M fetish
feto ['fɛtu] M (Med) foetus (BRIT),
fetus (US)
fevereiro [feve'rejru] M February
fez [fez] VB ver **fazer**
fezes ['fɛzis] FPL faeces (BRIT),
feces (US)

fiado, -a ['fjadu, a] ADV: **comprar/
vender ~** to buy/sell on credit
fiador, a [fja'dor(a)] (Jur)
guarantor; (Com) backer
fiambre ['fjãbri] M cold meat;
(presunto) ham
fiança ['fjãsa] F guarantee; (Jur)
bail; **prestar ~ por** to stand bail for;
sob ~ on bail
fiar ['fjar] VT (algodão etc) to spin;
(confiar) to entrust; (vender a crédito)
to sell on credit; **fiar-se** VR: **~-se em**
to trust
fibra ['fibra] F fibre (BRIT), fiber (US)

PALAVRA-CHAVE

ficar [fi'kar] VI **1** (permanecer) to
stay; (sobrar) to be left; **ficar
perguntando/olhando** etc to keep
asking/looking etc; **ficar por fazer**
to have still to be done; **ficar para
trás** to be left behind
2 (tornar-se) to become; **ficar cego/
surdo/louco** to go blind/deaf/
mad; **fiquei contente ao saber da
notícia** I was happy when I heard
the news; **ficar com raiva/medo**
to get angry/frightened; **ficar de
bem/mal com alguém** (col) to
make up/fall out with sb
3 (posição) to be; **a casa fica ao
lado da igreja** the house is next to
the church; **ficar sentado/deitado**
to be sitting down/lying down
4 (tempo: durar): **ele ficou duas
horas para resolver** he took two
hours to decide; (: ser adiado): **a
reunião ficou para amanhã** the
meeting has been postponed until
tomorrow
5 (comportamento): **sua atitude
não ficou bem** his (ou her etc)
behaviour was inappropriate; (cor):
você fica bem em azul blue suits

you, you look good in blue; (*roupa*): **ficar bem para** to suit

6: **ficar bom** (*de saúde*) to be cured; (*trabalho, foto etc*) to turn out well

7: **ficar de fazer algo** (*combinar*) to arrange to do sth; (*prometer*) to promise to do sth

8: **ficar de pé** to stand up

ficção [fik'sãw] F fiction

ficha ['fiʃa] F (*tb*: **~ de telefone**) token; (*tb*: **~ de jogo**) chip; (*de fichário*) (index) card; (*Polícia*) record; (*PT Elet*) plug; (*em loja, lanchonete*) ticket

fichário [fi'ʃarju] M filing cabinet; (*caixa*) card index; (*caderno*) file

ficheiro [fi'ʃejru] (*PT*) M = **fichário**

fidelidade [fideli'dadʒi] F fidelity, loyalty; (*exatidão*) accuracy

fiel [fjew] (*pl* **-éis**) ADJ (*leal*) faithful, loyal; (*acurado*) accurate; (*que não falha*) reliable

figa ['figa] F talisman; **fazer uma ~** to make a *figa*, ≈ cross one's fingers; **de uma ~** (*col*) damned

fígado ['figadu] M liver

figo ['figu] M fig; **figueira** [fi'gejra] F fig tree

figura [fi'gura] F figure; (*forma*) form, shape; (*Ling*) figure of speech; (*aspecto*) appearance

figurino [figu'rinu] M model; (*revista*) fashion magazine

fila ['fila] F row, line; (*BR: fileira de pessoas*) queue (*BRIT*), line (*US*); (*num teatro, cinema*) row; **em ~** in a row; **fazer ~** to form a line, queue; **~ indiana** single file

filé [fi'lɛ] M (*bife*) steak; (*peixe*) fillet

fileira [fi'lejra] F row, line; **fileiras** FPL (*serviço militar*) military service *sg*

filho, -a ['fiʎu, a] M/F son/daughter; **filhos** MPL children; (*de*

animais) young; **~ da mãe, ~ da puta** (*!*) bastard (*!*)

filhote [fi'ʎɔtʃi] M (*de leão, urso etc*) cub; (*cachorro*) pup(py)

filial [fi'ljaw] (*pl* **-ais**) F (*sucursal*) branch

filipeta [fili'peta] F flyer

Filipinas [fili'pinas] FPL: **as ~** the Philippines

filmadora [fiwma'dora] F video camera

filmar [fiw'mar] VT, VI to film

filme ['fiwmi] M film (*BRIT*), movie (*US*)

filosofia [filozo'fia] F philosophy; **filósofo, -a** [fi'lɔzofu, a] M/F philosopher

filtrar [fiw'trar] VT to filter; **filtrar-se** VR to filter; (*infiltrar-se*) to infiltrate

filtro ['fiwtru] M (*Tec*) filter

fim [fĩ] (*pl* **-ns**) M end; (*motivo*) aim, purpose; (*de história, filme*) ending; **a ~ de** in order to; **no ~ das contas** after all; **por ~** finally; **sem ~** endless; **levar ao ~** to carry through; **pôr** *ou* **dar ~ a** to put an end to; **ter ~** to come to an end; **~ de semana** weekend

finado, -a [fi'nadu, a] ADJ, M/F deceased

The day of **Finados**, 2 November, a holiday throughout Brazil, is dedicated to remembering the dead. On this day, people usually gather in cemeteries to remember their family dead, and also to worship at the graves of popular figures from Brazilian culture and society, such as singers, actors and other personalities. It is popularly believed that these people can work miracles.

final [fi'naw] (pl **-ais**) ADJ final, last ▶ M end; (Mús) finale ▶ F (Esporte) final; **finalista** [fina'lista] M/F finalist; **finalizar** [finali'zar] VT to finish, conclude

finanças [fi'nãsas] FPL finance sg; **financeiro, -a** [finã'sejru, a] ADJ financial ▶ M/F financier; **financiar** [finã'sjar] VT to finance

fingimento [fĩ3i'mẽtu] M pretence (BRIT), pretense (US)

fingir [fĩ'3ir] VT to feign ▶ VI to pretend; **fingir-se** VR: **~-se de** to pretend to be

finito, -a [fi'nitu, a] ADJ finite

finlandês, -esa [fĩlã'des, eza] ADJ Finnish ▶ M/F Finn ▶ M (Ling) Finnish

Finlândia [fĩ'lãd3ja] F: **a ~** Finland

fino, -a ['finu, a] ADJ fine; (delgado) slender; (educado) polite; (som, voz) shrill; (elegante) refined ▶ ADV: **falar ~** to talk in a high voice

fins [fĩs] MPL de **fim**

fio ['fiu] M thread; (Bot) fibre (BRIT), fiber (US); (Elet) wire; (Tel) line; (de líquido) trickle; (gume) edge; (encadeamento) series; **horas/dias a ~** hours/days on end; **sem ~** (Comput) wireless

firewall [fajau'aw] M firewall

firma ['firma] F signature; (Com) firm, company

firmar [fir'mar] VT to secure, make firm; (assinar) to sign; (estabelecer) to establish; (basear) to base ▶ VI (tempo) to settle; **firmar-se** VR: **~-se em** (basear-se) to rest on, be based on

firme ['firmi] ADJ firm; (estável) stable; (sólido) solid; (tempo) settled ▶ ADV firmly; **firmeza** [fir'meza] F firmness; (estabilidade) stability; (solidez) solidity

fiscal [fis'kaw] (pl **-ais**) M/F supervisor; (aduaneiro) customs officer; (de impostos) tax inspector; **fiscalizar** [fiskali'zar] VT to supervise; (examinar) to inspect, check

fisco ['fisku] M: **o ~** ≈ the Inland Revenue (BRIT), ≈ the Internal Revenue Service (US)

física ['fizika] F physics sg; ver tb **físico**

físico, -a ['fiziku, a] ADJ physical ▶ M/F (cientista) physicist ▶ M (corpo) physique

fisionomia [fizjono'mia] F (rosto) face; (ar) expression, look; (aspecto de algo) appearance

fissura [fi'sura] F crack

fita ['fita] F (tira) strip, band; (filme) film; (para máquina de escrever) ribbon; (magnética, adesiva) tape; **~ durex**® adhesive tape, Sellotape® (BRIT), Scotch tape® (US); **~ métrica** tape measure

fitar [fi'tar] VT to stare at, gaze at

fivela [fi'vɛla] F buckle

fixar [fik'sar] VT to fix; (colar, prender) to stick; (data, prazo, regras) to set; (atenção) to concentrate; **fixar-se** VR: **~-se em** (assunto) to concentrate on; (detalhe) to fix on; (apegar-se a) to be attached to; **~ os olhos em** to stare at; **~ residência** to set up house

fixo, -a ['fiksu, a] ADJ fixed; (firme) firm; (permanente) permanent; (cor) fast ▶ M (tb: **telefone ~**) landline

fiz [fiz] VB ver **fazer**

flagelado, -a [fla3e'ladu, a] M/F: **os ~s** the afflicted, the victims

flagrante [fla'grãtfi] ADJ flagrant; **apanhar em ~ (delito)** to catch red-handed ou in the act

flagrar [fla'grar] VT to catch

flanela [fla'nɛla] F flannel

flash [flaʃ] M (*Foto*) flash

flauta ['flawta] F flute

flecha ['flɛʃa] F arrow

fleuma ['flewma] F phlegm

floco ['flɔku] M flake; **~ de milho** cornflake; **~ de neve** snowflake

flor [flor] F flower; (*o melhor*) cream, pick; **em ~** in bloom; **à ~ da pele** on edge

florescente [flore'sētʃi] ADJ (*Bot*) in flower; (*próspero*) flourishing

florescer [flore'ser] VI (*Bot*) to flower; (*prosperar*) to flourish

floresta [flo'rɛsta] F forest; **florestal** [flores'taw] (*pl* **florestais**) ADJ forest *atr*

florido, -a [flo'ridu, a] ADJ (*jardim*) in flower

fluente [flu'ētʃi] ADJ fluent

fluido, -a ['flwidu, a] ADJ fluid ▶ M fluid

fluir [flwir] VI to flow

fluminense [flumi'nēsi] ADJ from the state of Rio de Janeiro ▶ M/F native *ou* inhabitant of the state of Rio de Janeiro

flutuar [flu'twar] VI to float; (*bandeira*) to flutter; (*fig: vacilar*) to waver

fluvial [flu'vjaw] (*pl* **-ais**) ADJ river *atr*

fluxo ['fluksu] M (*corrente*) flow; (*Elet*) flux; **~ de caixa** (*Com*) cash flow

fobia [fo'bia] F phobia

foca ['fɔka] F seal

foco ['fɔku] M focus; (*Med, fig*) seat, centre (*BRIT*), center (*US*); **fora de ~** out of focus

fofo, -a ['fofu, a] ADJ soft; (*col: pessoa*) cute

fofoca [fo'fɔka] F piece of gossip; **fofocas** FPL (*mexericos*) gossip *sg*;

fofocar [fofo'kar] VI to gossip

fogão [fo'gãw] (*pl* **-ões**) M stove, cooker

fogareiro [foga'rejru] M stove

foge ['fɔʒi] VB *ver* **fugir**

fogo ['fogu] M fire; (*fig*) ardour (*BRIT*), ardor (*US*); **você tem ~?** have you got a light?; **~s de artifício** fireworks; **pôr ~ a** to set fire to

fogões [fo'gõjs] MPL *de* **fogão**

fogueira [fo'gejra] F bonfire

foguete [fo'getʃi] M rocket

foi [foj] VB *ver* **ir, ser**

folclore [fowk'lɔri] M folklore

folclórico, -a [fowk'lɔriku, a] ADJ (*música etc*) folk *atr*; (*comida, roupa*) ethnic

fôlego ['folegu] M breath; (*folga*) breathing space; **perder o ~** to get out of breath

folga ['fɔwga] F rest, break; (*espaço livre*) clearance; (*ócio*) inactivity; (*col: atrevimento*) cheek; **dia de ~** day off; **folgado, -a** [fow'gadu, a] ADJ (*roupa*) loose; (*vida*) leisurely; (*col: atrevido*) cheeky; **folgar** [fow'gar] VT to loosen ▶ VI (*descansar*) to rest; (*divertir-se*) to have fun

folha ['foʎa] F leaf; (*de papel, de metal*) sheet; (*página*) page; (*de faca*) blade; (*jornal*) paper; **novo em ~** brand new; **~ de estanho** tinfoil (*BRIT*), aluminum foil (*US*); **~ de exercícios** worksheet

folhagem [fo'ʎaʒē] F foliage

folheto [fo'ʎetu] M booklet, pamphlet

fome ['fɔmi] F hunger; (*escassez*) famine; (*fig: avidez*) longing; **passar ~** to go hungry; **estar com** *ou* **ter ~** to be hungry

fone ['fɔni] M telephone, phone; (*peça do telefone*) receiver

fonte ['fõtʃi] F (*nascente*) spring; (*chafariz*) fountain; (*origem*) source; (*Anat*) temple

for [for] VB *ver* **ir, ser**

fora¹ ['fɔra] ADV out, outside ▶ PREP (*além de*) apart from ▶ M: **dar o ~** (*bateria, radio*) to give out; (*pessoa*) to leave, be off; **dar um ~** to slip up; **dar um ~ em alguém** (*namorado*) to chuck sb, dump sb; (*esnobar*) to snub sb; **levar um ~** (*de namorado*) to be given the boot; (*ser esnobado*) to get the brush-off; **~ de** outside; **~ de si** beside o.s.; **estar ~** (*viajando*) to be away; **estar ~ (de casa)** to be out; **lá ~** outside; (*no exterior*) abroad; **jantar ~** to eat out; **com os braços de ~** with bare arms; **ser de ~** to be from out of town; **ficar de ~** not to join in; **lá para ~** outside; **ir para ~** (*viajar*) to go out of town; **com a cabeça para ~ da janela** with one's head sticking out of the window; **costurar/cozinhar para ~** to do sewing/cooking for other people; **por ~** on the outside; **cobrar por ~** to charge extra; **~ de dúvida** beyond doubt; **~ de propósito** irrelevant

fora² VB *ver* **ir, ser**

foragido, -a [fora'ʒidu, a] ADJ, M/F fugitive; **estar ~** to be on the run

forasteiro, -a [foras'tejru, a] M/F outsider, stranger; (*de outro país*) foreigner

força ['forsa] F strength; (*Tec, Elet*) power; (*esforço*) effort; (*coerção*) force; **à ~** by force; **à ~ de** by dint of; **com ~** hard; **por ~** of necessity; **fazer ~** to try (hard); **~ de trabalho** workforce

forçado, -a [for'sadu, a] ADJ forced; (*afetado*) false

forçar [for'sar] VT to force; (*olhos, voz*) to strain

forma ['fɔrma] F form; (*de um objeto*) shape; (*físico*) figure; (*maneira*) way; (*Med*) fitness; **desta ~** in this way; **de qualquer ~** anyway; **manter a ~** to keep fit

fôrma ['fɔrma] F (*Culin*) cake tin; (*molde*) mould (BRIT), mold (US)

formação [forma'sãw] (*pl* **-ões**) F formation; (*antecedentes*) background; (*caráter*) make-up; (*profissional*) training

formado, -a [for'madu, a] ADJ (*modelado*): **ser ~ de** to consist of ▶ M/F graduate

formal [for'maw] (*pl* **-ais**) ADJ formal; **formalidade** [formali'dadʒi] F formality

formar [for'mar] VT to form; (*constituir*) to constitute, make up; (*educar*) to train; **formar-se** VR to form; (*Educ*) to graduate

formatar [forma'tar] VT (*Comput*) to format

formidável [formi'davew] (*pl* **-eis**) ADJ tremendous, great

formiga [for'miga] F ant

formigar [formi'gar] VI to abound; (*sentir comichão*) to itch

formoso, -a [for'mozu, ɔza] ADJ beautiful; (*esplêndido*) superb

fórmula ['fɔrmula] F formula

formular [formu'lar] VT to formulate; (*queixas*) to voice

formulário [formu'larju] M form; **formulários** MPL: **~s contínuos** (*Comput*) continuous stationery *sg*

fornecedor, a [fornese'dor(a)] M/F supplier ▶ F (*empresa*) supplier

fornecer [forne'ser] VT to supply, provide; **fornecimento** [fornesi'mẽtu] M supply

forno ['fornu] M (*Culin*) oven; (*Tec*) furnace; (*para cerâmica*) kiln; **alto ~** blast furnace

foro ['foru] M forum; (Jur) Court of Justice; **foros** MPL (privilégios) privileges

forro ['fohu] M covering; (interior) lining

forró [fo'hɔ] M see note

> **Forró** is a style of popular music and dance that originated in the north-east of Brazil, but which is now popular all over the country. The instruments which feature in **forró** are the accordion, the bass drum and the triangle, and it is danced with a partner. There are a number of different styles of **forró**, such as the faster-paced forró universitário, which has attracted a considerable following among the younger generation in Brazil's cities.

fortalecer [fortale'ser] VT to strengthen

fortaleza [forta'leza] F fortress; (força) strength; (moral) fortitude

forte ['fɔrtʃi] ADJ strong; (pancada) hard; (chuva) heavy; (som) loud; (dor) sharp ▶ ADV strongly; (som) loud(ly) ▶ M fort; (talento) strength; **ser ~ em algo** (versado) to be good at sth ou strong in sth

fortuito, -a [for'twitu, a] ADJ accidental

fortuna [for'tuna] F fortune, (good) luck; (riqueza) fortune, wealth

fórum ['fɔrũ] (pl **-ns**) M (Comput) forum; **~ de discussão** discussion forum, message board

fosco, -a ['fosku, a] ADJ dull; (opaco) opaque

fósforo ['fɔsforu] M match

fossa ['fɔsa] F pit

fosse ['fosi] VB ver **ir, ser**

fóssil ['fɔsiw] (pl **-eis**) M fossil

fosso ['fosu] M trench, ditch

foto ['fɔtu] F photo

fotocópia [foto'kɔpja] F photocopy; **fotocopiadora** [fotokopja'dora] F photocopier; **fotocopiar** [fotoko'pjar] VT to photocopy

fotografar [fotogra'far] VT to photograph

fotografia [fotogra'fia] F photography; (uma foto) photograph

fotógrafo, -a [fo'tɔgrafu, a] M/F photographer

foz [fɔz] F mouth (of river)

fração [fra'sãw] (pl **-ões**) F fraction

fracassar [fraka'sar] VI to fail; **fracasso** [fra'kasu] M failure

fraco, -a ['fraku, a] ADJ weak; (sol, som) faint

frágil ['fraʒiw] (pl **-eis**) ADJ (débil) fragile; (Com) breakable; (pessoa) frail; (saúde) delicate, poor

fragmento [frag'mẽtu] M fragment

fragrância [fra'grãsja] F fragrance, perfume

fralda ['frawda] F (da camisa) shirt tail; (para bebê) nappy (BRIT), diaper (US); (de montanha) foot

framboesa [frãbo'eza] F raspberry

França ['frãsa] F France

francamente [frãka'mẽtʃi] ADV (abertamente) frankly; (realmente) really

francês, -esa [frã'ses, eza] ADJ French ▶ M/F Frenchman/woman ▶ M (Ling) French

franco, -a ['frãku, a] ADJ frank; (isento de pagamento) free; (óbvio) clear ▶ M franc; **entrada franca** free admission

frango ['frãgu] M chicken
franja ['frãʒa] F fringe (BRIT), bangs pl (US)
franquia [frã'kia] F (Com) franchise; (isenção) exemption
franzino, -a [frã'zinu, a] ADJ skinny
fraqueza [fra'keza] F weakness
frasco ['frasku] M bottle
frase ['frazi] F sentence; **~ feita** set phrase
fratura [fra'tura] F fracture, break; **fraturar** [fratu'rar] VT to fracture
freada [fre'ada] (BR) F: **dar uma ~** to slam on the brakes
frear [fre'ar] (BR) VT to curb, restrain; (veículo) to stop ▶ VI (veículo) to brake
freezer ['frizer] M freezer
freguês, -guesa [fre'ges, 'geza] M/F customer; (PT) parishioner; **freguesia** [frege'zia] F customers pl; (PT) parish
freio ['freju] M (BR: veículo) brake; (de cavalo) bridle; (bocado do freio) bit; **~ de mão** handbrake
freira ['frejra] F nun
frenesi [frene'zi] M frenzy; **frenético, -a** [fre'nɛtʃiku, a] ADJ frantic, frenzied
frente ['frẽtʃi] F front; (rosto) face; (fachada) façade; **~ a ~** face to face; **de ~ para** facing; **em ~ de** in front of; (de fronte a) opposite; **para a ~** ahead, forward; **porta da ~** front door; **seguir em ~** to go straight on; **na minha (ou sua etc) ~** in front of me (ou you etc); **sair da ~** to get out of the way; **pra ~ (**col) fashionable, trendy
frequência [fre'kwẽsja] F frequency; **com ~** often, frequently
frequentar [frekwẽ'tar] VT to frequent
frequente [fre'kwẽtʃi] ADJ frequent

fresco, -a ['fresku, a] ADJ fresh; (vento, tempo) cool; (col: efeminado) camp; (: afetado) pretentious; (: cheio de luxo) fussy ▶ M (ar) fresh air
frescobol [fresko'bɔw] M (kind of) racketball (played mainly on the beach)
frescura [fres'kura] F freshness; (frialdade) coolness; (col: luxo) fussiness; (: afetaçao) pretentiousness
frete ['frɛtʃi] M (carregamento) freight, cargo; (tarifa) freightage
frevo ['frevu] M improvised Carnival dance
fria ['fria] F: **dar uma ~ em alguém** to give sb the cold shoulder; **estar/ entrar numa ~** (col) to be in/get into a mess
fricção [frik'sãw] F friction; (ato) rubbing; (Med) massage; **friccionar** [friksjo'nar] VT to rub
frieza ['frjeza] F coldness; (indiferença) coolness
frigideira [friʒi'dejra] F frying pan
frigorífico [frigo'rifiku] M refrigerator; (congelador) freezer
frio, -a ['friu, a] ADJ cold ▶ M coldness; **frios** MPL (Culin) cold meats; **estou com ~** I'm cold; **faz ou está ~** it's cold
frisar [fri'zar] VT (encrespar) to curl; (salientar) to emphasize
fritar [fri'tar] VT to fry
fritas ['fritas] FPL French fries, chips (BRIT)
frito, -a ['fritu, a] ADJ fried; (col): **estar ~** to be done for
frívolo, -a ['frivolu, a] ADJ frivolous
fronha ['froɲa] F pillowcase
fronteira [frõ'tejra] F frontier, border
frota ['frɔta] F fleet

frouxo, -a ['froʃu, a] ADJ loose; (*corda*) slack; (*fraco*) weak; (*col: condescendente*) soft

frustrar [frus'trar] VT to frustrate

fruta ['fruta] F fruit; **frutífero, -a** [fru'tʃiferu, a] ADJ (*proveitoso*) fruitful; (*árvore*) fruit-bearing

fruto ['frutu] M (*Bot*) fruit; (*resultado*) result, product; **dar ~** (*fig*) to bear fruit

fubá [fu'ba] M corn meal

fugir [fu'ʒir] VI to flee, escape; (*prisioneiro*) to escape

fui [fuj] VB *ver* **ir, ser**

fulano, -a [fu'lanu, a] M/F so-and-so

fulminante [fuwmi'nãtʃi] ADJ devastating; (*palavras*) scathing

fulo, -a ['fulu, a] ADJ: **estar** *ou* **ficar ~ de raiva** to be furious

fumaça [fu'masa] (BR) F (*de fogo*) smoke; (*de gás*) fumes *pl*

fumador, a [fuma'dor(a)] (PT) M/F smoker

fumante [fu'mãtʃi] M/F smoker

fumar [fu'mar] VT, VI to smoke

fumo ['fumu] M (PT: *de fogo*) smoke; (: *de gás*) fumes *pl*; (BR: *tabaco*) tobacco; (*fumar*) smoking

função [fũ'sãw] (*pl* **-ões**) F function; (*ofício*) duty; (*papel*) role; (*espetáculo*) performance

funcionalismo [fũsjona'lizmu] M: **~ público** civil service

funcionamento [fũsjona'mẽtu] M functioning, working; **pôr em ~** to set going, start

funcionar [fũsjo'nar] VI to function; (*máquina*) to work, run; (*dar bom resultado*) to work

funcionário, -a [fũsjo'narju, a] M/F official; **~ (público)** civil servant

funções [fũ'sõjs] FPL *de* **função**

fundação [fũda'sãw] (*pl* **-ões**) F foundation

fundamental [fũdamẽ'taw] (*pl* **-ais**) ADJ fundamental, basic

fundamento [fũda'mẽtu] M (*fig*) foundation, basis; (*motivo*) motive

fundar [fũ'dar] VT to establish, found; (*basear*) to base; **fundar-se** VR: **~-se em** to be based on

fundir [fũ'dʒir] VT to fuse; (*metal*) to smelt, melt down; (*Com: empresas*) to merge; (*em molde*) to cast; **fundir-se** VR to melt; (*juntar-se*) to merge

fundo, -a ['fũdu, a] ADJ deep; (*fig*) profound ▶ M (*do mar, jardim*) bottom; (*profundidade*) depth; (*base*) basis; (*da loja, casa, do papel*) back; (*de quadro*) background; (*de dinheiro*) fund ▶ ADV deeply; **fundos** MPL (*Com*) funds; (*da casa etc*) back *sg*; **a ~** thoroughly; **no ~** at the bottom; (*da casa etc*) at the back; (*fig*) basically

fúnebre ['funebri] ADJ funeral *atr*, funereal; (*fig*) gloomy

funeral [fune'raw] (*pl* **-ais**) M funeral

funil [fu'niw] (*pl* **-is**) M funnel

furacão [fura'kãw] (*pl* **-ões**) M hurricane

furado, -a [fu'radu, a] ADJ perforated; (*pneu*) flat; (*orelha*) pierced

furão, -rona [fu'rãw, 'rɔna] (*pl* **-ões/-s**) M ferret ▶ M/F (*col*) go-getter ▶ ADJ (*col*) hard-working, dynamic

furar [fu'rar] VT to perforate; (*penetrar*) to penetrate; (*frustrar*) to foil; (*fila*) to jump ▶ VI (*col: programa*) to fall through

fúria ['furja] F fury, rage; **furioso, -a** [fu'rjozu, ɔza] ADJ furious

furo ['furu] M hole; (num pneu) puncture

furões [fu'rõjs] MPL de **furão**

furona [fu'rɔna] F de **furão**

furor [fu'ror] M fury, rage; **fazer ~** to be all the rage

furtar [fur'tar] VT, VI to steal; **furtar-se** VR: **~-se a** to avoid

furtivo, -a [fur'tʃivu, a] ADJ furtive, stealthy

furto ['furtu] M theft

fusível [fu'zivew] (pl **-eis**) M (Elet) fuse

fuso ['fuzu] M (Tec) spindle; **~ horário** time zone

futebol [futʃi'bɔw] M football; **~ de salão** indoor football

futevôlei [futʃi'volej] M see note

> **Futevôlei** is a type of volleyball in which the ball is allowed to touch only the feet, legs, trunk and head of the players. It is very popular on the beaches of Rio de Janeiro, where tournaments take place during the summer, in which many famous footballers take part.

fútil ['futʃiw] (pl **-eis**) ADJ (pessoa) shallow; (insignificante) trivial

futilidade [futʃili'dadʒi] F (de pessoa) shallowness; (insignificância) triviality; (coisa fútil) trivial thing

futuro, -a [fu'turu, a] ADJ future ▶ M future; **no ~** in the future

fuzil [fu'ziw] (pl **-is**) M rifle; **fuzilar** [fuzi'lar] VT to shoot

fuzis [fu'zis] MPL de **fuzil**

g

g. ABR (= grama) gr.

gabar [ga'bar] VT to praise; **gabar-se** VR: **~-se de** to boast about

gabinete [gabi'netʃi] M (Com) office; (escritório) study; (Pol) cabinet

gado ['gadu] M livestock; (bovino) cattle; **~ leiteiro** dairy cattle; **~ suíno** pigs pl

gafanhoto [gafa'ɲotu] M grasshopper

gafe ['gafi] F gaffe, faux pas

gagueira [ga'gejra] F stutter

gaguejar [gage'ʒar] VI to stammer, stutter

gaiato, -a [ga'jatu, a] ADJ funny

gaiola [ga'jɔla] F cage; (cadeia) jail ▶ M (barco) riverboat

gaita ['gajta] F harmonica; **~ de foles** bagpipes pl

gaivota [gaj'vɔta] F seagull

gajo ['gaʒu] (PT col) M guy, fellow

gala ['gala] F: **traje de ~** evening dress; **festa de ~** gala

galão [ga'lãw] (pl **-ões**) M (Mil) stripe; (medida) gallon; (PT: café) white coffee; (passamanaria) braid

Galápagos [ga'lapagus] N: **(as) Ilhas ~** (the) Galapagos Islands

galáxia [ga'laksja] M galaxy

galera [ga'lɛra] F (Náut) galley; (col: pessoas, público) crowd

galeria [gale'ria] F gallery; (Teatro) circle

Gales ['galis] M: **País de ~** Wales

galho ['gaʎu] M (de árvore) branch

galinha [ga'liɲa] F hen; (Culin) chicken; **galinheiro** [gali'ɲejru] M hen-house

galo ['galu] M cock, rooster; (inchação) bump; **missa do ~** midnight mass

galões [ga'lõjs] MPL de **galão**

galopar [galo'par] VI to gallop; **galope** [ga'lɔpi] M gallop

gama ['gama] F (Mús) scale; (fig) range; (Zool) doe

gambá [gã'ba] M (Zool) opossum

game ['geimi] M computer game

Gana ['gana] M Ghana

gana ['gana] F craving, desire; (ódio) hate; **ter ~s de (fazer) algo** to feel like (doing) sth; **ter ~ de alguém** to hate sb

ganância [ga'nãsja] F greed; **ganancioso, -a** [ganã'sjozu, ɔza] ADJ greedy

gancho ['gãʃu] M hook; (de calça) crotch

gangue ['gãgi] (col) F gang

ganhador, a [gaɲa'dor(a)] ADJ winning ▶ M/F winner

ganha-pão ['gaɲa-] (pl **-pães**) M living, livelihood

ganhar [ga'ɲar] VT to win; (salário) to earn; (adquirir) to get; (lugar) to reach; (lucrar) to gain ▶ VI to win; **~ de alguém** (num jogo) to beat sb; **ganho** ['gaɲu] PP de **ganhar** ▶ M profit, gain; **ganhos** MPL (ao jogo) winnings

ganso, -a ['gãsu, a] M/F goose

garagem [ga'raʒẽ] (pl **-ns**) F garage

garantia [garã'tʃia] F guarantee; (de dívida) surety

garçom [gar'sõ] (BR) (pl **-ns**) M waiter

garçonete [garso'netʃi] (BR) F waitress

garçons [gar'sõs] MPL de **garçom**

garfo ['garfu] M fork

gargalhada [garga'ʎada] F burst of laughter; **rir às ~s** to roar with laughter; **dar** ou **soltar uma ~** to burst out laughing

gargalo [gar'galu] M (tb fig) bottleneck

garganta [gar'gãta] F throat; (Geo) gorge, ravine

gargarejo [garga'reʒu] M (ato) gargling; (líquido) gargle

gari [ga'ri] M/F (na rua) road sweeper (BRIT), street sweeper (US); (lixeiro) dustman (BRIT), garbage man (US)

garoa [ga'roa] F drizzle; **garoar** [ga'rwar] VI to drizzle

garotada [garo'tada] F: **a ~** the kids pl

garoto, -a [ga'rotu, a] M/F boy/girl ▶ M (BR: chope) small beer; (PT: café) coffee with milk

garoupa [ga'ropa] F (peixe) grouper

garrafa [ga'hafa] F bottle

garupa [ga'rupa] F (de cavalo) hindquarters pl; (de moto) back seat; **andar na ~** (de moto) to ride pillion

gás [gajs] M gas; **gases** MPL (do

intestino) wind *sg*; **~ natural** natural gas; **~ de efeito estufa** greenhouse gas

gasóleo [ga'zɔlju] M diesel oil

gasolina [gazo'lina] F petrol (BRIT), gas(oline) (US)

gasosa [ga'zɔza] F fizzy drink

gasoso, -a [ga'zozu, ɔza] ADJ (*água*) sparkling; (*bebida*) fizzy

gastador, -deira [gasta'dor, 'dejra] ADJ, M/F spendthrift

gastar [gas'tar] VT to spend; (*gasolina, electricidade*) to use; (*roupa, sapato*) to wear out; (*salto, piso etc*) to wear down; (*saúde*) to damage; (*desperdiçar*) to waste ▶ VI to spend; to wear out; to wear down; **gastar-se** VR to wear out; to wear down

gástrico, -a ['gastriku, a] ADJ gastric

gata ['gata] F (she-)cat

gatilho [ga'tʃiʎu] M trigger

gato ['gatu] M cat; **~ montês** wild cat

gatuno, -a [ga'tunu, a] ADJ thieving ▶ M/F thief

gaveta [ga'veta] F drawer

geada ['ʒjada] F frost

geladeira [ʒela'dejra] (BR) F refrigerator, icebox (US)

gelado, -a [ʒe'ladu, a] ADJ frozen ▶ M (PT: *sorvete*) ice cream

gelar [ʒe'lar] VT to freeze; (*vinho etc*) to chill ▶ VI to freeze

gelatina [ʒela'tʃina] F gelatine; (*sobremesa*) jelly (BRIT), Jell-O® (US)

geleia [ʒe'lɛja] F jam

gélido, -a ['ʒɛlidu, a] ADJ chill, icy

gelo ['ʒelu] ADJ INV light grey (BRIT) *ou* gray (US) ▶ M ice; (*cor*) light grey (BRIT) *ou* gray (US)

gema ['ʒɛma] F yolk; (*pedra preciosa*) gem

gêmeo, -a ['ʒemju, a] ADJ, M/F twin; **Gêmeos** MPL (*Astrologia*) Gemini *sg*

gemer [ʒe'mer] VI (*de dor*) to groan, moan; (*lamentar-se*) to wail; (*animal*) to whine; (*vento*) to howl;

gemido [ʒe'midu] M groan, moan; (*lamento*) wail; (*de animal*) whine

gene ['ʒeni] M gene

Genebra [ʒe'nɛbra] N Geneva

general [ʒene'raw] (*pl* -**ais**) M general

generalizar [ʒenerali'zar] VT to propagate ▶ VI to generalize; **generalizar-se** VR to become general, spread

gênero ['ʒeneru] M type, kind; (*Bio*) genus; (*Ling*) gender; **gêneros** MPL (*produtos*) goods; **~s alimentícios** foodstuffs; **~ humano** humankind, human race

generosidade [ʒenerozi'dadʒi] F generosity

generoso, -a [ʒene'rozu, ɔza] ADJ generous

genética [ʒe'nɛtʃika] F genetics *sg*

gengibre [ʒẽ'ʒibri] M ginger

gengiva [ʒẽ'ʒiva] F (*Anat*) gum

genial [ʒe'njaw] (*pl* -**ais**) ADJ inspired, brilliant; (*col*) terrific, fantastic

gênio ['ʒenju] M (*temperamento*) nature; (*irascibilidade*) temper; (*talento, pessoa*) genius; **de bom ~** good-natured; **de mau ~** bad-tempered

genital [ʒeni'taw] (*pl* -**ais**) ADJ: **órgãos genitais** genitals *pl*

genoma [ʒe'noma] M genome

genro ['ʒẽhu] M son-in-law

gente ['ʒẽtʃi] F people *pl*; (*col*) folks *pl*; (*col: alguém*): **tem ~ batendo à porta** there's somebody knocking at the door; **a ~** (*nós: suj*) we; (*: obj*) us; **a casa da ~** our house; **toda a ~** everybody; **~ grande** grown-ups pl

gentil [ʒẽ'tʃiw] (pl **-is**) ADJ kind; **gentileza** [ʒẽtʃi'leza] F kindness; **por gentileza** if you please; **tenha a gentileza de fazer …** would you be so kind as to do …?

genuíno, -a [ʒe'nwinu, a] ADJ genuine

geografia [ʒeogra'fia] F geography

geometria [ʒeome'tria] F geometry

geração [ʒera'sãw] (pl **-ões**) F generation

gerador, a [ʒera'dor(a)] M/F (produtor) creator ▶ M (Tec) generator

geral [ʒe'raw] (pl **-ais**) ADJ general ▶ F (Teatro) gallery; **em ~** in general, generally; **de um modo ~** on the whole; **geralmente** [ʒeraw'mẽtʃi] ADV generally, usually

gerânio [ʒe'ranju] M geranium

gerar [ʒe'rar] VT to produce; (eletricidade) to generate

gerência [ʒe'rẽsja] F management; **gerenciar** [ʒerẽ'sjar] VT, VI to manage

gerente [ʒe'rẽtʃi] ADJ managing ▶ M/F manager

gerir [ʒe'rir] VT to manage, run

germe ['ʒɛrmi] M (embrião) embryo; (micróbio) germ

gesso ['ʒesu] M plaster (of Paris)

gesticular [ʒestʃiku'lar] VI to make gestures, gesture

gesto ['ʒɛstu] M gesture

Gibraltar [ʒibraw'tar] F Gibraltar

gigabyte [ʒiga'bajtʃi] M gigabyte

gigante, -a [ʒi'gãtʃi, a] ADJ gigantic, huge ▶ M giant;

gigantesco, -a [ʒigã'tesku, a] ADJ gigantic

gim [ʒĩ] (pl **-ns**) M gin

ginásio [ʒi'nazju] M gymnasium; (escola) secondary (BRIT) ou high (US) school

ginástica [ʒi'nastʃika] F gymnastics sg; (para fortalecer o corpo) keep-fit

ginecologia [ʒinekolo'ʒia] F gynaecology (BRIT), gynecology (US)

ginecologista [ʒinekolo'ʒista] M/F gynaecologist (BRIT), gynecologist (US)

ginjinha [ʒĩ'ʒiɲa] (PT) F cherry brandy

gira-discos (PT) M INV record-player

girafa [ʒi'rafa] F giraffe

girar [ʒi'rar] VT to turn, rotate; (como pião) to spin ▶ VI to go round; to spin; (vaguear) to wander

girassol [ʒira'sɔw] (pl **-óis**) M sunflower

gíria ['ʒirja] F (calão) slang; (jargão) jargon

giro¹ ['ʒiru] M turn; **dar um ~** to go for a wander; (em veículo) to go for a spin; **que ~!** (PT) great!

giro² VB ver **gerir**

giz [ʒiz] M chalk

glacê [gla'se] M icing

glacial [gla'sjaw] (pl **-ais**) ADJ icy

glamouroso, -a [glamu'rozu, ɔza] ADJ glamorous

glândula ['glãdula] F gland

global [glo'baw] (pl **-ais**) ADJ global; (total) overall; **quantia ~** lump sum; **globalização** [globaliza'sãw] F globalization

globo ['globu] M globe; **~ ocular** eyeball

glória ['glɔrja] F glory; **glorificar**

[glorifi'kar] vt to glorify; **glorioso, -a** [glo'rjozu, ɔza] ADJ glorious
glossário [glo'sarju] M glossary
gnomo ['gnomu] M gnome
goiaba [go'jaba] F guava; **goiabada** [goja'bada] F guava jelly
gol [gow] (pl **gols**) M goal
gola ['gɔla] F collar
gole ['gɔli] M gulp, swallow; (pequeno) sip; **dar um ~** to have a sip
goleiro [go'lejru] (BR) M goalkeeper; (col) goalie
golfe ['gowfi] M golf; **campo de ~** golf course
golfinho [gow'fiɲu] M (Zool) dolphin
golfo ['gowfu] M gulf
golinho [go'liɲu] M sip; **beber algo aos ~s** to sip sth
golo ['golu] (PT) M = **gol**
golpe ['gɔwpi] M (tb fig) blow; (de mão) smack; (de punho) punch; (manobra) ploy; (de vento) gust; **de um só ~** at a stroke; **dar um ~ em alguém** to hit sb; (fig: trapacear) to trick sb; **~ (de estado)** coup (d'état); **~ de mestre** masterstroke; **golpear** [gow'pjar] vt to hit; (com navalha) to stab; (com o punho) to punch
goma ['gɔma] F gum, glue; (de roupa) starch; **~ de mascar** chewing gum
gomo ['gomu] M (de laranja) slice
gordo, -a ['gordu, a] ADJ fat; (gordurento) greasy; (carne) fatty; (fig: quantia) considerable, ample ▶ M/F fat man/woman
gordura [gor'dura] F fat; (derretida) grease; (obesidade) fatness; **gorduroso, -a** [gordu'rozu, ɔza] ADJ (pele) greasy; (comida) fatty
gorila [go'rila] M gorilla
gorjeta [gor'ʒeta] F tip, gratuity

gorro ['gohu] M cap; (de lã) hat
gosma ['gɔzma] F spittle; (fig) slime
gostar [gos'tar] vi: **~ de** to like; (férias, viagem etc) to enjoy; **gostar-se** vr to like each other; **~ mais de ...** to prefer ..., to like ... better
gosto ['gostu] M taste; (prazer) pleasure; **a seu ~** to your liking; **com ~** willingly; (vestir-se) tastefully; (comer) heartily; **de bom/mau ~** in good/bad taste; **ter ~ de** to taste of; **gostoso, -a** [gos'tozu, ɔza] ADJ tasty; (agradável) pleasant; (cheiro) lovely; (risada) good; (col: pessoa) gorgeous
gota ['gota] F drop; (de suor) bead; (Med) gout; **~ a ~** drop by drop
goteira [go'tejra] F (cano) gutter; (buraco) leak
gourmet [gur'me] (pl **-s**) M/F gourmet
governador, a [governador(a)] M/F governor
governamental [governamẽ'taw] (pl **-ais**) ADJ government atr
governante [gover'nãtʃi] ADJ ruling ▶ M/F ruler ▶ F governess
governar [gover'nar] vt to govern, rule; (barco) to steer
governo [go'vernu] M government; (controle) control
gozação [goza'sãw] (pl **-ões**) F enjoyment; (zombaria) teasing; (uma gozação) joke
gozado, -a [go'zadu, a] ADJ funny; (estranho) strange, odd
gozar [go'zar] vt to enjoy; (col: rir de) to make fun of ▶ vi to enjoy o.s.; **~ de** to enjoy; to make fun of; **gozo** ['gozu] M (prazer) pleasure; (uso) enjoyment, use; (orgasmo) orgasm

GPS ABR M (= *global positioning system*) GPS

Grã-Bretanha [grã-bre'taɲa] F Great Britain

graça ['grasa] F (*Rel*) grace; (*charme*) charm; (*gracejo*) joke; (*Jur*) pardon; **de ~** (*grátis*) for nothing; (*sem motivo*) for no reason; **sem ~** dull, boring; **fazer** *ou* **ter ~** to be funny; **ficar sem ~** to be embarrassed; **~s a** thanks to

gracejar [grase'ʒar] VI to joke; **gracejo** [gra'seʒu] M joke

gracioso, -a [gra'sjozu, ɔza] ADJ (*pessoa*) charming; (*gestos*) gracious

grade ['gradʒi] F (*no chão*) grating; (*grelha*) grill; (*na janela*) bars *pl*; (*col: cadeia*) prison

gradear [gra'dʒjar] VT (*janela*) to put bars up at; (*jardim*) to fence off

graduação [gradwa'sãw] (*pl* **-ões**) F (*classificação*) grading; (*Educ*) graduation; (*Mil*) rank

gradual [gra'dwaw] (*pl* **-ais**) ADJ gradual

graduar [gra'dwar] VT (*classificar*) to grade; (*luz, fogo*) to regulate; **graduar-se** VR to graduate

gráfica ['grafika] F graphics *sg*; *ver tb* **gráfico**

gráfico, -a ['grafiku, a] ADJ graphic ▶ M/F printer ▶ M (*Mat*) graph; (*diagrama*) diagram, chart; **gráficos** MPL (*Comput*) graphics; **~ de barras** bar chart

grã-fino, -a [grã'finu, a] (*col*) ADJ posh ▶ M/F nob, toff

grama ['grama] M gramme ▶ F (*BR: capim*) grass

gramado [gra'madu] (*BR*) M lawn; (*Futebol*) pitch

gramática [gra'matʃika] F grammar

grampear [grã'pjar] VT to staple

grampo ['grãpu] M staple; (*no cabelo*) hairgrip; (*de carpinteiro*) clamp; (*de chapéu*) hatpin

grande ['grãdʒi] ADJ big, large; (*alto*) tall; (*notável, intenso*) great; (*longo*) long; (*adulto*) grown-up; **mulher ~** big woman; **~ mulher** great woman; **grandeza** [grã'deza] F size; (*fig*) greatness; (*ostentação*) grandeur

grandioso, -a [grã'dʒjozu, ɔza] ADJ magnificent, grand

granito [gra'nitu] M granite

granizo [gra'nizu] M hailstone; **chover ~** to hail; **chuva de ~** hailstorm

granulado, -a [granu'ladu, a] ADJ grainy; (*açúcar*) granulated

grão ['grãw] (*pl* **grãos**) M grain; (*semente*) seed; (*de café*) bean; **grão-de-bico** (*pl* **grãos-de-bico**) M chickpea

gratidão [gratʃi'dãw] F gratitude

gratificar [gratʃifi'kar] VT to tip; (*dar bônus a*) to give a bonus to; (*recompensar*) to reward

grátis ['gratʃis] ADJ free

grato, -a ['gratu, a] ADJ grateful; (*agradável*) pleasant

gratuito, -a [gra'twitu, a] ADJ (*grátis*) free; (*infundado*) gratuitous

grau [graw] M degree; (*nível*) level; (*Educ*) class; **em alto ~** to a high degree; **ensino de primeiro/ segundo ~** primary (*BRIT*) *ou* elementary (*US*) /secondary education

gravação [grava'sãw] F (*em madeira*) carving; (*em disco, fita*) recording

gravador, a [grava'dor(a)] M tape

recorder ▶ M/F engraver; **~ de CD/ DVD** CD/DVD burner, CD/DVD writer

gravar [gra'var] VT to carve; (*metal, pedra*) to engrave; (*na memória*) to fix; (*disco, fita*) to record

gravata [gra'vata] F tie; **~ borboleta** bow tie

grave ['gravi] ADJ serious; (*tom*) deep; **gravemente** [grave'mẽtʃi] ADV (*doente, ferido*) seriously

grávida ['gravida] ADJ pregnant

gravidade [gravi'dadʒi] F gravity

gravidez [gravi'deʒ] F pregnancy

gravura [gra'vura] F (*em madeira*) engraving; (*estampa*) print

graxa ['graʃa] F (*para sapatos*) polish; (*lubrificante*) grease

Grécia ['grɛsja] F: **a ~** Greece; **grego, -a** ['gregu, a] ADJ, M/F Greek ▶ M (*Ling*) Greek

grelha ['grɛʎa] F grill; (*de fornalha*) grate; **bife na ~** grilled steak; **grelhado, -a** [gre'ʎadu, a] ADJ grilled ▶ M (*prato*) grill

grêmio ['gremju] M (*associação*) guild; (*clube*) club

grená [gre'na] ADJ, M dark red

greve ['grɛvi] F strike; **fazer ~** to go on strike; **~ branca** go-slow; **grevista** [gre'vista] M/F striker

grilo ['grilu] M cricket; (*Auto*) squeak; (*col: de pessoa*) hang-up; **qual é o ~?** what's the matter?; **não tem ~!** (*col*) (there's) no problem!

gringo, -a ['grĩgu, a] (*col, pej*) M/F foreigner

gripado, -a [gri'padu, a] ADJ: **estar/ficar ~** to have/get a cold

gripe ['gripi] F flu, influenza; **~ aviária** bird flu; **~ suína** swine flu

grisalho, -a [gri'zaʎu, a] ADJ (*cabelo*) grey (BRIT), gray (US)

gritante [gri'tãtʃi] ADJ (*hipocrisia*) glaring; (*desigualdade*) gross; (*mentira*) blatant; (*cor*) loud, garish

gritar [gri'tar] VT to shout, yell ▶ VI to shout; (*de dor, medo*) to scream; **~ com alguém** to shout at sb; **gritaria** [grita'ria] F shouting, din; **grito** ['gritu] M shout; (*de medo*) scream; (*de dor*) cry; (*de animal*) call; **dar um grito** to cry out; **falar/ protestar aos gritos** to shout/ shout protests

Groenlândia [grwẽ'lãdʒja] F: **a ~** Greenland

grosseiro, -a [gro'sejru, a] ADJ rude; (*piada*) crude; (*modos*) coarse; **grosseria** [grose'ria] F rudeness; (*ato*): **fazer uma grosseria** to be rude; (*dito*): **dizer uma grosseria** to be rude, say something rude

grosso, -a ['grosu, 'grɔsa] ADJ thick; (*áspero*) rough; (*voz*) deep; (*col: pessoa, piada*) rude ▶ M: **o ~ de** the bulk of; **grossura** [gro'sura] F thickness

grotesco, -a [gro'tesku, a] ADJ grotesque

grudar [gru'dar] VT to glue, stick ▶ VI to stick

grude ['grudʒi] F glue; **grudento, -a** [gru'dẽtu, a] ADJ sticky

grunhir [gru'ɲir] VI (*porco*) to grunt; (*tigre*) to growl; (*resmungar*) to grumble

grupo ['grupu] M group

guarda ['gwarda] M/F policeman/ woman ▶ F (*vigilância*) guarding; (*de objeto*) safekeeping ▶ M (*Mil*) guard; **estar de ~** to be on guard; **pôr-se em ~** to be on one's guard; **a G~ Civil** the Civil Guard; **guarda- chuva** (*pl* **-s**) M umbrella; **guarda-costas** M INV (*Náut*) coastguard boat; (*capanga*) bodyguard; **guardados**

[gwar'dadus] MPL keepsakes, valuables; **guarda-fogo** (*pl* **-s**) M fireguard; **guarda-louça** [gwarda'losa] (*pl* **-s**) M sideboard; **guardanapo** [gwarda'napu] M napkin; **guarda-noturno** (*pl* **guardas-noturnos**) M night watchman; **guardar** [gwar'dar] VT to put away; (*zelar por*) to guard; (*lembrança, segredo*) to keep; **guardar-se** VR (*defender-se*) to protect o.s.; **guardar-se de** (*acautelar-se*) to guard against; **guarda-redes** (*PT*) M INV goalkeeper; **guarda-roupa** (*pl* **-s**) M wardrobe; **guarda-sol** (*pl* **-sóis**) M sunshade, parasol

guardião, -diã [gwar'dʒjãw, 'dʒjã] (*pl* **-ães/-s**) M/F guardian

guarnição [gwarni'sãw] (*pl* **-ões**) F (*Mil*) garrison; (*Náut*) crew; (*Culin*) garnish

Guatemala [gwate'mala] F: **a ~** Guatemala

gude ['gudʒi] M: **bola de ~** marble; (*jogo*) marbles *pl*

guerra ['gɛha] F war; **em ~** at war; **fazer ~** to wage war; **~ civil** civil war; **~ mundial** world war; **guerreiro, -a** [ge'hejru, a] ADJ (*espírito*) fighting; (*belicoso*) warlike ▶ M warrior

guerrilha [ge'hiʎa] F (*luta*) guerrilla warfare; (*tropa*) guerrilla band; **guerrilheiro, -a** [gehi'ʎejru, a] M/F guerrilla

guia ['gia] F guidance; (*Com*) permit, bill of lading; (*formulário*) advice slip ▶ M (*livro*) guide(book) ▶ M/F (*pessoa*) guide

Guiana ['gjana] F: **a ~** Guyana

guiar [gjar] VT to guide; (*Auto*) to drive ▶ VI to drive; **guiar-se** VR: **~-se por** to go by

guichê [gi'ʃe] M ticket window; (*em banco, repartição*) window, counter

guinada [gi'nada] F: **dar uma ~** (*com o carro*) to swerve

guindaste [gĩ'dastʃi] M hoist, crane

guisado [gi'zadu] M stew

guitarra [gi'taha] F (electric) guitar

guloso, -a [gu'lozu, ɔza] ADJ greedy

h

há [a] VB *ver* **haver**
hábil ['abiw] (*pl* **-eis**) ADJ
competent, capable; (*astucioso, esperto*) clever; (*sutil*) diplomatic;
em tempo ~ in reasonable time;
habilidade [abili'dadʒi] F skill,
ability; (*astúcia, esperteza*)
shrewdness; (*tato*) discretion;
habilidoso, -a [abili'dozu, ɔza] ADJ
skilful (BRIT), skillful (US), clever
habilitação [abilita'sãw] (*pl* **-ões**)
F competence; (*ato*) qualification;
habilitações FPL (*conhecimentos*)
qualifications
habilitar [abili'tar] VT to enable;
(*dar direito a*) to qualify, entitle;
(*preparar*) to prepare
habitação [abita'sãw] (*pl* **-ões**) F
dwelling, residence; (*alojamento*)
housing
habitante [abi'tãtʃi] M/F
inhabitant
habitar [abi'tar] VT to live in;
(*povoar*) to inhabit ▶ VI to live
hábito ['abitu] M habit; (*social*)
custom; (*Rel: traje*) habit
habituado, -a [abi'twadu, a] ADJ:
~ a (fazer) algo used to (doing) sth
habituar [abi'twar] VT: **~ alguém
a** to get sb used to, accustom sb to;
habituar-se VR: **~-se a** to get used
to
hacker ['haker] (*pl* **-s**) M (*Comput*)
hacker
Haia ['aja] N the Hague
haja ['aʒa] VB *ver* **haver**
hálito ['alitu] M breath
hall [hɔw] (*pl* **halls**) M hall; (*de
teatro, hotel*) foyer; **~ de entrada**
entrance hall
hambúrguer [ã'burger] (*pl* **-s**) M
hamburger
hão [ãw] VB *ver* **haver**
hardware ['hadwer] M (*Comput*)
hardware
harmonia [armo'nia] F harmony
harmonioso, -a [armo'njozu, ɔza]
ADJ harmonious
harmonizar [armoni'zar] VT (*Mús*)
to harmonize; (*conciliar*): **~ algo
(com algo)** to reconcile sth (with
sth); **harmonizar-se** VR: **~(-se)
(com algo)** (*ideias etc*) to coincide
(with sth); (*pessoas*) to be in
agreement (with sth)
harpa ['arpa] F harp
Havaí [avaj'i] M: **o ~** Hawaii

(PALAVRA-CHAVE)

haver [a'ver] VB AUX **1** (*ter*) to have;
ele havia saído/comido he had
left/eaten
2: **quem haveria de dizer que ...**
who would have thought that ...
▶ VB IMPESS **1** (*existência*): **há** (*sg*)
there is; (*pl*) there are; **o que é que
há?** what's the matter?; **o que é
que houve?** what happened?, what
was that?; **não há de quê** don't

mention it, you're welcome; **haja o que houver** come what may **2** (*tempo*): **há séculos/cinco dias que não o vejo** I haven't seen him for ages/five days; **há um ano que ela chegou** it's a year since she arrived; **há cinco dias (atrás)** five days ago

haver-se VR: **haver-se com alguém** to sort things out with sb ▶ M (*Com*) credit; **haveres** MPL (*pertences*) property *sg*, possessions; (*riqueza*) wealth *sg*

haxixe [a'ʃiʃi] M hashish

hebraico, -a [e'brajku, a] ADJ Hebrew ▶ M (*Ling*) Hebrew

Hébridas ['ɛbridas] FPL: **as (ilhas) ~** the Hebrides

hediondo, -a [e'dʒjõdu, a] ADJ vile, revolting; (*crime*) heinous

hei [ej] VB *ver* **haver**

hélice ['ɛlisi] F propeller

helicóptero [eli'kɔpteru] M helicopter

hematoma [ema'tɔma] M bruise

hemorragia [emoha'ʒia] F haemorrhage (*BRIT*), hemorrhage (*US*); **~ nasal** nosebleed

hemorróidas [emo'hɔjdas] FPL haemorrhoids (*BRIT*), hemorrhoids (*US*), piles

hepatite [epa'tʃitʃi] F hepatitis

hera ['ɛra] F ivy

herança [e'rãsa] F inheritance; (*fig*) heritage

herdar [er'dar] VT: **~ algo (de)** to inherit sth (from); **~ a** to bequeath to

herdeiro, -a [er'dejru, a] M/F heir(ess)

herói [e'rɔj] M hero

heroína [ero'ina] F heroine; (*droga*) heroin

hesitação [ezita'sãw] (*pl* -**ões**) F hesitation

hesitante [ezi'tãtʃi] ADJ hesitant

hesitar [ezi'tar] VI to hesitate

heterossexual [eterosek'swaw] (*pl* -**ais**) ADJ, M/F heterosexual

híbrido, -a ['ibridu, a] ADJ hybrid

hidratante [idra'tãtʃi] M moisturizer

hidrato [i'dratu] M: **~ de carbono** carbohydrate

hidráulico, -a [i'drawliku, a] ADJ hydraulic

hidrelétrico, -a [idre'lɛtriku, a] ADJ hydroelectric

hidro... [idru] PREFIXO hydro..., water... *atr*

hidrogênio [idro'ʒenju] M hydrogen

hidroginástica [idroʒi'nastʃika] F aquaerobics

hífen ['ifẽ] (*pl* **hífens**) M hyphen

higiene [i'ʒjeni] F hygiene; **higiênico, -a** [i'ʒjeniku, a] ADJ hygienic; (*pessoa*) clean; **papel higiênico** toilet paper

hindu [ĩ'du] ADJ, M/F Hindu

hino ['inu] M hymn; **~ nacional** national anthem

hipermercado [ipermer'kadu] M hypermarket

hipertensão [ipertẽ'sãw] F high blood pressure

hipismo [i'pizmu] M (*turfe*) horse racing; (*equitação*) (horse) riding

hipocrisia [ipokri'zia] F hypocrisy; **hipócrita** [i'pɔkrita] ADJ hypocritical ▶ M/F hypocrite

hipódromo [i'pɔdromu] M racecourse

hipopótamo [ipo'pɔtamu] M hippopotamus

hipoteca [ipo'tɛka] F mortgage; **hipotecar** [ipote'kar] VT to mortgage

hipótese [i'pɔtezi] F hypothesis; **na ~ de** in the event of; **em ~ alguma** under no circumstances; **na melhor/pior das ~s** at best/worst

hispânico, -a [is'paniku, a] ADJ Hispanic

histeria [iste'ria] F hysteria; **histérico, -a** [is'tɛriku, a] ADJ hysterical

história [is'tɔrja] F history; (conto) story; **histórias** FPL (chateação) bother sg, fuss sg; **isso é outra ~** that's a different matter; **que ~ é essa?** what's going on?; **historiador, a** [istorja'dor(a)] M/F historian; **histórico, -a** [is'tɔriku, a] ADJ historical; (fig: notável) historic ▶ M history

hobby ['hɔbi] (pl -bies) M hobby

hoje ['oʒi] ADV today; (atualmente) now(adays); **~ à noite** tonight

Holanda [o'lãda] F: **a ~** Holland; **holandês, -esa** [olã'des, eza] ADJ Dutch ▶ M/F Dutchman/woman ▶ M (Ling) Dutch

holocausto [olo'kawstu] M holocaust

homem ['omẽ] (pl -ns) M man; (a humanidade) mankind; **~ de empresa** ou **negócios** businessman; **~ de estado** statesman; **homem-bomba** (pl **homens-bomba**) M suicide bomber

homenagear [omena'ʒjar] VT (pessoa) to pay tribute to, honour (BRIT), honor (US)

homenagem [ome'naʒẽ] F tribute; (Rel) homage; **prestar ~ a alguém** to pay tribute to sb

homens ['omẽs] MPL de **homem**

homeopático, -a [omjo'patʃiku, a] ADJ homoeopathic (BRIT), homeopathic (US)

homicida [omi'sida] ADJ homicidal ▶ M/F murderer; **homicídio** [omi'sidʒju] M murder; **homicídio involuntário** manslaughter

homologar [omolo'gar] VT to ratify

homólogo, -a [o'mɔlogu, a] ADJ homologous; (fig) equivalent ▶ M/F opposite number

homossexual [omosek'swaw] (pl -ais) ADJ, M/F homosexual

Honduras [õ'duras] F Honduras

honestidade [onestʃi'dadʒi] F honesty; (decência) decency; (justeza) fairness

honesto, -a [o'nɛstu, a] ADJ honest; (decente) decent; (justo) fair, just

honorário, -a [ono'rarju, a] ADJ honorary; **honorários** [ono'rarjus] MPL fees

honra ['õha] F honour (BRIT), honor (US); **em ~ de** in hono(u)r of

honrado, -a [õ'hadu, a] ADJ honest; (respeitado) honourable (BRIT), honorable (US)

honrar [õ'har] VT to honour (BRIT), honor (US)

honroso, -a [õ'hozu, ɔza] ADJ honourable (BRIT), honorable (US)

hóquei ['hɔkej] M hockey; **~ sobre gelo** ice hockey

hora ['ɔra] F (60 minutos) hour; (momento) time; **a que ~s?** (at) what time?; **que ~s são?** what time is it?; **são duas ~s** it's two o'clock; **você tem as ~s?** have you got the time?; **fazer ~** to kill time; **de ~ em ~** every hour; **na ~** on the spot; **chegar na ~** to be on time; **de última** ~ adj last-minute; adv at the last minute; **~ do almoço** lunch hour; **meia ~** half an hour; **~s extras** overtime sg; **horário, -a** [o'rarju, a] ADJ: **100 km horários**

100 km an hour ▶ M timetable; (*hora*) time; **horário de expediente** working hours *pl*; (*de um escritório*) office hours *pl*

horizontal [orizõ'taw] (*pl* **-ais**) ADJ horizontal

horizonte [ori'zõtʃi] M horizon

horóscopo [o'rɔskopu] M horoscope

horrível [o'hivew] (*pl* **-eis**) ADJ awful, horrible

horror [o'hor] M horror; **que ~!** how awful!; **ter ~ a algo** to hate sth; **horrorizar** [ohori'zar] VT to horrify, frighten; **horroroso, -a** [oho'rozu, ɔza] ADJ horrible, ghastly

hortaliças [orta'lisas] FPL vegetables

hortelã [orte'lã] F mint; **~ pimenta** peppermint

horticultor, a [ortʃikuw'tor(a)] M/F market gardener (BRIT), truck farmer (US)

hortifrutigranjeiros [ortʃifrutʃigrã'ʒejrus] MPL fruit and vegetables

horto ['ortu] M market garden (BRIT), truck farm (US)

hospedagem [ospe'daʒẽ] F guest house

hospedar [ospe'dar] VT to put up; **hospedar-se** VR to stay, lodge; **hospedaria** [ospeda'ria] F guest house

hóspede ['ɔspedʒi] M (*amigo*) guest; (*estranho*) lodger

hospedeira [ospe'dejra] F landlady; (PT: *de bordo*) stewardess, air hostess (BRIT)

hospício [os'pisju] M mental hospital

hospital [ospi'taw] (*pl* **-ais**) M hospital

hospitalidade [ospitali'dadʒi] F hospitality

hostil [os'tʃiw] (*pl* **-is**) ADJ hostile; **hostilizar** [ostʃili'zar] VT to antagonize; (*Mil*) to wage war on

hotel [o'tɛw] (*pl* **-éis**) M hotel; **hoteleiro, -a** [ote'lejru, a] M/F hotelier

houve ['ovi] VB *ver* **haver**

humanidade [umani'dadʒi] F (*os homens*) man(kind); (*compaixão*) humanity

humanitário, -a [umani'tarju, a] ADJ humane

humano, -a [u'manu, a] ADJ human; (*bondoso*) humane

humildade [umiw'dadʒi] F humility; (*pobreza*) poverty

humilde [u'miwdʒi] ADJ humble; (*pobre*) poor

humilhar [umi'ʎar] VT to humiliate

humor [u'mor] M mood, temper; (*graça*) humour (BRIT), humor (US); **de bom/mau ~** in a good/bad mood; **humorista** [umo'rista] M/F comedian; **humorístico, -a** [umo'ristʃiku, a] ADJ humorous

húngaro, -a ['ũgaru, a] ADJ, M/F Hungarian

Hungria [ũ'gria] F: **a ~** Hungary

hurra ['uha] M cheer ▶ EXCL hurrah!

h

ia ['ia] VB *ver* **ir**

iate ['jatʃi] M yacht; **~ clube** yacht club

ibérico, -a [i'bεriku, a] ADJ, M/F Iberian

ibero-americano, -a [iberu-] ADJ, M/F Ibero-American

ICMS (BR) ABR M (= *Imposto sobre Circulação de Mercadorias e Prestação de Serviços*) ≈ VAT

icone ['ikoni] M (*ger, Comput*) icon

ida ['ida] F going, departure; **~ e volta** round trip, return; **a (viagem de) ~** the outward journey; **na ~** on the way there

idade [i'dadʒi] F age; **ter cinco anos de ~** to be five (years old); **de meia ~** middle-aged; **qual é a ~ dele?** how old is he?; **na minha ~** at my age; **ser menor/maior de ~** to be under/of age; **pessoa de ~** elderly person; **I~ Média** Middle Ages *pl*

ideal [ide'jaw] (*pl* **-ais**) ADJ, M ideal; **idealista** [idea'lista] ADJ idealistic ▶ M/F idealist

ideia [i'dεja] F idea; (*mente*) mind; **mudar de ~** to change one's mind; **não ter a mínima ~** to have no idea; **não faço ~** I can't imagine; **estar com ~ de fazer** to plan to do

idem ['idẽ] PRON ditto

idêntico, -a [i'dẽtʃiku, a] ADJ identical

identidade [idẽtʃi'dadʒi] F identity

identificação [idẽtʃifika'sãw] F identification

identificar [idẽtʃifi'kar] VT to identify; **identificar-se** VR: **~-se com** to identify with

idioma [i'dʒɔma] M language

idiota [i'dʒɔta] ADJ idiotic ▶ M/F idiot

ido, -a ['idu, a] ADJ past

ídolo ['idolu] M idol

idoso, -a [i'dozu, ɔza] ADJ elderly, old

ignorado, -a [igno'radu, a] ADJ unknown

ignorância [igno'rãsja] F ignorance; **ignorante** [igno'rãtʃi] ADJ ignorant, uneducated ▶ M/F ignoramus

ignorar [igno'rar] VT not to know; (*não dar atenção a*) to ignore

igreja [i'greʒa] F church

igual [i'gwaw] (*pl* **-ais**) ADJ equal; (*superfície*) even ▶ M/F equal

igualar [igwa'lar] VT to equal; (*fazer igual*) to make equal; (*nivelar*) to level ▶ VI: **~ a** *ou* **com** to be equal to, be the same as; (*ficar no mesmo nível*) to be level with; **igualar-se** VR: **~-se a alguém** to be sb's equal

igualdade [igwaw'dadʒi] F equality; (*uniformidade*) uniformity

igualmente [igwaw'mẽtʃi] ADV equally; (*também*) likewise, also; **~!** (*saudação*) the same to you!

ilegal [ile'gaw] (pl **-ais**) ADJ illegal

ilegítimo, -a [ile'ʒitʃimu, a] ADJ illegitimate; (ilegal) unlawful

ilegível [ile'ʒivew] (pl **-eis**) ADJ illegible

iletrado, -a [ile'tradu, a] ADJ illiterate

ilha ['iʎa] F island; **ilhéu, ilhoa** [i'ʎɛw, i'ʎoa] M/F islander

ilícito, -a [i'lisitu, a] ADJ illicit

ilimitado, -a [ilimi'tadu, a] ADJ unlimited

iluminar [ilumi'nar] VT to light up; (estádio etc) to floodlight; (fig) to enlighten

ilusão [ilu'zãw] (pl **-ões**) F illusion; (quimera) delusion; **ilusório, -a** [ilu'zɔrju, a] ADJ deceptive

ilustração [ilustra'sãw] (pl **-ões**) F illustration

ilustrado, -a [ilus'tradu, a] ADJ illustrated; (instruído) learned

ilustrar [ilus'trar] VT to illustrate; (instruir) to instruct

ilustre [i'lustri] ADJ illustrious; **um ~ desconhecido** a complete stranger

ímã ['imã] M magnet

imagem [i'maʒẽ] (pl **-ns**) F image; (semelhança) likeness; (TV) picture; **imagens** FPL (Literatura) imagery sg

imaginação [imaʒina'sãw] (pl **-ões**) F imagination

imaginar [imaʒi'nar] VT to imagine; (supor) to suppose; **imaginar-se** VR to imagine o.s.; **imagine só!** just imagine!; **imaginário, -a** [imaʒi'narju, a] ADJ imaginary

imaturo, -a [ima'turu, a] ADJ immature

imbatível [ĩba'tʃivew] (pl **-eis**) ADJ invincible

imbecil [ĩbe'siw] (pl **-is**) ADJ stupid ▶ M/F imbecile; **imbecilidade** [ĩbesili'dadʒi] F stupidity

imediações [imedʒa'sõjs] FPL vicinity sg, neighbourhood sg (BRIT), neighborhood sg (US)

imediatamente [imedʒata'mẽtʃi] ADV immediately, right away

imediato, -a [ime'dʒatu, a] ADJ immediate; (seguinte) next; **~ a** next to; **de ~** straight away

imenso, -a [i'mẽsu, a] ADJ immense, huge; (ódio, amor) great

imigração [imigra'sãw] (pl **-ões**) F immigration

imigrante [imi'grãtʃi] ADJ, M/F immigrant

iminente [imi'nẽtʃi] ADJ imminent

imitação [imita'sãw] (pl **-ões**) F imitation

imitar [imi'tar] VT to imitate; (assinatura) to copy

imobiliária [imobi'ljarja] F estate agent's (BRIT), real estate broker's (US)

imobiliário, -a [imobi'ljarju, a] ADJ property atr

imobilizar [imobili'zar] VT to immobilize; (fig) to bring to a standstill

imoral [imo'raw] (pl **-ais**) ADJ immoral

imortal [imor'taw] (pl **-ais**) ADJ immortal

imóvel [i'mɔvew] (pl **-eis**) ADJ motionless, still; (não movediço) immovable ▶ M property; (edifício) building; **imóveis** MPL (propriedade) real estate sg, property sg

impaciência [ĩpa'sjẽsja] F impatience; **impacientar-se**

[ĩpasjē'tarsi] vʀ to lose one's patience; **impaciente** [ĩpa'sjētʃi] ADJ impatient

impacto [ĩ'paktu], (PT) **impacte** M impact

ímpar ['ĩpar] ADJ (*número*) odd; (*sem igual*) unique, unequalled

imparcial [ĩpar'sjaw] (*pl* -**ais**) ADJ fair, impartial

impecável [ĩpe'kavew] (*pl* -**eis**) ADJ perfect, impeccable

impeço [ĩ'pɛsu] vʙ *ver* **impedir**

impedido, -a [ĩpe'dʒidu, a] ADJ (*Futebol*) offside; (PT *Tel*) engaged (BRIT), busy (US)

impedimento [ĩpedʒi'mētu] M impediment

impedir [ĩpe'dʒir] vт to obstruct; (*estrada, passagem, tráfego*) to block; (*movimento, execução, progresso*) to impede; **~ alguém de fazer algo** to prevent sb from doing sth; (*proibir*) to forbid sb to do sth; **~ (que aconteça) algo** to prevent sth (happening)

impenetrável [ĩpene'travew] (*pl* -**eis**) ADJ impenetrable

impensado, -a [ĩpē'sadu, a] ADJ thoughtless; (*não calculado*) unpremeditated; (*imprevisto*) unforeseen

imperador [ĩpera'dor] M emperor

imperativo, -a [ĩpera'tʃivu, a] ADJ imperative ▶ M imperative

imperatriz [ĩpera'triz] F empress

imperdoável [ĩper'dwavew] (*pl* -**eis**) ADJ unforgivable, inexcusable

imperfeito, -a [ĩper'fejtu, a] ADJ imperfect ▶ M (*Ling*) imperfect (tense)

imperial [ĩpe'rjaw] (*pl* -**ais**) ADJ imperial

imperícia [ĩpe'risja] F inability; (*inexperiência*) inexperience

império [ĩ'pɛrju] M empire

impermeável [ĩper'mjavew] (*pl* -**eis**) ADJ: **~ a** (*tb fig*) impervious to; (*à água*) waterproof ▶ M raincoat

impessoal [ĩpe'swaw] (*pl* -**ais**) ADJ impersonal

ímpeto ['ĩpetu] M (*Tec*) impetus; (*movimento súbito*) start; (*de cólera*) fit; (*de emoção*) surge; (*de chamas*) fury; **agir com ~** to act on impulse; **levantar-se num ~** to get up with a start

impiedoso, -a [ĩpje'dozu, ɔza] ADJ merciless, cruel

implacável [ĩpla'kavew] (*pl* -**eis**) ADJ (*pessoa*) unforgiving

implantação [ĩplãta'sãw] (*pl* -**ões**) F introduction; (*Med*) implant

implementar [ĩplemē'tar] vт to implement

implicar [ĩpli'kar] vт (*envolver*) to implicate; (*pressupor*) to imply ▶ vı: **~ com alguém** (*chatear*) to tease sb, pick on sb; **implicar-se** vʀ to get involved; **~ (em) algo** to involve sth

implícito, -a [ĩ'plisitu, a] ADJ implicit

implorar [ĩplo'rar] vт: **~ (algo a alguém)** to beg *ou* implore (sb for sth)

impopular [ĩpopu'lar] ADJ unpopular; **impopularidade** [ĩpopulari'dadʒi] F unpopularity

impor [ĩ'por] (*irreg: como* **pôr**) vт to impose; (*respeito*) to command; **impor-se** vʀ to assert o.s.; **~ algo a alguém** to impose sth on sb

importação [importa'sãw] (*pl* -**ões**) F (*ato*) importing; (*mercadoria*) import

importador, a [ĩporta'dor(a)] ADJ import *atr* ▶ M/F importer

importância [ĩpor'tãsja] F importance; (*de dinheiro*) sum, amount; **não tem ~** it doesn't matter, never mind; **ter ~** to be important; **sem ~** unimportant; **importante** [īpor'tãtʃi] ADJ important ▶ M: **o (mais) importante** the (most) important thing

importar [īpor'tar] VT (Com) to import; (trazer) to bring in; (causar: prejuízos etc) to cause; (implicar) to imply, involve ▶ VI to matter, be important; **importar-se** VR: **~-se com algo** to mind sth; **não me importo** I don't care

importunar [īportu'nar] VT to bother, annoy

importuno, -a [īpor'tunu, a] ADJ annoying; (inoportuno) inopportune ▶ M/F nuisance

impossibilitado, -a [īposibili'tadu, a] ADJ: **~ de fazer** unable to do

impossibilitar [īposibili'tar] VT: **~ algo** to make sth impossible; **~ alguém de fazer, ~ a alguém fazer** to prevent sb doing; **~ algo a alguém, ~ alguém para algo** to make sth impossible for sb

impossível [īpo'sivew] (pl **-eis**) ADJ impossible; (insuportável: pessoa) insufferable; (incrível) incredible

imposto [ī'postu] M tax; **antes/ depois de ~s** before/after tax; **~ ambiental** green tax, environmental tax; **~ de renda** (BR) income tax; **~ predial** rates pl; **I~ sobre Circulação de Mercadorias (e Serviços)** (BR), **~ sobre valor agregado** value added tax (BRIT), sales tax (US)

impotente [īpo'tẽtʃi] ADJ powerless; (Med) impotent

impraticável [īpratʃi'kavew] (pl

-eis) ADJ impracticable; (rua, rio etc) impassable

impreciso, -a [īpre'sizu, a] ADJ vague; (falta de rigor) inaccurate

imprensa [ī'prẽsa] F printing; (máquina, jornais) press

imprescindível [īpresĩ'dʒivew] (pl **-eis**) ADJ essential, indispensable

impressão [impre'sãw] (pl **-ões**) F impression; (de livros) printing; (marca) imprint; **causar boa ~** to make a good impression; **ficar com/ter a ~ (de) que** to get/ have the impression that

impressionante [īpresjo'nãtʃi] ADJ impressive

impressionar [īpresjo'nar] VT to affect ▶ VI to be impressive; (pessoa) to make an impression; **impressionar-se** VR: **~-se (com algo)** (comover-se) to be moved (by sth)

impresso, -a [ī'presu, a] PP de **imprimir** ▶ ADJ printed ▶ M (para preencher) form; (folheto) leaflet; **impressos** MPL (formulário) printed matter sg

impressões [impre'sõjs] FPL de **impressão**

impressora [īpre'sora] F (Comput) printer; **~ jato de tinta** ink-jet printer

imprestável [īpres'tavew] (pl **-eis**) ADJ (inútil) useless; (pessoa) unhelpful

imprevisível [īprevi'zivew] (pl **-eis**) ADJ unforeseeable

imprevisto, -a [īpre'vistu, a] ADJ unexpected, unforeseen ▶ M: **um ~** something unexpected

imprimir [īpri'mir] VT to print; (marca) to stamp; (infundir) to instil (BRIT), instill (US)

impróprio, -a [ĩ'prɔprju, a] ADJ
inappropriate; (*indecente*) improper
improvável [ĩpro'vavew] (*pl* **-eis**)
ADJ unlikely
improviso [ĩpro'vizu] M: **de ~** (*de repente*) suddenly; (*sem preparação*)
without preparation
imprudente [ĩpru'dẽtʃi] ADJ
(*irrefletido*) rash; (*motorista*) careless
impulsivo, -a [ĩpuw'sivu, a] ADJ
impulsive
impulso [ĩ'puwsu] M impulse; (*fig: estímulo*) urge, impulse
impune [ĩ'puni] ADJ unpunished;
impunidade [ĩpuni'dadʒi] F
impunity
imundície [imũ'dʒisji] F filth;
imundo, -a [i'mũdu, a] ADJ filthy;
(*obsceno*) dirty
imune [i'muni] ADJ: **~ a** immune
to; **imunidade** [imuni'dadʒi] F
immunity
inábil [i'nabiw] (*pl* **-eis**) ADJ
incapable; (*desajeitado*) clumsy
inabitado, -a [inabi'tadu, a] ADJ
uninhabited
inacabado, -a [inaka'badu, a] ADJ
unfinished
inacreditável [inakredʒi'tavew]
(*pl* **-eis**) ADJ unbelievable, incredible
inadequado, -a [inade'kwadu, a]
ADJ inadequate; (*impróprio*)
unsuitable
inadiável [ina'dʒjavew] (*pl* **-eis**)
ADJ pressing
inadimplência [inadʒĩ'plẽsja] F
(*Jur*) breach of contract, default
inaptidão [inaptʃi'dãw] (*pl* **-ões**) F
inability
inatingível [inatʃĩ'ʒivew] (*pl* **-eis**)
ADJ unattainable
inativo, -a [ina'tʃivu, a] ADJ
inactive; (*aposentado, reformado*)
retired

inauguração [inawgura'sãw] (*pl* **-ões**) F inauguration; (*de exposição*)
opening; **inaugural** [inawgu'raw]
(*pl* **-ais**) ADJ inaugural; **inaugurar**
[inawgu'rar] VT to inaugurate;
(*exposição*) to open
incapacidade [ĩkapasi'dadʒi] F
incapacity; (*incompetência*)
incompetence
incapacitado, -a [ĩkapasi'tadu, a]
ADJ (*inválido*) disabled, handicapped
▶ M/F handicapped person; **estar ~ de fazer** to be unable to do
incapaz [ĩka'pajz] ADJ, M/F
incompetent; **~ de fazer** incapable
of doing; **~ para** unfit for
incendiar [ĩsẽ'dʒjar] VT to set fire
to; (*fig*) to inflame; **incendiar-se** VR
to catch fire
incêndio [ĩ'sẽdʒju] M fire;
~ criminoso *ou* **premeditado**
arson
incenso [ĩ'sẽsu] M incense
incentivar [ĩsẽtʃi'var] VT to
stimulate, encourage
incentivo [ĩsẽ'tʃivu] M incentive;
~ fiscal tax incentive
incerteza [ĩser'teza] F uncertainty
incerto, -a [ĩ'sɛrtu, a] ADJ
uncertain
incesto [ĩ'sɛstu] M incest
inchado, -a [ĩ'ʃadu, a] ADJ swollen;
(*fig*) conceited
inchar [ĩ'ʃar] VT, VI to swell
incidência [ĩsi'dẽsja] F incidence,
occurrence
incidente [ĩsi'dẽtʃi] M incident
incisivo, -a [ĩsi'zivu, a] ADJ cutting,
sharp; (*fig*) incisive
incitar [ĩsi'tar] VT to incite; (*pessoa, animal*) to drive on
inclinação [ĩklina'sãw] (*pl* **-ões**) F
inclination; **~ da cabeça** nod
inclinar [ĩkli'nar] VT to tilt; (*cabeça*)

to nod ▶ vi to slope; (*objeto*) to tilt; **inclinar-se** vr to tilt; (*dobrar o corpo*) to bow, stoop; **~-se sobre algo** to lean over sth

incluir [ĩ'klwir] vt to include; (*em carta*) to enclose; **incluir-se** vr to be included

inclusão [ĩklu'zãw] f inclusion; **inclusive** [ĩklu'zivi] prep including ▶ adv inclusive; (*até mesmo*) even

incoerente [ĩkoe'rẽtʃi] adj incoherent; (*contraditório*) inconsistent

incógnita [ĩ'kɔgnita] f (*Mat*) unknown; (*fato incógnito*) mystery

incógnito, -a [ĩ'kɔgnitu, a] adj unknown ▶ adv incógnito

incolor [ĩko'lor] adj colourless (BRIT), colorless (US)

incomodar [ĩkomo'dar] vt to bother, trouble; (*aborrecer*) to annoy ▶ vi to be bothersome; **incomodar-se** vr to bother, put o.s. out; **~-se com algo** to be bothered by sth, mind sth; **não se incomode!** don't worry!

incômodo, -a [ĩ'komodu, a] adj uncomfortable; (*incomodativo*) troublesome; (*inoportuno*) inconvenient

incompetente [ĩkõpe'tẽtʃi] adj, m/f incompetent

incompreendido, -a [ĩkõprjẽ'dʒidu, a] adj misunderstood

incomum [ĩko'mũ] adj uncommon

incomunicável [ĩkomuni'kavew] (*pl* -eis) adj cut off; (*privado de comunicação, fig*) incommunicado; (*preso*) in solitary confinement

inconformado, -a [ĩkõfor'madu, a]

adj bitter; **~ com** unreconciled to

inconfundível [ĩkõfũ'dʒivew] (*pl* -eis) adj unmistakeable

inconsciência [ĩkõ'sjẽsja] f (*Med*) unconsciousness; (*irreflexão*) thoughtlessness

inconsciente [ĩkõ'sjẽtʃi] adj unconscious ▶ m unconscious

inconsequente [ĩkõse'kwẽtʃi] adj inconsistent; (*contraditório*) illogical; (*irresponsável*) irresponsible

inconsistente [ĩkõsis'tẽtʃi] adj inconsistent; (*sem solidez*) runny

inconstante [ĩkõs'tãtʃi] adj fickle; (*tempo*) changeable

incontrolável [ĩkõtro'lavew] (*pl* -eis) adj uncontrollable

inconveniência [ĩkõve'njẽsja] f inconvenience; (*impropriedade*) inappropriateness

inconveniente [ĩkõve'njẽtʃi] adj inconvenient; (*inoportuno*) awkward; (*grosseiro*) rude; (*importuno*) annoying ▶ m disadvantage; (*obstáculo*) difficulty, problem

incorreto, -a [ĩko'hɛtu, a] adj incorrect; (*desonesto*) dishonest

incrédulo, -a [ĩ'krɛdulu, a] adj incredulous; (*cético*) sceptical (BRIT), skeptical (US) ▶ m/f sceptic (BRIT), skeptic (US)

incrível [ĩ'krivew] (*pl* -eis) adj incredible

incumbência [ĩkũ'bẽsja] f task, duty

incumbir [ĩkũ'bir] vt: **~ alguém de algo** *ou* **algo a alguém** to put sb in charge of sth ▶ vi: **~ a alguém** to be sb's duty; **incumbir-se** vr: **~-se de** to undertake, take charge of

indagação [ĩdaga'sãw] (*pl* -ões) f

investigation; (*pergunta*) inquiry, question

indagar [ĩda'gar] VT to investigate ▶ VI to inquire; **indagar-se** VR: **~-se a si mesmo** to ask o.s.; **~ algo de alguém** to ask sb about sth

indecente [ĩde'sẽtʃi] ADJ indecent, improper; (*obsceno*) rude, vulgar

indecoroso, -a [ĩdeko'rozu, ɔza] ADJ indecent, improper

indefinido, -a [ĩdefi'nidu, a] ADJ indefinite; (*vago*) vague, undefined; **por tempo ~** indefinitely

indelicado, -a [ĩdeli'kadu, a] ADJ impolite, rude

indenização [indeniza'sãw], (*PT*) **indemnização** (*pl* **-ões**) F compensation; (*Com*) indemnity

indenizar [ĩdeni'zar], (*PT*) **indemnizar** VT: **~ alguém por** *ou* **de algo** (*compensar*) to compensate sb for sth; (*por gastos*) to reimburse sb for sth

independência [ĩdepẽ'dẽsja] F independence; **independente** [ĩdepẽ'dẽtʃi] ADJ independent

indesejável [ĩdeze'ʒavew] (*pl* **-eis**) ADJ undesirable

indevido, -a [ĩde'vidu, a] ADJ (*imerecido*) unjust; (*impróprio*) inappropriate

Índia ['ĩdʒa] F: **a ~** India; **as ~s Ocidentais** the West Indies; **indiano, -a** [ĩ'dʒjanu, a] ADJ, M/F Indian

indicação [indʒika'sãw] (*pl* **-ões**) F indication; (*de termômetro*) reading; (*para um cargo, prêmio*) nomination; (*recomendação*) recommendation; (*de um caminho*) directions *pl*

indicado, -a [ĩdʒi'kadu, a] ADJ appropriate

indicador, a [ĩdʒika'dor(a)] ADJ: **~ de** indicative of ▶ M indicator;

(*Tec*) gauge; (*dedo*) index finger; (*ponteiro*) pointer

indicar [ĩdʒi'kar] VT to indicate; (*apontar*) to point to; (*temperatura*) to register; (*recomendar*) to recommend; (*para um cargo*) to nominate; (*determinar*) to determine; **~ o caminho a alguém** to give sb directions

índice ['ĩdʒisi] M (*de livro*) index; (*taxa*) rate

indício [in'dʒisju] M (*sinal*) sign; (*vestígio*) trace; (*Jur*) clue

indiferença [ĩdʒife'rẽsa] F indifference; **indiferente** [ĩdʒife'rẽtʃi] ADJ: **indiferente (a)** indifferent (to); **isso me é indiferente** it's all the same to me

indígena [ĩ'dʒiʒena] ADJ, M/F native; (*índio: da América*) Indian

indigência [ĩdʒi'ʒẽsja] F poverty; (*fig*) lack, need

indigestão [ĩdʒiʒes'tãw] F indigestion

indigesto, -a [ĩdʒi'ʒɛstu, a] ADJ indigestible

indignação [ĩdʒigna'sãw] F indignation; **indignado, -a** [ĩdʒig'nadu, a] ADJ indignant

indignar [ĩdʒig'nar] VT to anger, incense; **indignar-se** VR to get angry

índio, -a ['ĩdʒju, a] ADJ, M/F (*da América*) Indian; **o Oceano Í~** the Indian Ocean

indireto, -a [ĩdʒi'rɛtu, a] ADJ indirect

indiscreto, -a [ĩdʒis'krɛtu, a] ADJ indiscreet

indiscutível [ĩdʒisku'tʃivew] (*pl* **-eis**) ADJ indisputable

indispensável [ĩdʒispẽ'savew] (*pl* **-eis**) ADJ essential, vital ▶ M: **o ~** the essentials *pl*

indispor [ĩdʒis'por] (*irreg: como* **pôr**) VT (*de saúde*) to make ill; (*aborrecer*) to upset; **indisposto, -a** [ĩdʒis'postu, 'pɔsta] ADJ unwell, poorly

indistinto, -a [ĩdʒis'tʃĩtu, a] ADJ indistinct

individual [ĩdʒivi'dwaw] (*pl* -**ais**) ADJ individual

indivíduo [ĩdʒi'vidwu] M individual; (*col: sujeito*) person

indócil [ĩ'dɔsiw] (*pl* -**eis**) ADJ unruly, wayward; (*impaciente*) restless

índole ['ĩdoli] F (*temperamento*) nature; (*tipo*) sort, type

indolor [ĩdo'lor] ADJ painless

Indonésia [ĩdo'nɛzja] F: **a ~** Indonesia

indústria [ĩ'dustrja] F industry; **industrial** [ĩdus'trjaw] (*pl* -**ais**) ADJ industrial ▸ M/F industrialist; **industrializar** [ĩdustrjali'zar] VT (*país*) to industrialize; (*aproveitar*) to process

induzir [ĩdu'zir] VT to induce; (*persuadir*): **~ alguém a fazer** to persuade sb to do

inédito, -a [i'nɛdʒitu, a] ADJ (*livro*) unpublished; (*incomum*) unheard-of, rare

inegável [ine'gavew] (*pl* -**eis**) ADJ undeniable

inelutável [inelu'tavew] (*pl* -**eis**) ADJ inescapable

inepto, -a [i'nɛptu, a] ADJ inept, incompetent

inequívoco, -a [ine'kivoku, a] ADJ (*evidente*) clear; (*inconfundível*) unmistakeable

inércia [i'nɛrsja] F lethargy; (*Fís*) inertia

inerente [ine'rẽtʃi] ADJ: **~ a** inherent in *ou* to

inerte [i'nɛrtʃi] ADJ lethargic; (*Fís*) inert

inesgotável [inezgo'tavew] (*pl* -**eis**) ADJ inexhaustible; (*superabundante*) boundless

inesperado, -a [inespe'radu, a] ADJ unexpected, unforeseen ▸ M: **o ~** the unexpected

inesquecível [ineske'sivew] (*pl* -**eis**) ADJ unforgettable

inestimável [inestʃi'mavew] (*pl* -**eis**) ADJ invaluable

inexato, -a [ine'zatu, a] ADJ inaccurate

inexistência [inezis'tẽsja] F lack

inexperiência [inespe'rjẽsja] F inexperience; **inexperiente** [inespe'rjẽtʃi] ADJ inexperienced; (*ingênuo*) naive

inexpressivo, -a [inespre'sivu, a] ADJ expressionless

infância [ĩ'fãsja] F childhood

infantil [ĩfã'tʃiw] (*pl* -**is**) ADJ (*ingênuo*) childlike; (*pueril*) childish; (*para crianças*) children's

infarto [ĩ'fartu] M heart attack

infecção [ĩfek'sãw] (*pl* -**ões**) F infection; **infeccionar** [ĩfeksjo'nar] VT (*ferida*) to infect; **infeccioso, -a** [ĩfek'sjozu, ɔza] ADJ infectious

infelicidade [ĩfelisi'dadʒi] F unhappiness; (*desgraça*) misfortune

infeliz [ĩfe'liz] ADJ unhappy; (*infausto*) unlucky; (*ação, medida*) unfortunate; (*sugestão, ideia*) inappropriate ▸ M/F unhappy person; **infelizmente** [ĩfeliz'mẽtʃi] ADV unfortunately

inferior [ĩfe'rjor] ADJ: **~ (a)** (*em valor, qualidade*) inferior (to); (*mais baixo*) lower (than) ▸ M/F inferior, subordinate; **inferioridade** [ĩferjori'dadʒi] F inferiority

infernal [ĩfer'naw] (*pl* **-ais**) ADJ
infernal

inferno [ĩ'fεrnu] M hell; **vá pro ~!**
(*col*) piss off!

infetar [ĩfe'tar] VT to infect

infiel [ĩ'fjεw] (*pl* **-éis**) ADJ disloyal;
(*marido*) unfaithful; (*texto*)
inaccurate ▶ M/F (*Rel*) non-believer

ínfimo, -a [ĩfimu, a] ADJ lowest;
(*qualidade*) poorest

infindável [ĩfĩ'davew] (*pl* **-eis**) ADJ
unending, constant

infinidade [ĩfini'dadʒi] F infinity;
uma ~ de countless

infinitivo, -a [ĩfini'tʃivu, a] ADJ, M
(*Ling*) infinitive

inflação [ĩfla'sãw] F inflation;
inflacionário, -a [ĩflasjo'narju, a]
ADJ inflationary

inflamação [ĩflama'sãw] (*pl* **-ões**)
F inflammation; **inflamado, -a**
[ĩfla'madu, a] ADJ (*Med*) inflamed;
(*discurso*) heated

inflamar [ĩfla'mar] VT (*madeira,
pólvora*) to set fire to; (*Med, fig*) to
inflame; **inflamar-se** VR to catch
fire; (*fig*) to get worked up; **~-se de
algo** to be consumed with sth

inflamável [ĩfla'mavew] (*pl* **-eis**)
ADJ inflammable

inflar [ĩ'flar] VT to inflate, blow up;
inflar-se VR to swell (up)

inflexível [ĩflek'sivew] (*pl* **-eis**) ADJ
stiff, rigid; (*fig*) unyielding

influência [ĩ'flwẽsja] F influence;
sob a ~ de under the influence of;
influenciar [ĩflwẽ'sjar] VT to
influence ▶ VI: **influenciar em algo**
to influence sth, have an influence
on sth; **influenciar-se** VR:
influenciar-se por to be influenced
by; **influente** [ĩ'flwẽtʃi] ADJ
influential; **influir** [ĩ'flwir] VI to
matter, be important; **influir em** *ou*

sobre to influence, have an
influence on

informação [ĩforma'sãw] (*pl* **-ões**)
F (piece of) information; (*notícia*)
news; **informações** FPL (*detalhes*)
information *sg*; **Informações** FPL
(*Tel*) directory enquiries (BRIT),
information (US); **pedir
informações sobre** to ask about,
inquire about

informal [ĩfor'maw] (*pl* **-ais**) ADJ
informal

informar [ĩfor'mar] VT: **~ alguém
(de/sobre algo)** to inform sb (of/
about sth) ▶ VI to inform, be
informative; **informar-se** VR: **~-se
de** to find out about, inquire about;
~ de to report on

informática [ĩfor'matʃika] F IT,
information technology

informativo, -a [ĩforma'tʃivu, a]
ADJ informative

informatizar [ĩformatʃi'zar] VT to
computerize

infortúnio [ĩfor'tunju] M
misfortune

infração [ĩfra'sãw] (*pl* **-ões**) F
breach, infringement; (*Esporte*) foul

infrator, a [ĩfra'tor(a)] M/F
offender

infrutífero, -a [ĩfru'tʃiferu, a] ADJ
fruitless

ingênuo, -a [ĩ'ʒenwu, a] ADJ
ingenuous, naïve; (*comentário*)
harmless ▶ M/F naïve person

ingerir [ĩʒe'rir] VT to ingest;
(*engolir*) to swallow

Inglaterra [ĩgla'tɛha] F: **a ~**
England; **inglês, -esa** [ĩ'gles, eza]
ADJ English ▶ M/F Englishman/
woman ▶ M (*Ling*) English; **os
ingleses** MPL the English

ingrediente [ĩgre'dʒjẽtʃi] M
ingredient

íngreme [ˈĩgremi] ADJ steep

ingressar [ĩgreˈsar] VI: **~ em** to enter, go into; (*um clube*) to join

ingresso [ĩˈgrɛsu] M (*entrada*) entry; (*admissão*) admission; (*bilhete*) ticket

inibição [inibiˈsãw] (*pl* **-ões**) F inhibition

inibido, -a [iniˈbidu, a] ADJ inhibited

inibir [iniˈbir] VT to inhibit

inicial [iniˈsjaw] (*pl* **-ais**) ADJ, F initial

iniciar [iniˈsjar] VT, VI (*começar*) to begin, start; **~ alguém em algo** (*arte, seita*) to initiate sb into sth

iniciativa [inisjaˈtʃiva] F initiative; **a ~ privada** (*Econ*) private enterprise

início [iˈnisju] M beginning, start; **no ~** at the start

inimigo, -a [iniˈmigu, a] ADJ, M/F enemy

injeção [inʒeˈsãw] (*pl* **-ões**) F injection

injetar [ĩʒeˈtar] VT to inject

injúria [ĩˈʒurja] F insult

injustiça [ĩʒusˈtʃisa] F injustice

inocência [inoˈsẽsja] F innocence

inocentar [inoseˈtar] VT: **~ alguém (de algo)** to clear sb (of sth)

inocente [inoˈsẽtʃi] ADJ innocent ▶ M/F innocent man/woman

inofensivo, -a [inofẽˈsivu, a] ADJ harmless, inoffensive

inovação [inovaˈsãw] (*pl* **-ões**) F innovation

inquérito [ĩˈkɛritu] M inquiry; (*Jur*) inquest

inquietação [ĩkjetaˈsãw] F anxiety, uneasiness; (*agitação*) restlessness

inquietante [ĩkjeˈtãtʃi] ADJ worrying, disturbing

inquietar [ĩkjeˈtar] VT to worry, disturb; **inquietar-se** VR to worry, bother; **inquieto, -a** [ĩˈkjɛtu, a] ADJ anxious, worried; (*agitado*) restless

inquilino, -a [ĩkiˈlinu, a] M/F tenant

insalubre [ĩsaˈlubri] ADJ unhealthy

insanidade [ĩsaniˈdadʒi] F madness, insanity; **insano, -a** [ĩˈsanu, a] ADJ insane

insatisfatório, -a [ĩsatʃisfaˈtɔrju, a] ADJ unsatisfactory

insatisfeito, -a [ĩsatʃisˈfejtu, a] ADJ dissatisfied, unhappy

inscrever [ĩskreˈver] VT to inscribe; (*aluno*) to enrol (BRIT), enroll (US); (*em registro*) to register

inscrito, -a [ĩˈskritu, a] PP *de* **inscrever**

insegurança [ĩseguˈrãsa] F insecurity; **inseguro, -a** [ĩseˈguru, a] ADJ insecure

insensato, -a [ĩsẽˈsatu, a] ADJ unreasonable, foolish

inserir [ĩseˈrir] VT to insert, put in; (*Comput: dados*) to enter

inseticida [ĩsetʃiˈsida] M insecticide

inseto [ĩˈsetu] M insect

insípido, -a [ĩˈsipidu, a] ADJ insipid

insiro [ĩˈsiru] VB *ver* **inserir**

insistência [ĩsisˈtẽsja] F: **~ (em)** insistence (on); (*obstinação*) persistence (in); **insistente** [ĩsisˈtẽtʃi] ADJ (*pessoa*) insistent; (*apelo*) urgent

insistir [ĩsisˈtʃir] VI: **~ (em)** to insist (on); (*perseverar*) to persist (in); **~ (em) que** to insist that

insolação [insola'sãw] F
sunstroke; **pegar uma ~** to get
sunstroke

insólito, -a [ĩ'sɔlitu, a] ADJ unusual

insônia [ĩ'sonja] F insomnia

insosso, -a [ĩ'sosu, a] ADJ unsalted;
(sem sabor) tasteless; (pessoa)
uninteresting, dull

inspeção [ĩspe'sãw] (pl -ões) F
inspection, check; **inspecionar**
[ĩspesjo'nar] VT to inspect

inspetor, a [ĩspe'tor(a)] M/F
inspector

inspirar [ĩspi'rar] VT to inspire;
(Med) to inhale; **inspirar-se** VR to be
inspired

INSS (BR) ABR M (= Instituto Nacional
do Seguro Social) ≈ DSS (BRIT),
≈ Welfare Dept (US)

instalação [ĩstala'sãw] (pl -ões) F
installation; **~ elétrica** (de casa)
wiring

instalar [ĩsta'lar] VT to install;
(estabelecer) to set up; **instalar-se**
VR (numa cadeira) to settle down

instantâneo, -a [ĩstã'tanju, a] ADJ
instant, instantaneous ▶ M (Foto)
snap

instante [ĩs'tãtʃi] ADJ urgent ▶ M
moment; **num ~** in an instant,
quickly; **só um ~!** just a moment!

instável [ĩs'tavew] (pl -eis) ADJ
unstable; (tempo) unsettled

instintivo, -a [ĩstʃĩ'tʃivu, a] ADJ
instinctive

instinto [ĩs'tʃĩtu] M instinct; **por ~**
instinctively

instituição [ĩstʃitwi'sãw] (pl -ões)
F institution

instituto [ĩstʃi'tutu] M (escola)
institute; (instituição) institution;
~ de beleza beauty salon

instrução [ĩstru'sãw] (pl -ões) F
education; (erudição) learning;

(diretriz) instruction; (Mil) training;
instruções FPL (para o uso)
instructions (for use)

instruído, -a [ĩs'trwidu, a] ADJ
educated

instruir [ĩs'trwir] VT to instruct;
(Mil) to train; **instruir-se** VR: **~-se
em algo** to learn sth; **~ alguém de**
ou **sobre algo** to inform sb about sth

instrumento [ĩstru'mẽtu] M
instrument; (ferramenta)
implement; (Jur) deed, document;
~ de cordas/percussão/sopro
stringed/percussion/wind
instrument; **~ de trabalho** tool

instrutivo, -a [ĩstru'tʃivu, a] ADJ
instructive

instrutor, a [ĩstru'tor(a)] M/F
instructor; (Esporte) coach

insubordinação
[ĩsubordʒina'sãw] F rebellion; (Mil)
insubordination

insubstituível [ĩsubistʃi'twivew]
(pl -eis) ADJ irreplaceable

insuficiência [ĩsufi'sjẽsja] F
inadequacy; (carência) shortage;
(Med) deficiency; **~ cardíaca** heart
failure; **insuficiente** [ĩsufi'sjẽtʃi]
ADJ insufficient; (Educ: nota) ≈ fail;
(pessoa) incompetent

insulina [ĩsu'lina] F insulin

insultar [ĩsuw'tar] VT to insult;
insulto [ĩ'suwtu] M insult

insuportável [ĩsupor'tavew] (pl
-eis) ADJ unbearable

insurgir-se [ĩsur'ʒirsi] VR to rebel,
revolt

insurreição [ĩsuhej'sãw] (pl -ões)
F rebellion, insurrection

intato, -a [ĩ'tatu, a] ADJ intact

íntegra ['ĩtegra] F: **na ~** in full

integral [ĩte'graw] (pl -ais) ADJ
whole ▶ F (Mat) integral; **pão ~**
wholemeal (BRIT) ou wholewheat

(us) bread; **integralmente** [ĩtegraw'mẽtʃi] ADV in full, fully

integrar [ĩte'grar] VT to unite, combine; (*completar*) to form, make up; (*Mat, raças*) to integrate; **integrar-se** VR to become complete; **~-se em** *ou* **a algo** to join sth; (*adaptar-se*) to integrate into sth

integridade [ĩtegri'dadʒi] F entirety; (*fig: de pessoa*) integrity

íntegro, -a [ˈĩtegru, a] ADJ entire; (*honesto*) upright, honest

inteiramente [ĩtejra'mẽtʃi] ADV completely

inteirar [ĩtej'rar] VT (*completar*) to complete; **inteirar-se** VR: **~-se de** to find out about; **~ alguém de** to inform sb of

inteiro, -a [ĩ'tejru, a] ADJ whole, entire; (*ileso*) unharmed; (*não quebrado*) undamaged

intelecto [ĩte'lɛktu] M intellect; **intelectual** [ĩtelek'twaw] (*pl* -**ais**) ADJ, M/F intellectual

inteligência [ĩteli'ʒẽsja] F intelligence; **inteligente** [ĩteli'ʒẽtʃi] ADJ intelligent

inteligível [ĩteli'ʒivew] (*pl* -**eis**) ADJ intelligible

intenção [ĩtẽ'sãw] (*pl* -**ões**) F intention; **segundas intenções** ulterior motives; **ter a ~ de** to intend to; **intencionado, -a** [ĩtẽsjo'nadu, a] ADJ: **bem intencionado** well-meaning; **mal intencionado** spiteful; **intencional** [ĩtẽsjo'naw] (*pl* -**ais**) ADJ intentional, deliberate; **intencionar** [ĩtẽsjo'nar] VT to intend

intensificar [ĩtẽsifi'kar] VT to intensify; **intensificar-se** VR to intensify

intensivo, -a [ĩtẽ'sivu, a] ADJ intensive

intenso, -a [ĩ'tẽsu, a] ADJ intense; (*emoção*) deep; (*impressão*) vivid; (*vida social*) full

interação [ĩtera'sãw] F interaction

interativo, -a [ĩtera'tʃivu, a] ADJ (*Comput*) interactive

intercâmbio [ĩter'kãbju] M exchange

interdição [ĩterdʒi'sãw] (*pl* -**ões**) F (*de estrada, porta*) closure; (*Jur*) injunction

interditar [ĩterdʒi'tar] VT (*importação etc*) to ban; (*estrada, praia*) to close off; (*cinema etc*) to close down

interessado, -a [ĩtere'sadu, a] ADJ interested; (*amizade*) self-seeking

interessante [ĩtere'sãtʃi] ADJ interesting

interessar [ĩtere'sar] VT to interest ▶ VI to be interesting; **interessar-se** VR: **~-se em** *ou* **por** to take an interest in, be interested in; **a quem possa ~** to whom it may concern

interesse [ĩte'resi] M interest; (*próprio*) self-interest; (*proveito*) advantage; **no ~ de** for the sake of; **por ~ (próprio)** for one's own ends; **interesseiro, -a** [ĩtere'sejru, a] ADJ self-seeking

interface [ĩter'fasi] F (*Comput*) interface

interferência [ĩterfe'rẽsja] F interference

interferir [ĩterfe'rir] VI: **~ em** to interfere in; (*rádio*) to jam

interfone [ĩter'fɔni] M intercom

interior [ĩte'rjor] ADJ inner, inside; (*Com*) domestic, internal ▶ M inside, interior; (*do país*): **no ~**

inland; **Ministério do I~** ≈ Home Office (BRIT), ≈ Department of the Interior (US)

interjeição [ĩterʒej'sãw] (pl **-ões**) F interjection

interlocutor, a [ĩterloku'tor(a)] M/F speaker; **meu ~** the person I was speaking to

intermediário, -a [ĩterme'dʒjarju, a] ADJ intermediary ▶ M/F (Com) middleman; (mediador) intermediary, mediator

intermédio [ĩter'mɛdʒu] M: **por ~ de** through

internação [ĩterna'sãw] (pl **-ões**) F (de doente) admission

internacional [ĩternasjo'naw] (pl **-ais**) ADJ international

internações [ĩterna'sõjs] FPL de **internação**

internar [ĩter'nar] VT (aluno) to put into boarding school; (doente) to take into hospital; (Mil, Pol) to intern

internauta [ĩter'nawta] M/F internet user, web ou net surfer (col)

Internet [ĩter'nɛtʃi] F internet

interno, -a [ĩ'tɛrnu, a] ADJ internal; (Pol) domestic ▶ M/F (tb: **aluno ~**) boarder; (Med: estudante) houseman (BRIT), intern (US); **de uso ~** (Med) for internal use

interpretação [ĩterpreta'sãw] (pl **-ões**) F interpretation; (Teatro) performance

interpretar [ĩterpre'tar] VT to interpret; (um papel) to play; **intérprete** [ĩ'tɛrpretʃi] M/F interpreter; (Teatro) performer, artist

interrogação [ĩterhoga'sãw] (pl **-ões**) F interrogation; **ponto de ~** question mark

interrogar [ĩterho'gar] VT to question, interrogate; (Jur) to cross-examine

interromper [ĩtehõ'per] VT to interrupt; (parar) to stop; (Elet) to cut off

interruptor [ĩtehup'tor] M (Elet) switch

interseção [ĩterse'sãw] (pl **-ões**) F intersection

interurbano, -a [ĩterur'banu, a] ADJ (Tel) long-distance ▶ M long-distance ou trunk call

intervalo [ĩter'valu] M interval; (descanso) break; **a ~s** every now and then

intervir [ĩter'vir] (irreg: como **vir**) VI to intervene; (sobrevir) to come up

intimação [ĩtʃima'sãw] (pl **-ões**) F (ordem) order; (Jur) summons

intimar [ĩtʃi'mar] VT (Jur) to summon; **~ alguém a fazer** ou **a alguém que faça** to order sb to do

íntimo, -a [ĩ'tʃimu, a] ADJ intimate; (sentimentos) innermost; (amigo) close; (vida) private ▶ M/F close friend; **no ~** at heart

intolerante [ĩtole'ratʃi] ADJ intolerant

intolerável [ĩtole'ravew] (pl **-eis**) ADJ intolerable, unbearable

intoxicação [ĩtoksika'sãw] F poisoning; **~ alimentar** food poisoning

intoxicar [ĩtoksi'kar] VT to poison

intranet [ĩtra'nɛtʃi] F intranet

intransitável [ĩtrãsi'tavew] (pl **-eis**) ADJ impassable

intratável [ĩtra'tavew] (pl **-eis**) ADJ (pessoa) contrary, awkward; (doença) untreatable; (problema) insurmountable

intriga [ĩ'triga] F intrigue; (enredo) plot; (fofoca) piece of gossip; **intrigas** FPL (fofocas) gossip sg;

~ amorosa (*PT*) love affair;
intrigante [ĩtriˈgãtʃi] M/F
troublemaker ▶ ADJ intriguing;
intrigar [ĩtriˈgar] VT to intrigue
▶ VI to be intriguing
introdução [ĩtroduˈsãw] (*pl* **-ões**)
F introduction
introduzir [ĩtroduˈzir] VT to
introduce
intrometer-se [ĩtromeˈtersi] VR
to interfere, meddle;
intrometido, -a [ĩtromeˈtʃidu, a]
ADJ interfering; (*col*) nosey ▶ M/F
busybody
introvertido, -a [ĩtroverˈtʃidu, a]
ADJ introverted ▶ M/F introvert
intruso, -a [ĩˈtruzu, a] M/F
intruder
intuição [ĩtwiˈsãw] (*pl* **-ões**) F
intuition
intuito [ĩˈtuito] M intention, aim
inúmero, -a [iˈnumeru, a] ADJ
countless, innumerable
inundação [inũdaˈsãw] (*pl* **-ões**)
F (*enchente*) flood; (*ato*) flooding
inundar [inũˈdar] VT to flood; (*fig*)
to inundate ▶ VI to flood
inusitado, -a [inuziˈtadu, a] ADJ
unusual
inútil [iˈnutʃiw] (*pl* **-eis**) ADJ
useless; (*esforço*) futile;
(*desnecessário*) pointless; **inutilizar**
[inutʃiliˈzar] VT to make useless,
render useless; (*incapacitar*) to put
out of action; (*danificar*) to ruin;
(*esforços*) to thwart; **inutilmente**
[inutʃiwˈmẽtʃi] ADV in vain
invadir [ĩvaˈdʒir] VT to invade;
(*suj: água*) to overrun; (*: sentimento*)
to overcome
inválido, -a [ĩˈvalidu, a] ADJ, M/F
invalid
invasão [ĩvaˈzãw] (*pl* **-ões**) F
invasion

inveja [ĩˈvɛʒa] F envy; **invejar**
[ĩveˈʒar] VT to envy; (*cobiçar*) to
covet ▶ VI to be envious; **invejoso,
-a** [ĩveˈʒozu, ɔza] ADJ envious
invenção [ĩvẽˈsãw] (*pl* **-ões**) F
invention
inventado, -a [ĩvẽˈtadu, a] ADJ
(*história, personagem*) made-up
inventar [ĩvẽˈtar] VT to invent
inventivo, -a [ĩvẽˈtʃivu, a] ADJ
inventive
inventor, a [ĩvẽˈtor(a)] M/F
inventor
inverno [ĩˈvɛrnu] M winter
inverossímil [ĩveroˈsimiw],
(*PT*) **inverosímil** (*pl* **-eis**) ADJ
unlikely, improbable; (*inacreditável*)
implausible
invés [ĩˈvɛs] M: **ao ~ de** instead of
investigação [ĩvestʃigaˈsãw] (*pl*
-ões) F investigation; (*pesquisa*)
research
investigar [ĩvestʃiˈgar] VT to
investigate; (*examinar*) to examine
investimento [ĩvestʃiˈmẽtu] M
investment
investir [ĩvesˈtʃir] VT (*dinheiro*) to
invest
inviável [ĩˈvjavew] (*pl* **-eis**) ADJ
impracticable
invisível [ĩviˈzivew] (*pl* **-eis**) ADJ
invisible
invisto [ĩˈvistu] VB *ver* **investir**
invocar [ĩvoˈkar] VT to invoke
ioga [ˈjɔga] F yoga
iogurte [joˈgurtʃi] M yogurt
IR (*BR*) ABR M = **imposto de renda**

PALAVRA-CHAVE

ir [ir] VI **1** to go; (*a pé*) to walk; (*a
cavalo*) to ride; (*viajar*) to travel; **ir
caminhando** to walk; **fui de
trem** I went *ou* travelled by train;
vamos (embora)!, vamos nessa!

(*col*) let's go!; **já vou!** I'm coming!; **ir atrás de alguém** (*seguir*) to follow sb; (*confiar*) to take sb's word for it 2 (*progredir: pessoa, coisa*) to go; **o trabalho vai muito bem** work is going very well; **como vão as coisas?** how are things going?; **vou muito bem** I'm very well; (*na escola etc*) I'm getting on very well ▶ VB AUX 1 (+ *infin*): **vou fazer** I will do, I am going to do 2 (+ *gerúndio*): **ir fazendo** to keep on doing **ir-se** VR to go away, leave

ira ['ira] F anger, rage
Irã [i'rã] M: **o ~** Iran
iraniano, -a [ira'njanu, a] ADJ, M/F Iranian
Irão [i'rãw] (*PT*) M = **Irã**
Iraque [i'raki] M: **o ~** Iraq; **iraquiano, -a** [ira'kjanu, a] ADJ, M/F Iraqi
ir e vir M INV comings and goings *pl*
Irlanda [ir'lãda] F: **a ~** Ireland; **a ~ do Norte** Northern Ireland; **irlandês, -esa** [irlã'des, eza] ADJ Irish ▶ M/F Irishman/woman ▶ M (*Ling*) Irish
irmã [ir'mã] F sister; **~ gêmea** twin sister; **~ de criação** adoptive sister
irmão [ir'mãw] (*pl* **irmãos**) M brother; (*fig: similar*) twin; (*col: companheiro*) mate; **~ de criação** adoptive brother; **~ gêmeo** twin brother
ironia [iro'nia] F irony
irra! ['iha] (*PT*) EXCL damn!
irracional [ihasjo'naw] (*pl* **-ais**) ADJ irrational
irreal [ihe'aw] (*pl* **-ais**) ADJ unreal
irregular [ihegu'lar] ADJ irregular; (*vida*) unconventional; (*feições*) unusual; (*aluno, gênio*) erratic

irremediável [iheme'dʒjavew] (*pl* **-eis**) ADJ irremediable; (*sem remédio*) incurable
irrequieto, -a [ihe'kjɛtu, a] ADJ restless
irresistível [ihezis'tʃivew] (*pl* **-eis**) ADJ irresistible
irresponsável [ihespõ'savew] (*pl* **-eis**) ADJ irresponsible
irrigar [ihi'gar] VT to irrigate
irritação [ihita'sãw] (*pl* **-ões**) F irritation
irritadiço, -a [ihita'dʒisu, a] ADJ irritable
irritante [ihi'tãtʃi] ADJ irritating, annoying
irritar [ihi'tar] VT to irritate; **irritar-se** VR to get angry, get annoyed
irromper [ihõ'per] VI (*entrar subitamente*): **~ (em)** to burst in(to)
isca ['iska] F (*Pesca*) bait; (*fig*) lure, bait
isenção [izẽ'sãw] (*pl* **-ões**) F exemption
isentar [izẽ'tar] VT to exempt; (*livrar*) to free
Islã [iz'lã] M Islam
Islândia [iz'lãdʒa] F: **a ~** Iceland
isolado, -a [izo'ladu, a] ADJ isolated; (*solitário*) lonely
isolamento [izola'mẽtu] M isolation; (*Elet*) insulation
isotônico, -a [izo'toniku, a] ADJ isotonic
isqueiro [is'kejru] M (*cigarette*) lighter
Israel [izha'ɛw] M Israel; **israelense** [izhae'lẽsi] ADJ, M/F Israeli
isso ['isu] PRON that; (*col: isto*) this; **~ mesmo** exactly; **por ~** therefore, so; **por ~ mesmo** for that very reason; **só ~?** is that all?

isto ['istu] PRON this; **~ é** that is, namely

Itália [i'talja] F: **a ~** Italy; **italiano, -a** [ita'ljanu, a] ADJ, M/F Italian ▶ M (*Ling*) Italian

Itamarati [itamara'tʃi] M: **o ~** the Brazilian Foreign Ministry

> The Palace of **Itamarati** was built in 1855 in Rio de Janeiro. It became the seat of government when Brazil became a republic in 1889, and was later the Foreign Ministry. It ceased to be this when the Brazilian capital was transferred to Brasília, but **Itamarati** is still used to refer to the Foreign Ministry.

item ['itẽ] (*pl* **-ns**) M item

itinerário [itʃine'rarju] M itinerary; (*caminho*) route

j

já [ʒa] ADV already; (*em perguntas*) yet; (*agora*) now; (*imediatamente*) right away; (*agora mesmo*) right now ▶ CONJ on the other hand; **até já** bye; **desde já** from now on; **já não** no longer; **já que** as, since; **já se vê** of course; **já vou** I'm coming; **já até** even; **já, já** right away

jabuti [ʒabu'tʃi] M giant tortoise

jabuticaba [ʒabutʃi'kaba] F jaboticaba (*type of berry*)

jaca ['ʒaka] F jack fruit

jacaré [ʒaka'rɛ] (BR) M alligator

jaguar [ʒa'gwar] M jaguar

jaguatirica [ʒagwatʃi'rika] F leopard cat

Jamaica [ʒa'majka] F: **a ~** Jamaica

jamais [ʒa'majs] ADV never; (*com palavra negativa*) ever

janeiro [ʒa'nejru] M January

janela [ʒa'nɛla] F window

jangada [ʒã'gada] F raft

jantar [ʒã'tar] M dinner ▶ VT to have for dinner ▶ VI to have dinner

Japão [ʒa'pãw] M: **o ~** Japan;
japonês, -esa [ʒapo'nes, eza] ADJ,
M/F Japanese ▶ M (Ling) Japanese
jararaca [ʒara'raka] F jararaca
(snake)
jardim [ʒar'dʒĩ] (pl -ns) M garden;
~ de infância kindergarten;
~ zoológico ZOO; **jardinagem**
[ʒardʒi'naʒẽ] F gardening
jardineira [ʒardʒi'nejra] F (caixa)
trough; (calça) dungarees pl; ver tb
jardineiro
jardineiro, -a [ʒardʒi'nejru, a] M/F
gardener
jardins [ʒar'dʒĩs] MPL de **jardim**
jargão [ʒar'gãw] M jargon
jarra ['ʒaha] F pot
jarro ['ʒahu] M jug
jasmim [ʒaz'mĩ] M jasmine
jato ['ʒatu] M jet; (de luz) flash; (de
ar) blast; **a ~** at top speed
jaula ['ʒawla] F cage
jazigo [ʒa'zigu] M grave;
(monumento) tomb
jazz [dʒɛz] M jazz
jeito ['ʒejtu] M (maneira) way;
(aspecto) appearance; (aptidão,
habilidade) skill, knack; (modos
pessoais) manner; **ter ~ de** to look
like; **não ter ~** (pessoa) to be
awkward; (situação) to be hopeless;
dar um ~ em algo (pé) to twist sth;
(quarto, casa, papéis) to tidy sth up;
(consertar) to fix sth; **dar um ~** to
find a way; **o ~ é ...** the thing to do
is ...; **é o ~** it's the best way; **ao ~ de**
in the style of; **com ~** tactfully;
daquele ~ (in) that way; (col: em
desordem, mal) anyhow; **de
qualquer ~** anyway; **de ~
nenhum!** no way!
jejuar [ʒe'ʒwar] VI to fast
jejum [ʒe'ʒũ] (pl -ns) M fast; **em ~**
fasting

Jesus [ʒe'zus] M Jesus ▶ EXCL
heavens!
jiboia [ʒi'bɔja] F boa (constrictor)
jiló [ʒi'lɔ] M kind of vegetable
jingle ['dʒĩgew] M jingle
joalheria [ʒoaʎe'ria] F jeweller's
(shop) (BRIT), jewelry store (US)
joaninha [ʒwa'niɲa] F ladybird
(BRIT), ladybug (US)
joelho [ʒo'eʎu] M knee; **de ~s**
kneeling; **ficar de ~s** to kneel down
jogada [ʒo'gada] F move; (lanço)
throw; (negócio) scheme; move
jogador, a [ʒoga'dor(a)] M/F
player; (de jogo de azar) gambler
jogar [ʒo'gar] VT to play; (em jogo de
azar) to gamble; (atirar) to throw;
(indiretas) to drop ▶ VI to play; to
gamble; (barco) to pitch; **~ fora** to
throw away
jogging ['ʒɔgĩŋ] M jogging; (roupa)
track suit; **fazer ~** to go jogging, jog
jogo ['ʒogu] M game; (jogar) play;
(de azar) gambling; (conjunto) set;
(artimanha) trick; **~ de computador**
computer game; **J~s Olímpicos**
Olympic Games
joia ['ʒɔja] F jewel
Jordânia [ʒor'danja] F: **a ~** Jordan;
Jordão [ʒor'dãw] M: **o (rio) Jordão**
the Jordan (River)
jornada [ʒor'nada] F journey; **~ de
trabalho** working day
jornal [ʒor'naw] (pl -ais) M
newspaper; (TV, Rádio) news sg;
jornaleiro, -a [ʒorna'lejru, a] M/F
newsagent (BRIT), newsdealer (US)
jornalismo [ʒorna'lizmu] M
journalism; **jornalista** [ʒorna'lista]
M/F journalist
jovem ['ʒɔvẽ] (pl -ns) ADJ young
▶ M/F young person
jovial [ʒo'vjaw] (pl -ais) ADJ jovial,
cheerful

Jr ABR = **Júnior**

judaico, -a [ʒu'dajku, a] ADJ Jewish

judeu, judia [ʒu'dew, ʒu'dʒia] ADJ Jewish ▶ M/F Jew

judiar [ʒu'dʒjar] VI: **~ de alguém/algo** to ill-treat sb/sth

judicial [ʒudʒi'sjaw] (pl **-ais**) ADJ judicial

judiciário, -a [ʒudʒi'sjarju, a] ADJ judicial; **o (poder) ~** the judiciary

judô [ʒu'do] M judo

juiz, juíza [ʒwiz, -'iza] M/F judge; (em jogos) referee; **~ de paz** justice of the peace; **juizado** [ʒwi'zado] M court

juízo ['ʒwizu] M judgement; (parecer) opinion; (siso) common sense; (foro) court; **perder o ~** to lose one's mind; **não ter ~** to be foolish; **tomar** ou **criar ~** to come to one's senses; **chamar/levar a ~** to summon/take to court; **~!** behave yourself!

julgamento [ʒuwga'mẽtu] M judgement; (audiência) trial; (sentença) sentence

julgar [ʒuw'gar] VT to judge; (achar) to think; (Jur: sentenciar) to sentence; **julgar-se** VR: **~-se algo** to consider o.s. sth, think of o.s. as sth

julho ['ʒuʎu] M July

jumento, -a [ʒu'mẽtu, a] M/F donkey

junção [ʒũ'sãw] (pl **-ões**) F (ato) joining; (junta) join

junco ['ʒũku] M reed, rush

junções [ʒũ'sõjs] FPL de **junção**

junho ['ʒuɲu] M June

júnior ['ʒunjor] (pl **juniores**) ADJ younger, junior ▶ M/F (Esporte) junior; **Eduardo Autran J~** Eduardo Autran Junior

juntar [ʒũ'tar] VT to join; (reunir) to bring together; (aglomerar) to gather together; (recolher) to collect up; (acrescentar) to add; (dinheiro) to save up ▶ VI to gather; **juntar-se** VR to gather; (associar-se) to join up; **~-se a alguém** to join sb

junto, -a ['ʒũtu, a] ADJ joined; (chegado) near; **ir ~s** to go together; **~ a/de** near/next to; **segue ~** (Com) please find enclosed

jura ['ʒura] F vow

jurado, -a [ʒu'radu, a] ADJ sworn ▶ M/F juror

juramento [ʒura'mẽtu] M oath

jurar [ʒu'rar] VT, VI to swear; **jura?** really?

júri ['ʒuri] M jury

jurídico, -a [ʒu'ridʒiku, a] ADJ legal

juros ['ʒurus] MPL (Econ) interest sg; **~ simples/compostos** simple/compound interest

justamente [ʒusta'mẽtʃi] ADV fairly, justly; (precisamente) exactly

justiça [ʒus'tʃisa] F justice; (poder judiciário) judiciary; (equidade) fairness; (tribunal) court; **com ~** justly, fairly; **ir à ~** to go to court

justificar [ʒustʃifi'kar] VT to justify

justo, -a ['ʒustu, a] ADJ just, fair; (legítimo: queixa) legitimate, justified; (exato) exact; (apertado) tight ▶ ADV just

juvenil [ʒuve'niw] (pl **-is**) ADJ youthful; (roupa) young; (livro) for young people; (Esporte: equipe, campeonato) youth atr, junior

juventude [ʒuvẽ'tudʒi] F youth; (jovialidade) youthfulness; (jovens) young people pl, youth

k l

kg ABR (= *quilograma*) kg
kit ['kitʃi] (*pl* **-s**) M kit
kitchenette [kitʃe'nɛtʃi] F studio flat
km ABR (= *quilômetro*) km
km/h ABR (= *quilômetros por hora*) km/h

lá [la] ADV there ▶ M (*Mús*) A; **lá fora** outside; **lá em baixo** down there; **por lá** (*direção*) that way; (*situação*) over there; **até lá** (*no espaço*) there; (*no tempo*) until then
lã [lã] F wool
-la [la] PRON her; (*você*) you; (*coisa*) it
labia ['labja] F (*astúcia*) cunning; **ter ~** to have the gift of the gab
lábio ['labju] M lip
labirinto [labi'rĩtu] M labyrinth, maze
laboratório [labora'tɔrju] M laboratory
laca ['laka] F lacquer
laçar [la'sar] VT to bind, tie
laço ['lasu] M bow; (*de gravata*) knot; (*armadilha*) snare; (*fig*) bond, tie; **dar um ~** to tie a bow
lacrar [la'krar] VT to seal (with wax); **lacre** ['lakri] M sealing wax
lacuna [la'kuna] F gap; (*omissão*) omission; (*espaço em branco*) blank
ladeira [la'dejra] F slope
lado ['ladu] M side; (*Mil*) flank; (*rumo*) direction; **ao ~** (*perto*) close

by; **a casa ao ~** the house next door; **ao ~ de** beside; **deixar de ~** to set aside; (fig) to leave out; **de um ~ para outro** back and forth

ladra ['ladra] F thief, robber; (picareta) crook

ladrão, -ona [la'drãw, ɔna] (pl **-ões/-s**) ADJ thieving ▶ M/F thief, robber; (picareta) crook

ladrilho [la'driʎu] M tile; (chão) tiled floor, tiles pl

ladrões [la'drõjs] MPL de **ladrão**

lagarta [la'garta] F caterpillar

lagartixa [lagar'tʃiʃa] F gecko

lagarto [la'gartu] M lizard

lago ['lagu] M lake; (de jardim) pond

lagoa [la'goa] F pool, pond; (lago) lake

lagosta [la'gosta] F lobster

lagostim [lagos'tʃĩ] (pl **-ns**) M crayfish

lágrima ['lagrima] F tear

lama ['lama] F mud

lamaçal [lama'saw] (pl **-ais**) M quagmire; (pântano) bog, marsh

lamber [lã'ber] VT to lick; **lambida** [lã'bida] F: **dar uma lambida em algo** to lick sth

lambuzar [lãbu'zar] VT to smear

lamentar [lamẽ'tar] VT to lament; (sentir) to regret; **lamentar-se** VR: **~-se (de algo)** to lament (sth); **~ (que)** to be sorry that; **lamentável** [lamẽ'tavew] (pl **-eis**) ADJ regrettable; (deplorável) deplorable; **lamento** [la'mẽtu] M lament; (gemido) moan

lâmina ['lamina] F (chapa) sheet; (placa) plate; (de faca) blade; (de persiana) slat

lâmpada ['lãpada] F lamp; (tb: **~ elétrica**) light bulb; **~ de mesa** table lamp

lançar [lã'sar] VT to throw; (navio, produto, campanha) to launch; (disco, filme) to release; (Com: em livro) to enter; (em leilão) to bid

lancha ['lãʃa] F launch; **~ torpedeira** torpedo boat

lanchar [lã'ʃar] VI to have a snack ▶ VT to have as a snack; **lanche** ['lãʃi] M snack

lanchonete [lãʃo'nɛtʃi] (BR) F snack bar

LAN house [lã'hawzi] F internet café

lanterna [lã'tɛrna] F lantern; (portátil) torch (BRIT), flashlight (US)

lápide ['lapidʒi] F (tumular) tombstone; (comemorativa) memorial stone

lápis ['lapis] M INV pencil; **~ de cor** coloured (BRIT) ou colored (US) pencil, crayon; **~ de olho** eyebrow pencil; **lapiseira** [lapi'zejra] F propelling (BRIT) ou mechanical (US) pencil; (caixa) pencil case

lapso ['lapsu] M lapse; (de tempo) interval; (erro) slip

lar [lar] M home

laranja [la'rãʒa] ADJ INV orange ▶ F orange ▶ M (cor) orange; **laranjada** [larã'ʒada] F orangeade; **laranjeira** [larã'ʒejra] F orange tree

lareira [la'rejra] F hearth, fireside

larga ['larga] F: **à ~** lavishly; **dar ~ s a** to give free rein to; **viver à ~** to lead a lavish life

largada [lar'gada] F start; **dar a ~** to start; (fig) to make a start

largar [lar'gar] VT to let go of, release; (deixar) to leave; (deixar cair) to drop; (risada) to let out; (velas) to unfurl; (piada) to tell; (pôr em liberdade) to let go ▶ VI (Náut) to set sail; **largar-se** VR (desprender-se) to free o.s.; (*ir-se*) to go off; (*pôr-se*) to proceed

largo, -a ['largu, a] ADJ wide, broad; (*amplo*) extensive; (*roupa*) loose, baggy; (*conversa*) long ▶ M (*praça*) square; (*alto-mar*) open sea; **ao ~** at a distance, far off; **passar de ~ sobre um assunto** to gloss over a subject; **passar ao ~ de algo** (*fig*) to sidestep sth; **largura** [lar'gura] F width, breadth

laringite [larĩ'ʒitʃi] F laryngitis

lasanha [la'zaɲa] F lasagna

laser ['lejzer] M laser; **raio ~** laser beam

lástima ['lastʃima] F pity, compassion; (*infortúnio*) misfortune; **é uma ~ (que)** it's a shame (that); **lastimar** [lastʃi'mar] VT to lament; **lastimar-se** VR to complain, feel sorry for o.s.

lata ['lata] F can, tin (*BRIT*); (*material*) tin-plate; **~ de lixo** rubbish bin (*BRIT*), garbage can (*US*); **~ velha** (*col: carro*) old banger (*BRIT*) ou clunker (*US*)

latão [la'tãw] M brass

lataria [lata'ria] F (*Auto*) bodywork; (*enlatados*) canned food

latejar [late'ʒar] VI to throb

latente [la'tẽtʃi] ADJ latent

lateral [late'raw] (*pl* -**ais**) ADJ side, lateral ▶ F (*Futebol*) sideline ▶ M (*Futebol*) throw-in

latido [la'tʃidu] M bark(ing), yelp(ing)

latifundiário, -a [latʃifũ'dʒjarju, a] M/F landowner

latifúndio [latʃi'fũdʒju] M large estate

latim [la'tʃĩ] M (*Ling*) Latin; **gastar o seu ~** to waste one's breath

latino, -a [la'tʃinu, a] ADJ Latin; **latino-americano, -a** ADJ, M/F Latin-American

latir [la'tʃir] VI to bark, yelp

latitude [latʃi'tudʒi] F latitude; (*largura*) breadth; (*fig*) scope

latrocínio [latro'sinju] M armed robbery

laudo ['lawdu] M (*Jur*) decision; (*resultados*) findings *pl*; (*peça escrita*) report

lava ['lava] F lava

lavabo [la'vabu] M toilet

lavadeira [lava'dejra] F washerwoman

lavagem [la'vaʒẽ] F washing; **~ a seco** dry cleaning; **~ cerebral** brainwashing

lavanda [la'vãda] F (*Bot*) lavender; (*colônia*) lavender water; (*para lavar os dedos*) finger bowl

lavar [la'var] VT to wash; (*culpa*) to wash away; **~ a seco** to dry clean

lavatório [lava'tɔrju] M washbasin; (*aposento*) toilet

lavoura [la'vora] F tilling; (*agricultura*) farming; (*terreno*) plantation

laxativo, -a [laʃa'tʃivu, a] ADJ, M laxative

lazer [la'zer] M leisure

leal [le'aw] (*pl* -**ais**) ADJ loyal; **lealdade** [leaw'dadʒi] F loyalty

leão [le'ãw] (*pl* -**ões**) M lion; **L~** (*Astrologia*) Leo

lebre ['lɛbri] F hare

lecionar [lesjo'nar] VT, VI to teach

legal [le'gaw] (*pl* -**ais**) ADJ legal, lawful; (*col*) fine; (: *pessoa*) nice ▶ ADV (*col*) well; **(tá) ~!** OK!; **legalidade** [legali'dadʒi] F legality, lawfulness; **legalizar** [legali'zar] VT to legalize; (*documento*) to authenticate

legendado, -a [leʒẽ'dadu, a] ADJ (*filme*) subtitled

legendário, -a [leʒẽ'darju, a] ADJ legendary

legislação [leʒizla'sãw] F legislation

legislar [leʒiz'lar] VI to legislate ▶ VT to pass

legislativo, -a [leʒizla'tʃivu, a] ADJ legislative ▶ M legislature

legitimar [leʒitʃi'mar] VT to legitimize; (justificar) to legitimate

legume [le'gumi] M vegetable

lei [lej] F law; (regra) rule; (metal) standard

leigo, -a ['lejgu, a] ADJ (Rel) lay, secular ▶ M layman; **ser ~ em algo** (fig) to be no expert at sth, be unversed in sth

leilão [lej'lãw] (pl -**ões**) M auction; **vender em ~** to sell by auction, auction off; **leiloar** [lej'lwar] VT to auction

leio ['leju] VB ver **ler**

leitão, -toa [lej'tãw, 'toa] (pl -**ões/-s**) M/F sucking (BRIT) ou suckling (US) pig

leite ['lejtʃi] M milk; **~ em pó** powdered milk; **~ desnatado** ou **magro** skimmed milk; **~ de magnésia** milk of magnesia; **~ semidesnatado** semi-skimmed milk; **leiteira** [lej'tejra] F (para ferver) milk pan; (para servir) milk jug; **leiteiro, -a** [lej'tejru, a] ADJ (vaca, gado) dairy ▶ M/F milkman/woman

leitões [lej'tõjs] MPL de **leitão**

leitor, a [lej'tor(a)] M/F (pessoa) reader; (professor) lector ▶ M (objeto) reader; **~ de livros digitais** e-reader

leitura [lej'tura] F reading; (livro etc) reading matter

lema ['lɛma] M motto; (Pol) slogan

lembrança [lẽ'brãsa] F recollection, memory; (presente) souvenir; **lembranças** FPL (recomendações): **~s a sua mãe!** regards to your mother!

lembrar [lẽ'brar] VT, VI to remember; **lembrar-se** VR: **~(-se) de** to remember; **~(-se) (de) que** to remember that; **~ algo a alguém, ~ alguém de algo** to remind sb of sth; **~ alguém de que, ~ a alguém que** to remind sb that; **ele lembra meu irmão** he reminds me of my brother, he is like my brother; **lembrete** [lẽ'bretʃi] M reminder

leme ['lɛmi] M rudder; (Náut) helm; (fig) control

lenço ['lẽsu] M handkerchief; (de pescoço) scarf; (de cabeça) headscarf; **~ de papel** tissue; **~ umedecido** baby wipe

lençol [lẽ'sɔw] (pl -**óis**) M sheet; **estar em maus lençóis** to be in a fix

lenda ['lẽda] F legend; (fig: mentira) lie; **lendário, -a** [lẽ'darju, a] ADJ legendary

lenha ['lɛɲa] F firewood

lente ['lẽtʃi] F lens sg; **~ de aumento** magnifying glass; **~s de contato** contact lenses

lentidão [lẽtʃi'dãw] F slowness

lento, -a ['lẽtu, a] ADJ slow

leoa [le'oa] F lioness

leões [le'õjs] MPL de **leão**

leopardo [ljo'pardu] M leopard

lepra ['lɛpra] F leprosy

leque ['lɛki] M fan; (fig) array

ler [ler] VT, VI to read

lesão [le'zãw] (pl -**ões**) F harm, injury; (Jur) violation; (Med) lesion; **~ corporal** (Jur) bodily harm

lesar [le'zar] VT to harm, damage; (direitos) to violate

lésbica ['lɛzbika] F lesbian
lesma ['lezma] F slug; (*fig: pessoa*) slowcoach
lesões [le'zõjs] FPL *de* **lesão**
lesse ['lesi] VB *ver* **ler**
leste ['lɛstʃi] M east
letal [le'taw] (*pl* **-ais**) ADJ lethal
letargia [letar'ʒia] F lethargy
letivo, -a [le'tʃivu, a] ADJ school *atr*; **ano ~** academic year
letra ['letra] F letter; (*caligrafia*) handwriting; (*de canção*) lyrics *pl*; **Letras** FPL (*curso*) language and literature; **à ~** literally; **ao pé da ~** literally, word for word; **~ de câmbio** (*Com*) bill of exchange; **~ de imprensa** print; **letrado, -a** [le'tradu, a] ADJ learned, erudite ▶ M/F scholar; **letreiro** [le'trejru] M sign, notice; (*inscrição*) inscription; (*Cinema*) subtitle
leu [lew] VB *ver* **ler**
léu [lɛw] M: **ao ~** (*à toa*) aimlessly; (*à mostra*) uncovered
leucemia [lewse'mia] F leukaemia (*BRIT*), leukemia (*US*)
levado, -a [le'vadu, a] ADJ mischievous; (*criança*) naughty
levantador, a [levãta'dor(a)] ADJ lifting ▶ M/F: **~ de pesos** weightlifter
levantamento [levãta'mẽtu] M lifting, raising; (*revolta*) uprising, rebellion; (*arrolamento*) survey
levantar [levã'tar] VT to lift, raise; (*voz, capital*) to raise; (*apanhar*) to pick up; (*suscitar*) to arouse; (*ambiente*) to brighten up ▶ VI to stand up; (*da cama*) to get up; (*dar vida*) to brighten; **levantar-se** VR to stand up; (*da cama*) to get up; (*rebelar-se*) to rebel
levar [le'var] VT to take; (*portar*) to carry; (*tempo*) to pass, spend;

(*roupa*) to wear; (*lidar com*) to handle; (*induzir*) to lead; (*filme*) to show; (*peça teatral*) to put on; (*vida*) to lead ▶ VI to get a beating; **~ a** to lead to; **~ a mal** to take amiss
leve ['lɛvi] ADJ light; (*insignificante*) slight; **de ~** lightly, softly
leviandade [levjã'dadʒi] F frivolity
leviano, -a [le'vjanu, a] ADJ frivolous
lha [ʎa] = **lhe** + **a**
lhas [ʎas] = **lhe** + **as**
lhe [ʎi] PRON (*a ele*) to him; (*a ela*) to her; (*a você*) to you
lhes [ʎis] PRON PL (*a eles/elas*) to them; (*a vocês*) to you
lho [ʎu] = **lhe** + **o**
lhos [ʎus] = **lhe** + **os**
li [li] VB *ver* **ler**
Líbano ['libanu] M: **o ~** Lebanon
libélula [li'bɛlula] F dragonfly
liberação [libera'sãw] F liberation
liberal [libe'raw] (*pl* **-ais**) ADJ, M/F liberal
liberar [libe'rar] VT to release; (*permitir*) to allow
liberdade [liber'dadʒi] F freedom; **liberdades** FPL (*direitos*) liberties; **pôr alguém em ~** to set sb free; **~ condicional** probation; **~ de palavra** freedom of speech; **~ sob palavra** parole
libertação [liberta'sãw] F release
libertino, -a [liber'tʃinu, a] ADJ loose-living ▶ M/F libertine
Líbia ['libja] F: **a ~** Libya
libidinoso, -a [libidʒi'nozu, ɔza] ADJ lecherous, lustful
líbio, -a ['libju, a] ADJ, M/F Libyan
libra ['libra] F pound; **L~** (*Astrologia*) Libra
lição [li'sãw] (*pl* **-ões**) F lesson
licença [li'sẽsa] F licence (*BRIT*), license (*US*); (*permissão*) permission;

(*do trabalho, Mil*) leave; **com ~** excuse me; **estar de ~** to be on leave; **dá ~?** may I?

licenciado, -a [lisẽ'sjadu, a] M/F graduate

licenciar [lisẽ'sjar] VT to license; **licenciar-se** VR (*Educ*) to graduate; (*ficar de licença*) to take leave; **licenciatura** [lisẽsja'tura] F (*título*) degree; (*curso*) degree course

liceu [li'sew] (*PT*) M secondary school (*BRIT*) ou high (*US*) school

lições [li'sõjs] FPL *de* **lição**

licor [li'kor] M liqueur

lidar [li'dar] VI: **~ com** (*ocupar-se*) to deal with; (*combater*) to struggle against; **~ em algo** to work in sth

líder ['lider] M/F leader; **liderança** [lide'rãsa] F leadership; (*Esporte*) lead; **liderar** [lide'rar] VT to lead

ligado, -a [li'gadu, a] ADJ (*Tec*) connected; (*luz, rádio etc*) on; (*metal*) alloy

ligadura [liga'dura] F bandage

ligamento [liga'mẽtu] M ligament

ligar [li'gar] VT to tie, bind; (*unir*) to join, connect; (*luz, TV*) to switch on; (*afetivamente*) to bind together; (*carro*) to start (up) ▶ VI (*telefonar*) to ring; **ligar-se** VR to join; **~-se com alguém** to join with sb; **~-se a algo** to be connected with sth; **~ para alguém** to ring sb up; **~ para** *ou* **a algo** (*dar atenção*) to take notice of sth; (*dar importância*) to care about sth; **eu nem ligo** it doesn't bother me; **não ligo a mínima (para)** I couldn't care less (about)

ligeiro, -a [li'ʒejru, a] ADJ light; (*ferimento*) slight; (*referência*) passing; (*conhecimentos*) scant;

(*rápido*) quick, swift; (*ágil*) nimble ▶ ADV swiftly, nimbly

lilás [li'las] ADJ, M lilac

lima ['lima] F (*laranja*) type of orange; (*ferramenta*) file; **~ de unhas** nailfile

limão [li'mãw] (*pl* **-ões**) M lime; (*tb*: **~-galego**) lemon

limiar [li'mjar] M threshold

limitação [limita'sãw] (*pl* **-ões**) F limitation, restriction

limitar [limi'tar] VT to limit, restrict; **limitar-se** VR: **~-se a** to limit o.s. to; **~(-se) com** to border on; **limite** [li'mitʃi] M limit, boundary; (*fig*) limit; **passar dos limites** to go too far

limo ['limu] M (*Bot*) water weed; (*lodo*) slime

limoeiro [li'mwejru] M lemon tree

limões [li'mõjs] MPL *de* **limão**

limonada [limo'nada] F lemonade (*BRIT*), lemon soda (*US*)

limpar [lĩ'par] VT to clean; (*lágrimas, suor*) to wipe away; (*polir*) to shine, polish; (*fig*) to clean up; (*roubar*) to rob

limpo, -a ['lĩpu, a] PP *de* **limpar** ▶ ADJ clean; (*céu, consciência*) clear; (*Com*) net; (*fig*) pure; (*col: pronto*) ready; **passar a ~** to make a fair copy; **tirar a ~** to find out the truth about, clear up; **estar ~ com alguém** (*col*) to be in with sb

linchar [lĩ'ʃar] VT to lynch

lindo, -a ['lĩdu, a] ADJ lovely

lingerie [lĩʒe'ri] M lingerie

língua ['lĩgwa] F tongue; (*linguagem*) language; **botar a ~ para fora** to stick out one's tongue; **dar com a ~ nos dentes** to let the cat out of the bag; **estar na ponta da ~** to be on the tip of one's tongue

linguado [lĩ'gwadu] M (peixe) sole
linguagem [lĩ'gwaʒẽ] (pl **-ns**) F (tb: Comput) language; **~ de máquina** (Comput) machine language
linguarudo, -a [lĩgwa'rudu, a] ADJ gossiping ▶ M/F gossip
linguiça [lĩ'gwisa] F sausage
linha ['liɲa] F line; (para costura) thread; (barbante) string, cord; **linhas** FPL (carta) letter sg; **em ~** in line, in a row; (Comput) on line; **fora de ~** out of production; **manter/perder a ~** to keep/lose one's cool; **o telefone não deu ~** the line was dead; **~ aérea** airline; **~ de apoio** (PT) helpline; **~ de mira** sights pl; **~ de montagem** assembly line; **~ férrea** railway (BRIT), railroad (US)
linho ['liɲu] M linen; (planta) flax
liquidação [likida'sãw] (pl **-ões**) F liquidation; (em loja) (clearance) sale; (de conta) settlement; **em ~** on sale
liquidar [liki'dar] VT to liquidate; (conta) to settle; (mercadoria) to sell off; (assunto) to lay to rest ▶ VI (loja) to have a sale; **liquidar-se** VR (destruir-se) to be destroyed; **~ (com) alguém** (fig: arrasar) to destroy sb; (: matar) to do away with sb
liquidificador [likwidʒifika'dor] M liquidizer
líquido, -a ['likidu, a] ADJ liquid, fluid; (Com) net ▶ M liquid
lira ['lira] F lyre; (moeda) lira
lírio ['lirju] M lily
Lisboa [liz'boa] N Lisbon; **lisboeta** [liz'bweta] ADJ Lisbon atr ▶ M/F inhabitant ou native of Lisbon
liso, -a ['lizu, a] ADJ smooth; (tecido) plain; (cabelo) straight; (col: sem dinheiro) broke
lisonjear [lizõ'ʒjar] VT to flatter

lista ['lista] F list; (listra) stripe; (PT: menu) menu; **~ negra** blacklist; **~ telefônica** telephone directory; **listar** [lis'tar] VT to list
listra ['listra] F stripe; **listrado, -a** [lis'tradu, a] ADJ striped
literal [lite'raw] (pl **-ais**) ADJ literal
literário, -a [lite'rarju, a] ADJ literary
literatura [litera'tura] F literature; **Literatura de cordel** see note

> **Literatura de cordel** is a type of literature typical of the north-east of Brazil, and published in the form of cheaply printed booklets. Their authors hang these booklets from wires attached to walls in the street so that people can look at them. While they do this, the authors sing their stories aloud. **Literatura de cordel** deals both with local events and people, and with everyday public life, almost always in an irreverent manner.

litoral [lito'raw] (pl **-ais**) ADJ coastal ▶ M coast, seaboard
litro ['litru] M litre (BRIT), liter (US)
livrar [li'vrar] VT to release, liberate; (salvar) to save; **livrar-se** VR to escape; **~-se de** to get rid of; (compromisso) to get out of; **Deus me livre!** Heaven forbid!
livraria [livra'ria] F bookshop (BRIT), bookstore (US)
livre ['livri] ADJ free; (lugar) unoccupied; (desimpedido) clear, open; **~ de impostos** tax-free; **livre-arbítrio** M free will
livro ['livru] M book; **~ brochado** paperback; **~ de bolso** pocket-sized book; **~ de cheques** cheque book (BRIT), check book (US); **~ de consulta** reference book;

~ eletrônico e-book;
~ encadernado *ou* **de capa dura**
hardback

lixa ['liʃa] F sandpaper; *(de unhas)*
nailfile; *(peixe)* dogfish; **lixar**
[li'ʃar] VT to sand

lixeira [li'ʃejra] F dustbin (BRIT),
garbage can (US)

lixeiro [li'ʃejru] M dustman (BRIT),
garbage man (US)

lixo ['liʃu] M rubbish, garbage (US);
ser um ~ *(col)* to be rubbish;
~ atômico nuclear waste

-lo [lu] PRON him; *(você)* you;
(coisa) it

lobo ['lobu] M wolf

locação [loka'sãw] *(pl* **-ões)** F
lease; *(de vídeo etc)* rental

locador, a [loka'dor(a)] M/F *(de
casa)* landlord; *(de carro, filme)*
rental agent ▶ F rental company;
~a de vídeo video rental shop

local [lo'kaw] *(pl* **-ais)** ADJ local ▶ M
site, place ▶ F *(notícia)* story;
localidade [lokali'dadʒi] F *(lugar)*
locality; *(povoação)* town;
localização [lokaliza'sãw] *(pl*
-ões) F location; **localizar**
[lokali'zar] VT to locate; *(situar)* to
place; **localizar-se** VR to be
located; *(orientar-se)* to get one's
bearings

loção [lo'sãw] *(pl* **-ões)** F lotion;
~ após-barba aftershave (lotion)

locatário, -a [loka'tarju, a] M/F
(de casa) tenant; *(de carro, filme)*
hirer

loções [lo'sõjs] FPL *de* **loção**

locomotiva [lokomo'tʃiva] F
railway (BRIT) *ou* railroad (US)
engine, locomotive

locomover-se [lokomo'versi]
VR to move around

locutor, a [loku'tor(a)] M/F

(TV, Rádio) announcer

lógica ['lɔʒika] F logic; **lógico, -a**
['lɔʒiku, a] ADJ logical; **(é) lógico!**
of course!

logo ['lɔgu] ADV *(imediatamente)*
right away, at once; *(em breve)*
soon; *(justamente)* just, right; *(mais
tarde)* later; **~, ~** in no time; **~ mais**
later; **~ no começo** right at the
start; **~ que, tão ~** as soon as; **até
~!** bye!; **~ antes/depois** just
before/shortly afterwards; **~ de
saída** *ou* **de cara** straightaway,
right away

logotipo [logo'tʃipu] M logo

lograr [lo'grar] VT *(alcançar)* to
achieve; *(obter)* to get, obtain;
(enganar) to cheat; **~ fazer** to
manage to do

loiro, -a ['lojru, a] ADJ = **louro**

loja ['lɔʒa] F shop; **~ de presentes**
gift shop (BRIT), gift store (US);
lojista [lo'ʒista] M/F shopkeeper

lombo ['lõbu] M back; *(carne)* loin

lona ['lɔna] F canvas

Londres ['lõdris] N London;
londrino, -a [lõ'drinu, a] ADJ
London *atr* ▶ M/F Londoner

longa-metragem *(pl*
longas-metragens) M: **(filme
de) ~** feature (film)

longe ['lõʒi] ADV far, far away ▶ ADJ
distant; **ao ~** in the distance; **de ~**
from far away; *(sem dúvida)* by a
long way; **~ de** a long way *ou* far
from; **~ disso** far from it; **ir ~
demais** *(fig)* to go too far

longínquo, -a [lõ'ʒĩkwu, a] ADJ
distant, remote

longitude [lõʒi'tudʒi] F *(Geo)*
longitude

longo, -a ['lõgu, a] ADJ long ▶ M
(vestido) long dress, evening dress;
ao ~ de along, alongside

lotação [lota'sãw] F capacity; (de funcionários) complement; (BR: ônibus) bus; ~ **completa** ou **esgotada** (Teatro) sold out

lotado, -a [lo'tadu, a] ADJ (Teatro) full; (ônibus) full up; (bar, praia) packed, crowded

lotar [lo'tar] VT to fill, pack; (funcionário) to place ▶ VI to fill up

lote ['lɔtʃi] M portion, share; (em leilão) lot; (terreno) plot; (de ações) parcel, batch

loteria [lote'ria] F lottery; ~ **esportiva** football pools pl (BRIT), lottery (US)

louça ['losa] F china; (conjunto) crockery; (tb: ~ **sanitária**) bathroom suite; **de** ~ china atr; ~ **de barro** earthenware; ~ **de jantar** dinner service; **lavar a** ~ to do the washing up (BRIT) ou the dishes

louco, -a ['loku, a] ADJ crazy, mad; (sucesso) runaway; (frio) freezing ▶ M/F lunatic; ~ **varrido** raving mad; ~ **de fome/raiva** ravenous/hopping mad; ~ **por** crazy about; **deixar alguém** ~ to drive sb crazy; **loucura** [lo'kura] F madness; (ato) crazy thing; **ser loucura (fazer)** to be crazy (to do); **ser uma loucura** to be crazy; (col: ser muito bom) to be fantastic

louro, -a ['loru, a] ADJ blond, fair ▶ M laurel; (Culin) bay leaf; (papagaio) parrot; **louros** MPL (fig) laurels

louva-a-deus ['lova-] M INV praying mantis

louvar [lo'var] VT, VI: ~ **(a)** to praise; **louvável** [lo'vavew] (pl -eis) ADJ praiseworthy

louvor [lo'vor] M praise

LP ABR M LP (record)

Ltda. ABR (= Limitada) Ltd

lua ['lua] F moon; **estar** ou **viver no mundo da** ~ to have one's head in the clouds; **estar de** ~ (col) to be in a mood; **ser de** ~ (col) to be moody; ~ **cheia/nova** full/new moon; ~ **de mel** honeymoon

luar ['lwar] M moonlight

lubrificante [lubrifi'kãtʃi] M lubricant

lúcido, -a ['lusidu, a] ADJ lucid

lúcio ['lusju] M (peixe) pike

lucrar [lu'krar] VT (tirar proveito) to profit from ou by; (dinheiro) to make; (gozar) to enjoy ▶ VI to make a profit; ~ **com** ou **em** to profit by

lucrativo, -a [lukra'tʃivu, a] ADJ lucrative, profitable

lucro ['lukru] M gain; (Com) profit; ~**s e perdas** (Com) profit and loss

lugar [lu'gar] M place; (espaço) space, room; (para sentar) seat; (emprego) job; (ocasião) opportunity; **em** ~ **de** instead of; **dar** ~ **a** (causar) to give rise to; ~ **comum** commonplace; **em primeiro** ~ in the first place; **em algum/nenhum/todo** ~ somewhere/nowhere/everywhere; **em outro** ~ somewhere else, elsewhere; **ter** ~ (acontecer) to take place; ~ **de nascimento** place of birth; **lugarejo** [luga'reʒu] M village

lula ['lula] F squid

lume ['lumi] M fire; (luz) light

luminária [lumi'narja] F lamp; **luminárias** FPL (iluminações) illuminations

luminosidade [luminozi'dadʒi] F brightness

luminoso, -a [lumi'nozu, ɔza] ADJ luminous; (fig: raciocínio) clear; (: ideia, talento) brilliant; (letreiro) illuminated

lunar [lu'nar] ADJ lunar ▶ M (*na pele*) mole

lunático, -a [lu'natʃiku, a] ADJ mad

lusitano, -a [luzi'tanu, a] ADJ Portuguese, Lusitanian

luso, -a ['luzu, a] ADJ Portuguese; **luso-brasileiro, -a** (*pl* **luso-brasileiros**) ADJ Luso-Brazilian

lustre ['lustri] M gloss, sheen; (*fig*) lustre (BRIT), luster (US); (*luminária*) chandelier

luta ['luta] F fight, struggle; **~ de boxe** boxing; **~ livre** wrestling; **lutador, a** [luta'dor(a)] M/F fighter; (*atleta*) wrestler; **lutar** [lu'tar] VI to fight, struggle; (*luta livre*) to wrestle ▶ VT (*caratê, judô*) to do; **lutar contra/por algo** to fight against/for sth; **lutar para fazer algo** to fight *ou* struggle to do sth; **lutar com** (*dificuldades*) to struggle against; (*competir*) to fight with

luto ['lutu] M mourning; (*tristeza*) grief; **de ~** in mourning; **pôr ~** to go into mourning

luva ['luva] F glove; **luvas** FPL (*pagamento*) payment *sg*; (*ao locador*) fee *sg*

Luxemburgo [luʃē'burgu] M: **o ~** Luxembourg

luxo ['luʃu] M luxury; **de ~** luxury *atr*; **dar-se ao ~ de** to allow o.s. to; **luxuoso, -a** [lu'ʃwozu, ɔza] ADJ luxurious

luxúria [lu'ʃurja] F lust

luz [luz] F light; (*eletricidade*) electricity; **à ~ de** by the light of; (*fig*) in the light of; **a meia ~** with subdued lighting; **dar à ~ (um filho)** to give birth (to a son); **deu-me uma ~** I had an idea

ma [ma] PRON = **me + a**

má [ma] ADJ F *de* **mau**

maca ['maka] F stretcher

maçã [ma'sã] F apple; **~ do rosto** cheekbone

macabro, -a [ma'kabru, a] ADJ macabre

macacão [maka'kãw] (*pl* **-ões**) M (*de trabalhador*) overalls *pl* (BRIT), coveralls *pl* (US); (*da moda*) jump-suit

macaco, -a [ma'kaku, a] M/F monkey ▶ M (*Mecânica*) jack; **(fato) ~** (PT) overalls *pl* (BRIT), coveralls *pl* (US); **~ velho** (*fig*) old hand

macacões [maka'kõjs] MPL *de* **macacão**

maçador, a [masa'dor(a)] (PT) ADJ boring

maçaneta [masa'neta] F knob

maçante [ma'sãtʃi] (BR) ADJ boring

macarrão [maka'hãw] M pasta; (*em forma de canudo*) spaghetti;

macarronada [makaho'nada] F pasta with cheese and tomato sauce

macete [ma'setʃi] M mallet

machado [ma'ʃadu] M axe (BRIT), ax (US)

machista [ma'ʃista] ADJ chauvinistic, macho ▶ M male chauvinist

macho ['maʃu] ADJ male; (fig) virile, manly; (valentão) tough ▶ M male; (Tec) tap

machucado, -a [maʃu'kadu, a] ADJ hurt; (pé, braço) bad ▶ M injury; (área machucada) sore patch

machucar [maʃu'kar] VT to hurt; (produzir contusão) to bruise ▶ VI to hurt; **machucar-se** VR to hurt o.s.

maciço, -a [ma'sisu, a] ADJ solid; (espesso) thick; (quantidade) massive

macio, -a [ma'siu, a] ADJ soft; (liso) smooth

maço ['masu] M (de folhas, notas) bundle; (de cigarros) packet

maçom [ma'sõ] (pl **-ns**) M (free)mason

maconha [ma'kɔɲa] F dope; **cigarro de ~** joint

maçons [ma'sõs] MPL de **maçom**

má-criação (pl **-ões**) F rudeness; (ato, dito) rude thing

mácula ['makula] F stain, blemish

macumba [ma'kũba] F ≈ voodoo; (despacho) macumba offering;

macumbeiro, -a [makũ'bejru, a] ADJ ≈ voodoo atr ▶ M/F follower of macumba

madama [ma'dama] F = **madame**

madame [ma'dami] F (senhora) lady; (col: dona de casa) lady of the house

madeira [ma'dejra] F wood ▶ M Madeira (wine); **de ~** wooden; **bater na ~** (fig) to touch (BRIT) ou knock on (US) wood;

~ compensada plywood

madeirense [madej'rẽsi] ADJ, M/F Madeiran

madeixa [ma'dejʃa] F (de cabelo) lock

madrasta [ma'drasta] F stepmother

madrepérola [madre'pɛrola] F mother of pearl

Madri [ma'dri] N Madrid

Madrid [ma'drid] (PT) N Madrid

madrinha [ma'driɲa] F godmother

madrugada [madru'gada] F (early) morning; (alvorada) dawn, daybreak

madrugar [madru'gar] VI to get up early; (aparecer cedo) to be early

maduro, -a [ma'duro, a] ADJ ripe; (fig) mature; (: prudente) prudent

mãe [mãj] F mother; **~ adotiva** ou **de criação** adoptive mother

maestro, -trina [ma'ɛstru, 'trina] M/F conductor

má-fé F malicious intent

magia [ma'ʒia] F magic

mágica ['maʒika] F magic; (truque) magic trick; ver tb **mágico**

mágico, -a ['maʒiku, a] ADJ magic ▶ M/F magician

magistério [maʒis'tɛrju] M (ensino) teaching; (profissão) teaching profession; (professorado) teachers pl

magnético, -a [mag'nɛtʃiku, a] ADJ magnetic

magnífico, -a [mag'nifiku, a] ADJ splendid, magnificent

mago ['magu] M magician; **os reis ~s** the Three Wise Men, the Three Kings

mágoa ['magwa] F (tristeza) sorrow, grief; (fig: desagrado) hurt

magoado, -a [ma'gwadu, a] ADJ hurt

magoar [ma'gwar] VT, VI to hurt;
  magoar-se VR: **~-se com algo** to
  be hurt by sth
magro, -a ['magru, a] ADJ (pessoa)
  slim; (carne) lean; (fig: parco)
  meagre (BRIT), meager (US); (leite)
  skimmed
maio ['maju] M May
maiô [ma'jo] (BR) M swimsuit
maionese [majo'nɛzi] F
  mayonnaise
maior [ma'jɔr] ADJ (compar: de
  tamanho) bigger; (: de importância)
  greater; (superl: de tamanho)
  biggest; (: de importância) greatest
  ▶ M/F adult; **~ de idade** of age,
  adult; **~ de 21 anos** over 21;
maioria [majo'ria] F majority; **a**
  maioria de most of; **maioridade**
  [majori'dadʒi] F adulthood

PALAVRA-CHAVE

mais [majs] ADV 1 (compar): **mais**
  magro/inteligente (do que)
  thinner/more intelligent (than);
  ele trabalha mais (do que eu) he
  works more (than me)
  2 (superl): **o mais ...** the most ...; **o**
  mais magro/inteligente the
  thinnest/most intelligent
  3 (negativo): **ele não trabalha**
  mais aqui he doesn't work here
  any more; **nunca mais** never
  again
  4 (+ adj, valor intensivo): **que livro**
  mais chato! what a boring book!
  5: **por mais que** however much;
  por mais que se esforce ... no
  matter how hard you try ...; **por**
  mais que eu quisesse ... much as
  I should like to ...
  6: **a mais, temos um a mais**
  we've got one extra
  7 (tempo): **mais cedo ou mais**
  tarde sooner or later; **a mais**
  tempo sooner; **logo mais** later
  on; **no mais tardar** at the latest
  8 (frases): **mais ou menos** more or
  less; **mais uma vez** once more;
  cada vez mais more and more;
  sem mais nem menos out of the
  blue
  ▶ ADJ 1 (compar): **mais (do que)**
  more (than); **ele tem mais**
  dinheiro (do que o irmão) he's
  got more money (than his brother)
  2 (superl): **ele é quem tem mais**
  dinheiro he's got most money
  3 (+ números): **ela tem mais de dez**
  bolsas she's got more than ten
  bags
  4 (negativo): **não tenho mais**
  dinheiro I haven't got any more
  money
  5 (adicional) else; **mais alguma**
  coisa? anything else?; **nada/**
  ninguém mais nothing/no-one
  else
  ▶ PREP: **2 mais 2 são 4** 2 and 2 ou
  plus 2 is 4
  ▶ M: **o mais** the rest

maisena [maj'zena] F cornflour
  (BRIT), corn starch (US)
maiúscula [ma'juskula] F capital
  letter
majestade [maʒes'tadʒi] F
  majesty; **majestoso, -a**
  [maʒes'tozu, ɔza] ADJ majestic
major [ma'ʒɔr] M (Mil) major
majoritário, -a [maʒori'tarju, a]
  ADJ majority atr
mal [maw] (pl **males**) M harm;
  (Med) illness ▶ ADV badly; (quase
  não) hardly ▶ CONJ hardly;
  ~ desliguei o fone, a campainha
  tocou I had hardly put the phone
  down when the doorbell rang;

falar ~ de alguém to speak ill of sb, run sb down; **não faz ~** never mind; **estar ~** (*doente*) to be ill; **passar ~** to be sick; **estar de ~ com alguém** not to be speaking to sb; **~ de Alzheimer** Alzheimer's (disease)

mal- [maw] PREFIXO badly, mis-

mala ['mala] F suitcase; (*BR Auto*) boot, trunk (*US*); **malas** FPL (*bagagem*) luggage *sg*; **fazer as ~s** to pack

malabarismo [malaba'rizmu] M juggling; **malabarista** [malaba'rista] M/F juggler

mal-acabado, -a ADJ badly finished; (*pessoa*) deformed

malagueta [mala'geta] F chilli (*BRIT*) *ou* chili (*US*) pepper

Malaísia [mala'izja] F: **a ~** Malaysia

malandragem [malã'draʒẽ] F (*patifaria*) double-dealing; (*preguiça*) idleness; (*esperteza*) cunning

malária [ma'larja] F malaria

mal-arrumado, -a [-ahu'madu, a] ADJ untidy

malcomportado, -a [mawkõpor'tadu, a] ADJ badly behaved

malcriado, -a [maw'krjadu, a] ADJ rude ▶ M/F slob

maldade [maw'dadʒi] F cruelty; (*malícia*) malice

maldição [mawdʒi'sãw] (*pl* -ões) F curse

maldizer [mawdʒi'zer] (*irreg: como* **dizer**) VT to curse

maldoso, -a [maw'dozu, ɔza] ADJ wicked; (*malicioso*) malicious

maledicência [maledʒi'sẽsja] F slander

mal-educado, -a ADJ rude ▶ M/F slob

malefício [male'fisju] M harm;

maléfico, -a [ma'lɛfiku, a] ADJ (*pessoa*) malicious; (*prejudicial*) harmful

mal-entendido, -a ADJ misunderstood ▶ M misunderstanding

mal-estar M indisposition; (*embaraço*) awkward situation

malfeito, -a [maw'fejtu, a] ADJ (*roupa*) poorly made; (*corpo*) misshapen

malfeitor, -a [mawfej'tor(a)] M/F wrongdoer

malha ['maʎa] F (*de rede*) mesh; (*tecido*) jersey; (*suéter*) sweater; (*de ginástica*) leotard; **fazer ~** (*PT*) to knit; **artigos de ~** knitwear; **vestido de ~** jersey dress

malhar [ma'ʎar] VT (*bater*) to beat; (*cereais*) to thresh; (*col: criticar*) to knock, run down

mal-humorado, -a [-umo'radu, a] ADJ grumpy, sullen

maligno, -a [ma'lignu, a] ADJ evil, malicious; (*danoso*) harmful; (*Med*) malignant

malograr [malo'grar] VT (*planos*) to upset; (*frustrar*) to thwart, frustrate ▶ VI (*planos*) to fall through; (*fracassar*) to fail; **malograr-se** VR to fall through; to fail

malpassado, -a [mawpa'sadu, a] ADJ underdone; (*bife*) rare

malsucedido, -a [mawsuse'dʒidu, a] ADJ unsuccessful

Malta ['mawta] F Malta

malta ['mawta] (*PT*) F gang, mob

maltrapilho, -a [mawtra'piʎu, a] ADJ in rags, ragged ▶ M/F ragamuffin

maluco, -a [ma'luku, a] ADJ crazy, daft ▶ M/F madman/woman

malvadeza [mawva'deza] F

wickedness; (*ato*) wicked thing
malvado, -a [maw'vadu, a] ADJ
wicked
Malvinas [maw'vinas] FPL: **as
(ilhas) ~** the Falklands, the
Falkland Islands
mama ['mama] F breast
mamadeira [mama'dejra] (BR) F
feeding bottle
mamãe [ma'mãj] F mum,
mummy
mamão [ma'mãw] (*pl* **-ões**) M
papaya
mamar [ma'mar] VT to suck;
(*dinheiro*) to extort ▶ VI to be
breastfed; **dar de ~ a um bebê** to
(breast)feed a baby
mamífero [ma'miferu] M
mammal
mamilo [ma'milu] M nipple
mamões [ma'mõjs] MPL *de*
mamão
manada [ma'nada] F herd, drove
mancada [mã'kada] F (*erro*)
mistake; (*gafe*) blunder; **dar uma
~** to blunder
mancar [mã'kar] VT to cripple ▶ VI
to limp; **mancar-se** VR (*col*) to get
the message, take the hint
Mancha ['mãʃa] F: **o canal da ~**
the English Channel
mancha ['mãʃa] F stain; (*na pele*)
mark, spot; **sem ~s** (*reputação*)
spotless; **manchado, -a** [mã'ʃadu,
a] ADJ soiled; (*malhado*) mottled,
spotted; **manchar** [mã'ʃar] VT to
stain, mark; (*reputação*) to soil
manchete [mã'ʃetʃi] F headline
manco, -a ['mãku, a] ADJ crippled,
lame ▶ M/F cripple
mandado [mã'dadu] M order;
(*Jur*) writ; (*tb*: **~ de segurança**)
injunction; **~ de prisão/busca**
arrest/search warrant; **~ de**

segurança injunction
mandão, -dona [mã'dãw, 'dona]
(*pl* **-ões/-s**) ADJ bossy, domineering
mandar [mã'dar] VT (*ordenar*) to
order; (*enviar*) to send ▶ VI to be in
charge; **mandar-se** VR (*col: partir*)
to make tracks, get going; (*fugir*)
to take off; **~ buscar** *ou* **chamar**
to send for; **~ fazer um vestido** to
have a dress made; **~ que alguém
faça, ~ alguém fazer** to tell sb to
do; **o que é que você manda?**
(*col*) what can I do for you?; **~ em
alguém** to boss sb around
mandato [mã'datu] M mandate;
(*ordem*) order; (*Pol*) term of office
mandioca [mã'dʒjɔka] F cassava,
manioc
mandões [mã'dõjs] MPL *de*
mandão
mandona [mã'dɔna] F *de*
mandão
maneira [ma'nejra] F (*modo*) way;
(*estilo*) style, manner; **maneiras**
FPL (*modos*) manners; **à ~ de** like;
de ~ que so that; **de ~ alguma** *ou*
nenhuma not at all; **desta ~** in
this way; **de qualquer ~** anyway;
não houve ~ de convencê-lo it
was impossible to convince him
maneiro, -a [ma'nejru, a] ADJ
(*ferramenta*) easy to use; (*roupa*)
attractive; (*trabalho*) easy; (*pessoa*)
capable; (*col: bacana*) great,
brilliant
manejar [mane'ʒar] VT
(*instrumento*) to handle; (*máquina*)
to work; **manejo** [ma'neʒu] M
handling
manequim [mane'kĩ] (*pl* **-ns**) M
(*boneco*) dummy ▶ M/F model
manga ['mãga] F sleeve; (*fruta*)
mango; **em ~s de camisa** in
(one's) shirt sleeves

m

mangueira [mã'gejra] F hose(pipe); (*árvore*) mango tree

manha ['maɲa] F guile, craftiness; (*destreza*) skill; (*ardil*) trick; (*birra*) tantrum; **fazer ~** to have a tantrum

manhã [ma'ɲã] F morning; **de** *ou* **pela ~** in the morning; **amanhã/ hoje de ~** tomorrow/this morning

manhoso, -a [ma'ɲozu, ɔza] ADJ crafty, sly; (*criança*) whining

mania [ma'nia] F (*Med*) mania; (*obsessão*) craze; **estar com ~ de ...** to have a thing about ...; **maníaco, -a** [ma'niaku, a] ADJ manic ▶ M/F maniac

manicômio [mani'komju] M asylum, mental hospital

manifestação [manifesta'sãw] (*pl* **-ões**) F show, display; (*expressão*) expression, declaration; (*política*) demonstration

manifestante [manifes'tãtʃi] M/F demonstrator

manifestar [manifes'tar] VT to show, display; (*declarar*) to express, declare

manifesto, -a [mani'fɛstu, a] ADJ obvious, clear ▶ M manifesto

manipulação [manipula'sãw] F handling; (*fig*) manipulation

manipular [manipu'lar] VT to manipulate; (*manejar*) to handle

manjericão [mãʒeri'kãw] M basil

manobra [ma'nɔbra] F manoeuvre (*BRIT*), maneuver (*US*); (*de mecanismo*) operation; (*de trens*) shunting; **manobrar** [mano'brar] VT to manoeuvre (*BRIT*), maneuver (*US*); (*mecanismo*) to operate, work; (*governar*) to take charge of; (*manipular*) to manipulate ▶ VI to manoeuvre *ou* maneuver

manso, -a ['mãsu, a] ADJ gentle; (*mar*) calm; (*animal*) tame

manta ['mãta] F blanket; (*xale*) shawl; (*agasalho*) cloak

manteiga [mã'tejga] F butter; **~ de cacau** cocoa butter

manter [mã'ter] (*irreg: como* **ter**) VT to maintain; (*num lugar*) to keep; (*uma família*) to support; (*a palavra*) to keep; (*princípios*) to abide by; **manter-se** VR to support o.s.; (*permanecer*) to remain; **mantimento** [mãtʃi'mẽtu] M maintenance; **mantimentos** MPL (*alimentos*) provisions

manual [ma'nwaw] (*pl* **-ais**) ADJ manual ▶ M handbook, manual

manufatura [manufa'tura] F manufacture; **manufaturar** [manufatu'rar] VT to manufacture

manusear [manu'zjar] VT to handle; (*livro*) to leaf through

mão [mãw] (*pl* **mãos**) F hand; (*de animal*) paw; (*de pintura*) coat; (*de direção*) flow of traffic; **à ~** by hand; (*perto*) at hand; **de segunda ~** second-hand; **em ~** by hand; **dar a ~ a alguém** to hold sb's hand; (*cumprimentar*) to shake hands with sb; **dar uma ~ a alguém** to give sb a hand, help sb out; **~ única/dupla** one-way/two-way traffic; **rua de duas ~s** two-way street; **~ de obra** labour (*BRIT*), labor (*US*)

mapa ['mapa] M map; (*gráfico*) chart

maquiagem [ma'kjaʒẽ] F = **maquilagem**

maquiar [ma'kjar] VT to make up; **maquiar-se** VR to make o.s. up, put on one's make-up

maquilagem [maki'laʒẽ], (*PT*) **maquilhagem** F make-up; (*ato*) making up

máquina ['makina] F machine; (*de trem*) engine; (*fig*) machinery; **~ de**

costura sewing machine; **~ fotográfica** camera; **~ de lavar (roupa)** washing machine; **~ de lavar louça** dishwasher; **escrito à ~** typewritten

maquinar [maki'nar] VT to plot ▶ VI to conspire

maquinista [maki'nista] M (*Ferro*) engine driver; (*Náut*) engineer

mar [mar] M sea; **por ~** by sea; **fazer-se ao ~** to set sail; **pleno ~, ~ alto** high sea; **o ~ Morto** the Dead Sea; **o ~ Negro** the Black Sea

maracujá [maraku'ʒa] M passion fruit; **pé de ~** passion flower

maratona [mara'tona] F marathon

maravilha [mara'viʎa] F marvel, wonder; **maravilhoso, -a** [maravi'ʎozu, ɔza] ADJ wonderful

marca ['marka] F mark; (*Com*) make, brand; (*carimbo*) stamp; **~ de fábrica** trademark; **~ registrada** registered trademark

marcação [marka'sãw] (*pl* **-ões**) F marking; (*em jogo*) scoring; (*de instrumento*) reading; (*Teatro*) action; (*PT Tel*) dialling

marcador [marka'dor] M marker; (*de livro*) bookmark; (*Esporte: quadro*) scoreboard; (: *jogador*) scorer

marca-passo [marka'pasu] (*pl* **-s**) M (*Med*) pacemaker

marcar [mar'kar] VT to mark; (*hora, data*) to fix, set; (*PT Tel*) to dial; (*gol, ponto*) to score ▶ VI to make one's mark; **~ uma consulta, ~ hora** to make an appointment; **~ um encontro com alguém** to arrange to meet sb

marcha ['marʃa] F march; (*de acontecimentos*) course; (*passo*) pace; (*Auto*) gear; (*progresso*) progress; **à ré** (BR), **~ atrás** (PT) reverse (gear); **pôr-se em ~** to set off

marchar [mar'ʃar] VI to go; (*andar a pé*) to walk; (*Mil*) to march

marco ['marku] M landmark; (*de janela*) frame; (*fig*) frontier; (*moeda*) mark

março ['marsu] M March

maré [ma'rɛ] F tide

marechal [mare'ʃaw] (*pl* **-ais**) M marshal

maremoto [mare'mɔtu] M tidal wave

marfim [mar'fĩ] M ivory

margarida [marga'rida] F daisy

margarina [marga'rina] F margarine

margem ['marʒẽ] (*pl* **-ns**) F (*borda*) edge; (*de rio*) bank; (*litoral*) shore; (*de impresso*) margin; (*fig: tempo*) time; (: *lugar*) space; **à ~ de** alongside

marginal [marʒi'naw] (*pl* **-ais**) ADJ marginal ▶ M/F delinquent

marido [ma'ridu] M husband

marimbondo [marĩ'bõdu] M hornet

marinha [ma'riɲa] F (*tb*: **~ de guerra**) navy; **~ mercante** merchant navy; **marinheiro** [mari'ɲejru] M seaman, sailor

marinho, -a [ma'riɲu, a] ADJ sea *atr*, marine

mariposa [mari'poza] F moth

marítimo, -a [ma'ritʃimu, a] ADJ sea *atr*

marketing ['marketʃĩŋ] M marketing

marmelada [marme'lada] F quince jam

m

marmelo [mar'mɛlu] M quince
marmita [mar'mita] F (*vasilha*) pot
mármore ['marmori] M marble
marquês, -quesa [mar'kes, 'keza] M/F marquis/marchioness
marqueteiro, -a [marke'tejru, a] M/F (*col*) spin doctor
marquise [mar'kizi] F awning, canopy
Marrocos [ma'hɔkus] M: **o ~** Morocco
marrom [ma'hõ] (*pl* **-ns**) ADJ, M brown
martelar [marte'lar] VT to hammer; (*amolar*) to bother ▶ VI to hammer; (*insistir*): **~ (em algo)** to keep *ou* harp on (about sth); **martelo** [mar'tɛlu] M hammer
mártir ['martʃir] M/F martyr; **martírio** [mar'tʃirju] M martyrdom; (*fig*) torment
marxista [mar'ksista] ADJ, M/F Marxist
mas [ma(j)s] CONJ but ▶ PRON = **me + as**
mascar [mas'kar] VT to chew
máscara ['maskara] F mask; (*para limpeza de pele*) face pack; **sob a ~ de** under the guise of; **mascarar** [maska'rar] VT to mask; (*disfarçar*) to disguise; (*encobrir*) to cover up
mascote [mas'kɔtʃi] F mascot
masculino, -a [masku'linu, a] ADJ masculine; (*Bio*) male
massa ['masa] F (*Fís, fig*) mass; (*de tomate*) paste; (*Culin: de pão*) dough; (: *macarrão etc*) pasta
massacrar [masa'krar] VT to massacre; **massacre** [ma'sakri] F massacre
massagear [masa'ʒjar] VT to massage; **massagem** [ma'saʒẽ] (*pl* **-ns**) F massage
mastigar [mastʃi'gar] VT to chew

mastro ['mastru] M (*Náut*) mast; (*para bandeira*) flagpole
masturbar-se [mastur'barsi] VR to masturbate
mata ['mata] F forest, wood
matadouro [mata'doru] M slaughterhouse
matança [ma'tãsa] F massacre; (*de reses*) slaughter(ing)
matar [ma'tar] VT to kill; (*sede*) to quench; (*fome*) to satisfy; (*aula*) to skip; (*trabalho: não aparecer*) to skive off; (: *fazer rápido*) to dash off; (*adivinhar*) to guess ▶ VI to kill; **matar-se** VR to kill o.s.; (*esfalfar-se*) to wear o.s. out; **um calor/uma dor de ~** stifling heat/excruciating pain
mate ['matʃi] ADJ matt ▶ M (*chá*) maté tea; (*xeque-mate*) checkmate
matemática [mate'matʃika] F mathematics *sg*, maths *sg* (BRIT), math (US); **matemático, -a** [mate'matʃiku, a] ADJ mathematical ▶ M/F mathematician
matéria [ma'tɛrja] F matter; (*Tec*) material; (*Educ: assunto*) subject; (*tema*) topic; (*jornalística*) story, article; **em ~ de** on the subject of
material [mate'rjaw] (*pl* **-ais**) ADJ material; (*físico*) physical ▶ M material; (*Tec*) equipment; **materialista** [materja'lista] ADJ materialistic; **materializar** [materjali'zar] VT to materialize; **materializar-se** VR to materialize
maternal [mater'naw] (*pl* **-ais**) ADJ motherly, maternal; **escola ~** nursery (school); **maternidade** [materni'dadʒi] F motherhood, maternity; (*hospital*) maternity hospital
materno, -a [ma'tɛrnu, a] ADJ

motherly, maternal; (*língua*) native
matinê [matʃi'ne] F matinée
matiz [ma'tʃiz] M (*de cor*) shade
mato ['matu] M scrubland, bush;
(*plantas agrestes*) scrub; (*o campo*)
country
matraca [ma'traka] F rattle
matrícula [ma'trikula] F (*lista*)
register; (*inscrição*) registration;
(*pagamento*) enrolment (BRIT) *ou*
enrollment (US) fee; (PT Auto)
registration number (BRIT), license
number (US); **fazer a ~** to enrol
(BRIT), enroll (US)
matrimonial [matrimo'njaw] (*pl*
-ais) ADJ marriage *atr*, matrimonial
matrimônio [matri'monju] M
marriage
matriz [ma'triz] F (*Med*) womb;
(*fonte*) source; (*molde*) mould
(BRIT), mold (US); (*Com*) head office
maturidade [maturi'dadʒi] F
maturity
mau, má [maw, ma] ADJ bad;
(*malvado*) evil, wicked ▶ M bad;
(*Rel*) evil; **os ~s** bad people; (*num filme*) the baddies
maus-tratos MPL ill-treatment *sg*
maxila [mak'sila] F jawbone
maxilar [maksi'lar] M jawbone
máxima ['masima] F maxim
máximo, -a ['masimu, a] ADJ
(*maior que todos*) greatest; (*o maior possível*) maximum ▶ M maximum;
(*o cúmulo*) peak; (*temperature*) high;
no ~ at most; **ao ~** to the utmost
me [mi] PRON (*direto*) me; (*indireto*)
(to) me; (*reflexivo*) (to) myself
meado ['mjadu] M middle; **em** *ou*
nos ~s de julho in mid-July
Meca ['mɛka] N Mecca
mecânica [me'kanika] F (*ciência*)
mechanics *sg*; (*mecanismo*)
mechanism; *ver tb* **mecânico**

mecânico, -a [me'kaniku, a] ADJ
mechanical ▶ M/F mechanic
mecanismo [meka'nizmu] M
mechanism
meço ['mɛsu] VB *ver* **medir**
medalha [me'daʎa] F medal;
medalhão [meda'ʎãw] (*pl* **-ões**) M
medallion
média ['mɛdʒja] F average; (*café*)
coffee with milk; **em ~** on average
mediano, -a [me'dʒjanu, a] ADJ
medium; (*médio*) average;
(*medíocre*) mediocre
mediante [me'dʒjãtʃi] PREP by
(means of), through; (*a troco de*) in
return for
medicamento [medʒika'mẽtu]
M medicine
medicina [medʒi'sina] F
medicine
médico, -a ['mɛdʒiku, a] ADJ
medical ▶ M/F doctor; **receita
médica** prescription
medida [me'dʒida] F measure;
(*providência*) step; (*medição*)
measurement; (*moderação*)
prudence; **à ~ que** while, as; **na ~
em que** in so far as; **feito sob ~**
made to measure; **ir além da ~** to
go too far; **tirar as ~s de alguém**
to take sb's measurements; **tomar
~s** to take steps; **tomar as ~s de**
to measure
medieval [medʒje'vaw] (*pl* **-ais**)
ADJ medieval
médio, -a ['mɛdʒju, a] ADJ (*dedo,
classe*) middle; (*tamanho, estatura*)
medium; (*mediano*) average;
ensino ~ secondary education
medir [me'dʒir] VT to measure;
(*atos, palavras*) to weigh; (*avaliar:
consequências, distâncias*) to weigh
up ▶ VI to measure; **quanto você
mede? — meço 1.60 m** how tall

are you? — I'm 1.60 m (tall)

meditar [medʒi'tar] vɪ to meditate; **~ sobre algo** to ponder (on) sth

mediterrâneo, -a [medʒite'hanju, a] ADJ Mediterranean ▶ M: **o M~** the Mediterranean

medo ['medu] M fear; **com ~** afraid; **meter ~ em alguém** to frighten sb; **ter ~ de** to be afraid of

medonho, -a [me'doɲu, a] ADJ terrible, awful

medroso, -a [me'drozu, ɔza] ADJ (com medo) frightened; (tímido) timid

megabyte [mega'bajtʃi] M megabyte

meia ['meja] F stocking; (curta) sock; (meia-entrada) half-price ticket ▶ NUM six; **meia-idade** F middle age; **pessoa de meia-idade** middle-aged person; **meia-noite** F midnight

meigo, -a ['mejgu, a] ADJ sweet

meio, -a ['meju, a] ADJ half ▶ ADV a bit, rather ▶ M middle; (recurso) means; (social, profissional) environment; (tb: **~ ambiente**) environment; **meios** MPL (recursos) means pl; **~ quilo** half a kilo; **um mês e ~** one and a half months; **cortar ao ~** to cut in half; **dividir algo a ~** to divide sth in half ou fifty-fifty; **em ~ a** amid; **no ~ (de)** in the middle (of); **~s de comunicação (de massa)** (mass) media pl; **~s de comunicação social** social media pl; **por ~ de** through; **meio-dia** M midday, noon; **por meio-fios** M kerb (BRIT), curb (US); **meio-termo** (pl **meios-termos**) M (fig) compromise

mel [mɛw] M honey

melaço [me'lasu] M treacle (BRIT), molasses sg (US)

melancia [melã'sia] F watermelon

melancolia [melãko'lia] F melancholy, sadness; **melancólico, -a** [melã'kɔliku, a] ADJ melancholy, sad

melão [me'lãw] (pl **-ões**) M melon

melhor [me'ʎɔr] ADJ, ADV (compar) better; (superl) best; **~ que nunca** better than ever; **quanto mais ~** the more the better; **seria ~ começarmos** we had better begin; **tanto ~** so much the better; **ou ~ ...** (ou antes) or rather ...; **melhora** [me'ʎɔra] F improvement; **melhoras!** get well soon!; **melhorar** [meʎo'rar] vт to improve, make better; (doente) to cure ▶ vi to improve, get better

melodia [melo'dʒia] F melody; (composição) tune

melões [me'lõjs] MPL de **melão**

melro ['mɛwhu] M blackbird

membro ['mẽbru] M member; (Anat: braço, perna) limb

memória [me'mɔrja] F memory; **memórias** FPL (de autor) memoirs; **de ~** by heart

memorizar [memori'zar] vт to memorize

mencionar [mẽsjo'nar] vт to mention

mendigar [mẽdʒi'gar] vт to beg for ▶ vi to beg; **mendigo, -a** [mẽ'dʒigu, a] M/F beggar

menina [me'nina] F: **~ do olho** pupil; **ser a ~ dos olhos de alguém** (fig) to be the apple of sb's eye; ver tb **menino**

meninada [meni'nada] F kids pl

menino, -a [me'ninu, a] M/F boy/girl

menopausa [meno'pawza] F menopause

menor [me'nɔr] ADJ (mais pequeno: compar) smaller; (: superl) smallest; (mais jovem: compar) younger; (: superl) youngest; (o mínimo) least, slightest; (tb: ~ **de idade**) under age ▶ M/F juvenile, young person; (Jur) minor; **não tenho a ~ ideia** I haven't the slightest idea

(PALAVRA-CHAVE)

menos ['menus] ADJ 1(compar): **menos (do que)** (quantidade) less (than); (número) fewer (than); **com menos entusiasmo** with less enthusiasm; **menos gente** fewer people
2 (superl) least; **é o que tem menos culpa** he is the least to blame
▶ ADV 1(compar): **menos (do que)** less (than); **gostei menos do que do outro** I liked it less than the other one
2 (superl): **é o menos inteligente da classe** he is the least bright in his class; **de todas elas é a que menos me agrada** out of all of them she's the one I like least; **pelo menos** at (the very) least
3 (frases): **temos sete a menos** we are seven short; **não é para menos** it's no wonder; **isso é o de menos** that's nothing
▶ PREP (exceção) except; (números) minus; **todos menos eu** everyone except (for) me; **5 menos 2** 5 minus 2
▶ CONJ: **a menos que** unless; **a menos que ele venha amanhã** unless he comes tomorrow
▶ M: **o menos** the least

menosprezar [menuspre'zar] VT (subestimar) to underrate; (desprezar) to despise, scorn

mensageiro, -a [mêsa'zejru, a] M/F messenger

mensagem [mê'saʒẽ] (pl **-ns**) F message; ~ **de texto** text (message); **mandar uma ~ de texto para alguém** to text sb

mensal [mê'saw] (pl **-ais**) ADJ monthly; **ele ganha £2000 mensais** he earns £2000 a month; **mensalidade** [mêsali'dadʒi] F monthly payment; **mensalmente** [mêsaw'mẽtʃi] ADV monthly

menstruação [mêstrwa'sãw] F period; (Med) menstruation

menta ['mêta] F mint

mental [mê'taw] (pl **-ais**) ADJ mental; **mentalidade** [mêtali'dadʒi] F mentality

mente ['mêtʃi] F mind; **de boa ~** willingly; **ter em ~** to bear in mind

mentir [mê'tʃir] VI to lie

mentira [mê'tʃira] F lie; (ato) lying; **parece ~ que** it seems incredible that; **de ~** not for real; **~!** (acusação) that's a lie!, you're lying; (de surpresa) you don't say!, no!; **mentiroso, -a** [mêtʃi'rozu, ɔza] ADJ lying ▶ M/F liar

menu [me'nu] M (tb: Comput) menu

mercado [mer'kadu] M market; **M~ Comum** Common Market; ~ **negro** ou **paralelo** black market

mercadoria [merkado'ria] F commodity; **mercadorias** FPL (produtos) goods

mercearia [mersja'ria] F grocer's (shop) (BRIT), grocery store

mercúrio [mer'kurju] M mercury

merda ['mɛrda] (!) F shit (!) ▶ M/F (pessoa) jerk; **a ~ do carro** the bloody (BRIT) ou goddamn (US) car (!)

m

merecer [mere'ser] VT to deserve; (*consideração*) to merit; (*valer*) to be worth ▶ VI to be worthy; **merecido, -a** [mere'sidu, a] ADJ deserved; (*castigo, prêmio*) just

merenda [me'rẽda] F packed lunch

merengue [me'rẽgi] M meringue

mergulhador, a [merguʎa'dor(a)] M/F diver

mergulhar [mergu'ʎar] VI to dive; (*penetrar*) to plunge ▶ VT: **~ algo em algo** (*num líquido*) to dip sth into sth; (*na terra etc*) to plunge sth into sth; **mergulho** [mer'guʎu] M dip(ping), immersion; (*em natação*) dive; **dar um mergulho** (*na praia*) to go for a dip

mérito ['mɛritu] M merit

mero, -a ['mɛru, a] ADJ mere

mês [mes] M month

mesa ['meza] F table; (*de trabalho*) desk; (*comitê*) board; (*numa reunião*) panel; **pôr/tirar a ~** to lay/clear the table; **à ~** at the table; **~ de cabeceira** bedside table; **~ de toalete** dressing table; **~ telefônica** switchboard

mesada [me'zada] F monthly allowance; (*de criança*) pocket money

mesmo, -a ['mezmu, a] ADJ same; (*enfático*) very ▶ ADV (*exatamente*) right; (*até*) even; (*realmente*) really ▶ M/F: **o ~/a mesma** the same (one); **o ~** (*a mesma coisa*) the same (thing); **este ~ homem** this very man; **ele ~ o fez** he did it himself; **dá no ~** *ou* **na mesma** it's all the same; **aqui/agora/hoje ~** right here/right now/this very day; **~ que** even if; **é ~** it's true; **é ~?** really?; **(é) isso ~!** exactly!; **por isso ~** that's why; **nem ~** not even; **só ~** only; **por si ~** by oneself

mesquinho, -a [mes'kiɲu, a] ADJ mean

mesquita [mes'kita] F mosque

mestre, -a ['mɛstri, a] ADJ (*chave, viga*) master; (*linha, estrada*) main ▶ M/F master/mistress; (*professor*) teacher; **obra mestra** masterpiece

meta ['mɛta] F (*em corrida*) finishing post; (*gol*) goal; (*objetivo*) aim

metade [me'tadʒi] F half; (*meio*) middle

metáfora [me'tafora] F metaphor

metal [me'taw] (*pl* **-ais**) M metal; **metais** MPL (*Mús*) brass *sg*; **metálico, -a** [me'taliku, a] ADJ metallic; (*de metal*) metal *atr*

meteorologia [meteorolo'ʒia] F meteorology; **meteorologista** [meteorolo'ʒista] M/F meteorologist; (*TV, Rádio*) weather forecaster

meter [me'ter] VT (*colocar*) to put; (*envolver*) to involve; (*introduzir*) to introduce; **meter-se** VR (*esconder-se*) to hide; **~-se a fazer algo** to decide to have a go at sth; **~-se com** (*provocar*) to pick a quarrel with; (*associar-se*) to get involved with; **~-se em** to get involved in; (*intrometer-se*) to interfere in

meticuloso, -a [metʃiku'lozu, ɔza] ADJ meticulous

metido, -a [me'tʃidu, a] ADJ (*envolvido*) involved; (*intrometido*) meddling; **~ (a besta)** snobbish

metódico, -a [me'tɔdʒiku, a] ADJ methodical

método ['mɛtodu] M method

metralhadora [metraʎa'dora] F machine gun

métrico, -a ['mɛtriku, a] ADJ metric

metro ['mɛtru] M metre (*BRIT*), meter (*US*); (*PT: metropolitano*)

underground (BRIT), subway (US)
metrô [me'tro] (BR) M
underground (BRIT), subway (US)
metrópole [me'trɔpoli] F
metropolis; (capital) capital
meu, minha [mew, 'miɲa] ADJ
my ▶ PRON mine; **os meus** MPL
(minha família) my family ou folks
(col); **um amigo ~** a friend of mine
mexer [me'ʃer] VT to move;
(cabeça: dizendo sim) to nod;
(: dizendo não) to shake; (misturar)
to stir; (ovos) to scramble ▶ VI to
move; **mexer-se** VR to move;
(apressar-se) to get a move on;
~ em algo to touch sth; **mexa-se!**
get going!, move yourself!
mexerico [meʃe'riku] M piece of
gossip; **mexericos** MPL (fofocas)
gossip sg
México ['mɛʃiku] M: **o ~** Mexico
mexido, -a [me'ʃidu, a] ADJ
(papéis) mixed up; (ovos) scrambled
mexilhão [meʃi'ʎãw] (pl **-ões**) M
mussel
mi [mi] M (Mús) E
miau [mjaw] M miaow
micro... [mikru] PREFIXO micro...;
microblog, microblogue
[mikro'blɔgi] M microblog;
microfone [mikro'fɔni] M
microphone; **micro-ondas**
[mikro'õdas] M INV microwave;
microprocessador
[mikroprosesa'dor] M
microprocessor; **microscópio**
[mikro'skɔpju] M microscope
mídia ['midʒja] F media pl; **~s**
sociais social media pl
migalha [mi'gaʎa] F crumb;
migalhas FPL (restos, sobras) scraps
migrar [mi'grar] VI to migrate
mijar [mi'ʒar] (col) VI to pee;
mijar-se VR to wet o.s.

mil [miw] NUM thousand; **dois ~**
two thousand
milagre [mi'lagri] M miracle; **por**
~ miraculously; **milagroso, -a**
[mila'grozu, ɔza] ADJ miraculous
milhão [mi'ʎãw] (pl **-ões**) M
million; **um ~ de vezes** hundreds
of times
milhar [mi'ʎar] M thousand;
turistas aos ~es tourists in their
thousands
milho ['miʎu] M maize (BRIT), corn
(US)
milhões [mi'ʎõjs] MPL de **milhão**
miligrama [mili'grama] M
milligram(me)
milionário, -a [miljo'narju, a]
M/F millionaire
milionésimo, -a [miljo'nɛzimu,
a] NUM millionth
militar [mili'tar] ADJ military
▶ M soldier ▶ VI to fight; **~ em**
(Mil: regimento) to serve in; (Pol:
partido) to belong to, be active in;
(profissão) to work in
mim [mĩ] PRON me; (reflexivo)
myself; **de ~ para ~** to myself
mímica ['mimika] F mime
mimo ['mimu] M gift; (pessoa,
coisa encantadora) delight; (carinho)
tenderness; (gentileza) kindness;
cheio de ~s (criança) spoiled, spoilt
(BRIT); **mimoso, -a** [mi'mozu,
ɔza] ADJ (delicado) delicate;
(carinhoso) tender, loving;
(encantador) delightful
mina ['mina] F mine
mindinho [mĩ'dʒiɲu] M (tb: **dedo**
~) little finger
mineiro, -a [mi'nejru, a] ADJ
mining atr ▶ M/F miner
mineral [mine'raw] (pl **-ais**) ADJ,
M mineral
minério [mi'nɛrju] M ore

m

míngua ['mīgwa] F lack; **à ~ de** for want of; **viver à ~** to live in poverty; **minguado, -a** [mī'gwadu, a] ADJ scant; (*criança*) stunted; **minguado de algo** short of sth

minguar [mī'gwar] VI (*diminuir*) to decrease, dwindle; (*faltar*) to run short

minha ['miɲa] F *de* **meu**

minhoca [mi'ɲɔka] F (earth)worm

mini... [mini] PREFIXO mini...

miniatura [minja'tura] ADJ, F miniature

mínima ['minima] F (*temperatura*) low; (*Mús*) minim

mínimo, -a ['minimu, a] ADJ minimum ▶ M minimum; (*tb*: **dedo ~**) little finger; **não dou** *ou* **ligo a mínima para isso** I couldn't care less about it; **a mínima importância/ideia** the slightest importance/idea; **no ~** at least

minissaia [mini'saja] F miniskirt

ministério [mini'stɛrju] M ministry; **M~ da Fazenda** ≈ Treasury (BRIT), ≈ Treasury Department (US); **M~ das Relações Exteriores** ≈ Foreign Office (BRIT), ≈ State Department (US)

ministro, -a [mi'nistru, a] M/F minister

minoria [mino'ria] F minority

minto ['mĩtu] VB *ver* **mentir**

minucioso, -a [minu'sjozu, ɔza] ADJ (*indivíduo, busca*) thorough; (*explicação*) detailed

minúsculo, -a [mi'nuskulu, a] ADJ minute, tiny; **letra minúscula** lower case letter

minuta [mi'nuta] F draft

minuto [mi'nutu] M minute

miolo ['mjolu] M inside; (*polpa*) pulp; (*de maçã*) core; **miolos** MPL (*cérebro, inteligência*) brains

míope ['miopi] ADJ short-sighted

mira ['mira] F (*de fuzil*) sight; (*pontaria*) aim; (*fig*) aim, purpose; **à ~ de** on the lookout for; **ter em ~** to have one's eye on

miragem [mi'raʒẽ] (*pl* -**ns**) F mirage

miserável [mize'ravew] (*pl* -**eis**) ADJ (*digno de compaixão*) wretched; (*pobre*) impoverished; (*avaro*) stingy, mean; (*insignificante*) paltry; (*lugar*) squalid; (*infame*) despicable ▶ M wretch; (*coitado*) poor thing; (*pessoa infame*) rotter

miséria [mi'zɛrja] F misery; (*pobreza*) poverty; (*avareza*) stinginess

misericórdia [mizeri'kɔrdʒja] F (*compaixão*) pity, compassion; (*graça*) mercy

missa ['misa] F (*Rel*) mass

missão [mi'sãw] (*pl* -**ões**) F mission; (*dever*) duty

míssil ['misiw] (*pl* -**eis**) M missile

missionário, -a [misjo'narju, a] M/F missionary

missões [mi'sõjs] FPL *de* **missão**

mistério [mis'tɛrju] M mystery; **misterioso, -a** [miste'rjozu, ɔza] ADJ mysterious

mistificar [mistʃifi'kar] VT, VI to fool

misto, -a ['mistu, a] ADJ mixed; (*confuso*) mixed up ▶ M mixture; **misto-quente** (*pl* **mistos-quentes**) M toasted cheese and ham sandwich

mistura [mis'tura] F mixture; (*ato*) mixing; **misturar** [mistu'rar] VT to mix; (*confundir*) to mix up; **misturar-se** VR: **misturar-se com** to mingle with

mito ['mitu] M myth

miudezas [mju'dezas] FPL
minutiae; (*bugigangas*) odds and
ends; (*objetos pequenos*) trinkets

miúdo, -a ['mjudu, a] ADJ tiny,
minute ▶ M/F (*PT: criança*)
youngster, kid; **miúdos** MPL
(*dinheiro*) change sg; (*de aves*)
giblets; **dinheiro ~** small change

mm ABR (= *milímetro*) mm

mo [mu] PRON = **me + o**

moa ['moa] VB *ver* **moer**

móbil ['mɔbiw] (*pl* -**eis**) ADJ
= **móvel**

móbile ['mɔbili] M mobile

mobília [mo'bilja] F furniture;
mobiliar [mobi'ljar] (*BR*) VT to
furnish; **mobiliário** [mobi'ljarju]
M furnishings *pl*

moça ['mosa] F girl, young woman

Moçambique [mosã'biki] M
Mozambique

moção [mo'sãw] (*pl* -**ões**) F
motion

mochila [mo'ʃila] F rucksack

mochilão [moʃi'lãw] M
backpacking trip

mocidade [mosi'dadʒi] F youth;
(*os moços*) young people *pl*

moço, -a ['mosu, a] ADJ young ▶ M
young man, lad

moções [mo'sõjs] FPL *de* **moção**

moda ['mɔda] F fashion; **estar na
~** to be in fashion, be all the rage;
fora da ~ old-fashioned; **sair da
ou cair de ~** to go out of fashion

modalidade [modali'dadʒi] F
kind; (*Esporte*) event

modelo [mo'delu] M model;
(*criação de estilista*) design; (*pessoa
admirada*) role-model ▶ M/F
(*manequim*) model

modem ['modẽ] (*pl* -**ns**) M modem

moderar [mode'rar] VT to
moderate; (*violência*) to control,

restrain; (*velocidade*) to reduce;
(*voz*) to lower; (*gastos*) to cut down

modernizar [moderni'zar] VT to
modernize; **modernizar-se** VR to
modernize

moderno, -a [mo'dɛrnu, a] ADJ
modern; (*atual*) present-day

modéstia [mo'dɛstʃja] F modesty

módico, -a ['mɔdʒiku, a] ADJ
moderate; (*preço*) reasonable;
(*bens*) scant

modificar [modʒifi'kar] VT to
modify, alter

modista [mo'dʒista] F dressmaker

modo ['mɔdu] M (*maneira*) way,
manner; (*método*) way; (*Mús*)
mode; **modos** MPL
(*comportamento*) manners; **de (tal)
~ que** so (that); **de ~ nenhum** in
no way; **de qualquer ~** anyway,
anyhow; **~ de emprego**
instructions *pl* for use

módulo ['mɔdulu] M module

moeda ['mwɛda] F (*uma moeda*)
coin; (*dinheiro*) currency; **uma ~ de
50p** a 50p piece; **~ corrente**
currency; **Casa da M~** ≈ the
(Royal) Mint (*BRIT*), ≈ the (US) Mint
(*US*)

moedor [moe'dor] M (*de café*)
grinder; (*de carne*) mincer

moer [mwer] VT (*café*) to grind;
(*cana*) to crush

mofado, -a [mo'fadu, a] ADJ
mouldy (*BRIT*), moldy (*US*)

mofo ['mofu] M (*Bot*) mould (*BRIT*),
mold (*US*); **cheiro de ~** musty
smell

mogno ['mɔgnu] M mahogany

mói [mɔj] VB *ver* **moer**

moía [mo'ia] VB *ver* **moer**

moído, -a [mo'idu, a] ADJ (*café*)
ground; (*carne*) minced; (*cansado*)
tired out; (*corpo*) aching

m

moinho ['mwiɲu] M mill; (de café) grinder; **~ de vento** windmill

mola ['mɔla] F (Tec) spring; (fig) motive, motivation

moldar [mow'dar] VT to mould (BRIT), mold (US); (metal) to cast; **molde** ['mɔwdʒi] M mould (BRIT), mold (US); (de papel) pattern; (fig) model; **molde de vestido** dress pattern

moldura [mow'dura] F (de pintura) frame

mole ['mɔli] ADJ soft; (sem energia) listless; (carnes) flabby; (col: fácil) easy; (lento) slow; (preguiçoso) sluggish ▶ ADV (lentamente) slowly

moleque [mo'lɛki] M (de rua) urchin; (menino) youngster; (pessoa sem palavra) unreliable person; (canalha) scoundrel ▶ ADJ (levado) mischievous; (brincalhão) funny

molestar [moles'tar] VT to upset; (enfadar) to annoy; (importunar) to bother

moléstia [mo'lɛstʃa] F illness

moleza [mo'leza] F softness; (falta de energia) listlessness; (falta de força) weakness; **ser (uma) ~** (col) to be easy; **na ~** without exerting oneself

molhado, -a [mo'ʎadu, a] ADJ wet, damp

molhar [mo'ʎar] VT to wet; (de leve) to moisten, dampen; (mergulhar) to dip; **molhar-se** VR to get wet

molho¹ ['mɔʎu] M (de chaves) bunch; (de trigo) sheaf

molho² ['moʎu] M (Culin) sauce; (: de salada) dressing; (: de carne) gravy; **pôr de ~** to soak; **estar/deixar de ~** (roupa etc) to be/leave to soak

momentâneo, -a [momē'tanju, a] ADJ momentary

momento [mo'mētu] M moment; (Tec) momentum; **a todo ~** constantly; **de um ~ para outro** suddenly; **no ~ em que** just as

Mônaco ['monaku] M Monaco

monarquia [monar'kia] F monarchy

monitor [moni'tor] M monitor

monopólio [mono'pɔlju] M monopoly; **monopolizar** [monopoli'zar] VT to monopolize

monotonia [monoto'nia] F monotony; **monótono, -a** [mo'nɔtonu, a] ADJ monotonous

monstro, -a ['mõstru, a] ADJ INV giant ▶ M (tb fig) monster; **monstruoso, -a** [mõ'strwozu, ɔza] ADJ monstrous; (enorme) gigantic, huge

montagem [mõ'taʒē] (pl **-ns**) F assembly; (Arq) erection; (Cinema) editing; (Teatro) production

montanha [mõ'taɲa] F mountain; **montanha-russa** F roller coaster

montante [mõ'tãtʃi] M amount, sum; **a ~** (nadar) upstream

montar [mõ'tar] VT (cavalo) to mount, get on; (colocar em) to put on; (cavalgar) to ride; (peças) to assemble, put together; (loja, máquina) to set up; (casa) to put up; (peça teatral) to put on ▶ VI to ride; **~ a** ou **em** (animal) to get on; (cavalgar) to ride; (despesa) to come to

monte ['mõtʃi] M hill; (pilha) heap, pile; **um ~ de** (muitos) a lot of, lots of; **gente aos ~s** loads of people

montra ['mõtra] (PT) F shop window

monumento [monu'mētu] M monument

moqueca [mo'kɛka] F fish or seafood simmered in coconut cream and palm oil; **~ de camarão** prawn moqueca

morada [mo'rada] F home, residence; (PT: *endereço*) address; **moradia** [mora'dʒia] F home, dwelling; **morador, a** [mora'dor(a)] M/F resident; (*de casa alugada*) tenant

moral [mo'raw] (*pl* -**ais**) ADJ moral ▶ F (*ética*) ethics *pl*; (*conclusão*) moral ▶ M (*de pessoa*) sense of morality; (*ânimo*) morale; **moralidade** [morali'dadʒi] F morality

morango [mo'rãgu] M strawberry

morar [mo'rar] VI to live, reside

mórbido, -a ['mɔrbidu, a] ADJ morbid

morcego [mor'segu] M (*Bio*) bat

mordaça [mor'dasa] F (*de animal*) muzzle; (*fig*) gag

morder [mor'der] VT to bite; (*corroer*) to corrode; **mordida** [mor'dʒida] F bite

mordomia [mordo'mia] F (*de executivos*) perk; (*col: regalia*) luxury, comfort

mordomo [mor'dɔmu] M butler

moreno, -a [mo'renu, a] ADJ dark(-skinned); (*de cabelos*) dark(-haired); (*de tomar sol*) brown ▶ M/F dark person

mormaço [mor'masu] M sultry weather

morno, -a ['mornu, 'mɔrna] ADJ lukewarm, tepid

morrer [mo'her] VI to die; (*luz, cor*) to fade; (*fogo*) to die down; (*Auto*) to stall

morro ['mohu] M hill; (*favela*) slum

mortadela [morta'dɛla] F salami

mortal [mor'taw] (*pl* -**ais**) ADJ mortal; (*letal, insuportável*) deadly ▶ M mortal

mortalidade [mortali'dadʒi] F mortality

morte ['mɔrtʃi] F death

mortífero, -a [mor'tʃiferu, a] ADJ deadly, lethal

morto, -a ['mortu, 'mɔrta] PP *de* **matar, morrer** ▶ ADJ dead; (*cor*) dull; (*exausto*) exhausted; (*inexpressivo*) lifeless ▶ M/F dead man/woman; **estar ~** to be dead; **ser ~** to be killed; **estar ~ de inveja** to be green with envy; **estar ~ de vontade de** to be dying to

mos [mus] PRON = **me + os**

mosca ['moska] F fly; **estar às ~s** (*bar etc*) to be deserted

Moscou [mos'kow] (BR) N Moscow

Moscovo [mos'kovu] (PT) N Moscow

mosquito [mos'kitu] M mosquito

mostarda [mos'tarda] F mustard

mosteiro [mos'tejru] M monastery; (*de monjas*) convent

mostrador [mostra'dor] M (*de relógio*) face, dial

mostrar [mos'trar] VT to show; (*mercadorias*) to display; (*provar*) tó demonstrate, prove; **mostrar-se** VR to show o.s. to be; (*exibir-se*) to show off

motel [mo'tɛw] (*pl* -**éis**) M motel

motivar [motʃi'var] VT (*causar*) to cause, bring about; (*estimular*) to motivate; **motivo** [mo'tʃivu] M (*causa*): **motivo (de** *ou* **para)** cause (of), reason (for); (*fim*) motive; (*Arte, Mús*) motif; **por motivo de** because of, owing to

moto ['mɔtu] F motorbike ▶ M (*lema*) motto

motoboy [moto'bɔj] M motorcycle courier

motocicleta [motosi'kleta] F motorcycle, motorbike

motociclista [motosi'klista] M/F
motorcyclist

motociclo [moto'siklu] (PT) M
= **motocicleta**

motor, motriz [mo'tor, mo'triz]
ADJ, M motor; (de carro, avião)
engine; **força motriz** driving force;
~ de explosão internal combustion
engine; **~ diesel** diesel engine; **~ de
pesquisa** (PT Comput) search engine

motorista [moto'rista] M/F driver

móvel ['mɔvew] (pl **-eis**) ADJ
movable ▶ M piece of furniture;
móveis MPL (mobília) furniture sg

mover [mo'ver] VT to move;
(cabeça) to shake; (mecanismo) to
drive; (campanha) to start (up);
mover-se VR to move

movimentado, -a [movimē'tadu,
a] ADJ (rua, lugar) busy; (pessoa)
active; (show, música) up-tempo

movimentar [movimē'tar] VT to
move; (animar) to liven up

movimento [movi'mētu] M
movement; (Tec) motion; (na rua)
activity, bustle; **de muito ~** busy

MST (BR) ABR M (= Movimento dos
Trabalhadores Rurais Sem Terra)
pressure group for land reform

muamba ['mwãba] (col) F
(contrabando) contraband; (objetos
roubados) loot

muçulmano, -a [musuw'manu,
a] ADJ, M/F Moslem

muda ['muda] F (planta) seedling;
(vestuário) outfit; **~ de roupa**
change of clothes

mudança [mu'dãsa] F change; (de
casa) move; (Auto) gear; **~s
climáticas** climate change

mudar [mu'dar] VT to change;
(deslocar) to move ▶ VI to change;
(ave) to moult (BRIT), molt (US);
mudar-se VR (de casa) to move

(away); **~ de roupa/de assunto** to
change clothes/the subject; **~ de
casa** to move (house); **~ de ideia**
to change one's mind

mudo, -a ['mudu, a] ADJ dumb;
(calado, filme) silent; (telefone) dead
▶ M/F mute

muito, -a ['mwĩtu, a] ADJ
(quantidade) a lot of; (em frase
negativa ou interrogativa) much;
(número) lots of, a lot of, many;
muito esforço a lot of effort; **faz
muito calor** it's very hot; **muito
tempo** a long time; **muitas
amigas** lots ou a lot of friends;
muitas vezes often
▶ PRON a lot; (em frase negativa ou
interrogativa: sg) much; (: pl) many;
tenho muito que fazer I've got a
lot to do; **muitos dizem que ...** a
lot of people say that ...
▶ ADV **1** a lot; (+ adj) very; (+ compar):
muito melhor much ou far ou a lot
better; **gosto muito disto** I like it a
lot; **sinto muito** I'm very sorry;
muito interessante very
interesting
2 (resposta) very; **está cansado?
— muito** are you tired? — very
3 (tempo): **muito depois** long after;
há muito a long time ago; **não
demorou muito** it didn't take long

mula ['mula] F mule

mulato, -a [mu'latu, a] ADJ, M/F
mulatto

muleta [mu'leta] F crutch; (fig)
support

mulher [mu'ʎer] F woman; (esposa)
wife; **mulher-bomba** (pl **mulheres-
bomba**) F suicide bomber

multa ['muwta] F fine; **levar uma**

~ to be fined; **multar** [muw'tar]
vt to fine; **multar alguém em
$1000** to fine sb $1000
multi... [muwtʃi] PREFIXO multi...
multidão [muwtʃi'dãw] (pl **-ões**)
F crowd; **uma ~ de** (muitos) lots of
multimídia [muwtʃi'midʒja] ADJ
multimedia
multinacional
[muwtʃinasjo'naw] (pl **-ais**) ADJ, F
multinational
multiplicar [muwtʃipli'kar] vt to
multiply; (aumentar) to increase
múltiplo, -a ['muwtʃiplu, a] ADJ,
M multiple
múmia ['mumja] F mummy
mundial [mũ'dʒjaw] (pl **-ais**) ADJ
worldwide; (guerra, recorde) world
atr ▶ M world championship
mundo ['mũdu] M world; **todo o
~** everybody; **um ~ de** lots of, a
great many
munição [muni'sãw] (pl **-ões**) F
(de armas) ammunition; (chumbo)
shot; (Mil) munitions pl, supplies pl
municipal [munisi'paw] (pl **-ais**)
ADJ municipal
município [muni'sipju] M local
authority; (cidade) town; (condado)
county
munições [muni'sõjs] FPL de
munição
munir [mu'nir] vt: **~ de** to
provide with, supply with;
munir-se vr: **~-se de** (provisões) to
equip o.s. with
muralha [mu'raʎa] F (de fortaleza)
rampart; (muro) wall
murchar [mur'ʃar] vt (Bot) to
wither; (sentimentos) to dull;
(pessoa) to sadden ▶ vi to wither,
wilt; (fig) to fade
murmurar [murmu'rar] vi to
murmur, whisper; (queixar-se) to

mutter, grumble; (água) to ripple;
(folhagem) to rustle ▶ vt to
murmur; **murmúrio** [mur'murju]
M murmuring, whispering;
(queixa) grumbling; (de água)
rippling; (de folhagem) rustling
muro ['muru] M wall
murro ['muhu] M punch; **dar um
~ em alguém** to punch sb
musa ['muza] F muse
musculação [muskula'sãw] F
weight training
músculo ['muskulu] M muscle;
musculoso, -a [musku'lozu, ɔza]
ADJ muscular
museu [mu'zew] M museum; (de
pintura) gallery
musgo ['muzgu] M moss
música ['muzika] F music;
(canção) song; ver tb **músico**;
músico, -a ['muziku, a] ADJ
musical ▶ M/F musician
mútuo, -a ['mutwu, a] ADJ mutual

m

N ABR (= *norte*) N
na [na] = **em + a**
-na [na] PRON her; (*coisa*) it
nabo ['nabu] M turnip
nação [na'sãw] (*pl* **-ões**) F nation
nacional [nasjo'naw] (*pl* **-ais**) ADJ national; (*carro, vinho etc*) domestic, home-produced; **nacionalidade** [nasjonali'dadʒi] F nationality; **nacionalismo** [nasjona'lizmu] M nationalism; **nacionalista** [nasjona'lista] ADJ, M/F nationalist
nações [na'sõjs] FPL *de* **nação**
nada ['nada] PRON nothing ▶ ADV at all; **antes de mais** ~ first of all; **não é** ~ **difícil** it's not at all hard, it's not hard at all; ~ **mais** nothing else; ~ **de novo** nothing new; **obrigado** — **de** ~ thank you — not at all *ou* don't mention it
nadador, a [nada'dor(a)] M/F swimmer
nadar [na'dar] VI to swim
nádegas ['nadegas] FPL buttocks
nado ['nadu] M: **atravessar a** ~ to swim across; ~ **borboleta** butterfly (stroke); ~ **de costas** backstroke; ~ **de peito** breaststroke
naipe ['najpi] M (*cartas*) suit
namorado, -a [namo'radu, a] M/F boyfriend/girlfriend
namorar [namo'rar] VT (*ser namorado de*) to be going out with
namoro [na'moru] M relationship
não [nãw] ADV not; (*resposta*) no ▶ M no; ~ **sei** I don't know; ~ **muito** not much; ~ **só ... mas também** not only ... but also; **agora** ~ not now; ~ **tem de quê** don't mention it; ~ **é?** isn't it?, won't you?; **eles são brasileiros, ~ é?** they're Brazilian, aren't they?
não... [nãw] PREFIXO non-
naquele(s), naquela(s) [na'keli(s), na'kɛla(s)] = **em + aquele(s), aquela(s)**
naquilo [na'kilu] = **em + aquilo**
narina [na'rina] F nostril
nariz [na'riz] M nose
narração [naha'sãw] (*pl* **-ões**) F narration; (*relato*) account
narrar [na'har] VT to narrate
narrativa [naha'tʃiva] F narrative; (*história*) story
nas [nas] = **em + as**
-nas [nas] PRON them
nascença [na'sẽsa] F birth; **de** ~ by birth; **ele é surdo de** ~ he was born deaf
nascente [na'sẽtʃi] M East, Orient ▶ F (*fonte*) spring
nascer [na'ser] VI to be born; (*plantas*) to sprout; (*o sol*) to rise; (*ave*) to hatch; (*fig: ter origem*) to come into being ▶ M: ~ **do sol** sunrise; **ele nasceu para médico** *etc* he was born to be a doctor *etc*; **nascimento** [nasi'mẽtu] M birth; (*fig*) origin; (*estirpe*) descent

nata ['nata] F cream

natação [nata'sãw] F swimming

natais [na'tajs] ADJ PL de **natal**

Natal [na'taw] M Christmas; **Feliz ~!** Merry Christmas!

natal [na'taw] (pl -**ais**) ADJ (relativo ao nascimento) natal; (país) native; **cidade ~** home town

natalino, -a [nata'linu, a] ADJ Christmas atr

nativo, -a [na'tʃivu, a] ADJ, M/F native

natural [natu'raw] (pl -**ais**) ADJ natural; (nativo) native ▶ M/F native; **ao ~** (Culin) fresh, uncooked; **naturalidade** [naturali'dadʒi] F naturalness; **de naturalidade paulista** etc born in São Paulo etc; **naturalizar** [naturali'zar] VT to naturalize; **naturalizar-se** VR to become naturalized; **naturalmente** [naturaw'mẽtʃi] ADV naturally; **naturalmente!** of course!

natureza [natu'reza] F nature; (espécie) kind, type

nau [naw] F (literário) ship

náusea ['nawzea] F nausea; **dar ~s a alguém** to make sb feel sick; **sentir ~s** to feel sick

náutico, -a ['nawtʃiku, a] ADJ nautical

naval [na'vaw] (pl -**ais**) ADJ naval; **construção ~** shipbuilding

navalha [na'vaʎa] F (de barba) razor; (faca) knife

nave ['navi] F (de igreja) nave

navegação [navega'sãw] F navigation, sailing; **~ aérea** air traffic; **companhia de ~** shipping line

navegar [nave'gar] VT to navigate; (mares) to sail ▶ VI to sail; (dirigir o rumo) to navigate

navio [na'viu] M ship; **~ cargueiro** cargo ship, freighter; **~ de guerra** warship; **~ petroleiro** oil tanker

nazi [na'zi] (PT) ADJ, M/F = **nazista**

nazista [na'zista] (BR) ADJ, M/F Nazi

NB ABR (= note bem) NB

neblina [ne'blina] F fog, mist

nebuloso, -a [nebu'lozu, ɔza] ADJ foggy, misty; (céu) cloudy; (fig) vague

necessário, -a [nese'sarju, a] ADJ necessary ▶ M: **o ~** the necessities pl

necessidade [nesesi'dadʒi] F need, necessity; (o que se necessita) need; (pobreza) poverty, need; **ter ~ de** to need; **em caso de ~** if need be

necessitado, -a [nesesi'tadu, a] ADJ needy, poor; **~ de** in need of

necessitar [nesesi'tar] VT to need, require ▶ VI: **~ de** to need

neerlandês, -esa [neerlã'des, eza] ADJ Dutch ▶ M/F Dutchman/woman

Neerlândia [neer'lãdʒa] F the Netherlands pl

negar [ne'gar] VT to deny; (recusar) to refuse; **negar-se** VR: **~-se a** to refuse to

negativa [nega'tʃiva] F (Ling) negative; (recusa) denial

negativo, -a [nega'tʃivu, a] ADJ negative ▶ M (Tec, Foto) negative ▶ EXCL (col) nope!

negligência [negli'ʒẽsja] F negligence, carelessness; **negligente** [negli'ʒẽtʃi] ADJ negligent, careless

negociação [negosja'sãw] (pl -**ões**) F negotiation

negociante [nego'sjãtʃi] M/F businessman/woman

negociar [nego'sjar] VT to negotiate; (*Com*) to trade ▶ VI: **~ (com)** to trade *ou* deal (in); to negotiate (with)

negócio [ne'gɔsju] M (*Com*) business; (*transação*) deal; (*questão*) matter; (*col: troço*) thing; (*assunto*) affair, business; **homem de ~s** businessman; **a ~s** on business; **fechar um ~** to make a deal

negro, -a ['negru, a] ADJ black; (*raça*) Black; (*fig: lúgubre*) black, gloomy ▶ M/F Black man/woman

nele(s), nela(s) ['neli(s), 'nɛla(s)] = **em + ele(s), ela(s)**

nem [nēj] CONJ nor, neither; **~ (sequer)** not even; **~ que** even if; **~ bem** hardly; **~ um só** not a single one; **~ estuda ~ trabalha** he neither studies nor works; **~ eu** nor me; **sem ~** without even; **~ todos** not all; **~ tanto** not so much; **~ sempre** not always

nenê [ne'ne] M/F baby

neném [ne'nēj] (*pl* **-ns**) M/F = **nenê**

nenhum, a [ne'nũ, 'numa] ADJ no, not any ▶ PRON (*nem um só*) none, not one; (*de dois*) neither; **~ lugar** nowhere

nervo ['nervu] M (*Anat*) nerve; (*fig*) energy, strength; (*em carne*) sinew; **nervosismo** [nervo'zizmu] M (*nervosidade*) nervousness; (*irritabilidade*) irritability; **nervoso, -a** [ner'vozu, ɔza] ADJ nervous; (*irritável*) touchy, on edge; (*exaltado*) worked up; **isso/ele me deixa nervoso** he gets on my nerves

nesse(s), nessa(s) ['nesi(s), 'nɛsa(s)] = **em + esse(s), essa(s)**

neste(s), nesta(s) ['nestʃi(s), 'nɛsta(s)] = **em + este(s), esta(s)**

neto, -a ['nɛtu, a] M/F grandson/ daughter; **netos** MPL grandchildren

neurose [new'rɔzi] F neurosis; **neurótico, -a** [new'rɔtʃiku, a] ADJ, M/F neurotic

neutro, -a ['newtru, a] ADJ (*Ling*) neuter; (*imparcial*) neutral

nevar [ne'var] VI to snow; **nevasca** [ne'vaska] F snowstorm; **neve** ['nɛvi] F snow

névoa ['nɛvoa] F fog; **nevoeiro** [nevo'ejru] M thick fog

nexo ['nɛksu] M connection, link; **sem ~** disconnected, incoherent

Nicarágua [nika'ragwa] F: **a ~** Nicaragua

nicotina [niko'tʃina] F nicotine

Nigéria [ni'ʒɛrja] F: **a ~** Nigeria

Nilo ['nilu] M: **o ~** the Nile

ninguém [nĩ'gēj] PRON nobody, no-one

ninho ['niɲu] M nest; (*toca*) lair; (*lar*) home

nisso ['nisu] = **em + isso**

nisto ['nistu] = **em + isto**

nitidez [nitʃi'dez] F (*clareza*) clarity; (*brilho*) brightness; (*imagem*) sharpness

nítido, -a ['nitʃidu, a] ADJ clear, distinct; (*brilhante*) bright; (*imagem*) sharp, clear

nível ['nivew] (*pl* **-eis**) M level; (*fig: padrão*) standard; (: *ponto*) point, pitch; **~ de vida** standard of living

nº ABR (= *número*) no.

no [nu] = **em + o**

nó [nɔ] M knot; (*de uma questão*) crux; **nós dos dedos** knuckles; **dar um nó** to tie a knot

-no [nu] PRON him; (*coisa*) it

nobre ['nɔbri] ADJ, M/F noble; **horário ~** prime time; **nobreza** [no'breza] F nobility

noção [no'sãw] (*pl* **-ões**) F notion; **noções** FPL (*rudimentos*) rudiments, basics; **~ vaga** inkling; **não ter a**

menor ~ de algo not to have the slightest idea about sth

nocaute [no'kawtʃi] M knockout
▶ ADV: **pôr alguém ~** to knock sb out

nocivo, -a [no'sivu, a] ADJ harmful

noções [no'sõjs] FPL *de* **noção**

nódoa ['nɔdwa] F spot; (*mancha*) stain

nogueira [no'gejra] F (*árvore*) walnut tree; (*madeira*) walnut

noite ['nojtʃi] F night; **à** *ou* **de ~** at night, in the evening; **boa ~** good evening; (*despedida*) good night; **da ~ para o dia** overnight; **tarde da ~** late at night

noivado [noj'vadu] M engagement

noivo, -a ['nojvu, a] M/F (*prometido*) fiancé/fiancée; (*no casamento*) bridegroom/bride; **os noivos** MPL (*prometidos*) the engaged couple; (*no casamento*) the bride and groom; (*recém-casados*) the newly-weds

nojento, -a [no'ʒẽtu, a] ADJ disgusting

nojo ['noʒu] M nausea; (*repulsão*) disgust, loathing; **ela é um ~** she's horrible; **este trabalho está um ~** this work is messy

no-la(s) = **nos** + **a(s)**

no-lo(s) = **nos** + **o(s)**

nome ['nomi] M name; (*fama*) fame; **de ~** by name; **escritor de ~** famous writer; **um restaurante de ~** a restaurant with a good reputation; **em ~ de** in the name of; **~ de batismo** Christian name

nomear [no'mjar] VT to nominate; (*conferir um cargo a*) to appoint; (*dar nome a*) to name

nono, -a ['nonu, a] NUM ninth

nora ['nɔra] F daughter-in-law

nordeste [nor'dɛstʃi] M, ADJ northeast

norma ['nɔrma] F standard, norm; (*regra*) rule; **como ~** as a rule

normal [nor'maw] (*pl* **-ais**) ADJ normal; (*habitual*) usual; **normalizar** [normali'zar] VT to bring back to normal; **normalizar-se** VR to return to normal

noroeste [nor'wɛstʃi] ADJ northwest, northwestern ▶ M northwest

norte ['nɔrtʃi] ADJ northern, north; (*vento, direção*) northerly ▶ M north; **norte-americano, -a** ADJ, M/F (North) American

Noruega [nor'wega] F Norway; **norueguês, -esa** [norwe'ges, geza] ADJ, M/F Norwegian ▶ M (*Ling*) Norwegian

nos¹ [nus] = **em** + **os**

nos² [nus] PRON (*direto*) us; (*indireto*) us, to us, for us; (*reflexivo*) (to) ourselves; (*recíproco*) (to) each other

nós [nɔs] PRON we; (*depois de prep*) us; **~ mesmos** we ourselves

-nos [nus] PRON them

nosso, -a ['nɔsu, a] ADJ our ▶ PRON ours; **um amigo ~** a friend of ours; **Nossa Senhora** (*Rel*) Our Lady

nostalgia [nostaw'ʒia] F nostalgia; **nostálgico, -a** [nos'tawʒiku, a] ADJ nostalgic

nota ['nɔta] F note; (*Educ*) mark; (*conta*) bill; (*cédula*) banknote; **~ de venda** sales receipt; **~ fiscal** receipt

notar [no'tar] VT to notice, note; **notar-se** VR to be obvious; **fazer ~** to call attention to; **notável** [no'tavew] (*pl* **-eis**) ADJ notable, remarkable

notícia [no'tʃisja] F (*uma notícia*) piece of news; (*TV etc*) news item; **notícias** FPL (*informações*) news *sg*; **pedir ~s de** to inquire about; **ter ~s de** to hear from; **noticiário** [notʃi'sjarju] M (*de jornal*) news section; (*Cinema*) newsreel; (*TV, Rádio*) news bulletin

notório, -a [no'tɔrju, a] ADJ well-known

noturno, -a [no'turnu, a] ADJ nocturnal, nightly; (*trabalho*) night *atr* ▶ M (*trem*) night train

nova ['nɔva] F piece of news; **novas** FPL (*novidades*) news *sg*

novamente [nova'mẽtʃi] ADV again

novato, -a [no'vatu, a] ADJ inexperienced, raw ▶ M/F beginner, novice; (*Educ*) fresher

nove ['nɔvi] NUM nine

novela [no'vɛla] F short novel, novella; (*Rádio, TV*) soap opera

novelo [no'velu] M ball of thread

novembro [no'vẽbru] M November

noventa [no'vẽta] NUM ninety

novidade [novi'dadʒi] F novelty; (*notícia*) piece of news; **novidades** FPL (*notícias*) news *sg*

novilho, -a [no'viʎu, a] M/F young bull/heifer

novo, -a ['novu, 'nɔva] ADJ new; (*jovem*) young; (*adicional*) further; **de ~** again

noz [nɔz] F nut; (*da nogueira*) walnut; **~ moscada** nutmeg

nu, a [nu, 'nua] ADJ naked; (*braço, arvore, sala, parede*) bare ▶ M nude

nublado, -a [nu'bladu, a] ADJ cloudy, overcast

nuclear [nu'kljar] ADJ nuclear

núcleo ['nuklju] M nucleus *sg*; (*centro*) centre (BRIT), center (US)

nudez [nu'dez] F nakedness, nudity; (*de paredes etc*) bareness

nudista [nu'dʒista] ADJ, M/F nudist

nulo, -a ['nulu, a] ADJ (*Jur*) null, void; (*nenhum*) non-existent; (*sem valor*) worthless; (*esforço*) vain, useless

num [nũ] = **em** + **um**

numa(s) ['numa(s)] = **em** + **uma(s)**

numeral [nume'raw] (*pl* -**ais**) M numeral

numerar [nume'rar] VT to number

numérico, -a [nu'mɛriku, a] ADJ numerical

número ['numeru] M number; (*de jornal*) issue; (*Teatro etc*) act; (*de sapatos, roupa*) size; **sem ~** countless; **~ de matrícula** registration (BRIT) *ou* license plate (US) number; **numeroso, -a** [nume'rozu, ɔza] ADJ numerous

nunca ['nũka] ADV never; **~ mais** never again; **quase ~** hardly ever; **mais que ~** more than ever

nuns [nũs] = **em** + **uns**

núpcias ['nupsjas] FPL nuptials, wedding *sg*

nutrição [nutri'sãw] F nutrition

nuvem ['nuvẽj] (*pl* -**ns**) F cloud; (*de insetos*) swarm

O

que mais gostar take the one you like best
2 (*def*): **o que comprei ontem** the one I bought yesterday; **os que sairam** those who left
3: **o que** what; **o que eu acho/mais gosto** what I think/like most
▶ PRON PESSOAL 1 (*pessoa: m*) him; (: *f*) her; (: *pl*) them; **não consigo vê-lo(s)** I can't see him/them; **vemo-la todas as semanas** we see her every week
2 (*animal, coisa: sg*) it; (: *pl*) them; **não consigo vê-lo(s)** I can't see it/them; **acharam-nos na praia** they found them on the beach

(PALAVRA-CHAVE)

o, a [u, a] ART DEF 1 the; **o livro/a mesa/os estudantes** the book/table/students
2 (*com n abstrato, não se traduz*): **o amor/a juventude** love/youth
3 (*posse, traduz-se muitas vezes por adj possessivo*): **quebrar o braço** to break one's arm; **ele levantou a mão** he put his hand up; **ela colocou o chapéu** she put her hat on
4 (*valor descritivo*): **ter a boca grande/os olhos azuis** to have a big mouth/blue eyes
▶ PRON DEMONSTRATIVO: **meu livro e o seu** my book and yours; **as de Pedro são melhores** Pedro's are better; **não a(s) branca(s) mas a(s) verde(s)** not the white one(s) but the green one(s); **o que** (*etc*)
▶ PRON RELATIVO 1 (*indef*): **os que quiserem podem sair** anyone who wants to can leave; **leve o**

obedecer [obede'ser] VI: **~ a** to obey; **obediência** [obe'dʒẽsja] F obedience; **obediente** [obe'dʒẽtʃi] ADJ obedient
óbito ['ɔbitu] M death; **atestado de ~** death certificate
objeção [obʒe'sãw] (*pl* -**ões**) F objection; **fazer** *ou* **pôr objeções a** to object to
objetivo, -a [obʒe'tʃivu, a] ADJ objective ▶ M objective
objeto [ob'ʒɛtu] M object
obra ['ɔbra] F work; (*Arq*) building, construction; (*Teatro*) play; **em ~s** under repair; **ser ~ de alguém** to be the work of sb; **~ de arte** work of art; **~s públicas** public works; **obra-prima** (*pl* **obras-primas**) F masterpiece
obrigação [obriga'sãw] (*pl* -**ões**) F obligation; (*Com*) bond
obrigado, -a [obri'gadu, a] ADJ obliged, compelled ▶ EXCL thank you; (*recusa*) no, thank you
obrigar [obri'gar] VT to oblige, compel; **obrigar-se** VR: **~-se a**

fazer algo to undertake to do sth; **obrigatório, -a** [obriga'tɔrju, a] ADJ compulsory, obligatory

obsceno, -a [obi'sɛnu, a] ADJ obscene

obscurecer [obiskure'ser] VT to darken; (*entendimento, verdade etc*) to obscure ▶ VI to get dark

obscuro, -a [obi'skuru, a] ADJ dark; (*fig*) obscure

observação [obiserva'sãw] (*pl* **-ões**) F observation; (*comentário*) remark, comment; (*de leis, regras*) observance

observador, a [obiserva'dor(a)] M/F observer

observar [obiser'var] VT to observe; (*notar*) to notice; **~ algo a alguém** to point sth out to sb

observatório [obiserva'tɔrju] M observatory

obsessão [obise'sãw] (*pl* **-ões**) F obsession; **obsessivo, -a** [obise'sivu, a] ADJ obsessive

obsoleto, -a [obiso'lɛtu, a] ADJ obsolete

obstinado, -a [obistʃi'nadu, a] ADJ obstinate, stubborn

obstrução [obistru'sãw] (*pl* **-ões**) F obstruction; **obstruir** [obi'strwir] VT to obstruct; (*impedir*) to impede

obter [obi'ter] (*irreg: como* **ter**) VT to obtain, get; (*alcançar*) to gain

obturação [obitura'sãw] (*pl* **-ões**) F (*de dente*) filling

obtuso, -a [obi'tuzu, a] ADJ (*ger*) obtuse; (*fig: pessoa*) thick

óbvio, -a ['ɔbvju, a] ADJ obvious; **(é) ~!** of course!

ocasião [oka'zjãw] (*pl* **-ões**) F opportunity, chance; (*momento, tempo*) occasion; **ocasionar** [okazjo'nar] VT to cause, bring about

oceano [o'sjanu] M ocean

ocidental [oside'taw] (*pl* **-ais**) ADJ western ▶ M/F westerner

ocidente [osi'dẽtʃi] M west

ócio ['ɔsju] M (*lazer*) leisure; (*inação*) idleness; **ocioso, -a** [o'sjozu, ɔza] ADJ idle; (*vaga*) unfilled

oco, -a ['oku, a] ADJ hollow, empty

ocorrência [oko'hẽsja] F incident, event; (*circunstância*) circumstance

ocorrer [oko'her] VI to happen, occur; (*vir ao pensamento*) to come to mind; **~ a alguém** to happen to sb; (*vir ao pensamento*) to occur to sb

octogésimo, -a [okto'ʒezimu, a] NUM eightieth

oculista [oku'lista] M/F optician

óculo ['ɔkulu] M spyglass; **óculos** MPL glasses, spectacles; **~s de proteção** goggles

ocultar [okuw'tar] VT to hide, conceal; **oculto, -a** [o'kuwtu, a] ADJ hidden; (*desconhecido*) unknown; (*secreto*) secret; (*sobrenatural*) occult

ocupação [okupa'sãw] (*pl* **-ões**) F occupation

ocupado, -a [oku'padu, a] ADJ (*pessoa*) busy; (*lugar*) taken, occupied; (BR: *telefone*) engaged (BRIT), busy (US); **sinal de ~** (BR *Tel*) engaged tone (BRIT), busy signal (US)

ocupar [oku'par] VT to occupy; (*tempo*) to take up; (*pessoa*) to keep busy; **ocupar-se** VR: **~-se com** *ou* **de** *ou* **em algo** (*cuidar de*) to look after sth; (*passar seu tempo com*) to occupy o.s. with sth

odiar [o'dʒjar] VT to hate; **ódio** ['ɔdʒju] M hate, hatred; **odioso, -a** [o'dʒjozu, ɔza] ADJ hateful

odor [o'dor] M smell

oeste ['wɛstʃi] M west ▶ ADJ INV (*região*) western; (*direção, vento*) westerly

ofegante [ofe'gãtʃi] ADJ
breathless, panting

ofender [ofẽ'der] VT to offend;
ofender-se VR to take offence
(BRIT) *ou* offense (US)

ofensa [o'fẽsa] F insult; (*à lei,
moral*) offence (BRIT), offense (US);
ofensiva [ofẽ'siva] F offensive;
ofensivo, -a [ofẽ'sivu, a] ADJ
offensive

oferecer [ofere'ser] VT to offer;
(*dar*) to give; (*jantar*) to give;
(*propor*) to propose; (*dedicar*) to
dedicate; **oferecer-se** VR (*pessoa*)
to offer o.s., volunteer;
(*oportunidade*) to present itself,
arise; **~-se para fazer** to offer to
do; **oferecimento** [oferesi'mẽtu]
M offer; **oferta** [o'fɛrta] F offer;
(*dádiva*) gift; (*Com*) bid; (*em loja*)
special offer

oficial [ofi'sjaw] (*pl* **-ais**) ADJ
official ▶ M/F official; (*Mil*) officer;
~ de justiça bailiff

oficina [ofi'sina] F workshop;
~ mecânica garage

ofício [o'fisju] M trade; (*Rel*)
service; (*carta*) official letter;
(*função*) function; (*encargo*) job,
task

oitavo, -a [oj'tavu, a] NUM eighth

oitenta [oj'tẽta] NUM eighty

oito ['ojtu] NUM eight

olá [o'la] EXCL hello!

olaria [ola'ria] F (*fábrica: de louças
de barro*) pottery; (: *de tijolos*)
brickworks *sg*

óleo ['ɔlju] M (*lubricante*) oil; **~ de
bronzear** suntan oil; **~ diesel**
diesel oil; **oleoso, -a** [o'ljozu, ɔza]
ADJ oily; (*gorduroso*) greasy

olfato [ow'fatu] M sense of smell

olhada [o'ʎada] F glance, look;
dar uma ~ to have a look

olhadela [oʎa'dɛla] F peep

olhar [o'ʎar] VT to look at;
(*observar*) to watch; (*ponderar*) to
consider; (*cuidar de*) to look after
▶ VI to look ▶ M look; **olhar-se** VR
to look at o.s.; (*duas pessoas*) to
look at each other; **~ fixamente**
to stare at; **~ para** to look at;
~ por to look after; **~ fixo** stare

olho ['oʎu] M (*Anat, de agulha*) eye;
(*vista*) eyesight; **~ nele!** watch
him!; **~ vivo!** keep your eyes
open!; **a ~** (*medir, calcular etc*) by
eye; **~ mágico** (*na porta*) peephole;
~ roxo black eye; **num abrir e
fechar de ~s** in a flash

olimpíada [olĩ'piada] F: **as O~s**
the Olympics

oliveira [oli'vejra] F olive tree

ombro ['õbru] M shoulder;
encolher os ~s, dar de ~s to
shrug one's shoulders

omelete [ome'letʃi] F omelette
(BRIT), omelet (US)

omissão [omi'sãw] (*pl* **-ões**) F
omission; (*negligência*) negligence

omitir [omi'tʃir] VT to omit

omoplata [omo'plata] F shoulder
blade

onça ['õsa] F ounce; (*animal*)
jaguar

onda ['õda] F wave; (*moda*)
fashion; **~ curta/média/longa**
short/medium/long wave; **~ de
calor** heat wave

onde ['õdʒi] ADV where ▶ CONJ
where, in which; **de ~ você é?**
where are you from?; **por ~**
through which; **por ~?** which
way?; **~ quer que** wherever

ondulado, -a [õdu'ladu, a] ADJ
wavy

ônibus ['onibus] (*BR*) M INV bus;
ponto de ~ bus stop

ontem ['ōtē] ADV yesterday; **~ à noite** last night

ONU ['onu] ABR F (= *Organização das Nações Unidas*) UNO

ônus ['onus] M INV onus; (*obrigação*) obligation; (*Com*) charge; (*encargo desagradável*) burden

onze ['ōzi] NUM eleven

opaco, -a [o'paku, a] ADJ opaque; (*obscuro*) dark

opção [op'sāw] (*pl* **-ões**) F option, choice; (*preferência*) first claim, right

ópera ['ɔpera] F opera

operação [opera'sāw] (*pl* **-ões**) F operation; (*Com*) transaction

operador, a [opera'dor(a)] M/F operator; (*cirurgião*) surgeon; (*num cinema*) projectionist

operar [ope'rar] VT to operate; (*produzir*) to effect, bring about; (*Med*) to operate on ▶ VI to operate; (*agir*) to act, function; **operar-se** VR (*suceder*) to take place; (*Med*) to have an operation

operário, -a [ope'rarju, a] ADJ working ▶ M/F worker; **classe operária** working class

opinar [opi'nar] VT to think ▶ VI to give one's opinion

opinião [opi'njāw] (*pl* **-ões**) F opinion; **mudar de ~** to change one's mind

oponente [opo'nētʃi] ADJ opposing ▶ M/F opponent

opor [o'por] (*irreg: como* **pôr**) VT to oppose; (*resistência*) to put up, offer; (*objeção, dificuldade*) to raise; **opor-se** VR: **~-se a** to object to; (*resistir*) to oppose

oportunidade [oportuni'dadʒi] F opportunity

oportunista [oportu'nista] ADJ, M/F opportunist

oportuno, -a [opor'tunu, a] ADJ (*momento*) opportune, right; (*oferta de ajuda*) well-timed; (*conveniente*) convenient, suitable

oposição [opozi'sāw] F opposition; **em ~ a** against; **fazer ~ a** to oppose

opressão [opre'sāw] (*pl* **-ões**) F oppression; **opressivo, -a** [opre'sivu, a] ADJ oppressive

oprimir [opri'mir] VT to oppress; (*comprimir*) to press

optar [op'tar] VI to choose; **~ por** to opt for; **~ por fazer** to opt to do

ora ['ɔra] ADV now ▶ CONJ well; **por ~** for the time being; **~ ..., ~ ...** one moment ..., the next ...; **~ bem** now then

oração [ora'sāw] (*pl* **-ões**) F prayer; (*discurso*) speech; (*Ling*) clause

oral [o'raw] (*pl* **-ais**) ADJ oral ▶ F oral (exam)

orar [o'rar] VI (*Rel*) to pray

órbita ['ɔrbita] F orbit; (*do olho*) socket

Órcades ['ɔrkadʒis] FPL: **as ~** the Orkneys

orçamento [orsa'mētu] M (*do estado etc*) budget; (*avaliação*) estimate

orçar [or'sar] VT to value, estimate ▶ VI: **~ em** (*gastos etc*) to be valued at, be put at

ordem ['ɔrdē] (*pl* **-ns**) F order; **até nova ~** until further notice; **de primeira ~** first-rate; **estar em ~** to be tidy; **por ~** in order, in turn; **~ do dia** agenda; **~ pública** public order, law and order

ordenado, -a [orde'nadu, a] ADJ (*posto em ordem*) in order; (*metódico*) orderly ▶ M salary, wages *pl*

ordens ['ɔrdēs] FPL *de* **ordem**

ordinário, -a [ordʒi'narju, a] ADJ ordinary; (*comum*) usual; (*medíocre*) mediocre; (*grosseiro*) coarse, vulgar; (*de má qualidade*) inferior; **de ~** usually

orelha [o'reʎa] F ear; (*aba*) flap

orelhão [ore'ʎãw] (*pl* -**ões**) M payphone

órfão, -fã ['ɔrfãw, fã] (*pl* -**s/-s**) ADJ, M/F orphan

orgânico, -a [or'ganiku, a] ADJ organic

organismo [orga'nizmu] M organism; (*entidade*) organization

organização [organiza'sãw] (*pl* -**ões**) F organization; **organizar** [organi'zar] VT to organize

órgão ['ɔrgãw] (*pl* -**s**) M organ; (*governamental etc*) institution, body

orgasmo [or'gazmu] M orgasm

orgia [or'ʒia] F orgy

orgulho [or'guʎu] M pride; **orgulhoso, -a** [orgu'ʎozu, ɔza] ADJ proud

orientação [orjẽta'sãw] F guidance; (*posição*) position; **~ educacional** training, guidance

oriental [orjẽ'taw] (*pl* -**ais**) ADJ eastern; (*do Extremo Oriente*) oriental

orientar [orjẽ'tar] VT to orientate; (*indicar o rumo*) to direct; (*aconselhar*) to guide; **orientar-se** VR to get one's bearings; **~-se por algo** to follow sth

oriente [o'rjẽtʃi] M: **o O~** the East; **Extremo O~** Far East; **O~ Médio** Middle East

origem [o'riʒẽ] (*pl* -**ns**) F origin; (*ascendência*) lineage, descent; **lugar de ~** birthplace

original [oriʒi'naw] (*pl* -**ais**) ADJ original; (*estranho*) strange, odd ▸ M original; **originalidade** [oriʒinali'dadʒi] F originality;

(*excentricidade*) eccentricity

originar [oriʒi'nar] VT to give rise to, start; **originar-se** VR to arise; **~-se de** to originate from

oriundo, -a [o'rjũdu, a] ADJ: **~ de** arising from; (*natural*) native of

orla ['ɔrla] F: **~ marítima** seafront

ornamento [orna'mẽtu] M adornment, decoration

orquestra [or'kɛstra], (PT) **orquesta** F orchestra

orquídea [or'kidʒja] F orchid

ortodoxo, -a [orto'dɔksu, a] ADJ orthodox

ortografia [ortogra'fia] F spelling

orvalho [or'vaʎu] M dew

os [us] ART DEF *ver* **o**

osso ['osu] M bone

ostensivo, -a [ostẽ'sivu, a] ADJ ostensible

ostentar [ostẽ'tar] VT to show; (*alardear*) to show off, flaunt

ostra ['ostra] F oyster

OTAN ['otã] ABR F (= *Organização do Tratado do Atlântico Norte*) NATO

ótica ['ɔtʃika] F optics *sg*; (*loja*) optician's; (*fig: ponto de vista*) viewpoint; *ver tb* **ótico**

ótico, -a ['ɔtʃiku, a] ADJ optical ▸ M/F optician

otimista [otʃi'mista] ADJ optimistic ▸ M/F optimist

ótimo, -a ['ɔtʃimu, a] ADJ excellent, splendid ▸ EXCL great!, super!

ou [o] CONJ or; **ou este ou aquele** either this one or that one; **ou seja** in other words

ouço ['osu] VB *ver* **ouvir**

ouriço [o'risu] M (*europeu*) hedgehog; (*casca*) shell

ouro ['oru] M gold; **ouros** MPL (*Cartas*) diamonds

ousadia [oza'dʒia] F daring;

ousado, -a [o'zadu, a] ADJ daring, bold
ousar [o'zar] VT, VI to dare
outono [o'tɔnu] M autumn

(PALAVRA-CHAVE)

outro, -a ['otru, a] ADJ **1** (distinto: sg) another; (: pl) other; **outra coisa** something else; **de outro modo, de outra maneira** otherwise; **no outro dia** the next day; **ela está outra** (mudada) she's changed **2** (adicional): **quer outro café?** would you like another coffee?; **outra vez** again
▶ PRON **1**: **o outro** the other one; **(os) outros** (the) others; **de outro** somebody else's
2 (recíproco): **odeiam-se uns aos outros** they hate one another ou each other
3: **outro tanto** the same again; **comer outro tanto** to eat the same ou as much again; **ele recebeu uma dezena de telegramas e outras tantas chamadas** he got about ten telegrams and as many calls

outubro [o'tubru] M October
ouvido [o'vidu] M (Anat) ear; (sentido) hearing; **de ~** by ear; **dar ~s a** to listen to
ouvinte [o'vĩtʃi] M/F listener; (estudante) auditor
ouvir [o'vir] VT to hear; (com atenção) to listen to; (missa) to attend ▶ VI to hear; to listen; **~ dizer que ...** to hear that ...; **~ falar de** to hear of
ova ['ɔva] F roe
oval [o'vaw] (pl **-ais**) ADJ, F oval
ovário [o'varju] M ovary
ovelha [o'veʎa] F sheep

óvni ['ɔvni] M flying saucer
ovo ['ovu] M egg; **~ pochê** (BR) ou **escalfado** (PT) poached egg; **~ estrelado** ou **frito** fried egg; **~s mexidos** scrambled eggs; **~ cozido** ou **quente** boiled egg; **~s de granja** free-range eggs
oxidar [oksi'dar] VT to rust; **oxidar-se** VR to rust, go rusty
oxigenado, -a [oksiʒe'nadu, a] ADJ (cabelo) bleached; **água oxigenada** peroxide
oxigênio [oksi'ʒenju] M oxygen
ozônio [o'zonju] M ozone; **camada de ~** ozone layer

P

P. ABR (= *Praça*) Sq.

pá [pa] F shovel; (*de remo, hélice*) blade ▶ M (*PT*) pal, mate; **pá de lixo** dustpan

paca ['paka] F (*Zool*) paca

pacato, -a [pa'katu, a] ADJ (*pessoa*) quiet; (*lugar*) peaceful

paciência [pa'sjēsja] F patience; **paciente** [pa'sjētʃi] ADJ, M/F patient

pacífico, -a [pa'sifiku, a] ADJ (*pessoa*) peace-loving; (*aceito sem discussão*) undisputed; (*sossegado*) peaceful; **o (Oceano) P~** the Pacific (Ocean)

pacote [pa'kɔtʃi] M packet; (*embrulho*) parcel; (*Econ, Comput, Turismo*) package

pacto ['paktu] M pact; (*ajuste*) agreement

padaria [pada'ria] F bakery, baker's (shop)

padeiro [pa'dejru] M baker

padiola [pa'dʒjɔla] F stretcher

padrão [pa'drãw] (*pl* **-ões**) M standard; (*medida*) gauge; (*desenho*) pattern; (*fig: modelo*) model; **~ de vida** standard of living

padrasto [pa'drastu] M stepfather

padre ['padri] M priest

padrinho [pa'driɲu] M godfather; (*de noivo*) best man; (*patrono*) sponsor

padroeiro, -a [pa'drwejru, a] M/F patron; (*santo*) patron saint

padrões [pa'drõjs] MPL *de* **padrão**

pães [pãjs] MPL *de* **pão**

pagador, a [paga'dor(a)] ADJ paying ▶ M/F payer; (*de salário*) pay clerk; (*de banco*) teller

pagamento [paga'mētu] M payment; **~ a prazo** *ou* **em prestações** payment in instal(l)ments; **~ à vista** cash payment; **~ contra entrega** (*Com*) COD, cash on delivery

pagar [pa'gar] VT to pay; (*compras, pecados*) to pay for; (*o que devia*) to pay back; (*retribuir*) to repay ▶ VI to pay; **~ por algo** (*tb fig*) to pay for sth; **~ a prestações** to pay in instal(l)ments; **~ de contado** (*PT*) to pay cash

página ['paʒina] F page; **~ (da) web** web page; **~ inicial** home page; **P~s Amarelas** Yellow Pages®

pago, -a ['pagu, a] PP *de* **pagar** ▶ ADJ paid; (*fig*) even ▶ M pay

pai [paj] M father; **pais** MPL parents

painel [paj'nɛw] (*pl* **-éis**) M panel; (*quadro*) picture; (*Auto*) dashboard; (*de avião*) instrument panel; **~ solar** solar panel

país [pa'jis] M country; (*região*) land; **~ natal** native land

paisagem [paj'zaʒẽ] (pl **-ns**) F
scenery; landscape

paisano, -a [paj'zanu, a] ADJ
civilian ▶ M/F (não militar) civilian;
(compatriota) fellow countryman

Países Baixos MPL: **os ~** the
Netherlands

paixão [paj'ʃãw] (pl **-ões**) F passion

palácio [pa'lasju] M palace; **~ da
justiça** courthouse; **Palácio do
Planalto** see note

> **Palácio de Planalto** is the seat
> of the Brazilian government, in
> Brasília. The name comes from
> the fact that the Brazilian capital
> is situated on a plateau. It has
> come to be a byword for central
> government.

paladar [pala'dar] M taste; (Anat)
palate

palafita [pala'fita] F (estacaria)
stilts pl; (habitação) stilt house

palavra [pa'lavra] F word; (fala)
speech; (promessa) promise; (direito
de falar) right to speak; **dar a ~ a
alguém** to give sb the chance to
speak; **ter ~** (pessoa) to be reliable;
~s cruzadas crossword (puzzle) sg;
palavrão [pala'vrãw] (pl **-ões**) M
swearword

palco ['pawku] M (Teatro) stage;
(fig: local) scene

Palestina [pales'tʃina] F: **a ~**
Palestine; **palestino, -a**
[pales'tʃinu, a] ADJ, M/F Palestinian

palestra [pa'lɛstra] F chat, talk;
(conferência) lecture

paletó [pale'tɔ] M jacket

palha ['paʎa] F straw

palhaço [pa'ʎasu] M clown

pálido, -a ['palidu, a] ADJ pale

palito [pa'litu] M stick; (para os
dentes) toothpick

palma ['pawma] F (folha) palm leaf;
(da mão) palm; **bater ~s** to clap;
palmada [paw'mada] F slap

palmeira [paw'mejra] F palm tree

palmo ['pawmu] M span; **~ a ~** inch
by inch

palpável [paw'pavew] (pl **-eis**) ADJ
tangible; (fig) obvious

pálpebra ['pawpebra] F eyelid

palpitação [pawpita'sãw] (pl **-ões**)
F beating, throbbing; **palpitações**
FPL (batimentos cardíacos)
palpitations

palpitante [pawpi'tãtʃi] ADJ
beating, throbbing; (fig:
emocionante) thrilling; (: de interesse
atual) sensational

palpitar [pawpi'tar] VI (coração) to
beat

palpite [paw'pitʃi] M (intuição)
hunch; (Jogo, Turfe) tip; (opinião)
opinion

pampa ['pãpa] F pampas

Panamá [pana'ma] M: **o ~**
Panama; **o canal do ~** the Panama
Canal

pancada [pã'kada] F (no corpo)
blow, hit; (choque) knock; (de relógio)
stroke; **dar ~ em alguém** to hit sb;
pancadaria [pãkada'ria] F (surra)
beating; (tumulto) fight

pandeiro [pã'dejru] M tambourine

pandemia [pãde'mia] F pandemic

pane ['pani] F breakdown

panela [pa'nɛla] F (de barro) pot; (de
metal) pan; (de cozinhar) saucepan;
(no dente) hole; **~ de pressão**
pressure cooker

panfleto [pã'fletu] M pamphlet

pânico ['paniku] M panic; **entrar
em ~** to panic

pano ['panu] M cloth; (Teatro)
curtain; (vela) sheet, sail; **~ de
pratos** tea towel; **~ de pó** duster;
~ de fundo (tb fig) backdrop

panorama [pano'rama] M view

panqueca [pã'kɛka] F pancake

pantanal [pãta'naw] (pl **-ais**) M swampland

pântano ['pãtanu] M marsh, swamp

pantera [pã'tɛra] F panther

pão [pãw] (pl **pães**) M bread; **o P~ de Açúcar** (no Rio) Sugarloaf Mountain; **~ árabe** pitta (BRIT) ou pita (US) bread; **~ torrado** toast; **pão-duro** (pl **pães-duros**) (col) ADJ mean, stingy ▶ M/F miser;

pãozinho [pãw'ziɲu] M roll

papa ['papa] M Pope

papagaio [papa'gaju] M parrot; (pipa) kite

papai [pa'paj] M dad, daddy; **P~ Noel** Santa Claus, Father Christmas

papel [pa'pɛw] (pl **-éis**) M paper; (Teatro) part; (função) role; **~ de embrulho** wrapping paper; **~ de escrever/de alumínio** writing paper/tinfoil; **~ de parede** wallpaper; **~ de seda/ transparente** tissue paper/ tracing paper; **~ filme** Clingfilm® (BRIT), Saran Wrap® (US); **~ higiénico** toilet paper; **papelada** [pape'lada] F pile of papers; (burocracia) paperwork, red tape; **papelão** [pape'lãw] M cardboard; (fig) fiasco; **papelaria** [papela'ria] F stationer's (shop); **papel-carbono** M carbon paper

papinha [pa'piɲa] F: **~ de bebê** baby food

papo ['papu] M (col) double chin; (: conversa) chat; (: papo furado) hot air; **bater** ou **levar um ~** (col) to have a chat; **bater ~** (col) to chat (also internet); **ficar de ~ para o ar** (fig) to laze around

paquerar [pake'rar] (col) VI to flirt ▶ VT to chat up

paquistanês, -esa [pakista'nes, eza] ADJ, M/F Pakistani

Paquistão [pakis'tãw] M: **o ~** Pakistan

par [par] ADJ (igual) equal; (número) even ▶ M pair; (casal) couple; (pessoa na dança) partner; **~ a ~** side by side, level; **sem ~** incomparable

para ['para] PREP for; (direção) to, towards; **~ que** so that, in order that; **~ quê?** what for?, why?; **ir ~ casa** to go home; **~ com** (atitude) towards; **de lá ~ cá** since then; **~ a semana** next week; **estar ~** to be about to; **é ~ nós ficarmos aqui?** should we stay here?

parabéns [para'bẽjs] MPL congratulations; (no aniversário) happy birthday; **dar ~ a** to congratulate

para-brisa ['para-] (pl **-s**) M windscreen (BRIT), windshield (US)

para-choque ['para-] (pl **-s**) M (Auto) bumper

parada [pa'rada] F stop; (Com) stoppage; (militar, colegial) parade

parado, -a [pa'radu, a] ADJ (imóvel) standing still; (sem vida) lifeless; (carro) stationary; (máquina) out of action; (olhar) fixed; (trabalhador, fábrica) idle

paradoxo [para'dɔksu] M paradox

parafuso [para'fuzu] M screw

paragem [pa'raʒẽ] (pl **-ns**) F (PT) stop; **paragens** FPL (lugares) parts; **~ de eléctrico** (PT) tram (BRIT) ou streetcar (US) stop

parágrafo [pa'ragrafu] M paragraph

Paraguai [para'gwaj] M: **o ~**

P

Paraguay; **paraguaio, -a**
[para'gwaju, a] ADJ, M/F
Paraguayan

paraíso [para'izu] M paradise

para-lama ['para-] (pl **-s**) M wing
(BRIT), fender (US); (de bicicleta)
mudguard

paralelepípedo [paralele'pipedu]
M cobblestone

paralelo, -a [para'lɛlu, a] ADJ

parapeito [para'pejtu] M wall,
parapet; (da janela) windowsill

parapente [para'pẽjtʃi] M (Esporte)
paragliding; (equipamento)
paraglider

paraquedas [para'kɛdas] M INV
parachute

parar [pa'rar] VI to stop; (ficar) to
stay ▶ VT to stop; **fazer ~** (deter) to
stop; **~ na cadeia** to end up in jail;
~ de fazer to stop doing

para-raios ['para-] M INV lightning
conductor

parasita [para'zita] M parasite

parceiro, -a [par'sejru, a] ADJ
matching ▶ M/F partner

parcela [par'sɛla] F piece, bit; (de
pagamento) instalment (BRIT),
installment (US); (de terra) plot; (do
eleitorado etc) section; (Mat) item

parceria [parse'ria] F partnership

parcial [par'sjaw] (pl **-ais**) ADJ
partial; (feito por partes) in parts;
(pessoa) biased; (Pol) partisan;
parcialidade [parsjali'dadʒi] F
bias, partiality

pardal [par'daw] (pl **-ais**) M
sparrow

pardieiro [par'dʒjejru] M ruin,
heap

pardo, -a ['pardu, a] ADJ (cinzento)
grey (BRIT), gray (US); (castanho)
brown; (mulato) mulatto

parecer [pare'ser] VI (ter a aparência

de) to look, seem; **parecer-se** VR:
~-se com alguém to look like sb;
~ alguém/algo to look like sb/sth;
ao que parece apparently;
parece-me que I think that, it
seems to me that; **que lhe parece?**
what do you think?; **parece que**
(pelo visto) it looks as if; (segundo
dizem) apparently

parecido, -a [pare'sidu, a] ADJ
alike, similar; **~ com** like

parede [pa'redʒi] F wall

parente [pa'rẽtʃi] M/F relative,
relation; **parentesco** [parẽ'tesku]
M relationship; (fig) connection

parêntese [pa'rẽtezi] M
parenthesis; (na escrita) bracket;
(fig: digressão) digression

páreo ['parju] M race; (fig)
competition

parir [pa'rir] VT to give birth to ▶ VI
to give birth; (mulher) to have a baby

Paris [pa'ris] N Paris; **parisiense**
[pari'zjẽsi] ADJ, M/F Parisian

parlamentar [parlamẽ'tar] ADJ
parliamentary ▶ M/F member of
parliament

parlamento [parla'mẽtu] M
parliament

paróquia [pa'rɔkja] F (Rel) parish

parque ['parki] M park;
~ industrial industrial estate;
~ nacional national park; **~ de
diversões** amusement park

parte ['partʃi] F part; (quinhão)
share; (lado) side; (ponto) point;
(Jur) party; (papel) role; **a maior ~
de** most of; **à ~** aside; (separado)
separate; (separadamente)
separately; (além de) apart from; **da
~ de alguém** on sb's part; **em
alguma/qualquer ~** somewhere/
anywhere; **em ~ alguma** nowhere;
por toda (a) ~ everywhere; **pôr de ~**

to set aside; **tomar ~ em** to take part in; **dar ~ de alguém à polícia** to report sb to the police

participar [partʃisi'par] VT to announce, notify of ▶ VI: **~ de** ou **em** to participate in, take part in; (*compartilhar*) to share in

particípio [partʃi'sipju] M participle

particular [partʃiku'lar] ADJ particular, special; (*privativo, pessoal*) private ▶ M particular; (*indivíduo*) individual; **particulares** MPL (*pormenores*) details; **em ~** in private; **particularmente** [partʃikular'mẽtʃi] ADV privately; (*especialmente*) particularly

partida [par'tʃida] F (*saída*) departure; (*Esporte*) game, match

partidário, -a [partʃi'darju, a] ADJ supporting ▶ M/F supporter, follower

partido, -a [par'tʃidu, a] ADJ broken ▶ M (*Pol*) party; **tirar ~ de** to profit from; **tomar o ~ de** to side with

partilhar [partʃi'ʎar] VT to share; (*distribuir*) to share out

partir [par'tʃir] VT to break; (*dividir*) to split ▶ VI (*pôr-se a caminho*) to set off, set out; (*ir-se embora*) to leave, depart; **partir-se** VR to break; **a ~ de** (*starting*) from; **~ para outra** (*col*) to move on

parto ['partu] M (child)birth; **estar em trabalho de ~** to be in labour (*BRIT*) ou labor (*US*)

Páscoa ['paskwa] F Easter; (*dos judeus*) Passover

pasmo, -a ['pazmu, a] ADJ astonished ▶ M amazement

passa ['pasa] F raisin

passadeira [pasa'dejra] F (*tapete*) stair carpet; (*mulher*) ironing lady;

(*PT: para peões*) zebra crossing (*BRIT*), crosswalk (*US*)

passado, -a [pa'sadu, a] ADJ past; (*antiquado*) old-fashioned; (*fruta*) bad; (*peixe*) off ▶ M past; **o ano ~** last year; **bem ~** (*carne*) well done

passageiro, -a [pasa'ʒejru, a] ADJ passing ▶ M/F passenger

passagem [pa'saʒẽ] (*pl* **-ns**) F passage; (*preço de condução*) fare; (*bilhete*) ticket; **~ de ida e volta** return ticket, round trip ticket (*US*); **~ de nível** level (*BRIT*) ou grade (*US*) crossing; **~ de pedestres** pedestrian crossing (*BRIT*), crosswalk (*US*); **~ subterrânea** underpass, subway (*BRIT*)

passaporte [pasa'pɔrtʃi] M passport

passar [pa'sar] VT to pass; (*exceder*) to go beyond, exceed; (*a ferro*) to iron; (*o tempo*) to spend; (*a outra pessoa*) to pass on; (*pomada*) to put on ▶ VI to pass; (*na rua*) to go past; (*tempo*) to go by; (*dor*) to wear off; (*terminar*) to be over; **passar-se** VR (*acontecer*) to go on, happen; **~ bem** (*de saúde*) to be well; **passava das dez horas** it was past ten o'clock; **~ alguém para trás** to con sb; (*cônjuge*) to cheat on sb; **~ por algo** (*sofrer*) to go through sth; (*transitar, estrada*) to go along sth; (*ser considerado como*) to be thought of as sth; **~ sem** to do without

passarela [pasa'rɛla] F footbridge

pássaro ['pasaru] M bird

passatempo [pasa'tẽpu] M pastime

passe ['pasi] M pass

passear [pa'sjar] VT to take for a walk ▶ VI (*a pé*) to go for a walk; (*sair*) to go out; **~ a cavalo/de**

carro to go for a ride/a drive;
passeata [pa'sjata] F (*marcha coletiva*) protest march; **passeio** [pa'seju] M walk; (*de carro*) drive, ride; (*excursão*) outing; (*calçada*) pavement (BRIT), sidewalk (US); **dar um passeio** to go for a walk; (*de carro*) to go for a drive ou ride
passível [pa'sivew] (*pl* **-eis**) ADJ: **~ de** (*dor etc*) susceptible to; (*pena, multa*) subject to
passivo, -a [pa'sivu, a] ADJ passive ▶ M (*Com*) liabilities *pl*
passo ['pasu] M step; (*medida*) pace; (*modo de andar*) walk; (*ruído dos passos*) footstep; (*sinal de pé*) footprint; **ao ~ que** while; **ceder o ~ a** to give way to
pasta ['pasta] F paste; (*de couro*) briefcase; (*de cartolina*) folder; (*de ministro*) portfolio; **~ dentifrícia** ou **de dentes** toothpaste
pastar [pas'tar] VT to graze on ▶ VI to graze
pastel [pas'tɛw] (*pl* **-éis**) ADJ INV (*cor*) pastel ▶ M samosa
pastelão [paste'lãw] M slapstick
pastelaria [pastela'ria] F cake shop; (*comida*) pastry
pasteurizado, -a [pastewri'zadu, a] ADJ pasteurized
pastilha [pas'tʃiʎa] F (*Med*) tablet; (*doce*) pastille
pastor, a [pas'tor(a)] M/F shepherd(ess) ▶ M (*Rel*) clergyman, pastor
pata ['pata] F (*pé de animal*) foot, paw; (*ave*) duck; (*col: pé*) foot
patamar [pata'mar] M (*de escada*) landing; (*fig*) level
pateta [pa'tɛta] ADJ stupid, daft ▶ M/F idiot
patético, -a [pa'tɛtʃiku, a] ADJ pathetic, moving

patife [pa'tʃifi] M scoundrel, rogue
patim [pa'tʃĩ] (*pl* **-ns**) M skate; **~ de rodas** roller skate; **patins em linha** Rollerblades®; **patinar** [patʃi'nar] VI to skate; (*Auto: derrapar*) to skid
patins [pa'tʃĩs] MPL *de* **patim**
pátio ['patʃju] M (*de uma casa*) patio, backyard; (*espaço cercado de edifícios*) courtyard; (*tb: ~ de recreio*) playground; (*Mil*) parade ground
pato ['patu] M duck; (*macho*) drake
patologia [patolo'ʒia] F pathology; **patológico, -a** [pato'lɔʒiku, a] ADJ pathological
patrão [pa'trãw] (*pl* **-ões**) M (*Com*) boss; (*dono de casa*) master; (*proprietário*) landlord; (*Náut*) skipper
pátria ['patrja] F homeland
patrimônio [patri'monju] M (*herança*) inheritance; (*fig*) heritage; (*bens*) property
patriota [pa'trjɔta] M/F patriot
patrocinar [patrosi'nar] VT to sponsor; (*proteger*) to support; **patrocínio** [patro'sinju] M sponsorship, backing; (*proteção*) support
patrões [pa'trõjs] MPL *de* **patrão**
patrulha [pa'truʎa] F patrol; **patrulhar** [patru'ʎar] VT, VI to patrol
pau [paw] M (*madeira*) wood; (*vara*) stick; **paus** MPL (*Cartas*) clubs; **~ a ~** neck and neck; **~ de bandeira** flagpole
pausa ['pawza] F pause; (*intervalo*) break; (*descanso*) rest
pauta ['pawta] F (*linha*) (guide)line; (*ordem do dia*) agenda; (*indicações*) guidelines *pl*; **sem ~** (*papel*) plain; **em ~** on the agenda
pavão, -voa [pa'vãw, 'voa] (*pl* **-ões/-s**) M/F peacock/peahen

pavilhão [pavi'ʎãw] (pl **-ões**) M tent; (de madeira) hut; (no jardim) summerhouse; (em exposição) pavilion; (bandeira) flag

pavimento [pavi'mẽtu] M (chão, andar) floor; (da rua) road surface

pavões [pa'võjs] MPL de **pavão**

pavor [pa'vor] M dread, terror; **ter ~ de** to be terrified of; **pavoroso, -a** [pavo'rozu, ɔza] ADJ dreadful, terrible

paz [pajz] F peace; **fazer as ~es** to make up, be friends again

PC ABR M PC

Pça. ABR (= *Praça*) Sq.

pé [pɛ] M foot; (da mesa) leg; (fig: base) footing; (de milho, café) plant; **ir a pé** to walk, go on foot; **ao pé de** near, by; **ao pé da letra** literally; **estar de pé** (festa etc) to be on; **em** ou **de pé** standing (up); **dar no pé** (col) to run away, take off; **não ter pé nem cabeça** (fig) to make no sense

peão [pjãw] (pl **-ões**) M (PT) pedestrian

peça ['pɛsa] F piece; (Auto) part; (aposento) room; (Teatro) play; **~ de reposição** spare part; **~ de roupa** garment

pecado [pe'kadu] M sin

pecar [pe'kar] VI to sin; **~ por excesso de zelo** to be over-zealous

pechincha [pe'ʃiʃa] F (vantagem) godsend; (coisa barata) bargain; **pechinchar** [peʃi'ʃar] VI to bargain, haggle

peço ['pɛsu] VB ver **pedir**

peculiar [peku'ljar] ADJ special, peculiar; (particular) particular; **peculiaridade** [pekuljari'dadʒi] F peculiarity

pedaço [pe'dasu] M piece; (fig:

trecho) bit; **aos ~s** in pieces

pedágio [pe'daʒju] (BR) M (pagamento) toll

pedal [pe'daw] (pl **-ais**) M pedal; **pedalar** [peda'lar] VT, VI to pedal

pedante [pe'dãtʃi] ADJ pretentious ▶ M/F pseud

pedestre [pe'dɛstri] (BR) M pedestrian

pedicuro, -a [pedʒi'kuru, a] M/F chiropodist (BRIT), podiatrist (US)

pedido [pe'dʒidu] M request; (Com) order; **~ de demissão** resignation; **~ de desculpa** apology

pedinte [pe'dʒĩtʃi] M/F beggar

pedir [pe'dʒir] VT to ask for; (Com, comida) to order; (exigir) to demand ▶ VI to ask; (num restaurante) to order; **~ algo a alguém** to ask sb for sth; **~ a alguém que faça, ~ para alguém fazer** to ask sb to do

pedófilo, -a [pe'dɔfilu, a] M/F paedophile (BRIT), pedophile (US)

pedra ['pedra] F stone; (rochedo) rock; (de granizo) hailstone; (de açúcar) lump; (quadro-negro) slate; **~ de gelo** ice cube; **pedreiro** [pe'drejru] M stonemason

pegada [pe'gada] F (de pé) footprint; (Futebol) save; **~ de carbono** carbon footprint

pegado, -a [pe'gadu, a] ADJ stuck; (unido) together

pegajoso, -a [pega'ʒozu, ɔza] ADJ sticky

pegar [pe'gar] VT to catch; (selos) to stick (on); (segurar) to take hold of; (hábito, mania) to get into; (compreender) to take in; (trabalho) to take on; (estação de rádio) to pick up, get ▶ VI to stick; (planta) to take; (moda) to catch on; (doença) to be catching; (motor) to start;

P

~ em (*segurar*) to grab, pick up; **ir ~** (*buscar*) to go and get; **~ um emprego** to get a job; **~ fogo a algo** to set fire to sth; **~ no sono** to get to sleep

pego, -a ['pɛgu, a] pp de **pegar**

peito ['pejtu] M (*Anat*) chest; (*de ave, mulher*) breast; (*fig*) courage

peitoril [pejto'riw] (*pl* **-is**) M windowsill

peixada [pej'ʃada] F *fish cooked in a seafood sauce*

peixaria [pejʃa'ria] F fish shop, fishmonger's (*BRIT*)

peixe ['pejʃi] M fish; **Peixes** MPL (*Astrologia*) Pisces *sg*

pela ['pɛla] = **por + a**

pelada [pe'lada] F football game

> **Pelada** is an improvised, generally short, game of football, which in the past was played with a ball made out of socks, or an inflatable rubber ball. It is still played today on any piece of open land, or even in the street.

pelado, -a [pe'ladu, a] ADJ (*sem pele*) skinned; (*sem pelo, cabelo*) shorn; (*nu*) naked, in the nude; (*sem dinheiro*) broke

pelar [pe'lar] VT (*tirar a pele*) to skin; (*tirar o pelo*) to shear

pelas ['pɛlas] = **por + as**

pele ['pɛli] F skin; (*couro*) leather; (*como agasalho*) fur; (*de animal*) hide

película [pe'likula] F film

pelo¹ ['pɛlu] = **por + o**

pelo² ['pelu] M hair; (*de animal*) fur, coat; **nu em ~** stark naked

pelos ['pɛlus] = **por + os**

peludo, -a [pe'ludu, a] ADJ hairy; (*animal*) furry

pena ['pena] F feather; (*de caneta*) nib; (*escrita*) writing; (*Jur*) penalty,

punishment; (*sofrimento*) suffering; (*piedade*) pity; **que ~!** what a shame!; **dar ~** to be upsetting; **ter ~ de** to feel sorry for; **~ de morte** death penalty

pênalti ['penawtʃi] M (*Futebol*) penalty (kick)

penar [pe'nar] VT to grieve ▶ VI to suffer

pendência [pē'dēsja] F dispute, quarrel

pendente [pē'dētʃi] ADJ hanging; (*por decidir*) pending; (*inclinado*) sloping; (*dependent*): **~ de** dependent on ▶ M pendant

pêndulo ['pēdulu] M pendulum

pendurar [pēdu'rar] VT to hang

penedo [pe'nedu] M rock, boulder

peneira [pe'nejra] F sieve; **peneirar** [penej'rar] VT to sift, sieve ▶ VI (*chover*) to drizzle

penetrar [pene'trar] VT to get into, penetrate; (*compreender*) to understand ▶ VI: **~ em** *ou* **por** *ou* **entre** to penetrate

penhasco [pe'ɲasku] M cliff, crag

penhorar [peɲo'rar] VT (*dar em penhor*) to pledge, pawn

penicilina [penisi'lina] F penicillin

península [pe'nĩsula] F peninsula

pênis ['penis] M INV penis

penitência [peni'tēsja] F penitence; (*expiação*) penance; **penitenciária** [penitē'sjarja] F prison

penoso, -a [pe'nozu, ɔza] ADJ (*assunto, tratamento*) painful; (*trabalho*) hard

pensamento [pēsa'mētu] M thought; (*mente*) mind; (*opinião*) way of thinking; (*ideia*) idea

pensão [pē'sāw] (*pl* **-ões**) F (*tb*: **casa de ~**) boarding house; (*comida*) board; **~ completa** full board; **~ de**

aposentadoria (retirement) pension

pensar [pẽ'sar] vi to think; (*imaginar*) to imagine; **~ em** to think of ou about; **~ fazer** to intend to do; **pensativo, -a** [pẽsa'tʃivu, a] ADJ thoughtful, pensive

pensionista [pẽsjo'nista] M/F pensioner

pensões [pẽ'sõjs] FPL de **pensão**

pente ['pẽtʃi] M comb; **penteado, -a** [pẽ'tʃjadu, a] ADJ (*cabelo*) in place; (*pessoa*) smart ▶ M hairdo, hairstyle; **pentear** [pẽ'tʃjar] vt to comb; (*arranjar o cabelo*) to do, style; **pentear-se** VR to comb one's hair; to do one's hair

penúltimo, -a [pe'nuwtʃimu, a] ADJ last but one, penultimate

penumbra [pe'nũbra] F twilight, dusk; (*sombra*) shadow; (*meia-luz*) half-light

penúria [pe'nurja] F poverty

peões [pjõjs] MPL de **peão**

pepino [pe'pinu] M cucumber

pequeno, -a [pe'kenu, a] ADJ small; (*mesquinho*) petty ▶ M boy

Pequim [pe'kĩ] N Beijing

pera ['pera] F pear

perambular [perãbu'lar] vi to wander

perante [pe'rãtʃi] PREP before, in the presence of

per capita [pɛr'kapita] ADV, ADJ per capita

perceber [perse'ber] vt to realize; (*por meio dos sentidos*) to perceive; (*compreender*) to understand; (*ver*) to see; (*ouvir*) to hear; (*ver ao longe*) to make out; (*dinheiro: receber*) to receive

percentagem [persẽ'taʒẽ] F percentage

percepção [persep'sãw] F perception; **perceptível** [persep'tʃivew] (*pl* **-eis**) ADJ perceptible, noticeable; (*som*) audible

percevejo [perse'veʒu] M (*inseto*) bug; (*prego*) drawing pin (BRIT), thumbtack (US)

perco ['perku] vB ver **perder**

percorrer [perko'her] vt (*viajar por*) to travel (across ou over); (*passar por*) to go through, traverse; (*investigar*) to search through

percurso [per'kursu] M (*espaço percorrido*) distance (covered); (*trajeto*) route; (*viagem*) journey

percussão [perku'sãw] F (*Mús*) percussion

perda ['perda] F loss; (*desperdício*) waste; **~s e danos** damages, losses

perdão [per'dãw] M pardon, forgiveness; **~!** sorry!, I beg your pardon!

perder [per'der] vt to lose; (*tempo*) to waste; (*trem, show, oportunidade*) to miss ▶ vi to lose; **perder-se** VR to get lost; (*arruinar-se*) to be ruined; (*desaparecer*) to disappear; **~-se de alguém** to lose sb

perdido, -a [per'dʒidu, a] ADJ lost; **~s e achados** lost and found, lost property

perdiz [per'dʒiz] F partridge

perdoar [per'dwar] vt to forgive

perdurar [perdu'rar] vi to last a long time; (*continuar a existir*) to still exist

perecível [pere'sivew] (*pl* **-eis**) ADJ perishable

peregrinação [peregrina'sãw] (*pl* **-ões**) F (*viagem*) travels *pl*; (*Rel*) pilgrimage

peregrino, -a [pere'grinu, a] M/F pilgrim

peremptório, -a [perẽp'tɔrju, a] ADJ final; (*decisivo*) decisive

perene [pe'rɛni] ADJ everlasting; (*Bot*) perennial

perfeição [perfej'sãw] F perfection

perfeitamente [perfejta'mẽtʃi] ADV perfectly ▶ EXCL exactly!

perfeito, -a [per'fejtu, a] ADJ perfect ▶ M (*Ling*) perfect

perfil [per'fiw] (*pl* -**is**) M profile; (*silhueta*) silhouette, outline; (*Arq*) (*cross*) section

perfume [per'fumi] M perfume; scent

perfurar [perfu'rar] VT (*o chão*) to drill a hole in; (*papel*) to punch (a hole in)

pergunta [per'gũta] F question; **fazer uma ~ a alguém** to ask sb a question; **perguntar** [pergũ'tar] VT to ask; (*interrogar*) to question ▶ VI: **perguntar por alguém** to ask after sb; **perguntar-se** VR to wonder; **perguntar algo a alguém** to ask sb sth

perícia [pe'risja] F expertise; (*destreza*) skill; (*exame*) investigation

periferia [perife'ria] F periphery; (*da cidade*) outskirts *pl*

perigo [pe'rigu] M danger; **perigoso, -a** [peri'gozu, ɔza] ADJ dangerous; (*arriscado*) risky

período [pe'riodu] M period; (*estação*) season

periquito [peri'kitu] M parakeet

perito, -a [pe'ritu, a] ADJ expert ▶ M/F expert; (*quem faz perícia*) investigator

permanecer [permane'ser] VI to remain; (*num lugar*) to stay; (*continuar a ser*) to remain, keep; **~ parado** to keep still

permanência [perma'nẽsja] F permanence; (*estada*) stay;

permanente [perma'nẽtʃi] ADJ (*dor*) constant; (*cor*) fast; (*residência, pregas*) permanent ▶ M (*cartão*) pass ▶ F perm

permissão [permi'sãw] F permission, consent; **permissivo, -a** [permi'sivu, a] ADJ permissive

permitir [permi'tʃir] VT to allow, permit

perna ['pɛrna] F leg; **~s tortas** bow legs

pernil [per'niw] (*pl* -**is**) M (*de animal*) haunch; (*Culin*) leg

pernilongo [perni'lõgu] M mosquito

pernis [per'nis] MPL *de* **pernil**

pernoitar [pernoj'tar] VI to spend the night

pérola ['pɛrola] F pearl

perpendicular [perpẽdʒiku'lar] ADJ, F perpendicular

perpetuar [perpe'twar] VT to perpetuate; **perpétuo, -a** [per'pɛtwu, a] ADJ perpetual

persa ['pɛrsa] ADJ, M/F Persian

perseguição [persegi'sãw] F pursuit; (*Rel, Pol*) persecution

perseguir [perse'gir] VT to pursue; (*correr atrás*) to chase (after); (*Rel, Pol*) to persecute; (*importunar*) to harass, pester

perseverante [perseve'rãtʃi] ADJ persistent

perseverar [perseve'rar] VI to persevere

Pérsia ['pɛrsja] F: **a ~** Persia

persiana [per'sjana] F blind

Pérsico, -a ['pɛrsiku, a] ADJ: **o golfo ~** the Persian Gulf

persigo [per'sigu] VB *ver* **perseguir**

persistir [persis'tʃir] VI to persist

personagem [perso'naʒẽ] (*pl* -**ns**) M/F famous person, celebrity; (*num livro, filme*) character

personalidade [personali'dadʒi] F personality

perspectiva [perspek'tʃiva] F perspective; (*panorama*) view; (*probabilidade*) prospect

perspicácia [perspi'kasja] F insight, perceptiveness; **perspicaz** [perspi'kajʒ] ADJ perceptive; (*sagaz*) shrewd

persuadir [perswa'dʒir] VT to persuade; **persuadir-se** VR to convince o.s.; **persuasão** [perswa'zãw] F persuasion; **persuasivo, -a** [perswa'zivu, a] ADJ persuasive

pertencente [pertẽ'sẽtʃi] ADJ: **~ a** pertaining to

pertencer [pertẽ'ser] VI: **~ a** to belong to; (*referir-se*) to concern

pertences [per'tẽsis] MPL (*de uma pessoa*) belongings

pertinência [pertʃi'nẽsja] F relevance; **pertinente** [pertʃi'nẽtʃi] ADJ relevant; (*apropriado*) appropriate

perto, -a ['pɛrtu, a] ADJ nearby ▶ ADV near; **~ de** near to; (*em comparação com*) next to; **de ~** closely; (*ver*) close up; (*conhecer*) very well

perturbar [pertur'bar] VT to disturb; (*abalar*) to upset, trouble; (*atrapalhar*) to put off; (*andamento, trânsito*) to disrupt; (*envergonhar*) to embarrass; (*alterar*) to affect

Peru [pe'ru] M: **o ~** Peru

peru, a [pe'ru(a)] M/F turkey

peruca [pe'ruka] F wig

perverso, -a [per'vɛrsu, a] ADJ perverse; (*malvado*) wicked

perverter [perver'ter] VT to corrupt, pervert; **pervertido, -a** [perver'tʃidu, a] ADJ perverted ▶ M/F pervert

pesadelo [peza'delu] M nightmare

pesado, -a [pe'zadu, a] ADJ heavy; (*ambiente*) tense; (*trabalho*) hard; (*estilo*) dull, boring; (*andar*) slow; (*piada*) coarse; (*comida*) stodgy; (*tempo*) sultry ▶ ADV heavily

pêsames ['pezamis] MPL condolences, sympathy sg

pesar [pe'zar] VT to weigh; (*fig*) to weigh up ▶ VI to weigh; (*ser pesado*) to be heavy; (*influir*) to carry weight; (*causar mágoa*): **~ a** to hurt, grieve ▶ M grief; **~ sobre** (*recair*) to fall upon

pesaroso, -a [peza'rozu, ɔza] ADJ sorrowful, sad; (*arrependido*) regretful, sorry

pesca ['pɛska] F fishing; (*os peixes*) catch; **ir à ~** to go fishing

pescada [pes'kada] F whiting

pescado [pes'kadu] M fish

pescador, a [peska'dor(a)] M/F fisherman/woman; **~ à linha** angler

pescar [pes'kar] VT (*peixe*) to catch; (*tentar apanhar*) to fish for; (*retirar da água*) to fish out ▶ VI to fish

pescoço [pes'kosu] M neck

peso ['pezu] M weight; (*fig: ônus*) burden; (*importância*) importance; **~ bruto/líquido** gross/net weight

pesquisa [pes'kiza] F research; **uma ~** a study; **pesquisar** [peski'zar] VT, VI to research

pêssego ['pesegu] M peach

pessimista [pesi'mista] ADJ pessimistic ▶ M/F pessimist

péssimo, -a ['pɛsimu, a] ADJ very bad, awful

pessoa [pe'soa] F person; **pessoas** FPL people; **pessoal** [pe'swaw] (*pl* **-ais**) ADJ personal ▶ M personnel *pl*, staff *pl*; (*col*) people *pl*, folks *pl*

pestana [pes'tana] F eyelash

peste ['pɛstʃi] F epidemic; (bubônica) plague; (fig) pest, nuisance

pétala ['pɛtala] F petal

petição [petʃi'sãw] (pl -ões) F request; (documento) petition

petisco [pe'tʃisku] M savoury (BRIT), savory (US), titbit (BRIT), tidbit (US)

petróleo [pe'trɔlju] M oil, petroleum; **~ bruto** crude oil

peúga ['pjuga] (PT) F sock

pevide [pe'vidʒi] (PT) F (de melão) seed; (de maçã) pip

p. ex. ABR (= por exemplo) e.g.

pia ['pia] F wash basin; (da cozinha) sink; **~ batismal** font

piada ['pjada] F joke

pianista [pja'nista] M/F pianist

piano ['pjanu] M piano

piar [pjar] VI (pinto) to cheep; (coruja) to hoot

picada [pi'kada] F (de agulha etc) prick; (de abelha) sting; (de mosquito, cobra) bite; (de avião) dive; (de navalha) stab; (atalho) path, trail

picante [pi'kãtʃi] ADJ (tempero) hot

picar [pi'kar] VT to prick; (suj: abelha) to sting; (: mosquito) to bite; (: pássaro) to peck; (um animal) to goad; (carne) to mince; (papel) to shred; (fruta) to chop up ▶ VI (comichar) to prickle

picareta [pika'reta] F pickaxe (BRIT), pickax (US) ▶ M/F crook

pico ['piku] M (cume) peak; (ponta aguda) sharp point; (PT: um pouco) a bit; **mil e ~** just over a thousand

picolé [piko'lɛ] M lolly

picotar [piko'tar] VT to perforate; (bilhete) to punch

piedade [pje'dadʒi] F piety; (compaixão) pity; **ter ~ de** to have pity on; **piedoso, -a** [pje'dozu, ɔza] ADJ pious; (compassivo) merciful

piercing ['pirsĩ] (pl -s) M piercing

pifar [pi'far] (col) VI (carro) to break down; (rádio etc) to go wrong; (plano, programa) to fall through

pijama [pi'ʒama] M pyjamas pl (BRIT), pajamas pl (US)

pilantra [pi'lãtra] (col) M/F crook

pilar [pi'lar] VT to pound, crush ▶ M pillar

pilha ['piʎa] F (Elet) battery; (monte) pile, heap

pilhar [pi'ʎar] VT to plunder, pillage; (roubar) to rob; (surpreender) to catch

pilotar [pilo'tar] VT (avião) to fly

piloto [pi'lotu] M pilot; (motorista) (racing) driver; (bico de gás) pilot light ▶ ADJ INV (usina, plano) pilot; (peça) sample atr

pílula ['pilula] F pill; **a ~ (anticoncepcional)** the pill

pimenta [pi'mẽta] F (Culin) pepper; **~ de Caiena** cayenne pepper; **pimenta-do-reino** F black pepper; **pimenta-malagueta** (pl **pimentas-malagueta**) F chilli (BRIT) ou chili (US) pepper; **pimentão** [pimẽ'tãw] (pl -ões) M (Bot) pepper

pinça ['pĩsa] F (de sobrancelhas) tweezers pl; (de casa) tongs pl; (Med) callipers pl (BRIT), calipers pl (US)

pincel [pĩ'sɛw] (pl -éis) M brush; (para pintar) paintbrush; **pincelar** [pĩse'lar] VT to paint

pinga ['pĩga] F (cachaça) rum; (PT: trago) drink

pingar [pĩ'gar] VI to drip

pingo ['pĩgu] M (gota) drop

pingue-pongue [pĩgi-'põgi] M ping-pong

pinguim [pĩ'gwĩ] (pl -ns) M penguin

pinheiro [pi'ɲejru] M pine (tree)

pinho ['piɲu] M pine

pino ['pinu] M (*peça*) pin; (*Auto: na porta*) lock; **a ~** upright

pinta ['pĩta] F (*mancha*) spot

pintar [pĩ'tar] VT to paint; (*cabelo*) to dye; (*rosto*) to make up; (*descrever*) to describe; (*imaginar*) to picture ▶ VI to paint; **pintar-se** VR to make o.s. up

pintarroxo [pĩta'hoʃu] M (BR) linnet; (PT) robin

pinto ['pĩtu] M chick; (!) prick (!)

pintor, a [pĩ'tor(a)] M/F painter

pintura [pĩ'tura] F painting; (*maquiagem*) make-up

piolho ['pjoʎu] M louse

pioneiro, -a [pjo'nejru, a] M/F pioneer

pior ['pjɔr] ADJ, ADV (*compar*) worse; (*superl*) worst ▶ M: **o ~** worst of all; **piorar** [pjo'rar] VT to make worse, worsen ▶ VI to get worse

pipa ['pipa] F barrel, cask; (*de papel*) kite

pipi [pi'pi] (*col*) M pee; **fazer ~** to have a pee

pipoca [pi'pɔka] F popcorn

pipocar [pipo'kar] VI to pop up

piquenique [piki'niki] M picnic

pirâmide [pi'ramidʒi] F pyramid

piranha [pi'raɲa] F piranha (fish)

pirata [pi'rata] M pirate

pires ['piris] M INV saucer

Pirineus [piri'news] MPL: **os ~** the Pyrenees

pirulito [piru'litu] (BR) M lollipop

pisar [pi'zar] VT to tread on; (*esmagar, subjugar*) to crush ▶ VI to step, tread

pisca-pisca [piska-'piska] (*pl* -**s**) M (*Auto*) indicator

piscar [pis'kar] VT to blink; (*dar sinal*) to wink; (*estrelas*) to twinkle

▶ M: **num ~ de olhos** in a flash

piscina [pi'sina] F swimming pool

piso ['pizu] M floor

pisotear [pizo'tʃjar] VT to trample (on)

pista ['pista] F (*vestígio*) trace; (*indicação*) clue; (*de corridas*) track; (*Aer*) runway; (*de estrada*) lane; (*de dança*) (dance) floor

pistola [pis'tɔla] F pistol

pitada [pi'tada] F (*porção*) pinch

pivete [pi'vetʃi] M child thief

pivô [pi'vo] M pivot; (*fig*) central figure, prime mover

pizza ['pitsa] F pizza

placa ['plaka] F plate; (*Auto*) number plate (BRIT), license plate (US); (*comemorativa*) plaque; (*na pele*) blotch; **~ de sinalização** road sign

placar [pla'kar] M scoreboard

plácido, -a ['plasidu, a] ADJ calm; (*manso*) placid

plágio ['plaʒu] M plagiarism

planalto [pla'nawtu] M tableland, plateau

planar [pla'nar] VI to glide

planear [pla'njar] (PT) VT = **planejar**

planejamento [planeʒa'mẽtu] M planning; **~ familiar** family planning

planejar [plane'ʒar] (BR) VT to plan; (*edifício*) to design

planeta [pla'neta] M planet

planície [pla'nisi] F plain

planilha [pla'niʎa] F spreadsheet

plano, -a ['planu, a] ADJ flat, level; (*liso*) smooth ▶ M plan; **~ de saúde** health insurance; **em primeiro/ em último ~** in the foreground/ background

planta ['plãta] F plant; (*de pé*) sole; (*Arq*) plan

p

plantação [plãta'sãw] F (*ato*) planting; (*terreno*) planted land; (*safra*) crops *pl*

plantão [plã'tãw] (*pl* **-ões**) M duty; (*noturno*) night duty; (*plantonista*) person on duty; (*Mil: serviço*) sentry duty; (: *pessoa*) sentry; **estar de ~** to be on duty

plantar [plã'tar] VT to plant; (*estaca*) to drive in; (*estabelecer*) to set up

plantões [plã'tõjs] MPL *de* **plantão**

plástico, -a ['plastʃiku, a] ADJ, M plastic

plataforma [plata'fɔrma] F platform; **~ de exploração de petróleo** oil rig; **~ de lançamento** launch pad

plateia [pla'tɛja] F (*Teatro etc*) stalls *pl* (BRIT), orchestra (US); (*espectadores*) audience

platina [pla'tʃina] F platinum

platinados [platʃi'nadus] MPL (*Auto*) points

plausível [plaw'zivew] (*pl* **-eis**) ADJ credible, plausible

playground [plej'grãwdʒi] (*pl* **-s**) M play area

plenamente [plena'mẽtʃi] ADV fully, completely

pleno, -a ['plenu, a] ADJ full; (*completo*) complete; **em ~ dia** in broad daylight; **em ~ inverno** in the middle *ou* depths of winter

plural [plu'raw] (*pl* **-ais**) ADJ, M plural

pneu ['pnew] M tyre (BRIT), tire (US)

pneumonia [pnewmo'nia] F pneumonia

pó [pɔ] M powder; (*sujeira*) dust; **pó de arroz** face powder; **sabão em pó** soap powder; **tirar o pó (de algo)** to dust (sth)

pobre ['pɔbri] ADJ poor ▶ M/F poor person; **pobreza** [po'breza] F poverty

poça ['posa] F puddle, pool

poção [po'sãw] (*pl* **-ões**) F potion

poço ['posu] M well; (*de mina, elevador*) shaft

poções [po'sõjs] FPL *de* **poção**

pôde ['podʒi] VB *ver* **poder**

(PALAVRA-CHAVE)

poder [po'der] VI **1** (*capacidade*) can, be able to; **não posso fazê-lo** I can't do it, I'm unable to do it **2** (*ter o direito de*) can, may, be allowed to; **posso fumar aqui?** can I smoke here?; **pode entrar?** (*posso?*) can I come in? **3** (*possibilidade*) may, might, could; **pode ser** maybe; **pode ser que** it may be that; **ele poderá vir amanhã** he might come tomorrow **4**: **não poder com: não posso com ele** I cannot cope with him **5** (*col: indignação*): **pudera!** no wonder!; **como é que pode?** you're joking!

▶ M power; (*autoridade*) authority; **poder aquisitivo** purchasing power; **estar no poder** to be in power; **em poder de alguém** in sb's hands

poderoso, -a [pode'rozu, ɔza] ADJ powerful

podre ['podri] ADJ rotten; **podridão** [podri'dãw] F decay, rottenness; (*fig*) corruption

põe [põj] VB *ver* **pôr**

poeira ['pwejra] F dust; **~ radioativa** fall-out; **poeirento, -a** [pwej'rẽtu, a] ADJ dusty

poema ['pwɛma] M poem

poesia [poe'zia] F poetry; (*poema*) poem

poeta ['pwɛta] M poet; **poético, -a** ['pwɛtʃiku, a] ADJ poetic; **poetisa** [pwe'tʃiza] F (woman) poet

pois [pojs] ADV (*portanto*) so; (*PT: assentimento*) yes ▶ CONJ as, since; (*mas*) but; **~ bem** well then; **~ é** that's right; **~ não!** (BR) of course!; **~ não?** (BR: *numa loja*) can I help you?; (*PT*) isn't it?, aren't you?, didn't they? *etc*; **~ sim!** certainly not!; **~ (então)** then

polaco, -a [po'laku, a] ADJ Polish ▶ M/F Pole ▶ M (*Ling*) Polish

polar [po'lar] ADJ polar

polegada [pole'gada] F inch

polegar [pole'gar] M (*tb*: **dedo ~**) thumb

polêmica [po'lemika] F controversy; **polêmico, -a** [po'lemiku, a] ADJ controversial

pólen ['polẽ] M pollen

polícia [po'lisja] F police, police force ▶ M/F policeman/woman; **policial** [poli'sjaw] (*pl* **-ais**) ADJ police *atr* ▶ M/F (BR) policeman/ woman; **novela** *ou* **romance policial** detective novel; **policiar** [poli'sjar] VT to police; (*instintos, modos*) to control, keep in check

polidez [poli'dez] F good manners *pl*, politeness

polido, -a [po'lidu, a] ADJ polished, shiny; (*cortês*) well-mannered, polite

pólio ['pɔlju] F polio

polir [po'lir] VT to polish

política [po'litʃika] F politics *sg*; (*programa*) policy; **político, -a** [po'litʃiku, a] ADJ political ▶ M/F politician

polo ['pɔlu] M pole; (*Esporte*) polo; **P~ Norte/Sul** North/South Pole

polonês, -esa [polo'nes, eza] ADJ Polish ▶ M/F Pole ▶ M (*Ling*) Polish

Polônia [po'lonja] F: **a ~** Poland

polpa ['powpa] F pulp

poltrona [pow'trona] F armchair

poluição [polwi'sãw] F pollution; **poluir** [po'lwir] VT to pollute

polvo ['powvu] M octopus

pólvora ['pɔwvora] F gunpowder

pomada [po'mada] F ointment

pomar [po'mar] M orchard

pomba ['põba] F dove

pombo ['põbu] M pigeon

ponderação [põdera'sãw] F consideration, meditation; (*prudência*) prudence

ponderado, -a [põde'radu, a] ADJ prudent

ponderar [põde'rar] VT to consider, weigh up ▶ VI to meditate, muse

ponho ['poɲu] VB *ver* **pôr**

ponta ['põta] F tip; (*de faca*) point; (*de sapato*) toe; (*extremidade*) end; (*Futebol: posição*) wing; (: *jogador*) winger; **uma ~ de** (*um pouco*) a touch of; **~ do dedo** fingertip; **de ~** (*tecnologia*) cutting-edge

pontapé [põta'pɛ] M kick; **dar ~s em alguém** to kick sb

pontaria [põta'ria] F aim; **fazer ~** to take aim

ponte ['põtʃi] F bridge; **~ aérea** air shuttle, airlift; **~ de safena** (heart) bypass operation

ponteiro [põ'tejru] M (*indicador*) pointer; (*de relógio*) hand

pontiagudo, -a [põtʃja'gudu, a] ADJ sharp, pointed

ponto ['põtu] M point; (*Med, Costura, Tricô*) stitch; (*pequeno sinal, do i*) dot; (*na pontuação*) full stop (BRIT), period (US); (*na pele*) spot; (*de ônibus*) stop; (*de táxi*) rank (BRIT), stand (US); (*matéria escolar*)

P

subject; **estar a ~ de fazer** to be on the point of doing; **às cinco em ~** at five o'clock on the dot; **dois ~s** colon *sg*; **~ de admiração** (PT) exclamation mark; **~ de exclamação/interrogação** exclamation/question mark; **~ de vista** point of view, viewpoint; **~ e vírgula** semicolon

pontuação [põtwa'sãw] F punctuation

pontual [põ'twaw] (*pl* **-ais**) ADJ punctual

pontudo, -a [põ'tudu, a] ADJ pointed

popa ['popa] F stern

população [popula'sãw] (*pl* **-ões**) F population

popular [popu'lar] ADJ popular; **popularidade** [populari'dadʒi] F popularity

pôquer ['poker] M poker

PALAVRA-CHAVE

por [por] (*por* + *o*(*s*)/*a*(*s*) = *pelo*(*s*)/*a*(*s*)) PREP **1** (*objetivo*) for; **lutar pela pátria** to fight for one's country
2 (+ *infin*): **está por acontecer** it is about to happen, it is yet to happen; **está por fazer** it is still to be done
3 (*causa*) out of, because of; **por falta de fundos** through lack of funds; **por hábito/natureza** out of habit/by nature; **faço isso por ela** I do it for her; **por isso** therefore; **a razão pela qual …** the reason why …; **pelo amor de Deus!** for Heaven's sake!
4 (*tempo*): **pela manhã** in the morning; **por volta das duas horas** at about two o'clock; **ele vai ficar por uma semana** he's staying for a week
5 (*lugar*): **por aqui** this way;

viemos pelo parque we came through the park; **passar por São Paulo** to pass through São Paulo; **por fora/dentro** outside/inside
6 (*troca, preço*) for; **trocar o velho pelo novo** to change old for new; **comprei o livro por dez libras** I bought the book for ten pounds
7 (*valor proporcional*): **por cento** per cent; **por hora/dia/semana/mês/ano** hourly/daily/weekly/monthly/yearly; **por cabeça** a *ou* per head; **por mais difícil que seja** however difficult *etc* it is
8 (*modo, meio*) by; **por correio/avião** by post/air; **por sí** by o.s.; **por escrito** in writing; **entrar pela entrada principal** to go in through the main entrance
9: **por que** why; **por quê?** why?
10: **por mim tudo bem** as far as I'm concerned that's OK

PALAVRA-CHAVE

pôr [por] VT **1** (*colocar*) to put; (*roupas*) to put on; (*objeções, dúvidas*) to raise; (*ovos, mesa*) to lay; (*defeito*) to find; **põe mais forte** turn it up; **você põe açúcar?** do you take sugar?; **pôr de lado** to set aside
2 (+ *adj*) to make; **você está me pondo nervoso** you're making me nervous
pôr-se VR **1** (*sol*) to set
2 (*colocar-se*): **pôr-se de pé** to stand up; **ponha-se no meu lugar** put yourself in my position
3: **pôr-se a** to start to; **ela pôs-se a chorar** she started crying
▶ M: **o pôr do sol** sunset

porão [po'rãw] (*pl* **-ões**) M (*de casa*) basement; (: *armazém*) cellar

porca ['pɔrka] F (*animal*) sow

porção [por'sãw] (pl -**ões**) F portion, piece; **uma ~ de** a lot of

porcaria [porka'ria] F filth; (dito sujo) obscenity; (coisa ruim) piece of junk

porcelana [porse'lana] F porcelain

porcentagem [porsẽ'taʒẽ] (pl -**ns**) F percentage

porco, -a ['porku, 'pɔrka] ADJ filthy ▶ M (animal) pig; (carne) pork

porções [por'sõjs] FPL de **porção**

porém [po'rẽ] CONJ however

pormenor [porme'nor] M detail

pornografia [pornogra'fia] F pornography

poro ['pɔru] M pore

porões [po'rõjs] MPL de **porão**

porque [por'ke] CONJ because; (interrogativo: PT) why

porquê [por'ke] ADV (PT) why ▶ M reason, motive; **~?** (PT) why?

porrete [po'hetʃi] M club

porta ['pɔrta] F door; (vão da porta) doorway; (de um jardim) gate

portador, a [porta'dor(a)] M/F bearer

portagem [por'taʒẽ] (PT) (pl -**ns**) F toll

portal [por'taw] (pl -**ais**) M doorway

porta-luvas M INV (Auto) glove compartment

porta-malas M INV (Auto) boot (BRIT), trunk (US)

porta-níqueis M INV purse

portanto [por'tãtu] CONJ so, therefore

portão [por'tãw] (pl -**ões**) M gate

portar [por'tar] VT to carry; **portar-se** VR to behave

portaria [porta'ria] F (de um edifício) entrance hall; (recepção) reception desk; (do governo) edict, decree

portátil [por'tatʃiw] (pl -**eis**) ADJ portable

porta-voz (pl -**es**) M/F (pessoa) spokesman, spokesperson

porte ['pɔrtʃi] M transport; (custo) freight charge, carriage; **~ pago** post paid; **de grande ~** far-reaching, important

porteiro, -a [por'tejru, a] M/F caretaker; **~ eletrônico** entry phone

pórtico ['pɔrtʃiku] M porch, portico

porto ['portu] M (do mar) port, harbour (BRIT), harbor (US); (vinho) port; **o P~** Oporto

portões [por'tõjs] MPL de **portão**

Portugal [portu'gaw] M Portugal; **português, -guesa** [portu'ges, 'geza] ADJ Portuguese ▶ M/F Portuguese inv ▶ M (Ling) Portuguese

porventura [porvẽ'tura] ADJ by chance; **se ~ você ...** if you happen to ...

pôs [pos] VB ver **pôr**

posar [po'zar] VI (Foto) to pose

posição [pozi'sãw] (pl -**ões**) F position; (social) standing, status; **posicionar** [pozisjo'nar] VT to position

positivo, -a [pozi'tʃivu, a] ADJ positive

possante [po'sãtʃi] ADJ powerful, strong; (carro) flashy

possessão [pose'sãw] F possession; **possessivo, -a** [pose'sivu, a] ADJ possessive

possibilidade [posibili'dadʒi] F

possibility; **possibilidades** FPL (*recursos*) means

possibilitar [posibili'tar] VT to make possible, permit

possível [po'sivew] (*pl* **-eis**) ADJ possible; **fazer todo o ~** to do one's best

posso ['posu] VB *ver* **poder**

possuidor, a [poswi'dor(a)] M/F owner

possuir [po'swir] VT (*casa, livro etc*) to own; (*dinheiro, talento*) to possess

post [post] (*pl* **-s**) M (*Comput*) post

postal [pos'taw] (*pl* **-ais**) ADJ postal ▶ M postcard

postar [pos'tar] VT to place, post; (*Comput*) to post

poste ['pɔstʃi] M pole, post

posterior [poste'rjor] ADJ (*mais tarde*) subsequent, later; (*traseiro*) rear, back; **posteriormente** [posterjor'mẽtʃi] ADV later, subsequently

postiço, -a [pos'tʃisu, a] ADJ false, artificial

posto, -a ['postu, 'pɔsta] PP *de* **pôr** ▶ M post, position; (*emprego*) job; **~ de gasolina** service *ou* petrol station; **~ que** although; **~ de saúde** health centre *ou* center

póstumo, -a ['pɔstumu, a] ADJ posthumous

postura [pos'tura] F posture; (*aspecto físico*) appearance

potável [po'tavew] (*pl* **-eis**) ADJ drinkable; **água ~** drinking water

pote ['pɔtʃi] M jug, pitcher; (*de geleia*) jar; (*de creme*) pot; **chover a ~s** (PT) to rain cats and dogs

potência [po'tẽsja] F power

potencial [potẽ'sjaw] (*pl* **-ais**) ADJ, M potential

potente [po'tẽtʃi] ADJ powerful, potent

pouco, -a ['poku, a] ADJ **1** (*sg*) little, not much; **pouco tempo** little *ou* not much time; **de pouco interesse** of little interest, not very interesting; **pouca coisa** not much **2** (*pl*) few, not many; **uns poucos** a few, some; **poucas vezes** rarely; **poucas crianças comem o que devem** few children eat what they should
▶ ADV **1** little, not much; **custa pouco** it doesn't cost much; **dentro em pouco, daqui a pouco** shortly; **pouco antes** shortly before
2 (*+ adj, negativo*): **ela é pouco inteligente/simpática** she's not very bright/friendly
3: **por pouco eu não morri** I almost died
4: **pouco a pouco** little by little
5: **aos poucos** gradually
▶ M: **um pouco** a little, a bit; **nem um pouco** not at all

poupador, a [popa'dor(a)] ADJ thrifty

poupança [po'pãsa] F thrift; (*economias*) savings pl; (*tb*: **caderneta de ~**) savings bank

poupar [po'par] VT to save; (*vida*) to spare

pousada [po'zada] F (*hospedagem*) lodging; (*hospedaria*) inn

pousar [po'zar] VT to place; (*mão*) to rest ▶ VI (*avião, pássaro*) to land; (*pernoitar*) to spend the night

povo ['povu] M people; (*raça*) people pl, race; (*plebe*) common people pl; (*multidão*) crowd

povoação [povwa'sãw] (*pl* **-ões**) F (*aldeia*) village, settlement; (*habitantes*) population

povoado [po'vwadu] M village
povoar [po'vwar] VT (de habitantes) to people, populate; (de animais etc) to stock
pra [pra] (col) PREP = **para a**; ver **para**
praça ['prasa] F (largo) square; (mercado) marketplace; (soldado) soldier; **~ de touros** bullring
praga ['praga] F nuisance; (maldição) curse; (desgraça) misfortune; (erva daninha) weed
pragmático, -a [prag'matʃiku, a] ADJ pragmatic
praia ['praja] F beach
prancha ['prãʃa] F plank; (de surfe) board
prata ['prata] F silver; (col: cruzeiro) ≈ quid (BRIT), ≈ buck (US)
prateleira [prate'lejra] F shelf
prática ['pratʃika] F practice; (experiência) experience, know-how; (costume) habit, custom; ver tb **prático**
praticante [pratʃi'kãtʃi] ADJ practising (BRIT), practicing (US) ▶ M/F apprentice; (de esporte) practitioner
praticar [pratʃi'kar] VT to practise (BRIT), practice (US); (roubo, operação) to carry out; **prático, -a** ['pratʃiku, a] ADJ practical ▶ M/F expert
prato ['pratu] M plate; (comida) dish; (de uma refeição) course; (de toca-discos) turntable; **pratos** MPL (Mús) cymbals
praxe ['praʃi] F custom, usage; **de ~** usually; **ser de ~** to be the norm
Student life in Portugal follows the traditions set out in a written set of rules known as the 'código da **praxe**'. It begins in freshers' week, where freshers are jeered at by their seniors, and are subjected to a number of humiliating practical jokes, such as having their hair cut against their will and being made to walk around town in fancy dress.

prazer [pra'zer] M pleasure; **muito ~ em conhecê-lo** pleased to meet you
prazo ['prazu] M term, period; (vencimento) expiry date, time limit; **a curto/médio/longo ~** in the short/medium/long term; **comprar a ~** to buy on hire purchase (BRIT) ou on the installment plan (US)
precário, -a [pre'karju, a] ADJ precarious; (escasso) failing
precaução [prekaw'sãw] (pl **-ões**) F precaution
precaver-se [preka'versi] VR: **~ (contra** ou **de)** to be on one's guard (against); **precavido, -a** [preka'vidu, a] ADJ cautious
prece ['prɛsi] F prayer; (súplica) entreaty
precedente [prese'dẽtʃi] ADJ preceding ▶ M precedent
preceder [prese'der] VT, VI to precede; **~ a algo** to precede sth; (ter primazia) to take precedence over sth
precioso, -a [pre'sjozu, ɔza] ADJ precious
precipício [presi'pisju] M precipice; (fig) abyss
precipitação [presipita'sãw] F haste; (imprudência) rashness
precipitado, -a [presipi'tadu, a] ADJ hasty; (imprudente) rash
precisamente [presiza'mẽtʃi] ADV precisely
precisar [presi'zar] VT to need;

P

(*especificar*) to specify; **precisar-se**
VR: **"precisa-se"** "needed"; **~ de** to
need; **não precisa você se
preocupar** you needn't worry
preciso, -a [pre'sizu, a] ADJ precise,
accurate; (*necessário*) necessary;
(*claro*) concise; **é ~ você ir** you must
go
preço ['presu] M price; (*custo*) cost;
(*valor*) value; **a ~ de banana** (BR) ou
de chuva (PT) dirt cheap
preconceito [prekõ'sejtu] M
prejudice
predador [preda'dor] M predator
predileto, -a [predʒi'lɛtu, a] ADJ
favourite (BRIT), favorite (US)
prédio ['prɛdʒju] M building; **~ de
apartamentos** block of flats (BRIT),
apartment house (US)
predispor [predʒis'por] (*irreg: como*
pôr) VT: **~ alguém contra** to
prejudice sb against; **predispor-se**
VR: **~-se a/para** to get o.s. in the
mood to/for
predominar [predomi'nar] VI to
predominate, prevail
preencher [preẽ'ʃer] VT (*formulário*)
to fill in (BRIT) ou out, complete;
(*requisitos*) to fulfil (BRIT), fulfill (US),
meet; (*espaço, vaga, tempo, cargo*) to
fill
prefácio [pre'fasju] M preface
prefeito, -a [pre'fejtu, a] M/F
mayor; **prefeitura** [prefej'tura] F
town hall
preferência [prefe'rẽsja] F
preference; (*Auto*) priority; **de ~**
preferably; **ter ~ por** to have a
preference for; **preferencial**
[preferẽ'sjaw] (*pl* **-ais**) ADJ (*rua*)
main ▶ F main road (*with priority*)
preferido, -a [prefe'ridu, a] ADJ
favourite (BRIT), favorite (US)
preferir [prefe'rir] VT to prefer

prefiro [pre'firu] VB *ver* **preferir**
prefixo [pre'fiksu] M (*Ling*) prefix;
(*Tel*) code
prega ['prɛga] F pleat, fold
pregar¹ [pre'gar] VT, VI to preach
pregar² [pre'gar] VT (*com prego*) to
nail; (*fixar*) to pin, fasten; (*cosendo*)
to sew on; **~ uma peça** to play a
trick; **~ um susto em alguém** to
give sb a fright
prego ['prɛgu] M nail; (*col: casa de
penhor*) pawn shop
preguiça [pre'gisa] F laziness;
(*animal*) sloth; **estar com ~** to feel
lazy; **preguiçoso, -a** [pregi'sozu,
ɔza] ADJ lazy
pré-histórico, -a ADJ prehistoric
preia-mar (PT) F high tide
prejuízo [pre'ʒwizu] M damage,
harm; (*em dinheiro*) loss; **em ~ de** to
the detriment of
prematuro, -a [prema'turu, a] ADJ
premature
premiado, -a [pre'mjadu, a] ADJ
prize-winning; (*bilhete*) winning
▶ M/F prize-winner
premiar [pre'mjar] VT to award a
prize to; (*recompensar*) to reward
prêmio ['premju] M prize;
(*recompensa*) reward; (*Seguros*)
premium
prenda ['prẽda] F gift, present; (*em
jogo*) forfeit; **~s domésticas**
housework *sg*
prendedor [prẽde'dor] M fastener;
(*de cabelo, gravata*) clip; **~ de roupa**
clothes peg; **~ de papéis** paper clip
prender [prẽ'der] VT to fasten, fix;
(*roupa*) to pin; (*cabelo*) to tie back;
(*capturar*) to arrest; (*atar, ligar*) to
tie; (*atenção*) to catch;
(*afetivamente*) to tie, bind; (*reter:
doença, compromisso*) to keep;
(*movimentos*) to restrict; **prender-se**

VR to get caught, stick; **~-se a alguém** (*por amizade*) to be attached to sb

preocupação [preokupa'sãw] (*pl* **-ões**) F preoccupation; (*inquietação*) worry, concern

preocupar [preoku'par] VT to preoccupy; (*inquietar*) to worry; **preocupar-se** VR: **~-se com** to worry about, be worried about

preparação [prepara'sãw] (*pl* **-ões**) F preparation

preparar [prepa'rar] VT to prepare; **preparar-se** VR to get ready; **preparativos** [prepara'tʃivus] MPL preparations, arrangements

preponderante [prepõde'rãtʃi] ADJ predominant

preposição [prepozi'sãw] (*pl* **-ões**) F preposition

prepotente [prepo'tẽtʃi] ADJ predominant; (*despótico*) despotic; (*atitude*) overbearing

prescrever [preskre'ver] VT to prescribe; (*prazo*) to set

presença [pre'zẽsa] F presence; (*frequência*) attendance; **ter boa ~** to be presentable; **presenciar** [prezẽ'sjar] VT to be present at; (*testemunhar*) to witness

presente [pre'zẽtʃi] ADJ present; (*fig: interessado*) attentive; (*: evidente*) clear, obvious ▶ M present ▶ F (*Com: carta*): **a ~** this letter; **os presentes** MPL (*pessoas*) those present; **presentear** [prezẽ'tʃjar] VT: **presentear alguém (com algo)** to give sb (sth as) a present

preservação [prezerva'sãw] F preservation

presidente, -a [prezi'dẽtʃi, ta] M/F president

presidiário, -a [prezi'dʒjarju, a] M/F convict

presídio [pre'zidʒju] M prison

presidir [prezi'dʒir] VT, VI: **~ (a)** to preside over; (*reunião*) to chair; (*suj: leis, critérios*) to govern

preso, -a ['prezu, a] ADJ imprisoned; (*capturado*) under arrest; (*atado*) tied ▶ M/F prisoner; **estar ~ a alguém** to be attached to sb

pressa ['presa] F haste, hurry; (*rapidez*) speed; (*urgência*) urgency; **às ~s** hurriedly; **estar com ~** to be in a hurry; **ter ~ de** *ou* **em fazer** to be in a hurry to do

presságio [pre'sazu] M omen, sign; (*pressentimento*) premonition

pressão [pre'sãw] (*pl* **-ões**) F pressure; **(colchete de) ~** press stud, popper

pressentimento [presẽtʃi'mẽtu] M premonition

pressentir [presẽ'tʃir] VT to foresee; (*suspeitar*) to sense

pressionar [presjo'nar] VT (*botão*) to press; (*coagir*) to pressure ▶ VI to press, put on pressure

pressões [pre'sõjs] FPL *de* **pressão**

pressupor [presu'por] (*irreg: como* **pôr**) VT to presuppose

prestação [presta'sãw] (*pl* **-ões**) F instalment (BRIT), installment (US); (*por uma casa*) repayment

prestar [pres'tar] VT (*cuidados*) to give; (*favores, serviços*) to do; (*contas*) to render; (*informações*) to supply; (*uma qualidade a algo*) to lend ▶ VI: **~ a alguém para algo** to be of use to sb for sth; **prestar-se** VR: **~-se a** to be suitable for; (*admitir*) to lend o.s. to; (*dispor-se*) to be willing to;

P

~ atenção to pay attention

prestes ['prɛstʃis] ADJ INV ready; *(a ponto de)*: **~ a partir** about to leave

prestígio [pres'tʃiʒu] M prestige

presunção [prezũ'sãw] *(pl* **-ões)** F presumption; *(vaidade)* conceit, self-importance; **presunçoso, -a** [prezũ'sozu, ɔza] ADJ vain, self-important

presunto [pre'zũtu] M ham

pretender [pretẽ'der] VT to claim; *(cargo, emprego)* to go for; **~ fazer** to intend to do

pretensão [pretẽ'sãw] *(pl* **-ões)** F claim; *(vaidade)* pretension; *(propósito)* aim; *(aspiração)* aspiration; **pretensioso, -a** [pretẽ'sjozu, ɔza] ADJ pretentious

pretérito [pre'tɛritu] M *(Ling)* preterite

pretexto [pre'testu] M pretext

preto, -a ['pretu, a] ADJ black

prevalecer [prevale'ser] VI to prevail; **prevalecer-se** VR: **~-se de** *(aproveitar-se)* to take advantage of

prevenção [prevẽ'sãw] *(pl* **-ões)** F prevention; *(preconceito)* prejudice; *(cautela)* caution; **estar de ~ com** *ou* **contra alguém** to be bias(s)ed against sb

prevenido, -a [preve'nidu, a] ADJ cautious, wary

prevenir [preve'nir] VT to prevent; *(avisar)* to warn; *(preparar)* to prepare

prever [pre'ver] *(irreg: como* **ver)** VT to predict, foresee; *(pressupor)* to presuppose

prévio, -a ['prɛvju, a] ADJ prior; *(preliminar)* preliminary

previsão [previ'zãw] *(pl* **-ões)** F foresight; *(prognóstico)* prediction, forecast; **~ do tempo** weather forecast

previsível [previ'zivew] *(pl* **-eis)** ADJ predictable

previsões [previ'zõjs] FPL de **previsão**

prezado, -a [pre'zadu, a] ADJ esteemed; *(numa carta)* dear

prezar [pre'zar] VT *(amigos)* to value highly; *(autoridade)* to respect; *(gostar de)* to appreciate

primário, -a [pri'marju, a] ADJ primary; *(elementar)* basic, rudimentary; *(primitivo)* primitive ▶ M *(curso)* elementary education

primavera [prima'vɛra] F spring; *(planta)* primrose

primeira [pri'mejra] F *(Auto)* first (gear)

primeiro, -a [pri'mejru, a] ADJ, ADV first; **de primeira** first-class

primo, -a ['primu, a] M/F cousin; **~ irmão** first cousin

princesa [prĩ'seza] F princess

principal [prĩsi'paw] *(pl* **-ais)** ADJ principal; *(entrada, razão, rua)* main ▶ M head, principal; *(essencial, de dívida)* principal

príncipe ['prĩsipi] M prince

principiante [prĩsi'pjãtʃi] M/F beginner

principiar [prĩsi'pjar] VT, VI to begin

princípio [prĩ'sipju] M beginning, start; *(origem)* origin; *(legal, moral)* principle; **princípios** MPL *(de matéria)* rudiments

prioridade [prjori'dadʒi] F priority

prisão [pri'zãw] *(pl* **-ões)** F imprisonment; *(cadeia)* prison, jail; *(detenção)* arrest; **~ de ventre** constipation; **prisioneiro, -a** [prizjo'nejru, a] M/F prisoner

privacidade [privasi'dadʒi] F privacy

privada [pri'vada] F toilet

privado, -a [pri'vadu, a] ADJ
private; (*carente*) deprived

privar [pri'var] VT to deprive

privativo, -a [priva'tʃivu, a] ADJ
(*particular*) private; **~ de** peculiar
to

privilegiado, -a [privile'ʒjadu, a]
ADJ privileged; (*excepcional*) unique,
exceptional

privilegiar [privile'ʒjar] VT to
privilege; (*favorecer*) to favour
(BRIT), favor (US)

privilégio [privi'lɛʒu] M privilege

pró [prɔ] ADV for, in favour (BRIT) *ou*
favor (US) ▶ M advantage; **os ~s e
os contras** the pros and cons; **em
~ de** in favo(u)r of

pró- [prɔ] PREFIXO pro-

proa ['proa] F prow, bow

probabilidade [probabili'dadʒi]
F probability; **probabilidades** FPL
(*chances*) odds

problema [prob'lema] M problem

procedência [prose'dēsja] F
origin, source; (*lugar de saída*) point
of departure

proceder [prose'der] VI to
proceed; (*comportar-se*) to behave;
(*agir*) to act ▶ M conduct;
procedimento [prosedʒi'mētu] M
conduct, behaviour (BRIT),
behavior (US); (*processo*)
procedure; (*Jur*) proceedings *pl*

processamento [prosesa'mētu]
M processing; (*Jur*) prosecution;
(*verificação*) verification; **~ de
texto** word processing

processar [prose'sar] VT (*Jur*) to
take proceedings against,
prosecute; (*requerimentos, dados*)
to process

processo [pro'sɛsu] M process;
(*procedimento*) procedure; (*Jur*)
lawsuit, legal proceedings *pl*;

(: *autos*) record; (*conjunto de
documentos*) documents *pl*

procissão [prosi'sāw] (*pl* **-ões**) F
procession

Proclamação da República *see
note*

> Commemorated on 15
> November, which is a public
> holiday, the proclamation of the
> republic in 1889 was a military
> coup, led by Marshal Deodoro
> da Fonseca. It brought down
> the empire which had been
> established after independence
> and installed a federal republic
> in Brazil.

proclamar [prokla'mar] VT to
proclaim

procura [pro'kura] F search;
(*Com*) demand

procuração [prokura'sāw] (*pl*
-ões) F: **por ~** by proxy

procurador, a [prokura'dor(a)]
M/F attorney; **P~ Geral da
República** Attorney General

procurar [proku'rar] VT to look
for, seek; (*emprego*) to apply for; (*ir
visitar*) to call on; (*contatar*) to get
in touch with; **~ fazer** to try to do

produção [produ'sāw] (*pl* **-ões**) F
production; (*volume de produção*)
output; (*produto*) product; **~ em
massa** *ou* **série** mass production

produtivo, -a [produ'tʃivu, a] ADJ
productive; (*rendoso*) profitable

produto [pro'dutu] M product;
(*renda*) proceeds *pl*, profit

produtor, a [produ'tor(a)] ADJ
producing ▶ M/F producer

produzir [produ'zir] VT to
produce; (*ocasionar*) to cause,
bring about; (*render*) to bring in

proeminente [proemi'nētʃi] ADJ
prominent

p

proeza [pro'eza] F achievement, feat

profanar [profa'nar] VT to desecrate, profane; **profano, -a** [pro'fanu, a] ADJ profane ▶ M/F layman/woman

profecia [profe'sia] F prophecy

professor, a [profe'sor(a)] M/F teacher; (*universitário*) lecturer

profeta, -tisa [pro'fɛta, profe'tʃiza] M/F prophet; **profetizar** [profetʃi'zar] VT, VI to prophesy, predict

profissão [profi'sãw] (*pl* -**ões**) F profession; **profissional** [profisjo'naw] (*pl* -**ais**) ADJ, M/F professional; **profissionalizante** [profisjonali'zatʃi] ADJ (*ensino*) vocational

profundidade [profũdʒi'dadʒi] F depth

profundo, -a [pro'fũdu, a] ADJ deep; (*fig*) profound

profusão [profu'zãw] F profusion, abundance

prognóstico [prog'nɔstʃiku] M prediction, forecast

programa [pro'grama] M programme (*BRIT*), program (*US*); (*Comput*) program; (*plano*) plan; (*diversão*) thing to do; (*de um curso*) syllabus; **programação** [programa'sãw] F planning; (*TV, Rádio, Comput*) programming; **programador, a** [programa'dor(a)] M/F programmer; **programar** [progra'mar] VT to plan; (*Comput*) to program

progredir [progre'dʒir] VI to progress; (*avançar*) to move forward; (*infecção*) to progress

progressista [progre'sista] ADJ, M/F progressive

progressivo, -a [progre'sivu, a] ADJ progressive; (*gradual*) gradual

progresso [pro'grɛsu] M progress

progrido [pro'gridu] VB *ver* **progredir**

proibição [proibi'sãw] (*pl* -**ões**) F prohibition, ban

proibir [proi'bir] VT to prohibit; (*livro, espetáculo*) to ban; **"é proibido fumar"** "no smoking"; **~ alguém de fazer, ~ que alguém faça** to forbid sb to do

projeção [proʒe'sãw] (*pl* -**ões**) F projection

projetar [proʒe'tar] VT to project

projétil [pro'ʒɛtʃiw] (*pl* -**eis**) M projectile, missile

projeto [pro'ʒɛtu] M project; (*plano*) plan; (*Tec*) design; **~ de lei** bill

projetor [proʒe'tor] M (*Cinema*) projector

proliferar [prolife'rar] VI to proliferate

prolongação [prolõga'sãw] F extension

prolongado, -a [prolõ'gadu, a] ADJ prolonged; (*alongado*) extended

prolongar [prolõ'gar] VT to extend, lengthen; (*decisão etc*) to postpone; (*vida*) to prolong; **prolongar-se** VR to extend; (*durar*) to last

promessa [pro'mɛsa] F promise

prometer [prome'ter] VT, VI to promise

promíscuo, -a [pro'miskwu, a] ADJ disorderly, mixed up; (*comportamento sexual*) promiscuous

promissor, a [promi'sor(a)] ADJ promising

promoção [promo'sãw] (*pl* -**ões**) F promotion; **fazer ~ de alguém/ algo** to promote sb/sth

promotor, a [promo'tor(a)] M/F promoter; (*Jur*) prosecutor

promover [promo'ver] VT to promote; (*causar*) to bring about

pronome [pro'nɔmi] M pronoun

pronto, -a [prõtu, a] ADJ ready; (*rápido*) quick, speedy; (*imediato*) prompt ▶ ADV promptly; **de ~** promptly; **estar ~ a ...** to be prepared *ou* willing to ...; **pronto-socorro** (*pl* **prontos-socorros**) M (BR) casualty (BRIT), emergency room (US); (PT: *reboque*) tow truck

pronúncia [pro'nũsja] F pronunciation; (*Jur*) indictment

pronunciar [pronũ'sjar] VT to pronounce; (*discurso*) to make, deliver; (*Jur: réu*) to indict; (: *sentença*) to pass

propaganda [propa'gãda] F (*Pol*) propaganda; (*Com*) advertising; (: *uma propaganda*) advert, advertisement; **fazer ~ de** to advertise

propagar [propa'gar] VT to propagate; (*fig: difundir*) to disseminate

propensão [propẽ'sãw] (*pl* -ões) F inclination, tendency; **propenso, -a** [pro'pẽsu, a] ADJ: **propenso a** inclined to; **ser propenso a** to be inclined to, have a tendency to

propina [pro'pina] F (*gorjeta*) tip; (PT: *cota*) fee

propor [pro'por] (*irreg: como* **pôr**) VT to propose; (*oferecer*) to offer; (*um problema*) to pose; **propor-se** VR: **~-se (a) fazer** (*pretender*) to intend to do; (*visar*) to aim to do; (*dispor-se*) to decide to do; (*oferecer-se*) to offer to do

proporção [propor'sãw] (*pl* -ões) F proportion; **proporções** FPL (*dimensões*) dimensions; **proporcional** [proporsjo'naw]

(*pl* -**ais**) ADJ proportional; **proporcionar** [proporsjo'nar] VT to provide, give; (*adaptar*) to adjust, adapt

proposição [propozi'sãw] (*pl* -ões) F proposition, proposal

proposital [propozi'taw] (*pl* -**ais**) ADJ intentional

propósito [pro'pɔzitu] M (*intenção*) purpose; (*objetivo*) aim; **a ~** by the way; **a ~ de** with regard to; **de ~** on purpose

proposta [pro'pɔsta] F proposal; (*oferecimento*) offer

propriamente [proprja'mẽtʃi] ADV properly, exactly; **~ falando** *ou* **dito** strictly speaking

propriedade [proprje'dadʒi] F property; (*direito de proprietário*) ownership; (*o que é apropriado*) propriety

proprietário, -a [proprje'tarju, a] M/F owner, proprietor

próprio, -a ['prɔprju, a] ADJ own, of one's own; (*mesmo*) very, selfsame; (*hora, momento*) opportune, right; (*nome*) proper; (*característico*) characteristic; (*sentido*) proper, true; (*depois de pronome*) -self; **~ (para)** suitable (for); **eu ~** I myself; **por si ~** of one's own accord; **ele é o ~ inglês** he's a typical Englishman; **é o ~** it's him himself

prorrogação [prohoga'sãw] (*pl* -ões) F extension

prosa ['prɔza] F prose; (*conversa*) chatter; (*fanfarrice*) boasting, bragging ▶ ADJ full of oneself

prospecto [pros'pɛktu] M leaflet; (*em forma de livro*) brochure

prosperar [prospe'rar] VI to prosper, thrive; **prosperidade** [prosperi'dadʒi] F prosperity;

P

(*bom êxito*) success; **próspero, -a** ['prɔsperu, a] ADJ prosperous; (*bem sucedido*) successful; (*favorável*) favourable (BRIT), favorable (US)

prosseguir [prose'gir] VT, VI to continue; **~ em** to continue (with)

prostíbulo [pros'tʃibulu] M brothel

prostituta [prostʃi'tuta] F prostitute

prostrado, -a [pros'tradu, a] ADJ prostrate

protagonista [protago'nista] M/F protagonist

proteção [prote'sãw] F protection

proteger [prote'ʒer] VT to protect; **protegido, -a** [prote'ʒidu, a] M/F protégé(e)

proteína [prote'ina] F protein

protejo [pro'teʒu] VB *ver* **proteger**

protestante [protes'tãtʃi] ADJ, M/F Protestant

protestar [protes'tar] VT, VI to protest; **protesto** [pro'testu] M protest

protetor, a [prote'tor(a)] ADJ protective ▶ M/F protector; **~ solar** sunscreen; **~ de tela** (*Comput*) screensaver

protuberância [protube'rãsja] F bump; **protuberante** [protube'rãtʃi] ADJ sticking out

prova ['prɔva] F proof; (*Tec: teste*) test, trial; (*Educ: exame*) examination; (*sinal*) sign; (*de comida, bebida*) taste; (*de roupa*) fitting; (*Esporte*) competition; (*Tip*) proof; **prova(s)** F(PL) (*Jur*) evidence *sg*; **à ~ de bala/fogo/água** bulletproof/fireproof/waterproof; **pôr à ~** to put to the test

provar [pro'var] VT to prove; (*comida*) to taste, try; (*roupa*) to try on ▶ VI to try

provável [pro'vavew] (*pl* **-eis**) ADJ probable, likely

provedor, a [prove'dor(a)] M/F provider; **~ de acesso à Internet** internet service provider

proveito [pro'vejtu] M advantage; (*ganho*) profit; **em ~ de** for the benefit of; **fazer ~ de** to make use of; **proveitoso, -a** [provej'tozu, ɔza] ADJ profitable, advantageous; (*útil*) useful

proveniente [prove'njẽtʃi] ADJ: **~ de** originating from; (*que resulta de*) arising from

prover [pro'ver] (*irreg: como* **ver**) VT to provide, supply; (*vaga*) to fill ▶ VI: **~ a** to take care of, see to

provérbio [pro'vɛrbju] M proverb

providência [provi'dẽsja] F providence; **providências** FPL (*medidas*) measures, steps; **providencial** [providẽ'sjaw] (*pl* **-ais**) ADJ opportune; **providenciar** [providẽ'sjar] VT to provide; (*tomar providências*) to arrange ▶ VI to make arrangements, take steps; **providenciar para que** to see to it that

província [pro'vĩsja] F province; **provinciano, -a** [provĩ'sjanu, a] ADJ provincial

provisório, -a [provi'zɔrju, a] ADJ provisional, temporary

provocador, a [provoka'dor(a)] ADJ provocative

provocante [provo'kãtʃi] ADJ provocative

provocar [provo'kar] VT to provoke; (*ocasionar*) to cause; (*atrair*) to tempt, attract; (*estimular*) to rouse, stimulate

próximo, -a ['prɔsimu, a] ADJ (*no espaço*) near, close; (*no tempo*) close; (*seguinte*) next; (*amigo, parente*)

close; (*vizinho*) neighbouring
(BRIT), neighboring (US) ▶ ADV near
▶ M fellow man; **~ a** *ou* **de** near
(to), close to; **até a próxima!** see
you again soon!

prudência [pru'dēsja] F care,
prudence; **prudente** [pru'dētʃi]
ADJ prudent

prurido [pru'ridu] M itch

psicanálise [psika'nalizi] F
psychoanalysis

psicologia [psikolo'ʒia] F
psychology; **psicológico, -a**
[psiko'lɔʒiku, a] ADJ psychological;
psicólogo, -a [psi'kɔlogu, a] M/F
psychologist

psique ['psiki] F psyche

psiquiatra [psi'kjatra] M/F
psychiatrist

psiquiatria [psikja'tria] F
psychiatry

psíquico, -a ['psikiku, a] ADJ
psychological

puberdade [puber'dadʒi] F
puberty

publicação [publika'sãw] F
publication

publicar [publi'kar] VT to publish;
(*divulgar*) to divulge; (*proclamar*) to
announce

publicidade [publisi'dadʒi] F
publicity; (Com) advertising;
publicitário, -a [publisi'tarju, a]
ADJ publicity *atr*; (Com) advertising
atr

público, -a ['publiku, a] ADJ public
▶ M public; (*Cinema, Teatro etc*)
audience

pude ['pudʒi] VB *ver* **poder**

pudera [pu'dɛra] VB *ver* **poder**

pudim [pu'dʒĩ] (*pl* **-ns**) M pudding

pudor [pu'dor] M bashfulness,
modesty; (*moral*) decency

pular [pu'lar] VI to jump; (*no
Carnaval*) to celebrate ▶ VT to jump
(over); (*páginas, trechos*) to skip;
~ Carnaval to celebrate Carnival;
~ corda to skip

pulga ['puwga] F flea

pulmão [puw'mãw] (*pl* **-ões**) M
lung

pulo¹ ['pulu] M jump; **dar um ~ em**
to stop off at

pulo² VB *ver* **polir**

pulôver [pu'lover] (BR) M pullover

pulsação [puwsa'sãw] F
pulsation, beating; (Med) pulse

pulseira [puw'sejra] F bracelet;
(*de sapato*) strap

pulso ['puwsu] M (Anat) wrist;
(Med) pulse; (*fig*) vigour (BRIT),
vigor (US), energy

punha ['puɲa] VB *ver* **pôr**

punhado [pu'ɲadu] M handful

punhal [pu'ɲaw] (*pl* **-ais**) M
dagger

punho ['puɲu] M fist; (*de manga*)
cuff; (*de espada*) hilt

punição [puni'sãw] (*pl* **-ões**) F
punishment

punir [pu'nir] VT to punish

pupila [pu'pila] F (Anat) pupil

purê [pu're] M purée; **~ de batatas**
mashed potatoes

pureza [pu'reza] F purity

purificar [purifi'kar] VT to purify

puritano, -a [puri'tanu, a] ADJ
puritanical; (*seita*) puritan ▶ M/F
puritan

puro, -a ['puru, a] ADJ pure; (*uísque
etc*) neat; (*verdade*) plain;
(*intenções*) honourable (BRIT),
honorable (US); (*estilo*) clear

pus¹ [pus] M pus

pus² [pujs] VB *ver* **pôr**

puser [pu'zer] VB *ver* **pôr**

puta ['puta] (!) F whore; *ver tb*
puto

P

puto, -a ['putu, a] (!) M/F
(*sem-vergonha*) bastard ▶ ADJ
(*zangado*) furious; (*incrível*): **um ~ ...**
a hell of a ...; **o ~ de ...** the bloody ...

pútrido, -a ['putridu, a] ADJ putrid,
rotten

puxador [puʃa'dor] M handle, knob

puxão [pu'ʃãw] (*pl* **-ões**) M tug, jerk

puxar [pu'ʃar] VT to pull; (*sacar*) to
pull out; (*assunto*) to bring up;
(*conversa*) to strike up; (*briga*) to pick
▶ VI: **~ de uma perna** to limp; **~ a**
to take after

puxões [pu'ʃõjs] MPL *de* **puxão**

QG ABR M (= *Quartel-General*) HQ

QI ABR M (= *Quociente de Inteligência*)
IQ

quadra ['kwadra] F (*quarteirão*)
block; (*de tênis etc*) court; (*período*)
time, period

quadrado, -a [kwa'dradu, a] ADJ
square ▶ M square ▶ M/F (*col*)
square

quadril [kwa'driw] (*pl* **-is**) M hip

quadrinho [kwa'driɲu] M:
história em ~s (*BR*) cartoon, comic
strip

quadris [kwa'dris] MPL *de* **quadril**

quadro ['kwadru] M painting;
(*gravura, foto*) picture; (*lista*) list;
(*tabela*) chart, table; (*Tec: painel*)
panel; (*pessoal*) staff; (*time*) team;
(*Teatro, fig*) scene; **~ branco**
whiteboard; **~ interativo**
interactive whiteboard;
quadro-negro (*pl* **quadros-
negros**) M blackboard

quadruplicar [kwadrupli'kar] VT,
VI to quadruple

qual [kwaw] (pl **-ais**) PRON which ▶ CONJ as, like ▶ EXCL what!; **o ~** which; (*pessoa: suj*) who; (*: objeto*) whom; **seja ~ for** whatever ou whichever it may be; **cada ~** each one

qualidade [kwali'dadʒi] F quality

qualificação [kwalifika'sãw] (pl **-ões**) F qualification

qualificado, -a [kwalifi'kadu, a] ADJ qualified

qualificar [kwalifi'kar] VT to qualify; (*avaliar*) to evaluate; **qualificar-se** VR to qualify; **~ de** ou **como** to classify as

qualquer [kwaw'ker] (pl **quaisquer**) ADJ, PRON any; **~ pessoa** anyone, anybody; **~ um dos dois** either; **~ que seja** whichever it may be; **a ~ momento** at any moment

quando ['kwãdu] ADV when ▶ CONJ when; (*interrogativo*) when?; (*ao passo que*) whilst; **~ muito** at most

quantia [kwã'tʃia] F sum, amount

quantidade [kwãtʃi'dadʒi] F quantity, amount

PALAVRA-CHAVE

quanto, -a ['kwãtu, a] ADJ
1 (*interrogativo: sg*) how much?; (*: pl*) how many?; **quanto tempo?** how long?
2 (*o que for necessário*) all that, as much as; **daremos quantos exemplares ele precisar** we'll give him as many copies as ou all the copies he needs
3: **tanto/tantos ... quanto** as much/many ... as
▶ PRON **1** how much?; how many?; **quanto custa?** how much is it?; **a quanto está o jogo?** what's the score?

2: **tudo quanto** everything that, as much as
3: **tanto/tantos quanto ...** as much/as many as ...
4: **um tanto quanto** somewhat, rather
▶ ADV **1**: **quanto a** as regards; **quanto a mim** as for me
2: **quanto antes** as soon as possible
3: **quanto mais** (*principalmente*) especially; (*muito menos*) let alone; **quanto mais cedo melhor** the sooner the better
4: **tanto quanto possível** as much as possible; **tão ... quanto ... as ... as ...**
▶ CONJ: **quanto mais trabalha, mais ele ganha** the more he works, the more he earns; **quanto mais, (tanto) melhor** the more, the better

quarenta [kwa'rẽta] NUM forty

quarentena [kwarẽ'tɛna] F quarantine

quaresma [kwa'rezma] F Lent

quarta ['kwarta] F (*tb: ~-feira*) Wednesday; (*parte*) quarter; (*Auto*) fourth (gear); **quarta-feira** (pl **quartas-feiras**) F Wednesday; **quarta-feira de cinzas** Ash Wednesday

quarteirão [kwartej'rãw] (pl **-ões**) M (*de casas*) block

quartel [kwar'tɛw] (pl **-éis**) M barracks sg; **quartel-general** M headquarters pl

quarteto [kwar'tetu] M quartet(te)

quarto, -a ['kwartu, a] NUM fourth ▶ M quarter; (*aposento*) bedroom; **~ de banho** bathroom; **~ de dormir** bedroom; **três ~s de**

q

hora three quarters of an hour
quase ['kwazi] ADV almost, nearly;
~ **nunca** hardly ever
quatorze [kwa'torzi] NUM
fourteen
quatro ['kwatru] NUM four

┌─────────────────┐
│ **PALAVRA-CHAVE** │
└─────────────────┘

que [ki] CONJ **1** (*com oração
subordinada: muitas vezes não se
traduz*) that; **ele disse que viria** he
said (that) he would come; **não há
nada que fazer** there's nothing to
be done; **espero que sim/não**
I hope so/not; **dizer que sim/não**
to say yes/no
2 (*consecutivo: muitas vezes não se
traduz*) that; **é tão pesado que não
consigo levantá-lo** it's so heavy
(that) I can't lift it
3 (*comparações*): **(do) que** than; *ver
tb* **mais, menos, mesmo**
▶ PRON **1** (*coisa*) which, that;
(*+ prep*) which; **o chapéu que você
comprou** the hat (that *ou* which)
you bought
2 (*pessoa: suj*) who, that;
(*: complemento*) whom, that; **o
amigo que me levou ao museu**
the friend who took me to the
museum; **a moça que eu convidei**
the girl (that *ou* whom) I invited
3 (*interrogativo*) what?; **o que você
disse?** what did you say?
4 (*exclamação*) what!; **que pena!**
what a pity!; **que lindo!** how lovely!

quê [ke] M (*col*) something ▶ PRON
what; **~!** what!; **não tem de ~**
don't mention it; **para ~?** what for?;
por ~? why?
quebra ['kɛbra] F break, rupture;
(*falência*) bankruptcy; (*de energia
elétrica*) cut; **de ~** in addition;

quebra-cabeça (*pl* **quebra-
cabeças**) M puzzle, problem; (*jogo*)
jigsaw puzzle
quebrado, -a [ke'bradu, a] ADJ
broken; (*cansado*) exhausted;
(*falido*) bankrupt; (*carro, máquina*)
broken down; (*telefone*) out of order
quebrar [ke'brar] VT to break ▶ VI
to break; (*carro*) to break down;
(*Com*) to go bankrupt; (*ficar sem
dinheiro*) to go broke
queda ['kɛda] F fall; (*fig*) downfall;
ter ~ para algo to have a bent for
sth; **~ de barreira** landslide;
queda-d'água (*pl* **quedas-d'água**)
F waterfall
queijo ['kejʒu] M cheese
queimado, -a [kej'madu, a] ADJ
burnt; (*de sol: machucado*) sunburnt;
(*: bronzeado*) brown, tanned;
(*plantas, folhas*) dried up
queimadura [kejma'dura] F burn;
(*de sol*) sunburn
queimar [kej'mar] VT to burn;
(*roupa*) to scorch; (*com líquido*) to
scald; (*bronzear a pele*) to tan;
(*planta, folha*) to wither ▶ VI to burn;
queimar-se VR (*pessoa*) to burn o.s.;
(*bronzear-se*) to tan
queima-roupa F: **à ~** point-blank,
at point-blank range
queira ['kejra] VB *ver* **querer**
queixa ['kejʃa] F complaint;
(*lamentação*) lament; **fazer ~ de
alguém** to complain about sb
queixar-se [kej'ʃarsi] VR to
complain; **~ de** to complain about;
(*dores etc*) to complain of
queixo ['kejʃu] M chin; (*maxilar*)
jaw; **bater o ~** to shiver
quem [kẽj] PRON who; (*como objeto*)
who(m); **de ~ é isto?** whose is this?;
~ diria! who would have thought
(it)!; **~ sabe** (*talvez*) perhaps

Quênia ['kenja] M: **o ~** Kenya
quente ['kẽtʃi] ADJ hot; (*roupa*) warm
quentinha [kẽ'tʃiɲa] F heatproof carton (*for food*); (*de restaurante*) doggy bag
quer [ker] CONJ: **~ ... ~ ...** whether ... or ...; **~ chova ~ não** whether it rains or not; **onde/quando/quem ~ que** wherever/whenever/whoever; **o que ~ que seja** whatever it is

(PALAVRA-CHAVE)

querer [ke'rer] VT **1** (*desejar*) to want; **quero mais dinheiro** I want more money; **queria um chá** I'd like a cup of tea; **quero ajudar/que vá** I want to help/you to go; **você vai querer sair amanhã?** do you want to go out tomorrow?; **eu vou querer uma cerveja** (*num bar etc*) I'd like a beer; **por/sem querer** intentionally/unintentionally; **como queira** as you wish

2 (*perguntas para pedir algo*): **você quer fechar a janela?** will you shut the window?; **quer me dar uma mão?** can you give me a hand?

3 (*amar*) to love

4 (*convite*): **quer entrar/sentar** do come in/sit down

5: **querer dizer** (*significar*) to mean; (*pretender dizer*) to mean to say; **quero dizer** I mean; **quer dizer** (*com outras palavras*) in other words

▶ VI: **querer bem a** to be fond of
querer-se VR to love one another
▶ M (*vontade*) wish; (*afeto*) affection

querido, -a [ke'ridu, a] ADJ dear

▶ M/F darling; **Q~ João** Dear John
querosene [kero'zɛni] M kerosene
questão [kes'tãw] (*pl* **-ões**) F question; (*problema*) issue, question; (*Jur*) case; (*contenda*) dispute, quarrel; **fazer ~ (de)** to insist (on); **em ~** in question; **há ~ de um ano** about a year ago; **questionar** [kestʃjo'nar] VI to question ▶ VT to question, call into question; **questionário** [kestʃjo'narju] M questionnaire; **questionável** [kestʃjo'navew] (*pl* **-eis**) ADJ questionable
quicar [ki'kar] VT, VI to bounce
quieto, -a ['kjɛtu, a] ADJ quiet; (*imóvel*) still; **quietude** [kje'tudʒi] F calm, tranquillity
quilate [ki'latʃi] M carat
quilo ['kilu] M kilo; **quilobyte** [kilo'bajtʃi] M kilobyte; **quilograma** [kilo'grama] M kilogram; **quilometragem** [kilome'traʒẽ] F number of kilometres *ou* kilometers travelled, ≈ mileage; **quilômetro** [ki'lometru] M kilometre (*BRIT*), kilometer (*US*); **quilowatt** [kilo'watʃi] M kilowatt
química ['kimika] F chemistry
químico, -a ['kimiku, a] ADJ chemical ▶ M/F chemist
quina ['kina] F corner; (*de mesa etc*) edge; **de ~** edgeways (*BRIT*), edgewise (*US*)
quindim [kĩ'dʒĩ] M *sweet made of egg yolks, coconut and sugar*
quinhão [ki'ɲãw] (*pl* **-ões**) M share, portion
quinhentos, -as [ki'ɲẽtus, as] NUM five hundred
quinhões [ki'ɲõjs] MPL *de* **quinhão**

q

quinquilharias [kĩkiʎa'riaʃ] FPL odds and ends; (*miudezas*) knick-knacks, trinkets

quinta ['kĩta] F (tb: **~-feira**) Thursday; (*propriedade*) estate; (PT) farm; **quinta-feira** ['kĩta-'fejra] (*pl* **quintas-feiras**) F Thursday

quintal [kĩ'taw] (*pl* -**ais**) M back yard

quinteto [kĩ'tetu] M quintet(te)

quinto, -a ['kĩtu, a] NUM fifth

quinze ['kĩzi] NUM fifteen; **duas e ~** a quarter past (BRIT) *ou* after (US) two; **~ para as sete** a quarter to (BRIT) *ou* of (US) seven

quinzena [kĩ'zɛna] F two weeks, fortnight (BRIT); **quinzenal** [kĩze'naw] (*pl* -**ais**) ADJ fortnightly; **quinzenalmente** [kĩzenaw'mẽtʃi] ADV fortnightly

quiosque ['kjɔski] M kiosk

quis [kiz] VB *ver* **querer**

quiser [ki'zer] VB *ver* **querer**

quisto ['kiʃtu] M cyst

quitanda [ki'tãda] F grocer's (shop) (BRIT), grocery store (US)

quitar [ki'tar] VT (*dívida: pagar*) to pay off; (: *perdoar*) to cancel; (*devedor*) to release

quite ['kitʃi] ADJ (*livre*) free; (*com um credor*) squared up; (*igualado*) even; **estar ~ (com alguém)** to be quits (with sb)

quitute [ki'tutʃi] M titbit (BRIT), tidbit (US)

quota ['kwɔta] F quota; (*porção*) share, portion

quotidiano, -a [kwotʃi'dʒjanu, a] ADJ everyday

r

R ABR (= *rua*) St

R$ ABR = **real**

rã [hã] F frog

rabanete [haba'netʃi] M radish

rabiscar [habiʃ'kar] VT to scribble; (*papel*) to scribble on ▶ VI to scribble; (*desenhar*) to doodle; **rabisco** [ha'biʃku] M scribble

rabo ['habu] M tail

rabugento, -a [habu'ʒẽtu, a] ADJ grumpy

raça ['hasa] F breed; (*grupo étnico*) race; **cão/cavalo de ~** pedigree dog/thoroughbred horse

racha ['haʃa] F (*fenda*) split; (*greta*) crack; **rachadura** [haʃa'dura] F crack; **rachar** [ha'ʃar] VT to crack; (*objeto, despesas*) to split; (*lenha*) to chop ▶ VI to split; (*cristal*) to crack; **rachar-se** VR to split; to crack

racial [ha'sjaw] (*pl* -**ais**) ADJ racial

raciocínio [hasjo'sinju] M reasoning

racional [hasjo'naw] (*pl* -**ais**) ADJ rational; **racionalizar**

[hasjonali'zar] vт to rationalize
racionamento [hasjona'mẽtu]
м rationing
racismo [ha'sizmu] м racism;
racista [ha'sista] ADJ, M/F racist
radar [ha'dar] м radar
radiação [hadʒja'sãw] ϝ radiation
radiador [hadʒja'dor] м radiator
radical [hadʒi'kaw] (pl **-ais**) ADJ
radical
radicar-se [hadʒi'karsi] vʀ to
take root; (fixar residência) to settle
rádio ['hadʒju] м radio; (Quím)
radium; **radioativo, -a**
[hadʒjua'tʃivu, a] ADJ radioactive;
radiodifusão [hadʒjodʒifu'zãw] ϝ
broadcasting; **radiografar**
[hadʒjogra'far] vт to X-ray;
radiografia [hadʒjogra'fia] ϝ
X-ray
raia ['haja] ϝ (risca) line; (fronteira)
boundary; (limite) limit; (de corrida)
lane; (peixe) ray
raiar [ha'jar] vι to shine
rainha [ha'iɲa] ϝ queen
raio ['haju] м (de sol) ray; (de luz)
beam; (de roda) spoke; (relâmpago)
flash of lightning; (distância)
range; (Mat) radius; **~s X** X-rays
raiva ['hajva] ϝ rage, fury; (Med)
rabies sg; **estar/ficar com ~ (de)**
to be/get angry (with); **ter ~ de** to
hate; **raivoso, -a** [haj'vozu, ɔza]
ADJ furious
raiz [ha'iz] ϝ root; (origem) source;
~ quadrada square root
rajada [ha'ʒada] ϝ (vento) gust
ralado, -a [ha'ladu, a] ADJ grated;
ralador [hala'dor] м grater
ralar [ha'lar] vт to grate
ralhar [ha'ʎar] vι to scold; **~ com
alguém** to tell sb off
rali [ha'li] м rally
ralo, -a ['halu, a] ADJ (cabelo)
thinning; (tecido) flimsy;
(vegetação) sparse; (sopa) thin,
watery; (café) weak ▶ м (de
regador) rose, nozzle; (de pia,
banheiro) drain
rama ['hama] ϝ branches pl,
foliage; **pela ~** superficially;
ramagem [ha'maʒẽ] ϝ branches
pl, foliage; **ramal** [ha'maw] (pl
-ais) м (Ferro) branch line; (Tel)
extension; (Auto) side road
ramificar-se [hamifi'karsi] vʀ to
branch out
ramo ['hamu] м branch;
(profissão, negócios) line; (de flores)
bunch; **Domingo de R~s** Palm
Sunday
rampa ['hãpa] ϝ ramp; (ladeira)
slope
ranger [hã'ʒer] vι to creak ▶ vт:
~ os dentes to grind one's teeth
ranhura [ha'ɲura] ϝ groove;
(para moeda) slot
rapar [ha'par] vт to scrape; (a
barba) to shave; (o cabelo) to shave
off
rapariga [hapa'riga] ϝ girl
rapaz [ha'pajz] м boy; (col) lad
rapidez [hapi'dez] ϝ speed
rápido, -a ['hapidu, a] ADJ quick,
fast ▶ ADV fast, quickly ▶ м (trem)
express
rapina [ha'pina] ϝ robbery; **ave
de ~** bird of prey
raptar [hap'tar] vт to kidnap;
rapto ['haptu] м kidnapping;
raptor [hap'tor] м kidnapper
raquete [ha'ketʃi] ϝ racquet
raquítico, -a [ha'kitʃiku, a] ADJ
(franzino) puny; (vegetação) poor
raramente [hara'mẽtʃi] ADV
rarely, seldom
raro, -a ['haru, a] ADJ rare ▶ ADV
rarely, seldom

r

rasgado, -a [haz'gadu, a] ADJ
(*roupa*) torn, ripped

rasgão [haz'gãw] (*pl* **-ões**) M tear,
rip

rasgar [haz'gar] VT to tear, rip;
(*destruir*) to tear up, rip up;
rasgar-se VR to split; **rasgo**
['hazgu] M tear, rip

rasgões [haz'gõjs] MPL *de* **rasgão**

raso, -a ['hazu, a] ADJ (*liso*) flat,
level; (*não fundo*) shallow; (*baixo*)
low; **soldado ~** private

raspa ['haspa] F (*de madeira*)
shaving; (*de metal*) filing

raspão [has'pãw] (*pl* **-ões**) M
scratch, graze

raspar [has'par] VT to scrape;
(*alisar*) to file; (*tocar de raspão*) to
graze; (*arranhar*) to scratch; (*pelos,
cabeça*) to shave; (*apagar*) to rub out
▶ VI: **~ em** to scrape

raspões [has'põjs] MPL *de* **raspão**

rasteira [has'tejra] F: **dar uma ~
em alguém** to trip sb up

rasteiro, -a [has'tejru, a] ADJ
crawling; (*planta*) creeping

rastejar [haste'ʒar] VI to crawl;
(*furtivamente*) to creep; (*fig:
rebaixar-se*) to grovel ▶ VT (*fugitivo
etc*) to track

rasto ['hastu] M (*pegada*) track; (*de
veículo*) trail; (*fig*) sign, trace; **andar
de ~s** to crawl

rastro ['hastru] M = **rasto**

rata ['hata] F rat; (*pequena*) mouse

ratificar [hatʃifi'kar] VT to ratify

rato ['hatu] M rat; (*rato pequeno*)
mouse; **~ de hotel/praia** hotel/
beach thief; **ratoeira** [ha'twejra] F
rat trap; (*pequena*) mousetrap

ravina [ha'vina] F ravine

razão [ha'zãw] (*pl* **-ões**) F reason;
(*argumento*) reasoning; (*Mat*) ratio
▶ M (*Com*) ledger; **à ~ de** at the rate

of; **em ~ de** on account of; **dar ~ a
alguém** to support sb; **ter/não ter
~** to be right/wrong; **razoável**
[ha'zwavew] (*pl* **-eis**) ADJ reasonable

r/c (PT) ABR = **rés do chão**

ré [hɛ] F (*Auto*) reverse (gear); **dar
(marcha à) ré** to reverse, back up;
ver tb **réu**

reabastecer [heabaste'ser] VT
(*avião*) to refuel; (*carro*) to fill up;
reabastecer-se VR: **~-se de** to
replenish one's supply of

reação [hea'sãw] (*pl* **-ões**) F
reaction

reagir [hea'ʒir] VI to react; (*doente,
time perdedor*) to fight back; **~ a**
(*resistir*) to resist; (*protestar*) to rebel
against

reais [he'ajs] ADJ PL *de* **real**

reaja [he'aʒa] VB *ver* **reagir**; **reaver**

reajuste [hea'ʒustʃi] M adjustment

real [he'aw] (*pl* **-ais**) ADJ real;
(*relativo à realeza*) royal ▶ M (*moeda*)
real

> The Brazilian currency, the **real**,
> was introduced in 1994 as part of
> a comprehensive economic
> stabilization package known as
> the **Plano Real**. This brought an
> end to some thirty years of
> hyperinflation which saw
> successive devaluations and
> name-changes to the Brazilian
> currency, from *cruzeiro* to *cruzado*
> (1986), to *cruzado novo* (1989),
> back to *cruzeiro* (1990), to *cruzeiro
> real* (1993) and finally to *real*
> (1994). The *real* is subdivided into
> 100 *centavos*. The currency
> symbol is R$ and a comma is
> used to separate *reais* and
> *centavos*, e.g. R$ 2,40 (two *reais*
> and forty *centavos*).

realçar [heaw'sar] VT to highlight;

realce [he'awsi] M emphasis; (*mais brilho*) highlight; **dar realce a** to enhance

realeza [hea'leza] F royalty

realidade [heali'dadʒi] F reality; **na ~** actually, in fact; **~ virtual** virtual reality

realista [hea'lista] ADJ realistic ▶ M/F realist

realização [healiza'sãw] F fulfilment (BRIT), fulfillment (US), realization; (*de projeto*) execution, carrying out

realizador, a [healiza'dor(a)] ADJ enterprising

realizar [heali'zar] VT to achieve; (*projeto*) to carry out; (*ambições, sonho*) to fulfil (BRIT), fulfill (US), realize; (*negócios*) to transact; (*perceber, convertir en dinheiro*) to realize; **realizar-se** VR to take place; (*ambições*) to be realized; (*sonhos*) to come true

realmente [heaw'mẽtʃi] ADV really; (*de fato*) actually

reanimar [heani'mar] VT to revive; (*encorajar*) to encourage; **reanimar-se** VR to cheer up

reatar [hea'tar] VT to resume, take up again

reaver [hea'ver] VT to recover, get back

rebaixar [hebaj'ʃar] VT to lower; (*reduzir*) to reduce; (*time*) to relegate; (*funcionário*) to demote; (*humilhar*) to put down ▶ VI to drop; **rebaixar-se** VR to demean o.s.

rebanho [he'baɲu] M (*de carneiros, fig*) flock; (*de gado, elefantes*) herd

rebelar-se [hebe'larsi] VR to rebel; **rebelde** [he'bɛwdʒi] ADJ rebellious; (*indisciplinado*) unruly, wild ▶ M/F rebel; **rebeldia**

[hebew'dʒia] F rebelliousness; (*fig: obstinação*) stubbornness; (: *oposição*) defiance

rebelião [hebe'ljãw] (*pl* **-ões**) F rebellion

rebentar [hebē'tar] VI (*guerra*) to break out; (*louça*) to smash; (*corda*) to snap; (*represa*) to burst; (*ondas*) to break ▶ VT to smash; to snap; (*porta, ponte*) to break down

rebocador [heboka'dor] M tug(boat)

rebocar [hebo'kar] VT (*paredes*) to plaster; (*dar reboque a*) to tow

rebolar [hebo'lar] VT to swing ▶ VI to sway

reboque¹ [he'bɔki] M tow; (*veículo: tb:* **carro ~**) trailer; (*cabo*) towrope; (BR: *de socorro*) tow truck; **a ~** on *ou* in (US) tow

reboque² VB *ver* **rebocar**

rebuçado [hebu'sadu] (PT) M sweet, candy (US)

recado [he'kadu] M message; **deixar ~** to leave a message

recair [heka'ir] VI (*doente*) to relapse

recalcar [hekaw'kar] VT to repress

recalque VB *ver* **recalcar**

recanto [he'kãtu] M corner, nook

recapitular [hekapitu'lar] VT to sum up, recapitulate; (*fatos*) to review; (*matéria escolar*) to revise

recarga [he'karga] F (*de celular*) top-up; **preciso fazer a ~ do meu celular** I need to top up my mobile

recarregar [hekahe'gar] VT (*celular*) to top up; (*bateria*) to recharge; (*cartucho*) to refill

recatado, -a [heka'tadu, a] ADJ (*modesto*) modest; (*reservado*) reserved

recauchutado, -a [hekawʃu'tadu, a] ADJ: **pneu ~**

r

(*Auto*) retread, remould (*BRIT*)
recear [he'sjar] VT to fear ▶ VI:
~ **por** to fear for; ~ **fazer/que** to be afraid to do/that
receber [hese'ber] VT to receive; (*ganhar*) to earn, get; (*hóspedes*) to take in; (*convidados*) to entertain; (*acolher bem*) to welcome ▶ VI (*receber convidados*) to entertain; **recebimento** [hesebi'mẽtu] (*BR*) M reception; (*de uma carta*) receipt; **acusar o recebimento de** to acknowledge receipt of
receio [he'seju] M fear; **ter ~ de que** to fear that
receita [he'sejta] F income; (*do Estado*) revenue; (*Med*) prescription; (*culinária*) recipe; **R~ Federal** ≈ Inland Revenue (*BRIT*), ≈ IRS (*US*); **receitar** [hesej'tar] VT to prescribe
recém [he'sẽ] ADV recently, newly; **recém-casado, -a** ADJ: **os recém-casados** the newlyweds; **recém-chegado, -a** M/F newcomer; **recém-nascido, -a** M/F newborn child
recente [he'sẽtʃi] ADJ recent; (*novo*) new ▶ ADV recently; **recentemente** [hesẽtʃi'mẽtʃi] ADV recently
receoso, -a [he'sjozu, ɔza] ADJ frightened, fearful; **estar ~ de (fazer)** to be afraid of (doing)
recepção [hesep'sãw] (*pl* -**ões**) F reception; (*PT: de uma carta*) receipt; **acusar a ~ de** (*PT*) to acknowledge receipt of; **recepcionista** [hesepsjo'nista] M/F receptionist
receptivo, -a [hesep'tʃivu, a] ADJ receptive; (*acolhedor*) welcoming
receptor [hesep'tor] M receiver
recessão [hese'sãw] (*pl* -**ões**) F recession
recessões [hese'sõjs] FPL *de* **recessão**

recheado, -a [he'ʃjadu, a] ADJ (*ave, carne*) stuffed; (*empada, bolo*) filled; (*cheio*) full, crammed
rechear [he'ʃjar] VT to fill; (*ave, carne*) to stuff; **recheio** [he'ʃeju] M stuffing; (*de empada, de bolo*) filling; (*o conteúdo*) contents pl
rechonchudo, -a [heʃõ'ʃudu, a] ADJ chubby, plump
recibo [he'sibu] M receipt
reciclar [hesi'klar] VT to recycle
reciclável [hesi'klavew] (*pl* -**eis**) ADJ recyclable
recinto [he'sĩtu] M enclosure; (*lugar*) area
recipiente [hesi'pjẽtʃi] M container, receptacle
recíproco, -a [he'siproku, a] ADJ reciprocal
recitar [hesi'tar] VT to recite
reclamação [heklama'sãw] (*pl* -**ões**) F complaint
reclamar [hekla'mar] VT to demand; (*herança*) to claim ▶ VI: ~ **(de)** (*comida etc*) to complain (about)
reclinar [hekli'nar] VT to rest, lean; **reclinar-se** VR to lie back; (*deitar-se*) to lie down
recobrar [heko'brar] VT to recover, get back; **recobrar-se** VR to recover
recolher [heko'ʎer] VT to collect; (*gado, roupa do varal*) to bring in; (*juntar*) to collect up; **recolhido, -a** [heko'ʎidu, a] ADJ (*lugar*) secluded; (*pessoa*) withdrawn; **recolhimento** [hekoʎi'mẽtu] M retirement; (*arrecadação*) collection; (*ato de levar*) taking
recomeçar [hekome'sar] VT, VI to restart
recomendação [hekomẽda'sãw] (*pl* -**ões**) F recommendation; **recomendações** FPL (*cumprimentos*) regards

recomendar [hekomẽ'dar] vt to recommend; **recomendável** [hekomẽ'davew] (pl **-eis**) ADJ advisable

recompensa [hekõ'pẽsa] F reward; **recompensar** [hekõpẽ'sar] vt to reward

recompor [hekõ'por] (irreg: como **pôr**) vt to reorganize; (restabelecer) to restore

reconciliar [hekõsi'ljar] vt to reconcile

reconhecer [hekoɲe'ser] vt to recognize; (Mil) to reconnoitre (BRIT), reconnoiter (US); **reconhecido, -a** [hekoɲe'sidu, a] ADJ recognized; (agradecido) grateful, thankful; **reconhecimento** [hekoɲesi'mẽtu] M recognition; (admissão) admission; (gratidão) gratitude; (Mil) reconnaissance; **reconhecível** [hekoɲe'sivew] (pl **-eis**) ADJ recognizable

reconstruir [hekõs'trwir] vt to rebuild

recordação [hekorda'sãw] (pl **-ões**) F (reminiscência) memory; (objeto) memento

recordar [hekor'dar] vt to remember; **recordar-se** vR: **~-se de** to remember; **~ algo a alguém** to remind sb of sth

recorde [he'kɔrdʒi] ADJ INV record atr ▶ M record

recorrer [heko'her] vi: **~ a** to turn to; (valer-se de) to resort to

recortar [hekor'tar] vt to cut out; **recorte** [he'kɔrtʃi] M (ato) cutting out; (de jornal) cutting, clipping

recreação [hekrja'sãw] F recreation

recreio [he'kreju] M recreation

recriminar [hekrimi'nar] vt to reproach, reprove

recrutamento [hekruta'mẽtu] M recruitment

recrutar [hekru'tar] vt to recruit

recuar [he'kwar] vt to move back ▶ vi to move back; (exército) to retreat

recuperar [hekupe'rar] vt to recover; (tempo perdido) to make up for; (reabilitar) to rehabilitate; **recuperar-se** vR to recover

recurso [he'kursu] M resource; (Jur) appeal; **recursos** MPL (financeiros) resources

recusa [he'kuza] F refusal; (negação) denial; **recusar** [heku'zar] vt to refuse; to deny; **recusar-se** vR: **recusar-se a** to refuse to

redação [heda'sãw] (pl **-ões**) F (ato) writing; (Educ) composition, essay; (redatores) editorial staff

redator, a [heda'tor(a)] M/F editor

rede ['hedʒi] F net; (de dormir) hammock; (Ferro, Tec, Comput, TV, fig) network; **a ~** (a Internet) the web; **~ de área local** local area network; **~ sem fio** wireless network; **~ social** social network, social networking site

rédea ['hɛdʒja] F rein

redentor, a [hedẽ'tor(a)] ADJ redeeming

redigir [hedʒi'ʒir] vt, vi to write

redobrar [hedo'brar] vt (aumentar) to increase; (esforços) to redouble

redondamente [hedõda'mẽtʃi] ADV (completamente) completely

redondeza [hedõ'deza] F roundness; **redondezas** FPL surroundings

redondo, -a [he'dõdu, a] ADJ round

r

redor [he'dor] M: **ao** *ou* **em ~ (de)** around, round about

redução [hedu'sãw] (*pl* **-ões**) F reduction

redundância [hedũ'dãsja] F redundancy; **redundante** [hedũ'dãtʃi] ADJ redundant

reduzido, -a [hedu'zidu, a] ADJ reduced; (*limitado*) limited; (*pequeno*) small

reduzir [hedu'zir] VT to reduce; **reduzir-se** VR: **~-se a** to be reduced to; (*fig: resumir-se em*) to come down to

reembolsar [heẽbow'sar] VT to recover; (*restituir*) to reimburse; (*depósito*) to refund; **reembolso** [heẽ'bowsu] M (*de depósito*) refund; (*de despesa*) reimbursement

reencontro [heẽ'kõtru] M reunion

refeição [hefej'sãw] (*pl* **-ões**) F meal; **refeitório** [hefej'tɔrju] M refectory

refém [he'fẽ] (*pl* **-ns**) M hostage

referência [hefe'rẽsja] F reference; **referências** FPL (*informaçoes para emprego*) references; **fazer ~ a** to make reference to, refer to

referente [hefe'rẽtʃi] ADJ: **~ a** concerning, regarding

referir [hefe'rir] VT to relate, tell; **referir-se** VR: **~-se a** to refer to

REFESA F (= *Rede Ferroviária SA*) *Brazilian rail network*

refinamento [hefina'mẽtu] M refinement

refinaria [hefina'ria] F refinery

refiro [he'firu] VB *ver* **referir**

refletir [hefle'tʃir] VT to reflect ► VI: **~ em** *ou* **sobre** to consider, think about

reflexão [heflek'sãw] (*pl* **-ões**) F reflection

reflexo, -a [he'flɛksu, a] ADJ (*luz*) reflected; (*ação*) reflex ► M reflection; (*Anat*) reflex; (*no cabelo*) streak

reflexões [heflek'sõjs] FPL *de* **reflexão**

reflito [he'flitu] VB *ver* **refletir**

reforçado, -a [hefor'sadu, a] ADJ reinforced; (*pessoa*) strong; (*café da manhã, jantar*) hearty

reforçar [hefor'sar] VT to reinforce; (*revigorar*) to invigorate; **reforço** [he'forsu] M reinforcement

reforma [he'fɔrma] F reform; (*Arq*) renovation; **reformado, -a** [hefor'madu, a] ADJ reformed; renovated; (*Mil*) retired; **reformar** [hefor'mar] VT to reform; to renovate; **reformar-se** VR to reform

refrão [he'frãw] (*pl* **-ões**) M chorus, refrain; (*provérbio*) saying

refratário, -a [hefra'tarju, a] ADJ (*Tec*) heat-resistant; (*Culin*) ovenproof

refrear [hefre'ar] VT (*cavalo*) to rein in; (*inimigo*) to contain, check; (*paixões, raiva*) to control; **refrear-se** VR to restrain o.s.

refrescante [hefres'kãtʃi] ADJ refreshing

refrescar [hefres'kar] VT (*ar, ambiente*) to cool; (*pessoa*) to refresh ► VI to cool down

refresco [he'fresku] M cool fruit drink, squash; **refrescos** MPL (*refrigerantes*) refreshments

refrigerador [hefriʒera'dor] M refrigerator, fridge (BRIT)

refrigerante [hefriʒe'rãtʃi] M soft drink

refugiado, -a [hefu'ʒjadu, a] ADJ, M/F refugee

refugiar-se [hefu'ʒjarsi] VR to take refuge; **refúgio** [he'fuʒju] M refuge

refugo [he'fugu] M rubbish,

garbage (US); (mercadoria) reject

rega ['hɛga] F (PT) irrigation

regador [hega'dor] M watering can

regalia [hega'lia] F privilege

regar [he'gar] VT (plantas, jardim) to water; (umedecer) to sprinkle

regatear [hega'tʃjar] VT (o preço) to haggle over, bargain for ▶ VI to haggle

regenerar [heʒene'rar] VT to regenerate

reger [he'ʒer] VT to govern; (orquestra) to conduct; (empresa) to run ▶ VI to rule; (maestro) to conduct

região [he'ʒjãw] (pl **-ões**) F region, area

regime [he'ʒimi] M (Pol) regime; (dieta) diet; (maneira) way; **estar de ~** to be on a diet

regimento [heʒi'mẽtu] M regiment

regiões [he'ʒjõjs] FPL de **região**

regional [heʒjo'naw] (pl **-ais**) ADJ regional

registrar [heʒis'trar], (PT) **registar** VT to register; (anotar) to record

registro [he'ʒistru], (PT) **registo** M (ato) registration; (: anotação) recording; (livro, Ling) register; (histórico, Comput) record; **~ civil** registry office

regra ['hɛgra] F rule; **regras** FPL (Med) periods

regravável [hegra'vavew] (pl **-eis**) ADJ rewritable

regressar [hegre'sar] VI to come (ou go) back, return; **regresso** [he'grɛsu] M return

régua ['hɛgwa] F ruler; **~ de calcular** slide rule

regulador [hegula'dor] M regulator

regulamento [hegula'mẽtu] M rules pl, regulations pl

regular [hegu'lar] ADJ regular; (estatura) average, medium; (tamanho) normal; (razoável) not bad ▶ VT to regulate; (reger) to govern; (máquina) to adjust; (carro, motor) to tune ▶ VI to work, function; **regularidade** [hegulari'dadʒi] F regularity

rei [hej] M king; **Dia de R~s** Epiphany; **R~ Momo** carnival king

reinado [hej'nadu] M reign

reinar [hej'nar] VI to reign

reino ['hejnu] M kingdom; (fig) realm; **o R~ Unido** the United Kingdom

reivindicação [hejvĩdʒika'sãw] (pl **-ões**) F claim, demand

reivindicar [hejvĩdʒi'kar] VT to claim; (aumento salarial, direitos) to demand

rejeição [heʒej'sãw] (pl **-ões**) F rejection

rejeitar [heʒej'tar] VT to reject; (recusar) to refuse

rejo ['heʒu] VB ver **reger**

rejuvenescer [heʒuvene'ser] VT to rejuvenate

relação [hela'sãw] (pl **-ões**) F relation; (conexão) connection; (relacionamento) relationship; (Mat) ratio; (lista) list; **com ou em ~ a** regarding, with reference to; **relações públicas** public relations; **relacionamento** [helasjona'mẽtu] M relationship; **relacionar** [helasjo'nar] VT to make a list of; (ligar): **relacionar algo com algo** to connect sth with sth, relate sth to sth; **relacionar-se** VR to be connected ou related

relâmpago [he'lãpagu] M flash of

lightning; **relâmpagos** MPL (*clarões*) lightning *sg*

relance [he'lãsi] M glance; **olhar de ~** to glance at

relapso, -a [he'lapsu, a] ADJ (*negligente*) negligent

relatar [hela'tar] VT to give an account of

relativo, -a [hela'tʃivu, a] ADJ relative

relato [he'latu] M account

relatório [hela'tɔrju] M report

relaxado, -a [hela'ʃadu, a] ADJ relaxed; (*desleixado*) slovenly, sloppy; (*relapso*) negligent

relaxante [hela'ʃãtʃi] ADJ relaxing

relaxar [hela'ʃar] VT, VI to relax

relegar [hele'gar] VT to relegate

relembrar [helẽ'brar] VT to recall

relevante [hele'vãtʃi] ADJ relevant

relevo [he'levu] M relief

religião [heli'ʒãw] (*pl* **-ões**) F religion; **religioso, -a** [heli'ʒozu, ɔza] ADJ religious ▶ M/F religious person; (*frade/freira*) monk/nun

relíquia [he'likja] F relic; **~ de família** family heirloom

relógio [he'lɔʒu] M clock; (*de gás*) meter; **~ (de pulso)** (wrist)watch; **~ de sol** sundial

relutante [helu'tãtʃi] ADJ reluctant

relva ['hɛwva] F grass; (*terreno gramado*) lawn

relvado [hew'vadu] (*PT*) M lawn

remar [he'mar] VT, VI to row

rematar [hema'tar] VT to finish off; **remate** [he'matʃi] M (*fim*) end; (*acabamento*) finishing touch

remediar [heme'dʒjar] VT to put right, remedy

remédio [he'mɛdʒu] M (*medicamento*) medicine; (*recurso, solução*) remedy; (*Jur*) recourse; **não tem ~** there's no way

remendar [hemẽ'dar] VT to mend; (*com pano*) to patch; **remendo** [he'mẽdu] M repair; patch

remessa [he'mɛsa] F shipment; (*de dinheiro*) remittance

remetente [heme'tẽtʃi] M/F sender

remexer [heme'ʃer] VT (*papéis*) to shuffle; (*sacudir: braços*) to wave; (*folhas*) to shake; (*revolver: areia, lama*) to stir up ▶ VI: **~ em** to rummage through

reminiscência [hemini'sẽsja] F reminiscence

remo ['hɛmu] M oar; (*Esporte*) rowing

remoção [hemo'sãw] F removal

remorso [he'mɔrsu] M remorse

remover [hemo'ver] VT to move; (*transferir*) to transfer; (*demitir*) to dismiss; (*retirar, afastar*) to remove; (*terra*) to churn up

renal [he'naw] (*pl* **-ais**) ADJ renal, kidney *atr*

Renascença [hena'sẽsa] F: **a ~** the Renaissance

renascer [hena'ser] VI to be reborn; (*fig*) to revive

renascimento [henasi'mẽtu] M rebirth; (*fig*) revival; **o R~** the Renaissance

renda ['hẽda] F income; (*nacional*) revenue; (*de aplicação, locação*) yield; (*tecido*) lace

render [hẽ'der] VT (*lucro, dinheiro*) to bring in, yield; (*preço*) to fetch; (*homenagem*) to pay; (*graças*) to give; (*serviços*) to render; (*armas*) to surrender; (*guarda*) to relieve; (*causar*) to bring ▶ VI (*dar lucro*) to pay; **render-se** VR to surrender; **rendição** [hẽdʒi'sãw] F surrender

rendimento [hẽdʒi'mẽtu] M income; (*lucro*) profit; (*juro*) yield, interest

renegar [hene'gar] VT (*crença*) to renounce; (*detestar*) to hate; (*trair*) to betray; (*negar*) to deny; (*desprezar*) to reject

renomado, -a [heno'madu, a] ADJ renowned

renovar [heno'var] VT to renew; (*Arq*) to renovate

rentabilidade [hētabili'dadʒi] F profitability

rentável [hē'tavew] (*pl* **-eis**) ADJ profitable

renúncia [he'nūsja] F resignation

renunciar [henū'sjar] VT to give up, renounce ▶ VI to resign; (*abandonar*): **~ a algo** to give sth up

reouve [he'ovi] VB *ver* **reaver**

reouver [heo'ver] VB *ver* **reaver**

reparação [hepara'sāw] (*pl* **-ões**) F mending, repairing; (*de mal, erros*) remedying; (*fig*) amends *pl*, reparation

reparar [hepa'rar] VT to repair; (*forças*) to restore; (*mal, erros*) to remedy; (*prejuizo, danos, ofensa*) to make amends for; (*notar*) to notice ▶ VI: **~ em** to notice; **reparo** [he'paru] M repair; (*crítica*) criticism; (*observação*) observation

repartição [hepartʃi'sāw] (*pl* **-ões**) F distribution

repartir [hepar'tʃir] VT (*distribuir*) to distribute; (*dividir entre vários*) to share out; (*dividir em várias porções*) to divide up

repelente [hepe'lētʃi] ADJ, M repellent

repente [he'pētʃi] M outburst; **de ~** suddenly; (*col: talvez*) maybe

repentino, -a [hepē'tʃinu, a] ADJ sudden

repercussão [heperku'sāw] (*pl* **-ões**) F repercussion

repercutir [heperku'tʃir] VT to

echo ▶ VI to reverberate, echo; (*fig*): **~ (em)** to have repercussions (on)

repertório [heper'tɔrju] M list; (*coleção*) collection; (*Mús*) repertoire

repetidamente [hepetʃida'mētʃi] ADV repeatedly

repetir [hepe'tʃir] VT to repeat ▶ VI (*ao comer*) to have seconds; **repetir-se** VR to happen again; (*pessoa*) to repeat o.s.; **repetitivo, -a** [hepetʃi'tʃivu, a] ADJ repetitive

repito [he'pitu] VB *ver* **repetir**

repleto, -a [he'plɛtu, a] ADJ replete, full up

réplica ['hɛplika] F replica; (*contestação*) reply, retort

replicar [hepli'kar] VT to answer, reply to ▶ VI to reply, answer back

repolho [he'poʎu] M cabbage

repor [he'por] (*irreg: como* **pôr**) VT to put back, replace; (*restituir*) to return; **repor-se** VR to recover

reportagem [hepor'taʒē] (*pl* **-ns**) F reporting; (*notícia*) report

repórter [he'pɔrter] M/F reporter

repousar [hepo'zar] VI to rest; **repouso** [he'pozu] M rest

representação [hepreze̊ta'sāw] (*pl* **-ões**) F representation; (*Teatro*) performance; **representante** [hepreze̊'tātʃi] M/F representative

representar [hepreze̊'tar] VT to represent; (*Teatro: papel*) to play ▶ VI to act; **representativo, -a** [hepreze̊ta'tʃivu, a] ADJ representative

repressão [hepre'sāw] (*pl* **-ões**) F repression

reprimir [hepri'mir] VT to repress

reprodução [heprodu'sāw] (*pl* **-ões**) F reproduction

reproduzir [heprodu'zir] vt to reproduce; (*repetir*) to repeat; **reproduzir-se** vr to breed

reprovar [hepro'var] vt to disapprove of; (*aluno*) to fail

réptil ['hɛptʃiw] (*pl* -**eis**) M reptile

república [he'publika] F republic; **republicano, -a** [hepubli'kanu, a] ADJ, M/F republican

repudiar [hepu'dʒjar] vt to repudiate; **repúdio** [he'pudʒju] M repudiation

repulsivo, -a [hepuw'sivu, a] ADJ repulsive

reputação [reputa'sãw] (*pl* -**ões**) F reputation

requeijão [hekej'ʒãw] M cheese spread

requerer [heke'rer] vt (*emprego*) to apply for; (*pedir*) to request; (*exigir*) to require; **requerimento** [hekeri'mẽtu] M application; request; (*petição*) petition

requintado, -a [hekĩ'tadu, a] ADJ refined, elegant

requinte [he'kĩtʃi] M refinement, elegance; (*cúmulo*) height

requisito [heki'zitu] M requirement

rés do chão [hɛzdu'ʃãw] (*PT*) M INV ground floor (*BRIT*), first floor (*US*)

reserva [he'zɛrva] F reserve; (*para hotel, fig*) reservation ▶ M/F (*Esporte*) reserve

reservado, -a [hezer'vadu, a] ADJ reserved

reservar [hezer'var] vt to reserve; (*guardar de reserva*) to keep; (*forças*) to conserve; **reservar-se** vr to save o.s.

reservatório [hezerva'tɔrju] M reservoir

resfriado, -a [hes'frjadu, a] (*BR*) ADJ: **estar ~** to have a cold ▶ M cold, chill; **ficar ~** to catch (a) cold

resgatar [hezga'tar] vt (*salvar*) to rescue; (*retomar*) to get back, recover; **resgate** [hez'gatʃi] M rescue; (*para livrar reféns*) ransom

residência [hezi'dẽsja] F residence; **residencial** [hezidẽ'sjaw] (*pl* -**ais**) ADJ residential; (*computador, telefone etc*) home *atr*; **residente** [hezi'dẽtʃi] ADJ, M/F resident

residir [hezi'dʒir] vi to live, reside

resíduo [he'zidwu] M residue

resignação [hezigna'sãw] (*pl* -**ões**) F resignation

resignar-se [hezig'narsi] vr: **~ com** to resign o.s. to

resina [he'zina] F resin

resistente [hezis'tẽtʃi] ADJ resistant; (*material, objeto*) hard-wearing, strong

resistir [hezis'tʃir] vi to hold; (*pessoa*) to hold out; **~ a** to resist; (*sobreviver*) to survive

resmungar [hezmũ'gar] vt, vi to mutter, mumble

resolução [hezolu'sãw] (*pl* -**ões**) F resolution; (*de um problema*) solution; **resoluto, -a** [hezo'lutu, a] ADJ decisive

resolver [hezow'ver] vt to sort out; (*problema*) to solve; (*questão*) to resolve; (*decidir*) to decide; **resolver-se** vr: **~-se (a fazer)** to make up one's mind (to do), decide (to do)

respectivo, -a [hespek'tʃivu, a] ADJ respective

respeitar [hespej'tar] vt to respect; **respeitável** [hespej'tavew] (*pl* -**eis**) ADJ respectable; (*considerável*) considerable

respeito [hes'pejtu] M: **~ (a ou por)**

respect (for); **respeitos** MPL (*cumprimentos*) regards; **a ~ de, com ~ a** as to, as regards; (*sobre*) about; **dizer ~ a** to concern; **em ~ a** with respect to

respiração [hespira'sãw] F breathing

respirar [hespi'rar] VT, VI to breathe

respiro [hes'piru] M breath

resplandecente [hesplãde'sẽtʃi] ADJ resplendent

responder [hespõ'der] VT to answer ▶ VI to answer; (*ser respondão*) to answer back; **~ por** to be responsible for, answer for

responsabilidade [hespõsabili'dadʒi] F responsibility

responsabilizar [hespõsabili'zar] VT: **~ alguém (por algo)** to hold sb responsible (for sth); **responsabilizar-se** VR: **~-se por** to take responsibility for

responsável [hespõ'savew] (*pl* **-eis**) ADJ: **~ (por)** responsible (for); **~ a** answerable to, accountable to

resposta [hes'posta] F answer, reply

resquício [hes'kisju] M (*vestígio*) trace

ressabiado, -a [hesa'bjadu, a] ADJ wary; (*ressentido*) resentful

ressaca [he'saka] F undertow; (*mar bravo*) rough sea; (*fig: de quem bebeu*) hangover

ressalva [he'sawva] F safeguard

ressentido, -a [hesẽ'tʃidu, a] ADJ resentful

ressentimento [hesẽtʃi'mẽtu] M resentment

ressentir-se [hesẽ'tʃirsi] VR: **~ de** (*ofender-se*) to resent; (*magoar-se*) to be hurt by; (*sofrer*) to suffer from,

feel the effects of

ressurgimento [hesurʒi'mẽtu] M resurgence, revival

ressuscitar [hesusi'tar] VT, VI to revive

restabelecer [hestabele'ser] VT to re-establish, restore; **restabelecer-se** VR to recover, recuperate; **restabelecimento** [hestabelesi'mẽtu] M re-establishment; restoration; recovery

restante [hes'tãtʃi] ADJ remaining ▶ M rest

restar [hes'tar] VI to remain, be left

restauração [hestawra'sãw] (*pl* **-ões**) F restoration; (*de costumes, usos*) revival

restaurante [hestaw'rãtʃi] M restaurant

restaurar [hestaw'rar] VT to restore

restituição [hestʃitwi'sãw] (*pl* **-ões**) F restitution, return; (*de dinheiro*) repayment

restituir [hestʃi'twir] VT to return; (*dinheiro*) to repay; (*forças, saúde*) to restore; (*usos*) to revive; (*reempossar*) to reinstate

resto ['hestu] M rest; (*Mat*) remainder; **restos** MPL (*sobras*) remains; (*de comida*) scraps

restrição [hestri'sãw] (*pl* **-ões**) F restriction

resultado [hezuw'tadu] M result

resultante [hezuw'tãtʃi] ADJ resultant; **~ de** resulting from

resultar [hezuw'tar] VI: **~ (de/ em)** to result (from/in) ▶ VI (*vir a ser*) to turn out to be

resumir [hezu'mir] VT to summarize; (*livro*) to abridge; (*reduzir*) to reduce; (*conter em resumo*) to sum up; **resumo**

r

[he'zumu] M summary, résumé; **em resumo** in short, briefly

retaguarda [heta'gwarda] F rearguard; (*posição*) rear

retaliação [hetalja'sãw] (*pl* -**ões**) F retaliation

retângulo [he'tãgulu] M rectangle

retardar [hetar'dar] VT to hold up, delay; (*adiar*) to postpone

reter [he'ter] (*irreg: como* **ter**) VT (*guardar, manter*) to keep; (*deter*) to stop; (*segurar*) to hold; (*ladrão, suspeito*) to detain; (*na memória*) to retain; (*lágrimas, impulsos*) to hold back; (*impedir de sair*) to keep back

reticente [hetʃi'sētʃi] ADJ reticent

retificar [hetʃifi'kar] VT to rectify

retirada [hetʃi'rada] F (*Mil*) retreat; (*salário, saque*) withdrawal

reto, -a ['hɛtu, a] ADJ straight; (*fig: justo*) fair; (: *honesto*) honest, upright ▶ M (*Anat*) rectum

retorcer [hetor'ser] VT to twist; **retorcer-se** VR to wriggle, writhe

retornar [hetor'nar] VI to return, go back; **retorno** [he'tornu] M return; **dar retorno** to do a U-turn; **retorno (do carro)** (*Comput*) (carriage) return

retraído, -a [hetra'idu, a] ADJ (*tímido*) reserved, timid

retrair [hetra'ir] VT to withdraw; (*contrair*) to contract; (*pessoa*) to make reserved

retrato [he'tratu] M portrait; (*Foto*) photo; (*fig: efígie*) likeness; (: *representação*) portrayal; **~ falado** Identikit® picture

retribuir [hetri'bwir] VT to reward, recompense; (*pagar*) to remunerate; (*hospitalidade, favor, sentimento, visita*) to return

retroceder [hetrose'der] VI to retreat, fall back; **retrocesso**

[hetro'sɛsu] M retreat; (*ao passado*) return

retrógrado, -a [he'trɔgradu, a] ADJ retrograde; (*reacionário*) reactionary

retrospecto [hetro'spɛktu] M: **em ~** in retrospect

retrovisor [hetrovi'zor] ADJ, M: **(espelho) ~** rear-view mirror

réu, ré [hɛw, hɛ] M/F defendant; (*culpado*) culprit, criminal

reumatismo [hewma'tʃizmu] M rheumatism

reunião [heu'njãw] (*pl* -**ões**) F meeting; (*ato, reencontro*) reunion; (*festa*) get-together, party; **~ de cúpula** summit (meeting)

revanche [he'vãʃi] F revenge

reveillon [heve'jõ] M New Year's Eve

revelação [hevela'sãw] (*pl* -**ões**) F revelation

revelar [heve'lar] VT to reveal; (*Foto*) to develop; **revelar-se** VR to turn out to be

revelia [heve'lia] F default; **à ~** by default; **à ~ de** without the knowledge *ou* consent of

revendedor, a [hevẽde'dor(a)] M/F dealer

rever [he'ver] (*irreg: como* **ver**) VT to see again; (*examinar*) to check; (*revisar*) to revise

reverência [heve'rẽsja] F reverence, respect; (*ato*) bow; (: *de mulher*) curtsey; **fazer uma ~** to bow; to curtsey

reverso [he'vɛrsu] M reverse

reverter [hever'ter] VT to revert

revestir [heves'tʃir] VT (*paredes etc*) to cover; (*interior de uma caixa etc*) to line

revezar [heve'zar] VT to take turns with ▶ VI to take turns; **revezar-se**

vr to take it in turns

revidar [hevi'dar] vt (*soco, insulto*) to return; (*retrucar*) to answer; (*crítica*) to rise to, respond to ▶ vi to hit back; (*retrucar*) to respond

revirar [hevi'rar] vt to turn round; (*gaveta*) to turn out, go through

revisão [hevi'zãw] (*pl* **-ões**) F revision; (*de máquina*) overhaul; (*de carro*) service; (*Jur*) appeal

revisar [hevi'zar] vt to revise

revisões [hevi'zõjs] FPL *de* **revisão**

revista [he'vista] F (*busca*) search; (*Mil, exame*) inspection; (*publicação*) magazine; (*: profissional, erudita*) journal; (*Teatro*) revue

revisto [he'vistu] vb *ver* **revestir**

revogar [hevo'gar] vt to revoke

revolta [he'vɔwta] F revolt; (*fig: indignação*) disgust; **revoltado, -a** [hevow'tadu, a] ADJ in revolt; (*indignado*) disgusted; (*amargo*) bitter; **revoltante** [hevow'tãtʃi] ADJ disgusting; revolting

revoltar [hevow'tar] vt to disgust; **revoltar-se** vr to rebel, revolt; (*indignar-se*) to be disgusted

revolto, -a [he'vowtu, a] PP *de* **revolver** ▶ ADJ (*década*) turbulent; (*mundo*) troubled; (*cabelo*) dishevelled; (*mar*) rough; (*desarrumado*) untidy

revolução [hevolu'sãw] (*pl* **-ões**) F revolution; **revolucionar** [hevolusjo'nar] vt to revolutionize; **revolucionário, -a** [hevolusjo'narju, a] ADJ, M/F revolutionary

revolver [hevow'ver] vi to revolve, rotate

revólver [he'vɔwver] M revolver

reza ['hɛza] F prayer; **rezar**

[he'zar] vi to pray

riacho ['hjaʃu] M stream, brook

ribeiro [hi'bejru] M brook, stream

rico, -a ['hiku, a] ADJ rich; (*PT: lindo*) beautiful; (*: excelente*) splendid ▶ M/F rich man/woman

ridicularizar [hidʒikulari'zar] vt to ridicule

ridículo, -a [hi'dʒikulu, a] ADJ ridiculous

rifa ['hifa] F raffle

rifle ['hifli] M rifle

rigidez [hiʒi'dez] F rigidity, stiffness; (*austeridade*) severity, strictness

rígido, -a ['hiʒidu, a] ADJ rigid, stiff; (*fig*) strict

rigor [hi'gor] M rigidity; (*meticulosidade*) rigour (BRIT), rigor (US); (*severidade*) harshness, severity; (*exatidão*) precision; **ser de ~** to be essential *ou* obligatory; **rigoroso, -a** [higo'rozu, ɔza] ADJ rigorous; (*severo*) strict; (*exigente*) demanding; (*minucioso*) precise, accurate; (*inverno*) hard, harsh

rijo, -a ['hiʒu, a] ADJ tough, hard; (*severo*) harsh, severe

rim [hĩ] (*pl* **-ns**) M kidney; **rins** MPL (*parte inferior das costas*) small sg of the back

rima ['hima] F rhyme; (*poema*) verse, poem; **rimar** [hi'mar] vt, vi to rhyme

rímel® ['himew] (*pl* **-eis**) M mascara

ringue ['hĩgi] M ring

rins [hĩs] MPL *de* **rim**

Rio ['hiu] M: **o ~ (de Janeiro)** Rio (de Janeiro)

rio ['hiu] M river

riqueza [hi'keza] F wealth, riches *pl*; (*qualidade*) richness

rir [hir] vi to laugh; **~ de** to laugh at

risada [hi'zada] F laughter
risca ['hiska] F stroke; (*listra*) stripe; (*no cabelo*) parting
riscar [his'kar] VT (*marcar*) to mark; (*apagar*) to cross out; (*desenhar*) to outline
risco ['hisku] M (*marca*) mark, scratch; (*traço*) stroke; (*desenho*) drawing, sketch; (*perigo*) risk; **correr o ~ de** to run the risk of
riso ['hizu] M laughter; **risonho, -a** [hi'zoɲu, a] ADJ smiling; (*contente*) cheerful
ríspido, -a ['hispidu, a] ADJ brusque; (*áspero*) harsh
ritmo ['hitʃmu] M rhythm
rito ['hitu] M rite
ritual [hi'twaw] (*pl* **-ais**) ADJ, M ritual
rival [hi'vaw] (*pl* **-ais**) ADJ, M/F rival; **rivalidade** [hivali'dadʒi] F rivalry; **rivalizar** [hivali'zar] VT to rival ▶ VI: **rivalizar com** to compete with, vie with
roa ['hoa] VB *ver* **roer**
robô [ho'bo] M robot
roça ['hɔsa] F plantation; (*no mato*) clearing; (*campo*) country
rocha ['hɔʃa] F rock; (*penedo*) crag
rochedo [ho'ʃedu] M crag, cliff
rock-and-roll [-ã'hɔw] M rock and roll
roda ['hɔda] F wheel; (*círculo, grupo de pessoas*) circle; **~ dentada** cog(wheel); **em** *ou* **à ~ de** round, around
rodada [ho'dada] F (*de bebidas, Esporte*) round
rodar [ho'dar] VT to turn, spin; (*viajar por*) to tour, travel round; (*quilômetros*) to do; (*filme*) to make; (*imprimir*) to print; (*Comput: programa*) to run ▶ VI to turn round; (*Auto*) to drive around; **~ por** (*a pé*) to wander

around; (*de carro*) to drive around
rodela [ho'dɛla] F (*pedaço*) slice
rodízio [ho'dʒizju] M rota; **em ~** on a rota basis
rodopiar [hodo'pjar] VI to whirl around, swirl
rodovia [hodo'via] F highway, ≈ motorway (BRIT), ≈ interstate (US)
rodoviária [hodo'vjarja] F (*tb:* **estação ~**) bus station; *ver tb* **rodoviário**
rodoviário, -a [hodo'vjarju, a] ADJ road *atr*; (*polícia*) traffic *atr*
roer [hwer] VT to gnaw, nibble; (*enferrujar*) to corrode; (*afligir*) to eat away
rogar [ho'gar] VI to ask, request; **~ a alguém que faça** to beg sb to do
rói [hɔj] VB *ver* **roer**
roía [ho'ia] VB *ver* **roer**
rolar [ho'lar] VT, VI to roll
roleta [ho'leta] F roulette; (*borboleta*) turnstile
rolha ['hoʎa] F cork
roliço, -a [ho'lisu, a] ADJ (*pessoa*) plump, chubby; (*objeto*) round, cylindrical
rolo ['holu] M (*de papel etc*) roll; (*para nivelar o solo, para pintura*) roller; (*para cabelo*) curler; (*col: briga*) brawl, fight; **cortina de ~** roller blind; **~ compressor** steamroller
Roma ['homa] N Rome
romã [ho'mã] F pomegranate
romance [ho'mãsi] M novel; (*caso amoroso*) romance; **~ policial** detective story
romano, -a [ho'manu, a] ADJ, M/F Roman
romântico, -a [ho'mãtʃiku, a] ADJ romantic
rombo ['hõbu] M (*buraco*) hole; (*fig: desfalque*) embezzlement; (: *prejuízo*) loss, shortfall

Romênia [ho'menja] F: **a ~** Romania; **romeno, -a** [ho'mɛnu, a] ADJ, M/F Rumanian ▶ M (*Ling*) Rumanian

romper [hõ'per] VT to break; (*rasgar*) to tear; (*relações*) to break off ▶ VI: **~ em pranto** *ou* **lágrimas** to burst into tears; **rompimento** [hõpi'mẽtu] M breakage; (*fenda*) break; (*de relações*) breaking off

roncar [hõ'kar] VI to snore; **ronco** ['hõku] M snore

ronda ['hõda] F patrol, beat; **fazer a ~** to go the rounds; **rondar** [hõ'dar] VT to patrol; (*espreitar*) to prowl ▶ VI to prowl, lurk; (*fazer a ronda*) to patrol; **a inflação ronda os 10% ao ano** inflation is in the region of 10% a year

rosa ['hɔza] ADJ INV pink ▶ F rose; **rosado, -a** [ho'zadu, a] ADJ rosy, pink

rosário [ho'zarju] M rosary

rosbife [hoz'bifi] M roast beef

roseira [ho'zejra] F rosebush

rosnar [hoz'nar] VI (*cão*) to growl, snarl; (*murmurar*) to mutter, mumble

rosto ['hostu] M face

rota ['hɔta] F route, course

roteiro [ho'tejru] M itinerary; (*ordem*) schedule; (*guia*) guidebook; (*de filme*) script

rotina [ho'tʃina] F routine; **rotineiro, -a** [hotʃi'nejru, a] ADJ routine

roto, -a ['hotu, a] ADJ broken; (*rasgado*) torn

rotular [hotu'lar] VT to label; **rótulo** ['hɔtulu] M label

roubar [ho'bar] VT to steal; (*loja, casa, pessoa*) to rob ▶ VI to steal; (*em jogo, no preço*) to cheat; **~ algo a alguém** to steal sth from sb;

roubo ['hobu] M theft, robbery

rouco, -a ['roku, a] ADJ hoarse

round ['hãwdʒi] (*pl* **-s**) M (*Boxe*) round

roupa ['hopa] F clothes *pl*, clothing; **~ de baixo** underwear; **~ de cama** bedclothes *pl*, bed linen

roupão [ho'pãw] (*pl* **-ões**) M dressing gown

rouxinol [hoʃi'nɔw] (*pl* **-óis**) M nightingale

roxo, -a ['hoʃu, a] ADJ purple, violet

royalty ['hɔjawtʃi] (*pl* **-ies**) M royalty

rua ['hua] F street; **~ principal** main street; **~ sem saída** no through road, cul-de-sac

rubéola [hu'bɛola] F (*Med*) German measles

rubi [hu'bi] M ruby

rubor [hu'bor] M blush; (*fig*) shyness, bashfulness

ruborizar-se [hubori'zarsi] VR to blush

rubrica [hu'brika] F (signed) initials *pl*

rubro, -a ['hubru, a] ADJ (*faces*) rosy, ruddy

ruço, -a ['husu, a] ADJ grey (BRIT), gray (US), dun; (*desbotado*) faded

rúcula ['hukula] F rocket (BRIT), arugula (US)

ruela ['hwɛla] F lane, alley

ruga ['huga] F (*na pele*) wrinkle; (*na roupa*) crease

ruge ['huʒi] M rouge

rugido [hu'ʒidu] M roar

rugir [hu'ʒir] VI to roar

ruído ['hwidu] M noise; **ruidoso, -a** [hwi'dozu, ɔza] ADJ noisy

ruim [hu'ĩ] (*pl* **-ns**) ADJ bad; (*defeituoso*) defective

ruína ['hwina] F ruin; (*decadência*) downfall

ruins [huˈĩs] ADJ PL *de* **ruim**

ruir [ˈhwir] VI to collapse, go to ruin

ruivo, -a [ˈhwivu, a] ADJ red-haired
▶ M/F redhead

rum [hũ] M rum

rumo [ˈhumu] M course, bearing;
(*fig*) course; **~ a** bound for; **sem ~**
adrift

rumor [huˈmor] M noise; (*notícia*)
rumour (BRIT), rumor (US), report

ruptura [hupˈtura] F break, rupture

rural [huˈraw] (*pl* **-ais**) ADJ rural

rush [hʌʃ] M rush; **(a hora do) ~**
rush hour

Rússia [ˈhusja] F: **a ~** Russia;
russo, -a [ˈhusu, a] ADJ, M/F
Russian ▶ M (*Ling*) Russian

S

S. ABR (= *Santo/a, São*) St

SA ABR (= *Sociedade Anônima*) plc
(BRIT), Inc. (US)

sã [sã] F *de* **são**

Saara [saˈara] M: **o ~** the Sahara

sábado [ˈsabadu] M Saturday

sabão [saˈbãw] (*pl* **-ões**) M soap

sabedoria [sabedoˈria] F wisdom;
(*erudição*) learning

saber [saˈber] VT, VI to know;
(*descobrir*) to find out ▶ M
knowledge; **a ~** namely; **~ fazer** to
know how to do, be able to do; **que
eu saiba** as far as I know

sabiá [saˈbja] M/F thrush

sabido, -a [saˈbidu, a] ADJ
knowledgeable; (*esperto*) shrewd

sabões [saˈbõjs] MPL *de* **sabão**

sabonete [saboˈnetʃi] M toilet soap

sabor [saˈbor] M taste, flavour
(BRIT), flavor (US); **saborear**
[saboˈrjar] VT to taste, savour (BRIT),
savor (US); **saboroso, -a**
[saboˈrozu, ɔza] ADJ tasty, delicious

sabotagem [saboˈtaʒẽ] F sabotage

sabotar [sabo'tar] vt to sabotage

SAC ['saki] ABR M (= *serviço de atendimento ao cliente*) customer service

saca ['saka] F sack

sacar [sa'kar] vt to take out; (*dinheiro*) to withdraw; (*arma, cheque*) to draw; (*Esporte*) to serve; (*col: entender*) to understand ▶ vi (*col: entender*) to understand

saca-rolhas M INV corkscrew

sacerdote [saser'dɔtʃi] M priest

saciar [sa'sjar] vt (*fome etc*) to satisfy; (*sede*) to quench

saco ['saku] M bag; (*enseada*) inlet; **~ de café** coffee filter; **~ de dormir** sleeping bag

sacode [sa'kɔdʒi] vB *ver* **sacudir**

sacola [sa'kɔla] F bag

sacramento [sakra'mẽtu] M sacrament

sacrificar [sakrifi'kar] vt to sacrifice; **sacrificar-se** vR to sacrifice o.s.; **sacrifício** [sakri'fisju] M sacrifice

sacrilégio [sakri'lɛʒju] M sacrilege

sacro, -a ['sakru, a] ADJ sacred

sacudida [saku'dʒida] F shake

sacudir [saku'dʒir] vt to shake; **sacudir-se** vR to shake

sádico, -a ['sadʒiku, a] ADJ sadistic

sadio, -a [sa'dʒiu, a] ADJ healthy

safado, -a [sa'fadu, a] ADJ shameless; (*imoral*) dirty; (*travesso*) mischievous ▶ M rogue

safira [sa'fira] F sapphire

safra ['safra] F harvest

Sagitário [saʒi'tarju] M Sagittarius

sagrado, -a [sa'gradu, a] ADJ sacred, holy

saia ['saja] F skirt

saiba ['sajba] vB *ver* **saber**

saída [sa'ida] F exit, way out; (*partida*) departure; (*ato: de pessoa*) going out; (*fig: solução*) way out; (*Comput: de programa*) exit; (: *de dados*) output; **~ de emergência** emergency exit

sair [sa'ir] vi to go (*ou* come) out; (*partir*) to leave; (*realizar-se*) to turn out; (*Comput*) to exit; **sair-se** vR: **~-se bem/mal de** to be successful/unsuccessful in

sal [saw] (*pl* **sais**) M salt; **sem ~** (*comida*) salt-free; (*pessoa*) lacklustre (BRIT), lackluster (US)

sala ['sala] F room; (*num edifício público*) hall; (*classe, turma*) class; **~ (de aula)** classroom; **~ de bate-papo** (*Internet*) chatroom; **~ de espera** waiting room; **~ (de estar)** living room; **~ de jantar** dining room; **~ de operação** (*Med*) operating theatre (BRIT) *ou* theater (US)

salada [sa'lada] F salad; (*fig*) confusion, jumble

sala e quarto (*pl* **-s, salas e quarto**) M two-room flat (BRIT) *ou* apartment (US)

salão [sa'lãw] (*pl* **-ões**) M large room, hall; (*exposição*) show; **~ de beleza** beauty salon

salário [sa'larju] M wages *pl*, salary

saldo ['sawdu] M balance; (*sobra*) surplus

saleiro [sa'lejru] M salt cellar

salgadinho [sawga'dʒiɲu] M savoury (BRIT), savory (US), snack

salgado, -a [saw'gadu, a] ADJ salty, salted

salgueiro [saw'gejru] M willow; **~ chorão** weeping willow

salientar [saljẽ'tar] vt to point out; (*acentuar*) to stress, emphasize; **saliente** [sa'ljẽtʃi] ADJ

S

prominent; (*evidente*) clear, conspicuous; (*importante*) outstanding; (*assanhado*) forward

saliva [sa'liva] F saliva

salmão [saw'mãw] (*pl* **-ões**) M salmon

salmoura [saw'mora] F brine

salões [sa'lõjs] MPL *de* **salão**

salsa ['sawsa] F parsley

salsicha [saw'siʃa] F sausage; **salsichão** [sawsi'ʃãw] (*pl* **-ões**) M sausage

saltar [saw'tar] VT to jump (over), leap (over); (*omitir*) to skip ▶ VI to jump, leap; (*sangue*) to spurt out; (*de ônibus, cavalo*): **~ de** to get off

salto ['sawtu] M jump, leap; (*de calçado*) heel; **~ de vara** pole vault; **~ em altura** high jump; **~ em distância** long jump

salubre [sa'lubri] ADJ healthy, salubrious

salvamento [sawva'mẽtu] M rescue; (*de naufrágio*) salvage

salvar [saw'var] VT to save; (*resgatar*) to rescue; (*objetos, de ruína*) to salvage; (*honra*) to defend; **salvar-se** VR to escape

salva-vidas M INV (*boia*) lifebuoy ▶ M/F INV (*pessoa*) lifeguard; **barco ~** lifeboat

salvo, -a ['sawvu, a] ADJ safe ▶ PREP except, save; **a ~** in safety

samba ['sãba] M samba

> The greatest form of musical expression of the Brazilian people, the **samba** is a type of music and dance of African origin. It embraces a number of rhythmic styles, such as *samba de breque*, *samba-enredo*, *samba-canção* and *pagode*, among others. Officially, the first samba, entitled *Pelo telefone*, was written in Rio in 1917.

SAMU (BR) ABR M (= *Serviço de Atendimento Móvel de Urgência*) emergency ambulance service

sanar [sa'nar] VT to cure; (*remediar*) to remedy

sanção [sã'sãw] (*pl* **-ões**) F sanction; **sancionar** [sansjo'nar] VT to sanction

sandália [sã'dalja] F sandal

sandes ['sãdas] (PT) F INV sandwich

sanduíche [sand'wiʃi] (BR) M sandwich

saneamento [sanja'mẽtu] M sanitation

sanear [sa'njar] VT to clean up

sangrar [sã'grar] VT, VI to bleed; **sangrento, -a** [sã'grẽtu, a] ADJ bloody; (*Culin: carne*) rare

sangue ['sãgi] M blood

sanguinário, -a [sãgi'narju, a] ADJ bloodthirsty

sanguíneo, -a [sã'ginju, a] ADJ: **grupo ~** blood group; **pressão sanguínea** blood pressure; **vaso ~** blood vessel

sanidade [sani'dadʒi] F (*saúde*) health; (*mental*) sanity

sanita [sa'nita] (PT) F toilet, lavatory

sanitário, -a [sani'tarju, a] ADJ sanitary; **vaso ~** toilet, lavatory (bowl); **sanitários** [sani'tarjus] MPL toilets

santo, -a ['sãtu, a] ADJ holy ▶ M/F saint

santuário [sã'twarju] M shrine, sanctuary

São [sãw] M Saint

são, sã [sãw, sã] (*pl* **-s/-s**) ADJ healthy; (*conselho*) sound; (*mentalmente*) sane; **~ e salvo** safe and sound

São Paulo [-'pawlu] N São Paulo

sapataria [sapata'ria] F shoe shop

sapateiro [sapa'tejru] M shoemaker; (*vendedor*) shoe salesman; (*que conserta*) shoe repairer; (*loja*) shoe repairer's

sapatilha [sapa'tʃiʎa] F (*de balé*) shoe; (*sapato*) pump; (*de atleta*) running shoe

sapato [sa'patu] M shoe

sapo ['sapu] M toad

saque¹ ['saki] M (*de dinheiro*) withdrawal; (*Com*) draft, bill; (*Esporte*) serve; (*pilhagem*) plunder, pillage; **~ a descoberto** (*Com*) overdraft

saque² VB *ver* **sacar**

saquear [sa'kjar] VT to pillage, plunder

sarampo [sa'rãpu] M measles *sg*

sarar [sa'rar] VT to cure; (*ferida*) to heal ▶ VI to recover

sarcasmo [sar'kazmu] M sarcasm

sarda ['sarda] F freckle

Sardenha [sar'deɲa] F: **a ~** Sardinia

sardinha [sar'dʒiɲa] F sardine

sargento [sar'ʒẽtu] M sergeant

sarjeta [sar'ʒeta] F gutter

Satã [sa'tã] M Satan

Satanás [sata'nas] M Satan

satélite [sa'telitʃi] M satellite

sátira ['satʃira] F satire

satisfazer [satʃisfa'zer] (*irreg: como* **fazer**) VT to satisfy ▶ VI to be satisfactory; **satisfazer-se** VR to be satisfied; (*saciar-se*) to fill o.s. up; **~ a** to satisfy; **satisfeito, -a** [satʃis'fejtu, a] ADJ satisfied; (*saciado*) full; **dar-se por satisfeito com algo** to be content with sth

saudação [sawda'sãw] (*pl* **-ões**) F greeting

saudade [saw'dadʒi] F longing, yearning; (*lembrança nostálgica*) nostalgia; **deixar ~s** to be greatly missed; **ter ~s de** (*desejar*) to long for; (*sentir falta de*) to miss; **~s (de casa** *ou* **da família** *ou* **da pátria)** homesickness *sg*

saudar [saw'dar] VT to greet; (*dar as boas vindas*) to welcome; (*aclamar*) to acclaim

saudável [saw'davew] (*pl* **-eis**) ADJ healthy; (*moralmente*) wholesome

saúde [sa'udʒi] F health; (*brinde*) toast; **~!** (*brindando*) cheers!; (*quando se espirra*) bless you!; **beber à ~ de** to drink to, toast; **estar bem/mal de ~** to be well/ill

saudosismo [sawdo'zizmu] M nostalgia

saudoso, -a [saw'dozu, ɔza] ADJ (*nostálgico*) nostalgic; (*da família ou terra natal*) homesick; (*de uma pessoa*) longing; (*que causa saudades*) much-missed

sauna ['sawna] F sauna

saxofone [sakso'fɔni] M saxophone

sazonal [sazo'naw] (*pl* **-ais**) ADJ seasonal

scanner ['skaner] M scanner

PALAVRA-CHAVE

se [si] PRON 1 (*reflexivo: impess*) oneself; (: *m*) himself; (: *f*) herself; (: *coisa*) itself; (: *você*) yourself; (: *pl*) themselves; (: *vocês*) yourselves; **ela está se vestindo** she's getting dressed
2 (*uso recíproco*) each other, one another; **olharam-se** they looked at each other
3 (*impess*): **come-se bem aqui** you can eat well here; **sabe-se que ...** it is known that ...; **vende(m)-se jornais naquela loja** they sell newspapers in that shop

▶ CONJ if; (*em pergunta indireta*) whether; **se bem que** even though

sê [se] VB *ver* **ser**

sebe ['sɛbi] (PT) F fence; **~ viva** hedge

sebo ['sebu] M tallow; **seboso, -a** [se'bozu, ɔza] ADJ greasy; (*sujo*) dirty

seca ['seka] F drought

secador [seka'dor] M: **~ de cabelo/roupa** hairdryer/clothes horse

seção [se'sãw] (*pl* -**ões**) F section; (*em loja, repartição*) department

secar [se'kar] VT to dry; (*planta*) to parch ▶ VI to dry; to wither; (*fonte*) to dry up

seco, -a ['seku, a] ADJ dry; (*ríspido*) curt, brusque; (*magro*) thin; (*pessoa: frio*) cold; (: *sério*) serious

seções [se'sõjs] FPL *de* **seção**

secretaria [sekreta'ria] F general office; (*de secretário*) secretary's office; (*ministério*) ministry

secretária [sekre'tarja] F writing desk; **~ eletrônica** answering machine; *ver tb* **secretário**

secretário, -a [sekre'tarju, a] M/F secretary; **S~ de Estado de ...** Secretary of State for ...

século ['sɛkulu] M century; (*época*) age

secundário, -a [sekũ'darju, a] ADJ secondary

seda ['seda] F silk

sedativo [seda'tʃivu] M sedative

sede¹ ['sɛdʒi] F (*de empresa, instituição*) headquarters *sg*; (*de governo*) seat; (*Rel*) see, diocese

sede² ['sedʒi] F thirst; **estar com** *ou* **ter ~** to be thirsty; **sedento, -a** [se'dẽtu, a] ADJ thirsty

sediar [se'dʒjar] VT to base

sedução [sedu'sãw] (*pl* -**ões**) F seduction

sedutor, a [sedu'tor(a)] ADJ seductive; (*oferta etc*) tempting

seduzir [sedu'zir] VT to seduce; (*fascinar*) to fascinate

segmento [seg'mẽtu] M segment

segredo [se'gredu] M secret; (*sigilo*) secrecy; (*de fechadura*) combination

segregar [segre'gar] VT to segregate

seguidamente [segida'mẽtʃi] ADV (*sem parar*) continuously; (*logo depois*) soon afterwards

seguido, -a [se'gidu, a] ADJ following; (*contínuo*) continuous, consecutive; **~ de** *ou* **por** followed by; **três dias ~s** three days running; **horas seguidas** for hours on end; **em seguida** next; (*logo depois*) soon afterwards; (*imediatamente*) immediately, right away

seguimento [segi'mẽtu] M continuation; **dar ~ a** to proceed with; **em ~ de** after

seguinte [se'gĩtʃi] ADJ following, next; **eu lhe disse o ~** this is what I said to him

seguir [se'gir] VT to follow; (*continuar*) to continue ▶ VI to follow; (*continuar*) to continue, carry on; (*ir*) to go; **seguir-se** VR: **~-se (a)** to follow; **logo a ~** next; **~-se (de)** to result (from)

segunda [se'gũda] F (*tb*: **~-feira**) Monday; (*Auto*) second (gear); **de ~** second-rate; **segunda-feira** (*pl* **segundas-feiras**) F Monday

segundo, -a [se'gũdu, a] ADJ second ▶ PREP according to ▶ CONJ as, from what ▶ ADV secondly ▶ M second; **de segunda mão** second-hand; **de segunda (classe)** second-class; **~ ele disse** according to what he said; **~ dizem** apparently; **~ me consta** as far as I know; **segundas intenções** ulterior motives

seguramente [segura'mētʃi] ADV certainly; (*muito provavelmente*) surely

segurança [segu'rāsa] F security; (*ausência de perigo*) safety; (*confiança*) confidence ▶ M/F security guard; **com ~** assuredly

segurar [segu'rar] VT to hold; (*amparar*) to hold up; (*Com: bens*) to insure ▶ VI: **~ em** to hold; **segurar-se** VR: **~-se em** to hold on to

seguro, -a [se'guru, a] ADJ safe; (*livre de risco, firme*) secure; (*certo*) certain, assured; (*confiável*) reliable; (*de si mesmo*) confident; (*tempo*) settled ▶ ADV confidently ▶ M (*Com*) insurance; **estar ~ de/ de que** to be sure of/that; **fazer ~** to take out an insurance policy; **~ contra acidentes/incêndio** accident/fire insurance; **seguro-saúde** (*pl* **seguros-saúde**) M health insurance

sei [sej] VB *ver* **saber**

seio ['seju] M breast, bosom; (*âmago*) heart; **~ paranasal** sinus

seis [sejs] NUM six

seita ['sejta] F sect

seixo ['sejʃu] M pebble

seja ['seʒa] VB *ver* **ser**

sela ['sɛla] F saddle

selar [se'lar] VT (*carta*) to stamp; (*documento oficial, pacto*) to seal; (*cavalo*) to saddle

seleção [sele'sāw] (*pl* **-ões**) F selection; (*Esporte*) team

selecionar [selesjo'nar] VT to select

seleções [sele'sōjs] FPL *de* **seleção**

seleto, -a [se'lɛtu, a] ADJ select

selim [se'lī] (*pl* **-ns**) M saddle

selo ['selu] M stamp; (*carimbo, sinete*) seal

selva ['sɛwva] F jungle

selvagem [sew'vaʒē] (*pl* **-ns**) ADJ wild; (*feroz*) fierce; (*povo*) savage; **selvageria** [sewvaʒe'ria] F savagery

sem [sē] PREP without ▶ CONJ: **~ que eu peça** without my asking; **estar/ficar ~ dinheiro/gasolina** to have no/have run out of money/ petrol

semáforo [se'maforu] M (*Auto*) traffic lights *pl*; (*Ferro*) signal

semana [se'mana] F week; **semanal** [sema'naw] (*pl* **-ais**) ADJ weekly; **semanário** [sema'narju] M weekly (publication)

semear [se'mjar] VT to sow; **semelhante** [seme'ʎātʃi] ADJ similar; (*tal*) such ▶ M fellow creature

sêmen ['semē] M semen

semente [se'mētʃi] F seed

semestral [semes'traw] (*pl* **-ais**) ADJ half-yearly, bi-annual

semestre [se'mɛstri] M six months; (*Educ*) semester

semi... [semi] PREFIXO semi..., half...; **semicírculo** [semi'sirkulu] M semicircle; **semifinal** [semi'finaw] (*pl* **-ais**) F semi-final

seminário [semi'narju] M seminar; (*Rel*) seminary

sem-número M: **um ~ de coisas** loads of things

sempre ['sēpri] ADV always; **você ~ vai?** (*PT*) are you still going?; **~ que** whenever; **como ~** as usual; **a comida/hora** *etc* **de ~** the usual food/time *etc*

sem-terra ADJ INV landless ▶ M/F

S

INV landless labourer (BRIT) *ou* laborer (US)
sem-teto ADJ INV homeless ▶ M/F INV homeless person; **os ~** the homeless
sem-vergonha ADJ INV shameless ▶ M/F INV (*pessoa*) rogue
senado [se'nadu] M senate; **senador, a** [sena'dor(a)] M/F senator
senão [se'nãw] (*pl* **-ões**) CONJ otherwise; (*mas sim*) but, but rather ▶ PREP except ▶ M flaw, defect
senha ['sɛɲa] F sign; (*palavra de passe, Comput*) password; (*de caixa eletrônico*) PIN number; (*recibo*) receipt; (*passe*) pass
senhor, a [se'ɲor(a)] M (*homem*) man; (*formal*) gentleman; (*homem idoso*) elderly man; (*Rel*) lord; (*dono*) owner; (*tratamento*) Mr(.); (*tratamento respeitoso*) sir ▶ F (*mulher*) lady; (*esposa*) wife; (*mulher idosa*) elderly lady; (*dona*) owner; (*tratamento*) Mrs(.), Ms(.); (*tratamento respeitoso*) madam; **o ~/a ~a** (*você*) you; **nossa ~a!** (*col*) gosh; **sim, ~(a)!** yes indeed
senhorita [seɲo'rita] F young lady; (*tratamento*) Miss, Ms(.); **a ~** (*você*) you
senil [se'niw] (*pl* **-is**) ADJ senile
senões [se'nõjs] MPL *de* **senão**
sensação [sẽsa'sãw] (*pl* **-ões**) F sensation; **sensacional** [sẽsasjo'naw] (*pl* **-ais**) ADJ sensational
sensível [sẽ'sivew] (*pl* **-eis**) ADJ sensitive; (*visível*) noticeable; (*considerável*) considerable; (*dolorido*) tender
senso ['sẽsu] M sense; (*juízo*) judgement
sensual [sẽ'swaw] (*pl* **-ais**) ADJ sensual

sentado, -a [sẽ'tadu, a] ADJ sitting
sentar [sẽ'tar] VT to seat ▶ VI to sit; **sentar-se** VR to sit down
sentença [sẽ'tẽsa] F (*Jur*) sentence; **sentenciar** [sẽtẽ'sjar] VT (*julgar*) to pass judgement on; (*condenar por sentença*) to sentence
sentido, -a [sẽ'tʃidu, a] ADJ (*magoado*) hurt; (*choro, queixa*) heartfelt ▶ M sense; (*direção*) direction; (*atenção*) attention; (*aspecto*) respect; **~!** (*Mil*) attention!; **em certo ~** in a sense; **"~ único"** (PT: *sinal*) "one-way"
sentimental [sẽtʃimẽ'taw] (*pl* **-ais**) ADJ sentimental; **vida ~** love life
sentimento [sẽtʃi'mẽtu] M feeling; (*senso*) sense; **sentimentos** MPL (*pêsames*) condolences
sentinela [sẽtʃi'nɛla] F sentry, guard
sentir [sẽ'tʃir] VT to feel; (*perceber, pressentir*) to sense; (*ser afetado por*) to be affected by; (*magoar-se*) to be upset by ▶ VI to feel; (*sofrer*) to suffer; **sentir-se** VR to feel; (*julgar-se*) to consider o.s. (to be); **~ (a) falta de** to miss; **~ cheiro/gosto (de)** to smell/taste; **~ vontade de** to feel like; **sinto muito** I am very sorry
separação [separa'sãw] (*pl* **-ões**) F separation
separado, -a [sepa'radu, a] ADJ separate; **em ~** separately, apart
separar [sepa'rar] VT to separate; (*dividir*) to divide; (*pôr de lado*) to put aside; **separar-se** VR to separate; to be divided
sepultamento [sepuwta'mẽtu] M burial
sepultar [sepuw'tar] VT to bury; **sepultura** [sepuw'tura] F grave, tomb

sequência [se'kwēsja] F
sequence

sequer [se'kɛr] ADV at least;
(nem) ~ not even

sequestrar [sekwes'trar] VT
(*bens*) to seize, confiscate; (*raptar*)
to kidnap; (*avião etc*) to hijack;
sequestro [se'kwɛstru] M seizure;
(*rapto*) abduction, kidnapping; (*de
avião etc*) hijack

⸢PALAVRA-CHAVE⸣

ser [ser] VI **1** (*descrição*) to be; **ela é
médica/muito alta** she's a
doctor/very tall; **é Ana** (*Tel*) Ana
speaking *ou* here; **ela é de uma
bondade incrível** she's incredibly
kind; **ele está é danado** he's really
angry; **ser de mentir/briga** to be
the sort to lie/fight

2 (*horas, datas, números*): **é uma
hora** it's one o'clock; **são seis e
meia** it's half past six; **é dia 1º de
junho** it's the first of June;
somos/são seis there are six of
us/them

3 (*origem, material*): **ser de** to be *ou*
come from; (*feito de*) to be made of;
(*pertencer*) to belong to; **sua
família é da Bahia** his (*ou* her *etc*)
family is from Bahia; **a mesa é de
mármore** the table is made of
marble; **é de Pedro** it's Pedro's, it
belongs to Pedro

4 (*em orações passivas*): **já foi
descoberto** it had already been
discovered

5 (*locuções com subjun*): **ou seja**
that is to say; **seja quem for**
whoever it may be; **se eu fosse
você** if I were you; **se não fosse
você, ...** if it hadn't been for you ...

6 (*locuções*): **a não ser** except; **a
não ser que** unless; **é** (*resposta*

afirmativa) yes; **..., não é?** isn't it?,
don't you? *etc*; **ah, é?** really?; **que
foi?** (*o que aconteceu?*) what
happened?; (*qual é o problema?*)
what's the problem?; **será que ...?**
I wonder if ...?
▶ M being; **seres** MPL (*criaturas*)
creatures

sereia [se'reja] F mermaid

série ['sɛri] F series; (*sequência*)
sequence, succession; (*Educ*)
grade; (*categoria*) category; **fora
de ~** out of order; (*fig*)
extraordinary

seriedade [serje'dadʒi] F
seriousness; (*honestidade*) honesty

seringa [se'rĩga] F syringe

sério, -a ['sɛrju, a] ADJ serious;
(*honesto*) honest, decent;
(*responsável*) responsible;
(*confiável*) reliable; (*roupa*) sober
▶ ADV seriously; **a ~** seriously; **~?**
really?

sermão [ser'mãw] (*pl* **-ões**) M
sermon; (*fig*) telling-off

serpente [ser'pẽtʃi] F snake

serra ['sɛha] F (*montanhas*)
mountains *pl*; (*Tec*) saw

serralheiro, -a [seha'ʎejru, a]
M/F locksmith

serrano, -a [se'hanu, a] ADJ
highland *atr* ▶ M/F highlander

serrar [se'har] VT to saw

sertanejo, -a [serta'neʒu, a] ADJ
rustic, country ▶ M/F inhabitant of
the *sertão*

sertão [ser'tãw] (*pl* **-ões**) M
backwoods *pl*, bush (country)

servente [ser'vẽtʃi] M/F servant;
(*operário*) labourer (BRIT), laborer
(US)

serviçal [servi'saw] (*pl* **-ais**) ADJ
obliging, helpful ▶ M/F servant;

S

(*trabalhador*) wage earner

serviço [ser'visu] M service; (*de chá etc*) set; **estar ~** to be on duty; **prestar ~** to help

servidor, a [servi'dor(a)] M/F servant; (*funcionário*) employee ▶ M (*Comput*) server; **~ público** civil servant

servil [ser'viw] (*pl* -**is**) ADJ servile

servir [ser'vir] VT to serve ▶ VI to serve; (*ser útil*) to be useful; (*ajudar*) to help; (*roupa: caber*) to fit; **servir-se** VR: **~-se (de)** (*comida, café*) to help o.s. (to); **~-se de** (*meios*) to use, make use of; **~ de** (*prover*) to supply with, provide with; **você está servido?** (*num bar*) are you all right for a drink?; **~ de algo** to serve as sth; **qualquer ônibus serve** any bus will do

servis [ser'vis] ADJ PL *de* **servil**

sessão [se'sãw] (*pl* -**ões**) F (*do parlamento etc*) session; (*reunião*) meeting; (*de cinema*) showing

sessenta [se'sẽta] NUM sixty

sessões [se'sõjs] FPL *de* **sessão**

sesta [' sɛsta] F siesta, nap

seta [' sɛta] F arrow

sete [' sɛtʃi] NUM seven

setembro [se'tẽbru] M September

> Brazil's independence from Portugal is commemorated on 7 September (**7 de setembro**). Independence was declared in 1822 by the Portuguese prince regent, Dom Pedro, who rebelled against several orders from the Portuguese crown, among them the order to swear loyalty to the Portuguese constitution. It is a national holiday and the occasion for processions and military parades through the main cities.

setenta [se'tẽta] NUM seventy

sétimo, -a [' sɛtʃimu, a] NUM seventh

setor [se'tor] M sector

seu, sua [sew, 'sua] ADJ (*dele*) his; (*dela*) her; (*de coisa*) its; (*deles, delas*) their; (*de você, vocês*) your ▶ PRON (*dele*) his; (*dela*) hers; (*deles, delas*) theirs; (*de você, vocês*) yours ▶ M (*senhor*) Mr(.)

severidade [severi'dadʒi] F severity

severo, -a [se'vɛru, a] ADJ severe

sexo [' sɛksu] M sex

sexta [' sɛsta] F (*tb*: **~-feira**) Friday; **sexta-feira** (*pl* **sextas-feiras**) F Friday; **Sexta-feira Santa** Good Friday

sexto, -a [' sɛstu, a] NUM sixth

sexual [se'kswaw] (*pl* -**ais**) ADJ sexual; (*vida, ato*) sex atr

sexualidade [sekswali'dadʒi] F sexuality

sexy [' sɛksi] (*pl* -**s**) ADJ sexy

s.f.f. (PT) ABR = **se faz favor**

short [' ʃortʃi] M (pair of) shorts pl

si [si] PRON oneself; (*ele*) himself; (*ela*) herself; (*coisa*) itself; (PT: *você*) yourself, you; (: *vocês*) yourselves; (*eles, elas*) themselves

SIDA [' sida] (PT) ABR F (= *síndrome de deficiência imunológica adquirida*) AIDS

siderúrgica [side'rurʒika] F steel industry

sigilo [si'ʒilu] M secrecy

sigla [' sigla] F acronym; (*abreviação*) abbreviation

significado [signifi'kadu] M meaning

significar [signifi'kar] VT to mean, signify; **significativo, -a** [signifika'tʃivu, a] ADJ significant

signo [' signu] M sign

sigo ['sigu] VB *ver* **seguir**

sílaba ['silaba] F syllable

silenciar [silẽ'sjar] VT to silence

silêncio [si'lẽsju] M silence, quiet;
silencioso, -a [silẽ'sjozu, ɔza] ADJ
silent, quiet ▶ M (*Auto*) silencer
(*BRIT*), muffler (*US*)

silhueta [si'ʎweta] F silhouette

silvestre [siw'vɛstri] ADJ wild

sim [sĩ] ADV yes; **creio que ~** I
think so

símbolo ['sĩbolu] M symbol

simetria [sime'tria] F symmetry

similar [simi'lar] ADJ similar

simpatia [sĩpa'tʃia] F liking;
(*afeto*) affection; (*afinidade,
solidariedade*) sympathy;
simpatias FPL (*inclinações*)
sympathies; **simpático, -a**
[sĩ'patʃiku, a] ADJ (*pessoa, decoração
etc*) nice; (*lugar*) pleasant, nice;
(*amável*) kind; **simpatizante**
[sĩpatʃi'zãtʃi] ADJ sympathetic
▶ M/F sympathizer; **simpatizar**
[sĩpatʃi'zar] VI: **simpatizar com**
(*pessoa*) to like; (*causa*) to
sympathize with

simples ['sĩplis] ADJ INV simple;
(*único*) single; (*fácil*) easy; (*mero*)
mere; (*ingênuo*) naïve ▶ ADV
simply; **simplicidade**
[sĩplisi'dadʒi] F simplicity;
simplificar [sĩplifi'kar] VT to
simplify

simular [simu'lar] VT to simulate

simultaneamente
[simuwtanja'mẽtʃi] ADV
simultaneously

simultâneo, -a [simuw'tanju, a]
ADJ simultaneous

sinagoga [sina'gɔga] F
synagogue

sinal [si'naw] (*pl* **-ais**) M sign;
(*gesto, Tel*) signal; (*na pele*) mole;
(: *de nascença*) birthmark; (*depósito*)
deposit; (*tb*: **~ de tráfego
luminoso**) traffic light; **por ~** (*por
falar nisso*) by the way; (*aliás*) as a
matter of fact; **~ de chamada** (*Tel*)
ringing tone; **~ de discar** (*BR*) *ou*
de marcar (*PT*) dialling tone
(*BRIT*), dial tone (*US*); **~ de
ocupado** (*BR*) *ou* **de impedido** (*PT*)
engaged tone (*BRIT*), busy signal
(*US*); **sinalização** [sinaliza'sãw] F
(*ato*) signalling; (*para motoristas*)
traffic signs *pl*

sincero, -a [sĩ'sɛru, a] ADJ sincere

sindicalista [sĩdʒika'lista] M/F
trade unionist

sindicato [sĩdʒi'katu] M trade
union; (*financeiro*) syndicate

síndrome ['sĩdromi] F syndrome;
~ de Down Down's syndrome

sinfonia [sĩfo'nia] F symphony

singular [sĩgu'lar] ADJ singular;
(*extraordinário*) exceptional;
(*bizarro*) odd, peculiar

sino ['sinu] M bell

sintaxe [sĩ'tasi] F syntax

síntese ['sĩtezi] F synthesis;
sintético, -a [sĩ'tɛtʃiku, a] ADJ
synthetic; **sintetizar** [sĩtetʃi'zar]
VT to synthesize

sinto ['sĩtu] VB *ver* **sentir**

sintoma [sĩ'tɔma] M symptom

sinuca [si'nuka] F snooker

sinuoso, -a [si'nwozu, ɔza] ADJ
(*caminho*) winding; (*linha*) wavy

siri [si'ri] M crab

sirvo ['sirvu] VB *ver* **servir**

sistema [sis'tɛma] M system;
(*método*) method; **~ imunológico**
immune system

site ['sajtʃi] M (*na Internet*) website;
~ de relacionamentos social
networking site

sítio ['sitʃju] M (*Mil*) siege;

S

(*propriedade rural*) small farm; (PT: *lugar*) place

situação [sitwa'sãw] (*pl* **-ões**) F situation; (*posição*) position

situado, -a [si'twadu, a] ADJ situated

situar [si'twar] VT to place, put; (*edifício*) to situate, locate; **situar-se** VR to position o.s.; (*estar situado*) to be situated

slogan [iz'lɔgã] (*pl* **-s**) M slogan

smoking [iz'mokĩs] (*pl* **-s**) M dinner jacket (BRIT), tuxedo (US)

só [sɔ] ADJ alone; (*único*) single; (*solitário*) solitary ▶ ADV only; **a sós** alone

soar [swar] VI to sound ▶ VT (*horas*) to strike; (*instrumento*) to play; **~ a** to sound like; **~ bem/mal** (*fig*) to go down well/badly

sob [sob] PREP under; **~ juramento** on oath; **~ medida** (*roupa*) made to measure

sobe ['sɔbi] VB *ver* **subir**

soberano, -a [sobe'ranu, a] ADJ sovereign; (*fig: supremo*) supreme ▶ M/F sovereign

sobra ['sɔbra] F surplus, remnant; **sobras** FPL remains; (*de tecido*) remnants; (*de comida*) leftovers; **ter algo de ~** to have sth extra; (*tempo, comida, motivos*) to have plenty of sth; **ficar de ~** to be left over

sobrado [so'bradu] M (*andar*) floor; (*casa*) house (*of two or more storeys*)

sobrancelha [sobrã'seʎa] F eyebrow

sobrar [so'brar] VI to be left; (*dúvidas*) to remain

sobre ['sobri] PREP on; (*por cima de*) over; (*acima de*) above; (*a respeito de*) about

sobrecarregar [sobrikahe'gar] VT to overload

sobremesa [sobri'meza] F dessert

sobrenatural [sobrinatu'raw] (*pl* **-ais**) ADJ supernatural

sobrenome [sobri'nɔmi] (BR) M surname, family name

sobrepor [sobri'por] (*irreg: como* **pôr**) VT: **~ algo a algo** to put sth on top of sth

sobressair [sobrisa'ir] VI to stand out; **sobressair-se** VR to stand out

sobressalente [sobrisa'lẽtʃi] ADJ, M spare

sobressalto [sobri'sawtu] M start; (*temor*) trepidation; **de ~** suddenly

sobretaxa [sobri'taʃa] F surcharge

sobretudo [sobri'tudu] M overcoat ▶ ADV above all, especially

sobrevivência [sobrivi'vẽsja] F survival; **sobrevivente** [sobrivi'vẽtʃi] ADJ surviving ▶ M/F survivor

sobreviver [sobrivi'ver] VI: **~ (a)** to survive

sobrinho, -a [so'briɲu, a] M/F nephew/niece

sóbrio, -a ['sɔbrju, a] ADJ sober; (*moderado*) moderate, restrained

socar [so'kar] VT (*esmurrar*) to hit, strike; (*calcar*) to crush, pound; (*massa de pão*) to knead

social [so'sjaw] (*pl* **-ais**) ADJ social; **socialista** [sosja'lista] ADJ, M/F socialist

sociedade [sosje'dadʒi] F society; (*Com: empresa*) company; (*associação*) association; **~ anônima** limited company (BRIT), incorporated company (US)

sócio, -a ['sɔsju, a] M/F (*Com*) partner; (*de clube*) member

soco ['soku] M punch; **dar um ~ em** to punch

socorrer [soko'her] VT to help, assist; (*salvar*) to rescue;

socorrer-se VR: **~-se de** to resort to, have recourse to; **socorro** [so'kohu] M help, assistance; (*reboque*) breakdown (BRIT) *ou* tow (US) truck; **socorro!** help!; **primeiros socorros** first aid *sg*

soda ['sɔda] F soda (water)

sofá [so'fa] M sofa, settee; **sofá-cama** (*pl* **sofás-camas**) M sofa-bed

sofisticado, -a [sofist∫i'kadu, a] ADJ sophisticated; (*afetado*) pretentious

sofrer [so'frer] VT to suffer; (*acidente*) to have; (*aguentar*) to bear, put up with; (*experimentar*) to undergo ▶ VI to suffer; **sofrido, -a** [so'fridu, a] ADJ long-suffering; **sofrimento** [sofri'mẽtu] M suffering

software [sof'twer] M (*Comput*) software

sogro, -a ['sogru, 'sɔgra] M/F father-in-law/mother-in-law

sóis [sɔjs] MPL *de* **sol**

soja ['sɔʒa] F soya (BRIT), soy (US)

sol [sɔw] (*pl* **sóis**) M sun; (*luz*) sunshine, sunlight; **fazer ~** to be sunny; **pegar ~** to get the sun

sola ['sɔla] F sole

solar [so'lar] ADJ solar; **energia/painel ~** solar energy/panel

soldado [sow'dadu] M soldier

soleira [so'lejra] F doorstep

solene [so'lɛni] ADJ solemn; **solenidade** [soleni'dadʒi] F solemnity; (*cerimônia*) ceremony

soletrar [sole'trar] VT to spell

solicitar [solisi'tar] VT to ask for; (*emprego etc*) to apply for; (*amizade, atenção*) to seek; **~ algo a alguém** to ask sb for sth

solícito, -a [so'lisitu, a] ADJ helpful

solidão [soli'dãw] F solitude; (*sensação*) loneliness

solidariedade [solidarje'dadʒi] F solidarity

solidário, -a [soli'darju, a] ADJ (*pessoa*) supportive; **ser ~ a** *ou* **com** (*pessoa*) to stand by; (*causa*) to be sympathetic to, sympathize with

sólido, -a ['sɔlidu, a] ADJ solid

solitário, -a [soli'tarju, a] ADJ lonely, solitary ▶ M hermit

solo ['sɔlu] M ground, earth; (*Mús*) solo

soltar [sow'tar] VT to set free; (*desatar*) to loosen; (*largar*) to let go of; (*emitir*) to emit; (*grito, risada*) to let out; (*cabelo*) to let down; (*freio, animais*) to release; **soltar-se** VR to come loose; (*desinibir-se*) to let o.s. go

solteirão, -rona [sowtej'rãw, rona] (*pl* **-ões/-s**) ADJ unmarried ▶ M/F bachelor/spinster

solteiro, -a [sow'tejru, a] ADJ single ▶ M/F single man/woman

solteirões [sowtej'rõjs] MPL *de* **solteirão**

solto, -a ['sowtu, a] PP *de* **soltar** ▶ ADJ loose; (*livre*) free; (*sozinho*) alone

solução [solu'sãw] (*pl* **-ões**) F solution

soluçar [solu'sar] VI (*chorar*) to sob; (*Med*) to hiccup

solucionar [solusjo'nar] VT to solve; (*decidir*) to resolve

soluço [so'lusu] M sob; (*Med*) hiccup

soluções [solu'sõjs] FPL *de* **solução**

som [sõ] (*pl* **-ns**) M sound; **~ cd** compact disc player

soma ['sɔma] F sum; **somar**

[so'mar] VT (*adicionar*) to add (up); (*chegar a*) to add up to, amount to ▶ VI to add up

sombra ['sõbra] F shadow; (*proteção*) shade; (*indício*) trace, sign

sombrinha [sõ'briɲa] F parasol, sunshade

some ['sɔmi] VB ver **sumir**

somente [sɔ'mẽtʃi] ADV only

somos ['somos] VB ver **ser**

sonâmbulo, -a [so'nãbulu, a] M/F sleepwalker

sondar [sõ'dar] VT to probe; (*opinião etc*) to sound out

soneca [so'nɛka] F nap, snooze

sonegar [sone'gar] VT (*dinheiro, valores*) to conceal, withhold; (*furtar*) to steal, pilfer; (*impostos*) to dodge, evade; (*informações, dados*) to withhold

soneto [so'netu] M sonnet

sonhar [so'ɲar] VT, VI to dream; **~ com** to dream about; **sonho** ['sɔɲu] M dream; (*Culin*) doughnut

sono ['sɔnu] M sleep; **estar com** *ou* **ter ~** to be sleepy

sonolento, -a [sono'lẽtu, a] ADJ sleepy, drowsy

sonoro, -a [so'nɔru, a] ADJ resonant

sons [sõs] MPL de **som**

sonso, -a ['sõsu, a] ADJ sly, artful

sopa ['sopa] F soup

soporífero, -a [sopo'riferu, a] ADJ soporific ▶ M sleeping drug

soprar [so'prar] VT to blow; (*balão*) to blow up; (*vela*) to blow out; (*dizer em voz baixa*) to whisper ▶ VI to blow; **sopro** ['sopru] M blow, puff; (*de vento*) gust

sórdido, -a ['sɔrdʒidu, a] ADJ sordid; (*imundo*) squalid

soro ['soru] M (*Med*) serum

sorridente [sohi'dẽtʃi] ADJ smiling

sorrir [so'hir] VI to smile; **sorriso** [so'hizu] M smile

sorte ['sɔrtʃi] F luck; (*casualidade*) chance; (*destino*) fate, destiny; (*condição*) lot; (*espécie*) sort, kind; **de ~ que** so that; **dar ~** (*trazer sorte*) to bring good luck; (*ter sorte*) to be lucky; **estar com** *ou* **ter ~** to be lucky

sortear [sor'tʃjar] VT to draw lots for; (*rifar*) to raffle; (*Mil*) to draft; **sorteio** [sor'teju] M draw; (*rifa*) raffle; (*Mil*) draft

sortido, -a [sor'tʃidu, a] ADJ (*abastecido*) supplied, stocked; (*variado*) assorted; (*loja*) well-stocked

sortudo, -a [sor'tudu, a] (*col*) ADJ lucky

sorvete [sor'vetʃi] (BR) M ice cream

SOS ABR SOS

sossegado, -a [sose'gadu, a] ADJ peaceful, calm

sossegar [sose'gar] VT to calm, quieten ▶ VI to quieten down

sossego [so'segu] M peace (and quiet)

sótão ['sɔtãw] (*pl* **-s**) M attic, loft

sotaque [so'taki] M accent

soterrar [sote'har] VT to bury

sou [so] VB ver **ser**

soube ['sobi] VB ver **saber**

soutien [su'tʃjã] M = **sutiã**

sova ['sɔva] F beating, thrashing

sovaco [so'vaku] M armpit

sovina [so'vina] ADJ mean, stingy ▶ M/F miser

sozinho, -a [sɔ'ziɲu, a] ADJ (all) alone, by oneself; (*por si mesmo*) by oneself

spam [is'pã] (*pl* **-s**) M (*Comput*) spam

squash [is'kwɛʃ] M squash

Sr. ABR (= *senhor*) Mr

Sra. (BR), **Sr.a** (PT) ABR (= *senhora*) Mrs

Srta. (BR), **Sr.ta** (PT) ABR (=*senhorita*) Miss

sua ['sua] F *de* **seu**

suar [swar] VT, VI to sweat

suave ['swavi] ADJ gentle; (*música, voz*) soft; (*sabor, vinho*) smooth; (*cheiro*) delicate; (*dor*) mild; (*trabalho*) light; **suavidade** [suavi'dadʒi] F gentleness; softness

subalterno, -a [subaw'tɛrnu, a] ADJ, M/F subordinate

subconsciente [subkõ'sjẽtʃi] ADJ, M subconscious

subdesenvolvido, -a [subdʒizẽvow'vidu, a] ADJ underdeveloped

subentender [subẽtẽ'der] VT to understand, assume; **subentendido, -a** [subẽtẽ'dʒidu, a] ADJ implied ▶ M implication

subestimar [subestʃi'mar] VT to underestimate

subida [su'bida] F ascent, climb; (*ladeira*) slope; (*de preços*) rise

subir [su'bir] VI to go up; (*preço, de posto etc*) to rise ▶ VT to raise; (*ladeira, escada, rio*) to climb, go up; **~ em** to climb, go up; (*cadeira, palanque*) to climb onto, get up onto; (*ônibus*) to get on

súbito, -a ['subitu, a] ADJ sudden ▶ ADV (*tb*: **de ~**) suddenly

subjetivo, -a [subʒe'tʃivu, a] ADJ subjective

subjuntivo, -a [subʒũ'tʃivu, a] ADJ, M subjunctive

sublime [su'blimi] ADJ sublime

sublinhar [subli'ɲar] VT to underline; (*destacar*) to emphasize, stress

submarino, -a [subma'rinu, a] ADJ underwater ▶ M submarine

submeter [subme'ter] VT to subdue; (*plano*) to submit; (*sujeitar*): **~ a** to subject to; **submeter-se** VR: **~-se a** to submit to; (*operação*) to undergo

submisso, -a [sub'misu, a] ADJ submissive

subnutrição [subnutri'sãw] F malnutrition

subornar [subor'nar] VT to bribe; **suborno** [su'bornu] M bribery

subsequente [subse'kwẽtʃi] ADJ subsequent

subserviente [subser'vjẽtʃi] ADJ obsequious, servile

subsidiária [subsi'dʒjarja] F (*Com*) subsidiary (company)

subsidiário, -a [subsi'dʒjarju, a] ADJ subsidiary

subsídio [sub'sidʒu] M subsidy; (*ajuda*) aid

subsistência [subsis'tẽsja] F subsistence

subsistir [subsis'tʃir] VI to exist; (*viver*) to subsist

subsolo [sub'sɔlu] M (*de prédio*) basement

substância [sub'stãsja] F substance; **substancial** [substã'sjaw] (*pl* **-ais**) ADJ substantial

substantivo, -a [substã'tʃivu, a] ADJ substantive ▶ M noun

substituir [substʃi'twir] VT to substitute

subtil [sub'tiw] (PT) = **sutil** *etc*

subtrair [subtra'ir] VT to steal; (*deduzir*) to subtract ▶ VI to subtract

subumano, -a [subu'manu, a] ADJ subhuman; (*desumano*) inhuman

suburbano, -a [subur'banu, a] ADJ suburban

subúrbio [su'burbju] M suburb

S

subvenção [subvẽ'sãw] (*pl* -**ões**) F subsidy, grant

subversivo, -a [subver'sivu, a] ADJ, M/F subversive

sucata [su'kata] F scrap metal

sucção [suk'sãw] F suction

suceder [suse'der] VI to happen ▶ VT to succeed; ~ **a** (*num cargo*) to succeed; (*seguir*) to follow

sucessão [suse'sãw] (*pl* -**ões**) F succession; **sucessivo, -a** [suse'sivu, a] ADJ successive

sucesso [su'sɛsu] M success; (*música, filme*) hit; **fazer** *ou* **ter** ~ to be successful

sucinto, -a [su'sĩtu, a] ADJ succinct

suco ['suku] (BR) M juice

suculento, -a [suku'lẽtu, a] ADJ succulent

sucumbir [sukũ'bir] VI to succumb; (*morrer*) to die, perish

sucursal [sukur'saw] (*pl* -**ais**) F (*Com*) branch

Sudão [su'dãw] M: **o** ~ (the) Sudan

sudeste [su'dɛstʃi] M south-east

súdito ['sudʒitu] M (*de rei etc*) subject

sudoeste [sud'wɛstʃi] M south-west

Suécia ['swɛsja] F: **a** ~ Sweden; **sueco, -a** ['swɛku, a] ADJ Swedish ▶ M/F Swede ▶ M (*Ling*) Swedish

suéter ['swɛter] (BR) M *ou* F sweater

suficiente [sufi'sjẽtʃi] ADJ sufficient, enough

sufixo [su'fiksu] M suffix

sufocar [sufo'kar] VT, VI to suffocate

sugar [su'gar] VT to suck

sugerir [suʒe'rir] VT to suggest

sugestão [suʒes'tãw] (*pl* -**ões**) F suggestion; **dar uma** ~ to make a suggestion; **sugestivo, -a** [suʒes'tʃivu, a] ADJ suggestive

sugiro [su'ʒiru] VB *ver* **sugerir**

Suíça ['swisa] F: **a** ~ Switzerland

suíças ['swisas] FPL sideburns; *ver tb* **suíço**

suicida [swi'sida] ADJ suicidal ▶ M/F suicidal person; (*morto*) suicide; **suicidar-se** [swisi'darsi] VR to commit suicide; **suicídio** [swi'sidʒju] M suicide

suíço, -a ['swisu, a] ADJ, M/F Swiss

suíte ['switʃi] F (*Mús, em hotel*) suite

sujar [su'ʒar] VT to dirty ▶ VI to make a mess; **sujar-se** VR to get dirty

sujeira [su'ʒejra] F dirt; (*estado*) dirtiness; (*col*) dirty trick

sujeito, -a [su'ʒejtu, a] ADJ: ~ **a** subject to ▶ M (*Ling*) subject ▶ M/F man/woman

sujo, -a ['suʒu, a] ADJ dirty; (*fig: desonesto*) dishonest ▶ M dirt

sul [suw] ADJ INV south, southern ▶ M: **o** ~ the south; **sul-africano, -a** ADJ, M/F South African; **sul-americano, -a** ADJ, M/F South American

sulco [suw'ku] M furrow

suma ['suma] F: **em** ~ in short

sumário, -a [su'marju, a] ADJ (*breve*) brief, concise; (*Jur*) summary; (*biquíni*) skimpy ▶ M summary

sumiço [su'misu] M disappearance

sumir [su'mir] VI to disappear, vanish

sumo, -a ['sumu, a] ADJ (*importância*) extreme; (*qualidade*) supreme ▶ M (*PT*) juice

sunga ['sũga] F swimming trunks *pl*

suor [swɔr] M sweat

super... [super-] PREFIXO super-, over-

superado, -a [supe'radu, a] ADJ (*ideias*) outmoded

superar [supe'rar] VT (*rival*) to

surpass; (*inimigo, dificuldade*) to overcome; (*expectativa*) to exceed

superfície [super'fisi] F surface; (*extensão*) area; (*fig: aparência*) appearance

supérfluo, -a [su'pɛrflwu, a] ADJ superfluous

superior [supe'rjor] ADJ superior; (*mais elevado*) higher; (*quantidade*) greater; (*mais acima*) upper ▶ M superior; **superioridade** [superjori'dadʒi] F superiority

superlotado, -a [superlo'tadu, a] ADJ crowded; (*excessivamente cheio*) overcrowded

supermercado [supermer'kadu] M supermarket

superpotência [superpo'tẽsja] F superpower

superstição [superstʃi'sãw] (*pl* **-ões**) F superstition; **supersticioso, -a** [superstʃi'sjozu, ɔza] ADJ superstitious

supervisão [supervi'zãw] F supervision; **supervisionar** [supervizjo'nar] VT to supervise; **supervisor, a** [supervi'zor(a)] M/F supervisor

suplemento [suple'mẽtu] M supplement

súplica ['suplika] F supplication, plea; **suplicar** [supli'kar] VT, VI to plead, beg

suplício [su'plisju] M torture

supor [su'por] (*irreg: como* **pôr**) VT to suppose; (*julgar*) to think

suportar [supor'tar] VT to hold up, support; (*tolerar*) to bear, tolerate; **suportável** [supor'tavew] (*pl* **-eis**) ADJ bearable; **suporte** [su'pɔrtʃi] M support

suposto, -a [su'postu, 'pɔsta] ADJ

supposed ▶ M assumption, supposition

supremo, -a [su'prɛmu, a] ADJ supreme

suprimir [supri'mir] VT to suppress

surdo, -a ['surdu, a] ADJ deaf; (*som*) muffled, dull ▶ M/F deaf person; **surdo-mudo, surda-muda** ADJ deaf and dumb ▶ M/F deaf-mute

surfe ['surfi] M surfing

surfista [sur'fista] M/F surfer

surgir [sur'ʒir] VI to appear; (*problema, dificuldade*) to arise

surjo ['surʒu] VB *ver* **surgir**

surpreendente [surprjẽ'dẽtʃi] ADJ surprising

surpreender [surprjẽ'der] VT to surprise; **surpreender-se** VR: **~-se (de)** to be surprised (at); **surpresa** [sur'preza] F surprise; **surpreso, -a** [sur'prezu, a] PP *de* **surpreender** ▶ ADJ surprised

surra ['suha] F: **dar uma ~ em** to thrash; **levar uma ~ (de)** to get thrashed (by); **surrar** [su'har] VT to beat, thrash

surtar [sur'tar] VI to freak out

surtir [sur'tʃir] VT to produce, bring about

surto ['surtu] M (*de doença*) outbreak; (*ataque*) outburst

SUS [sus] (BR) ABR M (= *Sistema Único de Saúde*) national health service

suspeita [sus'pejta] F suspicion; **suspeitar** [suspej'tar] VT to suspect ▶ VI: **suspeitar de algo** to suspect sth; **suspeito, -a** [sus'pejtu, a] ADJ, M/F suspect

suspender [suspẽ'der] VT (*levantar*) to lift; (*pendurar*) to hang; (*trabalho, pagamento etc*) to suspend; (*encomenda*) to cancel; (*sessão*) to adjourn, defer; (*viagem*) to put off; **suspensão** [suspē'sāw] (*pl* **-ões**) F (*ger, Auto*) suspension; (*de trabalho, pagamento*) stoppage; (*de viagem, sessão*) deferment; (*de encomenda*) cancellation; **suspense** [sus'pēsi] M suspense; **filme de suspense** thriller; **suspenso, -a** [sus'pēsu, a] PP *de* **suspender**

suspensórios [suspē'sɔrjus] MPL braces (BRIT), suspenders (US)

suspirar [suspi'rar] VI to sigh; **suspiro** [sus'piru] M sigh; (*doce*) meringue

sussurrar [susu'har] VT, VI to whisper; **sussurro** [su'suhu] M whisper

sustentar [sustē'tar] VT to sustain; (*prédio*) to hold up; (*padrão*) to maintain; (*financeiramente, acusação*) to support; **sustentável** [sustē'tavew] (*pl* **-eis**) ADJ sustainable; **sustento** [sus'tētu] M sustenance; (*subsistência*) livelihood; (*amparo*) support

susto ['sustu] M fright, scare

sutiã [su'tʃjã] M bra(ssiere)

sutil [su'tʃiw] (*pl* **-is**) ADJ subtle; **sutileza** [sutʃi'leza] F subtlety

t

ta [ta] = **te + a**

tabacaria [tabaka'ria] F tobacconist's (shop)

tabaco [ta'baku] M tobacco

tabela [ta'bɛla] F table, chart; (*lista*) list; **por ~** indirectly

taberna [ta'bɛrna] F tavern, bar

tablet [tablitʃ] (*pl* **-s**) M (*Comput*) tablet

tablete [ta'blɛtʃi] M (*de chocolate*) bar

tabu [ta'bu] ADJ, M taboo

tábua ['tabwa] F plank, board; (*Mat*) table; **~ de passar roupa** ironing board

tabuleiro [tabu'lejru] M tray; (*Xadrez*) board

tabuleta [tabu'leta] F (*letreiro*) sign, signboard

taça ['tasa] F cup

tacha ['taʃa] F tack

tachinha [ta'ʃiɲa] F drawing pin (BRIT), thumb tack (US)

taco ['taku] M (*Bilhar*) cue; (*Golfe*) club

tagarela [taga'rɛla] ADJ talkative ▶ M/F chatterbox; **tagarelar** [tagare'lar] VI to chatter

Tailândia [taj'lãdʒja] F: **a ~** Thailand

tal [taw] (pl **tais**) ADJ such; **~ e coisa** this and that; **um ~ de Sr. X** a certain Mr. X; **que ~?** what do you think?; (PT) how are things?; **que ~ um cafezinho?** what about a coffee?; **que ~ nós irmos ao cinema?** what about (us) going to the cinema?; **~ pai, ~ filho** like father, like son; **~ como** such as; (da maneira que) just as; **~ qual** just like; **o ~ professor** that teacher; **a ~ ponto** to such an extent; **de ~ maneira** in such a way; **e ~** and so on; **o/a ~** (col) the greatest; **o Pedro de ~** Peter what's-his-name; **na rua ~** in such and such a street; **foi um ~ de gente ligar lá para casa** there were people ringing home non-stop

talão [ta'lãw] (pl **-ões**) M (de recibo) stub; **~ de cheques** cheque book (BRIT), check book (US)

talco ['tawku] M talcum powder; **pó de ~** (PT) talcum powder

talento [ta'lẽtu] M talent; (aptidão) ability

talha ['taʎa] F carving; (vaso) pitcher; (Náut) tackle

talher [ta'ʎer] M set of cutlery; **talheres** MPL cutlery sg

talo ['talu] M stalk, stem

talões [ta'lõjs] MPL de **talão**

talvez [taw'vez] ADV perhaps, maybe

tamanco [ta'mãku] M clog, wooden shoe

tamanduá [tamã'dwa] M anteater

tamanho, -a [ta'maɲu, a] ADJ such (a) great ▶ M size

tâmara ['tamara] F date

também [tã'bẽj] ADV also, too, as well; (além disso) besides; **~ não** not ... either, nor

tambor [tã'bor] M drum

tamborim [tãbo'rĩ] (pl **-ns**) M tambourine

Tâmisa ['tamiza] M: **o ~** the Thames

tampa ['tãpa] F lid; (de garrafa) cap

tampão [tã'pãw] (pl **-ões**) M tampon

tampar [tã'par] VT (lata, garrafa) to put the lid on; (cobrir) to cover

tampinha [tã'piɲa] F lid, top

tampo ['tãpu] M lid

tampões [tã'põjs] MPL de **tampão**

tampouco [tã'poku] ADV nor, neither

tangerina [tãʒe'rina] F tangerine

tanque ['tãki] M tank; (de lavar roupa) sink

tanto, -a ['tãtu, a] ADJ, PRON (sg) so much; (: + interrogativa/negativa) as much; (pl) so many; (: + interrogativa/negativa) as many ▶ ADV so much; **~ ... como ...** both ... and ...; **~ ... quanto ...** as much ... as ...; **~ tempo** so long; **quarenta e ~s anos** forty-odd years; **~ faz** it's all the same to me, I don't mind; **um ~ (quanto)** (como adv) rather, somewhat; **~ (assim) que** so much so that

tão [tãw] ADV so; **~ rico quanto** as rich as; **~ só** only

tapa ['tapa] M slap

tapar [ta'par] VT to cover; (garrafa) to cork; (caixa) to put the lid on; (orifício) to block up; (encobrir) to block out

tapear [ta'pjar] VT, VI to cheat

tapeçaria [tapesa'ria] F tapestry

tapete [ta'petʃi] M carpet, rug

tardar [tar'dar] VI to delay; (*chegar tarde*) to be late ▶ VT to delay; **sem mais ~** without delay; **~ a** *ou* **em fazer** to take a long time to do; **o mais ~** at the latest

tarde ['tardʒi] F afternoon ▶ ADV late; **mais cedo ou mais ~** sooner or later; **antes ~ do que nunca** better late than never; **boa ~!** good afternoon!; **à** *ou* **de ~** in the afternoon

tardio, -a [tar'dʒiu, a] ADJ late

tarefa [ta'rɛfa] F task, job; (*faina*) chore

tarifa [ta'rifa] F tariff; (*para transportes*) fare; (*lista de preços*) price list; **~ alfandegária** customs duty

tartaruga [tarta'ruga] F turtle

tasca ['taska] (*PT*) F cheap eating place

tática ['tatʃika] F tactics *pl*

tático, -a ['tatʃiku, a] ADJ tactical

tato ['tatu] M touch; (*fig: diplomacia*) tact

tatu [ta'tu] M armadillo

tatuagem [ta'twaʒẽ] (*pl* **-ns**) F tattoo

taxa ['taʃa] F (*imposto*) tax; (*preço*) fee; (*índice*) rate; **~ de câmbio** exchange rate; **~ de juros** interest rate; **taxação** [taʃa'sãw] F taxation; **taxar** [ta'ʃar] VT (*fixar o preço de*) to fix the price of; (*lançar impostos sobre*) to tax

táxi ['taksi] M taxi

taxista [tak'sista] M/F taxi driver

tchau [tʃaw] EXCL bye!

tcheco, -a ['tʃɛku, a] ADJ, M/F Czech; **a República Tcheca** the Czech Republic

te [tʃi] PRON you; (*para você*) (to) you

teatro ['tʃjatru] M theatre (*BRIT*),

theater (*US*); (*obras*) plays *pl*, dramatic works *pl*; (*gênero, curso*) drama; **peça de ~** play

tecer [te'ser] VT, VI to weave; **tecido** [te'sidu] M cloth, material; (*Anat*) tissue

tecla ['tɛkla] F key; **teclado** [tek'ladu] M keyboard

técnica ['tɛknika] F technique; *ver tb* **técnico**

técnico, -a ['tɛkniku, a] ADJ technical ▶ M/F technician; (*especialista*) expert

tecnologia [teknolo'ʒia] F technology; **tecnológico, -a** [tekno'lɔʒiku, a] ADJ technological

tédio ['tɛdʒju] M tedium, boredom; **tedioso, -a** [te'dʒjozu, ɔza] ADJ tedious, boring

teia ['teja] F web; **~ de aranha** cobweb

teimar [tej'mar] VI to insist, keep on; **~ em** to insist on

teimosia [tejmo'zia] F stubbornness; **~ em fazer** insistence on doing

teimoso, -a [tej'mozu, ɔza] ADJ obstinate; (*criança*) wilful (*BRIT*), willful (*US*)

Tejo ['teʒu] M: **o (rio) ~** the (river) Tagus

tela ['tɛla] F fabric, material; (*de pintar*) canvas; (*Cinema, TV*) screen

tele... ['tele] PREFIXO tele...; **telecomunicações** [telekomunika'sõjs] FPL telecommunications; **teleconferência** [telekõfe'rẽsja] F teleconference

teleférico [tele'fɛriku] M cable car

telefonar [telefo'nar] VI: **~ para alguém** to (tele)phone sb

telefone [tele'fɔni] M phone, telephone; (*número*) (tele)phone number; (*telefonema*) phone call; **~ celular** cellphone, mobile phone; **~ de carro** carphone; **~ fixo** landline; **telefonema** [telefo'nɛma] M phone call; **dar um telefonema** to make a phone call; **telefônico, -a** [tele'foniku, a] ADJ telephone *atr*; **telefonista** [telefo'nista] M/F telephonist; (*na companhia telefônica*) operator

tele...: telegrama [tele'grama] M telegram, cable; **telejornal** [teleʒor'naw] (*pl* -**ais**) M television news *sg*; **telemóvel** [tele'mɔvel] (*PT*) (*pl* -**eis**) M mobile (phone) (*BRIT*), cellphone (*US*); **telenovela** [teleno'vɛla] F (TV) soap opera; **telescópio** [tele'skɔpju] M telescope; **telespectador, a** [telespekta'dor(a)] M/F viewer **televendas** [tele'vẽdas] FPL telesales; **televisão** [televi'zãw] F television; **~ por assinatura** pay television; **~ a cabo** cable television; **~ a cores** colo(u)r television; **~ digital** digital television; **~ via satélite** satellite television; **aparelho de ~** television set; **televisionar** [televizjo'nar] VT to televise; **televisivo, -a** [televi'zivu, a] ADJ television *atr*; **televisor** [televi'zor] M (*aparelho*) television (set), TV (set)

telha ['teʎa] F tile; (*col: cabeça*) head; **ter uma ~ de menos** to have a screw loose **telhado** [te'ʎadu] M roof

tema ['tɛma] M theme; (*assunto*) subject; **temática** [te'matʃika] F theme

temer [te'mer] VT to fear, be afraid of ▶ VI to be afraid

temeroso, -a [teme'rozu, ɔza] ADJ fearful, afraid; (*pavoroso*) dreadful

temido, -a [te'midu, a] ADJ fearsome, frightening

temível [te'mivew] (*pl* -**eis**) ADJ = **temido**

temor [te'mor] M fear

temperado, -a [tẽpe'radu, a] ADJ (*clima*) temperate; (*comida*) seasoned

temperamento [tẽpera'mẽtu] M temperament, nature

temperar [tẽpe'rar] VT to season

temperatura [tẽpera'tura] F temperature

tempero [tẽ'peru] M seasoning, flavouring (*BRIT*), flavoring (*US*)

tempestade [tẽpes'tadʒi] F storm; **tempestuoso, -a** [tẽpes'twozu, ɔza] ADJ stormy

templo ['tẽplu] M temple; (*igreja*) church

tempo ['tẽpu] M time; (*meteorológico*) weather; (*Ling*) tense; **o ~ todo** the whole time; **a ~** on time; **ao mesmo ~** at the same time; **a um ~** at once; **com ~** in good time; **de ~ em ~** from time to time; **nesse meio ~** in the meantime; **quanto ~?** how long?; **mais ~** longer; **há ~s** for ages; (*atrás*) ages ago; **~ livre** spare time; **primeiro/segundo ~** (*Esporte*) first/second half

temporada [tẽpo'rada] F season; (*tempo*) spell

temporal [tẽpo'raw] (*pl* -**ais**) M storm, gale

temporário, -a [tẽpo'rarju, a] ADJ temporary, provisional

tenacidade [tenasi'dadʒi] F tenacity

tencionar [tẽsjo'nar] VT to intend, plan

t

tenda ['tẽda] F tent
tendão [tẽ'dãw] (pl **-ões**) M tendon
tendões [tẽ'dõjs] MPL de **tendão**
tenebroso, -a [tene'brozu, ɔza]
ADJ dark, gloomy; (fig) horrible
tenho ['teɲu] VB ver **ter**
tênis ['tenis] M INV tennis; (sapatos)
training shoes pl; (um sapato)
training shoe; **~ de mesa** table
tennis; **tenista** [te'nista] M/F
tennis player
tenor [te'nor] M (Mús) tenor
tenro, -a ['tẽhu, a] ADJ tender;
(macio) soft; (delicado) delicate;
(novo) young
tensão [tẽ'sãw] F tension; (pressão)
pressure, strain; (rigidez) tightness;
(Elet: voltagem) voltage
tenso, -a ['tẽsu, a] ADJ tense; (sob
pressão) under stress, strained
tentação [tẽta'sãw] F temptation
tentáculo [tẽ'takulu] M tentacle
tentar [tẽ'tar] VT to try; (seduzir) to
tempt ▶ VI to try; **tentativa**
[tẽta'tʃiva] F attempt; **tentativa
de homicídio/suicídio/roubo**
attempted murder/suicide/
robbery; **por tentativas** by trial
and error
tênue ['tenwi] ADJ tenuous; (fino)
thin; (delicado) delicate; (luz, voz)
faint; (pequeníssimo) minute
teor [te'or] M (conteúdo) tenor;
(sentido) meaning, drift
teoria [teo'ria] F theory;
teoricamente [teorika'mẽtʃi] ADV
theoretically, in theory; **teórico, -a**
[te'ɔriku, a] ADJ theoretical ▶ M/F
theoretician
tépido, -a ['tɛpidu, a] ADJ tepid

PALAVRA-CHAVE

ter [ter] VT **1** (possuir, ger) to have;
(na mão) to hold; **você tem uma**
caneta? have you got a pen?; **ela
vai ter neném** she is going to have
a baby
2 (idade, medidas, estado) to be; **ela
tem 7 anos** she's 7 (years old); **a
mesa tem 1 metro de
comprimento** the table is 1 metre
long; **ter fome/sorte** to be
hungry/lucky; **ter frio/calor** to be
cold/hot
3 (conter) to hold, contain; **a caixa
tem um quilo de chocolates** the
box holds one kilo of chocolates
4: **ter que** ou **de fazer** to have to do
5: **ter a ver com** to have to do with
6: **ir ter com** to (go and) meet
▶ VB IMPESS **1**: **tem** (sg) there is; (pl)
there are; **tem 3 dias que não saio
de casa** I haven't been out for 3 days
2: **não tem de quê** don't mention it

terapeuta [tera'pewta] M/F
therapist
terapia [tera'pia] F therapy
terça ['tersa] F (tb: **~-feira**) Tuesday;
terça-feira (pl **terças-feiras**) F
Tuesday; **terça-feira gorda** Shrove
Tuesday
terceiro, -a [ter'sejru, a] NUM
third; **terceiros** MPL (os outros)
outsiders; ver tb **quinto**
terço ['tersu] M third (part)
termas ['tɛrmas] FPL bathhouse sg
térmico, -a ['tɛrmiku, a] ADJ
thermal; **garrafa térmica**
(Thermos®) flask
terminal [termi'naw] (pl **-ais**) ADJ
terminal ▶ M (de rede, Elet, Comput)
terminal ▶ F terminal; **~ (de vídeo)**
monitor, visual display unit
terminar [termi'nar] VT to finish
▶ VI (pessoa) to finish; (coisa) to end;
~ de fazer to finish doing; (ter feito
há pouco) to have just done; **~ por**

algo/fazer algo to end with sth/end up doing sth

término ['tɛrminu] M end, termination

termo ['tɛrmu] M term; (*fim*) end, termination; (*limite*) limit, boundary; (*prazo*) period; (*PT: garrafa*) (Thermos®) flask; **meio ~** compromise; **em ~s (de)** in terms (of)

termômetro [ter'mometru] M thermometer

terno, -a ['tɛrnu, a] ADJ gentle, tender ▶ M (BR: *roupa*) suit; **ternura** [ter'nura] F gentleness, tenderness

terra ['tɛha] F earth, world; (*Agr, propriedade*) land; (*pátria*) country; (*chão*) ground; (*Geo*) soil; (*pó*) dirt

terraço [te'hasu] M terrace

terramoto [teha'mɔtu] (PT) M = **terremoto**

terreiro [te'hejru] M yard, square

terremoto [tehe'mɔtu] M earthquake

terreno, -a [te'hɛnu, a] M ground, land; (*porção de terra*) plot of land ▶ ADJ earthly

térreo, -a ['tɛhju, a] ADJ: **andar ~** (BR) ground floor (BRIT), first floor (US)

terrestre [te'hɛstri] ADJ land atr

território [tehi'tɔrju] M territory

terrível [te'hivew] (*pl* -eis) ADJ terrible, dreadful

terror [te'hor] M terror, dread; **terrorista** [teho'rista] ADJ, M/F terrorist; **terrorista suicida** suicide bomber

tese ['tɛzi] F proposition, theory; (*Educ*) thesis; **em ~** in theory

teso, -a ['tezu, a] ADJ (*cabo*) taut; (*rígido*) stiff

tesouraria [tezora'ria] F treasury

tesouro [te'zoru] M treasure; (*erário*) treasury, exchequer; (*livro*) thesaurus

testa ['tɛsta] F brow, forehead

testar [tes'tar] VT to test; (*deixar em testamento*) to bequeath

teste ['tɛstʃi] M test

testemunha [teste'muɲa] F witness; **testemunhar** [testemu'ɲar] VI to testify ▶ VT to give evidence about; (*presenciar*) to witness; (*confirmar*) to demonstrate; **testemunho** [teste'muɲu] M evidence

testículo [tes'tʃikulu] M testicle

teta ['tɛta] F teat

tétano ['tɛtanu] M tetanus

teto ['tɛtu] M ceiling; (*telhado*) roof; (*habitação*) home

teu, tua [tew, 'tua] ADJ your ▶ PRON yours

teve ['tevi] VB *ver* **ter**

têxtil ['testʃiw] (*pl* -eis) M textile

texto ['testu] M text

textura [tes'tura] F texture

thriller ['triler] (*pl* -s) M thriller

ti [tʃi] PRON you

tia ['tʃia] F aunt

Tibete [tʃi'betʃi] M: **o ~** Tibet

TIC [tʃik] ABR F (= *Tecnologia de Informação e Comunicação*) ICT

tido, -a ['tʃidu, a] PP *de* **ter** ▶ ADJ: **~ como** *ou* **por** considered to be

tigela [tʃi'ʒɛla] F bowl

tigre ['tʃigri] M tiger

tijolo [tʃi'ʒolu] M brick

til [tʃiw] (*pl* **tis**) M tilde

timbre ['tʃibri] M insignia, emblem; (*selo*) stamp; (*Mús*) tone, timbre; (*de voz*) tone; (*em papel de carta*) heading

time ['tʃimi] (BR) M team; **de segundo ~** (*fig*) second-rate

tímido, -a ['tʃimidu, a] ADJ shy, timid

tímpano ['tʃĩpanu] M eardrum; (*Mús*) kettledrum

tingir [tʃĩ'ʒir] VT to dye; (*fig*) to tinge

tinha ['tʃiɲa] VB *ver* **ter**

tinjo ['tʃĩʒu] VB *ver* **tingir**

tinta ['tʃĩta] F (*de pintar*) paint; (*de escrever*) ink; (*para tingir*) dye; (*fig: vestígio*) shade, tinge

tinto, -a ['tʃĩtu, a] ADJ dyed; (*fig*) stained; **vinho ~** red wine

tintura [tʃĩ'tura] F dye; (*ato*) dyeing; (*fig*) tinge, hint

tinturaria [tʃĩtura'ria] F dry-cleaner's

tio ['tʃiu] M uncle

típico, -a ['tʃipiku, a] ADJ typical

tipo ['tʃipu] M type; (*de imprensa*) print; (*de impressora*) typeface; (*col: sujeito*) guy, chap; (*pessoa*) person

tipografia [tʃipogra'fia] F printing; (*estabelecimento*) printer's

tíquete ['tʃiketʃi] M ticket

tira ['tʃira] F strip ▶ M (BR *col*) cop

tira-gosto (*pl* **-s**) M snack, savoury (BRIT)

tirano, -a [tʃi'ranu, a] ADJ tyrannical ▶ M/F tyrant

tirar [tʃi'rar] VT to take away; (*de dentro*) to take out; (*de cima*) to take off; (*roupa, sapatos*) to take off; (*arrancar*) to pull out; (*férias*) to take, have; (*boas notas*) to get; (*salário*) to earn; (*curso*) to do, take; (*mancha*) to remove; (*foto, cópia*) to take; (*mesa*) to clear; **~ algo a alguém** to take sth from sb

tiritar [tʃiri'tar] VI to shiver

tiro ['tʃiru] M shot; (*ato de disparar*) shooting; **~ ao alvo** target practice; **trocar ~s** to fire at one another

tiroteio [tʃiro'teju] M shooting, exchange of shots

tis [tʃis] MPL *de* **til**

titular [tʃitu'lar] ADJ titular ▶ M/F holder

título ['tʃitulu] M title; (*Com*) bond; (*universitário*) degree; **~ de propriedade** title deed

tive ['tʃivi] VB *ver* **ter**

to [tu] = **te + o**

toa ['toa] F towrope; **à ~** at random; (*sem motivo*) for no reason; (*inutilmente*) for nothing

toalete [twa'letʃi] M (*banheiro*) toilet ▶ F: **fazer a ~** to have a wash

toalha [to'aʎa] F towel

toca ['tɔka] F burrow, hole

toca-discos (BR) M INV record-player

tocador [toka'dor] M player; **~ MP3** MP3 player

toca-fitas M INV cassette player

tocaia [to'kaja] F ambush

tocante [to'kãtʃi] ADJ moving, touching; **no ~ a** regarding, concerning

tocar [to'kar] VT to touch; (*Mús*) to play ▶ VI to touch; (*Mús*) to play; (*campainha, sino, telefone*) to ring; **tocar-se** VR to touch (each other); **~ a** (*dizer respeito a*) to concern, affect; **~ em** to touch; (*assunto*) to touch upon; **~ para alguém** (*telefonar*) to ring sb (up), call sb (up); **pelo que me toca** as far as I am concerned

tocha ['tɔʃa] F torch

todavia [toda'via] ADV yet, still, however

(PALAVRA-CHAVE)

todo, -a ['todu, 'tɔda] ADJ 1 (*com artigo sg*) all: **toda a carne** all the meat; **toda a noite** all night, the whole night; **todo o Brasil** the whole of Brazil; **a toda (velocidade)** at full speed; **todo o**

mundo (BR), **toda a gente** (PT) everybody, everyone; **em toda (a) parte** everywhere
2 (com artigo pl) all; (: cada) every; **todos os livros** all the books; **todos os dias/todas as noites** every day/night; **todos os que querem sair** all those who want to leave; **todos nós** all of us ▶ ADV: **ao todo** altogether; (no total) in all; **de todo** completely ▶ PRON: **todos** everybody sg, everyone sg

todo-poderoso, -a ADJ all-powerful ▶ M: **o T~** the Almighty
toicinho [toj'siɲu] M bacon fat
tolerância [tole'rãsja] F tolerance; **tolerante** [tole'rãtʃi] ADJ tolerant
tolerar [tole'rar] VT to tolerate; **tolerável** [tole'ravew] (pl **-eis**) ADJ tolerable, bearable; (satisfatório) passable; (falta) excusable
tolice [to'lisi] F stupidity, foolishness; (ato, dito) stupid thing
tom [tõ] (pl **-ns**) M tone; (Mús: altura) pitch; (: escala) key; (cor) shade
tomada [to'mada] F capture; (Elet) socket
tomar [to'mar] VT to take; (capturar) to capture, seize; (decisão) to make; (bebida) to drink; **~ café** (de manhã) to have breakfast
tomara [to'mara] EXCL: **~!** if only!; **~ que venha hoje** I hope he comes today
tomate [to'matʃi] M tomato
tombadilho [tõba'dʒiʎu] M deck
tombar [tõ'bar] VI to fall down, tumble down ▶ VT to knock down, knock over; **tombo** [ˈtõbu] M

tumble, fall
tomilho [to'miʎu] M thyme
tona ['tɔna] F surface; **vir à ~** to come to the surface; (fig) to emerge; **trazer à ~** to bring up; (recordações) to bring back
tonalidade [tonali'dadʒi] F (de cor) shade
tonelada [tone'lada] F ton
tônica ['tonika] F (água) tonic (water); (fig) keynote
tônico, -a ['toniku, a] ADJ tonic ▶ M tonic; **acento ~** stress
tons [tõs] MPL de **tom**
tonteira [tõ'tejra] F dizziness
tonto, -a ['tõtu, a] ADJ stupid, silly; (zonzo) dizzy, lightheaded; (atarantado) flustered
topar [to'par] VT to agree to ▶ VI: **~ com** to come across; **topar-se** VR (duas pessoas) to run into one another; **~ em** (tropeçar) to stub one's toe on; (esbarrar) to run into; (tocar) to touch
tópico, -a ['tɔpiku, a] ADJ topical ▶ M topic
topless [tɔp'lɛs] ADJ INV topless
topo ['topu] M top; (extremidade) end, extremity
toque VB ver **tocar**
Tóquio ['tɔkju] N Tokyo
tora ['tɔra] F (pedaço) piece; (de madeira) log; (sesta) nap
toranja [to'rãʒa] F grapefruit
torção [tor'sãw] (pl **-ões**) M twist; (Med) sprain
torcedor, a [torse'dor(a)] M/F supporter, fan
torcer [tor'ser] VT to twist; (Med) to sprain; (desvirtuar) to distort, misconstrue; (roupa: espremer) to wring; (: na máquina) to spin; (vergar) to bend ▶ VI: **~ por** (time) to support; **torcer-se** VR to

squirm, writhe

torcicolo [torsi'kɔlu] M stiff neck

torcida [tor'sida] F (pavio) wick; (Esporte: ato de torcer) cheering; (: torcedores) supporters pl

torções [tor'sõjs] MPL de **torção**

tormenta [tor'mẽta] F storm

tormento [tor'mẽtu] M torment; (angústia) anguish

tornar [tor'nar] VI to return, go back ▶ VT: **~ algo em algo** to turn ou make sth into sth; **tornar-se** VR to become; **~ a fazer algo** to do sth again

torneio [tor'neju] M tournament

torneira [tor'nejra] F tap (BRIT), faucet (US)

tornozelo [torno'zelu] M ankle

torpedo [tor'pedu] M (bomba) torpedo; (col: mensagem) text (message)

torrada [to'hada] F toast; **uma ~** a piece of toast; **torradeira** [toha'dejra] F toaster

torrão [to'hãw] (pl -**ões**) M turf, sod; (terra) soil, land; (de açúcar) lump

torrar [to'har] VT to toast; (café) to roast

torre ['tohi] F tower; (Xadrez) castle, rook; (Elet) pylon; **~ de controle** (Aer) control tower

tórrido, -a ['tɔhidu, a] ADJ torrid

torrões [to'hõjs] MPL de **torrão**

torso ['torsu] M torso

torta ['tɔrta] F pie, tart

torto, -a ['tortu, 'tɔrta] ADJ twisted, crooked; **a ~ e a direito** indiscriminately

tortuoso, -a [tor'twozu, ɔza] ADJ winding

tortura [tor'tura] F torture; (fig) anguish; **torturar** [tortu'rar] VT to torture; to torment

tos [tus] = **te + os**

tosco, -a ['tosku, a] ADJ rough, unpolished; (grosseiro) coarse, crude

tosse ['tɔsi] F cough; **~ de cachorro** whooping cough; **tossir** [to'sir] VI to cough

tosta ['tɔsta] (PT) F toast; **~ mista** toasted cheese and ham sandwich

tostão [tos'tãw] M cash

tostar [tos'tar] VT to toast; (pele, pessoa) to tan; **tostar-se** VR to get tanned

total [to'taw] (pl -**ais**) ADJ, M total

touca ['toka] F bonnet; **~ de banho** bathing cap

tourada [to'rada] F bullfight; **toureiro** [to'rejru] M bullfighter

touro ['toru] M bull; **T~** (Astrologia) Taurus

tóxico, -a ['tɔksiku, a] ADJ toxic ▶ M poison; (droga) drug; **toxicômano, -a** [toksi'komanu, a] M/F drug addict

TPM ABR F (= tensão pré-menstrual) PMT

trabalhador, a [trabaʎa'dor(a)] ADJ hard-working, industrious; (Pol: classe) working ▶ M/F worker

trabalhar [traba'ʎar] VI to work ▶ VT (terra) to till; (madeira, metal) to work; (texto) to work on; **~ com** (comerciar) to deal in; **~ de** ou **como** to work as; **trabalhista** [traba'ʎista] ADJ labour atr (BRIT), labor atr (US); **trabalho** [tra'baʎu] M work; (emprego, tarefa) job; (Educ: tarefa) assignment; **trabalho braçal** manual work; **trabalho doméstico** housework; **trabalhoso, -a** [traba'ʎozu, ɔza] ADJ laborious, arduous

traça ['trasa] F moth

traçado [tra'sadu] M sketch, plan

tração [tra'sãw] F traction

traçar [tra'sar] VT to draw; (*determinar*) to set out, outline; (*planos*) to draw up; (*escrever*) to compose

tradição [tradʒi'sãw] (*pl* -**ões**) F tradition; **tradicional** [tradʒisjo'naw] (*pl* -**ais**) ADJ traditional

tradução [tradu'sãw] (*pl* -**ões**) F translation

tradutor, a [tradu'tor(a)] M/F translator

traduzir [tradu'zir] VT to translate

trafegar [trafe'gar] VI to move, go

tráfego ['trafegu] M traffic

traficante [trafi'kãtʃi] M/F trafficker, dealer

traficar [trafi'kar] VI: **~ (com)** to deal (in)

tráfico ['trafiku] M traffic

tragar [tra'gar] VT to swallow; (*fumaça*) to inhale; (*suportar*) to tolerate ▶ VI to inhale

tragédia [tra'ʒɛdʒja] F tragedy; **trágico, -a** ['traʒiku, a] ADJ tragic

trago¹ ['tragu] M mouthful

trago² VB *ver* **trazer**

traiçoeiro, -a [traj'swejru, a] ADJ treacherous

traidor, a [traj'dor(a)] M/F traitor

trailer ['trejler] (*pl* -**s**) M trailer; (*tipo casa*) caravan (BRIT), trailer (US)

trair [tra'ir] VT to betray; (*mulher, marido*) to be unfaithful to; (*esperanças*) not to live up to; **trair-se** VR to give o.s. away

trajar [tra'ʒar] VT to wear

traje ['traʒi] M dress, clothes *pl*; **~ de banho** swimsuit

trajeto [tra'ʒetu] M course, path

trajetória [traʒe'tɔrja] F trajectory, path; (*fig*) course

tralha ['traʎa] F fishing net

trama ['trama] F (*tecido*) weft (BRIT), woof (US); (*enredo, conspiração*) plot

tramar [tra'mar] VT (*tecer*) to weave; (*maquinar*) to plot ▶ VI: **~ contra** to conspire against

trâmites ['tramitʃis] MPL procedure *sg*, channels

trampolim [trãpo'lĩ] (*pl* -**ns**) M trampoline; (*de piscina*) diving board; (*fig*) springboard

tranca ['trãka] F (*de porta*) bolt; (*de carro*) lock

trança ['trãsa] F (*cabelo*) plait; (*galão*) braid

trancar [trã'kar] VT to lock

tranquilidade [trãkwili'dadʒi] F tranquillity; (*paz*) peace

tranquilizante [trãkwili'zãtʃi] M (*Med*) tranquillizer

tranquilizar [trãkwili'zar] VT to calm, quieten; (*despreocupar*): **~ alguém** to reassure sb, put sb's mind at rest; **tranquilizar-se** VR to calm down

tranquilo, -a [trã'kwilu, a] ADJ peaceful; (*mar, pessoa*) calm; (*criança*) quiet; (*consciência*) clear; (*seguro*) sure, certain

transação [trãza'sãw] (*pl* -**ões**) F transaction

transar [trã'zar] (BR *col*) VI (*ter relação sexual*) to have sex

transbordar [trãzbor'dar] VI to overflow

transbordo [trãz'bordu] M (*de viajantes*) change, transfer

transe ['trãzi] M ordeal; (*lance*) plight; (*hipnótico*) trance

transeunte [trã'zjũtʃi] M/F passer-by

transferência [trãsfe'rẽsja] F transfer

transferir [trãsfe'rir] VT to

transformação | 594

transfer; (adiar) to postpone

transformação [trɐ̃sforma'sãw] (pl **-ões**) F transformation

transformador [trɐ̃sforma'dor] M (Elet) transformer

transformar [trɐ̃sfor'mar] VT to transform; **transformar-se** VR to turn

transfusão [trɐ̃sfu'zãw] (pl **-ões**) F transfusion

transgênico, -a [trɐ̃z'ʒeniku, a] ADJ (planta, alimento) genetically modified, GM

transição [trɐ̃zi'sãw] (pl **-ões**) F transition

transitivo, -a [trɐ̃zi'tʃivu, a] ADJ (Ling) transitive

trânsito ['trɐ̃zitu] M transit, passage; (na rua: veículos) traffic; (: pessoas) flow; **transitório, -a** [trɐ̃zi'tɔrju, a] ADJ transitory; (período) transitional

transmissão [trɐ̃zmi'sãw] (pl **-ões**) F transmission; (transferência) transfer; **~ ao vivo** live broadcast

transmissor, a [trɐ̃zmi'sor(a)] ADJ transmitting ▶ M transmitter

transmitir [trɐ̃zmi'tʃir] VT to transmit; (Rádio, TV) to broadcast; (transferir) to transfer; (recado, notícia) to pass on

transparente [trɐ̃spa'rẽtʃi] ADJ transparent; (roupa) see-through; clear

transpirar [trɐ̃spi'rar] VI to perspire; (divulgar-se) to become known; (verdade) to come out ▶ VT to exude

transplante [trɐ̃s'plɐ̃tʃi] M transplant

transportar [trɐ̃spor'tar] VT to transport; (levar) to carry; (enlevar) to entrance, enrapture

transporte [trɐ̃s'pɔrtʃi] M transport; (Com) haulage

transtorno [trɐ̃s'tornu] M upset, disruption

trapalhão, -lhona [trapa'ʎãw, 'ʎɔna] (pl **-ões/-s**) M/F bungler, blunderer

trapo ['trapu] M rag

trarei [tra'rej] VB ver **trazer**

trás [trajs] PREP, ADV: **para ~** backwards; **por ~ de** behind; **de ~** from behind

traseira [tra'zejra] F rear; (Anat) bottom

traste ['trastʃi] M thing; (coisa sem valor) piece of junk

tratado [tra'tadu] M treaty

tratamento [trata'mẽtu] M treatment

tratar [tra'tar] VT to treat; (tema) to deal with; (combinar) to agree ▶ VI: **~ com** to deal with; (combinar) to agree with; **~ de** to deal with; **de que se trata?** what is it about?

trato ['tratu] M treatment; (contrato) agreement, contract; **tratos** MPL (relações) dealings

trator [tra'tor] M tractor

trauma ['trawma] M trauma

travão [tra'vãw] (PT) (pl **-ões**) M brake

travar [tra'var] VT (roda) to lock; (iniciar) to engage in; (conversa) to strike up; (luta) to wage; (carro) to stop; (passagem) to block; (movimentos) to hinder ▶ VI (PT) to brake

trave ['travi] F beam; (Esporte) crossbar

través [tra'vɛs] M slant, incline; **de ~** across, sideways

travessa [tra'vesa] F crossbeam, crossbar; (rua) lane, alley; (prato) dish; (para o cabelo) comb, slide

travessão [trave'sãw] (pl **-ões**) M

(*de balança*) bar, beam; (*pontuação*) dash

travesseiro [trave'sejru] M pillow

travessia [trave'sia] F (*viagem*) journey, crossing

travessões [trave'sõjs] MPL *de* **travessão**

travessura [trave'sura] F mischief, prank

travões [tra'võjs] MPL *de* **travão**

trazer [tra'zer] VT to bring

trecho ['treʃu] M passage; (*de rua, caminho*) stretch; (*espaço*) space

trégua ['tregwa] F truce; (*descanso*) respite

treinador, a [trejna'dor(a)] M/F trainer

treinamento [trejna'mẽtu] M training

treinar [trej'nar] VT to train; **treinar-se** VR to train; **treino** ['trejnu] M training

trejeito [tre'ʒejtu] M gesture; (*careta*) grimace, face

trem [trẽj] (*pl* **-ns**) M train; **~ de aterrissagem** (*avião*) landing gear

tremendo, -a [tre'mẽdu, a] ADJ tremendous; (*terrível*) terrible, awful

tremer [tre'mer] VI to shudder, quake; (*terra*) to shake; (*de frio, medo*) to shiver

trêmulo, -a ['tremulu, a] ADJ shaky, trembling

trenó [tre'nɔ] M sledge, sleigh (BRIT), sled (US)

trens [trẽjs] MPL *de* **trem**

trepar [tre'par] VT to climb ▶ VI: **~ em** to climb

trepidar [trepi'dar] VI to tremble, shake

três [tres] NUM three; *ver tb* **cinco**

trevas ['trɛvas] FPL darkness *sg*

treze ['trezi] NUM thirteen

triângulo ['trjãgulu] M triangle

tribal [tri'baw] (*pl* **-ais**) ADJ tribal

tribo ['tribu] F tribe

tribuna [tri'buna] F platform, rostrum; (*Rel*) pulpit

tribunal [tribu'naw] (*pl* **-ais**) M court; (*comissão*) tribunal

tributo [tri'butu] M tribute; (*imposto*) tax

tricô [tri'ko] M knitting; **tricotar** [triko'tar] VT, VI to knit

trigo ['trigu] M wheat

trilha ['triʎa] F (*caminho*) path; (*rasto*) track, trail; **~ sonora** soundtrack

trilhão [tri'ʎãw] (*pl* **-ões**) M billion (BRIT), trillion (US)

trilho ['triʎu] M (BR Ferro) rail; (*vereda*) path, track

trilhões [tri'ʎõjs] MPL *de* **trilhão**

trimestral [trimes'traw] (*pl* **-ais**) ADJ quarterly; **trimestralmente** [trimestraw'mẽtʃi] ADV quarterly

trimestre [tri'mestri] M (*Educ*) term; (*Com*) quarter

trincar [trĩ'kar] VT to crunch; (*morder*) to bite; (*dentes*) to grit ▶ VI to crunch

trinco ['trĩku] M latch

trinta ['trĩta] NUM thirty

trio ['triu] M trio; **~ elétrico**

Trios elétricos are lorries, carrying floats equipped for sound and/or live music, which parade through the streets during *carnaval*, especially in Bahia. Bands and popular performers on the floats draw crowds by giving frenzied performances of various types of music.

tripa ['tripa] F gut, intestine; **tripas** FPL (*intestinos*) bowels; (*vísceras*) guts; (*Culin*) tripe *sg*

t

tripé ['tri'pɛ] M tripod

triplicar [tripli'kar] VT, VI to treble; **triplicar-se** VR to treble

tripulação [tripula'sãw] (pl **-ões**) F crew

tripulante [tripu'lãtʃi] M/F crew member

triste ['tristʃi] ADJ sad; (lugar) depressing

tristeza [tris'teza] F sadness; (de lugar) gloominess

triturar [tritu'rar] VT to grind

triunfar [trjũ'far] VI to triumph; **triunfo** ['trjũfu] M triumph

trivial [tri'vjaw] (pl **-ais**) ADJ common(place), ordinary; (insignificante) trivial

triz [triz] M: **por um ~** by a hair's breadth

troca ['trɔka] F exchange, swap

trocadilho [troka'dʒiʎu] M pun, play on words

trocado [tro'kadu] M: **~(s)** (small) change

trocador, a [troka'dor(a)] M/F (em ônibus) conductor

trocar [tro'kar] VT to exchange, swap; (mudar) to change; (inverter) to change ou swap round; (confundir) to mix up; **trocar-se** VR to change; **~ dinheiro** to change money

troco ['trɔku] M (dinheiro) change; (revide) retort, rejoinder

troféu [tro'fɛw] M trophy

tromba ['trõba] F (do elefante) trunk; (de outro animal) snout

trombeta [trõ'beta] F trumpet

trombone [trõ'bɔni] M trombone

trombose [trõ'bɔzi] F thrombosis

tronco ['trõku] M trunk; (ramo) branch; (de corpo) torso, trunk

trono ['trɔnu] M throne

tropa ['trɔpa] F troop; (exército) army; **ir para a ~** (PT) to join the army

tropeçar [trope'sar] VI to stumble, trip; (fig) to blunder

tropical [tropi'kaw] (pl **-ais**) ADJ tropical

trotar [tro'tar] VI to trot; **trote** ['trɔtʃi] M trot; (por telefone etc) hoax call

trouxe ['trosi] VB ver **trazer**

trovão [tro'vãw] (pl **-ões**) M clap of thunder; (trovoada) thunder; **trovejar** [trove'ʒar] VI to thunder; **trovoada** [tro'vwada] F thunderstorm

truque ['truki] M trick; (publicitário) gimmick

truta ['truta] F trout

tu [tu] PRON you

tua ['tua] F de **teu**

tuba ['tuba] F tuba

tubarão [tuba'rãw] (pl **-ões**) M shark

tuberculose [tuberku'lɔzi] F tuberculosis

tubo ['tubu] M tube, pipe; **~ de ensaio** test tube

tucano [tu'kanu] M toucan

tudo ['tudu] PRON everything; **~ quanto** everything that; **antes de ~** first of all; **acima de ~** above all

tufão [tu'fãw] (pl **-ões**) M typhoon

tuitar [twi'tar] VT, VI to tweet

tulipa [tu'lipa] F tulip

tumba ['tũba] F tomb; (lápide) tombstone

tumor [tu'mor] M tumour (BRIT), tumor (US)

túmulo ['tumulu] M tomb; (sepultura) burial

tumulto [tu'muwtu] M uproar, trouble; (grande movimento) bustle; (balbúrdia) hubbub; (motim) riot;

tumultuado, -a [tumuw'twadu, a] ADJ riotous, heated; **tumultuar** [tumuw'twar] VT to disrupt; (*amotinar*) to rouse, incite
túnel ['tunew] (*pl* **-eis**) M tunnel
túnica ['tunika] F tunic
Tunísia [tu'nizja] F: **a ~** Tunisia
tupi [tu'pi] M Tupi (tribe); (*Ling*) Tupi ▶ M/F Tupi Indian
tupi-guarani [-gwara'ni] M *see note*

> **Tupi-guarani** is an important branch of indigenous languages from the tropical region of South America. It takes in thirty indigenous peoples and includes Tupi, Guarani, and other languages. Before Brazil was discovered by the Portuguese it had 1,300 indigenous languages, 87% of which are now extinct due to the extermination of indigenous peoples and the loss of territory.

tupiniquim [tupini'kĩ] (*pej*) (*pl* **-ns**) ADJ Brazilian (Indian)
turbilhão [turbi'ʎãw] (*pl* **-ões**) M (*de vento*) whirlwind; (*de água*) whirlpool
turbina [tur'bina] F turbine; **~ eólica** wind turbine
turbulência [turbu'lẽsja] F turbulence; **turbulento, -a** [turbu'lẽtu, a] ADJ turbulent
turco, -a ['turku, a] ADJ Turkish ▶ M/F Turk ▶ M (*Ling*) Turkish
turismo [tu'rizmu] M tourism; **turista** [tu'rista] M/F tourist ▶ ADJ (*classe*) tourist *atr*
turma ['turma] F group; (*Educ*) class
turquesa [tur'keza] ADJ INV turquoise

Turquia [tur'kia] F: **a ~** Turkey
tusso ['tusu] VB *ver* **tossir**
tutela [tu'tɛla] F protection; (*Jur*) guardianship
tutor, a [tu'tor(a)] M/F guardian
tutu [tu'tu] M (*Culin*) beans, bacon and manioc flour
TV [te've] ABR F (= *televisão*) TV

u

UE ABR F (= *União Europeia*) EU
Uganda [u'gãda] M Uganda
uísque ['wiski] M whisky (BRIT), whiskey (US)
uivar [wi'var] VI to howl; (*berrar*) to yell; **uivo** ['wivu] M howl; (*fig*) yell
úlcera ['uwsera] F ulcer
ultimamente [uwtʃima'mẽtʃi] ADV lately
ultimato [uwtʃi'matu] M ultimatum
último, -a ['uwtʃimu, a] ADJ last; (*mais recente*) latest; (*qualidade*) lowest; (*fig*) final; **por ~** finally; **nos ~s anos** in recent years; **a última** (*notícia*) the latest (news)
ultra... [uwtra-] PREFIXO ultra-
ultrajar [uwtra'ʒar] VT to outrage; (*insultar*) to insult, offend; **ultraje** [uw'traʒi] M outrage; (*insulto*) insult, offence (BRIT), offense (US)
ultramar [uwtra'mar] M overseas
ultrapassado, -a [uwtrapa'sadu, a] ADJ (*ideias etc*) outmoded
ultrapassar [uwtrapa'sar] VT

(*atravessar*) to cross, go beyond; (*ir além de*) to exceed; (*transgredir*) to overstep; (*Auto*) to overtake (BRIT), pass (US); (*ser superior a*) to surpass ▶ VI (*Auto*) to overtake (BRIT), pass (US)
ultrassom [uwtra'sõ] M ultrasound
ultravioleta [uwtravjo'leta] ADJ ultraviolet

(PALAVRA-CHAVE)

um, a [ũ, 'uma] (*pl* **uns/umas**) NUM one; **um e outro** both; **um a um** one by one; **à uma (hora)** at one (o'clock)
  ▶ ADJ: **uns cinco** about five; **uns poucos** a few
  ▶ ART INDEF **1** (*sg*) a; (*antes de vogal ou 'h' mudo*) an; (*pl*) some; **um livro** a book; **uma maçã** an apple
  2 (*dando ênfase*): **estou com uma fome!** I'm so hungry!; **ela é de uma beleza incrível** she's incredibly beautiful
  3: **um ao outro** one another; (*entre dois*) each other

umbigo [ũ'bigu] M navel
umbilical [ũbili'kaw] (*pl* **-ais**) ADJ: **cordão ~** umbilical cord
umedecer [umede'ser] VT to moisten, wet; **umedecer-se** VR to get wet
umidade [umi'dadʒi] F dampness; (*clima*) humidity
úmido, -a ['umidu, a] ADJ wet, moist; (*roupa*) damp; (*clima*) humid
unânime [u'nanimi] ADJ unanimous
unha ['uɲa] F nail; (*garra*) claw; **unhada** [u'ɲada] F scratch
união [u'njãw] (*pl* **-ões**) F union; (*ato*) joining; (*unidade, solidariedade*)

unity; (*casamento*) marriage; (*Tec*) joint; **a U~ Europeia** the European Union

unicamente [unika'mētʃi] ADV only

único, -a ['uniku, a] ADJ only; (*sem igual*) unique; (*um só*) single

unidade [uni'dadʒi] F unity; (*Tec, Com*) unit; **~ central de processamento** (*Comput*) central processing unit; **~ de disco** (*Comput*) disk drive

unido, -a [u'nidu, a] ADJ joined, linked; (*fig*) united

unificar [unifi'kar] VT to unite; **unificar-se** VR to join together

uniforme [uni'fɔrmi] ADJ uniform; (*semelhante*) alike, similar; (*superfície*) even ▶ M uniform; **uniformizado, -a** [uniformi'zadu, a] ADJ uniform, standardized; (*vestido de uniforme*) in uniform; **uniformizar** [uniformi'zar] VT to standardize

uniões [u'njõjs] FPL *de* **união**

unir [u'nir] VT to join together; (*ligar*) to link; (*pessoas, fig*) to unite; (*misturar*) to mix together; **unir-se** VR to come together; (*povos etc*) to unite

uníssono [u'nisonu] M: **em ~** in unison

universal [univer'saw] (*pl* **-ais**) ADJ universal; (*mundial*) worldwide

universidade [universi'dadʒi] F university; **universitário, -a** [universi'tarju, a] ADJ university *atr* ▶ M/F (*professor*) lecturer; (*aluno*) university student

universo [uni'vɛrsu] M universe; (*mundo*) world

uns [ũs] MPL *de* **um**

untar [ũ'tar] VT (*esfregar*) to rub; (*com óleo, manteiga*) to grease

urbanismo [urba'nizmu] M town planning

urbano, -a [ur'banu, a] ADJ (*da cidade*) urban; (*fig*) urbane

urgência [ur'ʒēsja] F urgency; **com toda ~** as quickly as possible; **urgente** [ur'ʒētʃi] ADJ urgent

urina [u'rina] F urine; **urinar** [uri'nar] VI to urinate ▶ VT (*sangue*) to pass; (*cama*) to wet; **urinar-se** VR to wet o.s.; **urinol** [uri'nɔw] (*pl* **-óis**) M chamber pot

urna ['urna] F urn; **~ eleitoral** ballot box

urrar [u'har] VT, VI to roar; (*de dor*) to yell

ursa ['ursa] F bear

urso ['ursu] M bear

urtiga [ur'tʃiga] F nettle

Uruguai [uru'gwaj] M: **o ~** Uruguay

urze ['urzi] M heather

usado, -a [u'zadu, a] ADJ used; (*comum*) common; (*roupa*) worn; (*gasto*) worn out; (*de segunda mão*) second-hand

usar [u'zar] VT (*servir-se de*) to use; (*vestir*) to wear; (*gastar com o uso*) to wear out; (*barba, cabelo curto*) to have, wear ▶ VI: **~ de** to use; **modo de ~** directions *pl*

usina [u'zina] F (*fábrica*) factory; (*de energia*) plant

uso ['uzu] M use; (*utilização*) usage; (*prática*) practice

usual [u'zwaw] (*pl* **-ais**) ADJ usual; (*comum*) common

usuário, -a [u'zwarju, a] M/F user

usufruir [uzu'frwir] VT to enjoy ▶ VI: **~ de** to enjoy

úteis ['utejs] PL *de* **útil**

utensílio [utē'silju] M utensil

útero ['uteru] M womb, uterus

útil ['utʃiw] (*pl* **-eis**) ADJ useful;

u

(*vantajoso*) profitable, worthwhile;
utilidade [utʃili'dadʒi] F
usefulness; **utilização**
[utʃiliza'sãw] F use; **utilizador, a**
[utʃiliza'dor(a)] (PT) M/F user;
utilizar [utʃili'zar] VT to use;
utilizar-se VR: **utilizar-se de** to
make use of
uva ['uva] F grape

v ABR (= *volt*) v
vá [va] VB *ver* **ir**
vã [vã] F *de* **vão²**
vaca ['vaka] F cow; **carne de ~** beef
vacina [va'sina] F vaccine; **vacinar**
[vasi'nar] VT to vaccinate
vácuo ['vakwu] M vacuum; (*fig*)
void; (*espaço*) space
vaga ['vaga] F wave; (*em hotel,
trabalho*) vacancy
vagão [va'gãw] (*pl* **-ões**) M (*de
passageiros*) carriage; (*de cargas*)
wagon; **vagão-leito** (*pl*
vagões-leitos) (PT) M sleeping car;
vagão-restaurante (*pl*
vagões-restaurantes) M buffet car
vagar [va'gar] VI to wander about;
(*barco*) to drift; (*ficar vago*) to be
vacant
vagaroso, -a [vaga'rozu, ɔza] ADJ
slow
vagina [va'ʒina] F vagina
vago, -a ['vagu, a] ADJ vague;
(*desocupado*) vacant, free
vagões [va'gõjs] MPL *de* **vagão**

vai [vaj] VB *ver* **ir**

vaia ['vaja] F booing; **vaiar** [va'jar] VT, VI to boo, hiss

vaidade [vaj'dadʒi] F vanity; (*futilidade*) futility

vaidoso, -a [vaj'dozu, ɔza] ADJ vain

vaivém [vaj'vẽj] M to-ing and fro-ing

vala ['vala] F ditch

vale ['vali] M valley; (*escrito*) voucher; **~ postal** postal order

valer [va'ler] VI to be worth; (*ser válido*) to be valid; (*ter influência*) to carry weight; (*servir*) to serve; (*ser proveitoso*) to be useful; **valer-se** VR: **~-se de** to use, make use of; **~ a pena** to be worthwhile; **~ por** (*equivaler*) to be worth the same as; **para ~** (*muito*) very much, a lot; (*realmente*) for real, properly; **vale dizer** in other words; **mais vale ... (do que ...)** it would be better to ... (than ...)

valeta [va'leta] F gutter

valha ['vaʎa] VB *ver* **valer**

validade [vali'dadʒi] F validity; (*de cartão de crédito*) expiry date (BRIT), expiration date (US); (*de alimento*) best-before date

validar [vali'dar] VT to validate; **válido, -a** ['validu, a] ADJ valid

valioso, -a [va'ljozu, ɔza] ADJ valuable

valise [va'lizi] F case, grip

valor [va'lor] M value; (*mérito*) merit; (*coragem*) courage; (*preço*) price; (*importância*) importance; **valores** MPL (*morais*) values; (*num exame*) marks; (*Com*) securities; **dar ~ a** to value; **valorizar** [valori'zar] VT to value

valsa ['vawsa] F waltz

válvula ['vawvula] F valve

vampiro, -a [vã'piru, a] M/F vampire

vandalismo [vãda'lizmu] M vandalism

vândalo, -a ['vãdalu, a] M/F vandal

vangloriar-se [vãglo'rjarsi] VR: **~ de** to boast of *ou* about

vanguarda [vã'gwarda] F vanguard; (*arte*) avant-garde

vantagem [vã'taʒẽ] (*pl* **-ns**) F advantage; (*ganho*) profit, benefit; **tirar ~ de** to take advantage of; **vantajoso, -a** [vãta'ʒozu, ɔza] ADJ advantageous; (*lucrativo*) profitable; (*proveitoso*) beneficial

vão¹ [vãw] VB *ver* **ir**

vão², vã [vãw, vã] (*pl* **-s/-s**) ADJ vain; (*fútil*) futile ▶ M (*intervalo*) space; (*de porta etc*) opening

vaqueiro [va'kejru] M cowboy

vara ['vara] F stick; (*Tec*) rod; (*Jur*) jurisdiction; (*de porcos*) herd; **salto de ~** pole vault; **~ de condão** magic wand

varal [va'raw] (*pl* **-ais**) M clothes line

varanda [va'rãda] F verandah; (*balcão*) balcony

varar [va'rar] VT to pierce; (*passar*) to cross

varejista [vare'ʒista] (BR) M/F retailer ▶ ADJ (*mercado*) retail

varejo [va'reʒu] (BR) M (*Com*) retail trade; **a ~** retail

variação [varja'sãw] (*pl* **-ões**) F variation

variado, -a [va'rjadu, a] ADJ varied; (*sortido*) assorted

variar [va'rjar] VT, VI to vary; **variável** [va'rjavew] (*pl* **-eis**) ADJ variable; (*tempo, humor*) changeable

varicela [vari'sɛla] F chickenpox

V

variedade [varje'dadʒi] F variety

varinha [va'riɲa] F wand; **~ de condão** magic wand

vário, -a ['varju, a] ADJ (*diverso*) varied; (*pl*) various, several; (*Com*) sundry

varizes [va'rizis] FPL varicose veins

varrer [va'her] VT to sweep; (*fig*) to sweep away

vaselina® [vaze'lina] F Vaseline®

vasilha [va'ziʎa] F (*para líquidos*) jug; (*para alimentos*) dish; (*barril*) barrel

vaso ['vazu] M pot; (*para flores*) vase

vassoura [va'sora] F broom

vasto, -a ['vastu, a] ADJ vast

vatapá [vata'pa] M *fish or chicken with coconut milk, shrimps, peanuts, palm oil and spices*

Vaticano [vatʃi'kanu] M: **o ~** the Vatican

vazamento [vaza'mẽtu] M leak

vazão [va'zãw] (*pl* **-ões**) F flow; (*venda*) sale; **dar ~ a** (*expressar*) to give vent to; (*atender*) to deal with; (*resolver*) to attend to

vazar [va'zar] VT to empty; (*derramar*) to spill; (*verter*) to pour out ▶ VI to leak

vazio, -a [va'ziu, a] ADJ empty; (*pessoa*) empty-headed, frivolous; (*cidade*) deserted ▶ M emptiness; (*deixado por alguém/algo*) void

vazões [va'zõjs] FPL de **vazão**

vê [ve] VB ver **ver**

veado ['vjadu] M deer; **carne de ~** venison

vedado, -a [ve'dadu, a] ADJ (*proibido*) forbidden; (*fechado*) enclosed

vedar [ve'dar] VT to ban, prohibit; (*buraco*) to stop up; (*entrada, passagem*) to block; (*terreno*) to close off

vegetação [veʒeta'sãw] F vegetation

vegetal [veʒe'taw] (*pl* **-ais**) ADJ vegetable *atr*; (*reino, vida*) plant *atr* ▶ M vegetable

vegetalista [veʒeta'lista] ADJ, M/F vegan

vegetariano, -a [veʒeta'rjanu, a] ADJ, M/F vegetarian

veia ['veja] F vein

veículo [ve'ikulu] M (*tb: fig*) vehicle

veio¹ ['veju] M (*de rocha*) vein; (*na mina*) seam; (*de madeira*) grain

veio² VB ver **vir¹**

vejo ['veʒu] VB ver **ver**

vela ['vɛla] F candle; (*Auto*) spark plug; (*Náut*) sail; **barco à ~** sailing boat

velar [ve'lar] VT to veil; (*ocultar*) to hide; (*vigiar*) to keep watch over; (*um doente*) to sit up with ▶ VI (*não dormir*) to stay up; (*vigiar*) to keep watch; **~ por** to look after

veleiro [ve'lejru] M sailing boat

velejar [vele'ʒar] VI to sail

velhaco, -a [ve'ʎaku, a] ADJ crooked ▶ M/F crook

velhice [ve'ʎisi] F old age

velho, -a ['vɛʎu, a] ADJ old ▶ M/F old man/woman

velocidade [velosi'dadʒi] F speed, velocity; (*PT Auto*) gear

velório [ve'lɔrju] M wake

veloz [ve'lɔz] ADJ fast

vem [vẽj] VB ver **vir¹**

vêm [vẽj] VB ver **vir¹**

vencedor, a [vẽse'dor(a)] ADJ winning ▶ M/F winner

vencer [vẽ'ser] VT (*num jogo*) to beat; (*competição*) to win; (*inimigo*) to defeat; (*exceder*) to surpass; (*obstáculos*) to overcome; (*percorrer*) to pass ▶ VI (*num jogo*) to win;

vencido, -a [vẽ'sidu, a] ADJ: **dar-se**

por vencido to give in;
vencimento [vẽsi'mẽtu] M (Com)
expiry; (data) expiry date; (salário)
salary; (de gêneros alimentícios etc)
sell-by date; **vencimentos** MPL
(ganhos) earnings

venda ['vẽda] F sale; (pano)
blindfold; (mercearia) general
store; **à ~** on sale, for sale

vendaval [vẽda'vaw] (pl -**ais**) M
gale

vendedor, a [vẽde'dor(a)] M/F
seller; (em loja) sales assistant; (de
imóvel) vendor; **~ ambulante**
street vendor

vender [vẽ'der] VT, VI to sell; **~ por
atacado/a varejo** to sell
wholesale/retail

veneno [ve'nɛnu] M poison;
venenoso, -a [vene'nozu, ɔza] ADJ
poisonous

venerar [vene'rar] VT to revere;
(Rel) to worship

venéreo, -a [ve'nɛrju, a] ADJ:
doença venérea venereal disease

Venezuela [vene'zwɛla] F: **a ~**
Venezuela

venha ['vɛɲa] VB ver **vir¹**

ventania [vẽta'nia] F gale

ventar [vẽ'tar] VI: **está ventando**
it is windy

ventilação [vẽtʃila'sãw] F
ventilation

ventilador [vẽtʃila'dor] M
ventilator; (elétrico) fan

vento ['vẽtu] M wind; (brisa)
breeze; **ventoinha** [vẽ'twiɲa] F
weathercock, weather vane; (PT
Auto) fan

ventre ['vẽtri] M belly

ver [ver] VT to see; (olhar para,
examinar) to look at; (televisão) to
watch ▶ VI to see ▶ M: **a meu ~**
in my opinion; **vai ~ que ...**

maybe ...; **não tem nada a ~
(com)** it has nothing to do (with)

veracidade [verasi'dadʒi] F
truthfulness

veraneio [vera'neju] M summer
holidays pl (BRIT) ou vacation (US)

verão [ve'rãw] (pl -**ões**) M summer

verba ['vɛrba] F allowance;
verba(s) F(PL) (recursos) funds pl

verbal [ver'baw] (pl -**ais**) ADJ verbal

verbete [ver'betʃi] M (num
dicionário) entry

verbo ['vɛrbu] M verb

verdade [ver'dadʒi] F truth; **na ~**
in fact; **de ~** (falar) truthfully;
(ameaçar etc) really; **para falar a ~**
to tell the truth; **verdadeiro, -a**
[verda'dejru, a] ADJ true; (genuíno)
real; (pessoa) truthful

verde [ver'dʒi] ADJ green; (fruta)
unripe ▶ M green; (plantas etc)
greenery

verdura [ver'dura] F (hortaliça)
greens pl; (Bot) greenery; (cor
verde) greenness

verdureiro, -a [verdu'rejru, a]
M/F greengrocer (BRIT), produce
dealer (US)

vereador, a [verja'dor(a)] M/F
councillor (BRIT), councilor (US)

veredicto [vere'dʒiktu] M verdict

verga ['vɛrga] F (vara) stick; (de
metal) rod

vergonha [ver'goɲa] F shame;
(timidez) embarrassment;
(humilhação) humiliation; (ato
indecoroso) indecency; (brio)
self-respect; **ter ~** to be ashamed;
(tímido) to be shy; **vergonhoso, -a**
[vergo'ɲozu, ɔza] ADJ shameful;
(indecoroso) disgraceful

verídico, -a [ve'ridʒiku, a] ADJ
true, truthful

verificar [verifi'kar] VT to check;

V

(*confirmar, Comput*) to verify
verme ['vɛrmi] M worm
vermelho, -a [ver'meʎu, a] ADJ red
▶ M red
verniz [ver'niz] M varnish; (*couro*)
patent leather
verões [ve'rõjs] MPL *de* **verão**
verossímil [vero'simiw], (PT)
verosímil (*pl* -**eis**) ADJ likely,
probable; (*crível*) credible
verruga [ve'huga] F wart
versão [ver'sãw] (*pl* -**ões**) F version;
(*tradução*) translation
versátil [ver'satʃiw] (*pl* -**eis**) ADJ
versatile
verso ['vɛrsu] M verse; (*linha*) line of
poetry
versões [ver'sõjs] FPL *de* **versão**
verter [ver'ter] VT to pour; (*por
acaso*) to spill; (*traduzir*) to translate;
(*lágrimas, sangue*) to shed ▶ VI: **~ de**
to spring from; **~ em** (*rio*) to flow
into
vertical [vertʃi'kaw] (*pl* -**ais**) ADJ
vertical; (*de pé*) upright, standing
▶ F vertical
vespa ['vespa] F wasp
véspera ['vɛspera] F: **a ~ (de)** the
day before; **a ~ de Natal** Christmas
Eve
vestiário [ves'tʃjarju] M (*em casa,
teatro*) cloakroom; (*Esporte*)
changing room (BRIT), locker-room
(US); (*de ator*) dressing room
vestíbulo [ves'tʃibulu] M
hall(way), vestibule; (*Teatro*) foyer
vestido, -a [ves'tʃidu, a] ADJ: **~ de
branco** *etc* dressed in white *etc* ▶ M
dress
vestígio [ves'tʃiʒju] M (*rastro*) track;
(*fig*) sign, trace
vestimenta [vestʃi'mẽta] F
garment
vestir [ves'tʃir] VT (*uma criança*) to

dress; (*pôr sobre si*) to put on; (*trajar*)
to wear; (*comprar, dar roupa para*) to
clothe; (*fazer roupa para*) to make
clothes for; **vestir-se** VR to get
dressed
vestuário [ves'twarju] M clothing
veterano, -a [vete'ranu, a] ADJ,
M/F veteran
veterinário, -a [veteri'narju, a]
M/F vet(erinary surgeon)
veto ['vɛtu] M veto
véu [vɛw] M veil
vexame [ve'ʃami] F shame,
disgrace; (*tormento*) affliction;
(*humilhação*) humiliation; (*afronta*)
insult
vez [vez] F time; (*turno*) turn; **uma ~**
once; **algumas ~es, às ~es**
sometimes; **~ por outra**
sometimes; **cada ~ (que)** every
time; **de ~ em quando** from time
to time; **em ~ de** instead of; **uma ~
que** since; **3 ~es 6** 3 times 6; **de
uma ~ por todas** once and for all;
muitas ~es many times;
(*frequentemente*) often; **toda ~ que**
every time; **um de cada ~** one at a
time; **uma ~ ou outra** once in a
while
vi [vi] VB *ver* **ver**
via[1] ['via] F road, route; (*meio*) way;
(*documento*) copy; (*conduto*) channel
▶ PREP via, by way of; **em ~s de** in
the process of; **por ~ terrestre/
marítima** by land/sea
via[2] VB *ver* **ver**
viaduto [vja'dutu] M viaduct
viagem ['vjaʒẽ] (*pl* -**ns**) F journey,
trip; (*o viajar*) travel; (*Náut*) voyage;
viagens FPL (*jornadas*) travels; **~ de
ida e volta** return trip, round trip
viajante [vja'ʒãtʃi] ADJ travelling
(BRIT), traveling (US) ▶ M traveller
(BRIT), traveler (US)

viajar [vja'ʒar] vi to travel

viável ['vjavew] (pl **-eis**) ADJ feasible, viable

víbora ['vibora] F viper

vibração [vibra'sãw] (pl **-ões**) F vibration; (fig) thrill

vibrante [vi'brãtʃi] ADJ vibrant; (discurso) stirring

vibrar [vi'brar] vt to brandish; (fazer estremecer) to vibrate; (cordas) to strike ▶ vi to vibrate; (som) to echo

vice ['visi] M/F deputy

vice- [visi-] PREFIXO vice-; **vice-presidente, -a** M/F vice president; **vice-versa** [-'vɛrsa] ADV vice versa

viciado, -a [vi'sjadu, a] ADJ addicted; (ar) foul ▶ M/F addict; **~ em algo** addicted to sth

viciar [vi'sjar] vt (falsificar) to falsify; **viciar-se** VR: **~-se em algo** to become addicted to sth

vício ['visju] M vice; (defeito) failing; (costume) bad habit; (em entorpecentes) addiction

viço ['visu] M vigour (BRIT), vigor (US); (da pele) freshness

vida ['vida] F life; (duração) lifetime; (fig) vitality; **com ~** alive; **ganhar a ~** to earn one's living; **modo de ~** way of life; **dar a ~ por algo/fazer algo** to give one's right arm for sth/to do sth; **estar bem de ~** to be well off

videira [vi'dejra] F grapevine

vidente [vi'dẽtʃi] M/F clairvoyant

vídeo ['vidʒu] M video; **videocassete** [vidʒjuka'sɛtʃi] M video cassette ou tape; (aparelho) video (recorder); **videoteipe** [vidʒju'tejpi] M video tape

vidraça [vi'drasa] F window pane

vidrado, -a [vi'dradu, a] ADJ glazed; (porta) glass atr; (olhos) glassy

vidro ['vidru] M glass; (frasco) bottle; **fibra de ~** fibreglass (BRIT), fiberglass (US); **~ de aumento** magnifying glass

vier [vjer] VB ver **vir¹**

viés [vjɛs] M slant; **ao** ou **de ~** diagonally

vieste ['vjestʃi] VB ver **vir¹**

Vietnã [vjet'nã] M: **o ~** Vietnam; **vietnamita** [vjetna'mita] ADJ, M/F Vietnamese

vigiar [vi'ʒjar] vt to watch; (ocultamente) to spy on; (presos, fronteira) to guard ▶ vi to be on the lookout

vigilância [viʒi'lãsja] F vigilance; **vigilante** [viʒi'lãtʃi] ADJ vigilant; (atento) alert

vigor [vi'gor] M energy; **em ~** in force; **entrar/pôr em ~** to take effect/put into effect; **vigoroso, -a** [vigo'rozu, ɔza] ADJ vigorous

vil [viw] (pl **vis**) ADJ vile

vila ['vila] F town; (casa) villa

vilão, -lã [vi'lãw, 'lã] (pl **-ões/-s**) M/F villain

vilarejo [vila'reʒu] M village

vim [vĩ] VB ver **vir¹**

vime ['vimi] M wicker

vinagre [vi'nagri] M vinegar

vinco ['vĩku] M crease; (sulco) furrow; (no rosto) line

vincular [vĩku'lar] vt to link, tie; **vínculo** ['vĩkulu] M bond, tie; (relação) link

vinda ['vĩda] F arrival; (regresso) return; **dar as boas ~s a** to welcome

vingança [vĩ'gãsa] F vengeance, revenge; **vingar** [vĩ'gar] vt to avenge; **vingar-se** VR: **vingar-se de** to take revenge on; **vingativo, -a**

V

[vĩga'tʃivu, a] ADJ vindictive

vinha¹ ['viɲa] F vineyard; (*planta*) vine

vinha² VB *ver* **vir¹**

vinho ['viɲu] M wine; **~ branco/ rosado/tinto** white/rosé/red wine; **~ seco/doce** dry/sweet wine; **~ do Porto** port

vinte ['vĩtʃi] NUM twenty

viola ['vjɔla] F viola

violão [vjo'lãw] (*pl* **-ões**) M guitar

violar [vjo'lar] VT to violate; (*a lei*) to break

violência [vjo'lẽsja] F violence; **violentar** [vjolẽ'tar] VT to force; (*mulher*) to rape; **violento, -a** [vjo'lẽtu, a] ADJ violent

violeta [vjo'leta] F violet

violino [vjo'linu] M violin

violões [vjo'lõjs] MPL *de* **violão**

violoncelo [vjolõ'sɛlu] M cello

vir¹ [vir] VI to come; **~ a ser** to turn out to be; **a semana que vem** next week

vir² VB *ver* **ver**

viral [vi'raw] ADJ viral

vira-lata ['vira-] (*pl* **vira-latas**) M (*cão*) mongrel

virar [vi'rar] VT to turn; (*página, disco, barco*) to turn over; (*copo*) to empty; (*transformar-se em*) to become ▶ VI to turn; (*barco*) to capsize; (*mudar*) to change; **virar-se** VR to turn; (*voltar-se*) to turn round; (*defender-se*) to fend for o.s.

virgem ['virʒẽ] (*pl* **-ns**) F virgin; **V~** (*Astrologia*) Virgo

vírgula ['virgula] F comma; (*decimal*) point

viril [vi'riw] (*pl* **-is**) ADJ virile

virilha [vi'riʎa] F groin

viris [vi'ris] ADJ PL *de* **viril**

virtual [vir'twaw] (*pl* **-ais**) ADJ virtual; (*potencial*) potential

virtude [vir'tudʒi] F virtue; **em ~ de** owing to, because of; **virtuoso, -a** [vir'twozu, ɔza] ADJ virtuous

virulento, -a [viru'lẽtu, a] ADJ virulent

vírus ['virus] M INV virus

vis [vis] ADJ PL *de* **vil**

visão [vi'zãw] (*pl* **-ões**) F vision; (*Anat*) eyesight; (*vista*) sight; (*maneira de perceber*) view

visar [vi'zar] VT (*alvo*) to aim at; (*ter em vista*) to have in view; (*ter como objetivo*) to aim for

vísceras ['viseras] FPL innards, bowels

visita [vi'zita] F visit, call; (*pessoa*) visitor; (*na Internet*) hit; **fazer uma ~ a** to visit; **~ guiada** guided tour; **visitante** [vizi'tãtʃi] ADJ visiting ▶ M/F visitor; **visitar** [vizi'tar] VT to visit

visível [vi'zivew] (*pl* **-eis**) ADJ visible

vislumbrar [vizlũ'brar] VT to glimpse, catch a glimpse of; **vislumbre** [viz'lũbri] M glimpse

visões [vi'zõjs] FPL *de* **visão**

visse ['visi] VB *ver* **ver**

vista ['vista] F sight; (*Med*) eyesight; (*panorama*) view; **à** *ou* **em ~ de** in view of; **dar na ~** to attract attention; **dar uma ~ de olhos em** to glance at; **fazer ~ grossa (a)** to turn a blind eye (to); **ter em ~** to have in mind; **à ~** visible, showing; (*Com*) in cash; **até a ~!** see you!

visto¹, -a ['vistu, a] PP *de* **ver** ▶ ADJ seen ▶ M (*em passaporte*) visa; (*em documento*) stamp; **pelo ~** by the looks of things

visto² VB *ver* **vestir**

vistoria [visto'ria] F inspection

vistoso, -a [vis'tozu, ɔza] ADJ eye-catching

visual [viˈzwaw] (pl **-ais**) ADJ
visual; **visualizar** [vizwaliˈzar] VT
to visualize

vital [viˈtaw] (pl **-ais**) ADJ vital;
vitalício, -a [vitaˈlisju, a] ADJ for
life

vitamina [vitaˈmina] F vitamin;
(para beber) fruit crush

vitela [viˈtɛla] F calf; (carne) veal

vítima [ˈvitʃima] F victim

vitória [viˈtɔrja] F victory;
vitorioso, -a [vitoˈrjozu, ɔza] ADJ
victorious

vitrina [viˈtrina] F = **vitrine**

vitrine [viˈtrini] F shop window;
(armário) display case

viúvo, -a [ˈvjuvu, a] M/F widower/
widow

viva [ˈviva] M cheer; **~!** hurray!

viva-voz [vivaˈvɔz] M (BR Tel: em
telefone) speakerphone; (para
celular) hands-free kit

viveiro [viˈvejru] M nursery

vivência [viˈvẽsja] F existence;
(experiência) experience

vivenda [viˈvẽda] F (casa)
residence

viver [viˈver] VI, VT to live ▶ M life;
~ de to live on

vívido, -a [ˈvividu, a] ADJ vivid

vivo, -a [ˈvivu, a] ADJ living;
(esperto) clever; (cor) bright;
(criança, debate) lively ▶ M: **os ~s**
the living

vizinhança [viziˈɲãsa] F
neighbourhood (BRIT),
neighborhood (US)

vizinho, -a [viˈziɲu, a] ADJ
neighbouring (BRIT), neighboring
(US); (perto) nearby ▶ M/F
neighbour (BRIT), neighbor (US)

vó [vɔ] (col) F gran

vô [vo] (col) M grandad, grandpa

voar [voˈar] VI to fly; (explodir) to
blow up, explode

vocabulário [vokabuˈlarju] M
vocabulary

vocábulo [voˈkabulu] M word

vocal [voˈkaw] (pl **-ais**) ADJ vocal

você [voˈse] PRON you

vocês [voˈses] PRON PL you

vodca [ˈvɔdʒka] F vodka

vogal [voˈgaw] (pl **-ais**) F (Ling)
vowel

vol. ABR (= volume) vol

volante [voˈlãtʃi] M steering wheel

vôlei [ˈvolej] M volleyball

voleibol [volejˈbɔw] M = **vôlei**

volt [ˈvɔwtʃi] (pl **-s**) M volt

volta [ˈvɔwta] F turn; (regresso)
return; (curva) bend, curve;
(circuito) lap; (resposta) retort;
dar uma ~ (a pé) to go for a walk;
(de carro) to go for a drive; **estar
de ~** to be back; **na ~ do correio**
by return (post); **por ~ de** about,
around; **à** ou **em ~ de** around;
na ~ (no caminho de volta) on the
way back

voltagem [vowˈtaʒẽ] F voltage

voltar [vowˈtar] VT to turn ▶ VI to
return, go (ou come) back;
voltar-se VR to turn round; **~ a
fazer** to do again; **~ a si** to come
to; **~-se para** to turn to; **~-se
contra** to turn against

volume [voˈlumi] M volume;
(pacote) package; **volumoso, -a**
[voluˈmozu, ɔza] ADJ bulky, big

voluntário, -a [volũˈtarju, a] ADJ
voluntary ▶ M/F volunteer

volúvel [voˈluvew] (pl **-eis**) ADJ
fickle

vomitar [vomiˈtar] VT, VI to
vomit; **vômito** [ˈvomitu] M (ato)
vomiting; (efeito) vomit

vontade [võˈtadʒi] F will; (desejo)
wish; **com ~** (com prazer) with

pleasure; (*com gana*) with gusto;
estar com *ou* **ter ~ de fazer** to feel
like doing

voo ['vou] M flight; **levantar ~**
to take off; **~ livre** (*Esporte*)
hang-gliding

voraz [vo'rajz] ADJ voracious

vos [vus] PRON you

vós [vɔs] PRON you

vosso, -a ['vɔsu, a] ADJ your
▶ PRON: **(o) ~** yours

votação [vota'sãw] (*pl* -**ões**) F vote,
ballot; (*ato*) voting

votar [vo'tar] VT (*eleger*) to vote for;
(*aprovar*) to pass; (*submeter a
votação*) to vote on ▶ VI to vote;
voto ['vɔtu] M vote; (*promessa*) vow;
votos MPL (*desejos*) wishes

vou [vo] VB *ver* **ir**

vovó [vo'vɔ] F grandma

vovô [vo'vo] M grandad

voz [vɔz] F voice; (*clamor*) cry; **a
meia ~** in a whisper; **de viva ~**
orally; **ter ~ ativa** to have a say;
em ~ baixa in a low voice; **em ~
alta** aloud; **~ de comando**
command

vulcão [vuw'kãw] (*pl* -**ões**) M
volcano

vulgar [vuw'gar] ADJ common;
(*pej: pessoa etc*) vulgar

vulnerável [vuwne'ravew] (*pl* -**eis**)
ADJ vulnerable

vulto ['vuwtu] M figure; (*volume*)
mass; (*fig*) importance; (*pessoa
importante*) important person

walkie-talkie [wɔki'tɔki] (*pl* -**s**) M
walkie-talkie

watt ['wɔtʃi] (*pl* -**s**) M watt

web ['wɛbi] F, ADJ (*Comput*) web

webcam [wɛb'cã] F webcam

windsurfe M windsurfing

X

indigenous people. Situated in the north of the state of Mato Grosso, it aims to preserve indigenous culture. It brings together sixteen communities, a total of two thousand Indians.

xadrez [ʃa'dreʒ] M chess; (*tabuleiro*) chessboard; (*tecido*) checked cloth

xampu [ʃã'pu] M shampoo

xarope [ʃa'rɔpi] M syrup; (*para a tosse*) cough syrup

xeque ['ʃeki] M (*soberano*) sheikh; **pôr em ~** (*fig*) to call into question; **xeque-mate** (*pl* **xeques-mate**) M checkmate

xerocar [ʃero'kar] VT to photocopy, Xerox®

xerox® [ʃe'rɔks] M (*copia*) photocopy; (*máquina*) photocopier

xícara ['ʃikara] (BR) F cup

xingar [ʃĩ'gar] VT to swear at ▶ VI to swear

Xingu [ʃĩ'gu] M *see note*

The **Xingu** National Park was created in 1961 by the federal government and directed by the brothers Orlando and Cláudio Vilasboas, who were known internationally for their efforts to preserve Brazil's

Z

-zinho, -a [-'ziɲu, a] SUFIXO little; **florzinha** little flower
zíper ['ziper] M zip (BRIT), zipper (US)
zodíaco [zo'dʒiaku] M zodiac
zoeira ['zwejra] F din
zombar [zõ'bar] VI to mock; **~ de** to make fun of; **zombaria** [zõba'ria] F mockery, ridicule
zona ['zɔna] F area; (de cidade) district; (Geo) zone; (col: local de meretrício) red-light district; (: confusão) mess; (: tumulto) free-for-all; **~ eleitoral** electoral district, constituency
zonzo, -a ['zõzu, a] ADJ dizzy
zoo ['zou] M zoo
zoológico, -a [zo'lɔʒiku, a] ADJ zoological; **jardim ~** zoo
zumbido [zũ'bidu] M buzz(ing); (de tráfego) hum
zunzum [zũ'zũ] M buzz(ing)

zagueiro [za'gejru] M (Futebol) fullback
Zâmbia ['zãbja] F Zambia
zangado, -a [zã'gadu, a] ADJ angry; annoyed; (irritadiço) bad-tempered
zangar [zã'gar] VT to annoy, irritate ▶ VI to get angry; **zangar-se** VR (aborrecer-se) to get annoyed; **~-se com** to get cross with
zarpar [zar'par] VI (navio) to set sail; (ir-se) to set off; (fugir) to run away
zebra ['zebra] F zebra
zelador, a [zela'dor(a)] M/F caretaker
zelar [ze'lar] VT, VI: **~ (por)** to look after
zerar [ze'rar] VT (conta, inflação) to reduce to zero; (déficit) to pay off, wipe out
zero ['zɛru] M zero; (Esporte) nil; **zero-quilômetro** ADJ INV brand new
ziguezague [zigi'zagi] M zigzag
Zimbábue [zĩ'babwi] M: **o ~** Zimbabwe